SELECTED SECTIONS

UNITED STATES INTERNATIONAL TAXATION

2026 Edition

DANIEL J. LATHROPE
Distinguished E.L. Wiegand Professor of Law, Emeritus
University of San Francisco School of Law
Professor of Law, Emeritus
University of California Law, San Francisco

FOUNDATION PRESS

860 Blue Gentian Road, Suite 350
Eagan, MN 55121
1-877-888-1330

Published in the United States of America

ISBN: 979-8-31770-443-8

Preface

This volume is intended to provide a concise and compact set of materials for introductory courses covering United States international taxation. It includes all relevant provisions of the Internal Revenue Code and selected Treasury Regulations. It is specially geared for use in two or three-unit courses covering U.S. taxation of foreign taxpayers and domestic taxpayers whose income derives from outside the United States. The volume is not intended to be a complete reference for the Internal Revenue Code and regulations. The Appendix includes the United States Model Income Tax Convention of February 17, 2016, and Internal Revenue Service pronouncements setting cost-of-living and inflation adjustments for 2026.

The text is current through June 1, 2026. If you have any suggestions regarding the content of this volume, please contact me at djlathrope@usfca.edu.

Daniel J. Lathrope
San Francisco, California
June 2026

Contents

SELECTED SECTIONS

UNITED STATES INTERNATIONAL TAXATION

2026 Edition

SUBTITLE A—INCOME TAXES

Chapter 1—Normal Taxes or Surtaxes

Subchapter A—Determination of Tax Liability

Part I—Tax on Individuals

§ 1. Tax imposed*

(a) Married individuals filing joint returns and surviving spouses.—There is hereby imposed on the taxable income of—

(1) every married individual (as defined in section 7703) who makes a single return jointly with his spouse under section 6013, and

(2) every surviving spouse (as defined in section 2(a)), a tax determined in accordance with the following table:

If taxable income is:	*The tax is:*
Not over $36,900	15% of taxable income.
Over $36,900 but not over $89,150	$5,535, plus 28% of the excess over $36,900.
Over $89,150 but not over $140,000	$20,165, plus 31% of the excess over $89,150.
Over $140,000 but not over $250,000	$35,928.50, plus 36% of the excess over $140,000.
Over $250,000	$75,528.50, plus 39.6% of the excess over $250,000.

* * *

(c) Unmarried individuals (other than surviving spouses and heads of households).—There is hereby imposed on the taxable income of every individual (other than a surviving spouse as defined in section 2(a) or the head of a household as defined in section 2(b)) who is not a married individual (as defined in section 7703) a tax determined in accordance with the following table:

If taxable income is:	*The tax is:*
Not over $22,100	15% of taxable income.
Over $22,100 but not over $53,500	$3,315, plus 28% of the excess over $22,100.
Over $53,500 but not over $115,000	$12,107, plus 31% of the excess over $53,500.
Over $115,000 but not over $250,000	$31,172, plus 36% of the excess over $115,000.
Over $250,000	$79,772, plus 39.6% of the excess over $250,000.

* * *

(h) Maximum capital gains rate.—

(1) In general.—If a taxpayer has a net capital gain for any taxable year, the tax imposed by this section for such taxable year shall not exceed the sum of—

(A) a tax computed at the rates and in the same manner as if this subsection had not been enacted on the greater of—

* The rates in § 1 are subject to various special rules. For example, § 1(f) requires that the tables be adjusted annually for inflation and § 1(i) creates a 10% bracket. The I.R.S. annually publishes new rates to comply with these and other requirements.

(i) taxable income reduced by the net capital gain; or

(ii) the lesser of—

(I) the amount of taxable income taxed at a rate below 25 percent; or

(II) taxable income reduced by the adjusted net capital gain;

(B) 0 percent of so much of the adjusted net capital gain (or, if less, taxable income) as does not exceed the excess (if any) of—

(i) the amount of taxable income which would (without regard to this paragraph) be taxed at a rate below 25 percent, over

(ii) the taxable income reduced by the adjusted net capital gain;

(C) 15 percent of the lesser of—

(i) so much of the adjusted net capital gain (or, if less, taxable income) as exceeds the amount on which a tax is determined under subparagraph (B), or

(ii) the excess of—

(I) the amount of taxable income which would (without regard to this paragraph) be taxed at a rate below 39.6 percent, over

(II) the sum of the amounts on which a tax is determined under subparagraphs (A) and (B),

(D) 20 percent of the adjusted net capital gain (or, if less, taxable income) in excess of the sum of the amounts on which tax is determined under subparagraphs (B) and (C),

(E) 25 percent of the excess (if any) of—

(i) the unrecaptured section 1250 gain (or, if less, the net capital gain (determined without regard to paragraph (11))), over

(ii) the excess (if any) of—

(I) the sum of the amount on which tax is determined under subparagraph (A) plus the net capital gain, over

(II) taxable income; and

(F) 28 percent of the amount of taxable income in excess of the sum of the amounts on which tax is determined under the preceding subparagraphs of this paragraph.

(2) Net capital gain taken into account as investment income.—For purposes of this subsection, the net capital gain for any taxable year shall be reduced (but not below zero) by the amount which the taxpayer takes into account as investment income under section 163(d)(4)(B)(iii).

(3) Adjusted net capital gain.—For purposes of this subsection, the term "adjusted net capital gain" means the sum of—

(A) net capital gain (determined without regard to paragraph (11)) reduced (but not below zero) by the sum of—

(i) unrecaptured section 1250 gain; and

(ii) 28-percent rate gain, plus

(B) qualified dividend income (as defined in paragraph (11)).

(4) 28-percent rate gain.—For purposes of this subsection, the term "28-percent rate gain" means the excess (if any) of—

(A) the sum of—

(i) collectibles gain; and

(ii) section 1202 gain, over

(B) the sum of—

(i) collectibles loss;

(ii) the net short-term capital loss; and

(iii) the amount of long-term capital loss carried under section 1212(b)(1)(B) to the taxable year.

(5) Collectibles gain and loss.—For purposes of this subsection.

(A) In general.—The terms "collectibles gain" and "collectibles loss" mean gain or loss (respectively) from the sale or exchange of a collectible (as defined in section 408(m) without regard to paragraph (3) thereof) which is a capital asset held for more than 1 year but only to the extent such gain is taken into account in computing gross income and such loss is taken into account in computing taxable income.

(B) Partnerships, etc.—For purposes of subparagraph (A), any gain from the sale of an interest in a partnership, S corporation, or trust which is attributable to unrealized appreciation in the value of collectibles shall be treated as gain from the sale or exchange of a collectible. Rules similar to the rules of section 751 shall apply for purposes of the preceding sentence.

(6) Unrecaptured section 1250 gain.—For purposes of this subsection.

(A) In general.—The term "unrecaptured section 1250 gain" means the excess (if any) of—

(i) the amount of long-term capital gain (not otherwise treated as ordinary income) which would be treated as ordinary income if section 1250(b)(1) included all depreciation and the applicable percentage under section 1250(a) were 100 percent, over

(ii) the excess (if any) of—

(I) the amount described in paragraph (4)(B); over

(II) the amount described in paragraph (4)(A).

(B) Limitation with respect to section 1231 property.—The amount described in subparagraph (A)(i) from sales, exchanges, and conversions described in section 1231(a)(3)(A) for any taxable year shall not exceed the net section 1231 gain (as defined in section 1231(c)(3)) for such year.

(7) Section 1202 gain.—For purposes of this subsection, the term "section 1202 gain" means the excess of—

(A) the gain which would be excluded from gross income under section 1202 but for the percentage limitation in section 1202(a), over

(B) the gain excluded from gross income under section 1202.

(8) Coordination with recapture of net ordinary losses under section 1231.—If any amount is treated as ordinary income under section 1231(c), such amount shall be allocated among the separate categories of net section 1231 gain (as defined in section 1231(c)(3)) in such manner as the Secretary may by forms or regulations prescribe.

(9) Regulations.—The Secretary may prescribe such regulations as are appropriate (including regulations requiring reporting) to apply this subsection in the case of sales and exchanges by pass-thru entities and of interests in such entities.

(10) Pass-thru entity defined.—For purposes of this subsection, the term "pass-thru entity" means—

(A) a regulated investment company;

(B) a real estate investment trust;

(C) an S corporation;

(D) a partnership;

(E) an estate or trust;

(F) a common trust fund; and

(G) a qualified electing fund (as defined in section 1295).

(11) Dividends taxed as net capital gain.—

(A) In general.—For purposes of this subsection, the term "net capital gain" means net capital gain (determined without regard to this paragraph) increased by qualified dividend income.

(B) Qualified dividend income.—For purposes of this paragraph—

(i) In general.—The term "qualified dividend income" means dividends received during the taxable year from—

(I) domestic corporations, and

(II) qualified foreign corporations.

(ii) Certain dividends excluded.—Such term shall not include—

(I) any dividend from a corporation which for the taxable year of the corporation in which the distribution is made, or the preceding taxable year, is a corporation exempt from tax under section 501 or 521,

(II) any amount allowed as a deduction under section 591 (relating to deduction for dividends paid by mutual savings banks, etc.), and

(III) any dividend described in section 404(k).

(iii) Coordination with section 246(c).—Such term shall not include any dividend on any share of stock—

(I) with respect to which the holding period requirements of section 246(c) are not met (determined by substituting in section 246(c) "60 days" for "45 days" each place it appears and by substituting "121-day period" for "91-day period"), or

(II) to the extent that the taxpayer is under an obligation (whether pursuant to a short sale or otherwise) to make related payments with respect to positions in substantially similar or related property.

(C) Qualified foreign corporations.—

(i) In general.—Except as otherwise provided in this paragraph, the term "qualified foreign corporation" means any foreign corporation if—

(I) such corporation is incorporated in a possession of the United States, or

(II) such corporation is eligible for benefits of a comprehensive income tax treaty with the United States which the Secretary determines is satisfactory for purposes of this paragraph and which includes an exchange of information program.

(ii) Dividends on stock readily tradable on United States securities market.—A foreign corporation not otherwise treated as a qualified foreign corporation under clause (i) shall be so treated with respect to any dividend paid by such corporation if the stock with respect to which such dividend is paid is readily tradable on an established securities market in the United States.

(iii) Exclusion of dividends of certain foreign corporations.—Such term shall not include—

(I) any foreign corporation which for the taxable year of the corporation in which the dividend was paid, or the preceding taxable year, is a passive foreign investment company (as defined in section 1297), and

(II) any corporation which first becomes a surrogate foreign corporation (as defined in section 7874(a)(2)(B)) after the date of the enactment of this subclause, other than a foreign corporation which is treated as a domestic corporation under section 7874(b).

(iv) Coordination with foreign tax credit limitation.—Rules similar to the rules of section 904(b)(2)(B) shall apply with respect to the dividend rate differential under this paragraph.

(D) Special rules.—

(i) Amounts taken into account as investment income.—Qualified dividend income shall not include any amount which the taxpayer takes into account as investment income under section 163(d)(4)(B).

(ii) Extraordinary dividends.—If a taxpayer to whom this section applies receives, with respect to any share of stock, qualified dividend income from 1 or more dividends which are extraordinary dividends (within the meaning of section 1059(c)), any loss on the sale or exchange of such share shall, to the extent of such dividends, be treated as long-term capital loss.

(iii) Treatment of dividends from regulated investment companies and real estate investment trusts.—A dividend received from a regulated investment company or a real estate investment trust shall be subject to the limitations prescribed in sections 854 and 857.

* * *

(j) Modifications for taxable years beginning after December 31, 2017.—

(1) In general.—In the case of a taxable year beginning after December 31, 2017—

(A) subsection (i) shall not apply, and

(B) this section (other than subsection (i)) shall be applied as provided in paragraphs (2) through (6).

(2) Rate tables.—

(A) Married individuals filing joint returns and surviving spouses.—The following table shall be applied in lieu of the table contained in subsection (a):

If taxable income is:	The tax is:
Not over $19,050	10% of taxable income.
Over $19,050 but not over $77,400	$1,905, plus 12% of the excess over $19,050.
Over $77,400 but not over $165,000	$8,907, plus 22% of the excess over $77,400.
Over $165,000 but not over $315,000	$28,179, plus 24% of the excess over $165,000.
Over $315,000 but not over $400,000	$64,179, plus 32% of the excess over $315,000.
Over $400,000 but not over $600,000	$91,379, plus 35% of the excess over $400,000.
Over $600,000	$161,379, plus 37% of the excess over $600,000.

(B) Heads of households.—The following table shall be applied in lieu of the table contained in subsection (b):

If taxable income is:	The tax is:
Not over $13,600	10% of taxable income.
Over $13,600 but not over $51,800	$1,360, plus 12% of the excess over $13,600.
Over $51,800 but not over $82,500	$5,944, plus 22% of the excess over $51,800.
Over $82,500 but not over $157,500	$12,698, plus 24% of the excess over $82,500.
Over $157,500 but not over $200,000	$30,698, plus 32% of the excess over $157,500.
Over $200,000 but not over $500,000	$44,298, plus 35% of the excess over $200,000.
Over $500,000	$149,298, plus 37% of the excess over $500,000.

(C) Unmarried individuals other than surviving spouses and heads of households.—The following table shall be applied in lieu of the table contained in subsection (c):

If taxable income is:	The tax is:
Not over $9,525	10% of taxable income.
Over $9,525 but not over $38,700	$952.50, plus 12% of the excess over $9,525.
Over $38,700 but not over $82,500	$4,453.50, plus 22% of the excess over $38,700.
Over $82,500 but not over $157,500	$14,089.50, plus 24% of the excess over $82,500.
Over $157,500 but not over $200,000	$32,089.50, plus 32% of the excess over $157,500.
Over $200,000 but not over $500,000	$45,689.50, plus 35% of the excess over $200,000.
Over $500,000	$150,689.50, plus 37% of the excess over $500,000.

(D) Married individuals filing separate returns.—The following table shall be applied in lieu of the table contained in subsection (d):

If taxable income is:	The tax is:
Not over $9,525	10% of taxable income.
Over $9,525 but not over $38,700	$952.50, plus 12% of the excess over $9,525.
Over $38,700 but not over $82,500	$4,453.50, plus 22% of the excess over $38,700.
Over $82,500 but not over $157,500	$14,089.50, plus 24% of the excess over $82,500.
Over $157,500 but not over $200,000	$32,089.50, plus 32% of the excess over $157,500.
Over $200,000 but not over $300,000	$45,689.50, plus 35% of the excess over $200,000.
Over $300,000	$80,689.50, plus 37% of the excess over $300,000.

(E) Estates and trusts.—The following table shall be applied in lieu of the table contained in subsection (e):

If taxable income is:	The tax is:
Not over $2,550	10% of taxable income.
Over $2,550 but not over $9,150	$255, plus 24% of the excess over $2,550.
Over $9,150 but not over $12,500	$1,839, plus 35% of the excess over $9,150.
Over $12,500	$3,011.50, plus 37% of the excess over $12,500.

(F) References to rate tables.—Any reference in this title to a rate of tax under subsection (c) shall be treated as a reference to the corresponding rate bracket under subparagraph (C) of this paragraph, except that the reference in section 3402(q)(1) to the third lowest rate of tax applicable under subsection (c) shall be treated as a reference to the fourth lowest rate of tax under subparagraph (C).

(3) Adjustments.—

(A) No adjustment in 2018.—The tables contained in paragraph (2) shall apply without adjustment for taxable years beginning after December 31, 2017, and before January 1, 2019.

(B) Subsequent years.—For taxable years beginning after December 31, 2018, the Secretary shall prescribe tables which shall apply in lieu of the tables contained in paragraph (2) in the same manner as under paragraphs (1) and (2) of subsection (f) (applied without regard to clauses (i) and (ii) of subsection (f)(2)(A)), except that in prescribing such tables—

(i) solely for purposes of determining the dollar amounts at which any rate bracket higher than 12 percent ends and at which any rate bracket higher than 22 percent begins, subsection (f)(3) shall be applied by substituting "calendar year 2017" for "calendar year 2016" in subparagraph (A)(ii) thereof,

(ii) subsection (f)(7)(B) shall apply to any unmarried individual other than a surviving spouse or head of household, and

(iii) subsection (f)(8) shall not apply.

* * *

(5) Application of current income tax brackets to capital gains brackets.—

(A) In general.—Section 1(h)(1) shall be applied—

(i) by substituting "below the maximum zero rate amount" for "which would (without regard to this paragraph) be taxed at a rate below 25 percent" in subparagraph (B)(i), and

(ii) by substituting "below the maximum 15-percent rate amount" for "which would (without regard to this paragraph) be taxed at a rate below 39.6 percent" in subparagraph (C)(ii)(I).

(B) Maximum amounts defined.—For purposes of applying section 1(h) with the modifications described in subparagraph (A)—

(i) Maximum zero rate amount.—The maximum zero rate amount shall be—

(I) in the case of a joint return or surviving spouse, $77,200,

(II) in the case of an individual who is a head of household (as defined in section 2(b)), $51,700,

(III) in the case of any other individual (other than an estate or trust), an amount equal to ½ of the amount in effect for the taxable year under subclause (I), and

(IV) in the case of an estate or trust, $2,600.

(ii) Maximum 15-percent rate amount.—The maximum 15-percent rate amount shall be—

(I) in the case of a joint return or surviving spouse, $479,000 (½ such amount in the case of a married individual filing a separate return),

(II) in the case of an individual who is the head of a household (as defined in section 2(b)), $452,400,

(III) in the case of any other individual (other than an estate or trust), $425,800, and

(IV) in the case of an estate or trust, $12,700.

(C) Inflation adjustment.—In the case of any taxable year beginning after 2018, each of the dollar amounts in clauses (i) and (ii) of subparagraph (B) shall be increased by an amount equal to—

(i) such dollar amount, multiplied by

(ii) the cost-of-living adjustment determined under subsection (f)(3) for the calendar year in which the taxable year begins, determined by substituting "calendar year 2017" for "calendar year 2016" in subparagraph (A)(ii) thereof.

If any increase under this subparagraph is not a multiple of $50, such increase shall be rounded to the next lowest multiple of $50.

(6) Section 15 not to apply.—Section 15 shall not apply to any change in a rate of tax by reason of this subsection.

§ 2. Definitions and special rules

* * *

(d) Nonresident aliens.—In the case of a nonresident alien individual, the taxes imposed by sections 1 and 55 shall apply only as provided by section 871 or 877.

* * *

Part II—Tax on Corporations

§ 11. Tax imposed

(a) Corporations in general.—A tax is hereby imposed for each taxable year on the taxable income of every corporation.

(b) Amount of tax.—The amount of tax imposed by subsection (a) shall be 21 percent of taxable income.

* * *

(d) Foreign corporations.—In the case of a foreign corporation, the taxes imposed by subsection (a) and section 55 shall apply only as provided by section 882.

Part IV—Credits Against Tax

Subpart B—Other Credits

§ 27. Taxes of foreign countries and possessions of the United States; possession tax credit

The amount of taxes imposed by foreign countries and possessions of the United States shall be allowed as a credit against the tax imposed by this chapter to the extent provided in section 901.

Subpart C—Refundable Credits

§ 33. Tax withheld at source on nonresident aliens and foreign corporations

There shall be allowed as a credit against the tax imposed by this subtitle the amount of tax withheld at source under subchapter A of chapter 3 (relating to withholding of tax on nonresident aliens and on foreign corporations).

Part VI—Alternative Minimum Tax

§ 55. Alternative minimum tax imposed

(a) General rule.—There is hereby imposed (in addition to any other tax imposed by this subtitle) a tax equal to the excess (if any) of—

(1) the tentative minimum tax for the taxable year, over

(2) the regular tax for the taxable year plus, in the case of an applicable corporation, the tax imposed by section 59A.

(b) Tentative minimum tax.—For purposes of this part—

(1) Noncorporate taxpayers.—In the case of a taxpayer other than a corporation—

(A) In general.—The tentative minimum tax for the taxable year is the sum of—

(i) 26 percent of so much of the taxable excess as does not exceed $175,000, plus

(ii) 28 percent of so much of the taxable excess as exceeds $175,000.

The amount determined under the preceding sentence shall be reduced by the alternative minimum tax foreign tax credit for the taxable year.

(B) Taxable excess.—For purposes of this subsection, the term "taxable excess" means so much of the alternative minimum taxable income for the taxable year as exceeds the exemption amount.

(C) Married individual filing separate return.—In the case of a married individual filing a separate return, subparagraph (A) shall be applied by substituting 50 percent of the dollar amount otherwise applicable under clause (i) and clause (ii) thereof. For purposes of the preceding sentence, marital status shall be determined under section 7703.

(D) Alternative minimum taxable income.—The term "alternative minimum taxable income" means the taxable income of the taxpayer for the taxable year—

(i) determined with the adjustments provided in section 56 and section 58, and

(ii) increased by the amount of the items of tax preference described in section 57.

If a taxpayer is subject to the regular tax, such taxpayer shall be subject to the tax imposed by this section (and, if the regular tax is determined by reference to an amount other than taxable income, such amount shall be treated as the taxable income of such taxpayer for purposes of the preceding sentence).

(2) Corporations.—

(A) Applicable corporations.—In the case of an applicable corporation, the tentative minimum tax for the taxable year shall be the excess of—

(i) 15 percent of the adjusted financial statement income for the taxable year (as determined under section 56A), over

(ii) the corporate AMT foreign tax credit for the taxable year.

(B) Other corporations.—In the case of any corporation which is not an applicable corporation, the tentative minimum tax for the taxable year shall be zero.

(3) Maximum rate of tax on net capital gain of noncorporate taxpayers.—The amount determined under the first sentence of paragraph (1)(A) shall not exceed the sum of—

(A) the amount determined under such first sentence computed at the rates and in the same manner as if this paragraph had not been enacted on the taxable excess reduced by the lesser of—

(i) the net capital gain; or

(ii) the sum of—

(I) the adjusted net capital gain, plus

(II) the unrecaptured section 1250 gain, plus

(B) 0 percent of so much of the adjusted net capital gain (or, if less, taxable excess) as does not exceed an amount equal to the excess described in section 1(h)(1)(B), plus

(C) 15 percent of the lesser of—

(i) so much of the adjusted net capital gain (or, if less, taxable excess) as exceeds the amount on which tax is determined under subparagraph (B), or

(ii) the excess described in section 1(h)(1)(C)(ii), plus

(D) 20 percent of the adjusted net capital gain (or, if less, taxable excess) in excess of the sum of the amounts on which tax is determined under subparagraphs (B) and (C), plus

(E) 25 percent of the amount of taxable excess in excess of the sum of the amounts on which tax is determined under the preceding subparagraphs of this paragraph.

Terms used in this paragraph which are also used in section 1(h) shall have the respective meanings given such terms by section 1(h) but computed with the adjustments under this part.

(c) Regular tax.—

(1) In general.—For purposes of this section, the term "regular tax" means the regular tax liability for the taxable year (as defined in section 26(b)) reduced by the foreign tax credit allowable under section 27(a). Such term shall not include any increase in tax under section 45(e)(11)(C), 49(b) or 50 (a) or subsection (j) or (k) of section 42.

* * *

(3) Cross references.—

For provisions providing that certain credits are not allowable against the tax imposed by this section, see sections 30C(d)(2) and 38(c).

(d) Exemption amount.—For purposes of this section—

(1) Exemption amount for taxpayers other than corporations.—In the case of a taxpayer other than a corporation, the term "exemption amount" means—

(A) $78,750 in the case of—

(i) a joint return, or

(ii) a surviving spouse,

(B) $50,600 in the case of an individual who—

(i) is not a married individual, and

(ii) is not a surviving spouse,

(C) 50 percent of the dollar amount applicable under subparagraph (A) in the case of a married individual who files a separate return, and

(D) $22,500 in the case of an estate or trust.

For purposes of this paragraph, the term "surviving spouse" has the meaning given to such term by section 2(a), and marital status shall be determined under section 7703.

(2) Phase-out of exemption amount.—The exemption amount of any taxpayer shall be reduced (but not below zero) by an amount equal to 25 percent of the amount by which the alternative minimum taxable income of the taxpayer exceeds—

(A) $150,000 in the case of a taxpayer described in paragraph (1)(A),

(B) $112,500 in the case of a taxpayer described in paragraph (1)(B), and

(C) 50 percent of the dollar amount applicable under subparagraph (A) in the case of a taxpayer described in subparagraph (C) or (D) of paragraph (1).

In the case of a taxpayer described in paragraph (1)(C), alternative minimum taxable income shall be increased by the lesser of (i) 25 percent of the excess of alternative minimum taxable income (determined without regard to this sentence) over the minimum amount of such income (as so determined) for which the exemption amount under paragraph (1)(C) is zero, or (ii) such exemption amount (determined without regard to this paragraph).

(3) Inflation adjustment.—

(A) In general.—In the case of any taxable year beginning in a calendar year after 2012, the amounts described in subparagraph (B) shall each be increased by an amount equal to—

(i) such dollar amount, multiplied by

(ii) the cost-of-living adjustment determined under section 1(f)(3) for the calendar year in which the taxable year begins, determined by substituting "calendar year 2011" for "calendar year 2016" in subparagraph (A)(ii) thereof.

(B) Amounts described.—The amounts described in this subparagraph are—

(i) each of the dollar amounts contained in subsection (b)(1)(A),

(ii) each of the dollar amounts contained in subparagraphs (A), (B), and (D) of paragraph (1), and

(iii) each of the dollar amounts in subparagraphs (A) and (B) of paragraph (2).

(C) Rounding.—Any increased amount determined under subparagraph (A) shall be rounded to the nearest multiple of $100.

(4) Special rule for taxable years beginning after 2017.—

(A) In general.—In the case of any taxable year beginning after December 31, 2017—

(i) paragraph (1) shall be applied—

(I) by substituting "$109,400" for "$78,750" in subparagraph (A), and

(II) by substituting "$70,300" for "$50,600" in subparagraph (B),

(ii) paragraph (2) shall be applied—

(I) by substituting "$1,000,000" for "$150,000" in subparagraph (A),

(II) by substituting "50 percent of the dollar amount applicable under subparagraph (A)" for "$112,500" in subparagraph (B),

(III) in the case of a taxpayer described in paragraph (1)(D), without regard to the substitution under subclause (I), and

(IV) by substituting "50 percent" for "25 percent", and

(iii) subsection (j) of section 59 shall not apply.

(B) Inflation adjustment.—

(i) In general.—In the case of any taxable year beginning in a calendar year after 2018 (2026, in the case of the $1,000,000 amount in subparagraph (A)(ii)(I)), the amounts described in clause (ii) shall each be increased by an amount equal to—

(I) such dollar amount, multiplied by

(II) the cost-of-living adjustment determined under section 1(f)(3) for the calendar year in which the taxable year begins, determined by substituting for "calendar year 2016" in subparagraph (A)(ii) thereof—

(1) "calendar year 2017", in the case of the $109,400 amount in subparagraph (A)(i)(I) and the $70,300 amount in subparagraph (A)(i)(II), and

(2) "calendar year 2025", in the case of the $1,000,000 amount in subparagraph (A)(ii)(I).

(ii) Amounts described.—The amounts described in this clause are the $109,400 amount in subparagraph (A)(i)(I), the $70,300 amount in subparagraph (A)(i)(II), and the $1,000,000 amount in subparagraph (A)(ii)(I)

(iii) Rounding.—Any increased amount determined under clause (i) shall be rounded to the nearest multiple of $100.

(iv) Coordination with current adjustments.—In the case of any taxable year to which subparagraph (A) applies, no adjustment shall be made under paragraph (3) to any of the numbers which are substituted under subparagraph (A) and adjusted under this subparagraph.

§ 56A. Adjusted financial statement income

(a) In general.—For purposes of this part, the term "adjusted financial statement income" means, with respect to any corporation for any taxable year, the net income or loss of the taxpayer set forth on the taxpayer's applicable financial statement for such taxable year, adjusted as provided in this section.

(b) Applicable financial statement.—For purposes of this section, the term "applicable financial statement" means, with respect to any taxable year, an applicable financial statement (as defined in section 451(b)(3) or as specified by the Secretary in regulations or other guidance) which covers such taxable year.

(c) General adjustments.—

(1) Statements covering different taxable years.—Appropriate adjustments shall be made in adjusted financial statement income in any case in which an applicable financial statement covers a period other than the taxable year.

(2) Special rules for related entities.—

(A) Consolidated financial statements.—If the financial results of a taxpayer are reported on the applicable financial statement for a group of entities, rules similar to the rules of section 451(b)(5) shall apply.

* * *

(C) Treatment of dividends and other amounts.—In the case of any corporation which is not included on a consolidated return with the taxpayer, adjusted financial statement income of the taxpayer with respect to such other corporation shall be determined by only taking into account the dividends received from such other corporation (reduced to the extent provided by the Secretary in regulations or other guidance) and other amounts which are includible in gross income or deductible as a loss under this chapter (other than amounts required to be included under sections 951 and 951A or such other amounts as provided by the Secretary) with respect to such other corporation.

(D) Treatment of partnerships.—

(i) In general.—Except as provided by the Secretary, if the taxpayer is a partner in a partnership, adjusted financial statement income of the taxpayer with respect to such partnership shall be adjusted to only take into account the taxpayer's distributive share of adjusted financial statement income of such partnership.

* * *

(3) Adjustments to take into account certain items of foreign income.—

(A) In general.—If, for any taxable year, a taxpayer is a United States shareholder of one or more controlled foreign corporations, the adjusted financial statement income of such taxpayer with respect to such controlled foreign corporation (as determined under paragraph (2)(C)) shall be adjusted to also take into account such taxpayer's pro rata share (determined under rules similar to the rules under section 951(a)(2)) of items taken into account in computing the net income or loss set forth on the applicable financial statement (as adjusted under rules similar to those that apply in determining adjusted financial statement income) of each such controlled foreign corporation with respect to which such taxpayer is a United States shareholder.

(B) Negative adjustments.—In any case in which the adjustment determined under subparagraph (A) would result in a negative adjustment for such taxable year—

(i) no adjustment shall be made under this paragraph for such taxable year, and

(ii) the amount of the adjustment determined under this paragraph for the succeeding taxable year (determined without regard to this paragraph) shall be reduced by an amount equal to the negative adjustment for such taxable year.

(4) Effectively connected income.—In the case of a foreign corporation, to determine adjusted financial statement income, the principles of section 882 shall apply.

(5) Adjustments for certain taxes.—Adjusted financial statement income shall be appropriately adjusted to disregard any Federal income taxes, or income, war profits, or excess profits taxes (within the meaning of section 901) with respect to a foreign country or possession of the United States, which are taken into account on the taxpayer's applicable financial statement. To the extent provided by the Secretary, the preceding sentence shall not apply to income, war profits, or excess profits taxes (within the meaning of section 901) that are imposed by a foreign country or possession of the United States and taken into account on the taxpayer's applicable financial statement if the taxpayer does not choose to have the benefits of subpart A of part III of subchapter N for the taxable year. The Secretary shall prescribe such regulations or other guidance as may be necessary and appropriate to provide for the proper treatment of current and deferred taxes for purposes of this paragraph, including the time at which such taxes are properly taken into account.

(6) Adjustment with respect to disregarded entities.—Adjusted financial statement income shall be adjusted to take into account any adjusted financial statement income of a disregarded entity owned by the taxpayer.

* * *

(13) Depreciation.—Adjusted financial statement income shall be—

(A) reduced by—

(i) depreciation deductions allowed under section 167 with respect to property to which section 168 applies to the extent of the amount allowed as deductions in computing taxable income for the year, and

(ii) any deduction allowed for expenses under section 263(c) (including any deduction for such expenses under section 59(e) or 291(b)(2)) with respect to property described therein to the extent of the amount allowed as deductions in computing taxable income for the year, and

(B) appropriately adjusted—

(i) to disregard any amount of—

(I) depreciation expense that is taken into account on the taxpayer's applicable financial statement with respect to such property, and

(II) depletion expense that is taken into account on the taxpayer's applicable financial statement with respect to the intangible drilling and development costs of such property, and

(ii) to take into account any other item specified by the Secretary in order to provide that such property is accounted for in the same manner as it is accounted for under this chapter.

* * *

(d) Deduction for financial statement net operating loss.—

(1) In general.—Adjusted financial statement income (determined after application of subsection (c) and without regard to this subsection) shall be reduced by an amount equal to the lesser of—

(A) the aggregate amount of financial statement net operating loss carryovers to the taxable year, or

(B) 80 percent of adjusted financial statement income computed without regard to the deduction allowable under this subsection.

(2) Financial statement net operating loss carryover.—A financial statement net operating loss for any taxable year shall be a financial statement net operating loss carryover to each taxable year following the taxable year of the loss. The portion of such loss which shall be carried to subsequent taxable years shall be the amount of such loss remaining (if any) after the application of paragraph (1).

(3) Financial statement net operating loss defined.—For purposes of this subsection, the term "financial statement net operating loss" means the amount of the net loss (if any) set forth on the corporation's applicable financial statement (determined after application of subsection (c) and without regard to this subsection) for taxable years ending after December 31, 2019.

(e) Regulations and other guidance.—The Secretary shall provide for such regulations and other guidance as necessary to carry out the purposes of this section, including regulations and other guidance relating to the effect of the rules of this section on partnerships with income taken into account by an applicable corporation.

§ 59. Other definitions and special rules

(a) Alternative minimum tax foreign tax credit.—For purposes of this part—

(1) In general.—The alternative minimum tax foreign tax credit for any taxable year shall be the credit which would be determined under section 27 for such taxable year if—

(A) the pre-credit tentative minimum tax were the tax against which such credit was taken for purposes of section 904 for the taxable year and all prior taxable years beginning after December 31, 1986,

(B) section 904 were applied on the basis of alternative minimum taxable income instead of taxable income, and

(C) the determination of whether any income is high-taxed income for purposes of section 904(d)(2) were made on the basis of the applicable rate specified in section 55(b)(1) in lieu of the highest rate of tax specified in section 1.

(2) Pre-credit tentative minimum tax.—For purposes of this subsection, the term "pre-credit tentative minimum tax" means the amount determined under the first sentence of section 55(b)(1)(A).

(3) Election to use simplified section 904 limitation.—

(A) In general.—In determining the alternative minimum tax foreign tax credit for any taxable year to which an election under this paragraph applies—

(i) subparagraph (B) of paragraph (1) shall not apply, and

(ii) the limitation of section 904 shall be based on the proportion which—

(I) the taxpayer's taxable income (as determined for purposes of the regular tax) from sources without the United States (but not in excess of the taxpayer's entire alternative minimum taxable income), bears to

(II) the taxpayer's entire alternative minimum taxable income for the taxable year.

(B) Election.—

(i) In general.—An election under this paragraph may be made only for the taxpayer's first taxable year which begins after December 31, 1997, and for which the taxpayer claims an alternative minimum tax foreign tax credit.

(ii) Election revocable only with consent.—An election under this paragraph, once made, shall apply to the taxable year for which made and all subsequent taxable years unless revoked with the consent of the Secretary.

* * *

(k) Applicable corporation.—For purposes of this part—

(1) Applicable corporation defined.—

(A) In general.—The term "applicable corporation" means, with respect to any taxable year, any corporation (other than an S corporation, a regulated investment company, or a real estate investment trust) which meets the average annual adjusted financial statement income test of subparagraph (B) for one or more taxable years which—

(i) are prior to such taxable year, and

(ii) end after December 31, 2021.

(B) Average annual adjusted financial statement income test.—For purposes of this subsection—

(i) a corporation meets the average annual adjusted financial statement income test for a taxable year if the average annual adjusted financial statement income of such corporation (determined without regard to section 56A(d)) for the 3-taxable-year period ending with such taxable year exceeds $1,000,000,000, and

(ii) in the case of a corporation described in paragraph (2), such corporation meets the average annual adjusted financial statement income test for a taxable year if—

(I) the corporation meets the requirements of clause (i) for such taxable year (determined after the application of paragraph (2)), and

(II) the average annual adjusted financial statement income of such corporation (determined without regard to the application of paragraph (2) and without regard to section 56A(d)) for the 3-taxable-year-period ending with such taxable year is $100,000,000 or more.

(C) Exception.—Notwithstanding subparagraph (A), the term "applicable corporation" shall not include any corporation which otherwise meets the requirements of subparagraph (A) if—

(i) such corporation—

(I) has a change in ownership, or

(II) has a specified number (to be determined by the Secretary and which shall, as appropriate, take into account the facts and circumstances of the taxpayer) of consecutive taxable years, including the most recent taxable year, in which the corporation does not meet the average annual adjusted financial statement income test of subparagraph (B), and

(ii) the Secretary determines that it would not be appropriate to continue to treat such corporation as an applicable corporation.

The preceding sentence shall not apply to any corporation if, after the Secretary makes the determination described in clause (ii), such corporation meets the average annual adjusted financial statement income test of subparagraph (B) for any taxable year beginning after the first taxable year for which such determination applies.

* * *

(E) Other special rules.—

(i) Corporations in existence for less than 3 years.—If the corporation was in existence for less than 3-taxable years, subparagraph (B) shall be applied on the basis of the period during which such corporation was in existence.

(ii) Short taxable years.—Adjusted financial statement income for any taxable year of less than 12 months shall be annualized by multiplying the adjusted financial statement income for the short period by 12 and dividing the result by the number of months in the short period.

(iii) Treatment of predecessors.—Any reference in this subparagraph to a corporation shall include a reference to any predecessor of such corporation.

(2) Special rule for foreign-parented multinational groups.—

(A) In general.—If a corporation is a member of a foreign-parented multinational group for any taxable year, then, solely for purposes of determining whether such corporation meets the average annual adjusted financial statement income test under paragraph (1)(B)(ii)(I) for such taxable year, the adjusted financial statement income of such corporation for such taxable year shall include the adjusted financial statement income of all members of such group. Solely for purposes of this subparagraph, adjusted financial statement income shall be determined without regard to paragraphs (2)(D)(i), (3), (4), and (11) of section 56A(c).

(B) Foreign-parented multinational group.—For purposes of subparagraph (A), the term "foreign-parented multinational group" means, with respect to any taxable year, two or more entities if—

(i) at least one entity is a domestic corporation and another entity is a foreign corporation,

(ii) such entities are included in the same applicable financial statement with respect to such year, and

(iii) either—

(I) the common parent of such entities is a foreign corporation, or

(II) if there is no common parent, the entities are treated as having a common parent which is a foreign corporation under subparagraph (D).

(C) Foreign corporations engaged in a trade or business within the United States.—For purposes of this paragraph, if a foreign corporation is engaged in a trade or business within the United States, such trade or business shall be treated as a separate domestic corporation that is wholly owned by the foreign corporation.

(D) Other rules.—The Secretary shall, applying the principles of this section, prescribe rules for the application of this paragraph, including rules for the determination of—

(i) the entities (if any) which are to be to be treated under subparagraph (B)(iii)(II) as having a common parent which is a foreign corporation,

(ii) the entities to be included in a foreign-parented multinational group, and

(iii) the common parent of a foreign-parented multinational group.

(3) Regulations or other guidance.—The Secretary shall provide regulations or other guidance for the purposes of carrying out this subsection, including regulations or other guidance—

(A) providing a simplified method for determining whether a corporation meets the requirements of paragraph (1), and

(B) addressing the application of this subsection to a corporation that experiences a change in ownership.

(*l*) Corporate AMT foreign tax credit.—

(1) In general.—For purposes of this part, if an applicable corporation chooses to have the benefits of subpart A of part III of subchapter N for any taxable year, the corporate AMT foreign tax credit for the taxable year of the applicable corporation is an amount equal to sum of—

(A) the lesser of—

(i) the aggregate of the applicable corporation's pro rata share (as determined under section 56A(c)(3)) of the amount of income, war profits, and excess profits taxes (within the meaning of section 901) imposed by any foreign country or possession of the United States which are—

(I) taken into account on the applicable financial statement of each controlled foreign corporation with respect to which the applicable corporation is a United States shareholder, and

(II) paid or accrued (for Federal income tax purposes) by each such controlled foreign corporation, or

(ii) the product of the amount of the adjustment under section 56A(c)(3) and the percentage specified in section 55(b)(2)(A)(i), and

(B) in the case of an applicable corporation that is a domestic corporation, the amount of income, war profits, and excess profits taxes (within the meaning of section 901) imposed by any foreign country or possession of the United States to the extent such taxes are—

(i) taken into account on the applicable corporation's applicable financial statement, and

(ii) paid or accrued (for Federal income tax purposes) by the applicable corporation.

(2) Carryover of excess tax paid.—For any taxable year for which an applicable corporation chooses to have the benefits of subpart A of part III of subchapter N, the excess of the amount described in paragraph (1)(A)(i) over the amount described in paragraph (1)(A)(ii) shall increase the amount described in paragraph (1)(A)(i) in any of the first 5 succeeding taxable years to the extent not taken into account in a prior taxable year.

(3) Regulations or other guidance.—The Secretary shall provide for such regulations or other guidance as is necessary to carry out the purposes of this subsection.

Part VII—Base Erosion and Anti-Abuse Tax

§ 59A. Tax on base erosion payments of taxpayers with substantial gross receipts

(a) Imposition of tax.—There is hereby imposed on each applicable taxpayer for any taxable year a tax equal to the base erosion minimum tax amount for the taxable year. Such tax shall be in addition to any other tax imposed by this subtitle.

(b) Base erosion minimum tax amount.—For purposes of this section—

(1) In general.—Except as provided in paragraph (2), the term "base erosion minimum tax amount" means, with respect to any applicable taxpayer for any taxable year, the excess (if any) of—

(A) an amount equal to 10.5 percent (5 percent in the case of taxable years beginning in calendar year 2018) of the modified taxable income of such taxpayer for the taxable year, over

(B) an amount equal to the regular tax liability (as defined in section 26(b)) of the taxpayer for the taxable year, reduced (but not below zero) by the excess (if any) of—

(i) the credits allowed under this chapter against such regular tax liability, over

(ii) the sum of—

(I) the credit allowed under section 38 for the taxable year which is properly allocable to the research credit determined under section 41(a), plus

(II) the portion of the applicable section 38 credits not in excess of 80 percent of the lesser of the amount of such credits or the base erosion minimum tax amount (determined without regard to this subclause).

(2) Increased rate for certain banks and securities dealers.—

(A) In general.—In the case of a taxpayer described in subparagraph (B) who is an applicable taxpayer for any taxable year, the percentages otherwise in effect under paragraph (1)(A) shall be increased by one percentage point.

(B) Taxpayer described.—A taxpayer is described in this subparagraph if such taxpayer is a member of an affiliated group (as defined in section 1504(a)(1)) which includes—

(i) a bank (as defined in section 581), or

(ii) a securities dealer registered under section 15(a) of the Securities Exchange Act of 1934.

(3) Applicable section 38 credits.—For purposes of paragraph (1)(B)(ii)(II), the term "applicable section 38 credits" means the credit allowed under section 38 for the taxable year which is properly allocable to—

(A) the low-income housing credit determined under section 42(a),

(B) the renewable electricity production credit determined under section 45(a), and

(C) the investment credit determined under section 46, but only to the extent properly allocable to the energy credit determined under section 48.

(c) Modified taxable income.—For purposes of this section—

(1) In general.—The term "modified taxable income" means the taxable income of the taxpayer computed under this chapter for the taxable year, determined without regard to—

(A) any base erosion tax benefit with respect to any base erosion payment, or

(B) the base erosion percentage of any net operating loss deduction allowed under section 172 for the taxable year.

(2) Base erosion tax benefit.—

(A) In general.—The term "base erosion tax benefit" means—

(i) any deduction described in subsection (d)(1) which is allowed under this chapter for the taxable year with respect to any base erosion payment,

(ii) in the case of a base erosion payment described in subsection (d)(2), any deduction allowed under this chapter for the taxable year for depreciation (or amortization in lieu of depreciation) with respect to the property acquired with such payment,

(iii) in the case of a base erosion payment described in subsection (d)(3)—

(I) any reduction under section 803(a)(1)(B) in the gross amount of premiums and other consideration on insurance and annuity contracts for premiums and other consideration arising out of indemnity insurance, and

(II) any deduction under section 832(b)(4)(A) from the amount of gross premiums written on insurance contracts during the taxable year for premiums paid for reinsurance, and

(iv) in the case of a base erosion payment described in subsection (d)(4), any reduction in gross receipts with respect to such payment in computing gross income of the taxpayer for the taxable year for purposes of this chapter.

(B) Tax benefits disregarded if tax withheld on base erosion payment.—

(i) In general.—Except as provided in clause (ii), any base erosion tax benefit attributable to any base erosion payment—

(I) on which tax is imposed by section 871 or 881, and

(II) with respect to which tax has been deducted and withheld under section 1441 or 1442,

shall not be taken into account in computing modified taxable income under paragraph (1)(A) or the base erosion percentage under paragraph (4).

(ii) Exception.—The amount not taken into account in computing modified taxable income by reason of clause (i) shall be reduced under rules similar to the rules under section 163(j)(5)(B) (as in effect before the date of the enactment of the Tax Cuts and Jobs Act).

(3) Special rules for determining interest for which deduction allowed.—For purposes of applying paragraph (1), in the case of a taxpayer to which section 163(j) applies for the taxable year, the reduction in the amount of interest for which a deduction is allowed by reason of such subsection shall be treated as allocable first to interest paid or accrued to persons who are not related parties with respect to the taxpayer and then to such related parties.

(4) Base erosion percentage.—For purposes of paragraph (1)(B)—

(A) In general.—The term "base erosion percentage" means, for any taxable year, the percentage determined by dividing—

(i) the aggregate amount of base erosion tax benefits of the taxpayer for the taxable year, by

(ii) the sum of—

(I) the aggregate amount of the deductions (including deductions described in clauses (i) and (ii) of paragraph (2)(A)) allowable to the taxpayer under this chapter for the taxable year, plus

(II) the base erosion tax benefits described in clauses (iii) and (iv) of paragraph (2)(A) allowable to the taxpayer for the taxable year.

(B) Certain items not taken into account.—The amount under subparagraph (A)(ii) shall be determined by not taking into account—

(i) any deduction allowed under section 172, 245A, or 250 for the taxable year,

(ii) any deduction for amounts paid or accrued for services to which the exception under subsection (d)(5) applies, and

(iii) any deduction for qualified derivative payments which are not treated as a base erosion payment by reason of subsection (h).

(d) Base erosion payment.—For purposes of this section—

(1) In general.—The term "base erosion payment" means any amount paid or accrued by the taxpayer to a foreign person which is a related party of the taxpayer and with respect to which a deduction is allowable under this chapter.

(2) Purchase of depreciable property.—Such term shall also include any amount paid or accrued by the taxpayer to a foreign person which is a related party of the taxpayer in connection with the acquisition by the taxpayer from such person of property of a character subject to the allowance for depreciation (or amortization in lieu of depreciation).

(3) Reinsurance payments.—Such term shall also include any premium or other consideration paid or accrued by the taxpayer to a foreign person which is a related party of the taxpayer for any reinsurance payments which are taken into account under sections 803(a)(1)(B) or 832(b)(4)(A).

(4) Certain payments to expatriated entities.—

(A) In general.—Such term shall also include any amount paid or accrued by the taxpayer with respect to a person described in subparagraph (B) which results in a reduction of the gross receipts of the taxpayer.

(B) Person described.—A person is described in this subparagraph if such person is a—

(i) surrogate foreign corporation which is a related party of the taxpayer, but only if such person first became a surrogate foreign corporation after November 9, 2017, or

(ii) foreign person which is a member of the same expanded affiliated group as the surrogate foreign corporation.

(C) Definitions.—For purposes of this paragraph—

(i) Surrogate foreign corporation.—The term "surrogate foreign corporation" has the meaning given such term by section 7874(a)(2)(B) but does not include a foreign corporation treated as a domestic corporation under section 7874(b).

(ii) Expanded affiliated group.—The term "expanded affiliated group" has the meaning given such term by section 7874(c)(1).

(5) Exception for certain amounts with respect to services.—Paragraph (1) shall not apply to any amount paid or accrued by a taxpayer for services if—

(A) such services are services which meet the requirements for eligibility for use of the services cost method under section 482(determined without regard to the requirement that the services not contribute significantly to fundamental risks of business success or failure), and

(B) such amount constitutes the total services cost with no markup component.

(e) Applicable taxpayer.—For purposes of this section—

(1) In general.—The term "applicable taxpayer" means, with respect to any taxable year, a taxpayer—

(A) which is a corporation other than a regulated investment company, a real estate investment trust, or an S corporation,

(B) the average annual gross receipts of which for the 3-taxable-year period ending with the preceding taxable year are at least $500,000,000, and

(C) the base erosion percentage (as determined under subsection (c)(4)) of which for the taxable year is 3 percent (2 percent in the case of a taxpayer described in subsection (b)(2)(B)) or higher.

(2) Gross receipts.—

(A) Special rule for foreign persons.—In the case of a foreign person the gross receipts of which are taken into account for purposes of paragraph (1)(B), only gross receipts which are taken into account in determining income which is effectively connected with the conduct of a trade or business within the United States shall be taken into account. In the case of a taxpayer which is a foreign person, the preceding sentence shall not apply to the gross receipts of any United States person which are aggregated with the taxpayer's gross receipts by reason of paragraph (3).

(B) Other rules made applicable.—Rules similar to the rules of subparagraphs (B), (C), and (D) of section 448(c)(3) shall apply in determining gross receipts for purposes of this section.

(3) Aggregation rules.—All persons treated as a single employer under subsection (a) of section 52 shall be treated as 1 person for purposes of this subsection and subsection (c)(4), except that in applying section 1563 for purposes of section 52, the exception for foreign corporations under section 1563(b)(2)(C) shall be disregarded.

(f) Foreign person.—For purposes of this section, the term 'foreign person' has the meaning given such term by section 6038A(c)(3).

(g) Related party.—For purposes of this section—

(1) In general.—The term "related party" means, with respect to any applicable taxpayer—

(A) any 25-percent owner of the taxpayer,

(B) any person who is related (within the meaning of section 267(b) or 707(b)(1)) to the taxpayer or any 25-percent owner of the taxpayer, and

(C) any other person who is related (within the meaning of section 482) to the taxpayer.

(2) 25-percent owner.—The term "25-percent owner" means, with respect to any corporation, any person who owns at least 25 percent of—

(A) the total voting power of all classes of stock of a corporation entitled to vote, or

(B) the total value of all classes of stock of such corporation.

(3) Section 318 to apply.—Section 318 shall apply for purposes of paragraphs (1) and (2), except that—

(A) "10 percent" shall be substituted for "50 percent" in section 318(a)(2)(C), and

(B) subparagraphs (A), (B), and (C) of section 318(a)(3) shall not be applied so as to consider a United States person as owning stock which is owned by a person who is not a United States person.

(h) Exception for certain payments made in the ordinary course of trade or business.—For purposes of this section—

(1) In general.—Except as provided in paragraph (3), any qualified derivative payment shall not be treated as a base erosion payment.

(2) Qualified derivative payment.—

(A) In general.—The term "qualified derivative payment" means any payment made by a taxpayer pursuant to a derivative with respect to which the taxpayer—

(i) recognizes gain or loss as if such derivative were sold for its fair market value on the last business day of the taxable year (and such additional times as required by this title or the taxpayer's method of accounting),

(ii) treats any gain or loss so recognized as ordinary, and

(iii) treats the character of all items of income, deduction, gain, or loss with respect to a payment pursuant to the derivative as ordinary.

(B) Reporting requirement.—No payments shall be treated as qualified derivative payments under subparagraph (A) for any taxable year unless the taxpayer includes in the information required to be reported under section 6038A(b)(2) with respect to such taxable year such information as is necessary to identify the payments to be so treated and such other information as the Secretary determines necessary to carry out the provisions of this subsection.

(3) Exceptions for payments otherwise treated as base erosion payments.—This subsection shall not apply to any qualified derivative payment if—

(A) the payment would be treated as a base erosion payment if it were not made pursuant to a derivative, including any interest, royalty, or service payment, or

(B) in the case of a contract which has derivative and nonderivative components, the payment is properly allocable to the nonderivative component.

(4) Derivative defined.—For purposes of this subsection—

(A) In general.—The term "derivative" means any contract (including any option, forward contract, futures contract, short position, swap, or similar contract) the value of which, or any payment or other transfer with respect to which, is (directly or indirectly) determined by reference to one or more of the following:

(i) Any share of stock in a corporation.

(ii) Any evidence of indebtedness.

(iii) Any commodity which is actively traded.

(iv) Any currency.

(v) Any rate, price, amount, index, formula, or algorithm.

Such term shall not include any item described in clauses (i) through (v).

(B) Treatment of american depository receipts and similar instruments.—Except as otherwise provided by the Secretary, for purposes of this part, American depository receipts (and similar instruments) with respect to shares of stock in foreign corporations shall be treated as shares of stock in such foreign corporations.

(C) Exception for certain contracts.—Such term shall not include any insurance, annuity, or endowment contract issued by an insurance company to which subchapter L applies (or issued by any foreign corporation to which such subchapter would apply if such foreign corporation were a domestic corporation).

(i) Regulations.—The Secretary shall prescribe such regulations or other guidance as may be necessary or appropriate to carry out the provisions of this section, including regulations—

(1) providing for such adjustments to the application of this section as are necessary to prevent the avoidance of the purposes of this section, including through—

(A) the use of unrelated persons, conduit transactions, or other intermediaries, or

(B) transactions or arrangements designed, in whole or in part—

(i) to characterize payments otherwise subject to this section as payments not subject to this section, or

(ii) to substitute payments not subject to this section for payments otherwise subject to this section and

(2) for the application of subsection (h), including rules to prevent the avoidance of the exceptions under subsection (h)(3).

Subchapter B—Computation of Taxable Income

Part I—Definition of Gross Income, Adjusted Gross Income, Taxable Income, Etc.

§ 61. Gross income defined

(a) General definition.—Except as otherwise provided in this subtitle, gross income means all income from whatever source derived, including (but not limited to) the following items:

(1) Compensation for services, including fees, commissions, fringe benefits, and similar items;

(2) Gross income derived from business;

(3) Gains derived from dealings in property;

(4) Interest;

(5) Rents;

(6) Royalties;

(7) Dividends;

(8) Annuities;

(9) Income from life insurance and endowment contracts;

(10) Pensions;

(11) Income from discharge of indebtedness;

(12) Distributive share of partnership gross income;

(13) Income in respect of a decedent; and

(14) Income from an interest in an estate or trust.

(b) Cross references.—

For items specifically included in gross income, see part II (sec. 71 and following). For items specifically excluded from gross income, see part III (sec. 101 and following).

§ 62. Adjusted gross income defined

(a) General rule.—For purposes of this subtitle, the term "adjusted gross income" means, in the case of an individual, gross income minus the following deductions:

(1) Trade and business deductions.—The deductions allowed by this chapter (other than by part VII of this subchapter) which are attributable to a trade or business carried on by the taxpayer, if such trade or business does not consist of the performance of services by the taxpayer as an employee.

(2) Certain trade and business deductions of employees.—

(A) Reimbursed expenses of employees.—The deductions allowed by part VI (section 161 and following) which consist of expenses paid or incurred by the taxpayer, in connection with the performance by him of services as an employee, under a reimbursement or other expense allowance arrangement with his employer. The fact that the reimbursement may be provided by a third party shall not be determinative of whether or not the preceding sentence applies.

* * *

(3) Losses from sale or exchange of property.—The deductions allowed by part VI (sec. 161 and following) as losses from the sale or exchange of property.

(4) Deductions attributable to rents and royalties.—The deductions allowed by part VI (sec. 161 and following), by section 212 (relating to expenses for production of income), and by section 611 (relating to depletion) which are attributable to property held for the production of rents or royalties.

* * *

§ 63. Taxable income defined

(a) In general.—Except as provided in subsection (b), for purposes of this subtitle, the term "taxable income" means gross income minus the deductions allowed by this chapter (other than the standard deduction).

(b) Individuals who do not itemize their deductions.—In the case of an individual who does not elect to itemize his deductions for the taxable year, for purposes of this subtitle, the term "taxable income" means adjusted gross income, minus—

(1) the standard deduction,

(2) the deduction for personal exemptions provided in section 151,

(3) any deduction provided in section 199A,

(4) the deduction provided in section 170(p),

(5) the deduction provided in section 224,

(6) the deduction provided in section 225 and

(7) so much of the deduction allowed by section 163(a) as is attributable to the exception under section 163(h)(4)(A).

(c) Standard deduction.—For purposes of this subtitle—

(1) In general.—Except as otherwise provided in this subsection, the term "standard deduction" means the sum of—

(A) the basic standard deduction, and

(B) the additional standard deduction.

(2) Basic standard deduction.—For purposes of paragraph (1), the basic standard deduction is—

(A) 200 percent of the dollar amount in effect under subparagraph (C) for the taxable year in the case of—

(i) a joint return, or

(ii) a surviving spouse (as defined in section 2(a)),

(B) $4,400 in the case of a head of household (as defined in section 2(b)), or

(C) $3,000 in any other case.

(3) Additional standard deduction for aged and blind.—For purposes of paragraph (1), the additional standard deduction is the sum of each additional amount to which the taxpayer is entitled under subsection (f).

(4) Adjustments for inflation.—In the case of any taxable year beginning in a calendar year after 1988, each dollar amount contained in paragraph (2)(B), (2)(C), or (5) or subsection (f) shall be increased by an amount equal to—

(A) such dollar amount, multiplied by

(B) the cost-of-living adjustment determined under section 1(f)(3) for the calendar year in which the taxable year begins * * *.

* * *

(7) Special rules for taxable years beginning after 2017.—In the case of a taxable year beginning after December 31, 2017—

(A) Increase in standard deduction.—Paragraph (2) shall be applied—

(i) by substituting "$23,625" for "$4,400" in subparagraph (B), and

(ii) by substituting "$15,750" for "$3,000" in subparagraph (C).

(B) Adjustment for inflation.—

(i) In general.—Paragraph (4) shall not apply to the dollar amounts contained in paragraphs (2)(B) and (2)(C).

(ii) Adjustment of increased amounts.—In the case of a taxable year beginning after 2025, the $23,625 and $15,750 amounts in subparagraph (A) shall each be increased by an amount equal to—

(I) such dollar amount, multiplied by

(II) the cost-of-living adjustment determined under section 1(f)(3) for the calendar year in which the taxable year begins, determined by substituting "2024" for "2016" in subparagraph (A)(ii) thereof.

If any increase under this clause is not a multiple of $50, such increase shall be rounded to the next lowest multiple of $50.

* * *

Part II—Items Specifically Included in Gross Income

§ 78. Gross up for deemed paid foreign tax credit

If a domestic corporation chooses to have the benefits of subpart A of part III of subchapter N (relating to foreign tax credit) for any taxable year, an amount equal to the taxes deemed to be paid by such corporation under subsections (a) and (d) of section 960 (determined without regard to the phrase "90 percent of" in subsection (d)(1) thereof) for such taxable year shall be treated for purposes of this title (other than sections 245 and 245A) as a dividend received by such domestic corporation from the foreign corporation.

§ 91. Certain foreign branch losses transferred to specified 10-percent owned foreign corporations

(a) In general.—If a domestic corporation transfers substantially all of the assets of a foreign branch (within the meaning of section 367(a)(3)(C), as in effect before the date of the enactment of the Tax Cuts and Jobs Act) to a specified 10-percent owned foreign corporation (as defined in section 245A) with respect to which it is a United States shareholder after such transfer, such domestic corporation shall include in gross income for the taxable year which includes such transfer an amount equal to the transferred loss amount with respect to such transfer.

(b) Transferred loss amount.—For purposes of this section, the term "transferred loss amount" means, with respect to any transfer of substantially all of the assets of a foreign branch, the excess (if any) of—

(1) the sum of losses—

(A) which were incurred by the foreign branch after December 31, 2017, and before the transfer, and

(B) with respect to which a deduction was allowed to the taxpayer, over

(2) the sum of—

(A) any taxable income of such branch for a taxable year after the taxable year in which the loss was incurred and through the close of the taxable year of the transfer, and

(B) any amount which is recognized under section 904(f)(3) on account of the transfer.

(c) Reduction for recognized gains.—The transferred loss amount shall be reduced (but not below zero) by the amount of gain recognized by the taxpayer on account of the transfer (other than amounts taken into account under subsection (b)(2)(B)).

(d) Source of income.—Amounts included in gross income under this section shall be treated as derived from sources within the United States.

(e) Basis adjustments.—Consistent with such regulations or other guidance as the Secretary shall prescribe, proper adjustments shall be made in the adjusted basis of the taxpayer's stock in the specified 10-percent owned foreign corporation to which the transfer is made, and in the transferee's adjusted basis in the property transferred, to reflect amounts included in gross income under this section.

Part III—Items Specifically Excluded from Gross Income

§ 103. Interest on State and local bonds

(a) Exclusion.—Except as provided in subsection (b), gross income does not include interest on any State or local bond.

(b) Exceptions.—Subsection (a) shall not apply to—

(1) Private activity bond which is not a qualified bond.—Any private activity bond which is not a qualified bond (within the meaning of section 141).

(2) Arbitrage bond.—Any arbitrage bond (within the meaning of section 148).

(3) Bond not in registered form, etc.—Any bond unless such bond meets the applicable requirements of section 149.

(c) Definitions.—For purposes of this section and part IV—

(1) State or local bond.—The term "State or local bond" means an obligation of a State or political subdivision thereof.

(2) State.—The term "State" includes the District of Columbia and any possession of the United States.

Part VI—Itemized Deductions for Individuals and Corporations

§ 162. Trade or business expenses

(a) In general.—There shall be allowed as a deduction all the ordinary and necessary expenses paid or incurred during the taxable year in carrying on any trade or business, including—

(1) a reasonable allowance for salaries or other compensation for personal services actually rendered;

(2) traveling expenses (including amounts expended for meals and lodging other than amounts which are lavish or extravagant under the circumstances) while away from home in the pursuit of a trade or business; and

(3) rentals or other payments required to be made as a condition to the continued use or possession, for purposes of the trade or business, of property to which the taxpayer has not taken or is not taking title or in which he has no equity.

* * *

(c) Illegal bribes, kickbacks, and other payments.—

(1) Illegal payments to government officials or employees.—No deduction shall be allowed under subsection (a) for any payment made, directly or indirectly, to an official or employee of any government, or of any agency or instrumentality of any government, if the payment constitutes an illegal bribe or kickback or, if the payment is to an official or employee of a foreign government, the payment is unlawful under the Foreign Corrupt Practices Act of 1977. The burden of proof in respect of the issue, for the purposes of this paragraph, as to whether a payment constitutes an illegal bribe or kickback (or is unlawful under the Foreign Corrupt Practices Act of 1977) shall be upon the Secretary to the same extent as he bears the burden of proof under section 7454 (concerning the burden of proof when the issue relates to fraud).

* * *

§ 163. Interest

(a) General rule.—There shall be allowed as a deduction all interest paid or accrued within the taxable year on indebtedness.

* * *

(f) Denial of deduction for interest on certain obligations not in registered form.—

(1) In general.—Nothing in subsection (a) or in any other provision of law shall be construed to provide a deduction for interest on any registration-required obligation unless such obligation is in registered form.

(2) Registration-required obligation.—For purposes of this section—

(A) In general.—The term "registration-required obligation" means any obligation (including any obligation issued by a governmental entity) other than an obligation which—

(i) is issued by a natural person,

(ii) is not of a type offered to the public, or

(iii) has a maturity (at issue) of not more than 1 year.

(B) Authority to include other obligations.—Clauses (ii) and (iii) of subparagraph (A), and subparagraph (B), shall not apply to any obligation if—

(i) in the case of—

(I) subparagraph (A), such obligation is of a type which the Secretary has determined by regulations to be used frequently in avoiding Federal taxes, or

(II) subparagraph (B), such obligation is of a type specified by the Secretary in regulations, and

(ii) such obligation is issued after the date on which the regulations referred to in clause (i) take effect.

(3) Book entries permitted, etc.—For purposes of this subsection, rules similar to the rules of section 149(a)(3) shall apply.

* * *

(j) Limitation on business interest.—

(1) In general.—The amount allowed as a deduction under this chapter for any taxable year for business interest shall not exceed the sum of—

(A) the business interest income of such taxpayer for such taxable year,

(B) 30 percent of the adjusted taxable income of such taxpayer for such taxable year, plus

(C) the floor plan financing interest of such taxpayer for such taxable year.

The amount determined under subparagraph (B) shall not be less than zero.

(2) Carryforward of disallowed business interest.—The amount of any business interest not allowed as a deduction for any taxable year by reason of paragraph (1) shall be treated as business interest paid or accrued in the succeeding taxable year.

(3) Exemption for certain small businesses.—In the case of any taxpayer (other than a tax shelter prohibited from using the cash receipts and disbursements method of accounting under section 448(a)(3)) which meets the gross receipts test of section 448(c) for any taxable year, paragraph (1) shall not apply to such taxpayer for such taxable year. In the case of any taxpayer which is not a corporation or a partnership, the gross receipts test of section 448(c) shall be applied in the same manner as if such taxpayer were a corporation or partnership.

(4) Application to partnerships, etc.—

(A) In general.—In the case of any partnership—

(i) this subsection shall be applied at the partnership level and any deduction for business interest shall be taken into account in determining the non-separately stated taxable income or loss of the partnership, and

(ii) the adjusted taxable income of each partner of such partnership—

(I) shall be determined without regard to such partner's distributive share of any items of income, gain, deduction, or loss of such partnership, and

(II) shall be increased by such partner's distributive share of such partnership's excess taxable income.

For purposes of clause (ii)(II), a partner's distributive share of partnership excess taxable income shall be determined in the same manner as the partner's distributive share of nonseparately stated taxable income or loss of the partnership.

(B) Special rules for carryforwards.—

(i) In general.—The amount of any business interest not allowed as a deduction to a partnership for any taxable year by reason of paragraph (1) for any taxable year—

(I) shall not be treated under paragraph (2) as business interest paid or accrued by the partnership in the succeeding taxable year, and

(II) shall, subject to clause (ii), be treated as excess business interest which is allocated to each partner in the same manner as the non-separately stated taxable income or loss of the partnership.

(ii) Treatment of excess business interest allocated to partners.—If a partner is allocated any excess business interest from a partnership under clause (i) for any taxable year—

(I) such excess business interest shall be treated as business interest paid or accrued by the partner in the next succeeding taxable year in which the partner is allocated excess taxable income from such partnership, but only to the extent of such excess taxable income, and

(II) any portion of such excess business interest remaining after the application of subclause (I) shall, subject to the limitations of subclause (I), be treated as business interest paid or accrued in succeeding taxable years.

For purposes of applying this paragraph, excess taxable income allocated to a partner from a partnership for any taxable year shall not be taken into account under paragraph (1)(A) with respect to any business interest other than excess business interest from the partnership until all such excess business interest for such taxable year and all preceding taxable years has been treated as paid or accrued under clause (ii).

(iii) Basis adjustments.—

(I) In general.—The adjusted basis of a partner in a partnership interest shall be reduced (but not below zero) by the amount of excess business interest allocated to the partner under clause (i)(II).

(II) Special rule for dispositions.—If a partner disposes of a partnership interest, the adjusted basis of the partner in the partnership interest shall be increased immediately before the disposition by the amount of the excess (if any) of the amount of the basis reduction under subclause (I) over the portion of any excess business interest allocated to the partner under clause (i)(II) which has previously been treated under clause (ii) as business interest paid or accrued by the partner. The preceding sentence shall also apply to transfers of the partnership interest (including by reason of death) in a transaction in which gain is not recognized in whole or in part. No deduction shall be allowed to the transferor or transferee under this chapter for any excess business interest resulting in a basis increase under this subclause.

(C) Excess taxable income.—The term "excess taxable income" means, with respect to any partnership, the amount which bears the same ratio to the partnership's adjusted taxable income as—

(i) the excess (if any) of—

(I) the amount determined for the partnership under paragraph (1)(B), over

(II) the amount (if any) by which the business interest of the partnership, reduced by the floor plan financing interest, exceeds the business interest income of the partnership, bears to

(ii) the amount determined for the partnership under paragraph (1)(B).

(D) Application to S corporations.—Rules similar to the rules of subparagraphs (A) and (C) shall apply with respect to any S corporation and its shareholders.

(5) Business interest.—For purposes of this subsection, the term "business interest" means any interest paid or accrued on indebtedness properly allocable to a trade or business. Such term shall not include investment interest (within the meaning of subsection (d)). Such term shall not include any interest which is capitalized under section 263(g) or 263A(f).

(6) Business interest income.—For purposes of this subsection, the term "business interest income" means the amount of interest includible in the gross income of the taxpayer for the taxable year which is properly allocable to a trade or business. Such term shall not include investment income (within the meaning of subsection (d)).

(7) Trade or business.—For purposes of this subsection—

(A) In general.—The term 'trade or business' shall not include—

(i) the trade or business of performing services as an employee,

(ii) any electing real property trade or business,

(iii) any electing farming business, or

(iv) the trade or business of the furnishing or sale of—

(I) electrical energy, water, or sewage disposal services,

(II) gas or steam through a local distribution system, or

(III) transportation of gas or steam by pipeline,

if the rates for such furnishing or sale, as the case may be, have been established or approved by a State or political subdivision thereof, by any agency or instrumentality of the United States, by a public service or public utility commission or other similar body of any State or political subdivision thereof, or by the governing or ratemaking body of an electric cooperative.

(B) Electing real property trade or business.—For purposes of this paragraph, the term "electing real property trade or business" means any trade or business which is described in section 469(c)(7)(C) and which makes an election under this subparagraph. Any such election shall be made at such time and in such manner as the Secretary shall prescribe, and, once made, shall be irrevocable.

(C) Electing farming business.—For purposes of this paragraph, the term "electing farming business" means—

(i) a farming business (as defined in section 263A(e)(4)) which makes an election under this subparagraph, or

(ii) any trade or business of a specified agricultural or horticultural cooperative (as defined in section 199A(g)(2)3) with respect to which the cooperative makes an election under this subparagraph.

Any such election shall be made at such time and in such manner as the Secretary shall prescribe, and, once made, shall be irrevocable.

(8) Adjusted taxable income.—For purposes of this subsection, the term "adjusted taxable income" means the taxable income of the taxpayer—

(A) computed without regard to—

(i) any item of income, gain, deduction, or loss which is not properly allocable to a trade or business,

(ii) any business interest or business interest income,

(iii) the amount of any net operating loss deduction under section 172,

(iv) the amount of any deduction allowed under section 199A,

(v) any deduction allowable for depreciation, amortization, or depletion, and

(vi) the amounts included in gross income under sections 951(a), 951A(a), and 78 (and the portion of the deductions allowed under sections 245A(a) (by reason of section 964(e)(4)) and 250(a)(1)(B) by reason of such inclusions), and

(B) computed with such other adjustments as provided by the Secretary.

(9) Floor plan financing interest defined.—For purposes of this subsection—

(A) In general.—The term "floor plan financing interest" means interest paid or accrued on floor plan financing indebtedness.

(B) Floor plan financing indebtedness.—The term "floor plan financing indebtedness" means indebtedness—

(i) used to finance the acquisition of motor vehicles held for sale or lease, and

(ii) secured by the inventory so acquired.

(C) Motor vehicle.—The term "motor vehicle" means a motor vehicle that is any of the following:

(i) Any self-propelled vehicle designed for transporting persons or property on a public street, highway, or road.

(ii) A boat.

(iii) Farm machinery or equipment.

* * *

(11) Regulatory authority.—The Secretary shall issue such regulations or guidance as may be necessary or appropriate to carry out the purposes of this subsection, including regulations or guidance to determine which business interest is taken into account under this subsection and section 59A(c)(3).

* * *

(13) Cross references.—

(A) For requirement that an electing real property trade or business use the alternative depreciation system, see section 168(g)(1)(F).

(B) For requirement that an electing farming business use the alternative depreciation system, see section 168(g)(1)(G).

* * *

§ 164. Taxes

(a) General rule.—Except as otherwise provided in this section, the following taxes shall be allowed as a deduction for the taxable year within which paid or accrued:

(1) State and local, and foreign, real property taxes.

(2) State and local personal property taxes.

(3) State and local, and foreign, income, war profits, and excess profits taxes.

(4) The GST tax imposed on income distributions.

In addition, there shall be allowed as a deduction State and local, and foreign, taxes not described in the preceding sentence which are paid or accrued within the taxable year in carrying on a trade or business or an activity described in section 212 (relating to expenses for production of income). Notwithstanding the preceding sentence, any tax (not described in the first sentence of this subsection) which is paid or accrued by the taxpayer in connection with an acquisition or disposition of property shall be treated as part of the cost of the acquired property or, in the case of a disposition, as a reduction in the amount realized on the disposition.

* * *

(b) Definitions and special rules.—For purposes of this section—

* * *

(3) Foreign taxes.—A foreign tax includes only a tax imposed by the authority of a foreign country.

* * *

(6) Limitation on individual deductions for taxable years 2018 through 2025.—In the case of an individual and a taxable year beginning after December 31, 2017,—

(A) foreign real property taxes shall not be taken into account under subsection (a)(1), and

(B) the aggregate amount of taxes taken into account under paragraphs (1), (2), and (3) of subsection (a) and paragraph (5) of this subsection for any taxable year shall not exceed the applicable limitation amount (half the applicable limitation amount in the case of a married individual filing a separate return).

The preceding sentence shall not apply to any foreign taxes described in subsection (a)(3) or to any taxes described in paragraph (1) and (2) of subsection (a) which are paid or accrued in carrying on a trade or business or an activity described in section 212. For purposes of subparagraph (B), an amount paid in a taxable year beginning before January 1, 2018, with respect to a State or local income tax imposed for a taxable year beginning after December 31, 2017, shall be treated as paid on the last day of the taxable year for which such tax is so imposed.

(7) Applicable limitation amount.—

(A) In general.—For purposes of paragraph (6), the term "applicable limitation amount" means—

(i) in the case of any taxable year beginning in calendar year 2025, $40,000,

(ii) in the case of any taxable year beginning in calendar year 2026, $40,400,

(iii) in the case of any taxable year beginning after calendar year 2026 and before 2030, 101 percent of the dollar amount in effect under this subparagraph for taxable years beginning in the preceding calendar year, and

(iv) in the case of any taxable year beginning after calendar year 2029, $10,000.

(B) Phasedown based on modified adjusted gross income.—

(i) In general.—Except as provided in clause (iii), in the case of any taxable year beginning before January 1, 2030, the applicable limitation amount shall be reduced by 30 percent of the excess (if any) of the taxpayer's modified adjusted gross income over the threshold amount (half the threshold amount in the case of a married individual filing a separate return).

(ii) Threshold amount.—For purposes of this subparagraph, the term "threshold amount" means—

(I) in the case of any taxable year beginning in calendar year 2025, $500,000,

(II) in the case of any taxable year beginning in calendar year 2026, $505,000, and

(III) in the case of any taxable year beginning after calendar year 2026, 101 percent of the dollar amount in effect under this subparagraph for taxable years beginning in the preceding calendar year.

(iii) Limitation on reduction.—The reduction under clause (i) shall not result in the applicable limitation amount being less than $10,000.

(iv) Modified adjusted gross income.—For purposes of this paragraph, the term "modified adjusted gross income" means adjusted gross income increased by any amount excluded from gross income under section 911, 931, or 933.

* * *

(g) Cross references.—

(1) For provisions disallowing any deduction for certain taxes, see section 275.

* * *

§ 168. Accelerated cost recovery system

(a) General rule.—Except as otherwise provided in this section, the depreciation deduction provided by section 167(a) for any tangible property shall be determined by using—

(1) the applicable depreciation method,

(2) the applicable recovery period, and

(3) the applicable convention.

(b) Applicable depreciation method.—For purposes of this section—

(1) In general.—Except as provided in paragraphs (2) and (3), the applicable depreciation method is—

(A) the 200 percent declining balance method,

(B) switching to the straight line method for the 1st taxable year for which using the straight line method with respect to the adjusted basis as of the beginning of such year will yield a larger allowance.

(2) 150 percent declining balance method in certain cases.—Paragraph (1) shall be applied by substituting "150 percent" for "200 percent" in the case of—

(A) any 15-year or 20-year property not referred to in paragraph (3),

* * *

(C) any property (other than property described in paragraph (3)) with respect to which the taxpayer elects under paragraph (5) to have the provisions of this paragraph apply.

(3) Property to which straight line method applies.—The applicable depreciation method shall be the straight line method in the case of the following property:

(A) Nonresidential real property.

(B) Residential rental property.

(C) Any railroad grading or tunnel bore.

(D) Property with respect to which the taxpayer elects under paragraph (5) to have the provisions of this paragraph apply.

* * *

(G) Qualified improvement property described in subsection (e)(6).

(4) Salvage value treated as zero.—Salvage value shall be treated as zero.

(5) Election.—An election under paragraph (2)(D) or (3)(D) may be made with respect to 1 or more classes of property for any taxable year and once made with respect to any class shall apply to all property in such class placed in service during such taxable year. Such an election, once made, shall be irrevocable.

(c) Applicable recovery period.—For purposes of this section, the applicable recovery period shall be determined in accordance with the following table:

In the case of:	*The applicable recovery period is:*
3-year property	3 years

5-year property	5 years
7-year property	7 years
10-year property	10 years
15-year property	15 years
20-year property	20 years
Water utility property	25 years
Residential rental property	27.5 years
Nonresidential real property	39 years
Any railroad grading or tunnel bore	50 years.

(d) Applicable convention.—For purposes of this section—

(1) In general.—Except as otherwise provided in this subsection, the applicable convention is the half-year convention.

(2) Real property.—In the case of—

(A) nonresidential real property,

(B) residential rental property, and

(C) any railroad grading or tunnel bore, the applicable convention is the mid-month convention.

* * *

(4) Definitions.—

(A) Half-year convention.—The half-year convention is a convention which treats all property placed in service during any taxable year (or disposed of during any taxable year) as placed in service (or disposed of) on the mid-point of such taxable year.

(B) Mid-month convention.—The mid-month convention is a convention which treats all property placed in service during any month (or disposed of during any month) as placed in service (or disposed of) on the mid-point of such month.

* * *

(e) Classification of property.—For purposes of this section—

(1) In general.—Except as otherwise provided in this subsection, property shall be classified under the following table:

Property shall be treated as:	*If such property has a class life (in years) of:*
3-year property	4 or less
5-year property	More than 4 but less than 10
7-year property	10 or more but less than 16
10-year property	16 or more but less than 20

15-year property	20 or more but less than 25
20-year property	25 or more.

(2) Residential rental or nonresidential real property.—

(A) Residential rental property.—

(i) Residential rental property.—The term "residential rental property" means any building or structure if 80 percent or more of the gross rental income from such building or structure for the taxable year is rental income from dwelling units.

(ii) Definitions.—For purposes of clause (i)—

(I) the term "dwelling unit" means a house or apartment used to provide living accommodations in a building or structure, but does not include a unit in a hotel, motel, or other establishment more than one-half of the units in which are used on a transient basis, and

(II) if any portion of the building or structure is occupied by the taxpayer, the gross rental income from such building or structure shall include the rental value of the portion so occupied.

(B) Nonresidential real property.—The term "nonresidential real property" means section 1250 property which is not—

(i) residential rental property, or

(ii) property with a class life of less than 27.5 years.

* * *

(f) Property to which section does not apply.—This section shall not apply to—

(1) Certain methods of depreciation.—Any property if—

(A) the taxpayer elects to exclude such property from the application of this section, and

(B) for the 1st taxable year for which a depreciation deduction would be allowable with respect to such property in the hands of the taxpayer, the property is properly depreciated under the unit-of-production method or any method of depreciation not expressed in a term of years (other than the retirement-replacement-betterment method or similar method).

* * *

(g) Alternative depreciation system for certain property.—

(1) In general.—In the case of—

(A) any tangible property which during the taxable year is used predominantly outside the United States,

* * *

the depreciation deduction provided by section 167(a) shall be determined under the alternative depreciation system.

(2) Alternative depreciation system.—For purposes of paragraph (1), the alternative depreciation system is depreciation determined by using—

(A) the straight line method (without regard to salvage value),

(B) the applicable convention determined under subsection (d), and

(C) a recovery period determined under the following table:

In the case of:	*The recovery period shall be:*
(i) Property not described in clause (ii) or (iii)	The class life.
(ii) Personal property with no class life	12 years.
(iii) Residential rental property	30 years.
(iv) Nonresidential real property	40 years.

* * *

(7) Election to use alternative depreciation system.—

(A) In general.—If the taxpayer makes an election under this paragraph with respect to any class of property for any taxable year, the alternative depreciation system under this subsection shall apply to all property in such class placed in service during such taxable year. Notwithstanding the preceding sentence, in the case of nonresidential real property or residential rental property, such election may be made separately with respect to each property.

(B) Election irrevocable.—An election under subparagraph (A), once made, shall be irrevocable.

* * *

(i) Definitions and special rules.—For purposes of this section—

(1) Class life.—Except as provided in this section, the term "class life" means the class life (if any) which would be applicable with respect to any property as of January 1, 1986, under subsection (m) of section 167 (determined without regard to paragraph (4) and as if the taxpayer had made an election under such subsection). The Secretary, through an office established in the Treasury, shall monitor and analyze actual experience with respect to all depreciable assets. The reference in this paragraph to subsection (m) of section 167 shall be treated as a reference to such subsection as in effect on the day before the date of the enactment of the Revenue Reconciliation Act of 1990.

* * *

(k) Special allowance for certain property.—

(1) Additional allowance.—In the case of any qualified property—

(A) the depreciation deduction provided by section 167(a) for the taxable year in which such property is placed in service shall include an allowance equal to 100 percent of the adjusted basis of the qualified property, and

(B) the adjusted basis of the qualified property shall be reduced by the amount of such deduction before computing the amount otherwise allowable as a depreciation deduction under this chapter for such taxable year and any subsequent taxable year.

(2) Qualified property.—For purposes of this subsection—

(A) In general.—The term "qualified property" means property—

(i)(I) to which this section applies which has a recovery period of 20 years or less,

(II) which is computer software (as defined in section 167(f)(1)(B)) for which a deduction is allowable under section 167(a) without regard to this subsection,

* * *

(ii) the original use of which begins with the taxpayer or the acquisition of which by the taxpayer meets the requirements of clause (i) of subparagraph (E).

(B) Certain property having longer production periods treated as qualified property.—

(i) In general.—The term "qualified property" includes any property if such property—

(I) meets the requirements of clauses (i) and (ii) of subparagraph (A),

(II) has a recovery period of at least 10 years or is transportation property,

(III) is subject to section 263A, and

(IV) meets the requirements of clause (iii) of section 263A(f)(1)(B) (determined as if such clause also applies to property which has a long useful life (within the meaning of section 263A(f))).

(ii) Transportation property.—For purposes of this subparagraph, the term "transportation property" means tangible personal property used in the trade or business of transporting persons or property.

(iii) Application of subparagraph.—This subparagraph shall not apply to any property which is described in subparagraph (C).

* * *

(D) Exception for alternative depreciation property.—The term "qualified property" shall not include any property to which the alternative depreciation system under subsection (g) applies, determined—

(i) without regard to paragraph (7) of subsection (g) (relating to election to have system apply), and

(ii) after application of section 280F(b) (relating to listed property with limited business use).

(E) Special rules.—

(i) Acquisition requirements.—An acquisition of property meets the requirements of this clause if—

(I) such property was not used by the taxpayer at any time prior to such acquisition, and

(II) the acquisition of such property meets the requirements of paragraphs (2)(A), (2)(B), (2)(C), and (3) of section 179(d).

* * *

(G) Deduction allowed in computing minimum tax.—For purposes of determining alternative minimum taxable income under section 55, the deduction under section 167 for qualified property shall be determined without regard to any adjustment under section 56.

* * *

(7) Election out.—If a taxpayer makes an election under this paragraph with respect to any class of property for any taxable year, paragraphs (1) and (2)(F) shall not apply to any qualified property in such class placed in service during such taxable year. An election under this paragraph may be revoked only with the consent of the Secretary.

[**(8) Repealed.**]

(9) Exception for certain property.—The term "qualified property" shall not include—

(A) any property which is primarily used in a trade or business described in clause (iv) of section 163(j)(7)(A), or

(B) any property used in a trade or business that has had floor plan financing indebtedness (as defined in paragraph (9) of section 163(j)), if the floor plan financing interest related to such indebtedness was taken into account under paragraph (1)(C) of such section.

(10) Special rule for property placed in service during certain periods.—

(A) In general.—In the case of qualified property placed in service by the taxpayer during the first taxable year ending after January 19, 2025, if the taxpayer elects to have this paragraph apply for such taxable year, paragraph (1)(A) shall be applied—

(i) in the case of property which is not described in clause (ii), by substituting "40 percent" for "100 percent", or

(ii) in the case of property which is described in subparagraph (B) or (C) of paragraph (2), by substituting "60 percent" for "100 percent".

* * *

§ 172. Net operating loss deduction

(a) Deduction Allowed.—There shall be allowed as a deduction for the taxable year an amount equal to—

(1) in the case of a taxable year beginning before January 1, 2021, the aggregate of the net operating loss carryovers to such year, plus the net operating loss carrybacks to such year, and

(2) in the case of a taxable year beginning after December 31, 2020, the sum of—

(A) the aggregate amount of net operating losses arising in taxable years beginning before January 1, 2018, carried to such taxable year, plus

(B) the lesser of—

(i) the aggregate amount of net operating losses arising in taxable years beginning after December 31, 2017, carried to such taxable year, or

(ii) 80 percent of the excess (if any) of—

(I) taxable income computed without regard to the deductions under this section and sections 199A and 250, over

(II) the amount determined under subparagraph (A).

(b) Net Operating Loss Carrybacks and Carryovers.—

(1) Years to which loss may be carried.—

(A) General rule.—A net operating loss for any taxable year—

(i) shall be a net operating loss carryback to the extent provided in subparagraphs (B), (C)(i), and (D), and

(ii) except as provided in subparagraph (C)(ii), shall be a net operating loss carryover—

(I) in the case of a net operating loss arising in a taxable year beginning before January 1, 2018, to each of the 20 taxable years following the taxable year of the loss, and

(II) in the case of a net operating loss arising in a taxable year beginning after December 31, 2017, to each taxable year following the taxable year of the loss.

* * *

(D) Special rule for losses arising in 2018, 2019, and 2020.—

(i) In general.—In the case of any net operating loss arising in a taxable year beginning after December 31, 2017, and before January 1, 2021—

(I) such loss shall be a net operating loss carryback to each of the 5 taxable years preceding the taxable year of such loss, and

(II) subparagraphs (B) and (C)(i) shall not apply.

* * *

(c) Net operating loss defined.—For purposes of this section, the term "net operating loss" means the excess of the deductions allowed by this chapter over the gross income. Such excess shall be computed with the modifications specified in subsection (d).

(d) Modifications.—The modifications referred to in this section are as follows:

(1) Net operating loss deduction.—No net operating loss deduction shall be allowed.

(2) Capital gains and losses of taxpayers other than corporations.—In the case of a taxpayer other than a corporation—

(A) the amount deductible on account of losses from sales or exchanges of capital assets shall not exceed the amount includable on account of gains from sales or exchanges of capital assets; and

(B) the exclusion provided by section 1202 shall not be allowed.

(3) Deduction for personal exemptions.—No deduction shall be allowed under section 151 (relating to personal exemptions). No deduction in lieu of any such deduction shall be allowed.

(4) Nonbusiness deductions of taxpayers other than corporations.—In the case of a taxpayer other than a corporation, the deductions allowable by this chapter which are not attributable to a taxpayer's trade or business shall be allowed only to the extent of the amount of the gross income not derived from such trade or business. For purposes of the preceding sentence—

(A) any gain or loss from the sale or other disposition of—

(i) property, used in the trade or business, of a character which is subject to the allowance for depreciation provided in section 167, or

(ii) real property used in the trade or business,

shall be treated as attributable to the trade or business;

(B) the modifications specified in paragraphs (1), (2)(B), and (3) shall be taken into account;

(C) any deduction for casualty or theft losses allowable under paragraph (2) or (3) of section 165(c) shall be treated as attributable to the trade or business; and

(D) any deduction allowed under section 404 to the extent attributable to contributions which are made on behalf of an individual who is an employee within the meaning of section 401(c)(1) shall not be treated as attributable to the trade or business of such individual.

(5) Computation of deduction for dividends received.—The deductions allowed by section1 243 (relating to dividends received by corporations) and 245 (relating to dividends received from certain foreign corporations) shall be computed without regard to section 246(b) (relating to limitation on aggregate amount of deductions).

* * *

(8) Qualified business income deduction.—Any deduction under section 199A shall not be allowed.

(9) Deduction for foreign-derived deduction eligible income.—The deduction under section 250 shall not be allowed.

(e) Law applicable to computations.—In determining the amount of any net operating loss carryback or carryover to any taxable year, the necessary computations involving any other taxable year shall be made under the law applicable to such other taxable year.

* * *

(g) Cross references.—

(1) For treatment of net operating loss carryovers in certain corporate acquisitions, see section 381.

(2) For special limitation on net operating loss carryovers in case of a corporate change of ownership, see section 382.

§ 174. Amortization of research and experimental expenditures

(a) In general.—In the case of a taxpayer's foreign research or experimental expenditures for any taxable year—

(1) except as provided in paragraph (2), no deduction shall be allowed for such expenditures, and

(2) the taxpayer shall—

(A) charge such expenditures to capital account, and

(B) be allowed an amortization deduction of such expenditures ratably over the 15-year period beginning with the midpoint of the taxable year in which such expenditures are paid or incurred.

(b) Foreign research or experimental expenditures.—For purposes of this section, the term "foreign research or experimental expenditures" means, with respect to any taxable year, research or experimental expenditures which are paid or incurred by the taxpayer during such taxable year in connection with the taxpayer's trade or business and which are attributable to foreign research (within the meaning of section 41(d)(4)(F)).

(c) Special rules.—

(1) Land and other property.—This section shall not apply to any expenditure for the acquisition or improvement of land, or for the acquisition or improvement of property to be used in connection with the research or experimentation and of a character which is subject to the allowance under section 167 (relating to allowance for depreciation, etc.) or section 611 (relating to allowance for depletion); but for purposes of this section allowances under section 167, and allowances under section 611, shall be considered as expenditures.

(2) Exploration expenditures.—This section shall not apply to any expenditure paid or incurred for the purpose of ascertaining the existence, location, extent, or quality of any deposit of ore or other mineral (including oil and gas).

(3) Software development.—For purposes of this section, any amount paid or incurred in connection with the development of any software shall be treated as a research or experimental expenditure.

(d) Treatment upon disposition, retirement, or abandonment.—If any property with respect to which foreign research or experimental expenditures are paid or incurred is disposed, retired, or abandoned during the period during which such expenditures are allowed as an amortization deduction under this section, no deduction or reduction to amount realized shall be allowed with respect to such expenditures on account of such disposition, retirement, or abandonment and such amortization deduction shall continue with respect to such expenditures.

§ 174A. Domestic research or experimental expenditures

(a) Treatment as expenses.—Notwithstanding section 263, there shall be allowed as a deduction any domestic research or experimental expenditures which are paid or incurred by the taxpayer during the taxable year.

(b) Domestic research or experimental expenditures.—For purposes of this section, the term "domestic research or experimental expenditures" means research or experimental expenditures paid or incurred by the taxpayer in connection with the taxpayer's trade or business other than such expenditures which are attributable to foreign research (within the meaning of section 41(d)(4)(F)).

(c) Amortization of certain domestic research or experimental expenditures.—

(1) In general.—At the election of the taxpayer, made in accordance with regulations or other guidance provided by the Secretary, in the case of domestic research or experimental expenditures which would (but for subsection (a)) be chargeable to capital account but not chargeable to property of a character which is subject to the allowance under section 167 (relating to allowance for depreciation, etc.) or section 611 (relating to allowance for depletion), subsection (a) shall not apply and the taxpayer shall—

(A) charge such expenditures to capital account, and

(B) be allowed an amortization deduction of such expenditures ratably over such period of not less than 60 months as may be selected by the taxpayer (beginning with the month in which the taxpayer first realizes benefits from such expenditures).

(2) Time for and scope of election.—The election provided by paragraph (1) may be made for any taxable year, but only if made not later than the time prescribed by law for filing the return for such taxable year (including extensions thereof). The method so elected, and the period selected by the taxpayer, shall be adhered to in computing taxable income for the taxable year for which the election is made and for all subsequent taxable years unless, with the approval of the Secretary, a change to a different method (or to a different period) is authorized with respect to part or all of such expenditures. The election shall not apply to any expenditure paid or incurred during any taxable year before the taxable year for which the taxpayer makes the election.

(d) Special rules.—

(1) Land and other property.—This section shall not apply to any expenditure for the acquisition or improvement of land, or for the acquisition or improvement of property to be used in connection with the research or experimentation and of a character which is subject to the allowance under section 167 (relating to allowance for depreciation, etc.) or section 611 (relating to allowance for depletion); but for purposes of this section allowances under section 167, and allowances under section 611, shall be considered as expenditures.

(2) Exploration expenditures.—This section shall not apply to any expenditure paid or incurred for the purpose of ascertaining the existence, location, extent, or quality of any deposit of ore or other mineral (including oil and gas).

(3) Software development.—For purposes of this section, any amount paid or incurred in connection with the development of any software shall be treated as a research or experimental expenditure.

§ 199A. Qualified business income

(a) Allowance of deduction.—In the case of a taxpayer other than a corporation, except as provided in subsection (i), there shall be allowed as a deduction for any taxable year an amount equal to the lesser of—

(1) the combined qualified business income amount of the taxpayer, or

(2) an amount equal to 20 percent of the excess (if any) of—

(A) the taxable income of the taxpayer for the taxable year, over

(B) the net capital gain (as defined in section 1(h)) of the taxpayer for such taxable year.

(b) Combined qualified business income amount.—For purposes of this section—

(1) In general.—The term "combined qualified business income amount" means, with respect to any taxable year, an amount equal to—

(A) the sum of the amounts determined under paragraph (2) for each qualified trade or business carried on by the taxpayer, plus

(B) 20 percent of the aggregate amount of the qualified REIT dividends and qualified publicly traded partnership income of the taxpayer for the taxable year.

(2) Determination of deductible amount for each trade or business.—The amount determined under this paragraph with respect to any qualified trade or business is the lesser of—

(A) 20 percent of the taxpayer's qualified business income with respect to the qualified trade or business, or

(B) the greater of—

(i) 50 percent of the W-2 wages with respect to the qualified trade or business, or

(ii) the sum of 25 percent of the W-2 wages with respect to the qualified trade or business, plus 2.5 percent of the unadjusted basis immediately after acquisition of all qualified property.

(3) Modifications to limit based on taxable income.—

(A) Exception from limit.—In the case of any taxpayer whose taxable income for the taxable year does not exceed the threshold amount, paragraph (2) shall be applied without regard to subparagraph (B).

(B) Phase-in of limit for certain taxpayers.—

(i) In general.—If—

(I) the taxable income of a taxpayer for any taxable year exceeds the threshold amount, but does not exceed the sum of the threshold amount plus $75,000 ($150,000 in the case of a joint return), and

(II) the amount determined under paragraph (2)(B) (determined without regard to this subparagraph) with respect to any qualified trade or business carried on by the taxpayer is less than the amount determined under paragraph (2)(A) with respect such trade or business, then paragraph (2) shall be applied with respect to such trade or business without regard to subparagraph (B) thereof and by reducing the amount determined under subparagraph (A) thereof by the amount determined under clause (ii).

(ii) Amount of reduction.—The amount determined under this subparagraph is the amount which bears the same ratio to the excess amount as—

(I) the amount by which the taxpayer's taxable income for the taxable year exceeds the threshold amount, bears to

(II) $75,000 ($150,000 in the case of a joint return).

(iii) Excess amount.—For purposes of clause (ii), the excess amount is the excess of—

(I) the amount determined under paragraph (2)(A) (determined without regard to this paragraph), over

(II) the amount determined under paragraph (2)(B) (determined without regard to this paragraph).

(4) Wages, etc.—

(A) In general.—The term "W-2 wages" means, with respect to any person for any taxable year of such person, the amounts described in paragraphs (3) and (8) of section 6051(a) paid by such person with respect to employment of employees by such person during the calendar year ending during such taxable year.

(B) Limitation to wages attributable to qualified business income.—Such term shall not include any amount which is not properly allocable to qualified business income for purposes of subsection (c)(1).

(C) Return requirement.—Such term shall not include any amount which is not properly included in a return filed with the Social Security Administration on or before the 60th day after the due date (including extensions) for such return.

(5) Acquisitions, dispositions, and short taxable years.—The Secretary shall provide for the application of this subsection in cases of a short taxable year or where the taxpayer acquires, or disposes of, the major portion of a trade or business or the major portion of a separate unit of a trade or business during the taxable year.

(6) Qualified property.—For purposes of this section:

(A) In general.—The term "qualified property" means, with respect to any qualified trade or business for a taxable year, tangible property of a character subject to the allowance for depreciation under section 167—

(i) which is held by, and available for use in, the qualified trade or business at the close of the taxable year,

(ii) which is used at any point during the taxable year in the production of qualified business income, and

(iii) the depreciable period for which has not ended before the close of the taxable year.

(B) Depreciable period.—The term "depreciable period" means, with respect to qualified property of a taxpayer, the period beginning on the date the property was first placed in service by the taxpayer and ending on the later of—

(i) the date that is 10 years after such date, or

(ii) the last day of the last full year in the applicable recovery period that would apply to the property under section 168 (determined without regard to subsection (g) thereof).

* * *

(c) Qualified business income.—For purposes of this section—

(1) In general.—The term "qualified business income" means, for any taxable year, the net amount of qualified items of income, gain, deduction, and loss with respect to any qualified trade or business of the taxpayer. Such term shall not include any qualified REIT dividends or qualified publicly traded partnership income.

(2) Carryover of losses.—If the net amount of qualified income, gain, deduction, and loss with respect to qualified trades or businesses of the taxpayer for any taxable year is less than zero, such amount shall be treated as a loss from a qualified trade or business in the succeeding taxable year.

(3) Qualified items of income, gain, deduction, and loss.—For purposes of this subsection—

(A) In general.—The term "qualified items of income, gain, deduction, and loss" means items of income, gain, deduction, and loss to the extent such items are—

(i) effectively connected with the conduct of a trade or business within the United States (within the meaning of section 864(c), determined by substituting 'qualified trade or business (within the meaning of section 199A)' for 'nonresident alien individual or a foreign corporation' or for 'a foreign corporation' each place it appears), and

(ii) included or allowed in determining taxable income for the taxable year.

(B) Exceptions.—The following items shall not be taken into account as a qualified item of income, gain, deduction, or loss:

(i) Any item of short-term capital gain, short-term capital loss, long-term capital gain, or long-term capital loss.

(ii) Any dividend, income equivalent to a dividend, or payment in lieu of dividends described in section 954(c)(1)(G). * * *

(iii) Any interest income other than interest income which is properly allocable to a trade or business.

(iv) Any item of gain or loss described in subparagraph (C) or (D) of section 954(c)(1) (applied by substituting 'qualified trade or business' for 'controlled foreign corporation').

(v) Any item of income, gain, deduction, or loss taken into account under section 954(c)(1)(F) (determined without regard to clause (ii) thereof and other than items attributable to notional principal contracts entered into in transactions qualifying under section 1221(a)(7)).

(vi) Any amount received from an annuity which is not received in connection with the trade or business. **(c)**

(vii) Any item of deduction or loss properly allocable to an amount described in any of the preceding clauses.

(4) Treatment of reasonable compensation and guaranteed payments.—Qualified business income shall not include—

(A) reasonable compensation paid to the taxpayer by any qualified trade or business of the taxpayer for services rendered with respect to the trade or business,

(B) any guaranteed payment described in section 707(c) paid to a partner for services rendered with respect to the trade or business,

(C) to the extent provided in regulations, any payment described in section 707(a) to a partner for services rendered with respect to the trade or business, and

(D) any amount with respect to which a deduction is allowable to the taxpayer under section 224(a) for the taxable year.

(d) Qualified trade or business.—For purposes of this section—

(1) In general.—The term "qualified trade or business" means any trade or business other than—

(A) a specified service trade or business, or

(B) the trade or business of performing services as an employee.

(2) Specified service trade or business.—The term "specified service trade or business" means any trade or business—

(A) which is described in section 1202(e)(3)(A) (applied without regard to the words 'engineering, architecture,') or which would be so described if the term 'employees or owners' were substituted for 'employees' therein, or

(B) which involves the performance of services that consist of investing and investment management, trading, or dealing in securities (as defined in section 475(c)(2)), partnership interests, or commodities (as defined in section 475(e)(2)).

(3) Exception for specified service businesses based on taxpayer's income.—

(A) In general.—If, for any taxable year, the taxable income of any taxpayer is less than the sum of the threshold amount plus $75,000 ($150,000 in the case of a joint return), then—

(i) any specified service trade or business of the taxpayer shall not fail to be treated as a qualified trade or business due to paragraph (1)(A), but

(ii) only the applicable percentage of qualified items of income, gain, deduction, or loss, and the W-2 wages and the unadjusted basis immediately after acquisition of qualified property, of the taxpayer allocable to such specified service trade or business shall be taken into account in computing the qualified business income, W-2 wages, and the unadjusted basis immediately after acquisition of qualified property of the taxpayer for the taxable year for purposes of applying this section.

(B) Applicable percentage.—For purposes of subparagraph (A), the term "applicable percentage" means, with respect to any taxable year, 100 percent reduced (not below zero) by the percentage equal to the ratio of—

(i) the taxable income of the taxpayer for the taxable year in excess of the threshold amount, bears to

(ii) $75,000 ($150,000 in the case of a joint return).

(e) Other definitions.—For purposes of this section—

(1) Taxable income.—Except as otherwise provided in subsection (g)(2)(B), taxable income shall be computed without regard to section 68 and without regard to any deduction allowable under this section.

(2) Threshold amount.—

(A) In general.—The term "threshold amount" means $157,500 (200 percent of such amount in the case of a joint return).

(B) Inflation adjustment.—In the case of any taxable year beginning after 2018, the dollar amount in subparagraph (A) shall be increased by an amount equal to—

(i) such dollar amount, multiplied by

(ii) the cost-of-living adjustment determined under section 1(f)(3) for the calendar year in which the taxable year begins, determined by substituting 'calendar year 2017' for 'calendar year 2016' in subparagraph (A)(ii) thereof.

The amount of any increase under the preceding sentence shall be rounded as provided in section 1(f)(7).

(3) Qualified REIT dividend.—The term "qualified REIT dividend" means any dividend from a real estate investment trust received during the taxable year which—

(A) is not a capital gain dividend, as defined in section 857(b)(3), and

(B) is not qualified dividend income, as defined in section 1(h)(11).

(4) Qualified publicly traded partnership income.—The term "qualified publicly traded partnership income" means, with respect to any qualified trade or business of a taxpayer, the sum of—

(A) the net amount of such taxpayer's allocable share of each qualified item of income, gain, deduction, and loss (as defined in subsection (c)(3) and determined after the application of subsection (c)(4)) from a publicly traded partnership (as defined in section 7704(a)) which is not treated as a corporation under section 7704(c), plus

(B) any gain recognized by such taxpayer upon disposition of its interest in such partnership to the extent such gain is treated as an amount realized from the sale or exchange of property other than a capital asset under section 751(a).

(f) Special rules.—

(1) Application to partnerships and S corporations.—

(A) In general.—In the case of a partnership or S corporation—

(i) this section shall be applied at the partner or shareholder level,

(ii) each partner or shareholder shall take into account such person's allocable share of each qualified item of income, gain, deduction, and loss, and

(iii) each partner or shareholder shall be treated for purposes of subsection (b) as having W-2 wages and unadjusted basis immediately after acquisition of qualified property for the taxable year in an amount equal to such person's allocable share of the W-2 wages and the unadjusted basis immediately after acquisition of qualified property of the partnership or S corporation for the taxable year (as determined under regulations prescribed by the Secretary).

For purposes of clause (iii), a partner's or shareholder's allocable share of W-2 wages shall be determined in the same manner as the partner's or shareholder's allocable share of wage expenses. For purposes of such clause, partner's or shareholder's allocable share of the unadjusted basis immediately after acquisition of qualified property shall be determined in the same manner as the partner's or shareholder's allocable share of depreciation. For purposes of this subparagraph, in the case of an S corporation, an allocable share shall be the shareholder's pro rata share of an item.

(B) Application to trusts and estates.—Rules similar to the rules under section 199(d)(1)(B)(i) (as in effect on December 1, 2017) for the apportionment of W-2 wages shall apply to the apportionment of W-2 wages and the apportionment of unadjusted basis immediately after acquisition of qualified property under this section.

(C) Treatment of trades or business in Puerto Rico.—

(i) In general.—In the case of any taxpayer with qualified business income from sources within the commonwealth of Puerto Rico, if all such income is taxable under section 1 for such taxable year, then for purposes of determining the qualified business income of such taxpayer for such taxable year, the term 'United States' shall include the Commonwealth of Puerto Rico.

(ii) Special rule for applying limit.—In the case of any taxpayer described in clause (i), the determination of W-2 wages of such taxpayer with respect to any qualified trade or business conducted in Puerto Rico shall be made without regard to any exclusion under section 3401(a)(8) for remuneration paid for services in Puerto Rico.

(2) Coordination with minimum tax.—For purposes of determining alternative minimum taxable income under section 55, qualified business income shall be determined without regard to any adjustments under sections 56 through 59.

(3) Deduction limited to income taxes.—The deduction under subsection (a) shall only be allowed for purposes of this chapter.

(4) Regulations.—The Secretary shall prescribe such regulations as are necessary to carry out the purposes of this section, including regulations—

(A) for requiring or restricting the allocation of items and wages under this section and such reporting requirements as the Secretary determines appropriate, and

(B) for the application of this section in the case of tiered entities.

* * *

(h) Anti-abuse rules.—The Secretary shall—

(1) apply rules similar to the rules under section 179(d)(2) in order to prevent the manipulation of the depreciable period of qualified property using transactions between related parties, and

(2) prescribe rules for determining the unadjusted basis immediately after acquisition of qualified property acquired in like-kind exchanges or involuntary conversions.

(i) Minimum deduction for active qualified business income.—

(1) In general.—In the case of an applicable taxpayer for any taxable year, the deduction allowed under subsection (a) for the taxable year shall be equal to the greater of—

(A) the amount of such deduction determined without regard to this subsection, or

(B) $400.

(2) Applicable taxpayer.—For purposes of this subsection—

(A) In general.—The term "applicable taxpayer" means, with respect to any taxable year, a taxpayer whose aggregate qualified business income with respect to all active qualified trades or businesses of the taxpayer for such taxable year is at least $1,000.

(B) Active qualified trade or business.—The term "active qualified trade or business" means, with respect to any taxpayer for any taxable year, any qualified trade or business of the taxpayer in which the taxpayer materially participates (within the meaning of section 469(h)).

(3) Inflation adjustment.—In the case of any taxable year beginning after 2026, the $400 amount in paragraph (1)(B) and the $1,000 amount in paragraph (2)(A) shall each be increased by an amount equal to—

(A) such dollar amount, multiplied by

(B) the cost-of-living adjustment determined under section 1(f)(3) for the calendar year in which the taxable year begins, determined by substituting "calendar year 2025" for "calendar year 2016" in subparagraph (A)(ii) thereof.

If any increase under this paragraph is not a multiple of $5, such increase shall be rounded to the nearest multiple of $5.

Part VIII—Special Deductions for Corporations

§ 243. Dividends received by corporations

(a) General rule.—In the case of a corporation, there shall be allowed as a deduction an amount equal to the following percentages of the amount received as dividends from a domestic corporation which is subject to taxation under this chapter:

(1) 50 percent, in the case of dividends other than dividends described in paragraph (2) or (3);

(2) 100 percent, in the case of dividends received by a small business investment company operating under the Small Business Investment Act of 1958 (15 U.S.C. 661 and following); and

(3) 100 percent, in the case of qualifying dividends (as defined in subsection (b)(1)).

(b) Qualifying dividends.—

(1) In general.—For purposes of this section, the term "qualifying dividend" means any dividend received by a corporation—

(A) if at the close of the day on which such dividend is received, such corporation is a member of the same affiliated group as the corporation distributing such dividend, and

(B) if such dividend is distributed out of the earnings and profits of a taxable year of the distributing corporation which ends after December 31, 1963, and on each day of which the distributing corporation and the corporation receiving the dividend were members of such affiliated group.

(2) Affiliated group.—For purposes of this subsection:

(A) In general.—The term "affiliated group" has the meaning given such term by section 1504(a), except that for such purposes sections 1504(b)(2) and 1504(c) shall not apply.

(B) Group must be consistent in foreign tax treatment.—The requirements of paragraph (1)(A) shall not be treated as being met with respect to any dividend received by a corporation if, for any taxable year which includes the day on which such dividend is received—

(i) 1 or more members of the affiliated group referred to in paragraph (1)(A) choose to any extent to take the benefits of section 901, and

(ii) 1 or more other members of such group claim to any extent a deduction for taxes otherwise creditable under section 901.

* * *

(c) Increased percentage for dividends from 20-percent owned corporations.—

(1) In general.—In the case of any dividend received from a 20-percent owned corporation, subsection (a)(1) shall be applied by substituting "65 percent" for "50 percent".

(2) 20-percent owned corporation.—For purposes of this section, the term "20-percent owned corporation" means any corporation if 20 percent or more of the stock of such corporation (by vote and value) is owned by the taxpayer. For purposes of the preceding sentence, stock described in section 1504(a)(4) shall not be taken into account.

* * *

(e) Certain dividends from foreign corporations.—For purposes of subsection (a) and for purposes of section 245, any dividend from a foreign corporation from earnings and profits accumulated by a domestic corporation during a period with respect to which such domestic corporation was subject to taxation under this chapter (or corresponding provisions of prior law) shall be treated as a dividend from a domestic corporation which is subject to taxation under this chapter.

§ 245. Dividends received from certain foreign corporations

(a) Dividends from 10-percent owned foreign corporations.—

(1) In general.—In the case of dividends received by a corporation from a qualified 10-percent owned foreign corporation, there shall be allowed as a deduction an amount equal to the percent (specified in section 243 for the taxable year) of the U.S.-source portion of such dividends.

(2) Qualified 10-percent owned foreign corporation.—For purposes of this subsection, the term "qualified 10-percent owned foreign corporation" means any foreign corporation (other than a passive foreign investment company) if at least 10 percent of the stock of such corporation (by vote and value) is owned by the taxpayer.

(3) U.S.-source portion.—For purposes of this subsection, the U.S.-source portion of any dividend is an amount which bears the same ratio to such dividend as—

(A) the post-1986 undistributed U.S. earnings, bears to

(B) the total post-1986 undistributed earnings.

(4) Post-1986 undistributed earnings.—The term "post-1986 undistributed earnings" means the amount of the earnings and profits of the foreign corporation (computed in accordance with sections 964(a) and 986) accumulated in taxable years beginning after December 31, 1986—

(A) as of the close of the taxable year of the foreign corporation in which the dividend is distributed, and

(B) without diminution by reason of dividends distributed during such taxable year.

(5) Post-1986 undistributed U.S. earnings.—For purposes of this subsection, the term "post-1986 undistributed U.S. earnings" means the portion of the post-1986 undistributed earnings which is attributable to—

(A) income of the qualified 10-percent owned foreign corporation which is effectively connected with the conduct of a trade or business within the United States and subject to tax under this chapter, or

(B) any dividend received (directly or through a wholly owned foreign corporation) from a domestic corporation at least 80 percent of the stock of which (by vote and value) is owned (directly or through such wholly owned foreign corporation) by the qualified 10-percent owned foreign corporation.

(6) Special rule.—If the 1st day on which the requirements of paragraph (2) are met with respect to any foreign corporation is in a taxable year of such corporation beginning after December 31, 1986, the post-1986 undistributed earnings and the post-1986 undistributed U.S. earnings of such corporation shall be determined by only taking into account periods beginning on and after the 1st day of the 1st taxable year in which such requirements are met.

(7) Coordination with subsection (b).—Earnings and profits of any qualified 10-percent owned foreign corporation for any taxable year shall not be taken into account under this subsection if the deduction provided by subsection (b) would be allowable with respect to dividends paid out of such earnings and profits.

(8) Disallowance of foreign tax credit.—No credit shall be allowed under section 901 for any taxes paid or accrued (or treated as paid or accrued) with respect to the United States-source portion of any dividend received by a corporation from a qualified 10-percent-owned foreign corporation.**(a)**

(9) Coordination with section 904.—For purposes of section 904, the U.S.-source portion of any dividend received by a corporation from a qualified 10-percent owned foreign corporation shall be treated as from sources in the United States.

(10) Coordination with treaties.—If—

(A) any portion of a dividend received by a corporation from a qualified 10-percent-owned foreign corporation would be treated as from sources in the United States under paragraph (9),

(B) under a treaty obligation of the United States (applied without regard to this subsection), such portion would be treated as arising from sources outside the United States, and

(C) the taxpayer chooses the benefits of this paragraph,

this subsection shall not apply to such dividend (but subsections (a), (b), and (c) of section 904 and sections 907 and 960 shall be applied separately with respect to such portion of such dividend).

(11) Coordination with section 1248.—For purposes of this subsection, the term "dividend" does not include any amount treated as a dividend under section 1248.

(12) Dividends received from RICs and REITs ineligible for deduction.—Regulated investment companies and real estate investment trusts shall not be treated as domestic corporations for purposes of paragraph (5)(B).

(b) Certain dividends received from wholly owned foreign subsidiaries.—

(1) In general.—In the case of dividends described in paragraph (2) received from a foreign corporation by a domestic corporation which, for its taxable year in which such dividends are received, owns (directly or indirectly) all of the outstanding stock of such foreign corporation, there shall be allowed as a deduction (in lieu of the deduction provided by subsection (a)) an amount equal to 100 percent of such dividends.

(2) Eligible dividends.—Paragraph (1) shall apply only to dividends which are paid out of the earnings and profits of a foreign corporation for a taxable year during which—

(A) all of its outstanding stock is owned (directly or indirectly) by the domestic corporation to which such dividends are paid; and

(B) all of its gross income from all sources is effectively connected with the conduct of a trade or business within the United States.

(3) Exception.—Paragraph (1) shall not apply to any dividends if an election under section 1562 is effective for either—

(A) the taxable year of the domestic corporation in which such dividends are received, or

(B) the taxable year of the foreign corporation out of the earnings and profits of which such dividends are paid.

(c) Certain dividends received from FSC.—

(1) In general.—In the case of a domestic corporation, there shall be allowed as a deduction an amount equal to—

(A) 100 percent of any dividend received from another corporation which is distributed out of earnings and profits attributable to foreign trade income for a period during which such other corporation was a FSC, and

(B) 50 percent (65 percent in the case of dividends from a 20-percent owned corporation as defined in section 243(c)(2)) of any dividend received from another corporation which is distributed out of earnings and profits attributable to effectively connected income received or accrued by such other corporation while such other corporation was a FSC.

(2) Exception for certain dividends.—Paragraph (1) shall not apply to any dividend which is distributed out of earnings and profits attributable to foreign trade income which—

(A) is section 923(a)(2) nonexempt income (within the meaning of section 927(d)(6)), or

(B) would not, but for section 923(a)(4), be treated as exempt foreign trade income.

(3) No deduction under subsection (a) or (b).—No deduction shall be allowable under subsection (a) or (b) with respect to any dividend which is distributed out of earnings and profits of a corporation accumulated while such corporation was a FSC.

(4) Definitions.—For purposes of this subsection—

(A) Foreign trade income; exempt foreign trade income.—The terms "foreign trade income" and "exempt foreign trade income" have the respective meanings given such terms by section 923.

(B) Effectively connected income.—The term "effectively connected income" means any income which is effectively connected (or treated as effectively connected) with the conduct of a trade or business in the United States and is subject to tax under this chapter. Such term shall not include any foreign trade income.

(C) FSC.—The term "FSC" has the meaning given such term by section 922.

(5) References to prior law.—Any reference in this subsection to section 922, 923, or 927 shall be treated as a reference to such section as in effect before its repeal by the FSC Repeal and Extraterritorial Income Exclusion Act of 2007.

§ 245A. Deduction for foreign source-portion of dividends received by domestic corporations from specified 10-percent owned foreign corporations

(a) In general.—In the case of any dividend received from a specified 10-percent owned foreign corporation by a domestic corporation which is a United States shareholder with respect to such foreign corporation, there shall be allowed as a deduction an amount equal to the foreign-source portion of such dividend.

(b) Specified 10-percent owned foreign corporation.—For purposes of this section—

(1) In general.—The term "specified 10-percent owned foreign corporation" means any foreign corporation with respect to which any domestic corporation is a United States shareholder with respect to such corporation.

(2) Exclusion of passive foreign investment companies.—Such term shall not include any corporation which is a passive foreign investment company (as defined in section 1297) with respect to the shareholder and which is not a controlled foreign corporation.

(c) Foreign-source portion.—For purposes of this section—

(1) In general.—The foreign-source portion of any dividend from a specified 10-percent owned foreign corporation is an amount which bears the same ratio to such dividend as—

(A) the undistributed foreign earnings of the specified 10-percent owned foreign corporation, bears to

(B) the total undistributed earnings of such foreign corporation.

(2) Undistributed earnings.—The term "undistributed earnings" means the amount of the earnings and profits of the specified 10-percent owned foreign corporation (computed in accordance with sections 964(a) and 986)—

(A) as of the close of the taxable year of the specified 10-percent owned foreign corporation in which the dividend is distributed, and

(B) without diminution by reason of dividends distributed during such taxable year.

(3) Undistributed foreign earnings.—The term "undistributed foreign earnings" means the portion of the undistributed earnings which is attributable to neither—

(A) income described in subparagraph (A) of section 245(a)(5), nor

(B) dividends described in subparagraph (B) of such section (determined without regard to section 245(a)(12)).

(d) Disallowance of foreign tax credit, etc.—

(1) In general.—No credit shall be allowed under section 901 for any taxes paid or accrued (or treated as paid or accrued) with respect to any dividend for which a deduction is allowed under this section.

(2) Denial of deduction.—No deduction shall be allowed under this chapter for any tax for which credit is not allowable under section 901 by reason of paragraph (1) (determined by treating the taxpayer as having elected the benefits of subpart A of part III of subchapter N).

(e) Special rules for hybrid dividends.—

(1) In general.—Subsection (a) shall not apply to any dividend received by a United States shareholder from a controlled foreign corporation if the dividend is a hybrid dividend.

(2) Hybrid dividends of tiered corporations.—If a controlled foreign corporation with respect to which a domestic corporation is a United States shareholder receives a hybrid dividend from any other controlled foreign corporation with respect to which such domestic corporation is also a United States shareholder, then, notwithstanding any other provision of this title—

(A) the hybrid dividend shall be treated for purposes of section 951(a)(1)(A) as subpart F income of the receiving controlled foreign corporation for the taxable year of the controlled foreign corporation in which the dividend was received, and

(B) the United States shareholder shall include in gross income an amount equal to the shareholder's pro rata share (determined in the same manner as under section 951(a)(2)) of the subpart F income described in subparagraph (A).

(3) Denial of foreign tax credit, etc.—The rules of subsection (d) shall apply to any hybrid dividend received by, or any amount included under paragraph (2) in the gross income of, a United States shareholder.

(4) Hybrid dividend.—The term "hybrid dividend" means an amount received from a controlled foreign corporation—

(A) for which a deduction would be allowed under subsection (a) but for this subsection, and

(B) for which the controlled foreign corporation received a deduction (or other tax benefit) with respect to any income, war profits, or excess profits taxes imposed by any foreign country or possession of the United States.

(f) Special rule for purging distributions of passive foreign investment companies.—Any amount which is treated as a dividend under section 1291(d)(2)(B) shall not be treated as a dividend for purposes of this section.

(g) Regulations.—The Secretary shall prescribe such regulations or other guidance as may be necessary or appropriate to carry out the provisions of this section, including regulations for the treatment of United States shareholders owning stock of a specified 10 percent owned foreign corporation through a partnership.

§ 246. Rules applying to deductions for dividends received

(a) Deduction not allowed for dividends from certain corporations.—

(1) In general.—The deductions allowed by sections 243[1] 245, and 245A shall not apply to any dividend from a corporation which, for the taxable year of the corporation in which the distribution is made, or for the next preceding taxable year of the corporation, is a corporation exempt from tax under section 501 (relating to certain charitable, etc., organizations) or section 521 (relating to farmers' cooperative associations).

* * *

(b) Limitation on aggregate amount of deductions.—

(1) General rule.—Except as provided in paragraph (2), the aggregate amount of the deductions allowed by section[2] 199A, 243 (a)(1), subsection (a) and (b) of section 245, and section 250 shall not exceed the percentage determined under paragraph (3) of the taxable income computed without regard to the deductions allowed by sections 172, 199A, 243(a)(1), subsection (a) and (b) of section 245, and 250, without regard to any adjustment under section 1059, and without regard to any capital loss carryback to the taxable year under section 1212(a)(1).

(2) Effect of net operating loss.—Paragraph (1) shall not apply for any taxable year for which there is a net operating loss (as determined under section 172).

(3) Special rules.—The provisions of paragraph (1) shall be applied—

(A) first separately with respect to dividends from 20-percent owned corporations (as defined in section 243(c)(2)) and the percentage determined under this paragraph shall be 65 percent, and

(B) then separately with respect to dividends not from 20-percent owned corporations and the percentage determined under this paragraph shall be 50 percent and the taxable income shall be reduced by the aggregate amount of dividends from 20-percent owned corporations (as so defined).

(c) Exclusion of certain dividends.—

(1) In general.—No deduction shall be allowed under section 243 245, or 245A, in respect of any dividend on any share of stock—

(A) which is held by the taxpayer for 45 days or less during the 91-day period beginning on the date which is 45 days before the date on which such share becomes ex-dividend with respect to such dividend, or

(B) to the extent that the taxpayer is under an obligation (whether pursuant to a short sale or otherwise) to make related payments with respect to positions in substantially similar or related property.

(2) 90-day rule in the case of certain preference dividends.—In the case of stock having preference in dividends, if the taxpayer receives dividends with respect to such stock which are attributable to a period or periods aggregating in excess of 366 days, paragraph (1)(A) shall be applied—

(A) by substituting "90 days" for "45 days" each place it appears, and

(B) by substituting "181-day period" for "91-day period".

(3) Determination of holding periods.—For purposes of this subsection, in determining the period for which the taxpayer has held any share of stock—

(A) the day of disposition, but not the day of acquisition, shall be taken into account, and

(B) paragraph (3) of section 1223 shall not apply.

(4) Holding period reduced for periods where risk of loss diminished.—The holding periods determined for purposes of this subsection shall be appropriately reduced (in the manner provided in regulations prescribed by the Secretary) for any period (during such periods) in which—

(A) the taxpayer has an option to sell, is under a contractual obligation to sell, or has made (and not closed) a short sale of, substantially identical stock or securities,

(B) the taxpayer is the grantor of an option to buy substantially identical stock or securities, or

(C) under regulations prescribed by the Secretary, a taxpayer has diminished his risk of loss by holding 1 or more other positions with respect to substantially similar or related property.

The preceding sentence shall not apply in the case of any qualified covered call (as defined in section 1092(c)(4) but without regard to the requirement that gain or loss with respect to the option not be ordinary income or loss), other than a qualified covered call option to which section 1092(f) applies.

(5) Special rules for foreign source portion of dividends received from specified 10-percent owned foreign corporations.—

(A) 1-year holding period requirement.—For purposes of section 245A—

(i) paragraph (1)(A) shall be applied—

(I) by substituting "365 days" for "45 days" each place it appears, and

(II) by substituting "731-day period" for "91-day period", and

(ii) paragraph (2) shall not apply.

(B) Status must be maintained during holding period.—For purposes of applying paragraph (1) with respect to section 245A, the taxpayer shall be treated as holding the stock referred to in paragraph (1) for any period only if—

(i) the specified 10-percent owned foreign corporation referred to in section 245A(a) is a specified 10-percent owned foreign corporation at all times during such period, and

(ii) the taxpayer is a United States shareholder with respect to such specified 10-percent owned foreign corporation at all times during such period.

(d) Dividends from a DISC or former DISC.—No deduction shall be allowed under section 243 in respect of a dividend from a corporation which is a DISC or former DISC (as defined in section 992(a)) to the extent such dividend is paid out of the corporation's accumulated DISC income or previously taxed income, or is a deemed distribution pursuant to section 995(b)(1).

§ 250. Foreign-derived deduction eligible income and net CFC tested income

(a) Allowance of deduction.—

(1) In general.—In the case of a domestic corporation for any taxable year, there shall be allowed as a deduction an amount equal to the sum of—

(A) 33.34 percent of the foreign-derived deduction eligible income of such domestic corporation for such taxable year, plus

(B) 40 percent of—

(i) the net CFC tested income amount (if any) which is included in the gross income of such domestic corporation under section 951A for such taxable year, and

(ii) the amount treated as a dividend received by such corporation under section 78 which is attributable to the amount described in clause (i).

(2) Limitation based on taxable income.—

(A) In general.—If, for any taxable year—

(i) the sum of the foreign-derived deduction eligible income and the net CFC tested income amount otherwise taken into account by the domestic corporation under paragraph (1), exceeds **(a)**

(ii) the taxable income of the domestic corporation (determined without regard to this section),

then the amount of the foreign-derived deduction eligible income and the net CFC tested income amount so taken into account shall be reduced as provided in subparagraph (B).

(B) Reduction.—For purposes of subparagraph (A)—

(i) foreign-derived deduction eligible income shall be reduced by an amount which bears the same ratio to the excess described in subparagraph (A) as such foreign-derived deduction eligible income bears to the sum described in subparagraph (A)(i), and

(ii) the net CFC tested income amount shall be reduced by the remainder of such excess.

(b) Foreign-derived deduction eligible income.—For purposes of this section—

(1) Foreign-derived deduction eligible income.—The term "foreign-derived deduction eligible income" means, with respect to any taxpayer for any taxable year, any deduction eligible income of such taxpayer which is derived in connection with—

(A) property—

(i) which is sold by the taxpayer to any person who is not a United States person, and

(ii) which the taxpayer establishes to the satisfaction of the Secretary is for a foreign use,

or

(B) services provided by the taxpayer which the taxpayer establishes to the satisfaction of the Secretary are provided to any person, or with respect to property, not located within the United States.

(2) Rules relating to foreign use property or services.—For purposes of this subsection—

(A) Foreign use.—The term "foreign use" means any use, consumption, or disposition which is not within the United States.

(B) Property or services provided to domestic intermediaries.—

(i) Property.—If a taxpayer sells property to another person (other than a related party) for further manufacture or other modification within the United States, such property shall not be treated as sold for a foreign use even if such other person subsequently uses such property for a foreign use.

(ii) Services.—If a taxpayer provides services to another person (other than a related party) located within the United States, such services shall not be treated as described in paragraph (1)(B) even if such other person uses such services in providing services which are so described.

(C) Special rules with respect to related party transactions.—

(i) Sales to related parties.—If property is sold to a related party who is not a United States person, such sale shall not be treated as for a foreign use unless—

(I) such property is ultimately sold by a related party, or used by a related party in connection with property which is sold or the provision of services, to another person who is an unrelated party who is not a United States person, and

(II) the taxpayer establishes to the satisfaction of the Secretary that such property is for a foreign use.

For purposes of this clause, a sale of property shall be treated as a sale of each of the components thereof.

(ii) Service provided to related parties.—If a service is provided to a related party who is not located in the United States, such service shall not be treated described1 in subparagraph (A)(ii)2 unless the taxpayer established to the satisfaction of the Secretary that such service is not substantially similar to services provided by such related party to persons located within the United States.

(D) Related party.—For purposes of this paragraph, the term "related party" means any member of an affiliated group as defined in section 1504(a), determined—

(i) by substituting "more than 50 percent" for "at least 80 percent" each place it appears, and

(ii) without regard to paragraphs (2) and (3) of section 1504(b).

Any person (other than a corporation) shall be treated as a member of such group if such person is controlled by members of such group (including any entity treated as a member of such group by reason of this sentence) or controls any such member. For purposes of the preceding sentence, control shall be determined under the rules of section 954(d)(3).

(E) Sold.—For purposes of this subsection (other than paragraph (3)(A)(i)(VII)), the terms "sold", "sells", and "sale" shall include any lease, license, exchange, or other disposition.

(3) Deduction eligible income.—

(A) In general.—The term "deduction eligible income" means, with respect to any domestic corporation, the excess (if any) of—

(i) gross income of such corporation determined without regard to—

(I) any amount included in the gross income of such corporation under section 951(a)(1),

(II) the net CFC tested income included in the gross income of such corporation under section 951A,

(III) any financial services income (as defined in section 904(d)(2)(D)) of such corporation,

(IV) any dividend received from a corporation which is a controlled foreign corporation of such domestic corporation,

(V) any domestic oil and gas extraction income of such corporation,

(VI) any foreign branch income (as defined in section 904(d)(2)(J)), and

(VII) except as otherwise provided by the Secretary, any income and gain from the sale or other disposition (including pursuant to the deemed sale or other deemed disposition or a transaction subject to section 367(d)) of—

(aa) intangible property (as defined in section 367(d)(4)), and

(bb) any other property of a type that is subject to depreciation, amortization, or depletion by the seller, over

(ii) expenses and deductions (including taxes), other than interest expense and research or experimental expenditures, properly allocable to such gross income.

(B) Domestic oil and gas extraction income.—For purposes of subparagraph (A), the term "domestic oil and gas extraction income" means income described in section 907(c)(1), determined by substituting "within the United States" for "without the United States".

(c) Regulations.—The Secretary shall prescribe such regulations or other guidance as may be necessary or appropriate to carry out the provisions of this section.

Part IX—Items Not Deductible

§ 267. Losses, expenses, and interest with respect to transactions between related taxpayers

(a) In general.—

(1) Deduction for losses disallowed.—No deduction shall be allowed in respect of any loss from the sale or exchange of property, directly or indirectly, between persons specified in any of the paragraphs of subsection (b). The preceding sentence shall not apply to any loss of the distributing corporation (or the distributee) in the case of a distribution in complete liquidation.

(2) Matching of deduction and payee income item in the case of expenses and interest.—If—

(A) by reason of the method of accounting of the person to whom the payment is to be made, the amount thereof is not (unless paid) includible in the gross income of such person, and

(B) at the close of the taxable year of the taxpayer for which (but for this paragraph) the amount would be deductible under this chapter, both the taxpayer and the person to whom the payment is to be made are persons specified in any of the paragraphs of subsection (b),

then any deduction allowable under this chapter in respect of such amount shall be allowable as of the day as of which such amount is includible in the gross income of the person to whom the payment is made (or, if later, as of the day on which it would be so allowable but for this paragraph). For purposes of this paragraph, in the case of a personal service corporation (within the meaning of section 441(i)(2)), such corporation and any employee-owner (within the meaning of section 269A(b)(2), as modified by section 441(i)(2)) shall be treated as persons specified in subsection (b).

(3) Payments to foreign persons.—

(A) In general.—The Secretary shall by regulations apply the matching principle of paragraph (2) in cases in which the person to whom the payment is to be made is not a United States person.

(B) Special rule for certain foreign entities.—

(i) In general.—Notwithstanding subparagraph (A), in the case of any item payable to a controlled foreign corporation (as defined in section 957) or a passive foreign investment company (as defined in section 1297), a deduction shall be allowable to the payor with respect to such amount for any taxable year before the taxable year in which paid only to the extent that an amount attributable to such item is includible (determined without regard to properly allocable deductions and qualified deficits under section 952(c)(1)(B)) during such prior taxable year in the gross income of a United States person who owns (within the meaning of section 958(a)) stock in such corporation.

(ii) Secretarial authority.—The Secretary may by regulation exempt transactions from the application of clause (i), including any transaction which is entered into by a payor in the ordinary course of a trade or business in which the payor is predominantly engaged and in which the payment of the accrued amounts occurs within 8 1/2 months after accrual or within such other period as the Secretary may prescribe.

(b) Relationships.—The persons referred to in subsection (a) are:

(1) Members of a family, as defined in subsection (c)(4);

(2) An individual and a corporation more than 50 percent in value of the outstanding stock of which is owned, directly or indirectly, by or for such individual;

(3) Two corporations which are members of the same controlled group (as defined in subsection (f));

(4) A grantor and a fiduciary of any trust;

(5) A fiduciary of a trust and a fiduciary of another trust, if the same person is a grantor of both trusts;

(6) A fiduciary of a trust and a beneficiary of such trust;

(7) A fiduciary of a trust and a beneficiary of another trust, if the same person is a grantor of both trusts;

(8) A fiduciary of a trust and a corporation more than 50 percent in value of the outstanding stock of which is owned, directly or indirectly, by or for the trust or by or for a person who is a grantor of the trust;

(9) A person and an organization to which section 501 (relating to certain educational and charitable organizations which are exempt from tax) applies and which is controlled directly or indirectly by such person or (if such person is an individual) by members of the family of such individual;

(10) A corporation and a partnership if the same persons own—

(A) more than 50 percent in value of the outstanding stock of the corporation, and

(B) more than 50 percent of the capital interest, or the profits interest, in the partnership;

(11) An S corporation and another S corporation if the same persons own more than 50 percent in value of the outstanding stock of each corporation; **(b)**

(12) An S corporation and a C corporation, if the same persons own more than 50 percent in value of the outstanding stock of each corporation; or

(13) Except in the case of a sale or exchange in satisfaction of a pecuniary bequest, an executor of an estate and a beneficiary of such estate.

(c) Constructive ownership of stock.—For purposes of determining, in applying subsection (b), the ownership of stock—

(1) Stock owned, directly or indirectly, by or for a corporation, partnership, estate, or trust shall be considered as being owned proportionately by or for its shareholders, partners, or beneficiaries;

(2) An individual shall be considered as owning the stock owned, directly or indirectly, by or for his family;

(3) An individual owning (otherwise than by the application of paragraph (2)) any stock in a corporation shall be considered as owning the stock owned, directly or indirectly, by or for his partner;

(4) The family of an individual shall include only his brothers and sisters (whether by the whole or half blood), spouse, ancestors, and lineal descendants; and

(5) Stock constructively owned by a person by reason of the application of paragraph (1) shall, for the purpose of applying paragraph (1), (2), or (3), be treated as actually owned by such person, but stock constructively owned by an individual by reason of the application of paragraph (2) or (3) shall not be treated as owned by him for the purpose of again applying either of such paragraphs in order to make another the constructive owner of such stock.

(d) Amount of gain where loss previously disallowed.—

(1) In General.—If—

(A) in the case of a sale or exchange of property to the taxpayer a loss sustained by the transferor is not allowable to the transferor as a deduction by reason of subsection (a)(1), and

(B) the taxpayer sells or otherwise disposes of such property (or of other property the basis of which in the taxpayer's hands is determined directly or indirectly by reference to such property) at a gain,

then such gain shall be recognized only to the extent that it exceeds so much of such loss as is properly allocable to the property sold or otherwise disposed of by the taxpayer.

(2) Exception for wash sales.—Paragraph (1) shall not apply if the loss sustained by the transferor is not allowable to the transferor as a deduction by reason of section 1091 (relating to wash sales).

(3) Exception for transfers from tax indifferent parties.—Paragraph (1) shall not apply to the extent any loss sustained by the transferor (if allowed) would not be taken into account in determining a tax imposed under section 1 or 11 or a tax computed as provided by either of such sections.

(e) Special rules for pass-thru entities.—

(1) In general.—In the case of any amount paid or incurred by, to, or on behalf of, a pass-thru entity, for purposes of applying subsection (a)(2)—

(A) such entity,

(B) in the case of—

(i) a partnership, any person who owns (directly or indirectly) any capital interest or profits interest of such partnership, or

(ii) an S corporation, any person who owns (directly or indirectly) any of the stock of such corporation,

(C) any person who owns (directly or indirectly) any capital interest or profits interest of a partnership in which such entity owns (directly or indirectly) any capital interest or profits interest, and

(D) any person related (within the meaning of subsection (b) of this section or section 707(b)(1)) to a person described in subparagraph (B) or (C),

shall be treated as persons specified in a paragraph of subsection (b). Subparagraph (C) shall apply to a transaction only if such transaction is related either to the operations of the partnership described in such subparagraph or to an interest in such partnership.

(2) Pass-thru entity.—For purposes of this section, the term "pass-thru entity" means—

(A) a partnership, and

(B) an S corporation.

(3) Constructive ownership in the case of partnerships.—For purposes of determining ownership of a capital interest or profits interest of a partnership, the principles of subsection (c) shall apply, except that—

(A) paragraph (3) of subsection (c) shall not apply, and

(B) interests owned (directly or indirectly) by or for a C corporation shall be considered as owned by or for any shareholder only if such shareholder owns (directly or indirectly) 5 percent or more in value of the stock of such corporation.

(4) Subsection (a)(2) not to apply to certain guaranteed payments of partnerships.—In the case of any amount paid or incurred by a partnership, subsection (a)(2) shall not apply to the extent that section 707(c) applies to such amount.

* * *

(6) Cross reference.—

For additional rules relating to partnerships, see section 707(b).

(f) Controlled group defined; special rules applicable to controlled groups.—

(1) Controlled group defined.—For purposes of this section, the term "controlled group" has the meaning given to such term by section 1563(a), except that—

(A) "more than 50 percent" shall be substituted for "at least 80 percent" each place it appears in section 1563(a), and

(B) the determination shall be made without regard to subsections (a)(4) and (e)(3)

(C) of section 1563.

(2) Deferral (rather than denial) of loss from sale or exchange between members.—In the case of any loss from the sale or exchange of property which is between members of the same controlled group and to which subsection (a)(1) applies (determined without regard to this paragraph but with regard to paragraph (3))—

(A) subsections (a)(1) and (d) shall not apply to such loss, but

(B) such loss shall be deferred until the property is transferred outside such controlled group and there would be recognition of loss under consolidated return principles or until such other time as may be prescribed in regulations.

(3) Loss deferral rules not to apply in certain cases.—

(A) Transfer to DISC.—For purposes of applying subsection (a)(1), the term "controlled group" shall not include a DISC.

(B) Certain sales of inventory.—Except to the extent provided in regulations prescribed by the Secretary, subsection (a)(1) shall not apply to the sale or exchange of property between members of the same controlled group (or persons described in subsection (b)(10)) if—

(i) such property in the hands of the transferor is property described in section 1221(a)(1),

(ii) such sale or exchange is in the ordinary course of the transferor's trade or business,

(iii) such property in the hands of the transferee is property described in section 1221(a)(1), and

(iv) the transferee or the transferor is a foreign corporation.

(C) Certain foreign currency losses.—To the extent provided in regulations, subsection (a)(1) shall not apply to any loss sustained by a member of a controlled group on the repayment of a loan made to another member of such group if such loan is payable in a foreign currency or is denominated in such a currency and such loss is attributable to a reduction in value of such foreign currency.

* * *

(4) Determination of relationship resulting in disallowance of loss, for purposes of other provisions.—For purposes of any other section of this title which refers to a relationship which would result in a disallowance of losses under this section, deferral under paragraph (2) shall be treated as disallowance.

(g) Coordination with section 1041.—Subsection (a)(1) shall not apply to any transfer described in section 1041(a) (relating to transfers of property between spouses or incident to divorce).

§ 267A. Certain related party amounts paid or accrued in hybrid transactions or with hybrid entities

(a) In general.—No deduction shall be allowed under this chapter for any disqualified related party amount paid or accrued pursuant to a hybrid transaction or by, or to, a hybrid entity.

(b) Disqualified related party amount.—For purposes of this section—

(1) Disqualified related party amount.—The term "disqualified related party amount" means any interest or royalty paid or accrued to a related party to the extent that—

(A) such amount is not included in the income of such related party under the tax law of the country of which such related party is a resident for tax purposes or is subject to tax, or

(B) such related party is allowed a deduction with respect to such amount under the tax law of such country.

Such term shall not include any payment to the extent such payment is included in the gross income of a United States shareholder under section 951(a).

(2) Related party.—The term "related party" means a related person as defined in section 954(d)(3), except that such section shall be applied with respect to the person making the payment described in paragraph (1) in lieu of the controlled foreign corporation otherwise referred to in such section.

(c) Hybrid transaction.—For purposes of this section, the term "hybrid transaction" means any transaction, series of transactions, agreement, or instrument one or more payments with respect to which are treated as interest or royalties for purposes of this chapter and which are not so treated for purposes the tax law of the foreign country of which the recipient of such payment is resident for tax purposes or is subject to tax.

(d) Hybrid entity.—For purposes of this section, the term "hybrid entity" means any entity which is either—

(1) treated as fiscally transparent for purposes of this chapter but not so treated for purposes of the tax law of the foreign country of which the entity is resident for tax purposes or is subject to tax, or

(2) treated as fiscally transparent for purposes of such tax law but not so treated for purposes of this chapter.

(e) Regulations.—The Secretary shall issue such regulations or other guidance as may be necessary or appropriate to carry out the purposes of this section, including regulations or other guidance providing for—

(1) rules for treating certain conduit arrangements which involve a hybrid transaction or a hybrid entity as subject to subsection (a),

(2) rules for the application of this section to branches or domestic entities,

(3) rules for treating certain structured transactions as subject to subsection (a),

(4) rules for treating a tax preference as an exclusion from income for purposes of applying subsection (b)(1) if such tax preference has the effect of reducing the generally applicable statutory rate by 25 percent or more,

(5) rules for treating the entire amount of interest or royalty paid or accrued to a related party as a disqualified related party amount if such amount is subject to a participation exemption system or other system which provides for the exclusion or deduction of a substantial portion of such amount,

(6) rules for determining the tax residence of a foreign entity if the entity is otherwise considered a resident of more than one country or of no country,

(7) exceptions from subsection (a) with respect to—

(A) cases in which the disqualified related party amount is taxed under the laws of a foreign country other than the country of which the related party is a resident for tax purposes, and

(B) other cases which the Secretary determines do not present a risk of eroding the Federal tax base,

(8) requirements for record keeping and information reporting in addition to any requirements imposed by section 6038A.

§ 269B. Stapled entities

(a) General rule.—Except as otherwise provided by regulations, for purposes of this title—

(1) if a domestic corporation and a foreign corporation are stapled entities, the foreign corporation shall be treated as a domestic corporation.

(2) in applying section 1563, stock in a second corporation which constitutes a stapled interest with respect to stock of a first corporation shall be treated as owned by such first corporation, and

(3) in applying subchapter M for purposes of determining whether any stapled entity is a regulated investment company or a real estate investment trust, all entities which are stapled entities with respect to each other shall be treated as 1 entity.

(b) Secretary to prescribe regulations.—The Secretary shall prescribe such regulations as may be necessary to prevent avoidance or evasion of Federal income tax through the use of stapled entities. Such regulations may include (but shall not be limited to) regulations providing the extent to which 1 of such entities shall be treated as owning the other entity (to the extent of the stapled interest) and regulations providing that any tax imposed on the foreign corporation referred to in subsection (a)(1) may, if not paid by such corporation, be collected from the domestic corporation referred to in such subsection or the shareholders of such foreign corporation.

(c) Definitions.—For purposes of this section—

(1) Entity.—The term “entity” means any corporation, partnership, trust, association, estate, or other form of carrying on a business or activity.

(2) Stapled entities.—The term “stapled entities” means any group of 2 or more entities if more than 50 percent in value of the beneficial ownership in each of such entities consists of stapled interests.

(3) Stapled interests.—Two or more interests are stapled interests if, by reason of form of ownership, restrictions on transfer, or other terms or conditions, in connection with the transfer of 1 of such interests the other such interests are also transferred or required to be transferred.

(d) Special rule for treaties.—Nothing in section 894 or 7852(d) or in any other provision of law shall be construed as permitting an exemption, by reason of any treaty obligation of the United States heretofore or hereafter entered into, from the provisions of this section.

(e) Subsection (a)(1) not to apply in certain cases.—

(1) In general.—Subsection (a)(1) shall not apply if it is established to the satisfaction of the Secretary that the domestic corporation and the foreign corporation referred to in such subsection are foreign owned.

(2) Foreign owned.—For purposes of paragraph (1), a corporation is foreign owned if less than 50 percent of—

(A) the total combined voting power of all classes of stock of such corporation entitled to vote, and

(B) the total value of the stock of the corporation,

is held directly (or indirectly through applying paragraphs (2) and (3) of section 958(a) and paragraph (4) of section 318(a)) by United States persons (as defined in section 7701(a)(30)).

§ 275. Certain taxes

(a) General rule.—No deduction shall be allowed for the following taxes:

(1) Federal income taxes, including—

(A) the tax imposed by section 3101 (relating to the tax on employees under the Federal Insurance Contributions Act);

(B) the taxes imposed by sections 3201 and 3211 (relating to the taxes on railroad employees and railroad employee representatives); and

(C) the tax withheld at source on wages under section 3402.

(2) Federal war profits and excess profits taxes.

(3) Estate, inheritance, legacy, succession, and gift taxes.

(4) Income, war profits, and excess profits taxes imposed by the authority of any foreign country or possession of the United States if the taxpayer chooses to take to any extent the benefits of section 901.

(5) Taxes on real property, to the extent that section 164(d) requires such taxes to be treated as imposed on another taxpayer.

(6) Taxes imposed by chapters 41, 42, 43, 44, 45, 46, 50A, and 54.

Paragraph (1) shall not apply to any taxes to the extent such taxes are allowable as a deduction under section 164(f).

(b) Cross reference.—

For disallowance of certain other taxes, see section 164(c).

Subchapter C—Corporate Distributions and Adjustments

Part I—Distributions by Corporations

Subpart A—Effects on Recipients

§ 301. Distributions of property

(a) In general.—Except as otherwise provided in this chapter, a distribution of property (as defined in section 317(a)) made by a corporation to a shareholder with respect to its stock shall be treated in the manner provided in subsection (c).

* * *

(c) Amount taxable.—In the case of a distribution to which subsection (a) applies—

(1) Amount constituting dividend.—That portion of the distribution which is a dividend (as defined in section 316) shall be included in gross income.

(2) Amount applied against basis.—That portion of the distribution which is not a dividend shall be applied against and reduce the adjusted basis of the stock.

(3) Amount in excess of basis.—

(A) In general.—Except as provided in subparagraph (B), that portion of the distribution which is not a dividend, to the extent that it exceeds the adjusted basis of the stock, shall be treated as gain from the sale or exchange of property.

(B) Distributions out of increase in value accrued before March 1, 1913.—That portion of the distribution which is not a dividend, to the extent that it exceeds the adjusted basis of the stock and to the extent that it is out of increase in value accrued before March 1, 1913, shall be exempt from tax.

Subpart B—Effects on Corporation

§ 312. Effect on earnings and profits

(a) General rule.—Except as otherwise provided in this section, on the distribution of property by a corporation with respect to its stock, the earnings and profits of the corporation (to the extent thereof) shall be decreased by the sum of—

(1) the amount of money,

(2) the principal amount of the obligations of such corporation (or, in the case of obligations having original issue discount, the aggregate issue price of such obligations), and

(3) the adjusted basis of the other property, so distributed.

(b) Distributions of appreciated property.—On the distribution by a corporation, with respect to its stock, of any property (other than an obligation of such corporation) the fair market value of which exceeds the adjusted basis thereof—

(1) the earnings and profits of the corporation shall be increased by the amount of such excess, and

(2) subsection (a)(3) shall be applied by substituting "fair market value" for "adjusted basis".

For purposes of this subsection and subsection (a), the adjusted basis of any property is its adjusted basis as determined for purposes of computing earnings and profits.

* * *

(k) Effect of depreciation on earnings and profits.—

(1) General rule.—For purposes of computing the earnings and profits of a corporation for any taxable year beginning after June 30, 1972, the allowance for depreciation (and amortization, if any) shall be deemed to be the amount which would be allowable for such year if the straight line method of depreciation had been used for each taxable year beginning after June 30, 1972.

(2) Exception.—If for any taxable year a method of depreciation was used by the taxpayer which the Secretary has determined results in a reasonable allowance under section 167(a) and which is the unit-of-production method or other method not expressed in a term of years, then the adjustment to earnings and profits for depreciation for such year shall be determined under the method so used (in lieu of the straight line method).

(3) Exception for tangible property.—

(A) In general.—Except as provided in subparagraph (B), in the case of tangible property to which section 168 applies, the adjustment to earnings and profits for depreciation for any taxable year shall be determined under the alternative depreciation system (within the meaning of section 168(g)(2)).

(B) Treatment of amounts deductible under section 179, 179B, 179C, 179D or 179E.—

(i) In general—For purposes of computing the earnings and profits of a corporation, except as provided in clause (ii), any amount deductible under section 179, 179B, 179C, 179D or 179E shall be allowed as a deduction ratably over the period of 5 taxable years (beginning with the taxable year for which such amount is deductible under section 179, 179B, 179C, 179D or 179E, as the case may be).

* * *

(4) Certain foreign corporations.—The provisions of paragraph (1) shall not apply in computing the earnings and profits of a foreign corporation for any taxable year for which less than 20 percent of the gross income from all sources of such corporation is derived from sources within the United States.

* * *

Subpart C—Definitions; Constructive Ownership of Stock

§ 316. Dividend defined

(a) General rule.—For purposes of this subtitle, the term "dividend" means any distribution of property made by a corporation to its shareholders—

(1) out of its earnings and profits accumulated after February 28, 1913, or

(2) out of its earnings and profits of the taxable year (computed as of the close of the taxable year without diminution by reason of any distributions made during the taxable year), without regard to the amount of the earnings and profits at the time the distribution was made.

Except as otherwise provided in this subtitle, every distribution is made out of earnings and profits to the extent thereof, and from the most recently accumulated earnings and profits. To the extent that any distribution is, under any provision of this subchapter, treated as a distribution of property to which section 301 applies, such distribution shall be treated as a distribution of property for purposes of this subsection.

(b) Special rules.—

* * *

(2) Distributions by personal holding companies.—

(A) In the case of a corporation which—

(i) under the law applicable to the taxable year in which the distribution is made, is a personal holding company (as defined in section 542), or

(ii) for the taxable year in respect of which the distribution is made under section 563(b) (relating to dividends paid after the close of the taxable year), or section 547 (relating to deficiency dividends), or the corresponding provisions of prior law, is a personal holding company under the law applicable to such taxable year,

the term "dividend" also means any distribution of property (whether or not a dividend as defined in subsection (a)) made by the corporation to its shareholders, to the extent of its undistributed personal holding company income (determined under section 545 without regard to distributions under this paragraph) for such year.

(B) For purposes of subparagraph (A), the term "distribution of property" includes a distribution in complete liquidation occurring within 24 months after the adoption of a plan of liquidation, but—

(i) only to the extent of the amounts distributed to distributees other than corporate shareholders, and

(ii) only to the extent that the corporation designates such amounts as a dividend distribution and duly notifies such distributees of such designation, under regulations prescribed by the Secretary, but

(iii) not in excess of the sum of such distributees' allocable share of the undistributed personal holding company income for such year, computed without regard to this subparagraph or section 562(b).

* * *

§ 318. Constructive ownership of stock

(a) General rule.—For purposes of those provisions of this subchapter to which the rules contained in this section are expressly made applicable—

(1) Members of family.—

(A) In general.—An individual shall be considered as owning the stock owned, directly or indirectly, by or for—

(i) his spouse (other than a spouse who is legally separated from the individual under a decree of divorce or separate maintenance), and

(ii) his children, grandchildren, and parents.

(B) Effect of adoption.—For purposes of subparagraph (A)(ii), a legally adopted child of an individual shall be treated as a child of such individual by blood.

(2) Attribution from partnerships, estates, trusts, and corporations.—

(A) From partnerships and estates.—Stock owned, directly or indirectly, by or for a partnership or estate shall be considered as owned proportionately by its partners or beneficiaries.

(B) From trusts.—

(i) Stock owned, directly or indirectly, by or for a trust (other than an employees' trust described in section 401(a) which is exempt from tax under section 501(a)) shall be considered as owned by its beneficiaries in proportion to the actuarial interest of such beneficiaries in such trust.

(ii) Stock owned, directly or indirectly, by or for any portion of a trust of which a person is considered the owner under subpart E of part I of subchapter J (relating to grantors and others treated as substantial owners) shall be considered as owned by such person.

(C) From corporations.—If 50 percent or more in value of the stock in a corporation is owned, directly or indirectly, by or for any person, such person shall be considered as owning the stock owned, directly or indirectly, by or for such corporation, in that proportion which the value of the stock which such person so owns bears to the value of all the stock in such corporation.

(3) Attribution to partnerships, estates, trusts, and corporations.—

(A) To partnerships and estates.—Stock owned, directly or indirectly, by or for a partner or a beneficiary of an estate shall be considered as owned by the partnership or estate.

(B) To trusts.—

(i) Stock owned, directly or indirectly, by or for a beneficiary of a trust (other than an employees' trust described in section 401(a) which is exempt from tax under section 501(a)) shall be considered as owned by the trust, unless such beneficiary's interest in the trust is a remote contingent interest. For purposes of this clause, a contingent interest of a beneficiary in a trust shall be considered remote if, under the maximum exercise of discretion by the trustee in favor of such beneficiary, the value of such interest, computed actuarially, is 5 percent or less of the value of the trust property.

(ii) Stock owned, directly or indirectly, by or for a person who is considered the owner of any portion of a trust under subpart E of part I of subchapter J (relating to grantors and others treated as substantial owners) shall be considered as owned by the trust.

(C) To corporations.—If 50 percent or more in value of the stock in a corporation is owned, directly or indirectly, by or for any person, such corporation shall be considered as owning the stock owned, directly or indirectly, by or for such person.

(4) Options.—If any person has an option to acquire stock, such stock shall be considered as owned by such person. For purposes of this paragraph, an option to acquire such an option, and each one of a series of such options, shall be considered as an option to acquire such stock.

(5) Operating rules.—

(A) In general.—Except as provided in subparagraphs (B) and (C), stock constructively owned by a person by reason of the application of paragraph (1), (2), (3), or (4), shall, for purposes of applying paragraphs (1), (2), (3), and (4), be considered as actually owned by such person.

(B) Members of family.—Stock constructively owned by an individual by reason of the application of paragraph (1) shall not be considered as owned by him for purposes of again applying paragraph (1) in order to make another the constructive owner of such stock.

(C) Partnerships, estates, trusts, and corporations.—Stock constructively owned by a partnership, estate, trust, or corporation by reason of the application of paragraph (3) shall not be considered as owned by it for purposes of applying paragraph (2) in order to make another the constructive owner of such stock.

(D) Option rule in lieu of family rule.—For purposes of this paragraph, if stock may be considered as owned by an individual under paragraph (1) or (4), it shall be considered as owned by him under paragraph (4).

(E) S corporation treated as partnership.—For purposes of this subsection—

(i) an S corporation shall be treated as a partnership, and

(ii) any shareholder of the S corporation shall be treated as a partner of such partnership.

The preceding sentence shall not apply for purposes of determining whether stock in the S corporation is constructively owned by any person.

(b) Cross references.—

For provisions to which the rules contained in subsection (a) apply, see—

* * *

(7) section 958(b) (relating to constructive ownership rules with respect to controlled foreign corporations); and

(8) section 6038(e)(2) (relating to information with respect to certain foreign corporations).

Part II—Corporate Liquidations

Subpart A—Effects on Recipients

§ 331. Gain or loss to shareholder in corporate liquidations

(a) Distributions in complete liquidation treated as exchanges.—Amounts received by a shareholder in a distribution in complete liquidation of a corporation shall be treated as in full payment in exchange for the stock.

(b) Nonapplication of section 301.—Section 301 (relating to effects on shareholder of distributions of property) shall not apply to any distribution of property (other than a distribution referred to in paragraph (2)(B) of section 316(b)) in complete liquidation.

(c) Cross reference.—

For general rule for determination of the amount of gain or loss recognized, see section 1001.

§ 332. Complete liquidations of subsidiaries

(a) General rule.—No gain or loss shall be recognized on the receipt by a corporation of property distributed in complete liquidation of another corporation.

(b) Liquidations to which section applies.—For purposes of this section, a distribution shall be considered to be in complete liquidation only if—

(1) the corporation receiving such property was, on the date of the adoption of the plan of liquidation, and has continued to be at all times until the receipt of the property, the owner of stock (in such other corporation) meeting the requirements of section 1504(a)(2); and either

(2) the distribution is by such other corporation in complete cancellation or redemption of all its stock, and the transfer of all the property occurs within the taxable year; in such case the adoption by the shareholders of the resolution under which is authorized the distribution of all the assets of such corporation in complete cancellation or redemption of all its stock shall be considered an adoption of a plan of liquidation, even though no time for the completion of the transfer of the property is specified in such resolution; or

(3) such distribution is one of a series of distributions by such other corporation in complete cancellation or redemption of all its stock in accordance with a plan of liquidation under which the transfer of all the property under the liquidation is to be completed within 3 years from the close of the taxable year during which is made the first of the series of distributions under the plan, except that if such transfer is not completed within such period, or if the taxpayer does not continue qualified under paragraph (1) until the completion of such transfer, no distribution under the plan shall be considered a distribution in complete liquidation.

If such transfer of all the property does not occur within the taxable year, the Secretary may require of the taxpayer such bond, or waiver of the statute of limitations on assessment and collection, or both, as he may deem necessary to insure, if the transfer of the property is not completed within such 3-year period, or if the taxpayer does not continue qualified under paragraph (1) until the completion of such transfer, the assessment and collection of all income taxes then imposed by law for such taxable year or subsequent taxable years, to the extent attributable to property so received. A distribution otherwise constituting a distribution in complete liquidation within the meaning of this subsection shall not be considered as not constituting such a distribution merely because it does not constitute a distribution or liquidation within the meaning of the corporate law under which the distribution is made; and for purposes of this subsection a transfer of property of such other corporation to the taxpayer shall not be considered as not constituting a distribution (or one of a series of distributions) in complete cancellation or redemption of all the stock of such other corporation, merely because the carrying out of the plan involves (A) the transfer under the plan to the taxpayer by such other corporation of property, not attributable to shares owned by the taxpayer, on an exchange described in section 361, and (B) the complete cancellation or redemption under the plan, as a result of exchanges described in section 354, of the shares not owned by the taxpayer. **§ 332(b)**

* * *

§ 334. Basis of property received in liquidations

(a) General rule.—If property is received in a distribution in complete liquidation, and if gain or loss is recognized on receipt of such property, then the basis of the property in the hands of the distributee shall be the fair market value of such property at the time of the distribution.

(b) Liquidation of subsidiary.—

(1) In general.—If property is received by a corporate distributee in a distribution in a complete liquidation to which section 332 applies (or in a transfer described in section 337(b)(1)), the basis of such property in the hands of such distributee shall be the same as it would be in the hands of the transferor; except that, in the hands of such distributee—

(A) the basis of such property shall be the fair market value of the property at the time of the distribution in any case in which gain or loss is recognized by the liquidating corporation with respect to such property, and

(B) the basis of any property described in section 362(e)(1)(B) shall be the fair market value of the property at the time of the distribution in any case in which such distributee's aggregate adjusted basis of such property would (but for this subparagraph) exceed the fair market value of such property immediately after such liquidation.

(2) Corporate distributee.—For purposes of this subsection, the term "corporate distributee" means only the corporation which meets the stock ownership requirements specified in section 332(b).

Subpart B—Effects on Corporation

§ 336. Gain or loss recognized on property distributed in complete liquidation

(a) **General rule.**—Except as otherwise provided in this section or section 337, gain or loss shall be recognized to a liquidating corporation on the distribution of property in complete liquidation as if such property were sold to the distributee at its fair market value.

(b) Treatment of liabilities.—If any property distributed in the liquidation is subject to a liability or the shareholder assumes a liability of the liquidating corporation in connection with the distribution, for purposes of subsection (a) and section 337, the fair market value of such property shall be treated as not less than the amount of such liability.

(c) Exception for liquidations which are part of a reorganization.—For provision providing that this subpart does not apply to distributions in pursuance of a plan of reorganization, see section 361(c)(4).

(d) Limitations on recognition of loss.—

(1) No loss recognized in certain distributions to related persons.—

(A) In general.—No loss shall be recognized to a liquidating corporation on the distribution of any property to a related person (within the meaning of section 267) if—

(i) such distribution is not pro rata, or

(ii) such property is disqualified property.

(B) Disqualified property.—For purposes of subparagraph (A), the term "disqualified property" means any property which is acquired by the liquidating corporation in a transaction to which section 351 applied, or as a contribution to capital, during the 5-year period ending on the date of the distribution. Such term includes any property if the adjusted basis of such property is determined (in whole or in part) by reference to the adjusted basis of property described in the preceding sentence.

(2) Special rule for certain property acquired in certain carryover basis transactions.—

(A) In general.—For purposes of determining the amount of loss recognized by any liquidating corporation on any sale, exchange, or distribution of property described in subparagraph (B), the adjusted basis of such property shall be reduced (but not below zero) by the excess (if any) of—

(i) the adjusted basis of such property immediately after its acquisition by such corporation, over

(ii) the fair market value of such property as of such time.

(B) Description of property.—

(i) In general.—For purposes of subparagraph (A), property is described in this subparagraph if—

(I) such property is acquired by the liquidating corporation in a transaction to which section 351 applied or as a contribution to capital, and

(II) the acquisition of such property by the liquidating corporation was part of a plan a principal purpose of which was to recognize loss by the liquidating corporation with respect to such property in connection with the liquidation.

Other property shall be treated as so described if the adjusted basis of such other property is determined (in whole or in part) by reference to the adjusted basis of property described in the preceding sentence.

(ii) Certain acquisitions treated as part of plan.—For purposes of clause (i), any property described in clause (i)(I) acquired by the liquidated corporation after the date 2 years before the date of the adoption of the plan of complete liquidation shall, except as provided in regulations, be treated as acquired as part of a plan described in clause (i)(II). **§ 336(d)**

(C) Recapture in lieu of disallowance.—The Secretary may prescribe regulations under which, in lieu of disallowing a loss under subparagraph (A) for a prior taxable year, the gross income of the liquidating corporation for the taxable year in which the plan of complete liquidation is adopted shall be increased by the amount of the disallowed loss.

(3) Special rule in case of liquidation to which section 332 applies.—In the case of any liquidation to which section 332 applies, no loss shall be recognized to the liquidating corporation on any distribution in such liquidation. The preceding sentence shall apply to any distribution to the 80-percent distributee only if subsection (a) or (b)(1) of section 337 applies to such distribution.

(e) Certain stock sales and distributions may be treated as asset transfers.—Under regulations prescribed by the Secretary, if—

(1) a corporation owns stock in another corporation meeting the requirements of section 1504(a)(2), and

(2) such corporation sells, exchanges, or distributes all of such stock, an election may be made to treat such sale, exchange, or distribution as a disposition of all of the assets of such other corporation, and no gain or loss shall be recognized on the sale, exchange, or distribution of such stock.

§ 337. Nonrecognition for property distributed to parent in complete liquidation of subsidiary

(a) In general.—No gain or loss shall be recognized to the liquidating corporation on the distribution to the 80-percent distributee of any property in a complete liquidation to which section 332 applies.

(b) Treatment of indebtedness of subsidiary, etc.—

(1) Indebtedness of subsidiary to parent.—If—

(A) a corporation is liquidated in a liquidation to which section 332 applies, and

(B) on the date of the adoption of the plan of liquidation, such corporation was indebted to the 80-percent distributee,

for purposes of this section and section 336, any transfer of property to the 80-percent distributee in satisfaction of such indebtedness shall be treated as a distribution to such distributee in such liquidation.

* * *

(c) 80-percent distributee.—For purposes of this section, the term "80-percent distributee" means only the corporation which meets the 80-percent stock ownership requirements specified in section 332(b). For purposes of this section, the determination of whether any corporation is an 80-percent distributee shall be made without regard to any consolidated return regulation.

(d) Regulations.—The Secretary shall prescribe such regulations as may be necessary or appropriate to carry out the purposes of the amendments made by subtitle D of title VI of the Tax Reform Act of 1986, including—

(1) regulations to ensure that such purposes may not be circumvented through the use of any provision of law or regulations (including the consolidated return regulations and part III of this subchapter) or through the use of a regulated investment company, real estate investment trust, or tax-exempt entity, and

(2) regulations providing for appropriate coordination of the provisions of this section with the provisions of this title relating to taxation of foreign corporations and their shareholders.

Part III—Corporate Organizations and Reorganizations

Subpart A—Corporate Organizations

§ 351. Transfer to corporation controlled by transferor

(a) General rule.—No gain or loss shall be recognized if property is transferred to a corporation by one or more persons solely in exchange for stock in such corporation and immediately after the exchange such person or persons are in control (as defined in section 368(c)) of the corporation.

(b) Receipt of property.—If subsection (a) would apply to an exchange but for the fact that there is received, in addition to the stock permitted to be received under subsection (a), other property or money, then—

(1) gain (if any) to such recipient shall be recognized, but not in excess of—

(A) the amount of money received, plus

(B) the fair market value of such other property received; and **(2)** no loss to such recipient shall be recognized.

* * *

(d) Services, certain indebtedness, and accrued interest not treated as property.—For purposes of this section, stock issued for—

(1) services,

(2) indebtedness of the transferee corporation which is not evidenced by a security, or

(3) interest on indebtedness of the transferee corporation which accrued on or after the beginning of the transferor's holding period for the debt, shall not be considered as issued in return for property.

* * *

Subpart B—Effects on Shareholders and Security Holders

§ 354. Exchanges of stock and securities in certain reorganizations

(a) General rule.—

(1) In general.—No gain or loss shall be recognized if stock or securities in a corporation a party to a reorganization are, in pursuance of the plan of reorganization, exchanged solely for stock or securities in such corporation or in another corporation a party to the reorganization.

(2) Limitations.—

(A) Excess principal amount.—Paragraph (1) shall not apply if—

(i) the principal amount of any such securities received exceeds the principal amount of any such securities surrendered, or

(ii) any such securities are received and no such securities are surrendered.

(B) Property attributable to accrued interest.—Neither paragraph (1) nor so much of section 356 as relates to paragraph (1) shall apply to the extent that any stock (including nonqualified preferred stock, as defined in section 351(g)(2)), securities, or other property received is attributable to interest which has accrued on securities on or after the beginning of the holder's holding period.

* * *

(3) Cross references.—

(A) For treatment of the exchange if any property is received which is not permitted to be received under this subsection (including nonqualified preferred stock and an excess principal amount of securities received over securities surrendered, but not including property to which paragraph (2)(B) applies), see section 356.

(B) For treatment of accrued interest in the case of an exchange described in paragraph (2)(B), see section 61.

(b) Exception.—

(1) In general.—Subsection (a) shall not apply to an exchange in pursuance of a plan of reorganization within the meaning of subparagraph (D) or (G) of section 368(a)(1), unless—

(A) the corporation to which the assets are transferred acquires substantially all of the assets of the transferor of such assets; and

(B) the stock, securities, and other properties received by such transferor, as well as the other properties of such transferor, are distributed in pursuance of the plan of reorganization.

(2) Cross reference.—

For special rules for certain exchanges in pursuance of plans of reorganization within the meaning of subparagraph (D) or (G) of section 368(a)(1), see section 355.

* * *

§ 355. Distribution of stock and securities of a controlled corporation

(a) Effect on distributees.—

(1) General rule.—If—

(A) a corporation (referred to in this section as the "distributing corporation")—

(i) distributes to a shareholder, with respect to its stock, or

(ii) distributes to a security holder, in exchange for its securities,

solely stock or securities of a corporation (referred to in this section as "controlled corporation") which it controls immediately before the distribution,

(B) the transaction was not used principally as a device for the distribution of the earnings and profits of the distributing corporation or the controlled corporation or both (but the mere fact that subsequent to the distribution stock or securities in one or more of such corporations are sold or exchanged by all or some of the distributees (other than pursuant to an arrangement negotiated or agreed upon prior to such distribution) shall not be construed to mean that the transaction was used principally as such a device),

(C) the requirements of subsection (b) (relating to active businesses) are satisfied,

and

(D) as part of the distribution, the distributing corporation distributes—

(i) all of the stock and securities in the controlled corporation held by it immediately before the distribution, or

(ii) an amount of stock in the controlled corporation constituting control within the meaning of section 368(c), and it is established to the satisfaction of the Secretary that the retention by the distributing corporation of stock (or stock and securities) in the controlled corporation was not in pursuance of a plan having as one of its principal purposes the avoidance of Federal income tax, then no gain or loss shall be recognized to (and no amount shall be includible in the income of) such shareholder or security holder on the receipt of such stock or securities.

(2) Non pro rata distributions, etc.—Paragraph (1) shall be applied without regard to the following:

(A) whether or not the distribution is pro rata with respect to all of the shareholders of the distributing corporation,

(B) whether or not the shareholder surrenders stock in the distributing corporation, and

(C) whether or not the distribution is in pursuance of a plan of reorganization (within the meaning of section 368(a)(1)(D)).

(3) Limitations.—

(A) Excess principal amount.—Paragraph (1) shall not apply if—

(i) the principal amount of the securities in the controlled corporation which are received exceeds the principal amount of the securities which are surrendered in connection with such distribution, or

(ii) securities in the controlled corporation are received and no securities are surrendered in connection with such distribution.

(B) Stock acquired in taxable transactions within 5 years treated as boot.—For purposes of this section (other than paragraph (1)(D) of this subsection) and so much of section 356 as relates to this section, stock of a controlled corporation acquired by the distributing corporation by reason of any transaction— **(a)**

(i) which occurs within 5 years of the distribution of such stock, and

(ii) in which gain or loss was recognized in whole or in part, shall not be treated as stock of such controlled corporation, but as other property.

(C) Property attributable to accrued interest.—Neither paragraph (1) nor so much of section 356 as relates to paragraph (1) shall apply to the extent that any stock (including nonqualified preferred stock, as defined in section 351(g)(2)), securities, or other property received is attributable to interest which has accrued on securities on or after the beginning of the holder's holding period.

(D) Nonqualified preferred stock.—Nonqualified preferred stock (as defined in section 351(g)(2)) received in a distribution with respect to stock other than nonqualified preferred stock (as so defined) shall not be treated as stock or securities.

(4) Cross references.—

(A) For treatment of the exchange if any property is received which is not permitted to be received under this subsection (including nonqualified preferred stock and an excess principal amount of securities received over securities surrendered, but not including property to which paragraph (3)(C) applies), see section 356.

(B) For treatment of accrued interest in the case of an exchange described in paragraph (3)(C), see section 61.

(b) Requirements as to active business.—

(1) In general.—Subsection (a) shall apply only if either—

(A) the distributing corporation, and the controlled corporation (or, if stock of more than one controlled corporation is distributed, each of such corporations), is engaged immediately after the distribution in the active conduct of a trade or business, or

(B) immediately before the distribution, the distributing corporation had no assets other than stock or securities in the controlled corporations and each of the controlled corporations is engaged immediately after the distribution in the active conduct of a trade or business.

(2) Definition.—For purposes of paragraph (1), a corporation shall be treated as engaged in the active conduct of a trade or business if and only if—

(A) it is engaged in the active conduct of a trade or business,

(B) such trade or business has been actively conducted throughout the 5-year period ending on the date of the distribution,

(C) such trade or business was not acquired within the period described in subparagraph (B) in a transaction in which gain or loss was recognized in whole or in part, and

(D) control of a corporation which (at the time of acquisition of control) was conducting such trade or business—

(i) was not acquired by any distributee corporation directly (or through 1 or more corporations, whether through the distributing corporation or otherwise) within the period described in subparagraph (B) and was not acquired by the distributing corporation directly (or through 1 or more corporations) within such period, or

(ii) was so acquired by any such corporation within such period, but, in each case in which such control was so acquired, it was so acquired, only by reason of transactions in which gain or loss was not recognized in whole or in part, or only by reason of such transactions combined with acquisitions before the beginning of such period.

For purposes of subparagraph (D), all distributee corporations which are members of the same affiliated group (as defined in section 1504(a) without regard to section 1504(b)) shall be treated as 1 distributee corporation.

(3) Special rules for determining active conduct in the case of affiliated groups.—

(A) In general.—For purposes of determining whether a corporation meets the requirements of paragraph (2)(A), all members of such corporation's separate affiliated group shall be treated as one corporation.

(B) Separate affiliated group.—For purposes of this paragraph, the term 'separate affiliated group' means, with respect to any corporation, the affiliated group which would be determined under section 1504(a) if such corporation were the common parent and section 1504(b) did not apply.

(C) Treatment of trade or business conducted by acquired member.—If a corporation became a member of a separate affiliated group as a result of one or more transactions in which gain or loss was recognized in whole or in part, any trade or business conducted by such corporation (at the time that such corporation became such a member) shall be treated for purposes of paragraph (2) as acquired in a transaction in which gain or loss was recognized in whole or in part.

(D) Regulations.—The Secretary shall prescribe such regulations as are necessary or appropriate to carry out the purposes of this paragraph, including regulations which provide for the proper application of subparagraphs (B), (C), and (D) of paragraph (2), and modify the application of subsection (a)(3)(B), in connection with the application of this paragraph.

(c) Taxability of corporation on distribution.—

(1) In general.—Except as provided in paragraph (2), no gain or loss shall be recognized to a corporation on any distribution to which this section (or so much of section 356 as relates to this section) applies and which is not in pursuance of a plan of reorganization.

(2) Distribution of appreciated property.—

(A) In general.—If—

(i) in a distribution referred to in paragraph (1), the corporation distributes property other than qualified property, and

(ii) the fair market value of such property exceeds its adjusted basis (in the hands of the distributing corporation),

then gain shall be recognized to the distributing corporation as if such property were sold to the distributee at its fair market value.

(B) Qualified property.—For purposes of subparagraph (A), the term "qualified property" means any stock or securities in the controlled corporation.

(C) Treatment of liabilities.—If any property distributed in the distribution referred to in paragraph (1) is subject to a liability or the shareholder assumes a liability of the distributing corporation in connection with the distribution, then, for purposes of subparagraph (A), the fair market value of such property shall be treated as not less than the amount of such liability.

(3) Coordination with sections 311 and 336(a).—Sections 311 and 336(a) shall not apply to any distribution referred to in paragraph (1).

(d) Recognition of gain on certain distributions of stock or securities in controlled corporation.—

(1) In general.—In the case of a disqualified distribution, any stock or securities in the controlled corporation shall not be treated as qualified property for purposes of subsection (c)(2) of this section or section 361(c)(2).

(2) Disqualified distribution.—For purposes of this subsection, the term "disqualified distribution" means any distribution to which this section (or so much of section 356 as relates to this section) applies if, immediately after the distribution—

(A) any person holds disqualified stock in the distributing corporation which constitutes a 50-percent or greater interest in such corporation, or

(B) any person holds disqualified stock in the controlled corporation (or, if stock of more than 1 controlled corporation is distributed, in any controlled corporation) which constitutes a 50-percent or greater interest in such corporation.

(3) Disqualified stock.—For purposes of this subsection, the term "disqualified stock" means—

(A) any stock in the distributing corporation acquired by purchase during the 5-year period ending on the date of the distribution, and

(B) any stock in any controlled corporation—

(i) acquired by purchase during the 5-year period ending on the date of the distribution, or

(ii) received in the distribution to the extent attributable to distributions on—

(I) stock described in subparagraph (A), or

(II) any securities in the distributing corporation acquired by purchase during the 5-year period ending on the date of the distribution.

(4) 50-percent or greater interest.—For purposes of this subsection, the term "50-percent or greater interest" means stock possessing at least 50 percent of the total combined voting power of all classes of stock entitled to vote or at least 50 percent of the total value of shares of all classes of stock.

(5) Purchase.—For purposes of this subsection—

(A) In general.—Except as otherwise provided in this paragraph, the term "purchase" means any acquisition but only if—

(i) the basis of the property acquired in the hands of the acquirer is not determined (I) in whole or in part by reference to the adjusted basis of such property in the hands of the person from whom acquired, or (II) under section 1014(a), and

(ii) the property is not acquired in an exchange to which section 351, 354, 355, or 356 applies.

(B) Certain section 351 exchanges treated as purchases.—The term "purchase" includes any acquisition of property in an exchange to which section 351 applies to the extent such property is acquired in exchange for—

(i) any cash or cash item,

(ii) any marketable stock or security, or

(iii) any debt of the transferor.

(C) Carryover basis transactions.—If—

(i) any person acquires property from another person who acquired such property by purchase (as determined under this paragraph with regard to this subparagraph), and

(ii) the adjusted basis of such property in the hands of such acquirer is determined in whole or in part by reference to the adjusted basis of such property in the hands of such other person,

such acquirer shall be treated as having acquired such property by purchase on the date it was so acquired by such other person.

(6) Special rule where substantial diminution of risk.—

(A) In general.—If this paragraph applies to any stock or securities for any period, the running of any 5-year period set forth in subparagraph (A) or (B) of paragraph (3) (whichever applies) shall be suspended during such period.

(B) Property to which suspension applies.—This paragraph applies to any stock or securities for any period during which the holder's risk of loss with respect to such stock or securities, or with respect to any portion of the activities of the corporation, is (directly or indirectly) substantially diminished by—

(i) an option,

(ii) a short sale,

(iii) any special class of stock, or

(iv) any other device or transaction.

(7) Aggregation rules.—

(A) In general.—For purposes of this subsection, a person and all persons related to such person (within the meaning of section 267(b) or 707(b)(1)) shall be treated as one person.

(B) Persons acting pursuant to plans or arrangements.—If two or more persons act pursuant to a plan or arrangement with respect to acquisitions of stock or securities in the distributing corporation or controlled corporation, such persons shall be treated as one person for purposes of this subsection.

(8) Attribution from entities.—

(A) In general.—Paragraph (2) of section 318(a) shall apply in determining whether a person holds stock or securities in any corporation (determined by substituting "10 percent" for "50 percent" in subparagraph (C) of such paragraph (2) and by treating any reference to stock as including a reference to securities).

(B) Deemed purchase rule.—If—

(i) any person acquires by purchase an interest in any entity, and

(ii) such person is treated under subparagraph (A) as holding any stock or securities by reason of holding such interest,

such stock or securities shall be treated as acquired by purchase by such person on the later of the date of the purchase of the interest in such entity or the date such stock or securities are acquired by purchase by such entity.

(9) Regulations.—The Secretary shall prescribe such regulations as may be necessary to carry out the purposes of this subsection, including—

(A) regulations to prevent the avoidance of the purposes of this subsection through the use of related persons, intermediaries, pass-thru entities, options, or other arrangements, and

(B) regulations modifying the definition of the term "purchase".

(e) Recognition of gain on certain distributions of stock or securities in connection with acquisitions.—

(1) General rule.—If there is a distribution to which this subsection applies, any stock or securities in the controlled corporation shall not be treated as qualified property for purposes of subsection (c)(2) of this section or section 361(c)(2).

(2) Distributions to which subsection applies.—

(A) In general.—This subsection shall apply to any distribution—

(i) to which this section (or so much of section 356 as relates to this section) applies, and

(ii) which is part of a plan (or series of related transactions) pursuant to which 1 or more persons acquire directly or indirectly stock representing a 50-percent or greater interest in the distributing corporation or any controlled corporation.

(B) Plan presumed to exist in certain cases.—If 1 or more persons acquire directly or indirectly stock representing a 50-percent or greater interest in the distributing corporation or any controlled corporation during the 4-year period beginning on the date which is 2 years before the date of the distribution, such acquisition shall be treated as pursuant to a plan described in subparagraph (A)(ii) unless it is established that the distribution and the acquisition are not pursuant to a plan or series of related transactions.

(C) Certain plans disregarded.—A plan (or series of related transactions) shall not be treated as described in subparagraph (A)(ii) if, immediately after the completion of such plan or transactions, the distributing corporation and all controlled corporations are members of a single affiliated group (as defined in section 1504 without regard to subsection (b) thereof).

(D) Coordination with subsection (d).—This subsection shall not apply to any distribution to which subsection (d) applies.

(3) Special rules relating to acquisitions.—

(A) Certain acquisitions not taken into account.—Except as provided in regulations, the following acquisitions shall not be taken into account in applying paragraph (2)(A)(ii):

(i) The acquisition of stock in any controlled corporation by the distributing corporation.

(ii) The acquisition by a person of stock in any controlled corporation by reason of holding stock or securities in the distributing corporation.

(iii) The acquisition by a person of stock in any successor corporation of the distributing corporation or any controlled corporation by reason of holding stock or securities in such distributing or controlled corporation.

(iv) The acquisition of stock in the distributing corporation or any controlled corporation to the extent that the percentage of stock owned directly or indirectly in such corporation by each person owning stock in such corporation immediately before the acquisition does not decrease.

This subparagraph shall not apply to any acquisition if the stock held before the acquisition was acquired pursuant to a plan (or series of related transactions) described in paragraph (2)(A)(ii).

(B) Asset acquisitions.—Except as provided in regulations, for purposes of this subsection, if the assets of the distributing corporation or any controlled corporation are acquired by a successor corporation in a transaction described in subparagraph (A), (C), or (D) of section 368(a)(1) or any other transaction specified in regulations by the Secretary, the shareholders (immediately before the acquisition) of the corporation acquiring such assets shall be treated as acquiring stock in the corporation from which the assets were acquired.

(4) Definition and special rules.—For purposes of this subsection—

(A) 50-percent or greater interest.—The term "50-percent or greater interest" has the meaning given such term by subsection (d)(4).

(B) Distributions in title 11 or similar case.—Paragraph (1) shall not apply to any distribution made in a title 11 or similar case (as defined in section 368(a)(3)).

(C) Aggregation and attribution rules.—

(i) Aggregation.—The rules of paragraph (7)(A) of subsection (d) shall apply.

(ii) Attribution.—Section 318(a)(2) shall apply in determining whether a person holds stock or securities in any corporation. Except as provided in regulations, section 318(a)(2)(C) shall be applied without regard to the phrase "50 percent or more in value" for purposes of the preceding sentence.

(D) Successors and predecessors.—For purposes of this subsection, any reference to a controlled corporation or a distributing corporation shall include a reference to any predecessor or successor of such corporation.

(E) Statute of limitations.—If there is a distribution to which paragraph (1) applies—

(i) the statutory period for the assessment of any deficiency attributable to any part of the gain recognized under this subsection by reason of such distribution shall not expire before the expiration of 3 years from the date the Secretary is notified by the taxpayer (in such manner as the Secretary may by regulations prescribe) that such distribution occurred, and

(ii) such deficiency may be assessed before the expiration of such 3-year period notwithstanding the provisions of any other law or rule of law which would otherwise prevent such assessment.

(5) Regulations.—The Secretary shall prescribe such regulations as may be necessary to carry out the purposes of this subsection, including regulations—

(A) providing for the application of this subsection where there is more than 1 controlled corporation,

(B) treating 2 or more distributions as 1 distribution where necessary to prevent the avoidance of such purposes, and

(C) providing for the application of rules similar to the rules of subsection (d)(6) where appropriate for purposes of paragraph (2)(B).

(f) Section not to apply to certain intragroup distributions.—Except as provided in regulations, this section (or so much of section 356 as relates to this section) shall not apply to the distribution of stock from 1 member of an affiliated group (as defined in section 1504(a)) to another member of such group if such distribution is part of a plan (or series of related transactions) described in subsection (e)(2)(A)(ii) (determined after the application of subsection (e)).

(g) Section not to apply to distributions involving disqualified investment corporations.—

(1) In general.—This section (and so much of section 356 as relates to this section) shall not apply to any distribution which is part of a transaction if—

(A) either the distributing corporation or controlled corporation is, immediately after the transaction, a disqualified investment corporation, and

(B) any person holds, immediately after the transaction, a 50-percent or greater interest in any disqualified investment corporation, but only if such person did not hold such an interest in such corporation immediately before the transaction.

(2) Disqualified investment corporation.—For purposes of this subsection—

(A) In general.—The term "disqualified investment corporation" means any distributing or controlled corporation if the fair market value of the investment assets of the corporation is—

(i) in the case of distributions after the end of the 1-year period beginning on the date of the enactment of this subsection, 2/3 or more of the fair market value of all assets of the corporation, and

(ii) in the case of distributions during such 1-year period, 3/4 or more of the fair market value of all assets of the corporation.

(B) Investment assets.—

(i) In general.—Except as otherwise provided in this subparagraph, the term "investment assets" means—

(I) cash,

(II) any stock or securities in a corporation,

(III) any interest in a partnership,

(IV) any debt instrument or other evidence of indebtedness,

(V) any option, forward or futures contract, notional principal contract, or derivative,

(VI) foreign currency, or

(VII) any similar asset.

(ii) Exception for assets used in active conduct of certain financial trades or businesses.—Such term shall not include any asset which is held for use in the active and regular conduct of—

(I) a lending or finance business (within the meaning of section 954(h)(4)),

(II) a banking business through a bank (as defined in section 581), a domestic building and loan association (within the meaning of section 7701(a)(19)), or any similar institution specified by the Secretary, or

(III) an insurance business if the conduct of the business is licensed, authorized, or regulated by an applicable insurance regulatory body.

This clause shall only apply with respect to any business if substantially all of the income of the business is derived from persons who are not related (within the meaning of section 267(b) or 707(b)(1)) to the person conducting the business.

(iii) Exception for securities marked to market.—Such term shall not include any security (as defined in section 475(c)(2)) which is held by a dealer in securities and to which section 475(a) applies.

(iv) Stock or securities in a 20-percent controlled entity.—

(I) In general.—Such term shall not include any stock and securities in, or any asset described in subclause (IV) or (V) of clause (i) issued by, a corporation which is a 20-percent controlled entity with respect to the distributing or controlled corporation.

(II) Look-thru rule.—The distributing or controlled corporation shall, for purposes of applying this subsection, be treated as owning its ratable share of the assets of any 20-percent controlled entity.

(III) 20-percent controlled entity.—For purposes of this clause, the term "20- percent controlled entity" means, with respect to any distributing or controlled corporation, any corporation with respect to which the distributing or controlled corporation owns directly or indirectly stock meeting the requirements of section 1504(a)(2), except that such section shall be applied by substituting "20 percent" for "80 percent" and without regard to stock described in section 1504(a)(4).

(v) Interests in certain partnerships.—

(I) In general.—Such term shall not include any interest in a partnership, or any debt instrument or other evidence of indebtedness, issued by the partnership, if 1 or more of the trades or businesses of the partnership are (or, without regard to the 5-year requirement under subsection (b)(2)(B), would be) taken into account by the distributing or controlled corporation, as the case may be, in determining whether the requirements of subsection (b) are met with respect to the distribution.

(II) Look-thru rule.—The distributing or controlled corporation shall, for purposes of applying this subsection, be treated as owning its ratable share of the assets of any partnership described in subclause (I).

(3) 50-percent or greater interest.—For purposes of this subsection—

(A) In general.—The term "50-percent or greater interest" has the meaning given such term by subsection (d)(4).

(B) Attribution rules.—The rules of section 318 shall apply for purposes of determining ownership of stock for purposes of this paragraph.

(4) Transaction.—For purposes of this subsection, the term "transaction" includes a series of transactions.

(5) Regulations.—The Secretary shall prescribe such regulations as may be necessary to carry out, or prevent the avoidance of, the purposes of this subsection, including regulations—

(A) to carry out, or prevent the avoidance of, the purposes of this subsection in cases involving—

(i) the use of related persons, intermediaries, pass-thru entities, options, or other arrangements, and

(ii) the treatment of assets unrelated to the trade or business of a corporation as investment assets if, prior to the distribution, investment assets were used to acquire such unrelated assets,

(B) which in appropriate cases exclude from the application of this subsection a distribution which does not have the character of a redemption which would be treated as a sale or exchange under section 302, and

(C) which modify the application of the attribution rules applied for purposes of this subsection.

* * *

§ 356. Receipt of additional consideration

(a) Gain on exchanges.—

(1) Recognition of gain.—If—

(A) section 354 or 355 would apply to an exchange but for the fact that

(B) the property received in the exchange consists not only of property permitted by section 354 or 355 to be received without the recognition of gain but also of other property or money,

then the gain, if any, to the recipient shall be recognized, but in an amount not in excess of the sum of such money and the fair market value of such other property.

(2) Treatment as dividend.—If an exchange is described in paragraph (1) but has the effect of the distribution of a dividend (determined with the application of section 318(a)), then there shall be treated as a dividend to each distributee such an amount of the gain recognized under paragraph (1) as is not in excess of his ratable share of the undistributed earnings and profits of the corporation accumulated after February 28, 1913. The remainder, if any, of the gain recognized under paragraph (1) shall be treated as gain from the exchange of property.

(b) Additional consideration received in certain distributions.—If—

(1) section 355 would apply to a distribution but for the fact that

(2) the property received in the distribution consists not only of property permitted by section 355 to be received without the recognition of gain, but also of other property or money,

then an amount equal to the sum of such money and the fair market value of such other property shall be treated as a distribution of property to which section 301 applies.

(c) Loss.—If—

(1) section 354 would apply to an exchange, or section 355 would apply to an exchange or distribution, but for the fact that

(2) the property received in the exchange or distribution consists not only of property permitted by section 354 or 355 to be received without the recognition of gain or loss, but also of other property or money,

then no loss from the exchange or distribution shall be recognized.

(d) Securities as other property.—For purposes of this section—

(1) In general.—Except as provided in paragraph (2), the term "other property" includes securities.

(2) Exceptions.—

(A) Securities with respect to which nonrecognition of gain would be permitted.—The term "other property" does not include securities to the extent that, under section 354 or 355, such securities would be permitted to be received without the recognition of gain.

(B) Greater principal amount in section 354 exchange.—If—

(i) in an exchange described in section 354 (other than subsection (c) thereof), securities of a corporation a party to the reorganization are surrendered and securities of any corporation a party to the reorganization are received, and

(ii) the principal amount of such securities received exceeds the principal amount of such securities surrendered,

then, with respect to such securities received, the term "other property" means only the fair market value of such excess. For purposes of this subparagraph and subparagraph (C), if no securities are surrendered, the excess shall be the entire principal amount of the securities received.

(C) Greater principal amount in section 355 transaction.—If, in an exchange or distribution described in section 355, the principal amount of the securities in the controlled corporation which are received exceeds the principal amount of the securities in the distributing corporation which are surrendered, then, with respect to such securities received, the term "other property" means only the fair market value of such excess.

(e) Nonqualified preferred stock treated as other property.—For purposes of this section—

(1) In general.—Except as provided in paragraph (2), the term "other property" includes nonqualified preferred stock (as defined in section 351(g)(2)).

(2) Exception.—The term "other property" does not include nonqualified preferred stock (as so defined) to the extent that, under section 354 or 355, such preferred stock would be permitted to be received without the recognition of gain.

(f) Exchanges for section 306 stock.—Notwithstanding any other provision of this section, to the extent that any of the other property (or money) is received in exchange for section 306 stock, an amount equal to the fair market value of such other property (or the amount of such money) shall be treated as a distribution of property to which section 301 applies.

(g) Transactions involving gift or compensation.—

For special rules for a transaction described in section 354, 355, or this section, but which—

(1) results in a gift, see section 2501 and following, or

(2) has the effect of the payment of compensation, see section 61(a)(1).

§ 358. Basis to distributees

(a) General rule.—In the case of an exchange to which section 351, 354, 355, 356, or 361 applies—

(1) Nonrecognition property.—The basis of the property permitted to be received under such section without the recognition of gain or loss shall be the same as that of the property exchanged—

(A) decreased by—

(i) the fair market value of any other property (except money) received by the taxpayer,

(ii) the amount of any money received by the taxpayer, and

(iii) the amount of loss to the taxpayer which was recognized on such exchange, and

(B) increased by—

(i) the amount which was treated as a dividend, and

(ii) the amount of gain to the taxpayer which was recognized on such exchange (not including any portion of such gain which was treated as a dividend).

(2) Other property.—The basis of any other property (except money) received by the taxpayer shall be its fair market value.

(b) Allocation of basis.—

(1) In general.—Under regulations prescribed by the Secretary, the basis determined under subsection (a)(1) shall be allocated among the properties permitted to be received without the recognition of gain or loss.

(2) Special rule for section 355.—In the case of an exchange to which section 355 (or so much of section 356 as relates to section 355) applies, then in making the allocation under paragraph (1) of this subsection, there shall be taken into account not only the property so permitted to be received without the recognition of gain or loss, but also the stock or securities (if any) of the distributing corporation which are retained, and the allocation of basis shall be made among all such properties.

(c) Section 355 transactions which are not exchanges.—For purposes of this section, a distribution to which section 355 (or so much of section 356 as relates to section 355) applies shall be treated as an exchange, and for such purposes the stock and securities of the distributing corporation which are retained shall be treated as surrendered, and received back, in the exchange.

(d) Assumption of liability.—

(1) In general.—Where, as part of the consideration to the taxpayer, another party to the exchange assumed a liability of the taxpayer, such assumption shall, for purposes of this section, be treated as money received by the taxpayer on the exchange.

(2) Exception.—Paragraph (1) shall not apply to the amount of any liability excluded under section 357(c)(3).

(e) Exception.—This section shall not apply to property acquired by a corporation by the exchange of its stock or securities (or the stock or securities of a corporation which is in control of the acquiring corporation) as consideration in whole or in part for the transfer of the property to it.

(f) Definition of nonrecognition property in case of section 361 exchange.—For purposes of this section, the property permitted to be received under section 361 without the recognition of gain or loss shall be treated as consisting only of stock or securities in another corporation a party to the reorganization.

* * *

Subpart C—Effects on Corporation

§ 361. Nonrecognition of gain or loss to corporations; treatment of distributions

(a) General rule.—No gain or loss shall be recognized to a corporation if such corporation is a party to a reorganization and exchanges property, in pursuance of the plan of reorganization, solely for stock or securities in another corporation a party to the reorganization.

(b) Exchanges not solely in kind.—

(1) Gain.—If subsection (a) would apply to an exchange but for the fact that the property received in exchange consists not only of stock or securities permitted by subsection (a) to be received without the recognition of gain, but also of other property or money, then—

(A) Property distributed.—If the corporation receiving such other property or money distributes it in pursuance of the plan of reorganization, no gain to the corporation shall be recognized from the exchange, but

(B) Property not distributed.—If the corporation receiving such other property or money does not distribute it in pursuance of the plan of reorganization, the gain, if any, to the corporation shall be recognized.

The amount of gain recognized under subparagraph (B) shall not exceed the sum of the money and the fair market value of the other property so received which is not so distributed.

(2) Loss.—If subsection (a) would apply to an exchange but for the fact that the property received in exchange consists not only of property permitted by subsection (a) to be received without the recognition of gain or loss, but also of other property or money, then no loss from the exchange shall be recognized.

(3) Treatment of transfers to creditors.—For purposes of paragraph (1), any transfer of the other property or money received in the exchange by the corporation to its creditors in connection with the reorganization shall be treated as a distribution in pursuance of the plan of reorganization. The Secretary may prescribe such regulations as may be necessary to prevent avoidance of tax through abuse of the preceding sentence or subsection (c)(3). In the case of a reorganization described in section 368(a)(1)(D) with respect to which stock or securities of the corporation to which the assets are transferred are distributed in a transaction which qualifies under section 355, this paragraph shall apply only to the extent that the sum of the money and the fair market value of other property transferred to such creditors does not exceed the adjusted bases of such assets transferred (reduced by the amount of the liabilities assumed (within the meaning of section 357(c))).

(c) Treatment of distributions.—

(1) In general.—Except as provided in paragraph (2), no gain or loss shall be recognized to a corporation a party to a reorganization on the distribution to its shareholders of property in pursuance of the plan of reorganization.

(2) Distributions of appreciated property.—

(A) In general.—If—

(i) in a distribution referred to in paragraph (1), the corporation distributes property other than qualified property, and

(ii) the fair market value of such property exceeds its adjusted basis (in the hands of the distributing corporation),

then gain shall be recognized to the distributing corporation as if such property were sold to the distributee at its fair market value.

(B) Qualified property.—For purposes of this subsection, the term "qualified property" means—

(i) any stock in (or right to acquire stock in) the distributing corporation or obligation of the distributing corporation, or

(ii) any stock in (or right to acquire stock in) another corporation which is a party to the reorganization or obligation of another corporation which is such a party if such stock (or right) or obligation is received by the distributing corporation in the exchange.

(C) Treatment of liabilities.—If any property distributed in the distribution referred to in paragraph (1) is subject to a liability or the shareholder assumes a liability of the distributing corporation in connection with the distribution, then, for purposes of **sub**paragraph (A), the fair market value of such property shall be treated as not less than the amount of such liability.

(3) Treatment of certain transfers to creditors.—For purposes of this subsection, any transfer of qualified property by the corporation to its creditors in connection with the reorganization shall be treated as a distribution to its shareholders pursuant to the plan of reorganization.

(4) Coordination with other provisions.—Section 311 and subpart B of part II of this subchapter shall not apply to any distribution referred to in paragraph (1).

(5) Cross Reference.—

For provision providing for recognition of gain in certain distributions, see section 355(d).

§ 362. Basis to corporations

(a) Property acquired by issuance of stock or as paid-in surplus.—If property was acquired by a corporation—

(1) in connection with a transaction to which section 351 (relating to transfer of property to corporation controlled by transferor) applies, or

(2) as paid-in surplus or as a contribution to capital,

then the basis shall be the same as it would be in the hands of the transferor, increased in the amount of gain recognized to the transferor on such transfer.

(b) Transfers to corporations.—If property was acquired by a corporation in connection with a reorganization to which this part applies, then the basis shall be the same as it would be in the hands of the transferor, increased in the amount of gain recognized to the transferor on such transfer. This subsection shall not apply if the property acquired consists of stock or securities in a corporation a party to the reorganization, unless acquired by the exchange of stock or securities of the transferee (or of a corporation which is in control of the transferee) as the consideration in whole or in part for the transfer.

(c) Special rule for certain contributions to capital.—

(1) Property other than money.—Notwithstanding subsection (a)(2), if property other than money—

(A) is acquired by a corporation, on or after June 22, 1954, as a contribution to capital, and

(B) is not contributed by a shareholder as such, then the basis of such property shall be zero.

(2) Money.—Notwithstanding subsection (a)(2), if money—

(A) is received by a corporation as a contribution to capital, and

(B) is not contributed by a shareholder as such,

then the basis of any property acquired with such money during the 12-month period beginning on the day the contribution is received shall be reduced by the amount of such contribution. The excess (if any) of the amount of such contribution over the amount of the reduction under the preceding sentence shall be applied to the reduction (as of the last day of the period specified in the preceding sentence) of the basis of any other property held by the taxpayer. The particular properties to which the reductions required by this paragraph shall be allocated shall be determined under regulations prescribed by the Secretary.

(d) Limitation on basis increase attributable to assumption of liability.—

(1) In general.—In no event shall the basis of any property be increased under subsection (a) or (b) above the fair market value of such property (determined without regard to section 7701(g)) by reason of any gain recognized to the transferor as a result of the assumption of a liability.

(2) Treatment of gain not subject to tax.—Except as provided in regulations, if—

(A) gain is recognized to the transferor as a result of an assumption of a nonrecourse liability by a transferee which is also secured by assets not transferred to such transferee; and

(B) no person is subject to tax under this title on such gain,

then, for purposes of determining basis under subsections (a) and (b), the amount of gain recognized by the transferor as a result of the assumption of the liability shall be determined as if the liability assumed by the transferee equaled such transferee's ratable portion of such liability determined on the basis of the relative fair market values (determined without regard to section 7701(g)) of all the assets subject to such liability.

(e) Limitations on built-in losses.—

(1) Limitation on importation of built-in losses.—

(A) In general.—If in any transaction described in subsection (a) or (b) there would (but for this subsection) be an importation of a net built-in loss, the basis of each property described in subparagraph (B) which is acquired in such transaction shall (notwithstanding subsections (a) and (b)) be its fair market value immediately after such transaction.

(B) Property described.—For purposes of subparagraph (A), property is described in this subparagraph if—

(i) gain or loss with respect to such property is not subject to tax under this subtitle in the hands of the transferor immediately before the transfer, and

(ii) gain or loss with respect to such property is subject to such tax in the hands of the transferee immediately after such transfer.

In any case in which the transferor is a partnership, the preceding sentence shall be applied by treating each partner in such partnership as holding such partner's proportionate share of the property of such partnership.

(C) Importation of net built-in loss.—For purposes of subparagraph (A), there is an importation of a net built-in loss in a transaction if the transferee's aggregate adjusted bases of property described in subparagraph (B) which is transferred in such transaction would (but for this paragraph) exceed the fair market value of such property immediately after such transaction.

(2) Limitation on transfer of built-in losses in section 351 transactions.—

(A) In general.—If—

(i) property is transferred by a transferor in any transaction which is described in subsection (a) and which is not described in paragraph (1) of this subsection, and

(ii) the transferee's aggregate adjusted bases of such property so transferred would (but for this paragraph) exceed the fair market value of such property immediately after such transaction,

then, notwithstanding subsection (a), the transferee's aggregate adjusted bases of the property so transferred shall not exceed the fair market value of such property immediately after such transaction.

(B) Allocation of basis reduction.—The aggregate reduction in basis by reason of subparagraph (A) shall be allocated among the property so transferred in proportion to their respective built-in losses immediately before the transaction.

(C) Election to apply limitation to transferor's stock basis.—

(i) In general.—If the transferor and transferee of a transaction described in subparagraph (A) both elect the application of this subparagraph—

(I) subparagraph (A) shall not apply, and

(II) the transferor's basis in the stock received for property to which subparagraph (A) does not apply by reason of the election shall not exceed its fair market value immediately after the transfer.

(ii) Election.—An election under clause (i) shall be made at such time and in such form and manner as the Secretary may prescribe, and, once made, shall be irrevocable.

Subpart D—Special Rule; Definitions

§ 367. Foreign corporations

(a) Transfers of property from the United States.—

(1) General rule.—If, in connection with any exchange described in section 332, 351, 354, 356, or 361, a United States person transfers property to a foreign corporation, such foreign corporation shall not, for purposes of determining the extent to which gain shall be recognized on such transfer, be considered to be a corporation.

(2) Exception for certain stock or securities.—Except to the extent provided in regulations, paragraph (1) shall not apply to the transfer of stock or securities of a foreign corporation which is a party to the exchange or a party to the reorganization.

(3) Special rule for transfer of partnership interests.—Except as provided in regulations prescribed by the Secretary, a transfer by a United States person of an interest in a partnership to a foreign corporation in an exchange described in paragraph (1) shall, for purposes of this subsection, be treated as a transfer to such corporation of such person's pro rata share of the assets of the partnership.

(4) Paragraph (2) not to apply to certain section 361 transactions.—Paragraph (2) shall not apply in the case of an exchange described in subsection (a) or (b) of section 361. Subject to such basis adjustments and such other conditions as shall be provided in regulations, the preceding sentence shall not apply if the transferor corporation is controlled (within the meaning of section 368(c)) by 5 or fewer domestic corporations. For purposes of the preceding sentence, all members of the same affiliated group (within the meaning of section 1504) shall be treated as 1 corporation.

(5) Secretary may exempt certain transactions from application of this subsection.— Paragraph (1) shall not apply to the transfer of any property which the Secretary, in order to carry out the purposes of this subsection, designates by regulation.

(b) Other transfers.—

(1) Effect of section to be determined under regulations.—In the case of any exchange described in section 332, 351, 354, 355, 356, or 361 in connection with which there is no transfer of property described in subsection (a)(1), a foreign corporation shall be considered to be a corporation except to the extent provided in regulations prescribed by the Secretary which are necessary or appropriate to prevent the avoidance of Federal income taxes.

(2) Regulations relating to sale or exchange of stock in foreign corporations.—The regulations prescribed pursuant to paragraph (1) shall include (but shall not be limited to) regulations dealing with the sale or exchange of stock or securities in a foreign corporation by a United States person, including regulations providing—

(A) the circumstances under which—

(i) gain shall be recognized currently, or amounts included in gross income currently as a dividend, or both, or

(ii) gain or other amounts may be deferred for inclusion in the gross income of a shareholder (or his successor in interest) at a later date, and

(B) the extent to which adjustments shall be made to earnings and profits, basis of stock or securities, and basis of assets.

(c) Transactions to be treated as exchanges.—

(1) Section 355 distribution.—For purposes of this section, any distribution described in section 355 (or so much of section 356 as relates to section 355) shall be treated as an exchange whether or not it is an exchange.

(2) Contribution of capital to controlled corporations.—For purposes of this chapter, any transfer of property to a foreign corporation as a contribution to the capital of such corporation by one or more persons who, immediately after the transfer, own (within the meaning of section 318) stock possessing at least 80 percent of the total combined voting power of all classes of stock of such corporation entitled to vote shall be treated as an exchange of such property for stock of the foreign corporation equal in value to the fair market value of the property transferred.

(d) Special rules relating to transfers of intangibles.—

(1) In general.—Except as provided in regulations prescribed by the Secretary, if a United States person transfers any intangible property to a foreign corporation in an exchange described in section 351 or 361—

(A) subsection (a) shall not apply to the transfer of such property, and

(B) the provisions of this subsection shall apply to such transfer.

(2) Transfer of intangibles treated as transfer pursuant to sale of contingent payments.—

(A) In general.—If paragraph (1) applies to any transfer, the United States person transferring such property shall be treated as—

(i) having sold such property in exchange for payments which are contingent upon the productivity, use, or disposition of such property, and

(ii) receiving amounts which reasonably reflect the amounts which would have been received—

(I) annually in the form of such payments over the useful life of such property, or

(II) in the case of a disposition following such transfer (whether direct or indirect), at the time of the disposition.

The amounts taken into account under clause (ii) shall be commensurate with the income attributable to the intangible.

(B) Effect on earnings and profits.—For purposes of this chapter, the earnings and profits of a foreign corporation to which the intangible property was transferred shall be reduced by the amount required to be included in the income of the transferor of the intangible property under subparagraph (A)(ii).

(C) Amounts received treated as ordinary income.—For purposes of this chapter, any amount included in gross income by reason of this subsection shall be treated as ordinary income. For purposes of applying section 904(d), any such amount shall be treated in the same manner as if such amount were a royalty.

(D) Regulatory authority.—For purposes of the last sentence of subparagraph (A), the Secretary shall require—

(i) the valuation of transfers of intangible property, including intangible property transferred with other property or services, on an aggregate basis, or

(ii) the valuation of such a transfer on the basis of the realistic alternatives to such a transfer,

if the Secretary determines that such basis is the most reliable means of valuation of such transfers.

(3) Regulations relating to transfers of intangibles to partnerships.—The Secretary may provide by regulations that the rules of paragraph (2) also apply to the transfer of intangible property by a United States person to a partnership in circumstances consistent with the purposes of this subsection.

(4) Intangible property.—For purposes of this subsection, the term "intangible property" means any—

(A) patent, invention, formula, process, design, pattern, or know-how,

(B) copyright, literary, musical, or artistic composition,

(C) trademark, trade name, or brand name,

(D) franchise, license, or contract,

(E) method, program, system, procedure, campaign, survey, study, forecast, estimate, customer list, or technical data,

(F) goodwill, going concern value, or workforce in place (including its composition and terms and conditions (contractual or otherwise) of its employment), or

(G) other item the value or potential value of which is not attributable to tangible property or the services of any individual.

(e) Treatment of distributions described in section 355 or liquidations under section 332.—

(1) Distributions described in section 355.—In the case of any distribution described in section 355 (or so much of section 356 as relates to section 355) by a domestic corporation to a person who is not a United States person, to the extent provided in regulations, gain shall be recognized under principles similar to the principles of this section.

(2) Liquidations under section 332.—In the case of any liquidation to which section 332 applies, except as provided in regulations, subsections (a) and (b)(1) of section 337 shall not apply where the 80-percent distributee (as defined in section 337(c)) is a foreign corporation.

(f) Other transfers.—To the extent provided in regulations, if a United States person transfers property to a foreign corporation as paid-in surplus or as a contribution to capital (in a transaction not otherwise described in this section), such transfer shall be treated as a sale or exchange for an amount equal to the fair market value of the property transferred, and the transferor shall recognize as gain the excess of—

(1) the fair market value of the property so transferred, over

(2) the adjusted basis (for purposes of determining gain) of such property in the hands of the transferor.

§ 368. Definitions relating to corporate reorganizations

(a) Reorganization.—

(1) In general.—For purposes of parts I and II and this part, the term "reorganization" means—

(A) a statutory merger or consolidation;

(B) the acquisition by one corporation, in exchange solely for all or a part of its voting stock (or in exchange solely for all or a part of the voting stock of a corporation which is in control of the acquiring corporation), of stock of another corporation if, immediately after the acquisition, the acquiring corporation has control of such other corporation (whether or not such acquiring corporation had control immediately before the acquisition);

(C) the acquisition by one corporation, in exchange solely for all or a part of its voting stock (or in exchange solely for all or a part of the voting stock of a corporation which is in control of the acquiring corporation), of substantially all of the properties of another corporation, but in determining whether the exchange is solely for stock the assumption by the acquiring corporation of a liability of the other shall be disregarded;

(D) a transfer by a corporation of all or a part of its assets to another corporation if immediately after the transfer the transferor, or one or more of its shareholders (including persons who were shareholders immediately before the transfer), or any combination thereof, is in control of the corporation to which the assets are transferred; but only if, in pursuance of the plan, stock or securities of the corporation to which the assets are transferred are distributed in a transaction which qualifies under section 354, 355, or 356;

(E) a recapitalization;

(F) a mere change in identity, form, or place of organization of one corporation, however effected; or

(G) a transfer by a corporation of all or part of its assets to another corporation in a title 11 or similar case; but only if, in pursuance of the plan, stock or securities of the corporation to which the assets are transferred are distributed in a transaction which qualifies under section 354, 355, or 356.

(2) Special rules relating to paragraph (1).—

(A) Reorganizations described in both paragraph (1)(C) and paragraph (1)(D).—If a transaction is described in both paragraph (1)(C) and paragraph (1)(D), then, for purposes of this subchapter (other than for purposes of subparagraph (C)), such transaction shall be treated as described only in paragraph (1)(D).

(B) Additional consideration in certain paragraph (1)(C) cases.—If—

(i) one corporation acquires substantially all of the properties of another corporation,

(ii) the acquisition would qualify under paragraph (1)(C) but for the fact that the acquiring corporation exchanges money or other property in addition to voting stock, and

(iii) the acquiring corporation acquires, solely for voting stock described in paragraph (1)(C), property of the other corporation having a fair market value which is at least 80 percent of the fair market value of all of the property of the other corporation,

then such acquisition shall (subject to subparagraph (A) of this paragraph) be treated as qualifying under paragraph (1)(C). Solely for the purpose of determining whether clause (iii) of the preceding sentence applies, the amount of any liability assumed by the acquiring corporation shall be treated as money paid for the property.

(C) Transfers of assets or stock to subsidiaries in certain paragraph (1)(A), (1)(B), (1)(C), and (1)(G) cases.—A transaction otherwise qualifying under paragraph (1)(A), (1)(B), or (1)(C) shall not be disqualified by reason of the fact that part or all of the assets or stock which were acquired in the transaction are transferred to a corporation controlled by the corporation acquiring such assets or stock. A similar rule shall apply to a transaction otherwise qualifying under paragraph (1)(G) where the requirements of subparagraphs (A) and (B) of section 354(b)(1) are met with respect to the acquisition of the assets.

(D) Use of stock of controlling corporation in paragraph (1)(A) and (1)(G) cases.— The acquisition by one corporation, in exchange for stock of a corporation (referred to in this subparagraph as "controlling corporation") which is in control of the acquiring corporation, of substantially all of the properties of another corporation shall not disqualify a transaction under paragraph (1)(A) or (1)(G) if—

(i) no stock of the acquiring corporation is used in the transaction, and

(ii) in the case of a transaction under paragraph (1)(A), such transaction would have qualified under paragraph (1)(A) had the merger been into the controlling corporation.

(E) Statutory merger using voting stock of corporation controlling merged corporation.—A transaction otherwise qualifying under paragraph (1)(A) shall not be disqualified by reason of the fact that stock of a corporation (referred to in this subparagraph as the "controlling corporation") which before the merger was in control of the merged corporation is used in the transaction, if—

(i) after the transaction, the corporation surviving the merger holds substantially all of its properties and of the properties of the merged corporation (other than stock of the controlling corporation distributed in the transaction); and

(ii) in the transaction, former shareholders of the surviving corporation exchanged, for an amount of voting stock of the controlling corporation, an amount of stock in the surviving corporation which constitutes control of such corporation.

* * *

(G) Distribution requirement for paragraph (1)(C).—

(i) In general.—A transaction shall fail to meet the requirements of paragraph (1)(C) unless the acquired corporation distributes the stock, securities, and other properties it receives, as well as its other properties, in pursuance of the plan of reorganization. For purposes of the preceding sentence, if the acquired corporation is liquidated pursuant to the plan of reorganization, any distribution to its creditors in connection with such liquidation shall be treated as pursuant to the plan of reorganization.

(ii) Exception.—The Secretary may waive the application of clause (i) to any transaction subject to any conditions the Secretary may prescribe.

(H) Special rules for determining whether certain transactions are qualified under paragraph (1)(D).—For purposes of determining whether a transaction qualifies under paragraph (1)(D)—

(i) in the case of a transaction with respect to which the requirements of subparagraphs (A) and (B) of section 354(b)(1) are met, the term "control" has the meaning given such term by section 304(c), and

(ii) in the case of a transaction with respect to which the requirements of section 355 (or so much of section 356 as relates to section 355) are met, the fact that the shareholders of the distributing corporation dispose of part or all of the distributed stock, or the fact that the corporation whose stock was distributed issues additional stock, shall not be taken into account.

(3) Additional rules relating to title 11 and similar cases.—

(A) Title 11 or similar case defined.—For purposes of this part, the term "title 11 or similar case" means—

(i) a case under title 11 of the United States Code, or

(ii) a receivership, foreclosure, or similar proceeding in a Federal or State court.

(B) Transfer of assets in a title 11 or similar case.—In applying paragraph (1)(G), a transfer of the assets of a corporation shall be treated as made in a title 11 or similar case if and only if—

(i) any party to the reorganization is under the jurisdiction of the court in such case, and

(ii) the transfer is pursuant to a plan of reorganization approved by the court.

(C) Reorganizations qualifying under paragraph (1)(G) and another provision.—If a transaction would (but for this subparagraph) qualify both—

(i) under subparagraph (G) of paragraph (1), and

(ii) under any other subparagraph of paragraph (1) or under section 332 or 351,

then, for purposes of this subchapter (other than section 357(c)(1)), such transaction shall be treated as qualifying only under subparagraph (G) of paragraph (1).

(D) Agency receivership proceedings which involve financial institutions.—For purposes of subparagraphs (A) and (B), in the case of a receivership, foreclosure, or similar proceeding before a Federal or State agency involving a financial institution referred to in section 581 or 591, the agency shall be treated as a court.

(E) Application of paragraph (2)(E)(ii).—In the case of a title 11 or similar case, the requirement of clause (ii) of paragraph (2)(E) shall be treated as met if—

(i) no former shareholder of the surviving corporation received any consideration for his stock, and

(ii) the former creditors of the surviving corporation exchanged, for an amount of voting stock of the controlling corporation, debt of the surviving corporation which had a fair market value equal to 80 percent or more of the total fair market value of the debt of the surviving corporation.

(b) Party to a reorganization.—For purposes of this part, the term "a party to a reorganization" includes—

(1) a corporation resulting from a reorganization, and

(2) both corporations, in the case of a reorganization resulting from the acquisition by one corporation of stock or properties of another.

In the case of a reorganization qualifying under paragraph (1)(B) or (1)(C) of subsection (a), if the stock exchanged for the stock or properties is stock of a corporation which is in control of the acquiring corporation, the term "a party to a reorganization" includes the corporation so controlling the acquiring corporation. In the case of a reorganization qualifying under paragraph (1)(A), (1)(B), (1)(C), or (1)(G) of subsection (a) by reason of paragraph (2)(C) of subsection (a), the term "a party to a reorganization" includes the corporation controlling the corporation to which the acquired assets or stock are transferred. In the case of a reorganization qualifying under paragraph (1)(A) or (1)(G) of subsection (a) by reason of paragraph (2)(D) of that subsection, the term "a party to a reorganization" includes the controlling corporation referred to in such paragraph (2)(D). In the case of a reorganization qualifying under subsection (a)(1)(A) by reason of subsection (a)(2)(E), the term "party to a reorganization" includes the controlling corporation referred to in subsection (a)(2)(E).

(c) Control defined.—For purposes of part I (other than section 304), part II, this part, and part V, the term "control" means the ownership of stock possessing at least 80 percent of the total combined voting power of all classes of stock entitled to vote and at least 80 percent of the total number of shares of all other classes of stock of the corporation.

Subchapter E—Accounting Periods and Methods of Accounting

Part II—Methods of Accounting

Subpart B—Taxable Year for Which Items of Gross Income Included

§ 453. Installment method

(a) General rule.—Except as otherwise provided in this section, income from an installment sale shall be taken into account for purposes of this title under the installment method.

(b) Installment sale defined.—For purposes of this section—

(1) In general.—The term "installment sale" means a disposition of property where at least 1 payment is to be received after the close of the taxable year in which the disposition occurs.

(2) Exceptions.—The term "installment sale" does not include—

(A) Dealer dispositions.—Any dealer disposition (as defined in subsection (*l*)).

(B) Inventories of personal property.—A disposition of personal property of a kind which is required to be included in the inventory of the taxpayer if on hand at the close of the taxable year.

(c) Installment method defined.—For purposes of this section, the term "installment method" means a method under which the income recognized for any taxable year from a disposition is that proportion of the payments received in that year which the gross profit (realized or to be realized when payment is completed) bears to the total contract price.

(d) Election out.—

(1) In general.—Subsection (a) shall not apply to any disposition if the taxpayer elects to have subsection (a) not apply to such disposition.

* * *

(*l*) Dealer dispositions.—For purposes of subsection (b)(2)(A)—

(1) In general.—The term "dealer disposition" means any of the following dispositions:

(A) Personal property.—Any disposition of personal property by a person who regularly sells or otherwise disposes of personal property of the same type on the installment plan.

(B) Real property.—Any disposition of real property which is held by the taxpayer for sale to customers in the ordinary course of the taxpayer's trade or business.

* * *

Part III—Adjustments

§ 482. Allocation of income and deductions among taxpayers

In any case of two or more organizations, trades, or businesses (whether or not incorporated, whether or not organized in the United States, and whether or not affiliated) owned or controlled directly or indirectly by the same interests, the Secretary may distribute, apportion, or allocate gross income, deductions, credits, or allowances between or among such organizations, trades, or businesses, if he determines that such distribution, apportionment, or allocation is necessary in order to prevent evasion of taxes or clearly to reflect the income of any of such organizations, trades, or businesses. In the case of any transfer (or license) of intangible property (within the meaning of section 367(d)(4)), the income with respect to such transfer or license shall be commensurate with the income attributable to the intangible. For purposes of this section, the Secretary shall require the valuation of transfers of intangible property (including intangible property transferred with other property or services) on an aggregate basis or the valuation of such a transfer on the basis of the realistic alternatives to such a transfer, if the Secretary determines that such basis is the most reliable means of valuation of such transfers.

§ 483. Interest on certain deferred payments

(a) Amount constituting interest.—For purposes of this title, in the case of any payment—

(1) under any contract for the sale or exchange of any property, and

(2) to which this section applies,

there shall be treated as interest that portion of the total unstated interest under such contract which, as determined in a manner consistent with the method of computing interest under section 1272(a), is properly allocable to such payment.

(b) Total unstated interest.—For purposes of this section, the term "total unstated interest" means, with respect to a contract for the sale or exchange of property, an amount equal to the excess of—

(1) the sum of the payments to which this section applies which are due under the contract, over

(2) the sum of the present values of such payments and the present values of any interest payments due under the contract.

For purposes of the preceding sentence, the present value of a payment shall be determined under the rules of section 1274(b)(2) using a discount rate equal to the applicable Federal rate determined under section 1274(d).

(c) Payments to which subsection (a) applies.—

(1) In general.—Except as provided in subsection (d), this section shall apply to any payment on account of the sale or exchange of property which constitutes part or all of the sales price and which is due more than 6 months after the date of such sale or exchange under a contract—

(A) under which some or all of the payments are due more than 1 year after the date of such sale or exchange, and

(B) under which there is total unstated interest.

(2) Treatment of other debt instruments.—For purposes of this section, a debt instrument of the purchaser which is given in consideration for the sale or exchange of property shall not be treated as a payment, and any payment due under such debt instrument shall be treated as due under the contract for the sale or exchange.

(3) Debt instrument defined.—For purposes of this subsection, the term "debt instrument" has the meaning given such term by section 1275(a)(1).

(d) Exceptions and limitations.—

(1) Coordination with original issue discount rules.—This section shall not apply to any debt instrument for which an issue price is determined under section 1273(b) (other than paragraph (4) thereof) or section 1274.

(2) Sales prices of $3,000 or less.—This section shall not apply to any payment on account of the sale or exchange of property if it can be determined at the time of such sale or exchange that the sales price cannot exceed $3,000.

(3) Carrying charges.—In the case of the purchaser, the tax treatment of amounts paid on account of the sale or exchange of property shall be made without regard to this section if any such amounts are treated under section 163(b) as if they included interest.

(4) Certain sales of patents.—In the case of any transfer described in section 1235(a) (relating to sale or exchange of patents), this section shall not apply to any amount contingent on the productivity, use, or disposition of the property transferred.

(e) Maximum rate of interest on certain transfers of land between related parties.—

(1) In general.—In the case of any qualified sale, the discount rate used in determining the total unstated interest rate under subsection (b) shall not exceed 6 percent, compounded semiannually.

(2) Qualified sale.—For purposes of this subsection, the term "qualified sale" means any sale or exchange of land by an individual to a member of such individual's family (within the meaning of section 267(c)(4)).

(3) $500,000 limitation.—Paragraph (1) shall not apply to any qualified sale between individuals made during any calendar year to the extent that the sales price for such sale (when added to the aggregate sales price for prior qualified sales between such individuals during the calendar year) exceeds $500,000.

(4) Nonresident alien individuals.—Paragraph (1) shall not apply to any sale or exchange if any party to such sale or exchange is a nonresident alien individual.

(f) Regulations.—The Secretary shall prescribe such regulations as may be necessary or appropriate to carry out the purposes of this section including regulations providing for the application of this section in the case of—

(1) any contract for the sale or exchange of property under which the liability for, or the amount or due date of, a payment cannot be determined at the time of the sale or exchange, or

(2) any change in the liability for, or the amount or due date of, any payment (including interest) under a contract for the sale or exchange of property.

(g) Cross references.—

(1) For treatment of assumptions, see section 1274(c)(4).

(2) For special rules for certain transactions where stated principal amount does not exceed $2,800,000, see section 1274A.

(3) For special rules in case of the borrower under certain loans for personal use, see section 1275(b).

Subchapter G—Corporations Used to Avoid Income Tax on Shareholders

Part I—Corporations Improperly Accumulating Surplus

§ 531. Imposition of accumulated earnings tax

In addition to other taxes imposed by this chapter, there is hereby imposed for each taxable year on the accumulated taxable income (as defined in section 535) of each corporation described in section 532, an accumulated earnings tax equal to 20 percent of the accumulated taxable income.

§ 532. Corporations subject to accumulated earnings tax

(a) General rule.—The accumulated earnings tax imposed by section 531 shall apply to every corporation (other than those described in subsection (b)) formed or availed of for the purpose of avoiding the income tax with respect to its shareholders or the shareholders of any other corporation, by permitting earnings and profits to accumulate instead of being divided or distributed.

(b) Exceptions.—The accumulated earnings tax imposed by section 531 shall not apply to—

(1) a personal holding company (as defined in section 542),

(2) a corporation exempt from tax under subchapter F (section 501 and following), or

(3) a passive foreign investment company (as defined in section 1297).

(c) Application determined without regard to number of shareholders.—The application of this part to a corporation shall be determined without regard to the number of shareholders of such corporation.

§ 533. Evidence of purpose to avoid income tax

(a) Unreasonable accumulation determinative of purpose.—For purposes of section 532, the fact that the earnings and profits of a corporation are permitted to accumulate beyond the reasonable needs of the business shall be determinative of the purpose to avoid the income tax with respect to shareholders, unless the corporation by the preponderance of the evidence shall prove to the contrary.

(b) Holding or investment company.—The fact that any corporation is a mere holding or investment company shall be prima facie evidence of the purpose to avoid the income tax with respect to shareholders.

§ 534. Burden of proof

(a) General rule.—In any proceeding before the Tax Court involving a notice of deficiency based in whole or in part on the allegation that all or any part of the earnings and profits have been permitted to accumulate beyond the reasonable needs of the business, the burden of proof with respect to such allegation shall—

(1) if notification has not been sent in accordance with subsection (b), be on the Secretary, or

(2) if the taxpayer has submitted the statement described in subsection (c), be on the Secretary with respect to the grounds set forth in such statement in accordance with the provisions of such subsection.

(b) Notification by Secretary.—Before mailing the notice of deficiency referred to in subsection (a), the Secretary may send by certified mail or registered mail a notification informing the taxpayer that the proposed notice of deficiency includes an amount with respect to the accumulated earnings tax imposed by section 531.

(c) Statement by taxpayer.—Within such time (but not less than 30 days) after the mailing of the notification described in subsection (b) as the Secretary may prescribe by regulations, the taxpayer may submit a statement of the grounds (together with facts sufficient to show the basis thereof) on which the taxpayer relies to establish that all or any part of the earnings and profits have not been permitted to accumulate beyond the reasonable needs of the business.

(d) Jeopardy assessment.—If pursuant to section 6861(a) a jeopardy assessment is made before the mailing of the notice of deficiency referred to in subsection (a), for purposes of this section such notice of deficiency shall, to the extent that it informs the taxpayer that such deficiency includes the accumulated earnings tax imposed by section 531, constitute the notification described in subsection (b), and in that event the statement described in subsection (c) may be included in the taxpayer's petition to the Tax Court.

§ 535. Accumulated taxable income

(a) Definition.—For purposes of this subtitle, the term "accumulated taxable income" means the taxable income, adjusted in the manner provided in subsection (b), minus the sum of the dividends paid deduction (as defined in section 561) and the accumulated earnings credit (as defined in subsection (c)).

(b) Adjustments to taxable income.—For purposes of subsection (a), taxable income shall be adjusted as follows:

(1) Taxes.—There shall be allowed as a deduction Federal income and excess profits taxes and income, war profits, and excess profits taxes of foreign countries and possessions of the United States (to the extent not allowable as a deduction under section 275(a)(4)), accrued during the taxable year or deemed to be paid by a domestic corporation under section 960 for the taxable year, but not including the accumulated earnings tax imposed by section 531 or the personal holding company tax imposed by section 541.

(2) Charitable contributions.—The deduction for charitable contributions provided under section 170 shall be allowed without regard to section 170(b)(2).

(3) Special deductions disallowed.—The special deductions for corporations provided in part VIII (except section 248) of subchapter B (section 241 and following, relating to the deduction for dividends received by corporations, etc.) shall not be allowed.

(4) Net operating loss.—The net operating loss deduction provided in section 172 shall not be allowed.

(5) Capital losses.—

(A) In general.—Except as provided in subparagraph (B), there shall be allowed as a deduction an amount equal to the net capital loss for the taxable year (determined without regard to paragraph (7)(A)).

(B) Recapture of previous deductions for capital gains.—The aggregate amount allowable as a deduction under subparagraph (A) for any taxable year shall be reduced by the lesser of—

(i) the nonrecaptured capital gains deductions, or

(ii) the amount of the accumulated earnings and profits of the corporation as of the close of the preceding taxable year.

(C) Nonrecaptured capital gains deductions.—For purposes of subparagraph (B), the term "nonrecaptured capital gains deductions" means the excess of—

(i) the aggregate amount allowable as a deduction under paragraph (6) for preceding taxable years beginning after July 18, 1984, over

(ii) the aggregate of the reductions under subparagraph (B) for preceding taxable years.

(6) Net capital gains.—

(A) In general.—There shall be allowed as a deduction—

(i) the net capital gain for the taxable year (determined with the application of paragraph (7)), reduced by

(ii) the taxes attributable to such net capital gain.

(B) Attributable taxes.—For purposes of subparagraph (A), the taxes attributable to the net capital gain shall be an amount equal to the difference between—

(i) the taxes imposed by this subtitle (except the tax imposed by this part) for the taxable year, and

(ii) such taxes computed for such year without including in taxable income the net capital gain for the taxable year (determined without the application of paragraph (7)).

(7) Capital loss carryovers.—

(A) Unlimited carryforward.—The net capital loss for any taxable year shall be treated as a short-term capital loss in the next taxable year.

(B) Section 1212 inapplicable.—No allowance shall be made for the capital loss carryback or carryforward provided in section 1212.

(8) Special rules for mere holding or investment companies.—In the case of a mere holding or investment company—

(A) Capital loss deduction, etc., not allowed.—Paragraphs (5) and (7)(A) shall not apply.

(B) Deduction for certain offsets.—There shall be allowed as a deduction the net short-term capital gain for the taxable year to the extent such gain does not exceed the amount of any capital loss carryover to such taxable year under section 1212 (determined without regard to paragraph (7)(B)).

(C) Earnings and profits.—For purposes of subchapter C, the accumulated earnings and profits at any time shall not be less than they would be if this subsection had applied to the computation of earnings and profits for all taxable years beginning after July 18, 1984.

(9) Special rule for capital gains and losses of foreign corporations.—In the case of a foreign corporation, paragraph (6) shall be applied by taking into account only gains and losses which are effectively connected with the conduct of a trade or business within the United States and are not exempt from tax under treaty.

(10) Controlled foreign corporations.—There shall be allowed as a deduction the amount of the corporation's income for the taxable year which is included in the gross income of a United States shareholder under section 951(a). In the case of any corporation the accumulated taxable income of which would (but for this sentence) be determined without allowance of any deductions, the deduction under this paragraph shall be allowed and shall be appropriately adjusted to take into account any deductions which reduced such inclusion.

(c) Accumulated earnings credit.—

(1) General rule.—For purposes of subsection (a), in the case of a corporation other than a mere holding or investment company the accumulated earnings credit is (A) an amount equal to such part of the earnings and profits for the taxable year as are retained for the reasonable needs of the business, minus (B) the deduction allowed by subsection (b)(6). For purposes of this paragraph, the amount of the earnings and profits for the taxable year which are retained is the amount by which the earnings and profits for the taxable year exceed the dividends paid deduction (as defined in section 561) for such year.

(2) Minimum credit.—

(A) In general.—The credit allowable under paragraph (1) shall in no case be less than the amount by which $250,000 exceeds the accumulated earnings and profits of the corporation at the close of the preceding taxable year.

(B) Certain service corporations.—In the case of a corporation the principal function of which is the performance of services in the field of health, law, engineering, architecture, accounting, actuarial science, performing arts, or consulting, subparagraph (A) shall be applied by substituting "$150,000" for "$250,000".

(3) Holding and investment companies.—In the case of a corporation which is a mere holding or investment company, the accumulated earnings credit is the amount (if any) by which $250,000 exceeds the accumulated earnings and profits of the corporation at the close of the preceding taxable year.

(4) Accumulated earnings and profits.—For purposes of paragraphs (2) and (3), the accumulated earnings and profits at the close of the preceding taxable year shall be reduced by the dividends which under section 563(a) (relating to dividends paid after the close of the taxable year) are considered as paid during such taxable year.

(5) Cross reference.—For limitation on credit provided in paragraph (2) or (3) in the case of certain controlled corporations, see section 1561.

(d) Income distributed to United States-owned foreign corporation retains United States connection.—

(1) In general.—For purposes of this part, if 10 percent or more of the earnings and profits of any foreign corporation for any taxable year—

(A) is derived from sources within the United States, or

(B) is effectively connected with the conduct of a trade or business within the United States,

any distribution out of such earnings and profits (and any interest payment) received (directly or through 1 or more other entities) by a United States-owned foreign corporation shall be treated as derived by such corporation from sources within the United States.

(2) United States-owned foreign corporation.—The term "United States-owned foreign corporation" has the meaning given to such term by section 904(g)(6).

§ 536. Income not placed on annual basis

Section 443(b) (relating to computation of tax on change of annual accounting period) shall not apply in the computation of the accumulated earnings tax imposed by section 531.

§ 537. Reasonable needs of the business

(a) General rule.—For purposes of this part, the term "reasonable needs of the business" includes—

(1) the reasonably anticipated needs of the business,

(2) the section 303 redemption needs of the business, and

(3) the excess business holdings redemption needs of the business.

(b) Special rules.—For purposes of subsection (a)—

(1) Section 303 redemption needs.—The term "section 303 redemption needs" means, with respect to the taxable year of the corporation in which a shareholder of the corporation died or any taxable year thereafter, the amount needed (or reasonably anticipated to be needed) to make a redemption of stock included in the gross estate of the decedent (but not in excess of the maximum amount of stock to which section 303(a) may apply).

* * *

(3) Obligations incurred to make redemptions.—In applying paragraphs (1) and (2), the discharge of any obligation incurred to make a redemption described in such paragraphs shall be treated as the making of such redemption.

* * *

(5) No inference as to prior taxable years.—The application of this part to any taxable year before the first taxable year specified in paragraph (1) shall be made without regard to the fact that distributions in redemption coming within the terms of such paragraphs were subsequently made.

Part II—Personal Holding Companies

§ 541. Imposition of personal holding company tax

In addition to other taxes imposed by this chapter, there is hereby imposed for each taxable year on the undistributed personal holding company income (as defined in section 545) of every personal holding company (as defined in section 542) a personal holding company tax equal to 20 percent of the undistributed personal holding company income.

§ 542. Definition of personal holding company

(a) General rule.—For purposes of this subtitle, the term "personal holding company" means any corporation (other than a corporation described in subsection (c)) if—

(1) Adjusted ordinary gross income requirement.—At least 60 percent of its adjusted ordinary gross income (as defined in section 543(b)(2)) for the taxable year is personal holding company income (as defined in section 543(a)), and

(2) Stock ownership requirement.—At any time during the last half of the taxable year more than 50 percent in value of its outstanding stock is owned, directly or indirectly, by or for not more than 5 individuals. For purposes of this paragraph, an organization described in section 401(a), 501(c)(17), or 509(a) or a portion of a trust permanently set aside or to be used exclusively for the purposes described in section 642(c) or a corresponding provision of a prior income tax law shall be considered an individual.

* * *

(c) Exceptions.—The term "personal holding company" as defined in subsection (a) does not include—

* * *

(5) a foreign corporation;

* * *

Subchapter I—Natural Resources

Part V—Continental Shelf Areas

§ 638. Continental shelf areas

For purposes of applying the provisions of this chapter (including sections 861(a)(3) and 862(a)(3) in the case of the performance of personal services) with respect to mines, oil and gas wells, and other natural deposits—

(1) the term "United States" when used in a geographical sense includes the seabed and subsoil of those submarine areas which are adjacent to the territorial waters of the United States and over which the United States has exclusive rights, in accordance with international law, with respect to the exploration and exploitation of natural resources; and **§ 638.**

(2) the terms "foreign country" and "possession of the United States" when used in a geographical sense include the seabed and subsoil of those submarine areas which are adjacent to the territorial waters of the foreign country or such possession and over which the foreign country (or the United States in case of such possession) has exclusive rights, in accordance with international law, with respect to the exploration and exploitation of natural resources, but this paragraph shall apply in the case of a foreign country only if it exercises, directly or indirectly, taxing jurisdiction with respect to such exploration or exploitation.

No foreign country shall, by reason of the application of this section, be treated as a country contiguous to the United States.

Subchapter J—Estates, Trusts, Beneficiaries, and Decedents

Part I—Estates, Trusts, and Beneficiaries

Subpart F—Miscellaneous

§ 684. Recognition of gain on certain transfers to certain foreign trusts and estates

(a) In general.—Except as provided in regulations, in the case of any transfer of property by a United States person to a foreign estate or trust, for purposes of this subtitle, such transfer shall be treated as a sale or exchange for an amount equal to the fair market value of the property transferred, and the transferor shall recognize as gain the excess of—

(1) the fair market value of the property so transferred, over

(2) the adjusted basis (for purposes of determining gain) of such property in the hands of the transferor.

(b) Exceptions.—Subsection (a) shall not apply to a transfer to a trust by a United States person to the extent that any such person is treated as the owner of such trust under section 671.

(c) Treatment of trusts which become foreign trusts.—If a trust which is not a foreign trust becomes a foreign trust, such trust shall be treated for purposes of this section as having transferred, immediately before becoming a foreign trust, all of its assets to a foreign trust.

Subchapter K—Partners and Partnerships

Part I—Determination of Tax Liability

§ 701. Partners, not partnership, subject to tax

A partnership as such shall not be subject to the income tax imposed by this chapter. Persons carrying on business as partners shall be liable for income tax only in their separate or individual capacities.

§ 702. Income and credits of partner

(a) General rule.—In determining his income tax, each partner shall take into account separately his distributive share of the partnership's—

(1) gains and losses from sales or exchanges of capital assets held for not more than 1 year,

(2) gains and losses from sales or exchanges of capital assets held for more than 1 year,

(3) gains and losses from sales or exchanges of property described in section 1231 (relating to certain property used in a trade or business and involuntary conversions),

(4) charitable contributions (as defined in section 170(c)),

(5) dividends with respect to which section 1(h)(11) or part VIII of subchapter B applies,

(6) taxes, described in section 901, paid or accrued to foreign countries and to possessions of the United States,

(7) other items of income, gain, loss, deduction, or credit, to the extent provided by regulations prescribed by the Secretary, and

(8) taxable income or loss, exclusive of items requiring separate computation under other paragraphs of this subsection.

(b) Character of items constituting distributive share.—The character of any item of income, gain, loss, deduction, or credit included in a partner's distributive share under paragraphs (1) through (7) of subsection (a) shall be determined as if such item were realized directly from the source from which realized by the partnership, or incurred in the same manner as incurred by the partnership.

(c) Gross income of a partner.—In any case where it is necessary to determine the gross income of a partner for purposes of this title, such amount shall include his distributive share of the gross income of the partnership.

(d) Cross reference.—

For rules relating to procedures for determining the tax treatment of partnership items see subchapter C of chapter 63 (section 6221 and following).

§ 704. Partner's distributive share

(a) Effect of partnership agreement.—A partner's distributive share of income, gain, loss, deduction, or credit shall, except as otherwise provided in this chapter, be determined by the partnership agreement.

(b) Determination of distributive share.—A partner's distributive share of income, gain, loss, deduction, or credit (or item thereof) shall be determined in accordance with the partner's interest in the partnership (determined by taking into account all facts and circumstances), if—

(1) the partnership agreement does not provide as to the partner's distributive share of income, gain, loss, deduction, or credit (or item thereof), or

(2) the allocation to a partner under the agreement of income, gain, loss, deduction, or credit (or item thereof) does not have substantial economic effect.

(c) Contributed property.—

(1) In general.—Under regulations prescribed by the Secretary—

(A) income, gain, loss, and deduction with respect to property contributed to the partnership by a partner shall be shared among the partners so as to take account of the variation between the basis of the property to the partnership and its fair market value at the time of contribution,

(B) if any property so contributed is distributed (directly or indirectly) by the partnership (other than to the contributing partner) within 7 years of being contributed—

(i) the contributing partner shall be treated as recognizing gain or loss (as the case may be) from the sale of such property in an amount equal to the gain or loss which would have been allocated to such partner under subparagraph (A) by reason of the variation described in subparagraph (A) if the property had been sold at its fair market value at the time of the distribution,

(ii) the character of such gain or loss shall be determined by reference to the character of the gain or loss which would have resulted if such property had been sold by the partnership to the distributee, and

(iii) appropriate adjustments shall be made to the adjusted basis of the contributing partner's interest in the partnership and to the adjusted basis of the property distributed to reflect any gain or loss recognized under this subparagraph, and

(C) if any property so contributed has a built-in loss—

(i) such built-in loss shall be taken into account only in determining the amount of items allocated to the contributing partner, and

(ii) except as provided in regulations, in determining the amount of items allocated to other partners, the basis of the contributed property in the hands of the partnership shall be treated as being equal to its fair market value at the time of contribution.

For purposes of subparagraph (C), the term "built-in loss" means the excess of the adjusted basis of the property (determined without regard to subparagraph (C)(ii)) over its fair market value at the time of contribution.

(2) Special rule for distributions where gain or loss would not be recognized outside partnerships.—Under regulations prescribed by the Secretary, if—

(A) property contributed by a partner (hereinafter referred to as the "contributing partner") is distributed by the partnership to another partner, and

(B) other property of a like kind (within the meaning of section 1031) is distributed by the partnership to the contributing partner not later than the earlier of—

(i) the 180th day after the date of the distribution described in subparagraph (A), or

(ii) the due date (determined with regard to extensions) for the contributing partner's return of the tax imposed by this chapter for the taxable year in which the distribution described in subparagraph (A) occurs, then to the extent of the value of the property described in subparagraph (B), paragraph (1)(B) shall be applied as if the contributing partner had contributed to the partnership the property described in subparagraph (B).

(3) Other rules.—Under regulations prescribed by the Secretary, rules similar to the rules of paragraph (1) shall apply to contributions by a partner (using the cash receipts and disbursements method of accounting) of accounts payable and other accrued but unpaid items. Any reference in paragraph (1) or (2) to the contributing partner shall be treated as including a reference to any successor of such partner.

* * *

§ 707. Transactions between partner and partnership

* * *

(b) Certain sales or exchanges of property with respect to controlled partnerships.—

(1) Losses disallowed.—No deduction shall be allowed in respect of losses from sales or exchanges of property (other than an interest in the partnership), directly or indirectly, between—

(A) a partnership and a person owning, directly or indirectly, more than 50 percent of the capital interest, or the profits interest, in such partnership, or

(B) two partnerships in which the same persons own, directly or indirectly, more than 50 percent of the capital interests or profits interests.

In the case of a subsequent sale or exchange by a transferee described in this paragraph, section 267(d) shall be applicable as if the loss were disallowed under section 267(a)(1). For purposes of section 267(a)(2), partnerships described in subparagraph (B) of this paragraph shall be treated as persons specified in section 267(b).

(2) Gains treated as ordinary income.—In the case of a sale or exchange, directly or indirectly, of property, which in the hands of the transferee, is property other than a capital asset as defined in section 1221—

(A) between a partnership and a person owning, directly or indirectly, more than 50 percent of the capital interest, or profits interest, in such partnership, or

(B) between two partnerships in which the same persons own, directly or indirectly, more than 50 percent of the capital interests or profits interests, any gain recognized shall be considered as ordinary income.

(3) Ownership of a capital or profits interest.—For purposes of paragraphs (1) and (2) of this subsection, the ownership of a capital or profits interest in a partnership shall be determined in accordance with the rules for constructive ownership of stock provided in section 267(c) other than paragraph (3) of such section.

* * *

Part II—Contributions, Distributions, and Transfers

Subpart A—Contributions to a Partnership

§ 721. Nonrecognition of gain or loss on contribution

(a) General rule.—No gain or loss shall be recognized to a partnership or to any of its partners in the case of a contribution of property to the partnership in exchange for an interest in the partnership.

(b) Special rule.—Subsection (a) shall not apply to gain realized on a transfer of property to a partnership which would be treated as an investment company (within the meaning of section 351) if the partnership were incorporated.

(c) Regulations relating to certain transfers to partnerships.—The Secretary may provide by regulations that subsection (a) shall not apply to gain realized on the transfer of property to a partnership if such gain, when recognized, will be includible in the gross income of a person other than a United States person.

(d) Transfers of intangibles.—For regulatory authority to treat intangibles transferred to a partnership as sold, see section 367(d)(3).

§ 722. Basis of contributing partner's interest

The basis of an interest in a partnership acquired by a contribution of property, including money, to the partnership shall be the amount of such money and the adjusted basis of such property to the contributing partner at the time of the contribution increased by the amount (if any) of gain recognized under section 721(b) to the contributing partner at such time.

§ 723. Basis of property contributed to partnership

The basis of property contributed to a partnership by a partner shall be the adjusted basis of such property to the contributing partner at the time of the contribution increased by the amount (if any) of gain recognized under section 721(b) to the contributing partner at such time.

Subpart C—Transfers of Interests in a Partnership

§ 741. Recognition and character of gain or loss on sale or exchange

In the case of a sale or exchange of an interest in a partnership, gain or loss shall be recognized to the transferor partner. Such gain or loss shall be considered as gain or loss from the sale or exchange of a capital asset, except as otherwise provided in section 751 (relating to unrealized receivables and inventory items).

Subpart D—Provisions Common to Other Subparts

§ 751. Unrealized receivables and inventory items

(a) Sale or exchange of interest in partnership.—The amount of any money, or the fair market value of any property, received by a transferor partner in exchange for all or a part of his interest in the partnership attributable to—

(1) unrealized receivables of the partnership, or

(2) inventory items of the partnership,

shall be considered as an amount realized from the sale or exchange of property other than a capital asset.

* * *

(c) Unrealized receivables.—For purposes of this subchapter, the term "unrealized receivables" includes, to the extent not previously includible in income under the method of accounting used by the partnership, any rights (contractual or otherwise) to payment for—

(1) goods delivered, or to be delivered, to the extent the proceeds therefrom would be treated as amounts received from the sale or exchange of property other than a capital asset, or

(2) services rendered, or to be rendered.

For purposes of this section and sections 731, 732, and 741 (but not for purposes of section 736), such term also includes mining property (as defined in section 617(f)(2)), stock in a DISC (as described in section 992(a)), section 1245 property (as defined in section 1245(a)(3)), stock in certain foreign corporations (as described in section 1248), section 1250 property (as defined in section 1250(c)), farm land (as defined in section 1252(a)), franchises, trademarks, or trade names (referred to in section 1253(a)), and an oil, gas, or geothermal property (described in section 1254) but only to the extent of the amount which would be treated as gain to which section 617(d)(1), 995(c), 1245(a), 1248(a), 1250(a), 1252(a), 1253(a), or 1254(a) would apply if (at the time of the transaction described in this section or section 731, 732, or 741, as the case may be) such property had been sold by the partnership at its fair market value. For purposes of this section and sections 731, 732, and 741 (but not for purposes of section 736), such term also includes any market discount bond (as defined in section 1278) and any short-term obligation (as defined in section 1283) but only to the extent of the amount which would be treated as ordinary income if (at the time of the transaction described in this section or section 731, 732, or 741, as the case may be) such property had been sold by the partnership.

* * *

Part III—Definitions

§ 761. Terms defined

(a) Partnership.—For purposes of this subtitle, the term "partnership" includes a syndicate, group, pool, joint venture, or other unincorporated organization through or by means of which any business, financial operation, or venture is carried on, and which is not, within the meaning of this title, a corporation or a trust or estate. Under regulations the Secretary may, at the election of all the members of an unincorporated organization, exclude such organization from the application of all or part of this subchapter, if it is availed of—

(1) for investment purposes only and not for the active conduct of a business,

(2) for the joint production, extraction, or use of property, but not for the purpose of selling services or property produced or extracted, or

(3) by dealers in securities for a short period for the purpose of underwriting, selling, or distributing a particular issue of securities,

if the income of the members of the organization may be adequately determined without the computation of partnership taxable income.

(b) Partner.—For purposes of this subtitle, the term "partner" means a member of a partnership. In the case of a capital interest in a partnership in which capital is a material income-producing factor, whether a person is a partner with respect to such interest shall be determined without regard to whether such interest was derived by gift from any other person.

(c) Partnership agreement.—For purposes of this subchapter, a partnership agreement includes any modifications of the partnership agreement made prior to, or at, the time prescribed by law for the filing of the partnership return for the taxable year (not including extensions) which are agreed to by all the partners, or which are adopted in such other manner as may be provided by the partnership agreement.

* * *

Subchapter N—Tax Based on Income From Sources Within or Without the United States

Part I—Source Rules and Other General Rules Relating to Foreign Income

§ 861. Income from sources within the United States

(a) Gross income from sources within United States.—The following items of gross income shall be treated as income from sources within the United States:

(1) Interest.—Interest from the United States or the District of Columbia, and interest on bonds, notes, or other interest-bearing obligations of noncorporate residents or domestic corporations, not including—

(A) interest—

(i) on deposits with a foreign branch of a domestic corporation or a domestic partnership if such branch is engaged in the commercial banking business, and

(ii) on amounts satisfying the requirements of subparagraph (B) of section 871(i)(3) which are paid by a foreign branch of a domestic corporation or a domestic partnership, and

(B) in the case of a foreign partnership, which is predominantly engaged in the active conduct of a trade or business outside the United States, any interest not paid by a trade or business engaged in by the partnership in the United States and not allocable to income which is effectively connected (or treated as effectively connected) with the conduct of a trade or business in the United States.

(2) Dividends.—The amount received as dividends—

(A) from a domestic corporation, or

(B) from a foreign corporation unless less than 25 percent of the gross income from all sources of such foreign corporation for the 3-year period ending with the close of its taxable year preceding the declaration of such dividends (or for such part of such period as the corporation has been in existence) was effectively connected (or treated as effectively connected other than income described in section 884(d)(2)) with the conduct of a trade or business within the United States; but only in an amount which bears the same ratio to such dividends as the gross income of the corporation for such period which was effectively connected (or treated as effectively connected other than income described in section 884(d)(2)) with the conduct of a trade or business within the United States bears to its gross income from all sources; but dividends (other than dividends for which a deduction is allowable under section 245(b)) from a foreign corporation shall, for purposes of subpart A of part III (relating to foreign tax credit), be treated as income from sources without the United States to the extent (and only to the extent) exceeding the amount which is 100/50 th of the amount of the deduction allowable under section 245 in respect of such dividends, or

(C) from a foreign corporation to the extent that such amount is required by section 243(e) (relating to certain dividends from foreign corporations) to be treated as dividends from a domestic corporation which is subject to taxation under this chapter, and to such extent subparagraph (B) shall not apply to such amount, or

(D) from a DISC or former DISC (as defined in section 992(a)) except to the extent attributable (as determined under regulations prescribed by the Secretary) to qualified export receipts described in section 993(a)(1) (other than interest and gains described in section 995(b)(1)).

In the case of any dividend from a 20-percent owned corporation (as defined in section 243(c)(2)), subparagraph (B) shall be applied by substituting "100/65 th" for "100/50 th".

(3) Personal services.—Compensation for labor or personal services performed in the United States; except that compensation for labor or services performed in the United States shall not be deemed to be income from sources within the United States if—

(A) the labor or services are performed by a nonresident alien individual temporarily present in the United States for a period or periods not exceeding a total of 90 days during the taxable year,

(B) such compensation does not exceed $3,000 in the aggregate, and

(C) the compensation is for labor or services performed as an employee of or under a contract with—

(i) a nonresident alien, foreign partnership, or foreign corporation, not engaged in trade or business within the United States, or

(ii) an individual who is a citizen or resident of the United States, a domestic partnership, or a domestic corporation, if such labor or services are performed for an office or place of business maintained in a foreign country or in a possession of the United States by such individual, partnership, or corporation.

In addition, compensation for labor or services performed in the United States shall not be deemed to be income from sources within the United States if the labor or services are performed by a nonresident alien individual in connection with the individual's temporary presence in the United States as a regular member of the crew of a foreign vessel engaged in transportation between the United States and a foreign country or a possession of the United States.

(4) Rentals and royalties.—Rentals or royalties from property located in the United States or from any interest in such property, including rentals or royalties for the use of or for the privilege of using in the United States patents, copyrights, secret processes and formulas, good will, trade-marks, trade brands, franchises, and other like property.

(5) Disposition of United States real property interest.—Gains, profits, and income from the disposition of a United States real property interest (as defined in section 897(c)).

(6) Sale or exchange of inventory property.—Gains, profits, and income derived from the purchase of inventory property (within the meaning of section 865(i)(1)) without the United States (other than within a possession of the United States) and its sale or exchange within the United States.

(7) Amounts received as underwriting income (as defined in section 832(b)(3)) derived from the issuing (or reinsuring) of any insurance or annuity contract.—

(A) in connection with property in, liability arising out of an activity in, or in connection with the lives or health of residents of, the United States, or

(B) in connection with risks not described in subparagraph (A) as a result of any arrangement whereby another corporation receives a substantially equal amount of premiums or other consideration in respect to issuing (or reinsuring) any insurance or annuity contract in connection with property in, liability arising out of activity in, or in connection with the lives or health of residents of, the United States.

(8) Social Security Benefits.—Any social security benefit (as defined in section 86(d)).

(9) Guarantees.—Amounts received, directly or indirectly, from—

(A) a noncorporate resident or domestic corporation for the provision of a guarantee of any indebtedness of such resident or corporation, or

(B) any foreign person for the provision of a guarantee of any indebtedness of such person, if such amount is connected with income which is effectively connected (or treated as effectively connected) with the conduct of a trade or business in the United States.

(b) Taxable income from sources within United States.—From the items of gross income specified in subsection (a) as being income from sources within the United States there shall be deducted the expenses, losses, and other deductions properly apportioned or allocated thereto and a ratable part of any expenses, losses, or other deductions which cannot definitely be allocated to some item or class of gross income. The remainder, if any, shall be included in full as taxable income from sources within the United States. In the case of an individual who does not itemize deductions, an amount equal to the standard deduction shall be considered a deduction which cannot definitely be allocated to some item or class of gross income.

(c) Special rule for application of subsection (a)(2)(B).—For purposes of subsection (a)(2)(B), if the foreign corporation has no gross income from any source for the 3-year period (or part thereof) specified, the requirements of such subsection shall be applied with respect to the taxable year of such corporation in which the payment of the dividend is made.

(d) Income from certain railroad rolling stock treated as income from sources within the United States.—

(1) General rule.—For purposes of subsection (a) and section 862(a), if—

(A) a taxpayer leases railroad rolling stock which is section 1245 property (as defined in section 1245(a)(3)) to a domestic common carrier by railroad or a corporation which is controlled, directly or indirectly, by one or more such common carriers, and

(B) the use under such lease is expected to be use within the United States,

all amounts includible in gross income by the taxpayer with respect to such railroad rolling stock (including gain from sale or other disposition of such railroad rolling stock) shall be treated as income from sources within the United States. The requirements of subparagraph (B) of the preceding sentence shall be treated as satisfied if the only expected use outside the United States is use by a person (whether or not a United States person) in Canada or Mexico on a temporary basis which is not expected to exceed a total of 90 days in any taxable year.

(2) Paragraph (1) not to apply where lessor is a member of controlled group which includes a railroad.—Paragraph (1) shall not apply to a lease between two members of the same controlled group of corporations (as defined in section 1563) if any member of such group is a domestic common carrier by railroad or a switching or terminal company all of whose stock is owned by one or more domestic common carriers by railroad.

(3) Denial of foreign tax credit.—No credit shall be allowed under section 901 for any payments to foreign countries with respect to any amount received by the taxpayer with respect to railroad rolling stock which is subject to paragraph (1).

(e) Cross reference.—

For treatment of interest paid by the branch of a foreign corporation, see section 884(f).

§ 862. Income from sources without the United States

(a) Gross income from sources without United States.—The following items of gross income shall be treated as income from sources without the United States:

(1) interest other than that derived from sources within the United States as provided in section 861(a)(1);

(2) dividends other than those derived from sources within the United States as provided in section 861(a)(2);

(3) compensation for labor or personal services performed without the United States;

(4) rentals or royalties from property located without the United States or from any interest in such property, including rentals or royalties for the use of or for the privilege of using without the

United States patents, copyrights, secret processes and formulas, good will, trade-marks, trade brands, franchises, and other like properties;

(5) gains, profits, and income from the sale or exchange of real property located without the United States;

(6) gains, profits, and income derived from the purchase of inventory property (within the meaning of section 865(i)(1)) within the United States and its sale or exchange without the United States;

(7) underwriting income other than that derived from sources within the United States as provided in section 861(a)(7);

(8) gains, profits, and income from the disposition of a United States real property interest (as defined in section 897(c)) when the real property is located in the Virgin Islands; and

(9) amounts received, directly or indirectly, from a foreign person for the provision of a guarantee of indebtedness of such person other than amounts which are derived from sources within the United States as provided in section 861(a)(9).

(b) Taxable income from sources without United States.—From the items of gross income specified in subsection (a) there shall be deducted the expenses, losses, and other deductions properly apportioned or allocated thereto, and a ratable part of any expenses, losses, or other deductions which cannot definitely be allocated to some item or class of gross income. The remainder, if any, shall be treated in full as taxable income from sources without the United States. In the case of an individual who does not itemize deductions, an amount equal to the standard deduction shall be considered a deduction which cannot definitely be allocated to some item or class of gross income.

§ 863. Special rules for determining source

(a) Allocation under regulations.—Items of gross income, expenses, losses, and deductions, other than those specified in sections 861(a) and 862(a), shall be allocated or apportioned to sources within or without the United States, under regulations prescribed by the Secretary. Where items of gross income are separately allocated to sources within the United States, there shall be deducted (for the purpose of computing the taxable income therefrom) the expenses, losses, and other deductions properly apportioned or allocated thereto and a ratable part of other expenses, losses, or other deductions which cannot definitely be allocated to some item or class of gross income. The remainder, if any, shall be included in full as taxable income from sources within the United States.

(b) Income partly from within and partly from without the United States.—In the case of gross income derived from sources partly within and partly without the United States, the taxable income may first be computed by deducting the expenses, losses, or other deductions apportioned or allocated thereto and a ratable part of any expenses, losses, or other deductions which cannot definitely be allocated to some item or class of gross income; and the portion of such taxable income attributable to sources within the United States may be determined by processes or formulas of general apportionment prescribed by the Secretary. Gains, profits, and income—

(1) from services rendered partly within and partly without the United States,

(2) from the sale or exchange of inventory property (within the meaning of section 865(i)(1)) produced (in whole or in part) by the taxpayer within and sold or exchanged without the United States, or produced (in whole or in part) by the taxpayer without and sold or exchanged within the United States, or

(3) derived from the purchase of inventory property (within the meaning of section 865(i)(1)) within a possession of the United States and its sale or exchange within the United States,

shall be treated as derived partly from sources within and partly from sources without the United States. Gains, profits, and income from the sale or exchange of inventory property described in paragraph (2) shall be allocated and apportioned between sources within and without the United States solely on the basis of the production activities with respect to the property.

(c) Source rule for certain transportation income.—

(1) Transportation beginning and ending in the United States.—All transportation income attributable to transportation which begins and ends in the United States shall be treated as derived from sources within the United States.

(2) Other transportation having United States connection.—

(A) In general.—50 percent of all transportation income attributable to transportation which—

(i) is not described in paragraph (1), and

(ii) begins or ends in the United States, shall be treated as from sources in the United States.

(B) Special rule for personal service income.—Subparagraph (A) shall not apply to any transportation income which is income derived from personal services performed by the taxpayer, unless such income is attributable to transportation which—

(i) begins in the United States and ends in a possession of the United States, or

(ii) begins in a possession of the United States and ends in the United States.

In the case of transportation income derived from, or in connection with, a vessel, this subparagraph shall only apply if the taxpayer is a citizen or resident alien.

(3) Transportation income.—For purposes of this subsection, the term "transportation income" means any income derived from, or in connection with—

(A) the use (or hiring or leasing for use) of a vessel or aircraft, or

(B) the performance of services directly related to the use of a vessel or aircraft.

For purposes of the preceding sentence the term "vessel or aircraft" includes any container used in connection with a vessel or aircraft.

(d) Source rules for space and certain ocean activities.—

(1) In general.—Except as provided in regulations, any income derived from a space or ocean activity—

(A) if derived by a United States person, shall be sourced in the United States, and

(B) if derived by a person other than a United States person, shall be sourced outside the United States.

(2) Space or ocean activity.—For purposes of paragraph (1)—

(A) In general.—The term "space or ocean activity" means—

(i) any activity conducted in space, and

(ii) any activity conducted on or under water not within the jurisdiction (as recognized by the United States) of a foreign country, possession of the United States, or the United States.

Such term includes any activity conducted in Antarctica.

(B) Exception for certain activities.—The term "space or ocean activity" shall not include—

(i) any activity giving rise to transportation income (as defined in section 863(c)),

(ii) any activity giving rise to international communications income (as defined in subsection (e)(2)), and

(iii) any activity with respect to mines, oil and gas wells, or other natural deposits to the extent within the United States or any foreign country or possession of the United States (as defined in section 638).

For purposes of applying section 638, the jurisdiction of any foreign country shall not include any jurisdiction not recognized by the United States.

(e) International communications income.—

(1) Source rules.—

(A) United States persons.—In the case of any United States person, 50 percent of any international communications income shall be sourced in the United States and 50 percent of such income shall be sourced outside the United States.

(B) Foreign persons.—

(i) In general.—Except as provided in regulations or clause (ii), in the case of any person other than a United States person, any international communications income shall be sourced outside the United States.

(ii) Special rule for income attributable to office or fixed place of business in the United States.—In the case of any person (other than a United States person) who maintains an office or other fixed place of business in the United States, any international communications income attributable to such office or other fixed place of business shall be sourced in the United States.

(2) Definition.—For purposes of this section, the term "international communications income" includes all income derived from the transmission of communications or data from the United States to any foreign country (or possession of the United States) or from any foreign country (or possession of the United States) to the United States.

§ 864. Definitions and special rules

(a) Produced.—For purposes of this part, the term "produced" includes created, fabricated, manufactured, extracted, processed, cured, or aged.

(b) Trade or business within the United States.—For purposes of this part, part II, and chapter 3, the term "trade or business within the United States" includes the performance of personal services within the United States at any time within the taxable year, but does not include—

(1) Performance of personal services for foreign employer.—The performance of personal services—

(A) for a nonresident alien individual, foreign partnership, or foreign corporation, not engaged in trade or business within the United States, or

(B) for an office or place of business maintained in a foreign country or in a possession of the United States by an individual who is a citizen or resident of the United States or by a domestic partnership or a domestic corporation,

by a nonresident alien individual temporarily present in the United States for a period or periods not exceeding a total of 90 days during the taxable year and whose compensation for such services does not exceed in the aggregate $3,000.

(2) Trading in securities or commodities.—

(A) Stocks and securities.—

(i) In general.—Trading in stocks or securities through a resident broker, commission agent, custodian, or other independent agent.

(ii) Trading for taxpayer's own account.—Trading in stocks or securities for the taxpayer's own account, whether by the taxpayer or his employees or through a resident broker, commission agent, custodian, or other agent, and whether or not any such employee or agent has discretionary authority to make decisions in effecting the transactions. This clause shall not apply in the case of a dealer in stocks or securities.

(B) Commodities.—

(i) In general.—Trading in commodities through a resident broker, commission agent, custodian, or other independent agent.

(ii) Trading for taxpayer's own account.—Trading in commodities for the taxpayer's own account, whether by the taxpayer or his employees or through a resident broker, commission agent, custodian, or other agent, and whether or not any such employee or agent has discretionary authority to make decisions in effecting the transactions. This clause shall not apply in the case of a dealer in commodities.

(iii) Limitation.—Clauses (i) and (ii) shall apply only if the commodities are of a kind customarily dealt in on an organized commodity exchange and if the transaction is of a kind customarily consummated at such place.

(C) Limitation.—Subparagraphs (A)(i) and (B)(i) shall apply only if, at no time during the taxable year, the taxpayer has an office or other fixed place of business in the United States through which or by the direction of which the transactions in stocks or securities, or in commodities, as the case may be, are effected.

(c) Effectively connected income, etc.—

(1) General rule.—For purposes of this title—

(A) In the case of a nonresident alien individual or a foreign corporation engaged in trade or business within the United States during the taxable year, the rules set forth in paragraphs (2), (3), (4), (6), (7), and (8) shall apply in determining the income, gain, or loss which shall be treated as effectively connected with the conduct of a trade or business within the United States.

(B) Except as provided in paragraph (6), (7) or (8) or in section 871(d) or sections 882(d) and (e), in the case of a nonresident alien individual or a foreign corporation not engaged in trade or business within the United States during the taxable year, no income, gain, or loss shall be treated as effectively connected with the conduct of a trade or business within the United States.

(2) Periodical, etc., income from sources within United States—Factors.—In determining whether income from sources within the United States of the types described in section 871(a)(1), section 871(h), section 881(a), or section 881(c), or whether gain or loss from sources within the United States from the sale or exchange of capital assets, is effectively connected with the conduct of a trade or business within the United States, the factors taken into account shall include whether—

(A) the income, gain, or loss is derived from assets used in or held for use in the conduct of such trade or business, or

(B) the activities of such trade or business were a material factor in the realization of the income, gain, or loss.

In determining whether an asset is used in or held for use in the conduct of such trade or business or whether the activities of such trade or business were a material factor in realizing an item of income, gain, or loss, due regard shall be given to whether or not such asset or such income, gain, or loss was accounted for through such trade or business.

(3) Other income from sources within United States.—All income, gain, or loss from sources within the United States (other than income, gain, or loss to which paragraph (2) applies) shall be treated as effectively connected with the conduct of a trade or business within the United States.

(4) Income from sources without United States.—

(A) Except as provided in subparagraphs (B) and (C), no income, gain, or loss from sources without the United States shall be treated as effectively connected with the conduct of a trade or business within the United States.

(B) Income, gain, or loss from sources without the United States shall be treated as effectively connected with the conduct of a trade or business within the United States by a nonresident alien individual or a foreign corporation if such person has an office or other fixed place of business within the United States to which such income, gain, or loss is attributable and such income, gain, or loss—

(i) consists of rents or royalties for the use of or for the privilege of using intangible property described in section 862(a)(4) derived in the active conduct of such trade or business;

(ii) consists of dividends, interest, or amounts received for the provision of guarantees of indebtedness, and either is derived in the active conduct of a banking, financing, or similar business within the United States or is received by a corporation the principal business of which is trading in stocks or securities for its own account; or

(iii) is derived from the sale or exchange (outside the United States) through such office or other fixed place of business of personal property described in section 1221(a)(1), except that this clause shall not apply if the property is sold or exchanged for use, consumption, or disposition outside the United States and an office or other fixed place of business of the taxpayer in a foreign country participated materially in such sale.

Any income or gain which is equivalent to any item of income or gain described in clause (i), (ii), or (iii) shall be treated in the same manner as such item for purposes of this subparagraph.

(C) In the case of a foreign corporation taxable under part I or part II of subchapter L, any income from sources without the United States which is attributable to its United States business shall be treated as effectively connected with the conduct of a trade or business within the United States.

(D) No income from sources without the United States shall be treated as effectively connected with the conduct of a trade or business within the United States if it either—

(i) consists of dividends, interest, or royalties paid by a foreign corporation in which the taxpayer owns (within the meaning of section 958(a)), or is considered as owning (by applying the ownership rules of section 958(b)), more than 50 percent of the total combined voting power of all classes of stock entitled to vote, or

(ii) is subpart F income within the meaning of section 952(a).

(5) Rules for application of paragraph (4)(B).—For purposes of subparagraph (B) of paragraph (4)—

(A) in determining whether a nonresident alien individual or a foreign corporation has an office or other fixed place of business, an office or other fixed place of business of an agent shall be disregarded unless such agent (i) has the authority to negotiate and conclude contracts in the name of the nonresident alien individual or foreign corporation and regularly exercises that authority or has a stock of merchandise from which he regularly fills orders on behalf of such individual or foreign corporation, and (ii) is not a general commission agent, broker, or other agent of independent status acting in the ordinary course of his business,

(B) income, gain, or loss shall not be considered as attributable to an office or other fixed place of business within the United States unless such office or fixed place of business is a material factor in the production of such income, gain, or loss and such office or fixed place of business regularly carries on activities of the type from which such income, gain, or loss is derived, and

(C) the income, gain, or loss which shall be attributable to an office or other fixed place of business within the United States shall be the income, gain, or loss property allocable thereto, but, in the case of a sale or exchange described in clause (iii) of such subparagraph, the income which shall be treated as attributable to an office or other fixed place of business within the United States shall not exceed the income which would be derived from sources within the United States if the sale or exchange were made in the United States.

(6) Treatment of certain deferred payments, etc.—For purposes of this title, in the case of any income or gain of a nonresident alien individual or a foreign corporation which—

(A) is taken into account for any taxable year, but

(B) is attributable to a sale or exchange of property or the performance of services (or any other transaction) in any other taxable year,

the determination of whether such income or gain is taxable under section 871(b) or 882 (as the case may be) shall be made as if such income or gain were taken into account in such other taxable year and without regard to the requirement that the taxpayer be engaged in a trade or business within the United States during the taxable year referred to in subparagraph (A).

(7) Treatment of certain property transactions.—For purposes of this title, if—

(A) any property ceases to be used or held for use in connection with the conduct of a trade or business within the United States, and

(B) such property is disposed of within 10 years after such cessation,

the determination of whether any income or gain attributable to such disposition is taxable under section 871(b) or 882 (as the case may be) shall be made as if such sale or exchange occurred immediately before such cessation and without regard to the requirement that the taxpayer be engaged in a trade or business within the United States during the taxable year for which such income or gain is taken into account.

(8) Gain or loss of foreign persons from sale or exchange of certain partnership interests.—

(A) In general.—Notwithstanding any other provision of this subtitle, if a nonresident alien individual or foreign corporation owns, directly or indirectly, an interest in a partnership which is engaged in any trade or business within the United States, gain or loss on the sale or exchange of all (or any portion of) such interest shall be treated as effectively connected with the conduct of such trade or business to the extent such gain or loss does not exceed the amount determined under subparagraph (B).

(B) Amount treated as effectively connected.—The amount determined under this subparagraph with respect to any partnership interest sold or exchanged—

(i) in the case of any gain on the sale or exchange of the partnership interest, is—

(I) the portion of the partner's distributive share of the amount of gain which would have been effectively connected with the conduct of a trade or business within the United States if the partnership had sold all of its assets at their fair market value as of the date of the sale or exchange of such interest, or

(II) zero if no gain on such deemed sale would have been so effectively connected, and

(ii) in the case of any loss on the sale or exchange of the partnership interest, is—

(I) the portion of the partner's distributive share of the amount of loss on the deemed sale described in clause (i)(I) which would have been so effectively connected, or

(II) zero if no loss on such deemed sale would be have been so effectively connected.

For purposes of this subparagraph, a partner's distributive share of gain or loss on the deemed sale shall be determined in the same manner as such partner's distributive share of the non-separately stated taxable income or loss of such partnership.

(C) Coordination with United States real property interests.—If a partnership described in subparagraph (A) holds any United States real property interest (as defined in section 897(c)) at the time of the sale or exchange of the partnership interest, then the gain or loss treated as effectively connected income under subparagraph (A) shall be reduced by the amount so treated with respect to such United States real property interest under section 897.

(D) Sale or exchange.—For purposes of this paragraph, the term "sale or exchange" means any sale, exchange, or other disposition.

(E) Secretarial authority.—The Secretary shall prescribe such regulations or other guidance as the Secretary determines appropriate for the application of this paragraph, including with respect to exchanges described in section 332, 351, 354, 355, 356, or 361.

(d) Treatment of related person factoring income.—

(1) In general.—For purposes of the provisions set forth in paragraph (2), if any person acquires (directly or indirectly) a trade or service receivable from a related person, any income of such person from the trade or service receivable so acquired shall be treated as if it were interest on a loan to the obligor under the receivable.

(2) Provisions to which paragraph (1) applies.—The provisions set forth in this paragraph are as follows:

(A) Section 904 (relating to limitation on foreign tax credit).

(B) Subpart F of part III of this subchapter (relating to controlled foreign corporations).

(3) Trade or service receivable.—For purposes of this subsection, the term "trade or service receivable" means any account receivable or evidence of indebtedness arising out of—

(A) the disposition by a related person of property described in section 1221(a)(1), or

(B) the performance of services by a related person.

(4) Related person.—For purposes of this subsection, the term "related person" means—

(A) any person who is a related person (within the meaning of section 267(b)), and

(B) any United States shareholder (as defined in section 951(b)) and any person who is a related person (within the meaning of section 267(b)) to such a shareholder.

(5) Certain provisions not to apply.—The following provisions shall not apply to any amount treated as interest under paragraph (1) or (6):

(A) Section 904(d)(2)(B)(iii)(1) (relating to exceptions for export financing interest).

(B) Subparagraph (A) of section 954(b)(3) (relating to exception where foreign base company income is less than 5 percent or $1,000,000).

(C) Subparagraph (B) of section 954(c)(2) (relating to certain export financing).

(D) Clause (i) of section 954(c)(3)(A) (relating to certain income received from related persons).

(6) Special rule for certain income from loans of a controlled foreign corporation.—Any income of a controlled foreign corporation (within the meaning of section 957(a)) from a loan to a person for the purpose of financing—

(A) the purchase of property described in section 1221(a)(1) of a related person, or

(B) the payment for the performance of services by a related person, shall be treated as interest described in paragraph (1).

(7) Exception for certain related persons doing business in same foreign country.—Paragraph (1) shall not apply to any trade or service receivable acquired by any person from a related person if—

(A) the person acquiring such receivable and such related person are created or organized under the laws of the same foreign country and such related person has a substantial part of its assets used in its trade or business located in such same foreign country, and

(B) such related person would not have derived any foreign base company income (as defined in section 954(a), determined without regard to section 954(b)(3)(A)), or any income effectively connected with the conduct of a trade or business within the United States, from such receivable if it had been collected by such related person.

(8) Regulations.—The Secretary shall prescribe such regulations as may be necessary to prevent the avoidance of the provisions of this subsection or section 956(c)(3).

(e) Rules for allocating interest, etc.—For purposes of this subchapter—

(1) Treatment of affiliated groups.—The taxable income of each member of an affiliated group shall be determined by allocating and apportioning interest expense of each member as if all members of such group were a single corporation.

(2) Gross income and fair market value methods may not be used for interest.—All allocations and apportionments of interest expense shall be determined using the adjusted bases of assets rather than on the basis of the fair market value of the assets or gross income.

(3) Tax-exempt assets not taken into account.—For purposes of allocating and apportioning any deductible expense, any tax-exempt asset (and any income from such an asset) shall not be taken into account. A similar rule shall apply in the case of the portion of any dividend (other than a qualifying dividend as defined in section 243(b)) equal to the deduction allowable under section 243 or 245(a) with respect to such dividend and in the case of a like portion of any stock the dividends on which would be so deductible and would not be qualifying dividends (as so defined).

(4) Basis of stock in nonaffiliated 10-percent owned corporations adjusted for earnings and profits changes.—

(A) In general.—For purposes of allocating and apportioning expenses on the basis of assets, the adjusted basis of any stock in a nonaffiliated 10-percent owned corporation shall be—

(i) increased by the amount of the earnings and profits of such corporation attributable to such stock and accumulated during the period the taxpayer held such stock, or

(ii) reduced (but not below zero) by any deficit in earnings and profits of such corporation attributable to such stock for such period.

(B) Nonaffiliated 10-percent owned corporation.—For purposes of this paragraph, the term "nonaffiliated 10-percent owned corporation" means any corporation if—

(i) such corporation is not included in the taxpayer's affiliated group, and

(ii) members of such affiliated group own 10 percent or more of the total combined voting power of all classes of stock of such corporation entitled to vote.

(C) Earnings and profits of lower tier corporations taken into account.—

(i) In general.—If, by reason of holding stock in a nonaffiliated 10-percent owned corporation, the taxpayer is treated under clause (iii) as owning stock in another corporation with respect to which the stock ownership requirements of clause (ii) are met, the adjustment under subparagraph (A) shall include an adjustment for the amount of the earnings and profits (or deficit therein) of such other corporation which are attributable to the stock the taxpayer is so treated as owning and to the period during which the taxpayer is treated as owning such stock.

(ii) Stock ownership requirements.—The stock ownership requirements of this clause are met with respect to any corporation if members of the taxpayer's affiliated group own (directly or through the application of clause (iii)) 10 percent or more of the total combined voting power of all classes of stock of such corporation entitled to vote.

(iii) Stock owned through entities.—For purposes of this subparagraph, stock owned (directly or indirectly) by a corporation, partnership, or trust shall be treated as being owned proportionately by its shareholders, partners, or beneficiaries. Stock considered to be owned by a person by reason of the application of the preceding sentence, shall, for purposes of applying such sentence, be treated as actually owned by such person.

(D) Coordination with subpart F, etc.—For purposes of this paragraph, proper adjustment shall be made to the earnings and profits of any corporation to take into account any earnings and profits included in gross income under section 951 or under any other provision of this title and reflected in the adjusted basis of the stock.

(5) Affiliated group.—For purposes of this subsection—

(A) In general.—Except as provided in subparagraph (B), the term "affiliated group" has the meaning given such term by section 1504. Notwithstanding the preceding sentence, a foreign corporation shall be treated as a member of the affiliated group if

(i) more than 50 percent of the gross income of such foreign corporation for the taxable year is effectively connected with the conduct of a trade or business within the United States, and

(ii) at least 80 percent of either the vote or value of all outstanding stock of such foreign corporation is owned directly or indirectly by members of the affiliated group (determined with regard to this sentence).

(B) Treatment of certain financial institutions.—For purposes of subparagraph (A), any corporation described in subparagraph (C) shall be treated as an includible corporation for purposes of section 1504 only for purposes of applying such section separately to corporations so described. This subparagraph shall not apply for purposes of paragraph (6).

(C) Description.—A corporation is described in this subparagraph if—

(i) such corporation is a financial institution described in section 581 or 591,

(ii) the business of such financial institution is predominantly with persons other than related persons (within the meaning of subsection (d)(4)) or their customers, and

(iii) such financial institution is required by State or Federal law to be operated separately from any other entity which is not such an institution.

(D) Treatment of bank holding companies.—To the extent provided in regulations—

(i) a bank holding company (within the meaning of section 2(a) of the Bank Holding Company Act of 1956), and

(ii) any subsidiary of a financial institution described in section 581 or 591 or of any bank holding company if such subsidiary is predominantly engaged (directly or indirectly) in the active conduct of a banking, financing, or similar business,

shall be treated as a corporation described in subparagraph (C).

(6) Allocation and apportionment of other expenses.—Expenses other than interest which are not directly allocable or apportioned to any specific income producing activity shall be allocated and apportioned as if all members of the affiliated group were a single corporation.

(7) Regulations.—The Secretary shall prescribe such regulations as may be necessary or appropriate to carry out the purposes of this section, including regulations providing—

(A) for the resourcing of income of any member of an affiliated group or modifications to the consolidated return regulations to the extent such resourcing or modification is necessary to carry out the purposes of this section,

(B) for direct allocation of interest expense incurred to carry out an integrated financial transaction to any interest (or interest-type income) derived from such transaction and in other circumstances where such allocation would be appropriate to carry out the purposes of this subsection,

(C) for the apportionment of expenses allocated to foreign source income among the members of the affiliated group and various categories of income described in section 904(d)(1),

(D) for direct allocation of interest expense in the case of indebtedness resulting in a disallowance under section 246A,

(E) for appropriate adjustments in the application of paragraph (3) in the case of an insurance company,

(F) preventing assets or interest expense from being taken into account more than once, and

(G) that this subsection shall not apply for purposes of any provision of this subchapter to the extent the Secretary determines that the application of this subsection for such purposes would not be appropriate.

(f) Repealed.

(g) Allocation of research and experimental expenditures.—

(1) In general.—For purposes of sections 861(b), 862(b), and 863(b), qualified research and experimental expenditures shall be allocated and apportioned as follows:

(A) Any qualified research and experimental expenditures expended solely to meet legal requirements imposed by a political entity with respect to the improvement or marketing of specific products or processes for purposes not reasonably expected to generate gross income (beyond de minimis amounts) outside the jurisdiction of the political entity shall be allocated only to gross income from sources within such jurisdiction.

(B) In the case of any qualified research and experimental expenditures (not allocated under subparagraph (A)) to the extent—

(i) that such expenditures are attributable to activities conducted in the United States, 50 percent of such expenditures shall be allocated and apportioned to income from sources within the United States and deducted from such income in determining the amount of taxable income from sources within the United States, and

(ii) that such expenditures are attributable to activities conducted outside the United States, 50 percent of such expenditures shall be allocated and apportioned to income from sources outside the United States and deducted from such income in determining the amount of taxable income from sources outside the United States.

(C) The remaining portion of qualified research and experimental expenditures (not allocated under subparagraphs (A) and (B)) shall be apportioned, at the annual election of the taxpayer, on the basis of gross sales or gross income, except that, if the taxpayer elects to apportion on the basis of gross income, the amount apportioned to income from sources outside the United States shall at least be 30 percent of the amount which would be so apportioned on the basis of gross sales.

(2) Qualified research and experimental expenditures.—For purposes of this section, the term "qualified research and experimental expenditures" means amounts which are foreign research or experimental expenditures within the meaning of section 174 or domestic research or experimental expenditures within the meaning of section 174A. For purposes of this paragraph, rules similar to the rules of subsection (c) of section 174 shall apply. Any qualified research and experimental expenditures allowed as an amortization deduction under section 174(a) or section 174A(c), shall be taken into account under this subsection for the taxable year for which such expenditures are allowed as a deduction under such section (as the case may be).

(3) Special rules for expenditures attributable to activities conducted in space, etc.—

(A) In general.—Any qualified research and experimental expenditures described in subparagraph (B)—

(i) if incurred by a United States person, shall be allocated and apportioned under this section in the same manner as if they were attributable to activities conducted in the United States, and

(ii) if incurred by a person other than a United States person, shall be allocated and apportioned under this section in the same manner as if they were attributable to activities conducted outside the United States.

(B) Description of expenditures.—For purposes of subparagraph (A), qualified research and experimental expenditures are described in this subparagraph if such expenditures are attributable to activities conducted—

(i) in space,

(ii) on or under water not within the jurisdiction (as recognized by the United States) of a foreign country, possession of the United States, or the United States, or

(iii) in Antarctica.

(4) Affiliated group.—

(A) Except as provided in subparagraph (B), the allocation and apportionment required by paragraph (1) shall be determined as if all members of the affiliated group (as defined in subsection (e)(5)) were a single corporation.

(B) For purposes of the allocation and apportionment required by paragraph (1)—

(i) sales and gross income from products produced in whole or in part in a possession by an electing corporation (within the meaning of section 936(h)(5)(E)), and

(ii) dividends from an electing corporation,

shall not be taken into account, except that this subparagraph shall not apply to sales of (and gross income and dividends attributable to sales of) products with respect to which an election under section 936(h)(5)(F) is not in effect.

(C) The qualified research and experimental expenditures taken into account for purposes of paragraph (1) shall be adjusted to reflect the amount of such expenditures included in computing the cost-sharing amount (determined under section 936(h)(5)(C)(i)(I)).

(D) The Secretary may prescribe such regulations as may be necessary to carry out the purposes of this paragraph, including regulations providing for the source of gross income and the allocation and apportionment of deductions to take into account the adjustments required by subparagraph (B) or (C).

(E) Paragraph (6) of subsection (e) shall not apply to qualified research and experimental expenditures.

(5) Regulations.—The Secretary shall prescribe such regulations as may be appropriate to carry out the purposes of this subsection, including regulations relating to the determination of whether any expenses are attributable to activities conducted in the United States or outside the United States and regulations providing such adjustments to the provisions of this subsection as may be appropriate in the case of cost-sharing arrangements and contract research.

(6) Applicability.—This subsection shall apply to the taxpayer's first taxable year (beginning on or before August 1, 1994) following the taxpayer's last taxable year to which Revenue Procedure 92–56 applies or would apply if the taxpayer elected the benefits of such Revenue Procedure.

§ 865. Source rules for personal property sales

(a) General rule.—Except as otherwise provided in this section, income from the sale of personal property—

(1) by a United States resident shall be sourced in the United States, or

(2) by a nonresident shall be sourced outside the United States.

(b) Exception for inventory property.—In the case of income derived from the sale of inventory property—

(1) this section shall not apply, and

(2) such income shall be sourced under the rules of sections 861(a)(6), 862(a)(6), and 863.

Notwithstanding the preceding sentence, any income from the sale of any unprocessed timber which is a softwood and was cut from an area in the United States shall be sourced in the United States and the rules of sections 862(a)(6) and 863(b) shall not apply to any such income. For purposes of the preceding sentence, the term "unprocessed timber" means any log, cant, or similar form of timber.

(c) Exception for depreciable personal property.—

(1) In general.—Gain (not in excess of the depreciation adjustments) from the sale of depreciable personal property shall be allocated between sources in the United States and sources outside the United States—

(A) by treating the same proportion of such gain as sourced in the United States as the United States depreciation adjustments with respect to such property bear to the total depreciation adjustments, and

(B) by treating the remaining portion of such gain as sourced outside the United States.

(2) Gain in excess of depreciation.—Gain (in excess of the depreciation adjustments) from the sale of depreciable personal property shall be sourced as if such property were inventory property.

(3) United States depreciation adjustments.—For purposes of this subsection—

(A) In general.—The term "United States depreciation adjustments" means the portion of the depreciation adjustments to the adjusted basis of the property which are attributable to the depreciation deductions allowable in computing taxable income from sources in the United States.

(B) Special rule for certain property.—Except in the case of property of a kind described in section 168(g)(4), if, for any taxable year—

(i) such property is used predominantly in the United States, or

(ii) such property is used predominantly outside the United States,

all of the depreciation deductions allowable for such year shall be treated as having been allocated to income from sources in the United States (or, where clause (ii) applies, from sources outside the United States).

(4) Other definitions.—For purposes of this subsection—

(A) Depreciable personal property.—The term "depreciable personal property" means any personal property if the adjusted basis of such property includes depreciation adjustments.

(B) Depreciation adjustments.—The term "depreciation adjustments" means adjustments reflected in the adjusted basis of any property on account of depreciation deductions (whether allowed with respect to such property or other property and whether allowed to the taxpayer or to any other person).

(C) Depreciation deductions.—The term "depreciation deductions" means any deductions for depreciation or amortization or any other deduction allowable under any provision of this chapter which treats an otherwise capital expenditure as a deductible expense.

(d) Exception for intangibles.—

(1) In general.—In the case of any sale of an intangible—

(A) this section shall apply only to the extent the payments in consideration of such sale are not contingent on the productivity, use, or disposition of the intangible, and

(B) to the extent such payments are so contingent, the source of such payments shall be determined under this part in the same manner as if such payments were royalties.

(2) Intangible.—For purposes of paragraph (1), the term "intangible" means any patent, copyright, secret process or formula, goodwill, trademark, trade brand, franchise, or other like property.

(3) Special rule in the case of goodwill.—To the extent this section applies to the sale of goodwill, payments in consideration of such sale shall be treated as from sources in the country in which such goodwill was generated.

(4) Coordination with subsection (c).—

(A) Gain not in excess of depreciation adjustments sourced under subsection (c).—Notwithstanding paragraph (1), any gain from the sale of an intangible shall be sourced under subsection (c) to the extent such gain does not exceed the depreciation adjustments with respect to such intangible.

(B) Subsection (c)(2) not to apply to intangibles.—Paragraph (2) of subsection (c) shall not apply to any gain from the sale of an intangible.

(e) Special rules for sales through offices or fixed places of business.—

(1) Sales by residents.—

(A) In general.—In the case of income not sourced under subsection (b), (c), (d)(1)(B) or (3), or (f), if a United States resident maintains an office or other fixed place of business in a foreign country, income from sales of personal property attributable to such office or other fixed place of business shall be sourced outside the United States.

(B) Tax must be imposed.—Subparagraph (A) shall not apply unless an income tax equal to at least 10 percent of the income from the sale is actually paid to a foreign country with respect to such income.

(2) Sales by nonresidents.—

(A) In general.—Notwithstanding any other provisions of this part, if a nonresident maintains an office or other fixed place of business in the United States, income from any sale of personal property (including inventory property) attributable to such office or other fixed place of business shall be sourced in the United States. The preceding sentence shall not apply for purposes of section 971 (defining export trade corporation).

(B) Exception.—Subparagraph (A) shall not apply to any sale of inventory property which is sold for use, disposition, or consumption outside the United States if an office or other fixed place of business of the taxpayer in a foreign country materially participated in the sale.

(3) Sales attributable to an office or other fixed place of business.—The principles of section 864(c)(5) shall apply in determining whether a taxpayer has an office or other fixed place of business and whether a sale is attributable to such an office or other fixed place of business.

(f) Stock of affiliates.—If—

(1) a United States resident sells stock in an affiliate which is a foreign corporation,

(2) such sale occurs in a foreign country in which such affiliate is engaged in the active conduct of a trade or business, and

(3) more than 50 percent of the gross income of such affiliate for the 3-year period ending with the close of such affiliate's taxable year immediately preceding the year in which the sale occurred was derived from the active conduct of a trade or business in such foreign country,

any gain from such sale shall be sourced outside the United States. For purposes of paragraphs (2) and (3), the United States resident may elect to treat an affiliate and all other corporations which are wholly owned (directly or indirectly) by the affiliate as one corporation.

(g) United States resident; nonresident.—For purposes of this section—

(1) In general.—Except as otherwise provided in this subsection—

(A) United States resident.—The term "United States resident" means—

(i) any individual who—

(I) is a United States citizen or a resident alien and does not have a tax home (as defined in section 911(d)(3)) in a foreign country, or

(II) is a nonresident alien and has a tax home (as so defined) in the United States, and

(ii) any corporation, trust, or estate which is a United States person (as defined in section 7701(a)(30)).

(B) Nonresident.—The term "nonresident" means any person other than a United States resident.

(2) Special rules for United States citizens and resident aliens.—For purposes of this section, a United States citizen or resident alien shall not be treated as a nonresident with respect to any sale of personal property unless an income tax equal to at least 10 percent of the gain derived from such sale is actually paid to a foreign country with respect to that gain.

(3) Special rule for certain stock sales by residents of Puerto Rico.—Paragraph (2) shall not apply to the sale by an individual who was a bona fide resident of Puerto Rico during the entire taxable year of stock in a corporation if—

(A) such corporation is engaged in the active conduct of a trade or business in Puerto Rico, and

(B) more than 50 percent of its gross income for the 3-year period ending with the close of such corporation's taxable year immediately preceding the year in which such sale occurred was derived from the active conduct of a trade or business in Puerto Rico.

For purposes of the preceding sentence, the taxpayer may elect to treat a corporation and all other corporations which are wholly owned (directly or indirectly) by such corporation as one corporation.

(h) Treatment of gains from sale of certain stock or intangibles and from certain liquidations.—

(1) In general.—In the case of gain to which this subsection applies—

(A) such gain shall be sourced outside the United States, but

(B) subsections (a), (b), and (c) of section 904 and sections 907 and 960 shall be applied separately with respect to such gain.

(2) Gain to which subsection applies.—This subsection shall apply to—

(A) Gain from sale of certain stock or intangibles.—Any gain—

(i) which is from the sale of stock in a foreign corporation or an intangible (as defined in subsection (d)(2)) and which would otherwise be sourced in the United States under this section,

(ii) which, under a treaty obligation of the United States (applied without regard to this section), would be sourced outside the United States, and

(iii) with respect to which the taxpayer chooses the benefits of this subsection.

(B) Gain from liquidation in possession.—Any gain which is derived from the receipt of any distribution in liquidation of a corporation—

(i) which is organized in a possession of the United States, and

(ii) more than 50 percent of the gross income of which during the 3-taxable year period ending with the close of the taxable year immediately preceding the taxable year in which the distribution is received is from the active conduct of a trade or business in such possession.

(i) Other definitions.—For purposes of this section—

(1) Inventory property.—The term "inventory property" means personal property described in paragraph (1) of section 1221(a).

(2) Sale includes exchange.—The term "sale" includes an exchange or any other disposition.

(3) Treatment of possessions.—Any possession of the United States shall be treated as a foreign country.

(4) Affiliate.—The term "affiliate" means a member of the same affiliated group (within the meaning of section 1504(a) without regard to section 1504(b)).

(5) Treatment of partnerships.—In the case of a partnership, except as provided in regulations, this section shall be applied at the partner level.

(j) Regulations.—The Secretary shall prescribe such regulations as may be necessary or appropriate to carry out the purpose of this section, including regulations—

(1) relating to the treatment of losses from sales of personal property,

(2) applying the rules of this section to income derived from trading in futures contracts, forward contracts, options contracts, and other instruments, and

(3) providing that, subject to such conditions (which may include provisions comparable to section 877) as may be provided in such regulations, subsections (e)(1)(B) and (g)(2) shall not apply for purposes of sections 931 and 933.

(k) Cross references.—

(1) For provisions relating to the characterization as dividends for source purposes of gains from the sale of stock in certain foreign corporations, see section 1248.

(2) For sourcing of income from certain foreign currency transactions, see section 988.

Part II—Nonresident Aliens and Foreign Corporations

Subpart A—Nonresident Alien Individuals

§ 871. Tax on nonresident alien individuals

(a) Income not connected with United States business—30 percent tax.—

(1) Income other than capital gains.—Except as provided in subsection (h), there is hereby imposed for each taxable year a tax of 30 percent of the amount received from sources within the United States by a nonresident alien individual as—

(A) interest (other than original issue discount as defined in section 1273), dividends, rents, salaries, wages, premiums, annuities, compensations, remunerations, emoluments, and other fixed or determinable annual or periodical gains, profits, and income,

(B) gains described in subsection (b) or (c) of section 631.

(C) in the case of—

(i) a sale or exchange of an original issue discount obligation, the amount of the original issue discount accruing while such obligation was held by the nonresident alien individual (to the extent such discount was not theretofore taken into account under clause (ii)), and

(ii) a payment on an original issue discount obligation, an amount equal to the original issue discount accruing while such obligation was held by the nonresident alien individual (except that such original issue discount shall be taken into account under this clause only to the extent such discount was not theretofore taken into account under this clause and only to the extent that the tax thereon does not exceed the payment less the tax imposed by subparagraph (A) thereon), and

(D) gains from the sale or exchange after October 4, 1966, of patents, copyrights, secret processes and formulas, good will, trademarks, trade brands, franchises, and other like property, or of any interest in any such property, to the extent such gains are from payments which are contingent on the productivity, use, or disposition of the property or interest sold or exchanged,

but only to the extent the amount so received is not effectively connected with the conduct of a trade or business within the United States.

(2) Capital gains of aliens present in the United States 183 days or more.—In the case of a nonresident alien individual present in the United States for a period or periods aggregating 183 days or more during the taxable year, there is hereby imposed for such year a tax of 30 percent of the amount by which his gains, derived from sources within the United States, from the sale or exchange at any time during such year of capital assets exceed his losses, allocable to sources within the United States, from the sale or exchange at any time during such year of capital assets. For purposes of this paragraph, gains and losses shall be taken into account only if, and to the extent that, they would be recognized and taken into account if such gains and losses were effectively connected with the conduct of a trade or business within the United States, except that such gains and losses shall be determined without regard to section 1202 and such losses shall be determined without the benefits of the capital loss carryover provided in section 1212. Any gain or loss which is taken into account in determining the tax under paragraph (1) or subsection (b) shall not be taken into account in determining the tax under this paragraph. For purposes of the 183-day requirement of this paragraph, a nonresident alien individual not engaged in trade or business within the United States who has not established a taxable year for any prior period shall be treated as having a taxable year which is the calendar year.

(3) Taxation of social security benefits.—For purposes of this section and section 1441—

(A) 85 percent of any social security benefit (as defined in section 86(d)) shall be included in gross income (notwithstanding section 207 of the Social Security Act), and

(B) section 86 shall not apply.

(b) Income connected with the United States business.—Graduated rate of tax.—

(1) Imposition of tax.—A nonresident alien individual engaged in trade or business within the United States during the taxable year shall be taxable as provided in section 1 or 55 on his taxable income which is effectively connected with the conduct of a trade or business within the United States.

(2) Determination of taxable income.—In determining taxable income for purposes of paragraph (1), gross income includes only gross income which is effectively connected with the conduct of a trade or business within the United States.

(c) Participants in certain exchange or training programs.—For purposes of this section, a nonresident alien individual who (without regard to this subsection) is not engaged in trade or business within the United States and who is temporarily present in the United States as a nonimmigrant under subparagraph (F), (J), (M), or (Q) of section 101(a)(15) of the Immigration and Nationality Act, as amended (8 U.S.C. 1101a(a)(15) (F), (J), (M), or (Q)), shall be treated as a nonresident alien individual engaged in trade or business within the United States, and any income described in the second sentence of section 1441(b) which is received by such individual shall, to the extent derived from sources within the United States, be treated as effectively connected with the conduct of a trade or business within the United States.

(d) Election to treat real property income as income connected with United States business.—

(1) In general.—A nonresident alien individual who during the taxable year derives any income—

(A) from real property held for the production of income and located in the United States, or from any interest in such real property, including (i) gains from the sale or exchange of such real property or an interest therein, (ii) rents or royalties from mines, wells, or other natural deposits, and (iii) gains described in section 631(b) or (c), and

(B) which, but for this subsection, would not be treated as income which is effectively connected with the conduct of a trade or business within the United States,

may elect for such taxable year to treat all such income as income which is effectively connected with the conduct of a trade or business within the United States. In such case, such income shall be taxable as provided in subsection (b)(1) whether or not such individual is engaged in trade or business within the United States during the taxable year. An election under this paragraph for any taxable year shall remain in effect for all subsequent taxable years, except that it may be revoked with the consent of the Secretary with respect to any taxable year.

(2) Election after revocation.—If an election has been made under paragraph (1) and such election has been revoked, a new election may not be made under such paragraph for any taxable year before the 5th taxable year which begins after the first taxable year for which such revocation is effective, unless the Secretary consents to such new election.

(3) Form and time of election and revocation.—An election under paragraph (1), and any revocation of such an election, may be made only in such manner and at such time as the Secretary may by regulations prescribe.

* * *

(f) Certain annuities received under qualified plans.—

(1) In general.—For purposes of this section, gross income does not include any amount received as an annuity under a qualified annuity plan described in section 403(a)(1), or from a qualified trust described in section 401(a) which is exempt from tax under section 501(a), if—

(A) All of the personal services by reason of which the annuity is payable were either—

(i) personal services performed outside the United States by an individual who, at the time of performance of such personal services, was a nonresident alien, or

(ii) personal services described in section 864(b)(1) performed within the United States by such individual, and

(B) at the time the first amount is paid as an annuity under the annuity plan or by the trust, 90 percent or more of the employees for whom contributions or benefits are provided under such annuity plan, or under the plan or plans of which the trust is a part, are citizens or residents of the United States.

(2) Exclusion.—Income received during the taxable year which would be excluded from gross income under this subsection but for the requirement of paragraph (1)(B) shall not be included in gross income if—

(A) the recipient's country of residence grants a substantially equivalent exclusion to residents and citizens of the United States; or

(B) the recipient's country of residence is a beneficiary developing country under title V of the Trade Act of 1974 (19 U.S.C. 2461 et seq.).

(g) Special rules for original issue discount.—For purposes of this section and section 881—

(1) Original issue discount obligation.—

(A) In general.—Except as provided in subparagraph (B), the term "original issue discount obligation" means any bond or other evidence of indebtedness having original issue discount (within the meaning of section 1273).

(B) Exceptions.—The term "original issue discount obligation" shall not include—

(i) Certain short-term obligations.—Any obligation payable 183 days or less from the date of original issue (without regard to the period held by the taxpayer).

(ii) Tax-exempt obligations.—Any obligation the interest on which is exempt from tax under section 103 or under any other provision of law without regard to the identity of the holder.

(2) Determination of portion of original issue discount accruing during any period.—The determination of the amount of the original issue discount which accrues during any period shall be made under the rules of section 1272 (or the corresponding provisions of prior law) without regard to any exception for short-term obligations.

(3) Source of original issue discount.—Except to the extent provided in regulations prescribed by the Secretary, the determination of whether any amount described in subsection (a)(1)(C) is from sources within the United States shall be made at the time of the payment (or sale or exchange) as if such payment (or sale or exchange) involved the payment of interest.

(4) Stripped bonds.—The provisions of section 1286 (relating to the treatment of stripped bonds and stripped coupons as obligations with original issue discount) shall apply for purposes of this section.

(h) Repeal of tax on interest of nonresident alien individuals received from certain portfolio debt investments.—

(1) In general.—In the case of any portfolio interest received by a nonresident individual from sources within the United States, no tax shall be imposed under paragraph (1)(A) or (1)(C) of subsection (a).

(2) Portfolio interest.—For purposes of this subsection, the term "portfolio interest" means any interest (including original issue discount) which—

(A) would be subject to tax under subsection (a) but for this subsection, and

(B) is paid on an obligation—

(i) which is in registered form, and

(ii) with respect to which—

(I) the United States person who would otherwise be required to deduct and withhold tax from such interest under section 1441(a) receives a statement (which meets the requirements of paragraph (5)) that the beneficial owner of the obligation is not a United States person, or

(II) the Secretary has determined that such a statement is not required in order to carry out the purposes of this subsection.

(3) Portfolio interest not to include interest received by 10-percent shareholders.—For purposes of this subsection—

(A) In general.—The term "portfolio interest" shall not include any interest described in paragraph (2) which is received by a 10-percent shareholder.

(B) 10-percent shareholder.—The term "10-percent shareholder" means—

(i) in the case of an obligation issued by a corporation, any person who owns 10 percent or more of the total combined voting power of all classes of stock of such corporation entitled to vote, or

(ii) in the case of an obligation issued by a partnership, any person who owns 10 percent or more of the capital or profits interest in such partnership.

(C) Attribution rules.—For purposes of determining ownership of stock under subparagraph (B)(i) the rules of section 318(a) shall apply, except that—

(i) section 318(a)(2)(C) shall be applied without regard to the 50-percent limitation therein,

(ii) section 318(a)(3)(C) shall be applied—

(I) without regard to the 50-percent limitation therein; and

(II) in any case where such section would not apply but for subclause (I), by considering a corporation as owning the stock (other than stock in such corporation) which is owned by or for any shareholder of such corporation in that proportion which the value of the stock which such shareholder owns in such corporation bears to the value of all stock in such corporation, and

(iii) any stock which a person is treated as owning after application of section 318(a)(4) shall not, for purposes of applying paragraphs (2) and (3) of section 318(a), be treated as actually owned by such person.

Under regulations prescribed by the Secretary, rules similar to the rules of the preceding sentence shall be applied in determining the ownership of the capital or profits interest in a partnership for purposes of subparagraph (B)(ii).

(4) Portfolio interest not to include certain contingent interest.—For purposes of this subsection—

(A) In general.—Except as otherwise provided in this paragraph, the term "portfolio interest" shall not include—

(i) any interest if the amount of such interest is determined by reference to—

(I) any receipts, sales or other cash flow of the debtor or a related person,

(II) any income or profits of the debtor or a related person,

(III) any change in value of any property of the debtor or a related person, or

(IV) any dividend, partnership distributions, or similar payments made by the debtor or a related person, or

(ii) any other type of contingent interest that is identified by the Secretary by regulation, where a denial of the portfolio interest exemption is necessary or appropriate to prevent avoidance of Federal income tax.

(B) Related person.—The term "related person" means any person who is related to the debtor within the meaning of section 267(b) or 707(b)(1), or who is a party to any arrangement undertaken for a purpose of avoiding the application of this paragraph.

(C) Exceptions.—Subparagraph (A)(i) shall not apply to—

(i) any amount of interest solely by reason of the fact that the timing of any interest or principal payment is subject to a contingency,

(ii) any amount of interest solely by reason of the fact that the interest is paid with respect to nonrecourse or limited recourse indebtedness,

(iii) any amount of interest all or substantially all of which is determined by reference to any other amount of interest not described in subparagraph (A) (or by reference to the principal amount of indebtedness on which such other interest is paid),

(iv) any amount of interest solely by reason of the fact that the debtor or a related person enters into a hedging transaction to manage the risk of interest rate or currency fluctuations with respect to such interest,

(v) any amount of interest determined by reference to—

(I) changes in the value of property (including stock) that is actively traded (within the meaning of section 1092(d)) other than property described in section 897(c)(1) or (g),

(II) the yield on property described in subclause (I), other than a debt instrument that pays interest described in subparagraph (A), or stock or other property that represents a beneficial interest in the debtor or a related person, or

(III) changes in any index of the value of property described in subclause (I) or of the yield on property described in subclause (II), and

(vi) any other type of interest identified by the Secretary by regulation.

(D) Exception for certain existing indebtedness.—Subparagraph (A) shall not apply to any interest paid or accrued with respect to any indebtedness with a fixed term—

(i) which was issued on or before April 7, 1993, or

(ii) which was issued after such date pursuant to a written binding contract in effect on such date and at all times thereafter before such indebtedness was issued.

(5) Certain statements.—A statement with respect to any obligation meets the requirements of this paragraph if such statement is made by—

(A) the beneficial owner of such obligation, or

(B) a securities clearing organization, a bank, or other financial institution that holds customers' securities in the ordinary course of its trade or business.

The preceding sentence shall not apply to any statement with respect to payment of interest on any obligation by any person if, at least one month before such payment, the Secretary has published a determination that any statement from such person (or any class including such person) does not meet the requirements of this paragraph.

(6) Secretary may provide subsection not to apply in cases of inadequate information exchange.—

(A) In general.—If the Secretary determines that the exchange of information between the United States and a foreign country is inadequate to prevent evasion of the United States income tax by United States persons, the Secretary may provide in writing (and publish a statement) that the provisions of this subsection shall not apply to payments of interest to any person within such foreign country (or payments addressed to, or for the account of, persons within such foreign country) during the period—

(i) beginning on the date specified by the Secretary, and

(ii) ending on the date that the Secretary determines that the exchange of information between the United States and the foreign country is adequate to prevent the evasion of United States income tax by United States persons.

(B) Exception for certain obligations.—Subparagraph (A) shall not apply to the payment of interest on any obligation which is issued on or before the date of the publication of the Secretary's determination under such subparagraph.

(7) Registered form.—For purposes of this subsection, the term "registered form" has the same meaning given such term by section 163(f).

(i) Tax not to apply to certain interest and dividends.—

(1) In general.—No tax shall be imposed under paragraph (1)(A) or (1)(C) of subsection (a) on any amount described in paragraph (2).

(2) Amounts to which paragraph (1) applies.—The amounts described in this paragraph are as follows:

(A) Interest on deposits, if such interest is not effectively connected with the conduct of a trade or business within the United States.

(B) The active foreign business percentage of—

(i) any dividend paid by an existing 80/20 company, and

(ii) any interest paid by an existing 80/20 company.

(C) Income derived by a foreign central bank of issue from bankers' acceptances.

(D) Dividends paid by a foreign corporation which are treated under section 861(a)(2)(B) as income from sources within the United States.

(3) Deposits.—For purposes of paragraph (2), the term "deposits" means amounts which are—

(A) deposits with persons carrying on the banking business,

(B) deposits or withdrawable accounts with savings institutions chartered and supervised as savings and loan or similar associations under Federal or State law, but only to the extent that amounts paid or credited on such deposits or accounts are deductible under section 591 (determined without regard to sections 265 and 291) in computing the taxable income of such institutions, and

(C) amounts held by an insurance company under an agreement to pay interest thereon.

(j) Exemption for certain gambling winnings.—No tax shall be imposed under paragraph (1)(A) of subsection (a) on the proceeds from a wager placed in any of the following games: blackjack, baccarat, craps, roulette, or big-6 wheel. The preceding sentence shall not apply in any case where the Secretary determines by regulation that the collection of the tax is administratively feasible.

(k) Exemption for certain dividends of regulated investment companies.—

(1) Interest-related dividends.—

(A) In general.—Except as provided in subparagraph (B), no tax shall be imposed under paragraph (1)(A) of subsection (a) on any interest-related dividend received from a regulated investment company which meets the requirements of section 852(a) for the taxable year with respect to which the dividend is paid.

(B) Exceptions.—Subparagraph (A) shall not apply—

(i) to any interest-related dividend received from a regulated investment company by a person to the extent such dividend is attributable to interest (other than interest described in subparagraph (E)(i) or (iii)) received by such company on indebtedness issued by such person or by any corporation or partnership with respect to which such person is a 10-percent shareholder,

(ii) to any interest-related dividend with respect to stock of a regulated investment company unless the person who would otherwise be required to deduct and withhold tax from such dividend under chapter 3 receives a statement (which meets requirements similar to the requirements of subsection (h)(5)) that the beneficial owner of such stock is not a United States person, and

(iii) to any interest-related dividend paid to any person within a foreign country (or any interest-related dividend payment addressed to, or for the account of, persons within such foreign country) during any period described in subsection (h)(6) with respect to such country.

Clause (iii) shall not apply to any dividend with respect to any stock which was acquired on or before the date of the publication of the Secretary's determination under subsection (h)(6).

(C) Interest-related dividend.—For purposes of this paragraph—

(i) In general.—Except as provided in clause (ii), an interest related dividend is any dividend, or part thereof, which is reported by the company as an interest related dividend in written statements furnished to its shareholders.

(ii) Excess reported amounts.—If the aggregate reported amount with respect to the company for any taxable year exceeds the qualified net interest income of the company for such taxable year, an interest related dividend is the excess of—

(I) the reported interest related dividend amount, over

(II) the excess reported amount which is allocable to such reported Interest related dividend amount.

(iii) Allocation of excess reported amount.—

(I) In general.—Except as provided in subclause (II), the excess reported amount (if any) which is allocable to the reported interest related dividend amount is that portion of the excess reported amount which bears the same ratio to the excess reported amount as the reported interest related dividend amount bears to the aggregate reported amount.

(II) Special rule for noncalendar year taxpayers.—In the case of any taxable year which does not begin and end in the same calendar year, if the post-December reported amount equals or exceeds the excess reported amount for such taxable year, subclause (I) shall be applied by substituting "post-December reported amount" for "aggregate reported amount" and no excess reported amount shall be allocated to any dividend paid on or before December 31 of such taxable year.

(iv) Definitions.—For purposes of this subparagraph—

(I) Reported interest related dividend amount.—The term "reported interest related dividend amount" means the amount reported to its shareholders under clause (i) as an interest related dividend.

(II) Excess reported amount.—The term "excess reported amount" means the excess of the aggregate reported amount over the qualified net interest income of the company for the taxable year.

(III) Aggregate reported amount.—The term "aggregate reported amount" means the aggregate amount of dividends reported by the company under clause (i) as interest related dividends for the taxable year (including interest related dividends paid after the close of the taxable year described in section 855).

(IV) Post-December reported amount.—The term "post-December reported amount" means the aggregate reported amount determined by taking into account only dividends paid after December 31 of the taxable year.

(D) Qualified net interest income.—For purposes of subparagraph (C), the term "qualified net interest income" means the qualified interest income of the regulated investment company reduced by the deductions properly allocable to such income.

(E) Qualified interest income.—For purposes of subparagraph (D), the term "qualified interest income" means the sum of the following amounts derived by the regulated investment company from sources within the United States:

(i) Any amount includible in gross income as original issue discount (within the meaning of section 1273) on an obligation payable 183 days or less from the date of original issue (without regard to the period held by the company).

(ii) Any interest includible in gross income (including amounts recognized as ordinary income in respect of original issue discount or market discount or acquisition discount under part V of subchapter P and such other amounts as regulations may provide) on an obligation which is in registered form; except that this clause shall not apply to—

(I) any interest on an obligation issued by a corporation or partnership if the regulated investment company is a 10-percent shareholder in such corporation or partnership, and

(II) any interest which is treated as not being portfolio interest under the rules of subsection (h)(4).

(iii) Any interest referred to in subsection (i)(2)(A) (without regard to the trade or business of the regulated investment company).

(iv) Any interest-related dividend includable in gross income with respect to stock of another regulated investment company.

(F) 10-percent shareholder.—For purposes of this paragraph, the term "10-percent shareholder" has the meaning given such term by subsection (h)(3)(B).

(2) Short-term capital gain dividends.—

(A) In general.—Except as provided in subparagraph (B), no tax shall be imposed under paragraph (1)(A) of subsection (a) on any short-term capital gain dividend received from a regulated investment company which meets the requirements of section 852(a) for the taxable year with respect to which the dividend is paid.

(B) Exception for aliens taxable under subsection (a)(2).—Subparagraph (A) shall not apply in the case of any nonresident alien individual subject to tax under subsection (a)(2).

(C) Short-term capital gain dividend.—For purposes of this paragraph—

(i) In general.—Except as provided in clause (ii), the term "short-term capital gain dividend" means any dividend, or part thereof, which is reported by the company as a short-term capital gain dividend in written statements furnished to its shareholders.

(ii) Excess reported amounts.—If the aggregate reported amount with respect to the company for any taxable year exceeds the qualified short-term gain of the company for such taxable year, the term "short-term capital gain dividend" means the excess of—

(I) the reported short-term capital gain dividend amount, over

(II) the excess reported amount which is allocable to such reported short-term capital gain dividend amount.

(iii) Allocation of excess reported amount.—

(I) In general.—Except as provided in subclause (II), the excess reported amount (if any) which is allocable to the reported short-term capital gain dividend amount is that portion of the excess reported amount which bears the same ratio to the excess reported amount as the reported short-term capital gain dividend amount bears to the aggregate reported amount.

(II) Special rule for noncalendar year taxpayers.—In the case of any taxable year which does not begin and end in the same calendar year, if the post-December reported amount equals or exceeds the excess reported amount for such taxable year, subclause (I) shall be applied by substituting "post-December reported amount" for "aggregate reported amount" and no excess reported amount shall be allocated to any dividend paid on or before December 31 of such taxable year.

(iv) Definitions.—For purposes of this subparagraph—

(I) Reported short-term capital gain dividend amount.—The term "reported short-term capital gain dividend amount" means the amount reported to its shareholders under clause (i) as a short-term capital gain dividend.

(II) Excess reported amount.—The term "excess reported amount" means the excess of the aggregate reported amount over the qualified short-term gain of the company for the taxable year.

(III) Aggregate reported amount.—The term "aggregate reported amount" means the aggregate amount of dividends reported by the company under clause (i) as short-term capital gain dividends for the taxable year (including short-term capital gain dividends paid after the close of the taxable year described in section 855).

(IV) Post-December reported amount.—The term "post-December reported amount" means the aggregate reported amount determined by taking into account only dividends paid after December 31 of the taxable year.

(D) Qualified short-term gain.—For purposes of subparagraph (C), the term "qualified short-term gain" means the excess of the net short-term capital gain of the regulated investment company for the taxable year over the net long-term capital loss (if any) of such company for such taxable year. For purposes of this subparagraph, the net short-term capital gain of the regulated investment company shall be computed by treating any short-term capital gain dividend includible in gross income with respect to stock of another regulated investment company as a short-term capital gain.

(E) Certain distributions.—In the case of a distribution to which section 897 does not apply by reason of the second sentence of section 897(h)(1), the amount which would be treated as a short-term capital gain dividend to the shareholder (without regard to this subparagraph)—

(i) shall not be treated as a short-term capital gain dividend, and

(ii) shall be included in such shareholder's gross income as a dividend from the regulated investment company.

(l) **Rules relating to existing 80/20 companies.**—For purposes of this subsection and subsection (i)(2)(B)—

(1) Existing 80/20 company—

(A) In general.—The term "existing 80/20 company" means any corporation if—

(i) such corporation met the 80-percent foreign business requirements of section 861(c)(1) (as in effect before the date of the enactment of this subsection) for such corporation's last taxable year beginning before January 1, 2011,

(ii) such corporation meets the 80-percent foreign business requirements of subparagraph (B) with respect to each taxable year after the taxable year referred to in clause (i), and

(iii) there has not been an addition of a substantial line of business with respect to such corporation after the date of the enactment of this subsection.

(B) Foreign business requirements.—

(i) In general.—Except as provided in clause (iv), a corporation meets the 80-percent foreign business requirements of this subparagraph if it is shown to the satisfaction of the Secretary that at least 80 percent of the gross income from all sources of such corporation for the testing period is active foreign business income.

(ii) Active foreign business income.—For purposes of clause (i), the term "active foreign business income" means gross income which—

(I) is derived from sources outside the United States (as determined under this subchapter), and

(II) is attributable to the active conduct of a trade or business in a foreign country or possession of the United States.

(iii) Testing period.—For purposes of this subsection, the term "testing period" means the 3-year period ending with the close of the taxable year of the corporation preceding the payment (or such part of such period as may be applicable). If the corporation has no gross income for such 3-year period (or part thereof), the testing period shall be the taxable year in which the payment is made.

(iv) Transition rule.—In the case of a taxable year for which the testing period includes 1 or more taxable years beginning before January 1, 2011—

(I) a corporation meets the 80-percent foreign business requirements of this subparagraph if and only if the weighted average of—

(aa) the percentage of the corporation's gross income from all sources that is active foreign business income (as defined in subparagraph (B) of section 861(c)(1) (as in effect before the date of the enactment of this subsection)) for the portion of the testing period that includes taxable years beginning before January 1, 2011, and

(bb) the percentage of the corporation's gross income from all sources that is active foreign business income (as defined in clause (ii) of this subparagraph) for the portion of the testing period, if any, that includes taxable years beginning on or after January 1, 2011, is at least 80 percent, and

(II) the active foreign business percentage for such taxable year shall equal the weighted average percentage determined under subclause (I).

(2) Active foreign business percentage.—Except as provided in paragraph (1)(B)(iv), the term "active foreign business percentage" means, with respect to any existing 80/20 company, the percentage which—

(A) the active foreign business income of such company for the testing period, is of

(B) the gross income of such company for the testing period from all sources.

(3) Aggregation rules.—For purposes of applying paragraph (1) (other than subparagraphs (A)(i) and (B)(iv) thereof) and paragraph (2)—

(A) In general.—The corporation referred to in paragraph (1)(A) and all of such corporation's subsidiaries shall be treated as one corporation.

(B) Subsidiaries.—For purposes of subparagraph (A), the term "subsidiary" means any corporation in which the corporation referred to in subparagraph (A) owns (directly or indirectly) stock meeting the requirements of section 1504(a)(2) (determined by substituting '50 percent' for '80 percent' each place it appears and without regard to section 1504(b)(3)).

(4) Regulations.—The Secretary may issue such regulations or other guidance as is necessary or appropriate to carry out the purposes of this section, including regulations or other guidance which provide for the proper application of the aggregation rules described in paragraph (3).

(m) Treatment of dividend equivalent payments.—

(1) In general.—For purposes of subsection (a), sections 881 and 4948(a), and chapters 3 and 4, a dividend equivalent shall be treated as a dividend from sources within the United States.

(2) Dividend equivalent.—For purposes of this subsection, the term "dividend equivalent" means—

(A) any substitute dividend made pursuant to a securities lending or a sale-repurchase transaction that (directly or indirectly) is contingent upon, or determined by reference to, the payment of a dividend from sources within the United States,

(B) any payment made pursuant to a specified notional principal contract that (directly or indirectly) is contingent upon, or determined by reference to, the payment of a dividend from sources within the United States, and

(C) any other payment determined by the Secretary to be substantially similar to a payment described in subparagraph (A) or (B).

(3) Specified notional principal contract.—For purposes of this subsection, the term "specified notional principal contract" means—

(A) any notional principal contract if—

(i) in connection with entering into such contract, any long party to the contract transfers the underlying security to any short party to the contract,

(ii) in connection with the termination of such contract, any short party to the contract transfers the underlying security to any long party to the contract,

(iii) the underlying security is not readily tradable on an established securities market,

(iv) in connection with entering into such contract, the underlying security is posted as collateral by any short party to the contract with any long party to the contract, or

(v) such contract is identified by the Secretary as a specified notional principal contract,

(B) in the case of payments made after the date which is 2 years after the date of the enactment of this subsection, any notional principal contract unless the Secretary determines that such contract is of a type which does not have the potential for tax avoidance.

(4) Definitions.—For purposes of paragraph (3)(A)—

(A) Long party.—The term "long party" means, with respect to any underlying security of any notional principal contract, any party to the contract which is entitled to receive any payment pursuant to such contract which is contingent upon, or determined by reference to, the payment of a dividend from sources within the United States with respect to such underlying security.

(B) Short party.—The term "short party" means, with respect to any underlying security of any notional principal contract, any party to the contract which is not a long party with respect to such underlying security.

(C) Underlying security.—The term "underlying security" means, with respect to any notional principal contract, the security with respect to which the dividend referred to in paragraph (2)(B) is paid. For purposes of this paragraph, any index or fixed basket of securities shall be treated as a single security.

(5) Payments determined on gross basis.—For purposes of this subsection, the term "payment" includes any gross amount which is used in computing any net amount which is transferred to or from the taxpayer.

(6) Prevention of over-withholding.—In the case of any chain of dividend equivalents one or more of which is subject to tax under subsection (a) or section 881, the Secretary may reduce such tax, but only to the extent that the taxpayer can establish that such tax has been paid with respect to another dividend equivalent in such chain, or is not otherwise due, or as the Secretary determines is appropriate to address the role of financial intermediaries in such chain. For purposes of this paragraph, a dividend shall be treated as a dividend equivalent.

(7) Coordination with chapters 3 and 4.—For purposes of chapters 3 and 4, each person that is a party to any contract or other arrangement that provides for the payment of a dividend equivalent shall be treated as having control of such payment.

(n) Cross references.—

(1) For tax treatment of certain amounts distributed by the United States to nonresident alien individuals, see section 402(e)(2).

(2) For taxation of nonresident alien individuals who are expatriate United States citizens, see section 877.

(3) For doubling of tax on citizens of certain foreign countries, see section 891.

(4) For adjustment of tax in case of nationals or residents of certain foreign countries, see section 896.

(5) For withholding of tax at source on nonresident alien individuals, see section 1441.

(6) For election to treat married nonresident alien individual as resident of United States in certain cases, see subsections (g) and (h) of section 6013.

(7) For special tax treatment of gain or loss from the disposition by a nonresident alien individual of a United States real property interest, see section 897.

§ 872. Gross income

(a) General rule.—In the case of a nonresident alien individual, except where the context clearly indicates otherwise, gross income includes only—

(1) gross income which is derived from sources within the United States and which is not effectively connected with the conduct of a trade or business within the United States, and

(2) gross income which is effectively connected with the conduct of a trade or business within the United States.

(b) Exclusions.—The following items shall not be included in gross income of a nonresident alien individual, and shall be exempt from taxation under this subtitle:

(1) Ships operated by certain nonresidents.—Gross income derived by an individual resident of a foreign country from the international operation of a ship or ships if such foreign country grants an equivalent exemption to individual residents of the United States.

(2) Aircraft operated by certain nonresidents.—Gross income derived by an individual resident of a foreign country from the international operation of aircraft if such foreign country grants an equivalent exemption to individual residents of the United States.

(3) Compensation of participants in certain exchange or training programs.—Compensation paid by a foreign employer to a nonresident alien individual for the period he is temporarily present in the United States as a nonimmigrant under subparagraph (F), (J) or (Q) of section 101(a)(15) of the Immigration and Nationality Act, as amended. For purposes of this paragraph, the term "foreign employer" means—

(A) a nonresident alien individual, foreign partnership, or foreign corporation, or

(B) an office or place of business maintained in a foreign country or in a possession of the United States by a domestic corporation, a domestic partnership, or an individual who is a citizen or resident of the United States.

(4) Certain bond income of residents of the Ryukyu Islands or the Trust Territory of the Pacific Islands.—Income derived by a nonresident alien individual from a series E or series H United States savings bond, if such individual acquired such bond while a resident of the Ryukyu Islands or the Trust Territory of the Pacific Islands.

(5) Income derived from wagering transactions in certain parimutuel pools.—Gross income derived by a nonresident alien individual from a legal wagering transaction initiated outside the United States in a parimutuel pool with respect to a live horse race or dog race in the United States.

(6) Certain rental income.—Income to which paragraphs (1) and (2) apply shall include income which is derived from the rental on a full or bareboat basis of a ship or ships or aircraft, as the case may be.

(7) Application to different types of transportation.—The Secretary may provide that this subsection be applied separately with respect to income from different types of transportation.

(8) Treatment of possessions.—To the extent provided in regulations, a possession of the United States shall be treated as a foreign country for purposes of this subsection.

§ 873. Deductions

(a) General rule.—In the case of a nonresident alien individual, the deductions shall be allowed only for purposes of section 871(b) and (except as provided by subsection (b)) only if and to the extent that they are connected with income which is effectively connected with the conduct of a trade or business within the United States; and the proper apportionment and allocation of the deductions for this purpose shall be determined as provided in regulations prescribed by the Secretary.

(b) Exceptions.—The following deductions shall be allowed whether or not they are connected with income which is effectively connected with the conduct of a trade or business within the United States:

(1) Losses.—The deduction allowed by section 165 for casualty or theft losses described in paragraph (2) or (3) of section 165(c), but only if the loss is of property located within the United States.

(2) Charitable contributions.—The deduction for charitable contributions and gifts allowed by section 170.

(3) Personal exemption.—The deduction for personal exemptions allowed by section 151, except that only one exemption shall be allowed under section 151 unless the taxpayer is a resident of a contiguous country or is a national of the United States.

(c) Cross reference.—

For rule that certain foreign taxes are not to be taken into account in determining deduction or credit, see section 906(b)(1).

§ 874. Allowance of deductions and credits

(a) Return prerequisite to allowance.—A nonresident alien individual shall receive the benefit of the deductions and credits allowed to him in this subtitle only by filing or causing to be filed with the Secretary a true and accurate return, in the manner prescribed in subtitle F (sec. 6001 and following, relating to procedure and administration), including therein all the information which the Secretary may deem necessary for the calculation of such deductions and credits. This subsection shall not be construed to deny the credits provided by sections 31 and 33 for tax withheld at source or the credit provided by section 34 for certain uses of gasoline and special fuels.

(b) Tax withheld at source.—The benefit of the deduction for exemptions under section 151 may, in the discretion of the Secretary, and under regulations prescribed by the Secretary, be received by a nonresident alien individual entitled thereto, by filing a claim therefor with the withholding agent.

(c) Foreign tax credit.—Except as provided in section 906, a nonresident alien individual shall not be allowed the credits against the tax for taxes of foreign countries and possessions of the United States allowed by section 901.

§ 875. Partnerships; beneficiaries of estates and trusts

For purposes of this subtitle—

(1) a nonresident alien individual or foreign corporation shall be considered as being engaged in a trade or business within the United States if the partnership of which such individual or corporation is a member is so engaged, and

(2) a nonresident alien individual or foreign corporation which is a beneficiary of an estate or trust which is engaged in any trade or business within the United States shall be treated as being engaged in such trade or business within the United States.

§ 877. Expatriation to avoid tax

(a) Treatment of expatriates.—

(1) In general.—Every nonresident alien individual to whom this section applies and who, within the 10-year period immediately preceding the close of the taxable year, lost United States citizenship shall be taxable for such taxable year in the manner provided in subsection (b) if the tax imposed pursuant to such subsection (after any reduction in such tax under the last sentence of such subsection) exceeds the tax which, without regard to this section, is imposed pursuant to section 871.

(2) Individuals subject to this section.—This section shall apply to any individual if—

(A) the average annual net income tax (as defined in section 38(c)(1)) of such individual for the period of 5 taxable years ending before the date of the loss of United States citizenship is greater than $124,000,

(B) the net worth of the individual as of such date is $2,000,000 or more, or

(C) such individual fails to certify under penalty of perjury that he has met the requirements of this title for the 5 preceding taxable years or fails to submit such evidence of such compliance as the Secretary may require.

In the case of the loss of United States citizenship in any calendar year after 2004, such $124,000 amount shall be increased by an amount equal to such dollar amount multiplied by the cost-of-living adjustment determined under section 1(f)(3) for such calendar year by substituting "2003" for "1992" in subparagraph (B) thereof. Any increase under the preceding sentence shall be rounded to the nearest multiple of $1,000. [See the Appendix for the increased amount.]

(b) Alternative tax.—A nonresident alien individual described in subsection (a) shall be taxable for the taxable year as provided in section 1 or 55 except that—

(1) the gross income shall include only the gross income described in section 872(a) (as modified by subsection (d) of this section), and

(2) the deductions shall be allowed if and to the extent that they are connected with the gross income included under this section, except that the capital loss carryover provided by section 1212(b) shall not be allowed; and the proper allocation and apportionment of the deductions for this purpose shall be determined as provided under regulations prescribed by the Secretary.

For purposes of paragraph (2), the deductions allowed by section 873(b) shall be allowed; and the deduction (for losses not connected with the trade or business if incurred in transactions entered into for profit) allowed by section 165(c)(2) shall be allowed, but only if the profit, if such transaction had resulted in a profit, would be included in gross income under this section. The tax imposed solely by reason of this section shall be reduced (but not below zero) by the amount of any income, war profits, and excess profits taxes (within the meaning of section 903) paid to any foreign country or possession of the United States on any income of the taxpayer on which tax is imposed solely by reason of this section.

(c) Exceptions.—

(1) In general.—Subparagraphs (A) and (B) of subsection (a)(2) shall not apply to an individual described in paragraph (2) or (3).

(2) Dual citizens.—

(A) In general.—An individual is described in this paragraph if—

(i) the individual became at birth a citizen of the United States and a citizen of another country and continues to be a citizen of such other country, and

(ii) the individual has had no substantial contacts with the United States.

(B) Substantial contacts.—An individual shall be treated as having no substantial contacts with the United States only if the individual—

(i) was never a resident of the United States (as defined in section 7701(b)),

(ii) has never held a United States passport, and

(iii) was not present in the United States for more than 30 days during any calendar year which is 1 of the 10 calendar years preceding the individual's loss of United States citizenship.

(3) Certain minors.—An individual is described in this paragraph if—

(A) the individual became at birth a citizen of the United States,

(B) neither parent of such individual was a citizen of the United States at the time of such birth,

(C) the individual's loss of United States citizenship occurs before such individual attains age 18 1/2, and

(D) the individual was not present in the United States for more than 30 days during any calendar year which is 1 of the 10 calendar years preceding the individual's loss of United States citizenship.

(d) Special rules for source, etc.—For purposes of subsection (b)—

(1) Source rules.—The following items of gross income shall be treated as income from sources within the United States:

(A) Sale of property.—Gains on the sale or exchange of property (other than stock or debt obligations) located in the United States.

(B) Stock or debt obligations.—Gains on the sale or exchange of stock issued by a domestic corporation or debt obligations of United States persons or of the United States, a State or political subdivision thereof, or the District of Columbia.

(C) Income or gain derived from controlled foreign corporation.—Any income or gain derived from stock in a foreign corporation but only—

(i) if the individual losing United States citizenship owned (within the meaning of section 958(a)), or is considered as owning (by applying the ownership rules of section 958(b)), at any time during the 2-year period ending on the date of the loss of United States citizenship, more than 50 percent of—

(I) the total combined voting power of all classes of stock entitled to vote of such corporation, or

(II) the total value of the stock of such corporation, and

(ii) to the extent such income or gain does not exceed the earnings and profits attributable to such stock which were earned or accumulated before the loss of citizenship and during periods that the ownership requirements of clause (i) are met.

(2) Gain recognition on certain exchanges.—

(A) In general.—In the case of any exchange of property to which this paragraph applies, notwithstanding any other provision of this title, such property shall be treated as sold for its fair market value on the date of such exchange, and any gain shall be recognized for the taxable year which includes such date.

(B) Exchanges to which paragraph applies.—This paragraph shall apply to any exchange during the 10-year period beginning on the date the individual loses United States citizenship if—

(i) gain would not (but for this paragraph) be recognized on such exchange in whole or in part for purposes of this subtitle,

(ii) income derived from such property was from sources within the United States (or, if no income was so derived, would have been from such sources), and

(iii) income derived from the property acquired in the exchange would be from sources outside the United States.

(C) Exception.—Subparagraph (A) shall not apply if the individual enters into an agreement with the Secretary which specifies that any income or gain derived from the property acquired in the exchange (or any other property which has a basis determined in whole or part by reference to such property) during such 10-year period shall be treated as from sources within the United States. If the property transferred in the exchange is disposed of by the person acquiring such property, such agreement shall terminate and any gain which was not recognized by reason of such agreement shall be recognized as of the date of such disposition.

(D) Secretary may extend period.—To the extent provided in regulations prescribed by the Secretary, subparagraph (B) shall be applied by substituting the 15-year period beginning 5 years before the loss of United States citizenship for the 10-year period referred to therein. In the case of any exchange occurring during such 5 years, any gain recognized under this subparagraph shall be recognized immediately after such loss of citizenship.

(E) Secretary may require recognition of gain in certain cases.—To the extent provided in regulations prescribed by the Secretary—

(i) the removal of appreciated tangible personal property from the United States, and

(ii) any other occurrence which (without recognition of gain) results in a change in the source of the income or gain from property from sources within the United States to sources outside the United States,

shall be treated as an exchange to which this paragraph applies.

(3) Substantial diminishing of risks of ownership.—For purposes of determining whether this section applies to any gain on the sale or exchange of any property, the running of the 10-year period described in subsection (a) and the period applicable under paragraph (2) shall be suspended for any period during which the individual's risk of loss with respect to the property is substantially diminished by—

(A) the holding of a put with respect to such property (or similar property),

(B) the holding by another person of a right to acquire the property, or

(C) a short sale or any other transaction.

(4) Treatment of property contributed to controlled foreign corporations.—

(A) In general.—If—

(i) an individual losing United States citizenship contributes property during the 10-year period beginning on the date the individual loses United States citizenship to any corporation which, at the time of the contribution, is described in subparagraph (B), and

(ii) income derived from such property immediately before such contribution was from sources within the United States (or, if no income was so derived, would have been from such sources),

any income or gain on such property (or any other property which has a basis determined in whole or part by reference to such property) received or accrued by the corporation shall be treated as received or accrued directly by such individual and not by such corporation. The preceding sentence shall not apply to the extent the property has been treated under subparagraph (C) as having been sold by such corporation.

(B) Corporation described.—A corporation is described in this subparagraph with respect to an individual if, were such individual a United States citizen—

(i) such corporation would be a controlled foreign corporation (as defined in section 957), and

(ii) such individual would be a United States shareholder (as defined in section 951(b)) with respect to such corporation.

(C) Disposition of stock in corporation.—If stock in the corporation referred to in subparagraph (A) (or any other stock which has a basis determined in whole or part by reference to such stock) is disposed of during the 10-year period referred to in subsection (a) and while the property referred to in subparagraph (A) is held by such corporation, a pro rata share of such property (determined on the basis of the value of such stock) shall be treated as sold by the corporation immediately before such disposition.

(D) Anti-abuse rules.—The Secretary shall prescribe such regulations as may be necessary to prevent the avoidance of the purposes of this paragraph, including where—

(i) the property is sold to the corporation, and

(ii) the property taken into account under subparagraph (A) is sold by the corporation.

(E) Information reporting.—The Secretary shall require such information reporting as is necessary to carry out the purposes of this paragraph.

(e) Comparable treatment of lawful permanent residents who cease to be taxed as residents.—

(1) In general.—Any long term resident of the United States who ceases to be a lawful permanent resident of the United States (within the meaning of section 7701(b)(6)) shall be treated for purposes of this section and sections 2107, 2501, and 6039G in the same manner as if such resident were a citizen of the United States who lost United States citizenship on the date of such cessation or commencement.

(2) Long-term resident.—For purposes of this subsection, the term "long-term resident" means any individual (other than a citizen of the United States) who is a lawful permanent resident of the United States in at least 8 taxable years during the period of 15 taxable years ending with the taxable year during which the event described in paragraph (1) occurs. For purposes of the preceding sentence, an individual shall not be treated as a lawful permanent resident for any taxable year if such individual is treated as a resident of a foreign country for the taxable year under the provisions of a tax treaty between the United States and the foreign country and does not waive the benefits of such treaty applicable to residents of the foreign country.

(3) Special rules.—

(A) Exceptions not to apply.—Subsection (c) shall not apply to an individual who is treated as provided in paragraph (1).

(B) Step-up in basis.—Solely for purposes of determining any tax imposed by reason of this subsection, property which was held by the long-term resident on the date the individual first became a resident of the United States shall be treated as having a basis on such date of not less than the fair market value of such property on such date. The preceding sentence shall not apply if the individual elects not to have such sentence apply. Such an election, once made, shall be irrevocable.

(4) Authority to exempt individuals.—This subsection shall not apply to an individual who is described in a category of individuals prescribed by regulation by the Secretary.

(5) Regulations.—The Secretary shall prescribe such regulations as may be appropriate to carry out this subsection, including regulations providing for the application of this subsection in cases where an alien individual becomes a resident of the United States during the 10-year period after being treated as provided in paragraph (1).

(f) Burden of proof.—If the Secretary establishes that it is reasonable to believe that an individual's loss of United States citizenship would, but for this section, result in a substantial reduction for the taxable year in the taxes on his probable income for such year, the burden of proving for such taxable year that such loss of citizenship did not have for one of its principal purposes the avoidance of taxes under this subtitle or subtitle B shall be on such individual.

(g) Physical presence.—

(1) In general.—This section shall not apply to any individual to whom this section would otherwise apply for any taxable year during the 10-year period referred to in subsection (a) in which such individual is physically present in the United States at any time on more than 30 days in the calendar year ending in such taxable year, and such individual shall be treated for purposes of this title as a citizen or resident of the United States, as the case may be, for such taxable year.

(2) Exception.—

(A) In general.—In the case of an individual described in any of the following subparagraphs of this paragraph, a day of physical presence in the United States shall be disregarded if the individual is performing services in the United States on such day for an employer. The preceding sentence shall not apply if—

(i) such employer is related (within the meaning of section 267 and 707) to such individual, or

(ii) such employer fails to meet such requirements as the Secretary may prescribe by regulations to prevent the avoidance of the purposes of this paragraph.

Not more than 30 days during any calendar year may be disregarded under this subparagraph.

(B) Individuals with ties to other countries.—An individual is described in this subparagraph if—

(i) the individual becomes (not later than the close of a reasonable period after loss of United States citizenship or termination of residency) a citizen or resident of the country in which—

(I) such individual was born,

(II) if such individual is married, such individual's spouse was born, or

(III) either of such individual's parents were born, and

(ii) the individual becomes fully liable for income tax in such country.

(C) Minimal prior physical presence in the United States.—An individual is described in this subparagraph if, for each year in the 10-year period ending on the date of loss of United

States citizenship or termination of residency, the individual was physically present in the United States for 30 days or less. The rule of section 7701(b)(3)(D) shall apply for purposes of this subparagraph.

(h) Termination.—This section shall not apply to any individual whose expatriation date (as defined in section 877A(g)(3)) is on or after the date of the enactment of this subsection [June 17, 2008. Ed.].

§ 877A. Tax responsibilities of expatriation

(a) General rules.—For purposes of this subtitle—

(1) Mark to market.—All property of a covered expatriate shall be treated as sold on the day before the expatriation date for its fair market value.

(2) Recognition of gain or loss.—In the case of any sale under paragraph (1)—

(A) notwithstanding any other provision of this title, any gain arising from such sale shall be taken into account for the taxable year of the sale, and

(B) any loss arising from such sale shall be taken into account for the taxable year of the sale to the extent otherwise provided by this title, except that section 1091 shall not apply to any such loss.

Proper adjustment shall be made in the amount of any gain or loss subsequently realized for gain or loss taken into account under the preceding sentence, determined without regard to paragraph (3).

(3) Exclusion for certain gain.—

(A) In general.—The amount which would (but for this paragraph) be includible in the gross income of any individual by reason of paragraph (1) shall be reduced (but not below zero) by $600,000.

(B) Adjustment for inflation.—

(i) In general.—In the case of any taxable year beginning in a calendar year after 2008, the dollar amount in subparagraph (A) shall be increased by an amount equal to—

(I) such dollar amount, multiplied by

(II) the cost of living adjustment determined under section 1(f)(3) for the calendar year in which the taxable year begins, by substituting "calendar year 2007" for "calendar year 2016" in subparagraph (A)(ii) thereof.

(ii) Rounding.—If any amount as adjusted under clause (i) is not a multiple of $1,000, such amount shall be rounded to the nearest multiple of $1,000.

(b) Election to defer tax.—

(1) In general.—If the taxpayer elects the application of this subsection with respect to any property treated as sold by reason of subsection (a), the time for payment of the additional tax attributable to such property shall be extended until the due date of the return for the taxable year in which such property is disposed of (or, in the case of property disposed of in a transaction in which gain is not recognized in whole or in part, until such other date as the Secretary may prescribe).

(2) Determination of tax with respect to property.—For purposes of paragraph (1), the additional tax attributable to any property is an amount which bears the same ratio to the additional tax imposed by this chapter for the taxable year solely by reason of subsection (a) as the gain taken into account under subsection (a) with respect to such property bears to the total gain taken into account under subsection (a) with respect to all property to which subsection (a) applies.

(3) Termination of extension.—The due date for payment of tax may not be extended under this subsection later than the due date for the return of tax imposed by this chapter for the taxable year which includes the date of death of the expatriate (or, if earlier, the time that the security provided with respect to the property fails to meet the requirements of paragraph (4), unless the taxpayer corrects such failure within the time specified by the Secretary).

(4) Security.—

(A) In general.—No election may be made under paragraph (1) with respect to any property unless adequate security is provided with respect to such property.

(B) Adequate security.—For purposes of subparagraph (A), security with respect to any property shall be treated as adequate security if—

(i) it is a bond which is furnished to, and accepted by, the Secretary, which is conditioned on the payment of tax (and interest thereon), and which meets the requirements of section 6325, or

(ii) it is another form of security for such payment (including letters of credit) that meets such requirements as the Secretary may prescribe.

(5) Waiver of certain rights.—No election may be made under paragraph (1) unless the taxpayer makes an irrevocable waiver of any right under any treaty of the United States which would preclude assessment or collection of any tax imposed by reason of this section.

(6) Elections.—An election under paragraph (1) shall only apply to property described in the election and, once made, is irrevocable.

(7) Interest.—For purposes of section 6601, the last date for the payment of tax shall be determined without regard to the election under this subsection.

(c) Exception for certain property.—Subsection (a) shall not apply to—

(1) any deferred compensation item (as defined in subsection (d)(4)),

(2) any specified tax deferred account (as defined in subsection (e)(2)), and

(3) any interest in a nongrantor trust (as defined in subsection (f)(3)).

(d) Treatment of deferred compensation items.—

(1) Withholding on eligible deferred compensation items.—

(A) In general.—In the case of any eligible deferred compensation item, the payor shall deduct and withhold from any taxable payment to a covered expatriate with respect to such item a tax equal to 30 percent thereof.

(B) Taxable payment.—For purposes of subparagraph (A), the term "taxable payment" means with respect to a covered expatriate any payment to the extent it would be includible in the gross income of the covered expatriate if such expatriate continued to be subject to tax as a citizen or resident of the United States. A deferred compensation item shall be taken into account as a payment under the preceding sentence when such item would be so includible.

(2) Other deferred compensation items.—In the case of any deferred compensation item which is not an eligible deferred compensation item—

(A) (i) with respect to any deferred compensation item to which clause (ii) does not apply, an amount equal to the present value of the covered expatriate's accrued benefit shall be treated as having been received by such individual on the day before the expatriation date as a distribution under the plan, and

(ii) with respect to any deferred compensation item referred to in paragraph (4) (D), the rights of the covered expatriate to such item shall be treated as becoming transferable and not subject to a substantial risk of forfeiture on the day before the expatriation date,

(B) no early distribution tax shall apply by reason of such treatment, and

(C) appropriate adjustments shall be made to subsequent distributions from the plan to reflect such treatment.

(3) Eligible deferred compensation items.—For purposes of this subsection, the term "eligible deferred compensation item" means any deferred compensation item with respect to which—

(A) the payor of such item is—

(i) a United States person, or

(ii) a person who is not a United States person but who elects to be treated as a United States person for purposes of paragraph (1) and meets such requirements as the Secretary may provide to ensure that the payor will meet the requirements of paragraph (1), and

(B) the covered expatriate—

(i) notifies the payor of his status as a covered expatriate, and

(ii) makes an irrevocable waiver of any right to claim any reduction under any treaty with the United States in withholding on such item.

(4) Deferred compensation item.—For purposes of this subsection, the term "deferred compensation item" means—

(A) any interest in a plan or arrangement described in section 219(g)(5),

(B) any interest in a foreign pension plan or similar retirement arrangement or program,

(C) any item of deferred compensation, and

(D) any property, or right to property, which the individual is entitled to receive in connection with the performance of services to the extent not previously taken into account under section 83 or in accordance with section 83.

(5) Exception.—Paragraphs (1) and (2) shall not apply to any deferred compensation item to the extent attributable to services performed outside the United States while the covered expatriate was not a citizen or resident of the United States.

(6) Special rules.—

(A) Application of withholding rules.—Rules similar to the rules of subchapter B of chapter 3 shall apply for purposes of this subsection.

(B) Application of tax.—Any item subject to the withholding tax imposed under paragraph (1) shall be subject to tax under section 871.

(C) Coordination with other withholding requirements.—Any item subject to withholding under paragraph (1) shall not be subject to withholding under section 1441 or chapter 24.

(e) Treatment of specified tax deferred accounts.—

(1) Account treated as distributed.—In the case of any interest in a specified tax deferred account held by a covered expatriate on the day before the expatriation date—

(A) the covered expatriate shall be treated as receiving a distribution of his entire interest in such account on the day before the expatriation date,

(B) no early distribution tax shall apply by reason of such treatment, and

(C) appropriate adjustments shall be made to subsequent distributions from the account to reflect such treatment.

(2) Specified tax deferred account.—For purposes of paragraph (1), the term "specified tax deferred account" means an individual retirement plan (as defined in section 7701(a)(37)) other than any arrangement described in subsection (k) or (p) of section 408, a qualified tuition program (as defined in section 529), a qualified ABLE program (as defined in section 529A), a Coverdell education savings account (as defined in section 530), a health savings account (as defined in section 223), and an Archer MSA (as defined in section 220).

(f) Special rules for nongrantor trusts.—

(1) In general.—In the case of a distribution (directly or indirectly) of any property from a nongrantor trust to a covered expatriate—

(A) the trustee shall deduct and withhold from such distribution an amount equal to 30 percent of the taxable portion of the distribution, and

(B) if the fair market value of such property exceeds its adjusted basis in the hands of the trust, gain shall be recognized to the trust as if such property were sold to the expatriate at its fair market value.

(2) Taxable portion.—For purposes of this subsection, the term "taxable portion" means, with respect to any distribution, that portion of the distribution which would be includible in the gross income of the covered expatriate if such expatriate continued to be subject to tax as a citizen or resident of the United States.

(3) Nongrantor trust.—For purposes of this subsection, the term "nongrantor trust" means the portion of any trust that the individual is not considered the owner of under subpart E of part I of subchapter J. The determination under the preceding sentence shall be made immediately before the expatriation date.

(4) Special rules relating to withholding.—For purposes of this subsection—

(A) rules similar to the rules of subsection (d)(6) shall apply, and

(B) the covered expatriate shall be treated as having waived any right to claim any reduction under any treaty with the United States in withholding on any distribution to which paragraph (1)(A) applies unless the covered expatriate agrees to such other treatment as the Secretary determines appropriate.

(5) Application.—This subsection shall apply to a nongrantor trust only if the covered expatriate was a beneficiary of the trust on the day before the expatriation date.

(g) Definitions and special rules relating to expatriation.—For purposes of this section—

(1) Covered expatriate.—

(A) In general.—The term "covered expatriate" means an expatriate who meets the requirements of subparagraph (A), (B), or (C) of section 877(a)(2).

(B) Exceptions.—An individual shall not be treated as meeting the requirements of subparagraph (A) or (B) of section 877(a)(2) if

(i) the individual—

(I) became at birth a citizen of the United States and a citizen of another country and, as of the expatriation date, continues to be a citizen of, and is taxed as a resident of, such other country, and

(II) has been a resident of the United States (as defined in section 7701(b)(1)(A)(ii)) for not more than 10 taxable years during the 15 taxable year period ending with the taxable year during which the expatriation date occurs, or

(ii)(I) the individual's relinquishment of United States citizenship occurs before such individual attains age 18 1/2, and

(II) the individual has been a resident of the United States (as so defined) for not more than 10 taxable years before the date of relinquishment.

(C) Covered expatriates also subject to tax as citizens or residents.—In the case of any covered expatriate who is subject to tax as a citizen or resident of the United States for any period beginning after the expatriation date, such individual shall not be treated as a covered expatriate during such period for purposes of subsections (d)(1) and (f) and section 2801.

(2) Expatriate.—The term "expatriate" means—

(A) any United States citizen who relinquishes his citizenship, and

(B) any long term resident of the United States who ceases to be a lawful permanent resident of the United States (within the meaning of section 7701(b)(6)).

(3) Expatriation date.—The term "expatriation date" means—

(A) the date an individual relinquishes United States citizenship, or

(B) in the case of a long term resident of the United States, the date on which the individual ceases to be a lawful permanent resident of the United States (within the meaning of section 7701(b)(6)).

(4) Relinquishment of citizenship.—A citizen shall be treated as relinquishing his United States citizenship on the earliest of—

(A) the date the individual renounces his United States nationality before a diplomatic or consular officer of the United States pursuant to paragraph (5) of section 349(a) of the Immigration and Nationality Act (8 U.S.C. 1481(a)(5)),

(B) the date the individual furnishes to the United States Department of State a signed statement of voluntary relinquishment of United States nationality confirming the performance of an act of expatriation specified in paragraph (1), (2), (3), or (4) of section 349(a) of the Immigration and Nationality Act (8 U.S.C. 1481(a)(1)–(4)),

(C) the date the United States Department of State issues to the individual a certificate of loss of nationality, or

(D) the date a court of the United States cancels a naturalized citizen's certificate of naturalization.

Subparagraph (A) or (B) shall not apply to any individual unless the renunciation or voluntary relinquishment is subsequently approved by the issuance to the individual of a certificate of loss of nationality by the United States Department of State.

(5) Long-term resident.—The term "long-term resident" has the meaning given to such term by section 877(e)(2).

(6) Early distribution tax.—The term "early distribution tax" means any increase in tax imposed under section 72(t), 220(f)(4), 223(f)(4), 409A(a)(1)(B), 529(c)(6), 529A(c)(3), or 530(d)(4).

(h) Other rules.—

(1) Termination of deferrals, etc.—In the case of any covered expatriate, notwithstanding any other provision of this title

(A) any time period for acquiring property which would result in the reduction in the amount of gain recognized with respect to property disposed of by the taxpayer shall terminate on the day before the expatriation date, and

(B) any extension of time for payment of tax shall cease to apply on the day before the expatriation date and the unpaid portion of such tax shall be due and payable at the time and in the manner prescribed by the Secretary.

(2) Step-up in basis.—Solely for purposes of determining any tax imposed by reason of subsection (a), property which was held by an individual on the date the individual first became a resident of the

United States (within the meaning of section 7701(b)) shall be treated as having a basis on such date of not less than the fair market value of such property on such date. The preceding sentence shall not apply if the individual elects not to have such sentence apply. Such an election, once made, shall be irrevocable.

(3) Coordination with section 684.—If the expatriation of any individual would result in the recognition of gain under section 684, this section shall be applied after the application of section 684.

(i) Regulations.—The Secretary shall prescribe such regulations as may be necessary or appropriate to carry out the purposes of this section.

§ 879. Tax treatment of certain community income in the case of nonresident alien individuals

(a) General rule.—In the case of a married couple 1 or both of whom are nonresident alien individuals and who have community income for the taxable year, such community income shall be treated as follows:

(1) Earned income (within the meaning of section 911(d)(2)), other than trade or business income and a partner's distributive share of partnership income, shall be treated as the income of the spouse who rendered the personal services,

(2) Trade or business income, and a partner's distributive share of partnership income, shall be treated as provided in section 1402(a)(5),

(3) Community income not described in paragraph (1) or (2) which is derived from the separate property (as determined under the applicable community property law) of one spouse shall be treated as the income of such spouse, and

(4) All other such community income shall be treated as provided in the applicable community property law.

(b) Exception where election under section 6013(g) is in effect.—Subsection (a) shall not apply for any taxable year for which an election under subsection (g) or (h) of section 6013 (relating to election to treat nonresident alien individual as resident of the United States) is in effect.

(c) Definitions and special rules.—For purposes of this section—

(1) Community income.—The term "community income" means income which, under applicable community property laws, is treated as community income.

(2) Community property laws.—The term "community property laws" means the community property laws of a State, a foreign country, or a possession of the United States.

(3) Determination of marital status.—The determination of marital status shall be made under section 7703(a).

Subpart B—Foreign Corporations

§ 881. Tax on income of foreign corporations not connected with United States business

(a) Imposition of tax.—Except as provided in subsection (c), there is hereby imposed for each taxable year a tax of 30 percent of the amount received from sources within the United States by a foreign corporation as—

(1) interest (other than original issue discount as defined in section 1273), dividends, rents, salaries, wages, premiums, annuities, compensations, remunerations, emoluments, and other fixed or determinable annual or periodical gains, profits, and income,

(2) gains described in section 631(b) or (c),

(3) in the case of—

(A) a sale or exchange of an original issue discount obligation, the amount of the original issue discount accruing while such obligation was held by the foreign corporation (to the extent such discount was not theretofore taken into account under subparagraph (B)), and

(B) a payment on an original issue discount obligation, an amount equal to the original issue discount accruing while such obligation was held by the foreign corporation (except that such original issue discount shall be taken into account under this subparagraph only to the extent such discount was not theretofore taken into account under this subparagraph and only to the extent that the tax thereon does not exceed the payment less the tax imposed by paragraph (1) thereon), and

(4) gains from the sale or exchange after October 4, 1966, of patents, copyrights, secret processes and formulas, good will, trademarks, trade brands, franchises, and other like property, or of any interest in any such property, to the extent such gains are from payments which are contingent on the productivity, use, or disposition of the property or interest sold or exchanged,

but only to the extent the amount so received is not effectively connected with the conduct of a trade or business within the United States.

(b) Exception for certain possessions.—

(1) Guam, American Samoa, the Northern Mariana Islands, and the Virgin Islands.—For purposes of this section and section 884, a corporation created or organized in Guam, American Samoa, the Northern Mariana Islands, or the Virgin Islands or under the law of any such possession shall not be treated as a foreign corporation for any taxable year if—

(A) at all times during such taxable year less than 25 percent in value of the stock of such corporation is beneficially owned (directly or indirectly) by foreign persons,

(B) at least 65 percent of the gross income of such corporation is shown to the satisfaction of the Secretary to be effectively connected with the conduct of a trade or business in such a possession or the United States for the 3-year period ending with the close of the taxable year of such corporation (or for such part of such period as the corporation or any predecessor has been in existence), and

(C) no substantial part of the income of such corporation is used (directly or indirectly) to satisfy obligations to persons who are not bona fide residents of such a possession or the United States.

(2) Commonwealth of Puerto Rico.—

(A) In general.—If dividends are received during a taxable year by a corporation—

(i) created or organized in, or under the law of, the Commonwealth of Puerto Rico, and

(ii) with respect to which the requirements of subparagraphs (A), (B), and (C) of paragraph (1) are met for the taxable year,

subsection (a) shall be applied for such taxable year by substituting "10 percent" for "30 percent".

(B) Applicability.—If, on or after the date of the enactment of this paragraph, an increase in the rate of the Commonwealth of Puerto Rico's withholding tax which is generally applicable to dividends paid to United States corporations not engaged in a trade or business in the Commonwealth to a rate greater than 10 percent takes effect, this paragraph shall not apply to dividends received on or after the effective date of the increase.

(3) Definitions.—

(A) Foreign person.—For purposes of paragraph (1), the term "foreign person" means any person other than—

(i) a United States person, or

(ii) a person who would be a United States person if references to the United States in section 7701 included references to a possession of the United States.

(B) Indirect ownership rules.—For purposes of paragraph (1), the rules of section 318(a)(2) shall apply except that "5 percent" shall be substituted for "50 percent" in subparagraph (C) thereof.

(c) Repeal of tax on interest of foreign corporations received from certain portfolio debt investments.—

(1) In general.—In the case of any portfolio interest received by a foreign corporation from sources within the United States, no tax shall be imposed under paragraph (1) or (3) of subsection (a).

(2) Portfolio interest.—For purposes of this subsection, the term "portfolio interest" means any interest (including original issue discount) which—

(A) would be subject to tax under subsection (a) but for this subsection, and

(B) is paid on an obligation—

(i) which is in registered form, and

(ii) with respect to which—

(I) the person who would otherwise be required to deduct and withhold tax from such interest under section 1442(a) receives a statement which meets the requirements of section 871(h)(5) that the beneficial owner of the obligation is not a United States person, or

(II) the Secretary has determined that such a statement is not required in order to carry out the purposes of this subsection.

(3) Portfolio interest shall not include interest received by certain persons.—For purposes of this subsection, the term "portfolio interest" shall not include any portfolio interest which—

(A) except in the case of interest paid on an obligation of the United States, is received by a bank on an extension of credit made pursuant to a loan agreement entered into in the ordinary course of its trade or business,

(B) is received by a 10-percent shareholder (within the meaning of section 871(h)(3)(B)), or

(C) is received by a controlled foreign corporation from a related person (within the meaning of section 864(d)(4)).

(4) Portfolio interest not to include certain contingent interest.—For purposes of this subsection, the term "portfolio interest" shall not include any interest which is treated as not being portfolio interest under the rules of section 871(h)(4).

(5) Special rules for controlled foreign corporations.—

(A) In general.—In the case of any portfolio interest received by a controlled foreign corporation, the following provisions shall not apply:

(i) Subparagraph (A) of section 954(b)(3) (relating to exception where foreign base company income is less than 5 percent or $1,000,000).

(ii) Paragraph (4) of section 954(b) (relating to exception for certain income subject to high foreign taxes).

(iii) Clause (i) of section 954(c)(3)(A) (relating to certain income received from related persons).

(B) Controlled foreign corporation.—For purposes of this subsection, the term "controlled foreign corporation" has the meaning given to such term by section 957(a).

(6) Secretary may cease application of this subsection.—Under rules similar to the rules of section 871(h)(6), the Secretary may provide that this subsection shall not apply to payments of interest described in section 871(h)(6).

(7) Registered form.—For purposes of this subsection, the term "registered form" has the meaning given such term by section 163(f).

(d) Tax not to apply to certain interest and dividends.—No tax shall be imposed under paragraph (1) or (3) of subsection (a) on any amount described in section 871(i)(2).

(e) Tax not to apply to certain dividends of regulated investment companies.—

(1) Interest-related dividends.—

(A) In general.—Except as provided in subparagraph (B), no tax shall be imposed under paragraph (1) of subsection (a) on any interest-related dividend (as defined in section 871(k)(1)) received from a regulated investment company.

(B) Exception.—Subparagraph (A) shall not apply—

(i) to any dividend referred to in section 871(k)(1)(B), and

(ii) to any interest-related dividend received by a controlled foreign corporation (within the meaning of section 957(a)) to the extent such dividend is attributable to interest received by the regulated investment company from a person who is a related person (within the meaning of section 864(d)(4)) with respect to such controlled foreign corporation.

(C) Treatment of dividends received by controlled foreign corporations.—The rules of subsection (c)(5)(A) shall apply to any interest-related dividend received by a controlled foreign corporation (within the meaning of section 957(a)) to the extent such dividend is attributable to interest received by the regulated investment company which is described in clause (ii) of section 871(k)(1)(E) (and not described in clause (i) or (iii) of such section).

(2) Short-term capital gain dividends.—No tax shall be imposed under paragraph (1) of subsection (a) on any short-term capital gain dividend (as defined in section 871(k)(2)) received from a regulated investment company.

(f) Cross reference.—

For doubling of tax on corporations of certain foreign countries, see section 891. For special rules for original issue discount, see section 871(g).

§ 882. Tax on income of foreign corporations connected with United States business

(a) Imposition of tax.—

(1) In general.—A foreign corporation engaged in trade or business within the United States during the taxable year shall be taxable as provided in section 11, 55, or 59A on its taxable income which is effectively connected with the conduct of a trade or business within the United States.

(2) Determination of taxable income.—In determining taxable income for purposes of paragraph (1), gross income includes only gross income which is effectively connected with the conduct of a trade or business within the United States.

(3) For special tax treatment of gain or loss from the disposition by a foreign corporation of a United States real property interest, see section 897.

(b) Gross income.—In the case of a foreign corporation, except where the context clearly indicates otherwise, gross income includes only—

(1) gross income which is derived from sources within the United States and which is not effectively connected with the conduct of a trade or business within the United States, and

(2) gross income which is effectively connected with the conduct of a trade or business within the United States.

(c) Allowance of deductions and credits.—

(1) Allocation of deductions.—

(A) General rule.—In the case of a foreign corporation, the deductions shall be allowed only for purposes of subsection (a) and (except as provided by subparagraph (B)) only if and to the extent that they are connected with income which is effectively connected with the conduct of a trade or business within the United States; and the proper apportionment and allocation of the deductions for this purpose shall be determined as provided in regulations prescribed by the Secretary.

(B) Charitable contributions.—The deduction for charitable contributions and gifts provided by section 170 shall be allowed whether or not connected with income which is effectively connected with the conduct of a trade or business within the United States.

(2) Deductions and credits allowed only if return filed.—A foreign corporation shall receive the benefit of the deductions and credits allowed to it in this subtitle only by filing or causing to be filed with the Secretary a true and accurate return, in the manner prescribed in subtitle F, including therein all the information which the Secretary may deem necessary for the calculation of such deductions and credits. The preceding sentence shall not apply for purposes of the tax imposed by section 541 (relating to personal holding company tax), and shall not be construed to deny the credit provided by section 33 for tax withheld at source or the credit provided by section 34 for certain uses of gasoline.

(3) Foreign tax credit.—Except as provided by section 906, foreign corporations shall not be allowed the credit against the tax for taxes of foreign countries and possessions of the United States allowed by section 901.

(4) Cross reference.—

For rule that certain foreign taxes are not to be taken into account in determining deduction or credit, see section 906(b)(1).

(d) Election to treat real property income as income connected with United States business.—

(1) In general.—A foreign corporation which during the taxable year derives any income—

(A) from real property located in the United States, or from any interest in such real property, including (i) gains from the sale or exchange of real property or an interest therein, (ii) rents or royalties from mines, wells, or other natural deposits, and (iii) gains described in section 631(b) or (c), and

(B) which, but for this subsection, would not be treated as income effectively connected with the conduct of a trade or business within the United States,

may elect for such taxable year to treat all such income as income which is effectively connected with the conduct of a trade or business within the United States. In such case, such income shall be taxable as provided in subsection (a)(1) whether or not such corporation is engaged in trade or business within the United States during the taxable year. An election under this paragraph for any taxable year shall remain in effect for all subsequent taxable years, except that it may be revoked with the consent of the Secretary with respect to any taxable year.

(2) Election after revocation, etc.—Paragraphs (2) and (3) of section 871(d) shall apply in respect of elections under this subsection in the same manner and to the same extent as they apply in respect of elections under section 871(d).

(e) Interest on United States obligations received by banks organized in possessions.—In the case of a corporation created or organized in, or under the law of, a possession of the United States which is carrying on the banking business in a possession of the United States, interest on obligations of the United States which is not portfolio interest (as defined in section 881(c)(2)) shall—

(1) for purposes of this subpart, be treated as income which is effectively connected with the conduct of a trade or business within the United States, and

(2) shall be taxable as provided in subsection (a)(1) whether or not such corporation is engaged in trade or business within the United States during the taxable year.

(f) Returns of tax by agent.—If any foreign corporation has no office or place of business in the United States but has an agent in the United States, the return required under section 6012 shall be made by the agent.

§ 883. Exclusions from gross income

(a) Income of foreign corporations from ships and aircraft.—The following items shall not be included in gross income of a foreign corporation, and shall be exempt from taxation under this subtitle:

(1) Ships operated by certain foreign corporations.—Gross income derived by a corporation organized in a foreign country from the international operation of a ship or ships if such foreign country grants an equivalent exemption to corporations organized in the United States.

(2) Aircraft operated by certain foreign corporations.—Gross income derived by a corporation organized in a foreign country from the international operation of aircraft if such foreign country grants an equivalent exemption to corporations organized in the United States.

(3) Railroad rolling stock of foreign corporations.—Earnings derived from payments by a common carrier for the use on a temporary basis (not expected to exceed a total of 90 days in any taxable year) of railroad rolling stock owned by a corporation of a foreign country which grants an equivalent exemption to corporations organized in the United States.

(4) Special rules.—The rules of paragraphs (6), (7), and (8) of section 872(b) shall apply for purposes of this subsection.

(5) Special rule for countries which tax on residence basis.—For purposes of this subsection, there shall not be taken into account any failure of a foreign country to grant an exemption to a corporation organized in the United States if such corporation is subject to tax by such foreign country on a residence basis pursuant to provisions of foreign law which meets such standards (if any) as the Secretary may prescribe.

(b) Earnings derived from communications satellite system.—The earnings derived from the ownership or operation of a communications satellite system by a foreign entity designated by a foreign government to participate in such ownership or operation shall be exempt from taxation under this subtitle, if the United States, through its designated entity, participates in such system pursuant to the Communications Satellite Act of 1962 (47 U.S.C. 701 and following).

(c) Treatment of certain foreign corporations.—

(1) In general.—Paragraph (1) or (2) of subsection (a) (as the case may be) shall not apply to any foreign corporation if 50 percent or more of the value of the stock of such corporation is owned by individuals who are not residents of such foreign country or another foreign country meeting the requirements of such paragraph.

(2) Treatment of controlled foreign corporations.—Paragraph (1) shall not apply to any foreign corporation which is a controlled foreign corporation (as defined in section 957(a)).

(3) Special rules for publicly traded corporations.—

(A) Exception.—Paragraph (1) shall not apply to any corporation which is organized in a foreign country meeting the requirements of paragraph (1) or (2) of subsection (a) (as the case may be) and the stock of which is primarily and regularly traded on an established securities market in such foreign country, another foreign country meeting the requirements of such paragraph, or the United States.

(B) Treatment of stock owned by publicly traded corporation.—Any stock in another corporation which is owned (directly or indirectly) by a corporation meeting the requirements of subparagraph (A) shall be treated as owned by individuals who are residents of the foreign country in which the corporation meeting the requirements of subparagraph (A) is organized.

(4) Stock ownership through entities.—For purposes of paragraph (1), stock owned (directly or indirectly) by or for a corporation, partnership, trust, or estate shall be treated as being owned proportionately by its shareholders, partners, or beneficiaries. Stock considered to be owned by a person by reason of the application of the preceding sentence shall, for purposes of applying such sentence, be treated as actually owned by such person.

§ 884. Branch profits tax

(a) Imposition of tax.—In addition to the tax imposed by section 882 for any taxable year, there is hereby imposed on any foreign corporation a tax equal to 30 percent of the dividend equivalent amount for the taxable year.

(b) Dividend equivalent amount.—For purposes of subsection (a), the term "dividend equivalent amount" means the foreign corporation's effectively connected earnings and profits for the taxable year adjusted as provided in this subsection:

(1) Reduction for increase in U.S. net equity.—If—

(A) the U.S. net equity of the foreign corporation as of the close of the taxable year, exceeds

(B) the U.S. net equity of the foreign corporation as of the close of the preceding taxable year,

the effectively connected earnings and profits for the taxable year shall be reduced (but not below zero) by the amount of such excess.

(2) Increase for decrease in net equity.—

(A) In general.—If—

(i) the U.S. net equity of the foreign corporation as of the close of the preceding taxable year, exceeds

(ii) the U.S. net equity of the foreign corporation as of the close of the taxable year, the effectively connected earnings and profits for the taxable year shall be increased by the amount of such excess.

(B) Limitation.—

(i) In general.—The increase under subparagraph (A) for any taxable year shall not exceed the accumulated effectively connected earnings and profits as of the close of the preceding taxable year.

(ii) Accumulated effectively connected earnings and profits.—For purposes of clause (i), the term "accumulated effectively connected earnings and profits" means the excess of—

(I) the aggregate effectively connected earnings and profits for preceding taxable years beginning after December 31, 1986, over

(II) the aggregate dividend equivalent amounts determined for such preceding taxable years.

(c) U.S. net equity.—For purposes of this section—

(1) In general.—The term "U.S. net equity" means—

(A) U.S. assets, reduced (including below zero) by

(B) U.S. liabilities.

(2) U.S. assets and U.S. liabilities.—For purposes of paragraph (1)—

(A) U.S. assets.—The term "U.S. assets" means the money and aggregate adjusted bases of property of the foreign corporation treated as connected with the conduct of a trade or business in the United States under regulations prescribed by the Secretary. For purposes of the preceding sentence, the adjusted basis of any property shall be its adjusted basis for purposes of computing earnings and profits.

(B) U.S. liabilities.—The term "U.S. liabilities" means the liabilities of the foreign corporation treated as connected with the conduct of a trade or business in the United States under regulations prescribed by the Secretary.

(C) Regulations to be consistent with allocation of deductions.—The regulations prescribed under subparagraphs (A) and (B) shall be consistent with the allocation of deductions under section 882(c)(1).

(d) Effectively connected earnings and profits.—For purposes of this section—

(1) In general.—The term "effectively connected earnings and profits" means earnings and profits (without diminution by reason of any distributions made during the taxable year) which are attributable to income which is effectively connected (or treated as effectively connected) with the conduct of a trade or business within the United States.

(2) Exception for certain income.—The term "effectively connected earnings and profits" shall not include any earnings and profits attributable to—

(A) income not includible in gross income under paragraph (1) or (2) of section 883(a),

(B) income treated as effectively connected with the conduct of a trade or business within the United States under section 921(d) or 926(b) (as in effect before repeal * * *),

(C) gain on the disposition of a United States real property interest described in section 897(c)(1)(A)(ii),

(D) income treated as effectively connected with the conduct of a trade or business within the United States under section 953(c)(3)(C), or

(E) income treated as effectively connected with the conduct of a trade or business within the United States under section 882(e).

Property and liabilities of the foreign corporation treated as connected with such income under regulations prescribed by the Secretary shall not be taken into account in determining the U.S. assets or U.S. liabilities of the foreign corporation.

(e) Coordination with income tax treaties; etc.—

(1) Limitation on treaty exemption.—No treaty between the United States and a foreign country shall exempt any foreign corporation from the tax imposed by subsection (a) (or reduce the amount thereof) unless—

(A) such treaty is an income tax treaty, and

(B) such foreign corporation is a qualified resident of such foreign country.

(2) Treaty modifications.—If a foreign corporation is a qualified resident of a foreign country with which the United States has an income tax treaty—

(A) the rate of tax under subsection (a) shall be the rate of tax specified in such treaty—

(i) on branch profits if so specified, or

(ii) if not so specified, on dividends paid by a domestic corporation to a corporation resident in such country which wholly owns such domestic corporation, and

(B) any other limitations under such treaty on the tax imposed by subsection (a) shall apply.

(3) Coordination with withholding tax.—

(A) In general.—If a foreign corporation is subject to the tax imposed by subsection (a) for any taxable year (determined after the application of any treaty), no tax shall be imposed by section 871(a), 881(a), 1441, or 1442 on any dividends paid by such corporation out of its earnings and profits for such taxable year.

(B) Limitation on certain treaty benefits.—If—

(i) any dividend described in section 861(a)(2)(B) is received by a foreign corporation, and

(ii) subparagraph (A) does not apply to such dividend,

rules similar to the rules of subparagraphs (A) and (B) of subsection (f)(3) shall apply to such dividend.

(4) Qualified resident.—For purposes of this subsection—

(A) In general.—Except as otherwise provided in this paragraph, the term "qualified resident" means, with respect to any foreign country, any foreign corporation which is a resident of such foreign country unless—

(i) 50 percent or more (by value) of the stock of such foreign corporation is owned (within the meaning of section 883(c)(4)) by individuals who are not residents of such foreign country and who are not United States citizens or resident aliens, or

(ii) 50 percent or more of its income is used (directly or indirectly) to meet liabilities to persons who are not residents of such foreign country or citizens or residents of the United States.

(B) Special rule for publicly traded corporations.—A foreign corporation which is a resident of a foreign country shall be treated as a qualified resident of such foreign country if—

(i) the stock of such corporation is primarily and regularly traded on an established securities market in such foreign country, or

(ii) such corporation is wholly owned (either directly or indirectly) by another foreign corporation which is organized in such foreign country and the stock of which is so traded.

(C) Corporations owned by publicly traded domestic corporations.—A foreign corporation which is a resident of a foreign country shall be treated as a qualified resident of such foreign country if—

(i) such corporation is wholly owned (directly or indirectly) by a domestic corporation, and

(ii) the stock of such domestic corporation is primarily and regularly traded on an established securities market in the United States.

(D) Secretarial authority.—The Secretary may, in his sole discretion, treat a foreign corporation as being a qualified resident of a foreign country if such corporation establishes to the satisfaction of the Secretary that such corporation meets such requirements as the Secretary may establish to ensure that individuals who are not residents of such foreign country do not use the treaty between such foreign country and the United States in a manner inconsistent with the purposes of this subsection.

(5) Exception for international organizations.—This section shall not apply to an international organization (as defined in section 7701(a)(18)).

(f) Treatment of interest allocable to effectively connected income.—

(1) In general.—In the case of a foreign corporation engaged in a trade or business in the United States (or having gross income treated as effectively connected with the conduct of a trade or business in the United States), for purposes of this subtitle—

(A) any interest paid by such trade or business in the United States shall be treated as if it were paid by a domestic corporation, and **§ 884(f)**

(B) to the extent that the allocable interest exceeds the interest described in subparagraph (A), such foreign corporation shall be liable for tax under section 881(a) in the same manner as if such excess were interest paid to such foreign corporation by a wholly owned domestic corporation on the last day of such foreign corporation's taxable year.

To the extent provided in regulations, subparagraph (A) shall not apply to interest in excess of the amounts reasonably expected to be allocable interest.

(2) Allocable interest.—For purposes of this subsection, the term "allocable interest" means any interest which is allocable to income which is effectively connected (or treated as effectively connected) with the conduct of a trade or business in the United States.

(3) Coordination with treaties.—

(A) Payor must be qualified resident.—In the case of any interest described in paragraph (1) which is paid or accrued by a foreign corporation, no benefit under any treaty between the United States and the foreign country of which such corporation is a resident shall apply unless—

(i) such treaty is an income tax treaty, and

(ii) such foreign corporation is a qualified resident of such foreign country.

(B) Recipient must be qualified resident.—In the case of any interest described in paragraph (1) which is received or accrued by any corporation, no benefit under any treaty between the United States and the foreign country of which such corporation is a resident shall apply unless—

(i) such treaty is an income tax treaty, and

(ii) such foreign corporation is a qualified resident of such foreign country.

(g) Regulations.—The Secretary shall prescribe such regulations as may be necessary or appropriate to carry out the purposes of this section, including regulations providing for appropriate adjustments in the determination of the dividend equivalent amount in connection with the distribution to shareholders or transfer to a controlled corporation of the taxpayer's U.S. assets and other adjustments in such determination as are necessary or appropriate to carry out the purposes of this section.

Subpart C—Tax on Gross Transportation Income

§ 887. Imposition of tax on gross transportation income of nonresident aliens and foreign corporations

(a) Imposition of tax.—In the case of any nonresident alien individual or foreign corporation, there is hereby imposed for each taxable year a tax equal to 4 percent of such individual's or corporation's United States source gross transportation income for such taxable year.

(b) United States source gross transportation income.—

(1) In general.—Except as provided in paragraphs (2) and (3), the term "United States source gross transportation income" means any gross income which is transportation income (as defined in section 863(c)(3)) to the extent such income is treated as from sources in the United States under section 863(c)(2). To the extent provided in regulations, such term does not include any income of a kind to which an exemption under paragraph (1) or (2) of section 883(a) would not apply.

(2) Exception for certain income effectively connected with business in the United States.— The term "United States source gross transportation income" shall not include any income taxable under section 871(b) or 882.

(3) Exception for certain income taxable in possessions.—The term "United States source gross transportation income" does not include any income taxable in a possession of the United States under the provisions of this title as made applicable in such possession.

(4) Determination of effectively connected income.—For purposes of this chapter, United States source gross transportation income of any taxpayer shall not be treated as effectively connected with the conduct of a trade or business in the United States unless—

(A) the taxpayer has a fixed place of business in the United States involved in the earning of United States source gross transportation income, and

(B) substantially all of the United States source gross transportation income (determined without regard to paragraph (2)) of the taxpayer is attributable to regularly scheduled transportation (or, in the case of income from the leasing of a vessel or aircraft, is attributable to a fixed place of business in the United States).

(c) Coordination with other provisions.—Any income taxable under this section shall not be taxable under section 871, 881, or 882.

Subpart D—Miscellaneous Provisions

§ 892. Income of foreign governments and of international organizations

(a) Foreign governments.—

(1) In general.—The income of foreign governments received from—

(A) investments in the United States in—

(i) stocks, bonds, or other domestic securities owned by such foreign governments, or

(ii) financial instruments held in the execution of governmental financial or monetary policy, or

(B) interest on deposits in banks in the United States of moneys belonging to such foreign governments,

shall not be included in gross income and shall be exempt from taxation under this subtitle.

(2) Income received directly or indirectly from commercial activities.—

(A) In general.—Paragraph (1) shall not apply to any income—

(i) derived from the conduct of any commercial activity (whether within or outside the United States),

(ii) received by a controlled commercial entity or received (directly or indirectly) from a controlled commercial entity.

(iii) derived from the disposition of any interest in a controlled commercial entity.

(B) Controlled commercial entity.—For purposes of subparagraph (A), the term "controlled commercial entity" means any entity engaged in commercial activities (whether within or outside the United States) if the government—

(i) holds (directly or indirectly) any interest in such entity which (by value or voting interest) is 50 percent or more of the total of such interests in such entity, or

(ii) holds (directly or indirectly) any other interest in such entity which provides the foreign government with effective control of such entity.

For purposes of the preceding sentence, a central bank of issue shall be treated as a controlled commercial entity only if engaged in commercial activities within the United States.

(3) Treatment as resident.—For purposes of this title, a foreign government shall be treated as a corporate resident of its country. A foreign government shall be so treated for purposes of any income tax treaty obligation of the United States if such government grants equivalent treatment to the Government of the United States.

(b) International organizations.—The income of international organizations received from investments in the United States in stocks, bonds, or other domestic securities owned by such international organizations, or from interest on deposits in banks in the United States of moneys belonging to such international organizations, or from any other source within the United States, shall not be included in gross income and shall be exempt from taxation under this subtitle.

(c) Regulations.—The Secretary shall prescribe such regulations as may be necessary or appropriate to carry out the purposes of this section.

§ 893. Compensation of employees of foreign governments or international organizations

(a) Rule for exclusion.—Wages, fees, or salary of any employee of a foreign government or of an international organization (including a consular or other officer, or a nondiplomatic representative), received as compensation for official services to such government or international organization shall not be included in gross income and shall be exempt from taxation under this subtitle if—

(1) such employee is not a citizen of the United States, or is a citizen of the Republic of the Philippines (whether or not a citizen of the United States); and

(2) in the case of an employee of a foreign government, the services are of a character similar to those performed by employees of the Government of the United States in foreign countries; and

(3) in the case of an employee of a foreign government, the foreign government grants an equivalent exemption to employees of the Government of the United States performing similar services in such foreign country.

(b) Certificate by Secretary of State.—The Secretary of State shall certify to the Secretary of the Treasury the names of the foreign countries which grant an equivalent exemption to the employees of the

Government of the United States performing services in such foreign countries, and the character of the services performed by employees of the Government of the United States in foreign countries.

(c) Limitation on exclusion.—Subsection (a) shall not apply to—

(1) any employee of a controlled commercial entity (as defined in section 892(a)(2)(B)), or

(2) any employee of a foreign government whose services are primarily in connection with a commercial activity (whether within or outside the United States) of the foreign government.

§ 894. Income affected by treaty

(a) Treaty provisions.—

(1) In general.—The provisions of this title shall be applied to any taxpayer with due regard to any treaty obligation of the United States which applies to such taxpayer.

(2) Cross reference.—

For relationship between treaties and this title, see section 7852(d).

(b) Permanent establishment in United States.—For purposes of applying any exemption from, or reduction of, any tax provided by any treaty to which the United States is a party with respect to income which is not effectively connected with the conduct of a trade or business within the United States, a nonresident alien individual or a foreign corporation shall be deemed not to have a permanent establishment in the United States at any time during the taxable year. This subsection shall not apply in respect of the tax computed under section 877(b).

(c) Denial of treaty benefits for certain payments through hybrid entities

(1) Application to certain payments.—A foreign person shall not be entitled under any income tax treaty of the United States with a foreign country to any reduced rate of any withholding tax imposed by this title on an item of income derived through an entity which is treated as a partnership (or is otherwise treated as fiscally transparent) for purposes of this title if—

(A) such item is not treated for purposes of the taxation laws of such foreign country as an item of income of such person,

(B) the treaty does not contain a provision addressing the applicability of the treaty in the case of an item of income derived through a partnership, and

(C) the foreign country does not impose tax on a distribution of such item of income from such entity to such person.

(2) Regulations.—The Secretary shall prescribe such regulations as may be necessary or appropriate to determine the extent to which a taxpayer to which paragraph (1) does not apply shall not be entitled to benefits under any income tax treaty of the United States with respect to any payment received by, or income attributable to any activities of, an entity organized in any jurisdiction (including the United States) that is treated as a partnership or is otherwise treated as fiscally transparent for purposes of this title (including a common investment trust under section 584, a grantor trust, or an entity that is disregarded for purposes of this title) and is treated as fiscally nontransparent for purposes of the tax laws of the jurisdiction of residence of the taxpayer.

§ 897. Disposition of investment in United States real property

(a) General rule.—

(1) Treatment as effectively connected with United States trade or business.—For purposes of this title, gain or loss of a nonresident alien individual or a foreign corporation from the disposition of a United States real property interest shall be taken into account—

(A) in the case of a nonresident alien individual, under section 871(b)(1), or

(B) in the case of a foreign corporation, under section 882(a)(1),

as if the taxpayer were engaged in a trade or business within the United States during the taxable year and as if such gain or loss were effectively connected with such trade or business.

(2) Minimum tax on nonresident alien individuals.—

(A) In general.—In the case of any nonresident alien individual, the taxable excess for purposes of section 55(b)(1) shall not be less than the lesser of—

(i) the individual's alternative minimum taxable income (as defined in section 55(b)(1)(D)) for the taxable year, or

(ii) the individual's net United States real property gain for the taxable year.

(B) Net United States real property gain.—For purposes of subparagraph (A), the term "net United States real property gain" means the excess of—

(i) the aggregate of the gains for the taxable year from dispositions of United States real property interests, over

(ii) the aggregate of the losses for the taxable year from dispositions of such interests.

(b) Limitation on losses of individuals.—In the case of an individual, a loss shall be taken into account under subsection (a) only to the extent such loss would be taken into account under section 165(c) (determined without regard to subsection (a) of this section).

(c) United States real property interest.—For purposes of this section—

(1) United States real property interest.—

(A) In general.—Except as provided in subparagraph (B) or subsection (k), the term "United States real property interest" means—

(i) an interest in real property (including an interest in a mine, well, or other natural deposit) located in the United States or the Virgin Islands, and

(ii) any interest (other than an interest solely as a creditor) in any domestic corporation unless the taxpayer establishes (at such time and in such manner as the Secretary by regulations prescribes) that such corporation was at no time a United States real property holding corporation during the shorter of—

(I) the period after June 18, 1980, during which the taxpayer held such interest, or

(II) the 5-year period ending on the date of the disposition of such interest.

(B) Exclusion for interest in certain corporations.—The term "United States real property interest" does not include any interest in a corporation if—

(i) as of the date of the disposition of such interest, such corporation did not hold any United States real property interests,

(ii) all of the United States real property interests held by such corporation at any time during the shorter of the periods described in subparagraph (A)(ii)—

(I) were disposed of in transactions in which the full amount of the gain (if any) was recognized, or

(II) ceased to be United States real property interests by reason of the application of this subparagraph to 1 or more other corporations, and

(iii) neither such corporation nor any predecessor of such corporation was a regulated investment company or a real estate investment trust at any time during the shorter of the periods described in subparagraph (A)(ii).

(2) United States real property holding corporation.—The term "United States real property holding corporation" means any corporation if—

(A) the fair market value of its United States real property interests equals or exceeds 50 percent of

(B) the fair market value of—

(i) its United States real property interests,

(ii) its interests in real property located outside the United States, plus

(iii) any other of its assets which are used or held for use in a trade or business.

(3) Exception for stock regularly traded on established securities markets.—If any class of stock of a corporation is regularly traded on an established securities market, stock of such class shall be treated as a United States real property interest only in the case of a person who, at some time during the shorter of the periods described in paragraph (1)(A)(ii), held more than 5 percent of such class of stock.

(4) Interests held by foreign corporations and by partnerships, trusts, and estates.—For purposes of determining whether any corporation is a United States real property holding corporation—

(A) Foreign corporations.—Paragraph (1)(A)(ii) shall be applied by substituting "any corporation (whether foreign or domestic)" for "any domestic corporation".

(B) Assets held by partnerships, etc.—Under regulations prescribed by the Secretary, assets held by a partnership, trust, or estate shall be treated as held proportionately by its partners or beneficiaries. Any asset treated as held by a partner or beneficiary by reason of this subparagraph which is used or held for use by the partnership, trust, or estate in a trade or business shall be treated as so used or held by the partner or beneficiary. Any asset treated as held by a partner or beneficiary by reason of this subparagraph shall be so treated for purposes of applying this subparagraph successively to partnerships, trusts, or estates which are above the first partnership, trust, or estate in a chain thereof.

(5) Treatment of controlling interests.—

(A) In general.—Under regulations, for purposes of determining whether any corporation is a United States real property holding corporation, if any corporation (hereinafter in this paragraph referred to as the "first corporation") holds a controlling interest in a second corporation—

(i) the stock which the first corporation holds in the second corporation shall not be taken into account,

(ii) the first corporation shall be treated as holding a portion of each asset of the second corporation equal to the percentage of the fair market value of the stock of the second corporation represented by the stock held by the first corporation, and

(iii) any asset treated as held by the first corporation by reason of clause (ii) which is used or held for use by the second corporation in a trade or business shall be treated as so used or held by the first corporation.

Any asset treated as held by the first corporation by reason of the preceding sentence shall be so treated for purposes of applying the preceding sentence successively to corporations which are above the first corporation in a chain of corporations.

(B) Controlling interest.—For purposes of subparagraph (A), the term "controlling interest" means 50 percent or more of the fair market value of all classes of stock of a corporation.

(6) Other special rules.—

(A) Interest in real property.—The term "interest in real property" includes fee ownership and co-ownership of land or improvements thereon, leaseholds of land or improvements thereon, options to acquire land or improvements thereon, and options to acquire leaseholds of land or improvements thereon.

(B) Real property includes associated personal property.—The term "real property" includes movable walls, furnishings, and other personal property associated with the use of the real property.

(C) Constructive ownership rules.—For purposes of determining under paragraph (3) whether any person holds more than 5 percent of any class of stock and of determining under paragraph (5) whether a person holds a controlling interest in any corporation, section 318(a) shall apply (except that paragraphs (2)(C) and (3)(C) of section 318(a) shall be applied by substituting "5 percent" for "50 percent").

(d) Treatment of distributions by foreign corporations.—

(1) In general.—Except to the extent otherwise provided in regulations, notwithstanding any other provision of this chapter, gain shall be recognized by a foreign corporation on the distribution (including a distribution in liquidation or redemption) of a United States real property interest in an amount equal to the excess of the fair market value of such interest (as of the time of the distribution) over its adjusted basis.

(2) Exceptions.—Gain shall not be recognized under paragraph (1)—

(A) if—

(i) at the time of the receipt of the distributed property, the distributee would be subject to taxation under this chapter on a subsequent disposition of the distributed property, and

(ii) the basis of the distributed property in the hands of the distributee is no greater than the adjusted basis of such property before the distribution, increased by the amount of gain (if any) recognized by the distributing corporation, or

(B) if such nonrecognition is provided in regulations prescribed by the Secretary under subsection (e)(2).

(e) Coordination with nonrecognition provisions.—

(1) In general.—Except to the extent otherwise provided in subsection (d) and paragraph (2) of this subsection, any nonrecognition provision shall apply for purposes of this section to a transaction only in the case of an exchange of a United States real property interest for an interest the sale of which would be subject to taxation under this chapter.

(2) Regulations.—The Secretary shall prescribe regulations (which are necessary or appropriate to prevent the avoidance of Federal income taxes) providing—

(A) the extent to which nonrecognition provisions shall, and shall not, apply for purposes of this section, and

(B) the extent to which—

(i) transfers of property in reorganization, and

(ii) changes in interests in, or distributions from, a partnership, trust, or estate, shall be treated as sales of property at fair market value.

(3) Nonrecognition provision defined.—For purposes of this subsection, the term "nonrecognition provision" means any provision of this title for not recognizing gain or loss.

* * *

(g) Special rule for sales of interest in partnerships, trusts, and estates.—Under regulations prescribed by the Secretary, the amount of any money, and the fair market value of any property, received by a nonresident alien individual or foreign corporation in exchange for all or part of its interest in a partnership, trust, or estate shall, to the extent attributable to United States real property interests, be considered as an amount received from the sale or exchange in the United States of such property.

(h) Special rules for certain investment entities.—For purposes of this section—

(1) Look-through of distributions.—Any distribution by a qualified investment entity to a nonresident alien individual, a foreign corporation, or other qualified investment entity shall, to the extent attributable to gain from sales or exchanges by the qualified investment entity of United States real property interests, be treated as gain recognized by such nonresident alien individual, foreign corporation, or other qualified investment entity from the sale or exchange of a United States real property interest. Notwithstanding the preceding sentence, any distribution by a qualified investment entity to a nonresident alien individual or a foreign corporation with respect to any class of stock which is regularly traded on an established securities market located in the United States shall not be treated as gain recognized from the sale or exchange of a United States real property interest if such individual or corporation did not own more than 5 percent of such class of stock at any time during the 1-year period ending on the date of such distribution.

(2) Sale of stock in domestically controlled entity not taxed.—The term "United States real property interest" does not include any interest in a domestically controlled qualified investment entity.

(3) Distributions by domestically controlled qualified investment entities.—In the case of a domestically controlled qualified investment entity, rules similar to the rules of subsection (d) shall apply to the foreign ownership percentage of any gain.

(4) Definitions and special rules.—

(A) Qualified investment entity.—The term "qualified investment entity" means—

(i) any real estate investment trust, and

(ii) any regulated investment company which is a United States real property holding corporation or which would be a United States real property holding corporation if the exceptions provided in subsections (c)(3) and (h)(2) did not apply to interests in any real estate investment trust and for purposes of determining whether a real estate investment trust is a domestically controlled qualified under this subsection or regulated investment company.

(B) Domestically controlled.—The term "domestically controlled qualified investment entity" means any qualified investment entity in which at all times during the testing period less than 50 percent in value of the stock was held directly or indirectly by foreign persons.

(C) Foreign ownership percentage.—The term "foreign ownership percentage" means that percentage of the stock of the qualified investment entity which was held (directly or indirectly) by foreign persons at the time during the testing period during which the direct and indirect ownership of stock by foreign persons was greatest.

(D) Testing period.—The term "testing period" means whichever of the following periods is the shortest:

(i) the period beginning on June 19, 1980, and ending on the date of the disposition or of the distribution, as the case may be,

(ii) the 5-year period ending on the date of the disposition or of the distribution, as the case may be, or

(iii) the period during which the qualified investment entity was in existence.

(E) Special ownership rules.—For purposes of determining the holder of stock under subparagraphs (B) and (C)—

(i) in the case of any class of stock of the qualified investment entity which is regularly traded on an established securities market in the United States, a person holding less than 5 percent of such class of stock at all times during the testing period shall be treated as a United States person unless the qualified investment entity has actual knowledge that such person is not a United States person,

(ii) any stock in the qualified investment entity held by another qualified investment entity—

(I) any class of stock of which is regularly traded on an established securities market, or

(II) which is a regulated investment company which issues redeemable securities (within the meaning of section 2 of the Investment Company Act of 1940),

shall be treated as held by a foreign person, except that if such other qualified investment entity is domestically controlled (determined after application of this subparagraph), such stock shall be treated as held by a United States person, and

(iii) any stock in the qualified investment entity held by any other qualified investment entity not described in subclause (I) or (II) of clause (ii) shall only be treated as held by a United States person in proportion to the stock of such other qualified investment entity which is (or is treated under clause (ii) or (iii) as) held by a United States person.

(5) Treatment of certain wash sale transactions.—

(A) In general.—If an interest in a domestically controlled qualified investment entity is disposed of in an applicable wash sale transaction, the taxpayer shall, for purposes of this section, be treated as having gain from the sale or exchange of a United States real property interest in an amount equal to the portion of the distribution described in subparagraph (B) with respect to such interest which, but for the disposition, would have been treated by the taxpayer as gain from the sale or exchange of a United States real property interest under paragraph (1).

(B) Applicable wash sales transaction.—For purposes of this paragraph—

(i) In general.—The term "applicable wash sales transaction" means any transaction (or series of transactions) under which a nonresident alien individual, foreign corporation, or qualified investment entity—

(I) disposes of an interest in a domestically controlled qualified investment entity during the 30-day period preceding the ex-dividend date of a distribution which is to be made with respect to the interest and any portion of which, but for the disposition, would have been treated by the taxpayer as gain from the sale or exchange of a United States real property interest under paragraph (1), and

(II) acquires, or enters into a contract or option to acquire, a substantially identical interest in such entity during the 61-day period beginning with the 1st day of the 30-day period described in subclause (I).

For purposes of subclause (II), a nonresident alien individual, foreign corporation, or qualified investment entity shall be treated as having acquired any interest acquired by a person related (within the meaning of section 267(b) or 707(b)(1)) to the individual, corporation, or entity, and any interest which such person has entered into any contract or option to acquire.

(ii) Application to substitute dividend and similar payments.—Subparagraph (A) shall apply to—

(I) any substitute dividend payment (within the meaning of section 861), or

(II) any other similar payment specified in regulations which the Secretary determines necessary to prevent avoidance of the purposes of this paragraph. **§ 897(h)**

The portion of any such payment treated by the taxpayer as gain from the sale or exchange of a United States real property interest under subparagraph (A) by reason of this clause shall be equal to the portion of the distribution such payment is in lieu of which would have been so treated but for the transaction giving rise to such payment.

(iii) Exception where distribution actually received.—A transaction shall not be treated as an applicable wash sales transaction if the nonresident alien individual, foreign corporation, or qualified investment entity receives the distribution described in clause (i)(I) with respect to either the interest which was disposed of, or acquired, in the transaction.

(iv) Exception for certain publicly traded stock.—A transaction shall not be treated as an applicable wash sales transaction if it involves the disposition of any class of stock in a qualified investment entity which is regularly traded on an established securities market within the United States but only if the nonresident alien individual, foreign corporation, or qualified investment entity did not own more than 5 percent of such class of stock at any time during the 1-year period ending on the date of the distribution described in clause (i)(I).

(i) Election by foreign corporation to be treated as domestic corporation.—

(1) In general.—If—

(A) a foreign corporation holds a United States real property interest, and

(B) under any treaty obligation of the United States the foreign corporation is entitled to nondiscriminatory treatment with respect to that interest,

then such foreign corporation may make an election to be treated as a domestic corporation for purposes of this section, section 1445, and section 6039C.

(2) Revocation only with consent.—Any election under paragraph (1), once made, may be revoked only with the consent of the Secretary.

(3) Making of election.—An election under paragraph (1) may be made only—

(A) if all of the owners of all classes of interests (other than interests solely as a creditor) in the foreign corporation at the time of the election consent to the making of the election and agree that gain, if any, from the disposition of such interest after June 18, 1980, which would be taken into account under subsection (a) shall be taxable notwithstanding any provision to the contrary in a treaty to which the United States is a party, and

(B) subject to such other conditions as the Secretary may prescribe by regulations with respect to the corporation or its shareholders.

In the case of a class of interest (other than an interest solely as a creditor) which is regularly traded on an established securities market, the consent described in subparagraph (A) need only be made by any person if such person held more than 5 percent of such class of interest at some time during the shorter of the periods described in subsection (c)(1)(A)(ii). The constructive ownership rules of subsection (c)(6)(C) shall apply in determining whether a person held more than 5 percent of a class of interest.

(4) Exclusive method of claiming nondiscrimination.—The election provided by paragraph (1) shall be the exclusive remedy for any person claiming discriminatory treatment with respect to this section, section 1445, and section 6039C.

(j) Certain contributions to capital.—Except to the extent otherwise provided in regulations, gain shall be recognized by a nonresident alien individual or foreign corporation on the transfer of a United States real property interest to a foreign corporation if the transfer is made as paid in surplus or as a contribution to capital, in the amount of the excess of—

(1) the fair market value of such property transferred, over

(2) the sum of—

(A) the adjusted basis of such property in the hands of the transferor, plus

(B) the amount of gain, if any, recognized to the transferor under any other provision at the time of the transfer.

(k) Special rules relating to real estate investment trusts.—

(1) Increase in percentage ownership for exceptions for persons holding publicly traded stock.—

(A) Dispositions.—In the case of any disposition of stock in a real estate investment trust, paragraphs (3) and (6)(C) of subsection (c) shall each be applied by substituting "more than 10 percent" for "more than 5 percent".

(B) Distributions.—In the case of any distribution from a real estate investment trust, subsection (h)(1) shall be applied by substituting "10 percent" for "5 percent".

(2) Stock held by qualified shareholders not treated as United States real property interest.—

(A) In general.—Except as provided in subparagraph (B)—

(i) stock of a real estate investment trust which is held directly (or indirectly through 1 or more partnerships) by a qualified shareholder shall not be treated as a United States real property interest, and

(ii) notwithstanding subsection (h)(1), any distribution to a qualified shareholder shall not be treated as gain recognized from the sale or exchange of a United States real property interest to the extent the stock of the real estate investment trust held by such qualified shareholder is not treated as a United States real property interest under clause (i).

(B) Exception.—In the case of a qualified shareholder with one or more applicable investors—

(i) subparagraph (A)(i) shall not apply to the applicable percentage of the stock of the real estate investment trust held by the qualified shareholder, and

(ii) the applicable percentage of the amounts realized by the qualified shareholder with respect to any disposition of stock in the real estate investment trust or with respect to any distribution from the real estate investment trust attributable to gain from sales or exchanges of a United States real property interest shall be treated as amounts realized from the disposition of United States real property interests.

(C) Special rule for certain distributions treated as sale or exchange.—If a distribution by a real estate investment trust is treated as a sale or exchange of stock under section 301(c)(3), 302, or 331 with respect to a qualified shareholder—

(i) in the case of an applicable investor, subparagraph (B) shall apply with respect to such distribution, and

(ii) in the case of any other person, such distribution shall be treated under section 857(b)(3)(F) as a dividend from a real estate investment trust notwithstanding any other provision of this title.

(D) Applicable investor.—For purposes of this subsection, the term "applicable investor" means, with respect to any qualified shareholder holding stock in a real estate investment trust, a person (other than a qualified shareholder) which—

(i) holds an interest (other than an interest solely as a creditor) in such qualified shareholder, and

(ii) holds more than 10 percent of the stock of such real estate investment trust (whether or not by reason of the person's ownership interest in the qualified shareholder).

(E) Constructive Ownership Rules.—For purposes of subparagraphs (B)(i) and (D), the constructive ownership rules under subsection (c)(6)(C) shall apply.

(F) Applicable percentage.—For purposes of subparagraph (B), the term "applicable percentage" means the percentage of the value of the interests (other than interests held solely as a creditor) in the qualified shareholder held by applicable investors.

(3) Qualified Shareholder.—For purposes of this subsection—

(A) In general.—The term "qualified shareholder" means a foreign person which—

(i) **(I)** is eligible for benefits of a comprehensive income tax treaty with the United States which includes an exchange of information program and the principal class of interests of which is listed and regularly traded on 1 or more recognized stock exchanges (as defined in such comprehensive income tax treaty), or

(II) is a foreign partnership that is created or organized under foreign law as a limited partnership in a jurisdiction that has an agreement for the exchange of information with respect to taxes with the United States and has a class of limited partnership units which is regularly traded on the New York Stock Exchange or Nasdaq Stock Market and such class of limited partnership units value is greater than 50 percent of the value of all the partnership units,

(ii) is a qualified collective investment vehicle, and

(iii) maintains records on the identity of each person who, at any time during the foreign person's taxable year, holds directly 5 percent or more of the class of interest described in subclause (I) or (II) of clause (i), as the case may be.

(B) Qualified collective investment vehicle.—For purposes of this subsection, the term "qualified collective investment vehicle" means a foreign person—

(i) which—

(I) is eligible for benefits under the comprehensive income tax treaty described in subparagraph (A)(i)(I), but only if the dividends article of such treaty imposes conditions on the benefits allowable in the case of dividends paid by a real estate investment trust, and

(II) is eligible under such treaty for a reduced rate of withholding with respect to ordinary dividends paid by a real estate investment trust even if such person holds more than 10 percent of the stock of such real estate investment trust,

(ii) which—

(I) is a publicly traded partnership (as defined in section 7704(b)) to which subsection (a) of section 7704 does not apply,

(II) is a withholding foreign partnership for purposes of chapters 3, 4, and 61, and

(III) if such foreign partnership were a domestic corporation, would be a United States real property holding corporation (determined without regard to paragraph (1)) at any time during the 5-year period ending on the date of disposition of, or distribution with respect to, such partnership's interests in a real estate investment trust, or

(iii) which is designated as a qualified collective investment vehicle by the Secretary and is either—

(I) fiscally transparent within the meaning of section 894, or

(II) required to include dividends in its gross income, but entitled to a deduction for distributions to persons holding interests (other than interests solely as a creditor) in such foreign person.

(4) Partnership allocations.—

(A) In general.—For the purposes of this subsection, in the case of an applicable investor who is a nonresident alien individual or a foreign corporation and is a partner in a partnership that is a qualified shareholder, if such partner's proportionate share of USRPI gain for the taxable year exceeds such partner's distributive share of USRPI gain for the taxable year, then

(i) such partner's distributive share of the amount of gain taken into account under subsection (a)(1) by the partner for the taxable year (determined without regard to this paragraph) shall be increased by the amount of such excess, and

(ii) such partner's distributive share of items of income or gain for the taxable year that are not treated as gain taken into account under subsection (a)(1) (determined without regard to this paragraph) shall be decreased (but not below zero) by the amount of such excess.

(B) USRPI gain.—For the purposes of this paragraph, the term "USRPI gain" means the excess (if any) of—

(i) the sum of—

(I) any gain recognized from the disposition of a United States real property interest, and

(II) any distribution by a real estate investment trust that is treated as gain recognized from the sale or exchange of a United States real property interest, over

(ii) any loss recognized from the disposition of a United States real property interest.

(C) Proportionate share of usrpi gain.—For purposes of this paragraph, an applicable investor's proportionate share of USRPI gain shall be determined on the basis of such investor's share of partnership items of income or gain (excluding gain allocated under section 704(c)), whichever results in the largest proportionate share. If the investor's share of partnership items of income or gain (excluding gain allocated under section 704(c)) may vary during the period such investor is a partner in the partnership, such share shall be the highest share such investor may receive.

(*l*) Exception for qualified foreign pension funds.—

(1) In general.—For purposes of this section, a qualified foreign pension fund shall not be treated as a nonresident alien individual or a foreign corporation. For purposes of the preceding sentence, an entity all the interests of which are held by a qualified foreign pension fund shall be treated as such a fund.

(2) Qualified foreign pension fund.—For purposes of this subsection, the term "qualified foreign pension fund" means any trust, corporation, or other organization or arrangement—

(A) which is created or organized under the law of a country other than the United States,

(B) which is established—

(i) by such country (or one or more political subdivisions thereof) to provide retirement or pension benefits to participants or beneficiaries that are current or former employees (including self-employed individuals) or persons designated by such employees, as a result of services rendered by such employees to their employers, or

(ii) by one or more employers to provide retirement or pension benefits to participants or beneficiaries that are current or former employees (including self-employed individuals) or persons designated by such employees in consideration for services rendered by such employees to such employers,

(C) which does not have a single participant or beneficiary with a right to more than five percent of its assets or income,

(D) which is subject to government regulation and with respect to which annual information about its beneficiaries is provided, or is otherwise available, to the relevant tax authorities in the country in which it is established or operates, and

(E) with respect to which, under the laws of the country in which it is established or operates—

(i) contributions to such trust, corporation, organization, or arrangement which would otherwise be subject to tax under such laws are deductible or excluded from the gross income of such entity or arrangement or taxed at a reduced rate, or

(ii) taxation of any investment income of such trust, corporation, organization or arrangement is deferred, or such income is excluded from the gross income of such entity or arrangement or is taxed at a reduced rate.

(3) Regulations.—The Secretary shall prescribe such regulations as may be necessary or appropriate to carry out the purposes of this subsection.

§ 898. Taxable year of certain foreign corporations

(a) General rule.—For purposes of this title, the taxable year of any specified foreign corporation shall be the required year determined under subsection (c).

(b) Specified Foreign Corporation.—For purposes of this section—

(1) In general.—The term "specified foreign corporation" means any foreign corporation—

(A) which is treated as a controlled foreign corporation for any purpose under subpart F of part III of this subchapter, and

(B) with respect to which the ownership requirements of paragraph (2) are met.

(2) Ownership requirements.—

(A) In general.—The ownership requirements of this paragraph are met with respect to any foreign corporation if a United States shareholder owns, on each testing day, more than 50 percent of—

(i) the total voting power of all classes of stock of such corporation entitled to vote, or

(ii) the total value of all classes of stock of such corporation.

(B) Ownership.—For purposes of subparagraph (A), the rules of subsections (a) and (b) of section 958 shall apply in determining ownership.

(3) United States shareholder.—The term "United States shareholder" has the meaning given to such term by section 951(b), except that, in the case of a foreign corporation having related person insurance income (as defined in section 953(c)(2)), the Secretary may treat any person as a United States shareholder for purposes of this section if such person is treated as a United States shareholder under section 953(c)(1).

(c) Determination of required year.—

(1) In general.—The required year is—

(A) the majority U.S. shareholder year, or

(B) if there is no majority U.S. shareholder year, the taxable year prescribed under regulations.

(2) Majority U.S. shareholder year.—

(A) In general.—For purposes of this subsection, the term "majority U.S. shareholder year" means the taxable year (if any) which, on each testing day, constituted the taxable year of—

(i) each United States shareholder described in subsection (b)(2)(A), and

(ii) each United States shareholder not described in clause (i) whose stock was treated as owned under subsection (b)(2)(B) by any shareholder described in such clause.

(B) Testing day.—The testing days shall be—

(i) the first day of the corporation's taxable year (determined without regard to this section), or

(ii) the days during such representative period as the Secretary may prescribe.

Part III—Income from Sources Without the United States

Subpart A—Foreign Tax Credit

§ 901. Taxes of foreign countries and of possessions of United States

(a) Allowance of credit.—If the taxpayer chooses to have the benefits of this subpart, the tax imposed by this chapter shall, subject to the limitation of section 904, be credited with the amounts provided in the applicable paragraph of subsection (b) plus, in the case of a corporation, the taxes deemed to have been paid under section 960. Such choice for any taxable year may be made or changed at any time before the expiration of the period prescribed for making a claim for credit or refund of the tax imposed by this chapter for such taxable year. The credit shall not be allowed against any tax treated as a tax not imposed by this chapter under section 26(b).

(b) Amount allowed.—Subject to the limitation of section 904, the following amounts shall be allowed as the credit under subsection (a):

(1) Citizens and domestic corporations.—In the case of a citizen of the United States and of a domestic corporation, the amount of any income, war profits, and excess profits taxes paid or accrued during the taxable year to any foreign country or to any possession of the United States; and

(2) Resident of the United States or Puerto Rico.—In the case of a resident of the United States and in the case of an individual who is a bona fide resident of Puerto Rico during the entire taxable year, the amount of any such taxes paid or accrued during the taxable year to any possession of the United States; and

(3) Alien resident of the United States or Puerto Rico.—In the case of an alien resident of the United States and in the case of an alien individual who is a bona fide resident of Puerto Rico during the entire taxable year, the amount of any such taxes paid or accrued during the taxable year to any foreign country; and

(4) Nonresident alien individuals and foreign corporations.—In the case of any nonresident alien individual not described in section 876 and in the case of any foreign corporation, the amount determined pursuant to section 906; and

(5) Partnerships and estates.—In the case of any person described in paragraph (1), (2), (3), or (4), who is a member of a partnership or a beneficiary of an estate or trust, the amount of his proportionate share of the taxes (described in such paragraph) of the partnership or the estate or trust paid or accrued during the taxable year to a foreign country or to any possession of the United States, as the case may be. Under rules or regulations prescribed by the Secretary, in the case of any foreign trust of which the settlor or another person would be treated as owner of any portion of the trust under subpart E but for section 672(f), the allocable amount of any income, war profits, and excess profits taxes imposed by any foreign country or possession of the United States on the settlor or such other person in respect of trust income.

(c) Similar credit required for certain alien residents.—Whenever the President finds that—

(1) a foreign country, in imposing income, war profits, and excess profits taxes, does not allow to citizens of the United States residing in such foreign country a credit for any such taxes paid or accrued to the United States or any foreign country, as the case may be, similar to the credit allowed under subsection (b)(3),

(2) such foreign country, when requested by the United States to do so, has not acted to provide such a similar credit to citizens of the United States residing in such foreign country, and

(3) it is in the public interest to allow the credit under subsection (b)(3) to citizens or subjects of such foreign country only if it allows such a similar credit to citizens of the United States residing in such foreign country,

the President shall proclaim that, for taxable years beginning while the proclamation remains in effect, the credit under subsection (b)(3) shall be allowed to citizens or subjects of such foreign country only if such foreign country, in imposing income, war profits, and excess profits taxes, allows to citizens of the United States residing in such foreign country such a similar credit.

(d) Treatment of dividends from a DISC or former DISC.—For purposes of this subpart, dividends from a DISC or former DISC (as defined in section 992(a)) shall be treated as dividends from a foreign corporation to the extent such dividends are treated under part I as income from sources without the United States.

(e) Foreign taxes on mineral income.—

(1) Reduction in amount allowed.—Notwithstanding subsection (b), the amount of any income, war profits, and excess profits taxes paid or accrued during the taxable year to any foreign country or possession of the United States with respect to foreign mineral income from sources within such country or possession which would (but for this paragraph) be allowed under such subsection shall be reduced by the amount (if any) by which—

(A) the amount of such taxes (or, if smaller, the amount of the tax which would be computed under this chapter with respect to such income determined without the deduction allowed under section 613), exceeds

(B) the amount of the tax computed under this chapter with respect to such income.

(2) Foreign mineral income defined.—For purposes of paragraph (1), the term "foreign mineral income" means income derived from the extraction of minerals from mines, wells, or other natural deposits, the processing of such minerals into their primary products, and the transportation, distribution, or sale of such minerals or primary products. Such term includes, but is not limited to that portion of the taxpayer's distributive share of the income of partnerships attributable to foreign mineral income.

(f) Certain payments for oil or gas not considered as taxes.—Notwithstanding subsection (b) and section 960, the amount of any income, or profits, and excess profits taxes paid or accrued during the taxable year to any foreign country in connection with the purchase and sale of oil or gas extracted in such country is not to be considered as tax for purposes of section 275(a) and this section if—

(1) the taxpayer has no economic interest in the oil or gas to which section 611(a) applies, and **§ 901(f)**

(2) either such purchase or sale is at a price which differs from the fair market value for such oil or gas at the time of such purchase or sale.

(g) Certain taxes paid with respect to distributions from possessions corporations.—

(1) In general.—For purposes of this chapter, any tax of a foreign country or possession of the United States which is paid or accrued with respect to any distribution from a corporation—

(A) to the extent that such distribution is attributable to periods during which such corporation is a possessions corporation, and

(B) (i) if a dividends received deduction is allowable with respect to such distribution under part VIII of subchapter B, or

(ii) to the extent that such distribution is received in connection with a liquidation or other transaction with respect to which gain or loss is not recognized,

shall not be treated as income, war profits, or excess profits taxes paid or accrued to a foreign country or possession of the United States, and no deduction shall be allowed under this title with respect to any amount so paid or accrued.

(2) Possessions corporation.—For purposes of paragraph (1), a corporation shall be treated as a possessions corporation for any period during which an election under section 936 (as in effect on the day before the enactment of the Tax Technical Corrections Act of 2018) applied to such corporation, during which section 931 (as in effect on the day before the date of the enactment of the Tax Reform Act of 1976) applied to such corporation, or during which section 957(c) (as in effect on the day before the date of the enactment of the Tax Reform Act of 1986) applied to such corporation.

(i) Taxes used to provide subsidies.—Any income, war profits, or excess profits tax shall not be treated as a tax for purposes of this title to the extent—

(1) the amount of such tax is used (directly or indirectly) by the country imposing such tax to provide a subsidy by any means to the taxpayer, a related person (within the meaning of section 482), or any party to the transaction or to a related transaction, and

(2) such subsidy is determined (directly or indirectly) by reference to the amount of such tax, or the base used to compute the amount of such tax.

(j) Denial of foreign tax credit, etc., with respect to certain foreign countries.—

(1) In general.—Notwithstanding any other provision of this part—

(A) no credit shall be allowed under subsection (a) for any income, war profits, or excess profits taxes paid or accrued (or deemed paid under section 960) to any country if such taxes are with respect to income attributable to a period during which this subsection applies to such country, and

(B) subsections (a), (b), and (c) of section 904 and section 960 shall be applied separately with respect to income attributable to such a period from sources within such country.

(2) Countries to which subsection applies.—

(A) In general.—This subsection shall apply to any foreign country—

(i) the government of which the United States does not recognize, unless such government is otherwise eligible to purchase defense articles or services under the Arms Export Control Act,

(ii) with respect to which the United States has severed diplomatic relations,

(iii) with respect to which the United States has not severed diplomatic relations but does not conduct such relations, or

(iv) which the Secretary of State has, pursuant to section 6(j) of the Export Administration Act of 1979, as amended, designated as a foreign country which repeatedly provides support for acts of international terrorisms.

(B) Period for which subsection applies.—This subsection shall apply to any foreign country described in subparagraph (A) during the period—

(i) beginning on the later of—

(I) January 1, 1987, or

(II) 6 months after such country becomes a country described in subparagraph (A), and

(ii) ending on the date the Secretary of State certifies to the Secretary of the Treasury that such country is no longer described in subparagraph (A).

(3) Taxes allowed as a deduction, etc.—Sections 275 and 78 shall not apply to any tax which is not allowable as a credit under subsection (a) by reason of this subsection.

(4) Regulations.—The Secretary shall prescribe such regulations as may be necessary or appropriate to carry out the purposes of this subsection, including regulations which treat income paid through 1 or more entities as derived from a foreign country to which this subsection applies if such income was, without regard to such entities, derived from such country.

(5) Waiver of denial.—

(A) In general.—Paragraph (1) shall not apply with respect to taxes paid or accrued to a country if the President—

(i) determines that a waiver of the application of such paragraph is in the national interest of the United States and will expand trade and investment opportunities for United States companies in such country; and

(ii) reports such waiver under subparagraph (B).

(B) Report.—Not less than 30 days before the date on which a waiver is granted under this paragraph, the President shall report to Congress—

(i) the intention to grant such waiver; and

(ii) the reason for the determination under subparagraph (A)(i).

(k) Minimum holding period for certain taxes on dividends.—

(1) Withholding taxes.—

(A) In general.—In no event shall a credit be allowed under subsection (a) for any withholding tax on a dividend with respect to stock in a corporation if—

(i) such stock is held by the recipient of the dividend for 15 days or less during the 31-day period beginning on the date which is 15 days before the date on which such share becomes ex-dividend with respect to such dividend, or

(ii) to the extent that the recipient of the dividend is under an obligation (whether pursuant to a short sale or otherwise) to make related payments with respect to positions in substantially similar or related property.

(B) Withholding tax.—For purposes of this paragraph, the term "withholding tax" includes any tax determined on a gross basis; but does not include any tax which is in the nature of a prepayment of a tax imposed on a net basis.

(2) Deemed paid taxes.—In the case of income, war profits, or excess profits taxes deemed paid under section 853 or 960 through a chain of ownership of stock in 1 or more corporations, no credit shall be allowed under subsection (a) for such taxes if—

(A) any stock of any corporation in such chain (the ownership of which is required to obtain credit under subsection (a) for such taxes) is held for less than the period described in paragraph (1)(A)(i), or

(B) the corporation holding the stock is under an obligation referred to in paragraph (1)(A)(ii).

(3) 45-Day rule in the case of certain preference dividends.—In the case of stock having preference in dividends and dividends with respect to such stock which are attributable to a period or periods aggregating in excess of 366 days, paragraph (1)(A)(i) shall be applied—

(A) by substituting "45 days" for "15 days" each place it appears, and

(B) by substituting "91-day period" for "31-day period".

(4) Exception for certain taxes paid by securities dealers.—

(A) In general.—Paragraphs (1) and (2) shall not apply to any qualified tax with respect to any security held in the active conduct in a foreign country of a business as a securities dealer of any person—

(i) who is registered as a securities broker or dealer under section 15(a) of the Securities Exchange Act of 1934,

(ii) who is registered as a Government securities broker or dealer under section 15C(a) of such Act, or

(iii) who is licensed or authorized in such foreign country to conduct securities activities in such country and is subject to bona fide regulation by a securities regulating authority of such country.

(B) Qualified tax.—For purposes of subparagraph (A), the term "qualified tax" means a tax paid to a foreign country (other than the foreign country referred to in subparagraph (A)) if—

(i) the dividend to which such tax is attributable is subject to taxation on a net basis by the country referred to in subparagraph (A), and

(ii) such country allows a credit against its net basis tax for the full amount of the tax paid to such other foreign country.

(C) Regulations.—The Secretary may prescribe such regulations as may be appropriate to carry out this paragraph, including regulations to prevent the abuse of the exception provided by this paragraph and to treat other taxes as qualified taxes.

(5) Certain rules to apply.—For purposes of this subsection, the rules of paragraphs (3) and (4) of section 246(c) shall apply.

(6) Treatment of bona fide sales.—If a person's holding period is reduced by reason of the application of the rules of section 246(c)(4) to any contract for the bona fide sale of stock, the determination of whether such person's holding period meets the requirements of paragraph (2) with respect to taxes deemed paid under section 960 shall be made as of the date such contract is entered into.

(7) Taxes allowed as deduction, etc.—Sections 275 and 78 shall not apply to any tax which is not allowable as a credit under subsection (a) by reason of this subsection.

(*l*) Minimum holding period for withholding taxes on gain and income other than dividends etc.—

(1) In general.—In no event shall a credit be allowed under subsection (a) for any withholding tax (as defined in subsection (k)) on any item of income or gain with respect to any property if—

(A) such property is held by the recipient of the item for 15 days or less during the 31-day period beginning on the date which is 15 days before the date on which the right to receive payment of such item arises, or

(B) to the extent that the recipient of the item is under an obligation (whether pursuant to a short sale or otherwise) to make related payments with respect to positions in substantially similar or related property.

This paragraph shall not apply to any dividend to which subsection (k) applies.

(2) Exception for taxes paid by dealers.—

(A) In general.—Paragraph (1) shall not apply to any qualified tax with respect to any property held in the active conduct in a foreign country of a business as a dealer in such property.

(B) Qualified tax.—For purposes of subparagraph (A), the term "qualified tax" means a tax paid to a foreign country (other than the foreign country referred to in subparagraph (A)) if—

(i) the item to which such tax is attributable is subject to taxation on a net basis by the country referred to in subparagraph (A), and

(ii) such country allows a credit against its net basis tax for the full amount of the tax paid to such other foreign country.

(C) Dealer.—For purposes of subparagraph (A), the term "dealer" means—

(i) with respect to a security, any person to whom paragraphs (1) and (2) of subsection (k) would not apply by reason of paragraph (4) thereof, and

(ii) with respect to any other property, any person with respect to whom such property is described in section 1221(a)(1).

(D) Regulations.—The Secretary may prescribe such regulations as may be appropriate to carry out this paragraph, including regulations to prevent the abuse of the exception provided by this paragraph and to treat other taxes as qualified taxes.

(3) Exceptions.—The Secretary may by regulation provide that paragraph (1) shall not apply to property where the Secretary determines that the application of paragraph (1) to such property is not necessary to carry out the purposes of this subsection.

(4) Certain rules to apply.—Rules similar to the rules of paragraphs (5), (6), and (7) of subsection (k) shall apply for purposes of this subsection.

(5) Determination of holding period.—Holding periods shall be determined for purposes of this subsection without regard to section 1235 or any similar rule.

(m) Denial of foreign tax credit with respect to foreign income not subject to United States taxation by reason of covered asset acquisitions.—

(1) In general.—In the case of a covered asset acquisition, the disqualified portion of any foreign income tax determined with respect to the income or gain attributable to the relevant foreign assets—

(A) shall not be taken into account in determining the credit allowed under subsection (a), and

(B) in the case of a foreign income tax paid by a foreign corporation, shall not be taken into account for purposes of section 960.

(2) Covered asset acquisition.—For purposes of this section, the term "covered asset acquisition" means—

(A) a qualified stock purchase (as defined in section 338(d)(3)) to which section 338(a) applies,

(B) any transaction which—

(i) is treated as an acquisition of assets for purposes of this chapter, and

(ii) is treated as the acquisition of stock of a corporation (or is disregarded) for purposes of the foreign income taxes of the relevant jurisdiction,

(C) any acquisition of an interest in a partnership which has an election in effect under section 754, and

(D) to the extent provided by the Secretary, any other similar transaction.

(3) Disqualified portion.—For purposes of this section—

(A) In general.—The term "disqualified portion" means, with respect to any covered asset acquisition, for any taxable year, the ratio (expressed as a percentage) of—

(i) the aggregate basis differences (but not below zero) allocable to such taxable year under subparagraph (B) with respect to all relevant foreign assets, divided by

(ii) the income on which the foreign income tax referred to in paragraph (1) is determined (or, if the taxpayer fails to substantiate such income to

the satisfaction of the Secretary, such income shall be determined by dividing the amount of such foreign income tax by the highest marginal tax rate applicable to such income in the relevant jurisdiction).

(B) Allocation of basis difference.—For purposes of subparagraph (A)(i)—

(i) In general.—The basis difference with respect to any relevant foreign asset shall be allocated to taxable years using the applicable cost recovery method under this chapter.

(ii) Special rule for disposition of assets.—Except as otherwise provided by the Secretary, in the case of the disposition of any relevant foreign asset—

(I) the basis difference allocated to the taxable year which includes the date of such disposition shall be the excess of the basis difference with respect to such asset over the aggregate basis difference with respect to such asset which has been allocated under clause (i) to all prior taxable years, and

(II) no basis difference with respect to such asset shall be allocated under clause (i) to any taxable year thereafter.

(C) Basis difference.—

(i) In general.—The term "basis difference" means, with respect to any relevant foreign asset, the excess of—

(I) the adjusted basis of such asset immediately after the covered asset acquisition, over

(II) the adjusted basis of such asset immediately before the covered asset acquisition.

(ii) Built-in loss assets.—In the case of a relevant foreign asset with respect to which the amount described in clause (i)(II) exceeds the amount described in clause (i)(I), such excess shall be taken into account under this subsection as a basis difference of a negative amount.

(iii) Special rule for section 338 elections.—In the case of a covered asset acquisition described in paragraph (2)(A), the covered asset acquisition shall be treated for purposes of this subparagraph as occurring at the close of the acquisition date (as defined in section 338(h)(2)).

(4) Relevant foreign assets.—For purposes of this section, the term "relevant foreign asset" means, with respect to any covered asset acquisition, any asset (including any goodwill, going concern value, or other intangible) with respect to such acquisition if income, deduction, gain, or loss attributable to such asset is taken into account in determining the foreign income tax referred to in paragraph (1).

(5) Foreign income tax.—For purposes of this section, the term "foreign income tax" means any income, war profits, or excess profits tax paid or accrued to any foreign country or to any possession of the United States.

(6) Taxes allowed as a deduction, etc.—Sections 275 and 78 shall not apply to any tax which is not allowable as a credit under subsection (a) by reason of this subsection.

(7) Regulations.—The Secretary may issue such regulations or other guidance as is necessary or appropriate to carry out the purposes of this subsection, including to exempt from the application of this subsection certain covered asset acquisitions, and relevant foreign assets with respect to which the basis difference is de minimis.

(n) Cross reference.—

(1) For deductions of income, war profits, and excess profits taxes paid to a foreign country or a possession of the United States, see sections 164 and 275.

(2) For right of each partner to make election under this section, see section 703(b).

(3) For right of estate or trust to the credit for taxes imposed by foreign countries and possessions of the United States under this section, see section 642(a).

(4) For reduction of credit for failure of a United States person to furnish certain information with respect to a foreign corporation or partnership controlled by him, see section 6038.

§ 903. Credit for taxes in lieu of income, etc., taxes

For purposes of this part and of sections 164(a) and 275(a), the term "income, war profits, and excess profits taxes" shall include a tax paid in lieu of a tax on income, war profits, or excess profits otherwise generally imposed by any foreign country or by any possession of the United States.

§ 904. Limitation on credit

(a) Limitation.—The total amount of the credit taken under section 901(a) shall not exceed the same proportion of the tax against which such credit is taken which the taxpayer's taxable income from sources without the United States (but not in excess of the taxpayer's entire taxable income) bears to his entire taxable income for the same taxable year.

(b) Taxable income for purpose of computing limitation.—

(1) Personal exemptions.—For purposes of subsection (a), the taxable income in the case of an individual, estate, or trust shall be computed without any deduction for personal exemptions under section 151 or 642(b).

(2) Capital gains.—For purposes of this section—

(A) In general.—Taxable income from sources outside the United States shall include gain from the sale or exchange of capital assets only to the extent of foreign source capital gain net income.

(B) Special rules where capital gain rate differential.—In the case of any taxable year for which there is a capital gain rate differential—

(i) in lieu of applying subparagraph (A), the taxable income from sources outside the United States shall include gain from the sale or exchange of capital assets only in an amount equal to foreign source capital gain net income reduced by the rate differential portion of foreign source net capital gain,

(ii) the entire taxable income shall include gain from the sale or exchange of capital assets only in an amount equal to capital gain net income reduced by the rate differential portion of net capital gain, and

(iii) for purposes of determining taxable income from sources outside the United States, any net capital loss (and any amount which is a short-term capital loss under section 1212(a)) from sources outside the United States to the extent taken into account in determining capital gain net income for the taxable year shall be reduced by an amount equal to the rate differential portion of the excess of net capital gain from sources within the United States over net capital gain.

(C) Coordination with capital gains rates.—The secretary may by regulations modify the application of this paragraph and paragraph (3) to the extent necessary to properly reflect any capital gain rate differential under section 1(h) and the computation of net capital gain.

(3) Definitions.—For purposes of this subsection—

(A) Foreign source capital gain net income.—The term "foreign source capital gain net income" means the lesser of—

(i) capital gain net income from sources without the United States, or

(ii) capital gain net income.

(B) Foreign source net capital gain.—The term "foreign source net capital gain" means the lesser of—

(i) net capital gain from sources without the United States, or

(ii) net capital gain.

(C) Section 1231 gains.—The term "gain from the sale or exchange of capital assets" includes any gain so treated under section 1231.

(D) Capital gain rate differential.—There is a capital gain rate differential for any year if subsection (h) of section 1 applies to such taxable year.

(E) Rate differential portion.—The rate differential portion of foreign source net capital gain, net capital gain, or the excess of net capital gain from sources within the United States over net capital gain, as the case may be, is the same proportion of such amount as—

(i) the excess of—

(I) the highest rate of tax set forth in subsection (a), (b), (c), (d), or (e) of section 1 (whichever applies), over

(II) the alternative rate of tax determined under section 1(h), bears to

(ii) that rate referred to in subclause (I).

(4) Treatment of dividends for which deduction is allowed under section 245a.—For purposes of subsection (a), in the case of a domestic corporation which is a United States shareholder with respect to a specified 10-percent owned foreign corporation, such shareholder's taxable income from sources without the United States (and entire taxable income) shall be determined without regard to—

(A) the foreign-source portion of any dividend received from such foreign corporation, and

(B) any deductions properly allocable or apportioned to—

(i) income (other than amounts includible under section 951(a)(1) or 951A(a)) with respect to stock of such specified 10-percent owned foreign corporation, or

(ii) such stock to the extent income with respect to such stock is other than amounts includible under section 951(a)(1) or 951A(a).

Any term which is used in section 245A and in this paragraph shall have the same meaning for purposes of this paragraph as when used in such section.

(5) Deductions treated as allocable to foreign source net CFC tested income.—Solely for purposes of the application of subsection (a) with respect to amounts described in subsection (d)(1)(A), the taxpayer's taxable income from sources without the United States shall be determined by allocating and apportioning—

(A) any deduction allowed under section 250(a)(1)(B) (and any deduction allowed under section 164(a)(3) for taxes imposed on amounts described in section 250(a)(1)(B)) to such income,

(B) no amount of interest expense or research and experimental expenditures to such income, and

(C) any other deduction to such income only if such deduction is directly allocable to such income.

Any amount or deduction which would (but for subparagraphs (B) and (C)) have been allocated or apportioned to such income shall only be allocated or apportioned to income which is from sources within the United States.

(6) Source rules for certain inventory produced in the United States and sold through foreign branches.—For purposes of this section, if a United States person maintains an office or other fixed place of business in a foreign country (determined under rules similar to the rules of section 864(c)(5)), the portion of income which—

(A) is from the sale or exchange outside the United States of inventory property (within the meaning of section 865(i)(1))—

(i) which is produced in the United States,

(ii) which is for use outside the United States, and

(iii) to which the third sentence of section 863(b) applies, and

(B) is attributable (determined under rules similar to the rules of section 864(c)(5)) to such office or other fixed place of business,

shall be treated as from sources without the United States, except that the amount so treated shall not exceed 50 percent of the income from the sale or exchange of such inventory property.

(c) Carryback and carryover of excess tax paid.—Any amount by which all taxes paid or accrued to foreign countries or possessions of the United States for any taxable year for which the taxpayer chooses to have the benefits of this subpart exceed the limitation under subsection (a) shall be deemed taxes paid or accrued to foreign countries or possessions of the United States in the first preceding taxable year and in any of the first 10 succeeding taxable years, in that order and to the extent not deemed taxes paid or accrued in a prior taxable year, in the amount by which the limitation under subsection (a) for such preceding or succeeding taxable year exceeds the sum of the taxes paid or accrued to foreign countries or possessions of the United States for such preceding or succeeding taxable year and the amount of the taxes for any taxable year earlier than the current taxable year which shall be deemed to have been paid or accrued in such preceding or subsequent taxable year (whether or not the taxpayer chooses to have the benefits of this subpart with respect to such earlier taxable year). Such amount deemed paid or accrued in any year may be availed of only as a tax credit and not as a deduction and only if the taxpayer for such year chooses to have the benefits of this subpart as to taxes paid or accrued for that year to foreign countries or possessions of the United States. This subsection shall not apply to taxes paid or accrued with respect to amounts described in subsection (d)(1)(A).

(d) Separate application of section with respect to certain categories of income.—

(1) In general.—The provisions of subsections (a), (b), and (c) and sections 902, 907, and 960 shall be applied separately with respect to—

(A) any amount includible in gross income under section 951A (other than passive category income),

(B) foreign branch income,

(C) passive category income, and

(D) general category income.

(2) Definitions and special rules.—For purposes of this subsection—

(A) Categories.—

(i) Passive category income.—The term "passive category income" means passive income and specified passive category income.

(ii) General category income.—The term "general category income" means income other than income described in paragraph (1)(A), foreign branch income, and passive category income.

(B) Passive income.—

(i) In general.—Except as otherwise provided in this subparagraph, the term "passive income" means any income received or accrued by any person which is of a kind which would be foreign personal holding company income (as defined in section 954(c)).

(ii) Certain amounts included.—Except as provided in clause (iii), subparagraph (E)(ii), or paragraph (3)(H), the term "passive income" includes any amount includible in gross income under section 1293 (relating to certain passive foreign investment companies).

(iii) Exceptions.—The term "passive income" shall not include—

(I) any export financing interest, and

(II) any high-taxed income.

(iv) Clarification of application of section 864(d)(6).—In determining whether any income is of a kind which would be foreign personal holding company income, the rules of section 864(d)(6) shall apply only in the case of income of a controlled foreign corporation.

(v) Specified passive category income.—The term "specified passive category income" means—

(I) dividends from a DISC or former DISC (as defined in section 992(a)) to the extent such dividends are treated as income from sources without the United States, and

(II) distributions from a former FSC (as defined in section 922) out of earnings and profits attributable to foreign trade income (within the meaning of section 923(b)) or interest or carrying charges (as defined in section 927(d)(1)) derived from a transaction which results in foreign trade income (as defined in section 923(b)).

Any reference in subclause (II) to section 922, 923, or 927 shall be treated as a reference to such section as in effect before its repeal by the FSC Repeal and Extraterritorial Income Exclusion Act of 2000.

(C) Treatment of financial services income and companies.—

(i) In general.—Financial services income shall be treated as general category income in the case of—

(I) a member of a financial services group, and

(II) any other person if such person is predominantly engaged in the active conduct of a banking, insurance, financing, or similar business.

(ii) Financial services group.—The term "financial services group" means any affiliated group (as defined in section 1504(a)without regard to paragraphs (2) and (3) of section 1504(b)) which is predominantly engaged in the active conduct of a banking, insurance, financing, or similar business. In determining whether such a group is so engaged, there shall be taken into account only the income of members of the group that are—

(I) United States corporations, or

(II) controlled foreign corporations in which such United States corporations own, directly or indirectly, at least 80 percent of the total voting power and value of the stock.

(iii) Pass-thru entities.—The Secretary shall by regulation specify for purposes of this subparagraph the treatment of financial services income received or accrued by partnerships and by other pass-thru entities which are not members of a financial services group.

(D) Financial services income.—

(i) In general.—Except as otherwise provided in this subparagraph, the term "financial services income" means any income which is received or accrued by any person predominantly engaged in the active conduct of a banking, insurance, financing, or similar business, and which is—

(I) described in clause (ii), or

(II) passive income (determined without regard to subparagraph (B)(iii)(II)).

(ii) General description of financial services income.—Income is described in this clause if such income is—

(I) derived in the active conduct of a banking, financing, or similar business,

(II) derived from the investment by an insurance company of its unearned premiums or reserves ordinary and necessary for the proper conduct of its insurance business, or

(III) of a kind which would be insurance income as defined in section 953(a) determined without regard to those provisions of paragraph (1)(A) of such section which limit insurance income to income from countries other than the country in which the corporation was created or organized.

(E) Noncontrolled section 902 corporation.—

(i) Noncontrolled 10-percent owned foreign corporation.—The term "noncontrolled 10-percent owned foreign corporation" means any foreign corporation which is—

(I) a specified 10-percent owned foreign corporation (as defined in section 245A(b)), or

(II) a passive foreign investment company (as defined in section 1297(a)) with respect to which the taxpayer meets the stock ownership requirements of section 902(a) (or, for purposes of applying paragraphs (3) and (4), the requirements of section 902(b)).

A controlled foreign corporation shall not be treated as a noncontrolled 10-percent owned foreign corporation with respect to any distribution out of its earnings and profits for periods during which it was a controlled foreign corporation. Any reference to section 902 in this clause shall be treated as a reference to such section as in effect before its repeal.

(ii) Treatment of inclusions under section 1293.—If any foreign corporation is a noncontrolled 10-percent owned foreign corporation with respect to the taxpayer, any inclusion under section 1293 with respect to such corporation shall be treated as a dividend from such corporation.

(F) High-taxed income.—The term "high-taxed income" means any income which (but for this subparagraph) would be passive income if the sum of—

(i) the foreign income taxes paid or accrued by the taxpayer with respect to such income, and

(ii) the foreign income taxes deemed paid by the taxpayer with respect to such income under section 902 or 960,

exceeds the highest rate of tax specified in section 1 or 11 (whichever applies) multiplied by the amount of such income (determined with regard to section 78). For purposes of the preceding sentence, the term "foreign income taxes" means any income, war profits, or excess profits tax imposed by any foreign country or possession of the United States.

(G) Export financing interest.—For purposes of this paragraph, the term "export financing interest" means any interest derived from financing the sale (or other disposition) for use or consumption outside the United States of any property—

(i) which is manufactured, produced, grown, or extracted in the United States by the taxpayer or a related person, and

(ii) not more than 50 percent of the fair market value of which is attributable to products imported into the United States.

For purposes of clause (ii), the fair market value of any property imported into the United States shall be its appraised value, as determined by the Secretary under section 402 of the Tariff Act of 1930 (19 U.S.C. 1401a) in connection with its importation.

(H) Treatment of income tax base differences.—

(i) In general.—In the case of taxable years beginning after December 31, 2006, tax imposed under the law of a foreign country or possession of the United States on an amount which does not constitute income under United States tax principles shall be treated as imposed on income described in paragraph (1)(D).

(ii) Special rule for years before 2007.—

(I) In general.—In the case of taxes paid or accrued in taxable years beginning after December 31, 2004, and before January 1, 2007, a taxpayer may elect to treat tax imposed under the law of a foreign country or possession of the United States on an amount which does not constitute income under United States tax principles as tax imposed on income described in subparagraph (C) or (I) of paragraph (1).

(II) Election irrevocable.—Any such election shall apply to the taxable year for which made and all subsequent taxable years described in subclause (I) unless revoked with the consent of the Secretary.

(I) Related person.—For purposes of this paragraph, the term "related person" has the meaning given such term by section 954(d)(3), except that such section shall be applied by substituting "the person with respect to whom the determination is being made" for "controlled foreign corporation" each place it appears.

(J) Foreign branch income.—

(i) In general.—The term "foreign branch income" means the business profits of such United States person which are attributable to 1 or more qualified business units (as defined in section 989(a)) in 1 or more foreign countries. For purposes of the preceding sentence, the amount of business profits attributable to a qualified business unit shall be determined under rules established by the Secretary.

(ii) Exception.—Such term shall not include any income which is passive category income.

(K) Transitional rules for 2007 changes.—For purposes of paragraph (1)—

(i) taxes carried from any taxable year beginning before January 1, 2007, to any taxable year beginning on or after such date, with respect to any item of income, shall be treated as described in the subparagraph of paragraph (1) in which such income would be described were such taxes paid or accrued in a taxable year beginning on or after such date, and

(ii) the Secretary may by regulations provide for the allocation of any carryback of taxes with respect to income from a taxable year beginning on or after January 1, 2007, to a taxable year beginning before such date for purposes of allocating such income among the separate categories in effect for the taxable year to which carried.

(3) Look-thru in case of controlled foreign corporations.—

(A) In general.—Except as otherwise provided in this paragraph, dividends, interest, rents, and royalties received or accrued by the taxpayer from a controlled foreign corporation in which the taxpayer is a United States shareholder shall not be treated as passive category income.

(B) Subpart F inclusions.—Any amount included in gross income under section 951(a)(1)(A) shall be treated as passive category income to the extent the amount so included is attributable to passive category income.

(C) Interest, rents, and royalties.—Any interest, rent, or royalty which is received or accrued from a controlled foreign corporation in which the taxpayer is a United States shareholder shall be treated as passive category income to the extent it is properly allocable (under regulations prescribed by the Secretary) to passive category income of the controlled foreign corporation.

(D) Dividends.—Any dividend paid out of the earnings and profits of any controlled foreign corporation in which the taxpayer is a United States shareholder shall be treated as passive category income in proportion to the ratio of—

(i) the portion of the earnings and profits attributable to passive category income, to

(ii) the total amount of earnings and profits.

(E) Look-thru applies only where subpart F applies.—If a controlled foreign corporation meets the requirements of section 954(b)(3)(A) (relating to de minimis rule) for any taxable year, for purposes of this paragraph, none of its foreign base company income (as defined in section 954(a) without regard to section 954(b)(5)) and none of its gross insurance income (as defined in section 954(b)(3)(C)) for such taxable year shall be treated as passive category income, except that this sentence shall not apply to any income which (without regard to this sentence) would be treated as financial services income. Solely for purposes of applying subparagraph (D), passive income of a controlled foreign corporation shall not be treated as passive category income if the requirements of section 954(b)(4) are met with respect to such income.

(F) Coordination with high-taxed income provisions.—

(i) In determining whether any income of a controlled foreign corporation is passive category income, subclause (II) of paragraph (2)(B)(iii) shall not apply.

(ii) Any income of the taxpayer which is treated as passive category income under this paragraph shall be so treated notwithstanding any provision of paragraph (2); except that the determination of whether any amount is high-taxed income shall be made after the application of this paragraph.

(G) Dividend.—For purposes of this paragraph, the term "dividend" includes any amount included in gross income in section 951(a)(1)(B). Any amount included in gross income under section 78 to the extent attributable to amounts included in gross income in section 951(a)(1)(A) shall not be treated as a dividend but shall be treated as included in gross income under section 951(a)(1)(A).

(H) Look-thru applies to passive foreign investment company inclusion.—If—

(i) a passive foreign investment company is a controlled foreign corporation, and

(ii) the taxpayer is a United States shareholder in such controlled foreign corporation, any amount included in gross income under section 1293 shall be treated as income in a separate category to the extent such amount is attributable to income in such category.

(4) Look-thru applies to dividends from noncontrolled 10-percent owned foreign corporations.—

(A) In general.—For purposes of this subsection, any dividend from a noncontrolled 10-percent owned foreign corporation with respect to the taxpayer shall be treated as income described in a subparagraph of paragraph (1) in proportion to the ratio of—

(i) the portion of earnings and profits attributable to income described in such subparagraph, to

(ii) the total amount of earnings and profits.

(B) Earnings and profits of controlled foreign corporations.—In the case of any distribution from a controlled foreign corporation to a United States shareholder, rules similar to the rules of subparagraph (A) shall apply in determining the extent to which earnings and profits of the controlled foreign corporation which are attributable to dividends received from a noncontrolled 10-percent owned foreign corporation may be treated as income in a separate category.

(C) Special rules.—For purposes of this paragraph—

(i) Earnings and profits.—

(I) In general.—The rules of section 316 shall apply.

(II) Regulations.—The Secretary may prescribe regulations regarding the treatment of distributions out of earnings and profits for periods before the taxpayer's acquisition of the stock to which the distributions relate.

(ii) Inadequate substantiation.—If the Secretary determines that the proper subparagraph of paragraph (1) in which a dividend is described has not been substantiated, such dividend shall be treated as income described in paragraph (1)(C).

(iii) Coordination with high-taxed income provisions.—Rules similar to the rules of paragraph (3)(F) shall apply for purposes of this paragraph.

(iv) Look-thru with respect to carryover of credit.—Rules similar to subparagraph (A) also shall apply to any carryforward under subsection (c) from a taxable year beginning before January 1, 2003, of tax allocable to a dividend from a noncontrolled 10-percent owned foreign corporation with respect to the taxpayer. The Secretary may by regulations provide for the allocation of any carryback of tax allocable to a dividend from a noncontrolled 10-percent owned foreign corporation from a taxable year beginning on or after January 1, 2003, to a taxable year beginning before such date for purposes of allocating such dividend among the separate categories in effect for the taxable year to which carried.

(5) Controlled foreign corporation; United States shareholder.—For purposes of this subsection—

(A) Controlled foreign corporation.—The term "controlled foreign corporation" has the meaning given such term by section 957 (taking into account section 953(c)).

(B) United States shareholder.—The term "United States shareholder" has the meaning given such term by section 951(b) (taking into account section 953(c)).

(6) Separate application to items resourced under treaties.—

(A) In general.—If—

(i) without regard to any treaty obligation of the United States, any item of income would be treated as derived from sources within the United States,

(ii) under a treaty obligation of the United States, such item would be treated as arising from sources outside the United States, and

(iii) the taxpayer chooses the benefits of such treaty obligation, subsections (a), (b), and (c) of this section and sections 907 and 960 shall be applied separately with respect to each such item.

(B) Coordination with other provisions.—This paragraph shall not apply to any item of income to which subsection (h)(10) or section 865(h) applies.

(C) Regulations.—The Secretary may issue such regulations or other guidance as is necessary or appropriate to carry out the purposes of this paragraph, including regulations or other guidance which provides that related items of income may be aggregated for purposes of this paragraph.

(7) Regulations.—The Secretary shall prescribe such regulations as may be necessary or appropriate for the purposes of this subsection, including regulations—

(A) for the application of paragraph (3) and subsection (f)(5) in the case of income paid (or loans made) through 1 or more entities or between 2 or more chains of entities,

(B) preventing the manipulation of the character of income the effect of which is to avoid the purposes of this subsection, and

(C) providing that rules similar to the rules of paragraph (3)(C) shall apply to interest, rents, and royalties received or accrued from entities which would be controlled foreign corporations if they were foreign corporations.

* * *

(f) Recapture of overall foreign loss.—

(1) General rule.—For purposes of this subpart, in the case of any taxpayer who sustains an overall foreign loss for any taxable year, that portion of the taxpayer's taxable income from sources without the United States for each succeeding taxable year which is equal to the lesser of—

(A) the amount of such loss (to the extent not used under this paragraph in prior taxable years), or

(B) 50 percent (or such larger percent as the taxpayer may choose) of the taxpayer's taxable income from sources without the United States for such succeeding taxable year,

shall be treated as income from sources within the United States (and not as income from sources without the United States).

(2) Overall foreign loss defined.—For purposes of this subsection, the term "overall foreign loss" means the amount by which the gross income for the taxable year from sources without the United States (whether or not the taxpayer chooses the benefits of this subpart for such taxable year) for such year is exceeded by the sum of the deductions properly apportioned or allocated thereto, except that there shall not be taken into account—

(A) any net operating loss deduction allowable for such year under section 172(a), and

(B) any—

(i) foreign expropriation loss for such year, as defined in section 172(h) (as in effect on the day before the date of the enactment of the Revenue Reconciliation Act of 1990), or

(ii) loss for such year which arises from fire, storm, shipwreck, or other casualty, or from theft,

to the extent such loss is not compensated for by insurance or otherwise.

(3) Dispositions.—

(A) In general.—For purposes of this chapter, if property which has been used predominantly without the United States in a trade or business is disposed of during any taxable year—

(i) the taxpayer, notwithstanding any other provision of this chapter (other than paragraph (1)), shall be deemed to have received and recognized taxable income from sources without the United States in the taxable year of the disposition, by reason of such disposition, in an amount equal to the lesser of the excess of the fair market value of such property over the taxpayer's adjusted basis in such property or the remaining amount of the overall foreign losses which were not used under paragraph (1) for such taxable year or any prior taxable year, and

(ii) paragraph (1) shall be applied with respect to such income by substituting "100 percent" for "50 percent".

In determining for purposes of this subparagraph whether the predominant use of any property has been without the United States, there shall be taken into account use during the 3-year period ending on the date of the disposition (or, if shorter, the period during which the property has been used in the trade or business).

(B) Disposition defined and special rules.—

(i) For purposes of this subsection, the term "disposition" includes a sale, exchange, distribution, or gift of property whether or not gain or loss is recognized on the transfer.

(ii) Any taxable income recognized solely by reason of subparagraph (A) shall have the same characterization it would have had if the taxpayer had sold or exchanged the property.

(iii) The Secretary shall prescribe such regulations as he may deem necessary to provide for adjustments to the basis of property to reflect taxable income recognized solely by reason of subparagraph (A).

(C) Exceptions.—Notwithstanding subparagraph (B), the term "disposition" does not include—

(i) a disposition of property which is not a material factor in the realization of income by the taxpayer, or

(ii) a disposition of property to a domestic corporation in a distribution or transfer described in section 381(a).

(D) Application to certain dispositions of stock in controlled foreign corporation.—

(i) In general.—This paragraph shall apply to an applicable disposition in the same manner as if it were a disposition of property described in subparagraph (A), except that the exception contained in subparagraph (C)(i) shall not apply.

(ii) Applicable disposition.—For purposes of clause (i), the term "applicable disposition" means any disposition of any share of stock in a controlled foreign corporation in a transaction or series of transactions if, immediately before such transaction or series of transactions, the taxpayer owned more than 50 percent (by vote or value) of the stock of the controlled foreign corporation. Such term shall not include a disposition described in clause (iii) or (iv), except that clause (i) shall apply to any gain recognized on any such disposition.

(iii) Exception for certain exchanges where ownership percentage retained.—A disposition shall not be treated as an applicable disposition under clause (ii) if it is part of a transaction or series of transactions—

(I) to which section 351 or 721 applies, or under which the transferor receives stock in a foreign corporation in exchange for the stock in the controlled foreign corporation and the stock received is exchanged basis property (as defined in section 7701(a)(44)), and

(II) immediately after which, the transferor owns (by vote or value) at least the same percentage of stock in the controlled foreign corporation (or, if the controlled foreign corporation is not in existence after such transaction or series of transactions, in another foreign corporation stock in which was received by the transferor in exchange for stock in the controlled foreign corporation) as the percentage of stock in the controlled foreign corporation which the taxpayer owned immediately before such transaction or series of transactions.

(iv) Exception for certain asset acquisitions.—A disposition shall not be treated as an applicable disposition under clause (ii) if it is part of a transaction or series of transactions in which the taxpayer (or any member of an affiliated group of corporations filing a consolidated return under section 1501 which includes the taxpayer) acquires the assets of a controlled foreign corporation in exchange for the shares of the controlled foreign corporation in a liquidation described in section 332 or a reorganization described in section 368(a)(1).

(v) Controlled foreign corporation.—For purposes of this subparagraph, the term "controlled foreign corporation" has the meaning given such term by section 957.

(vi) Stock ownership.—For purposes of this subparagraph, ownership of stock shall be determined under the rules of subsections (a) and (b) of section 958.

(4) Accumulation distributions of foreign trust.—For purposes of this chapter, in the case of amounts of income from sources without the United States which are treated under section 666 (without regard to subsections (b) and (c) thereof if the taxpayer chose to take a deduction with respect to the amounts described in such subsections under section 667(d)(1)(B)) as having been distributed by a foreign trust in a preceding taxable year, that portion of such amounts equal to the amount of any overall foreign loss sustained by the beneficiary in a year prior to the taxable year of the beneficiary in which such distribution is received from the trust shall be treated as income from sources within the United States (and not income from sources without the United States) to the extent that such loss was not used under this subsection in prior taxable years, or in the current taxable year, against other income of the beneficiary.

(5) Treatment of separate limitation losses.—

(A) In general.—The amount of the separate limitation losses for any taxable year shall reduce income from sources within the United States for such taxable year only to the extent the aggregate amount of such losses exceeds the aggregate amount of the separate limitation incomes for such taxable year.

(B) Allocation of losses.—The separate limitation losses for any taxable year (to the extent such losses do not exceed the separate limitation incomes for such year) shall be allocated among (and operate to reduce) such incomes on a proportionate basis.

(C) Recharacterization of subsequent income.—If—

(i) a separate limitation loss from any income category (hereinafter in this subparagraph referred to as "the loss category") was allocated to income from any other category under subparagraph (B), and

(ii) the loss category has income for a subsequent taxable year, such income (to the extent it does not exceed the aggregate separate limitation losses from the loss category not previously recharacterized under this subparagraph) shall be recharacterized as income from such other category in proportion to the prior reductions under subparagraph (B) in such other category not previously taken into account under this subparagraph. Nothing in the preceding sentence shall be construed as recharacterizing any tax.

(D) Special rules for losses from sources in the United States.—Any loss from sources in the United States for any taxable year (to the extent such loss does not exceed the separate limitation incomes from such year) shall be allocated among (and operate to reduce) such incomes on a proportionate basis. This subparagraph shall be applied after subparagraph (B).

(E) Definitions.—For purposes of this paragraph—

(i) Income category.—The term "income category" means each separate category of income described in subsection (d)(1).

(ii) Separate limitation income.—The term "separate limitation income" means, with respect to any income category, the taxable income from sources outside the United States, separately computed for such category.

(iii) Separate limitation loss.—The term "separate limitation loss" means, with respect to any income category, the loss from such category determined under the principles of section 907(c)(4)(B).

(F) Dispositions.—If any separate limitation laws for any taxable year is allocated against any separate limitation income for such taxable year, except to the extent provided in regulations, rules similar to the rules of paragraph (3) shall apply to any disposition of property if gain from such disposition would be in the income category with respect to which there was such separate limitation loss.

(g) Recharacterization of overall domestic loss.—

(1) General rule.—For purposes of this subpart and section 936, in the case of any taxpayer who sustains an overall domestic loss for any taxable year beginning after December 31, 2006, that portion of the taxpayer's taxable income from sources within the United States for each succeeding taxable year which is equal to the lesser of—

(A) the amount of such loss (to the extent not used under this paragraph in prior taxable years), or

(B) 50 percent of the taxpayer's taxable income from sources within the United States for such succeeding taxable year,

shall be treated as income from sources without the United States (and not as income from sources within the United States).

(2) Overall domestic loss.—For purposes of this subsection—

(A) In general.—The term "overall domestic loss" means—

(i) with respect to any qualified taxable year, the domestic loss for such taxable year to the extent such loss offsets taxable income from sources without the United States for the taxable year or for any preceding qualified taxable year by reason of a carryback, and

(ii) with respect to any other taxable year, the domestic loss for such taxable year to the extent such loss offsets taxable income from sources without the United States for any preceding qualified taxable year by reason of a carryback.

(B) Domestic loss.—For purposes of subparagraph (A), the term "domestic loss" means the amount by which the gross income for the taxable year from sources within the United States is exceeded by the sum of the deductions properly apportioned or allocated thereto (determined without regard to any carryback from a subsequent taxable year).

(C) Qualified taxable year.—For purposes of subparagraph (A), the term "qualified taxable year" means any taxable year for which the taxpayer chose the benefits of this subpart.

(3) Characterization of subsequent income.—

(A) In general.—Any income from sources within the United States that is treated as income from sources without the United States under paragraph (1) shall be allocated among and increase the income categories in proportion to the loss from sources within the United States previously allocated to those income categories.

(B) Income category.—For purposes of this paragraph, the term 'income category' has the meaning given such term by subsection (f)(5)(E)(i).

(4) Coordination with subsection (f).—The Secretary shall prescribe such regulations as may be necessary to coordinate the provisions of this subsection with the provisions of subsection (f).

(5) Election to increase percentage of taxable income treated as foreign source.—

(A) In general.—If any pre-2018 unused overall domestic loss is taken into account under paragraph (1) for any applicable taxable year, the taxpayer may elect to have such paragraph applied to such loss by substituting a percentage greater than 50 percent (but not greater than 100 percent) for 50 percent in subparagraph (B) thereof.

(B) Pre-2018 unused overall domestic loss.—For purposes of this paragraph, the term "pre-2018 unused overall domestic loss" means any overall domestic loss which—

(i) arises in a qualified taxable year beginning before January 1, 2018, and

(ii) has not been used under paragraph (1) for any taxable year beginning before such date.

(C) Applicable taxable year.—For purposes of this paragraph, the term "applicable taxable year" means any taxable year of the taxpayer beginning after December 31, 2017, and before January 1, 2028.

(h) Source rules in case of United States-owned foreign corporations.—

(1) In general.—The following amounts which are derived from a United States-owned foreign corporation and which would be treated as derived from sources outside the United States without regard to this subsection shall, for purposes of this section, be treated as derived from sources within the United States to the extent provided in this subsection:

(A) Any amount included in gross income under—

(i) section 951(a) (relating to amounts included in gross income of United States shareholders), or

(ii) section 1293 (relating to current taxation of income from qualified funds).

(B) Interest.

(C) Dividends.

(2) Subpart F and passive foreign investment company inclusions.—Any amount described in subparagraph (A) of paragraph (1) shall be treated as derived from sources within the United States to the extent such amount is attributable to income of the United States-owned foreign corporation from sources within the United States.

(3) Certain interest allocable to United States source income.—Any interest which—

(A) is paid or accrued by a United States-owned foreign corporation during any taxable year,

(B) is paid or accrued to a United States shareholder (as defined in section 951(b)) or a related person (within the meaning of section 267(b)) to such a shareholder, and

(C) is properly allocable (under regulations prescribed by the Secretary) to income of such foreign corporation for the taxable year from sources within the United States,

shall be treated as derived from sources within the United States.

(4) Dividends.—

(A) In general.—The United States source ratio of any dividend paid or accrued by a United States-owned foreign corporation shall be treated as derived from sources within the United States.

(B) United States source ratio.—For purposes of subparagraph (A), the term "United States source ratio" means, with respect to any dividend paid out of the earnings and profits for any taxable year, a fraction—

(i) the numerator of which is the portion of the earnings and profits for such taxable year from sources within the United States, and

(ii) the denominator of which is the total amount of earnings and profits for such taxable year.

(5) Exception where United States-owned foreign corporation has small amount of United States source income.—Paragraph (3) shall not apply to interest paid or accrued during any taxable year (and paragraph (4) shall not apply to any dividends paid out of the earnings and profits for such taxable year) if—

(A) the United States-owned foreign corporation has earnings and profits for such taxable year, and

(B) less than 10 percent of such earnings and profits is attributable to sources within the United States.

For purposes of the preceding sentence, earnings and profits shall be determined without any reduction for interest described in paragraph (3) (determined without regard to subparagraph (C) thereof).

(6) United States-owned foreign corporation.—For purposes of this subsection, the term "United States-owned foreign corporation" means any foreign corporation if 50 percent or more of—

(A) the total combined voting power of all classes of stock of such corporation entitled to vote, or

(B) the total value of the stock of such corporation,

is held directly (or indirectly through applying paragraphs (2) and (3) of section 958(a) and paragraph (4) of section 318(a)) by United States persons (as defined in section 7701(a)(30)).

(7) Dividend.—For purposes of this subsection, the term "dividend" includes any gain treated as a dividend under section 1248.

(8) Coordination with subsection (f).—This subsection shall be applied before subsection (f).

(9) Treatment of certain domestic corporations.—For purposes of this subsection—

(A) in the case of interest treated as not from sources within the United States under section 861(a)(1)(A), the corporation paying such interest shall be treated as a United States-owned foreign corporation, and

(B) in the case of any dividend treated as not from sources within the United States under section 861(a)(2)(A), the corporation paying such dividend shall be treated as a United States-owned foreign corporation.

(10) Coordination with treaties.—

(A) In general.—If—

(i) any amount derived from a United States-owned foreign corporation would be treated as derived from sources within the United States under this subsection by reason of an item of income of such United States-owned foreign corporation,

(ii) under a treaty obligation of the United States (applied without regard to this subsection and by treating any amount included in gross income under section 951(a)(1) as a dividend), such amount would be treated as arising from sources outside the United States, and

(iii) the taxpayer chooses the benefits of this paragraph,

this subsection shall not apply to such amount to the extent attributable to such item of income (but subsections (a), (b), and (c) of this section and sections 907 and 960 shall be applied separately with respect to such amount to the extent so attributable).

(B) Special rule.—Amounts included in gross income under section 951(a)(1) shall be treated as a dividend under subparagraph (A)(ii) only if dividends paid by each corporation (the stock in which is taken into account in determining whether the shareholder is a United States shareholder in the United States-owned foreign corporation), if paid to the United States shareholder, would be treated under a treaty obligation of the United States as arising from sources outside the United States (applied without regard to this subsection).

(11) Regulations.—The Secretary shall prescribe such regulations as may be necessary or appropriate for purposes of this subsection, including—

(A) regulations for the application of this subsection in the case of interest or dividend payments through 1 or more entities, and

(B) regulations providing that this subsection shall apply to interest paid or accrued to any person (whether or not a United States shareholder).

(i) Limitation on use of deconsolidation to avoid foreign tax credit limitations.—If 2 or more domestic corporations would be members of the same affiliated group if—

(1) section 1504(b) were applied without regard to the exceptions contained therein, and

(2) the constructive ownership rules of section 1563(e) applied for purposes of section 1504(a),

the Secretary may by regulations provide for resourcing the income of any of such corporations or for modifications to the consolidated return regulations to the extent that such resourcing or modifications are necessary to prevent the avoidance of the provisions of this subpart.

(j) Certain individuals exempt.—

(1) In general.—In the case of an individual to whom this subsection applies for any taxable year—

(A) the limitation of subsection (a) shall not apply,

(B) no taxes paid or accrued by the individual during such taxable year may be deemed paid or accrued under subsection (c) in any other taxable year, and

(C) no taxes paid or accrued by the individual during any other taxable year may be deemed paid or accrued under subsection (c) in such taxable year.

(2) Individuals to whom subsection applies.—This subsection shall apply to an individual for any taxable year if—

(A) the entire amount of such individual's gross income for the taxable year from sources without the United States consists of qualified passive income,

(B) the amount of the creditable foreign taxes paid or accrued by the individual during the taxable year does not exceed $300 ($600 in the case of a joint return), and

(C) such individual elects to have this subsection apply for the taxable year.

(3) Definitions.—For purposes of this subsection—

(A) Qualified passive income.—The term "qualified passive income" means any item of gross income if—

(i) such item of income is passive income (as defined in subsection (d)(2)(A) without regard to clause (iii) thereof), and

(ii) such item of income is shown on a payee statement furnished to the individual.

(B) Creditable foreign taxes.—The term "creditable foreign taxes" means any taxes for which a credit is allowable under section 901; except that such term shall not include any tax unless such tax is shown on a payee statement furnished to such individual.

(C) Payee statement.—The term "payee statement" has the meaning given to such term by section 6724(d)(2).

(D) Estates and trusts not eligible.—This subsection shall not apply to any estate or trust.

(k) Cross references.—For increase of limitation under subsection (a) for taxes paid with respect to amounts received which were included in the gross income of the taxpayer for a prior taxable year as a United States shareholder with respect to a controlled foreign corporation, see section 960(c).

§ 905. Applicable rules

(a) Year in which credit taken.—The credits provided in this subpart may, at the option of the taxpayer and irrespective of the method of accounting employed in keeping his books, be taken in the year in which the taxes of the foreign country or the possession of the United States accrued, subject, however, to the conditions prescribed in subsection (c). If the taxpayer elects to take such credits in the year in which the taxes of the foreign country or the possession of the United States accrued, the credits for all subsequent years shall be taken on the same basis, and no portion of any such taxes shall be allowed as a deduction in the same or any succeeding year.

(b) Proof of credits.—The credits provided in this subpart shall be allowed only if the taxpayer establishes to the satisfaction of the Secretary—

(1) the total amount of income derived from sources without the United States, determined as provided in part I,

(2) the amount of income derived from each country, the tax paid or accrued to which is claimed as a credit under this subpart, such amount to be determined under regulations prescribed by the Secretary, and

(3) all other information necessary for the verification and computation of such credits.

(c) Adjustments to accrued taxes.—

(1) In general.—If—

(A) accrued taxes when paid differ from the amounts claimed as credits by the taxpayer,

(B) accrued taxes are not paid before the date 2 years after the close of the taxable year to which such taxes relate, or

(C) any tax paid is refunded in whole or in part, the taxpayer shall notify the Secretary, who shall redetermine the amount of the tax for the year or years affected.

(2) Special rule for taxes not paid within 2 years.—

(A) In general.—Except as provided in subparagraph (B), in making the redetermination under paragraph (1), no credit shall be allowed for accrued taxes not paid before the date referred to in subparagraph (B) of paragraph (1).

(B) Taxes subsequently paid.—Any such taxes if subsequently paid—

(i) shall be taken into account for the taxable year to which such taxes relate, and

(ii) shall be translated as provided in section 986(a)(2)(A).

(3) Adjustments.—The amount of tax (if any) due on any redetermination under paragraph (1) shall be paid by the taxpayer on notice and demand by the Secretary, and the amount of tax overpaid (if any) shall be credited or refunded to the taxpayer in accordance with subchapter B of chapter 66 (section 6511 et seq.).

(4) Bond requirements.—In the case of any tax accrued but not paid, the Secretary, as a condition precedent to the allowance of the credit provided in this subpart, may require the taxpayer to give a bond, with sureties satisfactory to and approved by the Secretary, in such sum as the Secretary may require, conditioned on the payment by the taxpayer of any amount of tax found due on any such redetermination. Any such bond shall contain such further conditions as the Secretary may require.

(5) Other special rules.—In any redetermination under paragraph (1) by the Secretary of the amount of tax due from the taxpayer for the year or years affected by a refund, the amount of the taxes refunded for which credit has been allowed under this section shall be reduced by the amount of any tax described in section 901 imposed by the foreign country or possession of the United States with respect to such refund; but no credit under this subpart, or deduction under section 164, shall be allowed for any taxable year with respect to any such tax imposed on the refund. No interest shall be assessed or collected on any amount of tax due on any redetermination by the Secretary, resulting from a refund to the taxpayer, for any period before the receipt of such refund, except to the extent interest was paid by the foreign country or possession of the United States on such refund for such period.

§ 906. Nonresident alien individuals and foreign corporations

(a) Allowance of credit.—A nonresident alien individual or a foreign corporation engaged in trade or business within the United States during the taxable year shall be allowed a credit under section 901 for the amount of any income, war profits, and excess profits taxes paid or accrued during the taxable year to any foreign country or possession of the United States with respect to income effectively connected with the conduct of a trade or business within the United States.

(b) Special rules.—

(1) For purposes of subsection (a) and for purposes of determining the deductions allowable under sections 873(a) and 882(c), in determining the amount of any tax paid or accrued to any foreign country or possession there shall not be taken into account any amount of tax to the extent the tax so paid or accrued is imposed with respect to income from sources within the United States which would not be taxed by such foreign country or possession but for the fact that—

(A) in the case of a nonresident alien individual, such individual is a citizen or resident of such foreign country or possession, or

(B) in the case of a foreign corporation, such corporation was created or organized under the law of such foreign country or possession or is domiciled for tax purposes in such country or possession.

(2) For purposes of subsection (a), in applying section 904 the taxpayer's taxable income shall be treated as consisting only of the taxable income effectively connected with the taxpayer's conduct of a trade or business within the United States.

(3) The credit allowed pursuant to subsection (a) shall not be allowed against any tax imposed by section 871(a) (relating to income of nonresident alien individual not connected with United States business) or 881 (relating to income of foreign corporations not connected with United States business).

[**(4)**, **(5)** Repealed.]

(6) No credit shall be allowed under this section against the tax imposed by section 884.

§ 907. Special rules in case of foreign oil and gas income

(a) Reduction in amount allowed as foreign tax under section 901.—In applying section 901, the amount of any oil and gas taxes paid or accrued (or deemed to have been paid) during the taxable year which would (but for this subsection) be taken into account for purposes of section 901 shall be reduced by the amount (if any) by which the amount of such taxes exceeds the product of—

(1) the amount of the combined foreign oil and gas extraction income for the taxable year,

(2) multiplied by—

(A) in the case of a corporation, the percentage which is equal to the highest rate of tax specified under section 11(b), or

(B) in the case of an individual, a fraction the numerator of which is the tax against which the credit under section 901(a) is taken and the denominator of which is the taxpayer's entire taxable income.

(b) Combined foreign oil and gas income; foreign oil and gas taxes.—For purposes of this section—

(1) Combined foreign oil and gas income.—The term "combined foreign oil and gas income" means, with respect to any taxable year, the sum of—

(A) foreign oil and gas extraction income, and

(B) foreign oil related income.

(2) Foreign oil and gas taxes.—The term "foreign oil and gas taxes" means, with respect to any taxable year, the sum of—

(A) oil and gas extraction taxes, and

(B) any income, war profits, and excess profits taxes paid or accrued (or deemed to have been paid or accrued under section 960) during the taxable year with respect to foreign oil related income (determined without regard to subsection (c)(4)) or loss which would be taken into account for purposes of section 901 without regard to this section.

(c) Foreign income definitions and special rules.—For purposes of this section—

(1) Foreign oil and gas extraction income.—The term "foreign oil and gas extraction income" means the taxable income derived from sources without the United States and its possessions from—

(A) the extraction (by the taxpayer or any other person) of minerals from oil or gas wells, or

(B) the sale or exchange of assets used by the taxpayer in the trade or business described in subparagraph (A).

Such term does not include any dividend or interest income which is passive income (as defined in section 904(d)(2)(A)).

(2) Foreign oil related income.—The term "foreign oil related income" means the taxable income derived from sources outside the United States and its possessions from—

(A) the processing of minerals extracted (by the taxpayer or by any other person) from oil or gas wells into their primary products,

(B) the transportation of such minerals or primary products,

(C) the distribution or sale of such minerals or primary products,

(D) the disposition of assets used by the taxpayer in the trade or business described in subparagraph (A), (B), or (C), or

(E) the performance of any other related service.

Such term does not include any dividend or interest income which is passive income (as defined in section 904(d)(2)(A)).

(3) Dividends, interest, partnership distribution, etc.—The term "foreign oil and gas extraction income" and the term "foreign oil related income" include—

(A) interest, to the extent the category of income is determined under section 904(d)(3),

(B) amounts with respect to which taxes are deemed paid under section 960, and

(C) the taxpayer's distributive share of the income of partnerships,

to the extent such dividends, interest, amounts, or distributive share is attributable to foreign oil and gas extraction income, or to foreign oil related income, as the case may be; except that interest described in subparagraph (A) shall not be taken into account in computing foreign oil and gas extraction income but shall be taken into account in computing foreign oil-related income.

(4) Recapture of foreign oil and gas losses by recharacterizing later combined foreign oil and gas income.—

(A) In general.—The combined foreign oil and gas income of a taxpayer for a taxable year (determined without regard to this paragraph) shall be reduced—

(i) first by the amount determined under subparagraph (B), and

(ii) then by the amount determined under subparagraph (C).

The aggregate amount of such reductions shall be treated as income (from sources without the United States) which is not combined foreign oil and gas income.

(B) Reduction for pre-2009 foreign oil extraction losses.—The reduction under this paragraph shall be equal to the lesser of—

(i) the foreign oil and gas extraction income of the taxpayer for the taxable year (determined without regard to this paragraph), or

(ii) the excess of—

(I) the aggregate amount of foreign oil extraction losses for preceding taxable years beginning after December 31, 1982, and before January 1, 2009, over

(II) so much of such aggregate amount as was recharacterized under this paragraph (as in effect before and after the date of the enactment of the Energy Improvement and Extension Act of 2008) for preceding taxable years beginning after December 31, 1982.

(C) Reduction for post-2008 foreign oil and gas losses.—The reduction under this paragraph shall be equal to the lesser of—

(i) the combined foreign oil and gas income of the taxpayer for the taxable year (determined without regard to this paragraph), reduced by an amount equal to the reduction under subparagraph (A) for the taxable year, or

(ii) the excess of—

(I) the aggregate amount of foreign oil and gas losses for preceding taxable years beginning after December 31, 2008, over

(II) so much of such aggregate amount as was recharacterized under this paragraph for preceding taxable years beginning after December 31, 2008.

(D) Foreign oil and gas loss defined.—

(i) In general.—For purposes of this paragraph, the term "foreign oil and gas loss" means the amount by which

(I) the gross income for the taxable year from sources without the United States and its possessions (whether or not the taxpayer chooses the benefits of this subpart for such taxable year) taken into account in determining the combined foreign oil and gas income for such year, is exceeded by

(II) the sum of the deductions properly apportioned or allocated thereto.

(ii) Net operating loss deduction not taken into account.—For purposes of clause (i), the net operating loss deduction allowable for the taxable year under section 172(a) shall not be taken into account.

(iii) Expropriation and casualty losses not taken into account.—For purposes of clause (i), there shall not be taken into account—

(I) any foreign expropriation loss (as defined in section 172(h) (as in effect on the day before the date of the enactment of the Revenue Reconciliation Act of 1990)) for the taxable year, or

(II) any loss for the taxable year which arises from fire, storm, shipwreck, or other casualty, or from theft,

to the extent such loss is not compensated for by insurance or otherwise.

(iv) Foreign oil extraction loss.—For purposes of subparagraph (B)(ii)(I), foreign oil extraction losses shall be determined under this paragraph as in effect on the day before the date of the enactment of the Energy Improvement and Extension Act of 2008.

(5) Oil and gas extraction taxes.—The term "oil and gas extraction taxes" means any income, war profits, and excess profits tax paid or accrued (or deemed to have been paid under section 902 or 960) during the taxable year with respect to foreign oil and gas extraction income (determined without regard to paragraph (4)) or loss which would be taken into account for purposes of section 901 without regard to this section.

(d) Disregard of certain posted prices, etc.—For purposes of this chapter, in determining the amount of taxable income in the case of foreign oil and gas extraction income, if the oil or gas is disposed of, or is acquired other than from the government of a foreign country, at a posted price (or other pricing arrangement) which differs from the fair market value for such oil or gas, such fair market value shall be used in lieu of such posted price (or other pricing arrangement).

* * *

(f) Carryback and carryover of disallowed credits.—

(1) In general.—If the amount of the foreign oil and gas taxes paid or accrued during any taxable year exceeds the limitation provided by subsection (a) for such taxable year (hereinafter in this subsection referred to as the "unused credit year"), such excess shall be deemed to be foreign oil and gas taxes paid or accrued in the first preceding taxable year and in any of the first 10 succeeding taxable years, in that order and to the extent not deemed tax paid or accrued in a prior taxable year by reason of the limitation imposed by paragraph (2). Such amount deemed paid or accrued in any taxable year may be availed of only as a tax credit and not as a deduction and only if the taxpayer for such year chooses to have the benefits of this subpart as to taxes paid or accrued for that year to foreign countries or possessions.

(2) Limitation.—The amount of the unused foreign oil and gas taxes which under paragraph (1) may be deemed paid or accrued in any preceding or succeeding taxable year shall not exceed the lesser of

(A) the amount by which the limitation provided by subsection (a) for such taxable year exceeds the sum of—

(i) the foreign oil and gas taxes paid or accrued during such taxable year, plus

(ii) the amounts of the foreign oil and gas taxes which by reason of this subsection are deemed paid or accrued in such taxable year and are attributable to taxable years preceding the unused credit year; or

(B) the amount by which the limitation provided by section 904 for such taxable year exceeds the sum of—

(i) the taxes paid or accrued (or deemed to have been paid under section 960) to all foreign countries and possessions of the United States during such taxable year,

(ii) the amount of such taxes which were deemed paid or accrued in such taxable year under section 904(c) and which are attributable to taxable years preceding the unused credit year, plus

(iii) the amount of the foreign oil and gas taxes which by reason of this subsection are deemed paid or accrued in such taxable year and are attributable to taxable years preceding the unused credit year.

(3) Special rules.—

(A) In the case of any taxable year which is an unused credit year under this subsection and which is an unused credit year under section 904(c), the provisions of this subsection shall be applied before section 904(c).

(B) For purposes of determining the amount of taxes paid or accrued in any taxable year which may be deemed paid or accrued in a preceding or succeeding taxable year under section 904(c), any tax deemed paid or accrued in such preceding or succeeding taxable year under this subsection shall be considered to be tax paid or accrued in such preceding or succeeding taxable year.

(4) Transition rules for pre-2009 and 2009 disallowed credits.—

(A) Pre-2009 credits.—In the case of any unused credit year beginning before January 1, 2009, this subsection, as in effect on the day before the date of the enactment of the Energy

Improvement and Extension Act of 2008, shall apply to unused oil and gas extraction taxes carried from such unused credit year to a taxable year beginning after December 31, 2008.

(B) 2009 credits.—In the case of any unused credit year beginning in 2009, the amendments made to this subsection by the Energy Improvement and Extension Act of 2008 shall be treated as being in effect for any preceding year beginning before January 1, 2009, solely for purposes of determining how much of the unused foreign oil and gas taxes for such unused credit year may be deemed paid or accrued in such preceding year.

§ 908. Reduction of credit for participation in or cooperation with an international boycott

(a) In general.—If a person, or a member of a controlled group (within the meaning of section 993(a)(3)) which includes such person, participates in or cooperates with an international boycott during the taxable year (within the meaning of section 999(b)), the amount of the credit allowable under section 901 to such person, or under section 960 to United States shareholders of such person, for foreign taxes paid during the taxable year shall be reduced by an amount equal to the product of—

(1) the amount of the credit which, but for this section, would be allowed under section 901 for the taxable year, multiplied by

(2) the international boycott factor (determined under section 999).

(b) Application with sections 275(a)(4) and 78.—Section 275(a)(4) and section 78 shall not apply to any amount of taxes denied credit under subsection (a).

§ 909. Suspension of taxes and credits until related income taken into account

(a) In general.—If there is a foreign tax credit splitting event with respect to a foreign income tax paid or accrued by the taxpayer, such tax shall not be taken into account for purposes of this title before the taxable year in which the related income is taken into account under this chapter by the taxpayer.

(b) Special rules with respect to specified 10-percent owned foreign corporations.—If there is a foreign tax credit splitting event with respect to a foreign income tax paid or accrued by a specified 10-percent owned foreign corporation (as defined in section 245A(b)without regard to paragraph (2) thereof), such tax shall not be taken into account—

(1) for purposes of section 960, or

(2) for purposes of determining earnings and profits under section 964(a),

before the taxable year in which the related income is taken into account under this chapter by such specified 10-percent owned foreign corporation or a domestic corporation which is a United States shareholder with respect to such specified 10-percent owned foreign corporation.

(c) Special rules.—For purposes of this section—

(1) Application to partnerships, etc.—In the case of a partnership, subsections (a) and (b) shall be applied at the partner level. Except as otherwise provided by the Secretary, a rule similar to the rule of the preceding sentence shall apply in the case of any S corporation or trust.

(2) Treatment of foreign taxes after suspension.—In the case of any foreign income tax not taken into account by reason of subsection (a) or (b), except as otherwise provided by the Secretary, such tax shall be so taken into account in the taxable year referred to in such subsection (other than for purposes of section 986(a)) as a foreign income tax paid or accrued in such taxable year.

(d) Definitions.—For purposes of this section—

(1) Foreign tax credit splitting event.—There is a foreign tax credit splitting event with respect to a foreign income tax if the related income is (or will be) taken into account under this chapter by a covered person.

(2) Foreign income tax.—The term "foreign income tax" means any income, war profits, or excess profits tax paid or accrued to any foreign country or to any possession of the United States.

(3) Related income.—The term "related income" means, with respect to any portion of any foreign income tax, the income (or, as appropriate, earnings and profits) to which such portion of foreign income tax relates.

(4) Covered person.—The term "covered person" means, with respect to any person who pays or accrues a foreign income tax (hereafter in this paragraph referred to as the 'payor')—

(A) any entity in which the payor holds, directly or indirectly, at least a 10 percent ownership interest (determined by vote or value),

(B) any person which holds, directly or indirectly, at least a 10 percent ownership interest (determined by vote or value) in the payor,

(C) any person which bears a relationship to the payor described in section 267(b) or 707(b), and

(D) any other person specified by the Secretary for purposes of this paragraph.

(e) Regulations.—The Secretary may issue such regulations or other guidance as is necessary or appropriate to carry out the purposes of this section, including regulations or other guidance which provides—

(1) appropriate exceptions from the provisions of this section, and

(2) for the proper application of this section with respect to hybrid instruments.

Subpart B—Earned Income of Citizens or Residents of United States

§ 911. Citizens or residents of the United States living abroad

(a) Exclusion from gross income.—At the election of a qualified individual (made separately with respect to paragraphs (1) and (2)), there shall be excluded from the gross income of such individual, and exempt from taxation under this subtitle, for any taxable year—

(1) the foreign earned income of such individual, and

(2) the housing cost amount of such individual.

(b) Foreign earned income.—

(1) Definition.—For purposes of this section—

(A) In general.—The term "foreign earned income" with respect to any individual means the amount received by such individual from sources within a foreign country or countries which constitute earned income attributable to services performed by such individual during the period described in subparagraph (A) or (B) of subsection (d)(1), whichever is applicable.

(B) Certain amounts not included in foreign earned income.—The foreign earned income for an individual shall not include amounts—

(i) received as a pension or annuity,

(ii) paid by the United States or an agency thereof to an employee of the United States or an agency thereof,

(iii) included in gross income by reason of section 402(b) (relating to taxability of beneficiary of nonexempt trust) or section 403(c) (relating to taxability of beneficiary under a nonqualified annuity), or

(iv) received after the close of the taxable year following the taxable year in which the services to which the amounts are attributable are performed.

(2) Limitation on foreign earned income.—

(A) In general.—The foreign earned income of an individual which may be excluded under subsection (a)(1) for any taxable year shall not exceed the amount of foreign earned income computed on a daily basis at an annual rate equal to the exclusion amount for the calendar year in which such taxable year begins.

(B) Attribution to year in which services are performed.—For purposes of applying subparagraph (A), amounts received shall be considered received in the taxable year in which the services to which the amounts are attributable are performed.

(C) Treatment of community income.—In applying subparagraph (A) with respect to amounts received from services performed by a husband or wife which are community income under community property laws applicable to such income, the aggregate amount which may be excludable from the gross income of such husband and wife under subsection (a)(1) for any taxable year shall equal the amount which would be so excludable if such amounts did not constitute community income.

(D) Exclusion amount.—

(i) In general.—The exclusion amount for any calendar year is $80,000.

(ii) Inflation adjustment.—In the case of any taxable year beginning in a calendar year after 2005, the $80,000 amount in clause (i) shall be increased by an amount equal to the product of—

(I) such dollar amount, and

(II) the cost-of-living adjustment determined under section 1(f)(3) for the calendar year in which the taxable year begins, determined by substituting "2004" for "2016" in subparagraph (A)(ii) thereof.

If any increase determined under the preceding sentence is not a multiple of $100, such increase shall be rounded to the next lowest multiple of $100.

(c) Housing cost amount.—For purposes of this section—

(1) In general.—The term "housing cost amount" means an amount equal to the excess of—

(A) the housing expenses of an individual for the taxable year to the extent such expenses do not exceed the amount determined under paragraph (2), over

(B) an amount equal to the product of—

(i) 16 percent of the amount (computed on a daily basis) in effect under subsection (b)(2)(D) for the calendar year in which such taxable year begins, multiplied by

(ii) the number of days of such taxable year within the applicable period described in subparagraph (A) or (B) of subsection (d)(1).

(2) Limitation.—

(A) In general.—The amount determined under this paragraph is an amount equal to the product of—

(i) 30 percent (adjusted as may be provided under subparagraph (B)) of the amount (computed on a daily basis) in effect under subsection (b)(2)(D) for the calendar year in which the taxable year of the individual begins, multiplied by

(ii) the number of days of such taxable year within the applicable period described in subparagraph (A) or (B) of subsection (d)(1).

(B) Regulations.—The Secretary may issue regulations or other guidance providing for the adjustment of the percentage under subparagraph (A)(i) on the basis of geographic differences in housing costs relative to housing costs in the United States.

(3) Housing expenses.—

(A) In general.—The term "housing expenses" means the reasonable expenses paid or incurred during the taxable year by or on behalf of an individual for housing for the individual (and, if they reside with him, for his spouse and dependents) in a foreign country. The term—

(i) includes expenses attributable to the housing (such as utilities and insurance), but

(ii) does not include interest and taxes of the kind deductible under section 163 or 164 or any amount allowable as a deduction under section 216(a).

Housing expenses shall not be treated as reasonable to the extent such expenses are lavish or extravagant under the circumstances.

(B) Second foreign household.—

(i) In general.—Except as provided in clause (ii), only housing expenses incurred with respect to that abode which bears the closest relationship to the tax home of the individual shall be taken into account under paragraph (1).

(ii) Separate household for spouse and dependents.—If an individual maintains a separate abode outside the United States for his spouse and dependents and they do not reside with him because of living conditions which are dangerous, unhealthful, or otherwise adverse, then—

(I) the words "if they reside with him" in subparagraph (A) shall be disregarded, and

(II) the housing expenses incurred with respect to such abode shall be taken into account under paragraph (1).

(4) Special rules where housing expenses not provided by employer.—

(A) In general.—To the extent the housing cost amount of any individual for any taxable year is not attributable to employer provided amounts, such amount shall be treated as a deduction allowable in computing adjusted gross income to the extent of the limitation of subparagraph (B).

(B) Limitation.—For purposes of subparagraph (A), the limitation of this subparagraph is the excess of—

(i) the foreign earned income of the individual for the taxable year, over

(ii) the amount of such income excluded from gross income under subsection (a) for the taxable year.

(C) 1-year carryover of housing amounts not allowed by reason of subparagraph (B).—

(i) In general.—The amount not allowable as a deduction for any taxable year under subparagraph (A) by reason of the limitation of subparagraph (B) shall be treated as a deduction allowable in computing adjusted gross income for the succeeding taxable year (and only for the succeeding taxable year) to the extent of the limitation of clause (ii) for such succeeding taxable year.

(ii) Limitation.—For purposes of clause (i), the limitation of this clause for any taxable year is the excess of—

(I) the limitation of subparagraph (B) for such taxable year, over

(II) amounts treated as a deduction under subparagraph (A) for such taxable year.

(D) Employer provided amounts.—For purposes of this paragraph, the term "employer provided amounts" means any amount paid or incurred on behalf of the individual by the individual's employer which is foreign earned income included in the individual's gross income for the taxable year (without regard to this section).

(E) Foreign earned income.—For purposes of this paragraph, an individual's foreign earned income for any taxable year shall be determined without regard to the limitation of subparagraph (A) of subsection (b)(2).

(d) Definitions and special rules.—For purposes of this section—

(1) Qualified individual.—The term "qualified individual" means an individual whose tax home is in a foreign country and who is—

(A) a citizen of the United States and establishes to the satisfaction of the Secretary that he has been a bona fide resident of a foreign country or countries for an uninterrupted period which includes an entire taxable year, or

(B) a citizen or resident of the United States and who, during any period of 12 consecutive months, is present in a foreign country or countries during at least 330 full days in such period.

(2) Earned income.—

(A) In general.—The term "earned income" means wages, salaries, or professional fees, and other amounts received as compensation for personal services actually rendered, but does not include that part of the compensation derived by the taxpayer for personal services rendered by him to a corporation which represents a distribution of earnings or profits rather than a reasonable allowance as compensation for the personal services actually rendered.

(B) Taxpayer engaged in trade or business.—In the case of a taxpayer engaged in a trade or business in which both personal services and capital are material income-producing factors, under regulations prescribed by the Secretary, a reasonable allowance as compensation for the personal services rendered by the taxpayer, not in excess of 30 percent of his share of the net profits of such trade or business, shall be considered as earned income.

(3) Tax home.—The term "tax home" means, with respect to any individual, such individual's home for purposes of section 162(a)(2) (relating to traveling expenses while away from home). An individual shall not be treated as having a tax home in a foreign country for any period for which his abode is within the United States, unless such individual is serving in an area designated by the President of the United States by Executive order as a combat zone for purposes of section 112 in support of the Armed Forces of the United States.

(4) Waiver of period of stay in foreign country.—Notwithstanding paragraph (1), an individual who—

(A) is a bona fide resident of, or is present in, a foreign country for any period,

(B) leaves such foreign country after August 31, 1978—

(i) during any period during which the Secretary determines, after consultation with the Secretary of State or his delegate, that individuals were required to leave such foreign country because of war, civil unrest, or similar adverse conditions in such foreign country which precluded the normal conduct of business by such individuals, and

(ii) before meeting the requirements of such paragraph (1), and

(C) establishes to the satisfaction of the Secretary that such individual could reasonably have been expected to have met such requirements but for the conditions referred to in clause (i) of subparagraph (B),

shall be treated as a qualified individual with respect to the period described in subparagraph (A) during which he was a bona fide resident of, or was present in, the foreign country, and in applying subsections (b)(2)(A), (c)(1)(B)(ii), and (c)(2)(A)(ii) with respect to such individual, only the days within such period shall be taken into account.

(5) Test of bona fide residence.—If—

(A) an individual who has earned income from sources within a foreign country submits a statement to the authorities of that country that he is not a resident of that country, and

(B) such individual is held not subject as a resident of that country to the income tax of that country by its authorities with respect to such earnings,

then such individual shall not be considered a bona fide resident of that country for purposes of paragraph (1)(A).

(6) Denial of double benefits.—No deduction or exclusion from gross income under this subtitle or credit against the tax imposed by this chapter (including any credit or deduction for the amount of taxes paid or accrued to a foreign country or possession of the United States) shall be allowed to the extent such deduction, exclusion, or credit is properly allocable to or chargeable against amounts excluded from gross income under subsection (a).

(7) Aggregate benefit cannot exceed foreign earned income.—The sum of the amount excluded under subsection (a) and the amount deducted under subsection (c)(4)(A) for the taxable year shall not exceed the individual's foreign earned income for such year.

(8) Limitation on income earned in restricted country.—

(A) In general.—If travel (or any transaction in connection with such travel) with respect to any foreign country is subject to the regulations described in subparagraph (B) during any period—

(i) the term "foreign earned income" shall not include any income from sources within such country attributable to services performed during such period,

(ii) the term "housing expenses" shall not include any expenses allocable to such period for housing in such country or for housing of the spouse or dependents of the taxpayer in another country while the taxpayer is present in such country, and

(iii) an individual shall not be treated as a bona fide resident of, or as present in, a foreign country for any day during which such individual was present in such country during such period.

(B) Regulations.—For purposes of this paragraph, regulations are described in this subparagraph if such regulations—

(i) have been adopted pursuant to the Trading With the Enemy Act (50 U.S.C. 4301 et seq.), or the International Emergency Economic Powers Act (50 U.S.C. 1701 et seq.), and

(ii) include provisions generally prohibiting citizens and residents of the United States from engaging in transactions related to travel to, from, or within a foreign country.

(C) Exception.—Subparagraph (A) shall not apply to any individual during any period in which such individual's activities are not in violation of the regulations described in subparagraph (B).

(9) Regulations.—The Secretary shall prescribe such regulations as may be necessary or appropriate to carry out the purposes of this section, including regulations providing rules—

(A) for cases where a husband and wife each have earned income from sources outside the United States, and

(B) for married individuals filing separate returns.

(e) Election.—

(1) In general.—An election under subsection (a) shall apply to the taxable year for which made and to all subsequent taxable years unless revoked under paragraph (2).

(2) Revocation.—A taxpayer may revoke an election made under paragraph (1) for any taxable year after the taxable year for which such election was made. Except with the consent of the Secretary, any taxpayer who makes such a revocation for any taxable year may not make another election under this section for any subsequent taxable year before the 6th taxable year after the taxable year for which such revocation was made.

(f) Determination of tax liability.—

(1) In general.—If, for any taxable year, any amount is excluded from gross income of a taxpayer under subsection (a), then, notwithstanding sections 1 and 55—

(A) if such taxpayer has taxable income for such taxable year, the tax imposed by section 1 for such taxable year shall be equal to the excess (if any) of—

(i) the tax which would be imposed by section 1 for such taxable year if the taxpayer's taxable income were increased by the amount excluded under subsection (a) for such taxable year, over

(ii) the tax which would be imposed by section 1 for such taxable year if the taxpayer's taxable income were equal to the amount excluded under subsection (a) for such taxable year, and

(B) if such taxpayer has a taxable excess (as defined in section 55(b)(1)(B)) for such taxable year, the amount determined under the first sentence of section 55(b)(1)(A) for such taxable year shall be equal to the excess (if any) of—

(i) the amount which would be determined under such sentence for such taxable year (subject to the limitation of section 55(b)(3)) if the taxpayer's taxable excess (as so defined) were increased by the amount excluded under subsection (a) for such taxable year, over

(ii) the amount which would be determined under such sentence for such taxable year if the taxpayer's taxable excess (as so defined) were equal to the amount excluded under subsection (a) for such taxable year.

For purposes of this paragraph, the amount excluded under subsection (a) shall be reduced by the aggregate amount of any deductions or exclusions disallowed under subsection (d)(6) with respect to such excluded amount.

(2) Special rules.—

(A) Regular tax.—In applying section 1(h) for purposes of determining the tax under paragraph (1)(A)(i) for any taxable year in which, without regard to this subsection, the taxpayer's net capital gain exceeds taxable income (hereafter in this subparagraph referred to as the capital gain excess)—

(i) the taxpayer's net capital gain (determined without regard to section 1(h)(11)) shall be reduced (but not below zero) by such capital gain excess,

(ii) the taxpayer's qualified dividend income shall be reduced by so much of such capital gain excess as exceeds the taxpayer's net capital gain (determined without regard to section 1(h)(11) and the reduction under clause (i)), and

(iii) adjusted net capital gain, unrecaptured section 1250 gain, and 28-percent rate gain shall each be determined after increasing the amount described in section 1(h)(4)(B) by such capital gain excess.

(B) Alternative minimum tax.—In applying section 55(b)(3) for purposes of determining the tax under paragraph (1)(B)(i) for any taxable year in which, without regard to this subsection, the taxpayer's net capital gain exceeds the taxable excess (as defined in section 55(b)(1)(B))—

(i) the rules of subparagraph (A) shall apply, except that such subparagraph shall be applied by substituting 'the taxable excess (as defined in section 55(b)(1)(B))' for 'taxable income', and

(ii) the reference in section 55(b)(3)(B) to the excess described in section 1(h)(1)(B), and the reference in section 55(b)(3)(C)(ii) to the excess described in section 1(h)(1)(C)(ii), shall each be treated as a reference to each such excess as determined under the rules of subparagraph (A) for purposes of determining the tax under paragraph (1)(A)(i).

(C) Definitions.—Terms used in this paragraph which are also used in section 1(h) shall have the respective meanings given such terms by section 1(h), except that in applying subparagraph (B) the adjustments under part VI of subchapter A shall be taken into account.

(g) Cross references.—

For administrative and penal provisions relating to the exclusions provided for in this section, see sections 6001, 6011, 6012(c), and the other provisions of subtitle F.

§ 912. Exemption for certain allowances

The following items shall not be included in gross income, and shall be exempt from taxation under this subtitle:

(1) Foreign areas allowances.—In the case of civilian officers and employees of the Government of the United States, amounts received as allowances or otherwise (but not amounts received as post differentials) under—

(A) chapter 9 of title I of the Foreign Service Act of 1980,

(B) section 4 of the Central Intelligence Agency Act of 1949, as amended (50 U.S.C. 3505),

(C) title II of the Overseas Differentials and Allowances Act, or

(D) subsection (e) or (f) of the first section of the Administrative Expenses Act of 1946, as amended, or section 22 of such Act.

(2) Cost-of-living allowances.—In the case of civilian officers or employees of the Government of the United States stationed outside the continental United States (other than Alaska), amounts (other than amounts received under title II of the Overseas Differentials and Allowances Act) received as cost-of-living allowances in accordance with regulations approved by the President (or in the case of judicial officers or employees of the United States, in accordance with rules similar to such regulations).

(3) Peace Corps allowances.—In the case of an individual who is a volunteer or volunteer leader within the meaning of the Peace Corps Act and members of his family, amounts received as allowances under section 5 or 6 of the Peace Corps Act other than amounts received as—

(A) termination payments under section 5(c) or section 6(1) of such Act,

(B) leave allowances,

(C) if such individual is a volunteer leader training in the United States, allowances to members of his family, and

(D) such portion of living allowances as the President may determine under the Peace Corps Act as constituting basic compensation.

Subpart F—Controlled Foreign Corporations

§ 951. Amounts included in gross income of United States shareholders

(a) Amounts included.—

(1) In general.—If a foreign corporation is a controlled foreign corporation at any time during a taxable year of the foreign corporation (in this subsection referred to as the "CFC year")—

(A) each United States shareholder which owns (within the meaning of section 958(a)) stock in such corporation on any day during the CFC year shall include in gross income such shareholder's pro rata share (determined under paragraph (2)) of the corporation's subpart F income for the CFC year, and

(B) each United States shareholder which owns (within the meaning of section 958(a)) stock in such corporation on the last day, in the CFC year, on which such corporation is a controlled foreign corporation shall include in gross income the amount determined under section 956 with respect to such shareholder for the CFC year (but only to the extent not excluded from gross income under section 959(a)(2)).

(2) Pro rata share of subpart F income.—A United States shareholder's pro rata share of a controlled foreign corporation's subpart F income for a CFC year shall be the portion of such income which is attributable to—

(A) the stock of such corporation owned (within the meaning of section 958(a)) by such shareholder, and

(B) any period of the CFC year during which—

(i) such shareholder owned (within the meaning of section 958(a)) such stock,

(ii) such shareholder was a United States shareholder of such corporation, and

(iii) such corporation was a controlled foreign corporation.

(3) Taxable year of inclusion.—Any amount required to be included in gross income by a United States shareholder under paragraph (1) with respect to a CFC year shall be included in gross income for the shareholder's taxable year which includes the last day on which the shareholder owns (within the meaning of section 958(a)) stock in the controlled foreign corporation during such CFC year.

(4) Regulatory authority.—The Secretary shall prescribe such regulations or other guidance as may be necessary or appropriate to carry out the purposes of this subsection, including regulations or other guidance allowing taxpayers to elect, or requiring taxpayers, to close the taxable year of a controlled foreign corporation upon a direct or indirect disposition of stock of such corporation.

(b) United States shareholder defined.—For purposes of this title, the term "United States shareholder" means, with respect to any foreign corporation, a United States person (as defined in section 957(c)) who owns (within the meaning of section 958(a)), or is considered as owning by applying the rules of ownership of section 958(b), 10 percent or more of the total combined voting power of all classes of stock entitled to vote of such foreign corporation, or 10 percent or more of the total value of shares of all classes of stock of such foreign corporation.

(c) Coordination with passive foreign investment company provisions.—If, but for this subsection, an amount would be included in the gross income of a United States shareholder for any taxable year both under subsection (a)(1)(A)(i) and under section 1293 (relating to current taxation of income from certain passive foreign investment companies), such amount shall be included in the gross income of such shareholder only under subsection (a)(1)(A).

§ 951A. Net CFC tested income included in gross income of United States shareholders

(a) In general.—Each person who is a United States shareholder of any controlled foreign corporation for any taxable year of such United States shareholder shall include in gross income such shareholder's net CFC tested income for such taxable year.

(b) Net CFC tested income.—For purposes of this section—

(1) In general.—The term "net CFC tested income" means, with respect to any United States shareholder for any taxable year of such United States shareholder, the excess (if any) of—

(A) the aggregate of such shareholder's pro rata share of the tested income of each controlled foreign corporation with respect to which such shareholder is a United States shareholder for such taxable year of such United States shareholder, over

(B) the aggregate of such shareholder's pro rata share of the tested loss of each controlled foreign corporation with respect to which such shareholder is a United States shareholder for such taxable year of such United States shareholder.

(2) Tested income; tested loss.—For purposes of this section—

(A) Tested income.—The term "tested income" means, with respect to any controlled foreign corporation for any taxable year of such controlled foreign corporation, the excess (if any) of—

(i) the gross income of such corporation determined without regard to—

(I) any item of income described in section 952(b),

(II) any gross income taken into account in determining the subpart F income of such corporation,

(III) any gross income excluded from the foreign base company income (as defined in section 954) and the insurance income (as defined in section 953) of such corporation by reason of section 954(b)(4),

(IV) any dividend received from a related person (as defined in section 954(d)(3)), and

(V) any foreign oil and gas extraction income (as defined in section 907(c)(1)) of such corporation, over

(ii) the deductions (including taxes) properly allocable to such gross income under rules similar to the rules of section 954(b)(5) (or to which such deductions would be allocable if there were such gross income).

(B) Tested loss.—

(i) In general.—The term "tested loss" means, with respect to any controlled foreign corporation for any taxable year of such controlled foreign corporation, the excess (if any) of the amount described in subparagraph (A)(ii) over the amount described in subparagraph (A)(i).

(ii) Coordination with subpart F to deny double benefit of losses.—Section 952(c)(1)(A) shall be applied by increasing the earnings and profits of the controlled foreign corporation by the tested loss of such corporation.

(c) Determination of pro rata share, etc.—For purposes of this section—

(1) In general.—The pro rata shares referred to in subsections (b)(1)(A) and (b)(1)(B), respectively, shall be determined under the rules of section 951(a)(2) in the same manner as such section applies to subpart F income and shall be taken into account in the taxable year of the United States shareholder determined under section 951(a)(3).

(2) Treatment as United States shareholder.—A person shall be treated as a United States shareholder of a controlled foreign corporation for any taxable year of such person only if such person owns (within the meaning of section 958(a)) stock in such foreign corporation on any day in such taxable year.

(3) Treatment as controlled foreign corporation.—A foreign corporation shall be treated as a controlled foreign corporation for any taxable year if such foreign corporation is a controlled foreign corporation at any time during such taxable year.

(d) Treatment as subpart F income for certain purposes.—

(1) In general.—

(A) Application.—Except as provided in subparagraph (B), any net CFC tested income included in gross income under subsection (a) shall be treated in the same manner as an amount included under section 951(a)(1)(A) for purposes of applying sections 168(h)(2)(B), 535(b)(10),

851(b), 904(h), 959, 961, 962, 993(a)(1)(E), 996(f)(1), 1248(b)(1), 1248(d)(1), 6501(e)(1)(C), 6654(d)(2)(D), and 6655(e)(4).

(B) Exception.—The Secretary shall provide rules for the application of subparagraph (A) to other provisions of this title in any case in which the determination of subpart F income is required to be made at the level of the controlled foreign corporation.

(2) Allocation of net CFC tested income to controlled foreign corporations.—For purposes of the sections referred to in paragraph (1), with respect to any controlled foreign corporation any pro rata amount from which is taken into account in determining the net CFC tested income included in gross income of a United States shareholder under subsection (a), the portion of such net CFC tested income which is treated as being with respect to such controlled foreign corporation is—

(A) in the case of a controlled foreign corporation with no tested income, zero, and

(B) in the case of a controlled foreign corporation with tested income, the portion of such net CFC tested income which bears the same ratio to such net CFC tested income as—

(i) such United States shareholder's pro rata amount of the tested income of such controlled foreign corporation, bears to

(ii) the aggregate amount described in subsection (b)(1)(A) with respect to such United States shareholder.

§ 951B. Amounts included in gross income of foreign controlled United States shareholders

(a) In general.—In the case of any foreign controlled United States shareholder of a foreign controlled foreign corporation—

(1) this subpart (other than sections 951A, 951(b), and 957) shall be applied with respect to such shareholder (separately from, and in addition to, the application of this subpart without regard to this section)—

(A) by substituting "foreign controlled United States shareholder" for "United States shareholder" each place it appears therein, and

(B) by substituting "foreign controlled foreign corporation" for "controlled foreign corporation" each place it appears therein, and

(2) section 951A (and such other provisions of this subpart as provided by the Secretary) shall be applied with respect to such shareholder—

(A) by treating each reference to "United States shareholder" in such section as including a reference to such shareholder, and

(B) by treating each reference to "controlled foreign corporation" in such section as including a reference to such foreign controlled foreign corporation.

(b) Foreign controlled United States shareholder.—For purposes of this section, the term "foreign controlled United States shareholder" means, with respect to any foreign corporation, any United States person which would be a United States shareholder with respect to such foreign corporation if—

(1) section 951(b) were applied by substituting "more than 50 percent" for "10 percent or more", and

(2) section 958(b) were applied without regard to paragraph (4) thereof.

(c) Foreign controlled foreign corporation.—For purposes of this section, the term "foreign controlled foreign corporation" means a foreign corporation, other than a controlled foreign corporation, which would be a controlled foreign corporation if section 957(a) were applied—

(1) by substituting "foreign controlled United States shareholders" for "United States shareholders", and

(2) by substituting "section 958(b) (other than paragraph (4) thereof)" for "section 958(b)".

(d) Regulations.—The Secretary shall prescribe such regulations or other guidance as may be necessary or appropriate to carry out the purposes of this section, including regulations or other guidance—

(1) to treat a foreign controlled United States shareholder or a foreign controlled foreign corporation as a United States shareholder or as a controlled foreign corporation, respectively, for purposes of provisions of this title other than this subpart (including any reporting requirement), and

(2) with respect to the treatment of foreign controlled foreign corporations that are passive foreign investment companies (as defined in section 1297).

§ 952. Subpart F income defined

(a) In general.—For purposes of this subpart, the term "subpart F income" means, in the case of any controlled foreign corporation, the sum of—

(1) insurance income (as defined under section 953),

(2) the foreign base company income (as determined under section 954),

(3) an amount equal to the product of—

(A) the income of such corporation other than income which—

(i) is attributable to earnings and profits of the foreign corporation included in the gross income of a United States person under section 951 (other than by reason of this paragraph), or

(ii) is described in subsection (b), multiplied by

(B) the international boycott factor (as determined under section 999),

(4) the sum of the amounts of any illegal bribes, kickbacks, or other payments (within the meaning of section 162(c)) paid by or on behalf of the corporation during the taxable year of the corporation directly or indirectly to an official, employee, or agent in fact of a government, and

(5) the income of such corporation derived from any foreign country during any period during which section 901(j) applies to such foreign country.

The payments referred to in paragraph (4) are payments which would be unlawful under the Foreign Corrupt Practices Act of 1977 if the payor were a United States person. For purposes of paragraph (5), the income described therein shall be reduced, under regulations prescribed by the Secretary, so as to take into account deductions (including taxes) properly allocable to such income.

(b) Exclusion of United States income.—In the case of a controlled foreign corporation, subpart F income does not include any item of income from sources within the United States which is effectively connected with the conduct by such corporation of a trade or business within the United States unless such item is exempt from taxation (or is subject to a reduced rate of tax) pursuant to a treaty obligation of the United States. For purposes of this subsection, any exemption (or reduction) with respect to the tax imposed by section 884 shall not be taken into account.

(c) Limitation.—

(1) In general.—

(A) Subpart F income limited to current earnings and profits.—For purposes of subsection (a), the subpart F income of any controlled foreign corporation for any taxable year shall not exceed the earnings and profits of such corporation for such taxable year.

(B) Certain prior year deficits may be taken into account.—

(i) In general.—The amount included in the gross income of any United States shareholder under section 951(a)(1)(A) for any taxable year and attributable to a qualified activity shall be reduced by the amount of such shareholder's pro rata share of any qualified deficit.

(ii) Qualified deficit.—The term "qualified deficit" means any deficit in earnings and profits of the controlled foreign corporation for any prior taxable year which began after December 31, 1986, and for which the controlled foreign corporation was a controlled foreign corporation; but only to the extent such deficit—

(I) is attributable to the same qualified activity as the activity giving rise to the income being offset, and

(II) has not previously been taken into account under this subparagraph.

In determining the deficit attributable to qualified activities described in subclause (II) or (III) of clause (iii), deficits in earnings and profits (to the extent not previously taken into account under this section) for taxable years beginning after 1962 and before 1987 also shall be taken into account. In the case of the qualified activity described in clause (iii)(I), the rule of the preceding sentence shall apply, except that "1982" shall be substituted for "1962".

(iii) Qualified activity.—For purposes of this paragraph, the term "qualified activity" means any activity giving rise to—

(I) foreign base company sales income,

(II) foreign base company services income,

(III) in the case of a qualified insurance company, insurance income or foreign personal holding company income, or

(IV) in the case of a qualified financial institution, foreign personal holding company income.

(iv) Pro rata share.—For purposes of this paragraph, the shareholder's pro rata share of any deficit for any prior taxable year shall be determined under rules similar to rules under section 951(a)(2) for whichever of the following yields the smaller share:

(I) the close of the taxable year, or

(II) the close of the taxable year in which the deficit arose.

(v) Qualified insurance company.—For purposes of this subparagraph, the term "qualified insurance company" means any controlled foreign corporation predominantly engaged in the active conduct of an insurance business in the taxable year and in the prior taxable years in which the deficit arose.

(vi) Qualified financial institution.—For purposes of this paragraph, the term "qualified financial institution" means any controlled foreign corporation predominantly engaged in the active conduct of a banking, financing, or similar business in the taxable year and in the prior taxable year in which the deficit arose.

(vii) Special rules for insurance income.—

(I) In general.—An election may be made under this clause to have section 953(a) applied for purposes of this title without regard to the same country exception under paragraph (1)(A) thereof. Such election, once made, may be revoked only with the consent of the Secretary.

(II) Special rules for affiliated groups.—In the case of an affiliated group of corporations (within the meaning of section 1504 but without regard to section 1504(b)(3) and by substituting "more than 50 percent" for "at least 80 percent" each place it appears), no election may be made under subclause (I) for any controlled foreign corporation unless such election is made for all other controlled foreign corporations who are members of such group and who were created or organized under the laws of the same country as such controlled foreign corporation. For purposes of clause (v), in determining whether any controlled corporation described in the preceding sentence is a qualified insurance company, all such corporations shall be treated as 1 corporation.

(C) Certain deficits of member of the same chain of corporations may be taken into account.—

(i) In general.—A controlled foreign corporation may elect to reduce the amount of its subpart F income for any taxable year which is attributable to any qualified activity by the amount of any deficit in earnings and profits of a qualified chain member for a taxable year ending with (or within) the taxable year of such controlled foreign corporation to the extent such deficit is attributable to such activity. To the extent any deficit reduces subpart F income under the preceding sentence, such deficit shall not be taken into account under subparagraph (B).

(ii) Qualified chain member.—For purposes of this subparagraph, the term "qualified chain member" means, with respect to any controlled foreign corporation, any other corporation which is created or organized under the laws of the same foreign country as the controlled foreign corporation but only if—

(I) all the stock of such other corporation (other than directors' qualifying shares) is owned at all times during the taxable year in which the deficit arose (directly or through 1 or more corporations other than the common parent) by such controlled foreign corporation, or

(II) all the stock of such controlled foreign corporation (other than directors' qualifying shares) is owned at all times during the taxable year in which the deficit arose (directly or through 1 or more corporations other than the common parent) by such other corporation.

(iii) Coordination.—This subparagraph shall be applied after subparagraphs (A) and (B).

(2) Recharacterization in subsequent taxable years.—If the subpart F income of any controlled foreign corporation for any taxable year was reduced by reason of paragraph (1)(A), any excess of the earnings and profits of such corporation for any subsequent taxable year over the subpart F income of such foreign corporation for such taxable year shall be recharacterized as subpart F income under rules similar to the rules applicable under section 904(f)(5).

(3) Special rule for determining earnings and profits.—For purposes of this subsection, earnings and profits of any controlled foreign corporation shall be determined without regard to paragraphs (4), (5), and (6) of section 312(n). Under regulations, the preceding sentence shall not apply to the extent it would increase earnings and profits by an amount which was previously distributed by the controlled foreign corporation.

(d) Income derived from foreign country.—The Secretary shall prescribe such regulations as may be necessary or appropriate to carry out the purposes of subsection (a)(5), including regulations which treat income paid through 1 or more entities as derived from a foreign country to which section 901(j) applies if such income was, without regard to such entities, derived from such country.

§ 953. Insurance income

(a) Insurance income.—

(1) In general.—For purposes of section 952(a)(1), the term "insurance income" means any income which—

(A) is attributable to the issuing (or reinsuring) of an insurance or annuity contract, and

(B) would (subject to the modifications provided by subsection (b)) be taxed under subchapter L of this chapter if such income were the income of a domestic insurance company.

(2) Exception.—Such term shall not include any exempt insurance income (as defined in subsection (e)).

(b) Special rules.—For purposes of subsection (a)—

(1) The following provisions of subchapter L shall not apply:

(A) So much of section 805(a)(8) as relates to the deduction allowed under section 172.

(B) Section 832(c)(5) (relating to certain capital losses).

(2) The items referred to in—

(A) section 803(a)(1) (relating to gross amount of premiums and other considerations),

(B) section 803(a)(2) (relating to net decrease in reserves),

(C) section 805(a)(2) (relating to net increase in reserves), and

(D) section 832(b)(4) (relating to premiums earned on insurance contracts),

shall be taken into account only to the extent they are in respect of any reinsurance or the issuing of any insurance or annuity contract described in subsection (a)(1).

(3) Reserves for any insurance or annuity contract shall be determined in the same manner as under section 954(i).

(4) All items of income, expenses, losses, and deductions shall be properly allocated or apportioned under regulations prescribed by the Secretary.

(c) Special rule for certain captive insurance companies.—

(1) In general.—For purposes only of taking into account related person insurance income—

(A) the term "United States shareholder" means, with respect to any foreign corporation, a United States person (as defined in section 957(c)) who owns (within the meaning of section 958(a)) any stock of the foreign corporation,

(B) the term "controlled foreign corporation" has the meaning given to such term by section 957(a) determined by substituting "25 percent or more" for "more than 50 percent", and

(C) the pro rata share referred to in section 951(a)(1)(A) shall be determined under paragraph (5) of this subsection.

(2) Related person insurance income.—For purposes of this subsection, the term "related person insurance income" means any insurance income (within the meaning of subsection (a)) attributable to a policy of insurance or reinsurance with respect to which the person (directly or indirectly) insured is a United States shareholder in the foreign corporation or a related person to such a shareholder.

(3) Exceptions.—

(A) Corporations not held by insureds.—Paragraph (1) shall not apply to any foreign corporation if at all times during the taxable year of such foreign corporation—

(i) less than 20 percent of the total combined voting power of all classes of stock of such corporation entitled to vote, and

(ii) less than 20 percent of the total value of such corporation,

is owned (directly or indirectly under the principles of section 883(c)(4)) by persons who are (directly or indirectly) insured under any policy of insurance or reinsurance issued by such corporation or who are related persons to any such person.

(B) De minimis exception.—Paragraph (1) shall not apply to any foreign corporation for a taxable year of such corporation if the related person insurance income (determined on a gross basis) of such corporation for such taxable year is less than 20 percent of its insurance income (as so determined) for such taxable year determined without regard to those provisions of subsection (a)(1) which limit insurance income to income from countries other than the country in which the corporation was created or organized.

(C) Election to treat income as effectively connected.—Paragraph (1) shall not apply to any foreign corporation for any taxable year if—

(i) such corporation elects (at such time and in such manner as the Secretary may prescribe)—

(I) to treat its related person insurance income for such taxable year as income effectively connected with the conduct of a trade or business in the United States, and

(II) to waive all benefits (other than with respect to section 884) with respect to related person insurance income granted by the United States under any treaty between the United States and any foreign country, and

(ii) such corporation meets such requirements as the Secretary shall prescribe to ensure that the tax imposed by this chapter on such income is paid.

An election under this subparagraph made for any taxable year shall not be effective if the corporation (or any predecessor thereof) was a disqualified corporation for the taxable year for which the election was made or for any prior taxable year beginning after 1986.

(D) Special rules for subparagraph (C).—

(i) Period during which election in effect.—

(I) In general.—Except as provided in subclause (II), any election under subparagraph (C) shall apply to the taxable year for which made and all subsequent taxable years unless revoked with the consent of the Secretary.

(II) Termination.—If a foreign corporation which made an election under subparagraph (C) for any taxable year is a disqualified corporation for any subsequent taxable year, such election shall not apply to any taxable year beginning after such subsequent taxable year.

(ii) Exemption from tax imposed by section 4371.—The tax imposed by section 4371 shall not apply with respect to any related person insurance income treated as effectively connected with the conduct of a trade or business within the United States under subparagraph (C).

(E) Disqualified corporation.—For purposes of this paragraph the term "disqualified corporation" means, with respect to any taxable year, any foreign corporation which is a controlled foreign corporation for an uninterrupted period of 30 days or more during such taxable year (determined without regard to this subsection) but only if a United States shareholder (determined without regard to this subsection) owns (within the meaning of section 958(a)) stock in such corporation at some time during such taxable year.

(4) Treatment of mutual insurance companies.—In the case of a mutual insurance company—

(A) this subsection shall apply,

(B) policyholders of such company shall be treated as shareholders, and

(C) appropriate adjustments in the application of this subpart shall be made under regulations prescribed by the Secretary.

(5) Determination of pro rata share.—

(A) In general.—The pro rata share determined under this paragraph for any United States shareholder is the lesser of—

(i) the amount which would be determined under paragraph (2) of section 951(a) if—

(I) only related person insurance income were taken into account,

(II) stock owned (within the meaning of section 958(a)) by United States shareholders on the last day of the taxable year were the only stock in the foreign corporation, and

(III) only distributions received by United States shareholders were taken into account under subparagraph (B) of such paragraph (2), or

(ii) the amount which would be determined under paragraph (2) of section 951(a) if the entire earnings and profits of the foreign corporation for the taxable year were subpart F income.

(B) Coordination with other provisions.—The Secretary shall prescribe regulations providing for such modifications to the provisions of this subpart as may be necessary or appropriate by reason of subparagraph (A).

(6) Related person.—For purposes of this subsection—

(A) In general.—Except as provided in subparagraph (B), the term "related person" has the meaning given such term by section 954(d)(3).

(B) Treatment of certain liability insurance policies.—In the case of any policy of insurance covering liability arising from services performed as a director, officer, or employee of a corporation or as a partner or employee of a partnership, the person performing such services and the entity for which such services are performed shall be treated as related persons.

(7) Coordination with section 1248.—For purposes of section 1248, if any person is (or would be but for paragraph (3)) treated under paragraph (1) as a United States shareholder with respect to any foreign corporation which would be taxed under subchapter L if it were a domestic corporation and which is (or would be but for paragraph (3)) treated under paragraph (1) as a controlled foreign corporation—

(A) such person shall be treated as meeting the stock ownership requirements of section 1248(a)(2) with respect to such foreign corporation, and

(B) such foreign corporation shall be treated as a controlled foreign corporation.

(8) Regulations.—The Secretary shall prescribe such regulations as may be necessary to carry out the purposes of this subsection, including—

(A) regulations preventing the avoidance of this subsection through cross insurance arrangements or otherwise, and

(B) regulations which may provide that a person will not be treated as a United States shareholder under paragraph (1) with respect to any foreign corporation if neither such person (nor any related person to such person) is (directly or indirectly) insured under any policy of insurance or reinsurance issued by such foreign corporation.

(d) Election by foreign insurance company to be treated as domestic corporation.—

(1) In general.—If—

(A) a foreign corporation is a controlled foreign corporation (as defined in section 957(a) by substituting "25 percent or more" for "more than 50 percent" and by using the definition of United States shareholder under 953(c)(1)(A)),

(B) such foreign corporation would qualify under part I or II of subchapter L for the taxable year if it were a domestic corporation,

(C) such foreign corporation meets such requirements as the Secretary shall prescribe to ensure that the taxes imposed by this chapter on such foreign corporation are paid, and

(D) such foreign corporation makes an election to have this paragraph apply and waives all benefits to such corporation granted by the United States under any treaty,

for purposes of this title, such corporation shall be treated as a domestic corporation.

(2) Period during which election is in effect.—

(A) In general.—Except as provided in subparagraph (B), an election under paragraph (1) shall apply to the taxable year for which made and all subsequent taxable years unless revoked with the consent of the Secretary.

(B) Termination.—If a corporation which made an election under paragraph (1) for any taxable year fails to meet the requirements of subparagraphs (A), (B), and (C), of paragraph (1) for any subsequent taxable year, such election shall not apply to any taxable year beginning after such subsequent taxable year.

(3) Treatment of losses.—If any corporation treated as a domestic corporation under this subsection is treated as a member of an affiliated group for purposes of chapter 6 (relating to consolidated returns), any loss of such corporation shall be treated as a dual consolidated loss for purposes of section 1503(d) without regard to paragraph (2)(B) thereof.

(4) Effect of election.—

(A) In general.—For purposes of section 367, any foreign corporation making an election under paragraph (1) shall be treated as transferring (as of the 1st day of the 1st taxable year to which such election applies) all of its assets to a domestic corporation in connection with an exchange to which section 354 applies.

(B) Exception for pre-1988 earnings and profit.—

(i) In general.—Earnings and profits of the foreign corporation accumulated in taxable years beginning before January 1, 1988, shall not be included in the gross income of the persons holding stock in such corporation by reason of subparagraph (A).

(ii) Treatment of distributions.—For purposes of this title, any distribution made by a corporation to which an election under paragraph (1) applies out of earnings and profits accumulated in taxable years beginning before January 1, 1988, shall be treated as a distribution made by a foreign corporation.

(iii) Certain rules to continue to apply to pre-1988 earnings.—The provisions specified in clause (iv) shall be applied without regard to paragraph (1), except that, in the case of a corporation to which an election under paragraph (1) applies, only earnings and profits accumulated in taxable years beginning before January 1, 1988, shall be taken into account.

(iv) Specified provisions.—The provisions specified in this clause are:

(I) Section 1248 (relating to gain from certain sales or exchanges of stock in certain foreign corporations).

(II) Subpart F of part III of subchapter N to the extent such subpart relates to earnings invested in United States property.

(III) Section 884 to the extent the foreign corporation reinvested 1987 earnings and profits in United States assets.

(5) Effect of termination.—For purposes of section 367, if—

(A) an election is made by a corporation under paragraph (1) for any taxable year, and

(B) such election ceases to apply for any subsequent taxable year,

such corporation shall be treated as a domestic corporation transferring (as of the 1st day of such subsequent taxable year) all of its property to a foreign corporation in connection with an exchange to which section 354 applies.

(6) Additional tax on corporation making election.—

(A) In general.—If a corporation makes an election under paragraph (1), the amount of tax imposed by this chapter for the 1st taxable year to which such election applies shall be increased by the amount determined under subparagraph (B).

(B) Amount of tax.—The amount of tax determined under this paragraph shall be equal to the lesser of—

(i) 3/4 of 1 percent of the aggregate amount of capital and accumulated surplus of the corporation as of December 31, 1987, or

(ii) $1,500,000.

(e) Exempt insurance income.—For purposes of this section—

(1) Exempt insurance income defined.—

(A) In general.—The term "exempt insurance income" means income derived by a qualifying insurance company which—

(i) is attributable to the issuing (or reinsuring) of an exempt contract by such company or a qualifying insurance company branch of such company, and

(ii) is treated as earned by such company or branch in its home country for purposes of such country's tax laws.

(B) Exception for certain arrangements.—Such term shall not include income attributable to the issuing (or reinsuring) of an exempt contract as the result of any arrangement whereby another corporation receives a substantially equal amount of premiums or other consideration in respect of issuing (or reinsuring) a contract which is not an exempt contract.

(C) Determinations made separately.—For purposes of this subsection and section 954(i), the exempt insurance income and exempt contracts of a qualifying insurance company or any qualifying insurance company branch of such company shall be determined separately for such company and each such branch by taking into account—

(i) in the case of the qualifying insurance company, only items of income, deduction, gain, or loss, and activities of such company not properly allocable or attributable to any qualifying insurance company branch of such company, and

(ii) in the case of a qualifying insurance company branch, only items of income, deduction, gain, or loss and activities properly allocable or attributable to such branch.

(2) Exempt contract.—

(A) In general.—The term "exempt contract" means an insurance or annuity contract issued or reinsured by a qualifying insurance company or qualifying insurance company branch in connection with property in, liability arising out of activity in, or the lives or health of residents of, a country other than the United States.

(B) Minimum home country income required.—

(i) In general.—No contract of a qualifying insurance company or of a qualifying insurance company branch shall be treated as an exempt contract unless such company or branch derives more than 30 percent of its net written premiums from exempt contracts (determined without regard to this subparagraph)—

(I) which cover applicable home country risks, and

(II) with respect to which no policyholder, insured, annuitant, or beneficiary is a related person (as defined in section 954(d)(3)).

(ii) Applicable home country risks.—The term "applicable home country risks" means risks in connection with property in, liability arising out of activity in, or the lives or health of residents of, the home country of the qualifying insurance company or qualifying insurance company branch, as the case may be, issuing or reinsuring the contract covering the risks.

(C) Substantial activity requirements for cross border risks.—A contract issued by a qualifying insurance company or qualifying insurance company branch which covers risks other than applicable home country risks (as defined in subparagraph (B)(ii)) shall not be treated as an exempt contract unless such company or branch, as the case may be—

(i) conducts substantial activity with respect to an insurance business in its home country, and

(ii) performs in its home country substantially all of the activities necessary to give rise to the income generated by such contract.

(3) Qualifying insurance company.—The term "qualifying insurance company" means any controlled foreign corporation which—

(A) is subject to regulation as an insurance (or reinsurance) company by its home country, and is licensed, authorized, or regulated by the applicable insurance regulatory body for its home country to sell insurance, reinsurance, or annuity contracts to persons other than related persons (within the meaning of section 954(d)(3)) in such home country,

(B) derives more than 50 percent of its aggregate net written premiums from the issuance or reinsurance by such controlled foreign corporation and each of its qualifying insurance company branches of contracts—

(i) covering applicable home country risks (as defined in paragraph (2)) of such corporation or branch, as the case may be, and

(ii) with respect to which no policyholder, insured, annuitant, or beneficiary is a related person (as defined in section 954(d)(3)), except that in the case of a branch, such premiums shall only be taken into account to the extent such premiums are treated as earned by such branch in its home country for purposes of such country's tax laws, and

(C) is engaged in the insurance business and would be subject to tax under subchapter L if it were a domestic corporation.

(4) Qualifying insurance company branch.—The term "qualifying insurance company branch" means a qualified business unit (within the meaning of section 989(a)) of a controlled foreign corporation if—

(A) such unit is licensed, authorized, or regulated by the applicable insurance regulatory body for its home country to sell insurance, reinsurance, or annuity contracts to persons other than related persons (within the meaning of section 954(d)(3)) in such home country, and

(B) such controlled foreign corporation is a qualifying insurance company, determined under paragraph (3) as if such unit were a qualifying insurance company branch.

(5) Life insurance or annuity contract.—For purposes of this section and section 954, the determination of whether a contract issued by a controlled foreign corporation or a qualified business unit (within the meaning of section 989(a)) is a life insurance contract or an annuity contract shall be made without regard to sections 72(s), 101(f), 817(h), and 7702 if—

(A) such contract is regulated as a life insurance or annuity contract by the corporation's or unit's home country, and

(B) no policyholder, insured, annuitant, or beneficiary with respect to the contract is a United States person.

(6) Home country.—For purposes of this subsection, except as provided in regulations—

(A) Controlled foreign corporation.—The term "home country" means, with respect to a controlled foreign corporation, the country in which such corporation is created or organized.

(B) Qualified business unit.—The term "home country" means, with respect to a qualified business unit (as defined in section 989(a)), the country in which the principal office of such unit is located and in which such unit is licensed, authorized, or regulated by the applicable insurance regulatory body to sell insurance, reinsurance, or annuity contracts to persons other than related persons (as defined in section 954(d)(3)) in such country.

(7) Anti-abuse rules.—For purposes of applying this subsection and section 954(i)—

(A) the rules of section 954(h)(7) (other than subparagraph (B) thereof) shall apply,

(B) there shall be disregarded any item of income, gain, loss, or deduction of, or derived from, an entity which is not engaged in regular and continuous transactions with persons which are not related persons,

(C) there shall be disregarded any change in the method of computing reserves a principal purpose of which is the acceleration or deferral of any item in order to claim the benefits of this subsection or section 954(i),

(D) a contract of insurance or reinsurance shall not be treated as an exempt contract (and premiums from such contract shall not be taken into account for purposes of paragraph (2)(B) or (3)) if—

(i) any policyholder, insured, annuitant, or beneficiary is a resident of the United States and such contract was marketed to such resident and was written to cover a risk outside the United States, or

(ii) the contract covers risks located within and without the United States and the qualifying insurance company or qualifying insurance company branch does not maintain such contemporaneous records, and file such reports, with respect to such contract as the Secretary may require,

(E) the Secretary may prescribe rules for the allocation of contracts (and income from contracts) among 2 or more qualifying insurance company branches of a qualifying insurance company in order to clearly reflect the income of such branches, and

(F) premiums from a contract shall not be taken into account for purposes of paragraph (2)(B) or (3) if such contract reinsures a contract issued or reinsured by a related person (as defined in section 954(d)(3)).

For purposes of subparagraph (D), the determination of where risks are located shall be made under the principles of section 953.

(8) Coordination with subsection (c).—In determining insurance income for purposes of subsection (c), exempt insurance income shall not include income derived from exempt contracts which cover risks other than applicable home country risks.

(9) Regulations.—The Secretary shall prescribe such regulations as may be necessary or appropriate to carry out the purposes of this subsection and section 954(i).

(10) Cross reference.—

For income exempt from foreign personal holding company income, see section 954(i).

§ 954. Foreign base company income

(a) Foreign base company income.—For purposes of section 952(a)(2), the term "foreign base company income" means for any taxable year the sum of—

(1) the foreign personal holding company income for the taxable year (determined under subsection (c) and reduced as provided in subsection (b)(5)),

(2) the foreign base company sales income for the taxable year (determined under subsection (d) and reduced as provided in subsection (b)(5)), and

(3) the foreign base company services income for the taxable year (determined under subsection (e) and reduced as provided in subsection (b)(5)).

(b) Exclusions and special rules.—

* * *

(3) De minimis, etc., rules.—For purposes of subsection (a) and section 953—

(A) De minimis rule.—If the sum of foreign base company income (determined without regard to paragraph (5)) and the gross insurance income for the taxable year is less than the lesser of—

(i) 5 percent of gross income, or

(ii) $1,000,000,

no part of the gross income for the taxable year shall be treated as foreign base company income or insurance income.

(B) Foreign base company income and insurance income in excess of 70 percent of gross income.—If the sum of the foreign base company income (determined without regard to paragraph (5)) and the gross insurance income for the taxable year exceeds 70 percent of gross income, the entire gross income for the taxable year shall, subject to the provisions of paragraphs (4) and (5), be treated as foreign base company income or insurance income (whichever is appropriate).

(C) Gross insurance income.—For purposes of subparagraphs (A) and (B), the term "gross insurance income" means any item of gross income taken into account in determining insurance income under section 953.

(4) Exception for certain income subject to high foreign taxes.—For purposes of subsection (a) and section 953, foreign base company income and insurance income shall not include any item of income received by a controlled foreign corporation if the taxpayer establishes to the satisfaction of the Secretary that such income was subject to an effective rate of income tax imposed by a foreign country greater than 90 percent of the maximum rate of tax specified in section 11.

(5) Deductions to be taken into account.—For purposes of subsection (a), the foreign personal holding company income, the foreign base company sales income, and the foreign base company services income shall be reduced, under regulations prescribed by the Secretary, so as to take into account deductions (including taxes) properly allocable to such income. Except to the extent provided in regulations prescribed by the Secretary, any interest which is paid or accrued by the controlled foreign corporation to any United States shareholder in such corporation (or any controlled foreign corporation related to such a shareholder) shall be allocated first to foreign personal holding company income which is passive income (within the meaning of section 904(d)(2)) of such corporation to the extent thereof. The Secretary may, by regulations, provide that the preceding sentence shall apply also to interest paid or accrued to other persons.

(c) Foreign personal holding company income.—

(1) In general.—For purposes of subsection (a)(1), the term "foreign personal holding company income" means the portion of the gross income which consists of:

(A) Dividends, etc.—Dividends, interest, royalties, rents, and annuities.

(B) Certain property transactions.—The excess of gains over losses from the sale or exchange of property—

(i) which gives rise to income described in subparagraph (A) (after application of paragraph (2)(A)) other than property which gives rise to income not treated as foreign personal holding company income by reason of subsection (h) or (i) for the taxable year,

(ii) which is an interest in a trust, partnership, or REMIC, or

(iii) which does not give rise to any income.

Gains and losses from the sale or exchange of any property which, in the hands of the controlled foreign corporation, is property described in section 1221(a)(1) shall not be taken into account under this subparagraph.

(C) Commodities transactions.—The excess of gains over losses from transactions (including futures, forward, and similar transactions) in any commodities. This subparagraph shall not apply to gains or losses which—

(i) arise out of commodity hedging transactions (as defined in paragraph (5)(A)),

(ii) are active business gains or losses from the sale of commodities, but only if substantially all of the controlled foreign corporation's commodities are property described in paragraph (1), (2), or (8) of section 1221(a), or

(iii) are foreign currency gains or losses (as defined in section 988(b)) attributable to any section 988 transactions.

(D) Foreign currency gains.—The excess of foreign currency gains over foreign currency losses (as defined in section 988(b)) attributable to any section 988 transactions. This subparagraph shall not apply in the case of any transaction directly related to the business needs of the controlled foreign corporation.

(E) Income equivalent to interest.—Any income equivalent to interest, including income from commitment fees (or similar amounts) for loans actually made.

(F) Income from notional principal contracts.—

(i) In general.—Net income from notional principal contracts.

(ii) Coordination with other categories of foreign personal holding company income.—Any item of income, gain, deduction, or loss from a notional principal contract entered into for purposes of hedging any item described in any preceding subparagraph shall not be taken into account for purposes of this subparagraph but shall be taken into account under such other subparagraph.

(G) Payments in lieu of dividends.—Payments in lieu of dividends which are made pursuant to an agreement to which section 1058 applies.

(H) Personal service contracts.—

(i) Amounts received under a contract under which the corporation is to furnish personal services if—

(I) some person other than the corporation has the right to designate (by name or by description) the individual who is to perform the services, or

(II) the individual who is to perform the services is designated (by name or by description) in the contract, and

(ii) amounts received from the sale or other disposition of such a contract.

This subparagraph shall apply with respect to amounts received for services under a particular contract only if at some time during the taxable year 25 percent or more in value of the outstanding stock of the corporation is owned, directly or indirectly, by or for the individual who has performed, is to perform, or may be designated (by name or by description) as the one to perform, such services.

(2) Exception for certain amounts.—

(A) Rents and royalties derived in active business.—Foreign personal holding company income shall not include rents and royalties which are derived in the active conduct of a trade or business and which are received from a person other than a related person (within the meaning of subsection (d)(3)). For purposes of the preceding sentence, rents derived from leasing an aircraft or vessel in foreign commerce shall not fail to be treated as derived in the active conduct of a trade or business if, as determined under regulations prescribed by the Secretary, the active leasing expenses are not less than 10 percent of the profit on the lease.

(B) Certain export financing.—Foreign personal holding company income shall not include any interest which is derived in the conduct of a banking business and which is export financing interest (as defined in section 904(d)(2)(G)).

(C) Exception for dealers.—Except as provided by regulations, in the case of a regular dealer in property which is property described in paragraph (1)(B), forward contracts, option contracts, or similar financial instruments (including notional principal contracts and all instruments referenced to commodities), there shall not be taken into account in computing foreign personal holding company income—

(i) any item of income, gain, deduction, or loss (other than any item described in subparagraph (A), (E), or (G) of paragraph (1)) from any transaction (including hedging transactions and transactions involving physical settlement) entered into in the ordinary course of such dealer's trade or business as such a dealer, and

(ii) if such dealer is a dealer in securities (within the meaning of section 475), any interest or dividend or equivalent amount described in subparagraph (E) or (G) of paragraph (1) from any transaction (including any hedging transaction or transaction described in section 956(c)(2)(I)) entered into in the ordinary course of such dealer's trade or business as such a dealer in securities, but only if the income from the transaction is attributable to activities of the dealer in the country under the laws of which the dealer is created or organized (or in the case of a qualified business unit described in section 989(a), is attributable to activities of the unit in the country in which the unit both maintains its principal office and conducts substantial business activity).

(3) Certain income received from related persons.—

(A) In general.—Except as provided in subparagraph (B), the term "foreign personal holding company income" does not include—

(i) dividends and interest received from a related person which (I) is a corporation created or organized under the laws of the same foreign country under the laws of which the controlled foreign corporation is created or organized, and (II) has a substantial part of its assets used in its trade or business located in such same foreign country, and

(ii) rents and royalties received from a corporation which is a related person for the use of, or the privilege of using, property within the country under the laws of which the controlled foreign corporation is created or organized.

To the extent provided in regulations, payments made by a partnership with 1 or more corporate partners shall be treated as made by such corporate partners in proportion to their respective interests in the partnership.

(B) Exception not to apply to items which reduce subpart F income.—Subparagraph (A) shall not apply in the case of any interest, rent, or royalty to the extent such interest, rent, or royalty reduces the payor's subpart F income or creates (or increases) a deficit which under section 952(c) may reduce the subpart F income of the payor or another controlled foreign corporation.

(C) Exception for certain dividends.—Subparagraph (A)(i) shall not apply to any dividend with respect to any stock which is attributable to earnings and profits of the distributing corporation accumulated during any period during which the person receiving such dividend did not hold such stock either directly, or indirectly through a chain of one or more subsidiaries each of which meets the requirements of subparagraph (A)(i).

(4) Look-thru rule for certain partnership sales.—

(A) In general.—In the case of any sale by a controlled foreign corporation of an interest in a partnership with respect to which such corporation is a 25-percent owner, such corporation shall be treated for purposes of this subsection as selling the proportionate share of the assets of the partnership attributable to such interest. The Secretary shall prescribe such regulations as may be appropriate to prevent abuse of the purposes of this paragraph, including regulations providing for coordination of this paragraph with the provisions of subchapter K.

(B) 25-percent owner.—For purposes of this paragraph, the term "25-percent owner" means a controlled foreign corporation which owns directly 25 percent or more of the capital or profits interest in a partnership. For purposes of the preceding sentence, if a controlled foreign corporation is a shareholder or partner of a corporation or partnership, the controlled foreign corporation shall be treated as owning directly its proportionate share of any such capital or profits interest held directly or indirectly by such corporation or partnership. If a controlled foreign corporation is treated as owning a capital or profits interest in a partnership under constructive ownership rules similar to the rules of section 958(b), the controlled foreign corporation shall be treated as owning such interest directly for purposes of this subparagraph.

(5) Definition and special rules relating to commodity transactions.—

(A) Commodity hedging transactions.—For purposes of paragraph (1)(C)(i), the term "commodity hedging transaction" means any transaction with respect to a commodity if such transaction—

(i) is a hedging transaction as defined in section 1221(b)(2), determined—

(I) without regard to subparagraph (A)(ii) thereof,

(II) by applying subparagraph (A)(i) thereof by substituting "ordinary property or property described in section 1231(b)" for "ordinary property", and

(III) by substituting "controlled foreign corporation" for "taxpayer" each place it appears, and

(ii) is clearly identified as such in accordance with section 1221(a)(7).

(B) Treatment of dealer activities under paragraph (1)(c).—Commodities with respect to which gains and losses are not taken into account under paragraph (2)(C) in computing a controlled foreign corporation's foreign personal holding company income shall not be taken into account in applying the substantially all test under paragraph (1)(C)(ii) to such corporation.

(C) Regulations.—The Secretary shall prescribe such regulations as are appropriate to carry out the purposes of paragraph (1)(C) in the case of transactions involving related parties.

(6) Look-thru rule for related controlled foreign corporations.—

(A) In general.—For purposes of this subsection, dividends, interest, rents, and royalties received or accrued from a controlled foreign corporation which is a related person shall not be treated as foreign personal holding company income to the extent attributable or properly allocable (determined under rules similar to the rules of subparagraphs (C) and (D) of section 904(d)(3)) to income of the related person which is neither subpart F income nor income treated as effectively connected with the conduct of a trade or business in the United States. For purposes of this subparagraph, interest shall include factoring income which is treated as income equivalent to interest for purposes of paragraph (1)(E). The Secretary shall prescribe such regulations as may be necessary or appropriate to carry out this paragraph, including such regulations as may be necessary or appropriate to prevent the abuse of the purposes of this paragraph.

(B) Exception.—Subparagraph (A) shall not apply in the case of any interest, rent, or royalty to the extent such interest, rent, or royalty creates (or increases) a deficit which under section 952(c) may reduce the subpart F income of the payor or another controlled foreign corporation.

(C) Application.—Subparagraph (A) shall apply to taxable years of foreign corporations beginning after December 31, 2005, and to taxable years of United States shareholders with or within which such taxable years of foreign corporations end.

(d) Foreign base company sales income.—

(1) In general.—For purposes of subsection (a)(2), the term "foreign base company sales income" means income (whether in the form of profits, commissions, fees, or otherwise) derived in connection with the purchase of personal property from a related person and its sale to any person, the sale of personal property to any person on behalf of a related person, the purchase of personal property from any person and its sale to a related person, or the purchase of personal property from any person on behalf of a related person where—

(A) the property which is purchased (or in the case of property sold on behalf of a related person, the property which is sold) is manufactured, produced, grown, or extracted outside the country under the laws of which the controlled foreign corporation is created or organized, and

(B) the property is sold for use, consumption, or disposition outside such foreign country, or, in the case of property purchased on behalf of a related person, is purchased for use, consumption, or disposition outside such foreign country.

For purposes of this subsection, personal property does not include agricultural commodities which are not grown in the United States in commercially marketable quantities.

(2) Certain branch income.—For purposes of determining foreign base company sales income in situations in which the carrying on of activities by a controlled foreign corporation through a branch or similar establishment outside the country of incorporation of the controlled foreign corporation has substantially the same effect as if such branch or similar establishment were a wholly owned subsidiary corporation deriving such income, under regulations prescribed by the Secretary the income attributable to the carrying on of such activities of such branch or similar establishment shall be treated as income derived by a wholly owned subsidiary of the controlled foreign corporation and shall constitute foreign base company sales income of the controlled foreign corporation.

(3) Related person defined.—For purposes of this section, a person is a related person with respect to a controlled foreign corporation, if—

(A) such person is an individual, corporation, partnership, trust, or estate which controls, or is controlled by, the controlled foreign corporation, or

(B) such person is a corporation, partnership, trust, or estate which is controlled by the same person or persons which control the controlled foreign corporation.

For purposes of the preceding sentence, control means, with respect to a corporation, the ownership, directly or indirectly, of stock possessing more than 50 percent of the total voting power of all classes of stock entitled to vote or of the total value of stock of such corporation. In the case of a partnership, trust, or estate, control means the ownership, directly or indirectly, of more than 50 percent (by value) of the beneficial interests in such partnership, trust, or estate. For purposes of this paragraph, rules similar to the rules of section 958 shall apply.

(4) Special rule for certain timber products.—For purposes of subsection (a)(2), the term "foreign base company sales income" includes any income (whether in the form of profits, commissions, fees, or otherwise) derived in connection with—

(A) the sale of any unprocessed timber referred to in section 865(b), or

(B) the milling of any such timber outside the United States.

Subpart G shall not apply to any amount treated as subpart F income by reason of this paragraph.

(e) Foreign base company services income.—

(1) In general.—For purposes of subsection (a)(3), the term "foreign base company services income" means income (whether in the form of compensation, commissions, fees, or otherwise) derived in connection with the performance of technical, managerial, engineering, architectural, scientific, skilled, industrial, commercial, or like services which—

(A) are performed for or on behalf of any related person (within the meaning of subsection (d)(3)), and

(B) are performed outside the country under the laws of which the controlled foreign corporation is created or organized.

(2) Exception.—Paragraph (1) shall not apply to income derived in connection with the performance of services which are directly related to—

(A) the sale or exchange by the controlled foreign corporation of property manufactured, produced, grown, or extracted by it and which are performed before the time of the sale or exchange or

(B) an offer or effort to sell or exchange such property.

Paragraph (1) shall also not apply to income which is exempt insurance income (as defined in section 953(e)) or which is not treated as foreign personal holding income by reason of subsection (c)(2)(C)(ii), (h), or (i).

* * *

(h) Special rule for income derived in the active conduct of banking, financing, or similar businesses.—

(1) In general.—For purposes of subsection (c)(1), foreign personal holding company income shall not include qualified banking or financing income of an eligible controlled foreign corporation.

(2) Eligible controlled foreign corporation.—For purposes of this subsection—

(A) In general.—The term "eligible controlled foreign corporation" means a controlled foreign corporation which—

(i) is predominantly engaged in the active conduct of a banking, financing, or similar business, and

(ii) conducts substantial activity with respect to such business.

(B) Predominantly engaged.—A controlled foreign corporation shall be treated as predominantly engaged in the active conduct of a banking, financing, or similar business if—

(i) more than 70 percent of the gross income of the controlled foreign corporation is derived directly from the active and regular conduct of a lending or finance business from transactions with customers which are not related persons,

(ii) it is engaged in the active conduct of a banking business and is an institution licensed to do business as a bank in the United States (or is any other corporation not so licensed which is specified by the Secretary in regulations), or

(iii) it is engaged in the active conduct of a securities business and is registered as a securities broker or dealer under section 15(a) of the Securities Exchange Act of 1934 or is registered as a Government securities broker or dealer under section 15C(a) of such Act (or is any other corporation not so registered which is specified by the Secretary in regulations).

(3) Qualified banking or financing income.—For purposes of this subsection—

(A) In general.—The term "qualified banking or financing income" means income of an eligible controlled foreign corporation which—

(i) is derived in the active conduct of a banking, financing, or similar business by—

(I) such eligible controlled foreign corporation, or

(II) a qualified business unit of such eligible controlled foreign corporation,

(ii) is derived from one or more transactions—

(I) with customers located in a country other than the United States, and

(II) substantially all of the activities in connection with which are conducted directly by the corporation or unit in its home country, and

(iii) is treated as earned by such corporation or unit in its home country for purposes of such country's tax laws.

(B) Limitation on nonbanking and nonsecurities businesses.—No income of an eligible controlled foreign corporation not described in clause (ii) or (iii) of paragraph (2)(B) (or of a qualified business unit of such corporation) shall be treated as qualified banking or financing income unless more than 30 percent of such corporation's or unit's gross income is derived directly from the active and regular conduct of a lending or finance business from transactions with customers which are not related persons and which are located within such corporation's or unit's home country.

(C) Substantial activity requirement for cross border income.—The term "qualified banking or financing income" shall not include income derived from 1 or more transactions with customers located in a country other than the home country of the eligible controlled foreign corporation or a qualified business unit of such corporation unless such corporation or unit conducts substantial activity with respect to a banking, financing, or similar business in its home country.

(D) Determinations made separately.—For purposes of this paragraph, the qualified banking or financing income of an eligible controlled foreign corporation and each qualified business unit of such corporation shall be determined separately for such corporation and each such unit by taking into account—

(i) in the case of the eligible controlled foreign corporation, only items of income, deduction, gain, or loss and activities of such corporation not properly allocable or attributable to any qualified business unit of such corporation, and

(ii) in the case of a qualified business unit, only items of income, deduction, gain, or loss and activities properly allocable or attributable to such unit.

(E) Direct conduct of activities.—For purposes of subparagraph (A)(ii)(II), an activity shall be treated as conducted directly by an eligible controlled foreign corporation or qualified business unit in its home country if the activity is performed by employees of a related person and—

(i) the related person is an eligible controlled foreign corporation the home country of which is the same as the home country of the corporation or unit to which subparagraph (A)(ii)(II) is being applied,

(ii) the activity is performed in the home country of the related person, and

(iii) the related person is compensated on an arm's-length basis for the performance of the activity by its employees and such compensation is treated as earned by such person in its home country for purposes of the home country's tax laws.

(4) Lending or finance business.—For purposes of this subsection, the term "lending or finance business" means the business of—

(A) making loans,

(B) purchasing or discounting accounts receivable, notes, or installment obligations,

(C) engaging in leasing (including entering into leases and purchasing, servicing, and disposing of leases and leased assets),

(D) issuing letters of credit or providing guarantees,

(E) providing charge and credit card services, or

(F) rendering services or making facilities available in connection with activities described in subparagraphs (A) through (E) carried on by—

(i) the corporation (or qualified business unit) rendering services or making facilities available, or

(ii) another corporation (or qualified business unit of a corporation) which is a member of the same affiliated group (as defined in section 1504, but determined without regard to section 1504(b)(3)).

(5) Other definitions.—For purposes of this subsection—

(A) Customer.—The term "customer" means, with respect to any controlled foreign corporation or qualified business unit, any person which has a customer relationship with such corporation or unit and which is acting in its capacity as such.

(B) Home country.—Except as provided in regulations—

(i) Controlled foreign corporation.—The term "home country" means, with respect to any controlled foreign corporation, the country under the laws of which the corporation was created or organized.

(ii) Qualified business unit.—The term "home country" means, with respect to any qualified business unit, the country in which such unit maintains its principal office.

(C) Located.—The determination of where a customer is located shall be made under rules prescribed by the Secretary.

(D) Qualified business unit.—The term "qualified business unit" has the meaning given such term by section 989(a).

(E) Related person.—The term "related person" has the meaning given such term by subsection (d)(3).

(6) Coordination with exception for dealers.—Paragraph (1) shall not apply to income described in subsection (c)(2)(C)(ii) of a dealer in securities (within the meaning of section 475) which is an eligible controlled foreign corporation described in paragraph (2)(B)(iii).

(7) Anti-abuse rules.—For purposes of applying this subsection and subsection (c)(2)(C)(ii)—

(A) there shall be disregarded any item of income, gain, loss, or deduction with respect to any transaction or series of transactions one of the principal purposes of which is qualifying income or gain for the exclusion under this section, including any transaction or series of transactions a principal purpose of which is the acceleration or deferral of any item in order to claim the benefits of such exclusion through the application of this subsection,

(B) there shall be disregarded any item of income, gain, loss, or deduction of an entity which is not engaged in regular and continuous transactions with customers which are not related persons,

(C) there shall be disregarded any item of income, gain, loss, or deduction with respect to any transaction or series of transactions utilizing, or doing business with—

(i) one or more entities in order to satisfy any home country requirement under this subsection, or

(ii) a special purpose entity or arrangement, including a securitization, financing, or similar entity or arrangement,

if one of the principal purposes of such transaction or series of transactions is qualifying income or gain for the exclusion under this subsection, and

(D) a related person, an officer, a director, or an employee with respect to any controlled foreign corporation (or qualified business unit) which would otherwise be treated as a customer of such corporation or unit with respect to any transaction shall not be so treated if a principal purpose of such transaction is to satisfy any requirement of this subsection.

(8) Regulations.—The Secretary shall prescribe such regulations as may be necessary or appropriate to carry out the purposes of this subsection, subsection (c)(1)(B)(i), subsection (c)(2)(C)(ii), and the last sentence of subsection (e)(2).

(i) Special rule for income derived in the active conduct of insurance business.—

(1) In general.—For purposes of subsection (c)(1), foreign personal holding company income shall not include qualified insurance income of a qualifying insurance company.

(2) Qualified insurance income.—The term "qualified insurance income" means income of a qualifying insurance company which is—

(A) received from a person other than a related person (within the meaning of subsection (d)(3)) and derived from the investments made by a qualifying insurance company or a qualifying insurance company branch of its reserves allocable to exempt contracts or of 80 percent of its unearned premiums from exempt contracts (as both are determined in the manner prescribed under paragraph (4)), or

(B) received from a person other than a related person (within the meaning of subsection (d)(3)) and derived from investments made by a qualifying insurance company or a qualifying insurance company branch of an amount of its assets allocable to exempt contracts equal to—

(i) in the case of property, casualty, or health insurance contracts, one-third of its premiums earned on such insurance contracts during the taxable year (as defined in section 832(b)(4)), and

(ii) in the case of life insurance or annuity contracts, 10 percent of the reserves described in subparagraph (A) for such contracts.

(3) Principles for determining insurance income.—Except as provided by the Secretary, for purposes of subparagraphs (A) and (B) of paragraph (2)—

(A) in the case of any contract which is a separate account-type contract (including any variable contract not meeting the requirements of section 817), income credited under such contract shall be allocable only to such contract, and

(B) income not allocable under subparagraph (A) shall be allocated ratably among contracts not described in subparagraph (A).

(4) Methods for determining unearned premiums and reserves.—For purposes of paragraph (2)(A)—

(A) Property and casualty contracts.—The unearned premiums and reserves of a qualifying insurance company or a qualifying insurance company branch with respect to property, casualty, or health insurance contracts shall be determined using the same methods and interest rates which would be used if such company or branch were subject to tax under subchapter L, except that—

(i) the interest rate determined for the functional currency of the company or branch, and which, except as provided by the Secretary, is calculated in the same manner as the Federal mid-term rate under section 1274(d), shall be substituted for the applicable Federal interest rate, and

(ii) such company or branch shall use the appropriate foreign loss payment pattern.

(B) Life insurance and annuity contracts.—

(i) In general.—Except as provided in clause (ii), the amount of the reserve of a qualifying insurance company or qualifying insurance company branch for any life insurance or annuity contract shall be equal to the greater of—

(I) the net surrender value of such contract (as defined in section 807(e)(1)(A)), or

(II) the reserve determined under paragraph (5).

(ii) Ruling request, etc.—The amount of the reserve under clause (i) shall be the foreign statement reserve for the contract (less any catastrophe, deficiency, equalization, or similar reserves), if, pursuant to a ruling request submitted by the taxpayer or as provided in published guidance, the Secretary determines that the factors taken into account in determining the foreign statement reserve provide an appropriate means of measuring income.

(C) Limitation on reserves.—In no event shall the reserve determined under this paragraph for any contract as of any time exceed the amount which would be taken into account with respect to such contract as of such time in determining foreign statement reserves (less any catastrophe, deficiency, equalization, or similar reserves).

(5) Amount of reserve.—The amount of the reserve determined under this paragraph with respect to any contract shall be determined in the same manner as it would be determined if the qualifying insurance company or qualifying insurance company branch were subject to tax under subchapter L, except that in applying such subchapter—

(A) the interest rate determined for the functional currency of the company or branch, and which, except as provided by the Secretary, is calculated in the same manner as the Federal mid-term rate under section 1274(d), shall be substituted for the applicable Federal interest rate,

(B) the highest assumed interest rate permitted to be used in determining foreign statement reserves shall apply, and

(C) tables for mortality and morbidity which reasonably reflect the current mortality and morbidity risks in the company's or branch's home country shall be substituted for the mortality and morbidity tables otherwise used for such subchapter.

The Secretary may provide that the interest rate and mortality and morbidity tables of a qualifying insurance company may be used for 1 or more of its qualifying insurance company branches when appropriate.

(6) Definitions.—For purposes of this subsection, any term used in this subsection which is also used in section 953(e) shall have the meaning given such term by section 953.

§ 956. Investment of earnings in United States property

(a) General rule.—In the case of any controlled foreign corporation, the amount determined under this section with respect to any United States shareholder for any taxable year is the lesser of—

(1) the excess (if any) of—

(A) such shareholder's pro rata share of the average of the amounts of United States property held (directly or indirectly) by the controlled foreign corporation as of the close of each quarter of such taxable year, over

(B) the amount of earnings and profits described in section 959(c)(1)(A) with respect to such shareholder, or

(2) such shareholder's pro rata share of the applicable earnings of such controlled foreign corporation.

The amount taken into account under paragraph (1) with respect to any property shall be its adjusted basis as determined for purposes of computing earnings and profits, reduced by any liability to which the property is subject.

(b) Special rules.—

(1) Applicable earnings.—For purposes of this section, the term "applicable earnings" means, with respect to any controlled foreign corporation, the sum of—

(A) the amount (not including a deficit) referred to in section 316(a)(1) to the extent such amount was accumulated in prior taxable years, and

(B) the amount referred to in section 316(a)(2),

but reduced by distributions made during the taxable year and by earnings and profits described in section 959(c)(1).

(2) Special rule for U.S. property acquired before corporation is a controlled foreign corporation.—In applying subsection (a) to any taxable year, there shall be disregarded any item of United States property which was acquired by the controlled foreign corporation before the first day on which such corporation was treated as a controlled foreign corporation. The aggregate amount of property disregarded under the preceding sentence shall not exceed the portion of the applicable earnings of such controlled foreign corporation which were accumulated during periods before such first day.

(3) Special rule where corporation ceases to be controlled foreign corporation.—If any foreign corporation ceases to be a controlled foreign corporation during any taxable year—

(A) the determination of any United States shareholder's pro rata share shall be made on the basis of stock owned (within the meaning of section 958(a)) by such shareholder on the last day during the taxable year on which the foreign corporation is a controlled foreign corporation,

(B) the average referred to in subsection (a)(1)(A) for such taxable year shall be determined by only taking into account quarters ending on or before such last day, and

(C) in determining applicable earnings, the amount taken into account by reason of being described in paragraph (2) of section 316(a) shall be the portion of the amount so described which is allocable (on a pro rata basis) to the part of such year during which the corporation is a controlled foreign corporation.

(c) United States property defined.—

(1) In general.—For purposes of subsection (a), the term "United States property" means any property acquired after December 31, 1962, which is—

(A) tangible property located in the United States;

(B) stock of a domestic corporation;

(C) an obligation of a United States person; or

(D) any right to the use in the United States of—

(i) a patent or copyright,

(ii) an invention, model, or design (whether or not patented),

(iii) a secret formula or process, or

(iv) any other similar property right,

which is acquired or developed by the controlled foreign corporation for use in the United States.

(2) Exceptions.—For purposes of subsection (a), the term "United States property" does not include—

(A) obligations of the United States, money, or deposits with—

(i) any bank (as defined by section 2(c) of the Bank Holding Company Act of 1956 (12 U.S.C. 1841(c)), without regard to subparagraphs (C) and (G) of paragraph (2) of such section), or

(ii) any corporation not described in clause (i) with respect to which a bank holding company (as defined by section 2(a) of such Act) or financial holding company (as defined by section 2(p) of such Act) owns directly or indirectly more than 80 percent by vote or value of the stock of such corporation;

(B) property located in the United States which is purchased in the United States for export to, or use in, foreign countries;

(C) any obligation of a United States person arising in connection with the sale or processing of property if the amount of such obligation outstanding at no time during the taxable year exceeds the amount which would be ordinary and necessary to carry on the trade or business of both the other party to the sale or processing transaction and the United States person had the sale or processing transaction been made between unrelated persons;

(D) any aircraft, railroad rolling stock, vessel, motor vehicle, or container used in the transportation of persons or property in foreign commerce and used predominantly outside the United States;

(E) an amount of assets of an insurance company equivalent to the unearned premiums or reserves ordinary and necessary for the proper conduct of its insurance business attributable to contracts which are contracts described in section 953(e)(2);

(F) the stock or obligations of a domestic corporation which is neither a United States shareholder (as defined in section 951(b)) of the controlled foreign corporation, nor a domestic corporation, 25 percent or more of the total combined voting power of which, immediately after the acquisition of any stock in such domestic corporation by the controlled foreign corporation, is owned, or is considered as being owned, by such United States shareholders in the aggregate;

(G) any movable property (other than a vessel or aircraft) which is used for the purpose of exploring for, developing, removing, or transporting resources from ocean waters or under such waters when used on the Continental Shelf of the United States;

(H) an amount of assets of the controlled foreign corporation equal to the earnings and profits accumulated after December 31, 1962, and excluded from subpart F income under section 952(b);

(I) deposits of cash or securities made or received on commercial terms in the ordinary course of a United States or foreign person's business as a dealer in securities or in commodities, but only to the extent such deposits are made or received as collateral or margin for (i) a securities loan, notional principal contract, options contract, forward contract, or futures contract, or (ii) any other financial transaction in which the Secretary determines that it is customary to post collateral or margin;

(J) an obligation of a United States person to the extent the principal amount of the obligation does not exceed the fair market value of readily marketable securities sold or purchased pursuant to a sale and repurchase agreement or otherwise posted or received as collateral for the obligation in the ordinary course of its business by a United States or foreign person which is a dealer in securities or commodities;

(K) securities acquired and held by a controlled foreign corporation in the ordinary course of its business as a dealer in securities if—

(i) the dealer accounts for the securities as securities held primarily for sale to customers in the ordinary course of business, and

(ii) the dealer disposes of the securities (or such securities mature while held by the dealer) within a period consistent with the holding of securities for sale to customers in the ordinary course of business; and

(L) an obligation of a United States person which—

(i) is not a domestic corporation, and

(ii) is not—

(I) a United States shareholder (as defined in section 951(b)) of the controlled foreign corporation, or

(II) a partnership, estate, or trust in which the controlled foreign corporation, or any related person (as defined in section 954(d)(3)), is a partner, beneficiary, or trustee immediately after the acquisition of any obligation of such partnership, estate, or trust by the controlled foreign corporation.

For purposes of subparagraphs (I), (J), and (K), the term "dealer in securities" has the meaning given such term by section 475(c)(1), and the term "dealer in commodities" has the meaning given such term by section 475(e), except that such term shall include a futures commission merchant.

(3) Certain trade or service receivables acquired from related United States persons.—

(A) In general.—Notwithstanding paragraph (2) (other than subparagraph (H) thereof), the term "United States property" includes any trade or service receivable if— **§ 956(c)**

(i) such trade or service receivable is acquired (directly or indirectly) from a related person who is a United States person, and

(ii) the obligor under such receivable is a United States person.

(B) Definitions.—For purposes of this paragraph, the term "trade or service receivable" and "related person" have the respective meanings given to such terms by section 864(d).

(d) Pledges and guarantees.—For purposes of subsection (a), a controlled foreign corporation shall, under regulations prescribed by the Secretary, be considered as holding an obligation of a United States person if such controlled foreign corporation is a pledgor or guarantor of such obligation.

(e) Regulations.—The Secretary shall prescribe such regulations as may be necessary to carry out the purposes of this section, including regulations to prevent the avoidance of the provisions of this section through reorganizations or otherwise.

§ 957. Controlled foreign corporations; United States persons

(a) General rule.—For purposes of this title, the term "controlled foreign corporation" means any foreign corporation if more than 50 percent of—

(1) the total combined voting power of all classes of stock of such corporation entitled to vote, or

(2) the total value of the stock of such corporation,

is owned (within the meaning of section 958(a)), or is considered as owned by applying the rules of ownership of section 958(b), by United States shareholders on any day during the taxable year of such foreign corporation.

(b) Special rule for insurance.—For purposes only of taking into account income described in section 953(a) (relating to insurance income), the term "controlled foreign corporation" includes not only a foreign corporation as defined by subsection (a) but also one of which more than 25 percent of the total combined voting power of all classes of stock (or more than 25 percent of the total value of stock) is owned (within the meaning of section 958(a)), or is considered as owned by applying the rules of ownership of section 958(b), by United States shareholders on any day during the taxable year of such corporation, if the gross amount of premiums or other consideration in respect of the reinsurance or the issuing of insurance or annuity contracts not described in section 953(e)(2) exceeds 75 percent of the gross amount of all premiums or other consideration in respect of all risks.

(c) United States person.—For purposes of this subpart, the term "United States person" has the meaning assigned to it by section 7701(a)(30) except that—

(1) with respect to a corporation organized under the laws of the Commonwealth of Puerto Rico, such term does not include an individual who is a bona fide resident of Puerto Rico, if a dividend received by such individual during the taxable year from such corporation would, for purposes of section 933(1), be treated as income derived from sources within Puerto Rico, and

(2) with respect to a corporation organized under the laws of Guam, American Samoa, or the Northern Mariana Islands—

(A) 80 percent or more of the gross income of which for the 3-year period ending at the close of the taxable year (or for such part of such period as such corporation or any predecessor has been in existence) was derived from sources within such a possession or was effectively connected with the conduct of a trade or business in such a possession, and

(B) 50 percent or more of the gross income of which for such period (or part) was derived from the active conduct of a trade or business within such a possession,

such term does not include an individual who is a bona fide resident of Guam, American Samoa, or the Northern Mariana Islands.

For purposes of subparagraphs (A) and (B) of paragraph (2), the determination as to whether income was derived from the active conduct of a trade or business within a possession shall be made under regulations prescribed by the Secretary.

§ 958. Rules for determining stock ownership

(a) Direct and indirect ownership.—

(1) General rule.—For purposes of this subpart (other than section 960), stock owned means—

(A) stock owned directly, and

(B) stock owned with the application of paragraph (2).

(2) Stock ownership through foreign entities.—For purposes of subparagraph (B) of paragraph (1), stock owned, directly or indirectly, by or for a foreign corporation, foreign partnership, or foreign trust or foreign estate (within the meaning of section 7701(a)(31)) shall be considered as being owned proportionately by its shareholders, partners, or beneficiaries. Stock considered to be owned by a person by reason of the application of the preceding sentence shall, for purposes of applying such sentence, be treated as actually owned by such person.

(3) Special rule for mutual insurance companies.—For purposes of applying paragraph (1) in the case of a foreign mutual insurance company, the term "stock" shall include any certificate entitling the holder to voting power in the corporation.

(b) Constructive ownership.—For purposes of sections 951(b), 954(d)(3), 956(c)(2), and 957, section 318(a) (relating to constructive ownership of stock) shall apply to the extent that the effect is to treat any United States person as a United States shareholder within the meaning of section 951(b), to treat a person as a related person within the meaning of section 954(d)(3), to treat the stock of a domestic corporation as owned by a United States shareholder of the controlled foreign corporation for purposes of section 956(c)(2), or to treat a foreign corporation as a controlled foreign corporation under section 957, except that—

(1) In applying paragraph (1)(A) of section 318(a), stock owned by a nonresident alien individual (other than a foreign trust or foreign estate) shall not be considered as owned by a citizen or by a resident alien individual.

(2) In applying subparagraphs (A), (B), and (C) of section 318(a)(2), if a partnership, estate, trust, or corporation owns, directly or indirectly, more than 50 percent of the total combined voting power of all classes of stock entitled to vote of a corporation, it shall be considered as owning all the stock entitled to vote.

(3) In applying subparagraph (C) of section 318(a)(2), the phrase "10 percent" shall be substituted for the phrase "50 percent" used in subparagraph (C).

(4) Subparagraphs (A), (B), and (C) of section 318(a)(3) shall not be applied so as to consider a United States person as owning stock which is owned by a person who is not a United States person.

Paragraphs (1) and (4) shall not apply for purposes of section 956(c)(2) to treat stock of a domestic corporation as not owned by a United States shareholder.

§ 959. Exclusion from gross income of previously taxed earnings and profits

(a) Exclusion from gross income of United States persons.—For purposes of this chapter, the earnings and profits of a foreign corporation attributable to amounts which are, or have been, included in the gross income of a United States shareholder under section 951(a) shall not, when—

(1) such amounts are distributed to, or

(2) such amounts would, but for this subsection, be included under section 951(a)(1)(B) in the gross income of,

such shareholder (or any other United States person who acquires from any person any portion of the interest of such United States shareholder in such foreign corporation, but only to the extent of such portion, and subject to such proof of the identity of such interest as the Secretary may by regulations prescribe) directly or indirectly through a chain of ownership described under section 958(a), be again included in the gross income of such United States shareholder (or of such other United States person). The rules of subsection (c) shall apply for purposes of paragraph (1) of this subsection and the rules of subsection (f) shall apply for purposes of paragraph (2) of this subsection.

(b) Exclusion from gross income of certain foreign subsidiaries.—For purposes of section 951(a), the earnings and profits of a controlled foreign corporation attributable to amounts which are, or have been, included in the gross income of a United States shareholder under section 951(a), shall not, when distributed through a chain of ownership described under section 958(a), be also included in the gross income of another controlled foreign corporation in such chain for purposes of the application of section 951(a) to such other controlled foreign corporation with respect to such United States shareholder (or to any other United States shareholder who acquires from any person any portion of the interest of such United States shareholder in the controlled foreign corporation, but only to the extent of such portion, and subject to such proof of identity of such interest as the Secretary may prescribe by regulations).

(c) Allocation of distributions.—For purposes of subsections (a) and (b), section 316(a) shall be applied by applying paragraph (2) thereof, and then paragraph (1) thereof—

(1) first to the aggregate of—

(A) earnings and profits attributable to amounts included in gross income under section 951(a)(1)(B) (or which would have been included except for subsection (a)(2) of this section), and

(B) earnings and profits attributable to amounts included in gross income under section 951(a)(1)(C) (or which would have been included except for subsection (a)(3) of this section),

with any distribution being allocated between earnings and profits described in subparagraph (A) and earnings and profits described in subparagraph (B) proportionately on the basis of the respective amounts of such earnings and profits,

(2) then to earnings and profits attributable to amounts included in gross income under section 951(a)(1)(A) (but reduced by amounts not included under subparagraph (B) or (C) of section 951(a)(1) because of the exclusions in paragraphs (2) and (3) of subsection (a) of this section), and

(3) then to other earnings and profits.

References in this subsection to section 951(a)(1)(C) and subsection (a)(3) shall be treated as references to such provisions as in effect on the day before the date of the enactment of the Small Business Job Protection Act of 1996.

(d) Distributions excluded from gross income not to be treated as dividends.—Any distribution excluded from gross income under subsection (a) shall be treated, for purposes of this chapter, as a distribution which is not a dividend; except that such distributions shall immediately reduce earnings and profits.

(e) Coordination with amounts previously taxed under section 1248.—For purposes of this section and section 960(c), any amount included in the gross income of any person as a dividend by reason of subsection (a) or (f) of section 1248 shall be treated as an amount included in the gross income of such person (or, in any case to which section 1248(e) applies, of the domestic corporation referred to in section 1248(e)(2)) under section 951(a)(1)(A).

(f) Allocation rules for certain inclusions.—

(1) In general.—For purposes of this section, amounts that would be included under subparagraph (B) of section 951(a)(1) (determined without regard to this section) shall be treated as attributable first to earnings described in subsection (c)(2), and then to earnings described in subsection (c)(3).

(2) Treatment of distributions.—In applying this section, actual distributions shall be taken into account before amounts that would be included under section 951(a)(1)(B) (determined without regard to this section).

§ 960. Deemed paid credit for subpart F inclusions

(a) In general.—For purposes of subpart A of this part, if there is included in the gross income of a domestic corporation any item of income under section 951(a)(1) with respect to any controlled foreign corporation with respect to which such domestic corporation is a United States shareholder, such domestic corporation shall be deemed to have paid so much of such foreign corporation's foreign income taxes as are properly attributable to such item of income.

(b) Special rules for distributions from previously taxed earnings and profits.—For purposes of subpart A of this part—

(1) In general.—If any portion of a distribution from a controlled foreign corporation to a domestic corporation which is a United States shareholder with respect to such controlled foreign corporation is excluded from gross income under section 959(a), such domestic corporation shall be deemed to have paid so much of such foreign corporation's foreign income taxes as—

(A) are properly attributable to such portion, and

(B) have not been deemed to have to been paid by such domestic corporation under this section for the taxable year or any prior taxable year.

(2) Tiered controlled foreign corporations.—If section 959(b) applies to any portion of a distribution from a controlled foreign corporation to another controlled foreign corporation, such controlled foreign corporation shall be deemed to have paid so much of such other controlled foreign corporation's foreign income taxes as—

(A) are properly attributable to such portion, and

(B) have not been deemed to have been paid by a domestic corporation under this section for the taxable year or any prior taxable year.

(c) Special rules for foreign tax credit in year of receipt of previously taxed earnings and profits.—

(1) Increase in section 904 limitation.—In the case of any taxpayer who—

(A) either (i) chose to have the benefits of subpart A of this part for a taxable year beginning after September 30, 1993, in which he was required under section 951(a) to include any amount in his gross income, or (ii) did not pay or accrue for such taxable year any income, war profits, or excess profits taxes to any foreign country or to any possession of the United States,

(B) chooses to have the benefits of subpart A of this part for any taxable year in which he receives 1 or more distributions or amounts which are excludable from gross income under section 959(a) and which are attributable to amounts included in his gross income for taxable years referred to in subparagraph (A), and

(C) for the taxable year in which such distributions or amounts are received, pays, or is deemed to have paid, or accrues income, war profits, or excess profits taxes to a foreign country or to any possession of the United States with respect to such distributions or amounts,

the limitation under section 904 for the taxable year in which such distributions or amounts are received shall be increased by the lesser of the amount of such taxes paid, or deemed paid, or accrued with respect to such distributions or amounts or the amount in the excess limitation account as of the beginning of such taxable year.

(2) Excess limitation account.—

(A) Establishment of account.—Each taxpayer meeting the requirements of paragraph (1)(A) shall establish an excess limitation account. The opening balance of such account shall be zero.

(B) Increases in account.—For each taxable year beginning after September 30, 1993, the taxpayer shall increase the amount in the excess limitation account by the excess (if any) of—

(i) the amount by which the limitation under section 904(a) for such taxable year was increased by reason of the total amount of the inclusions in gross income under section 951(a) for such taxable year, over

(ii) the amount of any income, war profits, and excess profits taxes paid, or deemed paid, or accrued to any foreign country or possession of the United States which were allowable as a credit under section 901 for such taxable year and which would not have been allowable but for the inclusions in gross income described in clause (i).

Proper reductions in the amount added to the account under the preceding sentence for any taxable year shall be made for any increase in the credit allowable under section 901 for such taxable year by reason of a carryback if such increase would not have been allowable but for the inclusions in gross income described in clause (i).

(C) Decreases in account.—For each taxable year beginning after September 30, 1993, for which the limitation under section 904 was increased under paragraph (1), the taxpayer shall reduce the amount in the excess limitation account by the amount of such increase.

(3) Distributions of income previously taxed in years beginning before October 1, 1993.—If the taxpayer receives a distribution or amount in a taxable year beginning after September 30, 1993, which is excluded from gross income under section 959(a) and is attributable to any amount included in gross income under section 951(a) for a taxable year beginning before October 1, 1993, the limitation under section 904 for the taxable year in which such amount or distribution is received shall be increased by the amount determined under this subsection as in effect on the day before the date of the enactment of the Revenue Reconciliation Act of 1993.

(4) Cases in which taxes not to be allowed as deduction.—In the case of any taxpayer who—

(A) chose to have the benefits of subpart A of this part for a taxable year in which he was required under section 951(a) to include in his gross income an amount in respect of a controlled foreign corporation, and

(B) does not choose to have the benefits of subpart A of this part for the taxable year in which he receives a distribution or amount which is excluded from gross income under section 959(a) and which is attributable to earnings and profits of the controlled foreign corporation which was included in his gross income for the taxable year referred to in subparagraph (A),

no deduction shall be allowed under section 164 for the taxable year in which such distribution or amount is received for any income, war profits, or excess profits taxes paid or accrued to any foreign country or to any possession of the United States on or with respect to such distribution or amount.

(5) Insufficient taxable income.—If an increase in the limitation under this subsection exceeds the tax imposed by this chapter for such year, the amount of such excess shall be deemed an overpayment of tax for such year.

(d) Deemed paid credit for taxes properly attributable to tested income.—

(1) In general.—For purposes of subpart A of this part, if any amount is includible in the gross income of a domestic corporation under section 951A, such domestic corporation shall be deemed to have paid foreign income taxes equal to 90 percent of the product of—

(A) such domestic corporation's inclusion percentage, multiplied by **§ 960(d)**

(B) the aggregate tested foreign income taxes paid or accrued by controlled foreign corporations.

(2) Inclusion percentage.—For purposes of paragraph (1), the term "inclusion percentage" means, with respect to any domestic corporation, the ratio (expressed as a percentage) of—

(A) such corporation's net CFC tested income (as defined in section 951A(b)), divided by

(B) the aggregate amount described in section 951A(b)(1)(A) with respect to such corporation.

(3) Tested foreign income taxes.—For purposes of paragraph (1), the term "tested foreign income taxes" means, with respect to any domestic corporation which is a United States shareholder of a controlled foreign corporation, the foreign income taxes paid or accrued by such foreign corporation which are properly attributable to the tested income of such foreign corporation taken into account by such domestic corporation under section 951A.

(4) Disallowance of foreign tax credit with respect to distributions of previously taxed net CFC tested income.—No credit shall be allowed under section 901 for 10 percent of any foreign income taxes paid or accrued (or deemed paid under subsection (b)(1)) with respect to any amount excluded from gross income under section 959(a) by reason of an inclusion in gross income under section 951A(a).

(e) Foreign income taxes.—The term "foreign income taxes" means any income, war profits, or excess profits taxes paid or accrued to any foreign country or possession of the United States.

(f) Regulations.—The Secretary shall prescribe such regulations or other guidance as may be necessary or appropriate to carry out the provisions of this section.

§ 961. Adjustments to basis of stock in controlled foreign corporations and of other property

(a) Increase in basis.—Under regulations prescribed by the Secretary, the basis of a United States shareholder's stock in a controlled foreign corporation, and the basis of property of a United States shareholder by reason of which he is considered under section 958(a)(2) as owning stock of a controlled foreign corporation, shall be increased by the amount required to be included in his gross income under section 951(a) with respect to such stock or with respect to such property, as the case may be, but only to the extent to which such amount was included in the gross income of such United States shareholder. In the case of a United States shareholder who has made an election under section 962 for the taxable year, the increase in basis provided by this subsection shall not exceed an amount equal to the amount of tax paid under this chapter with respect to the amounts required to be included in his gross income under section 951(a).

(b) Reduction in basis.—

(1) In general.—Under regulations prescribed by the Secretary, the adjusted basis of stock or other property with respect to which a United States shareholder or a United States person receives an amount which is excluded from gross income under section 959(a) shall be reduced by the amount so excluded. In the case of a United States shareholder who has made an election under section 962 for any prior taxable year, the reduction in basis provided by this paragraph shall not exceed an amount equal to the amount received which is excluded from gross income under section 959(a) after the application of section 962(d).

(2) Amount in excess of basis.—To the extent that an amount excluded from gross income under section 959(a) exceeds the adjusted basis of the stock or other property with respect to which it is received, the amount shall be treated as gain from the sale or exchange of property.

(c) Basis adjustments in stock held by foreign corporations.—Under regulations prescribed by the Secretary, if a United States shareholder is treated under section 958(a)(2) as owning stock in a controlled foreign corporation which is owned by another controlled foreign corporation, then adjustments similar to the adjustments provided by subsections (a) and (b) shall be made to—

(1) the basis of such stock, and

(2) the basis of stock in any other controlled foreign corporation by reason of which the United States shareholder is considered under section 958(a)(2) as owning the stock described in paragraph (1),

but only for the purposes of determining the amount included under section 951 in the gross income of such United States shareholder (or any other United States shareholder who acquires from any person any portion of the interest of such United States shareholder by reason of which such shareholder was treated as owning such stock, but only to the extent of such portion, and subject to such proof of identity of such interest as the Secretary may prescribe by regulations). The preceding sentence shall not apply with respect to any stock to which a basis adjustment applies under subsection (a) or (b).

(d) Basis in specified 10-percent owned foreign corporation reduced by nontaxed portion of dividend for purposes of determining loss.—If a domestic corporation received a dividend from a specified 10-percent owned foreign corporation (as defined in section 245A) in any taxable year, solely for purposes of determining loss on any disposition of stock of such foreign corporation in such taxable year or any subsequent taxable year, the basis of such domestic corporation in such stock shall be reduced (but not below zero) by the amount of any deduction allowable to such domestic corporation under section 245A with respect to such stock except to the extent such basis was reduced under section 1059 by reason of a dividend for which such a deduction was allowable.

§ 962. Election by individuals to be subject to tax at corporate rates

(a) General rule.—Under regulations prescribed by the Secretary, in the case of a United States shareholder who is an individual and who elects to have the provisions of this section apply for the taxable year—

(1) the tax imposed under this chapter on amounts which are included in his gross income under section 951(a) shall (in lieu of the tax determined under sections 1 and 55) be an amount equal to the tax which would be imposed under sections 11 if such amounts were received by a domestic corporation, and

(2) for purposes of applying the provisions of section 960 (relating to foreign tax credit) such amounts shall be treated as if they were received by a domestic corporation.

(b) Election.—An election to have the provisions of this section apply for any taxable year shall be made by a United States shareholder at such time and in such manner as the Secretary shall prescribe by regulations. An election made for any taxable year may not be revoked except with the consent of the Secretary.

(c) Pro ration of each section 11 bracket amount.—For purposes of applying subsection (a)(1), the amount in each taxable income bracket in the tax table in section 11(b) shall not exceed an amount which bears the same ratio to such bracket amount as the amount included in the gross income of the United States shareholder under section 951(a) for the taxable year bears to such shareholder's pro rata share of the earnings and profits for the taxable year of all controlled foreign corporations with respect to which such shareholder includes any amount in gross income under section 951(a).

(d) Special rule for actual distributions.—The earnings and profits of a foreign corporation attributable to amounts which were included in the gross income of a United States shareholder under section 951(a) and with respect to which an election under this section applied shall, when such earnings and profits are distributed, notwithstanding the provisions of section 959(a)(1), be included in gross income to the extent that such earnings and profits so distributed exceed the amount of tax paid under this chapter on the amounts to which such election applied.

§ 964. Miscellaneous provisions

(a) Earnings and profits.—Except as provided in section 312(k)(4), for purposes of this subpart, the earnings and profits of any foreign corporation, and the deficit in earnings and profits of any foreign corporation, for any taxable year shall be determined according to rules substantially similar to those applicable to domestic corporations, under regulations prescribed by the Secretary. In determining such earnings and profits, or the deficit in such earnings and profits, the amount of any illegal bribe, kickback, or other payment (within the meaning of section 162(c)) shall not be taken into account to decrease such earnings and profits or to increase such deficit. The payments referred to in the preceding sentence are payments which would be unlawful under the Foreign Corrupt Practices Act of 1977 if the payor were a United States person.

(b) Blocked foreign income.—Under regulations prescribed by the Secretary, no part of the earnings and profits of a controlled foreign corporation for any taxable year shall be included in earnings and profits for purposes of sections 952 and 956, if it is established to the satisfaction of the Secretary that such part could not have been distributed by the controlled foreign corporation to United States shareholders who own (within the meaning of section 958(a)) stock of such controlled foreign corporation because of currency or other restrictions or limitations imposed under the laws of any foreign country.

(c) Records and accounts of United States shareholders.—

(1) Records and accounts to be maintained.—The Secretary may by regulations require each person who is, or has been, a United States shareholder of a controlled foreign corporation to maintain such records and accounts as may be prescribed by such regulations as necessary to carry out the provisions of this subpart and subpart G.

(2) Two or more persons required to maintain or furnish the same records and accounts with respect to the same foreign corporation.—Where, but for this paragraph, two or more United States persons would be required to maintain or furnish the same records and accounts as may by regulations be required under paragraph (1) with respect to the same controlled foreign corporation for the same period, the Secretary may by regulations provide that the maintenance or furnishing of such records and accounts by only one such person shall satisfy the requirements of paragraph (1) for such other persons.

(d) Treatment of certain branches.—

(1) In general.—For purposes of this chapter, section 6038, section 6046, and such other provisions as may be specified in regulations—

(A) a qualified insurance branch of a controlled foreign corporation shall be treated as a separate foreign corporation created under the laws of the foreign country with respect to which such branch qualifies under paragraph (2), and

(B) except as provided in regulations, any amount directly or indirectly transferred or credited from such branch to one or more other accounts of such controlled foreign corporation shall be treated as a dividend paid to such controlled foreign corporation.

(2) Qualified insurance branch.—For purposes of paragraph (1), the term "qualified insurance branch" means any branch of a controlled foreign corporation which is licensed and predominantly engaged on a permanent basis in the active conduct of an insurance business in a foreign country if—

(A) separate books and accounts are maintained for such branch,

(B) the principal place of business of such branch is in such foreign country,

(C) such branch would be taxable under subchapter L if it were a separate domestic corporation, and

(D) an election under this paragraph applies to such branch.

An election under this paragraph shall apply to the taxable year for which made and all subsequent taxable years unless revoked with the consent of the Secretary.

(3) Regulations.—The Secretary shall prescribe such regulations as may be necessary or appropriate to carry out the purposes of this subsection.

(e) Gain on certain stock sales by controlled foreign corporations treated as dividends.—

(1) In general.—If a controlled foreign corporation sells or exchanges stock in any other foreign corporation, gain recognized on such sale or exchange shall be included in the gross income of such controlled foreign corporation as a dividend to the same extent that it would have been so included under section 1248(a) if such controlled foreign corporation were a United States person. For purposes of determining the amount which would have been so includible, the determination of whether such other foreign corporation was a controlled foreign corporation shall be made without regard to the preceding sentence.

(2) Same country exception not applicable.—Clause (i) of section 954(c)(3)(A) shall not apply to any amount treated as a dividend by reason of paragraph (1).

(3) Clarification of deemed sales.—For purposes of this subsection, a controlled foreign corporation shall be treated as having sold or exchanged any stock if, under any provision of this subtitle, such controlled foreign corporation is treated as having gain from the sale or exchange of such stock.

(4) Coordination with dividends received deduction.—

(A) In general.—If, for any taxable year of a controlled foreign corporation beginning after December 31, 2017, any amount is treated as a dividend under paragraph (1) by reason of a sale or exchange by the controlled foreign corporation of stock in another foreign corporation held for 1 year or more, then, notwithstanding any other provision of this title—

(i) the foreign-source portion of such dividend shall be treated for purposes of section 951(a)(1)(A) as subpart F income of the selling controlled foreign corporation for such taxable year,

(ii) a United States shareholder with respect to the selling controlled foreign corporation shall include in gross income for the taxable year of the shareholder with or within which such taxable year of the controlled foreign corporation ends an amount equal to the shareholder's pro rata share (determined in the same manner as under section 951(a)(2)) of the amount treated as subpart F income under clause (i), and

(iii) the deduction under section 245A(a) shall be allowable to the United States shareholder with respect to the subpart F income included in gross income under clause (ii) in the same manner as if such subpart F income were a dividend received by the shareholder from the selling controlled foreign corporation.

(B) Application of basis or similar adjustment.—For purposes of this title, in the case of a sale or exchange by a controlled foreign corporation of stock in another foreign corporation in a taxable year of the selling controlled foreign corporation beginning after December 31, 2017, rules similar to the rules of section 961(d) shall apply.

(C) Foreign-source portion.—For purposes of this paragraph, the foreign-source portion of any amount treated as a dividend under paragraph (1) shall be determined in the same manner as under section 245A(c).

§ 965. Treatment of deferred foreign income upon transition to participation exemption system of taxation

(a) Treatment of deferred foreign income as subpart F income.—In the case of the last taxable year of a deferred foreign income corporation which begins before January 1, 2018, the subpart F income of such foreign corporation (as otherwise determined for such taxable year under section 952) shall be increased by the greater of—

(1) the accumulated post-1986 deferred foreign income of such corporation determined as of November 2, 2017, or

(2) the accumulated post-1986 deferred foreign income of such corporation determined as of December 31, 2017.

(b) Reduction in amounts included in gross income of United States shareholders of specified foreign corporations with deficits in earnings and profits.—

(1) In general.—In the case of a taxpayer which is a United States shareholder with respect to at least one deferred foreign income corporation and at least one E&P deficit foreign corporation, the amount which would (but for this subsection) be taken into account under section 951(a)(1) by reason of subsection (a) as such United States shareholder's pro rata share of the subpart F income of each deferred foreign income corporation shall be reduced by the amount of such United States shareholder's aggregate foreign E&P deficit which is allocated under paragraph (2) to such deferred foreign income corporation.

(2) Allocation of aggregate foreign E&P deficit.—The aggregate foreign E&P deficit of any United States shareholder shall be allocated among the deferred foreign income corporations of such United States shareholder in an amount which bears the same proportion to such aggregate as—

(A) such United States shareholder's pro rata share of the accumulated post-1986 deferred foreign income of each such deferred foreign income corporation, bears to

(B) the aggregate of such United States shareholder's pro rata share of the accumulated post-1986 deferred foreign income of all deferred foreign income corporations of such United States shareholder.

(3) Definitions related to E&P deficits.—For purposes of this subsection—

(A) Aggregate foreign E&P deficit.—

(i) In general.—The term "aggregate foreign E&P deficit" means, with respect to any United States shareholder, the lesser of—

(I) the aggregate of such shareholder's pro rata shares of the specified E&P deficits of the E&P deficit foreign corporations of such shareholder, or

(II) the amount determined under paragraph (2)(B).

(ii) Allocation of deficit.—If the amount described in clause (i)(II) is less than the amount described in clause (i)(I), then the shareholder shall designate, in such form and manner as the Secretary determines—

(I) the amount of the specified E&P deficit which is to be taken into account for each E&P deficit corporation with respect to the taxpayer, and

(II) in the case of an E&P deficit corporation which has a qualified deficit (as defined in section 952), the portion (if any) of the deficit taken into account under subclause (I) which is attributable to a qualified deficit, including the qualified activities to which such portion is attributable.

(B) E&P deficit foreign corporation.—The term "E&P deficit foreign corporation" means, with respect to any taxpayer, any specified foreign corporation with respect to which such taxpayer is a United States shareholder, if, as of November 2, 2017—

(i) such specified foreign corporation has a deficit in post-1986 earnings and profits,

(ii) such corporation was a specified foreign corporation, and

(iii) such taxpayer was a United States shareholder of such corporation.

(C) Specified E&P deficit.—The term "specified E&P deficit" means, with respect to any E&P deficit foreign corporation, the amount of the deficit referred to in subparagraph (B).

(4) Treatment of earnings and profits in future years.—

(A) Reduced earnings and profits treated as previously taxed income when distributed.— For purposes of applying section 959 in any taxable year beginning with the taxable year described in subsection (a), with respect to any United States shareholder of a deferred foreign income corporation, an amount equal to such shareholder's reduction under paragraph (1) which is allocated to such deferred foreign income corporation under this subsection shall be treated as an amount which was included in the gross income of such United States shareholder under section 951(a).

(B) E&P deficits.—For purposes of this title, with respect to any taxable year beginning with the taxable year described in subsection (a), a United States shareholder's pro rata share of the earnings and profits of any E&P deficit foreign corporation under this subsection shall be increased by the amount of the specified E&P deficit of such corporation taken into account by such shareholder under paragraph (1), and, for purposes of section 952, such increase shall be attributable to the same activity to which the deficit so taken into account was attributable.

(5) Netting among United States shareholders in same affiliated group.—

(A) In general.—In the case of any affiliated group which includes at least one E&P net surplus shareholder and one E&P net deficit shareholder, the amount which would (but for this paragraph) be taken into account under section 951(a)(1) by reason of subsection (a) by each such E&P net surplus shareholder shall be reduced (but not below zero) by such shareholder's applicable share of the affiliated group's aggregate unused E&P deficit.

(B) E&P net surplus shareholder.—For purposes of this paragraph, the term "E&P net surplus shareholder" means any United States shareholder which would (determined without regard to this paragraph) take into account an amount greater than zero under section 951(a)(1) by reason of subsection (a).

(C) E&P net deficit shareholder.—For purposes of this paragraph, the term "E&P net deficit shareholder" means any United States shareholder if—

(i) the aggregate foreign E&P deficit with respect to such shareholder (as defined in paragraph (3)(A) without regard to clause (i)(II) thereof), exceeds

(ii) the amount which would (but for this subsection) be taken into account by such shareholder under section 951(a)(1) by reason of subsection (a).

(D) Aggregate unused E&P deficit.—For purposes of this paragraph—

(i) In general.—The term "aggregate unused E&P deficit" means, with respect to any affiliated group, the lesser of—

(I) the sum of the excesses described in subparagraph (C), determined with respect to each E&P net deficit shareholder in such group, or

(II) the amount determined under subparagraph (E)(ii).

(ii) Reduction with respect to E&P net deficit shareholders which are not wholly owned by the affiliated group.—If the group ownership percentage of any E&P net deficit shareholder is less than 100 percent, the amount of the excess described in subparagraph (C) which is taken into account under clause (i)(I) with respect to such E&P net deficit shareholder shall be such group ownership percentage of such amount.

(E) Applicable share.—For purposes of this paragraph, the term "applicable share" means, with respect to any E&P net surplus shareholder in any affiliated group, the amount which bears the same proportion to such group's aggregate unused E&P deficit as—

(i) the product of—

(I) such shareholder's group ownership percentage, multiplied by

(II) the amount which would (but for this paragraph) be taken into account under section 951(a)(1) by reason of subsection (a) by such shareholder, bears to

(ii) the aggregate amount determined under clause (i) with respect to all E&P net surplus shareholders in such group.

(F) Group ownership percentage.—For purposes of this paragraph, the term "group ownership percentage" means, with respect to any United States shareholder in any affiliated group, the percentage of the value of the stock of such United States shareholder which is held by other includible corporations in such affiliated group. Notwithstanding the preceding sentence, the group ownership percentage of the common parent of the affiliated group is 100 percent. Any term used in this subparagraph which is also used in section 1504 shall have the same meaning as when used in such section.

(c) Application of participation exemption to included income.—

(1) In general.—In the case of a United States shareholder of a deferred foreign income corporation, there shall be allowed as a deduction for the taxable year in which an amount is included in the gross income of such United States shareholder under section 951(a)(1) by reason of this section an amount equal to the sum of—

(A) the United States shareholder's 8 percent rate equivalent percentage of the excess (if any) of—

(i) the amount so included as gross income, over

(ii) the amount of such United States shareholder's aggregate foreign cash position, plus

(B) the United States shareholder's 15.5 percent rate equivalent percentage of so much of the amount described in subparagraph (A)(ii) as does not exceed the amount described in subparagraph (A)(i).

(2) 8 And 15.5 percent rate equivalent percentages.—For purposes of this subsection—

(A) 8 Percent rate equivalent percentage.—The term "8 percent rate equivalent percentage" means, with respect to any United States shareholder for any taxable year, the percentage which would result in the amount to which such percentage applies being subject to a 8 percent rate of tax determined by only taking into account a deduction equal to such percentage of such amount and the highest rate of tax specified in section 11 for such taxable year. In the case of any taxable year of a United States shareholder to which section 15 applies, the highest rate of tax under section 11 before the effective date of the change in rates and the highest rate of tax under section 11 after the effective date of such change shall each be taken into account under the preceding sentence in the same proportions as the portion of such taxable year which is before and after such effective date, respectively.

(B) 15.5 Percent rate equivalent percentage.—The term "15.5 percent rate equivalent percentage" means, with respect to any United States shareholder for any taxable year, the percentage determined under subparagraph (A) applied by substituting "15.5 percent rate of tax" for "8 percent rate of tax".

(3) Aggregate foreign cash position.—For purposes of this subsection—

(A) In general.—The term "aggregate foreign cash position" means, with respect to any United States shareholder, the greater of—

(i) the aggregate of such United States shareholder's pro rata share of the cash position of each specified foreign corporation of such United States shareholder determined as of the close of the last taxable year of such specified foreign corporation which begins before January 1, 2018, or

(ii) one half of the sum of—

(I) the aggregate described in clause (i) determined as of the close of the last taxable year of each such specified foreign corporation which ends before November 2, 2017, plus

(II) the aggregate described in clause (i) determined as of the close of the taxable year of each such specified foreign corporation which precedes the taxable year referred to in subclause (I).

(B) Cash position.—For purposes of this paragraph, the cash position of any specified foreign corporation is the sum of—

(i) cash held by such foreign corporation,

(ii) the net accounts receivable of such foreign corporation, plus

(iii) the fair market value of the following assets held by such corporation:

(I) Personal property which is of a type that is actively traded and for which there is an established financial market.

(II) Commercial paper, certificates of deposit, the securities of the Federal government and of any State or foreign government.

(III) Any foreign currency.

(IV) Any obligation with a term of less than one year.

(V) Any asset which the Secretary identifies as being economically equivalent to any asset described in this subparagraph.

(C) Net accounts receivable.—For purposes of this paragraph, the term "net accounts receivable" means, with respect to any specified foreign corporation, the excess (if any) of—

(i) such corporation's accounts receivable, over

(ii) such corporation's accounts payable (determined consistent with the rules of section 461).

(D) Prevention of double counting.—Cash positions of a specified foreign corporation described in clause (ii), (iii)(I), or (iii)(IV) of subparagraph (B) shall not be taken into account by a United States shareholder under subparagraph (A) to the extent that such United States shareholder demonstrates to the satisfaction of the Secretary that such amount is so taken into account by such United States shareholder with respect to another specified foreign corporation.

(E) Cash positions of certain non-corporate entities taken into account.—An entity (other than a corporation) shall be treated as a specified foreign corporation of a United States shareholder for purposes of determining such United States shareholder's aggregate foreign cash position if any interest in such entity is held by a specified foreign corporation of such United States shareholder (determined after application of this subparagraph) and such entity would be a specified foreign corporation of such United States shareholder if such entity were a foreign corporation.

(F) Anti-abuse.—If the Secretary determines that a principal purpose of any transaction was to reduce the aggregate foreign cash position taken into account under this subsection, such transaction shall be disregarded for purposes of this subsection.

(d) Deferred foreign income corporation; accumulated post-1986 deferred foreign income.—For purposes of this section—

(1) Deferred foreign income corporation.—The term "deferred foreign income corporation" means, with respect to any United States shareholder, any specified foreign corporation of such United States shareholder which has accumulated post-1986 deferred foreign income (as of the date referred to in paragraph (1) or (2) of subsection (a)) greater than zero.

(2) Accumulated post-1986 deferred foreign income.—The term "accumulated post-1986 deferred foreign income" means the post-1986 earnings and profits except to the extent such earnings—

(A) are attributable to income of the specified foreign corporation which is effectively connected with the conduct of a trade or business within the United States and subject to tax under this chapter, or

(B) in the case of a controlled foreign corporation, if distributed, would be excluded from the gross income of a United States shareholder under section 959.

To the extent provided in regulations or other guidance prescribed by the Secretary, in the case of any controlled foreign corporation which has shareholders which are not United States shareholders, accumulated post-1986 deferred foreign income shall be appropriately reduced by amounts which would be described in subparagraph (B) if such shareholders were United States shareholders.

(3) Post-1986 earnings and profits.—The term "post-1986 earnings and profits" means the earnings and profits of the foreign corporation (computed in accordance with sections 964(a) and 986, and by only taking into account periods when the foreign corporation was a specified foreign corporation) accumulated in taxable years beginning after December 31, 1986, and determined—

(A) as of the date referred to in paragraph (1) or (2) of subsection (a), whichever is applicable with respect to such foreign corporation, and

(B) without diminution by reason of dividends distributed during the taxable year described in subsection (a) other than dividends distributed to another specified foreign corporation.

(e) Specified foreign corporation.—

(1) In general.—For purposes of this section, the term "specified foreign corporation" means—

(A) any controlled foreign corporation, and

(B) any foreign corporation with respect to which one or more domestic corporations is a United States shareholder.

(2) Application to certain foreign corporations.—For purposes of sections 951 and 961, a foreign corporation described in paragraph (1)(B) shall be treated as a controlled foreign corporation solely for purposes of taking into account the subpart F income of such corporation under subsection (a) (and for purposes of applying subsection (f)).

(3) Exclusion of passive foreign investment companies.—Such term shall not include any corporation which is a passive foreign investment company (as defined in section 1297) with respect to the shareholder and which is not a controlled foreign corporation.

(f) Determinations of pro rata share.—

(1) In general.—For purposes of this section, the determination of any United States shareholder's pro rata share of any amount with respect to any specified foreign corporation shall be determined under rules similar to the rules of section 951(a)(2) by treating such amount in the same manner as subpart F income (and by treating such specified foreign corporation as a controlled foreign corporation).

(2) Special rules.—The portion which is included in the income of a United States shareholder under section 951(a)(1) by reason of subsection (a) which is equal to the deduction allowed under subsection (c) by reason of such inclusion—

(A) shall be treated as income exempt from tax for purposes of sections 705(a)(1)(B) and 1367(a)(1)(A), and

(B) shall not be treated as income exempt from tax for purposes of determining whether an adjustment shall be made to an accumulated adjustment account under section 1368(e)(1)(A).

(g) Disallowance of foreign tax credit, etc.—

(1) In general.—No credit shall be allowed under section 901 for the applicable percentage of any taxes paid or accrued (or treated as paid or accrued) with respect to any amount for which a deduction is allowed under this section.

(2) Applicable percentage.—For purposes of this subsection, the term "applicable percentage" means the amount (expressed as a percentage) equal to the sum of—

(A) 0.771 multiplied by the ratio of—

(i) the excess to which subsection (c)(1)(A) applies, divided by

(ii) the sum of such excess plus the amount to which subsection (c)(1)(B) applies, plus

(B) 0.557 multiplied by the ratio of—

(i) the amount to which subsection (c)(1)(B) applies, divided by

(ii) the sum described in subparagraph (A)(ii).

(3) Denial of deduction.—No deduction shall be allowed under this chapter for any tax for which credit is not allowable under section 901 by reason of paragraph (1) (determined by treating the taxpayer as having elected the benefits of subpart A of part III of subchapter N).

(4) Coordination with section 78.—With respect to the taxes treated as paid or accrued by a domestic corporation with respect to amounts which are includible in gross income of such domestic corporation by reason of this section, section 78 shall apply only to so much of such taxes as bears the same proportion to the amount of such taxes as—

(A) the excess of—

(i) the amounts which are includible in gross income of such domestic corporation by reason of this section, over

(ii) the deduction allowable under subsection (c) with respect to such amounts, bears to

(B) such amounts.

(h) Election to pay liability in installments.—

(1) In general.—In the case of a United States shareholder of a deferred foreign income corporation, such United States shareholder may elect to pay the net tax liability under this section in 8 installments of the following amounts:

(A) 8 percent of the net tax liability in the case of each of the first 5 of such installments,

(B) 15 percent of the net tax liability in the case of the 6th such installment,

(C) 20 percent of the net tax liability in the case of the 7th such installment, and

(D) 25 percent of the net tax liability in the case of the 8th such installment.

(2) Date for payment of installments.—If an election is made under paragraph (1), the first installment shall be paid on the due date (determined without regard to any extension of time for filing the return) for the return of tax for the taxable year described in subsection (a) and each succeeding installment shall be paid on the due date (as so determined) for the return of tax for the taxable year following the taxable year with respect to which the preceding installment was made.

(3) Acceleration of payment.—If there is an addition to tax for failure to timely pay any installment required under this subsection, a liquidation or sale of substantially all the assets of the taxpayer (including in a title 11 or similar case), a cessation of business by the taxpayer, or any similar circumstance, then the unpaid portion of all remaining installments shall be due on the date of such event (or in the case of a title 11 or similar case, the day before the petition is filed). The preceding sentence shall not apply to the sale of substantially all the assets of a taxpayer to a buyer if such buyer enters into an agreement with the Secretary under which such buyer is liable for the remaining installments due under this subsection in the same manner as if such buyer were the taxpayer.

(4) Proration of deficiency to installments.—If an election is made under paragraph (1) to pay the net tax liability under this section in installments and a deficiency has been assessed with respect to such net tax liability, the deficiency shall be prorated to the installments payable under paragraph (1).

The part of the deficiency so prorated to any installment the date for payment of which has not arrived shall be collected at the same time as, and as a part of, such installment. The part of the deficiency so prorated to any installment the date for payment of which has arrived shall be paid upon notice and demand from the Secretary. This subsection shall not apply if the deficiency is due to negligence, to intentional disregard of rules and regulations, or to fraud with intent to evade tax.

(5) Election.—Any election under paragraph (1) shall be made not later than the due date for the return of tax for the taxable year described in subsection (a) and shall be made in such manner as the Secretary shall provide.

(6) Net tax liability under this section.—For purposes of this subsection—

(A) In general.—The net tax liability under this section with respect to any United States shareholder is the excess (if any) of—

(i) such taxpayer's net income tax for the taxable year in which an amount is included in the gross income of such United States shareholder under section 951(a)(1) by reason of this section, over

(ii) such taxpayer's net income tax for such taxable year determined—

(I) without regard to this section, and

(II) without regard to any income or deduction properly attributable to a dividend received by such United States shareholder from any deferred foreign income corporation.

(B) Net income tax.—The term "net income tax" means the regular tax liability reduced by the credits allowed under subparts A, B, and D of part IV of subchapter A.

(i) Special rules for S corporation shareholders.—

(1) In general.—In the case of any S corporation which is a United States shareholder of a deferred foreign income corporation, each shareholder of such S corporation may elect to defer payment of such shareholder's net tax liability under this section with respect to such S corporation until the shareholder's taxable year which includes the triggering event with respect to such liability. Any net tax liability payment of which is deferred under the preceding sentence shall be assessed on the return of tax as an addition to tax in the shareholder's taxable year which includes such triggering event.

(2) Triggering event.—

(A) In general.—In the case of any shareholder's net tax liability under this section with respect to any S corporation, the triggering event with respect to such liability is whichever of the following occurs first:

(i) Such corporation ceases to be an S corporation (determined as of the first day of the first taxable year that such corporation is not an S corporation).

(ii) A liquidation or sale of substantially all the assets of such S corporation (including in a title 11 or similar case), a cessation of business by such S corporation, such S corporation ceases to exist, or any similar circumstance.

(iii) A transfer of any share of stock in such S corporation by the taxpayer (including by reason of death, or otherwise).

(B) Partial transfers of stock.—In the case of a transfer of less than all of the taxpayer's shares of stock in the S corporation, such transfer shall only be a triggering event with respect to so much of the taxpayer's net tax liability under this section with respect to such S corporation as is properly allocable to such stock.

(C) Transfer of liability.—A transfer described in clause (iii) of subparagraph (A) shall not be treated as a triggering event if the transferee enters into an agreement with the Secretary under which such transferee is liable for net tax liability with respect to such stock in the same manner as if such transferee were the taxpayer.

(3) Net tax liability.—A shareholder's net tax liability under this section with respect to any S corporation is the net tax liability under this section which would be determined under subsection (h)(6) if the only subpart F income taken into account by such shareholder by reason of this section were allocations from such S corporation.

(4) Election to pay deferred liability in installments.—In the case of a taxpayer which elects to defer payment under paragraph (1)—

(A) subsection (h) shall be applied separately with respect to the liability to which such election applies,

(B) an election under subsection (h) with respect to such liability shall be treated as timely made if made not later than the due date for the return of tax for the taxable year in which the triggering event with respect to such liability occurs,

(C) the first installment under subsection (h) with respect to such liability shall be paid not later than such due date (but determined without regard to any extension of time for filing the return), and

(D) if the triggering event with respect to any net tax liability is described in paragraph (2)(A)(ii), an election under subsection (h) with respect to such liability may be made only with the consent of the Secretary.

(5) Joint and several liability of S corporation.—If any shareholder of an S corporation elects to defer payment under paragraph (1), such S corporation shall be jointly and severally liable for such payment and any penalty, addition to tax, or additional amount attributable thereto.

(6) Extension of limitation on collection.—Any limitation on the time period for the collection of a liability deferred under this subsection shall not be treated as beginning before the date of the triggering event with respect to such liability.

(7) Annual reporting of net tax liability.—

(A) In general.—Any shareholder of an S corporation which makes an election under paragraph (1) shall report the amount of such shareholder's deferred net tax liability on such shareholder's return of tax for the taxable year for which such election is made and on the return of tax for each taxable year thereafter until such amount has been fully assessed on such returns.

(B) Deferred net tax liability.—For purposes of this paragraph, the term "deferred net tax liability" means, with respect to any taxable year, the amount of net tax liability payment of which has been deferred under paragraph (1) and which has not been assessed on a return of tax for any prior taxable year.

(C) Failure to report.—In the case of any failure to report any amount required to be reported under subparagraph (A) with respect to any taxable year before the due date for the return of tax for such taxable year, there shall be assessed on such return as an addition to tax 5 percent of such amount.

(8) Election.—Any election under paragraph (1)—

(A) shall be made by the shareholder of the S corporation not later than the due date for such shareholder's return of tax for the taxable year which includes the close of the taxable year of such S corporation in which the amount described in subsection (a) is taken into account, and

(B) shall be made in such manner as the Secretary shall provide.

(j) Reporting by S corporation.—Each S corporation which is a United States shareholder of a specified foreign corporation shall report in its return of tax under section 6037(a) the amount includible in its gross income for such taxable year by reason of this section and the amount of the deduction allowable by subsection (c). Any copy provided to a shareholder under section 6037(b) shall include a statement of such shareholder's pro rata share of such amounts.

(k) Extension of limitation on assessment.—Notwithstanding section 6501, the limitation on the time period for the assessment of the net tax liability under this section (as defined in subsection (h)(6)) shall not expire before the date that is 6 years after the return for the taxable year described in such subsection was filed.

***(l)* Recapture for expatriated entities.**—

(1) In general.—If a deduction is allowed under subsection (c) to a United States shareholder and such shareholder first becomes an expatriated entity at any time during the 10-year period beginning on the date of the enactment of the Tax Cuts and Jobs Act (with respect to a surrogate foreign corporation which first becomes a surrogate foreign corporation during such period), then—

(A) the tax imposed by this chapter shall be increased for the first taxable year in which such taxpayer becomes an expatriated entity by an amount equal to 35 percent of the amount of the deduction allowed under subsection (c), and

(B) no credits shall be allowed against the increase in tax under subparagraph (A).

(2) Expatriated entity.—For purposes of this subsection, the term "expatriated entity" has the same meaning given such term under section 7874(a)(2), except that such term shall not include an entity if the surrogate foreign corporation with respect to the entity is treated as a domestic corporation under section 7874(b).

(3) Surrogate foreign corporation.—For purposes of this subsection, the term "surrogate foreign corporation" has the meaning given such term in section 7874(a)(2)(B).

(m) Special rules for United States shareholders which are real estate investment trusts.—

(1) In general.—If a real estate investment trust is a United States shareholder in 1 or more deferred foreign income corporations—

(A) any amount required to be taken into account under section 951(a)(1) by reason of this section shall not be taken into account as gross income of the real estate investment trust for purposes of applying paragraphs (2) and (3) of section 856(c) to any taxable year for which such amount is taken into account under section 951(a)(1), and

(B) if the real estate investment trust elects the application of this subparagraph, notwithstanding subsection (a), any amount required to be taken into account under section 951(a)(1) by reason of this section shall, in lieu of the taxable year in which it would otherwise be included in gross income (for purposes of the computation of real estate investment trust taxable income under section 857(b)), be included in gross income as follows:

(i) 8 percent of such amount in the case of each of the taxable years in the 5-taxable year period beginning with the taxable year in which such amount would otherwise be included.

(ii) 15 percent of such amount in the case of the 1st taxable year following such period.

(iii) 20 percent of such amount in the case of the 2nd taxable year following such period.

(iv) 25 percent of such amount in the case of the 3rd taxable year following such period.

(2) Rules for trusts electing deferred inclusion.—

(A) Election.—Any election under paragraph (1)(B) shall be made not later than the due date for the first taxable year in the 5-taxable year period described in clause (i) of paragraph (1)(B) and shall be made in such manner as the Secretary shall provide.

(B) Special rules.—If an election under paragraph (1)(B) is in effect with respect to any real estate investment trust, the following rules shall apply:

(i) Application of participation exemption.—For purposes of subsection (c)(1)—

(I) the aggregate amount to which subparagraph (A) or (B) of subsection (c)(1) applies shall be determined without regard to the election,

(II) each such aggregate amount shall be allocated to each taxable year described in paragraph (1)(B) in the same proportion as the amount included in the gross income of such United States shareholder under section 951(a)(1) by reason of this section is allocated to each such taxable year.

(III) No installment payments.—The real estate investment trust may not make an election under subsection (g) for any taxable year described in paragraph (1)(B).

(ii) Acceleration of inclusion.—If there is a liquidation or sale of substantially all the assets of the real estate investment trust (including in a title 11 or similar case), a cessation of business by such trust, or any similar circumstance, then any amount not yet included in gross income under paragraph (1)(B) shall be included in gross income as of the day before the date of the event and the unpaid portion of any tax liability with respect to such inclusion shall be due on the date of such event (or in the case of a title 11 or similar case, the day before the petition is filed).

(n) Election not to apply net operating loss deduction.—

(1) In general.—If a United States shareholder of a deferred foreign income corporation elects the application of this subsection for the taxable year described in subsection (a), then the amount described in paragraph (2) shall not be taken into account—

(A) in determining the amount of the net operating loss deduction under section 172 of such shareholder for such taxable year, or

(B) in determining the amount of taxable income for such taxable year which may be reduced by net operating loss carryovers or carrybacks to such taxable year under section 172.

(2) Amount described.—The amount described in this paragraph is the sum of—

(A) the amount required to be taken into account under section 951(a)(1) by reason of this section (determined after the application of subsection (c)), plus

(B) in the case of a domestic corporation which chooses to have the benefits of subpart A of part III of subchapter N for the taxable year, the taxes deemed to be paid by such corporation under subsections (a) and (b) of section 960 for such taxable year with respect to the amount described in subparagraph (A) which are treated as a dividends under section 78.

(3) Election.—Any election under this subsection shall be made not later than the due date (including extensions) for filing the return of tax for the taxable year and shall be made in such manner as the Secretary shall prescribe.

(*o*) Regulations.—The Secretary shall prescribe such regulations or other guidance as may be necessary or appropriate to carry out the provisions of this section, including—

(1) regulations or other guidance to provide appropriate basis adjustments, and

(2) regulations or other guidance to prevent the avoidance of the purposes of this section, including through a reduction in earnings and profits, through changes in entity classification or accounting methods, or otherwise.

Subpart I—Admissibility of Documentation Maintained in Foreign Countries

§ 982. Admissibility of documentation maintained in foreign countries

(a) General rule.—If the taxpayer fails to substantially comply with any formal document request arising out of the examination of the tax treatment of any item (hereinafter in this section referred to as the "examined item") before the 90th day after the date of the mailing of such request on motion by the Secretary, any court having jurisdiction of a civil proceeding in which the tax treatment of the examined item is an issue shall prohibit the introduction by the taxpayer of any foreign-based documentation covered by such request.

(b) Reasonable cause exception.—

(1) In general.—Subsection (a) shall not apply with respect to any documentation if the taxpayer establishes that the failure to provide the documentation as requested by the Secretary is due to reasonable cause.

(2) Foreign nondisclosure law not reasonable cause.—For purposes of paragraph (1), the fact that a foreign jurisdiction would impose a civil or criminal penalty on the taxpayer (or any other person) for disclosing the requested documentation is not reasonable cause.

(c) Formal document request.—For purposes of this section—

(1) Formal document request.—The term "formal document request" means any request (made after the normal request procedures have failed to produce the requested documentation) for the production of foreign-based documentation which is mailed by registered or certified mail to the taxpayer at his last known address and which sets forth—

(A) the time and place for the production of the documentation,

(B) a statement of the reason the documentation previously produced (if any) is not sufficient,

(C) a description of the documentation being sought, and

(D) the consequences to the taxpayer of the failure to produce the documentation described in subparagraph (C).

(2) Proceeding to quash.—

(A) In general.—Notwithstanding any other law or rule of law, any person to whom a formal document request is mailed shall have the right to begin a proceeding to quash such request not later than the 90th day after the day such request was mailed. In any such proceeding, the Secretary may seek to compel compliance with such request.

(B) Jurisdiction.—The United States district court for the district in which the person (to whom the formal document request is mailed) resides or is found shall have jurisdiction to hear any proceeding brought under subparagraph (A). An order denying the petition shall be deemed a final order which may be appealed.

(C) Suspension of 90-day period.—The running of the 90-day period referred to in subsection (a) shall be suspended during any period during which a proceeding brought under subparagraph (A) is pending.

(d) Definitions and special rules.—For purposes of this section—

(1) Foreign-based documentation.—The term "foreign-based documentation" means any documentation which is outside the United States and which may be relevant or material to the tax treatment of the examined item.

(2) Documentation.—The term "documentation" includes books and records.

(3) Authority to extend 90-day period.—The Secretary, and any court having jurisdiction over a proceeding under subsection (c)(2), may extend the 90-day period referred to in subsection (a).

(e) Suspension of statute of limitations.—If any person takes any action as provided in subsection (c)(2), the running of any period of limitations under section 6501 (relating to the assessment and collection of tax) or under section 6531 (relating to criminal prosecutions) with respect to such person shall be suspended for the period during which the proceeding under such subsection, and appeals therein, are pending.

Subpart J—Foreign Currency Transactions

§ 985. Functional currency

(a) In general.—Unless otherwise provided in regulations, all determinations under this subtitle shall be made in the taxpayer's functional currency.

(b) Functional currency.—

(1) In general.—For purposes of this subtitle, the term "functional currency" means—

(A) except as provided in subparagraph (B), the dollar, or

(B) in the case of a qualified business unit, the currency of the economic environment in which a significant part of such unit's activities are conducted and which is used by such unit in keeping its books and records.

(2) Functional currency where activities primarily conducted in dollars.—The functional currency of any qualified business unit shall be the dollar if activities of such unit are primarily conducted in dollars.

(3) Election.—To the extent provided in regulations, the taxpayer may elect to use the dollar as the functional currency for any qualified business unit if—

(A) such unit keeps its books and records in dollars, or

(B) the taxpayer uses a method of accounting that approximates a separate transactions method.

Any such election shall apply to the taxable year for which made and all subsequent taxable years unless revoked with the consent of the Secretary.

(4) Change in functional currency treated as a change in method of accounting.—Any change in the functional currency shall be treated as a change in the taxpayer's method of accounting for purposes of section 481 under procedures to be established by the Secretary.

§ 986. Determination of foreign taxes and foreign corporation's earnings and profits

(a) Foreign income taxes.—

(1) Translation of accrued taxes.—

(A) In general.—For purposes of determining the amount of the foreign tax credit, in the case of a taxpayer who takes foreign income taxes into account when accrued, the amount of any foreign income taxes (and any adjustment thereto) shall be translated into dollars by using the average exchange rate for the taxable year to which such taxes relate.

(B) Exception for certain taxes.—Subparagraph (A) shall not apply to any foreign income taxes—

(i) paid after the date 2 years after the close of the taxable year to which such taxes relate, or

(ii) paid before the beginning of the taxable year to which such taxes relate.

(C) Exception for inflationary currencies.—Subparagraph (a) shall not apply to any foreign income taxes the liability for which is denominated in any inflationary currency (as determined under regulations).

(D) Elective exception for taxes paid other than in functional currency.—

(i) In general.—At the election of the taxpayer, subparagraph (A) shall not apply to any foreign income taxes the liability for which is denominated in any currency other than in the taxpayer's functional currency.

(ii) Application to qualified business units.—An election under this subparagraph may apply to foreign income taxes attributable to a qualified business unit in accordance with regulations prescribed by the Secretary.

(iii) Election.—Any such election shall apply to the taxable year for which made and all subsequent taxable years unless revoked with the consent of the Secretary.

(E) Special rule for regulated investment companies.—In the case of a regulated investment company which takes into account income on an accrual basis, subparagraphs (A) through (D) shall not apply and foreign income taxes paid or accrued with respect to such income shall be translated into dollars using the exchange rate as of the date the income accrues.

(F) Cross reference.—

For adjustments where tax is not paid within 2 years, see section 905(c).

(2) Translation of taxes to which paragraph (1) does not apply.—For purposes of determining the amount of the foreign tax credit, in the case of any foreign income taxes to which subparagraph (A) or (E) of paragraph (1) does not apply—

(A) such taxes shall be translated into dollars using the exchange rates as of the time such taxes were paid to the foreign country or possession of the United States, and

(B) any adjustment to the amount of such taxes shall be translated into dollars using—

(i) except as provided in clause (ii), the exchange rate as of the time when such adjustment is paid to the foreign country or possession, or

(ii) in the case of any refund or credit of foreign income taxes, using the exchange rate as of the time of the original payment of such foreign income taxes.

(3) Authority to permit use of average rates.—To the extent prescribed in regulations, the average exchange rate for the period (specified in such regulations) during which the taxes or adjustment is paid may be used instead of the exchange rate as of the time of such payment.

(4) Foreign income taxes.—For purposes of this subsection, the term "foreign income taxes" means any income, war profits, or excess profits taxes paid or accrued to any foreign country or to any possession of the United States.

(b) Earnings and profits and distributions.—For purposes of determining the tax under this subtitle—

(1) of any shareholder of any foreign corporation, the earnings and profits of such corporation shall be determined in the corporation's functional currency, and

(2) in the case of any United States person, the earnings and profits determined under paragraph (1) (when distributed, deemed distributed, or otherwise taken into account under this subtitle) shall (if necessary) be translated into dollars using the appropriate exchange rate.

(c) Previously taxed earnings and profits.—

(1) In general.—Foreign currency gain or loss with respect to distributions of previously taxed earnings and profits (as described in section 959 or 1293(c)) attributable to movements in exchange rates between the times of deemed and actual distribution shall be recognized and treated as ordinary income or loss from the same source as the associated income inclusion.

(2) Distributions through tiers.—The Secretary shall prescribe regulations with respect to the treatment of distributions of previously taxed earnings and profits through tiers of foreign corporations.

§ 987. Branch transactions

In the case of any taxpayer having 1 or more qualified business units with a functional currency other than the dollar, taxable income of such taxpayer shall be determined—

(1) by computing the taxable income or loss separately for each such unit in its functional currency,

(2) by translating the income or loss separately computed under paragraph (1) at the appropriate exchange rate, and

(3) by making proper adjustments (as prescribed by the Secretary) for transfers of property between qualified business units of the taxpayer having different functional currencies, including—

(A) treating post-1986 remittances from each such unit as made on a pro rata basis out of post-1986 accumulated earnings, and

(B) treating gain or loss determined under this paragraph as ordinary income or loss, respectively, and sourcing such gain or loss by reference to the source of the income giving rise to post-1986 accumulated earnings.

§ 988. Treatment of certain foreign currency transactions

(a) General rule.—Notwithstanding any other provision of this chapter—

(1) Treatment as ordinary income or loss.—

(A) In general.—Except as otherwise provided in this section, any foreign currency gain or loss attributable to a section 988 transaction shall be computed separately and treated as ordinary income or loss (as the case may be).

(B) Special rule for forward contracts, etc.—Except as provided in regulations, a taxpayer may elect to treat any foreign currency gain or loss attributable to a forward contract, a futures contract, or option described in subsection (c)(1)(B)(iii) which is a capital asset in the hands of the taxpayer and which is not a part of a straddle (within the meaning of section 1092(c), without regard to paragraph (4) thereof) as capital gain or loss (as the case may be) if the taxpayer makes such election and identifies such transaction before the close of the day on which such transaction is entered into (or such earlier time as the Secretary may prescribe).

(2) Gain or loss treated as interest for certain purposes.—To the extent provided in regulations, any amount treated as ordinary income or loss under paragraph (1) shall be treated as interest income or expense (as the case may be).

(3) Source.—

(A) In general.—Except as otherwise provided in regulations, in the case of any amount treated as ordinary income or loss under paragraph (1) (without regard to paragraph (1)(B)), the source of such amount shall be determined by reference to the residence of the taxpayer or the qualified business unit of the taxpayer on whose books the asset, liability, or item of income or expense is properly reflected.

(B) Residence.—For purposes of this subpart—

(i) In general.—The residence of any person shall be—

(I) in the case of an individual, the country in which such individual's tax home (as defined in section 911(d)(3)) is located,

(II) in the case of any corporation, partnership, trust, or estate which is a United States person (as defined in section 7701(a)(30)), the United States, and

(III) in the case of any corporation, partnership, trust, or estate which is not a United States person, a country other than the United States.

If an individual does not have a tax home (as so defined), the residence of such individual shall be the United States if such individual is a United States citizen or a resident alien and shall be a country other than the United States if such individual is not a United States citizen or a resident alien.

(ii) Exception.—In the case of a qualified business unit of any taxpayer (including an individual), the residence of such unit shall be the country in which the principal place of business of such qualified business unit is located.

(iii) Special rule for partnerships.—To the extent provided in regulations, in the case of a partnership, the determination of residence shall be made at the partner level.

(C) Special rule for certain related party loans.—Except to the extent provided in regulations, in the case of a loan by a United States person or a related person to a 10-percent owned foreign corporation which is denominated in a currency other than the dollar and bears interest at a rate at least 10 percentage points higher than the Federal mid-term rate (determined under section 1274(d)) at the time such loan is entered into, the following rules shall apply:

(i) For purposes of section 904 only, such loan shall be marked to market on an annual basis.

(ii) Any interest income earned with respect to such loan for the taxable year shall be treated as income from sources within the United States to the extent of any loss attributable to clause (i).

For purposes of this subparagraph, the term "related person" has the meaning given such term by section 954(d)(3), except that such section shall be applied by substituting "United States person" for "controlled foreign corporation" each place such term appears.

(D) 10-percent owned foreign corporation.—The term "10-percent owned foreign corporation" means any foreign corporation in which the United States person owns directly or indirectly at least 10 percent of the voting stock.

(b) Foreign currency gain or loss.—For purposes of this section—

(1) Foreign currency gain.—The term "foreign currency gain" means any gain from a section 988 transaction to the extent such gain does not exceed gain realized by reason of changes in exchange rates on or after the booking date and before the payment date.

(2) Foreign currency loss.—The term "foreign currency loss" means any loss from a section 988 transaction to the extent such loss does not exceed the loss realized by reason of changes in exchange rates on or after the booking date and before the payment date.

(3) Special rule for certain contracts, etc.—In the case of any section 988 transaction described in subsection (c)(1)(B)(iii), any gain or loss from such transaction shall be treated as foreign currency gain or loss (as the case may be).

(c) Other definitions.—For purposes of this section

(1) Section 988 transaction.—

(A) In general.—The term "section 988 transaction" means any transaction described in subparagraph (B) if the amount which the taxpayer is entitled to receive (or is required to pay) by reason of such transaction—

(i) is denominated in terms of a nonfunctional currency, or

(ii) is determined by reference to the value of 1 or more nonfunctional currencies.

(B) Description of transactions.—For purposes of subparagraph (A), the following transactions are described in this subparagraph:

(i) The acquisition of a debt instrument or becoming the obligor under a debt instrument.

(ii) Accruing (or otherwise taking into account) for purposes of this subtitle any item of expense or gross income or receipts which is to be paid or received after the date on which so accrued or taken into account.

(iii) Entering into or acquiring any forward contract, futures contract, option, or similar financial instrument.

The Secretary may prescribe regulations excluding from the application of clause (ii) any class of items the taking into account of which is not necessary to carry out the purposes of this section by reason of the small amounts or short periods involved, or otherwise.

(C) Special rules for disposition of nonfunctional currency.—

(i) In general.—In the case of any disposition of any nonfunctional currency—

(I) such disposition shall be treated as a section 988 transaction, and

(II) any gain or loss from such transaction shall be treated as foreign currency gain or loss (as the case may be).

(ii) Nonfunctional currency.—For purposes of this section, the term "nonfunctional currency" includes coin or currency, and nonfunctional currency denominated demand or time deposits or similar instruments issued by a bank or other financial institution.

(D) Exception for certain instruments marked to market.—

(i) In general.—Clause (iii) of subparagraph (B) shall not apply to any regulated futures contract or nonequity option which would be marked to market under section 1256 if held on the last day of the taxable year.

(ii) Election out.—

(I) In general.—The taxpayer may elect to have clause (i) not apply to such taxpayer. Such an election shall apply to contracts held at any time during the taxable year for which such election is made or any succeeding taxable year unless such election is revoked with the consent of the Secretary.

(II) Time for making election.—Except as provided in regulations, an election under subclause (I) for any taxable year shall be made on or before the 1st day of such taxable year (or, if later, on or before the 1st day during such year on which the taxpayer holds a contract described in clause (i)).

(III) Special rule for partnerships, etc.—In the case of a partnership, an election under subclause (I) shall be made by each partner separately. A similar rule shall apply in the case of an S corporation.

(iii) Treatment of certain partnerships.—This subparagraph shall not apply to any income or loss of a partnership for any taxable year if such partnership made an election under subparagraph (E)(iii)(V) for such year or any preceding year.

(E) Special rules for certain funds.—

(i) In general.—In the case of a qualified fund, clause (iii) of subparagraph (B) shall not apply to any instrument which would be marked to market under section 1256 if held on the last day of the taxable year (determined after the application of clause (iv)).

(ii) Special rule where electing partnership does not qualify.—If any partnership made an election under clause (iii)(V) for any taxable year and such partnership has a net loss for such year or any succeeding year from instruments referred to in clause (i), the rules of clauses (i) and (iv) shall apply to any such loss year whether or not such partnership is a qualified fund for such year.

(iii) Qualified fund defined.—For purposes of this subparagraph, the term "qualified fund" means any partnership if—

(I) at all times during the taxable year (and during each preceding taxable year to which an election under subclause (V) applied), such partnership has at least 20 partners and no single partner owns more than 20 percent of the interests in the capital or profits of the partnership,

(II) the principal activity of such partnership for such taxable year (and each such preceding taxable year) consists of buying and selling options, futures, or forwards with respect to commodities,

(III) at least 90 percent of the gross income of the partnership for the taxable year (and for each such preceding taxable year) consisted of income or gains described in subparagraph (A), (B), or (G) of section 7704(d)(1) or gain from the sale or disposition of capital assets held for the production of interest or dividends,

(IV) no more than a de minimis amount of the gross income of the partnership for the taxable year (and each such preceding taxable year) was derived from buying and selling commodities, and

(V) an election under this subclause applies to the taxable year.

An election under subclause (V) for any taxable year shall be made on or before the 1st day of such taxable year (or, if later, on or before the 1st day during such year on which the partnership holds an instrument referred to in clause (i)). Any such election shall apply to the taxable year for which made and all succeeding taxable years unless revoked with the consent of the Secretary.

(iv) Treatment of certain currency contracts.—

(I) In general.—Except as provided in regulations, in the case of a qualified fund, any bank forward contract, any foreign currency futures contract traded on a foreign exchange, or to the extent provided in regulations any similar instrument, which is not otherwise a section 1256 contract shall be treated as a section 1256 contract for purposes of section 1256.

(II) Gains and losses treated as short-term.—In the case of any instrument treated as a section 1256 contract under subclause (I), subparagraph (A) of section 1256(a)(3) shall be applied by substituting "100 percent" for "40 percent" (and subparagraph (B) of such section shall not apply).

(v) Special rules for clause (iii)(I).—

(I) Certain general partners.—The interest of a general partner in the partnership shall not be treated as failing to meet the 20-percent ownership requirements of clause (iii)(I) for any taxable year of the partnership if, for the taxable year of the partner in which such partnership taxable year ends, such partner (and each corporation filing a consolidated return with such partner) had no ordinary income or loss from a section 988 transaction which is foreign currency gain or loss (as the case may be).

(II) Treatment of incentive compensation.—For purposes of clause (iii)(I), any income allocable to a general partner as incentive compensation based on profits rather than capital shall not be taken into account in determining such partner's interest in the profits of the partnership.

(III) Treatment of tax-exempt partners.—Except as provided in regulations, the interest of a partner in the partnership shall not be treated as failing to meet the 20-percent ownership requirements of clause (iii)(I) if none of the income of such partner from such partnership is subject to tax under this chapter (whether directly or through 1 or more pass-thru entities).

(IV) Look-thru rule.—In determining whether the requirements of clause (iii)(I) are met with respect to any partnership, except to the extent provided in regulations, any interest in such partnership held by another partnership shall be treated as held proportionately by the partners in such other partnership.

(vi) Other special rules.—For purposes of this subparagraph—

(I) Related persons.—Interests in the partnership held by persons related to each other (within the meaning of sections 267(b) and 707(b)) shall be treated as held by 1 person.

(II) Predecessors.—References to any partnership shall include a reference to any predecessor thereof.

(III) Inadvertent terminations.—Rules similar to the rules of section 7704(e) shall apply.

(IV) Treatment of certain debt instruments.—For purposes of clause (iii)(IV), any debt instrument which is a section 988 transaction shall be treated as a commodity.

(2) Booking date.—The term "booking date" means—

(A) in the case of a transaction described in paragraph (1)(B)(i), the date of acquisition or on which the taxpayer becomes the obligor, or

(B) in the case of a transaction described in paragraph (1)(B)(ii), the date on which accrued or otherwise taken into account.

(3) Payment date.—The term "payment date" means the date on which the payment is made or received.

(4) Debt instrument.—The term "debt instrument" means a bond, debenture, note, or certificate or other evidence of indebtedness. To the extent provided in regulations, such term shall include preferred stock.

(5) Special rules where taxpayer takes or makes delivery.—If the taxpayer takes or makes delivery in connection with any section 988 transaction described in paragraph (1)(B)(iii), any gain or loss (determined as if the taxpayer sold the contract, option, or instrument on the date on which he took or made delivery for its fair market value on such date) shall be recognized in the same manner as if such contract, option, or instrument were so sold.

(d) Treatment of 988 hedging transactions.—

(1) In general.—To the extent provided in regulations, if any section 988 transaction is part of a 988 hedging transaction, all transactions which are part of such 988 hedging transaction shall be integrated and treated as a single transaction or otherwise treated consistently for purposes of this subtitle. For purposes of the preceding sentence, the determination of whether any transaction is a section 988 transaction shall be determined without regard to whether such transaction would otherwise be marked-to-market under section 475 or 1256 and such term shall not include any transaction with respect to which an election is made under subsection (a)(1)(B). Sections 475, 1092, and 1256 shall not apply to a transaction covered by this subsection.

(2) 988 hedging transaction.—For purposes of paragraph (1), the term "988 hedging transaction" means any transaction—

(A) entered into by the taxpayer primarily—

(i) to manage risk of currency fluctuations with respect to property which is held or to be held by the taxpayer, or

(ii) to manage risk of currency fluctuations with respect to borrowings made or to be made, or obligations incurred or to be incurred, by the taxpayer, and **§ 988(d)**

(B) identified by the Secretary or the taxpayer as being a 988 hedging transaction.

(e) Application to individuals.—

(1) In general.—The preceding provisions of this section shall not apply to any section 988 transaction entered into by an individual which is a personal transaction.

(2) Exclusion for certain personal transactions.—If—

(A) nonfunctional currency is disposed of by an individual in any transaction, and

(B) such transaction is a personal transaction, no gain shall be recognized for purposes of this subtitle by reason of changes in exchange rates after such currency was acquired by such individual and before such disposition. The preceding sentence shall not apply if the gain which would otherwise be recognized on the transaction exceeds $200.

(3) Personal transactions.—For purposes of this subsection, the term "personal transaction" means any transaction entered into by an individual, except that such term shall not include any transaction to the extent that expenses properly allocable to such transaction meet the requirements of—

(A) section 162 (other than traveling expenses described in subsection (a)(2) thereof), or

(B) section 212 (other than that part of section 212 dealing with expenses incurred in connection with taxes).

§ 989. Other definitions and special rules

(a) Qualified business unit.—For purposes of this subpart, the term "qualified business unit" means any separate and clearly identified unit of a trade or business of a taxpayer which maintains separate books and records.

(b) Appropriate exchange rate.—Except as provided in regulations, for purposes of this subpart, the term "appropriate exchange rate" means—

(1) in the case of an actual distribution of earnings and profits, the spot rate on the date such distribution is included in income,

(2) in the case of an actual or deemed sale or exchange of stock in a foreign corporation treated as a dividend under section 1248, the spot rate on the date the deemed dividend is included in income,

(3) in the case of any amounts included in income under section 951(a)(1)(A) or 1293(a), the average exchange rate for the taxable year of the foreign corporation, or

(4) in the case of any other qualified business unit of a taxpayer, the average exchange rate for the taxable year of such qualified business unit.

For purposes of the preceding sentence, any amount included in income under section 951(a)(1)(B) shall be treated as an actual distribution made on the last day of the taxable year for which such amount was so included.

(c) Regulations.—The Secretary shall prescribe such regulations as may be necessary or appropriate to carry out the purposes of this subpart, including regulations—

(1) setting forth procedures to be followed by taxpayers with qualified business units using a net worth method of accounting before the enactment of this subpart,

(2) limiting the recognition of foreign currency loss on certain remittances from qualified business units,

(3) providing for the recharacterization of interest and principal payments with respect to obligations denominated in certain hyperinflationary currencies,

(4) providing for alternative adjustments to the application of section 905(c),

(5) providing for the appropriate treatment of related party transactions (including transactions between qualified business units of the same taxpayer), and

(6) setting forth procedures for determining the average exchange rate for any period.

Part IV—Domestic International Sales Corporations

Subpart A—Treatment of Qualifying Corporations

§ 993. Definitions and special rules

(a) Qualified export receipts.—

* * *

(3) Definition of controlled group.—For purposes of this part, the term "controlled group" has the meaning assigned to the term "controlled group of corporations" by section 1563(a), except that the phrase "more than 50 percent" shall be substituted for the phrase "at least 80 percent" each place it appears therein, and section 1563(b) shall not apply.

* * *

Part V—International Boycott Determinations

§ 999. Reports by taxpayers; determinations

(a) International boycott reports by taxpayers.—

(1) Report required.—If any person, or a member of a controlled group (within the meaning of section 993(a)(3)) which includes that person, has operations in, or related to—

(A) a country (or with the government, a company, or a national of a country) which is on the list maintained by the Secretary under paragraph (3), or

(B) any other country (or with the government, a company, or a national of that country) in which such person or such member had operations during the taxable year if such person (or, if such person is a foreign corporation, any United States shareholder of that corporation) knows or has reason to know that participation in or cooperation with an international boycott is required as a condition of doing business within such country or with such government, company, or national,

that person or shareholder (within the meaning of section 951(b)) shall report such operations to the Secretary at such time and in such manner as the Secretary prescribes, except that in the case of a foreign corporation such report shall be required only of a United States shareholder (within the meaning of such section) of such corporation.

(2) Participation and cooperation; request therefor.—A taxpayer shall report whether he, a foreign corporation of which he is a United States shareholder, or any member of a controlled group which includes the taxpayer or such foreign corporation has participated in or cooperated with an international boycott at any time during the taxable year, or has been requested to participate in or cooperate with such a boycott, and, if so, the nature of any operation in connection with which there was participation in or cooperation with such boycott (or there was a request to participate or cooperate).

(3) List to be maintained.—The Secretary shall maintain and publish not less frequently than quarterly a current list of countries which require or may require participation in or cooperation with an international boycott (within the meaning of subsection (b)(3)).

(b) Participation in or cooperation with an international boycott.—

(1) General rule.—If the person or a member of a controlled group (within the meaning of section 993(a)(3)) which includes the person participates in or cooperates with an international boycott in the taxable year, all operations of the taxpayer or such group in that country and in any other country which requires participation in or cooperation with the boycott as a condition of doing business within that country, or with the government, a company, or a national of that country, shall be treated as operations in connection with which such participation of cooperation occurred, except to the extent that the person can clearly demonstrate that a particular operation is a clearly separate and identifiable operation in connection with which there was no participation in or cooperation with an international boycott.

(2) Special rule.—

(A) Nonboycott operations.—A clearly separate and identifiable operation of a person, or of a member of the controlled group (within the meaning of section 993(a)(3)) which includes that person, in or related to any country within the group of countries referred to in paragraph (1) shall not be treated as an operation in or related to a group of countries associated in carrying out an international boycott if the person can clearly demonstrate that he, or that such member, did not participate in or cooperate with the international boycott in connection with that operation.

(B) Separate and identifiable operations.—A taxpayer may show that different operations within the same country, or operations in different countries, are clearly separate and identifiable operations.

(3) Definition of boycott participation and cooperation.—For purposes of this section, a person participates in or cooperates with an international boycott if he agrees—

(A) as a condition of doing business directly or indirectly within a country or with the government, a company, or a national of a country—

(i) to refrain from doing business with or in a country which is the object of the boycott or with the government, companies, or nationals of that country;

(ii) to refrain from doing business with any United States person engaged in trade in a country which is the object of the boycott or with the government, companies, or nationals of that country;

(iii) to refrain from doing business with any company whose ownership or management is made up, all or in part, of individuals of a particular nationality, race, or religion, or to remove (or refrain from selecting) corporate directors who are individuals of a particular nationality, race, or religion; or

(iv) to refrain from employing individuals of a particular nationality, race, or religion; or

(B) as a condition of the sale of a product to the government, a company, or a national of a country, to refrain from shipping or insuring that product on a carrier owned, leased, or operated by a person who does not participate in or cooperate with an international boycott (within the meaning of subparagraph (A)).

(4) Compliance with certain laws.—This section shall not apply to any agreement by a person (or such member)—

(A) to meet requirements imposed by a foreign country with respect to an international boycott if United States law or regulations, or an Executive Order, sanctions participation in, or cooperation with, that international boycott,

(B) to comply with a prohibition on the importation of goods produced in whole or in part in any country which is the object of an international boycott, or

(C) to comply with a prohibition imposed by a country on the exportation of products obtained in such country to any country which is the object of an international boycott.

(c) International boycott factor.—

(1) International boycott factor.—For purposes of sections 908(a), 952(a)(3), and 995(b)(1)(F)(ii), the international boycott factor is a fraction, determined under regulations prescribed by the Secretary, the numerator of which reflects the world-wide operations of a person (or, in the case of a controlled group (within the meaning of section 993(a)(3)) which includes that person, of the group) which are operations in or related to a group of countries associated in carrying out an international boycott in or with which that person or a member of that controlled group has participated or cooperated in the taxable year, and the denominator of which reflects the world-wide operations of that person or group.

(2) Specifically attributable taxes and income.—If the taxpayer clearly demonstrates that the foreign taxes paid and income earned for the taxable year are attributable to specific operations, then, in lieu of applying the international boycott factor for such taxable year, the amount of the credit disallowed under section 908(a), the addition to subpart F income under section 952(a)(3), and the amount of deemed distribution under section 995(b)(1)(F)(ii) for the taxable year, if any, shall be the amount specifically attributable to the operations in which there was participation in or cooperation with an international boycott under section 999(b)(1).

(3) World-wide operations.—For purposes of this subsection, the term "world-wide operations" means operations in or related to countries other than the United States.

(d) Determinations with respect to particular operations.—Upon a request made by the taxpayer, the Secretary shall issue a determination with respect to whether a particular operation of a person, or of a member of a controlled group which includes that person, constitutes participation in or cooperation with an international boycott. The Secretary may issue such a determination in advance of such operation in cases which are of such a nature that an advance determination is possible and appropriate under the circumstances. If the request is made before the operation is commenced, or before the end of a taxable year in which the operation is carried out, the Secretary may decline to issue such a determination before close of the taxable year.

(e) Participation or cooperation by related persons.—If a person controls (within the meaning of section 304(c)) a corporation—

(1) participation in or cooperation with an international boycott by such corporation shall be presumed to be such participation or cooperation by such person, and

(2) participation in or cooperation with such a boycott by such person shall be presumed to be such participation or cooperation by such corporation.

(f) Willful failure to report.—Any person (within the meaning of section 6671(b)) required to report under this section who willfully fails to make such report shall, in addition to other penalties provided by law, be fined not more than $25,000, imprisoned for not more than one year, or both.

Subchapter O—Gain or Loss on Disposition of Property

Part I—Determination of Amount of and Recognition of Gain or Loss

§ 1001. Determination of amount of and recognition of gain or loss

(a) Computation of gain or loss.—The gain from the sale or other disposition of property shall be the excess of the amount realized therefrom over the adjusted basis provided in section 1011 for determining gain, and the loss shall be the excess of the adjusted basis provided in such section for determining loss over the amount realized.

(b) Amount realized.—The amount realized from the sale or other disposition of property shall be the sum of any money received plus the fair market value of the property (other than money) received. In determining the amount realized—

(1) there shall not be taken into account any amount received as reimbursement for real property taxes which are treated under section 164(d) as imposed on the purchaser, and

(2) there shall be taken into account amounts representing real property taxes which are treated under section 164(d) as imposed on the taxpayer if such taxes are to be paid by the purchaser.

(c) Recognition of gain or loss.—Except as otherwise provided in this subtitle, the entire amount of the gain or loss, determined under this section, on the sale or exchange of property shall be recognized.

* * *

Part III—Common Nontaxable Exchanges

§ 1031. Exchange of real property held for productive use or investment

(a) Nonrecognition of gain or loss from exchanges solely in kind.—

(1) In general.—No gain or loss shall be recognized on the exchange of real property held for productive use in a trade or business or for investment if such real property is exchanged solely for real property of like kind which is to be held either for productive use in a trade or business or for investment.

(2) Exception for real property held for sale.—This subsection shall not apply to any exchange of real property held primarily for sale.

(3) Requirement that property be identified and that exchange be completed not more than 180 days after transfer of exchanged property.—For purposes of this subsection, any property received by the taxpayer shall be treated as property which is not like-kind property if—

(A) such property is not identified as property to be received in the exchange on or before the day which is 45 days after the date on which the taxpayer transfers the property relinquished in the exchange, or

(B) such property is received after the earlier of—

(i) the day which is 180 days after the date on which the taxpayer transfers the property relinquished in the exchange, or

(ii) the due date (determined with regard to extension) for the transferor's return of the tax imposed by this chapter for the taxable year in which the transfer of the relinquished property occurs.

(b) Gain from exchanges not solely in kind.—If an exchange would be within the provisions of subsection (a), of section 1035(a), of section 1036(a), or of section 1037(a), if it were not for the fact that the property received in exchange consists not only of property permitted by such provisions to be received without the recognition of gain, but also of other property or money, then the gain, if any, to the recipient shall be recognized, but in an amount not in excess of the sum of such money and the fair market value of such other property.

(c) Loss from exchanges not solely in kind.—If an exchange would be within the provisions of subsection (a), of section 1035(a), of section 1036(a), or of section 1037(a), if it were not for the fact that the property received in exchange consists not only of property permitted by such provisions to be received without the recognition of gain or loss, but also of other property or money, then no loss from the exchange shall be recognized.

(d) Basis.—If property was acquired on an exchange described in this section, section 1035(a), section 1036(a), or section 1037(a), then the basis shall be the same as that of the property exchanged, decreased in the amount of any money received by the taxpayer and increased in the amount of gain or decreased in the amount of loss to the taxpayer that was recognized on such exchange. If the property so acquired consisted in part of the type of property permitted by this section, section 1035(a), section 1036(a), or section 1037(a), to be received without the recognition of gain or loss, and in part of other property, the basis provided in this subsection shall be allocated between the properties (other than money) received, and for the purpose of the allocation there shall be assigned to such other property an amount equivalent to its fair market value at the date of the exchange. For purposes of this section, section 1035(a), and section 1036(a), where as part of the consideration to the taxpayer another party to the exchange assumed (as determined under section 357(d)) a liability of the taxpayer, such assumption shall be considered as money received by the taxpayer on the exchange.

* * *

(h) Special rules for foreign real property.—Real property located in the United States and real property located outside the United States are not property of a like kind.

Subchapter P—Capital Gains and Losses

Part III—General Rules for Determining Capital Gains and Losses

§ 1221. Capital asset defined

(a) In general.—For purposes of this subtitle, the term "capital asset" means property held by the taxpayer (whether or not connected with his trade or business), but does not include—

(1) stock in trade of the taxpayer or other property of a kind which would properly be included in the inventory of the taxpayer if on hand at the close of the taxable year, or property held by the taxpayer primarily for sale to customers in the ordinary course of his trade or business;

(2) property, used in his trade or business, of a character which is subject to the allowance for depreciation provided in section 167, or real property used in his trade or business;

(3) a patent, invention, model or design (whether or not patented), a secret formula or process, a copyright, a literary, musical, or artistic composition, a letter or memorandum, or similar property, held by—

(A) a taxpayer whose personal efforts created such property,

(B) in the case of a letter, memorandum, or similar property, a taxpayer for whom such property was prepared or produced, or

(C) a taxpayer in whose hands the basis of such property is determined, for purposes of determining gain from a sale or exchange, in whole or part by reference to the basis of such property in the hands of a taxpayer described in subparagraph (A) or (B);

(4) accounts or notes receivable acquired in the ordinary course of trade or business for services rendered or from the sale of property described in paragraph (1);

* * *

§ 1222. Other terms relating to capital gains and losses

For purposes of this subtitle—

(1) Short-term capital gain.—The term "short-term capital gain" means gain from the sale or exchange of a capital asset held for not more than 1 year, if and to the extent such gain is taken into account in computing gross income.

(2) Short-term capital loss.—The term "short-term capital loss" means loss from the sale or exchange of a capital asset held for not more than 1 year, if and to the extent that such loss is taken into account in computing taxable income.

(3) Long-term capital gain.—The term "long-term capital gain" means gain from the sale or exchange of a capital asset held for more than 1 year, if and to the extent such gain is taken into account in computing gross income.

(4) Long-term capital loss.—The term "long-term capital loss" means loss from the sale or exchange of a capital asset held for more than 1 year, if and to the extent that such loss is taken into account in computing taxable income.

(5) Net short-term capital gain.—The term "net short-term capital gain" means the excess of short-term capital gains for the taxable year over the short-term capital losses for such year.

(6) Net short-term capital loss.—The term "net short-term capital loss" means the excess of short-term capital losses for the taxable year over the short-term capital gains for such year.

(7) Net long-term capital gain.—The term "net long-term capital gain" means the excess of long-term capital gains for the taxable year over the long-term capital losses for such year.

(8) Net long-term capital loss.—The term "net long-term capital loss" means the excess of long-term capital losses for the taxable year over the long-term capital gains for such year.

(9) Capital gain net income.—The term "capital gain net income" means the excess of the gains from sales or exchanges of capital assets over the losses from such sales or exchanges.

(10) Net capital loss.—The term "net capital loss" means the excess of the losses from sales or exchanges of capital assets over the sum allowed under section 1211. In the case of a corporation, for the purpose of determining losses under this paragraph, amounts which are short-term capital losses under section 1212(a)(1) shall be excluded.

(11) Net capital gain.—The term "net capital gain" means the excess of the net long-term capital gain for the taxable year over the net short-term capital loss for such year.

Part IV—Special Rules for Determining Capital Gains and Losses

§ 1231. Property used in the trade or business and involuntary conversions

(a) General rule.—

(1) Gains exceed losses.—If—

(A) the section 1231 gains for any taxable year, exceed

(B) the section 1231 losses for such taxable year,

such gains and losses shall be treated as long-term capital gains or long-term capital losses, as the case may be.

(2) Gains do not exceed losses.—If—

(A) the section 1231 gains for any taxable year, do not exceed

(B) the section 1231 losses for such taxable year,

such gains and losses shall not be treated as gains and losses from sales or exchanges of capital assets.

(3) Section 1231 gains and losses.—For purposes of this subsection—

(A) Section 1231 gain.—The term "section 1231 gain" means—

(i) any recognized gain on the sale or exchange of property used in the trade or business, and

(ii) any recognized gain from the compulsory or involuntary conversion (as a result of destruction in whole or in part, theft or seizure, or an exercise of the power of requisition or condemnation or the threat or imminence thereof) into other property or money of—

(I) property used in the trade or business, or

(II) any capital asset which is held for more than 1 year and is held in connection with a trade or business or a transaction entered into for profit.

(B) Section 1231 loss.—The term "section 1231 loss" means any recognized loss from a sale or exchange or conversion described in subparagraph (A).

(4) Special rules.—For purposes of this subsection—

(A) In determining under this subsection whether gains exceed losses—

(i) the section 1231 gains shall be included only if and to the extent taken into account in computing gross income, and

(ii) the section 1231 losses shall be included only if and to the extent taken into account in computing taxable income, except that section 1211 shall not apply.

(B) Losses (including losses not compensated for by insurance or otherwise) on the destruction, in whole or in part, theft or seizure, or requisition or condemnation of—

(i) property used in the trade or business, or

(ii) capital assets which are held for more than 1 year and are held in connection with a trade or business or a transaction entered into for profit, shall be treated as losses from a compulsory or involuntary conversion.

(C) In the case of any involuntary conversion (subject to the provisions of this subsection but for this sentence) arising from fire, storm, shipwreck, or other casualty, or from theft, of any—

(i) property used in the trade or business, or

(ii) any capital asset which is held for more than 1 year and is held in connection with a trade or business or a transaction entered into for profit, this subsection shall not apply to such conversion (whether resulting in gain or loss) if during the taxable year the recognized losses from such conversions exceed the recognized gains from such conversions.

(b) Definition of property used in the trade or business.—For purposes of this section—

(1) General rule.—The term "property used in the trade or business" means property used in the trade or business, of a character which is subject to the allowance for depreciation provided in section 167, held for more than 1 year, and real property used in the trade or business, held for more than 1 year, which is not—

(A) property of a kind which would properly be includible in the inventory of the taxpayer if on hand at the close of the taxable year,

(B) property held by the taxpayer primarily for sale to customers in the ordinary course of his trade or business,

(C) a patent, invention, model or design (whether or not patented), a secret formula or process, a copyright, a literary, musical, or artistic composition, a letter or memorandum, or similar property, held by a taxpayer described in paragraph (3) of section 1221(a), or

(D) a publication of the United States Government (including the Congressional Record) which is received from the United States Government, or any agency thereof, other than by purchase at the price at which it is offered for sale to the public, and which is held by a taxpayer described in paragraph (5) of section 1221(a).

* * *

(c) Recapture of net ordinary losses.—

(1) In general.—The net section 1231 gain for any taxable year shall be treated as ordinary income to the extent such gain does not exceed the non-recaptured net section 1231 losses.

(2) Non-recaptured net section 1231 losses.—For purposes of this subsection, the term "non-recaptured net section 1231 losses" means the excess of—

(A) the aggregate amount of the net section 1231 losses for the 5 most recent preceding taxable years, over

(B) the portion of such losses taken into account under paragraph (1) for such preceding taxable years.

(3) Net section 1231 gain.—For purposes of this subsection, the term "net section 1231 gain" means the excess of—

(A) the section 1231 gains, over

(B) the section 1231 losses.

(4) Net section 1231 loss.—For purposes of this subsection, the term "net section 1231 loss" means the excess of—

(A) the section 1231 losses, over

(B) the section 1231 gains. **(c)**

(5) Special rules.—For purposes of determining the amount of the net section 1231 gain or loss for any taxable year, the rules of paragraph (4) of subsection (a) shall apply.

§ 1235. Sale or exchange of patents

(a) General.—A transfer (other than by gift, inheritance, or devise) of property consisting of all substantial rights to a patent, or an undivided interest therein which includes a part of all such rights, by any holder shall be considered the sale or exchange of a capital asset held for more than 1 year, regardless of whether or not payments in consideration of such transfer are—

(1) payable periodically over a period generally coterminous with the transferee's use of the patent, or

(2) contingent on the productivity, use, or disposition of the property transferred.

(b) "Holder" defined.—For purposes of this section, the term "holder" means—

(1) any individual whose efforts created such property, or

(2) any other individual who has acquired his interest in such property in exchange for consideration in money or money's worth paid to such creator prior to actual reduction to practice of the invention covered by the patent, if such individual is neither—

(A) the employer of such creator, nor

(B) related to such creator (within the meaning of subsection (c)).

(c) Related persons.—Subsection (a) shall not apply to any transfer, directly or indirectly, between persons specified within any one of the paragraphs of section 267(b) or persons described in section 707(b); except that, in applying section 267(b) and (c) and section 707(b) for purposes of this section—

(1) the phrase "25 percent or more" shall be substituted for the phrase "more than 50 percent" each place it appears in section 267(b) or 707(b), and

(2) paragraph (4) of section 267(c) shall be treated as providing that the family of an individual shall include only his spouse, ancestors, and lineal descendants.

(d) Cross reference.—

For special rule relating to nonresident aliens, see section 871(a).

§ 1248. Gain from certain sales or exchanges of stock in certain foreign corporations

(a) General rule.—If—

(1) a United States person sells or exchanges stock in a foreign corporation, and

(2) such person owns, within the meaning of section 958(a), or is considered as owning by applying the rules of ownership of section 958(b), 10 percent or more of the total combined voting power of all classes of stock entitled to vote of such foreign corporation at any time during the 5-year period ending on the date of the sale or exchange when such foreign corporation was a controlled foreign corporation (as defined in section 957), then the gain recognized on the sale or exchange of such stock shall be included in the gross income of such person as a dividend, to the extent of the earnings and profits of the foreign corporation attributable (under regulations prescribed by the Secretary) to such stock which were accumulated in taxable years of such foreign corporation beginning after December 31, 1962, and during the period or periods the stock sold or exchanged was held by such person while such foreign corporation was a controlled foreign corporation. For purposes of this section, a United States person shall be treated as having sold or exchanged any stock if, under any provision of this subtitle, such person is treated as realizing gain from the sale or exchange of such stock.

(b) Limitation on tax applicable to individuals.—In the case of an individual, if the stock sold or exchanged is a capital asset (within the meaning of section 1221) and has been held for more than 1 year, the tax attributable to an amount included in gross income as a dividend under subsection (a) shall not be greater than a tax equal to the sum of—

(1) a pro rata share of the excess of—

(A) the taxes that would have been paid by the foreign corporation with respect to its income had it been taxed under this chapter as a domestic corporation (but without allowance for deduction of, or credit for, taxes described in subparagraph (B)), for the period or periods the stock sold or exchanged was held by the United States person in taxable years beginning after December 31, 1962, while the foreign corporation was a controlled foreign corporation, adjusted for distributions and amounts previously included in gross income of a United States shareholder under section 951, over

(B) the income, war profits, or excess profits taxes paid by the foreign corporation with respect to such income; and

(2) an amount equal to the tax that would result by including in gross income, as gain from the sale or exchange of a capital asset held for more than 1 year, an amount equal to the excess of (A) the amount included in gross income as a dividend under subsection (a), over (B) the amount determined under paragraph (1).

(c) Determination of earnings and profits.—

(1) In general.—Except as provided in section 312(k)(4), for purposes of this section, the earnings and profits of any foreign corporation for any taxable year shall be determined according to rules substantially similar to those applicable to domestic corporations, under regulations prescribed by the Secretary.

(2) Earnings and profits of subsidiaries of foreign corporations.—If—

(A) subsection (a) or (f) applies to a sale, exchange, or distribution by a United States person of stock of a foreign corporation and, by reason of the ownership of the stock sold or exchanged, such person owned within the meaning of section 958(a)(2) stock of any other foreign corporation; and

(B) such person owned, within the meaning of section 958(a), or was considered as owning by applying the rules of ownership of section 958(b), 10 percent or more of the total combined voting power of all classes of stock entitled to vote of such other foreign corporation at any time during the 5-year period ending on the date of the sale or exchange when such other foreign corporation was a controlled foreign corporation (as defined in section 957), then, for purposes of this section, the earnings and profits of the foreign corporation the stock of which is sold or exchanged which are attributable to the stock sold or exchanged shall be deemed to include the earnings and profits of such other foreign corporation which— **(c)**

(C) are attributable (under regulations prescribed by the Secretary) to the stock of such other foreign corporation which such person owned within the meaning of section 958(a)(2) (by reason of his ownership within the meaning of section 958(a)(1)(A) of the stock sold or exchanged) on the date of such sale or exchange (or on the date of any sale or exchange of the stock of such other foreign corporation occurring during the 5-year period ending on the date of the sale or exchange of the stock of such foreign corporation, to the extent not otherwise taken into account under this section but not in excess of the fair market value of the stock of such other foreign corporation sold or exchanged over the basis of such stock (for determining gain) in the hands of the transferor); and

(D) were accumulated in taxable years of such other corporation beginning after December 31, 1962, and during the period or periods—

(i) such other corporation was a controlled foreign corporation, and

(ii) such person owned within the meaning of section 958(a) the stock of such other foreign corporation.

(d) Exclusions from earnings and profits.—For purposes of this section, the following amounts shall be excluded, with respect to any United States person, from the earnings and profits of a foreign corporation:

(1) Amounts included in gross income under section 951.—Earnings and profits of the foreign corporation attributable to any amount previously included in the gross income of such person under section 951, with respect to the stock sold or exchanged, but only to the extent the inclusion of such amount did not result in an exclusion of an amount from gross income under section 959.

* * *

(3) Less developed country corporations under prior law.—Earnings and profits of a foreign corporation which were accumulated during any taxable year beginning before January 1, 1976, while such corporation was a less developed country corporation under section 902(d) as in effect before the enactment of the Tax Reduction Act of 1975.

(4) United States income.—Any item includible in gross income of the foreign corporation under this chapter—

(A) for any taxable year beginning before January 1, 1967, as income derived from sources within the United States of a foreign corporation engaged in trade or business within the United States, or

(B) for any taxable year beginning after December 31, 1966, as income effectively connected with the conduct by such corporation of a trade or business within the United States.

This paragraph shall not apply with respect to any item which is exempt from taxation (or is subject to a reduced rate of tax) pursuant to a treaty obligation of the United States.

(5) Foreign trade income.—Earnings and profits of the foreign corporation attributable to foreign trade income of a FSC (as defined in section 922) other than foreign trade income which—

(A) is section 923(a)(2) non-exempt income (within the meaning of section 927(d)(6)), or

(B) would not (but for section 923(a)(4)) be treated as exempt foreign trade income.

For purposes of the preceding sentence, the terms "foreign trade income" and "exempt foreign trade income" have the respective meanings given such terms by section 923. Any reference in this paragraph to section 922, 923, or 927 shall be treated as a reference to such section as in effect before its repeal * * *.

(6) Amounts included in gross income under section 1293.—Earnings and profits of the foreign corporation attributable to any amount previously included in the gross income of such person under section 1293 with respect to the stock sold or exchanged, but only to the extent the inclusion of such amount did not result in an exclusion of an amount under section 1293(c).

(e) Sales or exchanges of stock in certain domestic corporations.—Except as provided in regulations prescribed by the Secretary, if—

(1) a United States person sells or exchanges stock of a domestic corporation, and

(2) such domestic corporation was formed or availed of principally for the holding, directly or indirectly, of stock of one or more foreign corporations,

such sale or exchange shall, for purposes of this section, be treated as a sale or exchange of the stock of the foreign corporation or corporations held by the domestic corporation.

(f) Certain nonrecognition transactions.—Except as provided in regulations prescribed by the Secretary—

(1) In general.—If—

(A) a domestic corporation satisfies the stock ownership requirements of subsection (a)(2) with respect to a foreign corporation, and

(B) such domestic corporation distributes stock of such foreign corporation in a distribution to which section 311(a), 337, 355(c)(1), or 361(c)(1) applies,

then, notwithstanding any other provision of this subtitle, an amount equal to the excess of the fair market value of such stock over its adjusted basis in the hands of the domestic corporation shall be included in the gross income of the domestic corporation as a dividend to the extent of the earnings and profits of the foreign corporation attributable (under regulations prescribed by the Secretary) to such stock which were accumulated in taxable years of such foreign corporation beginning after December 31, 1962, and during the period or periods the stock was held by such domestic corporation while such foreign corporation was a controlled foreign corporation. For purposes of subsections (c)(2), (d), and (h), a distribution of stock to which this subsection applies shall be treated as a sale of stock to which subsection (a) applies.

(2) Exception for certain distributions.—In the case of any distribution of stock of a foreign corporation, paragraph (1) shall not apply if such distribution is to a domestic corporation—

(A) which is treated under this section as holding such stock for the period for which the stock was held by the distributing corporation, and **(f)**

(B) which, immediately after the distribution, satisfies the stock ownership requirements of subsection (a)(2) with respect to such foreign corporation.

(3) Application to cases described in subsection (e).—To the extent that earnings and profits are taken into account under this subsection, they shall be excluded and not taken into account for purposes of subsection (e).

(g) Exceptions.—This section shall not apply to—

(1) distributions to which section 303 (relating to distributions in redemption of stock to pay death taxes) applies; or

(2) any amount to the extent that such amount is, under any other provision of this title, treated as—

(A) a dividend (other than an amount treated as a dividend under subsection (f)),

(B) ordinary income, or

(C) gain from the sale of an asset held for not more than 1 year.

(h) Taxpayer to establish earnings and profits.—Unless the taxpayer establishes the amount of the earnings and profits of the foreign corporation to be taken into account under subsection (a) or (f), all gain from the sale or exchange shall be considered a dividend under subsection (a) or (f), and unless the taxpayer establishes the amount of foreign taxes to be taken into account under subsection (b), the limitation of such subsection shall not apply.

(i) Treatment of certain indirect transfers.—

(1) In general.—If any shareholder of a 10-percent corporate shareholder of a foreign corporation exchanges stock of the 10-percent corporate shareholder for stock of the foreign corporation, such 10-percent corporate shareholder shall recognize gain in the same manner as if the stock of the foreign corporation received in such exchange had been—

(A) issued to the 10-percent corporate shareholder, and

(B) then distributed by the 10-percent corporate shareholder to such shareholder in redemption or liquidation (whichever is appropriate).

The amount of gain recognized by such 10-percent corporate shareholder under the preceding sentence shall not exceed the amount treated as a dividend under this section.

(2) 10-percent corporate shareholder defined.—For purposes of this subsection, the term "10-percent corporate shareholder" means any domestic corporation which, as of the day before the exchange referred to in paragraph (1), satisfies the stock ownership requirements of subsection (a)(2) with respect to the foreign corporation.

(j) Coordination with dividends received deduction.—In the case of the sale or exchange by a domestic corporation of stock in a foreign corporation held for 1 year or more, any amount received by the domestic corporation which is treated as a dividend by reason of this section shall be treated as a dividend for purposes of applying section 245A.

(k) Cross reference.—

For provision excluding amounts previously taxed under this section from gross income when subsequently distributed, see section 959(e).

§ 1249. Gain from certain sales or exchanges of patents, etc., to foreign corporations

(a) General rule.—Gain from the sale or exchange of a patent, an invention, model, or design (whether or not patented), a copyright, a secret formula or process, or any other similar property right to any foreign corporation by any United States person (as defined in section 7701(a)(30)) which controls such foreign corporation shall, if such gain would (but for the provisions of this subsection) be gain from the sale or exchange of a capital asset or of property described in section 1231, be considered as ordinary income.

(b) Control.—For purposes of subsection (a), control means, with respect to any foreign corporation, the ownership, directly or indirectly, of stock possessing more than 50 percent of the total combined voting power of all classes of stock entitled to vote. For purposes of this subsection, the rules for determining ownership of stock prescribed by section 958 shall apply.

§ 1253. Transfers of franchises, trademarks, and trade names

(a) General rule.—A transfer of a franchise, trademark, or trade name shall not be treated as a sale or exchange of a capital asset if the transferor retains any significant power, right, or continuing interest with respect to the subject matter of the franchise, trademark, or trade name.

(b) Definitions.—For purposes of this section—

(1) Franchise.—The term "franchise" includes an agreement which gives one of the parties to the agreement the right to distribute, sell, or provide goods, services, or facilities, within a specified area.

(2) Significant power, right, or continuing interest.—The term "significant power, right, or continuing interest" includes, but is not limited to, the following rights with respect to the interest transferred:

(A) A right to disapprove any assignment of such interest, or any part thereof.

(B) A right to terminate at will.

(C) A right to prescribe the standards of quality of products used or sold, or of services furnished, and of the equipment and facilities used to promote such products or services.

(D) A right to require that the transferee sell or advertise only products or services of the transferor.

(E) A right to require that the transferee purchase substantially all of his supplies and equipment from the transferor.

(F) A right to payments contingent on the productivity, use, or disposition of the subject matter of the interest transferred, if such payments constitute a substantial element under the transfer agreement. **(b)**

(3) Transfer.—The term "transfer" includes the renewal of a franchise, trademark, or trade name.

(c) Treatment of contingent payments by transferor.—Amounts received or accrued on account of a transfer, sale, or other disposition of a franchise, trademark, or trade name which are contingent on the productivity, use, or disposition of the franchise, trademark, or trade name transferred shall be treated as amounts received or accrued from the sale or other disposition of property which is not a capital asset.

(d) Treatment of payments by transferee.—

(1) Contingent serial payments.—

(A) In general.—Any amount described in subparagraph (B) which is paid or incurred during the taxable year on account of a transfer, sale, or other disposition of a franchise, trademark, or trade name shall be allowed as a deduction under section 162(a) (relating to trade or business expenses).

(B) Amounts to which paragraph applies.—An amount is described in this subparagraph if it—

(i) is contingent on the productivity, use, or disposition of the franchise, trademark, or trade name, and

(ii) is paid as part of a series of payments—

(I) which are payable not less frequently than annually throughout the entire term of the transfer agreement, and

(II) which are substantially equal in amount (or payable under a fixed formula).

(2) Other payments.—Any amount paid or incurred on account of a transfer, sale, or other disposition of a franchise, trademark, or trade name to which paragraph (1) does not apply shall be treated as an amount chargeable to capital account.

(3) Renewals, etc.—For purposes of determining the term of a transfer agreement under this section, there shall be taken into account all renewal options (and any other period for which the parties reasonably expect the agreement to be renewed).

Part V—Special Rules for Bonds and Other Debt Instruments

Subpart A—Original Issue Discount

§ 1274. Determination of issue price in the case of certain debt instruments issued for property

(a) In general.—In the case of any debt instrument to which this section applies, for purposes of this subpart, the issue price shall be—

(1) where there is adequate stated interest, the stated principal amount, or

(2) in any other case, the imputed principal amount.

(b) Imputed principal amount.—For purposes of this section—

(1) In general.—Except as provided in paragraph (3), the imputed principal amount of any debt instrument shall be equal to the sum of the present values of all payments due under such debt instrument.

(2) Determination of present value.—For purposes of paragraph (1), the present value of a payment shall be determined in the manner provided by regulations prescribed by the Secretary—

(A) as of the date of the sale or exchange, and

(B) by using a discount rate equal to the applicable Federal rate, compounded semiannually.

(3) Fair market value rule in potentially abusive situations.—

(A) In general.—In the case of any potentially abusive situation, the imputed principal amount of any debt instrument received in exchange for property shall be the fair market value of such property adjusted to take into account other consideration involved in the transaction.

(B) Potentially abusive situation defined.—For purposes of subparagraph (A), the term "potentially abusive situation" means—

(i) a tax shelter (as defined in section 6662(d)(2)(C)(ii)), and

(ii) any other situation which, by reason of—

(I) recent sales transactions,

(II) nonrecourse financing,

(III) financing with a term in excess of the economic life of the property, or

(IV) other circumstances,

is of a type which the Secretary specifies by regulations as having potential for tax avoidance.

(c) Debt instruments to which section applies.—

(1) In general.—Except as otherwise provided in this subsection, this section shall apply to any debt instrument given in consideration for the sale or exchange of property if—

(A) the stated redemption price at maturity for such debt instrument exceeds—

(i) where there is adequate stated interest, the stated principal amount, or

(ii) in any other case, the imputed principal amount of such debt instrument determined under subsection (b), and

(B) some or all of the payments due under such debt instrument are due more than 6 months after the date of such sale or exchange.

(2) Adequate stated interest.—For purposes of this section, there is adequate stated interest with respect to any debt instrument if the stated principal amount for such debt instrument is less than or equal to the imputed principal amount of such debt instrument determined under subsection (b).

(3) Exceptions.—This section shall not apply to—

(A) Sales for $1,000,000 or less of farms by individuals or small businesses.—

(i) In general.—Any debt instrument arising from the sale or exchange of a farm (within the meaning of section 6420(c)(2))—

(I) by an individual, estate, or testamentary trust,

(II) by a corporation which as of the date of the sale or exchange is a small business corporation (as defined in section 1244(c)(3)), or

(III) by a partnership which as of the date of the sale or exchange meets requirements similar to those of section 1244(c)(3).

(ii) $1,000,000 limitation.—Clause (i) shall apply only if it can be determined at the time of the sale or exchange that the sales price cannot exceed $1,000,000. For purposes of the preceding sentence, all sales and exchanges which are part of the same transaction (or a series of related transactions) shall be treated as 1 sale or exchange.

(B) Sales of principal residences.—Any debt instrument arising from the sale or exchange by an individual of his principal residence (within the meaning of section 121).

(C) Sales involving total payments of $250,000 or less.—

(i) In general.—Any debt instrument arising from the sale or exchange of property if the sum of the following amounts does not exceed $250,000:

(I) the aggregate amount of the payments due under such debt instrument and all other debt instruments received as consideration for the sale or exchange, and

(II) the aggregate amount of any other consideration to be received for the sale or exchange.

(ii) Consideration other than debt instrument taken into account at fair market value.—For purposes of clause (i), any consideration (other than a debt instrument) shall be taken into account at its fair market value.

(iii) Aggregation of transactions.—For purposes of this subparagraph, all sales and exchanges which are part of the same transaction (or a series of related transactions) shall be treated as 1 sale or exchange.

(D) Debt instruments which are publicly traded or issued for publicly traded property.—Any debt instrument to which section 1273(b)(3) applies.

(E) Certain sales of patents.—In the case of any transfer described in section 1235(a) (relating to sale or exchange of patents), any amount contingent on the productivity, use, or disposition of the property transferred.

(F) Sales or exchanges to which section 483(e) applies.—Any debt instrument to the extent section 483(e) (relating to certain land transfers between related persons) applies to such instrument.

(4) Exception for assumptions.—If any person—

(A) in connection with the sale or exchange of property, assumes any debt instrument, or

(B) acquires any property subject to any debt instrument, in determining whether this section or section 483 applies to such debt instrument, such assumption (or such acquisition) shall not be taken into account unless the terms and conditions of such debt instrument are modified (or the nature of the transaction is changed) in connection with the assumption (or acquisition).

(d) Determination of applicable federal rate.—For purposes of this section—

(1) Applicable federal rate.—

(A) In general.—

In the case of a debt instrument with a term of:	*The applicable Federal rate is:*
Not over 3 years	The Federal short-term rate.
Over 3 years but not over 9 years	The Federal mid-term rate.
Over 9 years	The Federal long-term rate.

(B) Determination of rates.—During each calendar month, the Secretary shall determine the Federal short-term rate mid-term rate and long-term rate which shall apply during the following calendar month.

(C) Federal rate for any calendar month.—For purposes of this paragraph—

(i) Federal short-term rate.—The Federal short-term rate shall be the rate determined by the Secretary based on the average market yield (during any 1-month period selected by the Secretary and ending in the calendar month in which the determination is made) on outstanding marketable obligations of the United States with remaining periods to maturity of 3 years or less.

(ii) Federal mid-term and long-term rates.—The Federal mid-term and long-term rate shall be determined in accordance with the principles of clause (i).

(D) Lower rate permitted in certain cases.—The Secretary may by regulations permit a rate to be used with respect to any debt instrument which is lower than the applicable Federal rate if the taxpayer establishes to the satisfaction of the Secretary that such lower rate is based on the same principles as the applicable Federal rate and is appropriate for the term of such instrument.

(2) Lowest 3-month rate applicable to any sale or exchange.—

(A) In general.—In the case of any sale or exchange, the applicable Federal rate shall be the lowest 3-month rate.

(B) Lowest 3-month rate.—For purposes of subparagraph (A), the term "lowest 3-month rate" means the lowest of the applicable Federal rates in effect for any month in the 3-calendar-month period ending with the 1st calendar month in which there is a binding contract in writing for such sale or exchange.

(3) Term of debt instrument.—In determining the term of a debt instrument for purposes of this subsection, under regulations prescribed by the Secretary, there shall be taken into account options to renew or extend.

(e) 110 Percent rate where sale-leaseback involved.—

(1) In general.—In the case of any debt instrument to which this subsection applies, the discount rate used under subsection (b)(2)(B) or section 483(b) shall be 110 percent of the applicable Federal rate, compounded semiannually.

(2) Lower discount rates shall not apply.—Section 1274A shall not apply to any debt instrument to which this subsection applies.

(3) Debt instruments to which this subsection applies.—This subsection shall apply to any debt instrument given in consideration for the sale or exchange of any property if, pursuant to a plan, the transferor or any related person leases a portion of such property after such sale or exchange.

Part VI—Treatment of Certain Passive Foreign Investment Companies

Subpart A—Interest on Tax Deferral

§ 1291. Interest on tax deferral

(a) Treatment of distributions and stock dispositions.—

(1) Distributions.—If a United States person receives an excess distribution in respect of stock in a passive foreign investment company, then—

(A) the amount of the excess distribution shall be allocated ratably to each day in the taxpayer's holding period for the stock,

(B) with respect to such excess distribution, the taxpayer's gross income for the current year shall include (as ordinary income) only the amounts allocated under subparagraph (A) to—

(i) the current year, or

(ii) any period in the taxpayer's holding period before the 1st day of the 1st taxable year of the company which begins after December 31, 1986, and for which it was a passive foreign investment company, and

(C) the tax imposed by this chapter for the current year shall be increased by the deferred tax amount (determined under subsection (c)).

(2) Dispositions.—If the taxpayer disposes of stock in a passive foreign investment company, then the rules of paragraph (1) shall apply to any gain recognized on such disposition in the same manner as if such gain were an excess distribution.

(3) Definitions.—For purposes of this section—

(A) Holding period.—The taxpayer's holding period shall be determined under section 1223; except that—

(i) for purposes of applying this section to an excess distribution, such holding period shall be treated as ending on the date of such distribution, and

(ii) if section 1296 applied to such stock with respect to the taxpayer for any prior taxable year, such holding period shall be treated as beginning on the first day of the first taxable year beginning after the last taxable year for which section 1296 so applied.

(B) Current year.—The term "current year" means the taxable year in which the excess distribution or disposition occurs.

(b) Excess distribution.—

(1) In general.—For purposes of this section, the term "excess distribution" means any distribution in respect of stock received during any taxable year to the extent such distribution does not exceed its ratable portion of the total excess distribution (if any) for such taxable year.

(2) Total excess distribution.—For purposes of this subsection—

(A) In general.—The term "total excess distribution" means the excess (if any) of—

(i) the amount of the distributions in respect of the stock received by the taxpayer during the taxable year, over

(ii) 125 percent of the average amount received in respect of such stock by the taxpayer during the 3 preceding taxable years (or, if shorter, the portion of the taxpayer's holding period before the taxable year).

For purposes of clause (ii), any excess distribution received during such 3-year period shall be taken into account only to the extent it was included in gross income under subsection (a)(1)(B).

(B) No excess for 1st year.—The total excess distributions with respect to any stock shall be zero for the taxable year in which the taxpayer's holding period in such stock begins.

(3) Adjustments.—Under regulations prescribed by the Secretary—

(A) determinations under this subsection shall be made on a share-by-share basis, except that shares with the same holding period may be aggregated,

(B) proper adjustments shall be made for stock splits and stock dividends,

(C) if the taxpayer does not hold the stock during the entire taxable year, distributions received during such year shall be annualized,

(D) if the taxpayer's holding period includes periods during which the stock was held by another person, distributions received by such other person shall be taken into account as if received by the taxpayer,

(E) if the distributions are received in a foreign currency, determinations under this subsection shall be made in such currency and the amount of any excess distribution determined in such currency shall be translated into dollars,

(F) proper adjustment shall be made for amounts not includible in gross income by reason of section 959(a) or 1293(c), and

(G) if a charitable deduction was allowable under section 642(c) to a trust for any distribution of its income, proper adjustments shall be made for the deduction so allowable to the extent allocable to distributions or gain in respect of stock in a passive foreign investment company.

(c) Deferred tax amount.—For purposes of this section—

(1) In general.—The term "deferred tax amount" means, with respect to any distribution or disposition to which subsection (a) applies, an amount equal to the sum of—

(A) the aggregate increases in taxes described in paragraph (2), plus **(c)**

(B) the aggregate amount of interest (determined in the manner provided under paragraph (3)) on such increases in tax.

Any increase in the tax imposed by this chapter for the current year under subsection (a) to the extent attributable to the amount referred to in subparagraph (B) shall be treated as interest paid under section 6601 on the due date for the current year.

(2) Aggregate increases in taxes.—For purposes of paragraph (1)(A), the aggregate increases in taxes shall be determined by multiplying each amount allocated under subsection (a)(1)(A) to any taxable year (other than any taxable year referred to in subsection (a)(1)(B)) by the highest rate of tax in effect for such taxable year under section 1 or 11, whichever applies.

(3) Computation of interest.—

(A) In general.—The amount of interest referred to in paragraph (1)(B) on any increase determined under paragraph (2) for any taxable year shall be determined for the period—

(i) beginning on the due date for such taxable year, and

(ii) ending on the due date for the taxable year with or within which the distribution or disposition occurs, by using the rates and method applicable under section 6621 for underpayments of tax for such period.

(B) Due date.—For purposes of this subsection, the term "due date" means the date prescribed by law (determined without regard to extensions) for filing the return of the tax imposed by this chapter for the taxable year.

(d) Coordination with subparts B and C.—

(1) In general.—This section shall not apply with respect to any distribution paid by a passive foreign investment company, or any disposition of stock in a passive foreign investment company, if such company is a qualified electing fund with respect to the taxpayer for each of its taxable years—

(A) which begins after December 31, 1986, and for which such company is a passive foreign investment company, and

(B) which includes any portion of the taxpayer's holding period.

Except as provided in section 1296(j), this section also shall not apply if an election under section 1296(k) is in effect for the taxpayer's taxable year. In the case of stock which is marked to market under section 475 or any other provision of this chapter, this section shall not apply, except that rules similar to the rules of section 1296(j) shall apply.

(2) Election to recognize gain where company becomes qualified electing fund.—

(A) In general.—If—

(i) a passive foreign investment company becomes a qualified electing fund with respect to the taxpayer for a taxable year which begins after December 31, 1986,

(ii) the taxpayer holds stock in such company on the first day of such taxable year, and

(iii) the taxpayer establishes to the satisfaction of the Secretary the fair market value of such stock on such first day,

the taxpayer may elect to recognize gain as if he sold such stock on such first day for such fair market value.

(B) Additional election for shareholder of controlled foreign corporations.—

(i) In general.—If—

(I) a passive foreign investment company becomes a qualified electing fund with respect to the taxpayer for a taxable year which begins after December 31, 1986,

(II) the taxpayer holds stock in such company on the first day of such taxable year, and

(III) such company is a controlled foreign corporation (as defined in section 957(a)),

the taxpayer may elect to include in gross income as a dividend received on such first day an amount equal to the portion of the post-1986 earnings and profits of such company attributable (under regulations prescribed by the Secretary) to the stock in such company held by the taxpayer on such first day. The amount treated as a dividend under the preceding sentence shall be treated as an excess distribution and shall be allocated under subsection (a)(1)(A) only to days during periods taken into account in determining the post-1986 earnings and profits so attributable.

(ii) Post-1986 earnings and profits.—For purposes of clause (i), the term "post-1986 earnings and profits" means earnings and profits which were accumulated in taxable years of such company beginning after December 31, 1986, and during the period or periods the stock was held by the taxpayer while the company was a passive foreign investment company.

(iii) Coordination with section 959(e).—For purposes of section 959(e), any amount included in gross income under this subparagraph shall be treated as included in gross income under section 1248(a).

(C) Adjustments.—In the case of any stock to which subparagraph (A) or (B) applies—

(i) the adjusted basis of such stock shall be increased by the gain recognized under subparagraph (A) or the amount treated as a dividend under subparagraph (B), as the case may be, and

(ii) the taxpayer's holding period in such stock shall be treated as beginning on the first day referred to in such subparagraph.

(e) Certain basis, etc., rules made applicable.—Except to the extent inconsistent with the regulations prescribed under subsection (f), rules similar to the rules of subsections (c), (d), and (e) of section 1246 (as in effect on the day before the date of the enactment of the American Jobs Creation Act of 2004) shall apply for purposes of this section; except that—

(1) the reduction under subsection (e) of such section shall be the excess of the basis determined under section 1014 over the adjusted basis of the stock immediately before the decedent's death, and

(2) such a reduction shall not apply in the case of a decedent who was a nonresident alien at all times during his holding period in the stock.

(f) Recognition of gain.—To the extent provided in regulations, in the case of any transfer of stock in a passive foreign investment company where (but for this subsection) there is not full recognition of gain, the excess (if any) of—

(1) the fair market value of such stock, over

(2) its adjusted basis,

shall be treated as gain from the sale or exchange of such stock and shall be recognized notwithstanding any provision of law. Proper adjustment shall be made to the basis of any such stock for gain recognized under the preceding sentence.

(g) Coordination with foreign tax credit rules.—

(1) In general.—If there are creditable foreign taxes with respect to any distribution in respect of stock in a passive foreign investment company—

(A) the amount of such distribution shall be determined for purposes of this section with regard to section 78,

(B) the excess distribution taxes shall be allocated ratably to each day in the taxpayer's holding period for the stock, and

(C) to the extent—

(i) that such excess distribution taxes are allocated to a taxable year referred to in subsection (a)(1)(B), such taxes shall be taken into account under section 901 for the current year, and

(ii) that such excess distribution taxes are allocated to any other taxable year, such taxes shall reduce (subject to the principles of section 904(d) and not below zero) the increase in tax determined under subsection (c)(2) for such taxable year by reason of such distribution (but such taxes shall not be taken into account under section 901).

(2) Definitions.—For purposes of this subsection—

(A) Creditable foreign taxes.—The term "creditable foreign taxes" means, with respect to any distribution, any withholding tax imposed with respect to such distribution, but only if the taxpayer chooses the benefits of section 901 and such taxes are creditable under section 901 (determined without regard to paragraph (1)(C)(ii)).

(B) Excess distribution taxes.—The term "excess distribution taxes" means, with respect to any distribution, the portion of the creditable foreign taxes with respect to such distribution which is attributable (on a pro rata basis) to the portion of such distribution which is an excess distribution.

(C) Section 1248 gain.—The rules of this subsection also shall apply in the case of any gain which but for this section would be includible in gross income as a dividend under section 1248.

Subpart B—Treatment of Qualified Electing Funds

§ 1293. Current taxation of income from qualified electing funds

(a) Inclusion.—

(1) In general.—Every United States person who owns (or is treated under section 1298(a) as owning) stock of a qualified electing fund at any time during the taxable year of such fund shall include in gross income—

(A) as ordinary income, such shareholder's pro rata share of the ordinary earnings of such fund for such year, and

(B) as long-term capital gain, such shareholder's pro rata share of the net capital gain of such fund for such year.

(2) Year of inclusion.—The inclusion under paragraph (1) shall be for the taxable year of the shareholder in which or with which the taxable year of the fund ends.

(b) Pro rata share.—The pro rata share referred to in subsection (a) in the case of any shareholder is the amount which would have been distributed with respect to the shareholder's stock if, on each day during the taxable year of the fund, the fund had distributed to each shareholder a pro rata share of that day's ratable share of the fund's ordinary earnings and net capital gain for such year. To the extent provided in regulations, if the fund establishes to the satisfaction of the Secretary that it uses a shorter period than the taxable year to determine shareholders' interests in the earnings of such fund, pro rata shares may be determined by using such shorter period.

(c) Previously taxed amounts distributed tax free.—If the taxpayer establishes to the satisfaction of the Secretary that any amount distributed by a passive foreign investment company is paid out of earnings and profits of the company which were included under subsection (a) in the income of any United States person, such amount shall be treated, for purposes of this chapter, as a distribution which is not a dividend; except that such distribution shall immediately reduce earnings and profits. If the passive foreign investment company is a controlled foreign corporation (as defined in section 957(a)), the preceding sentence shall not apply to any United States shareholder (as defined in section 951(b)) in such corporation, and, in applying section 959 to any such shareholder, any inclusion under this section shall be treated as an inclusion under section 951(a)(1)(A).

(d) Basis adjustments.—The basis of the taxpayer's stock in a passive foreign investment company shall be—

(1) increased by any amount which is included in the income of the taxpayer under subsection (a) with respect to such stock, and

(2) decreased by any amount distributed with respect to such stock which is not includible in the income of the taxpayer by reason of subsection (c).

A similar rule shall apply also in the case of any property if by reason of holding such property the taxpayer is treated under section 1298(a) as owning stock in a qualified electing fund.

(e) Ordinary earnings.—For purposes of this section—

(1) Ordinary earnings.—The term "ordinary earnings" means the excess of the earnings and profits of the qualified electing fund for the taxable year over its net capital gain for such taxable year.

(2) Limitation on net capital gain.—A qualified electing fund's net capital gain for any taxable year shall not exceed its earnings and profits for such taxable year.

(3) Determination of earnings and profits.—The earnings and profits of any qualified electing fund shall be determined without regard to paragraphs (4), (5), and (6) of section 312(n). Under regulations, the preceding sentence shall not apply to the extent it would increase earnings and profits by an amount which was previously distributed by the qualified electing fund.

(f) Foreign tax credit allowed in the case of 10-percent corporate shareholder.—For purposes of section 960—

(1) any amount included in the gross income under subsection (a) shall be treated as if it were included under section 951(a),

(2) any amount excluded from gross income under subsection (c) shall be treated in the same manner as amounts excluded from gross income under section 959, and

(3) a domestic corporation which owns (or is treated under section 1298(a) as owning) stock of a qualified electing fund shall be treated in the same manner as a United States shareholder of a controlled foreign corporation (and such qualified electing fund shall be treated in the same manner as such controlled foreign corporation) if such domestic corporation meets the stock ownership requirements of subsection (a) or (b) of section 902 (as in effect before its repeal) with respect to such qualified electing fund.

(g) Other special rules.—

(1) Exception for certain income.—For purposes of determining the amount included in the gross income of any person under this section, the ordinary earnings and net capital gain of a qualified electing fund shall not include any item of income received by such fund if—

(A) such fund is a controlled foreign corporation (as defined in section 957(a)) and such person is a United States shareholder (as defined in section 951(b)) in such fund, and

(B) such person establishes to the satisfaction of the Secretary that—

(i) such income was subject to an effective rate of income tax imposed by a foreign country greater than 90 percent of the maximum rate of tax specified in section 11, or

(ii) such income is—

(I) from sources within the United States,

(II) effectively connected with the conduct by the qualified electing fund of a trade or business in the United States, and

(III) not exempt from taxation (or subject to a reduced rate of tax) pursuant to a treaty obligation of the United States.

(2) Prevention of double inclusion.—The Secretary shall prescribe such adjustment to the provisions of this section as may be necessary to prevent the same item of income of a qualified electing fund from being included in the gross income of a United States person more than once.

§ 1294. Election to extend time for payment of tax on undistributed earnings

(a) Extension allowed by election.—

(1) In general.—At the election of the taxpayer, the time for payment of any undistributed PFIC earnings tax liability of the taxpayer for the taxable year shall be extended to the extent and subject to the limitations provided in this section.

(2) Election not permitted where amounts otherwise includible under section 951.—The taxpayer may not make an election under paragraph (1) with respect to the undistributed PFIC earnings tax liability attributable to a qualified electing fund for the taxable year if any amount is includible in the gross income of the taxpayer under section 951 with respect to such fund for such taxable year.

(b) Definitions.—For purposes of this section—

(1) Undistributed PFIC earnings tax liability.—The term "undistributed PFIC earnings tax liability" means, in the case of any taxpayer, the excess of—

(A) the tax imposed by this chapter for the taxable year, over

(B) the tax which would be imposed by this chapter for such year without regard to the inclusion in gross income under section 1293 of the undistributed earnings of a qualified electing fund.

(2) Undistributed earnings.—The term "undistributed earnings" means, with respect to any qualified electing fund, the excess (if any) of—

(A) the amount includible in gross income by reason of section 1293(a) for the taxable year, over

(B) the amount not includible in gross income by reason of section 1293(c) for such taxable year.

(c) Termination of extension.—

(1) Distributions.—

(A) In general.—If a distribution is not includible in gross income for the taxable year by reason of section 1293(c), then the extension under subsection (a) for payment of the undistributed PFIC earnings tax liability with respect to the earnings to which such distribution is attributable shall expire on the last date prescribed by law (determined without regard to extensions) for filing the return of tax for such taxable year.

(B) Ordering rule.—For purposes of subparagraph (A), a distribution shall be treated as made from the most recently accumulated earnings and profits.

(2) Transfers, etc.—If—

(A) stock in a passive foreign investment company is transferred during the taxable year, or

(B) a passive foreign investment company ceases to be a qualified electing fund,

all extensions under subsection (a) for payment of undistributed PFIC earnings tax liability attributable to such stock (or, in the case of such a cessation, attributable to any stock in such company) which had not expired before the date of such transfer or cessation shall expire on the last date prescribed by law (determined without regard to extensions) for filing the return of tax for the taxable year in which such transfer or cessation occurs. To the extent provided in regulations, the preceding sentence shall not apply in the case of a transfer in a transaction with respect to which gain or loss is not recognized (in whole or in part), and the transferee in such transaction shall succeed to the treatment under this section of the transferor.

(3) Jeopardy.—If the Secretary believes that collection of an amount to which an extension under this section relates is in jeopardy, the Secretary shall immediately terminate such extension with respect to such amount, and notice and demand shall be made by him for payment of such amount.

(d) Election.—The election under subsection (a) shall be made not later than the time prescribed by law (including extensions) for filing the return of tax imposed by this chapter for the taxable year.

(e) Authority to require bond.—Section 6165 shall apply to any extension under this section as though the Secretary were extending the time for payment of the tax.

(f) Treatment of loans to shareholder.—For purposes of this section and section 1293, any loan by a qualified electing fund (directly or indirectly) to a shareholder of such fund shall be treated as a distribution to such shareholder.

(g) Cross reference.—

For provisions providing for interest for the period of the extension under this section, see section 6601.

§ 1295. Qualified electing fund

(a) General rule.—For purposes of this part, any passive foreign investment company shall be treated as a qualified electing fund with respect to the taxpayer if—

(1) an election by the taxpayer under subsection (b) applies to such company for the taxable year, and

(2) such company complies with such requirements as the Secretary may prescribe for purposes of—

(A) determining the ordinary earnings and net capital gain of such company, and

(B) otherwise carrying out the purposes of this subpart.

(b) Election.—

(1) In general.—A taxpayer may make an election under this subsection with respect to any passive foreign investment company for any taxable year of the taxpayer. Such an election, once made with respect to any company, shall apply to all subsequent taxable years of the taxpayer with respect to such company unless revoked by the taxpayer with the consent of the Secretary.

(2) When made.—An election under this subsection may be made for any taxable year at any time on or before the due date (determined with regard to extensions) for filing the return of the tax imposed by this chapter for such taxable year. To the extent provided in regulations, such an election may be made later than as required in the preceding sentence where the taxpayer fails to make a timely election because the taxpayer reasonably believed that the company was not a passive foreign investment company.

Subpart C—Election of Mark to Market for Marketable Stock

§ 1296. Election of mark to market for marketable stock

(a) General rule.—In the case of marketable stock in a passive foreign investment company which is owned (or treated under subsection (g) as owned) by a United States person at the close of any taxable year of such person, at the election of such person—

(1) If the fair market value of such stock as of the close of such taxable year exceeds its adjusted basis, such United States person shall include in gross income for such taxable year an amount equal to the amount of such excess.

(2) If the adjusted basis of such stock exceeds the fair market value of such stock as of the close of such taxable year, such United States person shall be allowed a deduction for such taxable year equal to the lesser of—

(A) the amount of such excess, or

(B) the unreversed inclusions with respect to such stock.

(b) Basis adjustments.—

(1) In general.—The adjusted basis of stock in a passive foreign investment company—

(A) shall be increased by the amount included in the gross income of the United States person under subsection (a)(1) with respect to such stock, and

(B) shall be decreased by the amount allowed as a deduction to the United States person under subsection (a)(2) with respect to such stock.

(2) Special rule for stock constructively owned.—In the case of stock in a passive foreign investment company which the United States person is treated as owning under subsection (g)—

(A) the adjustments under paragraph (1) shall apply to such stock in the hands of the person actually holding such stock but only for purposes of determining the subsequent treatment under this chapter of the United States person with respect to such stock, and

(B) similar adjustments shall be made to the adjusted basis of the property by reason of which the United States person is treated as owning such stock.

(c) Character and source rules.—

(1) Ordinary treatment.—

(A) Gain.—Any amount included in gross income under subsection (a)(1), and any gain on the sale or other disposition of marketable stock in a passive foreign investment company (with respect to which an election under this section is in effect), shall be treated as ordinary income.

(B) Loss.—Any—

(i) amount allowed as a deduction under subsection (a)(2), and

(ii) loss on the sale or other disposition of marketable stock in a passive foreign investment company (with respect to which an election under this section is in effect) to the extent that the amount of such loss does not exceed the unreversed inclusions with respect to such stock,

shall be treated as an ordinary loss. The amount so treated shall be treated as a deduction allowable in computing adjusted gross income.

(2) Source.—The source of any amount included in gross income under subsection (a)(1) (or allowed as a deduction under subsection (a)(2)) shall be determined in the same manner as if such amount were gain or loss (as the case may be) from the sale of stock in the passive foreign investment company.

(d) Unreversed inclusions.—For purposes of this section, the term "unreversed inclusions" means, with respect to any stock in a passive foreign investment company, the excess (if any) of—

(1) the amount included in gross income of the taxpayer under subsection (a)(1) with respect to such stock for prior taxable years, over

(2) the amount allowed as a deduction under subsection (a)(2) with respect to such stock for prior taxable years.

The amount referred to in paragraph (1) shall include any amount which would have been included in gross income under subsection (a)(1) with respect to such stock for any prior taxable year but for section 1291. In the case of a regulated investment company which elected to mark to market the stock held by such company as of the last day of the taxable year preceding such company's first taxable year for which such company elects the application of this section, the amount referred to in paragraph (1) shall include amounts included in gross income under such mark to market with respect to such stock for prior taxable years.

(e) Marketable stock.—For purposes of this section—

(1) In general.—The term "marketable stock" means—

(A) any stock which is regularly traded on—

(i) a national securities exchange which is registered with the Securities and Exchange Commission or the national market system established pursuant to section 11A of the Securities and Exchange Act of 1934, or

(ii) any exchange or other market which the Secretary determines has rules adequate to carry out the purposes of this part,

(B) to the extent provided in regulations, stock in any foreign corporation which is comparable to a regulated investment company and which offers for sale or has outstanding any stock of which it is the issuer and which is redeemable at its net asset value, and

(C) to the extent provided in regulations, any option on stock described in subparagraph (A) or (B).

(2) Special rule for regulated investment companies.—In the case of any regulated investment company which is offering for sale or has outstanding any stock of which it is the issuer and which is redeemable at its net asset value, all stock in a passive foreign investment company which it owns directly or indirectly shall be treated as marketable stock for purposes of this section. Except as provided in regulations, similar treatment as marketable stock shall apply in the case of any other regulated investment company which publishes net asset valuations at least annually.

(f) Treatment of controlled foreign corporations which are shareholders in passive foreign investments companies.—In the case of a foreign corporation which is a controlled foreign corporation and which owns (or is treated under subsection (g) as owning) stock in a passive foreign investment company—

(1) this section (other than subsection (c)(2)) shall apply to such foreign corporation in the same manner as if such corporation were a United States person, and

(2) for purposes of subpart F of part III of subchapter N—

(A) any amount included in gross income under subsection (a)(1) shall be treated as foreign personal holding company income described in section 954(c)(1)(A), and

(B) any amount allowed as a deduction under subsection (a)(2) shall be treated as a deduction allocable to foreign personal holding company income so described.

(g) Stock owned through certain foreign entities.—Except as provided in regulations—

(1) In general.—For purposes of this section, stock owned, directly or indirectly, by or for a foreign partnership or foreign trust or foreign estate shall be considered as being owned proportionately by its partners or beneficiaries. Stock considered to be owned by a person by reason of the application of the preceding sentence shall, for purposes of applying such sentence, be treated as actually owned by such person.

(2) Treatment of certain dispositions.—In any case in which a United States person is treated as owning stock in a passive foreign investment company by reason of paragraph (1)—

(A) any disposition by the United States person or by any other person which results in the United States person being treated as no longer owning such stock, and

(B) any disposition by the person owning such stock, shall be treated as a disposition by the United States person of the stock in the passive foreign investment company.

(h) Coordination with section 851(b).—For purposes of section 851(b)(2), any amount included in gross income under subsection (a) shall be treated as a dividend.

(i) Stock acquired from a decedent.—In the case of stock of a passive foreign investment company which is acquired by bequest, devise, or inheritance (or by the decedent's estate) and with respect to which an election under this section was in effect as of the date of the decedent's death, notwithstanding section 1014, the basis of such stock in the hands of the person so acquiring it shall be the adjusted basis of such stock in the hands of the decedent immediately before his death (or, if lesser, the basis which would have been determined under section 1014 without regard to this subsection).

(j) Coordination with section 1291 for first year of election.—

(1) Taxpayers other that regulated investment companies.—

(A) In general.—If the taxpayer elects the application of this section with respect to any marketable stock in a corporation after the beginning of the taxpayer's holding period in such stock, and if the requirements of subparagraph (B) are not satisfied, section 1291 shall apply to—

(i) any distributions with respect to, or disposition of, such stock in the first taxable year of the taxpayer for which such election is made, and

(ii) any amount which, but for section 1291, would have been included in gross income under subsection (a) with respect to such stock for such taxable year in the same manner as if such amount were gain on the disposition of such stock.

(B) Requirements.—The requirements of this subparagraph are met if, with respect to each of such corporation's taxable years for which such corporation was a passive foreign investment company and which begin after December 31, 1986, and included any portion of the taxpayer's holding period in such stock, such corporation was treated as a qualified electing fund under this part with respect to the taxpayer.

(2) Special rules for regulated investment companies.—

(A) In general.—If a regulated investment company elects the application of this section with respect to any marketable stock in a corporation after the beginning of the taxpayer's holding period in such stock, then, with respect to such company's first taxable year for which such company elects the application of this section with respect to such stock—

(i) section 1291 shall not apply to such stock with respect to any distribution or disposition during, or amount included in gross income under this section for, such first taxable year, but

(ii) such regulated investment company's tax under this chapter for such first taxable year shall be increased by the aggregate amount of interest which would have been determined under section 1291(c)(3) if section 1291 were applied without regard to this subparagraph.

Clause (ii) shall not apply if for the preceding taxable year the company elected to mark to market the stock held by such company as of the last day of such preceding taxable year.

(B) Disallowance of deduction.—No deduction shall be allowed to any regulated investment company for the increase in tax under subparagraph (A)(ii).

(k) Election.—This section shall apply to marketable stock in a passive foreign investment company which is held by a United States person only if such person elects to apply this section with respect to such stock. Such an election shall apply to the taxable year for which made and all subsequent taxable years unless—

(1) such stock ceases to be marketable stock, or

(2) the Secretary consents to the revocation of such election.

***(l)* Transition rule for individuals becoming subject to United States tax.**—If any individual becomes a United States person in a taxable year beginning after December 31, 1997, solely for purposes of this section, the adjusted basis (before adjustments under subsection (b)) of any marketable stock in a passive foreign investment company owned by such individual on the first day of such taxable year shall be treated as being the greater of its fair market value on such first day or its adjusted basis on such first day.

Subpart D—General Provisions

§ 1297. Passive foreign investment company

(a) In general.—For purposes of this part, except as otherwise provided in this subpart, the term "passive foreign investment company" means any foreign corporation if—

(1) 75 percent or more of the gross income of such corporation for the taxable year is passive income, or

(2) the average percentage of assets (as determined in accordance with subsection (e)) held by such corporation during the taxable year which produce passive income or which are held for the production of passive income is at least 50 percent.

(b) Passive income.—For purposes of this section—

(1) In general.—Except as provided in paragraph (2), the term "passive income" means any income which is of a kind which would be foreign personal holding company income as defined in section 954(c).

(2) Exceptions.—Except as provided in regulations, the term "passive income" does not include any income—

(A) derived in the active conduct of a banking business by an institution licensed to do business as a bank in the United States (or, to the extent provided in regulations, by any other corporation),

(B) derived in the active conduct of an insurance business by a qualifying insurance corporation (as defined in subsection (f)),

(C) which is interest, a dividend, or a rent or royalty, which is received or accrued from a related person (within the meaning of section 954(d)(3)) to the extent such amount is properly allocable (under regulations prescribed by the Secretary) to income of such related person which is not passive income, or

(D) which is export trade income of an export trade corporation (as defined in section 971).

For purposes of subparagraph (C), the term "related person" has the meaning given such term by section 954(d)(3) determined by substituting "foreign corporation" for "controlled foreign corporation" each place it appears in section 954(d)(3).

(c) Look-thru in the case of 25-percent owned corporations.—If a foreign corporation owns (directly or indirectly) at least 25 percent (by value) of the stock of another corporation, for purposes of determining whether such foreign corporation is a passive foreign investment company, such foreign corporation shall be treated as if it—

(1) held its proportionate share of the assets of such other corporation, and

(2) received directly its proportionate share of the income of such other corporation.

(d) Exception for United States shareholder of controlled foreign corporations.—

(1) In general.—For purposes of this part, a corporation shall not be treated with respect to a shareholder as a passive foreign investment company during the qualified portion of such shareholder's holding period with respect to stock in such corporation.

(2) Qualified portion.—For purposes of this subsection, the term "qualified portion" means the portion of the shareholder's holding period—

(A) which is after December 31, 1997, and

(B) during which the shareholder is a United States shareholder (as defined in section 951(b)) of the corporation and the corporation is a controlled foreign corporation.

(3) New holding period if qualified portion ends.—

(A) In general.—Except as provided in subparagraph (B), if the qualified portion of a shareholder's holding period with respect to any stock ends after December 31, 1997, solely for purposes of this part, the shareholder's holding period with respect to such stock shall be treated as beginning as of the first day following such period.

(B) Exception.—Subparagraph (A) shall not apply if such stock was, with respect to such shareholder, stock in a passive foreign investment company at any time before the qualified portion of the shareholder's holding period with respect to such stock and no election under section 1298(b)(1) is made.

(4) Treatment of holders of options.—Paragraph (1) shall not apply to stock treated as owned by a person by reason of section 1298(a)(4) (relating to the treatment of a person that has an option to acquire stock as owning such stock) unless such person establishes that such stock is owned (within the meaning of section 958(a)) by a United States shareholder (as defined in section 951(b)) who is not exempt from tax under this chapter.

(e) Methods for measuring assets.—

(1) Determination using value.—The determination under subsection (a)(2) shall be made on the basis of the value of the assets of a foreign corporation if—

(A) such corporation is a publicly traded corporation for the taxable year, or

(B) paragraph (2) does not apply to such corporation for the taxable year.

(2) Determination using adjusted bases.—The determination under subsection (a)(2) shall be based on the adjusted bases (as determined for the purposes of computing earnings and profits) of the assets of a foreign corporation if such corporation is not described in paragraph (1)(A) and such corporation—

(A) is a controlled foreign corporation, or

(B) elects the application of this paragraph.

An election under subparagraph (B), once made, may be revoked only with the consent of the Secretary.

(3) Publicly traded corporation.—For purposes of this subsection, a foreign corporation shall be treated as a publicly traded corporation if the stock in the corporation is regularly traded on—

(A) a national securities exchange which is registered with the Securities and Exchange Commission or the national market system established pursuant to section 11A of the Securities and Exchange Act of 1934, or

(B) any exchange or other market which the Secretary determines has rules adequate to carry out the purposes of this subsection.

(f) Qualifying insurance corporation.—For purposes of subsection (b)(2)(B)—

(1) In general.—The term "qualifying insurance corporation" means, with respect to any taxable year, a foreign corporation—

(A) which would be subject to tax under subchapter L if such corporation were a domestic corporation, and

(B) the applicable insurance liabilities of which constitute more than 25 percent of its total assets, determined on the basis of such liabilities and assets as reported on the corporation's applicable financial statement for the last year ending with or within the taxable year.

(2) Alternative facts and circumstances test for certain corporations.—If a corporation fails to qualify as a qualified insurance corporation under paragraph (1) solely because the percentage determined under paragraph (1)(B) is 25 percent or less, a United States person that owns stock in such corporation may elect to treat such stock as stock of a qualifying insurance corporation if—

(A) the percentage so determined for the corporation is at least 10 percent, and

(B) under regulations provided by the Secretary, based on the applicable facts and circumstances—

(i) the corporation is predominantly engaged in an insurance business, and

(ii) such failure is due solely to runoff-related or rating-related circumstances involving such insurance business.

(3) Applicable insurance liabilities.—For purposes of this subsection—

(A) In general.—The term "applicable insurance liabilities" means, with respect to any life or property and casualty insurance business—

(i) loss and loss adjustment expenses, and

(ii) reserves (other than deficiency, contingency, or unearned premium reserves) for life and health insurance risks and life and health insurance claims with respect to contracts providing coverage for mortality or morbidity risks.

(B) Limitations on amount of liabilities.—Any amount determined under clause (i) or (ii) of subparagraph (A) shall not exceed the lesser of such amount—

(i) as reported to the applicable insurance regulatory body in the applicable financial statement described in paragraph (4)(A) (or, if less, the amount required by applicable law or regulation), or

(ii) as determined under regulations prescribed by the Secretary.

(4) Other definitions and rules.—For purposes of this subsection—

(A) Applicable financial statement.—The term "applicable financial statement" means a statement for financial reporting purposes which—

(i) is made on the basis of generally accepted accounting principles,

(ii) is made on the basis of international financial reporting standards, but only if there is no statement that meets the requirement of clause (i), or

(iii) except as otherwise provided by the Secretary in regulations, is the annual statement which is required to be filed with the applicable insurance regulatory body, but only if there is no statement which meets the requirements of clause (i) or (ii).

(B) Applicable insurance regulatory body.—The term "applicable insurance regulatory body" means, with respect to any insurance business, the entity established by law to license, authorize, or regulate such business and to which the statement described in subparagraph (A) is provided.

§ 1298. Special rules

(a) Attribution of ownership.—For purposes of this part—

(1) Attribution to United States persons.—This subsection—

(A) shall apply to the extent that the effect is to treat stock of a passive foreign investment company as owned by a United States person, and

(B) except to the extent provided in regulations, shall not apply to treat stock owned (or treated as owned under this subsection) by a United States person as owned by any other person.

(2) Corporations.—

(A) In general.—If 50 percent or more in value of the stock of a corporation is owned, directly or indirectly, by or for any person, such person shall be considered as owning the stock owned directly or indirectly by or for such corporation in that proportion which the value of the stock which such person so owns bears to the value of all stock in the corporation.

(B) 50-percent limitation not to apply to PFIC.—For purposes of determining whether a shareholder of a passive foreign investment company is treated as owning stock owned directly or indirectly by or for such company, subparagraph (A) shall be applied without regard to the 50-percent limitation contained therein. Section 1297(d) shall not apply in determining whether a corporation is a passive foreign investment company for purposes of this subparagraph.

(3) Partnerships, etc.—Stock owned, directly or indirectly, by or for a partnership, estate, or trust shall be considered as being owned proportionately by its partners or beneficiaries.

(4) Options.—To the extent provided in regulations, if any person has an option to acquire stock, such stock shall be considered as owned by such person. For purposes of this paragraph, an option to acquire such an option, and each one of a series of such options, shall be considered as an option to acquire such stock.

(5) Successive application.—Stock considered to be owned by a person by reason of the application of paragraph (2), (3), or (4) shall, for purposes of applying such paragraphs, be considered as actually owned by such person.

(b) Other special rules.—For purposes of this part—

(1) Time for determination.—Stock held by a taxpayer shall be treated as stock in a passive foreign investment company if, at any time during the holding period of the taxpayer with respect to such stock, such corporation (or any predecessor) was a passive foreign investment company which was not a qualified electing fund. The preceding sentence shall not apply if the taxpayer elects to recognize gain (as of the last day of the last taxable year for which the company was a passive foreign investment company (determined without regard to the preceding sentence)) under rules similar to the rules of section 1291(d)(2).

(2) Certain corporations not treated as PFIC's during start-up year.—A corporation shall not be treated as a passive foreign investment company for the first taxable year such corporation has gross income (hereinafter in this paragraph referred to as the "start-up year") if—

(A) no predecessor of such corporation was a passive foreign investment company,

(B) it is established to the satisfaction of the Secretary that such corporation will not be a passive foreign investment company for either of the 1st 2 taxable years following the start-up year, and

(C) such corporation is not a passive foreign investment company for either of the 1st 2 taxable years following the start-up year.

(3) Certain corporations changing businesses.—A corporation shall not be treated as a passive foreign investment company for any taxable year if—

(A) neither such corporation (nor any predecessor) was a passive foreign investment company for any prior taxable year,

(B) it is established to the satisfaction of the Secretary that—

(i) substantially all of the passive income of the corporation for the taxable year is attributable to proceeds from the disposition of 1 or more active trades or businesses, and

(ii) such corporation will not be a passive foreign investment company for either of the 1st 2 taxable years following such taxable year, and

(C) such corporation is not a passive foreign investment company for either of such 2 taxable years.

(4) Separate interests treated as separate corporations.—Under regulations prescribed by the Secretary, where necessary to carry out the purposes of this part, separate classes of stock (or other interests) in a corporation shall be treated as interests in separate corporations.

(5) Application of part where stock held by other entity.—

(A) In general.—Under regulations, in any case in which a United States person is treated as owning stock in a passive foreign investment company by reason of subsection (a)—

(i) any disposition by the United States person or the person owning such stock which results in the United States person being treated as no longer owning such stock, or

(ii) any distribution of property in respect of such stock to the person holding such stock,

shall be treated as a disposition by, or distribution to, the United States person with respect to the stock in the passive foreign investment company.

(B) Amount treated in same manner as previously taxed income.—Rules similar to the rules of section 959(b) shall apply to any amount described in subparagraph (A) and to any amount included in gross income under section 1293(a) (or which would have been so included but for section 951(c)) in respect of stock which the taxpayer is treated as owning under subsection (a).

(6) Dispositions.—Except as provided in regulations, if a taxpayer uses any stock in a passive foreign investment company as security for a loan, the taxpayer shall be treated as having disposed of such stock.

(7) Treatment of certain foreign corporations owning stock in 25-percent owned domestic corporation.—

(A) In general.—If—

(i) a foreign corporation is subject to the tax imposed by section 531 (or waives any benefit under any treaty which would otherwise prevent the imposition of such tax), and

(ii) such foreign corporation owns at least 25 percent (by value) of the stock of a domestic corporation,

for purposes of determining whether such foreign corporation is a passive foreign investment company, any qualified stock held by such domestic corporation shall be treated as an asset which does not produce passive income (and is not held for the production of passive income) and any amount included in gross income with respect to such stock shall not be treated as passive income.

(B) Qualified stock.—For purposes of subparagraph (A), the term "qualified stock" means any stock in a C corporation which is a domestic corporation and which is not a regulated investment company or real estate investment trust.

(8) Treatment of certain subpart F inclusions.—Any amount included in gross income under of section 951(a)(1)(B) shall be treated as a distribution received with respect to the stock.

(c) Treatment of stock held by pooled income fund.—If stock in a passive foreign investment company is owned (or treated as owned under subsection (a)) by a pooled income fund (as defined in section 642(c)(5)) and no portion of any gain from a disposition of such stock may be allocated to income under the terms of the governing instrument of such fund—

(1) section 1291 shall not apply to any gain on a disposition of such stock by such fund if (without regard to section 1291) a deduction would be allowable with respect to such gain under section 642(c)(3),

(2) section 1293 shall not apply with respect to such stock, and

(3) in determining whether section 1291 applies to any distribution in respect of such stock, subsection (d) of section 1291 shall not apply.

(d) Treatment of certain leased property.—For purposes of this part—

(1) In general.—Any tangible personal property with respect to which foreign corporation is the lessee under a lease with a term of at least 12 months shall be treated as an asset actually held by such corporation.

(2) Amount taken into account.—

(A) In general.—The amount taken into account under section 1297(a)(2) with respect to any asset to which paragraph (1) applies shall be the unamortized portion (as determined under regulations prescribed by the Secretary) of the present value of the payments under the lease for the use of such property.

(B) Present value.—For purposes of subparagraph (A), the present value of payments described in subparagraph (A) shall be determined in the manner provided in regulations prescribed by the Secretary—

(i) as of the beginning of the lease term, and

(ii) except as provided in such regulations, by using a discount rate equal to the applicable Federal rate determined under section 1274(d)—

(I) by substituting the lease term for the term of the debt instrument, and

(II) without regard to paragraph (2) or (3) thereof.

(3) Exceptions.—This subsection shall not apply in any case where—

(A) the lessor is a related person (as defined in section 954(d)(3)) with respect to the foreign corporation, or

(B) a principal purpose of leasing the property was to avoid the provisions of this part.

(e) Special rules for certain intangibles.—For purposes of this part—

(1) Research expenditures.—The adjusted basis of the total assets of a controlled foreign corporation shall be increased by the research or experimental expenditures (within the meaning of section 174) paid or incurred by such foreign corporation during the taxable year and the preceding 2 taxable years. Any expenditure otherwise taken into account under the preceding sentence shall be reduced by the amount of any reimbursement received by the controlled foreign corporation with respect to such expenditure.

(2) Certain licensed intangibles.—

(A) In general.—In the case of any intangible property (as defined in section 367(d)(4)) with respect to which a controlled foreign corporation is a licensee and which is used by such foreign corporation in the active conduct of a trade or business, the adjusted basis of the total assets of such foreign corporation shall be increased by an amount equal to 300 percent of the payments made during the taxable year by such foreign corporation for the use of such intangible property.

(B) Exceptions.—Subparagraph (A) shall not apply to—

(i) any payments to a foreign person if such foreign person is a related person (as defined in section 954(d)(3)) with respect to the controlled foreign corporation, and

(ii) any payments under a license if a principal purpose of entering into such license was to avoid the provisions of this part.

(3) Controlled foreign corporation.—For purposes of this subsection, the term "controlled foreign corporation" has the meaning given such term by section 957(a).

(f) Reporting requirement.—Except as otherwise provided by the Secretary, each United States person who is a shareholder of a passive foreign investment company shall file an annual report containing such information as the Secretary may require.

(g) Regulations.—The Secretary shall prescribe such regulations as may be necessary or appropriate to carry out the purposes of this part.

Chapter 3—Withholding of Tax on Nonresident Aliens and Foreign Corporations

Subchapter A—Nonresident Aliens and Foreign Corporations

§ 1441. Withholding of tax on nonresident aliens

(a) General rule.—Except as otherwise provided in subsection (c), all persons, in whatever capacity acting (including lessees or mortgagors of real or personal property, fiduciaries, employers, and all officers and employees of the United States) having the control, receipt, custody, disposal, or payment of any of the items of income specified in subsection (b) (to the extent that any of such items constitutes gross income from sources within the United States), of any nonresident alien individual or of any foreign partnership shall (except as otherwise provided in regulations prescribed by the Secretary under section 874) deduct and withhold from such items a tax equal to 30 percent thereof, except that in the case of any item of income specified in the second sentence of subsection (b), the tax shall be equal to 14 percent of such item.

(b) Income items.—The items of income referred to in subsection (a) are interest (other than original issue discount as defined in section 1273), dividends, rent, salaries, wages, premiums, annuities, compensations, remunerations, emoluments, or other fixed or determinable annual or periodical gains, profits, and income, gains described in section 631(b) or (c), amounts subject to tax under section 871(a)(1)(C), and gains subject to tax under section 871(a)(1)(D). The items of income referred to in subsection (a) from which tax shall be deducted and withheld at the rate of 14 percent are amounts which are received by a nonresident alien individual who is temporarily present in the United States as a nonimmigrant under subparagraph (F), (J), (M), or (Q) of section 101(a)(15) of the Immigration and Nationality Act and which are—

(1) incident to a qualified scholarship to which section 117(a) applies, but only to the extent includible in gross income; or

(2) in the case of an individual who is not a candidate for a degree at an educational organization described in section 170(b)(1)(A)(ii), granted by—

(A) an organization described in section 501(c)(3) which is exempt from tax under section 501(a),

(B) a foreign government,

(C) an international organization, or a binational or multinational educational and cultural foundation or commission created or continued pursuant to the Mutual Educational and Cultural Exchange Act of 1961, or

(D) the United States, or an instrumentality or agency thereof, or a State, or a possession of the United States, or any political subdivision thereof, or the District of Columbia,

as a scholarship or fellowship for study, training, or research in the United States. In the case of a nonresident alien individual who is a member of a domestic partnership, the items of income referred to in subsection (a) shall be treated as referring to items specified in this subsection included in his distributive share of the income of such partnership.

(c) Exceptions.—

(1) Income connected with United States business.—No deduction or withholding under subsection (a) shall be required in the case of any item of income (other than compensation for personal services) which is effectively connected with the conduct of a trade or business within the United States and which is included in the gross income of the recipient under section 871(b)(2) for the taxable year.

(2) Owner unknown.—The Secretary may authorize the tax under subsection (a) to be deducted and withheld from the interest upon any securities the owners of which are not known to the withholding agent.

(3) Bonds with extended maturity dates.—The deduction and withholding in the case of interest on bonds, mortgages, or deeds of trust or other similar obligations of a corporation, within subsections (a), (b), and (c) of section 1451 (as in effect before its repeal by the Tax Reform Act of 1984) were it not for the fact that the maturity date of such obligations has been extended on or after January 1, 1934, and the liability assumed by the debtor exceeds 27 1/2 percent of the interest, shall not exceed the rate of 27 1/2 percent per annum.

(4) Compensation of certain aliens.—Under regulations prescribed by the Secretary, compensation for personal services may be exempted from deduction and withholding under subsection (a).

(5) Special items.—In the case of gains described in section 631(b) or (c), and gains subject to tax under section 871(a)(1)(D), the amount required to be deducted and withheld shall, if the amount of such gain is not known to the withholding agent, be such amount, not exceeding 30 percent of the amount payable, as may be necessary to assure that the tax deducted and withheld shall not be less than 30 percent of such gain.

(6) Per diem of certain aliens.—No deduction or withholding under subsection (a) shall be required in the case of amounts of per diem for subsistence paid by the United States Government (directly or by contract) to any nonresident alien individual who is engaged in any program of training in the United States under the Mutual Security Act of 1954, as amended.

(7) Certain annuities received under qualified plans.—No deduction or withholding under subsection (a) shall be required in the case of any amount received as an annuity if such amount is, under section 871(f), exempt from the tax imposed by section 871(a).

(8) Original issue discount.—The Secretary may prescribe such regulations as may be necessary for the deduction and withholding of the tax on original issue discount subject to tax under section

871(a)(1)(C) including rules for the deduction and withholding of the tax on original issue discount from payments of interest.

(9) Interest income from certain portfolio debt investments.—In the case of portfolio interest (within the meaning of section 871(h)), no tax shall be required to be deducted and withheld from such interest unless the person required to deduct and withhold tax from such interest knows, or has reason to know, that such interest is not portfolio interest by reason of section 871(h)(3) or (4).

(10) Exception for certain interest and dividends.—No tax shall be required to be deducted and withheld under subsection (a) from any amount described in section 871(i)(2).

(11) Certain gambling winnings.—No tax shall be required to be deducted and withheld under subsection (a) from any amount exempt from the tax imposed by section 871(a)(1)(A) by reason of section 871(j).

(12) Certain dividends received from regulated investment companies.—

(A) In general.—No tax shall be required to be deducted and withheld under subsection (a) from any amount exempt from the tax imposed by section 871(a)(1)(A) by reason of section 871(k).

(B) Special rule.—For purposes of subparagraph (A), clause (i) of section 871(k)(1)(B) shall not apply to any dividend unless the regulated investment company knows that such dividend is a dividend referred to in such clause. A similar rule shall apply with respect to the exception contained in section 871(k)(2)(B).

(d) Exemption of certain foreign partnerships.—Subject to such terms and conditions as may be provided by regulations prescribed by the Secretary, subsection (a) shall not apply in the case of a foreign partnership engaged in trade or business within the United States if the Secretary determines that the requirements of subsection (a) impose an undue administrative burden and that the collection of the tax imposed by section 871(a) on the members of such partnership who are nonresident alien individuals will not be jeopardized by the exemption.

(e) Alien resident of Puerto Rico.—For purposes of this section, the term "nonresident alien individual" includes an alien resident of Puerto Rico.

(f) Continental shelf areas.—For sources of income derived from, or for services performed with respect to, the exploration or exploitation of natural resources on submarine areas adjacent to the territorial waters of the United States, see section 638.

(g) Cross reference.—For provision treating 85 percent of social security benefits as subject to withholding under this section, see section 871(a)(3).

§ 1442. Withholding of tax on foreign corporations

(a) General rule.—In the case of foreign corporations subject to taxation under this subtitle, there shall be deducted and withheld at the source in the same manner and on the same items of income as is provided in section 1441 a tax equal to 30 percent thereof. For purposes of the preceding sentence, the references in section 1441(b) to sections 871(a)(1)(C) and (D) shall be treated as referring to sections 881(a)(3) and (4), the reference in section 1441(c)(1) to section 871(b)(2) shall be treated as referring to section 842 or section 882(a)(2), as the case may be, the reference in section 1441(c)(5) to section 871(a)(1)(D) shall be treated as referring to section 881(a)(4), the reference in section 1441(c)(8) to section 871(a)(1)(C) shall be treated as referring to section 881(a)(3), the references in section 1441(c)(9) to sections 871(h) and 871(h)(3) or (4) shall be treated as referring to sections 881(c) and 881(c)(3) or (4), the reference in section 1441(c)(10) to section 871(i)(2) shall be treated as referring to section 881(d), and the references in section 1441(c)(12) to sections 871(a) and 871(k) shall be treated as referring to sections 881(a) and 881(e) (except that for purposes of applying subparagraph (A) of section 1441(c)(12), as so modified, clause (ii) of section 881(e)(1)(B) shall not apply to any dividend unless the regulated investment company knows that such dividend is a dividend referred to in such clause).

(b) Exemption.—Subject to such terms and conditions as may be provided by regulations prescribed by the Secretary, subsection (a) shall not apply in the case of a foreign corporation engaged in trade or business within the United States if the Secretary determines that the requirements of subsection (a) impose an undue administrative burden and that the collection of the tax imposed by section 881 on such corporation will not be jeopardized by the exemption.

(c) Exception for certain possessions corporations.—

(1) Guam, American Samoa, the Northern Mariana Islands, and the Virgin Islands.—For purposes of this section, the term "foreign corporation" does not include a corporation created or organized in Guam, American Samoa, the Northern Mariana Islands, or the Virgin Islands or under the law of any such possession if the requirements of subparagraphs (A), (B), and (C) of section 881(b)(1) are met with respect to such corporation.

(2) Commonwealth of Puerto Rico.—

(A) In general.—If dividends are received during a taxable year by a corporation—

(i) created or organized in, or under the law of, the Commonwealth of Puerto Rico, and

(ii) with respect to which the requirements of subparagraphs (A), (B), and (C) of section 881(b)(1) are met for the taxable year,

subsection (a) shall be applied for such taxable year by substituting "10 percent" for "30 percent".

(B) Applicability.—If, on or after the date of the enactment of this paragraph, an increase in the rate of the Commonwealth of Puerto Rico's withholding tax which is generally applicable to dividends paid to United States corporations not engaged in a trade or business in the Commonwealth to a rate greater than 10 percent takes effect, this paragraph shall not apply to dividends received on or after the effective date of the increase.

§ 1445. Withholding of tax on dispositions of United States real property interests

(a) General rule.—Except as otherwise provided in this section, in the case of any disposition of a United States real property interest (as defined in section 897(c)) by a foreign person, the transferee shall be required to deduct and withhold a tax equal to 15 percent of the amount realized on the disposition.

(b) Exemptions.—

(1) In general.—No person shall be required to deduct and withhold any amount under subsection (a) with respect to a disposition if paragraph (2), (3), (4), (5), or (6) applies to the transaction.

(2) Transferor furnishes nonforeign affidavit.—Except as provided in paragraph (7), this paragraph applies to the disposition if the transferor furnishes to the transferee an affidavit by the transferor stating, under penalty of perjury, the transferor's United States taxpayer identification number and that the transferor is not a foreign person.

(3) Nonpublicly traded domestic corporation furnishes affidavit that interests in corporation not United States real property interests.—Except as provided in paragraph (7), this paragraph applies in the case of a disposition of any interest in any domestic corporation if the domestic corporation furnishes to the transferee an affidavit by the domestic corporation stating, under penalty of perjury, that—

(A) the domestic corporation is not and has not been a United States real property holding corporation (as defined in section 897(c)(2)) during the applicable period specified in section 897(c)(1)(A)(ii), or

(B) as of the date of the disposition, interests in such corporation are not United States real property interests by reason of section 897(c)(1)(B).

(4) Transferee receives qualifying statement.—

(A) In general.—This paragraph applies to the disposition if the transferee receives a qualifying statement at such time, in such manner, and subject to such terms and conditions as the Secretary may by regulations prescribe.

(B) Qualifying statement.—For purposes of subparagraph (A), the term "qualifying statement" means a statement by the Secretary that—

(i) the transferor either—

(I) has reached agreement with the Secretary (or such agreement has been reached by the transferee) for the payment of any tax imposed by section 871(b)(1) or 882(a)(1) on any gain recognized by the transferor on the disposition of the United States real property interest, or

(II) is exempt from any tax imposed by section 871(b)(1) or 882(a)(1) on any gain recognized by the transferor on the disposition of the United States real property interest, and

(ii) the transferor or transferee has satisfied any transferor's unsatisfied withholding liability or has provided adequate security to cover such liability.

(5) Residence where amount realized does not exceed $300,000.—This paragraph applies to the disposition if—

(A) the property is acquired by the transferee for use by him as a residence, and

(B) the amount realized for the property does not exceed $300,000.

(6) Stock regularly traded on established securities market.—This paragraph applies if the disposition is of a share of a class of stock that is regularly traded on an established securities market.

(7) Special rules for paragraphs (2), (3), and (9).—Paragraph (2), (3), or (9) (as the case may be) shall not apply to any disposition—

(A) if—

(i) the transferee has actual knowledge that the affidavit referred to in such paragraph, or the statement referred to in paragraph (9)(A)(ii), is false, or

(ii) the transferee receives a notice (as described in subsection (d)) from a transferor's agent, a transferee's agent, or a qualified substitute that such affidavit is false, or

(B) if the Secretary by regulations requires the transferee or qualified substitute to furnish a copy of such affidavit or statement to the Secretary and the transferee or qualified substitute fails to furnish a copy of such affidavit or statement to the Secretary at such time and in such manner as required by such regulations.

(8) Applicable wash sales transactions.—No person shall be required to deduct and withhold any amount under subsection (a) with respect to a disposition which is treated as a disposition of a United States real property interest solely by reason of section 897(h)(5).

(9) Alternative procedure for furnishing nonforeign affidavit.—For purposes of paragraphs (2) and (7)—

(A) In general.—Paragraph (2) shall be treated as applying to a transaction if, in connection with a disposition of a United States real property interest—

(i) the affidavit specified in paragraph (2) is furnished to a qualified substitute, and

(ii) the qualified substitute furnishes a statement to the transferee stating, under penalty of perjury, that the qualified substitute has such affidavit in his possession.

(B) Regulations.—The Secretary shall prescribe such regulations as may be necessary or appropriate to carry out this paragraph.

(c) Limitations on amount required to be withheld.—

(1) Cannot exceed transferor's maximum tax liability.—

(A) In general.—The amount required to be withheld under this section with respect to any disposition shall not exceed the amount (if any) determined under subparagraph (B) as the transferor's maximum tax liability.

(B) Request.—At the request of the transferor or transferee, the Secretary shall determine, with respect to any disposition, the transferor's maximum tax liability.

(C) Refund of excess amounts withheld.—Subject to such terms and conditions as the Secretary may by regulations prescribe, a transferor may seek and obtain a refund of any amounts withheld under this section in excess of the transferor's maximum tax liability.

(2) Authority of secretary to prescribe reduced amount.—At the request of the transferor or transferee, the Secretary may prescribe a reduced amount to be withheld under this section if the Secretary determines that to substitute such reduced amount will not jeopardize the collection of the tax imposed by section 871(b)(1) or 882(a)(1).

(3) Procedural rules.—

(A) Regulations.—Requests for—

(i) qualifying statements under subsection (b)(4),

(ii) determinations of transferor's maximum tax liability under paragraph (1), and

(iii) reductions under paragraph (2) in the amount required to be withheld,

shall be made at the time and manner, and shall include such information, as the Secretary shall prescribe by regulations.

(B) Requests to be handled within 90 days.—The Secretary shall take action with respect to any request described in subparagraph (A) within 90 days after the Secretary receives the request.

(4) Reduced rate of withholding for residence where amount realized does not exceed $1,000,000.—In the case of a disposition—

(A) of property which is acquired by the transferee for use by the transferee as a residence,

(B) with respect to which the amount realized for such property does not exceed $1,000,000, and

(C) to which subsection (b)(5) does not apply,

subsection (a) shall be applied by substituting "10 percent" for "15 percent".

(d) Liability of transferor's agents or transferee's agents.—

(1) Notice of false affidavit; foreign corporations.—If—

(A) the transferor furnishes the transferee an affidavit described in paragraph (2) of subsection (b) or a domestic corporation furnishes the transferee an affidavit described in paragraph (3) of subsection (b), and

(B) in the case of—

(i) any transferor's agent—

(I) such agent has actual knowledge that such affidavit is false, or

(II) in the case of an affidavit described in subsection (b)(2) furnished by a corporation, such corporation is a foreign corporation, or

(ii) any transferee's agent, such agent has actual knowledge that such affidavit is false,

such agent shall so notify the transferee at such time and in such manner as the Secretary shall require by regulations.

(2) Failure to furnish notice.—

(A) In general.—If any transferor's agent or transferee's agent is required by paragraph (1) to furnish notice, but fails to furnish such notice at such time or times and in such manner as may be required by regulations, such agent shall have the same duty to deduct and withhold that the transferee would have had if such agent had complied with paragraph (1).

(B) Liability limited to amount of compensation.—An agent's liability under subparagraph (A) shall be limited to the amount of compensation the agent derives from the transaction.

(3) Transferor's agent.—For purposes of this subsection, the term "transferor's agent" means any person who represents the transferor—

(A) in any negotiation with the transferee or any transferee's agent related to the transaction, or

(B) in settling the transaction.

(4) Transferee's agent.—For purposes of this subsection, the term "transferee's agent" means any person who represents the transferee—

(A) in any negotiation with the transferor or any transferor's agent related to the transaction, or

(B) in settling the transaction.

(5) Settlement officer not treated as transferor's agent.—For purposes of this subsection, a person shall not be treated as a transferor's agent or transferee's agent with respect to any transaction merely because such person performs 1 or more of the following acts:

(A) The receipt and the disbursement of any portion of the consideration for the transaction.

(B) The recording of any document in connection with the transaction.

(e) Special rules relating to distributions, etc., by corporations, partnerships, trusts, or estates.—

(1) Certain domestic partnerships, trusts, and estates.—In the case of any disposition of a United States real property interest as defined in section 897(c) (other than a disposition described in paragraph (4) or (5)) by a domestic partnership, domestic trust, or domestic estate, such partnership, the trustee of such trust, or the executor of such estate (as the case may be) shall be required to deduct and withhold under subsection (a) a tax equal to the highest rate of tax in effect for the taxable year under section 11(b) (or, to the extent provided in regulations, 20 percent) multiplied by the gain realized to the extent such gain—

(A) is allocable to a foreign person who is a partner or beneficiary of such partnership, trust, or estate, or

(B) is allocable to a portion of the trust treated as owned by a foreign person under subpart E of part I of subchapter J.

(2) Certain distributions by foreign corporations.—In the case of any distribution by a foreign corporation on which gain is recognized under subsection (d) or (e) of section 897, the foreign corporation shall deduct and withhold under subsection (a) a tax equal to the highest rate of tax in effect for the taxable year under section 11(b) multiplied by the amount of gain recognized on such distribution under such subsection.

(3) Distributions by certain domestic corporations to foreign shareholders.—If a domestic corporation which is or has been a United States real property holding corporation (as defined in section 897(c)(2)) during the applicable period specified in section 897(c)(1)(A)(ii) distributes property to a foreign person in a transaction to which section 302 or part II of subchapter C applies, such corporation shall deduct and withhold under subsection (a) a tax equal to 10 percent of the amount realized by the foreign shareholder. The preceding sentence shall not apply if, as of the date of the distribution, interests in such corporation are not United States real property interests by reason of section 897(c)

(1)(B). Rules similar to the rules of the preceding provisions of this paragraph shall apply in the case of any distribution to which section 301 applies and which is not made out of the earnings and profits of such a domestic corporation.

(4) Taxable distributions by domestic or foreign partnerships, trusts, or estates.—A domestic or foreign partnership, the trustee of a domestic or foreign trust, or the executor of a domestic or foreign estate shall be required to deduct and withhold under subsection (a) a tax equal to 10 percent of the fair market value (as of the time of the taxable distribution) of any United States real property interest distributed to a partner of the partnership or a beneficiary of the trust or estate, as the case may be, who is a foreign person in a transaction which would constitute a taxable distribution under the regulations promulgated by the Secretary pursuant to section 897.

(5) Rules relating to dispositions of interest in partnerships, trusts, or estates.—To the extent provided in regulations, the transferee of a partnership interest or of a beneficial interest in a trust or estate shall be required to deduct and withhold under subsection (a) a tax equal to 10 percent of the amount realized on the disposition.

(6) Distributions by regulated investment companies and real estate investment trusts.—If any portion of a distribution from a qualified investment entity (as defined in section 897(h)(4)) to a nonresident alien individual or a foreign corporation is treated under section 897(h)(1) as gain realized by such individual or corporation from the sale or exchange of a United States real property interest, the qualified investment entity shall deduct and withhold under subsection (a) a tax equal to the highest rate of tax in effect for the taxable year under section 11(b) (or, to the extent provided in regulations, 20 percent) multiplied by the amount so treated.

(7) Regulations.—The Secretary shall prescribe such regulations as may be necessary to carry out the purposes of this subsection, including regulations providing for exceptions from provisions of this subsection and regulations for the application of this subsection in the case of payments through 1 or more entities.

(f) Definitions.—For purposes of this section—

(1) Transferor.—The term "transferor" means the person disposing of the United States real property interest.

(2) Transferee.—The term "transferee" means the person acquiring the United States real property interest.

(3) Foreign person.—The term "foreign person" means any person other than a United States person.

(4) Transferor's maximum tax liability.—The term "transferor's maximum tax liability" means, with respect to the disposition of any interest, the sum of—

(A) the maximum amount which the Secretary determines could be imposed as tax under section 871(b)(1) or 882(a)(1) by reason of the disposition, plus

(B) the amount the Secretary determines to be the transferor's unsatisfied withholding liability with respect to such interest.

(5) Transferor's unsatisfied withholding liability.—The term "transferor's unsatisfied withholding liability" means the withholding obligation imposed by this section on the transferor's acquisition of the United States real property interest or on the acquisition of a predecessor interest, to the extent such obligation has not been satisfied.

§ 1446. Withholding of tax on foreign partners' share of effectively connected income

(a) General rule.—If—

(1) a partnership has effectively connected taxable income for any taxable year, and

(2) any portion of such income is allocable under section 704 to a foreign partner, such partnership shall pay a withholding tax under this section at such time and in such manner as the Secretary shall by regulations prescribe.

(b) Amount of withholding tax.—

(1) In general.—The amount of the withholding tax payable by any partnership under subsection (a) shall be equal to the applicable percentage of the effectively connected taxable income of the partnership which is allocable under section 704 to foreign partners.

(2) Applicable percentage.—For purposes of paragraph (1), the term "applicable percentage" means—

(A) the highest rate of tax specified in section 1 in the case of the portion of the effectively connected taxable income which is allocable under section 704 to foreign partners who are not corporations, and

(B) the highest rate of tax specified in section 11(b) in the case of the portion of the effectively connected taxable income which is allocable under section 704 to foreign partners which are corporations.

(c) Effectively connected taxable income.—For purposes of this section, the term "effectively connected taxable income" means the taxable income of the partnership which is effectively connected (or treated as effectively connected) with the conduct of a trade or business in the United States computed with the following adjustments:

(1) Paragraph (1) of section 703(a) shall not apply.

(2) The partnership shall be allowed a deduction for depletion with respect to oil and gas wells but the amount of such deduction shall be determined without regard to sections 613 and 613A.

(3) There shall not be taken into account any item of income, gain, loss, or deduction to the extent allocable under section 704 to any partner who is not a foreign partner.

(d) Treatment of foreign partners.—

(1) Allowance of credit.—Each foreign partner of a partnership shall be allowed a credit under section 33 for such partner's share of the withholding tax paid by the partnership under this section. Such credit shall be allowed for the partner's taxable year in which (or with which) the partnership taxable year (for which such tax was paid) ends.

(2) Credit treated as distributed to partner.—Except as provided in regulations, a foreign partner's share of any withholding tax paid by the partnership under this section shall be treated as distributed to such partner by such partnership on the earlier of—

(A) the day on which such tax was paid by the partnership, or **(d)**

(B) the last day of the partnership's taxable year for which such tax was paid.

(e) Foreign partner.—For purposes of this section, the term "foreign partner" means any partner who is not a United States person.

(f) Special rules for withholding on dispositions of partnership interests.—

(1) In general.—Except as provided in this subsection, if any portion of the gain (if any) on any disposition of an interest in a partnership would be treated under section 864(c)(8) as effectively connected with the conduct of a trade or business within the United States, the transferee shall be required to deduct and withhold a tax equal to 10 percent of the amount realized on the disposition.

(2) Exception if nonforeign affidavit furnished.—

(A) In general.—No person shall be required to deduct and withhold any amount under paragraph (1) with respect to any disposition if the transferor furnishes to the transferee an affidavit by the transferor stating, under penalty of perjury, the transferor's United States taxpayer identification number and that the transferor is not a foreign person.

(B) False affidavit.—Subparagraph (A) shall not apply to any disposition if—

(i) the transferee has actual knowledge that the affidavit is false, or the transferee receives a notice (as described in section 1445(d)) from a transferor's agent or transferee's agent that such affidavit or statement is false, or

(ii) the Secretary by regulations requires the transferee to furnish a copy of such affidavit or statement to the Secretary and the transferee fails to furnish a copy of such affidavit or statement to the Secretary at such time and in such manner as required by such regulations.

(C) Rules for agents.—The rules of section 1445(d) shall apply to a transferor's agent or transferee's agent with respect to any affidavit described in subparagraph (A) in the same manner as such rules apply with respect to the disposition of a United States real property interest under such section.

(3) Authority of Secretary to prescribe reduced amount.—At the request of the transferor or transferee, the Secretary may prescribe a reduced amount to be withheld under this section if the Secretary determines that to substitute such reduced amount will not jeopardize the collection of the tax imposed under this title with respect to gain treated under section 864(c)(8) as effectively connected with the conduct of a trade or business with in the United States.

(4) Partnership to withhold amounts not withheld by the transferee.—If a transferee fails to withhold any amount required to be withheld under paragraph (1), the partnership shall be required to deduct and withhold from distributions to the transferee a tax in an amount equal to the amount the transferee failed to withhold (plus interest under this title on such amount).

(5) Definitions.—Any term used in this subsection which is also used under section 1445 shall have the same meaning as when used in such section.

(6) Regulations.—The Secretary shall prescribe such regulations or other guidance as may be necessary to carry out the purposes of this subsection, including regulations providing for exceptions from the provisions of this subsection.

(g) Regulations.—The Secretary shall prescribe such regulations as may be necessary to carry out the purposes of this section, including—

(1) regulations providing for the application of this section in the case of publicly traded partnerships, and

(2) regulations providing—

(A) that, for purposes of section 6655, the withholding tax imposed under this section shall be treated as a tax imposed by section 11 and any partnership required to pay such tax shall be treated as a corporation, and

(B) Appropriate adjustments in applying section 6655 with respect to such withholding tax.

Subchapter B—Application of Withholding Provisions

§ 1461. Liability for withheld tax

Every person required to deduct and withhold any tax under this chapter is hereby made liable for such tax and is hereby indemnified against the claims and demands of any person for the amount of any payments made in accordance with the provisions of this chapter.

§ 1462. Withheld tax as credit to recipient of income

Income on which any tax is required to be withheld at the source under this chapter shall be included in the return of the recipient of such income, but any amount of tax so withheld shall be credited against the amount of income tax as computed in such return.

§ 1463. Tax paid by recipient of income

If—

(1) any person, in violation of the provisions of this chapter, fails to deduct and withhold any tax under this chapter, and

(2) thereafter the tax against which such tax may be credited is paid, the tax so required to be deducted and withheld shall not be collected from such person; but this section shall in no case relieve such person from liability for interest or any penalties or additions to the tax otherwise applicable in respect of such failure to deduct and withhold.

§ 1464. Refunds and credits with respect to withheld tax

Where there has been an overpayment of tax under this chapter, any refund or credit made under chapter 65 shall be made to the withholding agent unless the amount of such tax was actually withheld by the withholding agent.

Chapter 4—Taxes to Enforce Reporting on Certain Foreign Accounts

§ 1471. Withholdable payments to foreign financial institutions

(a) In general.—In the case of any withholdable payment to a foreign financial institution which does not meet the requirements of subsection (b), the withholding agent with respect to such payment shall deduct and withhold from such payment a tax equal to 30 percent of the amount of such payment.

(b) Reporting requirements, etc.—

(1) In general.—The requirements of this subsection are met with respect to any foreign financial institution if an agreement is in effect between such institution and the Secretary under which such institution agrees—

(A) to obtain such information regarding each holder of each account maintained by such institution as is necessary to determine which (if any) of such accounts are United States accounts,

(B) to comply with such verification and due diligence procedures as the Secretary may require with respect to the identification of United States accounts,

(C) in the case of any United States account maintained by such institution, to report on an annual basis the information described in subsection (c) with respect to such account,

(D) to deduct and withhold a tax equal to 30 percent of—

(i) any passthru payment which is made by such institution to a recalcitrant account holder or another foreign financial institution which does not meet the requirements of this subsection, and

(ii) in the case of any passthru payment which is made by such institution to a foreign financial institution which has in effect an election under paragraph (3) with respect to such payment, so much of such payment as is allocable to accounts held by recalcitrant account holders or foreign financial institutions which do not meet the requirements of this subsection,

(E) to comply with requests by the Secretary for additional information with respect to any United States account maintained by such institution, and

(F) in any case in which any foreign law would (but for a waiver described in clause (i)) prevent the reporting of any information referred to in this subsection or subsection (c) with respect to any united states account maintained by such institution—

(i) to attempt to obtain a valid and effective waiver of such law from each holder of such account, and

(ii) if a waiver described in clause (i) is not obtained from each such holder within a reasonable period of time, to close such account.

Any agreement entered into under this subsection may be terminated by the Secretary upon a determination by the Secretary that the foreign financial institution is out of compliance with such agreement.

(2) Financial institutions deemed to meet requirements in certain cases.—A foreign financial institution may be treated by the Secretary as meeting the requirements of this subsection if—

(A) such institution

(i) complies with such procedures as the Secretary may prescribe to ensure that such institution does not maintain United States accounts, and

(ii) meets such other requirements as the Secretary may prescribe with respect to accounts of other foreign financial institutions maintained by such institution, or

(B) such institution is a member of a class of institutions with respect to which the Secretary has determined that the application of this section is not necessary to carry out the purposes of this section.

(3) Election to be withheld upon rather than withhold on payments to recalcitrant account holders and nonparticipating foreign financial institutions.—In the case of a foreign financial institution which meets the requirements of this subsection and such other requirements as the Secretary may provide and which elects the application of this paragraph—

(A) the requirements of paragraph (1)(D) shall not apply,

(B) the withholding tax imposed under subsection (a) shall apply with respect to any withholdable payment to such institution to the extent such payment is allocable to accounts held by recalcitrant account holders or foreign financial institutions which do not meet the requirements of this subsection, and

(C) the agreement described in paragraph (1) shall—

(i) require such institution to notify the withholding agent with respect to each such payment of the institution's election under this paragraph and such other information as may be necessary for the withholding agent to determine the appropriate amount to deduct and withhold from such payment, and

(ii) include a waiver of any right under any treaty of the United States with respect to any amount deducted and withheld pursuant to an election under this paragraph.

To the extent provided by the Secretary, the election under this paragraph may be made with respect to certain classes or types of accounts of the foreign financial institution.

(c) Information required to be reported on United States accounts.—

(1) In general.—The agreement described in subsection (b) shall require the foreign financial institution to report the following with respect to each United States account maintained by such institution:

(A) The name, address, and TIN of each account holder which is a specified United States person and, in the case of any account holder which is a United States owned foreign entity, the name, address, and TIN of each substantial United States owner of such entity.

(B) The account number.

(C) The account balance or value (determined at such time and in such manner as the Secretary may provide).

(D) Except to the extent provided by the Secretary, the gross receipts and gross withdrawals or payments from the account (determined for such period and in such manner as the Secretary may provide).

(2) Election to be subject to same reporting as United States financial institutions.—In the case of a foreign financial institution which elects the application of this paragraph—

(A) subparagraphs (C) and (D) of paragraph (1) shall not apply, and

(B) the agreement described in subsection (b) shall require such foreign financial institution to report such information with respect to each United States account maintained by such institution as such institution would be required to report under sections 6041, 6042, 6045, and 6049 if—

(i) such institution were a United States person, and

(ii) each holder of such account which is a specified United States person or United States owned foreign entity were a natural person and citizen of the United States.

An election under this paragraph shall be made at such time, in such manner, and subject to such conditions as the Secretary may provide.

(3) Separate requirements for qualified intermediaries.—In the case of a foreign financial institution which is treated as a qualified intermediary by the Secretary for purposes of section 1441 and the regulations issued thereunder, the requirements of this section shall be in addition to any reporting or other requirements imposed by the Secretary for purposes of such treatment.

(d) Definitions.—For purposes of this section—

(1) United States account.—

(A) In general.—The term "United States account" means any financial account which is held by one or more specified United States persons or United States owned foreign entities.

(B) Exception for certain accounts held by individuals.—Unless the foreign financial institution elects to not have this subparagraph apply, such term shall not include any depository account maintained by such financial institution if—

(i) each holder of such account is a natural person, and

(ii) with respect to each holder of such account, the aggregate value of all depository accounts held (in whole or in part) by such holder and maintained by the same financial institution which maintains such account does not exceed $50,000.

To the extent provided by the Secretary, financial institutions which are members of the same expanded affiliated group shall be treated for purposes of clause (ii) as a single financial institution.

(C) Elimination of duplicative reporting requirements.—Such term shall not include any financial account in a foreign financial institution if

(i) such account is held by another financial institution which meets the requirements of subsection (b), or

(ii) the holder of such account is otherwise subject to information reporting requirements which the Secretary determines would make the reporting required by this section with respect to United States accounts duplicative.

(2) Financial account.—Except as otherwise provided by the Secretary, the term "financial account" means, with respect to any financial institution—

(A) any depository account maintained by such financial institution,

(B) any custodial account maintained by such financial institution, and

(C) any equity or debt interest in such financial institution (other than interests which are regularly traded on an established securities market).

Any equity or debt interest which constitutes a financial account under subparagraph (C) with respect to any financial institution shall be treated for purposes of this section as maintained by such financial institution.

(3) United States owned foreign entity.—The term "United States owned foreign entity" means any foreign entity which has one or more substantial United States owners.

(4) Foreign financial institution.—The term "foreign financial institution" means any financial institution which is a foreign entity. Except as otherwise provided by the Secretary, such term shall not include a financial institution which is organized under the laws of any possession of the United States.

(5) Financial institution.—Except as otherwise provided by the Secretary, the term "financial institution" means any entity that

(A) accepts deposits in the ordinary course of a banking or similar business,

(B) as a substantial portion of its business, holds financial assets for the account of others, or

(C) is engaged (or holding itself out as being engaged) primarily in the business of investing, reinvesting, or trading in securities (as defined in section 475(c)(2) without regard to the last sentence thereof), partnership interests, commodities (as defined in section 475(e)(2)), or any interest (including a futures or forward contract or option) in such securities, partnership interests, or commodities.

(6) Recalcitrant account holder.—The term "recalcitrant account holder" means any account holder which—

(A) fails to comply with reasonable requests for the information referred to in subsection (b)(1)(A) or (c)(1)(A), or

(B) fails to provide a waiver described in subsection (b)(1)(F) upon request.

(7) Passthru payment.—The term "passthru payment" means any withholdable payment or other payment to the extent attributable to a withholdable payment.

(e) Affiliated groups.—

(1) In general.—The requirements of subsections (b) and (c)(1) shall apply—

(A) with respect to United States accounts maintained by the foreign financial institution, and

(B) except as otherwise provided by the Secretary, with respect to United States accounts maintained by each other foreign financial institution (other than any foreign financial institution which meets the requirements of subsection (b)) which is a member of the same expanded affiliated group as such foreign financial institution.

(2) Expanded affiliated group.—For purposes of this section, the term "expanded affiliated group" means an affiliated group as defined in section 1504(a), determined—

(A) by substituting "more than 50 percent" for "at least 80 percent" each place it appears, and

(B) without regard to paragraphs (2) and (3) of section 1504(b).

A partnership or any other entity (other than a corporation) shall be treated as a member of an expanded affiliated group if such entity is controlled (within the meaning of section 954(d)(3)) by members of such group (including any entity treated as a member of such group by reason of this sentence).

(f) Exception for certain payments.—Subsection (a) shall not apply to any payment to the extent that the beneficial owner of such payment is—

(1) any foreign government, any political subdivision of a foreign government, or any wholly owned agency or instrumentality of any one or more of the foregoing,

(2) any international organization or any wholly owned agency or instrumentality thereof,

(3) any foreign central bank of issue, or

(4) any other class of persons identified by the Secretary for purposes of this subsection as posing a low risk of tax evasion.

§ 1472. Withholdable payments to other foreign entities

(a) In general.—In the case of any withholdable payment to a nonfinancial foreign entity, if—

(1) the beneficial owner of such payment is such entity or any other nonfinancial foreign entity, and

(2) the requirements of subsection (b) are not met with respect to such beneficial owner,

then the withholding agent with respect to such payment shall deduct and withhold from such payment a tax equal to 30 percent of the amount of such payment.

(b) Requirements for waiver of withholding.—The requirements of this subsection are met with respect to the beneficial owner of a payment if—

(1) such beneficial owner or the payee provides the withholding agent with either

(A) a certification that such beneficial owner does not have any substantial United States owners, or

(B) the name, address, and TIN of each substantial United States owner of such beneficial owner,

(2) the withholding agent does not know, or have reason to know, that any information provided under paragraph (1) is incorrect, and

(3) the withholding agent reports the information provided under paragraph (1)(B) to the Secretary in such manner as the Secretary may provide.

(c) Exceptions.—Subsection (a) shall not apply to—

(1) except as otherwise provided by the Secretary, any payment beneficially owned by—

(A) any corporation the stock of which is regularly traded on an established securities market,

(B) any corporation which is a member of the same expanded affiliated group (as defined in section 1471(e)(2) without regard to the last sentence thereof) as a corporation described in subparagraph (A),

(C) any entity which is organized under the laws of a possession of the United States and which is wholly owned by one or more bona fide residents (as defined in section 937(a)) of such possession,

(D) any foreign government, any political subdivision of a foreign government, or any wholly owned agency or instrumentality of any one or more of the foregoing,

(E) any international organization or any wholly owned agency or instrumentality thereof,

(F) any foreign central bank of issue, or

(G) any other class of persons identified by the Secretary for purposes of this subsection, and

(2) any class of payments identified by the Secretary for purposes of this subsection as posing a low risk of tax evasion.

(d) Nonfinancial foreign entity.—For purposes of this section, the term "nonfinancial foreign entity" means any foreign entity which is not a financial institution (as defined in section 1471(d)(5)).

§ 1473. Definitions

For purposes of this chapter

(1) Withholdable payment.—Except as otherwise provided by the Secretary—

(A) In general.—The term "withholdable payment" means—

(i) any payment of interest (including any original issue discount), dividends, rents, salaries, wages, premiums, annuities, compensations, remunerations, emoluments, and other fixed or determinable annual or periodical gains, profits, and income, if such payment is from sources within the United States, and

(ii) any gross proceeds from the sale or other disposition of any property of a type which can produce interest or dividends from sources within the United States.

(B) Exception for income connected with United States business.—Such term shall not include any item of income which is taken into account under section 871(b)(1) or 882(a)(1) for the taxable year.

(C) Special rule for sourcing interest paid by foreign branches of domestic financial institutions.—Subparagraph (B) of section 861(a)(1) shall not apply.

(2) Substantial United States owner.—

(A) In general.—The term "substantial United States owner" means—

(i) with respect to any corporation, any specified United States person which owns, directly or indirectly, more than 10 percent of the stock of such corporation (by vote or value),

(ii) with respect to any partnership, any specified United States person which owns, directly or indirectly, more than 10 percent of the profits interests or capital interests in such partnership, and

(iii) in the case of a trust—

(I) any specified United States person treated as an owner of any portion of such trust under subpart E of part I of subchapter J of chapter 1, and

(II) to the extent provided by the Secretary in regulations or other guidance, any specified United States person which holds, directly or indirectly, more than 10 percent of the beneficial interests of such trust.

(B) Special rule for investment vehicles.—In the case of any financial institution described in section 1471(d)(5)(C), clauses (i), (ii), and (iii) of subparagraph (A) shall be applied by substituting "0 percent" for "10 percent".

(3) Specified United States person.—Except as otherwise provided by the Secretary, the term "specified United States person" means any United States person other than—

(A) any corporation the stock of which is regularly traded on an established securities market,

(B) any corporation which is a member of the same expanded affiliated group (as defined in section 1471(e)(2) without regard to the last sentence thereof) as a corporation the stock of which is regularly traded on an established securities market,

(C) any organization exempt from taxation under section 501(a) or an individual retirement plan,

(D) the United States or any wholly owned agency or instrumentality thereof,

(E) any State, the District of Columbia, any possession of the United States, any political subdivision of any of the foregoing, or any wholly owned agency or instrumentality of any one or more of the foregoing,

(F) any bank (as defined in section 581),

(G) any real estate investment trust (as defined in section 856),

(H) any regulated investment company (as defined in section 851),

(I) any common trust fund (as defined in section 584(a)), and

(J) any trust which—

(i) is exempt from tax under section 664(c), or

(ii) is described in section 4947(a)(1).

(4) Withholding agent.—The term "withholding agent" means all persons, in whatever capacity acting, having the control, receipt, custody, disposal, or payment of any withholdable payment.

(5) Foreign entity.—The term "foreign entity" means any entity which is not a United States person.

§ 1474. Special rules

(a) Liability for withheld tax.—Every person required to deduct and withhold any tax under this chapter is hereby made liable for such tax and is hereby indemnified against the claims and demands of any person for the amount of any payments made in accordance with the provisions of this chapter.

(b) Credits and refunds.—

(1) In general.—Except as provided in paragraph (2), the determination of whether any tax deducted and withheld under this chapter results in an overpayment by the beneficial owner of the payment to which such tax is attributable shall be made as if such tax had been deducted and withheld under subchapter A of chapter 3.

(2) Special rule where foreign financial institution is beneficial owner of payment.—

(A) In general.—In the case of any tax properly deducted and withheld under section 1471 from a specified financial institution payment—

(i) if the foreign financial institution referred to in subparagraph (B) with respect to such payment is entitled to a reduced rate of tax with respect to such payment by reason of any treaty obligation of the United States—

(I) the amount of any credit or refund with respect to such tax shall not exceed the amount of credit or refund attributable to such reduction in rate, and

(II) no interest shall be allowed or paid with respect to such credit or refund, and

(ii) if such foreign financial institution is not so entitled, no credit or refund shall be allowed or paid with respect to such tax.

(B) Specified financial institution payment.—The term "specified financial institution payment" means any payment if the beneficial owner of such payment is a foreign financial institution.

(3) Requirement to identify substantial United States owners.—No credit or refund shall be allowed or paid with respect to any tax properly deducted and withheld under this chapter unless the beneficial owner of the payment provides the Secretary such information as the Secretary may require to determine whether such beneficial owner is a United States owned foreign entity (as defined in section 1471(d)(3)) and the identity of any substantial United States owners of such entity.

(c) Confidentiality of information.—

(1) In general.—For purposes of this chapter, rules similar to the rules of section 3406(f) shall apply.

(2) Disclosure of list of participating foreign financial institutions permitted.—The identity of a foreign financial institution which meets the requirements of section 1471(b) shall not be treated as return information for purposes of section 6103. **(c)**

(d) Coordination with other withholding provisions.—The Secretary shall provide for the coordination of this chapter with other withholding provisions under this title, including providing for the proper crediting of amounts deducted and withheld under this chapter against amounts required to be deducted and withheld under such other provisions.

(e) Treatment of withholding under agreements.—Any tax deducted and withheld pursuant to an agreement described in section 1471(b) shall be treated for purposes of this title as a tax deducted and withheld by a withholding agent under section 1471(a).

(f) Regulations.—The Secretary shall prescribe such regulations or other guidance as may be necessary or appropriate to carry out the purposes of, and prevent the avoidance of, this chapter.

Chapter 6—Consolidated Returns

Subchapter A—Returns and Payment of Tax

§ 1501. Privilege to file consolidated returns

An affiliated group of corporations shall, subject to the provisions of this chapter, have the privilege of making a consolidated return with respect to the income tax imposed by chapter 1 for the taxable year in lieu of separate returns. The making of a consolidated return shall be upon the condition that all corporations which at any time during the taxable year have been members of the affiliated group consent to all the consolidated return regulations prescribed under section 1502 prior to the last day prescribed by law for the filing of such return. The making of a consolidated return shall be considered as such consent. In the case of a corporation which is a member of the affiliated group for a fractional part of the year, the consolidated return shall include the income of such corporation for such part of the year as it is a member of the affiliated group.

§ 1502. Regulations

The Secretary shall prescribe such regulations as he may deem necessary in order that the tax liability of any affiliated group of corporations making a consolidated return and of each corporation in the group, both during and after the period of affiliation, may be returned, determined, computed, assessed, collected, and adjusted, in such manner as clearly to reflect the income-tax liability and the various factors necessary for the determination of such liability, and in order to prevent avoidance of such tax liability. In carrying out the preceding sentence, the Secretary may prescribe rules that are different from the provisions of chapter 1 that would apply if such corporations filed separate returns.

§ 1503. Computation and payment of tax

(a) In any case in which a consolidated return is made or is required to be made, the tax shall be determined, computed, assessed, collected, and adjusted in accordance with the regulations under section 1502 prescribed before the last day prescribed by law for the filing of such return.

* * *

(d) Dual consolidated loss.—

(1) In general.—The dual consolidated loss for any taxable year of any corporation shall not be allowed to reduce the taxable income of any other member of the affiliated group for the taxable year or any other taxable year.

(2) Dual consolidated loss.—For purposes of this section—

(A) In general.—Except as provided in subparagraph (B), the term "dual consolidated loss" means any net operating loss of a domestic corporation which is subject to an income tax of a foreign country on its income without regard to whether such income is from sources in or outside of such foreign country, or is subject to such a tax on a residence basis.

(B) Special rule where loss not used under foreign law.—To the extent provided in regulations, the term "dual consolidated loss" shall not include any loss which, under the foreign income tax law, does not offset the income of any foreign corporation.

(3) Treatment of losses of separate business units.—To the extent provided in regulations, any loss of a separate unit of a domestic corporation shall be subject to the limitations of this subsection in the same manner as if such unit were a wholly owned subsidiary of such corporation.

(4) Income on assets acquired after the loss.—The Secretary shall prescribe such regulations as may be necessary or appropriate to prevent the avoidance of the purposes of this subsection by contributing assets to the corporation with the dual consolidated loss after such loss was sustained.

* * *

§ 1504. Definitions

(a) Affiliated group defined.—For purposes of this subtitle—

(1) In general.—The term "affiliated group" means—

(A) 1 or more chains of includible corporations connected through stock ownership with a common parent corporation which is an includible corporation, but only if—

(B) (i) the common parent owns directly stock meeting the requirements of paragraph (2) in at least 1 of the other includible corporations, and

(ii) stock meeting the requirements of paragraph (2) in each of the includible corporations (except the common parent) is owned directly by 1 or more of the other includible corporations.

(2) 80-percent voting and value test.—The ownership of stock of any corporation meets the requirements of this paragraph if it—

(A) possesses at least 80 percent of the total voting power of the stock of such corporation, and

(B) has a value equal to at least 80 percent of the total value of the stock of such corporation.

(3) 5 years must elapse before reconsolidation.—

(A) In general.—If—

(i) a corporation is included (or required to be included) in a consolidated return filed by an affiliated group, and

(ii) such corporation ceases to be a member of such group,

with respect to periods after such cessation, such corporation (and any successor of such corporation) may not be included in any consolidated return filed by the affiliated group (or by another affiliated group with the same common parent or a successor of such common parent) before the 61st month beginning after its first taxable year in which it ceased to be a member of such affiliated group.

(B) Secretary may waive application of subparagraph (A).—The Secretary may waive the application of subparagraph (A) to any corporation for any period subject to such conditions as the Secretary may prescribe.

(4) Stock not to include certain preferred stock.—For purposes of this subsection, the term "stock" does not include any stock which—

(A) is not entitled to vote,

(B) is limited and preferred as to dividends and does not participate in corporate growth to any significant extent,

(C) has redemption and liquidation rights which do not exceed the issue price of such stock (except for a reasonable redemption or liquidation premium), and

(D) is not convertible into another class of stock.

(5) Regulations.—The Secretary shall prescribe such regulations as may be necessary or appropriate to carry out the purposes of this subsection, including (but not limited to) regulations—

(A) which treat warrants, obligations convertible into stock, and other similar interests as stock, and stock as not stock,

(B) which treat options to acquire or sell stock as having been exercised,

(C) which provide that the requirements of paragraph (2)(B) shall be treated as met if the affiliated group, in reliance on a good faith determination of value, treated such requirements as met,

(D) which disregard an inadvertent ceasing to meet the requirements of paragraph (2)(B) by reason of changes in relative values of different classes of stock,

(E) which provide that transfers of stock within the group shall not be taken into account in determining whether a corporation ceases to be a member of an affiliated group, and

(F) which disregard changes in voting power to the extent such changes are disproportionate to related changes in value.

(b) Definition of "includible corporation".—As used in this chapter, the term "includible corporation" means any corporation except—

(1) Corporations exempt from taxation under section 501.

(2) Insurance companies subject to taxation under section 801.

(3) Foreign corporations.

(4) Regulated investment companies and real estate investment trusts subject to tax under subchapter M of chapter 1.

(5) A DISC (as defined in section 992(a)(1)).

(6) An S corporation.

* * *

(d) Subsidiary formed to comply with foreign law.—In the case of a domestic corporation owning or controlling, directly or indirectly, 100 percent of the capital stock (exclusive of directors' qualifying shares) of a corporation organized under the laws of a contiguous foreign country and maintained solely for the purpose of complying with the laws of such country as to title and operation of property, such foreign corporation may, at the option of the domestic corporation, be treated for the purpose of this subtitle as a domestic corporation.

* * *

Subchapter B—Related Rules

Part II—Certain Controlled Corporations

§ 1563. Definitions and special rules

(a) Controlled group of corporations.—For purposes of this part, the term "controlled group of corporations" means any group of—

(1) Parent-subsidiary controlled group.—One or more chains of corporations connected through stock ownership with a common parent corporation if—

(A) stock possessing at least 80 percent of the total combined voting power of all classes of stock entitled to vote or at least 80 percent of the total value of shares of all classes of stock of each of the corporations, except the common parent corporation, is owned (within the meaning of subsection (d)(1)) by one or more of the other corporations; and

(B) the common parent corporation owns (within the meaning of subsection (d)(1)) stock possessing at least 80 percent of the total combined voting power of all classes of stock entitled to vote or at least 80 percent of the total value of shares of all classes of stock of at least one of the other corporations, excluding, in computing such voting power or value, stock owned directly by such other corporations.

(2) Brother-sister controlled group.—Two or more corporations if 5 or fewer persons who are individuals, estates, or trusts own (within the meaning of subsection (d)(2)) stock possessing more than 50 percent of the total combined voting power of all classes of stock entitled to vote or more than 50 percent of the total value of shares of all classes of stock of each corporation, taking into account the stock ownership of each such person only to the extent such stock ownership is identical with respect to each such corporation.

(3) Combined group.—Three or more corporations each of which is a member of a group of corporations described in paragraph (1) or (2), and one of which—

(A) is a common parent corporation included in a group of corporations described in paragraph (1), and also

(B) is included in a group of corporations described in paragraph (2).

* * *

(d) Rules for determining stock ownership.—

(1) Parent-subsidiary controlled group.—For purposes of determining whether a corporation is a member of a parent-subsidiary controlled group of corporations (within the meaning of subsection (a)(1)), stock owned by a corporation means—

(A) stock owned directly by such corporation, and

(B) stock owned with the application of paragraphs (1), (2), and (3) of subsection (e).

(2) Brother-sister controlled group.—For purposes of determining whether a corporation is a member of a brother-sister controlled group of corporations (within the meaning of subsection (a)(2)), stock owned by a person who is an individual, estate, or trust means—

(A) stock owned directly by such person, and

(B) stock owned with the application of subsection (e).

(e) Constructive ownership.—

(1) Options.—If any person has an option to acquire stock, such stock shall be considered as owned by such person. For purposes of this paragraph, an option to acquire such an option, and each one of a series of such options, shall be considered as an option to acquire such stock.

(2) Attribution from partnerships.—Stock owned, directly or indirectly, by or for a partnership shall be considered as owned by any partner having an interest of 5 percent or more in either the capital or profits of the partnership in proportion to his interest in capital or profits, whichever such proportion is the greater.

(3) Attribution from estates or trusts.—

(A) Stock owned, directly or indirectly, by or for an estate or trust shall be considered as owned by any beneficiary who has an actuarial interest of 5 percent or more in such stock, to the extent of such actuarial interest. For purposes of this subparagraph, the actuarial interest of each beneficiary shall be determined by assuming the maximum exercise of discretion by the fiduciary in favor of such beneficiary and the maximum use of such stock to satisfy his rights as a beneficiary.

(B) Stock owned, directly or indirectly, by or for any portion of a trust of which a person is considered the owner under subpart E of part I of subchapter J (relating to grantors and others treated as substantial owners) shall be considered as owned by such person.

(C) This paragraph shall not apply to stock owned by any employees' trust described in section 401(a) which is exempt from tax under section 501(a).

(4) Attribution from corporations.—Stock owned, directly or indirectly, by or for a corporation shall be considered as owned by any person who owns (within the meaning of subsection (d)) 5 percent or more in value of its stock in that proportion which the value of the stock which such person so owns bears to the value of all the stock in such corporation.

(5) Spouse.—An individual shall be considered as owning stock in a corporation owned, directly or indirectly, by or for his spouse (other than a spouse who is legally separated from the individual under a decree of divorce whether interlocutory or final, or a decree of separate maintenance), except in the case of a corporation with respect to which each of the following conditions is satisfied for its taxable year—

(A) The individual does not, at any time during such taxable year, own directly any stock in such corporation;

(B) The individual is not a director or employee and does not participate in the management of such corporation at any time during such taxable year;

(C) Not more than 50 percent of such corporation's gross income for such taxable year was derived from royalties, rents, dividends, interest, and annuities; and

(D) Such stock in such corporation is not, at any time during such taxable year, subject to conditions which substantially restrict or limit the spouse's right to dispose of such stock and which run in favor of the individual or his children who have not attained the age of 21 years.

(6) Children, grandchildren, parents, and grandparents.—

(A) Minor children.—An individual shall be considered as owning stock owned, directly or indirectly, by or for his children who have not attained the age of 21 years, and, if the individual has not attained the age of 21 years, the stock owned, directly or indirectly, by or for his parents.

(B) Adult children and grandchildren.—An individual who owns (within the meaning of subsection (d)(2), but without regard to this subparagraph) more than 50 percent of the total combined voting power of all classes of stock entitled to vote or more than 50 percent of the total value of shares of all classes of stock in a corporation shall be considered as owning the stock in such corporation owned, directly or indirectly, by or for his parents, grandparents, grandchildren, and children who have attained the age of 21 years.

(C) Adopted child.—For purposes of this section, a legally adopted child of an individual shall be treated as a child of such individual by blood.

(f) Other definitions and rules.—

(1) Employee defined.—For purposes of this section the term "employee" has the same meaning such term is given by paragraphs (1) and (2) of section 3121(d).

(2) Operating rules.—

(A) In general.—Except as provided in subparagraph (B), stock constructively owned by a person by reason of the application of paragraph (1), (2), (3), (4), (5), or (6) of subsection (e) shall, for purposes of applying such paragraphs, be treated as actually owned by such person.

(B) Members of family.—Stock constructively owned by an individual by reason of the application of paragraph (5) or (6) of subsection (e) shall not be treated as owned by him for purposes of again applying such paragraphs in order to make another the constructive owner of such stock.

(3) Special rules.—For purposes of this section—

(A) If stock may be considered as owned by a person under subsection (e)(1) and under any other paragraph of subsection (e), it shall be considered as owned by him under subsection (e)(1).

(B) If stock is owned (within the meaning of subsection (d)) by two or more persons, such stock shall be considered as owned by the person whose ownership of such stock results in the corporation being a component member of a controlled group. If by reason of the preceding sentence, a corporation would (but for this sentence) become a component member of two controlled groups, it shall be treated as a component member of one controlled group. The determination as to the group of which such corporation is a component member shall be made under regulations prescribed by the Secretary which are consistent with the purposes of this part.

(C) If stock is owned by a person within the meaning of subsection (d) and such ownership results in the corporation being a component member of a controlled group, such stock shall not be treated as excluded stock under subsection (c)(2), if by reason of treating such stock as excluded stock the result is that such corporation is not a component member of a controlled group of corporations.

* * *

SUBTITLE D—MISCELLANEOUS EXCISE TAXES

Chapter 37—Repurchase of Corporate Stock

§ 4501. Repurchase of corporate stock

(a) General rule.—There is hereby imposed on each covered corporation a tax equal to 1 percent of the fair market value of any stock of the corporation which is repurchased by such corporation during the taxable year.

(b) Covered corporation.—For purposes of this section, the term "covered corporation" means any domestic corporation the stock of which is traded on an established securities market (within the meaning of section 7704(b)(1)).

(c) Repurchase.—For purposes of this section—

(1) In general.—The term "repurchase" means—

(A) a redemption within the meaning of section 317(b) with regard to the stock of a covered corporation, and

(B) any transaction determined by the Secretary to be economically similar to a transaction described in subparagraph (A).

(2) Treatment of purchases by specified affiliates.—

(A) In general.—The acquisition of stock of a covered corporation by a specified affiliate of such covered corporation, from a person who is not the covered corporation or a specified affiliate of such covered corporation, shall be treated as a repurchase of the stock of the covered corporation by such covered corporation.

(B) Specified affiliate.—For purposes of this section, the term "specified affiliate" means, with respect to any corporation—

(i) any corporation more than 50 percent of the stock of which is owned (by vote or by value), directly or indirectly, by such corporation, and

(ii) any partnership more than 50 percent of the capital interests or profits interests of which is held, directly or indirectly, by such corporation.

(3) Adjustment.—The amount taken into account under subsection (a) with respect to any stock repurchased by a covered corporation shall be reduced by the fair market value of any stock issued by the covered corporation during the taxable year, including the fair market value of any stock issued or provided to employees of such covered corporation or employees of a specified affiliate of such covered corporation during the taxable year, whether or not such stock is issued or provided in response to the exercise of an option to purchase such stock.

(d) Special rules for acquisition of stock of certain foreign corporations.—

(1) In general.—In the case of an acquisition of stock of an applicable foreign corporation by a specified affiliate of such corporation (other than a foreign corporation or a foreign partnership (unless such partnership has a domestic entity as a direct or indirect partner)) from a person who is not the applicable foreign corporation or a specified affiliate of such applicable foreign corporation, for purposes of this section—

(A) such specified affiliate shall be treated as a covered corporation with respect to such acquisition,

(B) such acquisition shall be treated as a repurchase of stock of a covered corporation by such covered corporation, and

(C) the adjustment under subsection (c)(3) shall be determined only with respect to stock issued or provided by such specified affiliate to employees of the specified affiliate.

(2) Surrogate foreign corporations.—In the case of a repurchase of stock of a covered surrogate foreign corporation by such covered surrogate foreign corporation, or an acquisition of stock of a covered surrogate foreign corporation by a specified affiliate of such corporation, for purposes of this section—

(A) the expatriated entity with respect to such covered surrogate foreign corporation shall be treated as a covered corporation with respect to such repurchase or acquisition,

(B) such repurchase or acquisition shall be treated as a repurchase of stock of a covered corporation by such covered corporation, and

(C) the adjustment under subsection (c)(3) shall be determined only with respect to stock issued or provided by such expatriated entity to employees of the expatriated entity.

(3) Definitions.—For purposes of this subsection—

(A) Applicable foreign corporation.—The term "applicable foreign corporation" means any foreign corporation the stock of which is traded on an established securities market (within the meaning of section 7704(b)(1)).

(B) Covered surrogate foreign corporation.—The term "covered surrogate foreign corporation" means any surrogate foreign corporation (as determined under section 7874(a)(2)(B) by substituting "September 20, 2021" for "March 4, 2003" each place it appears) the stock of which is traded on an established securities market (within the meaning of section 7704(b)(1)), but only with respect to taxable years which include any portion of the applicable period with respect to such corporation under section 7874(d)(1).

(C) Expatriated entity.—The term "expatriated entity" has the meaning given such term by section 7874(a)(2)(A).

(e) Exceptions.—Subsection (a) shall not apply—

(1) to the extent that the repurchase is part of a reorganization (within the meaning of section 368(a)) and no gain or loss is recognized on such repurchase by the shareholder under chapter 1 by reason of such reorganization,

(2) in any case in which the stock repurchased is, or an amount of stock equal to the value of the stock repurchased is, contributed to an employer-sponsored retirement plan, employee stock ownership plan, or similar plan,

(3) in any case in which the total value of the stock repurchased during the taxable year does not exceed $1,000,000,

(4) under regulations prescribed by the Secretary, in cases in which the repurchase is by a dealer in securities in the ordinary course of business,

(5) to repurchases by a regulated investment company (as defined in section 851) or a real estate investment trust, or

(6) to the extent that the repurchase is treated as a dividend for purposes of this title.

(f) Regulations and guidance.—The Secretary shall prescribe such regulations and other guidance as are necessary or appropriate to carry out, and to prevent the avoidance of, the purposes of this section, including regulations and other guidance—

(1) to prevent the abuse of the exceptions provided by subsection (e),

(2) to address special classes of stock and preferred stock, and

(3) for the application of the rules under subsection (d).

Chapter 45—Provisions Relating to Expatriated Entities

§ 4985. Stock compensation of insiders in expatriated corporations

(a) Imposition of tax.—In the case of an individual who is a disqualified individual with respect to any expatriated corporation, there is hereby imposed on such person a tax equal to—

(1) the rate of tax specified in section 1(h)(1)(D), multiplied by

(2) the value (determined under subsection (b)) of the specified stock compensation held (directly or indirectly) by or for the benefit of such individual or a member of such individual's family (as defined in section 267) at any time during the 12-month period beginning on the date which is 6 months before the expatriation date.

(b) Value.—For purposes of subsection (a)—

(1) In general.—The value of specified stock compensation shall be—

(A) in the case of a stock option (or other similar right) or a stock appreciation right, the fair value of such option or right, and

(B) in any other case, the fair market value of such compensation.

(2) Date for determining value.—The determination of value shall be made—

(A) in the case of specified stock compensation held on the expatriation date, on such date,

(B) in the case of such compensation which is canceled during the 6 months before the expatriation date, on the day before such cancellation, and

(C) in the case of such compensation which is granted after the expatriation date, on the date such compensation is granted.

(c) Tax to apply only if shareholder gain recognized.—Subsection (a) shall apply to any disqualified individual with respect to an expatriated corporation only if gain (if any) on any stock in such corporation is recognized in whole or part by any shareholder by reason of the acquisition referred to in section 7874(a)(2)(B)(i) with respect to such corporation.

(d) Exception where gain recognized on compensation.—Subsection (a) shall not apply to—

(1) any stock option which is exercised on the expatriation date or during the 6-month period before such date and to the stock acquired in such exercise, if income is recognized under section 83 on or before the expatriation date with respect to the stock acquired pursuant to such exercise, and

(2) any other specified stock compensation which is exercised, sold, exchanged, distributed, cashed-out, or otherwise paid during such period in a transaction in which income, gain, or loss is recognized in full.

(e) Definitions.—For purposes of this section—

(1) Disqualified individual.—The term "disqualified individual" means, with respect to a corporation, any individual who, at any time during the 12-month period beginning on the date which is 6 months before the expatriation date—

(A) is subject to the requirements of section 16(a) of the Securities Exchange Act of 1934 with respect to such corporation or any member of the expanded affiliated group which includes such corporation, or

(B) would be subject to such requirements if such corporation or member were an issuer of equity securities referred to in such section.

(2) Expatriated corporation; expatriation date.—

(A) Expatriated corporation.—The term "expatriated corporation" means any corporation which is an expatriated entity (as defined in section 7874(a)(2)). Such term includes any predecessor or successor of such a corporation.

(B) Expatriation date.—The term "expatriation date" means, with respect to a corporation, the date on which the corporation first becomes an expatriated corporation.

(3) Specified stock compensation.—

(A) In general.—The term "specified stock compensation" means payment (or right to payment) granted by the expatriated corporation (or by any member of the expanded affiliated group which includes such corporation) to any person in connection with the performance of services by a disqualified individual for such corporation or member if the value of such payment or right is based on (or determined by reference to) the value (or change in value) of stock in such corporation (or any such member).

(B) Exceptions.—Such term shall not include—

(i) any option to which part II of subchapter D of chapter 1 applies, or

(ii) any payment or right to payment from a plan referred to in section 280G(b)(6).

(4) Expanded affiliated group.—The term "expanded affiliated group" means an affiliated group (as defined in section 1504(a) without regard to section 1504(b)(3)); except that section 1504(a) shall be applied by substituting "more than 50 percent" for "at least 80 percent" each place it appears.

(f) Special rules.—For purposes of this section—

(1) Cancellation of restriction.—The cancellation of a restriction which by its terms will never lapse shall be treated as a grant.

(2) Payment or reimbursement of tax by corporation treated as specified stock compensation.—Any payment of the tax imposed by this section directly or indirectly by the expatriated corporation or by any member of the expanded affiliated group which includes such corporation—

(A) shall be treated as specified stock compensation, and

(B) shall not be allowed as a deduction under any provision of chapter 1.

(3) Certain restrictions ignored.—Whether there is specified stock compensation, and the value thereof, shall be determined without regard to any restriction other than a restriction which by its terms will never lapse.

(4) Property transfers.—Any transfer of property shall be treated as a payment and any right to a transfer of property shall be treated as a right to a payment.

(5) Other administrative provisions.—For purposes of subtitle F, any tax imposed by this section shall be treated as a tax imposed by subtitle A.

(g) Regulations.—The Secretary shall prescribe such regulations as may be necessary or appropriate to carry out the purposes of this section.

SUBTITLE F—PROCEDURE AND ADMINISTRATION

Chapter 61—Information and Returns

Subchapter A—Returns and Records

Part II—Tax Returns or Statements

Subpart B—Income Tax Returns

§ 6013. Joint returns of income tax by husband and wife

(a) Joint returns.—A husband and wife may make a single return jointly of income taxes under subtitle A, even though one of the spouses has neither gross income nor deductions, except as provided below:

(1) no joint return shall be made if either the husband or wife at any time during the taxable year is a nonresident alien;

(2) no joint return shall be made if the husband and wife have different taxable years; except that if such taxable years begin on the same day and end on different days because of the death of either or both, then the joint return may be made with respect to the taxable year of each. The above exception shall not apply if the surviving spouse remarries before the close of his taxable year, nor if the taxable year of either spouse is a fractional part of a year under section 443(a)(1);

(3) in the case of death of one spouse or both spouses the joint return with respect to the decedent may be made only by his executor or administrator; except that in the case of the death of one spouse the joint return may be made by the surviving spouse with respect to both himself and the decedent if no return for the taxable year has been made by the decedent, no executor or administrator has been appointed, and no executor or administrator is appointed before the last day prescribed by law for filing the return of the surviving spouse. If an executor or administrator of the decedent is appointed after the making of the joint return by the surviving spouse, the executor or administrator may disaffirm such joint return by making, within 1 year after the last day prescribed by law for filing the return of the surviving spouse, a separate return for the taxable year of the decedent with respect to which the joint return was made, in which case the return made by the survivor shall constitute his separate return.

* * *

(g) Election to treat nonresident alien individual as resident of the United States.—

(1) In general.—A nonresident alien individual with respect to whom this subsection is in effect for the taxable year shall be treated as a resident of the United States—

(A) for purposes of chapter 1 for all of such taxable year, and

(B) for purposes of chapter 24 (relating to wage withholding) for payments of wages made during such taxable year.

(2) Individuals with respect to whom this subsection is in effect.—This subsection shall be in effect with respect to any individual who, at the close of the taxable year for which an election under this subsection was made, was a nonresident alien individual married to a citizen or resident of the United States, if both of them made such election to have the benefits of this subsection apply to them.

(3) Duration of election.—An election under this subsection shall apply to the taxable year for which made and to all subsequent taxable years until terminated under paragraph (4) or (5); except that any such election shall not apply for any taxable year if neither spouse is a citizen or resident of the United States at any time during such year.

(4) Termination of election.—An election under this subsection shall terminate at the earliest of the following times:

(A) Revocation by taxpayers.—If either taxpayer revokes the election, as of the first taxable year for which the last day prescribed by law for filing the return of tax under chapter 1 has not yet occurred.

(B) Death.—In the case of the death of either spouse, as of the beginning of the first taxable year of the spouse who survives following the taxable year in which such death occurred; except that if the spouse who survives is a citizen or resident of the United States who is a surviving spouse entitled to the benefits of section 2, the time provided by this subparagraph shall be as of the close of the last taxable year for which such individual is entitled to the benefits of section 2.

(C) Legal separation.—In the case of the legal separation of the couple under a decree of divorce or of separate maintenance, as of the beginning of the taxable year in which such legal separation occurs.

(D) Termination by Secretary.—At the time provided in paragraph (5).

(5) Termination by Secretary.—The Secretary may terminate any election under this subsection for any taxable year if he determines that either spouse has failed—

(A) to keep such books and records,

(B) to grant such access to such books and records, or

(C) to supply such other information,

as may be reasonably necessary to ascertain the amount of liability for taxes under chapter 1 of either spouse for such taxable year.

(6) Only one election.—If any election under this subsection for any two individuals is terminated under paragraph (4) or (5) for any taxable year, such two individuals shall be ineligible to make an election under this subsection for any subsequent taxable year.

(h) Joint return, etc., for year in which nonresident alien becomes resident of United States.—

(1) In general.—If—

(A) any individual is a nonresident alien individual at the beginning of any taxable year but is a resident of the United States at the close of such taxable year,

(B) at the close of such taxable year, such individual is married to a citizen or resident of the United States, and

(C) both individuals elect the benefits of this subsection at the time and in the manner prescribed by the Secretary by regulation,

then the individual referred to in subparagraph (A) shall be treated as a resident of the United States for purposes of chapter 1 for all of such taxable year, and for purposes of chapter 24 (relating to wage withholding) for payments of wages made during such taxable year.

(2) Only one election.—If any election under this subsection applies for any 2 individuals for any taxable year, such 2 individuals shall be ineligible to make an election under this subsection for any subsequent taxable year.

Part III—Information Returns

Subpart A—Information Concerning Persons Subject to Special Provisions

§ 6038. Information reporting with respect to certain foreign corporations and partnerships

(a) Requirement.—

(1) In general.—Every United States person shall furnish, with respect to any foreign business entity which such person controls, such information as the Secretary may prescribe relating to—

(A) the name, the principal place of business, and the nature of business of such entity, and the country under whose laws such entity is incorporated (or organized in the case of a partnership);

(B) in the case of a foreign corporation, its post-1986 undistributed earnings (as defined in section 902(c));

(C) a balance sheet for such entity listing assets, liabilities, and capital;

(D) transactions between such entity and—

(i) such person,

(ii) any corporation or partnership which such person controls, and

(iii) any United States person owning, at the time the transaction takes place—

(I) in the case of a foreign corporation, 10 percent or more of the value of any class of stock outstanding of such corporation, and

(II) in the case of a foreign partnership, at least a 10-percent interest in such partnership; and

(E) (i) in the case of a foreign corporation, a description of the various classes of stock outstanding, and a list showing the name and address of, and number of shares held by, each United States person who is a shareholder of record owning at any time during the annual accounting period 5 percent or more in value of any class of stock outstanding of such foreign corporation, and

(ii) information comparable to the information described in clause (i) in the case of a foreign partnership.

The Secretary may also require the furnishing of any other information which is similar or related in nature to that specified in the preceding sentence or which the Secretary determines to be appropriate to carry out the provisions of this title.

(2) Period for which information is to be furnished, etc.—The information required under paragraph (1) shall be furnished for the annual accounting period of the foreign business entity ending with or within the United States person's taxable year. The information so required shall be furnished at such time and in such manner as the Secretary shall prescribe.

(3) Limitation.—No information shall be required to be furnished under this subsection with respect to any foreign business entity for any annual accounting period unless the Secretary has prescribed the furnishing of such information on or before the first day of such annual accounting period.

(4) Information required from certain shareholders in certain cases.—If any foreign corporation is treated as a controlled foreign corporation for any purpose under subpart F of part III of subchapter N of chapter 1, the Secretary may require any United States person treated as a United States shareholder of such foreign business entity for any purpose under subpart F to furnish the information required under paragraph (1).

(5) Information required from 10-percent partner of controlled foreign partnership.—In the case of a foreign partnership which is controlled by United States persons holding at least 10-percent interests (but not by any one United States person), the Secretary may require each United States person who holds a 10-percent interest in such partnership to furnish information relating to such partnership, including information relating to such partner's ownership interests in the partnership and allocations to such partner of partnership items.

(b) Dollar penalty for failure to furnish information.—

(1) In general.—If any person fails to furnish, within the time prescribed under paragraph (2) of subsection (a), any information with respect to any foreign business entity required under paragraph (1) of subsection (a), such person shall pay a penalty of $10,000 for each annual accounting period with respect to which such failure exists.

(2) Increase in penalty where failure continues after notification.—If any failure described in paragraph (1) continues for more than 90 days after the day on which the Secretary mails notice of such failure to the United States person, such person shall pay a penalty (in addition to the amount required under paragraph (1)) of $10,000 for each 30-day (or fraction thereof) during which such failure continues with respect to any annual accounting period after the expiration of such 90-day period. The increase in any penalty under this paragraph shall not exceed $50,000.

(c) Penalty of reducing foreign tax credit.—

(1) In general.—If a United States person fails to furnish, within the time prescribed under paragraph (2) of subsection (a), any information with respect to any foreign business entity required under paragraph (1) of subsection (a), then—

(A) in applying section 901 (relating to taxes of foreign countries and possessions of the United States) to such United States person for the taxable year, the amount of taxes (other than taxes reduced under subparagraph (B)) paid or deemed paid (other than those deemed paid under section 904(c)) to any foreign country or possession of the United States for the taxable year shall be reduced by 10 percent, and

(B) in the case of a foreign business entity which is a foreign corporation, in applying section 960 to any such United States person which is a corporation (or to any person who acquires from any other person any portion of the interest of such other person in any such foreign corporation, but only to the extent of such portion) for any taxable year, the amount of taxes paid or deemed paid by each foreign corporation with respect to which such person is required to furnish information during the annual accounting period or periods with respect to which such information is required under paragraph (2) of subsection (a) shall be reduced by 10 percent.

If such failure continues 90 days or more after notice of such failure by the Secretary to the United States person, then the amount of the reduction under this paragraph shall be 10 percent plus an additional 5 percent for each 3-month period, or fraction thereof, during which such failure to furnish information continues after the expiration of such 90-day period.

(2) Limitation.—The amount of the reduction under paragraph (1) for each failure to furnish information with respect to a foreign business entity required under subsection (a)(1) shall not exceed whichever of the following amounts is the greater:

(A) $10,000, or

(B) the income of the foreign business entity for its annual accounting period with respect to which the failure occurs.

(3) Coordination with subsection (b).—The amount of the reduction which (but for this paragraph) would be made under paragraph (1) with respect to any annual accounting period shall be reduced by the amount of the penalty imposed by subsection (b) with respect to such period.

(4) Special rules.—

(A) No taxes shall be reduced under this subsection more than once for the same failure.

(B) For purposes of this subsection and subsection (b), the time prescribed under paragraph (2) of subsection (a) to furnish information (and the beginning of the 90-day period after notice by the Secretary) shall be treated as being not earlier than the last day on which (as shown to the satisfaction of the Secretary) reasonable cause existed for failure to furnish such information.

(d) Two or more persons required to furnish information with respect to same foreign business entity.—Where, but for this subsection, two or more United States persons would be required to furnish information under subsection (a) with respect to the same foreign business entity for the same period, the Secretary may by regulations provide that such information shall be required only from one person. To the extent practicable, the determination of which person shall furnish the information shall be made on the basis of actual ownership of stock.

(e) Definitions.—For purposes of this section—

(1) Foreign business entity.—The term "foreign business entity" means a foreign corporation and a foreign partnership.

(2) Control of corporation.—A person is in control of a corporation if such person owns stock possessing more than 50 percent of the total combined voting power of all classes of stock entitled to vote, or more than 50 percent of the total value of shares of all classes of stock, of a corporation. If a person is in control (within the meaning of the preceding sentence) of a corporation which in turn owns more than 50 percent of the total combined voting power of all classes of stock entitled to vote of another corporation, or owns more than 50 percent of the total value of the shares of all classes of stock of another corporation, then such person shall be treated as in control of such other corporation. For purposes of this paragraph, the rules prescribed by section 318(a) for determining ownership of stock shall apply; except that—

(A) subparagraphs (A), (B), and (C) of section 318(a)(3) shall not be applied so as to consider a United States person as owning stock which is owned by a person who is not a United States person, and

(B) in applying subparagraph (C) of section 318(a)(2), the phrase "10 percent" shall be substituted for the phrase "50 percent" used in subparagraph (C).

(3) Partnership-related definitions.—

(A) Control.—A person is in control of a partnership if such person owns directly or indirectly more than a 50 percent interest in such partnership.

(B) 50-percent interest.—For purposes of subparagraph (A), a 50-percent interest in a partnership is—

(i) an interest equal to 50 percent of the capital interest, or 50 percent of the profits interest, in such partnership, or

(ii) to the extent provided in regulations, an interest to which 50 percent of the deductions or losses of such partnership are allocated.

For purposes of the preceding sentence, rules similar to the rules of section 267(c) (other than paragraph (3)) shall apply.

(C) 10-percent interest.—A 10-percent interest in a partnership is an interest which would be described in subparagraph (B) if "10 percent" were substituted for "50 percent" each place it appears.

(4) Annual accounting period.—The annual accounting period of a foreign business entity is the annual period on the basis of which such corporation regularly computes its income in keeping its books. In the case of a specified foreign business entity (as defined in section 898), the taxable year of such corporation shall be treated as its annual accounting period.

(f) Cross references.—

(1) For provisions relating to penalties for violations of this section, see section 7203.

(2) For definition of the term "United States person", see section 7701(a)(30).

§ 6038A. Information with respect to certain foreign-owned corporations

(a) Requirement.—If, at any time during a taxable year, a corporation (hereinafter in this section referred to as the "reporting corporation")—

(1) is a domestic corporation, and

(2) is 25-percent foreign-owned,

such corporation shall furnish, at such time and in such manner as the Secretary shall by regulations prescribe, the information described in subsection (b) and such corporation shall maintain (in the location, in the manner, and to the extent prescribed in regulations) such records as may be appropriate to determine the correct treatment of transactions with related parties as the Secretary shall by regulations prescribe (or shall cause another person to so maintain such records).

(b) Required information.—

(1) In general.—For purposes of subsection (a), the information described in this subsection is such information as the Secretary prescribes by regulations relating to—

(A) the name, principal place of business, nature of business, and country or countries in which organized or resident, of each person which—

(i) is a related party to the reporting corporation, and

(ii) had any transaction with the reporting corporation during its taxable year,

(B) the manner in which the reporting corporation is related to each person referred to in subparagraph (A), and

(C) transactions between the reporting corporation and each foreign person which is a related party to the reporting corporation.

(2) Additional information regarding base erosion payments.—For purposes of subsection (a) and section 6038C, if the reporting corporation or the foreign corporation to whom section 6038C applies is an applicable taxpayer, the information described in this subsection shall include—

(A) such information as the Secretary determines necessary to determine the base erosion minimum tax amount, base erosion payments, and base erosion tax benefits of the taxpayer for purposes of section 59A for the taxable year, and

(B) such other information as the Secretary determines necessary to carry out such section.

For purposes of this paragraph, any term used in this paragraph which is also used in section 59A shall have the same meaning as when used in such section.

(c) Definitions.—For purposes of this section—

(1) 25-percent foreign-owned.—A corporation is 25-percent foreign-owned if at least 25 percent of—

(A) the total voting power of all classes of stock of such corporation entitled to vote, or

(B) the total value of all classes of stock of such corporation,

is owned at any time during the taxable year by 1 foreign person (hereinafter in this section referred to as a "25-percent foreign shareholder").

(2) Related party.—The term "related party" means—

(A) any 25-percent foreign shareholder of the reporting corporation,

(B) any person who is related (within the meaning of section 267(b) or 707(b)(1)) to the reporting corporation or to a 25-percent foreign shareholder of the reporting corporation, and

(C) any other person who is related (within the meaning of section 482) to the reporting corporation.

(3) Foreign person.—The term "foreign person" means any person who is not a United States person. For purposes of the preceding sentence, the term "United States person" has the meaning given to such term by section 7701(a)(30), except that any individual who is a citizen of any possession of the United States (but not otherwise a citizen of the United States) and who is not a resident of the United States shall not be treated as a United States person.

(4) Records.—The term "records" includes any books, papers, or other data.

(5) Section 318 to apply.—Section 318 shall apply for purposes of paragraphs (1) and (2), except that—

(A) "10 percent" shall be substituted for "50 percent" in section 318(a)(2)(C), and

(B) subparagraphs (A), (B), and (C) of section 318(a)(3) shall not be applied so as to consider a United States person as owning stock which is owned by a person who is not a United States person.

(d) Penalty for failure to furnish information or maintain records.—

(1) In general.—If a reporting corporation—

(A) fails to furnish (within the time prescribed by regulations) any information described in subsection (b), or

(B) fails to maintain (or cause another to maintain) records as required by subsection (a),

such corporation shall pay a penalty of $25,000 for each taxable year with respect to which such failure occurs.

(2) Increase in penalty where failure continues after notification.—If any failure described in paragraph (1) continues for more than 90 days after the day on which the Secretary mails notice of such failure to the reporting corporation, such corporation shall pay a penalty (in addition to the amount required under paragraph (1)) of $25,000 for each 30-day period (or fraction thereof) during which such failure continues after the expiration of such 90-day period.

(3) Reasonable cause.—For purposes of this subsection, the time prescribed by regulations to furnish information or maintain records (and the beginning of the 90-day period after notice by the Secretary) shall be treated as not earlier than the last day on which (as shown to the satisfaction of the Secretary) reasonable cause existed for failure to furnish the information or maintain the records.

(e) Enforcement of requests for certain records.—

(1) Agreement to treat corporation as agent.—The rules of paragraph (3) shall apply to any transaction between the reporting corporation and any related party who is a foreign person unless such related party agrees (in such manner and at such time as the Secretary shall prescribe) to authorize the reporting corporation to act as such related party's limited agent solely for purposes of applying sections 7602, 7603, and 7604 with respect to any request by the Secretary to examine records or produce testimony related to any such transaction or with respect to any summons by the Secretary for such records or testimony. The appearance of persons or production of records by reason of the reporting corporation being such an agent shall not subject such persons or records to legal process for any purpose other than determining the correct treatment under this title of any transaction between the reporting corporation and such related party.

(2) Rules where information not furnished.—If—

(A) for purposes of determining the correct treatment under this title of any transaction between the reporting corporation and a related party who is a foreign person, the Secretary issues a summons to such corporation to produce (either directly or as agent for such related party) any records or testimony,

(B) such summons is not quashed in a proceeding begun under paragraph (4) and is not determined to be invalid in a proceeding begun under section 7604(b) to enforce such summons, and

(C) the reporting corporation does not substantially comply in a timely manner with such summons and the Secretary has sent by certified or registered mail a notice to such reporting corporation that such reporting corporation has not so substantially complied,

the Secretary may apply the rules of paragraph (3) with respect to such transaction (whether or not the Secretary begins a proceeding to enforce such summons). If the reporting corporation fails to maintain (or cause another to maintain) records as required by subsection (a), and by reason of that failure, the summons is quashed in a proceeding described in subparagraph (B) or the reporting corporation is not able to provide the records requested in the summons, the Secretary may apply the rules of paragraph (3) with respect to any transaction to which the records relate.

(3) Applicable rules in cases of noncompliance.—If the rules of this paragraph apply to any transaction—

(A) the amount of the deduction allowed under subtitle A for any amount paid or incurred by the reporting corporation to the related party in connection with such transaction, and

(B) the cost to the reporting corporation of any property acquired in such transaction from the related party (or transferred by such corporation in such transaction to the related party),

shall be the amount determined by the Secretary in the Secretary's sole discretion from the Secretary's own knowledge or from such information as the Secretary may obtain through testimony or otherwise.

(4) Judicial proceedings.—

(A) Proceedings to quash.—Notwithstanding any law or rule of law, any reporting corporation to which the Secretary issues a summons referred to in paragraph (2)(A) shall have the right to begin a proceeding to quash such summons not later than the 90th day after such summons was issued. In any such proceeding, the Secretary may seek to compel compliance with such summons.

(B) Review of Secretarial determination of noncompliance.—Notwithstanding any law or rule of law, any reporting corporation which has been notified by the Secretary that the Secretary has determined that such corporation has not substantially complied with a summons referred to in paragraph (2) shall have the right to begin a proceeding to review such determination not later than the 90th day after the day on which the notice referred to in paragraph (2)(C) was mailed. If such a proceeding is not begun on or before such 90th day, such determination by the Secretary shall be binding and shall not be reviewed by any court

(C) Jurisdiction.—The United States district court for the district in which the person (to whom the summons is issued) resides or is found shall have jurisdiction to hear any proceeding brought under subparagraph (A) or (B). Any order or other determination in such a proceeding shall be treated as a final order which may be appealed.

(D) Suspension of statute of limitations.—If the reporting corporation brings an action under subparagraph (A) or (B), the running of any period of limitations under section 6501 (relating to assessment and collection of tax) or under section 6531 (relating to criminal prosecutions) with respect to any affected taxable year shall be suspended for the period during which such proceeding, and appeals therein, are pending. In no event shall any such period expire before the 90th day after the day on which there is a final determination in such proceeding. For purposes of this subparagraph, the term "affected taxable year" means any taxable year if the determination of the amount of tax imposed for such taxable year is affected by the treatment of the transaction to which the summons relates.

(f) Cross reference.—

For provisions relating to criminal penalties for violation of this section, see section 7203.

§ 6038B. Notice of certain transfers to foreign persons

(a) In general.—Each United States person who—

(1) transfers property to—

(A) a foreign corporation in an exchange described in section 332, 351, 354, 355, 356, or 361, or

(B) a foreign partnership in a contribution described in section 721 or in any other contribution described in regulations prescribed by the Secretary, or

(2) makes a distribution described in section 336 to a person who is not a United States person,

shall furnish to the Secretary, at such time and in such manner as the Secretary shall by regulations prescribe, such information with respect to such exchange or distribution as the Secretary may require in such regulations.

(b) Exceptions for certain transfers to foreign partnerships; special rule.—

(1) Exceptions.—Subsection (a)(1)(B) shall apply to a transfer by a United States person to a foreign partnership only if—

(A) the United States person holds (immediately after the transfer) directly or indirectly at least a 10-percent interest (as defined in section 6046A(d)) in the partnership, or

(B) the value of the property transferred (when added to the value of the property transferred by such person or any related person to such partnership or a related partnership during the 12-month period ending on the date of the transfer) exceeds $100,000.

For purposes of the preceding sentence, the value of any transferred property is its fair market value at the time of its transfer.

(2) Special rule.—If by reason of an adjustment under section 482 or otherwise, a contribution described in subsection (a)(1) is deemed to have been made, such contribution shall be treated for purposes of this section as having been made not earlier than the date specified by the Secretary.

(c) Penalty for failure to furnish information.—

(1) In general.—If any United States person fails to furnish the information described in subsection (a) at the time and in the manner required by regulations, such person shall pay a penalty equal to 10 percent of the fair market value of the property at the time of the exchange (and, in the case of a contribution described in subsection (a)(1)(B), such person shall recognize gain as if the contributed property had been sold for such value at the time of such contribution).

(2) Reasonable cause exception.—Paragraph (1) shall not apply to any failure if the United States person shows such failure is due to reasonable cause and not to willful neglect.

(3) Limit on penalty.—The penalty under paragraph (1) with respect to any exchange shall not exceed $100,000 unless the failure with respect to such exchange was due to intentional disregard.

§ 6038C. Information with respect to foreign corporations engaged in U.S. business

(a) Requirement.—If a foreign corporation (hereinafter in this section referred to as the "reporting corporation") is engaged in a trade or business within the United States at any time during a taxable year—

(1) such corporation shall furnish (at such time and in such manner as the Secretary shall by regulations prescribe) the information described in subsection (b), and

(2) such corporation shall maintain (at the location, in the manner, and to the extent prescribed in regulations) such records as may be appropriate to determine the liability of such corporation for tax under this title as the Secretary shall by regulations prescribe (or shall cause another person to so maintain such records).

(b) Required information.—For purposes of subsection (a), the information described in this subsection is—

(1) the information described in section 6038A(b), and

(2) such other information as the Secretary may prescribe by regulations relating to any item not directly connected with a transaction for which information is required under paragraph (1).

(c) Penalty for failure to furnish information or maintain records.—The provisions of subsection (d) of section 6038A shall apply to—

(1) any failure to furnish (within the time prescribed by regulations) any information described in subsection (b), and

(2) any failure to maintain (or cause another to maintain) records as required by subsection (a),

in the same manner as if such failure were a failure to comply with the provisions of section 6038A.

(d) Enforcement of requests for certain records.—

(1) Agreement to treat corporation as agent.—The rules of paragraph (3) shall apply to any transaction between the reporting corporation and any related party who is a foreign person unless such related party agrees (in such manner and at such time as the Secretary shall prescribe) to authorize the reporting corporation to act as such related party's limited agent solely for purposes of applying sections 7602, 7603, and 7604 with respect to any request by the Secretary to examine records or produce testimony related to any such transaction or with respect to any summons by the Secretary for such records or testimony. The appearance of persons or production of records by reason of the reporting corporation being such an agent shall not subject such persons or records to legal process for any purpose other than determining the correct treatment under this title of any transaction between the reporting corporation and such related party.

(2) Rules where information not furnished.—If—

(A) for purposes of determining the amount of the reporting corporation's liability for tax under this title, the Secretary issues a summons to such corporation to produce (either directly or as an agent for a related party who is a foreign person) any records or testimony,

(B) such summons is not quashed in a proceeding begun under paragraph (4) of section 6038A(e) (as made applicable by paragraph (4) of this subsection) and is not determined to be invalid in a proceeding begun under section 7604(b) to enforce such summons, and

(C) the reporting corporation does not substantially comply in a timely manner with such summons and the Secretary has sent by certified or registered mail a notice to such reporting corporation that such reporting corporation has not so substantially complied,

the Secretary may apply the rules of paragraph (3) with respect to any transaction or item to which such summons relates (whether or not the Secretary begins a proceeding to enforce such summons). If the reporting corporation fails to maintain (or cause another to maintain) records as required by subsection (a), and by reason of that failure, the summons is quashed in a proceeding described in subparagraph (B) or the reporting corporation is not able to provide the records requested in the summons, the Secretary may apply the rules of paragraph (3) with respect to any transaction or item to which the records relate.

(3) Applicable rules.—If the rules of this paragraph apply to any transaction or item, the treatment of such transaction (or the amount and treatment of any such item) shall be determined by the Secretary in the Secretary's sole discretion from the Secretary's own knowledge or from such information as the Secretary may obtain through testimony or otherwise.

(4) Judicial proceedings.—The provisions of section 6038A(e)(4) shall apply with respect to any summons referred to in paragraph (2)(A); except that subparagraph (D) of such section shall be applied by substituting "transaction or item" for "transaction".

(e) Definitions.—For purposes of this section, the terms "related party", "foreign person", and "records" have the respective meanings given to such terms by section 6038A(c).

§ 6038D. Information with respect to foreign financial assets

(a) In general.—Any individual who, during any taxable year, holds any interest in a specified foreign financial asset shall attach to such person's return of tax imposed by subtitle A for such taxable year the information described in subsection (c) with respect to each such asset if the aggregate value of all such assets exceeds $50,000 (or such higher dollar amount as the Secretary may prescribe).

(b) Specified foreign financial assets.—For purposes of this section, the term 'specified foreign financial asset' means—

(1) any financial account (as defined in section 1471(d)(2)) maintained by a foreign financial institution (as defined in section 1471(d)(4)), and

(2) any of the following assets which are not held in an account maintained by a financial institution (as defined in section 1471(d)(5))—

(A) any stock or security issued by a person other than a United States person,

(B) any financial instrument or contract held for investment that has an issuer or counterparty which is other than a United States person, and

(C) any interest in a foreign entity (as defined in section 1473).

(c) Required information.—The information described in this subsection with respect to any asset is:

(1) In the case of any account, the name and address of the financial institution in which such account is maintained and the number of such account.

(2) In the case of any stock or security, the name and address of the issuer and such information as is necessary to identify the class or issue of which such stock or security is a part.

(3) In the case of any other instrument, contract, or interest—

(A) such information as is necessary to identify such instrument, contract, or interest, and

(B) the names and addresses of all issuers and counterparties with respect to such instrument, contract, or interest.

(4) The maximum value of the asset during the taxable year.

(d) Penalty for failure to disclose.—

(1) In general.—If any individual fails to furnish the information described in subsection (c) with respect to any taxable year at the time and in the manner described in subsection (a), such person shall pay a penalty of $10,000.

(2) Increase in penalty where failure continues after notification.—If any failure described in paragraph (1) continues for more than 90 days after the day on which the Secretary mails notice of such failure to the individual, such individual shall pay a penalty (in addition to the penalties under paragraph (1)) of $10,000 for each 30-day period (or fraction thereof) during which such failure continues after the expiration of such 90-day period. The penalty imposed under this paragraph with respect to any failure shall not exceed $50,000.

(e) Presumption that value of specified foreign financial assets exceeds dollar threshold.— If—

(1) the Secretary determines that an individual has an interest in one or more specified foreign financial assets, and

(2) such individual does not provide sufficient information to demonstrate the aggregate value of such assets,

then the aggregate value of such assets shall be treated as being in excess of $50,000 (or such higher dollar amount as the Secretary prescribes for purposes of subsection (a)) for purposes of assessing the penalties imposed under this section.

(f) Application to certain entities.—To the extent provided by the Secretary in regulations or other guidance, the provisions of this section shall apply to any domestic entity which is formed or availed of for purposes of holding, directly or indirectly, specified foreign financial assets, in the same manner as if such entity were an individual.

(g) Reasonable cause exception.—No penalty shall be imposed by this section on any failure which is shown to be due to reasonable cause and not due to willful neglect. The fact that a foreign jurisdiction would impose a civil or criminal penalty on the taxpayer (or any other person) for disclosing the required information is not reasonable cause.

(h) Regulations.—The Secretary shall prescribe such regulations or other guidance as may be necessary or appropriate to carry out the purposes of this section, including regulations or other guidance which provide appropriate exceptions from the application of this section in the case of—

(1) classes of assets identified by the Secretary, including any assets with respect to which the Secretary determines that disclosure under this section would be duplicative of other disclosures,

(2) nonresident aliens, and

(3) bona fide residents of any possession of the United States.

§ 6039C. Returns with respect to foreign persons holding direct investments in United States real property interests

(a) General rule.—To the extent provided in regulations, any foreign person holding direct investments in United States real property interests for the calendar year shall make a return setting forth—

(1) the name and address of such person,

(2) a description of all United States real property interests held by such person at any time during the calendar year, and

(3) such other information as the Secretary may by regulations prescribe.

(b) Definition of foreign persons holding direct investments in United States real property interests.—For purposes of this section, a foreign person shall be treated as holding direct investments in United States real property interests during any calendar year if—

(1) such person did not engage in a trade or business in the United States at any time during such calendar year, and

(2) the fair market value of the United States real property interests held directly by such person at any time during such year equals or exceeds $50,000.

(c) Definitions and special rules.—For purposes of this section—

(1) United States real property interests.—The term "United States real property interest" has the meaning given to such term by section 897(c).

(2) Foreign person.—The term "foreign person" means any person who is not a United States person.

(3) Attribution of ownership.—For purposes of subsection (b)(2)—

(A) Interests held by partnerships, etc.—United States real property interests held by a partnership, trust, or estate shall be treated as owned proportionately by its partners or beneficiaries.

(B) Interests held by family members.—United States real property interests held by the spouse or any minor child of an individual shall be treated as owned by such individual.

(4) Time and manner of filing return.—All returns required to be made under this section shall be made at such time and in such manner as the Secretary shall by regulations prescribe.

(d) Special rule for United States interest and Virgin Islands interest.—A nonresident alien individual or foreign corporation subject to tax under section 897(a) (and any person required to withhold tax under section 1445) shall pay any tax and file any return required by this title—

(1) to the United States, in the case of any interest in real property located in the United States and an interest (other than an interest solely as a creditor) in a domestic corporation (with respect to the United States) described in section 897(c)(1)(A)(ii), and

(2) to the Virgin Islands, in the case of any interest in real property located in the Virgin Islands and an interest (other than an interest solely as a creditor) in a domestic corporation (with respect to the Virgin Islands) described in section 897(c)(1)(A)(ii).

§ 6039E. Information concerning resident status

(a) General rule.—Notwithstanding any other provision of law, any individual who—

(1) applies for a United States passport (or a renewal thereof), or

(2) applies to be lawfully accorded the privilege of residing permanently in the United States as an immigrant in accordance with the immigration laws,

shall include with any such application a statement which includes the information described in subsection (b).

(b) Information to be provided.—Information required under subsection (a) shall include—

(1) the taxpayer's TIN (if any),

(2) in the case of a passport applicant, any foreign country in which such individual is residing,

(3) in the case of an individual seeking permanent residence, information with respect to whether such individual is required to file a return of the tax imposed by chapter 1 for such individual's most recent 3 taxable years, and

(4) such other information as the Secretary may prescribe.

(c) Penalty.—Any individual failing to provide a statement required under subsection (a) shall be subject to a penalty equal to $500 for each such failure, unless it is shown that such failure is due to reasonable cause and not to willful neglect.

(d) Information to be provided to Secretary.—Notwithstanding any other provision of law, any agency of the United States which collects (or is required to collect) the statement under subsection (a) shall—

(1) provide any such statement to the Secretary, and

(2) provide to the Secretary the name (and any other identifying information) of any individual refusing to comply with the provisions of subsection (a).

Nothing in the preceding sentence shall be construed to require the disclosure of information which is subject to section 245A of the Immigration and Nationality Act (as in effect on the date of the enactment of this sentence).

(e) Exemption.—The Secretary may by regulations exempt any class of individuals from the requirements of this section if he determines that applying this section to such individuals is not necessary to carry out the purposes of this section.

§ 6039G. Information on individuals losing United States citizenship

(a) In general.—Notwithstanding any other provision of law, any individual to whom section 877(b) or 877A applies for any taxable year shall provide a statement for such taxable year which includes the information described in subsection (b).

(b) Information to be provided.—Information required under subsection (a) shall include—

(1) the taxpayer's TIN,

(2) the mailing address of such individual's principal foreign residence,

(3) the foreign country in which such individual is residing,

(4) the foreign country of which such individual is a citizen,

(5) information detailing the income, assets, and liabilities of such individual,

(6) the number of days during any portion of which that the individual was physically present in the United States during the taxable year, and

(7) such other information as the Secretary may prescribe.

(c) Penalty.—If—

(1) an individual is required to file a statement under subsection (a) for any taxable year, and

(2) fails to file such a statement with the Secretary on or before the date such statement is required to be filed or fails to include all the information required to be shown on the statement or includes incorrect information,

such individual shall pay a penalty of $10,000 unless it is shown that such failure is due to reasonable cause and not to willful neglect.

(d) Information to be provided to Secretary.—Notwithstanding any other provision of law—

(1) any Federal agency or court which collects (or is required to collect) the statement under subsection (a) shall provide to the Secretary—

(A) a copy of any such statement, and

(B) the name (and any other identifying information) of any individual refusing to comply with the provisions of subsection (a),

(2) the Secretary of State shall provide to the Secretary a copy of each certificate as to the loss of American nationality under section 358 of the Immigration and Nationality Act which is approved by the Secretary of State, and

(3) the Federal agency primarily responsible for administering the immigration laws shall provide to the Secretary the name of each lawful permanent resident of the United States (within the meaning of section 7701(b)(6)) whose status as such has been revoked or has been administratively or judicially determined to have been abandoned.

Notwithstanding any other provision of law, not later than 30 days after the close of each calendar quarter, the Secretary shall publish in the Federal Register the name of each individual losing United States citizenship (within the meaning of section 877(a)) with respect to whom the Secretary receives information under the preceding sentence during such quarter.

Subpart B—Information Concerning Transactions with Other Persons

§ 6046. Returns as to organization or reorganization of foreign corporations and as to acquisitions of their stock

(a) Requirement of return.—

(1) In general.—A return complying with the requirements of subsection (b) shall be made by—

(A) each United States citizen or resident who becomes an officer or director of a foreign corporation if a United States person (as defined in section 7701(a)(30)) meets the stock ownership requirements of paragraph (2) with respect to such corporation,

(B) each United States person—

(i) who acquires stock which, when added to any stock owned on the date of such acquisition, meets the stock ownership requirements of paragraph (2) with respect to a foreign corporation, or

(ii) who acquires stock which, without regard to stock owned on the date of such acquisition, meets the stock ownership requirements of paragraph (2) with respect to a foreign corporation,

(C) each person (not described in subparagraph (B)) who is treated as a United States shareholder under section 953(c) with respect to a foreign corporation, and

(D) each person who becomes a United States person while meeting the stock ownership requirements of paragraph (2) with respect to stock of a foreign corporation.

In the case of a foreign corporation with respect to which any person is treated as a United States shareholder under section 953(c), subparagraph (A) shall be treated as including a reference to each United States person who is an officer or director of such corporation.

(2) Stock ownership requirements.—A person meets the stock ownership requirements of this paragraph with respect to any corporation if such person owns 10 percent or more of—

(A) the total combined voting power of all classes of stock of such corporation entitled to vote, or

(B) the total value of the stock of such corporation.

(b) Form and contents of returns.—The returns required by subsection (a) shall be in such form and shall set forth, in respect of the foreign corporation, such information as the Secretary prescribes by forms or regulations as necessary for carrying out the provisions of the income tax laws, except that in the case of persons described only in subsection (a)(1)(A) the information required shall be limited to the names and addresses of persons described in subparagraph (B) or (C) of subsection (a).

(c) Ownership of stock.—For purposes of subsection (a), stock owned directly or indirectly by a person (including, in the case of an individual, stock owned by members of his family) shall be taken into account. For purposes of the preceding sentence, the family of an individual shall be considered as including only his brothers and sisters (whether by the whole or half blood), spouse, ancestors, and lineal descendants.

(d) Time for filing.—Any return required by subsection (a) shall be filed on or before the 90th day after the day on which, under any provision of subsection (a), the United States citizen, resident, or person becomes liable to file such return (or on or before such later day as the Secretary may by forms or regulations prescribe).

(e) Limitation.—No information shall be required to be furnished under this section with respect to any foreign corporation unless such information was required to be furnished under regulations which have been in effect for at least 90 days before the date on which the United States citizen, resident, or person becomes liable to file a return required under subsection (a).

(f) Cross reference.—

For provisions relating to penalties for violations of this section, see sections 6679 and 7203.

§ 6046A. Returns as to interests in foreign partnerships

(a) Requirement of return.—Any United States person, except to the extent otherwise provided by regulations—

(1) who acquires any interest in a foreign partnership,

(2) who disposes of any portion of his interest in a foreign partnership, or

(3) whose proportional interest in a foreign partnership changes substantially,

shall file a return. Paragraphs (1) and (2) shall apply to any acquisition or disposition only if the United States person directly or indirectly holds at least a 10-percent interest in such partnership either before or after such acquisition or disposition, and paragraph (3) shall apply to any change only if the change is equivalent to at least a 10-percent interest in such partnership.

(b) Form and contents of return.—Any return required by subsection (a) shall be in such form and set forth such information as the Secretary shall by regulations prescribe.

(c) Time for filing return.—Any return required by subsection (a) shall be filed on or before the 90th day (or on or before such later day as the Secretary may by regulations prescribe) after the day on which the United States person becomes liable to file such return.

(d) 10-Percent interest.—For purposes of subsection (a), a 10-percent interest in a partnership is an interest described in section 6038(e)(3)(C).

(e) Cross reference.—

For provisions relating to penalties for violations of this section, see sections 6679 and 7203.

§ 6048. Information with respect to certain foreign trusts

(a) Notice of certain events.—

(1) General rule.—On or before the 90th day (or such later day as the Secretary may prescribe) after any reportable event, the responsible party shall provide written notice of such event to the Secretary in accordance with paragraph (2).

(2) Contents of notice.—The notice required by paragraph (1) shall contain such information as the Secretary may prescribe, including—

(A) the amount of money or other property (if any) transferred to the trust in connection with the reportable event, and

(B) the identity of the trust and of each trustee and beneficiary (or class of beneficiaries) of the trust.

(3) Reportable event.—For purposes of this subsection—

(A) In general.—The term "reportable event" means—

(i) the creation of any foreign trust by a United States person,

(ii) the transfer of any money or property (directly or indirectly) to a foreign trust by a United States person, including a transfer by reason of death, and

(iii) the death of a citizen or resident of the United States if—

(I) the decedent was treated as the owner of any portion of a foreign trust under the rules of subpart E of part I of subchapter J of chapter 1, or

(II) any portion of a foreign trust was included in the gross estate of the decedent.

(B) Exceptions.—

(i) Fair market value sales.—Subparagraph (A)(ii) shall not apply to any transfer of property to a trust in exchange for consideration of at least the fair market value of the transferred property. For purposes of the preceding sentence, consideration other than cash shall be taken into account at its fair market value and the rules of section 679(a)(3) shall apply.

(ii) Deferred compensation and charitable trusts.—Subparagraph (A) shall not apply with respect to a trust which is—

(I) described in section 402(b), 404(a)(4), or 404A, or

(II) determined by the Secretary to be described in section 501(c)(3).

(4) Responsible party.—For purposes of this subsection, the term "responsible party" means—

(A) the grantor in the case of the creation of an inter vivos trust,

(B) the transferor in the case of a reportable event described in paragraph (3)(A)(ii) other than a transfer by reason of death, and

(C) the executor of the decedent's estate in any other case.

(b) United States owner of foreign trust.—

(1) In general.—If, at any time during any taxable year of a United States person, such person is treated as the owner of any portion of a foreign trust under the rules of subpart E of part I of subchapter J of chapter 1, such person shall submit such information as the Secretary may prescribe with respect to such trust for such year and shall be responsible to ensure that—

(A) such trust makes a return for such year which sets forth a full and complete accounting of all trust activities and operations for the year, the name of the United States agent for such trust, and such other information as the Secretary may prescribe, and

(B) such trust furnishes such information as the Secretary may prescribe to each United States person (i) who is treated as the owner of any portion of such trust or (ii) who receives (directly or indirectly) any distribution from the trust.

(2) Trusts not having United States agent.—

(A) In general.—If the rules of this paragraph apply to any foreign trust, the determination of amounts required to be taken into account with respect to such trust by a United States person under the rules of subpart E of part I of subchapter J of chapter 1 shall be determined by the Secretary.

(B) United States agent required.—The rules of this paragraph shall apply to any foreign trust to which paragraph (1) applies unless such trust agrees (in such manner, subject to such conditions, and at such time as the Secretary shall prescribe) to authorize a United States person to act as such trust's limited agent solely for purposes of applying sections 7602, 7603, and 7604 with respect to—

(i) any request by the Secretary to examine records or produce testimony related to the proper treatment of amounts required to be taken into account under the rules referred to in subparagraph (A), or

(ii) any summons by the Secretary for such records or testimony.

The appearance of persons or production of records by reason of a United States person being such an agent shall not subject such persons or records to legal process for any purpose other than determining the correct treatment under this title of the amounts required to be taken into account under the rules referred to in subparagraph (A). A foreign trust which appoints an agent described in this subparagraph shall not be considered to have an office or a permanent establishment in the United States, or to be engaged in a trade or business in the United States, solely because of the activities of such agent pursuant to this subsection.

(C) Other rules to apply.—Rules similar to the rules of paragraphs (2) and (4) of section 6038A(e) shall apply for purposes of this paragraph.

(c) Reporting by United States beneficiaries of foreign trusts.—

(1) In general.—If any United States person receives (directly or indirectly) during any taxable year of such person any distribution from a foreign trust, such person shall make a return with respect to such trust for such year which includes—

(A) the name of such trust,

(B) the aggregate amount of the distributions so received from such trust during such taxable year, and

(C) such other information as the Secretary may prescribe.

(2) Inclusion in income if records not provided.—

(A) In general.—If adequate records are not provided to the Secretary to determine the proper treatment of any distribution from a foreign trust, such distribution shall be treated as an accumulation distribution includible in the gross income of the distributee under chapter 1. To the extent provided in regulations, the preceding sentence shall not apply if the foreign trust elects to be subject to rules similar to the rules of subsection (b)(2)(B).

(B) Application of accumulation distribution rules.—For purposes of applying section 668 in a case to which subparagraph (A) applies, the applicable number of years for purposes of section 668(a) shall be 1/2 of the number of years the trust has been in existence.

(d) Special rules.—

(1) Determination of whether United States person makes transfer or receives distribution.—For purposes of this section, in determining whether a United States person makes a transfer to, or receives a distribution from, a foreign trust, the fact that a portion of such trust is treated as owned by another person under the rules of subpart E of part I of subchapter J of chapter 1 shall be disregarded.

(2) Domestic trusts with foreign activities.—To the extent provided in regulations, a trust which is a United States person shall be treated as a foreign trust for purposes of this section and section 6677 if such trust has substantial activities, or holds substantial property, outside the United States.

(3) Time and manner of filing information.—Any notice or return required under this section shall be made at such time and in such manner as the Secretary shall prescribe.

(4) Modification of return requirements.—The Secretary is authorized to suspend or modify any requirement of this section if the Secretary determines that the United States has no significant tax interest in obtaining the required information.

(5) United States person's return must be consistent with trust return or Secretary notified of inconsistency.—Rules similar to the rules of section 6034A(c) shall apply to items reported by a trust under subsection (b)(1)(B) and to United States persons referred to in such subsection.

Part V—Time for Filing Returns and Other Documents

§ 6072. Time for filing income tax returns

* * *

(c) Returns by certain nonresident alien individuals and foreign corporations.—Returns made by nonresident alien individuals (other than those whose wages are subject to withholding under chapter 24) and foreign corporations (other than those having an office or place of business in the United States or a former FSC (as defined in section 922 as in effect before its repeal by the FSC Repeal and Extraterritorial Income Exclusion Act of 2000)) under section 6012 on the basis of a calendar year shall be filed on or before the 15th day of June following the close of the calendar year and such returns made on the basis of a fiscal year shall be filed on or before the 15th day of the 6th month following the close of the fiscal year.

* * *

Subchapter B—Miscellaneous Provisions

§ 6111. Disclosure of reportable transactions

(a) In general.—Each material advisor with respect to any reportable transaction shall make a return (in such form as the Secretary may prescribe) setting forth—

(1) information identifying and describing the transaction,

(2) information describing any potential tax benefits expected to result from the transaction, and

(3) such other information as the Secretary may prescribe.

Such return shall be filed not later than the date specified by the Secretary.

(b) Definitions.—For purposes of this section:

(1) Material advisor.—

(A) In general.—The term "material advisor" means any person—

(i) who provides any material aid, assistance, or advice with respect to organizing, managing, promoting, selling, implementing, insuring, or carrying out any reportable transaction, and

(ii) who directly or indirectly derives gross income in excess of the threshold amount (or such other amount as may be prescribed by the Secretary) for such aid, assistance, or advice.

(B) Threshold amount.—For purposes of subparagraph (A), the threshold amount is—

(i) $50,000 in the case of a reportable transaction substantially all of the tax benefits from which are provided to natural persons, and

(ii) $250,000 in any other case.

(2) Reportable transaction.—The term 'reportable transaction' has the meaning given to such term by section 6707A(c).

(c) Regulations.—The Secretary may prescribe regulations which provide—

(1) that only 1 person shall be required to meet the requirements of subsection (a) in cases in which 2 or more persons would otherwise be required to meet such requirements,

(2) exemptions from the requirements of this section, and

(3) such rules as may be necessary or appropriate to carry out the purposes of this section.

§ 6112. Material advisors of reportable transactions must keep lists of advisees, etc.

(a) In general.—Each material advisor (as defined in section 6111) with respect to any reportable transaction (as defined in section 6707A(c)) shall (whether or not required to file a return under section 6111 with respect to such transaction) maintain (in such manner as the Secretary may by regulations prescribe) a list—

(1) identifying each person with respect to whom such advisor acted as a material advisor with respect to such transaction, and

(2) containing such other information as the Secretary may by regulations require.

(b) Special rules.—

(1) Availability for inspection; retention of information on list.—Any person who is required to maintain a list under subsection (a) (or was required to maintain a list under subsection (a) as in effect before the enactment of the American Jobs Creation Act of 2004)—

(A) shall make such list available to the Secretary for inspection upon written request by the Secretary, and

(B) except as otherwise provided under regulations prescribed by the Secretary, shall retain any information which is required to be included on such list for 7 years.

(2) Lists which would be required to be maintained by 2 or more persons.—The Secretary may prescribe regulations which provide that, in cases in which 2 or more persons are required under subsection (a) to maintain the same list (or portion thereof), only 1 person shall be required to maintain such list (or portion).

§ 6114. Treaty-based return positions

(a) In general.—Each taxpayer who, with respect to any tax imposed by this title, takes the position that a treaty of the United States overrules (or otherwise modifies) an internal revenue law of the United States shall disclose (in such manner as the Secretary may prescribe) such position—

(1) on the return of tax for such tax (or any statement attached to such return), or

(2) if no return of tax is required to be filed, in such form as the Secretary may prescribe.

(b) Waiver authority.—The Secretary may waive the requirements of subsection (a) with respect to classes of cases for which the Secretary determines that the waiver will not impede the assessment and collection of tax.

Chapter 68—Additions to the Tax, Additional Amounts, and Assessable Penalties

Subchapter A—Additions to the Tax and Additional Amounts

Part II—Accuracy-Related and Fraud Penalties

§ 6662. Imposition of accuracy-related penalty on underpayments

(a) Imposition of penalty.—If this section applies to any portion of an underpayment of tax required to be shown on a return, there shall be added to the tax an amount equal to 20 percent of the portion of the underpayment to which this section applies.

(b) Portion of underpayment to which section applies.—This section shall apply to the portion of any underpayment which is attributable to 1 or more of the following:

(1) Negligence or disregard of rules or regulations.

(2) Any substantial understatement of income tax.

(3) Any substantial valuation misstatement under chapter 1.

(4) Any substantial overstatement of pension liabilities.

(5) Any substantial estate or gift tax valuation understatement.

(6) Any disallowance of claimed tax benefits by reason of a transaction lacking economic substance (within the meaning of section 7701(*o*)) or failing to meet the requirements of any similar rule of law.

(7) Any undisclosed foreign financial asset understatement.

* * *

This section shall not apply to any portion of an underpayment on which a penalty is imposed under section 6663. Except as provided in paragraph (1) or (2)(B) of section 6662A(e), this section shall not apply to the portion of any underpayment which is attributable to a reportable transaction understatement on which a penalty is imposed under section 6662A.

(c) Negligence.—For purposes of this section, the term "negligence" includes any failure to make a reasonable attempt to comply with the provisions of this title, and the term "disregard" includes any careless, reckless, or intentional disregard.

(d) Substantial understatement of income tax.—

(1) Substantial understatement.—

(A) In general.—For purposes of this section, there is a substantial understatement of income tax for any taxable year if the amount of the understatement for the taxable year exceeds the greater of—

(i) 10 percent of the tax required to be shown on the return for the taxable year, or

(ii) $5,000.

(B) Special rule for corporations.—In the case of a corporation other than an S corporation or a personal holding company (as defined in section 542), there is a substantial understatement of income tax for any taxable year if the amount of the understatement for the taxable year exceeds the lesser of—

(i) 10 percent of the tax required to be shown on the return for the taxable year (or, if greater, $10,000), or

(ii) $10,000,000.

(C) Special rule for taxpayers claiming section 199A deduction.—In the case of any taxpayer who claims any deduction allowed under section 199A for the taxable year, subparagraph (A) shall be applied by substituting "5 percent" for "10 percent".

(2) Understatement.—

(A) In general.—For purposes of paragraph (1), the term "understatement" means the excess of—

(i) the amount of the tax required to be shown on the return for the taxable year, over

(ii) the amount of the tax imposed which is shown on the return, reduced by any rebate (within the meaning of section 6211(b)(2)).

The excess under the preceding sentence shall be determined without regard to items to which section 6662A applies.

(B) Reduction for understatement due to position of taxpayer or disclosed item.—The amount of the understatement under subparagraph (A) shall be reduced by that portion of the understatement which is attributable to—

(i) the tax treatment of any item by the taxpayer if there is or was substantial authority for such treatment, or

(ii) any item if—

(I) the relevant facts affecting the item's tax treatment are adequately disclosed in the return or in a statement attached to the return, and

(II) there is a reasonable basis for the tax treatment of such item by the taxpayer.

For purposes of clause (ii)(II), in no event shall a corporation be treated as having a reasonable basis for its tax treatment of an item attributable to a multiple-party financing transaction if such treatment does not clearly reflect the income of the corporation.

(C) Reduction not to apply to tax shelters.—

(i) In general.—Subparagraph (B) shall not apply to any item attributable to a tax shelter.

(ii) Tax shelter.—For purposes of clause (i), the term "tax shelter" means—

(I) a partnership or other entity,

(II) any investment plan or arrangement, or

(III) any other plan or arrangement,

if a significant purpose of such partnership, entity, plan, or arrangement is the avoidance or evasion of Federal income tax.

(3) Secretarial list.—The Secretary may prescribe a list of positions which the Secretary believes do not meet 1 or more of the standards specified in paragraph (2)(B)(i), section 6664(d)(3), and section 6694(a)(1). Such list (and any revisions thereof) shall be published in the Federal Register or the Internal Revenue Bulletin.

(e) Substantial valuation misstatement under chapter 1.—

(1) In general.—For purposes of this section, there is a substantial valuation misstatement under chapter 1 if—

(A) the value of any property (or the adjusted basis of any property) claimed on any return of tax imposed by chapter 1 is 150 percent or more of the amount determined to be the correct amount of such valuation or adjusted basis (as the case may be), or

(B) **(i)** the price for any property or services (or for the use of property) claimed on any such return in connection with any transaction between persons described in section 482 is 200 percent or more (or 50 percent or less) of the amount determined under section 482 to be the correct amount of such price, or

(ii) the net section 482 transfer price adjustment for the taxable year exceeds the lesser of $5,000,000 or 10 percent of the taxpayer's gross receipts.

(2) Limitation.—No penalty shall be imposed by reason of subsection (b)(3) unless the portion of the underpayment for the taxable year attributable to substantial valuation misstatements under chapter 1 exceeds $5,000 ($10,000 in the case of a corporation other than an S corporation or a personal holding company (as defined in section 542)).

(3) Net section 482 transfer price adjustment.—For purposes of this subsection—

(A) In general.—The term "net section 482 transfer price adjustment" means, with respect to any taxable year, the net increase in taxable income for the taxable year (determined without regard to any amount carried to such taxable year from another taxable year) resulting from adjustments under section 482 in the price for any property or services (or for the use of property).

(B) Certain adjustments excluded in determining threshold.—For purposes of determining whether the threshold requirements of paragraph (1)(B)(ii) are met, the following shall be excluded:

(i) Any portion of the net increase in taxable income referred to in subparagraph (A) which is attributable to any redetermination of a price if—

(I) it is established that the taxpayer determined such price in accordance with a specific pricing method set forth in the regulations prescribed under section 482 and that the taxpayer's use of such method was reasonable,

(II) the taxpayer has documentation (which was in existence as of the time of filing the return) which sets forth the determination of such price in accordance with such a method and which establishes that the use of such method was reasonable, and

(III) the taxpayer provides such documentation to the Secretary within 30 days of a request for such documentation.

(ii) Any portion of the net increase in taxable income referred to in subparagraph (A) which is attributable to a redetermination of price where such price was not determined in accordance with such a specific pricing method if—

(I) the taxpayer establishes that none of such pricing methods was likely to result in a price that would clearly reflect income, the taxpayer used another pricing method to determine such price, and such other pricing method was likely to result in a price that would clearly reflect income,

(II) the taxpayer has documentation (which was in existence as of the time of filing the return) which sets forth the determination of such price in accordance with such other method and which establishes that the requirements of subclause(I) were satisfied, and

(III) the taxpayer provides such documentation to the Secretary within 30 days of request for such documentation.

(iii) Any portion of such net increase which is attributable to any transaction solely between foreign corporations unless, in the case of any such corporations, the treatment of such transaction affects the determination of income from sources within the United States or taxable income effectively connected with the conduct of a trade or business within the United States.

(C) Special rule.—If the regular tax (as defined in section 55(c)) imposed by chapter 1 on the taxpayer is determined by reference to an amount other than taxable income, such amount shall be treated as the taxable income of such taxpayer for purposes of this paragraph.

(D) Coordination with reasonable cause exception.—For purposes of section 6664(c) the taxpayer shall not be treated as having reasonable cause for any portion of an underpayment attributable to a net section 482 transfer price adjustment unless such taxpayer meets the requirements of clause (i), (ii), or (iii) of subparagraph (B) with respect to such portion.

* * *

(h) Increase in penalty in case of gross valuation misstatements.—

(1) In general.—To the extent that a portion of the underpayment to which this section applies is attributable to one or more gross valuation misstatements, subsection (a) shall be applied with respect to such portion by substituting "40 percent" for "20 percent".

(2) Gross valuation misstatements.—The term "gross valuation misstatements" means—

(A) any substantial valuation misstatement under chapter 1 as determined under subsection (e) by substituting—

(i) in paragraph (1)(A), "200 percent" for "150 percent",

(ii) in paragraph (1)(B)(i)—

(I) "400 percent" for "200 percent", and

(II) "25 percent" for "50 percent", and

(iii) in paragraph (1)(B)(ii)—

(I) "$20,000,000" for "$5,000,000", and

(II) "20 percent" for "10 percent".

(B) any substantial overstatement of pension liabilities as determined under subsection (f) by substituting "400 percent" for "200 percent", and

(C) any substantial estate or gift tax valuation understatement as determined under subsection (g) by substituting "40 percent" for "65 percent".

(i) Increase in Penalty in Case of Nondisclosed Noneconomic Substance Transactions.—

(1) In general.—In the case of any portion of an underpayment which is attributable to one or more nondisclosed noneconomic substance transactions, subsection (a) shall be applied with respect to such portion by substituting "40 percent" for "20 percent".

(2) Nondisclosed noneconomic substance transactions.—For purposes of this subsection, the term 'nondisclosed noneconomic substance transaction' means any portion of a transaction described in subsection (b)(6) with respect to which the relevant facts affecting the tax treatment are not adequately disclosed in the return nor in a statement attached to the return.

(3) Special rule for amended returns.—In no event shall any amendment or supplement to a return of tax be taken into account for purposes of this subsection if the amendment or supplement is filed after the earlier of the date the taxpayer is first contacted by the Secretary regarding the examination of the return or such other date as is specified by the Secretary.

(j) Undisclosed foreign financial asset understatement.—

(1) In general.—For purposes of this section, the term 'undisclosed foreign financial asset understatement' means, for any taxable year, the portion of the understatement for such taxable year which is attributable to any transaction involving an undisclosed foreign financial asset.

(2) Undisclosed foreign financial asset.—For purposes of this subsection, the term "undisclosed foreign financial asset" means, with respect to any taxable year, any asset with respect to which information was required to be provided under section 6038, 6038B, 6038D, 6046A, or 6048 for such taxable year but was not provided by the taxpayer as required under the provisions of those sections.

(3) Increase in penalty for undisclosed foreign financial asset understatements.—In the case of any portion of an underpayment which is attributable to any undisclosed foreign financial asset understatement, subsection (a) shall be applied with respect to such portion by substituting "40 percent" for "20 percent".

* * *

Subchapter B—Assessable Penalties

Part I—General Provisions

§ 6677. Failure to file information with respect to certain foreign trusts

(a) Civil penalty.—In addition to any criminal penalty provided by law, if any notice or return required to be filed by section 6048—

(1) is not filed on or before the time provided in such section, or

(2) does not include all the information required pursuant to such section or includes incorrect information,

the person required to file such notice or return shall pay a penalty equal to the greater of $10,000 or 35 percent of the gross reportable amount. If any failure described in the preceding sentence continues for more than 90 days after the day on which the Secretary mails notice of such failure to the person required to pay such penalty, such person shall pay a penalty (in addition to the amount determined under the preceding sentence) of $10,000 for each 30-day period (or fraction thereof) during which such failure continues after the expiration of such 90-day period. At such time as the gross reportable amount with respect to any failure can be determined by the Secretary, any subsequent penalty imposed under this subsection with respect to such failure shall be reduced as necessary to assure that the aggregate amount of such penalties do not exceed the gross reportable amount (and to the extent that such aggregate amount already exceeds the gross reportable amount the Secretary shall refund such excess to the taxpayer).

(b) Special rules for returns under section 6048(b).—In the case of a return required under section 6048(b)—

(1) the United States person referred to in such section shall be liable for the penalty imposed by subsection (a), and

(2) subsection (a) shall be applied by substituting "5 percent" for "35 percent".

(c) Gross reportable amount.—For purposes of subsection (a), the term "gross reportable amount" means—

(1) the gross value of the property involved in the event (determined as of the date of the event) in the case of a failure relating to section 6048(a),

(2) the gross value of the portion of the trust's assets at the close of the year treated as owned by the United States person in the case of a failure relating to section 6048(b)(1), and

(3) the gross amount of the distributions in the case of a failure relating to section 6048(c).

(d) Reasonable cause exception.—No penalty shall be imposed by this section on any failure which is shown to be due to reasonable cause and not due to willful neglect. The fact that a foreign jurisdiction would impose a civil or criminal penalty on the taxpayer (or any other person) for disclosing the required information is not reasonable cause.

(e) Deficiency procedures not to apply.—Subchapter B of chapter 63 (relating to deficiency procedures for income, estate, gift, and certain excise taxes) shall not apply in respect of the assessment or collection of any penalty imposed by subsection (a).

§ 6679. Failure to file returns, etc., with respect to foreign corporations or foreign partnerships

(a) Civil penalty.—

(1) In general.—In addition to any criminal penalty provided by law, any person required to file a return under section 6046 or 6046A who fails to file such return at the time provided in such section, or who files a return which does not show the information required pursuant to such section, shall pay a penalty of $10,000, unless it is shown that such failure is due to reasonable cause.

(2) Increase in penalty where failure continues after notification.—If any failure described in paragraph (1) continues for more than 90 days after the day on which the Secretary mails notice of such failure to the United States person, such person shall pay a penalty (in addition to the amount required under paragraph (1)) of $10,000 for each 30-day period (or fraction thereof) during which such failure continues after the expiration of such 90-day period. The increase in any penalty under this paragraph shall not exceed $50,000.

(b) Deficiency procedures not to apply.—Subchapter B of chapter 63 (relating to deficiency procedure for income, estate, gift, and certain excise taxes) shall not apply in respect of the assessment or collection of any penalty imposed by subsection (a).

§ 6707A. Penalty for failure to include reportable transaction information with return

(a) Imposition of penalty.—Any person who fails to include on any return or statement any information with respect to a reportable transaction which is required under section 6011 to be included with such return or statement shall pay a penalty in the amount determined under subsection (b).

(b) Amount of penalty.—

(1) In general.—Except as otherwise provided in this subsection, the amount of the penalty under subsection (a) with respect to any reportable transaction shall be 75 percent of the decrease in tax shown on the return as a result of such transaction (or which would have resulted from such transaction if such transaction were respected for Federal tax purposes).

(2) Maximum penalty.—The amount of the penalty under subsection (a) with respect to any reportable transaction shall not exceed—

(A) in the case of a listed transaction, $200,000 ($100,000 in the case of a natural person), or

(B) in the case of any other reportable transaction, $50,000 ($10,000 in the case of a natural person).

(3) Minimum penalty.—The amount of the penalty under subsection (a) with respect to any transaction shall not be less than $10,000 ($5,000 in the case of a natural person).

(c) Definitions.—For purposes of this section:

(1) Reportable transaction.—The term "reportable transaction" means any transaction with respect to which information is required to be included with a return or statement because, as determined under regulations prescribed under section 6011, such transaction is of a type which the Secretary determines as having a potential for tax avoidance or evasion.

(2) Listed transaction.—The term "listed transaction" means a reportable transaction which is the same as, or substantially similar to, a transaction specifically identified by the Secretary as a tax avoidance transaction for purposes of section 6011.

(d) Authority to rescind penalty.—

(1) In general.—The Commissioner of Internal Revenue may rescind all or any portion of any penalty imposed by this section with respect to any violation if—

(A) the violation is with respect to a reportable transaction other than a listed transaction, and

(B) rescinding the penalty would promote compliance with the requirements of this title and effective tax administration.

(2) No judicial appeal.—Notwithstanding any other provision of law, any determination under this subsection may not be reviewed in any judicial proceeding.

(3) Records.—If a penalty is rescinded under paragraph (1), the Commissioner shall place in the file in the Office of the Commissioner the opinion of the Commissioner with respect to the determination, including—

(A) a statement of the facts and circumstances relating to the violation,

(B) the reasons for the rescission, and

(C) the amount of the penalty rescinded.

(e) Penalty reported to SEC.—In the case of a person—

(1) which is required to file periodic reports under section 13 or 15(d) of the Securities Exchange Act of 1934 or is required to be consolidated with another person for purposes of such reports, and

(2) which—

(A) is required to pay a penalty under this section with respect to a listed transaction,

(B) is required to pay a penalty under section 6662A with respect to any reportable transaction at a rate prescribed under section 6662A(c), or

(C) is required to pay a penalty under section 6662(h) with respect to any reportable transaction and would (but for section 6662A(e)(2)(C)) have been subject to penalty under section 6662A at a rate prescribed under section 6662A(c),

the requirement to pay such penalty shall be disclosed in such reports filed by such person for such periods as the Secretary shall specify. Failure to make a disclosure in accordance with the preceding sentence shall be treated as a failure to which the penalty under subsection (b)(2) applies.

(f) Coordination with other penalties.—The penalty imposed by this section shall be in addition to any other penalty imposed by this title.

§ 6712. Failure to disclose treaty-based return positions

(a) General rule.—If a taxpayer fails to meet the requirements of section 6114, there is hereby imposed a penalty equal to $1,000 ($10,000 in the case of a C corporation) on each such failure.

(b) Authority to waive.—The Secretary may waive all or any part of the penalty provided by this section on a showing by the taxpayer that there was reasonable cause for the failure and that the taxpayer acted in good faith.

(c) Penalty in addition to other penalties.—The penalty imposed by this section shall be in addition to any other penalty imposed by law.

Chapter 75—Crimes, Other Offenses, and Forfeitures

Subchapter A—Crimes

Part I—General Provisions

§ 7203. Willful failure to file return, supply information, or pay tax

Any person required under this title to pay any estimated tax or tax, or required by this title or by regulations made under authority thereof to make a return, keep any records, or supply any information, who willfully fails to pay such estimated tax or tax, make such return, keep such records, or supply such information, at the time or times required by law or regulations, shall, in addition to other penalties provided by law, be guilty of a misdemeanor and, upon conviction thereof, shall be fined not more than $25,000 ($100,000 in the case of a corporation), or imprisoned not more than 1 year, or both, together with the costs of prosecution. In the case of any person with respect to whom there is a failure to pay any estimated tax, this section shall not apply to such person with respect to such failure if there is no addition to tax under section 6654 or 6655 with respect to such failure. In the case of a willful violation of any provision of section 6050I, the first sentence of this section shall be applied by substituting "felony" for "misdemeanor" and "5 years" for "1 year".

Subchapter D—Miscellaneous Penalty and Forfeiture Provisions

§ 7345. Revocation or denial of passport in case of certain tax delinquencies

(a) In general.—If the Secretary receives certification by the Commissioner of Internal Revenue that an individual has a seriously delinquent tax debt, the Secretary shall transmit such certification to the Secretary of State for action with respect to denial, revocation, or limitation of a passport pursuant to section 32101 of the FAST Act.

(b) Seriously delinquent tax debt.—

(1) In general.—For purposes of this section, the term "seriously delinquent tax debt" means an unpaid, legally enforceable Federal tax liability of an individual—

(A) which has been assessed,

(B) which is greater than $50,000, and

(C) with respect to which—

(i) a notice of lien has been filed pursuant to section 6323 and the administrative rights under section 6320 with respect to such filing have been exhausted or have lapsed, or

(ii) a levy is made pursuant to section 6331.

(2) Exceptions.—Such term shall not include—

(A) a debt that is being paid in a timely manner pursuant to an agreement to which the individual is party under section 6159 or 7122, and

(B) a debt with respect to which collection is suspended with respect to the individual—

(i) because a due process hearing under section 6330 is requested or pending, or

(ii) because an election under subsection (b) or (c) of section 6015 is made or relief under subsection (f) of such section is requested.

(c) Reversal of certification.—

(1) In general.—In the case of an individual with respect to whom the Commissioner makes a certification under subsection (a), the Commissioner shall notify the Secretary (and the Secretary shall subsequently notify the Secretary of State) if such certification is found to be erroneous or if the debt with respect to such certification is fully satisfied or ceases to be a seriously delinquent tax debt by reason of subsection (b)(2).

(2) Timing of notice.—

(A) Full satisfaction of debt.—In the case of a debt that has been fully satisfied or has become legally unenforceable, such notification shall be made not later than the date required for issuing the certificate of release of lien with respect to such debt under section 6325(a).

(B) Innocent spouse relief.—In the case of an individual who makes an election under subsection (b) or (c) of section 6015, or requests relief under subsection (f) of such section, such notification shall be made not later than 30 days after any such election or request.

(C) Installment agreement or offer-in-compromise.—In the case of an installment agreement under section 6159 or an offer-in-compromise under section 7122, such notification shall be made not later than 30 days after such agreement is entered into or such offer is accepted by the Secretary.

(D) Erroneous certification.—In the case of a certification found to be erroneous, such notification shall be made as soon as practicable after such finding.

(d) Contemporaneous notice to individual.—The Commissioner shall contemporaneously notify an individual of any certification under subsection (a), or any reversal of certification under subsection (c), with respect to such individual. Such notice shall include a description in simple and nontechnical terms of the right to bring a civil action under subsection (e).

(e) Judicial review of certification.—

(1) In general.—After the Commissioner notifies an individual under subsection (d), the taxpayer may bring a civil action against the United States in a district court of the United States, or against the Commission in the Tax Court, to determine whether the certification was erroneous or whether the Commissioner has failed to reverse the certification. For purposes of the preceding sentence, the court first acquiring jurisdiction over such an action shall have sole jurisdiction.

(2) Determination.—If the court determines that such certification was erroneous, then the court may order the Secretary to notify the Secretary of State that such certification was erroneous.

(f) Adjustment for inflation.—In the case of a calendar year beginning after 2016, the dollar amount in subsection (b)(1)(B) shall be increased by an amount equal to—

(1) such dollar amount, multiplied by

(2) the cost-of-living adjustment determined under section 1(f)(3) for the calendar year, determined by substituting 'calendar year 2015' for 'calendar year 2016' in subparagraph (A)(ii) thereof.

If any amount as adjusted under the preceding sentence is not a multiple of $1,000, such amount shall be rounded to the nearest multiple of $1,000.

(g) Delegation of certification.—A certification under subsection (a) or reversal of certification under subsection (c) may only be delegated by the Commissioner of Internal Revenue to the Deputy Commissioner for Services and Enforcement, or the Commissioner of an operating division, of the Internal Revenue Service.

Chapter 79—Definitions

§ 7701. Definitions

(a) When used in this title, where not otherwise distinctly expressed or manifestly incompatible with the intent thereof—

(1) Person.—The term "person" shall be construed to mean and include an individual, a trust, estate, partnership, association, company or corporation.

(2) Partnership and partner.—The term "partnership" includes a syndicate, group, pool, joint venture, or other unincorporated organization, through or by means of which any business, financial operation, or venture is carried on, and which is not, within the meaning of this title, a trust or estate or a corporation; and the term "partner" includes a member in such a syndicate, group, pool, joint venture, or organization.

(3) Corporation.—The term "corporation" includes associations, joint-stock companies, and insurance companies.

(4) Domestic.—The term "domestic" when applied to a corporation or partnership means created or organized in the United States or under the law of the United States or of any State unless, in the case of a partnership, the Secretary provides otherwise by regulations.

(5) Foreign.—The term "foreign" when applied to a corporation or partnership means a corporation or partnership which is not domestic.

* * *

(9) United States.—The term "United States" when used in a geographical sense includes only the States and the District of Columbia.

(10) State.—The term "State" shall be construed to include the District of Columbia, where such construction is necessary to carry out provisions of this title.

* * *

(18) International organization.—The term "international organization" means a public international organization entitled to enjoy privileges, exemptions, and immunities as an international organization under the International Organizations Immunities Act (22 U.S.C. 288–288f).

* * *

(30) United States person.—The term "United States person" means—

(A) a citizen or resident of the United States,

(B) a domestic partnership,

(C) a domestic corporation,

(D) any estate (other than a foreign estate, within the meaning of paragraph (31)), and

(E) any trust if—

(i) a court within the United States is able to exercise primary supervision over the administration of the trust, and

(ii) one or more United States persons have the authority to control all substantial decisions of the trust.

(31) Foreign estate or trust.—

(A) Foreign estate.—The term "foreign estate" means an estate the income of which, from sources without the United States which is not effectively connected with the conduct of a trade or business within the United States, is not includible in gross income under subtitle A.

(B) Foreign trust.—The term "foreign trust" means any trust other than a trust described in subparagraph (E) of paragraph (30).

* * *

(50) Termination of United States citizenship.—

(A) In general.—An individual shall not cease to be treated as a United States citizen before the date on which the individual's citizenship is treated as relinquished under section 877A(g)(4).

(B) Dual citizens.—Under regulations prescribed by the Secretary, subparagraph (A) shall not apply to an individual who became at birth a citizen of the United States and a citizen of another country.

(b) Definition of resident alien and nonresident alien.—

(1) In general.—For purposes of this title (other than subtitle B)—

(A) Resident alien.—An alien individual shall be treated as a resident of the United States with respect to any calendar year if (and only if) such individual meets the requirements of clause (i), (ii), or (iii):

(i) Lawfully admitted for permanent residence.—Such individual is a lawful permanent resident of the United States at any time during such calendar year.

(ii) Substantial presence test.—Such individual meets the substantial presence test of paragraph (3).

(iii) First year election.—Such individual makes the election provided in paragraph (4).

(B) Nonresident alien.—An individual is a nonresident alien if such individual is neither a citizen of the United States nor a resident of the United States (within the meaning of subparagraph (A)).

(2) Special rules for first and last year of residency.—

(A) First year of residency.—

(i) In general.—If an alien individual is a resident of the United States under paragraph (1)(A) with respect to any calendar year, but was not a resident of the United States at any time during the preceding calendar year, such alien individual shall be treated as a resident of the United States only for the portion of such calendar year which begins on the residency starting date.

(ii) Residency starting date for individuals lawfully admitted for permanent residence.—In the case of an individual who is a lawfully permanent resident of the United States at any time during the calendar year, but does not meet the substantial presence test of paragraph (3), the residency starting date shall be the first day in such calendar year on which he was present in the United States while a lawful permanent resident of the United States.

(iii) Residency starting date for individuals meeting substantial presence test.—In the case of an individual who meets the substantial presence test of paragraph (3) with respect to any calendar year, the residency starting date shall be the first day during such calendar year on which the individual is present in the United States.

(iv) Residency starting date for individuals making first year election.—In the case of an individual who makes the election provided by paragraph (4) with respect to any calendar year, the residency starting date shall be the 1st day during such calendar year on which the individual is treated as a resident of the United States under that paragraph.

(B) Last year of residency.—An alien individual shall not be treated as a resident of the United States during a portion of any calendar year if—

(i) such portion is after the last day in such calendar year on which the individual was present in the United States (or, in the case of an individual described in paragraph (1)(A)(i), the last day on which he was so described),

(ii) during such portion the individual has a closer connection to a foreign country than to the United States, and

(iii) the individual is not a resident of the United States at any time during the next calendar year.

(C) Certain nominal presence disregarded.—

(i) In general.—For purposes of subparagraphs (A)(iii) and (B), an individual shall not be treated as present in the United States during any period for which the individual establishes that he has a closer connection to a foreign country than to the United States.

(ii) Not more than 10 days disregarded.—Clause (i) shall not apply to more than 10 days on which the individual is present in the United States.

(3) Substantial presence test.—

(A) In general.—Except as otherwise provided in this paragraph, an individual meets the substantial presence test of this paragraph with respect to any calendar year (hereinafter in this subsection referred to as the "current year") if—

(i) such individual was present in the United States on at least 31 days during the calendar year, and

(ii) the sum of the number of days on which such individual was present in the United States during the current year and the 2 preceding calendar years (when multiplied by the applicable multiplier determined under the following table) equals or exceeds 183 days:

In the case of days in:	*The applicable multiplier is:*
Current year	1
1st preceding year	1/3
2nd preceding year	1/6

(B) Exception where individual is present in the United States during less than one-half of current year and closer connection to foreign country is established.—An individual shall not be treated as meeting the substantial presence test of this paragraph with respect to any current year if—

(i) such individual is present in the United States on fewer than 183 days during the current year, and

(ii) it is established that for the current year such individual has a tax home (as defined in section 911(d)(3) without regard to the second sentence thereof) in a foreign country and has a closer connection to such foreign country than to the United States.

(C) Subparagraph (B) not to apply in certain cases.—Subparagraph (B) shall not apply to any individual with respect to any current year if at any time during such year—

(i) such individual had an application for adjustment of status pending, or

(ii) such individual took other steps to apply for status as a lawful permanent resident of the United States.

(D) Exception for exempt individuals or for certain medical conditions.—An individual shall not be treated as being present in the United States on any day if—

(i) such individual is an exempt individual for such day, or

(ii) such individual was unable to leave the United States on such day because of a medical condition which arose while such individual was present in the United States.

(4) First-year election.—

(A) An alien individual shall be deemed to meet the requirements of this subparagraph if such individual—

(i) is not a resident of the United States under clause (i) or (ii) of paragraph (1)(A) with respect to a calendar year (hereinafter referred to as the "election year"),

(ii) was not a resident of the United States under paragraph (1)(A) with respect to the calendar year immediately preceding the election year,

(iii) is a resident of the United States under clause (ii) of paragraph (1)(A) with respect to the calendar year immediately following the election year, and

(iv) is both—

(I) present in the United States for a period of at least 31 consecutive days in the election year, and

(II) present in the United States during the period beginning with the first day of such 31-day period and ending with the last day of the election year (hereinafter referred to as the "testing period") for a number of days equal to or exceeding 75 percent of the number of days in the testing period (provided that an individual shall be treated for purposes of this subclause as present in the United States for a number of days during the testing period not exceeding 5 days in the aggregate, notwithstanding his absence from the United States on such days).

(B) An alien individual who meets the requirements of subparagraph (A) shall, if he so elects, be treated as a resident of the United States with respect to the election year.

(C) An alien individual who makes the election provided by subparagraph (B) shall be treated as a resident of the United States for the portion of the election year which begins on the 1st day of the earliest testing period during such year with respect to which the individual meets the requirements of clause (iv) of subparagraph (A).

(D) The rules of subparagraph (D)(i) of paragraph (3) shall apply for purposes of determining an individual's presence in the United States under this paragraph.

(E) An election under subparagraph (B) shall be made on the individual's tax return for the election year, provided that such election may not be made before the individual has met the substantial presence test of paragraph (3) with respect to the calendar year immediately following the election year.

(F) An election once made under subparagraph (B) remains in effect for the election year, unless revoked with the consent of the Secretary.

(5) Exempt individual defined.—For purposes of this subsection—

(A) In general.—An individual is an exempt individual for any day if, for such day, such individual is—

(i) a foreign government-related individual,

(ii) a teacher or trainee,

(iii) a student, or

(iv) a professional athlete who is temporarily in the United States to compete in a sports event—

(I) which is organized for the primary purpose of benefiting an organization which is described in section 501(c)(3) and exempt from tax under section 501(a),

(II) all of the net proceeds of which are contributed to such organization, and,

(III) which utilizes volunteers for substantially all of the work performed in carrying out such event.

(B) Foreign government-related individual.—The term "foreign government-related individual" means any individual temporarily present in the United States by reason of—

(i) diplomatic status, or a visa which the Secretary (after consultation with the Secretary of State) determines represents full-time diplomatic or consular status for purposes of this subsection,

(ii) being a full-time employee of an international organization, or

(iii) being a member of the immediate family of an individual described in clause (i) or (ii).

(C) Teacher or trainee.—The term "teacher or trainee" means any individual—

(i) who is temporarily present in the United States under subparagraph (J) or (Q) of section 101(15) of the Immigration and Nationality Act (other than as a student), and

(ii) who substantially complies with the requirements for being so present.

(D) Student.—The term "student" means any individual—

(i) who is temporarily present in the United States—

(I) under subparagraph (F) or (M) of section 101(15) of the Immigration and Nationality Act, or

(II) as a student under subparagraph (J) or (Q) of such section 101(15), and

(ii) who substantially complies with the requirements for being so present.

(E) Special rules for teachers, trainees, and students.—

(i) Limitation on teachers and trainees.—An individual shall not be treated as an exempt individual by reason of clause (ii) of subparagraph (A) for the current year if, for any 2 calendar years during the preceding 6 calendar years, such person was an exempt person under clause (ii) or (iii) of subparagraph (A). In the case of an individual all of whose compensation is described in section 872(b)(3), the preceding sentence shall be applied by substituting "4 calendar years" for "2 calendar years".

(ii) Limitation on students.—For any calendar year after the 5th calendar year for which an individual was an exempt individual under clause (ii) or (iii) of subparagraph (A), such individual shall not be treated as an exempt individual by reason of clause

(iii) of subparagraph (A), unless such individual establishes to the satisfaction of the Secretary that such individual does not intend to permanently reside in the United States and that such individual meets the requirements of subparagraph (D)(ii).

(6) Lawful permanent resident.—For purposes of this subsection, an individual is a lawful permanent resident of the United States at any time if—

(A) such individual has the status of having been lawfully accorded the privilege of residing permanently in the United States as an immigrant in accordance with the immigration laws, and

(B) such status has not been revoked (and has not been administratively or judicially determined to have been abandoned).

An individual shall cease to be treated as a lawful permanent resident of the United States if such individual commences to be treated as a resident of a foreign country under the provisions of a tax treaty between the United States and the foreign country, does not waive the benefits of such treaty applicable to residents of the foreign country, and notifies the Secretary of the commencement of such treatment.

(7) Presence in the United States.—For purposes of this subsection—

(A) In general.—Except as provided in subparagraph (B), (C), or (D) an individual shall be treated as present in the United States on any day if such individual is physically present in the United States at any time during such day.

(B) Commuters from Canada or Mexico.—If an individual regularly commutes to employment (or self-employment) in the United States from a place of residence in Canada or Mexico, such individual shall not be treated as present in the United States on any day during which he so commutes.

(C) Transit between 2 foreign points.—If an individual, who is in transit between 2 points outside the United States, is physically present in the United States for less than 24 hours, such individual shall not be treated as present in the United States on any day during such transit.

(D) Crew members temporarily present.—An individual who is temporarily present in the United States on any day as a regular member of the crew of a foreign vessel engaged in transportation between the United States and a foreign country or a possession of the United States shall not be treated as present in the United States on such day unless such individual otherwise engages in any trade or business in the United States on such day.

(8) Annual statements.—The Secretary may prescribe regulations under which an individual who (but for subparagraph (B) or (D) of paragraph (3)) would meet the substantial presence test of paragraph (3) is required to submit an annual statement setting forth the basis on which such individual claims the benefits of subparagraph (B) or (D) of paragraph (3), as the case may be.

(9) Taxable year.—

(A) In general.—For purposes of this title, an alien individual who has not established a taxable year for any prior period shall be treated as having a taxable year which is the calendar year.

(B) Fiscal year taxpayer.—If—

(i) an individual is treated under paragraph (1) as a resident of the United States for any calendar year, and

(ii) after the application of subparagraph (A), such individual has a taxable year other than a calendar year,

he shall be treated as a resident of the United States with respect to any portion of a taxable year which is within such calendar year.

(10) Coordination with section 877.—If—

(A) an alien individual was treated as a resident of the United States during any period which includes at least 3 consecutive calendar years (hereinafter referred to as the "initial residency period"), and

(B) such individual ceases to be treated as a resident of the United States but subsequently becomes a resident of the United States before the close of the 3rd calendar year beginning after the close of the initial residency period,

such individual shall be taxable for the period after the close of the initial residency period and before the day on which he subsequently became a resident of the United States in the manner provided in section 877(b). The preceding sentence shall apply only if the tax imposed pursuant to section 877(b) exceeds the tax which, without regard to this paragraph, is imposed pursuant to section 871.

(11) Regulations.—The Secretary shall prescribe such regulations as may be necessary or appropriate to carry out the purposes of this subsection.

* * *

(*l*) Regulations relating to conduit arrangements.—The Secretary may prescribe regulations recharacterizing any multiple-party financing transaction as a transaction directly among any 2 or more of such parties where the Secretary determines that such recharacterization is appropriate to prevent avoidance of any tax imposed by this title.

* * *

(*o*) Clarification of Economic Substance Doctrine.—

(1) Application of doctrine.—In the case of any transaction to which the economic substance doctrine is relevant, such transaction shall be treated as having economic substance only if—

(A) the transaction changes in a meaningful way (apart from Federal income tax effects) the taxpayer's economic position, and

(B) the taxpayer has a substantial purpose (apart from Federal income tax effects) for entering into such transaction.

(2) Special rule where taxpayer relies on profit potential.—

(A) In general.—The potential for profit of a transaction shall be taken into account in determining whether the requirements of subparagraphs (A) and (B) of paragraph (1) are met with respect to the transaction only if the present value of the reasonably expected pre-tax profit from the transaction is substantial in relation to the present value of the expected net tax benefits that would be allowed if the transaction were respected.

(B) Treatment of fees and foreign taxes.—Fees and other transaction expenses shall be taken into account as expenses in determining pre-tax profit under subparagraph (A). The Secretary shall issue regulations requiring foreign taxes to be treated as expenses in determining pre-tax profit in appropriate cases.

(3) State and local tax benefits.—For purposes of paragraph (1), any State or local income tax effect which is related to a Federal income tax effect shall be treated in the same manner as a Federal income tax effect.

(4) Financial accounting benefits.—For purposes of paragraph (1)(B), achieving a financial accounting benefit shall not be taken into account as a purpose for entering into a transaction if the origin of such financial accounting benefit is a reduction of Federal income tax.

(5) Definitions and special rules.—For purposes of this subsection—

(A) Economic substance doctrine.—The term "economic substance doctrine" means the common law doctrine under which tax benefits under subtitle A with respect to a transaction are not allowable if the transaction does not have economic substance or lacks a business purpose.

(B) Exception for personal transactions of individuals.—In the case of an individual, paragraph (1) shall apply only to transactions entered into in connection with a trade or business or an activity engaged in for the production of income.

(C) Determination of application of doctrine not affected.—The determination of whether the economic substance doctrine is relevant to a transaction shall be made in the same manner as if this subsection had never been enacted.

(D) Transaction.—The term "transaction" includes a series of transactions.

* * *

Chapter 80—General Rules

Subchapter B—Effective Date and Related Provisions

§ 7852. Other applicable rules

* * *

(d) Treaty obligations.—

(1) In general.—For purposes of determining the relationship between a provision of a treaty and any law of the United States affecting revenue, neither the treaty nor the law shall have preferential status by reason of its being a treaty or law.

(2) Savings clause for 1954 treaties.—No provision of this title (as in effect without regard to any amendment thereto enacted after August 16, 1954) shall apply in any case where its application would be contrary to any treaty obligation of the United States in effect on August 16, 1954.

* * *

Subchapter C—Provisions Affecting More Than One Subtitle

§ 7874. Rules relating to expatriated entities and their foreign parents

(a) Tax on inversion gain of expatriated entities.—

(1) In general.—The taxable income of an expatriated entity for any taxable year which includes any portion of the applicable period shall in no event be less than the inversion gain of the entity for the taxable year.

(2) Expatriated entity.—For purposes of this subsection—

(A) In general.—The term "expatriated entity" means—

(i) the domestic corporation or partnership referred to in subparagraph (B)(i) with respect to which a foreign corporation is a surrogate foreign corporation, and

(ii) any United States person who is related (within the meaning of section 267(b) or 707(b)(1)) to a domestic corporation or partnership described in clause (i).

(B) Surrogate foreign corporation.—A foreign corporation shall be treated as a surrogate foreign corporation if, pursuant to a plan (or a series of related transactions)—

(i) the entity completes after March 4, 2003, the direct or indirect acquisition of substantially all of the properties held directly or indirectly by a domestic corporation or substantially all of the properties constituting a trade or business of a domestic partnership,

(ii) after the acquisition at least 60 percent of the stock (by vote or value) of the entity is held—

(I) in the case of an acquisition with respect to a domestic corporation, by former shareholders of the domestic corporation by reason of holding stock in the domestic corporation, or

(II) in the case of an acquisition with respect to a domestic partnership, by former partners of the domestic partnership by reason of holding a capital or profits interest in the domestic partnership, and

(iii) after the acquisition the expanded affiliated group which includes the entity does not have substantial business activities in the foreign country in which, or under the law of which, the entity is created or organized, when compared to the total business activities of such expanded affiliated group.

An entity otherwise described in clause (i) with respect to any domestic corporation or partnership trade or business shall be treated as not so described if, on or before March 4, 2003, such entity acquired directly or indirectly more than half of the properties held directly or indirectly by such corporation or more than half of the properties constituting such partnership trade or business, as the case may be.

(3) Coordination with subsection (b).—A corporation which is treated as a domestic corporation under subsection (b) shall not be treated as a surrogate foreign corporation for purposes of paragraph (2)(A).

(b) Inverted corporations treated as domestic corporations.—Notwithstanding section 7701(a)(4), a foreign corporation shall be treated for purposes of this title as a domestic corporation if such corporation would be a surrogate foreign corporation if subsection (a)(2) were applied by substituting "80 percent" for "60 percent".

(c) Definitions and special rules.—

(1) Expanded affiliated group.—The term "expanded affiliated group" means an affiliated group as defined in section 1504(a) but without regard to section 1504(b)(3), except that section 1504(a) shall be applied by substituting "more than 50 percent" for "at least 80 percent" each place it appears.

(2) Certain stock disregarded.—There shall not be taken into account in determining ownership under subsection (a)(2)(B)(ii)—

(A) stock held by members of the expanded affiliated group which includes the foreign corporation, or

(B) stock of such foreign corporation which is sold in a public offering related to the acquisition described in subsection (a)(2)(B)(i).

(3) Plan deemed in certain cases.—If a foreign corporation acquires directly or indirectly substantially all of the properties of a domestic corporation or partnership during the 4-year period beginning on the date which is 2 years before the ownership requirements of subsection (a)(2)(B)(ii) are met, such actions shall be treated as pursuant to a plan.

(4) Certain transfers disregarded.—The transfer of properties or liabilities (including by contribution or distribution) shall be disregarded if such transfers are part of a plan a principal purpose of which is to avoid the purposes of this section.

(5) Special rule for related partnerships.—For purposes of applying subsection (a)(2)(B)(ii) to the acquisition of a trade or business of a domestic partnership, except as provided in regulations, all partnerships which are under common control (within the meaning of section 482) shall be treated as 1 partnership.

(6) Regulations.—The Secretary shall prescribe such regulations as may be appropriate to determine whether a corporation is a surrogate foreign corporation, including regulations—

(A) to treat warrants, options, contracts to acquire stock, convertible debt interests, and other similar interests as stock, and

(B) to treat stock as not stock.

(d) Other definitions.—For purposes of this section—

(1) Applicable period.—The term "applicable period" means the period—

(A) beginning on the first date properties are acquired as part of the acquisition described in subsection (a)(2)(B)(i), and

(B) ending on the date which is 10 years after the last date properties are acquired as part of such acquisition.

(2) Inversion gain.—The term "inversion gain" means the income or gain recognized by reason of the transfer during the applicable period of stock or other properties by an expatriated entity, and any income received or accrued during the applicable period by reason of a license of any property by an expatriated entity—

(A) as part of the acquisition described in subsection (a)(2)(B)(i), or

(B) after such acquisition if the transfer or license is to a foreign related person.

Subparagraph (B) shall not apply to property described in section 1221(a)(1) in the hands of the expatriated entity.

(3) Foreign related person.—The term "foreign related person" means, with respect to any expatriated entity, a foreign person which—

(A) is related (within the meaning of section 267(b) or 707(b)(1)) to such entity, or

(B) is under the same common control (within the meaning of section 482) as such entity.

(e) Special rules.—

(1) Credits not allowed against tax on inversion gain.—Credits (other than the credit allowed by section 901) shall be allowed against the tax imposed by this chapter on an expatriated entity for any taxable year described in subsection (a) only to the extent such tax exceeds the product of—

(A) the amount of the inversion gain for the taxable year, and

(B) the highest rate of tax specified in section 11(b).

For purposes of determining the credit allowed by section 901, inversion gain shall be treated as from sources within the United States.

(2) Special rules for partnerships.—In the case of an expatriated entity which is a partnership—

(A) subsection (a)(1) shall apply at the partner rather than the partnership level,

(B) the inversion gain of any partner for any taxable year shall be equal to the sum of—

(i) the partner's distributive share of inversion gain of the partnership for such taxable year, plus

(ii) gain recognized for the taxable year by the partner by reason of the transfer during the applicable period of any partnership interest of the partner in such partnership to the surrogate foreign corporation, and

(C) the highest rate of tax specified in the rate schedule applicable to the partner under this chapter shall be substituted for the rate of tax referred to in paragraph (1).

(3) Coordination with section 172 and minimum tax.—Rules similar to the rules of paragraphs (3) and (4) of section 860E(a) shall apply for purposes of subsection (a).

(4) Statute of limitations.—

(A) In general.—The statutory period for the assessment of any deficiency attributable to the inversion gain of any taxpayer for any pre-inversion year shall not expire before the expiration of 3 years from the date the Secretary is notified by the taxpayer (in such manner as the Secretary may prescribe) of the acquisition described in subsection (a)(2)(B)(i) to which such gain relates and such deficiency may be assessed before the expiration of such 3-year period notwithstanding the provisions of any other law or rule of law which would otherwise prevent such assessment.

(B) Pre-inversion year.—For purposes of subparagraph (A), the term "pre-inversion year" means any taxable year if—

(i) any portion of the applicable period is included in such taxable year, and

(ii) such year ends before the taxable year in which the acquisition described in subsection (a)(2)(B)(i) is completed.

(f) Special rule for treaties.—Nothing in section 894 or 7852(d) or in any other provision of law shall be construed as permitting an exemption, by reason of any treaty obligation of the United States heretofore or hereafter entered into, from the provisions of this section.

(g) Regulations.—The Secretary shall provide such regulations as are necessary to carry out this section, including regulations providing for such adjustments to the application of this section as are necessary to prevent the avoidance of the purposes of this section, including the avoidance of such purposes through—

(1) the use of related persons, pass-through or other noncorporate entities, or other intermediaries, or

(2) transactions designed to have persons cease to be (or not become) members of expanded affiliated groups or related persons.

Treasury Regulations

Income Taxes

Determination of Tax Liability

§ 1.1–1 Income tax on individuals.

* * *

(b) Citizens or residents of the United States liable to tax. In general, all citizens of the United States, wherever resident, and all resident alien individuals are liable to the income taxes imposed by the Code whether the income is received from sources within or without the United States. Pursuant to section 876, a nonresident alien individual who is a bona fide resident of a section 931 possession (as defined in § 1.931–1(c)(i) of this chapter) or Puerto Rico during the entire taxable year is, except as provided in section 931 or 933 with respect to Puerto Rican source income, subject to taxation in the same manner as a resident alien individual. As to tax on nonresident alien individuals, see sections 871 and 877.

(c) Who is a citizen. Every person born or naturalized in the United States and subject to its jurisdiction is a citizen. For other rules governing the acquisition of citizenship, see chapters 1 and 2 of title III of the Immigration and Nationality Act (8 U.S.C. 1401–1459). For rules governing loss of citizenship, see sections 349 to 357, inclusive, of such Act (8 U.S.C. 1481–1489), Schneider v. Rusk, (1964) 377 U.S. 163, and Rev. Rul. 70–506, C.B. 1970–2, 1. For rules pertaining to persons who are nationals but not citizens at birth, e.g., a person born in American Samoa, see section 308 of such Act (8 U.S.C. 1408). For special rules applicable to certain expatriates who have lost citizenship with a principal purpose of avoiding certain taxes, see section 877. A foreigner who has filed his declaration of intention of becoming a citizen but who has not yet been admitted to citizenship by a final order of a naturalization court is an alien.

[T.D. 6500, 25 FR 11402, Nov. 26, 1960, as amended by T.D. 7117, 36 FR 9396, May 25, 1971; T.D. 7332, 39 FR 44216, Dec. 23, 1974; T.D. 9391, 73 FR 19358, April 9, 2008]

§ 1.245A(d)–1 Disallowance of foreign tax credit or deduction.

(a) No foreign tax credit or deduction allowed under section 245A(d)—(1) Foreign income taxes paid or accrued by domestic corporations or successors. No credit under section 901 or deduction is allowed in any taxable year for:

(i) Foreign income taxes paid or accrued by a domestic corporation that are attributable to section 245A(d) income of the domestic corporation;

(ii) Foreign income taxes paid or accrued by a successor to a domestic corporation that are attributable to section 245A(d) income of the successor; and

(iii) Foreign income taxes paid or accrued by a domestic corporation that is a United States shareholder of a foreign corporation, other than a foreign corporation that is a passive foreign investment company (as defined in section 1297) with respect to the domestic corporation and that is not a controlled foreign corporation, that are attributable to non-inclusion income of the foreign corporation and are not otherwise disallowed under paragraph (a)(1)(i) or (ii) of this section.

(2) Foreign income taxes paid or accrued by foreign corporations. No credit under section 901 or deduction is allowed in any taxable year for foreign income taxes paid or accrued by a foreign corporation that are attributable to section 245A(d) income, and such taxes are not eligible to be deemed paid under section 960 in any taxable year.

(3) Effect of disallowance on earnings and profits. The disallowance of a credit or deduction for foreign income taxes under this paragraph (a) does not affect whether the foreign income taxes reduce earnings and profits of a corporation.

* * *

[T.D. 9959, 87 FR 317, Jan. 4, 2022; 87 FR 45018, July 27, 2022]

§ 1.250(b)–4 Foreign-derived deduction eligible income (FDDEI) sales.

* * *

(b) Definition of FDDEI sale. Except as provided in § 1.250(b)–6(c), the term FDDEI sale means a sale of general property or intangible property to a recipient that is a foreign person (see paragraph (c) of this section for presumption rules relating to determining foreign person status) and that is for a foreign use (as determined under paragraph (d) of this section). A sale of any property other than general property or intangible property is not a FDDEI sale.

(c) Presumption of foreign person status—(1) In general. The sale of property is presumed to be to a recipient that is a foreign person for purposes of paragraph (b) of this section if the sale is described in paragraph (c)(2) of this section. However, this presumption does not apply if the seller knows or has reason to know that the sale is not to a foreign person. A seller has reason to know that a sale is not to a foreign person if the information received as part of the sales process contains information that indicates that the recipient is not a foreign person and the seller fails to obtain evidence establishing that the recipient is in fact a foreign person. Information that indicates that a recipient is not a foreign person include, but are not limited to, a United States phone number, billing address, shipping address, or place of residence; and, with respect to an entity, evidence that the entity is incorporated, formed, or managed in the United States.

(2) Sales of property. A sale of a property is described in this paragraph **(c)**(2) if:

(i) The sale is a foreign retail sale;

(ii) In the case of a sale of general property that is not a foreign retail sale and

the general property is delivered (such as through a commercial carrier) to the recipient or an end user, the shipping address of the recipient or end user is outside the United States;

(iii) In the case of a sale of general property that is not described in either paragraph (c)(2)(i) or (ii) of this section, the billing address of the recipient is outside the United States; or

(iv) In the case of a sale of intangible property, the billing address of the recipient is outside the United States.

(d) Foreign use—(1) Foreign use for general property—(i) In general. The sale of general property is for a foreign use for purposes of paragraph (b) of this section if the seller determines that the sale is for a foreign use under the rules of paragraph (d)(1)(ii) or (iii) of this section and the exception in paragraph (d)(1)(iv) of this section does not apply.

(ii) Rules for determining foreign use—(A) Sales that are delivered to an end user by a carrier or freight forwarder. Except as otherwise provided in this paragraph (d)(1)(ii)(A), a sale of general property (other than a sale of general property described in paragraphs (d)(1)(ii)(D) through (F) of this section) that is delivered through a carrier or freight forwarder to a recipient that is an end user is for a foreign use if the end user receives delivery of the general property outside the United States. However, a sale described in the preceding sentence is not treated as a sale to an end user for a foreign use if the sale is made with a principal purpose of having the property transported from its location outside the United States to a location within the United States for ultimate use or consumption.

(B) Sales to an end user without the use of a carrier or freight forwarder. With respect to sales that are not delivered through the use of a carrier or freight forwarder, a sale of general property (other than a sale of general property described in paragraphs (d)(1)(ii)(D) through (F) of this section) to a recipient that is an end user is for a foreign use if the property is located outside the United States at the time of the sale (including as part of foreign retail sales).

(C) Sales for resale. A sale of general property (other than a sale of general property described in paragraphs (d)(1)(ii)(D) through (F) of this section) to a recipient (such as a distributor or retailer) that will resell the general property is for a foreign use if the general property will ultimately be sold to end users outside the United States (including in foreign retail sales) and such sales to end users outside the United States are substantiated under paragraph (d)(3)(ii) of this section. In the case of sales of a fungible mass of general property, the taxpayer may presume that the proportion of its sales that are ultimately sold to end users outside the United States is the same as the proportion of the recipient's resales of that fungible mass to end users outside the United States.

(D) Sales of digital content. A sale of general property that primarily contains digital content that is transferred electronically rather than in a physical medium is for a foreign use if the end user downloads, installs, receives, or accesses the purchased digital content on the end user's device outside the United States (see § 1.250(b)–5(d)(2) and (e)(2)(iii) for rules that apply in the case of digital content that is not purchased in a sale but is electronically supplied as a service). If information about where the digital content is downloaded, installed, received, or accessed (such as the devices IP address) is unavailable, and the gross receipts from all sales with respect to the end user (which may be a business) are in the aggregate less than $50,000 for the seller's taxable year, a sale of general property described in the preceding sentence is for a foreign use if it is to an end user that has a billing address located outside the United States.

(E) Sales of international transportation property used for compensation or hire. A sale of international transportation property used for compensation or hire is for a foreign use if the end user registers the property with a foreign jurisdiction.

(F) Sales of international transportation property not used for compensation or hire. A sale of international transportation property not used for compensation or hire is for a foreign use if the end user registers the property in a foreign jurisdiction and hangars or stores the property primarily outside the United States.

(iii) Sales for manufacturing, assembly, or other processing—(A) In general. A sale of general property is for a foreign use if the sale is to a foreign unrelated party that subjects the property to manufacture, assembly, or other processing outside the United States and such manufacturing, assembly, or other processing outside the United States is substantiated under paragraph (d)(3)(iii) of this section. Property is subject to manufacture, assembly, or other processing only if the property is physically and materially changed (as described in paragraph (d)(1)(iii)(B) of this section) or the property is incorporated as a component into another product (as described in paragraph (d)(1)(iii)(C) of this section).

(B) Property subject to a physical and material change. The determination of whether general property is subject to a physical and material change is made based on all the relevant facts and circumstances. General property is subject to a physical and material change if it is substantially transformed and is distinguishable from and cannot be readily returned to its original state.

(C) Property incorporated into a product as a component. General property is a component incorporated into another product if the incorporation of the general property into another product involves activities that are substantial in nature and generally considered to constitute the manufacture, assembly, or processing of property based on all the relevant facts and circumstances. However, general property is not considered a component incorporated into another product if it is subject only to packaging, repackaging, labeling, or minor assembly operations. In addition, general property is treated as a component if the seller expects, using reliable estimates, that the fair market value of the property when it is delivered to the recipient will constitute no more than 20 percent of the fair market value of the finished good into which the general property is directly or indirectly incorporated when the finished good is sold to end users (the "20-percent rule"). If the property could be incorporated into a number of different finished goods, a reliable estimate of the fair market value of the finished good may include the average fair market value of a representative range of such goods. For purposes of the 20-percent rule, all general property that is sold by the seller and incorporated into the finished good is treated as a single item of property if the seller sells the property to the recipient and the seller knows or has reason to know that the components will be incorporated into a single item of property (for example, where multiple components are sold as a kit). A seller knows or has reason to know that the components will be incorporated into a single item of property if the information received as part of the sales process indicates that the components will be included in the same second product or the nature of the components compels inclusion into the second product and the seller fails to obtain evidence to the contrary.

(iv) Sales of property subject to manufacturing, assembly, or other processing in the United States. If the seller sells general property to a recipient (other than a related party) for manufacturing, assembly, or other processing within the United States, such property is not sold for a foreign use even if the requirements of paragraph (d)(1)(ii) or (iii) of this section are subsequently satisfied. See § 1.250(b)–6(c) for rules governing sales of general property to a foreign person that is a related party. Property is subject to manufacture, assembly, or other processing only if the property is physically and materially changed (as described in paragraph (d)(1)(iii)(B) of this section) or the property is incorporated as a component into another product (as described in paragraph (d)(1)(iii)(C) of this section).

* * *

(2) Foreign use for intangible property—(i) In general. A sale of rights to exploit intangible property solely outside the United States is for a foreign use. A sale of rights to exploit intangible property solely within the United States is not for a foreign use. A sale of rights to exploit intangible property worldwide is partially for a foreign use and partially not for a foreign use. Whether intangible property is exploited within versus outside the United States is determined based on revenue earned from end users located within versus outside the United States. Therefore, a sale of rights to exploit intangible property both within and outside the United States is for a foreign use in proportion to the revenue earned from end users located outside the United States over the total revenue earned from the exploitation of the intangible property. A sale of intangible property will be treated as a FDDEI sale only if the substantiation requirements of paragraph (d)(3)(iv) of this section are satisfied. For rules specific to determining end users and revenue earned from end users for intangible property used in sales of general property, provision of services, research and development, or consisting of a manufacturing method or process, see paragraph (d)(2)(ii) of this section.

(ii) Determination of end users and revenue earned from end users—(A) Intangible property embedded in general property or used in connection with the sale of general property. If intangible property is embedded in general property that is sold, or used in connection with a sale of general property, then the end user of the intangible property is the end user of the general property. Revenue is earned from the end user of the general property outside the United States to the extent the sale of the general property is for a foreign use under paragraph (d)(1)(ii) or (iii) of this section.

(B) Intangible property used in providing a service. If intangible property is used to provide a service, then the end user of that intangible property is the recipient, consumer, or business recipient of the service or, in the case of a property service or a transportation service that involves the transportation of property, the end user is the owner of the property on which such service is being performed. Such end users are treated as located outside the United States only to the extent the service qualifies as a FDDEI service under § 1.250(b)–5. Therefore, in the case of a recipient of a sale of intangible property that uses such intangible property to provide a property service that qualifies as a FDDEI service to another person, that person is the end user and is treated as located outside the United States.

(C) Intangible property consisting of a manufacturing method or process—(1) In general. Except as provided in paragraph (d)(2)(ii)(C)(2) of this section, if intangible property consists of a manufacturing method or process (as defined in paragraph (d)(2)(ii)(C)(3) of this section) and is sold to a foreign unrelated party (including in a sale by a foreign related party), then the foreign unrelated party is treated as an end user located outside the United States, unless the seller knows or has reason to know that the manufacturing method or process will be used in the United States, in which case the foreign unrelated party is treated as an end user located within the United States. A seller has reason to know that the manufacturing method or process will be used in the United States if the information received from the recipient as part of the sales process contains information that indicates that the recipient intends to use the manufacturing method or process in the United States and the seller fails to obtain evidence establishing that the recipient does not intend to use the manufacturing method or process in the United States.

(2) Exception for certain manufacturing arrangements. A sale of intangible property consisting of a manufacturing method or process (including a sale by a foreign related party) to a foreign unrelated party for use in manufacturing products for or on behalf of the seller or any person related to the seller does not qualify as a sale to a foreign unrelated party for purposes of determining the end user under paragraph (d)(2)(ii)(C)(1) of this section.

(3) Manufacturing method or process. For purposes of this section, a manufacturing method or process consists of a sequence of actions or steps that comprise an overall method or process that is used to manufacture a product or produce a particular manufacturing result, which may be in the form of a patent or know-how. Intangible property consisting of the right to make and sell an item of property is not a manufacturing method or process, whereas intangible property consisting of the right to apply a series of actions or steps to be performed to achieve a particular manufacturing result is a manufacturing method or process. For example, a utility or design patent on an article of manufacture, machine, composition of matter, design, or providing the right to sell equipment to perform a process is not a manufacturing method or process, whereas a utility patent covering a method or process of manufacturing is a manufacturing method or process for purposes of this section.

(D) Intangible property used in research and development. If intangible property (primary IP) is used to develop new or modify other intangible property (secondary IP), then the end user of the primary IP is the end user (applying paragraph (d)(2)(ii)(A), (B), or (C) of this section) of the secondary IP.

(iii) Determination of revenue for periodic payments versus lump sums—

(A) Sales in exchange for periodic payments. In the case of a sale of intangible property, other than intangible property consisting of a manufacturing method or process that is sold to a foreign unrelated party, to a recipient in exchange for periodic payments, the extent to which the sale is for a foreign use is determined annually based on the actual revenue earned by the recipient from any use of the intangible property for the taxable year in which a periodic payment is received. If actual revenue earned by the recipient cannot be obtained after reasonable efforts, then estimated revenue earned by a recipient that is not a related party of the seller from the use of the intangible property may be used based on the principles of paragraph (d)(2)(iii)(B) of this section.

(B) Sales in exchange for a lump sum. In the case of a sale of intangible property, other than intangible property consisting of a manufacturing method or process that is sold to a foreign unrelated party, for a lump sum, the extent to which the sale is for a foreign use is determined based on the ratio of the total net present value of revenue the seller would have expected to earn from the exploitation of the intangible property outside the United States to the total net present value of revenue the seller would have expected to earn from the exploitation of the intangible property. In the case of a recipient that is a foreign unrelated party, net present values of revenue that the recipient expected to earn from the exploitation of the intangible property within and outside the United States may also be used if the seller obtained such revenue data from the recipient near the time of the sale and such revenue data was used to negotiate the lump sum price paid for the intangible property. Net present values must be determined using reliable inputs including, but not limited to, reliable revenue, expenses, and discount rates. The extent to which the inputs are used by the parties to determine the sales price agreed to between the seller and a foreign unrelated party purchasing the intangible property will be a factor in determining whether such inputs are reliable. If the intangible property is sold to a foreign related party, the reliability of the inputs used to determine net present values and the net present values are determined under section 482.

(C) Sales to a foreign unrelated party of intangible property consisting of a manufacturing method or process. In the case of a sale to an unrelated foreign party of intangible property consisting of a manufacturing method or process, the revenue earned from the end user is equal to the amount received from the recipient in exchange for the manufacturing method or process. In the case of a bundled sale of intangible property consisting of a manufacturing method or process and intangible property not consisting of a manufacturing method or process, the revenue earned from the intangible property consisting of the manufacturing method or process equals the total amount paid for the bundled sale multiplied by the proportion that the value of the manufacturing method or process bears to the total value of the intangible property. The value of the manufacturing method or process to the total value of the intangible property must be determined using the principles of section 482.

* * *

(3) Foreign use substantiation for certain sales of property—(i) In general. Except as provided in § 1.250(b)–3(f)(3) (relating to certain loss transactions), a sale of property described in paragraphs (d)(1)(ii)(C) of this section (foreign use for sale of general property for resale), (d)(1)(iii) of this section (foreign use for sale of general property subject to manufacturing, assembly, or processing outside the United States), or (d)(2) of this section (foreign use for sale of intangible property) is a FDDEI transaction only if the taxpayer satisfies the substantiation requirements described in paragraphs (d)(3)(ii), (iii), or (iv) of this section, as applicable.

(ii) Substantiation of foreign use for resale. A seller satisfies the substantiation requirements with respect to a sale of property described in paragraph (d)(1)(ii)(C) of this section (sales of general property for resale) only if the seller maintains one or more of the following items—

(A) A binding contract that specifically limits subsequent sales to sales outside the United States;

(B) Proof that property is specifically designed, labeled, or adapted for a foreign market;

(C) Proof that the cost of shipping the property back to the United States relative to the value of the property makes it impractical that the property will be resold in the United States;

(D) Credible evidence obtained or created in the ordinary course of business from the recipient evidencing that property will be sold to an end user outside the United States (or, in the case of sales of fungible mass property, stating what portion of the property will be sold to end users outside the United States); or

(E) A written statement prepared by the seller containing the information described in paragraphs (d)(3)(ii)(E)(1) through (7) of this section corroborated by evidence that is credible and sufficient to support the information provided.

(1) The name and address of the recipient;

(2) The date or dates the property was shipped or delivered to the recipient;

(3) The amount of gross income from the sale;

(4) A full description of the property subject to resale;

(5) A description of the method of sales to the end users, such as direct sales by the recipient or sales by the recipient to retail stores;

(6) If known, a description of the end users; and

(7) description of how the seller determined that property will be ultimately sold to an end user outside the United States (or, in the case of sales of fungible mass property, of how the taxpayer determined what portion of the property that will ultimately be sold to end users outside the United States).

(iii) Substantiation of foreign use for manufacturing, assembly, or other processing outside the United States. A seller satisfies the substantiation requirements with respect to a sale of property described in paragraph (d)(1)(iii) of this section (sales of general property subject to manufacturing, assembly, or other processing outside the United States) if the seller maintains one or more of the following items—

(A) Credible evidence that the property has been sold to a foreign unrelated party that is a manufacturer and such property generally cannot be sold to end users without being subject to a physical and material change (for example, the sale of raw materials that cannot be used except in a manufacturing process);

(B) Credible evidence obtained or created in the ordinary course of business from the recipient to support that the product purchased will be subject to manufacture, assembly, or other processing outside the United States within the meaning of paragraph (d)(1)(iii) of this section; or

(C) A written statement prepared by the seller containing the information described in paragraphs (d)(3)(iii)(C)(1) through (7) of this section corroborated by evidence that is credible and sufficient to support the information provided.

(1) The name and address of the manufacturer of the property;

(2) The date or dates the property was shipped or delivered to the recipient;

(3) The amount of gross income from the sale;

(4) A full description of the general property sold and the type or types of finished goods that will incorporate the general property the taxpayer sold;

(5) A description of the manufacturing, assembly, or other processing operations, including the location or locations of manufacture, assembly, or other processing; how the general property will be used in the finished good; and the nature of the finished good's manufacturing, assembly, or other processing operations as compared to the process used to make the general property used to make the finished good;

(6) A description of how the seller determined the general property was substantially transformed or the activities were substantial in nature within the meaning of paragraph (d)(1)(iii)(B) or (C) of this section, whichever the case may be; and,

(7) If the seller is relying on the rule described in paragraph (d)(1)(iii)(C) of this section (that the fair market value of the general property be no more than twenty percent of the fair market value when incorporated into the finished goods sold to end users), an explanation of how the seller satisfies the requirements in that paragraph.

(iv) Substantiation of foreign use of intangible property. A taxpayer satisfies the substantiation requirements with respect to a sale of property described in paragraph (d)(2) of this section (foreign use for intangible property) if the seller maintains one or more of the following items—

(A) A binding contract that specifically provides that the intangible property can be exploited solely outside the United States;

(B) Credible evidence obtained or created in the ordinary course of business from the recipient establishing the portion of its revenue for a taxable year that was derived from exploiting the intangible property outside the United States; or

(C) A written statement prepared by the seller containing the information described in paragraphs (d)(3)(iv)(C)(1) through (9) of this section corroborated by evidence that is credible and sufficient to support the information provided.

(1) The name and address of the recipient;

(2) The date of the sale;

(3) The amount of gross income from the sale;

(4) A description of the intangible property;

(5) An explanation of how the intangible property will be used by the recipient (embedded in general property, used to provide a service, used as a manufacturing method or process, or used in research and development);

(6) An explanation of how the seller determined what portion of the sale is a FDDEI sale;

(7) If the intangible property consists of a manufacturing method or process, an explanation of how the elements of paragraph (d)(2)(ii)(C) of this section are satisfied;

(8) If the sale is for periodic payments, an explanation of how the seller determined the extent of foreign use based on the actual revenue earned by the recipient from the use of the intangible property for the taxable year in which a periodic payment is received as required by paragraph (d)(2)(iii)(A) of this section, or, if actual revenue cannot be obtained after reasonable efforts, an explanation of why actual revenue is unavailable and how the seller determined the extent of foreign use based on estimated revenue; and

(9) If the sale is for a lump sum, an explanation of how the seller determined the total net present value of revenue it expected to earn from the exploitation of the intangible property outside the United States and the total net present value of revenue it expected to earn from the exploitation of the intangible property as required by paragraph (d)(2)(iii)(B) of this section.

* * *

[T.D. 9901, 85 FR 43080, 43095, July 15, 2020; 85 FR 60910, Sept. 29, 2020; 85 FR 68249, Oct. 28, 2020]

§ 1.250(b)–5 Foreign-derived deduction eligible income (FDDEI) services.

* * *

(b) Definition of FDDEI service. Except as provided in § 1.250(b)–6(d), the term FDDEI service means a provision of a service described in any one of paragraphs (b)(1) through (5) of this section. If only a portion of a service is treated as provided to a person, or with respect to property, outside the United States, the provision of the service is a FDDEI service only to the extent of the gross income derived with respect to such portion.

(1) The provision of a general service to a consumer located outside the United States (as determined under paragraph (d) of this section).

(2) The provision of a general service to a business recipient located outside the United States (as determined under paragraph (e) of this section).

(3) The provision of a proximate service to a recipient located outside the United States (as determined under paragraph (f) of this section).

(4) The provision of a property service with respect to tangible property located outside the United States (as determined under paragraph (g) of this section).

(5) The provision of a transportation service to a recipient, or with respect to property, located outside the United States (as determined under paragraph (h) of this section).

(c) Definitions. This paragraph (c) provides definitions that apply for purposes of this section and § 1.250(b)–6.

(1) Advertising service. The term advertising service means a general service that consists primarily of transmitting or displaying content (including via the internet) with a purpose to generate revenue based on the promotion of a product or service.

(2) Benefit. The term benefit has the meaning set forth in § 1.482–9(*l*)(3).

(3) Business recipient. The term business recipient means a recipient other than a consumer and includes all related parties of the recipient. However, if the recipient is a related party of the taxpayer, the term does not include the taxpayer.

(4) Consumer. The term consumer means a recipient that is an individual that purchases a general service for personal use.

(5) Electronically supplied service. The term electronically supplied service means, with respect to a general service other than an advertising service, a service that is delivered primarily over the internet or an electronic network and for which value of the service to the end user is derived primarily from automation or electronic delivery. Electronically supplied services include the provision of access to digital content (as defined in § 1.250(b)–3), such as streaming content; on-demand network access to computing resources, such as networks, servers, storage, and software; the provision or support of a business or personal presence on a network, such as a website or a web page; online intermediation platform services; services automatically generated from a computer via the internet or other network in response to data input by the recipient; and similar services. Electronically supplied services do not include services that primarily involve the application of human effort by the renderer (not considering the human effort involved in the development or maintenance of the technology enabling the electronically supplied services). Accordingly, electronically supplied services do not include certain services (such as legal, accounting, medical, or teaching services) involving primarily human effort that are provided electronically.

(6) General service. The term general service means any service other than a property service, proximate service, or transportation service. The term general service includes advertising services and electronically supplied services.

(7) Property service. The term property service means a service, other than a transportation service, provided with respect to tangible property, but only if substantially all of the service is performed at the location of the property and results in physical manipulation of the property such as through manufacturing, assembly, maintenance, or repair. Substantially all of a service is performed at the location of property only if the renderer spends more than 80 percent of the time providing the service at or near the location of the property.

(8) Proximate service. The term proximate service means a service, other than a property service or a transportation service, provided to a consumer or business recipient, but only if substantially all of the service is performed in the physical presence of the consumer or, in the case of a business recipient, substantially all of the service is performed in the physical presence of persons working for the business recipient such as employees, contractors, or agents. Substantially all of a service is performed in the physical presence of a consumer or persons working for a business recipient only if the renderer spends more than 80 percent of the time providing the service in the physical presence of such persons.

(9) Transportation service. The term transportation service means a service to transport a person or property using aircraft, railroad rolling stock, vessel, motor vehicle, or any other mode of transportation. Transportation services include freight forwarding and similar services.

(d) General services provided to consumers—(1) In general. A general service is provided to a consumer located outside the United States if the consumer of a general service resides outside of the United States when the service is provided. Except as provided in paragraph (d)(2) of this section, if the renderer does not have or cannot after reasonable efforts obtain the consumer's location of residence when the service is provided, the consumer of a general service is treated as residing at the location of the consumer's billing address. However, the rule in the preceding sentence allowing for the use of a consumer's billing address does not apply if the renderer knows or has reason to know that the consumer does not reside outside the United States. A renderer has reason to know that the consumer does not reside outside the United States if the information received as part of the provision of the service indicates that the consumer resides in the United States and the renderer fails to obtain evidence establishing that the consumer resides outside the United States.

(2) Electronically supplied services. The consumer of an electronically supplied service is deemed to reside at the location of the device used to receive the service. Such location may be determined based on the location of the IP address when the electronically supplied service is provided. However, if the renderer does not have or cannot after reasonable efforts obtain the consumer's device location, then the location of the device is treated as being outside the United States if the renderer's billing address for the consumer is outside of the United States, subject to the knowledge and reason to know standards described in paragraph (d)(1) of this section.

* * *

(e) General services provided to business recipients—(1) In general. A general service is provided to a business recipient located outside the United States to the extent that the service confers a benefit on the business recipient's operations outside the United States under the rules in paragraph (e)(2) of this section. The location of residence, incorporation, or formation of a business recipient is not relevant to determining the location of the business recipient's operations that benefit from a general service.

(2) Determination of business operations that benefit from the service—(i) In general. Except as otherwise provided in paragraph (e)(2)(ii) and (iii) of this section, the determination of which operations of the business recipient located outside the United States benefit from a general service, and the extent to which such operations benefit, is made under the principles of § 1.482–9 by treating the taxpayer as one controlled taxpayer, the portions of the business recipient's operations within the United States (if any) that may benefit from the general service as one or more controlled taxpayers, and the portions of the business recipient's operations outside the United States (if any) that may benefit from the general service, each as one or more controlled taxpayers. * * *

(ii) Advertising services. With respect to advertising services, the operations of the business recipient that benefit from the advertising service provided by the renderer are deemed to be located where the advertisements are viewed by individuals. If advertising services are displayed via the internet, the advertising services are viewed at the location of the device on which the advertisements are viewed. For this purpose, the IP address may be used to establish the location of a device on which an advertisement is viewed.

(iii) Electronically supplied services. With respect to an electronically supplied service, the operations of the business recipient that benefit from that service provided by the renderer are deemed to be located where the business recipient (including employees, contractors, or agents) accesses or otherwise uses the service. If it cannot be determined whether the location is within or outside the United States (such as where the location of access cannot be reliably determined using the location of the IP address of the device used to receive the service), and the gross receipts from all services with respect to the business recipient are in the aggregate less than $50,000 for the renderer's taxable year, the operations of the business recipient that benefit from the service provided by the renderer are deemed to be located at the recipient's billing address; otherwise, the operations of the business recipient that benefit are deemed to be located in the United States. If the renderer provides a service that is partially an electronically supplied service and partially a general service that is not an electronically supplied service (such as a service that is performed partially online and partially by mail or in person), the location of the business recipient is determined using the rule for electronically supplied services in this paragraph (e)(2)(iii) if the primary purpose of the service is to provide electronically supplied services; otherwise, the rule for general services described in paragraph (e)(2)(i) of this section applies.

(3) Identification of business recipient's operations—(i) In general. For purposes of this paragraph (e), except with respect to advertising services and electronically supplied services, a business recipient is treated as having operations where it maintains an office or other fixed place of business. In general, an office or other fixed place of business is a fixed facility, that is, a place, site, structure, or other similar facility, through which the business recipient engages in a trade or business. For purposes of making the determination in this paragraph (e)(3)(i), the renderer may make reliable assumptions based on the information available to it.

(ii) Advertising services and electronically supplied services. The location of a business recipient that receives advertising services or electronically supplied services will be determined under the rules of paragraph (e)(2)(ii) and (iii) of this section, respectively, even if the business recipient does not maintain an office or other fixed place of business in the locations where the advertisements are viewed (in the case of advertising services) or where the general service is accessed (in the case of electronically supplied services).

(iii) No office or fixed place of business. In the case of general services other than advertising services and other than electronically supplied services, if the business recipient does not have an identifiable office or fixed place of business (including the office of a principal manager or managing owner), the business recipient is deemed to be located at its primary billing address.

(4) Substantiation of the location of a business recipient's operations outside the United States. Except as provided in § 1.250(b)–3(f)(3) (relating to certain loss transactions), a general service provided to a business recipient is treated as a FDDEI service only if the renderer substantiates its determination of the extent to which the service benefits a business recipient's operations outside the United States. A renderer satisfies the preceding sentence if the renderer maintains one or more of the following items—

(i) Credible evidence obtained or created in the ordinary course of business from the business recipient establishing the extent to which operations of the business recipient outside the United States benefit from the service; or

(ii) A written statement prepared by the renderer containing the information described in paragraphs (e)(4)(ii)(A) through (F) of this section corroborated by evidence that is credible and sufficient to support the information provided.

(A) The name of the business recipient;

(B) The date or dates of the service;

(C) The amount of gross income from the service;

(D) A full description of the service;

(E) A description of how the service will benefit the business recipient; and

(F) An explanation of how the renderer determined what portion of the service will benefit the business recipient's operations located outside the United States.

* * *

(f) Proximate services. A proximate service is provided to a recipient located outside the United States if the proximate service is performed outside the United States. In the case of a proximate service performed partly within the United States and partly outside of the United States, a proportionate amount of the service is treated as provided to a recipient located outside the United States corresponding to the portion of time the renderer spends providing the service outside of the United States.

(g) Property services—(1) In general. Except as provided in paragraph (g)(2) of this section, a property service is provided with respect to tangible property located outside the United States only if the property is located outside the United States for the duration of the period the service is performed.

(2) Exception for services provided with respect to property temporarily in the United States. A property service is deemed to be provided with respect to tangible property located outside the United States if the following conditions are satisfied—

(i) The property is temporarily in the United States for the purpose of receiving the property service;

(ii) After the completion of the service, the property will be primarily hangared, stored, or used outside the United States;

(iii) The property is not used to generate revenue in the United States at any point during the duration of the service; and

(iv) The property is owned by a foreign person that resides or primarily operates outside the United States.

(h) Transportation services. Except as provided in this paragraph (h), a transportation service is provided to a recipient, or with respect to property, located outside the United States only if both the origin and the destination of the service are outside of the United States. However, in the case of a transportation service provided to a recipient, or with respect to property, where either the origin or the destination of the service is outside of the United States, but not both, then 50 percent of the gross income from the transportation service is considered derived from services provided to a recipient, or with respect to property, located outside the United States.

[T.D. 9901, 85 FR 43080, 43103, July 15, 2020; 85 FR 60910, Sept. 29, 2020; 85 FR 68249, Oct. 28, 2020; T.D. 9959, 87 FR 324, Jan. 4, 2022]

Corporate Distributions and Adjustments

§ 1.367(a)–1 Transfers to foreign corporations subject to section 367(a): In general.

(a) Scope. Section 367(a)(1) provides the general rule concerning certain transfers of property by a United States person (referred to at times in this section as the "U.S. person" or "U.S. transferor") to a foreign corporation. Paragraph (b) of this section provides general rules explaining the effect of section 367(a)(1). Paragraph (c) of this section describes transfers of property that are described in section 367(a)(1). Paragraph (d) of this section provides definitions that apply for purposes of sections 367(a) and (d) and the regulations thereunder. Paragraphs (e) and (f) of this section provide rules that apply to certain reorganizations described in section 368(a)(1)(F). Paragraph (g) of this section provides dates of applicability. For rules concerning the reporting requirements under section 6038B for certain transfers of property to a foreign corporation, see § 1.6038B–1.

(b) General rules—(1) Foreign corporation not considered a corporation for purposes of certain transfers. If a U.S. person transfers property to a foreign corporation in connection with an exchange described in section 351, 354, 356, or 361, then, pursuant to section 367(a)(1), the foreign corporation will not be considered to be a corporation for purposes of determining the extent to which gain is recognized on the transfer. Section 367(a)(1) denies nonrecognition treatment only to transfers of items of property on which gain is realized. Thus, the amount of gain recognized because of section 367(a)(1) is unaffected by the transfer of items of property on which loss is realized (but not recognized).

(2) Cases in which foreign corporate status is not disregarded. For circumstances in which section 367(a)(1) does not apply to a U.S. transferor's transfer of property to a foreign corporation, and thus the foreign corporation is considered to be a corporation, see §§ 1.367(a)–2, 1.367(a)–3, and 1.367(a)–7.

(3) Determination of value. In cases in which a U.S. transferor's transfer of property to a foreign corporation constitutes a controlled transaction as defined in § 1.482–1(i)(8), the value of the property transferred is determined in accordance with section 482 and the regulations thereunder.

(4) Character, source, and adjustments—(i) In general. If a U.S. person is required to recognize gain under section 367 upon a transfer of property to a foreign corporation, then—

(A) The character and source of such gain are determined as if the property had been disposed of in a taxable exchange with the transferee foreign corporation (unless otherwise provided by regulation); and

(B) Appropriate adjustments to earnings and profits, basis, and other affected items will be made according to otherwise applicable rules, taking into account the gain recognized under section 367(a)(1).

* * *

(5) Treatment of certain property as subject to section 367(d). A U.S. transferor may apply section 367(d) and § 1.367(d)–1, rather than section 367(a) and the regulations thereunder, to a transfer of property to a foreign corporation that otherwise would be subject to section 367(a), provided that the property is not eligible property, as defined in § 1.367(a)–2(b) but determined without regard to § 1.367(a)–2(c). A U.S. transferor and any other U.S. transferor that is related (within the meaning of section 267(b) or 707(b)(1)) to the U.S. transferor must consistently apply this paragraph (b)(5) to all property described in this paragraph (b)(5) that is transferred to one or more foreign corporations pursuant to a plan. A U.S. transferor applies the provisions of this paragraph (b)(5) in the form and manner set forth in § 1.6038B–1(d)(1)(iv) and (v).

(c)(1) through (c)(3)(i) reserved. For further guidance, see § 1.367(a)–1T(c)(1) through (c)(3)(i).

(ii) Transfer of partnership interest treated as transfer of proportionate share of assets—(A) In general. If a U.S. person transfers an interest as a partner in a partnership (whether foreign or domestic) in an exchange described in section 367(a)(1), then that person is treated as having transferred a proportionate share of the property of the partnership in an exchange described in section 367(a)(1). Accordingly, the applicability of the exception to section 367(a)(1) provided in § 1.367(a)–2 is determined with reference to the property of the partnership rather than the partnership interest itself. A U.S. person's proportionate share of partnership property is determined under the rules and principles of sections 701 through 761 and the regulations thereunder.

* * *

[T.D. 9441, 74 FR 348, Jan. 5, 2009; T.D. 9568, 76 FR 80087, Dec. 22, 2011; T.D. 9614, 78 FR 17030, March 19, 2013; T.D. 9739, 80 FR 56912, Sept. 21, 2015; T.D. 9803, 81 FR 91022, Dec. 16, 2016; 82 FR 52848, Nov. 15, 2017; T.D. 9994, 89 FR 82165, Oct. 10, 2024]

§ 1.367(a)–3 Treatment of transfers of stock or securities to foreign corporations.

(a) In general—(1) Overview. This section provides rules concerning the transfer of stock or securities by a U.S. person to a foreign corporation in an exchange described in section 367(a)(1). In general, a transfer of stock or securities (including an indirect stock transfer described in paragraph (d) of this section) by a U.S. person to a foreign corporation that is described in section 351, 354 (including a section 354 exchange pursuant to a reorganization described in section 368(a)(1)(B)), 356, or section 361(a) or (b) is subject to section 367(a)(1). Therefore, gain is recognized on such a transfer unless one of the exceptions set forth in paragraph (a)(2) of this section (regarding general exceptions for certain exchanges of stock or securities), paragraph (b) of this section (regarding transfers of foreign stock or securities), paragraph (c) of this section (regarding transfers of domestic stock or securities), or paragraph (e) of this section (regarding transfers of stock or securities in a section 361 exchange) applies to the transfer.* * *

(2) Exceptions for certain exchanges of stock or securities. Unless otherwise provided, the following exchanges are not subject to section 367(a)(1) and therefore gain is not recognized under section 367(a)(1).

(i) Section 368(a)(1)(E) reorganizations. In an exchange under section 354 or 356, a U.S. person exchanges stock or securities of a foreign corporation in a reorganization described in section 368(a)(1)(E).

(ii) Certain section 368(a)(1) asset reorganizations. In an exchange under section 354 or 356, a U.S. person exchanges stock or securities of a domestic or foreign corporation pursuant to an asset reorganization that is not treated as an indirect stock transfer under paragraph (d) of this section. See paragraph (d)(3) Example 16 of this section. For purposes of this section, an asset reorganization is defined as a reorganization described in section 368(a)(1) involving a transfer of property under section 361.

(iii) Certain reorganizations described in sections 368(a)(1)(A) and (a)(2)(E). If, in an exchange described in section 361, a domestic merging corporation transfers stock of a controlling corporation to a foreign surviving corporation in a reorganization described in section 368(a)(1)(A) and (a)(2)(E), the stock of the controlling corporation transferred in such section 361 exchange is not subject to section 367(a)(1) if the stock of the controlling corporation is provided to the merging corporation by the controlling corporation pursuant to the plan of reorganization. However, a section 361 exchange of other property, including stock of the controlling corporation not provided by the controlling corporation pursuant to the plan of reorganization, by the domestic merging corporation to the foreign surviving corporation pursuant to such a reorganization is described in section 367(a)(1) and therefore subject to section 367(a)(1) unless an exception to section 367(a)(1) applies.

(iv) Certain triangular reorganizations described in § 1.367(b)–10. If, in an exchange under section 354 or 356, one or more U.S. persons exchange stock or securities of T (as defined in § 1.367(b)–10(a)(3)(i)) in connection with a transaction described in § 1.367(b)–10 (applying to certain acquisitions of parent stock or securities for property in triangular reorganizations), section 367(a)(1) does not apply to such U.S. persons with respect to the exchange of the stock or securities of T if the condition in paragraph (a)(2)(iv)(A) or (B) of this section is satisfied. See § 1.367(b)–10(a)(2)(iii) (providing a similar rule that excludes certain transactions from the application of § 1.367(b)–10).

(A) The amount of gain in the T stock or securities that would otherwise be recognized under section 367(a)(1) (without regard to any exceptions thereto) pursuant to the indirect stock transfer rules of paragraph (d) of this section is less than the sum of the amount of the deemed distribution under § 1.367(b)–10 that would be treated and subject to U.S. tax as a dividend under section 301(c)(1) (or would give rise to an inclusion under section 951(a)(1)(A) or 951A(a) that would be subject to U.S. tax) and the amount of such deemed distribution that would be treated and subject to U.S. tax as gain from the sale or exchange of property under section 301(c)(3) (or would give rise to an inclusion under section 951(a)(1)(A) or 951A(a) that would be subject to U.S. tax) if § 1.367(b)–10 would otherwise apply to the triangular reorganization.

(B) T is a foreign corporation, but only to the extent that the stock or securities of T are exchanged for stock or securities of P that were acquired by S in exchange for property in the P acquisition (as the terms P, S, property, and P acquisition are defined in § 1.367(b)–10(a)). Such exchange of T stock or securities is subject to the rules under § 1.367(b)–4(g). Section 367(a) applies to the exchange of T stock or securities to the extent that such stock or securities are exchanged for P stock or securities that were not acquired by S in exchange for property in the P acquisition.

* * *

(b) Transfers of stock or securities of foreign corporations—(1) General rule. Except as provided in paragraph (e) of this section, a transfer of stock or securities of a foreign corporation by a U.S. person to a foreign corporation that would otherwise be subject to section 367(a)(1) under paragraph (a) of this section shall not be subject to section 367(a)(1) if either—

(i) Less than 5-percent shareholder. The U.S. person owns less than five percent (applying the attribution rules of section 318, as modified by section 958(b)) of both the total voting power and the total value of the stock of the transferee foreign corporation immediately after the transfer; or

(ii) 5-percent shareholder. The U.S. person enters into a five-year gain recognition agreement with respect to the transferred stock or securities as provided in § 1.367(a)–8.

(2) Certain transfers subject to sections 367(a) and (b)—(i) In general. A transfer of stock or securities described in section 367(a) or the regulations thereunder as well as in section 367(b) or the regulations thereunder shall be subject concurrently to sections 367(a) and (b) and the respective regulations thereunder, except as provided in paragraph (b)(2)(i)(A) through (C) of this section.* * *

(A) Section 367(b) and the regulations thereunder shall not apply if a foreign corporation is not treated as a corporation under section 367(a)(1). * * *

* * *

(c) Transfers of stock or securities of domestic corporations—(1) General rule. Except as provided in paragraph (e) of this section, a transfer of stock or securities of a domestic corporation by a U.S. person to a foreign corporation that would otherwise be subject to section 367(a)(1) under paragraph (a) of this section shall not be subject to section 367(a)(1) if the domestic corporation the stock or securities of which are transferred (referred to as the U.S. target company) complies with the reporting requirements in paragraph (c)(6) of this section and if each of the following four conditions is met:

(i) Fifty percent or less of both the total voting power and the total value of the stock of the transferee foreign corporation is received in the transaction, in the aggregate, by U.S. transferors (i.e., the amount of stock received does not exceed the 50-percent ownership threshold).

(ii) Fifty percent or less of each of the total voting power and the total value of the stock of the transferee foreign corporation is owned, in the aggregate, immediately after the transfer by U.S. persons that are either officers or directors of the U.S. target company or that are five-percent target shareholders (as defined in paragraph (c)(5)(iii) of this section) (i.e., there is no control group). For purposes of this paragraph (c)(1)(ii), any stock of the transferee foreign corporation owned by U.S. persons immediately after the transfer will be taken into account, whether or not it was received in the exchange for stock or securities of the U.S. target company.

(iii) Either—

(A) The U.S. person is not a five-percent transferee shareholder (as defined in paragraph (c)(5)(ii) of this section); or

(B) The U.S. person is a five-percent transferee shareholder and enters into a five-year agreement to recognize gain with respect to the U.S. target company stock or securities it exchanged in the form provided in § 1.367(a)–8; and

(iv) The active trade or business test (as defined in paragraph (c)(3) of this section) is satisfied.

(2) Ownership presumption. For purposes of paragraph (c)(1) of this section, persons who transfer stock or securities of the U.S. target company in exchange for stock of the transferee foreign corporation are presumed to be U.S. persons. This presumption may be rebutted in accordance with paragraph (c)(7) of this section.

(3) Active trade or business test—(i) In general. The tests of this paragraph (c)(3), collectively referred to as the active trade or business test, are satisfied if:

(A) The transferee foreign corporation or any qualified subsidiary (as defined in paragraph (c)(5)(vii) of this section) or any qualified partnership (as defined in paragraph (c)(5)(viii) of this section) is engaged in an active trade or business outside the United States, within the meaning of § 1.367(a)–2(b)(2), (3), and (4) for the entire 36-month period immediately before the transfer;

(B) At the time of the transfer, neither the transferors nor the transferee foreign corporation (and, if applicable, the qualified subsidiary or qualified partnership engaged in the active trade or business) have an intention to substantially dispose of or discontinue such trade or business; and

(C) The substantiality test (as defined in paragraph (c)(3)(iii) of this section) is satisfied.

* * *

(iii) Substantiality test—(A) General rule. A transferee foreign corporation will be deemed to satisfy the substantiality test if, at the time of the transfer, the fair market value of the transferee foreign corporation is at least equal to the fair market value of the U.S. target company.

* * *

(e) Transfers of stock or securities by a domestic corporation to a foreign corporation in a section 361 exchange—(1) Overview—(i) Scope and definitions. This paragraph (e) applies to a domestic corporation (U.S. transferor) that transfers stock or securities of a domestic or foreign corporation (transferred stock or securities) to a foreign corporation (foreign acquiring corporation) in a section 361 exchange. Except as otherwise provided in this paragraph (e), paragraphs (b) and (c) of this section do not apply to the U.S. transferor's transfer of the transferred stock or securities in the section 361 exchange. For purposes of this paragraph (e), the definitions of control group, control group member, and non-control group member in § 1.367(a)–7(f)(1), ownership interest percentage in § 1.367(a)–7(f)(7), section 361 exchange in § 1.367(a)–7(f)(8), and U.S. transferor shareholder in § 1.367(a)–7(f)(13), apply.

(ii) Ordering rules. Except as otherwise provided, this paragraph (e) applies to the transfer of the transferred stock or securities in the section 361 exchange prior to the application of any other provision of section 367 to such transfer. Furthermore, any gain recognized (including gain treated as a deemed dividend pursuant to section 1248(a)) by the U.S. transferor under this paragraph (e) shall be taken into account for purposes of applying any other provision of section 367 (including §§ 1.367(a)–6, 1.367(a)–7, and 1.367(b)–4) to the transfer of the transferred stock or securities.

(2) General rule. Except as provided in paragraph (e)(3) of this section, the transfer by the U.S. transferor of the transferred stock or securities to the foreign acquiring corporation in the section 361 exchange shall be subject to section 367(a)(1), and therefore the U.S. transferor shall recognize any gain (but not loss) realized with respect to the transferred stock or securities. Realized gain is recognized pursuant to the prior sentence notwithstanding that the transfer is described in any other nonrecognition provision enumerated in section 367(a)(1) (such as section 351 or 354).

(3) Exception. The general rule of paragraph (e)(2) of this section shall not apply if the conditions of paragraphs (e)(3)(i), (ii), and (iii) of this section are satisfied.

(i) The conditions set forth in § 1.367(a)–7(c) are satisfied with respect to the section 361 exchange.

(ii) If the transferred stock or securities are of a domestic corporation, the U.S. target company (as defined in paragraph (c)(1) of this section) complies with the reporting requirements of paragraph (c)(6) of this section, and the conditions of paragraphs (c)(1)(i), (ii), and (iv) of this section are satisfied with respect to the transferred stock or securities.

(iii) If the U.S. transferor owns (applying the attribution rules of section 318, as modified by section 958(b)) five percent or more of the total voting power or the total value of the stock of the transferee foreign corporation immediately after the transfer of the transferred stock or securities in the section 361 exchange, then the conditions set forth in paragraphs (e)(3)(iii)(A), (B), and (C) of this section are satisfied.

(A) Except as otherwise provided in this paragraph (e)(3)(iii)(A), each U.S. transferor shareholder that is a qualified U.S. person (as defined in paragraph (e)(6)(vii) of this section) owning (applying the attribution rules of section 318, as modified by section 958(b)) five percent or more of the total voting power or the total value of the stock of the transferee foreign corporation immediately after the reorganization enters into a gain recognition agreement that satisfies the conditions of paragraph (e)(6) of this section and § 1.367(a)–8. A U.S. transferor shareholder is not required to enter into a gain recognition agreement pursuant to this paragraph if the amount of gain that would be subject to the gain recognition agreement (as determined under paragraph (e)(6)(i) of this section) is zero.

(B) With respect to non-control group members that are not described in paragraph (e)(3)(iii)(A) of this section, the U.S. transferor recognizes gain equal to the product of the aggregate ownership interest percentage of such non-control group members multiplied by the gain realized by the U.S.

transferor on the transfer of the transferred stock or securities.

(C) With respect to each control group member that is not described in paragraph (e)(3)(iii)(A) of this section, the U.S. transferor recognizes gain equal to the product of the ownership interest percentage of such control group member multiplied by the gain realized by the U.S. transferor on the transfer of the transferred stock or securities.

(4) Application of certain rules at U.S. transferor-level. For purposes of paragraphs (c)(5)(iii) and (e)(3)(ii) and (iii) of this section, ownership of the stock of the transferee foreign corporation is determined by reference to stock owned by the U.S. transferor immediately after the transfer of the transferred stock or securities to the foreign acquiring corporation in the section 361 exchange, but prior to and without taking into account the U.S. transferor's distribution under section 361(c)(1) of the stock received.

(5) Transferee foreign corporation—(i) General rule. Except as provided in paragraph (e)(5)(ii) of this section, the transferee foreign corporation for purposes of applying paragraph (e) of this section and § 1.367(a)–8 shall be the foreign corporation that issues stock or securities to the U.S. transferor in the section 361 exchange.

(ii) Special rule for triangular asset reorganizations involving the receipt of stock or securities of a domestic corporation. In the case of a triangular asset reorganization described in § 1.358–(6)(b)(2)(i), (ii), or (iii) or (b)(2)(v) (triangular asset reorganization) in which the U.S. transferor receives stock or securities of a domestic corporation that is in control (within the meaning of section 368(c)) of the foreign acquiring corporation, the transferee foreign corporation shall be the foreign acquiring corporation.

(6) Special requirements for gain recognition agreements. A gain recognition agreement filed by a U.S. transferor shareholder pursuant to paragraph (e)(3)(iii)(A) of this section is, in addition to the terms and conditions of § 1.367(a)–8, subject to the conditions of this paragraph (e)(6).

(i) The amount of gain subject to the gain recognition agreement shall equal the product of the ownership interest percentage of the U.S. transferor shareholder multiplied by the gain realized by the U.S. transferor on the transfer of the transferred stock or securities, reduced (but not below zero) by the sum of the amounts described in paragraphs (e)(6)(i)(A), (B), (C), and (D) of this section.

(A) Gain recognized by the U.S. transferor with respect to the transferred stock or securities under section 367(a)(1) (including any portion treated as a deemed dividend under section 1248(a)) that is attributable to such U.S. transferor shareholder pursuant to § 1.367(a)–7(c)(2) or (e)(5).

(B) A deemed dividend included in the income of the U.S. transferor with respect to the transferred stock under § 1.367(b)–4(b)(1)(i) that is attributable to such U.S. transferor shareholder pursuant to § 1.367(a)–7(e)(4).

(C) If the U.S. transferor shareholder is subject to an election under § 1.1248(f)–2(c)(1), a deemed dividend included in the income of the U.S. transferor pursuant to § 1.1248(f)–2(c)(3) that is attributable to the U.S. transferor shareholder.

(D) If the U.S. transferor shareholder is not subject to an election under § 1.1248(f)–2(c)(1), the hypothetical section 1248 amount (as defined in § 1.1248(f)–1(c)(4)) with respect to the stock of each foreign corporation transferred in the section 361 exchange attributable to the U.S. transferor shareholder.

(ii) The gain recognition agreement shall include the election described in § 1.367(a)–8(c)(2)(vi).

(iii) The gain recognition agreement shall designate the U.S. transferor shareholder as the U.S. transferor for purposes of § 1.367(a)–8.

(iv) If the transfer of the transferred stock or securities in the section 361 exchange is pursuant to a triangular asset reorganization, the gain recognition agreement shall include appropriate provisions that are consistent with the principles of § 1.367(a)–8 for gain recognition agreements involving multiple parties. See § 1.367(a)–8(j)(9).

(v) The gain recognition agreement shall not be eligible for termination upon a taxable disposition pursuant to § 1.367(a)–8(*o*)(1) unless the value of the stock or securities received by the U.S. transferor shareholder in exchange for the stock or securities of the U.S. transferor under section 354 or 356 is at least equal to the amount of gain subject to the gain recognition agreement filed by such U.S. transferor shareholder.

(vi) Except as otherwise provided in this paragraph (e)(6)(vi), if gain is subsequently recognized by the U.S. transferor shareholder under the terms of the gain recognition agreement pursuant to § 1.367(a)–8(c)(1)(i), the increase in stock basis provided under § 1.367(a)–8(c)(4)(i) with respect to the stock received by the U.S. transferor shareholder shall not exceed the amount of the stock basis adjustment made pursuant to § 1.367(a)–7(c)(3) with respect to the stock received by the U.S. transferor shareholder. This paragraph (e)(6)(vi) shall not apply if the U.S. transferor shareholder and the U.S. transferor are members of the same consolidated group at the time of the reorganization.

(vii) For purposes of this section, a qualified U.S. person means a U.S. person, as defined in § 1.367(a)–1T(d)(1), but for this purpose does not include domestic partnerships, regulated investment companies (as defined in section 851(a)), real estate investment trusts (as defined in section 856(a)), and S corporations (as defined in section 1361(a)).

(7) Gain subject to section 1248(a). If the U.S. transferor recognizes gain under paragraphs (e)(3)(iii)(B) or (C) of this section with respect to transferred stock that is stock in a foreign corporation to which section 1248(a) applies, then the portion of such gain treated as a deemed dividend under section 1248(a) is the product of the amount of the gain multiplied by the section 1248(a) ratio. The section 1248(a) ratio is the ratio of the amount that would be treated as a deemed dividend under section 1248(a) if all the gain in the transferred stock were recognized to the amount of gain realized in all the transferred stock.

* * *

[T.D. 8702, 61 FR 68637, Dec. 30, 1996; T.D. 8770, 63 FR 33556, June 19, 1998; 64 FR 15687, April 1, 1999; T.D. 8850, 64 FR 72550, Dec. 28, 1999; T.D. 8862, 65 FR 3596, Jan. 24, 2000; T.D. 9243, 71 FR 4282, Jan. 26, 2006; T.D. 9250, 71 FR 8804, Feb. 21, 2006; T.D. 9311, 72 FR 5182, 5183, Feb. 5, 2007; T.D. 9400, 73 FR 30303, May 27, 2008; T.D. 9444, 74 FR 6826, Feb. 11, 2009; T.D. 9446, 74 FR 6957, 6958, Feb. 11, 2009; T.D. 9526, 76 FR 28892, May 19, 2011; T.D. 9614, 78 FR 17031, March 19, 2013; T.D. 9615, 78 FR 17024, March 19, 2013; T.D. 9704, 79 FR 68766, Nov. 19, 2014; T.D. 9760, 81 FR 15161, Mar. 22, 2016; T.D. 9761, 81 FR 20883, April 8, 2016; T.D. 9803, 81 FR 91027, Dec. 16, 2016; T.D. 9834, 83 FR 32524, July 12, 2018; T.D. 9614, 85 FR 51347, Aug. 20, 2020; T.D. 10004, 89 FR 58278, July 18, 2024]

§ 1.367(a)–4 Special rule applicable to U.S. depreciated property.

(a) Depreciated property used in the United States—(1) In general. A U.S. person that transfers U.S. depreciated property (as defined in paragraph (a)(2) of this section) to a foreign corporation in an exchange described in section 367(a)(1), must include in its gross income for the taxable year in which the transfer occurs ordinary income equal to the gain realized that would have been includible in the transferor's gross income as ordinary income under section 617(d)(1), 1245(a), 1250(a), 1252(a), 1254(a), or 1255(a), whichever is applicable, if at the time of the transfer the U.S. person had sold the property at its fair market value. Recapture of depreciation under this paragraph (a) is required regardless of whether the exception to section 367(a)(1) provided by § 1.367(a)–2(a)(2) applies to the transfer of the U.S. depreciated property.

However, the transfer of the U.S. depreciated property may qualify for the exception with respect to realized gain that is not included in ordinary income pursuant to this paragraph (a).

(2) U.S. depreciated property. U.S. depreciated property subject to the rules of this paragraph (a) is any property that—

(i) Is either mining property (as defined in section 617(f)(2)), section 1245 property (as defined in section 1245(a)(3)), section 1250 property (as defined in section 1250(c)), farm land (as defined in section 1252(a)(2)), section 1254 property (as defined in section 1254(a)(3)), or section 126 property (as defined in section 1255(a)(2)); and

(ii) Has been used in the United States or has been described in section 168(g)(4) before its transfer.

(3) Property used within and without the United States. (i) If U.S. depreciated property has been used partly within and partly without the United States, then the amount required to be included in ordinary income pursuant to this paragraph (a) is reduced to an amount determined in accordance with the following formula:

$$\text{Full recapture amount} \times \frac{\text{U.S. use}}{\text{Total use}}$$

(ii) For purposes of the fraction in paragraph (a)(3)(i) of this section, the "full recapture amount" is the amount that would otherwise be included in the transferor's income under paragraph (a)(1) of this section. "U.S. use" is the number of months that the property either was used within the United States or has been described in section 168(g)(4), and was subject to depreciation by the transferor or a related person. "Total use" is the total number of months that the property was used (or available for use), and subject to depreciation, by the transferor or a related person. For purposes of this paragraph (a)(3), property is not considered to have been in use outside of the United States during any period in which such property was, for purposes of section 168, treated as property not used predominantly outside the United States pursuant to section 168(g)(4). For purposes of this paragraph (a)(3), the term "related person" has the meaning set forth in § 1.367(d)–1(h).

* * *

[T.D. 9525, 76 FR 26179, May 6, 2011; T.D. 9803, 81 FR 91027, Dec. 16, 2016]

§ 1.367(a)–8 Gain recognition agreement requirements.

(a) Scope.—This section provides the terms and conditions for a gain recognition agreement entered into by a United States person pursuant to § 1.367(a)–3(b) through (e) in connection with a transfer of stock or securities to a foreign corporation pursuant to an exchange that would otherwise be subject to section 367(a)(1). Paragraph (b) of this section provides definitions and special rules. Paragraphs (c) through (h) of this section identify the form, content, and other conditions of a gain recognition agreement. Paragraph (i) of this section is reserved. Paragraph (j) of this section identifies certain events that may require gain to be recognized under a gain recognition agreement. Paragraph (k) of this section provides exceptions for certain events that would otherwise require gain to be recognized under a gain recognition agreement. Paragraph (*l*) of this section is reserved. Paragraph (m) of this section provides rules that require gain to be recognized under a gain recognition agreement in connection with certain events to which an exception under paragraph (k) of this section otherwise applies. Paragraph (n) of this section provides special rules in the case of a distribution of property with respect to stock to which section 301 applies. Paragraph (*o*) of this section provides rules for certain transactions that terminate or reduce the amount of gain subject to a gain recognition agreement. Paragraph (p) of this section provides relief for certain failures to file an initial gain recognition agreement (as defined in paragraph (b)(1)(vi) of this section) or to comply with the requirements of this section with respect to a gain recognition agreement (as described in paragraph (c) of this section). Paragraph (q) of this section provides examples that illustrate the rules of the section. Paragraph (r) of this section provides effective dates for the provisions of this section.

* * *

[T.D. 8770, 63 FR 33562, June 19, 1998; T.D. 9243, 71 FR 4288, Jan. 26, 2006; T.D. 9311, 72 FR 5184, Feb. 5, 2007; T.D. 9446, 74 FR 6960, Feb. 11, 2009; 74 FR 10175, March 10, 2009; 74 FR 13341, March 27, 2009; T.D. 9614, 78 FR 17031, March 19, 2013; T.D. 9704, 79 FR 68766, Nov. 19, 2014; T.D. 9760, 81 FR 15170, Mar. 22, 2016; T.D. 9803, 81 FR 91029, Dec. 16, 2016; T.D. 9908, 85 FR 59431, Sept. 22, 2020]

§ 1.367(b)–1 Other transfers.

(a) Scope. The regulations promulgated under section 367(b) (the section 367(b) regulations) set forth rules regarding the proper inclusions and adjustments that must be made as a result of an exchange described in section 367(b) (a section 367(b) exchange). A section 367(b) exchange is any exchange described in section 332, 351, 354, 355, 356 or 361, with respect to which the status of a foreign corporation as a corporation is relevant for determining the extent to which income shall be recognized or for determining the effect of the transaction on earnings and profits, basis of stock or securities, basis of assets, or other relevant tax attributes.* * *

(b) General rules—(1) Rules. The following general rules apply under the section 367(b) regulations—

(i) A foreign corporation in a section 367(b) exchange is considered to be a corporation and, as a result, all of the related provisions (e.g., section 381) shall apply, except to the extent provided in the section 367(b) regulations; and

(ii) Nothing in the section 367(b) regulations shall permit—

(A) The nonrecognition of income that would otherwise be required to be recognized under another provision of the Internal Revenue Code or the regulations thereunder; or

(B) The recognition of a loss or deduction that would otherwise not be recognized under another provision of the Internal Revenue Code or the regulations thereunder.

(2) Example. The following example illustrates the rules of this paragraph (b):

Example—(i) Facts. DC, a domestic corporation, owns 90 percent of P, a partnership. The remaining 10 percent of P is owned by a person unrelated to DC. P owns all of the outstanding stock of FC, a controlled foreign corporation. FC liquidates into P.

(ii) Result. FC's liquidation is not a transaction described in section 332. Nothing in the section 367(b) regulations, including § 1.367(b) 2(k), permits FC's liquidation to qualify as a liquidation described in section 332.

* * *

[T.D. 8770, 63 FR 33566, June 19, 1998; T.D. 8862, 65 FR 3597, Jan. 24, 2000; T.D. 8862, 65 FR 66501, Nov. 6, 2000; T.D. 9243, 71 FR 4288, Jan. 26, 2006; T.D. 9273, 71 FR 44894, Aug. 8, 2006; T.D. 10004, 89 FR 58278, July 18, 2024]

§ 1.367(b)–2 Definitions and special rules.

(a) Controlled foreign corporation. The term controlled foreign corporation means a controlled foreign corporation as defined in section 957 (taking into account section 953(c)).

(b) Section 1248 shareholder. The term section 1248 shareholder means any United States person that satisfies the ownership requirements of section 1248 (a)(2) or (c)(2) with respect to a foreign corporation.

(c) Section 1248 amount—(1) Rule. The term section 1248 amount with respect to stock in a foreign corporation means the net positive earnings and profits (if any) that would have been attributable to such stock and includible in income as a dividend under section 1248 and the regulations thereunder if the stock were sold by the shareholder. But see § 1.1411–10(c)(3)(ii), which for certain exchanges modifies the section 1248 amount for purposes of section 1411. In the case of a transaction in which the shareholder is a foreign corporation (foreign shareholder), the following additional rules shall apply—

(i) The foreign shareholder shall be deemed to be a United States person for purposes of this paragraph (c), except that the foreign shareholder shall not be considered a United States person for purposes of determining whether the stock owned by the foreign shareholder is stock of a controlled foreign corporation; and

(ii) The foreign shareholder's holding period in the stock of the foreign corporation shall be determined by reference to the period that the foreign shareholder's section 1248 shareholders held (directly or indirectly) an interest in the foreign corporation. This paragraph (c)(1)(ii) applies in addition to the section 1248 regulations' incorporation of section 1223 holding periods. See § 1.1248–8.

(2) Examples. The following examples illustrate the rules of this paragraph (c):

Example 1—(i) Facts. DC, a domestic corporation, owns all of the outstanding stock of FC1, a controlled foreign corporation (CFC). FC1 owns all of the outstanding stock of FC2, a CFC. DC has always owned all of the stock of FC1, and FC1 has always owned all of the stock of FC2.

(ii) Result. Under this paragraph (c), DC's section 1248 amount with respect to its FC1 stock is computed by reference to all of FC1's and FC2's earnings and profits. See section 1248(c)(2). Because FC1's section 1248 shareholder (DC) always indirectly held all of the stock of FC2, FC1's section 1248 amount with respect to its FC2 stock is computed by reference to all of FC2's earnings and profits.

* * *

(d) All earnings and profits amount—(1) General rule. The term all earnings and profits amount with respect to stock in a foreign corporation means the net positive earnings and profits (if any) determined as provided under paragraph (d)(2) of this section and attributable to such stock as provided under paragraph (d)(3) of this section. The all earnings and profits amount shall be determined without regard to the amount of gain that would be realized on a sale or exchange of the stock of the foreign corporation.

(2) Rules for determining earnings and profits—(i) Domestic rules generally applicable. For purposes of this paragraph (d), except as provided in sections 312(k)(4) and (n)(8), 964 and 986, the earnings and profits of a foreign corporation for any taxable year shall be determined according to principles substantially similar to those applicable to domestic corporations.

(ii) Certain adjustments to earnings and profits. Notwithstanding paragraph (d)(2)(i) of this section, for purposes of this paragraph (d), the earnings and profits of a foreign corporation for any taxable year shall not include the amounts specified in section 1248(d). In the case of amounts specified in section 1248(d)(4), the preceding sentence requires that the earnings and profits for any taxable year be decreased by the net positive amount (if any) of earnings and profits attributable to activities described in section 1248(d)(4), and increased by the net reduction (if any) in earnings and profits attributable to activities described in section 1248(d)(4). But see § 1.1411–10(c)(3)(ii), which for certain exchanges modifies the all earnings and profits amount for purposes of section 1411.

* * *

[T.D. 8397, 57 FR 6555, Feb. 26, 1992; T.D. 8862, 65 FR 3598, Jan. 24, 2000; T.D. 8862, 65 FR 66501,

Nov. 6, 2000; T.D. 9216, 70 FR 43760, July 29, 2005; T.D. 9273, 71 FR 44894, Aug. 8, 2006; T.D. 9345, 72 FR 41444, July 30, 2007; T.D. 9400, 73 FR 30303, May 27, 2008; T.D. 9959, 87 FR 325, Jan. 4, 2022; T.D. 10004, 89 FR 58279, July 18, 2024]

§ 1.367(b)–3 Repatriation of foreign corporate assets in certain nonrecognition transactions.

(a) Scope. This section applies to an acquisition by a domestic corporation (the domestic acquiring corporation) of the assets of a foreign corporation (the foreign acquired corporation) in a liquidation described in section 332 or an asset acquisition described in section 368(a)(1).

(b) Exchange of stock owned directly by a United States shareholder or by certain foreign corporate shareholders—(1) Scope. This paragraph (b) applies in the case of an exchanging shareholder that is either—

(i) A United States shareholder of the foreign acquired corporation; or

(ii) A foreign corporation with respect to which there are one or more United States shareholders.

(2) United States shareholder. For purposes of this section (and for purposes of the other section 367(b) regulation provisions that specifically refer to this paragraph (b)(2)), the term United States shareholder means any shareholder described in section 951(b) (without regard to whether the foreign corporation is a controlled foreign corporation), and also any shareholder described in section 953(c)(1)(A) (but only if the foreign corporation is a controlled foreign corporation as defined in section 953(c)(1)(B) subject to the rules of section 953(c)).

(3) Income inclusion—(i) Inclusion of all earnings and profits amount. An exchanging shareholder shall include in income as a deemed dividend the all earnings and profits amount with respect to its stock in the foreign acquired corporation.

* * *

[T.D. 8862, 65 FR 3601, Jan. 24, 2000; T.D. 8862, 65 FR 66501, Nov. 6, 2000; T.D. 9243, 71 FR 4288, Jan. 26, 2006; T.D. 9273, 71 FR 44895, Aug. 8, 2006; T.D. 9959, 87 FR 325, Jan. 4, 2022; T.D. 10004, 89 FR 58279, July 18, 2024]

§ 1.367(b)–4 Acquisition of foreign corporate stock or assets by a foreign corporation in certain nonrecognition transactions.

(a) Scope. This section applies to certain acquisitions by a foreign corporation of the stock or assets of a foreign corporation in an exchange described in section 351 or in a reorganization described in section 368(a)(1). Paragraph (b) of this section provides a rule regarding when an exchanging shareholder is required to include in income as a deemed dividend the section 1248 amount attributable to the stock that it exchanges. Paragraph (c) of this section provides a rule excluding deemed dividends from foreign personal holding company income. Paragraph (d) of this section provides rules for subsequent sales or exchanges. Paragraphs (e) and (f) of this section provide rules regarding certain exchanges following inversion transactions. Paragraph (g) of this section provides rules regarding exchanges that occur pursuant to a transaction described in § 1.367(b)–10(a)(1), without regard to the exceptions in § 1.367(b)–10(a)(2). Paragraph (h) of this section provides definitions and special rules, including special rules regarding triangular reorganizations and recapitalizations. Paragraph (i) of this section provides the applicability dates for certain paragraphs of this section. See also § 1.367(a)–3(b)(2) for transactions subject to the concurrent application of sections 367(a) and (b) and § 1.367(b)–2 for additional definitions that apply.

(b) Income inclusion. If a foreign corporation (the transferee foreign corporation) acquires the stock of a foreign corporation in an exchange described in section 351 or the stock or assets of a foreign corporation in a reorganization described in section 368(a)(1) (in either case, the foreign acquired corporation), then an exchanging shareholder must, if its exchange is described in paragraph (b)(1)(i), (b)(2)(i), or (b)(3) of this section, include in income as a deemed dividend the section 1248 amount attributable to the stock that it exchanges.

(1) Exchange that results in loss of status as section 1248 shareholder—(i) General rule. Except as provided in paragraph (b)(1)(ii) of this section, an exchange is described in this paragraph (b)(1)(i) if—

(A) Immediately before the exchange, the exchanging shareholder is—

(1) A United States person that is a section 1248 shareholder with respect to the foreign acquired corporation; or

(2) A foreign corporation, and a United States person is a section 1248 shareholder with respect to such foreign corporation and with respect to the foreign acquired corporation;

(B) Either of the following conditions is satisfied—

(1) Immediately after the exchange, the stock received in the exchange is not stock in a corporation that is a controlled foreign corporation as to which the United States person described in paragraph (b)(1)(i)(A) of this section is a section 1248 shareholder; or

(2) Immediately after the exchange, the foreign acquiring corporation or the foreign acquired corporation (in the case of the acquisition of the stock of a foreign acquired corporation) is not a controlled foreign corporation as to which the United States person described in paragraph (b)(1)(i)(A) of this section is a section 1248 shareholder; and

(C) The exchange is not a specified exchange to which paragraph (e)(1) of this section applies.

* * *

(2) Receipt by exchanging shareholder of preferred or other stock in certain instances—(i) Rule. An exchange is described in this paragraph (b)(2)(i) if—

(A) Immediately before the exchange, the foreign acquired corporation and the foreign acquiring corporations are not members of the same affiliated group (within the meaning of section 1504(a), but without regard to the exceptions set forth in section 1504(b), and substituting the words "more than 50" in place of the words "at least 80" in sections 1504(a)(2)(A) and (B));

(B) Immediately after the exchange, a domestic corporation directly or indirectly owns 10 percent or more of the voting power or value of the transferee foreign corporation; and

(C) The exchanging shareholder receives preferred stock (other than preferred stock that is fully participating with respect to dividends, redemptions and corporate growth) in consideration for common stock or preferred stock that is fully participating with respect to dividends, redemptions and corporate growth, or, in the discretion of the Commissioner or the Commissioner's delegate (and without regard to whether the stock exchanged is common stock or preferred stock), receives stock that entitles it to participate (through dividends, redemption payments or otherwise) disproportionately in the earnings generated by particular assets of the foreign acquired corporation or foreign acquiring corporation.

* * *

(e) Income inclusion and gain recognition in certain exchanges following an inversion transaction—(1) General rule. If a foreign corporation (the transferee foreign corporation) acquires stock of a foreign corporation in an exchange described in section 351 or stock or assets of a foreign corporation in a reorganization described in section 368(a)(1) (in either case, the foreign acquired corporation), then an exchanging shareholder must, if its exchange is a specified exchange and the exception in paragraph (e)(3) of this section does not apply—

(i) Include in income as a deemed dividend the section 1248 amount attributable to the stock that it exchanges; and

(ii) After taking into account the increase in basis provided in § 1.367(b)–2(e)(3)(ii) resulting from the deemed dividend (if any), recognize all realized gain with respect to the stock that would not otherwise be recognized.

(2) Specified exchanges. An exchange is a specified exchange if—

(i) Immediately before the exchange, the foreign acquired corporation is an expatriated foreign subsidiary and the exchanging shareholder is either an expatriated entity described in paragraph (b)(1)(i)(A)(1) of this section or an expatriated foreign subsidiary described in paragraph (b)(1)(i)(A)(2) of this section;

(ii) The stock received in the exchange is stock of a foreign corporation; and

(iii) The exchange occurs during the applicable period.

(3) De minimis exception. The exception in this paragraph (e)(3) applies if—

(i) Immediately after the exchange, the foreign acquired corporation (in the case of an acquisition of stock of the foreign acquired corporation) or the transferee foreign corporation (in the case of an acquisition of assets of the foreign acquired corporation) is a controlled foreign corporation;

(ii) The post-exchange ownership percentage with respect to the foreign acquired corporation (in the case of an acquisition of stock of the foreign acquired corporation) or the transferee foreign corporation (in the case of an acquisition of assets of the foreign acquired corporation) is at least 90 percent of the pre-exchange ownership percentage with respect to the foreign acquired corporation; and

(iii) The post-exchange ownership percentage with respect to each lower-tier expatriated foreign subsidiary of the foreign acquired corporation is at least 90 percent of the pre-exchange ownership percentage with respect to the lower-tier expatriated foreign subsidiary.

(4) Certain exceptions from foreign personal holding company not available. An income inclusion of a foreign corporation under paragraph (e)(1) of this section does not qualify for the exceptions from foreign personal holding company income provided by sections 954(c)(3)(A)(i) and 954(c)(6) (to the extent in effect).

(5) Examples. The following examples illustrate the application of this paragraph (e). For purposes of all of the examples, unless otherwise indicated: FP, a foreign corporation, owns all of the stock of USP, a domestic corporation, and all 40 shares of stock of FS, a controlled foreign corporation for its taxable year beginning January 1, 2017, but not for prior taxable years, except as a result of a transaction described in the facts of an example. USP owns all 50 shares of stock of FT1, a controlled foreign corporation, which, in turn, owns all 50 shares of FT2, a controlled foreign corporation. FP acquired all of the stock of USP in an inversion transaction that was completed on July 1, 2016. Therefore, with respect to that inversion transaction, USP is an expatriated entity; FT1 and FT2 are expatriated foreign subsidiaries; and FP and FS are each a non-EFS foreign related person. All entities have a calendar year tax year for U.S. tax purposes. All shares of stock have a fair market value of $1x, and each corporation has a single class of stock outstanding.

Example 1. Specified exchange to which general rule applies—(i) Facts. During the applicable period, and pursuant to a reorganization described in section 368(a)(1)(B), FT1 transfers all 50 shares of FT2 stock to FS in exchange solely for 50 newly issued voting shares of FS. Immediately before the exchange, USP is a section 1248 shareholder with respect to FT1 and FT2. At the time of the exchange, the FT2 stock owned by FT1 has a fair market value of $50x and an adjusted basis of $5x, such that the FT2 stock has a built-in gain of $45x. In addition, the earnings and profits of FT2 attributable to FT1's stock in FT2 for purposes of section 1248 is $30x, taking into account the rules of § 1.367(b)–2(c)(1)(i) and (ii), and therefore the section 1248 amount with respect to the FT2 stock is $30x (the lesser of the $45x of built-in gain and the $30x of earnings and profits attributable to the stock).

(ii) Analysis. FT1's exchange is a specified exchange because the requirements set forth in paragraphs (e)(2)(i) through (iii) of this section are satisfied. The requirement set forth in paragraph (e)(2)(i) of this section is satisfied because, immediately before the exchange, FT2 (the foreign acquired corporation) is an expatriated foreign subsidiary and FT1 (the exchanging shareholder) is an expatriated foreign subsidiary that is described in paragraph (b)(1)(i)(A)(2) of this section. The requirement set forth in paragraph (e)(2)(ii) of this section is also satisfied because the stock received in the exchange (FS stock) is stock of a foreign corporation. The requirement set forth in paragraph (e)(2)(iii) of this section is satisfied because the exchange occurs during the applicable period. Accordingly, under paragraph (e)(1)(i) of this section, FT1 must include in income as a deemed dividend $30x, the section 1248 amount with respect to its FT2 stock. In addition, under paragraph (e)(1)(ii) of this section, FT1 must, after taking into account the increase in basis provided in § 1.367(b)–2(e)(3)(ii) resulting from the deemed dividend (which increases FT1's basis in its FT2 stock from $5x to $35x), recognize $15x ($50x amount realized less $35x basis), the realized gain with respect to the FT2 stock that would not otherwise be recognized.

* * *

[T.D. 8770, 63 FR 33567, June 19, 1998; 64 FR 15687, April 1, 1999; T.D. 8862, 65 FR 3603, Jan. 24, 2000; T.D. 8862, 65 FR 66501, Nov. 6, 2000; T.D. 9243, 71 FR 4288, Jan. 26, 2006; T.D. 9250, 71 FR 8804, Feb. 21, 2006; T.D. 9311, 72 FR 5182, Feb. 5, 2007; T.D. 9345, 72 FR 41444, July 30, 2007; T.D. 9444, 74 FR 6827, Feb. 11, 2009; T.D. 9446, 74 FR 6957, Feb. 11, 2009; T.D. 9614, 78 FR 17031, March 19, 2013; T.D. 9760, 81 FR 15170, Mar. 22, 2016; T.D. 9761, 81 FR 20883, April 8, 2016; T.D. 9834, 83 FR 32524, July 12, 2018; T.D. 9959, 87 FR 324, Jan. 4, 2022; 87 FR 45019, July 27, 2022; T.D. 10004, 89 FR 58282, July 18, 2024]

§ 1.367(b)–5 Distributions of stock described in section 355.

(a) In general—(1) Scope. This section provides rules relating to a distribution described in section 355 (or so much of section 356 as relates to section 355) and to which section 367(b) applies. For purposes of this section, the terms distributing corporation, controlled corporation, and distributee have the same meaning as used in section 355 and the regulations thereunder.

(2) Treatment of distributees as exchanging shareholders. For purposes of the section 367(b) regulations, all distributees in a transaction described in paragraph (b), (c), or (d) of this section shall be treated as exchanging shareholders that realize income in a section 367(b) exchange.

(b) Distribution by a domestic corporation—(1) General rule. In a distribution described in section 355, if the distributing corporation is a domestic corporation and the controlled corporation is a foreign corporation, the following general rules shall apply—

(i) If the distributee is a corporation, then the controlled corporation shall be considered to be a corporation; and

(ii) If the distributee is an individual, then, solely for purposes of determining the gain recognized by the distributing corporation, the controlled corporation shall not be considered to be a corporation, and the distributing corporation shall recognize any gain (but not loss) realized on the distribution.

(2) Section 367(e) transactions. The rules of paragraph (b)(1) of this section shall not apply to a foreign distributee to the extent gain is recognized under section 367(e)(1) and the regulations thereunder.

(3) Determining whether distributees are individuals. All distributees in a distribution described in paragraph (b)(1) of this section are presumed to be individuals. However, the shareholder identification principles of § 1.367(e) 1(d) (including the reporting procedures in § 1.367(e)–1(d)(2) and (3)) shall apply for purposes of rebutting this presumption.

* * *

[T.D. 8862, 65 FR 3606, Jan. 24, 2000; T.D. 8862, 65 FR 66502, Nov. 6, 2000]

§ 1.367(d)–1 Transfers of intangible property to foreign corporations.

(a) [Reserved]. For further guidance, see § 1.367(d)–1T(a).

(b) Property subject to section 367(d). Section 367(d) and the rules of this section apply to the transfer of intangible property, as defined in § 1.367(a)–1(d)(5), by a U.S. person to a foreign corporation in an exchange described in section 351 or 361. See section 367(a) and the regulations thereunder for the rules that apply to the transfer of any property other than intangible property.

(c) Deemed payments upon transfer of intangible property to foreign corporation—(1) In general. For further guidance, see § 1.367(d)–1T(c)(1).

(2) Required adjustments. For further guidance, see § 1.367(d)–1T(c)(2) introductory text and (c)(2)(i).

(i) [Reserved]

(ii) The deemed payment is treated as an allowable deduction (whether or not that amount is paid) of the transferee foreign corporation properly allocated and apportioned to the appropriate classes of gross income in accordance with §§ 1.882–4(b)(1), 1.951A–2(c)(3), 1.954–1(c), and 1.960–1(c) and (d), as applicable.

(3) Useful life—(i) In general. For purposes of determining the period of inclusions for deemed payments under § 1.367(d)–1T(c)(1), the useful life of intangible property is the entire period during which exploitation of the intangible property is reasonably anticipated to affect the determination of taxable income, as of the time of transfer. Exploitation of intangible property includes any direct or indirect use or transfer of the intangible property, including use without further development, use in the further development of the intangible property itself (and any exploitation of the further developed intangible property), and use in the development of other intangible property (and any exploitation of the other developed intangible property).

(ii) Procedure to limit inclusions to 20 years. In cases where the useful life of the transferred property is indefinite or is reasonably anticipated to exceed twenty years, taxpayers may, in lieu of including amounts during the entire useful life of the intangible property, choose in the year of transfer to increase annual inclusions during the 20-year period beginning with the first year in which the U.S. transferor takes into account income pursuant to section 367(d), to reflect amounts that, but for this paragraph (c)(3)(ii), would have been required to be included following the end of the 20-year period. See § 1.6038B–1(d)(1)(iv) for guidance on reporting this choice of method. If the taxpayer applies this method during the 20-year period, no adjustments will be made for taxable years beginning after the conclusion of the 20-year period. However, for purposes of determining whether amounts included during the 20-year period are commensurate with the income attributable to the transferred intangible property, the Commissioner may take into account information with respect to taxable years after that period, such as the income attributable to the transferred property during those later years. The application of this paragraph (c)(3)(ii) must be reflected in a statement (titled "Application of 20-

Year Inclusion Period to Section 367(d) Transfers") attached to a timely filed original federal income tax return (including extensions) for the year of the transfer. An increase to the deemed payment rate made pursuant to this paragraph (c)(3)(ii) will be irrevocable, and a failure to timely file the statement under this paragraph (c)(3)(ii) may not be remedied.

(iii) Example. Property subject to section 367(d) is transferred from USP, a domestic corporation, to FA, a foreign corporation wholly owned by USP. The useful life of the transferred property, inclusive of derivative works, at the time of transfer is indefinite but is reasonably anticipated to exceed 20 years. In the first five years following the transfer, sales related to the property are expected to be $100x, $130x, $160x, $180x and $187.2x, respectively. Thereafter, for the remainder of the property's useful life, sales are expected to grow by four percent annually. In the first five years following the transfer, operating profits attributable to the property are expected to be $5x, $8x, $11x, $12.5x, and $13x, respectively. Thereafter, for the remainder of the property's useful life, operating profits are expected to grow by four percent annually. It is determined that the appropriate discount rate for sales and operating profits is 10 percent. The present value of operating profits through the property's indefinite useful life is $185x. The present value of sales through the property's indefinite useful life is $2698x. Accordingly, the sales based royalty rate during the property's useful life is 6.8 percent ($185x/$2698x). The taxpayer may choose to take income inclusions into account over a 20-year period. The present value of sales through the 20-year period is $1787x. Accordingly, the sales based royalty rate under the 20-year option is increased to 10.3 percent ($185x/$1787x).

* * *

[T.D. 9803, 81 FR 91029, Dec. 16, 2016; T.D. 9994, 89 FR 82165, Oct. 10, 2024]

§ 1.367(d)–1T Transfers of intangible property to foreign corporations (temporary).

(a) Purpose and scope. This section provides rules under section 367(d) concerning transfers of intangible property by U.S. persons to foreign corporations pursuant to section 351 or 361. Paragraph (b) of this section specifies the transfers that are subject to section 367(d) and the rules of this section, while paragraph (c) provides rules concerning the consequences of such a transfer. In general, the U.S. transferor will be treated as receiving annual payments contingent on productivity or use of the transferred property, over the useful life of the property (regardless of whether such payments are in fact made by the transferee). Paragraphs (d), (e), and (f) of this section provide rules for cases in which there is a later direct or indirect disposition of the intangible property transferred. In general, deemed annual license payments will continue if a transfer is made to a related person, while gain must be recognized immediately if the transfer is to an unrelated person. Paragraph (g) of this section provides several special rules, including a rule allowing appropriate adjustments where deemed payments under section 367(d) are not in fact received by the U.S. transferor of the intangible property, and a rule providing for a limited election to treat certain transfers of intangible property as sales at fair market value (in lieu of applying the general useful life-contingent payment rule). In addition, paragraph (g) of this section provides rules coordinating the application of section 367(d) with other relevant Code sections. Paragraph (h) of this section defines the term related person for purposes of this section. Finally, paragraph (i) of this section provides the effective date of this section. For rules concerning transfers of intangible property pursuant to section 332, see § 1.367(a)–5T(e). For purposes of determining whether a U.S. person has made a transfer of intangible property that is subject to the rules of section 367(d), the rules of § 1.367(a)–1T(c) shall apply.

* * *

(c) Deemed payments upon transfer of intangible property to foreign corporation—(1) In general. If a U.S. person transfers intangible property that is subject to section 367(d) and the rules of this section to a foreign corporation in an exchange described in section 351 or 361, then such person shall be treated as having transferred that property in exchange for annual payments contingent on the productivity or use of the property. Such person shall, over the useful life of the property, annually include in gross income an amount that represents an appropriate arms-length charge for the use of the property. The appropriate charge shall be determined in accordance with the provisions of section 482 and regulations thereunder. See § 1.482–2(d). The amount of the deemed payment thus calculated shall be reduced by any royalty or other periodic payment made or accrued by the transferee to an unrelated person during that taxable year for the right to use the intangible property. Amounts so included in the transferor's income shall be treated as ordinary income from sources within the United States. For purposes of computing estimated tax payments, deemed payments under this paragraph (c) shall be treated as received by the transferor on the last day of its taxable year.

* * *

(g) Special rules—* * *

* * *

(4) Coordination with section 482—(i) In general. Section 367(d) and the rules of this section shall not apply in the case of an actual sale or license of intangible property by a U.S. person to a foreign corporation. If an adjustment under section 482 is required with respect to an actual sale or license of intangible property, then section 367(d) and the rules of this section shall not apply with respect to the required adjustment. If a U.S. person transfers intangible property to a related foreign corporation without consideration, or in exchange for stock or securities of the transferee in a transaction described in sections 351 or 361, no sale or license subject to adjustment under section 482 will be deemed to have occurred. Instead, the U.S. person shall be treated as having made a transfer of the intangible property that is subject to section 367(d).

* * *

(6) Anti-abuse rule. If a U.S. person—

(i) Transfers intangible property to a domestic corporation with a principal purpose of avoiding the effect of section 367(d) and the rules of this section; and

(ii) Thereafter transfers the stock of that domestic corporation to a related foreign corporation,

then solely for purposes of section 367(d) that U.S. person shall be treated as having transferred the intangible property directly to the foreign corporation. A U.S. person shall be presumed to have transferred intangible property for a principal purpose of avoiding the effect of section 367(d) if the property is transferred to the domestic corporation less than two years prior to the transfer of the stock of that domestic corporation to a foreign corporation. The presumption created by the previous sentence may be rebutted by clear evidence that the subsequent transfer of the stock of the domestic transferee corporation was not contemplated at the time the intangible property was transferred to that corporation and that avoidance of section 367(d) and the rules of this section was not a principal purpose of the transaction. A transfer may have more than one principal purpose.

* * *

[T.D. 8087, 51 FR 17953, May 16, 1986; T.D. 8770, 63 FR 33568, June 19, 1998; T.D. 9803, 81 FR 91030, Dec. 16, 2016; T.D. 9994, 89 FR 82169, Oct. 10, 2024]

§ 1.367(e)–1 Distributions described in section 367(e)(1).

* * *

(b) Gain recognition—(1) General rule. If a domestic corporation makes a distribution of stock or securities of a corporation that qualifies for nonrecognition under section 355 to a person who is not a qualified U.S. person, then, except as provided in paragraph (c) of this section, the distributing corporation shall recognize gain (but not loss) on the distribution under section 367(e)(1). A distributing corporation shall not recognize gain under this section with respect to a section 355 distribution to a qualified U.S. person. For purposes of this section, a qualified U.S. person is—

(A) A citizen or resident of the United States; or

(B) A domestic corporation. * * *

* * *

(c) Nonrecognition of gain. A domestic distributing corporation shall not recognize gain under paragraph (b)(1) of this section on the distribution of stock or securities of a domestic corporation.

(d) Determining whether distributees are qualified U.S. persons—(1) General rule—presumption of foreign status. Except as provided in paragraphs (d)(2) and (3) of this section, all distributions of stock or securities in a distribution described in section 355 in which the distributing corporation is domestic and the controlled corporation is foreign are presumed to be to persons who are not qualified U.S. persons, as defined in paragraph (b)(1) of this section.

* * *

[T.D. 8834, 64 FR 43076, Aug. 9, 1999; 65 FR 11467, March 3, 2000; T.D. 9614, 78 FR 17031, March 19, 2013; T.D. 9760, 81 FR 15170, March 22, 2016]

§ 1.367(e)–2 Distributions described in section 367(e)(2).

(a) Purpose and scope—(1) In general.

* * *

(2) Nonapplicability of section 367(a). Section 367(a) shall not apply to a complete liquidation described in section 332 by a domestic liquidating corporation into a foreign corporation that meets the stock ownership requirements of section 332(b).

(b) Distribution by a domestic corporation—(1) General rule—(i) Recognition of gain and loss. If a domestic corporation (domestic liquidating corporation) makes a distribution of property in complete liquidation under section 332 to a foreign corporation (foreign distributee corporation) that meets the stock ownership requirements of section 332(b) with respect to stock in the domestic liquidating corporation, then—

(A) Section 337(a) and (b)(1) will not apply; and

(B) The domestic liquidating corporation will recognize gain or loss on the distribution of property to the foreign distributee corporation, except as provided in paragraph (b)(2) of this section.

(ii) Operating rules—(A) General rule. Except as provided in paragraphs (b)(1)(ii)(B) and (C) of this section, the rules contained in section 336 will apply to the gain and loss recognized pursuant to this section.

(B) Overall loss limitation—(1) Overall loss limitation rule. Loss in excess of gain from the distribution shall not be recognized. If realized losses exceed recognized losses, the losses shall be recognized on a pro rata basis with respect to the realized loss attributable to each distributed loss asset in the category of assets (i.e., capital or ordinary) to which the realized but unrecognized loss relates. For additional limitations on the recognition of losses, see, e.g., section 1211.

* * *

(2) Exceptions—(i) Distribution of property used in a U.S. trade or business—

(A) Conditions for nonrecognition. A domestic liquidating corporation shall not recognize gain or loss under paragraph (b)(1) of this section on its distribution of property (including inventory) used by the domestic liquidating corporation in the conduct of a trade or business within United States, if—

(1) The foreign distributee corporation, immediately thereafter and for the ten-year period beginning on the date of the distribution of such property, uses the property in the conduct of a trade or business within the United States;

(2) The domestic liquidating corporation attaches the statement described in paragraph (b)(2)(i)(C) of this section to its timely filed U.S. income tax returns for the taxable years that include the distributions in liquidation; and

(3) The foreign distributee corporation attaches a copy of the property description contained in paragraph (b)(2)(i)(C)(2) of this section to its timely filed U.S. income tax return for the tax year that includes the date of distribution.

(B) Qualifying property. Property is used by the foreign distributee corporation in the conduct of a trade or business in the United States within the meaning of this paragraph (b)(2)(i) only if all income from the use of the property and all income or gain from the sale or exchange of the property would be subject to taxation under section 882(a) as effectively connected income. Also, stock held by a dealer as inventory or for sale in the ordinary course of its trade or business shall be treated as inventory and not as stock in the hands of both the domestic liquidating corporation and the distributee foreign corporation. Notwithstanding the foregoing, the exception provided in this paragraph (b)(2)(i) shall not apply to intangibles described in section 367(d)(4).

* * *

(E) Operating rules. By the domestic liquidating corporation's claiming nonrecognition under this paragraph (b)(2)(i) and filing a statement described in paragraph (b)(2)(i)(C) of this section, the domestic liquidating corporation and the foreign distributee corporation agree to be subject to the rules of this paragraph (b)(2)(i)(E).

(1) Gain or loss recognition by the foreign distributee corporation—(i) Taxable dispositions. If, within the ten-year period from the date of a distribution of qualifying property, the foreign distributee corporation disposes of any qualifying property in a transaction subject to tax under section 882(a), then the foreign distributee corporation shall recognize such gain (or loss) and properly report it on a timely filed U.S. income tax return. If the foreign distributee corporation recognizes gain (or loss) under this paragraph (b)(2)(i)(E)(1)(i) and properly reports such gain (or loss) on its U.S. income tax return, then the domestic liquidating corporation shall not recognize gain attributable to such property under paragraph (b)(2)(i)(E)(2) of this section.

* * *

(c) Distribution by a foreign corporation—(1) General rule—gain and loss not recognized. If a foreign corporation (foreign liquidating) makes a distribution of property in complete liquidation under section 332 to a foreign corporation (foreign distributee) that meets the stock ownership requirements of section 332(b) with respect to stock in the foreign liquidating corporation, then, except as provided in paragraph (c)(2) of this section, section 337(a) and (b)(1) shall apply and the foreign liquidating corporation shall not recognize gain (or loss) on the distribution under section 367(e)(2). If a foreign liquidating corporation distributes a partnership interest (whether foreign or domestic), then such corporation shall be treated as having distributed a proportionate share of partnership property in accordance with the principles of paragraph (b)(1)(iii) of this section.

(2) Exceptions—(i) Property used in a U.S. trade or business—(A) General rule. A foreign liquidating corporation (including a corporation that has made an effective election under section 897(i)) that makes a distribution described in paragraph (c)(1) of this section shall recognize gain (or loss in accordance with principles contained in paragraph (b)(1)(ii) of this section) on the distribution of qualified property, as described in paragraph (b)(2)(i)(B) of this section (other than U.S. real property interests), that is used by the foreign liquidating corporation in the conduct of a trade or business within the United States at the time of distribution.

(B) Ten-year active U.S. business exception. A foreign liquidating corporation shall not recognize gain under paragraph (c)(2)(i)(A) of this section, if—

(1) The foreign distributee corporation, immediately thereafter and for the ten-year period beginning on the date of the distribution of such property, uses the property in the conduct of a trade or business in the United States;

(2) The foreign distributee corporation is not entitled to benefits under a comprehensive income tax treaty (this requirement shall apply only if the foreign liquidating corporation (or predecessor corporation) was not entitled to benefits under a comprehensive income tax treaty); and

(3) The foreign liquidating corporation and foreign distributee corporation attach the statement described in paragraph (c)(2)(i)(C) of this section to their timely filed U.S. income tax returns for their taxable years that include the distribution.

* * *

(d) Anti-abuse rule. The Commissioner may require a domestic liquidating corporation to recognize gain on a distribution in liquidation described in paragraph (b) of this section (or treat the liquidating corporation as if it had recognized loss on a distribution in liquidation), if a principal purpose of the liquidation is the avoidance of U.S. tax (including, but not limited to, the distribution of a liquidating corporation's earnings and profits with a principal purpose of avoiding U.S. tax). A liquidation may have a principal purpose of tax avoidance even though the tax avoidance purpose is outweighed by other purposes when taken together.

* * *

[T.D. 8834, 64 FR 43077, Aug. 9, 1999; 65 FR 11467, March 3, 2000; T.D. 9066, 68 FR 39453, July 2, 2003; T.D. 9704, 79 FR 68771, Nov. 19, 2014; 80 FR 167, Jan. 5, 2015; T.D. 9803, 81 FR 91030, Dec. 16, 2016; T.D. 9994, 89 FR 82169, Oct. 10, 2024]

Deferred Compensation, Etc.

§ 1.482–1 Allocation of income and deductions among taxpayers.

(a) In general—(1) Purpose and scope. The purpose of section 482 is to ensure that taxpayers clearly reflect income attributable to controlled transactions and to prevent the avoidance of taxes with respect to such transactions. Section 482 places a controlled taxpayer on a tax parity with an uncontrolled taxpayer by determining the true taxable income of the controlled taxpayer. This section sets forth general principles and guidelines to be followed under section 482. Section 1.482–2 provides rules for the determination of the true taxable income of controlled taxpayers in specific situations, including controlled transactions involving loans or advances or the use of tangible property. Sections 1.482–3 through 1.482–6 provide rules for the determination of the true taxable income of controlled taxpayers in cases involving the transfer of property. Section 1.482–7T sets forth the cost sharing provisions applicable to taxable years beginning on or after January 5, 2009. Section 1.482–8 provides examples illustrating the application of the best method rule. Finally, § 1.482–9 provides rules for the determination of the true taxable income of controlled taxpayers in cases involving the performance of services.

(2) Authority to make allocations. The district director may make allocations between or among the members of a controlled group if a controlled taxpayer has not reported its true taxable income. In such case, the district director may allocate income, deductions, credits, allowances, basis, or any other item or element affecting taxable income (referred to as allocations). The appropriate allocation may take the form of an increase or decrease in any relevant amount.

(3) Taxpayer's use of section 482. If necessary to reflect an arm's length result, a controlled taxpayer may report on a timely filed U.S. income tax return (including extensions) the results of its controlled transactions based upon prices different from those actually charged. Except as provided in this paragraph, section 482 grants no other right to a controlled taxpayer to apply the provisions of section 482 at will or to compel the district director to apply such provisions. * * *

(b) Arm's length standard—(1) In general. In determining the true taxable income of a controlled taxpayer, the standard to be applied in every case is that of a taxpayer dealing at arm's length with an uncontrolled taxpayer. A controlled transaction meets the arm's length standard if the results of the transaction are consistent with the results that would have been realized if uncontrolled taxpayers had engaged in the same transaction under the same circumstances (arm's length result). However, because identical transactions can rarely be located, whether a transaction produces an arm's length result generally will be determined by reference to the results of comparable transactions under comparable circumstances. See § 1.482–1(d)(2) (Standard of comparability). Evaluation of whether a controlled transaction produces an arm's length result is made pursuant to a method selected under the best method rule described in § 1.482–1(c).

(2) Arm's length methods—(i) Methods. Sections 1.482–2 through 1.482–7 and 1.482–9 provide specific methods to be used to evaluate whether transactions between or among members of the controlled group satisfy the arm's length standard, and if they do not, to determine the arm's length result. This section provides general principles applicable in determining arm's length results of such controlled transactions, but do not provide methods, for which reference must be made to those other sections in accordance with paragraphs (b)(2)(ii) and (iii) of this section. Section 1.482–7 provides the specific methods to be used to evaluate whether a cost sharing arrangement as defined in § 1.482–7 produces results consistent with an arm's length result.

(ii) Selection of category of method applicable to transaction. The methods listed in § 1.482–2 apply to different types of transactions, such as transfers of property, services, loans or advances, and rentals. Accordingly, the method or methods most appropriate to the calculation of arm's length results for controlled transactions must be selected, and different methods may be applied to interrelated transactions if such transactions are most reliably evaluated on a separate basis. For example, if services are provided in connection with the transfer of property, it may be appropriate to separately apply the methods applicable to services and property in order to determine an arm's length result. But see § 1.482–1(f)(2)(i) (Aggregation of transactions). In addition, other applicable provisions of the Code may affect the characterization of a transaction, and therefore affect the methods applicable under section 482. See for example section 467.

(iii) Coordination of methods applicable to certain intangible development arrangements. Section 1.482–7 provides the specific methods to be used to determine arm's length results of controlled transactions in connection with a cost sharing arrangement as defined in § 1.482–7. Sections 1.482–4 and 1.482–9, as appropriate, provide the specific methods to be used to determine arm's length results of arrangements, including partnerships, for sharing the costs and risks of developing intangibles, other than a cost sharing arrangement covered by § 1.482–7. See also §§ 1.482–4(g) (Coordination with rules governing cost sharing arrangements) and 1.482–9(m)(3) (Coordination with rules governing cost sharing arrangements).

(c) Best method rule—(1) In general. The arm's length result of a controlled transaction must be determined under the method that, under the facts and circumstances, provides the most reliable measure of an arm's length result. Thus, there is no strict priority of methods, and no method will invariably be considered to be more reliable than others. An arm's length result may be determined under any method without establishing the inapplicability of another method, but if another method subsequently is shown to produce a more reliable measure of an arm's length result, such other method must be used. Similarly, if two or more applications of a single method provide inconsistent results, the arm's length result must be determined under the application that, under the facts and circumstances, provides the most reliable measure of an arm's length result. See § 1.482–8 for examples of the application of the best method rule. See § 1.482–7 for the applicable methods in the case of a cost sharing arrangement.

(2) Determining the best method. Data based on the results of transactions between unrelated parties provides the most objective basis for determining whether the results of a controlled transaction are arm's length. Thus, in determining which of two or more available methods (or applications of a single method) provides the most reliable measure of an arm's length result, the two primary factors to take into account are the degree of comparability between the controlled transaction (or taxpayer) and any uncontrolled comparables, and the quality of the data and assumptions used in the analysis. In addition, in certain circumstances, it also may be relevant to consider whether the results of an analysis are consistent with the results of an analysis under another method. These factors are explained in paragraphs (c)(2)(i), (ii), and (iii) of this section.

(i) Comparability. The relative reliability of a method based on the results of transactions between unrelated parties depends on the degree of comparability between the controlled transaction or taxpayers and the uncontrolled comparables, taking into account the factors described in § 1.482–1(d)(3) (Factors for determining comparability), and after making adjustments for differences, as described in § 1.482–1(d)(2) (Standard of comparability). * * *

(ii) Data and assumptions. Whether a method provides the most reliable measure of an arm's length result also depends upon the completeness and accuracy of the underlying data, the reliability of the assumptions, and the sensitivity of the results to possible deficiencies in the data and assumptions. Such factors are particularly relevant in evaluating the degree of comparability between the controlled and uncontrolled transactions. * * *

(iii) Confirmation of results by another method. If two or more methods produce inconsistent results, the best method rule will be applied to select the method that provides the most reliable measure of an arm's length result. If the best method rule does not clearly indicate which method should be selected, an additional factor that may be taken into account in selecting a method is whether any of the competing methods produce results that are consistent with the results obtained from the appropriate application of another method. Further, in evaluating different applications of the same method, the fact that a second method (or another application of the first method) produces results that are consistent with one of the competing applications may be taken into account.

(d) Comparability—(1) In general. Whether a controlled transaction produces an arm's length result is generally evaluated by comparing the results of that transaction to results realized by uncontrolled taxpayers engaged in comparable transactions under comparable circumstances. For this purpose, the comparability of transactions and circumstances must be evaluated considering all factors that could affect prices or profits in arm's length dealings (comparability factors). While a specific comparability factor may be of particular importance in applying a method, each method requires analysis of all of the factors that affect comparability under that method. Such factors include the following—

(i) Functions;

(ii) Contractual terms;

(iii) Risks;

(iv) Economic conditions; and

(v) Property or services.

(2) Standard of comparability. In order to be considered comparable to a controlled transaction, an uncontrolled transaction need not be identical to the controlled transaction, but must be sufficiently similar that it provides a reliable measure of an arm's length result. If there are material differences between the controlled and uncontrolled transactions, adjustments must be made if the effect of such differences on prices or profits can be ascertained with sufficient accuracy to improve the reliability of the results. For purposes of this section, a material difference is one that would materially affect the measure of an arm's length result under the method being applied. If adjustments for material differences cannot be made, the uncontrolled transaction may be used as a measure of an arm's length result, but the reliability of the analysis will be reduced. Generally, such adjustments must be made to the results of the uncontrolled comparable and must be based on commercial practices, economic principles, or statistical analyses. The extent and reliability of any adjustments will affect the relative reliability of the analysis. See § 1.482–1(c)(1) (Best method rule). In any event, unadjusted industry average returns themselves cannot establish arm's length results.

(3) Factors for determining comparability. The comparability factors listed in § 1.482–1(d)(1) are discussed in this section. Each of these factors must be considered in determining the degree of comparability between transactions or taxpayers and the extent to which comparability adjustments may be necessary. In addition, in certain cases involving special circumstances, the rules under paragraph (d)(4) of this section must be considered.

(i) Functional analysis. Determining the degree of comparability between controlled and uncontrolled transactions requires a comparison of the functions performed, and associated resources employed, by the taxpayers in each transaction. This comparison is based on a functional analysis that identifies and compares the economically significant activities undertaken, or to be undertaken, by the taxpayers in both controlled and uncontrolled transactions. A functional analysis should also include consideration of the resources that are employed, or to be employed, in conjunction with the activities undertaken, including consideration of the type of assets used, such as plant and equipment, or the use of valuable intangibles. A functional analysis is not a pricing method and does not itself determine the arm's length result for the controlled transaction under review. Functions that may need to be accounted for in determining the comparability of two transactions include—

(A) Research and development;

(B) Product design and engineering;

(C) Manufacturing, production and process engineering;

(D) Product fabrication, extraction, and assembly;

(E) Purchasing and materials management;

(F) Marketing and distribution functions, including inventory management, warranty administration, and advertising activities;

(G) Transportation and warehousing; and

(H) Managerial, legal, accounting and finance, credit and collection, training, and personnel management services.

(ii) Contractual terms—(A) In general. Determining the degree of comparability between the controlled and uncontrolled transactions requires a comparison of the significant contractual terms that could affect the results of the two transactions. These terms include—

(1) The form of consideration charged or paid;

(2) Sales or purchase volume;

(3) The scope and terms of warranties provided;

(4) Rights to updates, revisions or modifications;

(5) The duration of relevant license, contract or other agreements, and termination or renegotiation rights;

(6) Collateral transactions or ongoing business relationships between the buyer and the seller, including arrangements for the provision of ancillary or subsidiary services; and

(7) Extension of credit and payment terms. Thus, for example, if the time for payment of the amount charged in a controlled transaction differs from the time for payment of the amount charged in an uncontrolled transaction, an adjustment to reflect the difference in payment terms should be made if such difference would have a material effect on price. Such comparability adjustment is required even if no interest would be allocated or imputed under § 1.482–2(a) or other applicable provisions of the Internal Revenue Code or regulations.

(B) Identifying contractual terms—(1) Written agreement. The contractual terms, including the consequent allocation of risks, that are agreed to in writing before the transactions are entered into will be respected if such terms are consistent with the economic substance of the underlying transactions. In evaluating economic substance, greatest weight will be given to the actual conduct of the parties, and the respective legal rights of the parties (see, for example, § 1.482–4(f)(3) (Ownership of intangible property)). If the contractual terms are inconsistent with the economic substance of the underlying transaction, the district director may disregard such terms and impute terms that are consistent with the economic substance of the transaction.

(2) No written agreement. In the absence of a written agreement, the district director may impute a contractual agreement between the controlled taxpayers consistent with the economic substance of the transaction. In determining the economic substance of the transaction, greatest weight will be given to the actual conduct of the parties and their respective legal rights (see, for example, § 1.482–4(f)(3) (Ownership of intangible property)). For example, if, without a written agreement, a controlled taxpayer operates at full capacity and regularly sells all of its output to another member of its controlled group, the district director may impute a purchasing contract from the course of conduct of the controlled taxpayers, and determine that the producer bears little risk that the buyer will fail to purchase its full output. Further, if an established industry convention or usage of trade assigns a risk or resolves an issue, that convention or usage will be followed if the conduct of the taxpayers is consistent with it. See UCC 1–205. For example, unless otherwise agreed, payment generally is due at the time and place at which the buyer is to receive goods. See UCC 2–310.

(C) Examples. The following examples illustrate this paragraph (d)(3)(ii).

Example 1. Differences in volume. USP, a United States agricultural exporter, regularly buys transportation services from FSub, its foreign subsidiary, to ship its products from the United States to overseas markets. Although FSub occasionally provides transportation services to URA, an unrelated domestic corporation, URA accounts for only 10% of the gross revenues of FSub, and the remaining 90% of FSub's gross revenues are attributable to FSub's transactions with USP. In determining the degree of comparability between FSub's uncontrolled transaction with URA and its controlled transaction with USP, the difference in volumes involved in the two transactions and the regularity with which these services are provided must be taken into account if such difference would have a material effect on the price charged. Inability to make reliable adjustments for these differences would affect the reliability of the results derived from the uncontrolled transaction as a measure of the arm's length result.

Example 2. Reliability of adjustment for differences in volume. (i) FS manufactures product XX and sells that product to its parent corporation, P. FS also sells product XX to uncontrolled taxpayers at a price of $100 per unit. Except for the volume of each transaction, the sales to P and to uncontrolled taxpayers take place under substantially the same economic conditions and contractual terms. In uncontrolled transactions, FS offers a 2% discount for quantities of 20 per order, and a 5% discount for quantities of 100 per order. If P purchases product XX in quantities of 60 per order, in the absence of other reliable information, it may reasonably be concluded that the arm's length price to P would be $100, less a discount of 3.5%.

(ii) If P purchases product XX in quantities of 1,000 per order, a reliable estimate of the appropriate volume discount must be based on proper economic or statistical analysis, not necessarily a linear extrapolation from the 2% and 5% catalog discounts applicable to sales of 20 and 100 units, respectively.

Example 3. Contractual terms imputed from economic substance. (i) FP, a foreign producer of wristwatches, is the registered holder of the YY trademark in the United States and in other countries worldwide. In year 1, FP enters the United States market by selling YY wristwatches to its newly organized United States subsidiary, USSub, for distribution in the United States market. USSub pays FP a fixed price per wristwatch. USSub and FP undertake, without separate compensation, marketing activities to establish the YY trademark in the United States market. Unrelated foreign producers of trademarked wristwatches and their authorized United States distributors respectively undertake similar marketing activities in independent arrangements involving distribution of trademarked wristwatches in the United States market. In years 1 through 6, USSub markets and sells YY wristwatches in the United States. Further, in years 1 through 6, USSub undertakes incremental marketing activities in addition to the activities similar to those observed in the independent distribution transactions in the United States market. FP does not directly or indirectly compensate US-Sub for performing these incremental activities during years 1 through 6. Assume that, aside from these incremental activities, and after any adjustments are made to improve the reliability of the comparison, the price paid per wristwatch by the independent, authorized distributors of wristwatches would provide the most reliable measure of the arm's length price paid per YY wristwatch by USSub.

(ii) By year 7, the wristwatches with the YY trademark generate a premium return in the United States market, as compared to wristwatches marketed by the independent distributors. In year 7, substantially all the premium return from the YY trademark in the United States market is attributed to FP, for example through an increase in the price paid per watch by USSub, or by some other means.

(iii) In determining whether an allocation of income is appropriate in year 7, the Commissioner may consider the economic substance of the arrangements between USSub and FP, and the parties' course of conduct throughout their relationship. Based on this analysis, the Commissioner determines that it is unlikely that, ex ante, an uncontrolled taxpayer operating at arm's length would engage in the incremental marketing activities to develop or enhance intangible property owned by another party unless it received contemporaneous compensation or otherwise had a reasonable anticipation of receiving a future benefit from those activities. In this case, USSub's undertaking the incremental marketing activities in years 1 through 6 is a course of conduct that is inconsistent with the parties' attribution to FP in year 7 of substantially all the premium return from the enhanced YY trademark in the United States market. Therefore, the Commissioner may impute one or more agreements between USSub and FP, consistent with the economic substance of their course of conduct, which would afford USSub an appropriate portion of the premium return from the YY trademark wristwatches. For example, the Commissioner may impute a separate services agreement that affords USSub contingent-payment compensation for its incremental marketing activities in years 1 through 6, which benefited FP by contributing to the value of the trademark owned by FP. In the alternative, the Commissioner may impute a long-term, exclusive agreement to exploit the YY trademark in the United States that allows USSub to benefit from the incremental marketing activities it performed. As another alternative, the Commissioner may require FP to compensate USSub for terminating USSub's imputed long-term, exclusive agreement to exploit the YY trademark in the United States, an agreement that USSub made more valuable at its own expense and risk. The taxpayer may present additional facts that could indicate which of these or other alternative agreements best reflects the economic substance of the underlying transactions, consistent with the parties' course of conduct in the particular case.

* * *

(iii) Risk—(A) Comparability. Determining the degree of comparability between controlled and uncontrolled transactions requires a comparison of the significant risks that could affect the prices that would be charged or paid, or the profit that would be earned, in the two transactions. Relevant risks to consider include—

(1) Market risks, including fluctuations in cost, demand, pricing, and inventory levels;

(2) Risks associated with the success or failure of research and development activities;

(3) Financial risks, including fluctuations in foreign currency rates of exchange and interest rates;

(4) Credit and collection risks;

(5) Product liability risks; and

(6) General business risks related to the ownership of property, plant, and equipment.

(B) Identification of taxpayer that bears risk. In general, the determination of which controlled taxpayer bears a particular risk will be made in accordance with the provisions of § 1.482–1(d)(3)(ii)(B) (Identifying contractual terms). Thus, the allocation of risks specified or implied by the taxpayer's contractual terms will generally be respected if it is consistent with the economic substance of the transaction. An allocation of risk between controlled taxpayers after the outcome of such risk is known or reasonably knowable lacks economic substance. In considering the economic substance of the transaction, the following facts are relevant—

(1) Whether the pattern of the controlled taxpayer's conduct over time is consistent with the purported allocation of risk between the controlled taxpayers; or where the pattern is changed, whether the relevant contractual arrangements have been modified accordingly;

(2) Whether a controlled taxpayer has the financial capacity to fund losses that might be expected to occur as the result of the assumption of a risk, or whether, at arm's length, another party to the controlled transaction would ultimately suffer the consequences of such losses; and

(3) The extent to which each controlled taxpayer exercises managerial or operational control over the business activities that directly influence the amount of income or loss realized. In arm's length dealings, parties ordinarily bear a greater share of those risks over which they have relatively more control.

(C) Examples. The following examples illustrate this paragraph (d)(3)(iii).

Example 1. FD, the wholly-owned foreign distributor of USM, a U.S. manufacturer, buys widgets from USM under a written contract. Widgets are a generic electronic appliance. Under the terms of the contract, FD must buy and take title to 20,000 widgets for each of the five years of the contract at a price of $10 per widget. The widgets will be sold under FD's label, and FD must finance any marketing strategies to promote sales in the foreign market. There are no rebate or buy back provisions. FD has adequate financial capacity to fund its obligations under the contract under any circumstances that could reasonably be expected to arise. In Years 1, 2 and 3, FD sold only 10,000 widgets at a price of $11 per unit. In Year 4, FD sold its entire inventory of widgets at a price of $25 per unit. Since the contractual terms allocating market risk were agreed to before the outcome of such risk was known or reasonably knowable, FD had the financial capacity to bear the market risk that it would be unable to sell all of the widgets it purchased currently, and its conduct was consistent over time, FD will be deemed to bear the risk.

Example 2. The facts are the same as in Example 1, except that in Year 1 FD had only $100,000 in total capital, including loans. In subsequent years USM makes no additional contributions to the capital of FD, and FD is unable to obtain any capital through loans from an unrelated party. Nonetheless, USM continues to sell 20,000 widgets annually to FD under the terms of the contract, and USM extends credit to FD to enable it to finance the purchase. FD does not have the financial capacity in Years 1, 2 and 3 to finance the purchase of the widgets given that it could not sell most of the widgets it purchased during those years. Thus, notwithstanding the terms of the contract, USM and not FD assumed the market risk that a substantial portion of the widgets could not be sold, since in that event FD would not be able to pay USM for all of the widgets it purchased.

Example 3. S, a Country X corporation, manufactures small motors that it sells to P, its U.S. parent. P incorporates the motors into various products and sells those products to uncontrolled customers in the United States. The contract price for the motors is expressed in U.S. dollars, effectively allocating the currency risk for these transactions to S for any currency fluctuations between the time the contract is signed and payment is made. As long as S has adequate financial capacity to bear this currency risk (including by hedging all or part of the risk) and the conduct of S and P is consistent with the terms of the contract (i.e., the contract price is not adjusted to reflect exchange rate movements), the agreement of the parties to allocate the exchange risk to S will be respected.

Example 4. USSub is the wholly-owned U.S. subsidiary of FP, a foreign manufacturer. USSub acts as a distributor of goods manufactured by FP. FP and USSub execute an agreement providing that FP will bear any ordinary product liability costs arising from defects in the goods manufactured by FP. In practice, however, when ordinary product liability claims are sustained against USSub and FP, USSub pays the resulting damages. Therefore, the district director disregards the contractual arrangement regarding product liability costs between FP and USSub, and treats the risk as having been assumed by USSub.

(iv) Economic conditions. Determining the degree of comparability between controlled and uncontrolled transactions requires a comparison of the significant economic conditions that could affect the prices that would be charged or paid, or the profit that would be earned in each of the transactions. These factors include—

(A) The similarity of geographic markets;

(B) The relative size of each market, and the extent of the overall economic development in each market;

(C) The level of the market (e.g., wholesale, retail, etc.);

(D) The relevant market shares for the products, properties, or services transferred or provided;

(E) The location-specific costs of the factors of production and distribution;

(F) The extent of competition in each market with regard to the property or services under review;

(G) The economic condition of the particular industry, including whether the market is in contraction or expansion; and

(H) The alternatives realistically available to the buyer and seller.

(v) Property or services. Evaluating the degree of comparability between controlled and uncontrolled transactions requires a comparison of the property or services transferred in the transactions. This comparison may include any intangible property that is embedded in tangible property or services being transferred (embedded intangibles). The comparability of the embedded intangibles will be analyzed using the factors listed in § 1.482–4(c)(2)(iii)(B)(1) (comparable intangible property). The relevance of product comparability in evaluating the relative reliability of the results will depend on the method applied. For guidance concerning the specific comparability considerations applicable to transfers of tangible and intangible property and performance of services, see §§ 1.482–3 through 1.482–6 and § 1.482–9; see also §§ 1.482–3(f), 1.482–4(f)(4), and 1.482–9(m), dealing with the coordination of intangible and tangible property and performance of services rules.

(4) Special circumstances—(i) Market share strategy. In certain circumstances, taxpayers may adopt strategies to enter new markets or to increase a product's share of an existing market (market share strategy). Such a strategy would be reflected by temporarily increased market development expenses or resale prices that are temporarily lower than the prices charged for comparable products in the same market. Whether or not the strategy is reflected in the transfer price depends on which party to the controlled transaction bears the costs of the pricing strategy. * * *

(ii) Different geographic markets—(A) In general. Uncontrolled comparables ordinarily should be derived from the geographic market in which the controlled taxpayer operates, because there may be significant differences in economic conditions in different markets. If information from the same market is not available, an uncontrolled comparable derived from a different geographic market may be considered if adjustments are made to account for differences between the two markets. * * *

(iii) Transactions ordinarily not accepted as comparables—(A) In general. Transactions ordinarily will not constitute reliable measures of an arm's length result for purposes of this section if—

(1) They are not made in the ordinary course of business; or

(2) One of the principal purposes of the uncontrolled transaction was to establish an arm's length result with respect to the controlled transaction.

* * *

(e) Arm's length range—(1) In general. In some cases, application of a pricing method will produce a single result that is the most reliable measure of an arm's length result. In other cases, application of a method may produce a number of results from which a range of reliable results may be derived. A taxpayer will not be subject to adjustment if its results fall within such range (arm's length range).

(2) Determination of arm's length range—(i) Single method. The arm's length range is ordinarily determined by applying a single pricing method selected under the best method rule to two or more uncontrolled transactions of similar comparability and reliability. Use of more than one method may be appropriate for the purposes described in paragraph (c)(2)(iii) of this section (Best method rule).

(ii) Selection of comparables. Uncontrolled comparables must be selected based upon the comparability criteria relevant to the method applied and must be sufficiently similar to the controlled transaction that they provide a reliable measure of an arm's length result. If material differences exist between the controlled and uncontrolled transactions, adjustments must be made to the results of the uncontrolled transaction if the effect of such differences on price or profits can be ascertained with sufficient accuracy to improve the reliability of the results. See § 1.482–1(d)(2) (Standard of comparability). The arm's length range will be derived only from those uncontrolled comparables that have, or through adjustments can be brought to, a similar level of comparability and reliability, and uncontrolled comparables that have a significantly lower level of comparability and reliability will not be used in establishing the arm's length range.

(iii) Comparables included in arm's length range—(A) In general. The arm's length range will consist of the results of all of the uncontrolled comparables that meet the following conditions: the information on the controlled transaction and the uncontrolled comparables is sufficiently complete that it is likely that all material differences have been identified, each such difference has a definite and reasonably ascertainable effect on price or profit, and an adjustment is made to eliminate the effect of each such difference.

(B) Adjustment of range to increase reliability. If there are no uncontrolled comparables described in paragraph (e)(2)(iii)(A) of this section, the arm's length range is derived from the results of all the uncontrolled comparables, selected pursuant to paragraph (e)(2)(ii) of this section, that achieve a similar level of comparability and reliability. In such cases the reliability of the analysis must be increased, where it is possible to do so, by adjusting the range through application of a valid statistical method to the results of all of the uncontrolled comparables so selected. The reliability of the analysis is increased when statistical methods are used to establish a range of results in which the limits of the range will be determined such that there is a 75 percent probability of a result falling above the lower end of the range and a 75 percent probability of a result falling below the upper end of the range. The interquartile range ordinarily provides an acceptable measure of this range; however a different statistical method may be applied if it provides a more reliable measure.

(C) Interquartile range. For purposes of this section, the interquartile range is the range from the 25th to the 75th percentile of the results derived from the uncontrolled comparables. For this purpose, the 25th percentile is the lowest result derived from an uncontrolled comparable such that at least 25 percent of the results are at or below the value of that result. However, if exactly 25 percent of the results are at or below a result, then the 25th percentile is equal to the average of that result and the next higher result derived from the uncontrolled comparables. The 75th percentile is determined analogously.

* * *

(f) Scope of review—(1) In general. The authority to determine true taxable income extends to any case in which either by inadvertence or design the taxable income, in whole or in part, of a controlled taxpayer is other than it would have been had the taxpayer, in the conduct of its affairs, been dealing at arm's length with an uncontrolled taxpayer.

(i) Intent to evade or avoid tax not a prerequisite. In making allocations under section 482, the district director is not restricted to the case of improper accounting, to the case of a fraudulent, colorable, or sham transaction, or to the case of a device designed to reduce or avoid tax by shifting or distorting income, deductions, credits, or allowances.

(ii) Realization of income not a prerequisite—(A) In general. The district director may make an allocation under section 482 even if the income ultimately anticipated from a series of transactions has not been or is never realized. For example, if a controlled taxpayer sells a product at less than an arm's length price to a related taxpayer in one taxable year and the second controlled taxpayer resells the product to an unrelated party in the next taxable year, the district director may make an appropriate allocation to reflect an arm's length price for the sale of the product in the first taxable year, even though the second controlled taxpayer had not realized any gross income from the resale of the product in the first year. Similarly, if a controlled taxpayer lends money to a related taxpayer in a taxable year, the district director may make an appropriate allocation to reflect an arm's length charge for interest during such taxable year even if the second controlled taxpayer does not realize income during such year. Finally, even if two controlled taxpayers realize an overall loss that is attributable to a particular controlled transaction, an allocation under section 482 is not precluded.

* * *

(g) Collateral adjustments with respect to allocations under section 482—(1) In general. The district director will take into account appropriate collateral adjustments with respect to allocations under section 482. Appropriate collateral adjustments may include correlative allocations, conforming adjustments, and setoffs, as described in this paragraph (g).

(2) Correlative allocations—(i) In general. When the district director makes an allocation under section 482 (referred to in this paragraph (g)(2) as the primary allocation), appropriate correlative allocations will also be made with respect to any other member of the group affected by the allocation. Thus, if the district director makes an allocation of income, the district director will not only increase the income of one member of the group, but correspondingly decrease the income of the other member. In addition, where appropriate, the district director may make such further correlative allocations as may be required by the initial correlative allocation.

* * *

(3) Adjustments to conform accounts to reflect section 482 allocations—(i) In general. Appropriate adjustments must be made to conform a taxpayer's accounts to reflect allocations made under section 482. Such adjustments may include the treatment of an allocated amount as a dividend or a capital contribution (as appropriate), * * *

(4) Setoffs—(i) In general. If an allocation is made under section 482 with respect to a transaction between controlled taxpayers, the Commissioner will take into account the effect of any other non-arm's length transaction between the same controlled taxpayers in the same taxable year which will result in a setoff against the original section 482 allocation. Such setoff, however, will be taken into account only if the requirements of paragraph (g)(4)(ii) of this section are satisfied. If the effect of the setoff is to change the characterization or source of the income or deductions, or otherwise distort taxable income, in such a manner as to affect the U.S. tax liability of any member, adjustments will be made to reflect the correct amount of each category of income or deductions. For purposes of this setoff provision, the term arm's length refers to the amount defined in paragraph (b) of this section (arm's length standard), without regard to the rules in § 1.482–2(a) that treat certain interest rates as arm's length rates of interest.

(ii) Requirements. The district director will take a setoff into account only if the taxpayer—

(A) Establishes that the transaction that is the basis of the setoff was not at arm's length and the amount of the appropriate arm's length charge;

(B) Documents, pursuant to paragraph (g)(2) of this section, all correlative adjustments resulting from the proposed setoff; and

(C) Notifies the district director of the basis of any claimed setoff within 30 days after the earlier of the date of a letter by which the district director transmits an examination report notifying the taxpayer of proposed adjustments or the date of the issuance of the notice of deficiency.

* * *

(h) Special rules—

* * *

(2) Effect of foreign legal restrictions—(i) In general. The district director will take into account the effect of a foreign legal restriction to the extent that such restriction affects the results of transactions at arm's length. Thus, a foreign legal restriction will be taken into account only to the extent that it is shown that the restriction affected an uncontrolled taxpayer under comparable circumstances for a comparable period of time. In the absence of evidence indicating the effect of the foreign legal restriction on uncontrolled taxpayers, the restriction will be taken into account only to the extent provided in paragraphs (h)(2)(iii) and (iv) of this section (Deferred income method of accounting).

(ii) Applicable legal restrictions. Foreign legal restrictions (whether temporary or permanent) will be taken into account for purposes of this paragraph (h)(2) only if, and so long as, the conditions set forth in paragraphs (h)(2)(ii)(A) through (D) of this section are met.

(A) The restrictions are publicly promulgated, generally applicable to all similarly situated persons (both controlled and uncontrolled), and not imposed as part of a commercial transaction between the taxpayer and the foreign sovereign;

(B) The taxpayer (or other member of the controlled group with respect to which the restrictions apply) has exhausted all remedies prescribed by foreign law or practice for obtaining a waiver of such restrictions (other than remedies that would have a negligible prospect of success if pursued);

(C) The restrictions expressly prevented the payment or receipt, in any form, of part or all of the arm's length amount that would otherwise be required under section 482 (for example, a restriction that applies only to the deductibility of an expense for tax purposes is not a restriction on payment or receipt for this purpose); and

(D) The related parties subject to the restriction did not engage in any arrangement with controlled or uncontrolled parties that had the effect of circumventing the restriction, and have not otherwise violated the restriction in any material respect.

(iii) Requirement for electing the deferred income method of accounting. If a foreign legal restriction prevents the payment or receipt of part or all of the arm's length amount that is due with respect to a controlled transaction, the restricted amount may be treated as deferrable if the following requirements are met—

(A) The controlled taxpayer establishes to the satisfaction of the district director that the payment or receipt of the arm's length amount was prevented because of a foreign legal restriction and circumstances described in paragraph (h)(2)(ii) of this section; and

(B) The controlled taxpayer whose U.S. tax liability may be affected by the foreign legal restriction elects the deferred income method of accounting, as described in paragraph (h)(2)(iv) of this section, on a written statement attached to a timely U.S. income tax return (or an amended return) filed before the IRS first contacts any member of the controlled group concerning an examination of the return for the taxable year to which the foreign legal restriction applies. A written statement furnished by a taxpayer subject to the Coordinated Examination Program will be considered an amended return for purposes of this paragraph (h)(2)(iii)(B) if it satisfies the requirements of a qualified amended return for purposes of § 1.6664–2(c)(3) as set forth in those regulations or as the Commissioner may prescribe by applicable revenue procedures. The election statement must identify the affected transactions, the parties to the transactions, and the applicable foreign legal restrictions.

(iv) Deferred income method of accounting. If the requirements of paragraph (h)(2)(ii) of this section are satisfied, any portion of the arm's length amount, the payment or receipt of which is prevented because of applicable foreign legal restrictions, will be treated as deferrable until payment or receipt of the relevant item ceases to be prevented by the foreign legal restriction. For purposes of the deferred income method of accounting under this paragraph (h)(2)(iv), deductions (including the cost or other basis of inventory and other assets sold or exchanged) and credits properly chargeable against any amount so deferred, are subject to deferral under the provisions of § 1.461–1(a)(4). In addition, income is deferrable under this deferred income method of accounting only to the extent that it exceeds the related deductions already claimed in open taxable years to which the foreign legal restriction applied.

* * *

(i) Definitions. The definitions set forth in paragraphs (i)(1) through (i)(10) of this section apply to this section and §§ 1.482–2 through 1.482–9.

(1) Organization includes an organization of any kind, whether a sole proprietorship, a partnership, a trust, an estate, an association, or a corporation (as each is defined or understood in the Internal Revenue Code or the regulations thereunder), irrespective of the place of organization, operation, or conduct of the trade or business, and regardless of whether it is a domestic or foreign organization, whether it is an exempt organization, or whether it is a member of an affiliated group that files a consolidated U.S. income tax return, or a member of an affiliated group that does not file a consolidated U.S. income tax return.

(2) Trade or business includes a trade or business activity of any kind, regardless of whether or where organized, whether owned individually or otherwise, and regardless of the place of operation. Employment for compensation will constitute a separate trade or business from the employing trade or business.

(3) Taxpayer means any person, organization, trade or business, whether or not subject to any internal revenue tax.

(4) Controlled includes any kind of control, direct or indirect, whether legally enforceable or not, and however exercisable or exercised, including control resulting from the actions of two or more taxpayers acting in concert or with a common goal or purpose. It is the reality of the control that is decisive, not its form or the mode of its exercise. A presumption of control arises if income or deductions have been arbitrarily shifted.

* * *

[T.D. 8552, 59 FR 34990, July 8, 1994; T.D. 9088, 68 FR 51177, Aug. 26, 2003; T.D. 9278, 71 FR 44481, Aug. 4, 2006; 71 FR 76903, Dec. 22, 2006; T.D. 9441, 74 FR 351, Jan. 5, 2009; T.D. 9456, 74 FR 38839, Aug. 4, 2009; 74 FR 46345, Sept. 9, 2009; T.D. 9568, 76 FR 80089, Dec. 22, 2011; 77 FR 3606, Jan. 25, 2012; 78 FR 18234, March 26, 2013; T.D. 9738, 80 FR 55541, Sept. 16, 2015]

§ 1.482–2 Determination of taxable income in specific situations.

(a) Loans or advances—(1) Interest on bona fide indebtedness—(i) In general. Where one member of a group of controlled entities makes a loan or advance directly or indirectly to, or otherwise becomes a creditor of, another member of such group and either charges no interest, or charges interest at a rate which is not equal to an arm's length rate of interest (as defined in paragraph (a)(2) of this section) with respect to such loan or advance, the district director may make appropriate allocations to reflect an arm's length rate of interest for the use of such loan or advance.

* * *

(2) Arm's length interest rate—(i) In general. For purposes of section 482 and paragraph (a) of this section, an arm's length rate of interest shall be a rate of interest which was charged, or would have been charged, at the time the indebtedness arose, in independent transactions with or between unrelated parties under similar circumstances. All relevant factors shall be considered, including the principal amount and duration of the loan, the security involved, the credit standing of the borrower, and the interest rate prevailing at the situs of the lender or creditor for comparable loans between unrelated parties.

* * *

(iii) Safe haven interest rates for certain loans and advances made after May 8, 1986—(A) Applicability—(1) General rule. Except as otherwise provided in paragraph (a)(2) of this section, paragraph (a)(2)(iii)(B) applies with respect to the rate of interest charged and to the amount of interest paid or accrued in any taxable year—

(i) Under a term loan or advance between members of a group of controlled entities where (except as provided in paragraph (a)(2)(iii)(A)(2)(ii) of this section) the loan or advance is entered into after May 8, 1986; and

(ii) After May 8, 1986 under a demand loan or advance between such controlled entities.

* * *

(B) Safe haven interest rate based on applicable Federal rate. Except as otherwise provided in this paragraph (a)(2), in the case of a loan or advance between members of a group of controlled entities, an arm's length rate of interest referred to in paragraph (a)(2)(i) of this section shall be for purposes of chapter 1 of the Internal Revenue Code—

(1) The rate of interest actually charged if that rate is—

(i) Not less than 100 percent of the applicable Federal rate (lower limit); and

(ii) Not greater than 130 percent of the applicable Federal rate (upper limit); or

(2) If either no interest is charged or if the rate of interest charged is less than the lower limit, then an arm's length rate of interest shall be equal to the lower limit, compounded semiannually; or

(3) If the rate of interest charged is greater than the upper limit, then an arm's length rate of interest shall be equal to the upper limit, compounded semiannually, unless the taxpayer establishes a more appropriate compound rate of interest under paragraph (a)(2)(i) of this section. * * *

* * *

(b) Rendering of services. For rules governing allocations under section 482 to reflect an arm's length charge for controlled transactions involving the rendering of services, see § 1.482–9.

(c) Use of tangible property—(1) General rule. Where possession, use, or occupancy of tangible property owned or leased by one member of a group of controlled entities (referred to in this paragraph as the owner) is transferred by lease or other arrangement to another member of such group (referred to in this paragraph as the user) without charge or at a charge which is not equal to an arm's length rental charge (as defined in paragraph (c)(2)(i) of this section) the district director may make appropriate allocations to properly reflect such arm's length charge. Where possession, use, or occupancy of only a portion of such property is transferred, the determination of the arm's length charge and the allocation shall be made with reference to the portion transferred.

(2) Arm's length charge—(i) In general. For purposes of paragraph (c) of this section, an arm's length rental charge shall be the amount of rent which was charged, or would have been charged for the use of the same or similar property, during the time it was in use, in independent transactions with or between unrelated parties under similar circumstances considering the period and location of the use, the owner's investment in the property or rent paid for the property, expenses of maintaining the property, the type of property involved, its condition, and all other relevant facts.

* * *

(iii) Subleases—(A) Except as provided in paragraph (c)(2)(iii)(B) of this section, where possession, use, or occupancy of tangible property, which is leased by the owner (lessee) from an unrelated party is transferred by sublease or other arrangement to the user, an arm's length rental charge shall be considered to be equal to all the deductions claimed by the owner (lessee) which are attributable to the property for the period such property is used by the user. * * *

(B) The provisions of paragraph (c)(2)(iii)(A) of this section shall not apply if either—

(1) The taxpayer establishes a more appropriate rental charge under the general rule set forth in paragraph (c)(2)(i) of this section; or

(2) During the taxable year, the owner (lessee) or the user was regularly engaged in the trade or business of renting property of the same general type as the property in question to unrelated persons.

(d) Transfer of property. For rules governing allocations under section 482 to reflect an arm's length consideration for controlled transactions involving the transfer of property, see §§ 1.482–3 through 1.482–6.

(e) Cost sharing arrangement. For rules governing allocations under section 482 to reflect an arm's length consideration for controlled transactions involving a cost sharing arrangement, see § 1.482–7.

* * *

[T.D. 8552, 59 FR 35002, July 8, 1994; 60 FR 16381, 16382, March 30, 1995; T.D. 9278, 71 FR 44484, Aug. 4, 2006; T.D. 9456, 74 FR 38842, Aug. 4, 2009; T.D. 9568, 76 FR 80090, Dec. 22, 2011]

§ 1.482–3 Methods to determine taxable income in connection with a transfer of tangible property.

(a) In general. The arm's length amount charged in a controlled transfer of tangible property must be determined under one of the six methods listed in this paragraph (a). Each of the methods must be applied in accordance with all of the provisions of § 1.482–1, including the best method rule of § 1.482–1(c), the comparability analysis of § 1.482–1(d), and the arm's length range of § 1.482–1(e). The methods are—

(1) The comparable uncontrolled price method, described in paragraph (b) of this section;

(2) The resale price method, described in paragraph (c) of this section;

(3) The cost plus method, described in paragraph (d) of this section;

(4) The comparable profits method, described in § 1.482–5;

(5) The profit split method, described in § 1.482–6; and

(6) Unspecified methods, described in paragraph (e) of this section.

(b) Comparable uncontrolled price method—(1) In general. The comparable uncontrolled price method evaluates whether the amount charged in a controlled transaction is arm's length by reference to the amount charged in a comparable uncontrolled transaction.

(2) Comparability and reliability considerations—(i) In general. Whether results derived from applications of this method are the most reliable measure of the arm's length result must be determined using the factors described under the best method rule in § 1.482–1(c). The application of these factors under the comparable uncontrolled price method is discussed in paragraph (b)(2)(ii) and (iii) of this section.

(ii) Comparability—(A) In general. The degree of comparability between controlled and uncontrolled transactions is determined by applying the provisions of § 1.482–1(d). Although all of the factors described in § 1.482–1(d)(3) must be considered, similarity of products generally will have the greatest effect on comparability under this method. In addition, because even minor differences in contractual terms or economic conditions could materially affect the amount charged in an uncontrolled transaction, comparability under this method depends on close similarity with respect to these factors, or adjustments to account for any differences. * * *

(B) Adjustments for differences between controlled and uncontrolled transactions. If there are differences between the controlled and uncontrolled transactions that would affect price, adjustments should be made to the price of the uncontrolled transaction according to the comparability provisions of § 1.482–1(d)(2). * * *

* * *

(4) Examples. The principles of this paragraph (b) are illustrated by the following examples.

Example 1. Comparable Sales of Same Product. USM, a U.S. manufacturer, sells the same product to both controlled and uncontrolled distributors. The circumstances surrounding the controlled and uncontrolled transactions are substantially the same, except that the controlled sales price is a delivered price and the uncontrolled sales are made f.o.b. USM's factory. Differences in the contractual terms of transportation and insurance generally have a definite and reasonably ascertainable effect on price, and adjustments are made to the results of the uncontrolled transaction to account for such differences. No other material difference has been identified between the controlled and uncontrolled transactions. Because USM sells in both the controlled and uncontrolled transactions, it is likely that all material differences between the two transactions have been identified. In addition, because the comparable uncontrolled price method is applied to an uncontrolled comparable with no product differences, and there are only minor contractual differences that have a definite and reasonably ascertainable effect on price, the results of this application of the comparable uncontrolled price method will provide the most direct and reliable measure of an arm's length result. See § 1.482–3(b)(2)(ii)(A).

Example 2. Effect of Trademark. The facts are the same as in Example 1, except that USM affixes its valuable trademark to the property sold in the controlled transactions, but does not affix its trademark to the property sold in the uncontrolled transactions. Under the facts of this case, the effect on price of the trademark is material and cannot be reliably estimated. Because there are material product differences for which reliable adjustments cannot be made, the comparable uncontrolled price method is unlikely to provide a reliable measure of the arm's length result. See § 1.482–3(b)(2)(ii)(A).

* * *

Example 4. Effect of Geographic Differences. FM, a foreign specialty radio manufacturer, sells its radios to a controlled U.S. distributor, AM, that serves the West Coast of the United States. FM sells its radios to uncontrolled distributors to serve other regions in the United States. The product in the controlled and uncontrolled transactions is the same, and all other circumstances surrounding the controlled and uncontrolled transactions are substantially the same, other than the geographic differences. If the geographic differences are unlikely to have a material effect on price, or they have definite and reasonably ascertainable effects for which adjustments are made, then the adjusted results of the uncontrolled sales may be used under the comparable uncontrolled price method to establish an arm's length range pursuant to § 1.482–1(e)(2)(iii)(A). If the effects of the geographic differences would be material but cannot be reliably ascertained, then the reliability of the results will be diminished. However, the comparable uncontrolled price method may still provide the most reliable measure of an arm's length result, pursuant to the best method rule of § 1.482–1(c), and, if so, an arm's length range may be established pursuant to § 1.482–1(e)(2)(iii)(B).

* * *

(c) Resale price method—(1) In general. The resale price method evaluates whether the amount charged in a controlled transaction is arm's length by reference to the gross profit margin realized in comparable uncontrolled transactions. The resale price method measures the value of functions performed, and is ordinarily used in cases involving the purchase and resale of tangible property in which the reseller has not added substantial value to the tangible goods by physically altering the goods before resale. For this purpose, packaging, repackaging, labelling, or minor assembly do not ordinarily constitute physical alteration. Further the resale price method is not ordinarily used in cases where the controlled taxpayer uses its intangible property to add substantial value to the tangible goods.

(2) Determination of arm's length price—(i) In general. The resale price method measures an arm's length price by subtracting the appropriate gross profit from the applicable resale price for the property involved in the controlled transaction under review.

(ii) Applicable resale price. The applicable resale price is equal to either the resale price of the particular item of property involved or the price at which contemporaneous resales of the same property are made. If the property purchased in the controlled sale is resold to one or more related parties in a series of controlled sales before being resold in an uncontrolled sale, the applicable resale price is the price at which the property is resold to an uncontrolled party, or the price at which contemporaneous resales of the same property are made. In such case, the determination of the appropriate gross profit will take into account the functions of all members of the group participating in the series of controlled sales and final uncontrolled resales, as well as any other relevant factors described in § 1.482–1(d)(3).

(iii) Appropriate gross profit. The appropriate gross profit is computed by multiplying the applicable resale price by the gross profit margin (expressed as a percentage of total revenue derived from sales) earned in comparable uncontrolled transactions.

* * *

(3) Comparability and reliability considerations—(i) In general. Whether results derived from applications of this method are the most reliable measure of the arm's length result must be determined using the factors described under the best method rule in § 1.482–1(c). The application of these factors under the resale price method is discussed in paragraphs (c)(3)(ii) and (iii) of this section.

(ii) Comparability—(A) Functional comparability. The degree of comparability between an uncontrolled transaction and a controlled transaction is determined by applying the comparability provisions of § 1.482–1(d). A reseller's gross profit provides compensation for the performance of resale functions related to the product or products under review, including an operating profit in return for the reseller's investment of capital and the assumption of risks. Therefore, although all of the factors described in § 1.482–1(d)(3) must be considered, comparability under this method is particularly dependent on similarity of functions performed, risks borne, and contractual terms, or adjustments to account for the effects of any such differences. * * *

(B) Other comparability factors. Comparability under this method is less dependent on close physical similarity between the products transferred than under the comparable uncontrolled price method. For example, distributors of a wide variety of consumer durables might perform comparable distribution functions without regard to the specific durable goods distributed. * * *

* * *

(d) Cost plus method—(1) In general. The cost plus method evaluates whether the amount charged in a controlled transaction is arm's length by reference to the gross profit markup realized in comparable uncontrolled transactions. The cost plus method is ordinarily used in cases involving the manufacture, assembly, or other production of goods that are sold to related parties.

(2) Determination of arm's length price—(i) In general. The cost plus method measures an arm's length price by adding the appropriate gross profit to the controlled taxpayer's costs of producing the property involved in the controlled transaction.

(ii) Appropriate gross profit. The appropriate gross profit is computed by multiplying the controlled taxpayer's cost of producing the transferred property by the gross profit markup, expressed as a percentage of cost, earned in comparable uncontrolled transactions.

* * *

(3) Comparability and reliability considerations—(i) In general. Whether results derived from the application of this method are the most reliable measure of the arm's length result must be determined using the factors described under the best method rule in § 1.482–1(c).

(ii) Comparability—(A) Functional comparability. The degree of comparability between controlled and uncontrolled transactions is determined by applying the comparability provisions of § 1.482–1(d). A producer's gross profit provides compensation for the performance of the production functions related to the product or products under review, including an operating profit for the producer's investment of capital and assumption of risks. Therefore, although all of the factors described in § 1.482–1(d)(3) must be considered, comparability under this method is particularly dependent on similarity of functions performed, risks borne, and contractual terms, or adjustments to account for the effects of any such differences. * * *

(B) Other comparability factors. Comparability under this method is less dependent on close physical similarity between the products transferred than under the comparable uncontrolled price method. Substantial differences in the products may, however, indicate significant functional differences between the controlled and uncontrolled taxpayers. * * *

(e) Unspecified methods—(1) In general. Methods not specified in paragraphs (a)(1), (2), (3), (4), and (5) of this section may be used to evaluate whether the amount charged in a controlled transaction is arm's length. Any method used under this paragraph (e) must be applied in accordance with the provisions of § 1.482–1. * * * As with any method, an unspecified method will not be applied unless it provides the most reliable measure of an arm's length result under the principles of the best method rule. See § 1.482–1(c). * * *

(f) Coordination with intangible property rules. The value of an item of tangible property may be affected by the value of intangible property, such as a trademark affixed to the tangible property (embedded intangible). Ordinarily, the transfer of tangible property with an embedded intangible will not be considered a transfer of such intangible if the controlled purchaser does not acquire any rights to exploit the intangible property other than rights relating to the resale of the tangible property under normal commercial practices. * * *

[T.D. 8552, 59 FR 35011, July 8, 1994; 60 FR 16382, March 30, 1995]

§ 1.482–4 Methods to determine taxable income in connection with a transfer of intangible property.

(a) In general. The arm's length amount charged in a controlled transfer of intangible property must be determined under one of the four methods listed in this paragraph (a). Each of the methods must be applied in accordance with all of the provisions of § 1.482–1, including the best method rule of § 1.482–1(c), the comparability analysis of § 1.482–1(d), and the arm's length range of § 1.482–1(e). The arm's length consideration for the transfer of an intangible determined under this section must be commensurate with the income attributable to the intangible. See § 1.482–4(f)(2) (Periodic adjustments). The available methods are—

(1) The comparable uncontrolled transaction method, described in paragraph (c) of this section;

(2) The comparable profits method, described in § 1.482–5;

(3) The profit split method, described in § 1.482–6; and

(4) Unspecified methods described in paragraph (d) of this section.

(b) Definition of intangible. For purposes of section 482, an intangible is an asset that comprises any of the following items and has substantial value independent of the services of any individual—

(1) Patents, inventions, formulae, processes, designs, patterns, or know-how;

(2) Copyrights and literary, musical, or artistic compositions;

(3) Trademarks, trade names, or brand names;

(4) Franchises, licenses, or contracts;

(5) Methods, programs, systems, procedures, campaigns, surveys, studies, forecasts, estimates, customer lists, or technical data; and

(6) Other similar items. For purposes of section 482, an item is considered similar to those listed in paragraph (b)(1) through (5) of this section if it derives its value not from its physical attributes but from its intellectual content or other intangible properties.

(c) Comparable uncontrolled transaction method—(1) In general. The comparable uncontrolled transaction method evaluates whether the amount charged for a controlled transfer of intangible property was arm's length by reference to the amount charged in a comparable uncontrolled transaction. The amount determined under this method may be adjusted as required by paragraph (f)(2) of this section (Periodic adjustments).

(2) Comparability and reliability considerations—(i) In general. Whether results derived from applications of this method are the most reliable measure of an arm's length result is determined using the factors described under the best method rule in § 1.482–1(c). The application of these factors under the comparable uncontrolled transaction method is discussed in paragraphs (c)(2)(ii), (iii), and (iv) of this section.

(ii) Reliability. If an uncontrolled transaction involves the transfer of the same intangible under the same, or substantially the same, circumstances as the controlled transaction, the results derived from applying the comparable uncontrolled transaction method will generally be the most direct and reliable measure of the arm's length result for the controlled transfer of an intangible. Circumstances between the controlled and uncontrolled transactions will be considered substantially the same if there are at most only minor differences that have a definite and reasonably ascertainable effect on the amount charged and for which appropriate adjustments are made. If such uncontrolled transactions cannot be identified, uncontrolled transactions that involve the transfer of comparable intangibles under comparable circumstances may be used to apply this method, but the reliability of the analysis will be reduced.

(iii) Comparability—(A) In general. The degree of comparability between controlled and uncontrolled transactions is determined by applying the comparability provisions of § 1.482–1(d). Although all of the factors described in § 1.482–1(d)(3) must be considered, specific factors may be particularly relevant to this method. In particular, the application of this method requires that the controlled and uncontrolled transactions involve either the same intangible property or comparable intangible property, as defined in paragraph (c)(2)(iii)(B)(1) of this section. In addition, because differences in contractual terms, or the economic conditions in which transactions take place, could materially affect the amount charged, comparability under this method also depends on similarity with respect to these factors, or adjustments to account for material differences in such circumstances.

(B) Factors to be considered in determining comparability—(1) Comparable intangible property. In order for the intangible property involved in an uncontrolled transaction to be considered comparable to the intangible property involved in the controlled transaction, both intangibles must—

(i) Be used in connection with similar products or processes within the same general industry or market; and

(ii) Have similar profit potential. The profit potential of an intangible is most reliably measured by directly calculating the net present value of the benefits to be realized (based on prospective profits to be realized or costs to be saved) through the use or subsequent transfer of the intangible, considering the capital investment and start-up expenses required, the risks to be assumed, and other relevant considerations. The need to reliably measure profit potential increases in relation to both the total amount of potential profits and the potential rate of return on investment necessary to exploit the intangible. If the information necessary to directly calculate net present value of the benefits to be realized is unavailable, and the need to reliably measure profit potential is reduced because the potential profits are relatively small in terms of total amount and rate of return, comparison of profit potential may be based upon the factors referred to in paragraph (c)(2)(iii)(B)(2) of this section. See Example 3 of § 1.482–4(c)(4). Finally, the reliability of a measure of profit potential is affected by the extent to which the profit attributable to the intangible can be isolated from the profit attributable to other factors, such as functions performed and other resources employed.

(2) Comparable circumstances. In evaluating the comparability of the circumstances of the controlled and uncontrolled transactions, although all of the factors described in § 1.482–1(d)(3) must be considered, specific factors that may be particularly relevant to this method include the following—

(i) The terms of the transfer, including the exploitation rights granted in the intangible, the exclusive or nonexclusive character of any rights granted, any restrictions on use, or any limitations on the geographic area in which the rights may be exploited;

(ii) The stage of development of the intangible (including, where appropriate, necessary governmental approvals, authorizations, or licenses) in the market in which the intangible is to be used;

(iii) Rights to receive updates, revisions, or modifications of the intangible;

(iv) The uniqueness of the property and the period for which it remains unique, including the degree and duration of protection afforded to the property under the laws of the relevant countries;

(v) The duration of the license, contract, or other agreement, and any termination or renegotiation rights;

(vi) Any economic and product liability risks to be assumed by the transferee;

(vii) The existence and extent of any collateral transactions or ongoing business relationships between the transferee and transferor; and

(vii) The functions to be performed by the transferor and transferee, including any ancillary or subsidiary services.

* * *

(f) Special rules for transfers of intangible property—(1) Form of consideration. If a transferee of an intangible pays nominal or no consideration and the transferor has retained a substantial interest in the property, the arm's length consideration shall be in the form of a royalty, unless a different form is demonstrably more appropriate.

(2) Periodic adjustments—(i) General rule. If an intangible is transferred under an arrangement that covers more than one year, the consideration charged in each taxable year may be adjusted to ensure that it is commensurate with the income attributable to the intangible. Adjustments made pursuant to this paragraph (f)(2) shall be consistent with the arm's length standard and the provisions of § 1.482–1. In determining whether to make such adjustments in the taxable year under examination, the district director may consider all relevant facts and circumstances throughout the period the intangible is used. The determination in an earlier year that the amount charged for an intangible was an arm's length amount will not preclude the district director in a subsequent taxable year from making an adjustment to the amount charged for the intangible in the subsequent year. A periodic adjustment under the commensurate with income requirement of section 482 may be made in a subsequent taxable year without regard to whether the taxable year of the original transfer remains open for statute of limitation purposes. For exceptions to this rule see paragraph (f)(2)(ii) of this section.

(ii) Exceptions—(A) Transactions involving the same intangible. If the same intangible was transferred to an uncontrolled taxpayer under substantially the same circumstances as those of the controlled transaction; this transaction serves as the basis for the application of the comparable uncontrolled transaction method in the first taxable year in which substantial periodic consideration was required to be paid; and the amount paid in that year was an arm's length amount, then no allocation in a subsequent year will be made under paragraph (f)(2)(i) of this paragraph for a controlled transfer of intangible property.

(B) Transactions involving comparable intangible. If the arm's length result is derived from the application of the comparable uncontrolled transaction method based on the transfer of a comparable intangible under comparable circumstances to those of the controlled transaction, no allocation will be made under paragraph (f)(2)(i) of this section if each of the following facts is established—

(1) The controlled taxpayers entered into a written agreement (controlled agreement) that provided for an amount of consideration with respect to each taxable year subject to such agreement, such consideration was an arm's length amount for the first taxable year in which substantial periodic consideration was required to be paid under the agreement, and such agreement remained in effect for the taxable year under review;

(2) There is a written agreement setting forth the terms of the comparable uncontrolled transaction relied upon to establish the arm's length consideration (uncontrolled agreement), which contains no provisions that would permit any change to the amount of consideration, a renegotiation, or a termination of the agreement, in circumstances comparable to those of the controlled transaction in the taxable year under review (or that contains provisions permitting only specified, non-contingent, periodic changes to the amount of consideration);

(3) The controlled agreement is substantially similar to the uncontrolled agreement, with respect to the time period for which it is effective and the provisions described in paragraph (f)(2)(ii)(B)(2) of this section;

(4) The controlled agreement limits use of the intangible to a specified field or purpose in a manner that is consistent with industry practice and any such limitation in the uncontrolled agreement;

(5) There were no substantial changes in the functions performed by the controlled transferee after the controlled agreement was executed, except changes required by events that were not foreseeable; and

(6) The aggregate profits actually earned or the aggregate cost savings actually realized by the controlled taxpayer from the exploitation of the intangible in the year under examination, and all past years, are not less than 80% nor more than 120% of the prospective profits or cost savings that were foreseeable when the comparability of the uncontrolled agreement was established under paragraph (c)(2) of this section.

(C) Methods other than comparable uncontrolled transaction. If the arm's length amount was determined under any method other than the comparable uncontrolled transaction method, no allocation will be made under paragraph (f)(2)(i) of this section if each of the following facts is established—

(1) The controlled taxpayers entered into a written agreement (controlled agreement) that provided for an amount of consideration with respect to each taxable year subject to such agreement, and such agreement remained in effect for the taxable year under review;

(2) The consideration called for in the controlled agreement was an arm's length amount for the first taxable year in which substantial periodic consideration was required to be paid, and relevant supporting documentation was prepared contemporaneously with the execution of the controlled agreement;

(3) There have been no substantial changes in the functions performed by the transferee since the controlled agreement was executed, except changes required by events that were not foreseeable; and

(4) The total profits actually earned or the total cost savings realized by the controlled transferee from the exploitation of the intangible in the year under examination, and all past years, are not less than 80% nor more than 120% of the prospective profits or cost savings that were foreseeable when the controlled agreement was entered into.

(D) Extraordinary events. No allocation will be made under paragraph (f)(2)(i) of this section if the following requirements are met—

(1) Due to extraordinary events that were beyond the control of the controlled taxpayers and that could not reasonably have been anticipated at the time the controlled agreement was entered into, the aggregate actual profits or aggregate cost savings realized by the taxpayer are less than 80% or more than 120% of the prospective profits or cost savings; and

(2) All of the requirements of paragraph (f)(2)(ii)(B) or (C) of this section are otherwise satisfied.

(E) Five-year period. If the requirements of § 1.482–4(f)(2)(ii)(B) or (f)(2)(ii)(C) are met for each year of the five-year period beginning with the first year in which substantial periodic consideration was required to be paid, then no periodic adjustment will be made under paragraph (f)(2)(i) of this section in any subsequent year.

(iii) Examples. The following examples illustrate this paragraph (f)(2).

Example 1. (i) USdrug, a U.S. pharmaceutical company, has developed a new drug, Nosplit, that is useful in treating migraine headaches and produces no significant side effects. A number of other drugs for treating migraine headaches are already on the market, but Nosplit can be expected rapidly to dominate the worldwide market for such treatments and to command a premium price since all other treatments produce side effects. Thus, USdrug projects that extraordinary profits will be derived from Nosplit in the U.S. and European markets.

(ii) USdrug licenses its newly established European subsidiary, Eurodrug, the rights to produce and market Nosplit for the European market for 5 years. In setting the royalty rate for this license, USdrug makes projections of the annual sales revenue and the annual profits to be derived from the exploitation of Nosplit by Eurodrug. Based on the projections, a royalty rate of 3.9% is established for the term of the license.

(iii) In Year 1, USdrug evaluates the royalty rate it received from Eurodrug. Given the high profit potential of Nosplit, USdrug is unable to locate any uncontrolled transactions dealing with licenses of comparable intangible property. USdrug therefore determines that the comparable uncontrolled transaction method will not provide a reliable measure of an arm's length royalty. However, applying the comparable profits method to Eurodrug, USdrug determines that a royalty rate of 3.9% will result in Eurodrug earning an arm's length return for its manufacturing and marketing functions.

(iv) In Year 5, the U.S. income tax return for USdrug is examined, and the district director must determine whether the royalty rate between USdrug and Eurodrug is commensurate with the income attributable to Nosplit. In making this determination, the district director considers whether any of the exceptions in § 1.482–4(f)(2)(ii) are applicable. In particular, the district director compares the profit projections attributable to Nosplit made by USdrug against the actual profits realized by Eurodrug. The projected and actual profits are as follows:

	Profit projections	*Actual profits*
Year 1	200	250
Year 2	250	300
Year 3	500	600
Year 4	350	200
Year 5	100	100
Total	1400	1450

(v) The total profits earned through Year 5 were not less than 80% nor more than 120% of the profits that were projected when the license was entered into. If the district director determines that the other requirements of § 1.482–4(f)(2)(ii)(C) were met, no adjustment will be made to the royalty rate between USdrug and Eurodrug for the license of Nosplit.

Example 2. (i) The facts are the same as in Example 1, except that Eurodrug's actual profits earned were much higher than the projected profits, as follows:

	Profit projections	*Actual profits*
Year 1	200	250
Year 2	250	500
Year 3	500	800
Year 4	350	700
Year 5	100	600
Total	1400	2850

(ii) In examining USdrug's tax return for Year 5, the district director considers the actual profits realized by Eurodrug in Year 5, and all past years. Accordingly, although Years 1 through 4 may be closed under the statute of limitations, for purposes of determining whether an adjustment should be made with respect to the royalty rate in Year 5 with respect to Nosplit, the district director aggregates the actual profits from those years with the profits of Year 5. However, the district director will make an adjustment, if any, only with respect to Year 5.

Example 3. (i) FP, a foreign corporation, licenses to USS, its U.S. subsidiary, a new air-filtering process that permits manufacturing plants to meet new environmental standards. The license runs for a 10-year period, and the profit derived from the new process is projected to be $15 million per year, for an aggregate profit of $150 million.

(ii) The royalty rate for the license is based on a comparable uncontrolled transaction involving a comparable intangible under comparable circumstances. The requirements of paragraphs (f)(2)(ii)(B)(1) through (5) of this section have been met. Specifically, FP and USS have entered into a written agreement that provides for a royalty in each year of the license, the royalty rate is considered arm's length for the first taxable year in which a substantial royalty was required to be paid, the license limited the use of the process to a specified field, consistent with industry practice, and there are no substantial changes in the functions performed by USS after the license was entered into.

(iii) In examining Year 4 of the license, the district director determines that the aggregate actual profits earned by USS through Year 4 are $30 million, less than 80% of the projected profits of $60 million. However, USS establishes to the satisfaction of the district director that the aggregate actual profits from the process are less than 80% of the projected profits in Year 3 because an earthquake severely damaged USS's manufacturing plant. Because the difference between the projected profits and actual profits was due to an extraordinary event that was beyond the control of USS, and could not reasonably have been anticipated at the time the license was entered into, the requirement under § 1.482–4(f)(2)(ii)(D) has been met, and no adjustment under this section is made.

(3) Ownership of intangible property—(i) Identification of owner—(A) In general. The legal owner of intangible property pursuant to the intellectual property law of the relevant jurisdiction, or the holder of rights constituting an intangible property pursuant to contractual terms (such as the terms of a license) or other legal provision, will be considered the sole owner of the respective intangible property for purposes of this section unless such ownership is inconsistent with the economic substance of the underlying transactions. See § 1.482–1(d)(3)(ii)(B) (identifying contractual terms). If no owner of the respective intangible property is identified under the intellectual property law of the relevant jurisdiction, or pursuant to contractual terms (including terms imputed pursuant to § 1.482–1(d)(3)(ii)(B)) or other legal provision, then the controlled taxpayer who has control of the intangible property, based on all the facts and circumstances, will be considered the sole owner of the intangible property for purposes of this section.

(B) Cost sharing arrangements. The rules in this paragraph (f)(3) regarding ownership with respect to cost shared intangibles and cost sharing arrangements will apply only as provided in § 1.482–7.

(ii) Examples. The principles of this paragraph (f)(3) are illustrated by the following examples:

Example 1. FP, a foreign corporation, is the registered holder of the AA trademark in the United States. FP licenses to its U.S. subsidiary, USSub, the exclusive rights to manufacture and market products in the United States under the AA trademark. FP is the owner of the trademark pursuant to intellectual property law. USSub is the owner of the license pursuant to the terms of the license, but is not the owner of the trademark. See paragraphs (b)(3) and (4) of this section (defining an intangible as, among other things, a trademark or a license).

Example 2. The facts are the same as in Example 1. As a result of its sales and marketing activities, USSub develops a list of several hundred creditworthy customers that regularly purchase AA trademarked products. Neither the terms of the contract between FP and USSub nor the relevant intellectual property law specify which party owns the customer list. Because USSub has knowledge of the contents of the list, and has practical control over its use and dissemination, USSub is considered the sole owner of the customer list for purposes of this paragraph (f)(3).

(4) Contribution to the value of intangible property owned by another—(i) In general. The arm's length consideration for a contribution by one controlled taxpayer that develops or enhances the value, or may be reasonably anticipated to develop or enhance the value, of intangible property owned by another controlled taxpayer will be determined in accordance with the applicable rules under section 482. If the consideration for such a contribution is embedded within the contractual terms for a controlled transaction that involves such intangible property, then ordinarily no separate allocation will be made with respect to such contribution.

In such cases, pursuant to § 1.482–1(d)(3), the contribution must be accounted for in evaluating the comparability of the controlled transaction to uncontrolled comparables, and accordingly in determining the arm's length consideration in the controlled transaction.

(ii) Examples. The principles of this paragraph (f)(4) are illustrated by the following examples:

Example 1. A, a member of a controlled group, allows B, another member of the controlled group, to use tangible property, such as laboratory equipment, in connection with B's development of an intangible that B owns. By furnishing tangible property, A makes a contribution to the development of intangible property owned by another controlled taxpayer, B. Pursuant to paragraph (f)(4)(i) of this section, the arm's length charge for A's furnishing of tangible property will be determined under the rules for use of tangible property in § 1.482–2(c).

Example 2. (i) Facts. FP, a foreign producer of wristwatches, is the registered holder of the YY trademark in the United States and in other countries worldwide. FP enters into an exclusive, five-year, renewable agreement with its newly organized U.S. subsidiary, USSub. The contractual terms of the agreement grant USSub the exclusive right to re-sell YY trademark wristwatches in the United States, obligate USSub to pay a fixed price per wristwatch throughout the entire term of the contract, and obligate both FP and USSub to undertake without separate compensation specified types and levels of marketing activities.

(ii) The consideration for FP's and USSub's marketing activities, as well as the consideration for the exclusive right to re-sell YY trademarked merchandise in the United States, are embedded in the transfer price paid for the wristwatches. Accordingly, pursuant to paragraph (f)(4)(i) of this section, ordinarily no separate allocation would be appropriate with respect to these embedded contributions.

(iii) Whether an allocation is warranted with respect to the transfer price for the wristwatches is determined under §§ 1.482–1, 1.482–3, and this section through § 1.482–6. The comparability analysis would include consideration of all relevant factors, including the nature of the intangible property embedded in the wristwatches and the nature of the marketing activities required under the agreement. This analysis would also take into account that the compensation for the activities performed by USSub and FP, as well as the consideration for USSub's use of the YY trademark, is embedded in the transfer price for the wristwatches, rather than provided for in separate agreements. See §§ 1.482–3(f) and 1.482–9(m)(4).

Example 3. (i) Facts. FP, a foreign producer of athletic gear, is the registered holder of the AA trademark in the United States and in other countries. In year 1, FP licenses to a newly organized U.S. subsidiary, USSub, the exclusive rights to use certain manufacturing and marketing intangible property to manufacture and market athletic gear in the United States under the AA trademark. The license agreement obligates USSub to pay a royalty based on sales of trademarked merchandise. The license agreement also obligates FP and USSub to perform without separate compensation specified types and levels of marketing activities. In year 1, USSub manufactures and sells athletic gear under the AA trademark in the United States.

(ii) The consideration for FP's and USSub's respective marketing activities is embedded in the contractual terms of the license for the AA trademark. Accordingly, pursuant to paragraph (f)(4)(i) of this section, ordinarily no separate allocation would be appropriate with respect to the embedded contributions in year 1. See § 1.482–9(m)(4).

(iii) Whether an allocation is warranted with respect to the royalty under the license agreement would be analyzed under § 1.482–1, and this section through § 1.482–6. The comparability analysis would include consideration of all relevant factors, such as the term and geographical exclusivity of the license, the nature of the intangible property subject to the license, and the nature of the marketing activities required to be undertaken pursuant to the license. Pursuant to paragraph (f)(4)(i) of this section, the analysis would also take into account the fact that the compensation for the marketing services is embedded in the royalty paid for use of the AA trademark, rather than provided for in a separate services agreement. For illustrations of application of the best method rule, see § 1.482–8 Examples 10, 11, and 12.

Example 4. (i) Facts. The year 1 facts are the same as in Example 3, with the following exceptions. In year 2, USSub undertakes certain incremental marketing activities in addition to those required by the contractual terms of the license for the AA trademark executed in year 1. The parties do not execute a separate agreement with respect to these incremental marketing activities performed by USSub. The license agreement executed in year 1 is of sufficient duration that it is reasonable to anticipate that USSub will obtain the benefit of its incremental activities, in the form of increased sales or revenues of trademarked products in the U.S. market.

(ii) To the extent that it was reasonable to anticipate that USSub's incremental marketing activities would increase the value only of USSub's intangible property (that is, USSub's license to use the AA trademark for a specified term), and not the value of the AA trademark owned by FP, USSub's incremental activities do not constitute a contribution for which an allocation is warranted under paragraph (f)(4)(i) of this section.

Example 5. (i) Facts. The year 1 facts are the same as in Example 3. In year 2, FP and USSub enter into a separate services agreement that obligates USSub to perform certain incremental marketing activities to promote AA trademark athletic gear in the United States, above and beyond the activities specified in the license agreement executed in year 1. In year 2, USSub begins to perform these incremental activities, pursuant to the separate services agreement with FP.

(ii) Whether an allocation is warranted with respect to USSub's incremental marketing activities covered by the separate services agreement would be evaluated under §§ 1.482–1 and 1.482–9, including a comparison of the compensation provided for the services with the results obtained under a method pursuant to § 1.482–9, selected and applied in accordance with the best method rule of § 1.482–1(c).

(iii) Whether an allocation is warranted with respect to the royalty under the license agreement is determined under § 1.482–1, and this section through § 1.482–6. The comparability analysis would include consideration of all relevant factors, such as the term and geographical exclusivity of the license, the nature of the intangible property subject to the license, and the nature of the marketing activities required to be undertaken pursuant to the license. The comparability analysis would take into account that the compensation for the incremental activities by USSub is provided for in the separate services agreement, rather than embedded in the royalty paid for use of the AA trademark. For illustrations of application of the best method rule, see § 1.482–8 Examples 10, 11, and 12.

Example 6. (i) Facts. The year 1 facts are the same as in Example 3. In year 2, FP and USSub enter into a separate services agreement that obligates FP to perform incremental marketing activities, not specified in the year 1 license, by advertising AA trademarked athletic gear in selected international sporting events, such as the Olympics and the soccer World Cup. FP's corporate advertising department develops and coordinates these special promotions. The separate services agreement obligates USSub to pay an amount to FP for the benefit to USSub that may reasonably be anticipated as the result of FP's incremental activities. The separate services agreement is not a qualified cost sharing arrangement under § 1.482–7T. FP begins to perform the incremental activities in year 2 pursuant to the separate services agreement.

(ii) Whether an allocation is warranted with respect to the incremental marketing activities performed by FP under the separate services agreement would be evaluated under § 1.482–9. Under the circumstances, it is reasonable to anticipate that FP's activities would increase the value of USSub's license as well as the value of FP's trademark. Accordingly, the incremental activities by FP may constitute in part a controlled services transaction for which USSub must compensate FP. The analysis of whether an allocation is warranted would include a comparison of the compensation provided for the services with the results obtained under a method pursuant to § 1.482–9, selected and applied in accordance with the best method rule of § 1.482–1(c).

(iii) Whether an allocation is appropriate with respect to the royalty under the license agreement would be evaluated under §§ 1.482–1 through 1.482–3, this section, and §§ 1.482–5 and 1.482–6. The comparability analysis would include consideration of all relevant factors, such as the term and geographical exclusivity of USSub's license, the nature of the intangible property subject to the license, and the marketing activities required to be undertaken by both FP and USSub pursuant to the license. This comparability analysis would take into account that the compensation for the incremental activities performed by FP was provided for in the separate services agreement, rather than embedded in the royalty paid for use of the AA trademark. For illustrations of application of the best method rule, see § 1.482–8, Example 10, Example 11, and Example 12.

(5) Consideration not artificially limited. The arm's length consideration for the controlled transfer of an intangible is not limited by the consideration paid in any uncontrolled transactions that do not meet the requirements of the comparable uncontrolled transaction method described in paragraph (c) of this section. Similarly, the arm's length consideration for an intangible is not limited by the prevailing rates of consideration paid for the use or transfer of intangibles within the same or similar industry.

(6) Lump sum payments—(i) In general. If an intangible is transferred in a controlled transaction for a lump sum, that amount must be commensurate with the income attributable to the intangible. A lump sum is commensurate with income in a taxable year if the equivalent royalty amount for that taxable year is equal to an arm's length royalty. The equivalent royalty amount for a taxable year is the amount determined by treating the lump sum as an advance payment of a stream of royalties over the useful life of the intangible (or the period covered by an agreement, if shorter), taking into account the projected sales of the licensee as of the date of the transfer. Thus, determining the equivalent royalty amount requires a present value calculation based on the lump sum, an appropriate discount rate, and the projected sales over the relevant period. The equivalent royalty amount is subject to periodic adjustments under § 1.482–4(f)(2)(i) to the same extent as an actual royalty payment pursuant to a license agreement.

(ii) Exceptions. No periodic adjustment will be made under paragraph (f)(2)(i) of this section if any of the exceptions to periodic adjustments provided in paragraph (f)(2)(ii) of this section apply.

(iii) Example. The following example illustrates the principle of this paragraph (f)(5).

Example. Calculation of the equivalent royalty amount. (i) FSub is the foreign subsidiary of USP, a U.S. company. USP licenses FSub the right to produce and sell the whopper-chopper, a patented new kitchen appliance, for the foreign market. The license is for a period of five years, and payment takes the form of a single lump-sum charge of $500,000 that is paid at the beginning of the period.

(ii) The equivalent royalty amount for this license is determined by deriving an equivalent royalty rate equal to the lump-sum payment divided by the present discounted value of FSub's projected sales of whopperchoppers over the life of the license. Based on the riskiness of the whopperchopper business, an appropriate discount rate is determined to be 10 percent. Projected sales of whopperchoppers for each year of the license are as follows:

Year	*Projected sales*
1	$2,500,000
2	2,600,000
3	2,700,000
4	2,700,000
5	2,750,000

(iii) Based on this information, the present discounted value of the projected whopper-chopper sales is approximately $10 million, yielding an equivalent royalty rate of approximately 5%. Thus, the equivalent royalty amounts for each year are as follows:

Year	*Projected sales*	*Equivalent royalty amount*
1	2,500,000	125,000
2	2,600,000	130,000
3	2,700,000	135,000
4	2,700,000	135,000
5	2,750,000	137,500

(iv) If in any of the five taxable years the equivalent royalty amount is determined not to be an arm's length amount, a periodic adjustment may be made pursuant to § 1.482–4(f)(2)(i). The adjustment in such case would be equal to the difference between the equivalent royalty amount and the arm's length royalty in that taxable year.

(7) [Reserved]. For further guidance, see § 1.482–4T(f)(7).

* * *

[T.D. 8552, 59 FR 35016, July 8, 1994; T.D. 9278, 71 FR 44484, Aug. 4, 2006; T.D. 9456, 74 FR 38842, Aug. 4, 2009; T.D. 9568, 76 FR 80090, Dec. 22, 2011]

§ 1.482–5 Comparable profits method.

(a) In general. The comparable profits method evaluates whether the amount charged in a controlled transaction is arm's length based on objective measures of profitability (profit level indicators) derived from uncontrolled taxpayers that engage in similar business activities under similar circumstances.

(b) Determination of arm's length result—(1) In general. Under the comparable profits method, the determination of an arm's length result is based on the amount of operating profit that the tested party would have earned on related party transactions if its profit level indicator were equal to that of an uncontrolled comparable (comparable operating profit). Comparable operating profit is calculated by determining a profit level indicator for an uncontrolled comparable, and applying the profit level indicator to the financial data related to the tested party's most narrowly identifiable business activity for which data incorporating the controlled transaction is available (relevant business activity). To the extent possible, profit level indicators should be applied solely to the tested party's financial data that is related to controlled transactions. The tested party's reported operating profit is compared to the comparable operating profits derived from the profit level indicators of uncontrolled comparables to determine whether the reported operating profit represents an arm's length result.

(2) Tested party—(i) In general. For purposes of this section, the tested party will be the participant in the controlled transaction whose operating profit attributable to the controlled transactions can be verified using the most reliable data and requiring the fewest and most reliable adjustments, and for which reliable data regarding uncontrolled comparables can be located. Consequently, in most cases the tested party will be the least complex of the controlled taxpayers and will not own valuable intangible property or unique assets that distinguish it from potential uncontrolled comparables.

(ii) Adjustments for tested party. The tested party's operating profit must first be adjusted to reflect all other allocations under section 482, other than adjustments pursuant to this section.

(3) Arm's length range. See § 1.482–1(e)(2) for the determination of the arm's length range. For purposes of the comparable profits method, the arm's length range will be established using comparable operating profits derived from a single profit level indicator.

(4) Profit level indicators. Profit level indicators are ratios that measure relationships between profits and costs incurred or resources employed. A variety of profit level indicators can be calculated in any given case. Whether use of a particular profit level indicator is appropriate depends upon a number of factors, including the nature of the activities of the tested party, the reliability of the available data with respect to uncontrolled comparables, and the extent to which the profit level indicator is likely to produce a reliable measure of the income that the tested party would have earned had it dealt with controlled taxpayers at arm's length, taking into account all of the facts and circumstances. The profit level indicators should be derived from a sufficient number of years of data to reasonably measure returns that accrue to uncontrolled comparables. Generally, such a period should encompass at least the taxable year under review and the preceding two taxable years. This analysis must be applied in accordance with § 1.482–1(f)(2)(iii)(D). Profit level indicators that may provide a reliable basis for comparing operating profits of the tested party and uncontrolled comparables include the following—

(i) Rate of return on capital employed. The rate of return on capital employed is the ratio of operating profit to operating assets. The reliability of this profit level indicator increases as operating assets play a greater role in generating operating profits for both the tested party and the uncontrolled comparable. In addition, reliability under this profit level indicator depends on the extent to which the composition of the tested party's assets is similar to that of the uncontrolled comparable. Finally, difficulties in properly valuing operating assets will diminish the reliability of this profit level indicator.

(ii) Financial ratios. Financial ratios measure relationships between profit and costs or sales revenue. Since functional differences generally have a greater effect on the relationship between profit and costs or sales revenue than the relationship between profit and operating assets, financial ratios are more sensitive to functional differences than the rate of return on capital employed. Therefore, closer functional comparability normally is required under a financial ratio than under the rate of return on capital employed to achieve a similarly reliable measure of an arm's length result. Financial ratios that may be appropriate include the following—

(A) Ratio of operating profit to sales; and

(B) Ratio of gross profit to operating expenses. Reliability under this profit level indicator also depends on the extent to which the composition of the tested party's operating expenses is similar to that of the uncontrolled comparables.

(iii) Other profit level indicators. Other profit level indicators not described in this paragraph (b)(4) may be used if they provide reliable measures of the income that the tested party would have earned had it dealt with controlled taxpayers at arm's length. However, profit level indicators based solely on internal data may not be used under this paragraph (b)(4) because they are not objective measures of profitability derived from operations of uncontrolled taxpayers engaged in similar business activities under similar circumstances.

(c) Comparability and reliability considerations—(1) In general. Whether results derived from application of this method are the most reliable measure of the arm's length result must be determined using the factors described under the best method rule in § 1.482–1(c).

(2) Comparability—(i) In general. The degree of comparability between an uncontrolled taxpayer and the tested party is determined by applying the provisions of § 1.482–1(d)(2). The comparable profits method compares the profitability of the tested party, measured by a profit level indicator (generally based on operating profit), to the profitability of uncontrolled taxpayers in similar circumstances. As with all methods that rely on external market benchmarks, the greater the degree of comparability between the tested party and the uncontrolled taxpayer, the more reliable will be the results derived from the application of this method. The determination of the degree of comparability between the tested party and the uncontrolled taxpayer depends upon all the relevant facts and circumstances, including the relevant lines of business, the product or service markets involved, the asset composition employed (including the nature and quantity of tangible assets, intangible assets and working capital), the size and scope of operations, and the stage in a business or product cycle.

(ii) Functional, risk and resource comparability. An operating profit represents a return for the investment of resources and assumption of risks. Therefore, although all of the factors described in § 1.482–1(d)(3) must be considered, comparability under this method is particularly dependent on resources employed and risks assumed. Moreover, because resources and risks usually are directly related to functions performed, it is also important to consider functions performed in determining the degree of comparability between the tested party and an uncontrolled taxpayer. The degree of functional comparability required to obtain a reliable result under the comparable profits method, however, is generally less than that required under the resale price or cost plus methods. For example, because differences in functions performed often are reflected in operating expenses, taxpayers performing different functions may have very different gross profit margins but earn similar levels of operating profit.

(iii) Other comparability factors. Other factors listed in § 1.482–1(d)(3) also may be particularly relevant under the comparable profits method. Because operating profit usually is less sensitive than gross profit to product differences, reliability under the comparable profits method is not as dependent on product similarity as the resale price or cost plus method. However, the reliability of profitability measures based on operating profit may be adversely affected by factors that have less effect on results under the comparable uncontrolled price, resale price, and cost plus methods. For example, operating profit may be affected by varying cost structures (as reflected, for example, in the age of plant and equipment), differences in business experience (such as whether the business is in a start-up phase or is mature), or differences in management efficiency (as indicated, for example, by objective evidence such as expanding or contracting sales or executive compensation over time). Accordingly, if material differences in these factors are identified based on objective evidence, the reliability of the analysis may be affected.

(iv) Adjustments for the differences between the tested party and the uncontrolled taxpayers. If there are differences between the tested party and an uncontrolled comparable that would materially affect the profits determined under the relevant profit level indicator, adjustments should be made according to the comparability provisions of § 1.482–1(d)(2). In some cases, the assets of an uncontrolled comparable may need to be adjusted to achieve greater comparability between the tested party and the uncontrolled comparable. In such cases, the uncontrolled comparable's operating income attributable to those assets must also be adjusted before computing a profit level indicator in order to reflect the income and expense attributable to the adjusted assets. In certain cases it may also be appropriate to adjust the operating profit of the tested party and comparable parties. For example, where there are material differences in accounts payable among the comparable parties and the tested party, it will generally be appropriate to adjust the operating profit of each party by increasing it to reflect an imputed interest charge on each party's accounts payable. As another example, it may be appropriate to adjust the operating profit of a party to account for material differences in the utilization of or accounting for stock-based compensation (as defined by § 1.482–7(d)(3)(i)) among the tested party and comparable parties.

(3) Data and assumptions—(i) In general. The reliability of the results derived from the comparable profits method is affected by the quality of the data and assumptions used to apply this method.

(ii) Consistency in accounting. The degree of consistency in accounting practices between the controlled transaction and the uncontrolled comparables that materially affect operating profit affects the reliability of the result. Thus, for example, if differences in inventory and other cost accounting practices would materially affect operating profit, the ability to make reliable adjustments for such differences would affect the reliability of the results.

* * *

(e) Examples. The following examples illustrate the application of this section.

Example 1. Transfer of tangible property resulting in no adjustment. (i) FP is a publicly traded foreign corporation with a U.S. subsidiary, USSub, that is under audit for its 1996 taxable year. FP manufactures a consumer product for worldwide distribution. USSub imports the assembled product and distributes it within the United States at the wholesale level under the FP name.

(ii) FP does not allow uncontrolled taxpayers to distribute the product. Similar products are produced by other companies but none of them is sold to uncontrolled taxpayers or to uncontrolled distributors.

(iii) Based on all the facts and circumstances, the district director determines that the comparable profits method will provide the most reliable measure of an arm's length result. USSub is selected as the tested party because it engages in activities that are less complex than those undertaken by FP.

There is data from a number of independent operators of wholesale distribution businesses. These potential comparables are further narrowed to select companies in the same industry segment that perform similar functions and bear similar risks to USSub. An analysis of the information available on these taxpayers shows that the ratio of operating profit to sales is the most appropriate profit level indicator, and this ratio is relatively stable where at least three years are included in the average. For the taxable years 1994 through 1996, USSub shows the following results:

	1994	1995	1996	Average
Sales	$500,000	$560,000	$500,000	$520,000
Cost of Goods Sold	393,000	412,400	400,000	401,800
Operating Expenses	80,000	110,000	104,600	98,200
Operating Profit	27,000	37,600	(4,600)	20,000

(iv) After adjustments have been made to account for identified material differences between USSub and the uncontrolled distributors, the average ratio of operating profit to sales is calculated for each of the uncontrolled distributors. Applying each ratio to USSub would lead to the following comparable operating profit (COP) for USSub:

Uncontrolled distributor	*OP/S (percent)*	*USSub COP*
A	1.7	$8,840
B	3.1	16,120
C	3.8	19,760
D	4.5	23,400
E	4.7	24,440
F	4.8	24,960
G	4.9	25,480

H....................	6.7	34,840
I......................	9.9	51,480
J......................	10.5	54,600

(v) The data is not sufficiently complete to conclude that it is likely that all material differences between USSub and the uncontrolled distributors have been identified. Therefore, an arm's length range can be established only pursuant to § 1.482–1(e)(2)(iii)(B). The district director measures the arm's length range by the interquartile range of results, which consists of the results ranging from $19,760 to $34,840. Although USSub's operating income for 1996 shows a loss of $4,600, the district director determines that no allocation should be made, because USSub's average reported operating profit of $20,000 is within this range.

Example 2. Transfer of tangible property resulting in adjustment. (i) The facts are the same as in Example 1 except that USSub reported the following income and expenses:

	1994	1995	1996	Average
Sales..................................	$500,000	$560,000	$500,000	$520,000
Cost of Goods Sold..............	370,000	460,000	400,000	410,000
Operating Expenses............	110,000	110,000	110,000	110,000
Operating Profit.....................	20,000	(10,000)	(10,000)	0

(ii) The interquartile range of comparable operating profits remains the same as derived in Example 1: $19,760 to $34,840. USSub's average operating profit for the years 1994 through 1996 ($0) falls outside this range. Therefore, the district director determines that an allocation may be appropriate.

(iii) To determine the amount, if any, of the allocation, the district director compares USSub's reported operating profit for 1996 to comparable operating profits derived from the uncontrolled distributors' results for 1996. The ratio of operating profit to sales in 1996 is calculated for each of the uncontrolled comparables and applied to USSub's 1996 sales to derive the following results:

Uncontrolled distributor	*OP/S (percent)*	*USSub COP*
C......................	0.5	$2,500
D......................	1.5	7,500
E......................	2.0	10,000
A......................	1.6	13,000
F......................	2.8	14,000
B......................	2.9	14,500
J......................	3.0	15,000
I......................	4.4	22,000
H......................	6.9	34,500
G......................	7.4	37,000

(iv) Based on these results, the median of the comparable operating profits for 1996 is $14,250. Therefore, USSub's income for 1996 is increased by $24,250, the difference between USSub's reported operating profit for 1996 and the median of the comparable operating profits for 1996.

* * *

[T.D. 8552, 59 FR 35021, July 8, 1994; 60 FR 16703, March 31, 1995; T.D. 9088, 68 FR 51177, Aug. 26, 2003; T.D. 9441, 74 FR 352, Jan. 5, 2009; T.D. 9568, 76 FR 80090, Dec. 22, 2011]

§ 1.482–6 Profit split method.

(a) In general. The profit split method evaluates whether the allocation of the combined operating profit or loss attributable to one or more controlled transactions is arm's length by reference to the relative value of each controlled taxpayer's contribution to that combined operating profit or loss. The combined operating profit or loss must be derived from the most narrowly identifiable business activity of the controlled taxpayers for which data is available that includes the controlled transactions (relevant business activity).

(b) Appropriate share of profits and losses. The relative value of each controlled taxpayer's contribution to the success of the relevant business activity must be determined in a manner that reflects the functions performed, risks assumed, and resources employed by each participant in the relevant business activity, consistent with the comparability provisions of § 1.482–1(d)(3). Such an allocation is intended to correspond to the division of profit or loss that would result from an arrangement between uncontrolled taxpayers, each performing functions similar to those of the various controlled taxpayers engaged in the relevant business activity. * * *

(c) Application—(1) In general. The allocation of profit or loss under the profit split method must be made in accordance with one of the following allocation methods—

(i) The comparable profit split, described in paragraph (c)(2) of this section; or

(ii) The residual profit split, described in paragraph (c)(3) of this section.

(2) Comparable profit split—(i) In general. A comparable profit split is derived from the combined operating profit of uncontrolled taxpayers whose transactions and activities are similar to those of the controlled taxpayers in the relevant business activity. Under this method, each uncontrolled taxpayer's percentage of the combined operating profit or loss is used to allocate the combined operating profit or loss of the relevant business activity.

(ii) Comparability and reliability considerations—(A) In general. Whether results derived from application of this method are the most reliable measure of the arm's length result is determined using the factors described under the best method rule in § 1.482–1(c).

(B) Comparability—(1) In general. The degree of comparability between the controlled and uncontrolled taxpayers is determined by applying the comparability provisions of § 1.482–1(d). The comparable profit split compares the division of operating profits among the controlled taxpayers to the division of operating profits among uncontrolled taxpayers engaged in similar activities under similar circumstances. Although all of the factors described in § 1.482–1(d)(3) must be considered, comparability under this method is particularly dependent on the considerations described under the comparable profits method in § 1.482–5(c)(2) or § 1.482–9(f)(2)(iii) because this method is based on a comparison of the operating profit of the controlled and uncontrolled taxpayers. In addition, because the contractual terms of the relationship among the participants in the relevant business activity will be a principal determinant of the allocation of functions and risks among them, comparability under this method also depends particularly on the degree of similarity of the contractual terms of the controlled and uncontrolled taxpayers. Finally, the comparable profit split may not be used if the combined operating profit (as a percentage of the combined assets) of the uncontrolled comparables varies significantly from that earned by the controlled taxpayers.

(2) Adjustments for differences between the controlled and uncontrolled taxpayers. If there are differences between the controlled and uncontrolled taxpayers that would materially affect the division of operating profit, adjustments must be made according to the provisions of § 1.482–1(d)(2).

(C) Data and assumptions. The reliability of the results derived from the comparable profit split is affected by the quality of the data and assumptions used to apply this method. * * *

* * *

(D) Other factors affecting reliability. Like the methods described in §§ 1.482–3, 1.482–4, 1.482–5, and 1.482–9, the comparable profit split relies exclusively on external market benchmarks. As indicated in § 1.482–1(c)(2)(i), as the degree of comparability between the controlled and uncontrolled transactions increases, the relative weight accorded the analysis under this method will increase. In addition, the reliability of the analysis under this method may be enhanced by the fact that all parties to the controlled transaction are evaluated under the comparable profit split. However, the reliability of the results of an analysis based on information from all parties to a transaction is affected by the reliability of the data and the assumptions pertaining to each party to the controlled transaction. Thus, if the data and assumptions are significantly more reliable with respect to one of the parties than with respect to the others, a different method, focusing solely on the results of that party, may yield more reliable results.

(3) Residual profit split—(i) In general. Under this method, the combined operating profit or loss from the relevant business activity is allocated between the controlled taxpayers following the two-step process set forth in paragraphs (c)(3)(i)(A) and (B) of this section.

(A) Allocate income to routine contributions. The first step allocates operating income to each party to the controlled transactions to provide a market return for its routine contributions to the relevant business activity. Routine contributions are contributions of the same or a similar kind to those made by uncontrolled taxpayers involved in similar business activities for which it is possible to identify market returns. Routine contributions ordinarily include contributions of tangible property, services and intangible property that are generally owned by uncontrolled taxpayers engaged in similar activities. A functional analysis is required to identify these contributions according to the functions performed, risks assumed, and resources employed by each of the controlled taxpayers. Market returns for the routine contributions should be determined by reference to the returns achieved by uncontrolled taxpayers engaged in similar activities, consistent with the methods described in §§ 1.482–3, 1.482–4, 1.482–5 and 1.482–9.

(B) Allocate residual profit—(1) Nonroutine contributions generally. The allocation of income to the controlled taxpayer's routine contributions will not reflect profits attributable to each controlled taxpayer's contributions to the relevant business activity that are not routine (nonroutine contributions). A nonroutine contribution is a contribution that is not accounted for as a routine contribution. Thus, in cases where such nonroutine contributions are present, there normally will be an unallocated residual profit after the allocation of income described in paragraph (c)(3)(i)(A) of this section. Under this second step, the residual profit generally should be divided among the controlled taxpayers based upon the relative value of their nonroutine contributions to the relevant business activity. The relative value of the nonroutine contributions of each taxpayer should be measured in a manner that most reliably reflects each nonroutine contribution made to the controlled transaction and each controlled taxpayer's role in the nonroutine contributions. If the nonroutine contribution by one of the controlled taxpayers is also used in other business activities (such as transactions with other controlled taxpayers), an appropriate allocation of the value of the nonroutine contribution must be made among all the business activities in which it is used.

(2) Nonroutine contributions of intangible property. In many cases, nonroutine contributions of a taxpayer to the relevant business activity may be contributions of intangible property. For purposes of paragraph (c)(3)(i)(B)(1) of this section, the relative value of nonroutine intangible property contributed by taxpayers may be measured by external market benchmarks that reflect the fair market value of such intangible property. Alternatively, the relative value of non-routine intangible property contributions may be estimated by the capitalized cost of developing the intangible property and all related improvements and updates, less an appropriate amount of amortization based on the useful life of each intangible property. Finally, if the intangible property development expenditures of the parties are relatively constant over time and the useful life of the intangible property contributed by all parties is approximately the same, the amount of actual expenditures in recent years may be used to estimate the relative value of nonroutine intangible property contributions.

(ii) Comparability and reliability considerations—(A) In general. Whether results derived from this method are the most reliable measure of the arm's length result is determined using the factors described under the best method rule in § 1.482–1(c). Thus, comparability and the quality of data and assumptions must be considered in determining whether this method provides the most reliable measure of an arm's length result. The application of these factors to the residual profit split is discussed in paragraph (c)(3)(ii)(B), (C), and (D) of this section.

(B) Comparability. The first step of the residual profit split relies on market benchmarks of profitability. Thus, the comparability considerations that are relevant for the first step of the residual profit split are those that are relevant for the methods that are used to determine market returns for the routine contributions. The second step of the residual profit split, however, may not rely so directly on market benchmarks. Thus, the reliability of the results under this method is reduced to the extent that the allocation of profits in the second step does not rely on market benchmarks.

(C) Data and assumptions. The reliability of the results derived from the residual profit split is affected by the quality of the data and assumptions used to apply this method. In particular, the following factors must be considered—

(1) The reliability of the allocation of costs, income, and assets as described in paragraph (c)(2)(ii)(C)(1) of this section;

(2) Accounting consistency as described in paragraph (c)(2)(ii)(C)(2) of this section;

(3) The reliability of the data used and the assumptions made in valuing the intangible property contributed by the participants. In particular, if capitalized costs of development are used to estimate the value of intangible property, the reliability of the results is reduced relative to the reliability of other methods that do not require such an estimate, for the following reasons. First, in any given case, the costs of developing the intangible may not be related to its market value. Second, the calculation of the capitalized costs of development may require the allocation of indirect costs between the relevant business activity and the controlled taxpayer's other activities, which may affect the reliability of the analysis. Finally, the calculation of costs may require assumptions regarding the useful life of the intangible property.

(D) Other factors affecting reliability. Like the methods described in §§ 1.482–3, 1.482–4, 1.482–5, and 1.482–9, the first step of the residual profit split relies exclusively on external market benchmarks. As indicated in § 1.482–1(c)(2)(i), as the degree of comparability between the controlled and uncontrolled transactions increases, the relative weight accorded the analysis under this method will increase. In addition, to the extent the allocation of profits in the second step is not based on external market benchmarks, the reliability of the analysis will be decreased in relation to an analysis under a method that relies on market benchmarks. Finally, the reliability of the analysis under this method may be enhanced by the fact that all parties to the controlled transaction are evaluated under the residual profit split. However, the reliability of the results of an analysis based on information from all parties to a transaction is affected by the reliability of the data and the assumptions pertaining to each party to the controlled transaction. Thus, if the data and assumptions are significantly more reliable with respect to one of the parties than with respect to the others, a different method, focusing solely on the results of that party, may yield more reliable results.

(iii) Example. The provisions of this paragraph (c)(3) are illustrated by the following example.

Example—Application of Residual Profit Split. (i) XYZ is a U.S. corporation that develops, manufactures and markets a line of products for police use in the United States. XYZ's research unit developed a bulletproof material for use in protective clothing and headgear (Nulon). XYZ obtains patent protection for the chemical formula for Nulon. Since its introduction in the U.S., Nulon has captured a substantial share of the U.S. market for bulletproof material.

(ii) XYZ licensed its European subsidiary, XYZ-Europe, to manufacture and market Nulon in Europe. XYZ-Europe is a well-established company that manufactures and markets XYZ products in Europe. XYZ-Europe has a research unit that adapts XYZ products for the defense market, as well as a well-developed marketing network that employs brand names that it developed.

(iii) XYZ-Europe's research unit alters Nulon to adapt it to military specifications and develops a high-intensity marketing campaign directed at the defense industry in several European countries. Beginning with the 1995 taxable year, XYZ-Europe manufactures and sells Nulon in Europe through its marketing network under one of its brand names.

(iv) For the 1995 taxable year, XYZ has no direct expenses associated with the license of Nulon to XYZ-Europe and incurs no expenses related to the marketing of Nulon in Europe. For the 1995 taxable year, XYZ-Europe's Nulon sales and pre-royalty expenses are $500 million and $300 million, respectively, resulting in net pre-royalty profit of $200 million related to the Nulon business. The operating assets employed in XYZ-Europe's Nulon business are $200 million. Given the facts and circumstances, the district director determines under the best method rule that a residual profit split will provide the most reliable measure of an arm's length result. Based on an examination of a sample of European companies performing functions similar to those of XYZ-Europe, the district director determines that an average market return on XYZ-Europe's operating assets in the Nulon business is 10 percent, resulting in a market return of $20 million (10% X $200 million) for XYZ-Europe's Nulon business, and a residual profit of $180 million.

(v) Since the first stage of the residual profit split allocated profits to XYZ-Europe's contributions other than those attributable to highly valuable intangible property, it is assumed that the residual profit of $180 million is attributable to the valuable intangibles related to Nulon, i.e., the European brand name for Nulon and the Nulon formula (including XYZ-Europe's modifications). To estimate the relative values of these intangibles, the district director compares the ratios of the capitalized value of expenditures as of 1995 on Nulon-related research and development and marketing over the 1995 sales related to such expenditures.

(vi) Because XYZ's protective product research and development expenses support the worldwide protective product sales of the XYZ group, it is necessary to allocate such expenses among the worldwide business activities to which they relate. The district director determines that it is reasonable to allocate the value of these expenses based on worldwide protective product sales. Using information on the average useful life of its investments in protective product research and development, the district director capitalizes and amortizes XYZ's protective product research and development expenses. This analysis indicates that the capitalized research and development expenditures have a value of $0.20 per dollar of global protective product sales in 1995.

(vii) XYZ-Europe's expenditures on Nulon research and development and marketing support only its sales in Europe. Using information on the average useful life of XYZ-Europe's investments in marketing and research and development, the district director capitalizes and amortizes XYZ-Europe's expenditures and determines that they have a value in 1995 of $0.40 per dollar of XYZ-Europe's Nulon sales.

(viii) Thus, XYZ and XYZ-Europe together contributed $0.60 in capitalized intangible development expenses for each dollar of XYZ-Europe's protective product sales for 1995, of which XYZ contributed one-third (or $0.20 per dollar of sales). Accordingly, the district director determines that an arm's length royalty for the Nulon license for the 1995 taxable year is $60 million, i.e., one-third of XYZ-Europe's $180 million in residual Nulon profit.

* * *

[T.D. 8552, 59 FR 35025, July 8, 1994; 60 FR 16382, March 30, 1995; T.D. 9278, 71 FR 44486, Aug. 4, 2006; T.D. 9456, 74 FR 38844, Aug. 4, 2009; 74 FR 46345, Sept. 9, 2009]

§ 1.482–7 Methods to determine taxable income in connection with a cost sharing arrangement.

(a) In general. The arm's length amount charged in a controlled transaction reasonably anticipated to contribute to developing intangibles pursuant to a cost sharing arrangement (CSA), as described in paragraph (b) of this section, must be determined under a method described in this section. Each method must be applied in accordance with the provisions of § 1.482–1, except as those provisions are modified in this section.

(1) RAB share method for cost sharing transactions (CSTs). See paragraph (b)(1)(i) of this section regarding the requirement that controlled participants, as defined in section (j)(1)(i) of this section, share intangible development costs (IDCs) in proportion to their shares of reasonably anticipated benefits (RAB shares) by entering into cost sharing transactions (CSTs).

(2) Methods for platform contribution transactions (PCTs). The arm's length amount charged in a platform contribution transaction (PCT) described in paragraph (b)(1)(ii) of this section must be determined under the method or methods applicable under the other section or sections of the section 482 regulations, as supplemented by paragraph (g) of this section. See § 1.482–1(b)(2)(ii) (Selection of category of method applicable to transaction), § 1.482–1(b)(2)(iii) (Coordination of methods applicable to certain intangible development arrangements), and paragraph (g) of this section (Supplemental guidance on methods applicable to PCTs).

(3) Methods for other controlled transactions—(i) Contribution to a CSA by a controlled taxpayer that is not a controlled participant. If a controlled taxpayer that is not a controlled participant contributes to developing a cost shared intangible, as defined in section (j)(1)(i) of this section, it must receive consideration from the controlled participants under the rules of § 1.482–4(f)(4) (Contribution to the value of an intangible owned by another). Such consideration will be treated as an intangible development cost for purposes of paragraph (d) of this section.

(ii) Transfer of interest in a cost shared intangible. If at any time (during the term, or upon or after the termination, of a CSA) a controlled participant transfers an interest in a cost shared intangible to another controlled taxpayer, the controlled participant must receive an arm's length amount of consideration from the transferee under the rules of §§ 1.482–4 through 1.482–6 as supplemented by paragraph (f)(4) of this section regarding arm's length consideration for a change in participation. For this purpose, a capability variation described in paragraph (f)(3) of this section is considered to be a controlled transfer of interests in cost shared intangibles.

(iii) Other controlled transactions in connection with a CSA. Controlled transactions between controlled participants that are not PCTs or CSTs and are not described in paragraph (a)(3)(ii) of this section (for example, provision of a cross operating contribution, as defined in paragraph (j)(1)(i) of this section, or make-or-sell rights, as defined in paragraph (c)(4) of this section) require arm's length consideration under the rules of §§ 1.482–1 through 1.482–6, and 1.482–9 as supplemented by paragraph (g)(2)(iv) of this section.

(iv) Controlled transactions in the absence of a CSA. If a controlled transaction is reasonably anticipated to contribute to developing intangibles pursuant to an arrangement that is not a CSA described in paragraph (b)(1) or (5) of this section, whether the results of any such controlled transaction are consistent with an arm's length result must be determined under the applicable rules of the other sections of the regulations under section 482. For example, an arrangement for developing intangibles in which one controlled taxpayer's costs of developing the intangibles significantly exceeds its share of reasonably anticipated benefits from exploiting the developed intangibles would not in substance be a CSA, as described in paragraphs (b)(1)(i) through (iii) of this section or paragraph (b)(5)(i) of this section. In such a case, unless the rules of this section are applicable by reason of paragraph (b)(5) of this section, the arrangement must be analyzed under other applicable sections of regulations under section 482 to determine whether it achieves arm's length results, and if not, to determine any allocations by the Commissioner that are consistent with such other regulations under section 482. See § 1.482–1(b)(2)(ii) (Selection of category of method applicable to transaction) and (iii) (Coordination of methods applicable to certain intangible development arrangements).

(4) Coordination with the arm's length standard. A CSA produces results that are consistent with an arm's length result within the meaning of § 1.482–1(b)(1) if, and only if, each controlled participant's IDC share (as determined under paragraph (d)(4) of this section) equals its RAB share, each controlled participant compensates its RAB share of the value of all platform contributions by other controlled participants, and all other requirements of this section are satisfied.

(b) Cost sharing arrangement. A cost sharing arrangement is an arrangement by which controlled participants share the costs and risks of developing cost shared intangibles in proportion to their RAB shares. An arrangement is a CSA if and only if the requirements of paragraphs (b)(1) through (4) of this section are met.

(1) Substantive requirements—(i) CSTs. All controlled participants must commit to, and in fact, engage in cost sharing transactions. In CSTs, the controlled participants make payments to each other (CST Payments) as appropriate, so that in each taxable year each controlled participant's IDC share is in proportion to its respective RAB share.

(ii) PCTs. All controlled participants must commit to, and in fact, engage in platform contributions transactions to the extent that there are platform contributions pursuant to paragraph (c) of this section. In a PCT, each other controlled participant (PCT Payor) is obligated to, and must in fact, make arm's length payments (PCT Payments) to each controlled participant (PCT Payee) that provides a platform contribution. For guidance on determining such arm's length obligation, see paragraph (g) of this section.

(iii) Divisional interests. Each controlled participant must receive a non-overlapping interest in the cost shared intangibles without further obligation to compensate another controlled participant for such interest.

(iv) Examples. The following examples illustrate the principles of this paragraph (b)(1):

Example 1. Company A and Company B, who are members of the same controlled group, execute an agreement to jointly develop vaccine X and own the exclusive rights to commercially exploit vaccine X in their respective territories, which together comprise the whole world. The agreement provides that they will share some, but not all, of the costs for developing Vaccine X in proportion to RAB share. Such agreement is not a CSA because Company A and Company B have not agreed to share all of the IDCs in proportion to their respective RAB shares.

Example 2. Company A and Company B agree to share all the costs of developing Vaccine X. The agreement also provides for employing certain resources and capabilities of Company A in this program including a skilled research team and certain research facilities, and provides for Company B to make payments to Company A in this respect. However, the agreement expressly provides that the program will not employ, and so Company B is expressly relieved of the payments in regard to, certain software developed by Company A as a medical research tool to model certain cellular processes expected to be implicated in the operation of Vaccine X even though such software would reasonably be anticipated to be relevant to developing Vaccine X and, thus, would be a platform contribution. See paragraph (c) of this section. Such agreement is not a CSA because Company A and Company B have not engaged in a necessary PCT for purposes of developing Vaccine X.

Example 3. Companies C and D, who are members of the same controlled group, enter into a CSA. In the first year of the CSA, C and D conduct the intangible development activity, as described in paragraph (d)(1) of this section. The total IDCs in regard to such activity are $3,000,000 of which C and D pay $2,000,000 and $1,000,000, respectively, directly to third parties. As between C and D, however, their CSA specifies that they will share all IDCs in accordance with their RAB shares (as described in paragraph (e)(1) of this section), which are 60% for C and 40% for D. It follows that C should bear $1,800,000 of the total IDCs (60% of total IDCs of $3,000,000) and D should bear $1,200,000 of the total IDCs (40% of total IDCs of $3,000,000). D makes a CST payment to C of $200,000, that is, the amount by which D's share of IDCs in accordance with its RAB share exceeds the amount of IDCs initially borne by D ($1,200,000–$1,000,000), and which also equals the amount by which the total IDCs initially borne by C exceeds its share of IDCS in accordance with its RAB share ($2,000,000– $1,800,000). As a result of D's CST payment to C, the IDC shares of C and D are in proportion to their respective RAB shares.

(2) Administrative requirements. The CSA must meet the requirements of paragraph (k) of this section.

(3) Date of a PCT. The controlled participants must enter into a PCT as of the earliest date on or after the CSA is entered into on which a platform contribution is reasonably anticipated to contribute to developing cost shared intangibles.

(4) Divisional interests—(i) In general. Pursuant to paragraph (b)(1)(iii) of this section, each controlled participant must receive a non-overlapping interest in the cost shared intangibles without further obligation to compensate another controlled participant for such interest. Each controlled participant must be entitled to the perpetual and exclusive right to the profits from transactions of any member of the controlled group that includes the controlled participant with uncontrolled taxpayers to the extent that such profits are attributable to such interest in the cost shared intangibles.

(ii) Territorial based divisional interests. The CSA may divide all interests in cost shared intangibles on a territorial basis as follows. The entire world must be divided into two or more non-overlapping geographic territories. Each controlled participant must receive at least one such territory, and in the aggregate all the participants must receive all such territories. Each controlled participant will be assigned the perpetual and exclusive right to exploit the cost shared intangibles through the use, consumption, or disposition of property or services in its territories. Thus, compensation will be required if other members of the controlled group exploit the cost shared intangibles in such territory.

(iii) Field of use based divisional interests. The CSA may divide all interests in cost shared intangibles on the basis of all uses (whether or not known at the time of the division) to which cost shared intangibles are to be put as follows. All anticipated uses of cost shared intangibles must be identified. Each controlled participant must be assigned at least one such anticipated use, and in the aggregate all the participants must be assigned all such anticipated uses. Each controlled participant will be assigned the perpetual and exclusive right to exploit the cost shared intangibles through the use or uses assigned to it and one controlled participant must be assigned the exclusive and perpetual right to exploit cost shared intangibles through any unanticipated uses.

(iv) Other divisional bases. (A) In the event that the CSA does not divide interests in the cost shared intangibles on the basis of exclusive territories or fields of use as described in paragraphs (b)(4)(ii) and (iii) of this section, the CSA may adopt some other basis on which to divide all interests in the cost shared intangibles among the controlled participants, provided that each of the following criteria is met:

(1) The basis clearly and unambiguously divides all interests in cost shared intangibles among the controlled participants.

(2) The consistent use of such basis for the division of all interests in the cost shared intangibles can be dependably verified from the records maintained by the controlled participants.

(3) The rights of the controlled participants to exploit cost shared intangibles are non-overlapping, exclusive, and perpetual.

(4) The resulting benefits associated with each controlled participant's interest in cost shared intangibles are predictable with reasonable reliability.

(B) See paragraph (f)(3) of this section for rules regarding the requirement of arm's length consideration for changes in participation in CSAs involving divisions of interest described in this paragraph (b)(4)(iv).

(v) Examples. The following examples illustrate the principles of this paragraph (b)(4):

Example 1. Companies P and S, both members of the same controlled group, enter into a CSA to develop product Z. Under the CSA, P receives the interest in product Z in the United States and S receives the interest in product Z in the rest of the world, as described in paragraph (b)(4)(ii) of this section. Both P and S have plants for manufacturing product Z located in their respective geographic territories. However, for commercial reasons, product Z is nevertheless manufactured by P in the United States for sale to customers in certain locations just outside the United States in close proximity to P's U.S. manufacturing plant. Because S owns the territorial rights outside the United States, P must compensate S to ensure that S realizes all the cost shared intangible profits from P's sales of product Z in S's territory. The pricing of such compensation must also ensure that P realizes an appropriate return for its manufacturing efforts. Benefits projected with respect to such sales will be included for purposes of estimating S's, but not P's, RAB share.

Example 2. The facts are the same as in Example 1 except that P and S agree to divide their interest in product Z based on site of manufacturing. P will have exclusive and perpetual rights in product Z manufactured in facilities owned by P. S will have exclusive and perpetual rights to product Z manufactured in facilities owned by S. P and S agree that neither will license manufacturing rights in product Z to any related or unrelated party. Both P and S maintain books and records that allow production at all sites to be verified. Both own facilities that will manufacture product Z and the relative capacities of these sites are known. All facilities are currently operating at near capacity and are expected to continue to operate at near capacity when product Z enters production so that it will not be feasible to shift production between P's and S's facilities. P and S have no plans to build new facilities and the lead time required to plan and build a manufacturing facility precludes the possibility that P or S will build a new facility during the period for which sales of Product Z are expected. Based on these facts, this basis for the division of interests in Product Z is a division described in paragraph (b)(4)(iv) of this section. The basis for the division of interest is unambiguous and clearly defined and its use can be dependably verified. P and S both have non-overlapping, exclusive and perpetual rights in Product Z. The division of interest results in the participant's relative benefits being predictable with reasonable reliability.

Example 3. The facts are the same as in Example 2 except that P's and S's manufacturing facilities are not expected to operate at full capacity when product Z enters production. Production of Product Z can be shifted at any time between sites owned by P and sites owned by S, although neither P nor S intends to shift production as a result of the agreement. The division of interests in Product Z between P and S based on manufacturing site is not a division described in paragraph (b)(4)(iv) of this section because their relative shares of benefits are not predictable with reasonable reliability. The fact that neither P nor S intends to shift production is irrelevant.

* * *

(c) Platform contributions—(1) In general. A platform contribution is any resource, capability, or right that a controlled participant has developed, maintained, or acquired externally to the intangible development activity (whether prior to or during the course of the CSA) that is reasonably anticipated to contribute to developing cost shared intangibles. The determination whether a resource, capability, or right is reasonably anticipated to contribute to developing cost shared intangibles is ongoing and based on the best available information. Therefore, a resource, capability, or right reasonably determined not to be a platform contribution as of an earlier point in time, may be reasonably determined to be a platform contribution at a later point in time. The PCT obligation regarding a resource or capability or right once determined to be a platform contribution does not terminate merely because it may later be determined that such resource or capability or right has not contributed, and no longer is reasonably anticipated to contribute, to developing cost shared intangibles. Notwithstanding the other provisions of this paragraph (c), platform contributions do not include rights in land or depreciable tangible property, and do not include rights in other resources acquired by IDCs. See paragraph (d)(1) of this section.

* * *

(d) Intangible development costs—(1) Determining whether costs are IDCs. Costs included in IDCs are determined by reference to the scope of the intangible development activity (IDA).

(i) Definition and scope of the IDA. For purposes of this section, the IDA means the activity under the CSA of developing or attempting to develop reasonably anticipated cost shared intangibles. The scope of the IDA includes all of the controlled participants' activities that could reasonably be anticipated to contribute to developing the reasonably anticipated cost shared intangibles. The IDA cannot be described merely by a list of particular resources, capabilities, or rights that will be used in the CSA, because such a list would not identify reasonably anticipated cost shared intangibles. Also, the scope of the IDA may change as the nature or identity of the reasonably anticipated cost shared intangibles changes or the nature of the activities necessary for their development become clearer. For example, the relevance of certain ongoing work to developing reasonably anticipated cost shared intangibles or the need for additional work may only become clear over time.

(ii) Reasonably anticipated cost shared intangible. For purposes of this section, reasonably anticipated cost shared intangible means any intangible, within the meaning of § 1.482–4(b), that, at the applicable point in time, the controlled participants intend to develop under the CSA. Reasonably anticipated cost shared intangibles may change over the course of the CSA. The controlled participants may at any time change the reasonably anticipated cost shared intangibles but must document any such change pursuant to paragraph (k)(2)(ii)(A)(1) of this section. Removal of reasonably anticipated cost shared intangibles does not affect the controlled participants' interests in cost shared intangibles already developed under the CSA. In addition, the reasonably anticipated cost shared intangibles automatically expand to include the intended result of any further development of a cost shared intangible already developed under the CSA, or applications of such an intangible. However, the controlled participants may override this automatic expansion in a particular case if they separately remove specified further development of such intangible (or specified applications of such intangible) from the IDA, and document such separate removal pursuant to paragraph (k)(2)(ii)(A)(3) of this section.

(iii) Costs included in IDCs. For purposes of this section, IDCs mean all costs, in cash or in kind (including stock-based compensation, as described in paragraph (d)(3) of this section), but excluding acquisition costs for land or depreciable property, in the ordinary course of business after the formation of a CSA that, based on analysis of the facts and circumstances, are directly identified with, or are reasonably allocable to, the IDA. Thus, IDCs include costs incurred in attempting to develop reasonably anticipated cost shared intangibles regardless of whether such costs ultimately lead to development of those intangibles, other intangibles developed unexpectedly, or no intangibles. IDCs shall also include the arm's length rental charge for the use of any land or depreciable tangible property (as determined under § 1.482–2(c) (Use of tangible property)) directly identified with, or reasonably allocable to, the IDA. Reference to generally accepted accounting principles or Federal income tax accounting rules may provide a useful starting point but will not be conclusive regarding inclusion of costs in IDCs. IDCs do not include interest expense, foreign income taxes (as defined in § 1.901–2(a)), or domestic income taxes.

(iv) Examples. The following examples illustrate the principles of this paragraph (d)(1):

Example 1. A contract that purports to be a CSA provides that the IDA to which the agreement applies consists of all research and development activity conducted at laboratories A, B, and C but not at other facilities maintained by the controlled participants. The contract does not describe the reasonably anticipated cost shared intangibles with respect to which research and development is to be undertaken. The contract fails to meet the requirements set forth in paragraph (k)(1)(ii)(B) of this section because it fails to adequately describe the scope of the IDA to be undertaken.

Example 2. A contract that purports to be a CSA provides that the IDA to which the agreement applies consists of all research and development activity conducted by any of the controlled participants with the goal of developing a cure for a particular disease. Such a cure is thus a reasonably anticipated cost shared intangible. The contract also contains a provision that the IDA will exclude any activity that builds on the results of the controlled participants' prior research concerning Enzyme X even though such activity could reasonably be anticipated to contribute to developing such cure. The contract fails to meet the requirement set forth in paragraph (d)(1)(i) of this section that the scope of the IDA include all of the controlled participants' activities that could reasonably be anticipated to contribute to developing reasonably anticipated cost shared intangibles.

(2) Allocation of costs. If a particular cost is directly identified with, or reasonably allocable to, a function the results of which will benefit both the IDA and other business activities, the cost must be allocated on a reasonable basis between the IDA and such other business activities in proportion to the relative economic value that the IDA and such other business activities are anticipated to derive from such results.

(3) Stock-based compensation—(i) In general. As used in this section, the term stock-based compensation means any compensation provided by a controlled participant to an employee or independent contractor in the form of equity instruments, options to acquire stock (stock options), or rights with respect to (or determined by reference to) equity instruments or stock options, including but not limited to property to which section 83 applies and stock options to which section 421 applies, regardless of whether ultimately settled in the form of cash, stock, or other property.

(ii) Identification of stock-based compensation with the IDA. The determination of whether stock-based compensation is directly identified with, or reasonably allocable to, the IDA is made as of the date that the stock-based compensation is granted. Accordingly, all stock-based compensation that is granted during the term of the CSA and, at date of grant, is directly identified with, or reasonably allocable to, the IDA is included as an IDC under paragraph (d)(1) of this section. In the case of a repricing or other modification of a stock option, the determination of whether the repricing or other modification constitutes the grant of a new stock option for purposes of this paragraph (d)(3)(ii) will be made in accordance with the rules of section 424(h) and related regulations.

* * *

(4) IDC share. A controlled participant's IDC share for a taxable year is equal to the controlled participant's cost contribution for the taxable year, divided by the sum of all IDCs for the taxable year. A controlled participant's cost contribution for a taxable year means all of the IDCs initially borne by the controlled participant, plus all of the CST Payments that the participant makes to other controlled participants, minus all of the CST Payments that the participant receives from other controlled participants.

(5) Examples. The following examples illustrate this paragraph (d):

Example 1. Foreign parent (FP) and its U.S. subsidiary (USS) enter into a CSA to develop a better mousetrap. USS and FP share the costs of FP's R & D facility that will be exclusively dedicated to this research, the salaries of the researchers at the facility, and overhead costs attributable to the project. They also share the cost of a conference facility that is at the disposal of the senior executive management of each company. Based on the facts and circumstances, the cost of the conference facility cannot be directly identified with, and is not reasonably allocable to, the IDA. In this case, the cost of the conference facility must be excluded from the amount of IDCs.

Example 2. U.S. parent (USP) and its foreign subsidiary (FS) enter into a CSA to develop intangibles for producing a new device. USP and FS share the costs of an R & D facility, the salaries of the facility's researchers, and overhead costs attributable to the project. Although USP also incurs costs related to field testing of the device, USP does not include those costs in the IDCs that USP and FS will share under the CSA. The Commissioner may determine, based on the facts and circumstances, that the costs of field testing are IDCs that the controlled participants must share.

Example 3. U.S. parent (USP) and its foreign subsidiary (FS) enter into a CSA to develop a new process patent. USP assigns certain employees to perform solely R & D to develop a new mathematical algorithm to perform certain calculations. That algorithm will be used both to develop the new process patent and to develop a new design patent the development of which is outside the scope of the CSA. During years covered by the CSA, USP compensates such employees with cash salaries, stock-based compensation, or a combination of both. USP and FS anticipate that the economic value attributable to the R & D will be derived from the process patent and the design patent in a relative proportion of 75% and 25%, respectively. Applying the principles of paragraph (d)(2) of this section, 75% of the compensation of such employees must be allocated to the development of the new process patent and, thus, treated as IDCs. With respect to the cash salary compensation, the IDC is 75% of the face value of the cash. With respect to the stock-based compensation, the IDC is 75% of the value of the stock-based compensation as determined under paragraph (d)(3)(iii) of this section.

Example 4. Foreign parent (FP) and its U.S. subsidiary (USS) enter into a CSA to develop a new computer source code. FP has an executive officer who oversees a research facility and employees dedicated solely to the IDA. The executive officer also oversees other research facilities and employees unrelated to the IDA, and performs certain corporate overhead functions.

The full amount of the costs of the research facility and employees dedicated solely to the IDA can be directly identified with the IDA and, therefore, are IDCs. In addition, based on the executive officer's records of time worked on various matters, the controlled participants reasonably allocate 20% of the executive officer's compensation to supervision of the facility and employees dedicated to the IDA, 50% of the executive officer's compensation to supervision of the facilities and employees unrelated to the IDA, and 30% of the executive officer's compensation to corporate overhead functions. The controlled participants also reasonably determine that the results of the executive officer's corporate overhead functions yield equal economic benefit to the IDA and the other business activities of FP. Applying the principles of paragraph (d)(1) of this section, the executive officer's compensation allocated to supervising the facility and employees dedicated to the IDA (amounting to 20% of the executive officer's total compensation) must be treated as IDCs. Applying the principles of paragraph (d)(2) of this section, half of the executive officer's compensation allocated to corporate overhead functions (that is, half of 30% of the executive officer's total compensation), must be treated as IDCs. Therefore, a total of 35% (20% plus 15%) of the executive officer's total compensation must be treated as IDCs.

(e) Reasonably anticipated benefits share—(1) Definition—(i) In general. A controlled participant's share of reasonably anticipated benefits is equal to its reasonably anticipated benefits divided by the sum of the reasonably anticipated benefits, as defined in paragraph (j)(1)(i) of this section, of all the controlled participants. RAB shares must be updated to account for changes in economic conditions, the business operations and practices of the participants, and the ongoing development of intangibles under the CSA. For purposes of determining RAB shares at any given time, reasonably anticipated benefits must be estimated over the entire period, past and future, of exploitation of the cost shared intangibles, and must reflect appropriate updates to take into account the most reliable data regarding past and projected future results available at such time. RAB shares determined for a particular purpose shall not be further updated for that purpose based on information not available at the time that determination needed to be made. For example, RAB shares determined in order to determine IDC shares for a particular taxable year (as set forth in paragraphs (b)(1)(i) and (d)(4) of this section) shall not be recomputed based on information not available at that time. Similarly, RAB shares determined for the purpose of using a particular method such as the acquisition price method (as set forth in paragraph (g)(5)(ii) of this section) to evaluate the arm's length amount charged in a PCT shall not be recomputed based on information not available at the date of that PCT. However, nothing in this paragraph (e)(1)(i) shall limit the Commissioner's use of subsequently available information for purposes of its allocation determinations in accordance with the provisions of paragraph (i) (Allocations by the Commissioner in connection with a CSA) of this section.

(ii) Reliability. A controlled participant's RAB share must be determined by using the most reliable estimate. In determining which of two or more available estimates is most reliable, the quality of the data and assumptions used in the analysis must be taken into account, consistent with § 1.482–1(c)(2)(ii) (Data and assumptions). Thus, the reliability of an estimate will depend largely on the completeness and accuracy of the data, the soundness of the assumptions, and the relative effects of particular deficiencies in data or assumptions on different estimates. If two estimates are equally reliable, no adjustment should be made based on differences between the estimates. The following factors will be particularly relevant in determining the reliability of an estimate of RAB shares:

(A) The basis used for measuring benefits, as described in paragraph (e)(2)(ii) of this section.

(B) The projections used to estimate benefits, as described in paragraph (e)(2)(iii) of this section.

(iii) Examples. The following examples illustrate the principles of this paragraph (e)(1):

Example 1. (i) USP and FS plan to conduct research to develop Product Lines A and B. USP and FS reasonably anticipate respective benefits from Product Line A of 100X and 200X and respective benefits from Product Line B, respectively, of 300X and 400X. USP and FS thus reasonably anticipate combined benefits from Product Lines A and B of 400X and 600X, respectively.

(ii) USP and FS could enter into a separate CSA to develop Product Line A with respective RAB shares of 33 1/3 percent and 66 2/3 percent (reflecting a ratio of 100X to 200X), and into a separate CSA to develop Product Line B with respective RAB shares of 42 6/7 percent and 57 1/7 percent (reflecting a ratio of 300X to 400X). Alternatively, USP and FS could enter into a single CSA to develop both Product Lines A and B with respective RAB shares of 40 percent and 60 percent (in the ratio of 400X to 600X). If the separate CSAs are chosen, then any costs for activities that contribute to developing both Product Line A and Product Line B will constitute IDCs of the respective CSAs as required by paragraphs (d)(1) and (2) of this section.

Example 2. (i) USP, a US company, wholly owns foreign subsidiary, FS. USP and FS enter into a CSA at the start of Year 1. The CSA's total IDCs are $100,000 in each year for Years 1 through 4. In Year 1, USP correctly estimates its RAB share as 50%, based on information available at the time, and therefore correctly computes $50,000 as its cost contribution for Year 1.

(ii) In Year 4, USP correctly estimates its RAB share to be 70%, based on information available at the time and, therefore, correctly computes $70,000 as its cost contribution for Year 4.

(iii) In Year 4, USP also files an amended return for Year 1 in which USP deducts a cost contribution of $70,000, asserting that, for this purpose, it should revise its Year 1 estimated RAB share to 70% based on the information that is now available to it in Year 4. The Commissioner determines that USP is incorrect for two reasons. First, a RAB share determined for a particular purpose (here, to determine USP's IDC shares and thus USP's cost contributions in Year 1) should not be revised based on information not available to USP until Year 4. See paragraph (e)(1)(i) of this section. Second, more generally, USP is not permitted to file an amended return for this purpose under § 1.482–1(a)(3). Therefore, for both of these reasons, Commissioner adjusts USP's amended return for Year 1 by disallowing $20,000 of the $70,000 deduction.

(2) Measure of benefits—(i) In general. In order to estimate a controlled participant's RAB share, the amount of each controlled participant's reasonably anticipated benefits must be measured on a basis that is consistent for all such participants. See paragraph (e)(2)(ii)(E) Example 9 of this section. If a controlled participant transfers a cost shared intangible to another controlled taxpayer, other than by way of a transfer described in paragraph (f) of this section, that controlled participant's benefits from the transferred intangible must be measured by reference to the transferee's benefits, disregarding any consideration paid by the transferee to the controlled participant (such as a royalty pursuant to a license agreement). Reasonably anticipated benefits are measured either on a direct basis, by reference to estimated benefits to be generated by the use of cost shared intangibles (generally based on additional revenues plus cost savings less any additional costs incurred), or on an indirect basis, by reference to certain measurements that reasonably can be assumed to relate to benefits to be generated. Such indirect bases of measurement of anticipated benefits are described in paragraph (e)(2)(ii) of this section. A controlled participant's reasonably anticipated benefits must be measured on the basis, whether direct or indirect, that most reliably determines RAB shares. In determining which of two bases of measurement is most reliable, the factors set forth in § 1.482–1(c)(2)(ii) (Data and assumptions) must be taken into account. It normally will be expected that the basis that provided the most reliable estimate for a particular year will continue to provide the most reliable estimate in subsequent years, absent a material change in the factors that affect the reliability of the estimate. Regardless of whether a direct or indirect basis of measurement is used, adjustments may be required to account for material differences in the activities that controlled participants undertake to exploit their interests in cost shared intangibles. See Examples 4 and 7 of paragraph (e)(2)(ii)(E) of this section.

(ii) Indirect bases for measuring anticipated benefits. Indirect bases for measuring anticipated benefits from participation in a CSA include the following:

(A) Units used, produced, or sold. Units of items used, produced, or sold by each controlled participant in the business activities in which cost shared intangibles are exploited may be used as an indirect basis for measuring its anticipated benefits. This basis of measurement will more reliably determine RAB shares to the extent that each controlled participant is expected to have a similar increase in net profit or decrease in net loss attributable to the cost shared intangibles per unit of the item or items used, produced, or sold. This circumstance is most likely to arise when the cost shared intangibles are exploited by the controlled participants in the use, production, or sale of substantially uniform items under similar economic conditions.

(B) Sales. Sales by each controlled participant in the business activities in which cost shared intangibles are exploited may be used as an indirect basis for measuring its anticipated benefits. This basis of measurement will more reliably determine RAB shares to the extent that each controlled participant is expected to have a similar increase in net profit or decrease in net loss attributable to cost shared intangibles per dollar of sales. This circumstance is most likely to arise if the costs of exploiting cost shared intangibles are not substantial relative to the revenues generated, or if the principal effect of using cost shared intangibles is to increase the controlled participants' revenues (for example, through a price premium on the products they sell) without affecting their costs substantially. Sales by each controlled participant are unlikely to provide a reliable basis for measuring RAB shares unless each controlled participant operates at the same market level (for example, manufacturing, distribution, etc.).

(C) Operating profit. Operating profit of each controlled participant from the activities in which cost shared intangibles are exploited, as determined before any expense (including amortization) on account of IDCs, may be used as an indirect basis for measuring anticipated benefits. This basis of measurement will more reliably determine RAB shares to the extent that such profit is largely attributable to the use of cost shared intangibles, or if the share of profits attributable to the use of cost shared intangibles is expected to be similar for each controlled participant. This circumstance is most likely to arise when cost shared intangibles are closely associated with the activity that generates the profit and the activity could not be carried on or would generate little profit without use of those intangibles.

(D) Other bases for measuring anticipated benefits. Other bases for measuring anticipated benefits may in some circumstances be appropriate, but only to the extent that there is expected to be a reasonably identifiable relationship between the basis of measurement used and additional revenue generated or net costs saved by the use of cost shared intangibles. For example, a division of costs based on employee compensation would be considered unreliable unless there were a relationship between the amount of compensation and the expected additional revenue generated or net costs saved by the controlled participants from using the cost shared intangibles.

(E) Examples. The following examples illustrates this paragraph (e)(2)(ii):

Example 1. Controlled parties A and B enter into a CSA to develop product and process intangibles for already existing Product P. Without such intangibles, A and B would each reasonably anticipate revenue, in present value terms, of $100M from sales of Product P until it becomes obsolete. With the intangibles, A and B each reasonably anticipate selling the same number of units each year, but reasonably anticipate that the price will be higher. Because the particular product intangible is more highly regarded in A's market, A reasonably anticipates an increase of $20M in present value revenue from the product intangible, while B reasonably anticipates an increase of only $10M in present value from the product intangible. Further, A and B each reasonably anticipate spending an additional amount equal to $5M in present value in production costs to include the feature embodying the product intangible. Finally, A and B each reasonably anticipate saving an amount equal to $2M in present value in production costs by using the process intangible. A and B reasonably anticipate no other economic effects from exploiting the cost shared intangibles. A's reasonably anticipated benefits from exploiting the cost shared intangibles equal its reasonably anticipated increase in revenue ($20M) plus its reasonably anticipated cost savings ($2M) less its reasonably anticipated increased costs ($5M), which equals $17M. Similarly, B's reasonably anticipated benefits from exploiting the cost shared intangibles equal its reasonably anticipated increase in revenue ($10M) plus its reasonably anticipated cost savings ($2M) less its reasonably anticipated increased costs ($5M), which equals $7M. Thus A's reasonably anticipated benefits are $17M and B's reasonably anticipated benefits are $7M.

Example 2. Foreign Parent (FP) and U.S. Subsidiary (USS) both produce a feedstock for the manufacture of various high-performance plastic products. Producing the feedstock requires large amounts of electricity, which accounts for a significant portion of its production cost. FP and USS enter into a CSA to develop a new process that will reduce the amount of electricity required to produce a unit of the feedstock. FP and USS currently both incur an electricity cost of $2 per unit of feedstock produced and rates for each are expected to remain similar in the future. The new process, if it is successful, will reduce the amount of electricity required by each company to produce a unit of the feedstock by 50%. Switching to the new process would not require FP or USS to incur significant investment or other costs. Therefore, the cost savings each company is expected to achieve after implementing the new process are $1 per unit of feedstock produced. Under the CSA, FP and USS divide the costs of developing the new process based on the units of the feedstock each is anticipated to produce in the future. In this case, units produced is the most reliable basis for measuring RAB shares and dividing the IDCs because each controlled participant is expected to have a similar $1 (50% of current charge of $2) decrease in costs per unit of the feedstock produced.

Example 3. The facts are the same as in Example 2, except that currently USS pays $3 per unit of feedstock produced for electricity while FP pays $6 per unit of feedstock produced. In this case, units produced is not the most reliable basis for measuring RAB shares and dividing the IDCs because the participants do not expect to have a similar decrease in costs per unit of the feedstock produced. The Commissioner determines that the most reliable measure of RAB shares may be based on units of the feedstock produced if FP's units are weighted relative to USS's units by a factor of 2. This reflects the fact that FP pays twice as much as USS for electricity and, therefore, FP's savings of $3 per unit of the feedstock (50% reduction of current charge of $6) would be twice USS's savings of $1.50 per unit of feedstock (50% reduction of current charge of $3) from any new process eventually developed.

Example 4. The facts are the same as in Example 3, except that to supply the particular needs of the U.S. market USS manufactures the feedstock with somewhat different properties than

FP's feedstock. This requires USS to employ a somewhat different production process than does FP. Because of this difference, USS would incur significant construction costs in order to adopt any new process that may be developed under the cost sharing agreement. In this case, units produced is not the most reliable basis for measuring RAB shares. In order to reliably determine RAB shares, the Commissioner measures the reasonably anticipated benefits of USS and FP on a direct basis. USS's reasonably anticipated benefits are its reasonably anticipated total savings in electricity costs, less its reasonably anticipated costs of adopting the new process. FS's reasonably anticipated benefits are its reasonably anticipated total savings in electricity costs.

Example 5. U.S. Parent (USP) and Foreign Subsidiary (FS) enter into a CSA to develop new anesthetic drugs. USP obtains the right to market any resulting drugs in the United States and FS obtains the right to market any resulting drugs in the rest of the world. USP and FS determine RAB shares on the basis of their respective total anticipated operating profit from all drugs under development. USP anticipates that it will receive a much higher profit than FS per unit sold because the price of the drugs is not regulated in the United States, whereas the price of the drugs is regulated in many non-U.S. jurisdictions. In both controlled participants' territories, the anticipated operating profits are almost entirely attributable to the use of the cost shared intangibles. In this case, the controlled participants' basis for measuring RAB shares is the most reliable.

* * *

Example 9. U.S. Parent (USP), Foreign Subsidiary 1 (FS1), and Foreign Subsidiary 2 (FS2) enter into a CSA to develop computer software that each will market and install on customers' computer systems. The controlled participants measure benefits on the basis of projected sales by USP, FS1, and FS2 of the software in their respective geographic areas. However, FS1 plans not only to sell but also to license the software to unrelated customers, and FS1's licensing income (which is a percentage of the licensees' sales) is not counted in the projected benefits. In this case, the basis used for measuring the benefits of each controlled participant is not the most reliable because all of the benefits received by controlled participants are not taken into account. In order to reliably determine RAB shares, FS1's projected benefits from licensing must be included in the measurement on a basis that is the same as that used to measure its own and the other controlled participants' projected benefits from sales (for example, all controlled participants might measure their benefits on the basis of operating profit).

(iii) Projections used to estimate benefits (A) In general. The reliability of an estimate of RAB shares also depends upon the reliability of projections used in making the estimate. Projections required for this purpose generally include a determination of the time period between the inception of the research and development activities under the CSA and the receipt of benefits, a projection of the time over which benefits will be received, and a projection of the benefits anticipated for each year in which it is anticipated that the cost shared intangible will generate benefits. A projection of the relevant basis for measuring anticipated benefits may require a projection of the factors that underlie it. For example, a projection of operating profits may require a projection of sales, cost of sales, operating expenses, and other factors that affect operating profits. If it is anticipated that there will be significant variation among controlled participants in the timing of their receipt of benefits, and consequently benefit shares are expected to vary significantly over the years in which benefits will be received, it normally will be necessary to use the present value of the projected benefits to reliably determine RAB shares. See paragraph (g)(2)(v) of this section for best method considerations regarding discount rates used for this purpose. If it is not anticipated that benefit shares will significantly change over time, current annual benefit shares may provide a reliable projection of RAB shares. This circumstance is most likely to occur when the CSA is a long-term arrangement, the arrangement covers a wide variety of intangibles, the composition of the cost shared intangibles is unlikely to change, the cost shared intangibles are unlikely to generate unusual profits, and each controlled participant's share of the market is stable.

(B) Examples. The following examples illustrate the principles of this paragraph (e)(2)(iii):

Example 1. (i) Foreign Parent (FP) and U.S. Subsidiary (USS) enter into a CSA to develop a new car model. The controlled participants plan to spend four years developing the new model and four years producing and selling the new model. USS and FP project total sales of $4 billion and $2 billion, respectively, over the planned four years of exploitation of the new model. The controlled participants determine RAB shares for each year of 66 2/3 % for USS and 33 1/3 % for FP, based on projected total sales.

(ii) USS typically begins producing and selling new car models a year after FP begins producing and selling new car models. In order to reflect USS's one-year lag in introducing new car models, a more reliable projection of each participant's RAB share would be based on a projection of all four years of sales for each participant, discounted to present value.

Example 2. U.S. Parent (USP) and Foreign Subsidiary (FS) enter into a CSA to develop new and improved household cleaning products. Both controlled participants have sold household cleaning products for many years and have stable worldwide market shares. The products under development are unlikely to produce unusual profits for either controlled participant. The controlled participants determine RAB shares on the basis of each controlled participant's current sales of household cleaning products. In this case, the controlled participants' RAB shares are reliably projected by current sales of cleaning products.

Example 3. The facts are the same as in Example 2, except that FS's market share is rapidly expanding because of the business failure of a competitor in its geographic area. The controlled participants' RAB shares are not reliably projected by current sales of cleaning products. FS's benefit projections should take into account its growth in market share.

* * *

(f) Changes in participation under a CSA—(1) In general. A change in participation under a CSA occurs when there is either a controlled transfer of interests or a capability variation. A change in participation requires arm's length consideration under paragraph (a)(3)(ii) of this section, and as more fully described in this paragraph (f).

* * *

(g) Supplemental guidance on methods applicable to PCTs—(1) In general. This paragraph (g) provides supplemental guidance on applying the methods listed in this paragraph (g)(1) for purposes of evaluating the arm's length amount charged in a PCT. Each method will yield a value for the compensation obligation of each PCT Payor consistent with the product of the combined pre-tax value to all controlled participants of the platform contribution that is the subject of the PCT and the PCT Payor's RAB share. Each method must yield results consistent with measuring the value of a platform contribution by reference to the future income anticipated to be generated by the resulting cost shared intangibles. The methods are—

(i) The comparable uncontrolled transaction method described in § 1.482–4(c), or the comparable uncontrolled services price method described in § 1.482–9(c), as further described in paragraph (g)(3) of this section;

(ii) The income method, described in paragraph (g)(4) of this section;

(iii) The acquisition price method, described in paragraph (g)(5) of this section;

(iv) The market capitalization method, described in paragraph (g)(6) of this section;

(v) The residual profit split method, described in paragraph (g)(7) of this section; and

(vi) Unspecified methods, described in paragraph (g)(8) of this section.

(2) Best method analysis applicable for evaluation of a PCT pursuant to a CSA—(i) In general. Each method must be applied in accordance with the provisions of § 1.482–1, including the best method rule of § 1.482–1(c), the comparability analysis of § 1.482–1(d), and the arm's length range of § 1.482–1(e), except as those provisions are modified in this paragraph (g).

* * *

(h) Form of payment rules—(1) CST Payments. CST Payments may not be paid in shares of stock in the payor (or stock in any member of the controlled group that includes the controlled participants).

(2) PCT Payments—(i) In general. The consideration under a PCT for a platform contribution may take one or a combination of both of the following forms:

(A) Payments of a fixed amount (fixed payments), either paid in a lump sum payment or in installment payments spread over a specified period, with interest calculated in accordance with § 1.482–2(a) (Loans or advances).

(B) Payments contingent on the exploitation of cost shared intangibles by the PCT Payor (contingent payments). Accordingly, controlled participants have flexibility to adopt a form and period of payment, provided that such form and period of payment are consistent with an arm's length charge as of the date of the PCT. See also paragraphs (h)(2)(iv) and (3) of this section.

(ii) No PCT Payor Stock. PCT Payments may not be paid in shares of stock in the PCT Payor (or stock in any member of the controlled group that includes the controlled participants).

(iii) Specified form of payment—(A) In general. The form of payment selected (subject to the rules of this paragraph (h)) for any PCT, including, in the case of contingent payments, the contingent base and structure of the payments as set forth in paragraph (h)(2)(iii)(B) of this section, must be specified no later than the due date of the applicable tax return (including extensions) for the later of the taxable year of the PCT Payor or PCT Payee that includes the date of that PCT.

(B) Contingent payments. In accordance with paragraph (k)(1)(iv)(A) of this section, a provision of a written contract described in paragraph (k)(1) of this section, or of the additional documentation described in paragraph (k)(2) of this section, that provides for payments for a PCT (or group of PCTs) to be contingent on the exploitation of cost shared intangibles will be respected as consistent with economic substance only if the allocation between the controlled participants of the risks attendant on such form of payment is determinable before the outcomes of such allocation that would have materially affected the PCT pricing are known or reasonably knowable. A contingent payment provision must clearly and unambiguously specify the basis on which the contingent payment obligations are to be determined. In particular, the contingent payment provision must clearly and unambiguously specify the events that give rise to an obligation to make PCT Payments, the royalty base (such as sales or revenues), and the computation used to determine the PCT Payments. The royalty base specified must be one that permits verification of its proper use by reference to books and records maintained by the controlled participants in the normal course of business (for example, books and records maintained for financial accounting or business management purposes).

* * *

(i) Allocations by the Commissioner in connection with a CSA—(1) In general. The

Commissioner may make allocations to adjust the results of a controlled transaction in connection with a CSA so that the results are consistent with an arm's length result, in accordance with the provisions of this paragraph (i).

(2) CST allocations—(i) In general. The Commissioner may make allocations to adjust the results of a CST so that the results are consistent with an arm's length result, including any allocations to make each controlled participant's IDC share, as determined under paragraph (d)(4) of this section, equal to that participant's RAB share, as determined under paragraph (e)(1) of this section. Such allocations may result from, for purposes of CST determinations, adjustments to—

(A) Redetermine IDCs by adding any costs (or cost categories) that are directly identified with, or are reasonably allocable to, the IDA, or by removing any costs (or cost categories) that are not IDCs;

(B) Reallocate costs between the IDA and other business activities;

(C) Improve the reliability of the selection or application of the basis used for measuring benefits for purposes of estimating a controlled participant's RAB share;

(D) Improve the reliability of the projections used to estimate RAB shares, including adjustments described in paragraph (i)(2)(ii) of this section; and

(E) Allocate among the controlled participants any unallocated interests in cost shared intangibles.

(ii) Adjustments to improve the reliability of projections used to estimate RAB shares (A) Unreliable projections. A significant divergence between projected benefit shares and benefit shares adjusted to take into account any available actual benefits to date (adjusted benefit shares) may indicate that the projections were not reliable for purposes of estimating RAB shares. In such a case, the Commissioner may use adjusted benefit shares as the most reliable measure of RAB shares and adjust IDC shares accordingly. The projected benefit shares will not be considered unreliable, as applied in a given taxable year, based on a divergence from adjusted benefit shares for every controlled participant that is less than or equal to 20% of the participant's projected benefits share. Further, the Commissioner will not make an allocation based on such divergence if the difference is due to an extraordinary event, beyond the control of the controlled participants, which could not reasonably have been anticipated at the time that costs were shared. The Commissioner generally may adjust projections of benefits used to calculate benefit shares in accordance with the provisions of § 1.482–1. In particular, if benefits are projected over a period of years, and the projections for initial years of the period prove to be unreliable, this may indicate that the projections for the remaining years of the period are also unreliable and thus should be adjusted. For purposes of this paragraph (i)(2)(ii)(A), all controlled participants that are not U.S. persons are treated as a single controlled participant. Therefore, an adjustment based on an unreliable projection of RAB shares will be made to the IDC shares of foreign controlled participants only if there is a matching adjustment to the IDC shares of controlled participants that are U.S. persons. Nothing in this paragraph (i)(2)(ii)(A) prevents the Commissioner from making an allocation if a taxpayer did not use the most reliable basis for measuring anticipated benefits. For example, if the taxpayer measures its anticipated benefits based on units sold, and the Commissioner determines that another basis is more reliable for measuring anticipated benefits, then the fact that actual units sold were within 20% of the projected unit sales will not preclude an allocation under this section.

(B) Foreign-to-foreign adjustments. Adjustments to IDC shares based on an unreliable projection also may be made among foreign controlled participants if the variation between actual and projected benefits has the effect of substantially reducing U.S. tax.

(C) Correlative adjustments to PCTs. Correlative adjustments will be made to any PCT

Payments of a fixed amount that were determined based on RAB shares that are subsequently adjusted on a finding that they were based on unreliable projections. No correlative adjustments will be made to contingent PCT Payments regardless of whether RAB shares were used as a parameter in the valuation of those payments.

(D) Examples. The following examples illustrate the principles of this paragraph (i)(2)(ii):

Example 1. U.S. Parent (USP) and Foreign Subsidiary (FS) enter into a CSA to develop new food products, dividing costs on the basis of projected sales two years in the future. In Year 1, USP and FS project that their sales in Year 3 will be equal, and they divide costs accordingly. In Year 3, the Commissioner examines the controlled participants' method for dividing costs. USP and FS actually accounted for 42% and 58% of total sales, respectively. The Commissioner agrees that sales two years in the future provide a reliable basis for estimating benefit shares. Because the differences between USP's and FS's adjusted and projected benefit shares are less than 20% of their projected benefit shares, the projection of future benefits for Year 3 is reliable.

Example 2. The facts are the same as in Example 1, except that in Year 3 USP and FS actually accounted for 35% and 65% of total sales, respectively. The divergence between USP's projected and adjusted benefit shares is greater than 20% of USP's projected benefit share and is not due to an extraordinary event beyond the control of the controlled participants. The Commissioner concludes that the projected benefit shares were unreliable, and uses adjusted benefit shares as the basis for an adjustment to the cost shares borne by USP and FS.

Example 3. U.S. Parent (USP), a U.S. corporation, and its foreign subsidiary (FS) enter into a CSA in Year 1. They project that they will begin to receive benefits from cost shared intangibles in Years 4 through 6, and that USP will receive 60% of total benefits and FS 40% of total benefits. In Years 4 through 6, USP and FS actually receive 50% each of the total benefits. In evaluating the reliability of the controlled participants' projections, the Commissioner compares the adjusted benefit shares to the projected benefit shares. Although USP's adjusted benefit share (50%) is within 20% of its projected benefit share (60%), FS's adjusted benefit share (50%) is not within 20% of its projected benefit share (40%). Based on this discrepancy, the Commissioner may conclude that the controlled participants' projections were unreliable and may use adjusted benefit shares as the basis for an adjustment to the cost shares borne by USP and FS.

* * *

(k) CSA administrative requirements. A controlled participant meets the requirements of this paragraph if it substantially complies, respectively, with the CSA contractual, documentation, accounting, and reporting requirements of paragraphs (k)(1) through (4) of this section.

* * *

[T.D. 9568, 76 FR 80090, Dec. 22, 2011; T.D. 9569, 76 FR 80250, Dec. 23, 2011; T.D. 9568, 77 FR 3606, Jan. 25, 2012; 77 FR 8144, Feb. 14, 2012; T.D. 9630, 78 FR 52855, April 27, 2013; 78 FR, Oct. 22, 2013]

§ 1.482–8 Examples of the best method rule.

(a) Introduction. In accordance with the best method rule of § 1.482–1(c), a method may be applied in a particular case only if the comparability, quality of data, and reliability of assumptions under that method make it more reliable than any other available measure of the arm's length result. The following examples illustrate the comparative analysis required to apply this rule. As with all of the examples in these regulations, these examples are based on simplified facts, are provided solely for purposes of illustrating the type of analysis required under the relevant rule, and do not provide rules of general application. Thus, conclusions reached in these examples as to the relative reliability of methods are based on the assumed facts of the examples, and are not general conclusions concerning the relative reliability of any method.

(b) Examples.

Example 1. Preference for comparable uncontrolled price method. Company A is the U.S. distribution subsidiary of Company B, a foreign manufacturer of consumer electrical appliances. Company A purchases toaster ovens from Company B for resale in the U.S. market. To exploit other outlets for its toaster ovens, Company B also sells its toaster ovens to Company C, an unrelated U.S. distributor of toaster ovens. The products sold to Company A and Company C are identical in every respect and there are no material differences between the transactions. In this case application of the CUP method, using the sales of toaster ovens to Company C, generally will provide a more reliable measure of an arm's length result for the controlled sale of toaster ovens to Company A than the application of any other method. See §§ 1.482–1(c)(2)(i) and –3(b)(2)(ii)(A).

Example 2. Resale price method preferred to comparable uncontrolled price method. The facts are the same as in Example 1, except that the toaster ovens sold to Company A are of substantially higher quality than those sold to Company C and the effect on price of such quality differences cannot be accurately determined. In addition, in order to round out its line of consumer appliances Company A purchases blenders from unrelated parties for resale in the United States. The blenders are resold to substantially the same customers as the toaster ovens, have a similar resale value to the toaster ovens, and are purchased under similar terms and in similar volumes. The distribution functions performed by Company A appear to be similar for toaster ovens and blenders. Given the product differences between the toaster ovens, application of the resale price method using the purchases and resales of blenders as the uncontrolled comparables is likely to provide a more reliable measure of an arm's length result than application of the comparable uncontrolled price method using Company B's sales of toaster ovens to Company C.

Example 3. Resale price method preferred to comparable profits method. (i) The facts are the same as in Example 2 except that Company A purchases all its products from Company B and Company B makes no uncontrolled sales into the United States. However, six uncontrolled U.S. distributors are identified that purchase a similar line of products from unrelated parties. The uncontrolled distributors purchase toaster ovens from unrelated parties, but there are significant differences in the characteristics of the toaster ovens, including the brandnames under which they are sold.

(ii) Under the facts of this case, reliable adjustments for the effect of the different brandnames cannot be made. Except for some differences in payment terms and inventory levels, the purchases and resales of toaster ovens by the three uncontrolled distributors are closely similar to the controlled purchases in terms of the markets in which they occur, the volume of the transactions, the marketing activities undertaken by the distributor, inventory levels, warranties, allocation of currency risk, and other relevant functions and risks. Reliable adjustments can be made for the differences in payment terms and inventory levels. In addition, sufficiently detailed accounting information is available to permit adjustments to be made for differences in accounting methods or in reporting of costs between cost of goods sold and operating expenses. There are no other material differences between the controlled and uncontrolled transactions.

(iii) Because reliable adjustments for the differences between the toaster ovens, including the trademarks under which they are sold, cannot be made, these uncontrolled transactions will not serve as reliable measures of an arm's length result under the comparable uncontrolled price method. There is, however, close functional similarity between the controlled and uncontrolled transactions and reliable adjustments have been made for material differences that would be likely to affect gross profit. Under these circumstances, the gross profit margins derived under the resale price method are less likely to be susceptible to any unidentified differences than the operating profit measures used under the comparable profits method. Therefore, given the close functional comparability between the controlled and uncontrolled transactions, and the high quality of the data, the resale price method achieves a higher degree of comparability and will provide a more reliable measure of an arm's length result. See § 1.482–1(c) (Best method rule).

Example 4. Comparable profits method preferred to resale price method. The facts are the same as in Example 3, except that the accounting information available for the uncontrolled comparables is not sufficiently detailed to ensure consistent reporting between cost of goods sold and operating expenses of material items such as discounts, insurance, warranty costs, and supervisory, general and administrative expenses. These expenses are significant in amount. Therefore, whether these expenses are treated as costs of goods sold or operating expenses would have a significant effect on gross margins. Because in this case reliable adjustments can not be made for such accounting differences, the reliability of the resale price method is significantly reduced. There is, however, close functional similarity between the controlled and uncontrolled transactions and reliable adjustments have been made for all material differences other than the potential accounting differences. Because the comparable profits method is not adversely affected by the potential accounting differences, under these circumstances the comparable profits method is likely to produce a more reliable measure of an arm's length result than the resale price method. See § 1.482–1(c) (Best method rule).

Example 5. Cost plus method preferred to comparable profits method. **(i)** USS is a U.S. company that manufactures machine tool parts and sells them to its foreign parent corporation, FP. Four U.S. companies are identified that also manufacture various types of machine tool parts but sell them to uncontrolled purchasers.

(ii) Except for some differences in payment terms, the manufacture and sales of machine tool parts by the four uncontrolled companies are closely similar to the controlled transactions in terms of the functions performed and risks assumed. Reliable adjustments can be made for the differences in payment terms. In addition, sufficiently detailed accounting information is available to permit adjustments to be made for differences between the controlled transaction and the uncontrolled comparables in accounting methods and in the reporting of costs between cost of goods sold and operating expenses.

(iii) There is close functional similarity between the controlled and uncontrolled transactions and reliable adjustments can be made for material differences that would be likely to affect gross profit. Under these circumstances, the gross profit markups derived under the cost plus method are less likely to be susceptible to any unidentified differences than the operating profit measures used under the comparable profits method. Therefore, given the close functional comparability between the controlled and uncontrolled transactions, and the high quality of the data, the cost plus method achieves a higher degree of comparability and will provide a more reliable measure of an arm's length result. See § 1.482–1(c) (Best method rule).

Example 6. Comparable profits method preferred to cost plus method. The facts are the same as in Example 5, except that there are significant differences between the controlled and uncontrolled transactions in terms of the types of parts and components manufactured and the complexity of the manufacturing process. The resulting functional differences are likely to materially affect gross profit margins, but it is not possible to identify the specific differences and reliably adjust for their effect on gross profit. Because these functional differences would be reflected in differences in operating expenses, the operating profit measures used under the comparable profits method implicitly reflect to some extent these functional differences. Therefore, because in this case the comparable profits method is less sensitive than the cost plus method to the potentially significant functional differences between the controlled and uncontrolled transactions, the comparable profits method is likely to produce a more reliable measure of an arm's length result than the cost plus method. See § 1.482–1(c) (Best method rule).

Example 7. Preference for comparable uncontrolled transaction method. (i) USpharm, a U.S. pharmaceutical company, develops a new drug Z that is a safe and effective treatment for the disease zeezee. USpharm has obtained patents covering drug Z in the United States and in various foreign countries. USpharm has also obtained the regulatory authorizations necessary to market drug Z in the United States and in foreign countries.

(ii) USpharm licenses its subsidiary in country X, Xpharm, to produce and sell drug Z in country X. At the same time, it licenses an unrelated company, Ydrug, to produce and sell drug Z in country Y, a neighboring country. Prior to licensing the drug, USpharm had obtained patent protection and regulatory approvals in both countries and both countries provide similar protection for intellectual property rights. Country X and country Y are similar countries in terms of population, per capita income and the incidence of disease zeezee. Consequently, drug Z is expected to sell in similar quantities and at similar prices in both countries. In addition, costs of producing drug Z in each country are expected to be approximately the same.

(iii) USpharm and Xpharm establish terms for the license of drug Z that are identical in every material respect, including royalty rate, to the terms established between USpharm and Ydrug. In this case the district director determines that the royalty rate established in the Ydrug license agreement is a reliable measure of the arm's length royalty rate for the Xpharm license agreement. Given that the same property is transferred in the controlled and uncontrolled transactions, and that the circumstances under which the transactions occurred are substantially the same, in this case the comparable uncontrolled transaction method is likely to provide a more reliable measure of an arm's length result than any other method. See § 1.482–4(c)(2)(ii).

Example 8. Residual profit split method preferred to other methods. (i) USC is a U.S. company that develops, manufactures and sells communications equipment. EC is the European subsidiary of USC. EC is an established company that carries out extensive research and development activities and develops, manufactures and sells communications equipment in Europe. There are extensive transactions between USC and EC. USC licenses valuable technology it has developed to EC for use in the European market but EC also licenses valuable technology it has developed to USC. Each company uses components manufactured by the other in some of its products and purchases products from the other for resale in its own market.

(ii) Detailed accounting information is available for both USC and EC and adjustments can be made to achieve a high degree of consistency in accounting practices between them. Relatively reliable allocations of costs, income and assets can be made between the business activities that are related to the controlled transactions and those that are not. Relevant marketing and research and development expenditures can be identified and reasonable estimates of the useful life of the related intangibles are available so that the capitalized value of the intangible development expenses of USC and EC can be calculated. In this case there is no reason to believe that the relative value of these capitalized expenses is substantially different from the relative value of the intangible property of USC and EC. Furthermore, comparables are identified that could be used to estimate a market return for the routine contributions of USC and EC. Based on these facts, the residual profit split could provide a reliable measure of an arm's length result.

(iii) There are no uncontrolled transactions involving property that is sufficiently comparable to much of the tangible and intangible property transferred between USC and EC to permit use of the comparable uncontrolled price method or the comparable uncontrolled transaction method. Uncontrolled companies are identified in Europe and the United States that perform somewhat similar activities to USC and EC; however, the activities of none of these companies are as complex as those of USC and EC and they do not use similar levels of highly valuable intangible property that they have developed themselves. Under these circumstances, the uncontrolled companies may be useful in determining a market return for the routine contributions of USC and EC, but that return would not reflect the value of the intangible property employed by USC and EC. Thus, none of the uncontrolled companies is sufficiently similar so that reliable results would be obtained using the resale price, cost plus, or comparable profits methods. Moreover, no uncontrolled companies can be identified that engaged in sufficiently similar activities and transactions with each other to employ the comparable profit split method.

(iv) Given the difficulties in applying the other methods, the reliability of the internal data on USC and EC, and the fact that acceptable comparables are available for deriving a market return for the routine contributions of USC and EC, the residual profit split method is likely to provide the most reliable measure of an arm's length result in this case.

Example 9. Comparable profits method preferred to profit split. (i) Company X is a large, complex U.S. company that carries out extensive research and development activities and manufactures and markets a variety of products. Company X has developed a new process by which compact disks can be fabricated at a fraction of the cost previously required. The process is expected to prove highly profitable, since there is a large market for compact disks. Company X establishes a new foreign subsidiary, Company Y, and licenses it the rights to use the process to fabricate compact disks for the foreign market as well as continuing technical support and improvements to the process. Company Y uses the process to fabricate compact disks which it supplies to related and unrelated parties.

(ii) The process licensed to Company Y is unique and highly valuable and no uncontrolled transfers of intangible property can be found that are sufficiently comparable to permit reliable application of the comparable uncontrolled transaction method. Company X is a large, complex company engaged in a variety of activities that owns unique and highly valuable intangible property. Consequently, no uncontrolled companies can be found that are similar to Company X. Furthermore, application of the profit split method in this case would involve the difficult and problematic tasks of allocating Company X's costs and assets between the relevant business activity and other activities and assigning a value to Company X's intangible contributions. On the other hand, Company Y performs relatively routine manufacturing and marketing activities and there are a number of similar uncontrolled companies. Thus, application of the comparable profits method using Company Y as the tested party is likely to produce a more reliable measure of an arm's length result than a profit split in this case.

Example 10. Cost of services plus method preferred to other methods. (i) FP designs and manufactures consumer electronic devices that incorporate advanced technology. In year 1, FP introduces Product X, an entertainment device targeted primarily at the youth market. FP's wholly-owned, exclusive U.S. distributor, USSub, sells Product X in the U.S. market. USSub hires an independent marketing firm, Agency A, to promote Product X in the U.S. market. Agency A has successfully promoted other electronic products on behalf of other uncontrolled parties. USSub executes a one-year, renewable contract with Agency A that requires it to develop the market for Product X, within an annual budget set by USSub. In years 1 through 3, Agency A develops advertising, buys media, and sponsors events featuring Product X. Agency A receives a markup of 25% on all expenses of promoting Product X, with the exception of media buys, which are reimbursed at cost. During year 3, sales of Product X decrease sharply, as Product X is displaced by competitors' products. At the end of year 3, sales of Product X are discontinued.

(ii) Prior to the start of year 4, FP develops a new entertainment device, Product Y. Like Product X, Product Y is intended for sale to the youth market, but it is marketed under a new trademark distinct from that used for Product X. USSub decides to perform all U.S. market promotion for Product Y. USSub hires key Agency A staff members who handled the successful Product X campaign. To promote Product Y, USSub intends to use methods similar to those used successfully by Agency A to promote Product X (print advertising, media, event sponsorship, etc.). FP and USSub enter into a one-year, renewable agreement concerning promotion of Product Y in the U.S. market. Under the agreement, FP compensates USSub for promoting Product Y, based on a cost of services plus markup of A%. Third-party media buys by USSub in connection with Product Y are reimbursed at cost.

(iii) Assume that under the contractual arrangements between FP and USSub, the arm's length consideration for Product Y and the trademark or other intangible property may be determined reliably under one or more transfer pricing methods. At issue in this example is the separate evaluation of the arm's length compensation for the year 4 promotional activities performed by USSub pursuant to its contract with FP.

(iv) USSub's accounting records contain reliable data that separately state the costs incurred to promote Product Y. A functional analysis indicates that USSub's activities to promote Product Y in year 4 are similar to activities performed by Agency A during years 1 through 3 under the contract with USSub. In other respects, no material differences exist in the market conditions or the promotional activities performed in year 4, as compared to those in years 1 through 3.

(v) It is possible to identify uncontrolled distributors or licensees of electronic products that perform, as one component of their business activities, promotional activities similar to those performed by USSub. However, it is unlikely that publicly available accounting data from these companies would allow computation of the comparable transactional costs or total services costs associated with the marketing or promotional activities that these entities perform, as one component of business activities. If that were possible, the comparable profits method for services might provide a reliable measure of an arm's length result. The functional analysis of the marketing activities performed by USSub in year 4 indicates that they are similar to the activities performed by Agency A in years 1 through 3 for Product X. Because reliable information is available concerning the markup on costs charged in a comparable uncontrolled transaction, the most reliable measure of an arm's length price is the cost of services plus method in § 1.482–9(e).

Example 11. CPM for services preferred to other methods. (i) FP manufactures furniture and accessories for residential use. FP sells its products to retailers in Europe under the trademark, "Moda." FP holds all worldwide rights to the trademark, including in the United States. USSub is FP's wholly-owned subsidiary in the U.S. market and the exclusive U.S. distributor of FP's merchandise. Historically, USSub dealt only with specialized designers in the U.S. market and advertised in trade publications targeted to this market. Although items sold in the U.S. and Europe are physically identical, USSub's U.S. customers generally resell the merchandise as non-branded merchandise.

(ii) FP retains an independent firm to evaluate the feasibility of selling FP's trademarked merchandise in the general wholesale and retail market in the United States. The study concludes that this segment of the U.S. market, which is not exploited by USSub, may generate substantial profits. Based on this study, FP enters into a separate agreement with USSub, which provides that USSub will develop this market in the United States for the benefit of FP. USSub separately accounts for personnel expenses, overhead, and out-of-pocket costs attributable to the initial stage of the marketing campaign (Phase I). US-Sub receives as compensation its costs, plus a markup of X%, for activities in Phase I. At the end of Phase I, FP will evaluate the program. If success appears likely, USSub will begin full-scale distribution of trademarked merchandise in the new market segment, pursuant to agreements negotiated with FP at that time.

(iii) Assume that under the contractual arrangements in effect between FP and USSub, the arm's length consideration for the merchandise and the trademark or other intangible property may be determined reliably under one or more transfer pricing methods. At issue in this example is the separate evaluation of the arm's length compensation for the marketing activities conducted by USSub in years 1 and following.

(iv) A functional analysis reveals that USSub's activities consist primarily of modifying the promotional materials created by FP, negotiating media buys, and arranging promotional events. FP separately compensates USSub for all Phase I activities, and detailed accounting information is available regarding the costs of these activities. The Phase I activities of USSub are similar to those of uncontrolled companies that perform, as their primary business activity, a range of advertising and media relations activities on a contract basis for uncontrolled parties.

(v) No information is available concerning the comparable uncontrolled prices for services in transactions similar to those engaged in by FP and USSub. Nor is any information available concerning uncontrolled transactions that would allow application of the cost of services plus method. It is possible to identify uncontrolled distributors or licensees of home furnishings that perform, as one component of their business activities, promotional activities similar to those performed by USSub. However, it is unlikely that publicly available accounting data from these companies would allow computation of the comparable transactional costs or total services costs associated with the marketing or promotional activities that these entities performed, as one component of their business activities. On the other hand, it is possible to identify uncontrolled advertising and media relations companies, the principal business activities of which are similar to the Phase I activities of USSub. Under these circumstances, the most reliable measure of an arm's length price is the comparable profits method of § 1.482–9(f). The uncontrolled advertising comparables' treatment of material items, such as classification of items as cost of goods sold or selling, general, and administrative expenses, may differ from that of USSub. Such inconsistencies in accounting treatment between the uncontrolled comparables and the tested party, or among the comparables, are less important when using the ratio of operating profit to total services costs under the comparable profits method for services in § 1.482–9(f). Under this method, the operating profit of US-Sub from the Phase I activities is compared to the operating profit of uncontrolled parties that perform general advertising and media relations as their primary business activity.

Example 12. Residual profit split preferred to other methods. (i) USP is a manufacturer of athletic apparel sold under the AA trademark, to which FP owns the worldwide rights. USP sells AA trademark apparel in countries throughout the world, but prior to year 1, USP did not sell its merchandise in Country X. In year 1, USP acquires an uncontrolled Country X company which becomes its wholly-owned subsidiary, XSub. USP enters into an exclusive distribution arrangement with XSub in Country X. Before being acquired by USP in year 1, XSub distributed athletic apparel purchased from uncontrolled suppliers and resold that merchandise to retailers. After being acquired by USP in year

1, XSub continues to distribute merchandise from uncontrolled suppliers and also begins to distribute AA trademark apparel. Under a separate agreement with USP, XSub uses its best efforts to promote the AA trademark in Country X, with the goal of maximizing sales volume and revenues from AA merchandise.

(ii) Prior to year 1, USP executed long-term endorsement contracts with several prominent professional athletes. These contracts give USP the right to use the names and likenesses of the athletes in any country in which AA merchandise is sold during the term of the contract. These contracts remain in effect for five years, starting in year 1. Before being acquired by USP, XSub renewed a long-term agreement with SportMart, an uncontrolled company that owns a nationwide chain of sporting goods retailers in Country X. XSub has been SportMart's primary supplier from the time that SportMart began operations. Under the agreement, SportMart will provide AA merchandise preferred shelf-space and will feature AA merchandise at no charge in its print ads and seasonal promotions. In consideration for these commitments, USP and XSub grant SportMart advance access to new products and the right to use the professional athletes under contract with USP in SportMart advertisements featuring AA merchandise (subject to approval of content by USP).

(iii) Assume that it is possible to segregate all transactions by XSub that involve distribution of merchandise acquired from uncontrolled distributors (non-controlled transactions). In addition, assume that, apart from the activities undertaken by USP and XSub to promote AA apparel in Country X, the arm's length compensation for other functions performed by USP and XSub in the Country X market in years 1 and following can be reliably determined. At issue in this Example 12 is the application of the residual profit split analysis to determine the appropriate division between USP and XSub of the balance of the operating profits from the Country X market, that is the portion attributable to nonroutine contributions to the marketing and promotional activities.

(iv) A functional analysis of the marketing and promotional activities conducted in the Country X market, as described in this example, indicates that both USP and XSub made nonroutine contributions to the business activity. USP contributed the long-term endorsement contracts with professional athletes. XSub contributed its long-term contractual rights with SportMart, which were made more valuable by its successful, long-term relationship with SportMart.

(v) Based on the facts and circumstances, including the fact that both USP and XSub made valuable nonroutine contributions to the marketing and promotional activities and an analysis of the availability (or lack thereof) of comparable and reliable market benchmarks, the Commissioner determines that the most reliable measure of an arm's length result is the residual profit split method in § 1.482–9(g). The residual profit split analysis would take into account both routine and nonroutine contributions by USP and XSub, in order to determine an appropriate allocation of the combined operating profits in the Country X market from the sale of AA merchandise and from related promotional and marketing activities.

Example 13. Preference for acquisition price method. (i) USP develops, manufacturers, and distributes pharmaceutical products. USP and FS, USP's wholly-owned subsidiary, enter into a CSA to develop a new oncological drug, Oncol. Immediately prior to entering into the CSA, USP acquires Company X, an unrelated U.S. pharmaceutical company. Company X is solely engaged in oncological pharmaceutical research, and its only significant resources and capabilities are its workforce and its sole patent, which is associated with Compound X, a promising molecular compound derived from a rare plant, which USP reasonably anticipates will contribute to developing Oncol. All of Company X researchers will be engaged solely in research that is reasonably anticipated to contribute to developing Oncol as well. The rights in the Compound X and the commitment of Company X's researchers to the development of Oncol are platform contributions for which compensation is due from FS as part of a PCT.

(ii) In this case, the acquisition price method, based on the lump sum price paid by USP for Company X, is likely to provide a more reliable measure of an arm's length PCT Payment due to USP than the application of any other method. See §§ 1.482–4(c)(2) and 1.482–7(g)(5)(iv)(A).

Example 14. Preference for market capitalization method. (i) Company X is a publicly traded U.S. company solely engaged in oncological pharmaceutical research and its only significant resources and capabilities are its workforce and its sole patent, which is associated with Compound Y, a promising molecular compound derived from a rare plant. Company X has no marketable products. Company X enters into a CSA with FS, a newly-formed foreign subsidiary, to develop a new oncological drug, Oncol, derived from Compound Y. Compound Y is reasonably anticipated to contribute to developing Oncol. All of Company X researchers will be engaged solely in research that is reasonably anticipated to contribute to developing Oncol under the CSA. The rights in Compound Y and the commitment of Company X's researchers are platform contributions for which compensation is due from FS as part of a PCT.

(ii) In this case, given that Company X's platform contributions covered by PCTs relate to its entire economic value, the application of the market capitalization method, based on the market capitalization of Company X, provides a reliable measure of an arm's length result for Company X's PCTs to the CSA. See §§ 1.482–4(c)(2) and 1.482–7(g)(6)(v)(A).

Example 15. Preference for market capitalization method. (i) MicroDent, Inc. (MDI) is a publicly traded company that developed a new dental surgical microscope ScopeX-1, which drastically shortens many surgical procedures. On January 1 of Year 1, MDI entered into a CSA with a wholly-owned foreign subsidiary (FS) to develop ScopeX-2, the next generation of ScopeX-1. In the CSA, divisional interests are divided on a territorial basis. The rights associated with ScopeX-1, as well as MDI's research capabilities are reasonably anticipated to contribute to the development of ScopeX-2 and are therefore platform contributions for which compensation is due from FS as part of a PCT. At the time of the PCT, MDI's only product was the ScopeX-1 microscope, although MDI was in the process of developing ScopeX-2. Concurrent with the CSA, MDI separately transfers exclusive and perpetual exploitation rights associated with ScopeX-1 to FS in the same territory as assigned to FS in the CSA.

(ii) Although the transactions between MDI and FS under the CSA are distinct from the transactions between MDI and FS relating to the exploitation rights for ScopeX-1, it is likely to be more reliable to evaluate the combined effect of the transactions than to evaluate them in isolation. This is because the combined transactions between MDI and FS relate to all of the economic value of MDI (that is, the exploitation rights and research rights associated with ScopeX-1, as well as the research capabilities of MDI). In this case, application of the market capitalization method, based on the enterprise value of MDI on January 1 of Year 1, is likely to provide a reliable measure of an arm's length payment for the aggregated transactions. See §§ 1.482–4(c)(2) and 1.482–7(g)(6)(v)(A).

(iii) Notwithstanding that the market capitalization method provides the most reliable measure of the aggregated transactions between MDI and FS, see § 1.482–7(g)(2)(iv) for further considerations of when further analysis may be required to distinguish between the remuneration to MDI associated with PCTs under the CSA (for research rights and capabilities associated with ScopeX-1) and the remuneration to MDI for the exploitation rights associated with ScopeX-1.

Example 16. Income method (applied using CPM) preferred to acquisition price method. The facts are the same as in Example 13, except that the acquisition occurred significantly in advance of formation of the CSA, and reliable adjustments cannot be made for this time difference. In addition, Company X has other valuable molecular patents and associated research capabilities, apart from Compound X, that are not reasonably anticipated to contribute to the development of Oncol and that cannot be reliably valued. The CSA divides divisional interests on a territorial basis. Under the terms of the CSA, USP will undertake all R & D (consisting of laboratory research and clinical testing) and manufacturing associated with Oncol, as well as the distribution activities for its territory (the United States). FS will distribute Oncol in its territory (the rest of the world). FS's distribution activities are routine in nature, and the profitability from its activities may be reliably determined from third-party comparables. FS does not furnish any platform contributions. At the time of the PCT, reliable (ex ante) financial projections associated with the development of Oncol and its separate exploitation in each of USP's and FSub's assigned geographical territories are undertaken. In this case, application of the income method using CPM is likely to provide a more reliable measure of an arm's length result than application of the acquisition price method based on the price paid by USP for Company X. See § 1.482–7(g)(4)(vi) and (5)(iv)(C).

Example 17. Evaluation of alternative methods. (i) The facts are the same as in Example 13, except that the acquisition occurred sometime prior to the CSA, and Company X has some areas of promising research that are not reasonably anticipated to contribute to developing Oncol. For purposes of this example, the CSA is assumed to divide divisional interests on a territorial basis. In general, the Commissioner determines that the acquisition price data is useful in informing the arm's length price, but not necessarily determinative. Under the terms of the CSA, USP will undertake all R & D (consisting of laboratory research and clinical testing) and manufacturing associated with Oncol, as well as the distribution activities for its territory (the United States). FS will distribute Oncol in its territory (the rest of the world). FS's distribution activities are routine in nature, and the profitability from its activities may be reliably determined from third-party comparables. At the time of the PCT, financial projections associated with the development of Oncol and its separate exploitation in each of USP's and FSub's assigned geographical territories are undertaken.

(ii) Under the facts, it is possible that the acquisition price method or the income method using CPM might reasonably be applied. Whether the acquisition price method or the income method provides the most reliable evidence of the arm's length price of USP's contributions depends on a number of factors, including the reliability of the financial projections, the reliability of the discount rate chosen, and the extent to which the acquisition price of Company X can be reliably adjusted to account for changes in value over the time period between the acquisition and the formation of the CSA and to account for the value of the in-process research done by Company X that does not constitute platform contributions to the CSA. See § 1.482–7(g)(4)(vi) and (5)(iv)(A) and (C).

Example 18. Evaluation of alternative methods. (i) The facts are the same as in Example 17, except that FS has a patent on Compound Y, which the parties reasonably anticipate will be useful in mitigating potential side effects associated with Compound X and thereby contribute to the development of Oncol. The rights in Compound Y constitute a platform contribution for which compensation is due from USP as part of a PCT. The value of FS's platform contribution cannot be reliably measured by market benchmarks.

(ii) Under the facts, it is possible that either the acquisition price method and the income method together or the residual profit split method might reasonably be applied to determine the arm's length

PCT Payments due between USP and FS. Under the first option the PCT Payment for the platform contributions related to Company X's workforce and Compound X would be determined using the acquisition price method referring to the lump sum price paid by USP for Company X. Because the value of these platform contributions can be determined by reference to a market benchmark, they are considered routine platform contributions. Accordingly, under this option, the platform contribution related to Compound Y would be the only nonroutine platform contribution and the relevant PCT Payment is determined using the income method. Under the second option, rather than looking to the acquisition price for Company X, all the platform contributions are considered nonroutine and the RPSM is applied to determine the PCT Payments for each platform contribution. Under either option, the PCT Payments will be netted against each other.

(iii) Whether the acquisition price method together with the income method or the residual profit split method provides the most reliable evidence of the arm's length price of the platform contributions of USP and FS depends on a number of factors, including the reliability of the determination of the relative values of the platform contributions for purposes of the RPSM, and the extent to which the acquisition price of Company X can be reliably adjusted to account for changes in value over the time period between the acquisition and the formation of the CSA and to account for the value of the rights in the in-process research done by Company X that does not constitute platform contributions to the CSA. In these circumstances, it is also relevant to consider whether the results of each method are consistent with each other, or whether one or both methods are consistent with other potential methods that could be applied. See § 1.482–7(g)(4)(vi), (5)(iv), and (7)(iv).

* * *

[T.D. 8552, 59 FR 35028, July 8, 1994; T.D. 9278, 71 FR 44487, Aug. 4, 2006; T.D. 9441, 74 FR 388, Jan. 5, 2009; T.D. 9456, 74 FR 38845, Aug. 4, 2009; 74 FR 46345, Sept. 9, 2009; T.D. 9568, 76 FR 80134, Dec. 22, 2011]

§ 1.482–9 Methods to determine taxable income in connection with a controlled services transaction.

(a) In general. The arm's length amount charged in a controlled services transaction must be determined under one of the methods provided for in this section. Each method must be applied in accordance with the provisions of § 1.482–1, including the best method rule of § 1.482–1(c), the comparability analysis of § 1.482–1(d), and the arm's length range of § 1.482–1(e), except as those provisions are modified in this section. The methods are—

(1) The services cost method, described in paragraph (b) of this section;

(2) The comparable uncontrolled services price method, described in paragraph (c) of this section;

(3) The gross services margin method, described in paragraph (d) of this section;

(4) The cost of services plus method, described in paragraph (e) of this section;

(5) The comparable profits method, described in § 1.482–5 and in paragraph (f) of this section;

(6) The profit split method, described in § 1.482–6 and in paragraph (g) of this section; and

(7) Unspecified methods, described in paragraph (h) of this section.

(b) Services cost method—(1) In general. The services cost method evaluates whether the amount charged for certain services is arm's length by reference to the total services costs (as defined in paragraph (j) of this section) with no markup. If a taxpayer applies the services cost method in accordance with the rules of this paragraph (b), then it will be considered the best method for purposes of

§ 1.482–1(c), and the Commissioner's allocations will be limited to adjusting the amount charged for such services to the properly determined amount of such total services costs.

(2) Eligibility for the services cost method. To apply the services cost method to a service in accordance with the rules of this paragraph (b), all of the following requirements must be satisfied with respect to the service—

(i) The service is a covered service as defined in paragraph (b)(3) of this section;

(ii) The service is not an excluded activity as defined in paragraph (b)(4) of this section;

(iii) The service is not precluded from constituting a covered service by the business judgment rule described in paragraph (b)(5) of this section; and

(iv) Adequate books and records are maintained as described in paragraph (b)(6) of this section.

(3) Covered services. For purposes of this paragraph (b), covered services consist of a controlled service transaction or a group of controlled service transactions (see § 1.482–1(f)(2)(i) (aggregation of transactions)) that meet the definition of specified covered services or low margin covered services.

(i) Specified covered services. Specified covered services are controlled services transactions that the Commissioner specifies by revenue procedure. Services will be included in such revenue procedure based upon the Commissioner's determination that the specified covered services are support services common among taxpayers across industry sectors and generally do not involve a significant median comparable markup on total services costs. For the definition of the median comparable markup on total services costs, see paragraph (b)(3)(ii) of this section. The Commissioner may add to, subtract from, or otherwise revise the specified covered services described in the revenue procedure by subsequent revenue procedure, which amendments will ordinarily be prospective only in effect.

(ii) Low margin covered services. Low margin covered services are controlled services transactions for which the median comparable markup on total services costs is less than or equal to seven percent. For purposes of this paragraph (b), the median comparable markup on total services costs means the excess of the arm's length price of the controlled services transaction determined under the general section 482 regulations without regard to this paragraph (b), using the interquartile range described in § 1.482–1(e)(2)(iii)(C) and as necessary adjusting to the median of such interquartile range, over total services costs, expressed as a percentage of total services costs.

(4) Excluded activity. The following types of activities are excluded activities:

(i) Manufacturing.

(ii) Production.

(iii) Extraction, exploration, or processing of natural resources.

(iv) Construction.

(v) Reselling, distribution, acting as a sales or purchasing agent, or acting under a commission or other similar arrangement.

(vi) Research, development, or experimentation.

(vii) Engineering or scientific.

(viii) Financial transactions, including guarantees.

(ix) Insurance or reinsurance.

(5) Not services that contribute significantly to fundamental risks of business success or failure. A service cannot constitute a covered service unless the taxpayer reasonably concludes in its business judgment that the service does not contribute significantly to key competitive advantages, core capabilities, or fundamental risks of success or failure in one or more trades or businesses of the controlled group, as defined in § 1.482–1(i)(6). In evaluating the reasonableness of the conclusion required by this paragraph (b)(5), consideration will be given to all the facts and circumstances.

(6) Adequate books and records. Permanent books of account and records are maintained for as long as the costs with respect to the covered services are incurred by the renderer. Such books and records must include a statement evidencing the taxpayer's intention to apply the services cost method to evaluate the arm's length charge for such services. Such books and records must be adequate to permit verification by the Commissioner of the total services costs incurred by the renderer, including a description of the services in question, identification of the renderer and the recipient of such services, and sufficient documentation to allow verification of the methods used to allocate and apportion such costs to the services in question in accordance with paragraph (k) of this section.

(7) Shared services arrangement—(i) In general. If the services cost method is used to evaluate the amount charged for covered services, and such services are the subject of a shared services arrangement, then the arm's length charge to each participant for such services will be the portion of the total costs of the services otherwise determined under the services cost method of this paragraph (b) that is properly allocated to such participant pursuant to the arrangement.

(ii) Requirements for shared services arrangement. A shared services arrangement must meet the requirements described in this paragraph (b)(7).

(A) Eligibility. To be eligible for treatment under this paragraph (b)(7), a shared services arrangement must—

(1) Include two or more participants;

(2) Include as participants all controlled taxpayers that reasonably anticipate a benefit (as defined under paragraph (*l*)(3)(i) of this section) from one or more covered services specified in the shared services arrangement; and

(3) Be structured such that each covered service (or each reasonable aggregation of services within the meaning of paragraph (b)(7)(iii)(B) of this section) confers a benefit on at least one participant in the shared services arrangement.

(B) Allocation. The costs for covered services must be allocated among the participants based on their respective shares of the reasonably anticipated benefits from those services, without regard to whether the anticipated benefits are in fact realized. Reasonably anticipated benefits are benefits as defined in paragraph (*l*)(3)(i) of this section. The allocation of costs must provide the most reliable measure of the participants' respective shares of the reasonably anticipated benefits under the principles of the best method rule. See § 1.482–1(c). The allocation must be applied on a consistent basis for all participants and services. The allocation to each participant in each taxable year must reasonably reflect that participant's respective share of reasonably anticipated benefits for such taxable year. If the taxpayer reasonably concluded that the shared services arrangement (including any aggregation pursuant to paragraph (b)(7)(iii)(B) of this section) allocated costs for covered services on a basis that most reliably reflects the participants' respective shares of the reasonably anticipated benefits attributable to such services, as provided for in this paragraph (b)(7), then the Commissioner may not adjust such allocation basis.

(C) Documentation. The taxpayer must maintain sufficient documentation to establish that the requirements of this paragraph (b)(7) are satisfied, and include—

(1) A statement evidencing the taxpayer's intention to apply the services cost method to evaluate the arm's length charge for covered services pursuant to a shared services arrangement;

(2) A list of the participants and the renderer or renderers of covered services under the shared services arrangement;

(3) A description of the basis of allocation to all participants, consistent with the participants' respective shares of reasonably anticipated benefits; and

(4) A description of any aggregation of covered services for purposes of the shared services arrangement, and an indication whether this aggregation (if any) differs from the aggregation used to evaluate the median comparable markup for any low margin covered services described in paragraph (b)(3)(ii) of this section.

(iii) Definitions and special rules—(A) Participant. A participant is a controlled taxpayer that reasonably anticipates benefits from covered services subject to a shared services arrangement that substantially complies with the requirements described in this paragraph (b)(7).

(B) Aggregation. Two or more covered services may be aggregated in a reasonable manner taking into account all the facts and circumstances, including whether the relative magnitude of reasonably anticipated benefits of the participants sharing the costs of such aggregated services may be reasonably reflected by the allocation basis employed pursuant to paragraph (b)(7)(ii)(B) of this section. The aggregation of services under a shared services arrangement may differ from the aggregation used to evaluate the median comparable markup for any low margin covered services described in paragraph (b)(3)(ii) of this section, provided that such alternative aggregation can be implemented on a reasonable basis, including appropriately identifying and isolating relevant costs, as necessary.

(C) Coordination with cost sharing arrangements. To the extent that an allocation is made to a participant in a shared services arrangement that is also a participant in a cost sharing arrangement subject to § 1.482–7T, such amount with respect to covered services is first allocated pursuant to the shared services arrangement under this paragraph (b)(7). Costs allocated pursuant to a shared services arrangement may (if applicable) be further allocated between the intangible property development activity under § 1.482–7T and other activities of the participant.

(8) Examples. The application of this section is illustrated by the following examples. No inference is intended whether the presence or absence of one or more facts is determinative of the conclusion in any example. For purposes of Examples 1 through 14, assume that Company P and its subsidiaries, Company Q and Company R, are corporations and members of the same group of controlled entities (PQR Controlled Group). For purposes of Example 15, assume that Company P and its subsidiary, Company S, are corporations and members of the same group of controlled entities (PS Controlled Group). For purposes of Examples 16 through 24, assume that Company P and its subsidiaries, Company X, Company Y, and Company Z, are corporations and members of the same group of controlled entities (PXYZ Group) and that Company P and its subsidiaries satisfy all of the requirements for a shared services arrangement specified in paragraphs (b)(7)(ii) and (iii) of this section.

* * *

Example 5. Credit analysis services. **(i)** Company P is a manufacturer and distributor of clothing for retail stores. Company Q and Company R are distributors of clothing for retail stores. As part of its operations, personnel in Company P perform credit analysis on its customers. Most of the customers have a history of purchases from Company P, and the credit analysis involves a review of the recent payment history of the customer's account. For new customers, the personnel in Company P perform a basic credit check of the customer using reports from a credit reporting agency. On behalf of Company Q and Company R, Company P performs credit analysis on customers who order clothing from Company Q and Company R using the same method as Company P uses for itself.

(ii) Assume that these services relating to credit analysis are specified covered services within the meaning of paragraph (b)(3)(i) of this section. Under the facts and circumstances of the business of the PQR Controlled Group, the taxpayer could reasonably conclude that these services do not contribute significantly to the controlled group's key competitive advantages, core capabilities, or fundamental risks of success or failure in the group's business. If these services meet the other requirements of this paragraph (b), Company P will be eligible to charge these services to Company Q and Company R in accordance with the services cost method.

Example 6. Credit analysis services. (i) Company P, Company Q, and Company R lease furniture to retail customers who present a significant credit risk and are generally unable to lease furniture from other providers. As part of its leasing operations, personnel in Company P perform credit analysis on each of the potential lessees. The personnel have developed special expertise in determining whether a particular customer who presents a significant credit risk (as indicated by credit reporting agencies) will be likely to make the requisite lease payments on a timely basis. Also, as part of its operations, Company P performs similar credit analysis services for Company Q and Company R, which charge correspondingly high monthly lease payments.

(ii) Assume that these services relating to credit analysis are specified covered services within the meaning of paragraph (b)(3)(i) of this section. Under the facts and circumstances, the taxpayer is unable to reasonably conclude that these services do not contribute significantly to the controlled group's key competitive advantages, core capabilities, or fundamental risks of success or failure in the group's business. Company P is not eligible to charge these services to Company Q and Company R in accordance with the services cost method.

Example 7. Credit analysis services. (i) Company P is a large full-service bank, which provides products and services to corporate and consumer markets, including unsecured loans, secured loans, lines of credit, letters of credit, conversion of foreign currency, consumer loans, trust services, and sales of certificates of deposit. Company Q makes routine consumer loans to individuals, such as auto loans and home equity loans. Company R makes only business loans to small businesses.

(ii) Company P performs credit analysis and prepares credit reports for itself, as well as for Company Q and Company R. Company P, Company Q and Company R regularly employ these credit reports in the ordinary course of business in making decisions regarding extensions of credit to potential customers (including whether to lend, rate of interest, and loan terms).

(iii) Assume that these services relating to credit analysis are specified covered services within the meaning of paragraph (b)(3)(i) of this section. Under the facts and circumstances, the credit analysis services constitute part of a "financial transaction" described in paragraph (b)(4)(viii) of this section. Company P is not eligible to charge these services to Company Q and Company R in accordance with the services cost method.

* * *

(c) Comparable uncontrolled services price method—(1) In general. The comparable uncontrolled services price method evaluates whether the amount charged in a controlled services transaction is arm's length by reference to the amount charged in a comparable uncontrolled services transaction.

(2) Comparability and reliability considerations—(i) In general. Whether results derived from application of this method are the most reliable measure of the arm's length result must be determined using the factors described under the best method rule in § 1.482–1(c). The application of these factors under the comparable uncontrolled services price method is discussed in paragraphs (c)(2)(ii) and (iii) of this section.

(ii) Comparability—(A) In general. The degree of comparability between controlled and uncontrolled transactions is determined by applying the provisions of § 1.482–1(d). Although all of the factors described in § 1.482–1(d)(3) must be considered, similarity of the services rendered, and of the intangible property (if any) used in performing the services, generally will have the greatest effects on comparability under this method. In addition, because even minor differences in contractual terms or economic conditions could materially affect the amount charged in an uncontrolled transaction, comparability under this method depends on close similarity with respect to these factors, or adjustments to account for any differences. The results derived from applying the comparable uncontrolled services price method generally will be the most direct and reliable measure of an arm's length price for the controlled transaction if an uncontrolled transaction has no differences from the controlled transaction that would affect the price, or if there are only minor differences that have a definite and reasonably ascertainable effect on price and for which appropriate adjustments are made. If such adjustments cannot be made, or if there are more than minor differences between the controlled and uncontrolled transactions, the comparable uncontrolled services price method may be used, but the reliability of the results as a measure of the arm's length price will be reduced. Further, if there are material differences for which reliable adjustments cannot be made, this method ordinarily will not provide a reliable measure of an arm's length result.

* * *

(d) Gross services margin method—(1) In general. The gross services margin method evaluates whether the amount charged in a controlled services transaction is arm's length by reference to the gross profit margin realized in comparable uncontrolled transactions. This method ordinarily is used in cases where a controlled taxpayer performs services or functions in connection with an uncontrolled transaction between a member of the controlled group and an uncontrolled taxpayer. This method may be used where a controlled taxpayer renders services (agent services) to another member of the controlled group in connection with a transaction between that other member and an uncontrolled taxpayer. This method also may be used in cases where a controlled taxpayer contracts to provide services to an uncontrolled taxpayer (intermediary function) and another member of the controlled group actually performs a portion of the services provided.

* * *

(e) Cost of services plus method—(1) In general. The cost of services plus method evaluates whether the amount charged in a controlled services transaction is arm's length by reference to the gross services profit markup realized in comparable uncontrolled transactions. The cost of services plus method is ordinarily used in cases where the controlled service renderer provides the same or similar services to both controlled and uncontrolled parties. This method is ordinarily not used in cases where the controlled services transaction involves a contingent-payment arrangement, as described in paragraph (i)(2) of this section.

* * *

(f) Comparable profits method—(1) In general. The comparable profits method evaluates whether the amount charged in a controlled transaction is arm's length, based on objective measures of profitability (profit level indicators) derived from uncontrolled taxpayers that engage in similar business activities under similar circumstances. The rules in § 1.482–5 relating to the comparable profits method apply to controlled services transactions, except as modified in this paragraph (f).

* * *

(g) Profit split method—(1) In general. The profit split method evaluates whether the allocation of the combined operating profit or loss attributable to one or more controlled transactions is arm's length by reference to the relative value of each controlled taxpayer's contribution to that combined operating profit or loss. The relative value of each controlled taxpayer's contribution is determined in a manner that reflects the functions performed, risks assumed and resources employed by such controlled taxpayer in the relevant business activity. For application of the profit split method (both the comparable profit split and the residual profit split), see § 1.482–6. The residual profit split method may not be used where only one controlled taxpayer makes significant nonroutine contributions.

* * *

(h) Unspecified methods. Methods not specified in paragraphs (b) through (g) of this section may be used to evaluate whether the amount charged in a controlled services transaction is arm's length. Any method used under this paragraph (h) must be applied in accordance with the provisions of § 1.482–1. Consistent with the specified methods, an unspecified method should take into account the general principle that uncontrolled taxpayers evaluate the terms of a transaction by considering the realistic alternatives to that transaction, including economically similar transactions structured as other than services transactions, and only enter into a particular transaction if none of the alternatives is preferable to it. For example, the comparable uncontrolled services price method compares a controlled services transaction to similar uncontrolled transactions to provide a direct estimate of the price to which the parties would have agreed had they resorted directly to a market alternative to the controlled services transaction. Therefore, in establishing whether a controlled services transaction achieved an arm's length result, an unspecified method should provide information on the prices or profits that the controlled taxpayer could have realized by choosing a realistic alternative to the controlled services transaction (for example, outsourcing a particular service function, rather than performing the function itself). As with any method, an unspecified method will not be applied unless it provides the most reliable measure of an arm's length result under the principles of the best method rule. See § 1.482–1(c). Therefore, in accordance with § 1.482–1(d) (comparability), to the extent that an unspecified method relies on internal data rather than uncontrolled comparables, its reliability will be reduced. Similarly, the reliability of a method will be affected by the reliability of the data and assumptions used to apply the method, including any projections used.

* * *

(m) Coordination with transfer pricing rules for other transactions—(1) Services transactions that include other types of transactions. A transaction structured as a controlled services transaction may include other elements for which a separate category or categories of methods are provided, such as a loan or advance, a rental, or a transfer of tangible or intangible property. See §§ 1.482–1(b)(2) and 1.482–2(a), (c), and (d). Whether such an integrated transaction is evaluated as a controlled services transaction under this section or whether one or more elements should be evaluated separately under other sections of the section 482 regulations depends on which approach will provide the most reliable measure of an arm's length result. Ordinarily, an integrated transaction of this type may be evaluated under this section and its separate elements need not be evaluated separately, provided that each component of the transaction may be adequately accounted for in evaluating the comparability of the controlled transaction to the uncontrolled comparables and, accordingly, in determining the arm's length result in the controlled transaction. See § 1.482–1(d)(3).

(2) Services transactions that effect a transfer of intangible property. A transaction structured as a controlled services transaction may in certain cases include an element that constitutes the transfer of intangible property or may result in a transfer, in whole or in part, of intangible property. Notwithstanding paragraph (m)(1) of this section, if such element relating to intangible property is material to the evaluation, the arm's length result for the element of the transaction that involves intangible property must be corroborated or determined by an analysis under § 1.482–4.

(3) Coordination with rules governing cost sharing arrangements. Section 1.482–7 provides the specific methods to be used to determine arm's length results of controlled transactions in connection with a cost sharing arrangement. This section provides the specific methods to be used to determine arm's length results of a controlled service transaction, including in an arrangement for sharing the costs and risks of developing intangibles other than a cost sharing arrangement covered by § 1.482–7. In the case of such an arrangement, consideration of the principles, methods, comparability, and reliability considerations set forth in § 1.482–7 is relevant in determining the best method, including an unspecified method, under this section, as appropriately adjusted in light of the differences in the facts and circumstances between such arrangement and a cost sharing arrangement.

(4) Other types of transactions that include controlled services transactions. A transaction structured other than as a controlled services transaction may include one or more elements for which separate pricing methods are provided in this section. Whether such an integrated transaction is evaluated under another section of the section 482 regulations or whether one or more elements should be evaluated separately under this section depends on which approach will provide the most reliable measure of an arm's length result. Ordinarily, a single method may be applied to such an integrated transaction, and the separate services component of the transaction need not be separately analyzed under this section, provided that the controlled services may be adequately accounted for in evaluating the comparability of the controlled transaction to the uncontrolled comparables and, accordingly, in determining the arm's length results in the controlled transaction. See § 1.482–1(d)(3).

(5) Examples. The principles of this paragraph (m) are illustrated by the following examples:

* * *

Example 4. (i) Company X, a U.S. corporation, and Company Y, a foreign corporation, are members of a controlled group. Both companies perform research and development activities relating to integrated circuits. In addition, Company Y manufactures integrated circuits. In years 1 through 3, Company X engages in substantial research and development activities, gains significant know-how regarding the development of a particular high-temperature resistant integrated circuit, and memorializes that research in a written report. In years 1 through 3, Company X generates overall net operating losses as a result of the expenditures associated with this research and development effort. At the beginning of year 4, Company X enters into a technical assistance agreement with Company Y. As part of this agreement, the researchers from Company X responsible for this project meet with the researchers from Company Y and provide them with a copy of the written report. Three months later, the researchers from Company Y apply for a patent for a high-temperature resistant integrated circuit based in large part upon the know-how obtained from the researchers from Company X.

(ii) The controlled services transaction between Company X and Company Y includes an element that constitutes the transfer of intangible property (such as, know-how). Because the element relating to the intangible property is material to the arm's length evaluation, the arm's length result for that element must be corroborated or determined by an analysis under § 1.482–4.

* * *

[T.D. 9456, 74 FR 38846, Aug. 4, 2009; 74 FR 46345, Sept. 9, 2009; T.D. 9568, 76 FR 80136, Dec. 22, 2011]

Corporations Used to Avoid Income Tax on Shareholders

§ 1.532–1 Corporations subject to accumulated earnings tax.

* * *

(c) Foreign corporations. Section 531 is applicable to any foreign corporation, whether resident or nonresident, with respect to any income derived from sources, within the United States, if any of its shareholders are subject to income tax on the distributions of the corporation by reason of being (1) citizens or residents of the United States, or (2) nonresident alien individuals to whom section 871 is applicable, or (3) foreign corporations if a beneficial interest therein is owned directly or indirectly by any shareholder specified in subparagraph (1) or (2) of this paragraph.

[T.D. 6500, 25 FR 11402, Nov. 26, 1960; 25 FR 14021, Dec. 21, 1960]

Partners and Partnerships

Determination of Tax Liability

§ 1.702–1 Income and credits of partner.

(a) General rule. Each partner is required to take into account separately in his return his distributive share, whether or not distributed, of each class or item of partnership income, gain, loss, deduction, or credit described in subparagraphs (1) through (9) of this paragraph. (For the taxable year in which a partner includes his distributive share of partnership taxable income, see section 706(a) and § 1.706–1(a). Such distributive share shall be determined as provided in section 704 and § 1.704–1.) Accordingly, in determining his income tax:

(1) Each partner shall take into account, as part of his gains and losses from sales or exchanges of capital assets held for not more than 1 year (6 months for taxable years beginning before 1977; 9 months for taxable years beginning in 1977), his distributive share of the combined net amount of such gains and losses of the partnership.

(2) Each partner shall take into account, as part of his gains and losses from sales or exchanges of capital assets held for more than 1 year (6 months for taxable years beginning before 1977; 9 months for taxable years beginning in 1977), his distributive share of the combined net amount of such gains and losses of the partnership.

(3) Each partner shall take into account, as part of his gains and losses from sales or exchanges of property described in section 1231 (relating to property used in the trade or business and involuntary conversions), his distributive share of the combined net amount of such gains and losses of the partnership. The partnership shall not combine such items with items set forth in subparagraph (1) or (2) of this paragraph.

(4) Each partner shall take into account, as part of the charitable contributions paid by him, his distributive share of each class of charitable contributions paid by the partnership within the partnership's taxable year. Section 170 determines the extent to which such amount may be allowed as a deduction to the partner. For the definition of the term "charitable contribution", see section 170(c).

(5) Each partner shall take into account, as part of the dividends received by him from domestic corporations, his distributive share of dividends received by the partnership, with respect to which the partner is entitled to a credit under section 34 (for dividends received on or before December 31, 1964), an exclusion under section 116, or a deduction under part VIII, Subchapter B, Chapter 1 of the Code.

(6) Each partner shall take into account, as part of his taxes described in section 901 which have been paid or accrued to foreign countries or to possessions of the United States, his distributive share of such taxes which have been paid or accrued by the partnership, according to its method of treating such taxes. A partner may elect to treat his total amount of such taxes, including his distributive share of such taxes of the partnership, as a deduction under section 164 or as a credit under section 901, subject to the provisions of sections 901 through 905.

(7) Each partner shall take into account, as part of the partially tax-exempt interest received by him on obligations of the United States or on obligations of instrumentalities of the United States, as described in section 35 or section 242, his distributive share of such partially tax-exempt interest received by the partnership. However, if the partnership elects to amortize premiums on bonds as provided in section 171, the amount received on such obligations by the partnership shall be reduced by the amortizable bond premium applicable to such obligations as provided in section 171(a)(3).

(8)(i) Each partner shall take into account separately, as part of any class of income, gain, loss, deduction, or credit, his distributive share of the following items: Recoveries of bad debts, prior taxes, and delinquency amounts (section 111); gains and losses from wagering transactions (section 165(d)); soil and water conservation expenditures (section 175); nonbusiness expenses as described in section 212; medical, dental, etc., expenses (section 213); expenses for care of certain dependents (section 214); alimony, etc., payments (section 215); amounts representing taxes and interest paid to cooperative housing corporations (section 216); intangible drilling and developments costs (section 263(c)); pre-1970 exploration expenditures (section 615); certain mining exploration expenditures (section 617); income, gain, or loss to the partnership under section 751(b); and any items of income, gain, loss, deduction, or credit subject to a special allocation under the partnership agreement which differs from the allocation of partnership taxable income or loss generally.

(ii) Each partner must also take into account separately the partner's distributive share of any partnership item which, if separately taken into account by any partner, would result in an income tax liability for that partner, or for any other person, different from that which would result if that partner did not take the item into account separately. Thus, if any partner is a controlled foreign corporation, as defined in section 957, items of income that would be gross subpart F income if separately taken into account by the controlled foreign corporation must be separately stated for all partners. Under section 911(a), if any partner is a bona fide resident of a foreign country who may exclude from gross income the part of the partner's distributive share which qualifies as earned income, as defined in section 911(b), the earned income of the partnership for all partners must be separately stated. Similarly, all relevant items of income or deduction of the partnership must be separately stated for all partners in determining the applicability of section 183 (relating to activities not engaged in for profit) and the recomputation of tax thereunder for any partner. This paragraph (a)(8)(ii) applies to taxable years beginning on or after July 23, 2002.

(iii) Each partner shall aggregate the amount of his separate deductions or exclusions and his distributive share of partnership deductions or exclusions separately stated in determining the amount allowable to him of any deduction or exclusion under Subtitle A of the Code as to which a limitation is imposed. For example, partner A has individual domestic exploration expenditures of $300,000. He is also a member of the AB partnership which in 1971 in its first year of operation has foreign exploration expenditures of $400,000. A's distributable share of this item is $200,000. However, the total amount of his distributable share that A can deduct as exploration expenditures under section 617(a) is limited to $100,000 in view of the limitation provided in section 617(h). Therefore, the excess of $100,000 ($200,000 minus $100,000) is not deductible by A.

(9) Each partner shall also take into account separately his distributive share of the taxable income or loss of the partnership, exclusive of items requiring separate computations under subparagraphs (1) through (8) of this paragraph. For limitation on allowance of a partner's distributive share of partnership losses, see section 704(d) and paragraph (d) of § 1.704–1.

* * *

[T.D. 6500, 25 FR 11814, Nov. 26, 1960, as amended by T.D. 6605, 27 FR 8097, Aug. 15, 1962; T.D. 6777, 29 FR 17809, Dec. 16, 1964; T.D. 6885, 31 FR 7803, June 2, 1966; T.D. 7192, 37 FR 12949, June 30, 1972; T.D. 7564, 43 FR 40496, Sept. 12, 1978; T.D. 7728, 45 FR 72650, Nov. 3, 1980; T.D. 8247, 54 FR 13680, April 5, 1989; T.D. 8348, 56 FR 21952, May 13, 1991; T.D. 8348, 57 FR 4913, Feb. 10, 1992; T.D. 9008, 67 FR 48023, July 23, 2002; T.D. 9194, 70 FR 18928, April 11, 2005]

§ 1.704–1 Partner's distributive share.

* * *

(b) Determination of partner's distributive share—* * *

(1) In General—* * *

* * *

(4) Special rules—* * *

(viii) Allocation of creditable foreign taxes—(a) In general. Allocations of creditable foreign taxes do not have substantial economic effect within the meaning of paragraph (b)(2) of this section and, accordingly, such expenditures must be allocated in accordance with the partners' interests in the partnership. See paragraph (b)(3)(iv) of this section. An allocation of a creditable foreign tax expenditure (CFTE) will be deemed to be in accordance with the partners' interests in the partnership if—

(1) The CFTE is allocated (whether or not pursuant to an express provision in the partnership agreement) to each partner and reported on the partnership return in proportion to the partners' CFTE category shares of income to which the CFTE relates; and

(2) Allocations of all other partnership items that, in the aggregate, have a material effect on the amount of CFTEs allocated to a partner pursuant to paragraph (b)(4)(viii)(a)(1) of this section are valid.

(b) Creditable foreign tax expenditures (CFTEs). For purposes of this section, a CFTE is a foreign tax paid or accrued by a partnership that is eligible for a credit under section 901(a) or an applicable U.S. income tax treaty. A foreign tax is a CFTE for these purposes without regard to whether a partner receiving an allocation of such foreign tax elects to claim a credit for such tax. Foreign taxes paid or accrued by a partner with respect to a distributive share of partnership income, and foreign taxes deemed paid under section 902 or 960 by a corporate partner with respect to stock owned, directly or indirectly, by or for a partnership, are not taxes paid or accrued by a partnership and, therefore, are not CFTEs subject to the rules of this section. See paragraphs (e) and (f) of § 1.901–2 for rules for determining when and by whom a foreign tax is paid or accrued.

(c) Income to which CFTEs relate. (1) In general. For purposes of paragraph (b)(4)(viii)(a) of this section, CFTEs are related to net income in the partnership's CFTE category or categories to which the CFTE is allocated and apportioned in accordance with the rules of paragraph (b)(4)(viii)(d) of this section. Paragraph (b)(4)(viii)(c)(2) of this section provides rules for determining a partnership's CFTE categories. Paragraph (b)(4)(viii)(c)(3) of this section provides rules for determining the net income in each CFTE category. Paragraph (b)(4)(viii)(c)(4) of this section provides rules for determining a partner's CFTE category share of income, including rules that require adjustments to net income in a CFTE category for purposes of determining the partners' CFTE category share of income with respect to certain

CFTEs. Paragraph (b)(4)(viii)(c)(5) of this section provides a special rule for allocating CFTEs when a partnership has no net income in a CFTE category.

(2) CFTE category—(i) Income from activities. A CFTE category is a category of net income (or loss) attributable to one or more activities of the partnership. Net income (or loss) from all the partnership's activities shall be included in a single CFTE category unless the allocation of net income (or loss) from one or more activities differs from the allocation of net income (or loss) from other activities, in which case income from each activity or group of activities that is subject to a different allocation shall be treated as net income (or loss) in a separate CFTE category.

(ii) Different allocations. Different allocations of net income (or loss) generally will result from provisions of the partnership agreement providing for different sharing ratios for net income (or loss) from separate activities. Different allocations of net income (or loss) from separate activities generally will also result if any partnership item is shared in a different ratio than any other partnership item. A guaranteed payment described in paragraph (b)(4)(viii)(c)(4)(ii) of this section, gross income allocation, or other preferential allocation will result in different allocations of net income (or loss) from separate activities only if the amount of the payment or the allocation is determined by reference to income from less than all of the partnership's activities.

(iii) Activity. Whether a partnership has one or more activities, and the scope of each activity, is determined in a reasonable manner taking into account all the facts and circumstances. In evaluating whether aggregating or disaggregating income from particular business or investment operations constitutes a reasonable method of determining the scope of an activity, the principal consideration is whether the proposed determination has the effect of separating CFTEs from the related foreign income. Relevant considerations include whether the partnership conducts business in more than one geographic location or through more than one entity or branch, and whether certain types of income are exempt from foreign tax or subject to preferential foreign tax treatment. In addition, income from a divisible part of a single activity is treated as income from a separate activity if necessary to prevent separating CFTEs from the related foreign income, such as when income from divisible parts of a single activity is subject to different allocations. See, for example, paragraph (b)(4)(viii)(c)(3)(iv) of this section (special allocations related to disregarded payments can give rise to subdivision of an activity into divisible parts). A guaranteed payment, gross income allocation, or other preferential allocation of income that is determined by reference to all the income from a single activity generally will not result in the division of an activity into divisible parts. See Example 22 in paragraph (b)(5)(xxii) of this section and Example 1 in paragraph (b)(6)(i) of this section. The partnership's activities must be determined consistently from year to year absent a material change in facts and circumstances.

(3) Net income in a CFTE category—(i) In general. A partnership computes net income in a CFTE category as follows: First, the partnership determines for U.S. Federal income tax purposes all of its partnership items, including items of gross income, gain, loss, deduction, and expense, and items allocated pursuant to section 704(c). For the purpose of this paragraph (b)(4)(viii)(c)(3)(i), the items of the partnership are determined without regard to any adjustments under section 743(b) that its partners may have to the basis of property of the partnership. However, if the partnership is a transferee partner that has a basis adjustment under section 743(b) in its capacity as a direct or indirect partner in a lower-tier partnership, the partnership does take such basis adjustment into account. Second, the partnership must assign those partnership items to its activities pursuant to paragraph (b)(4)(viii)(c)(3)(ii) of this section. Third, partnership items attributable to each activity are aggregated within the relevant CFTE category as determined under paragraph (b)(4)(viii)(c)(2) of this section in order to compute the net income in a CFTE category.

(ii) Assignment of partnership items to activities. The items of gross income attributable to an activity must be determined in a consistent manner under any reasonable method taking into account all the facts and circumstances. Except as otherwise provided in paragraph (b)(4)(viii)(c)(3)(iii) of this section, expenses, losses, or other deductions must be allocated and apportioned to gross income attributable to an activity in accordance with the rules of §§ 1.861–8 and 1.861–8T. Under the rules §§ 1.861–8 and 1.861–8T, if an expense, loss, or other deduction is allocated to gross income from more than one activity, such expense, loss, or deduction must be apportioned among each such activity using a reasonable method that reflects to a reasonably close extent the factual relationship between the deduction and the gross income from such activities. See § 1.861–8T(c). For the effect of disregarded payments in determining the amount of net income attributable to an activity, see paragraph (b)(4)(viii)(c)(3)(iv) of this section.

(iii) Interest expense and research and experimental expenditures. The partnership's interest expense and research and experimental expenditures described in section 174 may be allocated and apportioned under any reasonable method, including but not limited to the methods prescribed in §§ 1.861–9 through 1.861–13T (interest expense) and § 1.861–17 (research and experimental expenditures).

(iv) Disregarded payments. An item of gross income is assigned to the activity that generates the item of income that is recognized for U.S. Federal income tax purposes. Consequently, disregarded payments are not taken into account in determining the amount of net income attributable to an activity, although a special allocation of income used to make a disregarded payment may result in the subdivision of an activity into divisible parts. See paragraph (b)(4)(viii)(c)(2)(iii) of this section, Example 24 in paragraph (b)(5)(xxiv) of this section, and Examples 2 and 3 in paragraphs (b)(6)(ii) and (iii), respectively, of this section (relating to inter-branch payments).

(4) CFTE category share of income—(i) In general. CFTE category share of income means the portion of the net income in a CFTE category, determined in accordance with paragraph (b)(4)(viii)(c)(3) of this section as modified by paragraphs (b)(4)(viii)(c)(4)(ii) through (iv) of this section, that is allocated to a partner. To the extent provided in paragraph (b)(4)(viii)(c)(4)(ii) of this section, a guaranteed payment is treated as an allocation to the recipient of the guaranteed payment for this purpose. If more than one partner receives positive income allocations (income in excess of expenses) from a CFTE category, which in the aggregate exceed the total net income in the CFTE category, then such partner's CFTE category share of income equals the partner's positive income allocation from the CFTE category, divided by the aggregate positive income allocations from the CFTE category, multiplied by the net income in the CFTE category. Paragraphs (b)(4)(viii)(c)(4)(ii) through (iv) of this section require adjustments to the net income in a CFTE category for purposes of determining the partners' CFTE category share of income if one or more foreign jurisdictions impose a tax that provides for certain exclusions or deductions from the foreign taxable base. Such adjustments apply only with respect to CFTEs attributable to the taxes that allow such exclusions or deductions. Thus, net income in a CFTE category may vary for purposes of applying paragraph (b)(4)(viii)(a)(1) of this section to different CFTEs within that CFTE category.

(ii) Guaranteed payments. Except as otherwise provided in this paragraph (b)(4)(viii)(c)(4)(ii), solely for purposes of applying the safe harbor provisions of paragraph (b)(4)(viii)(a)(1) of this section, net income in the CFTE category from which a guaranteed payment (within the meaning of section 707(c)) is made is increased by the amount of the guaranteed payment that is deductible for U.S. Federal income tax purposes, and such amount is treated as an allocation to the recipient of such guaranteed payment for purposes of determining the partners' CFTE category shares of income. If a foreign tax allows (whether in the current or in a different taxable year) a deduction from its taxable base for a guaranteed payment, then solely for purposes of applying the safe harbor provisions of paragraph (b)(4)(viii)(a)(1) of this section to allocations of CFTEs that are attributable to that foreign tax, net income in the CFTE category is increased only to the extent that the amount of the guaranteed payment that is deductible for U.S. Federal income tax purposes exceeds the amount allowed as a deduction for purposes of the foreign tax, and such excess is treated as an allocation to the recipient of the guaranteed payment for purposes of determining the partners' CFTE category shares of income. See Example 1 in paragraph (b)(6)(i) of this section.

(iii) Preferential allocations. To the extent that a foreign tax allows (whether in the current or in a different taxable year) a deduction from its taxable base for an allocation (or distribution of an allocated amount) to a partner, then solely for purposes of applying the safe harbor provisions of paragraph (b)(4)(viii)(a)(1) of this section to allocations of CFTEs that are attributable to that foreign tax, the net income in the CFTE category from which the allocation is made is reduced by the amount of the allocation, and that amount is not treated as an allocation for purposes of determining the partners' CFTE category shares of income. See Example 1 in paragraph (b)(6)(i) of this section.

(iv) Foreign law exclusions due to status of partner. If a foreign tax excludes an amount from its taxable base as a result of the status of a partner, then solely for purposes of applying the safe harbor provisions of paragraph (b)(4)(viii)(a)(1) of this section to allocations of CFTEs that are attributable to that foreign tax, the net income in the relevant CFTE category is reduced by the excluded amounts that are allocable to such partners. See Example 27 in paragraph (b)(5)(xxvii) of this section.

(v) Adjustments related to section 901(m). If one or more assets owned by a partnership are relevant foreign assets (or RFAs) with respect to a foreign income tax, then, solely for purposes of applying the safe harbor provisions of paragraph (b)(4)(viii)(a)(1) of this section to allocations of CFTEs with respect to that foreign income tax, the net income in a CFTE category that includes partnership items of income, deduction, gain, or loss attributable to the RFA shall be increased by the amount described in paragraph (b)(4)(viii)(c)(4)(vi) of this section and reduced by the amount described in paragraph (b)(4)(viii)(c)(4)(vii) of this section. Similarly, a partner's CFTE category share of income shall be increased by the portion of the amount described in paragraph (b)(4)(viii)(c)(4)(vi) of this section that is allocated to the partner under § 1.901(m)–5(d) and reduced by the portion of the amount described in paragraph (b)(4)(viii)(c)(4)(vii) of this section that is allocated to the partner under § 1.901(m)–5(d). The principles of this paragraph (b)(4)(viii)(c)(4)(v) apply similarly when a partnership owns an RFA indirectly through one or more other partnerships. For purposes of this paragraph (b)(4)(viii)(c)(4)(v) and paragraphs (b)(4)(viii)(c)(4)(vi) and (b)(4)(viii)(c)(4)(vii) of this section, basis difference is defined in § 1.901(m)–4, cost recovery amount is defined in § 1.901(m)–5(b)(2), disposition amount is defined in § 1.901(m)–5(c)(2), foreign income tax is defined in § 1.901(m)–1(a)(26), RFA is defined in § 1.901(m)–2(c), U.S. disposition gain is defined in § 1.901(m)–1(a)(52), and U.S. disposition loss is defined in § 1.901(m)–1(a)(53).

(vi) Adjustment amounts for RFAs with a positive basis difference. With respect to RFAs with a positive basis difference, the amount referenced in paragraph (b)(4)(viii)(c)(4)(v) of this section is the sum of any cost recovery amounts and disposition amounts attributable to U.S. disposition loss that correspond to partnership items that are included in the net income in the CFTE category and that are taken into account for the U.S. taxable year of the partnership under § 1.901(m)–5(d).

(vii) Adjustment amounts for RFAs with a negative basis difference. With respect to RFAs with a negative basis difference, the amount referenced in paragraph (b)(4)(viii)(c)(4)(v) of this section is the sum of any cost recovery amounts and disposition amounts attributable to U.S. disposition gain that correspond to partnership items that are included in the net income in the CFTE category and that are taken into account for the U.S. taxable year of the partnership under § 1.901(m)–5(d).

(5) No net income in a CFTE category. If a CFTE is allocated or apportioned to a CFTE category that does not have net income for the year in which the foreign tax is paid or accrued, the CFTE shall be deemed to relate to the aggregate of the net income (disregarding net losses) recognized by the partnership in that CFTE category in each of the three preceding taxable years. Accordingly, except as provided below, such CFTE must be allocated in the current taxable year in the same proportion as the allocation of the aggregate net income for the prior three-year period in order to satisfy the requirements of paragraph (b)(4)(viii)(a)(1) of this section. If the partnership does not have net income in the applicable CFTE category in either the current year or any of the previous three taxable years, the CFTE must be allocated in the same proportion that the partnership reasonably expects to allocate the aggregate net income (disregarding net losses) in the CFTE category for the succeeding three taxable years. If the partnership does not reasonably expect to have net income in the CFTE category for the succeeding three years and the partnership has net income in one or more other CFTE categories for the year in which the foreign tax is paid or accrued, the CFTE shall be deemed to relate to such other net income and must be allocated in proportion to the allocations of such other net income. If any CFTE is not allocated pursuant to the above provisions of this paragraph then the CFTE must be allocated in proportion to the partners' outstanding capital contributions.

(d) Allocation and apportionment of CFTEs to CFTE categories—(1) In general. CFTEs are allocated and apportioned to CFTE categories in accordance with § 1.861–20 by treating each CFTE category as a statutory grouping (with no residual grouping). See paragraphs (b)(6)(ii) and (iii) of this section (Examples 2 and 3), which illustrate the application of this paragraph (b)(4)(viii)(d)(1) in the case of serial disregarded payments subject to withholding tax. In addition, if as described in § 1.861–20(e), foreign law does not provide for the direct allocation or apportionment of expenses, losses or other deductions allowed under foreign law to a CFTE category of income, then such expenses, losses or other deductions must be allocated and apportioned to gross income as determined under foreign law in a manner that is consistent with the allocation and apportionment of such items for purposes of determining the net income in the CFTE categories for Federal income tax purposes pursuant to paragraph (b)(4)(viii)(c)(3) of this section.

(2) Timing and base differences. A foreign tax imposed on an item that would be income under U.S. tax principles in another year (a timing difference) is allocated to the CFTE category that would include the income if the income were recognized for U.S. tax purposes in the year in which the foreign tax is imposed. A foreign tax imposed on an item that would not constitute income under U.S. tax principles in any year (a base difference) is allocated to the CFTE category that includes the partnership items attributable to the activity with respect to which the foreign tax is imposed. See paragraph (b)(5) Example 23 of this section.

(3) Special rules for inter-branch payments. For rules relating to foreign tax paid or accrued in partnership taxable years beginning before January 1, 2012, in respect of certain inter-branch payments, see 26 CFR 1.704–1(b)(4)(viii)(d)(3) (revised as of April 1, 2011).

* * *

[T.D. 6500, 25 FR 11814, Nov. 26, 1960, as amended by T.D. 6771, 29 FR 15571, Nov. 20, 1964; T.D. 8065, 50 FR 53423, Dec. 31, 1985; 51 FR 10826, March 31, 1986; T.D. 8099, 51 FR

32062, 32068–32070, Sept. 9, 1986; 52 FR 10223, March 31, 1987; T.D. 8237, 53 FR 53173, Dec. 30, 1988; T.D. 8385, 56 FR 66983, Dec. 27, 1991; 57 FR 11430, April 3, 1992; T.D. 8500, 58 FR 67679, Dec. 22, 1993; T.D. 8585, 59 FR 66728, Dec. 28, 1994; T.D. 8717, 62 FR 25499, May 9, 1997; 64 FR 67763, Dec. 3, 1999; T.D. 9121, 69 FR 21407, April 21, 2004; T.D. 9126, 69 FR 25316, May 6, 2004; T.D. 9207, 70 FR 30341, May 26, 2005; T.D. 9292, 71 FR 61656, Oct. 19, 2006; 71 FR 70877, Dec. 7, 2006; T.D. 9398, 73 FR 28702, May 19, 2008; 73 FR 33301, June 12, 2008; T.D. 9577, 77 FR 8134, Feb. 14, 2012; T.D. 9607, 77 FR 76382, Dec. 28, 2012; T.D. 9612, 78 FR 8006, Feb. 5, 2013; 78 FR 17868, March 25, 2013; 78 FR 19100, March 29, 2013; 78 FR 35559, June 13, 2013; T.D. 9710, 80 FR 7326, Feb. 10, 2015; T.D. 9748, 81 FR 5911, Feb. 4, 2016; T.D. 9814, 82 FR 7597, Jan. 19, 2017; T.D. 9871, 84 FR 35540, July 24, 2019; T.D. 9874, 84 FR 50149, Sept. 24, 2019; T.D. 9877, 84 FR 54021, Oct. 9, 2019; T.D. 9891, 85 FR 3838, Jan. 23, 2020; T.D. 9895, 85 FR 16248, March 23, 2020; T.D. 9905, 85 FR 56842, Sept. 14, 2020; T.D. 9922, 85 FR 72033, Nov. 12, 2020]

Contribution to a Partnership

§ 1.721(c)–2 Recognition of gain on certain contributions of property to partnerships with related foreign partners.

* * *

(b) General rule for contributions of section 721(c) property. Except as provided in this paragraph (b), paragraph (c) of this section, and § 1.721(c)–3 (describing the gain deferral method), nonrecognition under section 721(a) will not apply to gain realized by the contributing partner upon a contribution of section 721(c) property to a section 721(c) partnership. This paragraph (b) does not apply to a direct contribution by a U.S. transferor if the U.S. transferor and related persons with respect to the U.S. transferor do not own 80 percent or more of the interests in partnership capital, profits, deductions, or losses.

* * *

[T.D. 9891, 85 FR 3841, Jan. 23, 2020]

§ 1.721(c)–3 Gain deferral method.

* * *

(b) Requirements of the gain deferral method. A contribution of section 721(c) property to a section 721(c) partnership that would be subject to § 1.721(c)–2(b) will not be subject to § 1.721(c)–2(b) if the conditions in paragraphs (b)(1) through (5) of this section are satisfied with respect to that property.

(1) Either—

(i) Both—

(A) The section 721(c) partnership adopts the remedial allocation method described in § 1.704–3(d) with respect to the section 721(c) property; and

(B) The section 721(c) partnership applies the consistent allocation method provided in paragraph (c) of this section; or

(ii) For the period beginning on the date of the contribution of the section 721(c) property and ending on the date on which there is no remaining built-in gain with respect to that property, all distributive shares of income and gain with respect to the section 721(c) property for all direct and indirect partners that are related foreign persons with respect to the U.S. transferor will be subject to taxation as income effectively connected with a trade or business within the United States (under either section 871 or 882), and neither the section 721(c) partnership nor a related foreign person that is a direct or indirect partner in the section 721(c) partnership claims benefits under an income tax convention that would exempt the income or gain from tax or reduce the rate of taxation to which the income or gain is subject.

(2) Upon an acceleration event, the U.S. transferor recognizes an amount of gain equal to the remaining built-in gain with respect to the section

721(c) property or an amount of gain required to be recognized under § 1.721(c)–5(d) or (e), as applicable.

(3) The procedural and reporting requirements provided in § 1.721(c)–6(b) are satisfied.

(4) The U.S. transferor consents to extend the period of limitations on assessment of tax as required by § 1.721(c)–6(b)(5).

(5) If the section 721(c) property is a partnership interest or property described in the partnership look-through rule provided in § 1.721(c)–2(d), the applicable tiered-partnership rules provided in paragraph (d) of this section are applied.

* * *

[T.D. 9891, 85 FR 3842, Jan. 23, 2020]

§ 1.721(c)–4 Acceleration events.

* * *

(b) Definition of an acceleration event—(1) General rules. Except as provided in this paragraph (b) and § 1.721(c)–5 (acceleration event exceptions), an acceleration event with respect to section 721(c) property is any event that either would reduce the amount of remaining built-in gain that a U.S. transferor would recognize under the gain deferral method if the event had not occurred or could defer the recognition of the remaining built-in gain. An acceleration event includes a contribution of section 721(c) property to another partnership by a section 721(c) partnership and a contribution of an interest in a section 721(c) partnership to another partnership. This paragraph (b) applies on a property-by-property basis.

(2) Failure to comply with a requirement of the gain deferral method—

(i) General rule. An acceleration event with respect to section 721(c) property occurs when any party fails to comply with a condition of the gain deferral method with respect to the section 721(c) property.

(ii) Certain failures to comply with procedural and reporting requirements. Notwithstanding paragraph (b)(2)(i) of this section, an acceleration event will not occur solely as a result of a failure to comply with a requirement of § 1.721(c)–3(b)(3) that is not willful. See §§ 1.721(c)–6(f) and 1.6038B–2(h)(3).

(3) Lower-tier partnership allocations. Notwithstanding paragraph (b)(1) of this section, an acceleration event will not occur because of a reduction in remaining built-in gain in an interest in a partnership that is section 721(c) property that occurs as a result of allocations of book items of deduction and loss, or tax items of income and gain.

(4) Deemed acceleration event. A U.S. transferor may treat an acceleration event as having occurred with respect to section 721(c) property by both recognizing gain in an amount equal to the remaining built-in gain that would have been allocated to the U.S. transferor if the section 721(c) partnership had sold the section 721(c) property immediately before the deemed acceleration event for fair market value and satisfying the reporting required by § 1.721(c)–6(b)(3)(i)(D). In this case, see paragraph (c) of this section regarding basis adjustments.

* * *

[T.D. 9891, 85 FR 3844, Jan. 23, 2020]

§ 1.721(c)–5 Acceleration event exceptions.

* * *

(b) Termination events—(1) In general. Notwithstanding § 1.721(c)–4(b)(1), a termination event with respect to section 721(c) property will not constitute an acceleration event. In these cases, the section 721(c) property will no longer be subject to the gain deferral method.

(2) Transfers of section 721(c) property (other than a partnership interest) to a domestic corporation described in section 351. A termination event occurs if a section 721(c) partnership transfers section 721(c) property (other than an interest in a partnership) to a domestic corporation in a transaction to which section 351 applies.

(3) Certain incorporations of a section 721(c) partnership. A termination event occurs upon an incorporation of a section 721(c) partnership into a domestic corporation by any method of incorporation (other than a method involving an actual distribution of partnership property to the partners, followed by a contribution of that property to a corporation), provided that the section 721(c) partnership is liquidated as part of the incorporation transaction.

(4) Certain distributions of section 721(c) property. A termination event occurs if a section 721(c) partnership distributes section 721(c) property either to the U.S. transferor or, if the U.S. transferor is a member of a consolidated group (as defined in § 1.1502–1(h)) at the time of the distribution and the distribution occurs outside the seven-year period described in section 704(c)(1)(B), to a member of the consolidated group.

(5) Partnership ceases to have a partner that is a related foreign person. A termination event occurs when a section 721(c) partnership ceases to have any direct or indirect partners that are related foreign persons with respect to the U.S. transferor, provided there is no plan for a related foreign person to subsequently become a direct or indirect partner in the partnership (or a successor). This paragraph (b)(5) does not apply to a distribution of section 721(c) property in redemption of a related foreign person's interest in a section 721(c) partnership.

(6) Fully taxable dispositions of section 721(c) property. A termination event occurs if a section 721(c) partnership disposes of section 721(c) property in a transaction in which all gain or loss, if any, is recognized.

(7) Fully taxable dispositions of an entire interest in a section 721(c) partnership. A termination event occurs if a U.S. transferor or a partnership in which a U.S. transferor is a direct or indirect partner disposes of its entire interest in a section 721(c) partnership that owns the section 721(c) property in a transaction in which all gain or loss, if any, is recognized. This paragraph (b)(7) does not apply if a U.S. transferor is a member of a consolidated group (as defined in § 1.1502–1(h)) and the interest in the section 721(c) partnership is transferred in an intercompany transaction (as defined in § 1.1502–13(b)(1)); see paragraph (c)(3) of this section for a successor event rule applicable to these intercompany transactions.

* * *

(d) Partial acceleration events—(1) In general. * * *

* * *

(3) Certain distributions of other partnership property to a partner that result in an adjustment under section 734. A partial acceleration event occurs with respect to section 721(c) property if there is a distribution of other property by the section 721(c) partnership that results in a positive basis adjustment to the section 721(c) property under section 734. In these cases, the U.S. transferor must recognize an amount of gain (but not in excess of the remaining built-in gain) equal to the positive basis adjustment to the section 721(c) property under section 734, reduced (but not below zero) by the amount of gain recognized by the U.S. transferor (or a member of its consolidated group (as defined in § 1.1502–1(h))) under section 731(a). In these cases, the partnership will not increase its basis under § 1.721(c)–4(c)(2) by the amount of gain recognized by the U.S. transferor.

* * *

[T.D. 9891, 85 FR 3844, Jan. 23, 2020]

Tax Based on Income from Sources Within or Without the United States

§ 1.861–1 Income from sources within the United States.

(a) Categories of income. Part I (section 861 and following), subchapter N, chapter 1 of the Code, and the regulations thereunder determine the sources of income for purposes of the income tax. These sections explicitly allocate certain important sources of income to the United States or to areas outside the United States, as the case may be; and, with respect to the remaining income (particularly that derived partly from sources within and partly from sources without the United States), authorize the Secretary or his delegate to determine the income derived from sources within the United States, either by rules of separate allocation or by processes or formulas of general apportionment. The statute provides for the following three categories of income:

(1) Within the United States. The gross income from sources within the United States, consisting of the items of gross income specified in section 861(a) plus the items of gross income allocated or apportioned to such sources in accordance with section 863(a). See §§ 1.861–2 to 1.861–7, inclusive, and § 1.863–1. The taxable income from sources within the United States, in the case of such income, shall be determined by deducting therefrom, in accordance with sections 861(b) and 863(a), the expenses, losses, and other deductions properly apportioned or allocated thereto and a ratable part of any other expenses, losses, or deductions which cannot definitely be allocated to some item or class of gross income. See §§ 1.861–8 and 1.863–1.

(2) Without the United States. The gross income from sources without the United States, consisting of the items of gross income specified in section 862(a) plus the items of gross income allocated or apportioned to such sources in accordance with section 863(a). See §§ 1.862–1 and 1.863–1. The taxable income from sources without the United States, in the case of such income, shall be determined by deducting therefrom, in accordance with sections 862(b) and 863(a), the expenses, losses, and other deductions properly apportioned or allocated thereto and a ratable part of any other expenses, losses, or deductions which cannot definitely be allocated to some item or class of gross income. See §§ 1.862–1 and 1.863–1.

(3) Partly within and partly without the United States. The gross income derived from sources partly within and partly without the United States, consisting of the items specified in section 863(b)(1), (2), and (3). The taxable income allocated or apportioned to sources within the United States, in the case of such income, shall be determined in accordance with section 863(a) or (b). See §§ 1.863–2 to 1.863–5, inclusive.

* * *

(b) Taxable income from sources within the United States. The taxable income from sources within the United States shall consist of the taxable income described in paragraph (a)(1) of this section plus the taxable income allocated or apportioned to such sources, as indicated in paragraph (a)(3) of this section.

(c) Computation of income. If a taxpayer has gross income from sources within or without the United States, together with gross income derived partly from sources within and partly from sources without the United States, the amounts thereof, together with the expenses and investment applicable thereto, shall be segregated; and the taxable income from sources within the United States shall be separately computed therefrom.

[T.D. 6500, 25 FR 11910, Nov. 26, 1960, as amended by T.D. 7635, 44 FR 46457, Aug. 8, 1979; T.D. 7928, 48 FR 55845, Dec. 16, 1983]

§ 1.861–2 Interest.

(a) In general. (1) Gross income consisting of interest from the United States or any agency or instrumentality thereof (other than a possession of the United States or an agency or instrumentality of a possession), a State or any political subdivision thereof, or the District of Columbia, and interest from a resident of the United States on a bond, note, or other interest-bearing obligation issued, assumed or incurred by such person shall be treated as income from sources within the United States. Thus, for example, income from sources within the United States includes interest received on any refund of income tax imposed by the United States, a State or any political subdivision thereof, or the District of Columbia. Interest other than that described in this paragraph is not to be treated as income from sources within the United States. See paragraph (a)(7) of this section for special rules concerning substitute interest paid or accrued pursuant to a securities lending transaction.

(2) The term "resident of the United States", as used in this paragraph, includes (i) an individual who at the time of payment of the interest is a resident of the United States, (ii) a domestic corporation, (iii) a domestic partnership which at any time during its taxable year is engaged in trade or business in the United States, or (iv) a foreign corporation or a foreign partnership, which at any time during its taxable year is engaged in trade or business in the United States.

(3) The method by which, or the place where, payment of the interest is made is immaterial in determining whether interest is derived from sources within the United States.

(4) For purposes of this section, the term "interest" includes all amounts treated as interest under section 483, and the regulations thereunder. It also includes original issue discount, as defined in section 1232(b)(1), whether or not the underlying bond, debenture, note, certificate, or other evidence of indebtedness is a capital asset in the hands of the taxpayer within the meaning of section 1221.

(5) If interest is paid on an obligation of a resident of the United States by a nonresident of the United States acting in the nonresident's capacity as a guarantor of the obligation of the resident, the interest will be treated as income from sources within the United States.

(6) In the case of interest received by a non-resident alien individual or foreign corporation this paragraph (a) applies whether or not the interest is effectively connected for the taxable year with the conduct of a trade or business in the United States by such individual or corporation.

(7) A substitute interest payment is a payment, made to the transferor of a security in a securities lending transaction or a sale-repurchase transaction, of an amount equivalent to an interest payment which the owner of the transferred security is entitled to receive during the term of the transaction. A securities lending transaction is a transfer of one or more securities that is described in section 1058(a) or a substantially similar transaction. A sale-repurchase transaction is an agreement under which a person transfers a security in exchange for cash and simultaneously agrees to receive substantially identical securities from the transferee in the future in exchange for cash. A substitute interest payment shall be sourced in the same manner as the interest accruing on the transferred security for purposes of this section and § 1.862–1. See also §§ 1.864–5(b)(2)(iii), 1.871–7(b)(2), 1.881–2(b)(2) and for the character of such payments and § 1.894–1(c) for the application tax treaties to these transactions.

* * *

[T.D. 6500, 25 FR 11910, Nov. 26, 1960, as amended by T.D. 6873, 31 FR 953, Jan. 25, 1966; T.D. 7314, 39 FR 18073, May 23, 1974; T.D. 7378, 40 FR 45429, Oct. 2, 1975; 40 FR 48508, Oct. 16, 1975; T.D. 8257, 54 FR 31819, Aug. 2, 1989; T.D. 8735, 62 FR 53500, Oct. 14, 1997]

§ 1.861–3 Dividends and income inclusions under sections 951, 951A, and 1293 and associated section 78 dividends.

(a) General—(1) Dividends included in gross income. Gross income from sources within the United States includes a dividend described in subparagraph (2), (3), (4), or (5) of this paragraph. For purposes of subparagraphs (2), (3), and (4) of this paragraph, the term "dividend" shall have the same meaning as set forth in section 316 and the regulations thereunder. * * * *

(2) Dividend from a domestic corporation. A dividend described in this paragraph (a)(2) is a dividend from a domestic corporation other than a corporation that has an election in effect under section 936. * * * *

* * *

(d) Source of income inclusions under sections 951, 951A, and 1293 and associated section 78 dividends. For purposes of sections 861 and 862 and §§ 1.861–1 and 1.862–1, and for purposes of applying this section, the amount included in gross income of a United States person under sections 951, 951A, and 1293 and the associated section 78 dividend for the taxable year with respect to a foreign corporation are treated as dividends received directly by the United States person from the foreign corporation that generated the inclusion. See section 904(h) and § 1.904–5(m) for rules concerning the resourcing of inclusions under sections 951, 951A, and 1293.

* * *

[T.D. 6500, 25 FR 11910, Nov. 26, 1960, as amended by T.D. 6830, 30 FR 8046, June 23, 1965; T.D. 7378, 40 FR 45432, Oct. 2, 1975; 40 FR 48508, Oct. 16, 1975; T.D. 7472, 42 FR 12179, March 3, 1977; T.D. 7591, 44 FR 5116, Jan. 25, 1979; T.D. 7854, 47 FR 51738, Nov. 17, 1982; T.D. 8735, 62 FR 53501, Oct. 14, 1997; T.D. 9194, 70 FR 18928, April 11, 2005; T.D. 9391, 73 FR 19358, April 9, 2008; T.D. 9959, 87 FR 325, Jan. 4, 2022]

§ 1.861–4 Compensation for labor or personal services.

(a) Compensation for labor or personal services performed wholly within the United States. (1) Generally, compensation for labor or personal services, including fees, commissions, fringe benefits, and similar items, performed wholly within the United States is gross income from sources within the United States. Gross income from sources within the United States includes compensation for labor or personal services performed in the United States irrespective of the residence of the payer, the place in which the contract for service was made, or the place or time of payment; * * *

(b) Compensation for labor or personal services performed partly within and partly without the United States—(1) Compensation for labor or personal services performed by persons other than individuals—(i) In general. In the case of compensation for labor or personal services performed partly within and partly without the United States by a person other than an individual, the part of that compensation that is attributable to the labor or personal services performed within the United States, and that is therefore included in gross income as income from sources within the United States, is determined on the basis that most correctly reflects the proper source of the income under the facts and circumstances of the particular case. In many cases, the facts and circumstances will be such that an apportionment on the time basis, as defined in paragraph (b)(2)(ii)(E) of this section, will be acceptable.

* * *

(2) Compensation for labor or personal services performed by an individual—(i) In general. Except as provided in paragraph (b)(2)(ii) of this section, in the case of compensation for labor or personal services performed partly within and partly without the United States by an individual, the part of such compensation that is attributable to the labor or personal services performed within the United States, and that is therefore included in gross income as income from sources within the United States, is determined on the basis that most correctly reflects the proper source of that income under the facts and circumstances of the particular case. In many cases, the facts and circumstances will be such that an apportionment on a time basis, as defined in paragraph (b)(2)(ii)(E) of this section, will be acceptable.

(ii) Employee compensation—(A) In general. Except as provided in paragraph (b)(2)(ii)(B) or (C) of this section, in the case of compensation for labor or personal services performed partly within and partly without the United States by an individual as an employee, the part of such compensation that is attributable to the labor or personal services performed within the United States, and that is therefore included in gross income as income from sources within the United States, is determined on a time basis, as defined in paragraph (b)(2)(ii)(E) of this section.

(B) Certain fringe benefits sourced on a geographical basis. Except as provided in paragraph (b)(2)(ii)(C) of this section, items of compensation of an individual as an employee for labor or personal services performed partly within and partly without the United States that are described in paragraphs (b)(2)(ii)(D)(1) through (6) of this section are sourced on a geographical basis in accordance with those paragraphs.

(C) Exceptions and special rules—(1) Alternative basis—(i) Individual as an employee generally. An individual may determine the source of his or her compensation as an employee for labor or personal services performed partly within and partly without the United States under an alternative basis if the individual establishes to the satisfaction of the Commissioner that, under the facts and circumstances of the particular case, the alternative basis more properly determines the source of the compensation than a basis described in paragraph (b)(2)(ii)(A) or (B), whichever is applicable, of this section. An individual that uses an alternative basis must retain in his or her records documentation setting forth why the alternative basis more properly determines the source of the compensation. In addition, the individual must provide the information related to the alternative basis required by applicable Federal tax forms and accompanying instructions.

(ii) Determination by Commissioner. The Commissioner may, under the facts and circumstances of the particular case, determine the source of compensation that is received by an individual as an employee for labor or personal services performed partly within and partly without the United States under an alternative basis other than a basis described in paragraph (b)(2)(ii)(A) or (B) of this section if such compensation either is not for a specific time period or constitutes in substance a fringe benefit described in paragraph (b)(2)(ii)(D) of this section notwithstanding a failure to meet any requirement of paragraph (b)(2)(ii)(D) of this section. The Commissioner may make this determination only if such alternative basis determines the source of compensation in a more reasonable manner than the basis used by the individual pursuant to paragraph (b)(2)(ii)(A) or (B) of this section.

(2) Ruling or other administrative pronouncement with respect to groups of taxpayers. The Commissioner may, by ruling or other administrative pronouncement applying to similarly situated taxpayers generally, permit individuals to determine the source of their compensation as an employee for labor or personal services performed partly within and partly without the United States under an alternative basis. Any such individual shall be treated as having met the requirement to establish such alternative basis to the satisfaction of the Commissioner under the facts and circumstances of the particular case, provided that the individual meets the other requirements of paragraph (b)(2)(ii)(C)(1)(i) of this section. The Commissioner also may, by ruling or other administrative pronouncement, indicate the circumstances in which he will require individuals to determine the source of certain compensation as an employee for labor or personal services performed partly within and partly without the United States under an alternative basis pursuant to the authority under paragraph (b)(2)(ii)(C)(1)(ii) of this section.

(3) Artists and athletes. [Reserved]

(D) Fringe benefits sourced on a geographical basis. Except as provided in paragraph (b)(2)(ii)(C) of this section, compensation of an individual as an employee for labor or personal services performed partly within and partly without the United States in the form of the following fringe benefits is sourced on a geographical basis as indicated in this paragraph (b)(2)(ii)(D). The amount of the compensation in the form of the fringe benefit must be reasonable, and the individual must substantiate such amounts by adequate records or by sufficient evidence under rules similar to those set forth in § 1.274–5T(c) or (h) or § 1.132–5. For purposes of this paragraph (b)(2)(ii)(D), the term principal place of work has the same meaning that it has for purposes of section 217 and § 1.217–2(c)(3).

(1) Housing fringe benefit. The source of compensation in the form of a housing fringe benefit is determined based on the location of the individual's principal place of work. For purposes of this paragraph (b)(2)(ii)(D)(1), a housing fringe benefit includes payments to or on behalf of an individual (and the individual's family if the family resides with the individual) only for rent, utilities (other than telephone charges), real and personal property insurance, occupancy taxes not deductible under section 164 or 216(a), nonrefundable fees paid for securing a leasehold, rental of furniture and accessories, household repairs, residential parking, and the fair rental value of housing provided in kind by the individual's employer. A housing fringe benefit does not include payments for expenses or items set forth in § 1.911–4(b)(2).

(2) Education fringe benefit. The source of compensation in the form of an education fringe benefit for the education expenses of the individual's dependents is determined based on the location of the individual's principal place of work. For purposes of this paragraph (b)(2)(ii)(D)(2), an education fringe benefit includes payments only for qualified tuition and expenses of the type described in section 530(b)(4)(A)(i) (regardless of whether incurred in connection with enrollment or attendance at a school) and expenditures for room and board and uniforms as described in section 530(b)(4)(A)(ii) with respect to education at an elementary or secondary educational institution.

(3) Local transportation fringe benefit. The source of compensation in the form of a local transportation fringe benefit is determined based on the location of the individual's principal place of work. For purposes of this paragraph (b)(2)(ii)(D)(3), an individual's local transportation fringe benefit is the amount that the individual receives as compensation for local transportation of the individual or the individual's spouse or dependents at the location of the individual's principal place of work. The amount treated as a local transportation fringe benefit is limited to the actual expenses incurred for local transportation and the fair rental value of any vehicle provided by the employer and used predominantly by the individual or the individual's spouse or dependents for local transportation. For this purpose, actual expenses incurred for local transportation do not include the cost (including interest) of the purchase by the individual, or on behalf of the individual, of an automobile or other vehicle.

(4) Tax reimbursement fringe benefit. The source of compensation in the form of a foreign tax reimbursement fringe benefit is determined based on the location of the jurisdiction that imposed the tax for which the individual is reimbursed.

(5) Hazardous or hardship duty pay fringe benefit. The source of compensation in the form of a hazardous or hardship duty pay fringe benefit is determined based on the location of the hazardous or hardship duty zone for which the hazardous or hardship duty pay fringe benefit is paid. For purposes of this paragraph (b)(2)(ii)(D)(5), a hazardous or hardship duty zone is any place in a foreign country which is either designated by the Secretary of State as a place where living conditions are extraordinarily difficult, notably unhealthy, or where excessive physical hardships exist, and for which a post differential of 15 percent or more would be provided under section 5925(b) of Title 5 of the U.S. Code to any officer or employee of the U.S. Government present at that place, or where a civil insurrection, civil war, terrorism, or wartime conditions threatens physical harm or imminent danger to the health and well-being of the individual. Compensation provided an employee during the period that the employee performs labor or personal services in a hazardous or hardship duty zone may be treated as a hazardous or hardship duty pay fringe benefit only if the employer provides the hazardous or hardship duty pay fringe benefit only to employees performing labor or personal services in a hazardous or hardship duty zone. The amount of compensation treated as a hazardous or hardship duty pay fringe benefit may not exceed the maximum amount that the U.S. government would allow its officers or employees present at that location.

(6) Moving expense reimbursement fringe benefit. Except as otherwise provided in this paragraph (b)(2)(ii)(D)(6), the source of compensation in the form of a moving expense reimbursement is determined based on the location of the employee's new principal place of work. The source of such compensation is determined based on the location of the employee's former principal place of work, however, if the individual provides sufficient evidence that such determination of source is more appropriate under the facts and circumstances of the particular case. For purposes of this paragraph (b)(2)(ii)(D)(6), sufficient evidence generally requires an agreement, between the employer and the employee, or a written statement of company policy, which is reduced to writing before the move and which is entered into or established to induce the employee or employees to move to another country. Such written statement or agreement must state that the employer will reimburse the employee for moving expenses that the employee incurs to return to the employee's former principal place of work regardless of whether he or she continues to work for the employer after returning to that location. The writing may contain certain conditions upon which the right to reimbursement is determined as long as those conditions set forth standards that are definitely ascertainable and can only be fulfilled prior to, or through completion of, the employee's return move to the employee's former principal place of work.

(E) Time basis. The amount of compensation for labor or personal services performed within the United States determined on a time basis is the amount that bears the same relation to the individual's total compensation as the number of days of performance of the labor or personal services by the individual within the United States bears to his or her total number of days of performance of labor or personal services. A unit of time less than a day may be appropriate for purposes of this calculation. The time period for which the compensation for labor or personal services is made is presumed to be the calendar year in which the labor or personal services are performed, unless the taxpayer establishes to the satisfaction of the Commissioner, or the Commissioner determines, that another distinct, separate, and continuous period of time is more appropriate. For example, a transfer during a year from a position in the United States to a foreign posting that lasted through the end of that year would generally establish two separate time periods within that taxable year. The first of these time periods would be the portion of the year preceding the start of the foreign posting, and the second of these time periods would be the portion of the year following the start of the foreign posting. However, in the case of a foreign posting that requires short-term returns to the United States to perform services for the employer, such short-term returns would not be sufficient to establish distinct, separate, and continuous time periods within the foreign posting time period but would be relevant to the allocation of compensation relating to the overall time period. In each case, the source of the compensation on a time basis is based upon the number of days (or unit of time less than a day, if appropriate) in that separate time period.

* * *

[T.D. 6500, 25 FR 11910, Nov. 26, 1960; 25 FR 14021, Dec. 31, 1960, as amended by T.D. 7378, 40 FR 45433, Oct. 2, 1975; 40 FR 48508, Oct. 16, 1975; T.D. 9212, 70 FR 40665, July 14, 2005]

§ 1.861–7 Sale of personal property.

(a) General. Gains, profits, and income derived from the purchase and sale of personal property shall be treated as derived entirely from the country in which the property is sold. Thus, gross income from sources within the United States includes gains, profits, and income derived from the purchase of personal property without the United States and its sale within the United States.

* * *

(c) Country in which sold. For purposes of part I (section 861 and following), subchapter N, chapter 1 of the Code, and the regulations thereunder, a sale of personal property is consummated at the time when, and the place where, the rights, title, and interest of the seller in the property are transferred to the buyer. Where bare legal title is retained by the seller, the sale shall be deemed to have occurred at the time and place of passage to the buyer of beneficial ownership and the risk of loss. However, in any case in which the sales transaction is arranged in a particular manner for the primary purpose of tax avoidance, the foregoing rules will not be applied. In such cases, all factors of the transaction, such as negotiations, the execution of the agreement, the location of the property, and the place of payment, will be considered, and the sale will be treated as having been consummated at the place where the substance of the sale occurred. For determining the place of sale of copyrighted articles transferred through an electronic medium, see § 1.861–18(f)(2)(ii).

(d) Production and sale. For provisions respecting the source of income derived from the sale of personal property produced by the taxpayer, see section 863(b)(2) and paragraphs (b) of §§ 1.863–1 and 1.863–2.

* * *

[T.D. 6500, 25 FR 11910, Nov. 26, 1960; T.D. 10022, 90 FR 2988, Jan. 14, 2025]

§ 1.861–8 Computation of taxable income from sources within the United States and from other sources and activities.

(a) In general—(1) Scope. Sections 861(b) and 863(a) state in general terms how to determine taxable income of a taxpayer from sources within the United States after gross income from sources within the United States has been determined. Sections 862(b) and 863(a) state in general terms how to determine taxable income of a taxpayer from sources without the United States after gross income from sources without the United States has been determined. This section provides specific guidance for applying the cited Code sections by prescribing rules for the allocation and apportionment of expenses, losses, and other deductions (referred to collectively in this section as “deductions”) of the taxpayer. The rules contained in this section apply in determining taxable income of the taxpayer from specific sources and activities under other sections of the Code, referred to in this section as operative sections. * * *

(2) Allocation and apportionment of deductions in general. A taxpayer to which this section applies is required to allocate deductions to a class of gross income and, then, if necessary to make the determination required by the operative section of the Code, to apportion deductions within the class of gross income between the statutory grouping of gross income (or among the statutory groupings) and the residual grouping of gross income. Except for deductions, if any, which are not definitely related to gross income (see paragraphs (c)

(3) and (e)(9) of this section) and which, therefore, are ratably apportioned to all gross income, all deductions of the taxpayer (except the deductions for personal exemptions enumerated in paragraph (e)(11) of this section) must be so allocated and apportioned. As further detailed below, allocations and apportionments are made on the basis of the factual relationship of deductions to gross income.

(3) Class of gross income. For purposes of this section, the gross income to which a specific deduction is definitely related is referred to as a "class of gross income" and may consist of one or more items (or subdivisions of these items) of gross income enumerated in section 61, namely:

(i) Compensation for services, including fees, commissions, and similar items;

(ii) Gross income derived from business;

(iii) Gains derived from dealings in property;

(iv) Interest;

(v) Rents;

(vi) Royalties;

(vii) Dividends;

(viii) Alimony and separate maintenance payments;

(ix) Annuities;

(x) Income from life insurance and endowment contracts;

(xi) Pensions;

(xii) Income from discharge of indebtedness;

(xiii) Distributive share of partnership gross income;

(xiv) Income in respect of a decedent;

(xv) Income from an interest in an estate or trust.

(4) Statutory grouping of gross income and residual grouping of gross income. For purposes of this section, the term "statutory grouping of gross income" or "statutory grouping" means the gross income from a specific source or activity which must first be determined in order to arrive at "taxable income" from which specific source or activity under an operative section. (See paragraph (f)(1) of this section.) Gross income from other sources or activities is referred to as the "residual grouping of gross income" or "residual grouping."
* * *

(b) Allocation—(1) In general. For purposes of this section, the gross income to which a specific deduction is definitely related is referred to as a "class of gross income" and may consist of one or more items of gross income. The rules emphasize the factual relationship between the deduction and a class of gross income. See paragraph (d)(1) of this section which provides that in a taxable year there may be no item of gross income in a class or less gross income than deductions allocated to the class, and paragraph (d)(2) of this section which provides that a class of gross income may include excluded income. Allocation is accomplished by determining, with respect to each deduction, the class of gross income to which the deduction is definitely related and then allocating the deduction to such class of gross income (without regard to the taxpayable year in which such gross income is received or accrued or is expected to be received or accrued). The classes of gross income are not predetermined but must be determined on the basis of the deductions to be allocated. Although most deductions will be definitely related to some class of a taxpayer's total gross income, some deductions are related to all gross income. In addition, some deductions are treated as not definitely related to any gross income and are ratably apportioned to all gross income. (See paragraph (e)(9) of this section.) In allocating deductions it is not necessary to differentiate between deductions related to one item of gross income and deductions related to another item of gross income where both items of gross income are exclusively within the same statutory grouping or exclusively within the residual grouping.

(2) Relationship to activity or property. A deduction shall be considered definitely related to a class of gross income and therefore allocable to such class if it is incurred as a result of, or incident to, an activity or in connection with property from which such class of gross income is derived. Where a deduction is incurred as a result of, or incident to, an activity or in connection with property, which activity or property generates, has generated, or could reasonably have been expected to generate gross income, such deduction shall be considered definitely related to such gross income as a class whether or not there is any item of gross income in such class which is received or accrued during the taxable year and whether or not the amount of deductions exceeds the amount of the gross income in such class. See paragraph (d)(1) of this section with respect to cases in which there is an excess of deductions. In some cases, it will be found that this subparagraph can most readily be applied by determining, with respect to a deduction, the categories of gross income to which it is not related and concluding that it is definitely related to a class consisting of all other gross income.

(3) Supportive functions. Deductions which are supportive in nature (such as overhead, general and administrative, and supervisory expenses) may relate to other deductions which can more readily be allocated to gross income. In such instance, such supportive deductions may be allocated and apportioned along with the deductions to which they relate. On the other hand, it would be equally acceptable to attribute supportive deductions on some reasonable basis directly to activities or property which generate, have generated or could reasonably be expected to generate gross income. This would ordinarily be accomplished by allocating the supportive expenses to all gross income or to another broad class of gross income and apportioning the expenses in accordance with paragraph (c)(1) of this section. For this purpose, reasonable departmental overhead rates may be utilized. For examples of the application of the principles of this paragraph (b)(3) to expenses other than expenses attributable to stewardship activities, see Examples 19 through 21 of paragraph (g) of this section. See paragraph (e)(4)(ii) of this section for the allocation and apportionment of deductions attributable to stewardship expenses. However, supportive deductions that are described in § 1.861–14T(e)(3) shall be allocated and apportioned in accordance with the rules of § 1.861–14T and shall not be allocated and apportioned by reference only to the gross income of a single member of an affiliated group of corporations as defined in § 1.861–14T(d).

(4) Deductions related to a class of gross income. See paragraph (e) of this section for rules relating to the allocation and apportionment of certain specific deductions definitely related to a class of gross income. See paragraph (c)(1) of this section for rules relating to the apportionment of deductions.

(5) Deductions related to all gross income. If a deduction does not bear a definite relationship to a class of gross income constituting less than all of gross income, it shall ordinarily be treated as definitely related and allocable to all of the taxpayer's gross income except where provided to the contrary under paragraph (e) of this section. Paragraph (e)(9) of this section lists various deductions which generally are not definitely related to any gross income and are ratably apportioned to all gross income.

(c) Apportionment of deductions—(1) Deductions definitely related to a class of gross income. [Reserved] For guidance, see § 1.861–8T(c)(1).

(2) Apportionment based on assets. Certain taxpayers are required by paragraph (e)(2) of this section and § 1.861–9T to apportion interest expense on the basis of assets. A taxpayer may apportion other deductions based on the comparative value of assets that generate income within each grouping, provided that this method reflects the factual relationship between the deduction and the groupings of income and is applied in accordance with the rules of § 1.861–9T(g). In general, such apportionments must be made either on the basis of the tax book value of those assets or, except in the case of interest expense, on the basis of their fair market value. See § 1.861–9(h). Taxpayers using the fair market value method for their last taxable year beginning before January 1, 2018, must change to the tax book value method (or the alternative tax book value method) for purposes of apportioning interest expense for their first taxable year beginning after December 31, 2017. The Commissioner's approval is not required for this change. In the case of any corporate taxpayer that both uses tax book value or alternative tax book value, and owns directly or indirectly (within the meaning of § 1.861–12T(c)(2)(ii)(B)) 10 percent or more of the total combined voting power of all classes of stock entitled to vote in any other corporation (domestic or foreign) that is not a member of the affiliated group (as defined in section 864(e)(5)), the taxpayer must adjust its basis in that stock in the manner described in § 1.861–12(c)(2). For the definition of related persons formerly contained in § 1.861–8T(c)(2), see paragraph (c)(4) of this section.

(3) Deductions not definitely related to any gross income. If a deduction is not definitely related to any gross income (see paragraph (e)(9) of this section), the deduction must be apportioned ratably between the statutory grouping (or among the statutory groupings) of gross income and the residual grouping. Thus, the amount apportioned to each statutory grouping shall be equal to the same proportion of the deduction which the amount of gross income in the statutory grouping bears to the total amount of gross income. The amount apportioned to the residual grouping shall be equal to the same proportion of the deduction which the amount of the gross income in the residual grouping bears to the total amount of gross income.

* * *

(d) Excess of deductions and excluded and eliminated income.—

* * *

(2) Allocation and apportionment to exempt, excluded, or eliminated income—(i) In general. For further guidance, see § 1.861–8T(d)(2)(i).

(ii) Exempt income and exempt asset defined—(A) In general. For purposes of this section, the term exempt income means any gross income to the extent that it is exempt, excluded, or eliminated for Federal income tax purposes. The term exempt asset means any asset to the extent income from the asset is (or is treated as under paragraph (d)(2)(ii)(B) or (C) of this section) exempt, excluded, or eliminated for Federal income tax purposes.

(B) Certain stock and dividends. The term exempt income includes the portion of the dividends that are deductible under section 243(a)(1) or (2) (relating to the dividends received deduction) or section 245(a) (relating to the dividends received deduction for dividends from certain foreign corporations). Thus, for purposes of apportioning deductions using a gross income method, gross income does not include a dividend to the extent that it gives rise to a dividends-received deduction under either section 243(a)(1), section 243(a)(2), or section 245(a). In addition, for purposes of apportioning deductions using an asset method, assets do not include that portion of the value of the stock (determined in accordance with § 1.861–9(g), and, as relevant, §§ 1.861–12 and 1.861–13) equal to the portion of dividends that would be offset by a deduction under either section 243(a)(1), section 243(a)(2), or section 245(a), to the extent the stock generates, has generated, or can reasonably be expected to generate such dividends. For example, in the case of stock for which all dividends would be allowed a deduction of 50 percent under section 243(a)(1), 50 percent of the value of the stock is treated as an exempt asset. In the case of stock which generates, has generated, or can reasonably be expected to generate qualifying dividends deductible under section 243(a)(3), such stock does not constitute an exempt asset. However, such stock and the qualifying dividends thereon are eliminated from consideration in the apportionment of interest expense under the affiliated group rule set forth in § 1.861–11T(c), and in the apportionment of other expenses under the affiliated group rules set forth in § 1.861–14T.

(C) Foreign-derived intangible income and inclusions under section 951A(a)—(1) Exempt income. The term "exempt income" includes an amount of a domestic corporation's gross income included in gross foreign-derived deduction eligible income (or gross FDDEI), and also includes an amount of a domestic corporation's gross income from an inclusion under section 951A(a) and the gross up under section 78 attributable to such an inclusion, in each case equal to the amount of the deduction allowed under section 250(a) for such gross income (taking into account the reduction under section 250(a)(2)(B), if any). Therefore, for purposes of apportioning deductions using a gross income method, gross income does not include gross income included in gross FDDEI, an inclusion under section 951A(a), or the gross up under section 78 attributable to an inclusion under section 951A(a), in an amount equal to the amount of the deduction allowed under section 250(a)(1)(A), (B)(i), or (B)(ii), respectively (taking into account the reduction under section 250(a)(2)(B), if any). The term gross foreign-derived deduction eligible income, or gross FDDEI, has the meaning provided in § 1.250(b)–1(c)(16).

(2) Exempt assets—(i) Assets that produce foreign-derived intangible income. The term "exempt asset" includes the portion of a domestic corporation's assets that produce gross FDDEI equal to the amount of such assets multiplied by the fraction that equals the amount of the domestic corporation's deduction allowed under section 250(a)(1)(A) (taking into account the reduction under section 250(a)(2)(B)(i), if any) divided by its gross FDDEI. No portion of the value of stock in a foreign corporation is treated as an exempt asset by reason of this paragraph (d)(2)(ii)(C)(2)(i), including by reason of a transfer of intangible property to a foreign corporation subject to section 367(d) that gives rise to gross FDDEI.

(ii) Controlled foreign corporation stock that gives rise to inclusions under section 951A(a). The term "exempt asset" includes a portion of the value of a United States shareholder's stock in a controlled foreign corporation if the United States shareholder is a domestic corporation that is eligible for a deduction under section 250(a) with respect to income described in section 250(a)(1)(B)(i) and all or a portion of the domestic corporation's stock in the controlled foreign corporation is characterized as GILTI inclusion stock. The portion of foreign corporation stock that is treated as an exempt asset for a taxable year equals the portion of the value of such foreign corporation stock (determined in accordance with §§ 1.861–9(g), 1.861–12, and 1.861–13) that is characterized as GILTI inclusion stock multiplied by a fraction that equals the amount of the domestic corporation's deduction allowed under section 250(a)(1)(B)(i) (taking into account the reduction under section 250(a)(2)(B)(ii), if any) divided by its GILTI inclusion amount (as defined in § 1.951A–1(c)(1) or, in the case of a member of a consolidated group, § 1.1502–51(b)) for such taxable year. The portion of controlled foreign corporation stock treated as an exempt asset under this paragraph (d)(2)(ii)(C)(2)(ii) is treated as attributable to the relevant categories of GILTI inclusion stock described in each of paragraphs (d)(2)(ii)(C)(3)(i) through (v) of this section based on the relative value of the portion of the stock in each such category.

(3) GILTI inclusion stock. For purposes of paragraph (d)(2)(ii)(C)(2)(ii) of this section, the term GILTI inclusion stock means the aggregate of the portions of the value of controlled foreign corporation stock that are—

(i) Assigned to the section 951A category under § 1.861–13(a)(2);

(ii) Assigned to a particular treaty category under § 1.861–13(a)(3)(i) (relating to resourced gross tested income stock);

(iii) Assigned under § 1.861–13(a)(1) to the gross tested income statutory grouping within the foreign source passive category less the amount described in § 1.861–13(a)(5)(iii)(A);

(iv) Assigned under § 1.861–13(a)(1) to the gross tested income statutory grouping within the U.S. source general category less the amount described in § 1.861–13(a)(5)(iv)(A); and

(v) Assigned under § 1.861–13(a)(1) to the gross tested income statutory grouping within the U.S. source passive category less the amount described in § 1.861–13(a)(5)(iv)(B).

(4) Non-applicability to section 250(b). Paragraphs (d)(2)(ii)(C)(1) through (3) of this section do not apply when apportioning deductions for purposes of determining deduction eligible income or foreign-derived deduction eligible income under the operative section of section 250(b).

* * *

(e) Allocation and apportionment of certain deductions—(1) In general.

* * *

(13) Foreign-derived intangible income. The portion of the deduction that is allowed for foreign-derived intangible income under section 250(a)(1)(A) (taking into account the reduction under section 250(a)(2)(B)(i), if any) is considered definitely related and allocable to the class of gross income included in the taxpayer's foreign-derived deduction eligible income (as defined in section 250(b)(4)). If necessary, the portion of the deduction is apportioned within the class ratably between the statutory grouping (or among the statutory groupings) of gross income and the residual grouping of gross income based on the relative amounts of foreign-derived deduction eligible income in each grouping.

(14) Global intangible low-taxed income and related section 78 gross up. The portion of the deduction (taking into account the reduction under section 250(a)(2)(B)(ii), if any) that is allowed for the global intangible low-taxed income amount described in section 250(a)(1)(B)(i), and that is allowed for the section 78 gross up under section 250(a)(1)(B)(ii), is considered definitely related and allocable to the class of gross income included under section 951A(a) and section 78, respectively. If necessary (for example, because a portion of the inclusion under section 951A(a) is passive category income or U.S. source income), the portion of the deduction is apportioned within the class ratably between the statutory grouping (or among the statutory groupings) of gross income and the residual grouping of gross income based on the relative amounts of gross income in each grouping.

* * *

(f) Miscellaneous matters—(1) Operative sections. The operative sections of the Code which require the determination of taxable income of the taxpayer from specific sources or activities and which give rise to statutory groupings to which this section is applicable include the sections described below.

* * *

(ii) Separate foreign tax credit limitations. Section 904(d)(1) and other sections described in § 1.904–4(m) require that a separate foreign tax credit limitation be determined with respect to each separate category of income specified in those sections. Accordingly, the foreign source income within each separate category described in § 1.904–5(a)(4)(v) constitutes a separate statutory grouping of income. U.S. source income is treated as income in the residual grouping for purposes of determining the limitation on the foreign tax credit.

* * *

(iv) Effectively connected taxable income. Nonresident alien individuals and foreign corporations engaged in trade or business within the United States, under sections 871(b)(1) and 882(a)(1), on taxable income which is effectively connected with the conduct of a trade or business within the United States. Such taxable income is determined in most instances by initially determining, under section 864(c), the amount of gross income which is effectively connected with the conduct of a trade or business within the United States. Pursuant to sections 873 and 882(c), this section is applicable for purposes of determining the deductions from such gross income (other than the deduction for interest expense allowed to foreign corporations (see § 1.882–5)) which are to be taken into account in determining taxable income. See example 21 of paragraph (g) of this section.

(v) Foreign base company income. Section 954 defines the term "foreign base company income" with respect to controlled foreign corporations. Section 954(b)(5) provides that in determining foreign base company income the gross income shall be reduced by the deductions of the controlled foreign corporation "properly allocable to such income". This section provides rules for identifying which deductions are properly allocable to foreign base company income.

(vi) Other operative sections. The rules provided in this section also apply in determining—

* * *

(2) Application to more than one operative section. (i) Where more than one operative section applies, it may be necessary for the taxpayer to apply this section separately for each applicable operative section. In such a case, the taxpayer is required to use the same method of allocation and the same principles of apportionment for all operative sections.

* * *

(3) Special rules of section 863(b)—(i) In general. Special rules under section 863(b) provide for the application of rules of general apportionment provided in §§ 1.863–3 to 1.863–5, to worldwide taxable income in order to attribute part of such worldwide taxable income to U.S. sources and the remainder of such worldwide taxable income to foreign sources. The activities specified in section 863(b) are—

(A) Transportation or other services rendered partly within and partly without the United States,

(B) Sales of personal property produced by the taxpayer within and sold without the United States, or produced by the taxpayer without and sold within the United States, and

(C) Sales within the United States of personal property purchased within a possession of the United States.

In the instances provided in §§ 1.863–3 and 1.863–4 with respect to the activities described in (A), (B), and (C) of this subdivision, this section is applicable only in determining worldwide taxable income attributable to these activities.

(ii) Relationship of sections 861, 862, 863(a), and 863(b). Sections 861, 862, 863(a), and 863(b) are the four provisions applicable in determining taxable income from specific sources. Each of these four provisions applies independently. Where a deduction has been allocated and apportioned to income under one of these four provisions, the deduction shall not again be allocated and apportioned to gross income under any of the other three provisions. However, two or more of these provisions may have to be applied at the same time to determine the proper allocation and apportionment of a deduction. The special rules under section 863(b) take precedence over the general rules of Code sections 861, 862 and 863(a). For example, where a deduction is allocable in whole or in part to gross income to which section 863(b) applies, such deduction or part thereof shall not otherwise be allocated under section 861, 862, or 863(a). However, where the gross income to which the deduction is allocable includes both gross income to which section 863(b) applies and gross income to which section 861, 862, or 863(a) applies, more than one section must be applied at the same time in order to determine the proper allocation and apportionment of the deduction.

(4) Adjustments made under other provisions of the Code—(i) In general. If an adjustment which affects the taxpayer is made under section 482 or any other provision of the Code, it may be necessary to recompute the allocations and apportionments required by this section in order to reflect changes resulting from the adjustment. The recomputation made by the Commissioner shall be made using the same method of allocation and apportionment as was originally used by the taxpayer, provided such method as originally used conformed with paragraph (a)(2) of this section and, in light of the adjustment, such method does not result in a material distortion. In addition to adjustments which would be made aside from this section, adjustments to the taxpayer's income and deductions which would not otherwise be made may be required before applying this section in order to prevent a distortion in determining taxable income from a particular source of activity. For example, if an item included as a part of the cost of goods sold has been improperly attributed to specific sales, and, as a result, gross income under one of the operative sections referred to in paragraph (f)(1) of this section is improperly determined, it may be necessary for the Commissioner to make an adjustment to the cost of goods sold, consistent with the principles of this section, before applying this section. Similarly, if a domestic corporation transfers the stock in its foreign subsidiaries to a domestic subsidiary and the parent corporation continues to incur expenses in connection with protecting its capital investment in the foreign subsidiaries (see paragraph (e)(4) of this section), it may be necessary for the Commissioner to make an allocation under section 482 with respect to such expenses before making allocations and apportionments required by this section, even though the section 482 allocation might not otherwise be made.

* * *

(5) Verification of allocations and apportionments. Since, under this section, allocations and apportionments are made on the basis of the factual relationship between deductions and gross income, the taxpayer is required to furnish, at the request of the District Director, information from which such factual relationships can be determined. In reviewing the overall limitation to the foreign tax credit of a domestic corporation, for example, the District Director should consider information which would enable him to determine the extent to which deductions attributable to functions performed in the United States are related to earning foreign source income, United States source income, or income from both sources. In addition to functions with a specific international purpose, consideration should be given to the functions of management, the direction and results of an acquisition program, the functions of operating units and personnel located at the head office, the functions of support units (including but not limited to engineering, legal, budget, accounting, and industrial relations), the functions of selling and advertising units and personnel, the direction and uses of research and development and the direction and uses of services furnished by independent contractors. Thus, for example when requested by the District Director, the taxpayer shall make available any of its organization charts, manuals, and other writings which relate to the manner in which its gross income arises and to the functions of organizational units, employees, and assets of the taxpayer and arrange for the interview of such of its employees as the District Director deems desirable in order to determine the gross income to which deductions relate. See section 7602 and the regulations thereunder which generally provide for the examination of books and witnesses. See also section 905(b) and the regulations thereunder which require proof of foreign tax credits to the satisfaction of the Secretary or his delegate.

* * *

[T.D. 6500, 25 FR 11910, Nov. 26, 1960, as amended by T.D. 6892, 31 FR 11144, Aug. 23, 1966, T.D. 7378, 40 FR 45434, Oct. 2, 1975; T.D. 7456, 42 FR 1195, Jan. 6, 1977; T.D. 7749, 46 FR 1683, Jan. 7, 1981; T.D. 7939, 49 FR 4207, Feb. 3, 1984; T.D. 8228, 53 FR 35474, Sept. 14, 1988; T.D. 8236, 53

FR 49874, Dec. 12, 1988; T.D. 8286, 55 FR 3052, Jan. 30, 1990; T.D. 8337, 56 FR 10369, March 12, 1991; 56 FR 22760, May 16, 1991; 56 FR 24001, May 28, 1991; T.D. 8228, 60 FR 36669, July 18, 1995; T.D. 8646, 60 FR 66503, Dec. 22, 1995; T.D. 8805, 64 FR 1509, Jan. 11, 1999; T.D. 8973, 66 FR 67083, Dec. 28, 2001; T.D. 9143, 69 FR 44931, July 28, 2004; T.D. 9194, 70 FR 18928, April 11, 2005; T.D. 9211, 70 FR 40662, July 14, 2005; T.D. 9278, 71 FR 44514, Aug. 4, 2006; T.D. 9391, 73 FR 19358, April 9, 2008; T.D. 9456, 74 FR 38872, Aug. 4, 2009; 74 FR 46346, Sept. 9, 2009; 78 FR 18235, March 26, 2013; T.D. 9882, 84 FR 69058, Dec. 17, 2019; 85 FR 29323, May 15, 2020; T.D. 9901, 85 FR 43109, July 15, 2020; 85 FR 68250, Oct. 28, 2020; T.D. 9922, 85 FR 72033, Nov. 12, 2020; 86 FR 54367, Oct. 1, 2021; T.D. 9959, 87 FR 326, Jan. 4, 2022; 87 FR 45019, July 27, 2022]

§ 1.861–9 Allocation and apportionment of interest expense and rules for asset-based apportionment.

(a) In general. For further guidance, see § 1.861–9T(a).

* * *

(g) Asset method—(1) In general. (i) For further guidance, see § 1.861–9T(g)(1)(i).

(ii) A taxpayer may elect to determine the value of its assets on the basis of either the tax book value or the fair market value of its assets. However, for taxable years beginning after December 31, 2017, the fair market value method is not allowed with respect to allocations and apportionments of interest expense. See section 864(e)(2). For rules concerning the application of an alternative method of valuing assets for purposes of the tax book value method, see paragraph (i) of this section. For rules concerning the application of the fair market value method, see paragraph (h) of this section.

* * *

(i) Alternative tax book value method—(1) Alternative value for certain tangible property. A taxpayer may elect to determine the tax book value of its tangible property that is depreciated under section 168 (section 168 property) using the rules provided in this paragraph (i)(1) (the alternative tax book value method). The alternative tax book value method applies solely for purposes of apportioning expenses (including the calculation of the alternative minimum tax foreign tax credit pursuant to section 59(a)) under the asset method described in paragraph (g) of this section.

(i) The tax book value of section 168 property placed in service during or after the first taxable year to which the election to use the alternative tax book value method applies shall be determined as though such property were subject to the alternative depreciation system set forth in section 168(g) (or a successor provision) for the entire period that such property has been in service.

(ii) In the case of section 168 property placed in service prior to the first taxable year to which the election to use the alternative tax book value method applies, the tax book value of such property shall be determined under the depreciation method, convention, and recovery period provided for under section 168(g) for the first taxable year to which the election applies.

(iii) If a taxpayer revokes an election to use the alternative tax book value method (the prior election) and later makes another election to use the alternative tax book value method (the subsequent election) that is effective for a taxable year that begins within 3 years of the end of the last taxable year to which the prior election applied, the taxpayer shall determine the tax book value of its section 168 property as though the prior election has remained in effect.

(iv) The tax book value of section 168 property shall be determined without regard to the election to expense certain depreciable assets under section 179.

* * *

[T.D. 8916, 66 FR 272, Jan. 3, 2001; T.D. 9120, 69 FR 15675, March 26, 2004; T.D. 9247, 71 FR 4814, Jan. 30, 2006; T.D. 9452, 74 FR 27873, June 11, 2009; T.D. 9676, 79 FR 41425, July 16, 2014; 79 FR 49683, Aug. 22, 2014; T.D. 9882, 84 FR 69064, Dec. 17, 2019; T.D. 9922, 85 FR 72038, Nov. 12, 2020; 86 FR 54367, Oct. 1, 2021; T.D. 9959, 87 FR 326, Jan. 4, 2022; T.D. 10016, 89 FR 100164, Dec. 11, 2024]

§ 1.861–9T Allocation and apportionment of interest expense (temporary).

(a) In general. * * * The method of allocation and apportionment for interest set forth in this section is based on the approach that, in general, money is fungible and that interest expense is attributable to all activities and property regardless of any specific purpose for incurring an obligation on which interest is paid. Exceptions to the fungibility rule are set forth in § 1.861–10T. The fungibility approach recognizes that all activities and property require funds and that management has a great deal of flexibility as to the source and use of funds. When borrowing will generally free other funds for other purposes, and it is reasonable under this approach to attribute part of the cost of borrowing to such other purposes. Consistent with the principles of fungibility, except as otherwise provided, the aggregate of deductions for interest in all cases shall be considered related to all income producing activities and assets of the taxpayer and, thus, allocable to all the gross income which the assets of the taxpayer generate, have generated, or could reasonably have been expected to generate. * * *

* * *

(g) Asset method—(1) In general. (i) Under the asset method, the taxpayer apportions interest expense to the various statutory groupings based on the average total value of assets within each such grouping for the taxable year, as determined under the asset valuation rules of this paragraph (g)(1) and paragraph (g)(2) of this section and the asset characterization rules of paragraph (g)(3) of this section and § 1.861–12T. Except to the extent otherwise provided (see, e.g., paragraph (d)(1)(iv) of this section), taxpayers must apportion interest expense only on the basis of asset values and may not apportion any interest deduction on the basis of gross income.

* * *

(iii) A taxpayer electing to apportion its interest expense on the basis of the fair market value of its assets must establish the fair market value to the satisfaction of the Commissioner. If a taxpayer fails to establish the fair market value of an asset to the satisfaction of the Commissioner, the Commissioner may determine the appropriate asset value. If a taxpayer fails to establish the value of a substantial portion of its assets to the satisfaction of the Commissioner, the Commissioner may require the taxpayer to use the tax book value method of apportionment.

* * *

[T.D. 8228, 53 FR 35477, Sept. 14, 1988; T.D. 8257, 54 FR 31819, Aug. 2, 1989; T.D. 8597, 60 FR 36679, July 18, 1995; T.D. 8658, 61 FR 9329, March 8, 1996; T.D. 8916, 66 FR 273, Jan. 3, 2001; T.D. 9120, 69 FR 15675, March 26, 2004; T.D. 9247, 71 FR 4815, Jan. 30, 2006; T.D. 9260, 71 FR 24525, April 25, 2006; T.D. 9452, 74 FR 27874, June 11, 2009; T.D. 9456, 74 FR 38874, Aug. 4, 2009; T.D. 9571, 77 FR 2227, Jan. 17, 2012; 77 FR 9844, Feb. 21, 2012; T.D. 9676, 79 FR 41426, July 16, 2014; T.D. 9794, 81 FR 88819, Dec. 8, 2016; T.D. 9849, 84 FR 923, Mar. 14, 2019; T.D. 9882, 84 FR 69022, Dec. 17, 2019; T.D. 9922, 85 FR 72040, Nov. 12, 2020; T.D. 10016, 89 FR 100164, Dec. 11, 2024]

§ 1.861–10T Special allocations of interest expense (temporary regulations).

(a) In general. This section applies to all taxpayers and provides three exceptions to the rules of § 1.861–9T that require the allocation and apportionment of interest expense on the basis of all assets of all members of the affiliated group. Paragraph (b) of this section describes the direct allocation of interest expense to the income generated by certain assets that are subject to qualified nonrecourse indebtedness. Paragraph (c) of this section describes the direct allocation of interest expense to income generated by certain assets that are acquired in integrated financial transaction. Paragraph (d) of this section provides special rules that are applicable to all transactions described in paragraphs (b) and (c) of this section. Paragraph (e) of this section requires the direct allocation of third party interest of an affiliated group to such group's investment in related controlled foreign corporations in cases involving excess related person indebtedness (as defined therein). See also § 1.861–9T(b)(5), which requires direct allocation of amortizable bond premium.

(b) Qualified nonrecourse indebtedness—(1) In general. In the case of qualified nonrecourse indebtedness (as defined in paragraph (b)(2) of this section), the deduction for interest shall be considered directly allocable solely to the gross income which the property acquired, constructed, or improved with the proceeds of the indebtedness generates, has generated, or could reasonably be expected to generate.

(2) Qualified nonrecourse indebtedness defined. The term "qualified nonrecourse indebtedness" means any borrowing that is not excluded by paragraph (b)(4) of this section if:

(i) The borrowing is specifically incurred for the purpose of purchasing, constructing, or improving identified property that is either depreciable tangible personal property or real property with a useful life of more than one year or for the purpose of purchasing amortizable intangible personal property with a useful life of more than one year;

(ii) The proceeds are actually applied to purchase, construct, or improve the identified property;

(iii) Except as provided in paragraph (b)(7)(ii) (relating to certain third party guarantees in leveraged lease transactions), the creditor can look only to the identified property (or any lease or other interest therein) as security for payment of the principal and interest on the loan and, thus, cannot look to any other property, the borrower, or any third party with respect to repayment of principal or interest on the loan;

(iv) The cash flow from the property, as defined in paragraph (b)(3) of this section, is reasonably expected to be sufficient in the first year of ownership as well as in each subsequent year of ownership to fulfill the terms and conditions of the loan agreement with respect to the amount and timing of payments of interest and original issue discount and periodic payments of principal in each such year; and

(v) There are restrictions in the loan agreement on the disposal or use of the property consistent with the assumptions described in subdivisions (iii) and (iv) of this paragraph (b)(2).

* * *

[T.D. 8228, 53 FR 35485, Sept. 14, 1988; T.D. 9456, 74 FR 38875, Aug. 4, 2009; T.D. 9882, 84 FR 69022, Dec. 17, 2019]

§ 1.861–17 Allocation and apportionment of research and experimental expenditures.

(a) Scope. This section provides rules for the allocation and apportionment of research and experimental expenditures that a taxpayer deducts, or amortizes and deducts, in a taxable year under section 174 or section 59(e) (applicable to expenditures that are allowable as a deduction under section 174(a)) (R&E expenditures). R&E expenditures do not include any expenditures that are not deductible expenses by reason of the second sentence under § 1.482–7(j)(3)(i) (relating to CST Payments (as defined in § 1.482–7(b)(1)) owed to a controlled participant in a cost sharing arrangement).

(b) Allocation—(1) In general. The method of allocation and apportionment of R&E expenditures set forth in this section recognizes that research and experimentation is an inherently speculative activity, that findings may contribute unexpected benefits, and that the gross income derived from successful research and experimentation must bear the cost of unsuccessful research and experimentation. In addition, the method set forth in this section recognizes that successful R&E expenditures ultimately result in the creation of intangible property that will be used to generate income. Therefore, R&E expenditures ordinarily are considered deductions that are definitely related to gross intangible income (as defined in paragraph (b)(2) of this section) reasonably connected with the relevant SIC code category (or categories) of the taxpayer and therefore allocable to gross intangible income as a class related to the SIC code category (or categories) and apportioned under the rules in this section. For purposes of the allocation under this paragraph (b)(1), a taxpayer's SIC code category (or categories) are determined in accordance with the provisions of paragraph (b)(3) of this section. For purposes of this section, the term intangible property means intangible property (as defined in section 367(d)(4)), including intangible property either created or acquired by the taxpayer, that is derived from R&E expenditures.

(2) Definition of gross intangible income. The term gross intangible income means all gross income earned by a taxpayer that is attributable to a sale or license of intangible property (including income from platform contribution transactions described in § 1.482–7(b)(1)(ii), royalty income from the licensing of intangible property, or amounts taken into account under section 367(d) by reason of a transfer of intangible property), and the full amount of gross income from sales or leases of products or services if the income is derived directly or indirectly (in whole or in part) from intangible property. Gross intangible income also includes a distributive share of any amounts described in the previous sentence, but does not include dividends or any amounts included in income under section 951, 951A, or 1293. See § 1.904–4(f)(2)(vi) for rules addressing the assignment of gross income, including gross intangible income, to a separate category by reason of certain disregarded payments to or from a taxpayer's foreign branch.

(3) SIC code categories—(i) Allocation based on SIC code categories. Ordinarily, a taxpayer's R&E expenditures are incurred to produce gross intangible income that is reasonably connected with one or more relevant SIC code categories. Except as provided in paragraph (b)(3)(iv) of this section, where research and experimentation is conducted with respect to more than one SIC code category, the taxpayer may aggregate the categories for purposes of allocation and apportionment, provided the categories are in the same Major Group. However, the taxpayer may not subdivide any categories. Where research and experimentation is not clearly related to any SIC code category (or categories), it will be considered conducted with respect to all of the taxpayer's SIC code categories.

(ii) Use of three digit standard industrial classification codes. A taxpayer determines the relevant Major Groups and SIC code categories by reference to the two digit and three digit classification, respectively, of the Standard Industrial Classification Manual (SIC code). The SIC Manual is available at https://www.osha.gov/pls/imis/sic_manual.html.

(iii) Consistency. Once a taxpayer selects a SIC code category or Major Group for the first taxable year for which this section applies to the taxpayer, it must continue to use that category in following years unless the taxpayer establishes to the satisfaction of the Commissioner that, due to changes in the relevant facts, a change in the category is appropriate. Therefore, once a taxpayer elects a permissible aggregation of three digit SIC code categories into a two digit Major Group, it must continue to use that two digit category in following years unless the taxpayer establishes to the satisfaction of the Commissioner that, due to changes in the relevant facts, a change is appropriate.

(iv) Wholesale trade and retail trade categories. A taxpayer must use a SIC code category within the divisions of "wholesale trade" or "retail trade" if it is engaged solely in sales-related activities with respect to a particular category of products. In the case of a taxpayer that conducts material non-sales-related activities with respect to a particular category of products, all R&E expenditures related to sales of the products must be allocated and apportioned as if the expenditures were reasonably connected to the most closely related three digit SIC code category other than those within the wholesale and retail trade divisions. For example, if a taxpayer engages in both the manufacturing and assembling of cars and trucks (SIC code 371) and in a wholesaling activity related to motor vehicles and motor vehicle parts and supplies (SIC code 501), the taxpayer must allocate and apportion all R&E expenditures related to both activities as if they relate solely to the manufacturing SIC code 371. By contrast, if the taxpayer engages only in the wholesaling activity related to motor vehicles and motor vehicle parts and supplies, the taxpayer must allocate and apportion all R&E expenditures to the wholesaling SIC code 501.

(c) Exclusive apportionment. Solely for purposes of applying this section to section 904 as the operative section, an amount equal to fifty percent of a taxpayer's R&E expenditures in a SIC code category (or categories) is apportioned exclusively to the residual grouping of U.S. source gross intangible income if research and experimentation that accounts for at least fifty percent of such R&E expenditures was performed in the United States. Similarly, an amount equal to fifty percent of a taxpayer's R&E expenditures in a SIC code category (or categories) is apportioned exclusively to the statutory grouping (or groupings) of foreign source gross intangible income in that SIC code category if research and experimentation that accounts for more than fifty percent of such R&E expenditures was performed outside the United States. If there are multiple separate categories with foreign source gross intangible income in the SIC code category, the fifty percent of R&E expenditures apportioned under the previous sentence is apportioned ratably to foreign source gross intangible income based on the relative amounts of gross receipts from gross intangible income in the SIC code category in each separate category, as determined under paragraph (d) of this section. Solely for purposes of determining whether fifty percent or more of R&E expenditures in a year are performed within or without the United States under this paragraph (c), a taxpayer's R&E expenditures with respect to a taxable year are determined by taking into account only the R&E expenditures incurred in such taxable year (without regard to whether such expenditures are capitalized under section 59(e) or any other provision in the Code), and do not include amounts that were capitalized in a prior taxable year and are deducted in such taxable year.

(d) Apportionment based on gross receipts from sales of products or services—(1) In general. A taxpayer's R&E expenditures not apportioned under paragraph (c) of this section are apportioned between the statutory grouping (or among the statutory groupings) within the class of gross intangible income and the residual grouping within such class according to the rules in paragraphs (d)(1)(i) through (iv) of this section. See paragraph (b) of this section for defining the class of gross intangible income in relation to SIC code categories.

(i) A taxpayer's R&E expenditures not apportioned under paragraph (c) of this section are apportioned in the same proportions that:

(A) The amounts of the taxpayer's gross receipts from sales and leases of products (as measured by gross receipts without regard to cost of goods sold) or services that are related to gross intangible income within the statutory grouping (or statutory groupings) and in the residual grouping bear, respectively; to

(B) The total amount of such gross receipts in the class.

(ii) For purposes of this paragraph (d), gross receipts from sales and leases of products are related to gross intangible income if intangible property is embedded or used in connection with the manufacture or sale of such products, and gross income from services is related to gross intangible income if intangible property is incorporated in or directly or indirectly benefits such services. See paragraph (g)(7) of this section (Example 7). The amount of the gross receipts used to apportion R&E expenditures also includes gross receipts from sales and leases of products or services of any controlled or uncontrolled party to the extent described in paragraphs (d)(3) and (4) of this section. A royalty or other amount paid to the taxpayer for intangible property constitutes gross intangible income, but is not considered part of gross receipts arising from the sale or lease of a product or service, and so is not taken into account in apportioning the taxpayer's R&E expenditures to its gross intangible income.

(iii) The statutory grouping (or groupings) or residual grouping to which the gross receipts are assigned is the grouping to which the gross intangible income related to the sale, lease, or service is assigned. In cases where the gross intangible income of the taxpayer is income not described in paragraph (d)(3) or (4) of this section, the grouping to which the taxpayer's gross receipts and the gross intangible income are assigned is the same. In cases where the taxpayer's gross intangible income is related to sales, leases, or services described in paragraph (d)(3) or (4) of this section, the gross receipts that will be used for purposes of this paragraph (d) are the gross receipts of the controlled and uncontrolled parties that are taken into account under paragraphs (d)(3) and (4) of this section. The grouping to which the controlled or uncontrolled parties' gross receipts are assigned is determined based on the grouping of the taxpayer's gross intangible income attributable to the license, sale, or other transfer of intangible property to such controlled or uncontrolled party as described in paragraph (d)(3)(i) or (d)(4)(i) of this section, and not the grouping to which the gross receipts would be assigned if the assignment were based on the income earned by the controlled or uncontrolled party. See paragraph (g)(1) of this section (Example 1). For purposes of applying this paragraph (d)(1)(iii) to section 250 or section 904 as the operative section, the assignment of gross receipts to the general and foreign branch categories is made after taking into account the assignment of gross intangible income to those categories as adjusted by reason of disregarded payments under the rules of § 1.904–4(f)(2)(vi), and by making similar adjustments to gross receipts under the principles of § 1.904–4(f)(2)(vi).

(iv) For purposes of applying this section to section 904 as the operative section, because a United States person's gross intangible income cannot include income assigned to the section 951A category, no R&E expenditures of a United States person are apportioned to foreign source income in the section 951A category.

(2) Apportionment in excess of gross income. Amounts apportioned under this section may exceed the amount of gross income related to the SIC code category within the statutory or residual grouping. In such case, the excess is applied against other gross income within the statutory or residual grouping. See § 1.861–8(d)(1) for applicable rules where the apportionment results in an excess of deductions over gross income within the statutory or residual grouping.

(3) Sales or services of uncontrolled parties—(i) In general. For purposes of the apportionment within a class under paragraph (d)(1) of this section, if a taxpayer reasonably expects an uncontrolled party to (through a license, purchase, or transfer): Acquire intangible property that would arise from the taxpayer's current R&E expenditures; acquire products in which such intangible property is embedded or used in connection with the manufacture or sale of such products; or receive services that incorporate or directly or indirectly benefit from such intangible property, then the gross receipts of the uncontrolled party from sales, licenses, leases, or services of the particular products or services in which the taxpayer's intangible property is embedded or incorporated or which the taxpayer's intangible property directly or indirectly benefitted are taken into account. If the taxpayer has previously licensed, sold, or transferred intangible property related to a SIC code category to an uncontrolled party, the taxpayer is presumed to expect to license, sell, or transfer to that uncontrolled party all future intangible property related to the same SIC code category. The presumption described in the preceding sentence may be rebutted by the taxpayer with facts that demonstrate that the taxpayer reasonably expects not to license, sell, or transfer future intangible property to the uncontrolled party.

(ii) Definition of uncontrolled party. For purposes of this paragraph (d)(3), the term uncontrolled party means a person that is not a controlled party as defined in paragraph (d)(4)(ii) of this section.

(iii) Sales of components. In the case of a sale or lease of a product by an uncontrolled party that is derived from the taxpayer's intangible property but is incorporated as a component of a larger product (for example, where the product incorporating the intangible property is a component of a large machine), only the portion of the gross receipts from the larger product that are attributable to the component derived from the intangible property is included. For purposes of the preceding sentence, a reasonable estimate based on the principles of section 482 must be made. See paragraph (g)(4)(ii)(B)(3) of this section (Example 4).

(iv) Reasonable estimates of gross receipts. If the amount of gross receipts of an uncontrolled party is unknown, a reasonable estimate of gross receipts must be made annually. Appropriate economic analyses, based on the principles of section 482, must be used to estimate gross receipts. See paragraph (g)(5)(ii)(B)(3)(ii) of this section (Example 5).

(4) Sales or services of controlled parties—(i) In general. For purposes of the apportionment within a class under paragraph (d)(1) of this section, if the controlled party is reasonably expected to (through a license, sale, or transfer): Acquire intangible property that would arise from the taxpayer's current R&E expenditures; acquire products in which such intangible property is embedded or used in connection with the manufacture or sale of such products; or receive services that incorporate or directly or indirectly benefit from such intangible property, then the gross receipts of the controlled party from all of its sales, licenses, leases, or services are taken into account. Except to the extent provided in paragraph (d)(4)(iv) of this section, if the taxpayer has previously licensed, sold, or transferred intangible property related to a SIC code category to a controlled party, the taxpayer is presumed to expect to license, sell, or transfer to that controlled party all future intangible property related to the same SIC code category. The presumption described in the preceding sentence may be rebutted by the taxpayer with facts that demonstrate that the taxpayer will not license, sell, or transfer future intangible property to the controlled party.

(ii) Definition of a controlled party. For purposes of this paragraph (d)(4), the term controlled party means any person that has a relationship to the taxpayer specified in section 267(b) or 707(b), or is a member of a controlled group of corporations (within the meaning of section 267(f)) to which the taxpayer belongs. Because an affiliated group is treated as a single taxpayer, a member of an affiliated group is not a controlled party. See paragraph (e) of this section.

(iii) Gross receipts not to be taken into account more than once. Sales, licenses, leases, or services among the taxpayer, controlled parties, and uncontrolled parties are not taken into account more than once; in such a situation, the amount of gross receipts of the selling person must be subtracted from the gross receipts of the buying person. Therefore, the gross receipts taken into account under paragraph (d)(4)(i) of this section generally reflect the gross receipts from sales made to end users.

(iv) Effect of cost sharing arrangements. If the controlled party has entered into a cost sharing arrangement, in accordance with the provisions of § 1.482–7, with the taxpayer for the purpose of developing intangible property, then ordinarily the controlled party is not reasonably expected to acquire rights in intangible property that would arise from the taxpayer's share of the R&E expenditures with respect to the cost shared intangibles as defined in § 1.482–7(j)(1)(i); acquire products in which such intangible property is embedded or used in connection with the manufacture or sale of such products; or receive services that incorporate or directly or indirectly benefit from such intangible property. Therefore, solely for purposes of apportioning a taxpayer's R&E expenditures (which do not include the amount of CST Payments received by the taxpayer; see paragraph (a) of this section) that are intangible development costs (as defined in § 1.482–7(d)) with respect to a cost sharing arrangement, the controlled party's gross receipts are not taken into account for purposes of paragraphs (d)(1) and (d)(4)(i) of this section. However, the rule in this paragraph (d)(4)(iv) does not apply, and the controlled party's sales are taken into account, to the extent the taxpayer licenses, or has licensed, to the controlled party intangible property resulting from a cost sharing arrangement with the controlled party.

(5) Application of section 864(e)(3). Section 864(e)(3) and § 1.861–8(d)(2) do not apply for purposes of this section.

(e) Affiliated groups. See § 1.861–14(e)(2) for rules on allocating and apportioning R&E expenditures of an affiliated group (as defined in § 1.861–14(d)).

(f) Special rules for partnerships—(1) R&E expenditures. For purposes of applying this section, if R&E expenditures are incurred by a partnership in which the taxpayer is a partner, the taxpayer's R&E expenditures include the taxpayer's distributive share of the partnership's R&E expenditures.

(2) Purpose and location of expenditures. In applying exclusive apportionment under paragraph (c) of this section, a partner's distributive share of R&E expenditures incurred by a partnership is treated as incurred by the partner for the same purpose and in the same location as incurred by the partnership.

(3) Apportionment based on gross receipts. In applying the remaining apportionment under paragraph (d) of this section, if a taxpayer is a partner in a partnership that incurs R&E expenditures described in paragraph (f)(1) of this section and the taxpayer is not reasonably expected to license, sell, or transfer to the partnership (directly or indirectly) intangible property that would arise from the taxpayer's current R&E expenditures, in the manner described in paragraph (d)(3)(i) or (d)(4)(i) of this section, then the taxpayer's gross receipts in a SIC code category include only the taxpayer's share of any gross receipts in the SIC code category of the partnership. For purposes of the preceding sentence, the taxpayer's share of gross receipts is proportionate to the taxpayer's distributive share of the partnership's gross income in the product category. However, if the taxpayer is reasonably expected to license, sell, or transfer to the partnership (directly or indirectly) intangible property that would arise from the taxpayer current R&E expenditures, in the manner described in paragraph (d)(3)(i) or (d)(4)(i) of this section, then the taxpayer's gross receipts in a SIC code category include the full amount of any gross receipts in the SIC code category of the partnership as provided in paragraph (d)(3)(i) or (d)(4)(i) of this section.

* * *

[T.D. 8646, 60 FR 66503, Dec. 22, 1995; T.D. 9441, 74 FR 390, Jan. 5, 2009; T.D. 9568, 76 FR 80136, Dec. 22, 2011; T. D. 9882, 84 FR 69074, Dec. 17, 2019; 85 FR 29323, May 15, 2020; T.D. 9922, 85 FR 72042, Nov. 12, 2020; 86 FR 54367, Oct. 1, 2021]

§ 1.861–18 Classification of, and source of gross income from, digital content transactions.

(a) General—(1) Scope. This section provides rules for classifying digital content transactions (as defined in paragraph (b)(1) of this section) for purposes of subchapter N of chapter 1 of the Internal Revenue Code, sections 59A, 245A, 250, 267A, 367, 404A, 482, 679, 1059A, chapters 3 and 4, sections 842 and 845 (to the extent involving a foreign person), and transfers to foreign trusts not covered by section 679.

(2) Digital content—(i) Digital content defined. For purposes of this section, digital content means a computer program or any other content, such as books, movies, and music, in digital format that is—

(A) Protected by copyright law; or

(B) Not protected by copyright law solely—

(1) Due to the passage of time; or

(2) Because the creator dedicated the content to the public domain.

(ii) Computer program defined. For purposes of this section, a computer program is a set of statements or instructions to be used directly or indirectly in a computer in order to bring about a certain result and includes any media, user manuals, documentation, data base, or similar item if the media, user manuals, documentation, data base, or other similar item is incidental to the operation of the computer program.

(b) Categories of transactions—(1) General. A transaction that constitutes a transfer of digital content, or the provision of services or of know-how with respect to digital content (each a digital content transaction), is treated as being solely one of the following—

(i) A transfer of a copyright right in the digital content;

(ii) A transfer of a copy of the digital content (a copyrighted article);

(iii) The provision of services for the development or modification of the digital content; or

(iv) The provision of know-how relating to development of digital content.

(2) Transaction with multiple elements. Taking into account the overall transaction and the surrounding facts and circumstances, a transaction that has multiple elements, one or more of which would be a digital content transaction if considered separately, is classified in its entirety as a digital content transaction under one of the categories described in paragraph (b)(1) of this section if the predominant character of the transaction is described in one of the categories in that paragraph.

(3) Determination of predominant character—(i) General rule. For purposes of paragraph (b)(2) of this section and § 1.861–19(c)(2), the predominant character of a transaction is determined by ascertaining the primary benefit or value received by the customer in the transaction.

(ii) Special rule. If the primary benefit or value received by the customer in the transaction is not reasonably ascertainable, the predominant character of a transaction is instead determined by ascertaining the primary benefit or value received by a typical customer in a substantially similar transaction as determined under paragraphs (b)(3)(ii)(A) and (B) of this section.

(A) The primary benefit or value received by a typical customer is determined by data on how a typical customer uses or accesses the digital content. See paragraph (h)(17) of this section (Example 17).

(B) If data described in paragraph (b)(3)(ii)(A) of this section is not available, then the predominant character of a transaction subject to the special rule in paragraph (b)(3)(ii) of this section is determined by examining other factors that are indicative of the primary benefit or value received by a typical customer, including the following—

(1) How the transferor or provider markets the transaction;

(2) The relative development costs to the transferor or provider of each element of the transaction; and

(3) The relative price paid in an uncontrolled transaction for one or more elements compared to the total contract price of the transaction in question.

(iii) Identification and development of data. A transferor or provider must use reasonable efforts to identify the data specified in paragraphs (b)(3)(i) and (ii)(A) of this section, or if necessary, to apply the factors relevant to paragraph (b)(3)(ii)(B) of this section. However, a transferor or provider is not required to develop any of the data specified in those paragraphs that it does not develop in the course of business.

(c) Transfers involving copyright rights and copyrighted articles—(1) Transfers treated as transfers of copyright rights. A digital content transaction involves a transfer of a copyright right if, as a result of the transaction, a person acquires one or more of the rights described in paragraphs (c)(2)(i) through (iv) of this section.

(2) Copyright rights. The copyright rights referred to in paragraph (c)(1) of this section are as follows—

(i) The right to make copies of the digital content for purposes of distribution to the public by sale or other transfer of ownership, or by rental, lease or lending;

(ii) The right to prepare derivative digital content based upon the digital content;

(iii) The right to make a public performance of digital content, other than a right to publicly perform digital content for the purpose of advertising the sale of the digital content performed; or

(iv) The right to publicly display digital content, other than a right to publicly display digital content for the purpose of advertising the sale of the digital content displayed.

(3) Copyrighted articles. A copyrighted article includes a copy of digital content from which the work can be perceived, reproduced, or otherwise communicated, either directly or with the aid of a machine or device. The copy of the digital content may be fixed in any medium.

(d) Provision of services. The determination of whether a transaction involving newly developed or modified digital content involves the provision of services described in paragraph (b)(1) of this section is based on all the facts and circumstances of the transaction, including, as appropriate, the intent of the parties (as evidenced by their agreement and conduct) as to which party is to own the copyright rights in the digital content and how the risks of loss are allocated between the parties. See paragraph (h)(15) of this section (Example 15).

(e) Provision of know-how. The provision of information with respect to digital content involves the provision of know-how for purposes of this section only if the information is—

(1) Information relating to the development of digital content;

(2) Furnished under conditions preventing unauthorized disclosure, specifically contracted for between the parties; and

(3) Considered property subject to trade secret protection.

(f) Further classification of transfers involving copyright rights and copyrighted articles—(1) Transfers of copyright rights. The determination of whether a transfer of a copyright right is a sale or exchange of property is made on the basis of whether, taking into account all facts and circumstances, there has been a transfer of all substantial rights in the copyright. A transfer of a copyright right that does not constitute a sale or exchange because not all substantial rights have been transferred will be classified as a license. For this purpose, the principles of sections 1222 and 1235 apply. Income derived from the sale or exchange of a copyright right will be sourced under section 865(a), (c), (d), (e), or (h), as appropriate. Income derived from the licensing of a copyright right will be sourced under section 861(a)(4) or 862(a)(4), as appropriate.

(2) Transfers of copyrighted articles—(i) Classification. The determination of whether a transfer of a copyrighted article is a sale or exchange is made on the basis of whether, taking into account all facts and circumstances, the benefits and burdens of ownership have been transferred. A transfer of a copyrighted article that does not constitute a sale or exchange because insufficient benefits and burdens of ownership of the copyrighted article have been transferred, such that a person other than the transferee is properly treated as the owner of the copyrighted article, will be classified as a lease.

(ii) Source. Income from transactions that are classified as sales or exchanges of copyrighted articles will be sourced under section 861(a)(6), 862(a)(6), 863, or 865(a), (b), (c), or (e), as appropriate. When a copyrighted article is sold and transferred through an electronic medium, the sale is deemed to have occurred at the location of the billing address of the purchaser for purposes of § 1.861–7(c). However, in any case in which the sales transaction is arranged in a particular manner for a principal purpose of tax avoidance, the foregoing rules will not be applied. In such a case, all of the facts and circumstances relevant to the transaction, such as the place where the copyrighted article will be used, the place where negotiations and the execution of the agreement occurred, and the terms of the agreement, will be considered, and the sale will be treated as having occurred where the substance of the sale occurred. Income derived from leasing a copyrighted article will be sourced under section 861(a)(4) or 862(a)(4), as appropriate.

(3) Special circumstances of digital content. In connection with determinations under this paragraph (f), consideration must be given as appropriate to the special characteristics of digital content in transactions that take advantage of these characteristics (such as the ability to make perfect copies at minimal cost). For example, a transaction in which a person acquires a copy of digital content on a disk subject to a requirement that the disk be destroyed after a specified period is generally the equivalent of a transaction subject to a requirement that the disk be returned after such period. Similarly, a transaction in which the digital content deactivates itself after a specified period is generally the equivalent of a transaction subject to a requirement that the disk be returned after a specified period.

(g) Rules of operation—(1) Term applied to transaction by parties. Neither the form adopted by the parties to a transaction, nor the classification of the transaction under copyright law, shall be determinative. Therefore, for example, if there is a transfer of a computer program on a single disk for a one-time payment with restrictions on transfer and reverse engineering, which the parties characterize as a license (including, but not limited to, agreements commonly referred to as shrink-wrap licenses), application of the rules of paragraphs (c) and (f) of this section may nevertheless result in the transaction being classified as the sale of a copyrighted article.

(2) Means of transfer not to be taken into account. The rules of this section shall be applied irrespective of the physical or electronic or other medium used to effectuate a digital content transaction.

(3) To the public—(i) In general. For purposes of paragraph (c)(2)(i) of this section, a transferee of digital content shall not be considered to have the right to distribute copies of the digital content to the public if it is permitted to distribute copies of the digital content to only either a related person, or to identified persons who may be identified by either name or by legal relationship to the original transferee. For purposes of this subparagraph, a related person is a person who bears a relationship to the transferee specified in section 267(b)(3), (10), (11), or (12), or section 707(b)(1)(B). In applying section 267(b), 267(f), 707(b)(1)(B), or 1563(a), "10 percent" shall be substituted for "50 percent."

(ii) Use by individuals. The number of employees of a transferee of digital content who are permitted to use the digital content in connection with their employment is not relevant for purposes of this paragraph (g)(3). In addition, the number of individuals with a contractual agreement to provide services to the transferee of digital content who are permitted to use the digital content in connection with the performance of those services is not relevant for purposes of this paragraph (g)(3).

(h) Examples. The examples in this paragraph (h) illustrate the provisions of this section. Unless otherwise specified, assume that Corp A is a domestic corporation, the digital content described in each example does not contain any online functionality, and all facts in each example occur as part of a single transaction.

(1) Example 1: Sale of a computer program on a disk—(i) Facts. Corp A owns the copyright in a computer program, Program X. It copies Program X onto disks. The disks are placed in boxes covered with a wrapper on which is printed what is generally referred to as a shrink-wrap license. The license is stated to be perpetual. Under the license no reverse engineering, decompilation, or disassembly of the computer program is permitted. The transferee receives, first, the right to use the program on two of its own computers (for example, a laptop and a desktop) provided that only one copy is in use at any one time, and second, the right to make one copy of the program on each machine as an essential step in the utilization of the program. The transferee is permitted by the shrink-wrap license to sell the copy so long as it destroys any other copies it has made and imposes the same terms and conditions of the license on the purchaser of its copy. These disks are made available for sale to the general public in Country Z. In return for valuable consideration, P, a Country Z resident, receives one such disk.

(ii) Analysis. (A) Under paragraph (b)(1) of this section, the transfer of a disk containing a copy of Program X from Corp A to P is a digital content transaction with one element, which is the transfer of a copy of Program X. Therefore, the transaction is treated solely as a transfer of a copyrighted article under paragraph (b)(1)(ii) of this section. Under paragraph (g)(1) of this section, the label license is not determinative.

(B) Taking into account all of the facts and circumstances, P is properly treated as the owner of a copyrighted article. Therefore, under paragraph (f)(2) of this section, there has been a sale of a copyrighted article rather than the grant of a lease.

(2) Example 2: Sale of a computer program via download from the internet—(i) Facts. The facts are the same as those in paragraph (h)(1) of this section (Example 1), except that instead of selling disks, Corp A decides to make Program X available, for a fee, on a World Wide Web home page on the internet. P, the Country Z resident, in return for payment made to Corp A, downloads Program X (via modem) onto the hard drive of his computer. As part of the electronic communication, P signifies his assent to a license agreement with terms identical to those in Example 1, except that in this case P may make a back-up copy of the program on to a disk.

(ii) Analysis. (A) Under paragraph (b)(1) of this section, the digital transfer of a copy of Program X from Corp A to P is a digital content transaction with one element, which is the transfer of a copy of Program X. Therefore, the transaction is treated solely as a transfer of a copyrighted article under paragraph (b)(1)(ii) of this section. Although P did not buy a physical copy of the disk with the program on it, paragraph (g)(2) of this section provides that the means of transferring the program is irrelevant.

(B) As in paragraph (h)(1) of this section (Example 1), P is properly treated as the owner of a copyrighted article. Therefore, under paragraph (f)(2) of this section, there has been a sale of a copyrighted article rather than the grant of a lease.

* * *

[T.D. 8785, 63 FR 52977, Oct. 2, 1998; 63 FR 64868, Nov. 24, 1998; T.D. 9870, 84 FR 33692, July 15, 2019; T.D. 10022, 90 FR 2988, Jan. 14, 2025]

§ 1.861–19 Classification of cloud transactions.

(a) In general. This section provides rules for classifying cloud transactions (as defined in paragraph (b) of this section). The rules of this section apply for purposes of Internal Revenue Code sections 59A, 245A, 250, 267A, 367, 404A, 482, 679, and 1059A; subchapter N of chapter 1; chapters 3 and 4; and sections 842 and 845 (to the extent involving a foreign person), and apply with respect to transfers to foreign trusts not covered by section 679.

(b) Cloud transaction defined. A cloud transaction is a transaction through which a person obtains on-demand network access to computer hardware, digital content (as defined in § 1.861–18(a)(2)), or other similar resources. A cloud transaction does not include network access to download digital content for storage and use on a person's computer or other electronic device.

(c) Classification of cloud transactions—(1) In general. A cloud transaction is classified as the provision of services.

(2) Transaction with multiple elements. Taking into account the overall transaction and the surrounding facts and circumstances, a transaction that has multiple elements, one or more of which would be a cloud transaction if considered separately, is classified in its entirety as a cloud transaction if the predominant character of the transaction as determined under § 1.861–18(b)(3) is a cloud transaction.

* * *

[T.D. 10022, 90 FR 2999, Jan. 14, 2025]

§ 1.861–20 Allocation and apportionment of foreign income taxes.

* * *

(c) General rule. A foreign income tax (other than certain in lieu of taxes described in paragraph (h) of this section) is allocated and apportioned to the statutory and residual groupings that include the items of foreign gross income included in the base on which the tax is imposed. Each such foreign income tax (that is, each separate levy) is allocated and apportioned separately under the rules in paragraphs (c) through (f) of this section. A foreign income tax is allocated and apportioned to or among the statutory and residual groupings under the following steps:

(1) First, by assigning the items of foreign gross income to the groupings under the rules of paragraph (d) of this section;

(2) Second, by allocating and apportioning the deductions that are allowed under foreign law to the foreign gross income in the groupings under the rules of paragraph (e) of this section; and

(3) Third, by allocating and apportioning the foreign income tax by reference to the foreign taxable income in the groupings under the rules of paragraph (f) of this section.

* * *

(f) Allocation and apportionment of foreign income tax. Foreign income tax is allocated to the statutory or residual grouping or groupings to which the items of foreign gross income are assigned under the rules of paragraph (d) of this section. If foreign gross income is assigned to more than one grouping, then the foreign income tax is apportioned among the statutory and residual groupings by multiplying the foreign income tax by a fraction, the numerator of which is the foreign taxable income in a grouping and the denominator of which is all foreign taxable income on which the foreign income tax is imposed. If foreign law, including by reason of an income tax convention, exempts certain types of income from tax, or if foreign taxable income is reduced to or below zero by foreign law deductions, then no foreign income tax is allocated and apportioned to that income. A withholding tax (as defined in section 901(k)(1)(B)) is allocated and apportioned to the foreign gross income from which it is withheld. If foreign law, including by reason of an income tax convention, provides for a specific rate of tax with respect to certain types of income (for example, capital gains), or allows credits only against tax on particular items or types of income (for example, credit for foreign withholding taxes), then such provisions are taken into account in determining the amount of foreign tax imposed on such foreign taxable income.

* * *

[T.D. 9922, 85 FR 72049, Nov. 12, 2020; 86 FR 54367, Oct. 1, 2021; T.D. 9959, 87 FR 327, Jan. 4, 2022; 87 FR 21743, April 13, 2022; 87 FR 45018, 45019, July 27, 2022]

§ 1.863–1 Allocation of gross income under section 863(a).

* * *

(d) Scholarships, fellowship grants, grants, prizes and awards—(1) In general. This paragraph (d) applies to scholarships, fellowship grants, grants, prizes and awards. The provisions of this paragraph (d) do not apply to amounts paid as salary or other compensation for services.

(2) Source of income. The source of income from scholarships, fellowship grants, grants, prizes and awards is determined as follows:

(i) United States source income. Except as provided in paragraph (d)(2)(iii) of this section, scholarships, fellowship grants, grants, prizes and awards made by a U.S. citizen or resident, a domestic partnership, a domestic corporation, an estate or trust (other than a foreign estate or trust within the meaning of section 7701(a)(31)), the United States (or an instrumentality or agency thereof), a State (or any political subdivision thereof), or the District of Columbia shall be treated as income from sources within the United States.

(ii) Foreign source income. Scholarships, fellowship grants, grants, prizes and awards made by a foreign government (or an instrumentality, agency, or any political subdivision thereof), an international organization (as defined in section 7701(a)(18)), or a person other than a U.S. person (as defined in section 7701(a)(30)) shall be treated as income from sources without the United States.

(iii) Certain activities conducted outside the United States. Scholarships, fellowship grants, targeted grants, and achievement awards received by a person other than a U.S. person (as defined in section 7701(a)(30)) with respect to activities previously conducted (in the case of achievement awards) or to be conducted (in the case of scholarships, fellowships grants, and targeted grants) outside the United States shall be treated as income from sources without the United States.

* * *

[T.D. 6500, 25 FR 11910, Nov. 26, 1960; T.D. 8615, 60 FR 44275, Aug. 25, 1995; T.D. 8687, 61 FR 60545, Nov. 29, 1996; 61 FR 65323, Dec. 12, 1996; T.D. 9128, 69 FR 26041, May 11, 2004; T.D. 9272, 71 FR 43366, Aug. 1, 2006; T.D. 9415,73 FR 40172, July 14, 2008; T.D. 9921, 85 FR 79845, Dec. 11, 2020]

§ 1.863–2 Allocation and apportionment of taxable income.

(a) Determination of taxable income. Section 863(b) provides an alternate method for determining taxable income from sources within the United States in the case of gross income derived from sources partly within and partly without the United States. Under this method, taxable income is determined by deducting from such gross income the expenses, losses, or other deductions properly apportioned or allocated thereto and a ratable part of any other expenses, losses, or deductions that cannot definitely be allocated to some item or class of gross income. The income to which this section applies will consist of gains, profits, and income:

(1) From certain transportation or other services rendered partly within and partly without the United States to the extent not within the scope of section 863(c) or other specific provisions of this title;

(2) From the sale of inventory property (within the meaning of section 865(i)) produced (in whole or in part) by the taxpayer in the United States and sold outside the United States or produced (in whole or in part) by the taxpayer outside the United States and sold in the United States; or

(3) Derived from the purchase of personal property within a possession of the United States and its sale within the United States, to the extent not excluded from the scope of these regulations under § 1.936–6(a)(5), Q&A 7.

(b) Determination of source of taxable income. Income treated as derived from sources partly within and partly without the United States under paragraph (a) of this section may be allocated or apportioned to sources within and without the United States pursuant to §§ 1.863–1, 1.863–3, 1.863–4, 1.863–8, and 1.863–9. To determine the source of certain types of income described in paragraph (a)(1) of this section, see § 1.863–4. To determine the source of gross income described in paragraph (a)(2) of this section, see § 1.863–1 for natural resources, § 1.863–3 for other sales of inventory property, and § 1.863–8 for source of gross income from space and ocean activity. Section 1.865–3 may apply instead of the provisions in this section to source gross income from sales of personal property (including inventory property) by nonresidents attributable to an office or other fixed place of business in the United States. To determine the source of income partly from sources within a possession of the United States, including income described in paragraph (a)(3) of this section, see § 1.863–3(e).

* * *

[T.D. 6500, 25 FR 11910, Nov. 26, 1960; T.D. 8687, 61 FR 60546, Nov. 29, 1996; 61 FR 65323, Dec. 12, 1996; T.D. 9921, 85 FR 79846, Dec. 11, 2020]

§ 1.863–3 Allocation and apportionment of income from certain sales of inventory.

(a) In general—(1) Scope. Subject to the rules of § 1.865–3, paragraphs (a) through (d) of this section apply to determine the source of income derived from the sale of inventory property (inventory) that a taxpayer produces (in whole or in part) within the United States and sells without the United States, or that a taxpayer produces (in whole or in part) without the United States and sells within the United States (collectively, Section 863(b)(2) Sales). See section 865(i)(1) for the definition of inventory. Paragraph (b) of this section provides that the source of gross income from Section 863(b)(2) Sales is based solely on the production activities with respect to the inventory. Paragraph (c) of this section describes how to determine source based on production activity, including when inventory is produced partly within the United States and partly without the United States. Paragraph (d) of this section determines taxable income from Section 863(b)(2) Sales. Paragraph (e) of this section applies to determine the source of certain income derived from a possession of the United States. Paragraph (f) of this section provides special rules for partnerships for all sales subject to §§ 1.863–1 through 1.863–3. Paragraph (g) of this section provides applicability dates for the rules in this section.

(2) Cross references. To determine the source of income derived from the sale of personal property (including inventory) by a nonresident that is attributable to the nonresident's office or other fixed place of business in the United States under section 865(e)(2) and § 1.865–3(c), the rules of § 1.865–3 apply, and the rules of this section do not apply except to the extent provided in § 1.865–3.
* * *

(b) Sourcing based solely on production activities. Subject to the rules of § 1.865–3, all income, gain, or loss derived from Section 863(b)(2) Sales is allocated and apportioned solely on the basis of the production activities with respect to the inventory.

(c) Determination of the source of gross income from production activity—(1) Production only within the United States or only within foreign countries—(i) Source of income. For purposes of this section, production activity means an activity that creates, fabricates, manufactures, extracts, processes, cures, or ages inventory. See § 1.864–1. Whether a taxpayer's activities constitute production activity is determined under the principles of § 1.954–3(a)(4) (except for § 1.954–3(a)(4)(iv)). Subject to the provisions in § 1.1502–13 or paragraph (f)(2)(ii) of this section, the only production activities that are taken into account for purposes of §§ 1.863–1, 1.863–2, and this section are those conducted directly by the taxpayer. Where the taxpayer's production assets are located only within the United States or only outside the United States, gross income is sourced where the taxpayer's production assets are located. For rules regarding the source of income when production assets are located both within the United States and without the United States, see paragraph (c)(2) of this section. * * *

(ii) Definition of production assets. Subject to the provisions of § 1.1502–13 and paragraph (f)(2)(ii) of this section, production assets include only tangible and intangible assets owned directly by the taxpayer that are directly used by the taxpayer to produce inventory described in paragraph (a) of this section. Production assets do not include assets that are not directly used to produce inventory described in paragraph (a) of this section. Thus, production assets do not include such assets as accounts receivables, intangibles not related to production of inventory (e.g., marketing intangibles, including trademarks and customer lists), transportation assets, warehouses, the inventory itself, raw materials, or work-in-process. In addition, production assets do not include cash or other liquid assets (including working capital), investment assets, prepaid expenses, or stock of a subsidiary.

(iii) Location of production assets. For purposes of this section, a tangible production asset will be considered located where the asset is physically located. An intangible production asset will be considered located where the tangible production assets owned by the taxpayer to which it relates are located.

(2) Production both within and without the United States—(i) Source of income. Where the taxpayer's production assets are located both within and without the United States, income from sources without the United States will be determined by multiplying the gross income by a fraction, the numerator of which is the average adjusted basis of production assets that are located outside the United States and the denominator of which is the average adjusted basis of all production assets within and without the United States. The remaining income is treated as from sources within the United States.

(ii) Adjusted basis of production assets—(A) In general. For purposes of paragraph (c)(2)(i) of this section, the adjusted basis of an asset is determined by using the alternative depreciation system under section 168(g)(2). The adjusted basis of all production assets for purposes of paragraph (c)(2)(i) of this section is determined as though the production assets were subject to the alternative depreciation system set forth in section 168(g)(2) for the entire period that such property has been in service. The adjusted basis of the production assets is determined without regard to the election to expense certain depreciable assets under section 179 and without regard to any additional first-year depreciation provision (for example, section 168(k), (*l*), and (m), and former sections 1400L(b) and 1400N(d)). The average adjusted basis of assets is computed by averaging the adjusted basis at the beginning and end of the taxable year, unless by reason of changes during the taxable year, as might be the case in the event of a major acquisition or disposition of assets, the average would materially distort the calculation in paragraph (c)(2)(i) of this section. In this event, the average adjusted basis is determined upon a more appropriate basis that is weighted to reasonably reflect the period for which the assets are held by the taxpayer during the taxable year.

(B) Production assets used to produce other property. If a production asset is used to produce inventory sold in Section 863(b)(2) Sales and also used to produce other property during the taxable year, the portion of its adjusted basis that is included in the fraction described in paragraph (c)(2)(i) of this section will be determined under any method that reasonably reflects the portion of the asset that produces inventory sold in Section 863(b)(2) Sales. For example, the portion of such an asset that is included in the formula may be determined by multiplying the asset's average adjusted basis by a fraction, the numerator of which is the gross receipts from sales of inventory from Section 863(b)(2) Sales produced by the asset, and the denominator of which is the gross receipts from all property produced by that asset.

(3) Anti-abuse rule. The purpose of paragraph (b) of this section and this paragraph (c) is to attribute the source of the taxpayer's gross income from certain sales of inventory property to the location of the taxpayer's production activity. Therefore, if the taxpayer has entered into or structured one or more transactions with a principal purpose of reducing its U.S. tax liability in a manner inconsistent with the purpose of paragraph (b) of this section or this paragraph (c), the Commissioner may make appropriate adjustments so that the source of the taxpayer's gross income more clearly reflects the location of production activity. For example, a taxpayer may be subject to the rule in this paragraph (c)(3) if domestic production assets are acquired by a related partnership (or a subsidiary of a related partnership) with a principal purpose of reducing its U.S. tax liability by claiming that the taxpayer's income from sales of inventory is subject to section 862(a)(6) rather than section 863(b).

(4) Examples. The following examples illustrate the rules of this paragraph (c):

(i) Example 1. Source of gross income—(A) Facts. A, a U.S. corporation, produces widgets that are sold both within the United States and within a foreign country. The initial manufacture of all widgets occurs in the United States. The second stage of production of widgets that are sold within a foreign country is completed within the country of sale. A's U.S. plant and machinery which is involved in the initial manufacture of the widgets has an average adjusted basis of $200, as determined using the alternative depreciation system under section 168(g)(2). A also owns warehouses used to store work-in-process. A owns foreign equipment with an average adjusted basis of $25. A's gross receipts from all sales of widgets is $100, and its gross receipts from export sales of widgets is $25. Assume that apportioning average adjusted basis using gross receipts is reasonable. Assume A's cost of goods sold from the sale of widgets in the foreign countries is $13 and thus, its gross income from widgets sold in foreign countries is $12.

(B) Analysis. A determines its gross income from sources without the United States by multiplying A's $12 of gross income from sales of widgets in foreign countries by a fraction, the numerator of which is all relevant foreign production assets, or $25, and the denominator of which is all relevant production assets, or $75 ($25 foreign assets + ($200 U.S. assets x $25 gross receipts from export sales/$100 gross receipts from all sales)). Therefore, A's gross income from sources without the United States is $4 ($12 x ($25/$75)).

(ii) Example 2. Location of intangible property. Assume the same facts as in paragraph (c)(4)(i)(A) of this section (the facts in Example 1), except that A employs a patented process that applies only to the initial production of widgets. In computing the formula used to determine the source of gross income, A's patent, if it has an average adjusted basis, would be located in the United States.

(iii) Example 3. Anti-abuse rule—(A) Facts. Assume the same facts as in paragraph (c)(4)(i)(A) of this section (the facts in Example 1). A sells its U.S. assets to B, an unrelated U.S. corporation, with a principal purpose of reducing its U.S. tax liability by manipulating the property fraction. A then leases these assets from B. After this transaction, under the general rule of paragraph (c)(2) of this section, all of A's gross income would be considered from sources without the United States, because all of A's relevant production assets are located within a foreign country. Since the leased property is not owned by the taxpayer, it is not included in the fraction.

(B) Analysis. Because A has entered into a transaction with a principal purpose of reducing its U.S. tax liability by manipulating the formula described in paragraph (c)(2)(i) of this section, A's income must be adjusted to more clearly reflect the source of that income. In this case, the Commissioner may redetermine the source of A's gross income by ignoring the sale-leaseback transactions.

(d) Determination of source of taxable income. Once the source of gross income has been determined under paragraph (c) of this section, the taxpayer must properly allocate and apportion its expenses, losses, and other deductions to its respective amounts of gross income from sources within and without the United States from its Section 863(b)(2) Sales. See §§ 1.861–8 through 1.861–14T and 1.861–17.

* * *

(f) Special rules for partnerships—(1) General rule. For purposes of § 1.863–1 and this section, a taxpayer's production activity does not include production activities conducted by a partnership of which the taxpayer is a partner either directly or through one or more partnerships, except as otherwise provided in paragraphs (c)(3) or (f)(2) of this section.

(2) Exceptions—(i) In general. For purposes of determining the source of the partner's distributive share of partnership income or determining the source of the partner's income from the sale of inventory property which the partnership distributes to the partner in kind, the partner's production activity includes an activity conducted by the partnership. In addition, the production activity of a partnership includes the production activity of a taxpayer that is a partner either directly or through one or more partnerships, to the extent that the partner's production activity is related to inventory that the partner contributes to the partnership in a transaction described under section 721.

(ii) Attribution of production assets to or from a partnership. A partner will be treated as owning its proportionate share of the partnership's production assets only to the extent that, under paragraph (f)(2)(i) of this section, the partner's activity includes production activity conducted through a partnership. A partner's share of partnership assets will be determined by reference to the partner's distributive share of partnership income for the year attributable to such production assets. Similarly, to the extent a partnership's activities include the production activities of a partner, the partnership will be treated as owning the partner's production assets related to the inventory that is contributed in kind to the partnership. See paragraph (c)(2)(ii) of this section for rules apportioning the basis of assets to Section 863 Sales.

(iii) Basis. For purposes of this section, in those cases where the partner is treated as owning its proportionate share of the partnership's production assets, the partner's basis in production assets held through a partnership shall be determined by reference to the partnership's adjusted basis in its assets (including a partner's special basis adjustment, if any, under section 743). Similarly, a partnership's basis in a partner's production assets is determined with reference to the partner's adjusted basis in its assets.

(3) Examples. The following examples illustrate the rules of this paragraph (f):

(i) Example 1. Distributive share of partnership income. A, a U.S. corporation, forms a partnership in the United States with B, a country X corporation. A and B each have a 50 percent interest in the income, gains, losses, deductions and credits of the partnership. The partnership is engaged in the manufacture and sale of widgets. The widgets are manufactured in the partnership's plant located in the United States and are sold by the partnership outside the United States. The partnership owns the manufacturing facility and all other production assets used to produce the widgets. A's distributive share of partnership income includes 50 percent of the sales income from these sales. In applying the rules of section 863 to determine the source of its distributive share of partnership income from the export sales of widgets, A is treated as carrying on the activity of the partnership related to production of these widgets and as owning a proportionate share of the partnership's assets related to production of the widgets, based upon its distributive share of partnership income.

* * *

[T.D. 8687, 61 FR 60547, Nov. 29, 1996; 61 FR 65323, Dec. 12, 1996; T.D. 8786, 63 FR 55023, Oct. 14, 1998; T.D. 9305, 71 FR 77603, Dec. 27, 2006; T.D. 9921, 85 FR 79846, Dec. 11, 2020]

§ 1.864–2 Trade or business within the United States.

(a) In general. As used in part I (section 861 and following) and part II (section 871 and following), subchapter N, chapter 1 of the Code, and chapter 3 (section 1441 and following) of the Code, and the regulations thereunder, the term "engaged in trade or business within the United States" does not include the activities described in paragraphs (c) and (d) of this section, but includes the performance of personal services within the United States at any time within the taxable year except to the extent otherwise provided in this section.

(b) Performance of personal services for foreign employer—(1) Excepted services. For purposes of paragraph (a) of this section, the term "engaged in trade or business within the United States" does not include the performance of personal services—

(i) For a nonresident alien individual, foreign partnership, or foreign corporation, not engaged in trade or business within the United States at any time during the taxable year, or

(ii) For an office or place of business maintained in a foreign country or in a possession of the United States by an individual who is a citizen or resident of the United States or by a domestic partnership or a domestic corporation, by a nonresident alien individual who is temporarily present in the United States for a period or periods not exceeding a total of 90 days during the taxable year and whose compensation for such services does not exceed in the aggregate gross amount of $3,000.

(2) Rules of application. (i) As a general rule, the term "day", as used in subparagraph (1) of this paragraph, means a calendar day during any portion of which the nonresident alien individual is physically present in the United States.

(ii) Solely for purposes of applying this paragraph, the nonresident alien individual, foreign partnership, or foreign corporation for which the nonresident alien individual is performing personal services in the United States shall not be considered to be engaged in trade or business in the United States by reason of the performance of such services by such individual.

(iii) In applying subparagraph (1) of this paragraph it is immaterial whether the services performed by the nonresident alien individual are performed as an employee for his employer or under any form of contract with the person for whom the services are performed.

(iv) In determining for purposes of subparagraph (1) of this paragraph whether compensation received by the nonresident alien individual exceeds in the aggregate a gross amount of $3,000, any amounts received by the individual from an employer as advances or reimbursements for travel expenses incurred on behalf of the employer shall be omitted from the compensation received by the individual, to the extent of expenses incurred, where he was required to account and did account to his employer for such expenses and has met the tests for such accounting provided in § 1.162–17 and paragraph (e)(4) of § 1.274–5. If advances or reimbursements exceed such expenses, the amount of the excess shall be included as compensation for personal services for purposes of such subparagraph. Pensions and retirement pay attributable to personal services performed in the United States are not to be taken into account for purposes of subparagraph (1) of this paragraph.

(v) See section 7701(a)(5) and § 301.7701–5 of this chapter (Procedure and Administration Regulations) for the meaning of "foreign" when applied to a corporation or partnership.

(vi) As to the source of compensation for personal services, see §§ 1.861–4 and 1.862–1.

* * *

(c) Trading in stocks or securities. For purposes of paragraph (a) of this section—

(1) In general. The term "engaged in trade or business within the United States" does not include the effecting of transactions in the United States in stocks or securities through a resident broker, commission agent, custodian, or other independent agent. This subparagraph shall apply to any taxpayer, including a broker or dealer in stocks or securities, except that it shall not apply if at any time during the taxable year the taxpayer has an office or other fixed place of business in the United States through which, or by the direction of which, the transactions in stocks or securities are effected. The volume of stock or security transactions effected during the taxable year shall not be taken into account in determining under this subparagraph whether the taxpayer is engaged in trade or business within the United States.

(2) Trading for taxpayer's own account—(i) In general. The term "engaged in trade or business within the United States" does not include the effecting of transactions in the United States in stocks or securities for the taxpayer's own account, irrespective of whether such transactions are effected by or through—

(a) The taxpayer himself while present in the United States,

(b) Employees of the taxpayer, whether or not such employees are present in the United States while effecting the transactions, or

(c) A broker, commission agent, custodian, or other agent of the taxpayer, whether or not such agent while effecting the transactions is (1) dependent or independent, or (2) resident, nonresident, or present, in the United States, and irrespective of whether any such employee or agent has discretionary authority to make decisions in effecting such transactions. For purposes of this paragraph, the term "securities" means any note, bond, debenture, or other evidence of indebtedness, or any evidence of an interest in or right to subscribe to or purchase any of the foregoing; and the effecting of transactions in stocks or securities includes buying, selling (whether or not by entering into short sales), or trading in stocks, securities, or contracts or options to buy or sell stocks or securities, on margin or otherwise, for the account and risk of the taxpayer, and any other activity closely related thereto (such as obtaining credit for the purpose of effectuating such buying, selling, or trading). The volume of stock of security transactions effected during the taxable year shall not be taken into account in determining under this subparagraph whether the taxpayer is engaged in trade or business within the United States. The application of this subdivision may be illustrated by the following example:

Example. A, a nonresident alien individual who is not a dealer in stocks or securities, authorizes B, an individual resident of the United States, as his agent to effect transactions in the United States in stocks and securities for the account of A. B is empowered with complete authority to trade in stocks and securities for the account of A and to use his own discretion as to when to buy or sell for A's account. This grant of discretionary authority from A to B is also communicated in writing by A to various domestic brokerage firms through which A ordinarily effects transactions in the United States in stocks or securities. Under the agency arrangement B has the authority to place orders with the brokers, and all confirmations are to be made by the brokers to B, subject to his approval. The brokers are authorized by A to make payments to B and to charge such payments to the account of A. In addition, B is authorized to obtain and advance the necessary funds, if any, to maintain credits with the brokerage firms. Pursuant to his authority B carries on extensive trading transactions in the United States during the taxable year through the various brokerage firms for the account of A. During the taxable year A makes several visits to the United States in order to discuss with B various aspects of his trading activities and to make necessary changes in his trading policy. A is not engaged in trade or business within the United States during the taxable year solely because of the effecting by B of transactions in the United States in stocks or securities during such year for the account of A.

(ii) Partnerships. A nonresident alien individual, foreign partnership, foreign estate, foreign trust, or foreign corporation shall not be considered to be engaged in trade or business within the United States solely because such person is a member of a partnership (whether domestic or foreign) which, pursuant to discretionary authority granted to such partnership by such person, effects transactions in the United States in stocks or securities for the partnership's own account or solely because an employee of such partnership, or a broker, commission agent, custodian, or other agent, pursuant to discretionary authority granted by such partnership, effects transactions in the United States in stocks or securities for the account of such partnership. This subdivision shall not apply, however, to any member of (a) a partnership which is a dealer in stocks or securities or (b) a partnership (other than a partnership in which, at any time during the last half of its taxable year, more than 50 percent of either the capital interest or the profits interest is owned, directly or indirectly, by five or fewer partners who are individuals) the principal business of which is trading in stocks or securities for its own account, if the principal office of such partnership is in the United States at any time during the taxable year. The principles of subdivision (iii) of this subparagraph for determining whether a foreign corporation has its principal office in the United States shall apply in determining under this subdivision whether a partnership has its principal office in the United States. See section 707(b)(3) and paragraph (b)(3) of § 1.707–1 for rules for determining the extent of the ownership by a partner of a capital interest or profits interest in a partnership. * * *

* * *

(iii) Dealers in stocks or securities and certain foreign corporations. This subparagraph shall not apply to the effecting of transactions in the United States for the account of (a) a dealer in stocks or securities or (b) a foreign corporation (other than a corporation which is, or but for section 542(c)(7) or 543(b)(1)(C) would be, a personal holding company) the principal business of which is trading in stocks or securities for its own account, if the principal office of such corporation is in the United States at any time during the taxable year. Whether a foreign corporation's principal office is in the United States for this purpose is to be determined by comparing the activities (other than trading in stocks or securities) which the corporation conducts from its office or other fixed place of business located in the United States with the activities it conducts from its offices or other fixed places of business located outside the United States. For purposes of this subdivision, a foreign corporation is considered to have only one principal office, and an office of such corporation will not be considered to be its principal office merely because it is a statutory office of such corporation. For example, a foreign corporation which carries on most or all of its investment activities in the United States but maintains a general business office or offices outside the United States in which its management is located will not be considered as having its principal office in the United States if all or a substantial portion of the following functions is carried on at or from an office or offices located outside the United States:

(1) Communicating with its shareholders (including the furnishing of financial reports),

(2) Communicating with the general public,

(3) Soliciting sales of its own stock,

(4) Accepting the subscriptions of new stockholders,

(5) Maintaining its principal corporate records and books of account,

(6) Auditing its books of account,

(7) Disbursing payments of dividends, legal fees, accounting fees, and officers' and directors' salaries,

(8) Publishing or furnishing the offering and redemption price of the shares of stock issued by it,

(9) Conducting meetings of its shareholders and board of directors, and

(10) Making redemptions of its own stock.

* * *

(iv) Definition of dealer in stocks or securities—(a) In general. For purposes of this subparagraph, a dealer in stocks or securities is a merchant of stocks or securities, with an established place of business, regularly engaged as a merchant in purchasing stocks or securities and selling them to customers with a view to the gains and profits that may be derived therefrom. Persons who buy and sell, or hold, stocks or securities for investment or speculation, irrespective of whether such buying or selling constitutes the carrying on of a trade or business, and officers of corporations, members of partnerships, or fiduciaries, who in their individual capacities buy and sell, or hold, stocks or securities for investment or speculation are not dealers in stocks or securities within the meaning of this subparagraph solely by reason of that activity. In determining under this subdivision whether a person is a dealer in stocks or securities such person's transactions in stocks or securities effected both in and outside the United States shall be taken into account.

* * *

[T.D. 6948, 33 FR 5090, March 28, 1968, as amended by T.D. 7378, 40 FR 45435, Oct. 2, 1975]

§ 1.864–3 Rules for determining income effectively connected with U.S. business of nonresident aliens or foreign corporations.

(a) In general. For purposes of the Internal Revenue Code, in the case of a nonresident alien individual or a foreign corporation that is engaged in a trade or business in the United States at any time during the taxable year, the rules set forth in §§ 1.864–4 through 1.864–7 and this section shall apply in determining whether income, gain, or loss shall be treated as effectively connected for a taxable year beginning after December 31, 1966, with the conduct of a trade or business in the United States. Except as provided in sections 871(c) and (d) and 882(d) and (e), and the regulations thereunder, in the case of a nonresident alien individual or a foreign corporation that is at no time during the taxable year engaged in a trade or business in the United States, no income, gain, or loss shall be treated as effectively connected for the taxable year with the conduct of a trade or business in the United States. The general rule prescribed by the preceding sentence shall apply even though the income, gain, or loss would have been treated as effectively connected with the conduct of a trade or business in the United States if such income or gain had been received or accrued, or such loss had been sustained, in an earlier taxable year when the taxpayer was engaged in a trade or business in the United States. In applying

§§ 1.864–4 through 1.864–7 and this section, the determination whether an item of income, gain, or loss is effectively connected with the conduct of a trade or business in the United States shall not be controlled by any administrative, judicial, or other interpretation made under the laws of any foreign country.

* * *

[T.D. 7216, 37 FR 23424, Nov. 3, 1972]

§ 1.864–4 U.S. source income effectively connected with U.S. business.

(a) In general. This section applies only to a nonresident alien individual or a foreign corporation that is engaged in a trade or business in the United States at some time during a taxable year beginning after December 31, 1966, and to the income, gain, or loss of such person from sources within the United States. If the income, gain, or loss of such person for the taxable year from sources within the United States consists of (1) gain or loss from the sale or exchange of capital assets or (2) fixed or determinable annual or periodical gains, profits, and income or certain other gains described in section 871(a)(1) or 881(a), certain factors must be taken into account, as prescribed by section 864(c)(2) and paragraph (c) of this section, in order to determine whether the income, gain, or loss is effectively connected for the taxable year with the conduct of a trade or business in the United States by that person. All other income, gain, or loss of such person for the taxable year from sources within the United States shall be treated as effectively connected for the taxable year with the conduct of a trade or business in the United States by that person, as prescribed by section 864(c)(3) and paragraph (b) of this section.

(b) Income other than fixed or determinable income and capital gains. All income, gain, or loss for the taxable year derived by a nonresident alien individual or foreign corporation engaged in a trade or business in the United States from sources within the United States which does not consist of income, gain, or loss described in section 871(a)(1) or 881(a), or of gain or loss from the sale or exchange of capital assets, shall, for purposes of paragraph (a) of this section, be treated as effectively connected for the taxable year with the conduct of a trade or business in the United States. This income, gain, or loss shall be treated as effectively connected for the taxable year with the conduct of a trade or business in the United States, whether or not the income, gain, or loss is derived from the trade or business being carried on in the United States during the taxable year. The application of this paragraph may be illustrated by the following examples:

* * *

Example 3. Foreign corporation S, which uses the calendar year as the taxable year, is engaged in the business of purchasing and selling electronic equipment. The home office of such corporation is also engaged in the business of purchasing and selling vintage wines. During 1968, S establishes a branch office in the United States to sell electronic equipment to customers, some of whom are located in the United States and the balance, in foreign countries. This branch office is not equipped to sell, and does not participate in sales of, wine purchased by the home office. Negotiations for the sales of the electronic equipment take place in the United States. By reason of the activity of its branch office in the United States, S is engaged in business in the United States during 1968. As a result of advertisements which the home office of S places in periodicals sold in the United States, customers in the United States frequently place orders for the purchase of wines with the home office in the foreign country, and the home office makes sales of wine in 1968 directly to such customers without routing the transactions through its branch office in the United States. The income or loss from sources within the United States for 1968 from sales of electronic equipment by the branch office, together with the income or loss from sources within the United States for that year from sales of wine by the home office, is treated as effectively connected for that year with the conduct of a business in the United States by S.

(c) Fixed or determinable income and capital gains—(1) Principal factors to be taken into account—(i) In general. In determining for purposes of paragraph (a) of this section whether any income for the taxable year from sources within the United States which is described in section 871(a)(1) or 881(a), relating to fixed or determinable annual or periodical gains, profits, and income and certain other gains, or whether gain or loss from sources within the United States for the taxable year from the sale or exchange of capital assets, is effectively connected for the taxable year with the conduct of a trade or business in the United States, the principal tests to be applied are (a) the asset-use test, that is, whether the income, gain, or loss is derived from assets used in, or held for use in, the conduct of the trade or business in the United States, and (b) the business-activities test, that is, whether the activities of the trade or business conducted in the United States were a material factor in the realization of the income, gain, or loss.

* * *

(2) Application of the asset-use test—(i) In general. For purposes of subparagraph (1) of this paragraph, the asset-use test ordinarily shall apply in making a determination with respect to income, gain, or loss of a passive type where the trade or business activities as such do not give rise directly to the realization of the income, gain, or loss. However, even in the case of such income, gain, or loss, any activities of the trade or business which materially contribute to the realization of such income, gain, or loss shall also be taken into account as a factor in determining whether the income, gain, or loss is effectively connected with the conduct of a trade or business in the United States. The asset-use test is of primary significance where, for example, interest income is derived from sources within the United States by a nonresident alien individual or foreign corporation that is engaged in the business of manufacturing or selling goods in the United States. See also subparagraph (5) of this paragraph for rules applicable to taxpayers conducting a banking, financing, or similar business in the United States.

(ii) Cases where applicable. Ordinarily, an asset shall be treated as used in, or held for use in, the conduct of a trade or business in the United States if the asset is—

(a) Held for the principal purpose of promoting the present conduct of the trade or business in the United States; or

(b) Acquired and held in the ordinary course of the trade or business conducted in the United States, as, for example, in the case of an account or note receivable arising from that trade or business; or

(c) Otherwise held in a direct relationship to the trade or business conducted in the United States, as determined under paragraph (c)(2)(iv) of this section.

(iii) Application of asset-use test to stock—(a) In general. Except as provided in paragraph (c)(2)(iii)(b) of this section, stock of a corporation (whether domestic or foreign) shall not be treated as an asset used in, or held for use in, the conduct of a trade or business in the United States.

* * *

(iv) Direct relationship between holding of asset and trade or business—(a) In general. In determining whether an asset is held in a direct relationship to the trade or business conducted in the United States, principal consideration shall be given to whether the asset is needed in that trade or business. An asset shall be considered needed in a trade or business, for this purpose, only if the asset is held to meet the present needs of that trade or business and not its anticipated future needs. An asset shall be considered as needed in the trade or business conducted in the United States if, for example, the asset is held to meet the operating expenses of that trade or business. Conversely, an asset shall be considered as not needed in the trade or business conducted in the United States if, for example, the asset is held for the purpose of providing for (1) future diversification into a new trade or business, (2) expansion of trade or business activities conducted outside of the United States,

(3) future plant replacement, or (4) future business contingencies.

(b) Presumption of direct relationship. Generally, an asset will be treated as held in a direct relationship to the trade or business if (1) the asset was acquired with funds generated by that trade or business, (2) the income from the asset is retained or reinvested in that trade or business, and (3) personnel who are present in the United States and actively involved in the conduct of that trade or business exercise significant management and control over the investment of such asset.

(v) Illustration. The application of paragraph (iv) may be illustrated by the following examples:

Example 1. M, a foreign corporation which uses the calendar year as the taxable year, is engaged in industrial manufacturing in a foreign country. M maintains a branch in the United States which acts as importer and distributor of the merchandise it manufactures abroad; by reason of these branch activities. M is engaged in business in the United States during 1968. The branch in the United States is required to hold a large current cash balance for business purposes, but the amount of the cash balance so required varies because of the fluctuating seasonal nature of the branch's business. During 1968 at a time when large cash balances are not required the branch invests the surplus amount in U.S. Treasury bills. Since these Treasury bills are held to meet the present needs of the business conducted in the United States they are held in a direct relationship to that business, and the interest for 1968 on these bills is effectively connected for that year with the conduct of the business in the United States by M.

Example 2. Foreign corporation M, which uses the calendar year as the taxable year, has a branch office in the United States where it sells to customers located in the United States various products which are manufactured by that corporation in a foreign country. By reason of this activity M is engaged in business in the United States during 1997. The U.S. branch establishes in 1997 a fund to which are periodically credited various amounts which are derived from the business carried on at such branch. The amounts in this fund are invested in various securities issued by domestic corporations by the managing officers of the U.S. branch, who have the responsibility for maintaining proper investment diversification and investment of the fund. During 1997, the branch office derives from sources within the United States interest on these securities, and gains and losses resulting from the sale or exchange of such securities. Since the securities were acquired with amounts generated by the business conducted in the United States, the interest is retained in that business, and the portfolio is managed by personnel actively involved in the conduct of that business, the securities are presumed under paragraph (c)(2)(iv)(b) of this section to be held in a direct relationship to that business. However, M is able to rebut this presumption by demonstrating that the fund was established to carry out a program of future expansion and not to meet the present needs of the business conducted in the United States. Consequently, the income, gains, and losses from the securities for 1997 are not effectively connected for that year with the conduct of a trade or business in the United States by M.

(3) Application of the business-activities test—(i) In general. For purposes of subparagraph (1) of this paragraph, the business-activities test shall ordinarily apply in making a determination with respect to income, gain, or loss which, even though generally of the passive type, arises directly from the active conduct of the taxpayer's trade or business in the United States. The business-activities test is of primary significance, for example, where (a) dividends or interest are derived by a dealer in stocks or securities, (b) gain or loss is derived from the sale or exchange of capital assets in the active conduct of a trade or business by an investment company, (c) royalties are derived in the active conduct of a business consisting of the licensing of patents or similar intangible property, or (d) service fees are derived in the active conduct of a servicing business. In applying the business-activities test, activities relating to the management of investment portfolios shall not be treated as activities of the trade or business conducted in the United States unless the maintenance of the investments constitutes the principal activity of that trade or business. See also subparagraph (5) of this paragraph for rules applicable to taxpayers conducting a banking, financing, or similar business in the United States.

(ii) Illustrations. The application of this subparagraph may be illustrated by the following examples:

* * *

Example 2. N, a foreign corporation which uses the calendar year as the taxable year, has a branch in the United States which acts as an importer and distributor of merchandise; by reason of the activities of that branch, N is engaged in business in the United States during 1968. N also carries on a business in which it licenses patents to unrelated persons in the United States for use in the United States. The businesses of the licensees in which these patents are used have no direct relationship to the business carried on in N's branch in the United States, although the merchandise marketed by the branch is similar in type to that manufactured under the patents. The negotiations and other activities leading up to the consummation of these licenses are conducted by employees of N who are not connected with the U.S. branch of that corporation, and the U.S. branch does not otherwise participate in arranging for the licenses. Royalties received by N during 1968 from these licenses are not effectively connected for that year with the conduct of its business in the United States because the activities of that business are not a material factor in the realization of such income.

(4) Method of accounting as a factor. In applying the asset-use test or the business-activities test described in subparagraph (1) of this paragraph, due regard shall be given to whether or not the asset, or the income, gain, or loss, is accounted for through the trade or business conducted in the United States, that is, whether or not the asset, or the income, gain, or loss, is carried on books of account separately kept for that trade or business, but this accounting test shall not by itself be controlling. In applying this subparagraph, consideration shall be given to whether the accounting treatment of an item reflects the consistent application of generally accepted accounting principles in a particular trade or business in accordance with accepted conditions or practices in that trade or business and whether there is a consistent accounting treatment of that item from year to year by the taxpayer.

* * *

[T.D. 7216, 37 FR 23425, Nov. 3, 1972, as amended by T.D. 7332, 39 FR 44232, Dec. 23, 1974; T.D. 7958, 49 FR 21052, May 18, 1984; T.D. 8657, 61 FR 9337, March 8, 1996; T.D. 9226, 70 FR 57510, Oct. 3, 2005]

§ 1.864–5 Foreign source income effectively connected with U.S. business.

(a) In general. This section applies only to a nonresident alien individual or a foreign corporation that is engaged in a trade or business in the United States at some time during a taxable year beginning after December 31, 1966, and to the income, gain, or loss of such person from sources without the United States. The income, gain, or loss of such person for the taxable year from sources without the United States which is specified in paragraph (b) of this section shall be treated as effectively connected for the taxable year with the conduct of a trade or business in the United States, only if he also has in the United States at some time during the taxable year, but not necessarily at the time the income, gain, or loss is realized, an office or other fixed place of business, as defined in § 1.864–7, to which such income, gain, or loss is attributable in accordance with § 1.864–6. The income of such person for the taxable year from sources without the United States which is specified in paragraph (c) of this section shall be treated as effectively connected for the taxable year with the conduct of a trade or business in the United States when derived by a foreign corporation carrying on a life insurance business in the United States. Except as provided in paragraphs (b) and (c) of this section, no income, gain, or loss of a nonresident alien individual or a foreign corporation for the taxable year from sources without the United States shall be treated as effectively connected for the taxable year with the conduct of a trade or business in the United States by that person. Any income, gain, or loss described in paragraph (b) or (c) of this section which, if it were derived by the taxpayer from sources within the United States for the taxable year, would not be treated under § 1.864–4 as effectively connected for the taxable year with the conduct of a trade or business in the United States shall not be treated under this section as effectively connected for the taxable year with the conduct of a trade or business in the United States. To determine the source of income, gain or loss from the sale of personal property (including inventory property) attributable to an office or other fixed place of business in the United States by nonresidents, as defined in section 865(g)(1)(B), see § 1.865–3.

(b) Income other than income attributable to U.S. life insurance business. Income, gain, or loss from sources without the United States other than income described in paragraph (c) of this section or income from section 865(e)(2) sales, as defined in § 1.865–3(c), shall be taken into account pursuant to paragraph (a) of this section in applying §§ 1.864–6 and 1.864–7 only if it consists of—

(1) Rents, royalties, or gains on sales of intangible property. (i) Rents or royalties for the use of, or for the privilege of using, intangible personal property located outside the United States or from any interest in such property, including rents or royalties for the use, or for the privilege of using, outside the United States, patents, copyrights, secret processes and formulas, good will, trademarks, trade brands, franchises, and other like properties, if such rents or royalties are derived in the active conduct of the trade or business in the United States.

(ii) Gains or losses on the sale or exchange of intangible personal property located outside the United States or from any interest in such property, including gains or losses on the sale or exchange of the privilege of using, outside the United States, patents, copyrights, secret processes and formulas, good will, trademarks, trade brands, franchises, and other like properties, if such gains or losses are derived in the active conduct of the trade or business in the United States.

(iii) Whether or not such an item of income, gain, or loss is derived in the active conduct of a trade or business in the United States shall be determined from the facts and circumstances of each case. The frequency with which a nonresident alien individual or a foreign corporation enters into transactions of the type from which the income, gain, or loss is derived shall not of itself determine that the income, gain, or loss is derived in the active conduct of a trade or business.

(iv) This subparagraph shall not apply to rents or royalties for the use of, or for the privilege of using, real property or tangible personal property, or to gain or loss from the sale or exchange of such property.

(2) Dividends or interest, or gains or loss from sales of stocks or securities—(i) In general. Dividends or interests from any transaction, or gains or losses on the sale or exchange of stocks or securities, realized by (a) a nonresident alien individual or a foreign corporation in the active conduct of a banking, financing, or similar business in the United States or (b) a foreign corporation engaged in business in the United States whose principal business is trading in stocks or securities for its own account. Whether the taxpayer is engaged in the active conduct of a banking, financing, or similar business in the United States for purposes of this subparagraph shall be determined in accordance with the principles of paragraph (c)(5)(i) of § 1.864–4.

* * *

[T.D. 7216, 37 FR 23429, Nov. 3, 1972, as amended by T.D. 7893, 48 FR 22507, May 19, 1983; T.D. 8735, 62 FR 53501, Oct. 14, 1997; T.D. 9921, 85 FR 79850, Dec. 11, 2020]

§ 1.864–6 Income, gain, or loss attributable to an office or other fixed place of business in the United States.

(a) In general. Income, gain, or loss from sources without the United States which is specified in paragraph (b) of § 1.864–5 and received by a nonresident alien individual or a foreign corporation engaged in a trade or business in the United States at some time during a taxable year beginning after December 31, 1966, shall be treated as effectively connected for the taxable year with the conduct of a trade or business in the United States only if the income, gain, or loss is attributable under paragraphs (b) and (c) of this section to an office or other fixed place of business, as defined in § 1.864–7, which the taxpayer has in the United States at some time during the taxable year.

(b) Material factor test—(1) In general. For purposes of paragraph (a) of this section, income, gain, or loss is attributable to an office or other fixed place of business which a nonresident alien individual or a foreign corporation has in the United States only if such office or other fixed place of business is a material factor in the realization of the income, gain, or loss, and if the income, gain, or loss is realized in the ordinary course of the trade or business carried on through that office or other fixed place of business. For this purpose, the activities of the office or other fixed place of business shall not be considered to be a material factor in the realization of the income, gain, or loss unless they provide a significant contribution to, by being an essential economic element in, the realization of the income, gain, or loss. Thus, for example, meetings in the United States of the board of directors of a foreign corporation do not of themselves constitute a material factor in the realization of income, gain, or loss. It is not necessary that the activities of the office or other fixed place of business in the United States be a major factor in the realization of the income, gain, or loss. An office or other fixed place of business located in the United States at some time during a taxable year may be a material factor in the realization of an item of income, gain, or loss for that year even though the office or other fixed place of business is not present in the United States when the income, gain, or loss is realized.

(2) Application of material factor test to specific classes of income. For purposes of paragraph (a) of this section, an office or other fixed place of business which a nonresident alien individual or a foreign corporation, engaged in a trade or business in the United States at some time during the taxable year, had in the United States, shall be considered a material factor in the realization of income, gain, or loss consisting of—

* * *

(iii) Sale of goods or merchandise through U.S. office. Income, gain, or loss from sales of goods or merchandise specified in paragraph (b)(3) of § 1.864–5, if the office or other fixed place of business actively participates in soliciting the order, negotiating the contract of sale, or performing other significant services necessary for the consummation of the sale which are not the subject of a separate agreement between the seller and the buyer. The office or other fixed place of business in the United States shall be considered a material factor in the realization of income, gain, or loss from a sale made as a result of a sales order received in such office or other fixed place of business except where the sales order is received unsolicited and that office or other fixed place of business is not held out to potential customers as the place to which such sales orders should be sent. The income, gain, or loss must be realized in the ordinary course of the trade or business carried on through the office or other fixed place of business in the United States. Thus, if a foreign corporation is engaged solely in a manufacturing business in the United States, the income derived by its office in the United States as a result of an occasional sale outside the United

States is not attributable to the U.S. office if the sales office of the manufacturing business is located outside the United States. On the other hand, if a foreign corporation establishes a sales office in the United States to sell for consumption in the Western Hemisphere merchandise which the corporation produces in Africa, the income derived by the sales office in the United States as a result of an occasional sale made by it in Europe shall be attributable to the U.S. sales office. An office or other fixed place of business in the United States shall not be considered to be a material factor in the realization of income, gain, or loss for purposes of this subdivision merely because of one or more of the following activities: (a) The sale is made subject to the final approval of such office or other fixed place of business, (b) the property sold is held in, and distributed from, such office or other fixed place of business, (c) samples of the property sold are displayed (but not otherwise promoted or sold) in such office or other fixed place of business, or (d) such office or other fixed place of business performs merely clerical functions incident to the sale. Activities carried on by employees of an office or other fixed place of business constitute activities of that office or other fixed place of business.

(3) Limitation where foreign office is a material factor in realization of income—(i) Goods or merchandise destined for foreign use, consumption, or disposition. Notwithstanding subparagraphs (1) and (2) of this paragraph, an office or other fixed place of business which a nonresident alien individual or a foreign corporation has in the United States shall not be considered, for purposes of paragraph (a) of this section, to be a material factor in the realization of income, gain, or loss from sales of goods or merchandise specified in paragraph (b)(3) of § 1.864–5 if the property is sold for use, consumption, or disposition outside the United States and an office or other fixed place of business, as defined in § 1.864–7, which such nonresident alien individual or foreign corporation has outside the United States participates materially in the sale. For this purpose an office or other fixed place of business which the taxpayer has outside the United States shall be considered to have participated materially in a sale made through the office or other fixed place of business in the United States if the office or other fixed place of business outside the United States actively participates in soliciting the order resulting in the sale, negotiating the contract of sale, or performing other significant services necessary for the consummation of the sale which are not the subject of a separate agreement between the seller and buyer. An office or other fixed place of business which the taxpayer has outside the United States shall not be considered to have participated materially in a sale merely because of one or more of the following activities: (a) The sale is made subject to the final approval of such office or other fixed place of business, (b) the property sold is held in, and distributed from, such office or other fixed place of business, (c) samples of the property sold are displayed (but not otherwise promoted or sold) in such office or other fixed place of business, (d) such office or other fixed place of business is used for purposes of having title to the property pass outside the United States, or (e) such office or other fixed place of business performs merely clerical functions incident to the sale.

* * *

(c) Amount of income, gain, or loss allocable to U.S. office—(1) In general. If, in accordance with paragraph (b) of this section, an office or other fixed place of business which a nonresident alien individual or a foreign corporation has in the United States at some time during the taxable year is a material factor in the realization for that year of an item of income, gain, or loss specified in paragraph (b) of § 1.864–5, such item of income, gain, or loss shall be considered to be allocable in its entirety to that office or other fixed place of business. In no case may any income, gain, or loss for the taxable year from sources without the United States, or part thereof, be allocable under this paragraph to an office or other fixed place of business which a nonresident alien individual or a foreign corporation has in the United States if the taxpayer is at no time during the taxable year engaged in a trade or business in the United States.

(2) Special limitation in case of sales of goods or merchandise through U.S. office. Notwithstanding paragraph (c)(1) of this section, the special rules described in this paragraph (c)(2) apply with respect to a sale of goods or merchandise specified in § 1.864–5(b)(3), to which paragraph (b)(3)(i) of this section does not apply. In the case of a nonresident alien with a tax home within the United States, as defined in section 911(d)(3), the amount of income from the sale of goods or merchandise that is properly allocable to the individual's U.S. office is determined under § 1.865–3(d).

(3) Examples. The application of this paragraph (c) may be illustrated by the following examples—

(i) Example 1. Sales of produced inventory through a U.S. sales office. Individual A, who is a nonresident alien within the meaning of section 7701(b)(1)(B) and has a tax home in the United States, manufactures machinery in a foreign country and sells the machinery outside the United States through A's sales office in the United States for use in foreign countries. A is not a nonresident within the meaning of section 865(g)(1)(B). Therefore, § 1.865–3 does not apply to A's sale of the machinery, except to the extent provided in paragraph (c)(2) of this section. Title to the property sold is transferred to the foreign purchaser outside the United States, but no office or other fixed place of business of A in a foreign country materially participates in the sale made through A's U.S. office. By reason of its sales activities in the United States, A is engaged in business in the United States during the taxable year. During the taxable year, A derives a total income of $250,000x from these sales. Under paragraph (c)(2) of this section, the amount of income that is allocable to A's U.S. office is determined under § 1.865–3(d)(2). The taxpayer does not allocate income from the sale under the books and records method described in § 1.865–3(d)(2)(ii). Thus, 50 percent of A's foreign source income of $250,000x, plus any additional income allocable based on the location of production activities under §§ 1.865–3(d)(2)(i) and 1.863–3 (in this case, $0x), is effectively connected for the taxable year with the conduct of A's U.S. trade or business, or $125,000x.

(ii) Example 2. Sales of inventory purchased and resold through a U.S. sales office by a nonresident alien with a tax home in the United States. Individual B, who is a nonresident alien within the meaning of section 7701(b)(1)(B) and has a tax home in the United States, has an office in a foreign country that purchases merchandise and sells it through B's sales office in the United States for use in various foreign countries, with title to the property passing outside the United States. B is not a nonresident within the meaning of section 865(g)(1)(B). Therefore, § 1.865–3 does not apply to B's sale of the merchandise, except to the extent provided in paragraph (c)(2) of this section. No other office of B materially participates in these sales made through its U.S. office. By reason of its sales activities in the United States, B is engaged in business in the United States during the taxable year. During the taxable year, B derives income of $300,000x from these sales made through its U.S. sales office. All of B's income from these sales is foreign source as B purchases the merchandise outside the United States and title to the merchandise also passes outside the United States. The amount of income properly allocable to B's U.S. office determined under § 1.865–3(d)(3) is $300,000x, and thus $300,000x is effectively connected for the taxable year with the conduct of B's U.S. trade or business.

(iii) Example 3. Foreign sales office also materially participates in sale. The facts are the same as in paragraph (c)(3)(ii) of this section (the facts in Example 2), except that B also has an office in a foreign country that is a material factor in the realization of income from the sales made through B's U.S. office. No income from the sale of merchandise is allocable to B's U.S. sales office for the taxable year, by reason of paragraph (b)(3)(i) of this section, and thus none of the $300,000x is effectively connected for the taxable year with the conduct of B's U.S. trade or business.

(iv) Example 4. Sales of inventory purchased and resold through a U.S. sales office by a foreign corporation. The facts are the same as in paragraph (c)(3)(ii) of this section (the facts in Example 2), except that B is a foreign corporation. B is a nonresident within the meaning of section 865(g)(1)(B). The income from such sales will be sourced in accordance with § 1.865–3(a) and (d)(3).

* * *

[T.D. 7216, 37 FR 23431, Nov. 3, 1972; T.D. 9921, 85 FR 79850, Dec. 11, 2020]

§ 1.864–7 Definition of office or other fixed place of business.

(a) In general. (1) This section applies for purposes of determining whether a nonresident alien individual or a foreign corporation that is engaged in a trade or business in the United States at some time during a taxable year beginning after December 31, 1966, has an office or other fixed place of business in the United States for purposes of applying section 864(c)(4)(B) and § 1.864–6 to income, gain, or loss specified in paragraph (b) of § 1.864–5 from sources without the United States or has an office or other fixed place of business outside the United States for purposes of applying section 864(c)(4)(B)(iii) and paragraph (b)(3)(i) of § 1.864–6 to sales of goods or merchandise for use, consumption, or disposition outside the United States.

(2) In making a determination under this section due regard shall be given to the facts and circumstances of each case, particularly to the nature of the taxpayer's trade or business and the physical facilities actually required by the taxpayer in the ordinary course of the conduct of his trade or business.

(3) The law of a foreign country shall not be controlling in determining whether a nonresident alien individual or a foreign corporation has an office or other fixed place of business.

(b) Fixed facilities—(1) In general. As a general rule, an office or other fixed place of business is a fixed facility, that is, a place, site, structure, or other similar facility, through which a nonresident alien individual or a foreign corporation engages in a trade or business. For this purpose an office or other fixed place of business shall include, but shall not be limited to, a factory; a store or other sales outlet; a workshop; or a mine, quarry, or other place of extraction of natural resources. A fixed facility may be considered an office or other fixed place of business whether or not the facility is continuously used by a nonresident alien individual or foreign corporation.

(2) Use of another person's office or other fixed place of business. A nonresident alien individual or a foreign corporation shall not be considered to have an office or other fixed place of business merely because such alien individual or foreign corporation uses another person's office or other fixed place of business, whether or not the office or place of business of a related person, through which to transact a trade or business, if the trade or business activities of the alien individual or foreign corporation in that office or other fixed place of business are relatively sporadic or infrequent, taking into account the overall needs and conduct of that trade or business.

(c) Management activity. A foreign corporation shall not be considered to have an office or other fixed place of business merely because a person controlling that corporation has an office or other fixed place of business from which general supervision and control over the policies of the foreign corporation are exercised. The fact that top management decisions affecting the foreign corporation are made in a country shall not of itself mean that the foreign corporation has an office or other fixed place of business in that country. For example, a foreign sales corporation which is a wholly owned subsidiary of a domestic corporation shall not be considered to have an office or other fixed place of business in the United States merely because of the presence in the United States of officers of the domestic parent corporation who are generally responsible only for the policy decisions affecting the foreign sales corporation, provided that the foreign corporation has a chief executive officer, whether or not he is also an officer of the domestic parent corporation, who conducts the day-to-day trade or business of the foreign corporation from a foreign office. The result in this example would be the same even if the executive officer should (1) regularly confer with the officers of the domestic parent corporation, (2) occasionally visit the U.S. office of the domestic parent corporation, and (3) during such visits to the United States temporarily conduct the business of the foreign subsidiary corporation out of the domestic parent corporation's office in the United States.

(d) Agent activity—(1) Dependent agents—(i) In general. In determining whether a nonresident alien individual or a foreign corporation has an office or other fixed place of business, the office or other fixed place of business of an agent who is not an independent agent, as defined in subparagraph (3) of this paragraph, shall be disregarded unless such agent (a) has the authority to negotiate and conclude contracts in the name of the nonresident alien individual or foreign corporation, and regularly exercises that authority, or (b) has a stock of merchandise belonging to the nonresident alien individual or foreign corporation from which orders are regularly filed on behalf of such alien individual or foreign corporation. A person who purchases goods from a nonresident alien individual or a foreign corporation shall not be considered to be an agent for such alien individual or foreign corporation for purposes of this paragraph where such person is carrying on such purchasing activities in the ordinary course of its own business, even though such person is related in some manner to the nonresident alien individual or foreign corporation. For example, a wholly owned domestic subsidiary corporation of a foreign corporation shall not be treated as an agent of the foreign parent corporation merely because the subsidiary corporation purchases goods from the foreign parent corporation and resells them in its own name. However, if the domestic subsidiary corporation regularly negotiates and concludes contracts in the name of its foreign parent corporation or maintains a stock of merchandise from which it regularly fills orders on behalf of the foreign parent corporation, the office or other fixed place of business of the domestic subsidiary corporation shall be treated as the office or other fixed place of business of the foreign parent corporation unless the domestic subsidiary corporation is an independent agent within the meaning of subparagraph (3) of this paragraph.

(ii) Authority to conclude contracts or fill orders. For purposes of subdivision (i) of this subparagraph, an agent shall be considered regularly to exercise authority to negotiate and conclude contracts or regularly to fill orders on behalf of his foreign principal only if the authority is exercised, or the orders are filled, with some frequency over a continuous period of time. This determination shall be made on the basis of the facts and circumstances in each case, taking into account the nature of the business of the principal; but, in all cases, the frequency and continuity tests are to be applied conjunctively. Regularity shall not be evidenced by occasional or incidental activity. An agent shall not be considered regularly to negotiate and conclude contracts on behalf of his foreign principal if the agent's authority to negotiate and conclude contracts is limited only to unusual cases or such authority must be separately secured by the agent from his principal with respect to each transaction effected.

(2) Independent agents. The office or other fixed place of business of an independent agent, as defined in subparagraph (3) of this paragraph, shall not be treated as the office or other fixed place of business of his principal who is a nonresident alien individual or a foreign corporation, irrespective of whether such agent has authority to negotiate and conclude contracts in the name of his principal, and regularly exercises that authority, or maintains a stock of goods from which he regularly fills orders on behalf of his principal.

(3) Definition of independent agent—(i) In general. For purposes of this paragraph, the term "independent agent" means a general commission agent, broker, or other agent of an independent status acting in the ordinary course of his business in that capacity. Thus, for example, an agent who, in pursuance of his usual trade or business, and for compensation, sells goods or merchandise consigned or entrusted to his possession, management, and control for that purpose by or for the owner of such goods or merchandise is an independent agent.

(ii) Related persons. The determination of whether an agent is an independent agent for purposes of this paragraph shall be made without regard to facts indicating that either the agent or the principal owns or controls directly or indirectly the other or that a third person or persons own or control directly or indirectly both. For example, a wholly owned domestic subsidiary corporation of a foreign corporation which acts as an agent for the foreign parent corporation may be treated as acting in the capacity of independent agent for the foreign parent corporation. The facts and circumstances of a specific case shall determine whether the agent, while acting for his principal, is acting in pursuance of his usual trade or business and in such manner as to constitute him an independent agent in his relations with the nonresident alien individual or foreign corporation.

(iii) Exclusive agents. Where an agent who is otherwise an independent agent within the meaning of subdivision (i) of this subparagraph acts in such capacity exclusively, or almost exclusively, for one principal who is a nonresident alien individual or a foreign corporation, the facts and circumstances of a particular case shall be taken into account in determining whether the agent, while acting in that capacity, may be classified as an independent agent.

(e) Employee activity. Ordinarily, an employee of a nonresident alien individual or a foreign corporation shall be treated as a dependent agent to whom the rules of paragraph (d)(1) of this section apply if such employer does not in and of itself have a fixed facility (as defined in paragraph (b) of this section) in the United States or outside the United States, as the case may be. However, where the employee, in the ordinary course of his duties, carries on the trade or business of his employer in or through a fixed facility of such employer which is regularly used by the employee in the course of carrying out such duties, such fixed facility shall be considered the office or other fixed place of business of the employer, irrespective of the rules of paragraph (d)(1) of this section. The application of this paragraph may be illustrated by the following example:

Example. M, a foreign corporation, opens a showroom office in the United States for the purpose of promoting its sales of merchandise which it purchases in foreign country X. The employees of the U.S. office, consisting of salesmen and general clerks, are empowered only to run the office, to arrange for the appointment of distributing agents for the merchandise offered by M, and to solicit orders generally. These employees do not have the authority to negotiate and conclude contracts in the name of M, nor do they have a stock of merchandise from which to fill orders on behalf of M. Any negotiations entered into by these employees are under M's instructions and subject to its approval as to any decision reached. The only independent authority which the employees have is in the appointment of distributors to whom M is to sell merchandise, but even this authority is subject to the right of M to approve or disapprove these buyers on receipt of information as to their business standing. Under the circumstances, this office used by a group of salesmen for sales promotion is a fixed place of business which M has in the United States.

(f) Office or other fixed place of business of a related person. The fact that a nonresident alien individual or a foreign corporation is related in some manner to another person who has an office or other fixed place of business shall not of itself mean that such office or other fixed place of business of the other person is the office or other fixed place of business of the nonresident alien individual or foreign corporation. Thus, for example, the U.S. office of foreign corporation M, a wholly owned subsidiary corporation of foreign corporation N, shall not be considered the office or other fixed place of business of N unless the facts and circumstances show that N is engaged in trade or business in the United States through that office or other fixed place of business. However, see paragraph (b)(2) of this section.

* * *

[T.D. 7216, 37 FR 23433, Nov. 3, 1972]

§ 1.864(c)(8)–1 Gain or loss by foreign persons on the disposition of certain partnership interests.

(a) Overview. This section provides rules and definitions under section 864(c)(8). Paragraph (b) of this section provides the general rule treating gain or loss recognized by a nonresident alien individual or foreign corporation from the sale or exchange of a partnership interest as effectively connected gain or effectively connected loss. Paragraph (c) of this section provides rules for determining the limitations on the amount of effectively connected gain or effectively connected loss under section 864(c)(8) and paragraph (b) of this section. Paragraph (d) of this section provides rules regarding coordination with section 897. Paragraph (e) of this section provides rules regarding certain tiered partnerships. Paragraph (f) of this section provides rules regarding U.S. income tax treaties. Paragraph (g) of this section provides definitions. Paragraph (h) of this section provides a rule regarding certain contributions of property to a partnership. Paragraph (i) of this section contains examples illustrating the rules set forth in this section. Paragraph (j) of this section provides the applicability date.

(b) Gain or loss treated as effectively connected gain or loss—(1) In general. Notwithstanding any other provision of subtitle A of the Internal Revenue Code, if a foreign transferor owns, directly or indirectly, an interest in a partnership that is engaged in the conduct of a trade or business within the United States, outside capital gain, outside capital loss, outside ordinary gain, or outside ordinary loss (each as defined in paragraph (b)(2) of this section) recognized by the foreign transferor on the transfer of all (or any portion) of the interest is treated as effectively connected gain or effectively connected loss, subject to the limitations described in paragraph (b)(3) of this section. Except as provided in paragraph (d) of this section, this section does not apply to prevent any portion of the gain or loss that is otherwise treated as effectively connected gain or effectively connected loss under provisions of the Internal Revenue Code other than section 864(c)(8) from being so treated.

(2) Determination of outside gain and loss—(i) In general. The amount of gain or loss recognized by the foreign transferor in connection with the transfer of its partnership interest is determined under all relevant provisions of the Internal Revenue Code and the regulations thereunder. See, e.g., §§ 1.741–1(a) and 1.751–1(a)(2). For purposes of this section, the amount of gain or loss that is treated as capital gain or capital loss under sections 741 and 751 is referred to as outside capital gain or outside capital loss, respectively. The amount of gain or loss that is treated as ordinary gain or ordinary loss under sections 741 and 751 is referred to as outside ordinary gain or outside ordinary loss, respectively.

(ii) Nonrecognition provisions. A foreign transferor's gain or loss recognized in connection with the transfer of its partnership interest does not include gain or loss to the extent that the gain or loss is not recognized by reason of one or more nonrecognition provisions of the Internal Revenue Code.

(3) Limitations. For purposes of applying this section, this paragraph (b)(3) limits the amount of gain or loss recognized by a foreign transferor that may be treated as effectively connected gain or effectively connected loss.

(i) Capital gain limitation. Outside capital gain recognized by a foreign transferor is treated as effectively connected gain to the extent it does not exceed aggregate deemed sale EC capital gain determined under paragraph (c)(3)(ii)(B) of this section.

(ii) Capital loss limitation. Outside capital loss recognized by a foreign transferor is treated as effectively connected loss to the extent it does not exceed aggregate deemed sale EC capital loss determined under paragraph (c)(3)(ii)(B) of this section.

(iii) Ordinary gain limitation. Outside ordinary gain recognized by a foreign transferor is treated as effectively connected gain to the extent it does not exceed aggregate deemed sale EC ordinary gain determined under paragraph (c)(3)(ii)(A) of this section.

(iv) Ordinary loss limitation. Outside ordinary loss recognized by a foreign transferor is treated as effectively connected loss to the extent it does not exceed aggregate deemed sale EC ordinary loss determined under paragraph (c)(3)(ii)(A) of this section.

* * *

[T.D. 9919, 85 FR 70965, Nov. 6, 2020]

§ 1.865–2 Loss with respect to stock.

(a) General rules for allocation of loss with respect to stock—(1) Allocation against gain. Except as otherwise provided in paragraph (b) of this section, loss recognized with respect to stock shall be allocated to the class of gross income and, if necessary, apportioned between the statutory grouping of gross income (or among the statutory groupings) and the residual grouping of gross income, with respect to which gain (other than gain treated as a dividend under section 964(e)(1) or 1248) from a sale of such stock would give rise in the hands of the seller (without regard to section 865(f)). For purposes of this section, loss includes loss on property that is marked-to-market (such as under section 475) and subject to the rules of this section. Thus, for example, loss recognized by a United States resident on the sale of stock generally is allocated to reduce United States source income.

(2) Stock attributable to foreign office. Except as otherwise provided in paragraph (b) of this section, in the case of loss recognized by a United States resident with respect to stock that is attributable to an office or other fixed place of business in a foreign country within the meaning of section 865(e)(3), the loss shall be allocated to reduce foreign source income if a gain on the sale of the stock would have been taxable by the foreign country and the highest marginal rate of tax imposed on such gains in the foreign country is at least 10 percent.

(3) Loss recognized by United States citizen or resident alien with foreign tax home—(i) In general. Except as otherwise provided in paragraph (b) of this section, in the case of loss with respect to stock that is recognized by a United States citizen or resident alien that has a tax home (as defined in section 911(d)(3)) in a foreign country, the loss shall be allocated to reduce foreign source income if a gain on the sale of the stock would have been taxable by a foreign country and the highest marginal rate of tax imposed on such gains in the foreign country is at least 10 percent.

* * *

(4) Stock constituting a United States real property interest. Loss recognized by a non-resident alien individual or a foreign corporation with respect to stock that constitutes a United States real property interest shall be allocated to reduce United States source income. For additional rules governing the treatment of such loss, see section 897 and the regulations thereunder.

* * *

[T.D. 8805, 64 FR 1511, Jan. 11, 1999; T.D. 8973, 66 FR 67086, Dec. 28, 2001; 67 FR 3812, Jan. 28, 2002]

§ 1.865–3 Source of gross income from sales of personal property (including inventory property) by a nonresident attributable to an office or other fixed place of business in the United States.

(a) In general. Notwithstanding any provision of section 861 through 865 or other regulations in this part, this section provides the sole sourcing rules for gross income, gain, or loss from section 865(e)(2) sales. Gross income, gain, or loss from a section 865(e)(2) sale is U.S. source income to the extent that the gross income, gain, or loss is properly allocable to an office or other fixed place of business in the United States under paragraph (d) of this section.

(b) Exception for certain inventory sales for use, disposition or consumption outside the United States. A section 865(e)(2) sale does not include any sale of inventory property that is sold for use, disposition, or consumption outside the United States if an office or other fixed place of business of the nonresident in a foreign country materially participates in the sale. See § 1.864–6(b)(3) to determine whether a foreign office materially participates in the sale and whether the property was destined for foreign use.

(c) Section 865(e)(2) sales. For purposes of this section, a "section 865(e)(2) sale" is a sale of personal property by a nonresident, including inventory property, other than a sale described in paragraph (b) of this section, that is attributable to an office or other fixed place of business in the United States under the principles of section 864(c)(5)(B) as prescribed in § 1.864–6(b)(1) and (2). In determining whether a nonresident maintains an office or other fixed place of business in the United States, the principles of section 864(c)(5)(A) as prescribed in § 1.864–7 apply, including the rules of paragraph (d) of that section regarding the office or other fixed place of business of a dependent agent of the nonresident. For purposes of this section, "inventory property" has the meaning provided in section 865(i)(1), and "nonresident" has the meaning provided in section 865(g)(1)(B).

(d) Amount of gross income, gain, or loss on sale of personal property properly allocable to a U.S. office—(1) In general. Except as otherwise provided in paragraphs (d)(2) through (4) of this section, the amount of gross income, gain, or loss from a section 865(e)(2) sale that is properly allocable to an office or other fixed place of business in the United States is determined under the principles of § 1.864–6(c)(1).

(2) Produced inventory property. Gross income, gain, or loss from a section 865(e)(2) sale of inventory property that is produced by the nonresident seller is properly allocable to an office or other fixed place of business in the United States or to production activities in accordance with the "50/50 method" described in paragraph (d)(2)(i) of this section. However, in lieu of the 50/50 method, the nonresident seller may elect to allocate the gross income, gain, or loss under the "books and records method" described in paragraph (d)(2)(ii)(A) of this section, provided that the nonresident satisfies all of the requirements described in paragraph (d)(2)(ii)(B) of this section to the satisfaction of the Commissioner. Gross income allocable to production activities under this paragraph (d)(2) is sourced in accordance with § 1.863–3. For purposes of this paragraph (d)(2), the term "produced" includes created, fabricated, manufactured, extracted, processed, cured, and aged, as determined under the principles of § 1.954–3(a)(4) (except for § 1.954–3(a)(4)(iv)). See section 864(a) and § 1.864–1.

(i) The 50/50 method. Fifty percent of the gross income, gain, or loss from a section 865(e)(2) sale of inventory property that is produced by the nonresident seller is properly allocable to an office or other fixed place of business in the United States, and the remaining 50 percent of the gross income, gain, or loss is properly allocable to production activities (the "50/50 method").

(ii) Books and records method—(A) Method. Subject to paragraph (d)(2)(ii)(B) of this section, a nonresident may elect to determine the amount of its gross income, gain, or loss from the sale of inventory property produced by the nonresident seller that is properly allocable to production activities and sales activities for the taxable year based upon its books of account (the "books and records method"). The gross income, gain, or loss allocable to sales activities under this method is treated as properly allocable to an office or other fixed place of business in the United States and the remaining gross income, gain, or loss is treated as properly allocable to production activities.

(B) Election and reporting rules—(1) In general. A nonresident may not make the election described in paragraph (d)(2)(ii)(A) of this section unless the requirements of paragraphs (d)(2)(ii)(B)(2) through (4) of this section are satisfied. Once the election is made, the nonresident must continue to satisfy the requirements of paragraphs (d)(2)(ii)(B)(2) through (4) of this section until the election is revoked. If the nonresident fails to satisfy the requirements in paragraphs (d)(2)(ii)(B)(2) through (4) of this section to the satisfaction of the Commissioner, the Commissioner may, in its sole discretion, apply the 50/50 method described in paragraph (d)(2)(i) of this section.

(2) Books of account. The nonresident must establish that it, in good faith and unaffected by considerations of tax liability, regularly employs in its books of account a detailed allocation of receipts and expenditures that, under the principles of section 482, clearly reflects both the amount of the nonresident's gross income, gain, or loss from its inventory sales that are attributable to its sales activities, and the amount of its gross income, gain, or loss from its inventory sales that are attributable to its production activities. For purposes of this paragraph (d)(2)(ii)(B)(2), section 482 principles apply as if the office or other fixed place of business in the United States were a separate organization, trade, or business (and, thus, a separate controlled taxpayer) from the nonresident (whether or not payments are made between the United States office or other fixed place of business and the nonresident's other offices, and whether or not the nonresident itself would otherwise constitute an organization, trade, or business).

(3) Required records. The nonresident must prepare and maintain the records described in paragraph (d)(2)(ii)(B)(2) of this section, which must be in existence when its return is filed. The nonresident must also prepare an explanation of how the allocation clearly reflects the nonresident's gross income, gain, or loss from production and sales activities under the principles of section 482. The nonresident must make available the explanation and records of the nonresident (including for the office or other fixed place of business in the United States and the offices or branches that perform the production activities) upon request of the Commissioner, within 30 days, unless some other period is agreed upon between the Commissioner and the nonresident.

(4) Making and revoking the books and records method election; disclosure of election. Except as otherwise provided in publications, forms, instructions, or other guidance, a nonresident makes or revokes the election to apply the books and records method by attaching a statement to its original timely filed Federal income tax return (including extensions) providing that it elects, or revokes the election, to apply the books and records method described in paragraph (d)(2)(ii)(A) of this section. For nonresidents making the election, the statement must provide that the nonresident has prepared the records described in paragraph (d)(2)(ii)(B)(2) and (3) of this section.

(5) Limitation on revoking the books and records method election. Once made, the books and records method election continues until revoked. An election cannot be revoked, without the consent of the Commissioner, for any taxable year beginning within 48 months of the last day of the taxable year for which the election was made.

(3) Purchased inventory property. All gross income, gain, or loss from a section 865(e)(2) sale of inventory property that is both purchased and sold by a nonresident is properly allocable to an office or other fixed place of business in the United States.

(4) Depreciable personal property. Gain from a section 865(e)(2) sale of depreciable personal property (as defined in section 865(c)(4)) is allocated under paragraphs (d)(4)(i) and (ii) of this section.

(i) The gain not in excess of the depreciation adjustments, if any, is properly allocable to an office or other fixed place of business in the United States to the same extent that the gain would be allocated to sources within the United States under the rules of section 865(c)(1). The remaining gain not in excess of the depreciation adjustments, if any, is allocated to sources without the United States in accordance with section 865(c)(1). However, notwithstanding the preceding sentences, if the property was predominantly used in the United States, within the meaning of section 865(c)(3)(B)(i), for a particular taxable year, all of the gain not in excess of depreciation for that year is properly allocable to the office or other fixed place of business in the United States.

(ii) The gain in excess of the depreciation adjustments, if any, is treated as if such gain was from the sale of inventory and the amount allocable to an office or fixed place of business in the United States is determined under paragraph (d)(2) or (3) of this section, as applicable.

(e) Determination of source of taxable income. For rules allocating and apportioning expenses to gross income effectively connected with the conduct of a trade or business of a foreign corporation in the United States (including gross income, gain, or loss sourced under this section), see section 882(c)(1). For rules allocating and apportioning expenses to gross income, gain, or loss effectively connected with the conduct of a trade or business of a nonresident alien in the United States (including gross income, gain, or loss sourced under this section), see section 873(a).

* * *

[T.D. 9921, 85 FR 79851, Dec. 11, 2020]

§ 1.871–2 Determining residence of alien individuals.

(a) General. The term nonresident alien individual means an individual whose residence is not within the United States, and who is not a citizen of the United States. The term includes a nonresident alien fiduciary. For such purpose the term fiduciary shall have the meaning assigned to it by section 7701(a)(6) and the regulations in part 301 of this chapter (Regulations on Procedure and Administration). For presumption as to an alien's nonresidence, see paragraph (b) of § 1.871–4.

(b) Residence defined. An alien actually present in the United States who is not a mere transient or sojourner is a resident of the United States for purposes of the income tax. Whether he is a transient is determined by his intentions with regard to the length and nature of his stay. A mere floating intention, indefinite as to time, to return to another country is not sufficient to constitute him a transient. If he lives in the United States and has no definite intention as to his stay, he is a resident. One who comes to the United States for a definite purpose which in its nature may be promptly accomplished is a transient; but, if his purpose is of such a nature that an extended stay may be necessary for its accomplishment, and to that end the alien makes his home temporarily in the United States, he becomes a resident, though it may be his intention at all times to return to his domicile abroad when the purpose for which he came has been consummated or abandoned. An alien whose stay in the United States is limited to a definite period by the immigration laws is not a resident of the United States within the meaning of this section, in the absence of exceptional circumstances.

* * *

[T.D. 6500, 25 FR 11910, Nov. 26, 1960; T.D. 8411, 57 FR 15241, April 27, 1992]

§ 1.871–7 Taxation of nonresident alien individuals not engaged in U.S. business.

(a) Imposition of tax. (1) This section applies for purposes of determining the tax of a nonresident alien individual who at no time during the taxable year is engaged in trade or business in the United States. However, see also § 1.871–8 where such individual is a student or trainee deemed to be engaged in trade or business in the United States or where he has an election in effect for the taxable year in respect to real property income. Except as otherwise provided in § 1.871–12, a nonresident alien individual to whom this section applies is not subject to the tax imposed by section 1 or section 1201(b) but, pursuant to the provision of section 871(a), is liable to a flat tax of 30 percent upon the aggregate of the amounts determined under paragraphs (b), (c), and (d) of this section which are received during the taxable year from sources within the United States. Except as specifically provided in such paragraphs, such amounts do not include gains from the sale or exchange of property. To determine the source of such amounts, see sections 861 through 863, and the regulations thereunder.

(2) The tax of 30 percent is imposed by section 871(a) upon an amount only to the extent the amount constitutes gross income. Thus, for example, the amount of an annuity which is subject to such tax shall be determined in accordance with section 72.

(3) Deductions shall not be allowed in determining the amount subject to tax under this section except that losses from sales or exchanges of capital assets shall be allowed to the extent provided in section 871(a)(2) and paragraph (d) of this section.

(4) Except as provided in §§ 1.871–9 and 1.871–10, a nonresident alien individual not engaged in trade or business in the United States during the taxable year has no income, gain, or loss for the taxable year which is effectively connected for the taxable year with the conduct of a trade or business in the United States. See section 864(c)(1)(B) and § 1.864–3.

(5) Gains and losses which, by reason of section 871(d) and § 1.871–10, are treated as gains or losses which are effectively connected for the taxable year with the conduct of a trade or business in the United States by the nonresident alien individual shall not be taken into account in determining the tax under this section. See, for example, paragraph (c)(2) of § 1.871–10.

(6) For special rules applicable in determining the tax of certain nonresident alien individuals, see paragraph (b) of § 1.871–1.

(b) Fixed or determinable annual or periodical income—(1) General rule. The tax of 30 percent imposed by section 871(a)(1) applies to the gross amount received from sources within the United States as fixed or determinable annual or periodical gains, profits, or income. Specific items of fixed or determinable annual or periodical income are enumerated in section 871(a)(1)(A) as interest, dividends, rents, salaries, wages, premiums, annuities, compensations, remunerations, and emoluments, but other items of fixed or determinable annual or periodical gains, profits, or income are also subject to the tax, as, for instance, royalties, including royalties for the use of patents, copyrights, secret processes and formulas, and other like property. As to the determination of fixed or determinable annual or periodical income see § 1.1441–2(b). For special rules treating gain on the disposition of section 306 stock as fixed or determinable annual or periodical income for purposes of section 871(a), see section 306(f) and paragraph (h) of § 1.306–3.

(2) Substitute payments. For purposes of this section, a substitute interest payment (as defined in § 1.861–2(a)(7)) received by a foreign person pursuant to a securities lending transaction or a sale-repurchase transaction (as defined in § 1.861–2(a)(7)) shall have the same character as interest income paid or accrued with respect to the terms of the transferred security. Similarly, for purposes of this section, a substitute dividend payment (as defined in § 1.861–3(a)(6)) received by a foreign person pursuant to a securities lending transaction or a sale-repurchase transaction (as defined in § 1.861–3(a)(6)) shall have the same character as a distribution received with respect to the transferred security. Where, pursuant to a securities lending transaction or a sale-repurchase transaction, a foreign person transfers to another person a security the interest on which would qualify as portfolio interest under section 871(h) in the hands of the lender, substitute interest payments made with respect to the transferred security will be treated as portfolio interest, provided that in the case of interest on an obligation in registered form (as defined in § 1.871–14(c)(1)(i)), the transferor complies with the documentation requirement described in § 1.871–14(c)(1)(ii)(C) with respect to the payment of the substitute interest and none of the exceptions to the portfolio interest exemption in sections 871(h)(3) and (4) apply. See also §§ 1.861–2(b)(2) and 1.894–1(c).

(c) Other income and gains—(1) Items subject to tax. The tax of 30 percent imposed by section 871(a)(1) also applies to the following gains received during the taxable year from sources within the United States:

(i) Gains described in section 402(a)(2), relating to the treatment of total distributions from certain employees' trusts; section 403(a)(2), relating to treatment of certain payments under certain employee annuity plans; and section 631(b) or (c), relating to treatment of gain on the disposal of timber, coal, or iron ore with a retained economic interest;

(ii) [Reserved]

(iii) Gains on transfers described in section 1235, relating to certain transfers of patent rights, made on or before October 4, 1966; and

(iv) Gains from the sale or exchange after October 4, 1966, of patents, copyrights, secret processes and formulas, good will, trademarks, trade brands, franchises, or other like property, or of any interest in any such property, to the extent the gains are from payments (whether in a lump sum or in installments) which are contingent on the productivity, use or disposition of the property or interest sold or exchanged, or from payments which are treated under section 871(e) and § 1.871–11 as being so contingent.

(2) Nonapplication of 183-day rule. The provisions of section 871(a)(2), relating to gains from the sale or exchange of capital assets, and paragraph (d)(2) of this section do not apply to the gains described in this paragraph; as a consequence, the taxpayer receiving gains described in subparagraph (1) of this paragraph during a taxable year is subject to the tax of 30 percent thereon without regard to the 183-day rule contained in such provisions.

(3) Determination of amount of gain. The tax of 30 percent imposed upon the gains described in subparagraph (1) of this paragraph applies to the full amount of the gains and is determined (i) without regard to the alternative tax imposed by section 1201(b) upon the excess of the net long-term capital gain over the net short-term capital loss; (ii) without regard to the deduction allowed by section 1202 in respect of capital gains; (iii) without regard to section 1231, relating to property used in the trade or business and involuntary conversions; and (iv), except in the case of gains described in subparagraph (1)(ii) of this paragraph, whether or not the gains are considered to be gains from the sale or exchange of property which is a capital asset.

(d) Gains from sale or exchange of capital assets—(1) Gains subject to tax. The tax of 30 percent imposed by section 871(a)(2) applies to the excess of gains derived from sources within the United States over losses allocable to sources within the United States, which are derived from the sale or exchange of capital assets, determined in accordance with the provisions of subparagraphs (2) through (4) of this paragraph.

(2) Presence in the United States 183 days or more. (i) If the nonresident alien individual has been present in the United States for a period or periods aggregating 183 days or more during the taxable year, he is liable to a tax of 30 percent upon the amount by which his gains, derived from sources within the United States, from sales or exchanges of capital assets effected at any time during the year exceed his losses, allocable to sources within the United States, from sales or exchanges of capital assets effected at any time during that year. Gains and losses from sales or exchanges effected at any time during such taxable year are to be taken into account for this purpose even though the nonresident alien individual is not present in the United States at the time the sales or exchanges are effected. In addition, if the nonresident alien individual has been present in the United States for a period or periods aggregating 183 days or more during the taxable year, gains and losses for such taxable year from sales or exchanges of capital assets effected during a previous taxable year beginning after December 31, 1966, are to be taken into account, but only if he was also present in the United States during such previous taxable year for a period or periods aggregating 183 days or more.

(ii) If the nonresident alien individual has not been present in the United States during the taxable year, or if he has been present in the United States for a period or periods aggregating less than 183 days during the taxable year, gains and losses from sales or exchanges of capital assets effected during the year are not to be taken into account, except as required by paragraph (c) of this section, in determining the tax of such individual even though the sales or exchanges are effected during his presence in the United States. Moreover, gains and losses for such taxable year from sales or exchanges of capital assets effected during a previous taxable year beginning after December 31, 1966, are not to be taken into account, even though the nonresident alien individual was present in the United States during such previous year for a period or periods aggregating 183 days or more.

(iii) For purposes of this subparagraph, a nonresident alien individual is not considered to be present in the United States by reason of the presence in the United States of a person who is an agent or partner of such individual or who is a fiduciary of an estate or trust of which such individual is a beneficiary or a grantor-owner to whom section 671 applies.

(iv) The application of this subparagraph may be illustrated by the following examples:

* * *

Example 3. D, a nonresident alien individual not engaged in trade or business in the United States and using the calendar year as the taxable year, is present in the United States from April 1, 1971, to August 31, 1971, a period of less than 183 days. While present in the United States, D effects for his own account on various dates a number of transactions in stocks and securities on the stock exchange, as a result of which he has recognized capital gains of $15,000. During the period from January 1, 1971, to March 31, 1971, he carries out similar transactions through an agent in the United States, as a result of which D has recognized capital gains of $8,000. On December 20, 1971, through an agent in the United States D sells a capital asset on the installment plan, no payments being made by the purchaser in 1971. During 1972, D receives installment payments of $200,000 on the installment sale made in 1971, and the capital gain from sources within the United States for 1972 attributable to such payments is $50,000. In addition, during the period from February 1, 1972, to August 15, 1972, a period of more than 182 days. D effects for his own account, through an agent in the United States, a number of transactions in stocks and securities on the stock exchange, as a result of which D has recognized capital gains of $25,000. At no time during 1972 is D present in the United States or engaged in trade or business in the United States. Accordingly, D is not subject to tax for 1971 or 1972 on any of his recognized capital gains.

Example 4. The facts are the same as in example 3 except that D is present in the United States from February 1, 1972, to August 15, 1972, a period of more than 182 days. Accordingly, D is not subject to tax for 1971 on his capital gains of $23,000 from the transactions in that year on the stock exchange. For 1972 he is subject to tax under section 871(a)(2) on his capital gains of $25,000 from the transactions in that year on the stock exchange, but he is not subject to the tax on the capital gain of $50,000 from the installment sale in 1971.

(3) Determination of 183-day period—(i) In general. In determining the total period of presence in the United States for a taxable year for purposes of subparagraph (2) of this paragraph, all separate periods of presence in the United States during the taxable year are to be aggregated. If the nonresident alien individual has not previously established a taxable year, as defined in section 441(b), he shall be treated as having a taxable year which is the calendar year, as defined in section 441(d). Subsequent adoption by such individual of a fiscal year as the taxable year will be treated as a change in the taxpayer's annual accounting period to which section 442 applies, and the change must be authorized under this part (Income Tax Regulations) or prior approval must be obtained by filing an application on Form 1128 in accordance with paragraph (b) of § 1.442–1. If in the course of his taxable year the nonresident alien individual changes his status from that of a citizen or resident of the United States to that of a nonresident alien individual, or vice versa, the determination of whether the individual has been present in the United States for 183 days or more during the taxable year shall be made by taking into account the entire taxable year, and not just that part of the taxable year during which he has the status of a nonresident alien individual.

(ii) Definition of "day". The term "day", as used in subparagraph (2) of this paragraph, means a calendar day during any portion of which the nonresident alien individual is physically present in the United States (within the meaning of sections 7701(a)(9) and 638) except that, in the case of an individual who is a resident of Canada or Mexico and, in the normal course of his employment in transportation service touching points within both Canada or Mexico and the United States, performs personal services in both the foreign country and the United States, the following rules shall apply:

(a) The performance of labor or personal services during 8 hours or more in any 1 day within the United States shall be considered as 1 day in the United States, except that if a period of more or less than 8 hours is considered a full workday in the transportation job involved, such period shall be considered as 1 day within the United States.

(b) The performance of labor or personal services during less than 8 hours in any day in the United States shall, except as provided in (a) of this subdivision, be considered as a fractional part of a day in the United States. The total number of hours during which such services are performed in the United States during the taxable year, when divided by eight, shall be the number of days during which such individual shall be considered present in the United States during the taxable year.

(c) The aggregate number of days determined under (a) and (b) of this subdivision shall be considered the total number of days during which such individual is present in the United States during the taxable year.

(4) Determination of amount of excess gains—(i) In general. For the purpose of determining the excess of gains over losses subject to tax under this paragraph, gains and losses shall be taken into account only if, and to the extent that, they would be recognized and taken into account if the nonresident alien individual were engaged in trade or business in the United States during the taxable year and such gains and losses were effectively connected for such year with the conduct of a trade or business in the United States by such individual. However, in determining such excess of gains over losses no deduction may be taken under section 1202, relating to the deduction for capital gains, or section 1212, relating to the capital loss carryover. Thus, for example, in determining such excess gains all amounts considered under chapter 1 of the

Code as gains or losses from the sale or exchange of capital assets shall be taken into account, except those gains which are described in section 871(a)(1)(B) or (D) and taken into account under paragraph (c) of this section and are considered to be gains from the sale or exchange of capital assets. Also, for example, a loss described in section 631 (b) or (c) which is considered to be a loss from the sale of a capital asset shall be taken into account in determining the excess gains which are subject to tax under this paragraph. In further illustration, in determining such excess gains no deduction shall be allowed, pursuant to the provisions of section 267, for losses from sales or exchanges of property between related taxpayers. Any gains which are taken into account under section 871(a)(1) and paragraph (c) of this section shall not be taken into account in applying section 1231 for purposes of this paragraph. Gains and losses are to be taken into account under this paragraph whether they are short-term or long-term capital gains or losses within the meaning of section 1222.

(ii) Gains not included. The provisions of this paragraph do not apply to any gains described in section 871(a)(1)(B) or (D), and in subdivision (i), (iii), or (iv) of paragraph (c)(1) of this section, which are considered to be gains from the sale or exchange of capital assets.

(iii) Allowance of losses. In determining the excess of gains over losses subject to tax under this paragraph losses shall be allowed only to the extent provided by section 165(c). Losses from sales or exchanges of capital assets in excess of gains from sales or exchanges of capital assets shall not be taken into account.

(e) Credits against tax. The credits allowed by section 31 (relating to tax withheld on wages), by section 32 (relating to tax withheld at source on nonresident aliens), by section 39 (relating to certain uses of gasoline and lubricating oil), and by section 6402 (relating to overpayments of tax) shall be allowed against the tax of a nonresident alien individual determined in accordance with this section.

* * *

[T.D. 7332, 39 FR 44219, Dec. 23, 1974; T.D. 8734, 62 FR 53416, Oct. 14, 1997; T.D. 8735, 62 FR 53501, Oct. 14, 1997; T.D. 8804, 63 FR 72183, Dec. 31, 1998; T.D. 8856, 64 FR 73408, Dec. 30, 1999]

§ 1.871–8 Taxation of nonresident alien individuals engaged in U.S. business or treated as having effectively connected income.

(a) Segregation of income. This section applies for purposes of determining the tax of a nonresident alien individual who at any time during the taxable year is engaged in trade or business in the United States. It also applies for purposes of determining the tax of a nonresident alien student or trainee who is deemed under section 871(c) and § 1.871–9 to be engaged in trade or business in the United States or of a nonresident alien individual who at no time during the taxable year is engaged in trade or business in the United States but has an election in effect for the taxable year under section 871(d) and § 1.871–10 in respect to real property income. A nonresident alien individual to whom this section applies must segregate his gross income for the taxable year into two categories, namely (1) the income which is effectively connected for the taxable year with the conduct of a trade or business in the United States by that individual, and (2) the income which is not effectively connected for the taxable year with the conduct of a trade or business in the United States by that individual. A separate tax shall then be determined upon each such category of income, as provided in paragraph (b) of this section. The determination of whether income or gain is or is not effectively connected for the taxable year with the conduct of a trade or business in the United States by the nonresident alien individual shall be made in accordance with section 864(c) and §§ 1.864–3 through 1.864–7. For purposes of this section income which is effectively connected for the taxable year with the conduct of a trade or business in the United States includes all income which is treated under section 871(c) or (d) and § 1.871–9 or § 1.871–10 as income which is effectively connected for such year with the conduct of a trade or business in the United States by the nonresident alien individual.

(b) Imposition of tax—(1) Income not effectively connected with the conduct of a trade or business in the United States. If a nonresident alien individual who is engaged in trade or business in the United States at any time during the taxable year derives during such year from sources within the United States income or gains described in section 871(a)(1), and paragraph (b) or (c) of § 1.871–7 or gains from the sale or exchange of capital assets determined as provided in section 871(a)(2) and paragraph (d) of § 1.871–7, which are not effectively connected for the taxable year with the conduct of a trade or business in the United States by that individual, such income or gains shall be subject to a flat tax of 30 percent of the aggregate amount of such items. This tax shall be determined in the manner, and subject to the same conditions, set forth in § 1.871–7 as though the income or gains were derived by a nonresident alien individual not engaged in trade or business in the United States during the taxable year, except that (i) the rule in paragraph (d)(3) of such section for treating the calendar year as the taxable year shall not apply and (ii) in applying paragraph (c) and (d)(4) of such section, there shall not be taken into account any gains or losses which are taken into account in determining the tax under section 871(b) and subparagraph (2) of this paragraph. A nonresident alien individual who has an election in effect for the taxable year under section 871(d) and § 1.871–10 and who at no time during the taxable year is engaged in trade or business in the United States must determine his tax under § 1.871–7 on his income which is not treated as effectively connected with the conduct of a trade or business in the United States, subject to the exception contained in subdivision (ii) of this subparagraph.

(2) Income effectively connected with the conduct of a trade or business in the United States—(i) In general. If a nonresident alien to whom this section applies derives income or gains which are effectively connected for the taxable year with the conduct of a trade or business in the United States by that individual, the taxable income or gains shall, except as provided in § 1.871–12, be taxed in accordance with section 1 or, in the alternative, section 1201(b). See section 871(b)(1). Any income of the nonresident alien individual which is not effectively connected for the taxable year with the conduct of a trade or business in the United States by that individual shall not be taken into account in determining either the rate or amount of such tax. See paragraph (b) of § 1.872–1.

(ii) Determination of taxable income. The taxable income for any taxable year for purposes of this subparagraph consists only of the nonresident alien individual's taxable income which is effectively connected for the taxable year with the conduct of a trade or business in the United States by that individual; and, for this purpose, it is immaterial that the trade or business with which that income is effectively connected is not the same as the trade or business carried on in the United States by that individual during the taxable year. See example 2 in § 1.864–4(b). In determining such taxable income all amounts constituting, or considered to be, gains or losses for the taxable year from the sale or exchange of capital assets shall be taken into account if such gains or losses are effectively connected for the taxable year with the conduct of a trade or business in the United States by that individual, and, for such purpose, the 183-day rule set forth in section 871(a)(2) and paragraph (d)(2) of § 1.871–7 shall not apply. Losses which are not effectively connected for the taxable year with the conduct of a trade or business in the United States by that individual shall not be taken into account in determining taxable income under this subdivision, except as provided in section 873(b)(1).

(iii) Cross references. For rules for determining the gross income and deductions for the taxable year, see sections 872 and 873, and the regulations thereunder.

(c) Change in trade or business status—(1) In general. The determination as to whether a nonresident alien individual is engaged in trade or business within the United States during the taxable year is to be made for each taxable year. If at any time during the taxable year he is engaged in a trade or business in the United States, he is considered to be engaged in trade or business within the United States during the taxable year for purposes of sections 864(c)(1) and 871(b), and the regulations thereunder. Income, gain, or loss of a nonresident alien individual is not treated as being effectively connected for the taxable year with the conduct of a trade or business in the United States if he is not engaged in trade or business within the United States during such year, even though such income, gain, or loss may have been effectively connected for a previous taxable year with the conduct of a trade or business in the United States. See § 1.864–3. However, income, gain, or loss which is treated as effectively connected for the taxable year with the conduct of a trade or business in the United States by a nonresident alien individual will generally be treated as effectively connected for a subsequent taxable year if he is engaged in a trade or business in the United States during such subsequent year, even though such income, gain, or loss is not effectively connected with the conduct of the trade or business carried on in the United States during such subsequent year. This subparagraph does not apply to income described in section 871 (c) or (d). It may not apply to a nonresident alien individual who for the taxable year uses an accrual method of accounting or to income which is constructively received in the taxable year within the meaning of § 1.451–2.

* * *

(d) Credits against tax. The credits allowed by section 31 (relating to tax withheld on wages), section 32 (relating to tax withheld at source on nonresident aliens), section 33 (relating to the foreign tax credit), section 35 (relating to partially tax-exempt interest), section 38 (relating to investment in certain depreciable property), section 39 (relating to certain uses of gasoline and lubricating oil), section 40 (relating to expenses of work incentive programs), and section 6402 (relating to overpayments of tax) shall be allowed against the tax determined in accordance with this section. However, the credits allowed by sections 33, 38, and 40 shall not be allowed against the flat tax of 30 percent imposed by section 871(a) and paragraph (b)(1) of this section. Moreover, no credit shall be allowed under section 35 to a nonresident alien individual with respect to whom a tax is imposed for the taxable year under section 871(a) and paragraph (b)(1) of this section, even though such individual has income for such year upon which tax is imposed under section 871(b) and paragraph (b)(2) of this section. For special rules applicable in determining the foreign tax credit, see section 906(b) and the regulations thereunder. For the disallowance of certain credits where a return is not filed for the taxable year, see section 874 and § 1.874–1.

* * *

[T.D. 7332, 39 FR 44221, Dec. 23, 1974]

§ 1.873–1 Deductions allowed nonresident alien individuals.

(a) General provisions—(1) Allocation of deductions. In computing the taxable income of a nonresident alien individual the deductions otherwise allowable shall be allowed only if, and to the extent that, they are connected with income from sources within the United States. No deduction shall be allowed in respect of any item, or portion thereof, which is not connected with income from such sources. For this purpose, the proper apportionment and allocation of the deductions with respect to sources of income within and without the United States shall be determined as provided in part I (section 861 and following), subchapter N, chapter 1 of the Code, and the regulations thereunder, except as may otherwise be provided by tax convention. Thus, from the items of gross income specifically from sources within the United States and from the items allocated thereto under the provisions of section 863(a), there shall be deducted (i) the expenses, losses, and other deductions which are connected with those items of income and are properly apportioned or allocated thereto, and (ii) a ratable part of any other expenses, losses, or deductions which are connected with those items of income but cannot definitely be allocated to some item or class of gross income. The ratable part shall be based upon the ratio of gross income from sources within the United States to the total gross income. See §§ 1.861–8 and 1.863–1. In the case of income partly from within and partly from without the United States the expenses, losses, and other deductions connected with income from sources within the United States shall also be deducted in the manner prescribed by §§ 1.863–2 through 1.863–5 in order to ascertain under section 863 the portion of the taxable income attributable to sources within the United States.

(2) Personal exemptions. The deductions for the personal exemptions allowed by section 151 or 642(b) shall not be taken into account for purposes of subparagraph (1) of this paragraph but shall be allowed to the extent provided by paragraphs (b) and (c) of this section.

(3) Adjusted gross income. The adjusted gross income of a nonresident alien individual shall be the gross income from sources within the United States, determined in accordance with § 1.871–7, minus the deductions prescribed by section 62 to the extent such deductions are allowed under this section in computing taxable income.

(4) Standard deduction. The standard deduction shall not be allowed in computing the taxable income of a nonresident alien individual. See section 142(b)(1) and the regulations thereunder.

(5) Exempt income. No deduction shall be allowed under this section for the amount of any item or part thereof allocable to a class or classes of exempt income, including income exempt by tax convention. See section 265 and the regulations thereunder.

* * *

[T.D. 6500, 25 FR 11910, Nov. 26, 1960]

§ 1.874–1 Allowance of deductions and credits to nonresident alien individuals.

(a) Return required. A nonresident alien individual shall receive the benefit of the deductions and credits otherwise allowable with respect to the income tax, only if the nonresident alien individual timely files or causes to be filed with the Philadelphia Service Center, in the manner prescribed in subtitle F, a true and accurate return of the income which is effectively connected, or treated as effectively connected, with the conduct of a trade or business within the United States by the nonresident alien individual. * * *

* * *

[T.D. 6500, 25 FR 11910, Nov. 26, 1960, as amended by T.D. 6669, 28 FR 9385, Aug. 27, 1963; T.D. 8322, 55 FR 50828, Dec. 11, 1990; T.D. 8322, 56 FR 1361, Jan. 14, 1991; T.D. 8981, 67 FR 4174, Jan. 29, 2002; T.D. 9043, 68 FR 11313, March 10, 2003]

§ 1.881–3 Conduit financing arrangements.

(a) General rules and definitions—(1) Purpose and scope. Pursuant to the authority of section 7701(*l*), this section provides rules that permit the director of field operations to disregard, for purposes of section 881, the participation of one or more intermediate entities in a financing arrangement where such entities are acting as conduit entities. * * *

* * *

(3) Disregard of participation of conduit entity—(i) Authority of director of field

operations. The director of field operations may determine that the participation of a conduit entity in a conduit financing arrangement should be disregarded for purposes of section 881. For this purpose, an intermediate entity will constitute a conduit entity if it meets the standards of paragraph (a)(4) of this section. The director of field operations has discretion to determine the manner in which the standards of paragraph (a)(4) of this section apply, including the financing transactions and parties composing the financing arrangement.

(ii) Effect of disregarding conduit entity (A) In general. If the director of field operations determines that the participation of a conduit entity in a financing arrangement should be disregarded, the financing arrangement is re-characterized as a transaction directly between the remaining parties to the financing arrangement (in most cases, the financed entity and the financing entity) for purposes of section 881. To the extent that a disregarded conduit entity actually receives or makes payments pursuant to a conduit financing arrangement, it is treated as an agent of the financing entity. * * *

(4) Standard for treatment as a conduit entity—(i) In general. An intermediate entity is a conduit entity with respect to a financing arrangement if—

(A) The participation of the intermediate entity (or entities) in the financing arrangement reduces the tax imposed by section 881 (determined by comparing the aggregate tax imposed under section 881 on payments made on financing transactions making up the financing arrangement with the tax that would have been imposed under paragraph (d) of this section);

(B) The participation of the intermediate entity in the financing arrangement is pursuant to a tax avoidance plan; and

(C) Either—

(1) The intermediate entity is related to the financing entity or the financed entity; or

(2) The intermediate entity would not have participated in the financing arrangement on substantially the same terms but for the fact that the financing entity engaged in the financing transaction with the intermediate entity.

* * *

(b) Determination of whether participation of intermediate entity is pursuant to a tax avoidance plan—(1) In general. A tax avoidance plan is a plan one of the principal purposes of which is the avoidance of tax imposed by section 881. Avoidance of the tax imposed by section 881 may be one of the principal purposes for such a plan even though it is outweighed by other purposes (taken together or separately). In this regard, the only relevant purposes are those pertaining to the participation of the intermediate entity in the financing arrangement and not those pertaining to the existence of a financing arrangement as a whole. The plan may be formal or informal, written or oral, and may involve any one or more of the parties to the financing arrangement. The plan must be in existence no later than the last date that any of the financing transactions comprising the financing arrangement is entered into. The director of field operations may infer the existence of a tax avoidance plan from the facts and circumstances. In determining whether there is a tax avoidance plan, the director of field operations will weigh all relevant evidence regarding the purposes for the intermediate entity's participation in the financing arrangement. * * *

(2) Factors taken into account in determining the presence or absence of a tax avoidance purpose. The factors described in paragraphs (b)(2)(i) through (iv) of this section are among the facts and circumstances taken into account in determining whether the participation of an intermediate entity in a financing arrangement has as one of its principal purposes the avoidance of tax imposed by section 881.

(i) Significant reduction in tax. The director of field operations will consider whether the participation of the intermediate entity (or entities) in the financing arrangement significantly reduces the tax that otherwise would have been imposed under section 881. The fact that an intermediate entity is a resident of a country that has an income tax treaty with the United States that significantly reduces the tax that otherwise would have been imposed under section 881 is not sufficient, by itself, to establish the existence of a tax avoidance plan. The determination of whether the participation of an intermediate entity significantly reduces the tax generally is made by comparing the aggregate tax imposed under section 881 on payments made on financing transactions making up the financing arrangement with the tax that would be imposed under paragraph (d) of this section. However, the taxpayer is not barred from presenting evidence that the financing entity, as determined by the director of field operations, was itself an intermediate entity and another entity should be treated as the financing entity for purposes of applying this test. A reduction in the absolute amount of tax may be significant even if the reduction in rate is not. A reduction in the amount of tax may be significant if the reduction is large in absolute terms or in relative terms. * * *

(ii) Ability to make the advance. The director of field operations will consider whether the intermediate entity had sufficient available money or other property of its own to have made the advance to the financed entity without the advance of money or other property to it by the financing entity (or in the case of multiple intermediate entities, whether each of the intermediate entities had sufficient available money or other property of its own to have made the advance to either the financed entity or another intermediate entity without the advance of money or other property to it by either the financing entity or another intermediate entity).

(iii) Time period between financing transactions. The director of field operations will consider the length of the period of time that separates the advances of money or other property, or the grants of rights to use property, by the financing entity to the intermediate entity (in the case of multiple intermediate entities, from one intermediate entity to another), and ultimately by the intermediate entity to the financed entity. A short period of time is evidence of the existence of a tax avoidance plan while a long period of time is evidence that there is not a tax avoidance plan. * * *

(iv) Financing transactions in the ordinary course of business. If the parties to the financing transaction are related, the director of field operations will consider whether the financing transaction occurs in the ordinary course of the active conduct of complementary or integrated trades or businesses engaged in by these entities. The fact that a financing transaction is described in this paragraph (b)(2)(iv) is evidence that the participation of the parties to that transaction in the financing arrangement is not pursuant to a tax avoidance plan. A loan will not be considered to occur in the ordinary course of the active conduct of complementary or integrated trades or businesses unless the loan is a trade receivable or the parties to the transaction are actively engaged in a banking, insurance, financing or similar trade or business and such business consists predominantly of transactions with customers who are not related persons. * * *

(3) Presumption if significant financing activities performed by a related intermediate entity—(i) General rule. It shall be presumed that the participation of an intermediate entity (or entities) in a financing arrangement is not pursuant to a tax avoidance plan if the intermediate entity is related to either or both the financing entity or the financed entity and the intermediate entity performs significant financing activities with respect to the financing transactions forming part of the financing arrangement to which it is a party. This presumption may be rebutted if the director of field operations establishes that the participation of the intermediate entity in the financing arrangement is pursuant to a tax avoidance plan. * * *

(ii) Significant financing activities. For purposes of this paragraph (b)(3), an intermediate entity performs significant financing activities with respect to such financing transactions only if the financing transactions satisfy the requirements of either paragraph (b)(3)(ii)(A) or (B) of this section.

(A) Active rents or royalties. An intermediate entity performs significant financing activities with respect to leases or licenses if rents or royalties earned with respect to such leases or licenses are derived in the active conduct of a trade or business within the meaning of section 954(c)(2)(A), to be applied by substituting the term intermediate entity for the term controlled foreign corporation.

(B) Active risk management—(1) In general. An intermediate entity is considered to perform significant financing activities with respect to financing transactions only if officers and employees of the intermediate entity participate actively and materially in arranging the intermediate entity's participation in such financing transactions (other than financing transactions described in paragraph (b)(3)(ii)(B)(3) of this section) and perform the business activity and risk management activities described in paragraph (b)(3)(ii)(B)(2) of this section with respect to such financing transactions, and the participation of the intermediate entity in the financing transactions produces (or reasonably can be expected to produce) efficiency savings by reducing transaction costs and overhead and other fixed costs.

* * *

[T.D. 8611, 60 FR 41005, Aug. 11, 1995; 60 FR 55312, Oct. 31, 1995; 63 FR 67578, Dec. 8, 1998; T.D. 9562, 76 FR 76896, Dec. 9, 2011; 77 FR 22480, April 16, 2012; T.D. 9922, 85 FR 72055, Nov. 12, 2020; 86 FR 54367, Oct. 1, 2021]

§ 1.882–1 Taxation of foreign corporations engaged in U.S. business or of foreign corporations treated as having effectively connected income.

(a) Segregation of income. This section applies for purposes of determining the tax of a foreign corporation which at any time during the taxable year is engaged in trade or business in the United States. It also applies for purposes of determining the tax of a foreign corporation which at no time during the taxable year is engaged in trade or business in the United States but has for the taxable year real property income or interest on obligations of the United States which, by reason of section 882(d) or (e) and § 1.882–2, is treated as effectively connected for the taxable year with the conduct of a trade or business in the United States by that corporation. A foreign corporation to which this section applies must segregate its gross income for the taxable year into two categories, namely, the income which is effectively connected for the taxable year with the conduct of a trade or business in the United States by that corporation and the income which is not effectively connected for the taxable year with the conduct of a trade or business in the United States by that corporation. A separate tax shall then be determined upon each such category of income, as provided in paragraph (b) of this section. The determination of whether income or gain is or is not effectively connected for the taxable year with the conduct of a trade or business in the United States by the foreign corporation shall be made in accordance with section 864(c) and §§ 1.864–3 through 1.864–7. For purposes of this section income which is effectively connected for the taxable year with the conduct of a trade or business in the United States includes all income which is treated under section 882(d) or (e) and § 1.882–2 as income which is effectively connected for the taxable year with the conduct of a trade or business in the United States by the foreign corporation.

(b) Imposition of tax—(1) Income not effectively connected with the conduct of a trade or business in the United States. If a foreign corporation to which this section applies derives during the taxable year from sources within the United States income or gains described in section 881(a) and paragraph (b) or (c) of § 1.881–2 which are not effectively connected for the taxable year with the conduct of a trade or business in the United

States by that corporation, such income or gains shall be subject to a flat tax of 30 percent of the aggregate amount of such items. This tax shall be determined in the manner, and subject to the same conditions, set forth in § 1.881–2 as though the income or gains were derived by a foreign corporation not engaged in trade or business in the United States during the taxable year, except that in applying paragraph (c) of such section there shall not be taken into account any gains which are taken into account in determining the tax under section 882(a)(1) and subparagraph (2) of this paragraph.

(2) Income effectively connected with the conduct of a trade or business in the United States—(i) In general. If a foreign corporation to which this section applies derives income or gains which are effectively connected for the taxable year with the conduct of a trade or business in the United States by that corporation, the taxable income or gains shall, except as provided in § 1.871–12, be taxed in accordance with section 11 or, in the alternative, section 1201(a). See sections 11(f) and 882(a)(1). Any income of the foreign corporation which is not effectively connected for the taxable year with the conduct of a trade or business in the United States by that corporation shall not be taken into account in determining either the rate or amount of such tax.

(ii) Determination of taxable income. The taxable income for any taxable year for purposes of this subparagraph consists only of the foreign corporation's taxable income which is effectively connected for the taxable year with the conduct of a trade or business in the United States by that corporation; and, for this purpose, it is immaterial that the trade or business with which that income is effectively connected is not the same as the trade or business carried on in the United States by that corporation during the taxable year. See example 2 in § 1.864–4(b). In determining such taxable income all amounts constituting, or considered to be, gains or losses for the taxable year from the sale or exchange of capital assets shall be taken into account if such gains or losses are effectively connected for the taxable year with the conduct of a trade or business in the United States by that corporation.

(iii) Cross references. For rules for determining the gross income and deductions for the taxable year, see section 882(b) and (c)(1) and the regulations thereunder.

(c) Change in trade or business status. The principles of paragraph (c) of § 1.871–8 shall apply to cases where there has been a change in the trade or business status of a foreign corporation.

(d) Credits against tax. The credits allowed by section 32 (relating to tax withheld at source on foreign corporations), section 33 (relating to the foreign tax credit), section 38 (relating to investment in certain depreciable property), section 39 (relating to certain uses of gasoline and lubricating oil), section 40 (relating to expenses of work incentive programs), and section 6042 (relating to overpayments of a tax) shall be allowed against the tax determined in accordance with this section. However, the credits allowed by sections 33, 38, and 40 shall not be allowed against the flat tax of 30 percent imposed by section 881(a) and paragraph (b)(1) of this section. For special rules applicable in determining the foreign tax credit, see section 906(b) and the regulations thereunder. For the disallowance of certain credits where a return is not filed for the taxable year see section 882(c)(2) and the regulations thereunder.

[T.D. 6500, 25 FR 11910, Nov. 26, 1960, as amended by T.D. 7244, 37 FR 28897, Dec. 30, 1972; T.D. 7293, 38 FR 32797, Nov. 28, 1973]

§ 1.882–5 Determination of interest deduction.

(a)(1) Overview—(i) In general. The amount of interest expense of a foreign corporation that is allocable under section 882(c) to income which is (or is treated as) effectively connected with the conduct of a trade or business within the United States (ECI) is the sum of the interest allocable by the foreign corporation under the three-step process set forth in paragraphs (b), (c), and (d) of this section and the specially allocated interest expense determined under paragraph (a)(1)(ii) of this section. The provisions of this section provide the exclusive rules for allocating interest expense to the ECI of a foreign corporation under section 882(c). Under the three-step process, the total value of the U.S. assets of a foreign corporation is first determined under paragraph (b) of this section (Step 1). Next, the amount of U.S.-connected liabilities is determined under paragraph (c) of this section (Step 2). Finally, the amount of interest paid or accrued on U.S.-booked liabilities, as determined under paragraph (d)(2) of this section, is adjusted for interest expense attributable to the difference between U.S.-connected liabilities and U.S.-booked liabilities (Step 3). Alternatively, a foreign corporation may elect to determine its interest rate on U.S.-connected liabilities by reference to its U.S. assets, using the separate currency pools method described in paragraph (e) of this section.

* * *

(b) * * *

(2) Determination of the value of a U.S. asset—(i) General rule. The value of a U.S. asset is the adjusted basis of the asset for determining gain or loss from the sale or other disposition of that item, further adjusted as provided in paragraph (b)(2)(iii) of this section.

* * *

[T.D. 6500, 25 FR 11910, Nov. 26, 1960, as amended by T.D. 7244, 37 FR 28897, Dec. 30, 1972; T.D. 7293, 38 FR 32797, Nov. 28, 1973; T.D. 8658, 61 FR 9329, March 8, 1996; 61 FR 15891, April 10, 1996; T.D. 9281, 71 FR 47448, Aug. 17, 2006; 71 FR 56868, Sept. 28, 2006; 74 FR 13340, March 27, 2009; T.D. 9465, 74 FR 49317, Sept. 28, 2009; 74 FR 57252, Nov. 5, 2009; 75 FR 13679, March 23, 2010; T.D. 9976, 88 FR 42234, June 30, 2023; T.D. 10042, 90 FR 57901, Dec.15, 2025]

§ 1.884–1 Branch profits tax.

(a) General rule. A foreign corporation shall be liable for a branch profits tax in an amount equal to 30 percent of the foreign corporation's dividend equivalent amount for the taxable year. The branch profits tax shall be in addition to the tax imposed by section 882 and shall be reported on a foreign corporation's income tax return for the taxable year. The tax shall be due and payable as provided in section 6151 and such other provisions of Subtitle F of the Internal Revenue Code as apply to the income tax liability of corporations. However, no estimated tax payments shall be due with respect to a foreign corporation's liability for the branch profits tax. See paragraph (g) of this section for the application of the branch profits tax to corporations that are residents of countries with which the United States has an income tax treaty, and § 1.884–2T for the effect on the branch profits tax of the termination or incorporation of a U.S. trade or business, or the liquidation or reorganization of a foreign corporation or its domestic subsidiary.

(b) Dividend equivalent amount—(1) Definition. The term "dividend equivalent amount" means a foreign corporation's effectively connected earnings and profits ("ECEP", as defined in paragraph (f)(1) of this section) for the taxable year, adjusted pursuant to paragraph (b)(2) or (3) of this section, as applicable. The dividend equivalent amount cannot be less than zero.

(2) Adjustment for increase in U.S. net equity. If a foreign corporation's U.S. net equity (as defined in paragraph (c) of this section) as of the close of the taxable year exceeds the foreign corporation's U.S. net equity as of the close of the preceding taxable year, then, for purposes of computing the foreign corporation's dividend equivalent amount for the taxable year, the foreign corporation's ECEP for the taxable year shall be reduced (but not below zero) by the amount of such excess.

(3) Adjustment for decrease in U.S. net equity—(i) In general. Except as provided in paragraph (b)(3)(ii) of this section, if a foreign corporation's U.S. net equity as of the close of the taxable year is less than the foreign corporation's U.S. net equity as of the close of the preceding taxable year, then, for purposes of computing the foreign corporation's dividend equivalent amount for the taxable year, the foreign corporation's ECEP for the taxable year shall be increased by the amount of such difference.

(ii) Limitation based on accumulated ECEP. The increase of a foreign corporation's ECEP under paragraph (b)(3)(i) of this section shall not exceed the accumulated ECEP of the foreign corporation as of the beginning of the taxable year. The term "accumulated ECEP" means the aggregate amount of ECEP of a foreign corporation for preceding taxable years beginning after December 31, 1986, minus the aggregate dividend equivalent amounts for such preceding taxable years. Accumulated ECEP may be less than zero.

* * *

[T.D. 8432, 57 FR 41651, Sept. 11, 1992; 57 FR 49117, Oct. 29, 1992; 57 FR 60126, Dec. 18, 1992; 58 FR 17166, April 1, 1993; T.D. 8657, 61 FR 9338, March 8, 1996; 61 FR 14247, April 1, 1996; T.D. 9281, 71 FR 47451, Aug. 17, 2006; T.D. 9465, 74 FR 49320, Sept. 28, 2009; 74 FR 57252, Nov. 5, 2009]

Miscellaneous Provisions

§ 1.894–1 Income affected by treaty.

* * *

(d) Special rule for items of income received by entities—(1) In general. The tax imposed by sections 871(a), 881(a), 1443, 1461, and 4948(a) on an item of income received by an entity, wherever organized, that is fiscally transparent under the laws of the United States and/or any other jurisdiction with respect to an item of income shall be eligible for reduction under the terms of an income tax treaty to which the United States is a party only if the item of income is derived by a resident of the applicable treaty jurisdiction. For this purpose, an item of income may be derived by either the entity receiving the item of income or by the interest holders in the entity or, in certain circumstances, both. An item of income paid to an entity shall be considered to be derived by the entity only if the entity is not fiscally transparent under the laws of the entity's jurisdiction, as defined in paragraph (d)(3)(ii) of this section, with respect to the item of income. An item of income paid to an entity shall be considered to be derived by the interest holder in the entity only if the interest holder is not fiscally transparent in its jurisdiction with respect to the item of income and if the entity is considered to be fiscally transparent under the laws of the interest holder's jurisdiction with respect to the item of income, as defined in paragraph (d)(3)(iii) of this section. Notwithstanding the preceding two sentences, an item of income paid directly to a type of entity specifically identified in a treaty as a resident of a treaty jurisdiction shall be treated as derived by a resident of that treaty jurisdiction.

* * *

(3) Definitions—(i) Entity. For purposes of this paragraph (d), the term entity shall mean any person that is treated by the United States or the applicable treaty jurisdiction as other than an individual. The term entity includes disregarded entities, including single member disregarded entities with individual owners.

(ii) Fiscally transparent under the law of the entity's jurisdiction—(A) General rule. For purposes of this paragraph (d), an entity is fiscally transparent under the laws of the entity's jurisdiction with respect to an item of income to the extent that the laws of that jurisdiction require the interest holder in the entity, wherever resident, to separately take into account on a current basis the interest holder's respective share of the item of income paid to the entity, whether or not distributed to the interest holder, and the character and source of the item in the hands of the interest holder are determined as if such item were realized directly from the source from which realized by the entity. However, the entity will be fiscally transparent with respect to the item of income even if the item of income is not separately taken into account by the interest holder, provided the item of income, if separately taken into account by the interest holder, would not result in an income tax liability for that interest holder different from that which would result if the interest holder did not take the item into account separately, and provided the interest holder is required to take into account on a current basis the interest holder's share of all such nonseparately stated items of income paid to the entity, whether or not distributed to the interest holder. In determining whether an entity is fiscally transparent with respect to an item of income in the entity's jurisdiction, it is irrelevant that, under the laws of the entity's jurisdiction, the entity is permitted to exclude such item from gross income or that the entity is required to include such item in gross income but is entitled to a deduction for distributions to its interest holders.

(B) Special definitions. For purposes of this paragraph (d)(3)(ii), an entity's jurisdiction is the jurisdiction where the entity is organized or incorporated or may otherwise be considered a resident under the laws of that jurisdiction. An interest holder will be treated as taking into account that person's share of income paid to an entity on a current basis even if such amount is taken into account by the interest holder in a taxable year other than the taxable year of the entity if the difference is due solely to differing taxable years.

(iii) Fiscally transparent under the law of an interest holder's jurisdiction—(A) General rule. For purposes of this paragraph (d), an entity is treated as fiscally transparent under the law of an interest holder's jurisdiction with respect to an item of income to the extent that the laws of the interest holder's jurisdiction require the interest holder resident in that jurisdiction to separately take into account on a current basis the interest holder's respective share of the item of income paid to the entity, whether or not distributed to the interest holder, and the character and source of the item in the hands of the interest holder are determined as if such item were realized directly from the source from which realized by the entity. However, an entity will be fiscally transparent with respect to the item of income even if the item of income is not separately taken into account by the interest holder, provided the item of income, if separately taken into account by the interest holder, would not result in an income tax liability for that interest holder different from that which would result if the interest holder did not take the item into account separately, and provided the interest holder is required to take into account on a current basis the interest holder's share of all such nonseparately stated items of income paid to the entity, whether or not distributed to the interest holder. An entity will not be treated as fiscally transparent with respect to an item of income under the laws of the interest holder's jurisdiction, however, if, under the laws of the interest holder's jurisdiction, the interest holder in the entity is required to include in gross income a share of all or a part of the entity's income on a current basis year under any type of anti-deferral or comparable mechanism. In determining whether an entity is fiscally transparent with respect to an item of income under the laws of an interest holder's jurisdiction, it is irrelevant how the entity is treated under the laws of the entity's jurisdiction.

(B) Special definitions. For purposes of this paragraph (d)(3)(iii), an interest holder's jurisdiction is the jurisdiction where the interest holder is organized or incorporated or may otherwise be considered a resident under the laws of that jurisdiction. An interest holder will be treated as taking into account that person's share of income paid to an entity on a current basis even if such amount is taken into account by such person in a taxable year other than the taxable year of the entity if the difference is due solely to differing taxable years.

(iv) Applicable treaty jurisdiction. The term applicable treaty jurisdiction means the jurisdiction whose income tax treaty with the United States is invoked for purposes of reducing the rate of tax imposed under sections 871(a), 881(a), 1461, and 4948(a).

(v) Resident. The term resident shall have the meaning assigned to such term in the applicable income tax treaty.

* * *

[T.D. 6500, 25 FR 11910, Nov. 26, 1960, as amended by T.D. 7293, 38 FR 32800, Nov. 28, 1973; T.D. 8735, 62 FR 53502, Oct. 14, 1997; T.D. 8889, 65 FR 40997, July 3, 2000; T.D. 8889, 65 FR 76932, Dec. 8, 2000; T.D. 8999, 67 FR 40160, June 12, 2002; T.D. 9648, 78 FR 73081, Dec. 5, 2013]

§ 1.897–1 Taxation of foreign investment in United States real property interests, definition of terms.

* * *

(b) Real property—(1) In general. The term "real property" includes the following three categories of property: Land and unserved natural products of the land, improvements, and personal property associated with the use of real property. The three categories of real property are defined in subparagraphs (2), (3), and (4) of this paragraph (b). Local law definitions will not be controlling for purposes of determining the meaning of the term "real property" as it is used in sections 897, 1445, and 6039C and the regulations thereunder.

(2) Land and unserved natural products of the land. The term "real property" includes land, growing crops and timber, and mines, wells, and other natural deposits. Crops and timber cease to be real property at the time that they are served from the land. Ores, minerals, and other natural deposits cease to be real property when they are extracted from the ground. The storage of severed or extracted crops, timber, or minerals in or upon real property will not cause such property to be recharacterized as real property.

(3) Improvements—(i) In general. The term "real property" includes improvements on land. An improvement is a building, any other inherently permanent structure, or the structural components of either, as defined in subdivisions (ii) through (iv) of this paragraph (b)(3).

(ii) Building. The term "building" generally means any structure or edifice enclosing a space within its walls, and usually covered by a roof, the purpose of which is, for example, to provide shelter or housing or to provide working, office, parking, display, or sales space. The term includes, for example, structures such as apartment houses, factory and office buildings, warehouses, barns, garages, railway or bus stations, and stores. Any structure that is classified as a building for purposes of section 48(a)(1)(B) and § 1.48–1 shall be treated as such for purposes of this section.

(iii) Inherently permanent structure—(A) In general. The term "inherently permanent structure" means any property not otherwise described in this paragraph (b)(3) that is affixed to real property and that will ordinarily remain affixed for an indefinite period of time. Property that is not classified as a building for purposes of section 48(a)(1)(B) and § 1.48–1 may nevertheless constitute an inherently permanent structure. For purposes of this section, affixation to real property may be accomplished by weight alone.

(B) Use of precedents under section 48. Any property not otherwise described in this paragraph (b)(3) that constitutes "other tangible property" under the principles of section 48(a)(1)(B) and § 1.48–1(c) and (d) shall be treated for purposes of this section as an inherently permanent structure. Thus, for example, the term includes swimming pools, paved parking areas and other pavements, special foundations for heavy equipment, wharves and docks, bridges, fences, inherently permanent advertising displays, inherently permanent outdoor lighting facilities, railroad tracks and signals, telephone poles, permanently installed telephone and television cables, broadcasting towers, oil derricks, oil and gas pipelines, oil and gas storage tanks, grain storage bins, and silos. However, property that is determined to be either property in the nature of machinery under § 1.48–1(c) or property which is essentially an item of machinery or equipment under § 1.48–1(e)(1)(i) shall not be treated as an inherently permanent structure.

(C) Absence of precedents under section 48. Where precedents developed under the principles of section 48 fail to provide adequate guidance with respect to the classification of particular property, the determination of whether such property constitutes an inherently permanent structure shall be made in view of all the facts and circumstances. In particular, the following factors must be taken into account:

(1) The manner in which the property is affixed to real property;

(2) Whether the property was designed to be easily removable or to remain in place indefinitely;

(3) Whether the property has been moved since its initial installation;

(4) Any circumstances that suggest the expected period of affixation (e.g., a lease that requires removal of the property upon its expiration);

(5) The amount of damage that removal of the property would cause to the property itself or to the real property to which it is affixed; and

(6) The extent of the effort that would be required to remove the property, in terms of time and expense.

(iv) Structural components of buildings and other inherently permanent structures. Structural components of buildings and other inherently permanent structures, as defined in § 1.48–1(e)(2), themselves constitute improvements. Structural components include walls, partitions, floors, ceilings, windows, doors, wiring, plumbing, central heating and central air conditioning systems, lighting fixtures, pipes, ducts, elevators, escalators, sprinkler systems, fire escapes and other components relating to the operation or maintenance of a building. However, the term "structural components" does not include machinery the sole justification for the installation of which is the fact that such machinery is required to meet temperature or humidity requirements which are essential for the operation of other machinery or the processing of materials or foodstuffs. Machinery may meet the "sole justification" test provided by the preceding sentence even though it incidentally provides for the comfort of employees or serves to an insubstantial degree areas where such temperature or humidity requirements are not essential.

(4) Personal property associated with the use of the real property—(i) In general. The term "real property" includes movable walls, furnishings, and other personal property associated with the use of the real property. Personal property is associated with the use of real property only if it is described in one of the categories set forth in subdivisions (A) through (D) of this paragraph (b)(4)(i). "Personal property" for purposes of this section means any property that constitutes "tangible personal property" under the principles of § 1.48–1(c), without regard to whether such property qualifies as section 38 property. Such property will be associated with the use of the real property only where both the personal property and the United States real property interest with which it is associated are held by the same person or by related persons within the meaning of § 1.897–1(i). For purposes of this paragraph (b)(4)(i), property is used "predominantly" in a named activity if it is devoted to that activity during at least half of the time in which it is in use during a calendar year.

(A) Property used in mining, farming, and forestry. Personal property is associated with the use of real property if it is predominantly used to exploit unsevered natural products in or upon the land. Such property includes mining equipment used to extract ores, minerals, and other natural deposits from the ground. It also includes any property used to cultivate the soil and harvest its products, such as farm machinery, draft animals, and equipment used in the growing and cutting of timber. However, personal property used to process or transport minerals, crops, or timber after they are severed from the land is not associated personal property.

(B) Property used in the improvement of real property. Personal property is associated with the use of real property if it is predominantly used to construct or otherwise carry out improvements to real property. Such property includes equipment used to alter the natural contours of the land, equipment used to clear and prepare raw land for construction, and equipment used to carry out the construction of improvements.

(C) Property used in the operation of a lodging facility. Personal property is associated with the use of real property if it is predominantly used in connection with the operation of a lodging facility. Property that is used in connection with the operation of a lodging facility includes property used in the living quarters of such facility, such as beds and other furniture, refrigerators, ranges and other equipment, as well as property used in the common areas of such facility, such as lobby furniture and laundry equipment. Such property constitutes personal property associated with the use of real property in the hands of the owner or operator of the facility, not of the tenant or guest. A lodging facility is an apartment house or apartment, hotel, motel, dormitory, residence, or any other facility (or part of a facility) predominantly used to provide, at a charge, living and/or sleeping accommodations, whether on daily, weekly, monthly, annual, or other basis. The term "lodging facility" does not include a personal residence occupied solely by its owner, or a facility used primarily as a means of transportation (such as an aircraft, vessel, or a railroad car) or used primarily to provide medical or convalescent services, even though sleeping accommodations are provided. Nor does the term include temporary living quarters provided by an employer due to the unavailability of lodgings within a reasonable distance of a work-site (such as a mine or construction project). The term "lodging facility" does not include any portion of a facility that constitutes a nonlodging commercial facility and that is available to persons not using the lodging facility on the same basis that it is available to tenants of the lodging facility. Examples of nonlodging commercial facilities include restaurants, drug stores, and grocery stores located in a lodging facility.

(D) Property used in the rental of furnished office and other work space. Personal property is associated with the use of real property if it is predominantly used by a lessor to provide furnished office or other work space to lessees. Property that is so used includes office furniture and equipment included in the rental of furnished space. Such property constitutes personal property associated with the use of real property in the hands of the lessor, not of the lessee.

(ii) Dispositions of associated personal property—(A) In general. Personal property that has become associated with the use of a real property interest shall itself be treated as a real property interest upon its disposition, unless either:

(1) The personal property is disposed of more than one year before the disposition of any present right to use or occupy the real property with which it was associated (and subject to the provisions of subdivision (B) of this paragraph (b)(4)(ii));

(2) The personal property is disposed of more than one year after the disposition of all present rights to use or occupy the real property with which it was associated (and subject to the provisions of subdivision (C) of this paragraph (b)(4)(ii)); or

(3) The personal property and the real property with which it was associated are separately sold to persons that are related neither to the transferor nor to one another (and subject to the provisions of subdivision (D) of this paragraph (b)(4)(ii)).

* * *

[T.D. 7999, 49 FR 50693, Dec. 31, 1984; 50 FR 12530, March 29, 1985; T.D. 8113, 51 FR 46626, Dec. 24, 1986; T.D. 8198, 53 FR 16217, May 5,

1988; T.D. 8657, 61 FR 9343, March 8, 1996; 61 FR 14248, April 1, 1996; T.D. 9082, 68 FR 46082, Aug. 5, 2003; T.D. 9992, 89 FR 31626, April 25, 2024; 89 FR 105451, Dec. 27, 2024]

§ 1.897–2 United States real property holding corporations.

(a) Purpose and scope. This section provides rules regarding the definition and consequences of U.S. real property holding corporation status. U.S. real property holding corporation status is important for determining whether gain from the disposition by a foreign person of an interest in a domestic corporation is taxable. Such status is also important for purposes of the withholding and reporting requirements of sections 1445 and 6039C. For example, a person that buys stock of a U.S. real property holding corporation from a foreign person is required to withhold under section 1445. In addition, for purposes of determining whether another corporation is a U.S. real property holding corporation, an interest in a foreign corporation is a U.S. real property interest unless it is established that the foreign corporation is not a U.S. real property holding corporation. The general definition of a U.S. real property holding corporation is provided in paragraph (b) of this section. Paragraph (c) provides rules regarding the dates on which U.S. real property holding corporation status must be determined. The assets that must be included in making the determination of a corporation's status are set forth in paragraph (d), while paragraph (e) provides special rules regarding the treatment of interests held by a corporation in partnerships, trusts, estates, and other corporations. Rules regarding the termination of U.S. real property holding corporation status are set forth in paragraph (f). Paragraph (g) explains the manner in which an interest-holder can establish that a corporation is not a U.S. real property holding corporation, and paragraph (h) provides rules regarding certain notification requirements applicable to corporations.

(b) U.S. real property holding corporation—(1) In general. A corporation is a U.S. real property holding corporation if the fair market value of the U.S. real property interests held by the corporation on any applicable determination date equals or exceeds 50 percent of the sum of the fair market values of its—

(i) U.S. real property interests;

(ii) Interests in real property located outside the United States; and

(iii) Assets other than those described in subdivision (i) or (ii) of this paragraph (b)(1) that are used or held for use in its trade or business.

See paragraphs (d) and (e) of this section for rules regarding the directly and indirectly held assets that must be included in the determination of whether a corporation is a U.S. real property holding corporation. The term "interest in real property located outside the United States" means an interest other than solely as a creditor (as defined in § 1.897–1(d)) in real property (as defined in § 1.897–(b)) that is located outside the United States or the Virgin Islands. If a corporation qualifies as a U.S. real property holding corporation on any applicable determination date after June 18, 1980, any interest in it shall be treated as a U.S. real property interest for a period of five years from that date, unless the provisions of paragraph (f)(2) of this section are applicable.

* * *

(c) Determination dates for applying U.S. real property holding corporation test—(1) In general. Whether a corporation is a U.S. real property holding corporation is to be determined as of the following dates:

(i) The last day of the corporation's taxable year;

(ii) The date on which the corporation acquires any U.S. real property interest;

(iii) The date on which the corporation disposes of an interest in real property located outside the United States or disposes of other assets used or held for use in a trade or business during the calendar year, subject to the provisions of paragraph (c)(2)(i) of this section; and

(iv) In the case of a corporation that is treated pursuant to paragraph (d)(4) or (5) of this section as owning a portion of the assets held by an entity in which the corporation directly or indirectly holds an interest, the date on which that entity either (A) acquires a U.S. real property interest, (B) disposes of an interest in real property located outside the United States or (C) disposes of other assets used or held for use in a trade or business during the calendar year, subject to the provisions of paragraph (c)(2)(ii) of this section. A determination that is triggered by a transaction described in subdivision (ii), (iii), or (iv) of this paragraph (c)(1) must take such transaction into account. However, the first determination of a corporation's status need not be made until the 120th day after the later of the date of incorporation or of the date on which the corporation first acquires a shareholder. In addition, no determination of a corporation's status need be made during the 12-month period beginning on the date on which a corporation adopts a plan of complete liquidation, provided that all the assets of the corporation (other than assets retained to meet claims) are distributed within such period.

[T.D. 7999, 49 FR 50702, Dec. 31, 1984, as amended by 50 FR 12531, March 29, 1985; T.D. 8113, 51 FR 46627, Dec. 24, 1986; 52 FR 3796, 3916, Feb. 6, 1987; T.D. 9082, 68 FR 46083, Aug. 5, 2003; T.D. 9751, 81 FR 8400, Feb. 19, 2016; T.D. 9992, 89 FR 31632, April 25, 2024]

§ 1.897–6T Nonrecognition exchanges applicable to corporations, their shareholders, and other taxpayers, and certain transfers of property in corporate reorganizations (temporary).

(a) Nonrecognition exchanges—(1) In general. Except as otherwise provided in this section and in § 1.897–5T, for purposes of section 897(e) any nonrecognition provision shall apply to a transfer by a foreign person of a U.S. real property interest on which gain is realized only to the extent that the transferred U.S. real property interest is exchanged for a U.S. real property interest which, immediately following the exchange, would be subject to U.S. taxation upon its disposition, and the transferor complies with the filing requirements of paragraph (d)(1)(iii) of § 1.897–5T. No loss shall be recognized pursuant to section 897(e) or the rules of this section unless such loss is otherwise permitted to be recognized. In the case of an exchange of a U.S. real property interest for stock in a domestic corporation (that is otherwise treated as a U.S. real property interest), such stock shall not be considered a U.S. real property interest unless the domestic corporation is a U.S. real property holding corporation immediately after the exchange. Whether an interest would be subject to U.S. taxation in the hands of the transferor upon its disposition shall be determined in accordance with the rules of § 1.897–5T(d)(1).

(2) Definition of "nonrecognition" provision. A "nonrecognition provision" is any provision of the Code which provides that gain or loss shall not be recognized if the requirements of that provision are met. Nonrecognition provisions relevant to this section include, but are not limited to, sections 332, 351, 354, 355, 361, 721, 731, 1031, 1033, and 1036. For purposes of section 897(e), sections 121 and 453 are not nonrecognition provisions.

(3) Consequence of nonapplication of nonrecognition provisions. If a nonrecognition provision does not apply to a transaction, then the U.S. real property interest transferred shall be considered exchanged pursuant to a transaction that is subject to U.S. taxation by reason of the operation of section 897. See, however, § 1.897–5T(d)(2) with respect to the treaty exceptions to the imposition of tax. If a U.S. real property interest is exchanged for an interest the disposition of which is only partially subject to taxation under chapter 1 of the Code (as modified by the provisions of any applicable U.S. income tax treaty), then any nonrecognition provision shall apply only to the extent that the interest received in the exchange would be subject to taxation under chapter 1 of the Code, as modified. For example, the exchange of a U.S. real property interest for an interest in a partnership will receive nonrecognition treatment pursuant to section 721 only to the extent that a disposition of the partnership interest will be subject to U.S. taxation by reason of the operation of section 897(g).

[T.D. 8198, 53 FR 16224, May 5, 1988; T.D. 8189, 53 FR 18022, May 19, 1988; T.D. 9082, 68 FR 46084, Aug. 5, 2003]

§ 1.901–1 Allowance of credit for foreign income taxes.

(a) In general. Citizens of the United States, domestic corporations, certain aliens resident in the United States or Puerto Rico, and certain estates and trusts may choose to claim a credit, as provided in section 901, against the tax imposed by chapter 1 of the Internal Revenue Code (Code) for certain taxes paid or accrued to foreign countries and possessions of the United States, subject to the conditions prescribed in this section.

(1) Citizen of the United States. A citizen of the United States, whether resident or nonresident, may claim a credit for—

(i) The amount of any foreign income taxes, as defined in § 1.901–2(a), paid or accrued (as the case may be, depending on the individual's method of accounting for such taxes) during the taxable year;

(ii) The individual's share of any such taxes of a partnership of which the individual is a member, or of an estate or trust of which the individual is a beneficiary; and

(iii) In the case of an individual who has made an election under section 962, the taxes deemed to have been paid under section 960 (see § 1.962–1(b)(2)).

(2) Domestic corporation. A domestic corporation may claim a credit for—

(i) The amount of any foreign income taxes, as defined in § 1.901–2(a), paid or accrued (as the case may be, depending on the corporation's method of accounting for such taxes) during the taxable year;

(ii) The corporation's share of any such taxes of a partnership of which the corporation is a member, or of an estate or trust of which the corporation is a beneficiary; and

(iii) The taxes deemed to have been paid under section 960.

(3) Alien resident of the United States or Puerto Rico. Except as provided in a Presidential proclamation described in section 901(c), an individual who is a resident alien of the United States (as defined in section 7701(b)), or an individual who is a bona fide resident of Puerto Rico (as defined in section 937(a)) during the entire taxable year, may claim a credit for—

(i) The amount of any foreign income taxes, as defined in § 1.901–2(a), paid or accrued (as the case may be, depending on the individual's method of accounting for such taxes) during the taxable year;

(ii) The individual's share of any such taxes of a partnership of which the individual is a member, or of an estate or trust of which the individual is a beneficiary; and

(iii) In the case of an individual who has made an election under section 962, the taxes deemed to have been paid under section 960 (see § 1.962–1(b)(2)).

* * *

(b) Limitations. Certain Code sections, including sections 245A(d) and (e)(3), 814, 901(e) through (m), 904, 906, 907, 908, 909, 911, 965(g), 999, and 6038, reduce, defer, or otherwise limit the credit against the tax imposed by chapter 1 of the Code for certain amounts of foreign income taxes.

(c) Deduction denied if credit claimed—(1) In general. Except as provided in paragraphs (c)(2) and (3) of this section, if a taxpayer chooses with respect to any taxable year to claim a credit under section 901 to any extent, such choice will apply to all of the foreign income taxes paid or accrued (as the case may be, depending on the taxpayer's method of accounting for such taxes) by the taxpayer in such taxable year, and no deduction from gross income is allowed for any portion of such taxes in any taxable year. See section 275(a)(4).

(2) Exception for taxes not subject to section 275. A deduction may be allowed under section 164(a)(3) for foreign income tax for which a credit is disallowed under any Code section and to which section 275 does not apply. See, for example, sections 901(f), 901(j)(3), 901(k)(7), 901(*l*)(4), 901(m)(6), and 908(b). For rules on the taxable year in which a deduction for foreign income taxes is allowed under section 164(a)(3), see §§ 1.446–1(c)(1)(ii), 1.461–2(a)(2), and 1.461–4(g)(6)(iii)(B).

* * *

(e) Joint return. In the case of spouses making a joint return, credit for taxes paid or accrued to any foreign country or to any possession of the United States shall be computed upon the basis of the total taxes so paid by or accrued against the spouses.

* * *

[T.D. 6500, 25 FR 11910, Nov. 26, 1960, as amended by T.D. 6780, 29 FR 18148, Dec. 22, 1964; T.D. 6789, 29 FR 19241, Dec. 31, 1964; T.D. 6795, 30 FR 934, Jan. 29, 1965; T.D. 7283, 38 FR 20824, Aug. 3, 1973; T.D. 7564, 43 FR 40496, Sept. 12, 1978; T.D. 7636, 44 FR 47058, Aug. 10, 1979; T.D. 7961, 49 FR 26225, June 27, 1984; T.D. 8160, 52 FR 33932, Sept. 9, 1987; T.D. 9194, 70 FR 18930, April 11, 2005; T.D. 9391, 73 FR 19360, April 9, 2008; T.D. 9416, 73 FR 40733, July 16, 2008; T.D. 9535, 76 FR 42043, July 18, 2011; T.D. 9959, 87 FR 334, Jan. 4, 2022]

§ 1.901–2 Income, war profits, or excess profits tax paid or accrued.

Editor's Note: In Notice 2023–55, 2023–30 I.R.B. 427, and Notice 2023–80, 2023–52 I.R.B. 1583, the Treasury and IRS have granted taxpayers temporary relief in determining whether a foreign tax meets the definition of a foreign income tax under §§ 901 and 903. During the relief period, taxpayers may apply former § 1.901–2(a) and (b) prior to amendment, with modifications.

(a) Definition of foreign income tax—(1) Overview and scope. Paragraphs (a) and (b) of this section define a foreign income tax for purposes of section 901. Paragraph (c) of this section is reserved. Paragraph (d) of this section contains rules describing what constitutes a separate levy. Paragraph (e) of this section provides rules for determining the amount of foreign income tax paid by a taxpayer. Paragraph (f) of this section contains rules for determining by whom foreign income tax is paid. Paragraph (g) of this section defines the terms used in this section, and in particular provides that the term "paid" means "paid" or "accrued," depending on the taxpayer's method of accounting for foreign income taxes. Paragraph (h) of this section provides the applicability date for this section.

(i) In general. Section 901 allows a credit for the amount of income, war profits, and excess profits taxes paid during the taxable year to any foreign country, and section 903 provides that for purposes of Part III of subchapter N of the Code and sections 164(a) and 275(a), such taxes include a tax paid in lieu of a tax on income, war profits or excess profits that is otherwise generally imposed by a foreign country (collectively, for purposes of this section, a "foreign income tax"). Whether a foreign levy is a foreign income tax is determined independently for each separate levy. A foreign tax either is or is not a foreign income tax, in its entirety, for all persons subject to the foreign tax.

(ii) Requirements. A foreign levy is a foreign income tax only if—

(A) It is a foreign tax; and

(B) Either:

(1) The foreign tax is a net income tax, as defined in paragraph (a)(3) of this section; or

(2) The foreign tax is a tax in lieu of an income tax, as defined in § 1.903–1(b).

(iii) Coordination with treaties. A foreign levy that is treated as an income tax under the relief from double taxation article of an income tax treaty entered into by the United States and the foreign country imposing the levy is a foreign income tax if the levy is, as determined under such income tax treaty, paid by a citizen or resident of the United States that elects benefits under the treaty. In addition, a foreign levy (including a foreign levy paid by a controlled foreign corporation) that is modified by an applicable income tax treaty to which the foreign country imposing the levy is a party may qualify as a foreign income tax notwithstanding that the unmodified foreign levy does not satisfy the requirements in paragraph (b) of this section or the requirements of § 1.903–1(b) if the levy, as modified by such treaty, satisfies the requirements of paragraph (b) of this section or the requirements of § 1.903–1(b). See paragraph (d)(1)(iv) of this section for rules treating as a separate levy a foreign tax that is limited in its application or otherwise modified by the terms of an income tax treaty to which the foreign country imposing the tax is a party.

(2) Tax—(i) In general. A foreign levy is a tax if it requires a compulsory payment pursuant to the authority of a foreign country to levy taxes. A penalty, fine, interest, or similar obligation is not a tax, nor is a customs duty a tax. Whether a foreign levy requires a compulsory payment pursuant to a foreign country's authority to levy taxes is determined by principles of U.S. law and not by principles of law of the foreign country. Therefore, the assertion by a foreign country that a levy is pursuant to the foreign country's authority to levy taxes is not determinative that, under U.S. principles, it is pursuant thereto. Notwithstanding any assertion of a foreign country to the contrary, a foreign levy is not pursuant to a foreign country's authority to levy taxes, and thus is not a tax, to the extent a person subject to the levy receives (or will receive), directly or indirectly, a specific economic benefit (as defined in paragraph (a)(2)(ii)(B) of this section) from the foreign country in exchange for payment pursuant to the levy. Rather, to that extent, such levy requires a compulsory payment in exchange for such specific economic benefit. If, applying U.S. principles, a foreign levy requires a compulsory payment pursuant to the authority of a foreign country to levy taxes and also requires a compulsory payment in exchange for a specific economic benefit, the levy is considered to have two distinct elements: A tax and a requirement of compulsory payment in exchange for such specific economic benefit. In such a situation, these two distinct elements of the foreign levy (and the amount paid pursuant to each such element) must be separated. No credit is allowable for a payment pursuant to a foreign levy by a dual capacity taxpayer (as defined in paragraph (a)(2)(ii)(A) of this section) unless the person claiming such credit establishes the amount that is paid pursuant to the distinct element of the foreign levy that is a tax. See paragraph (a)(2)(ii) of this section and § 1.901–2A.

(ii) Dual capacity taxpayers—(A) In general. For purposes of this section and §§ 1.901–2A and 1.903–1, a person who is subject to a levy of a foreign state or of a possession of the United States or of a political subdivision of such a state or possession and who also, directly or indirectly (within the meaning of paragraph (a)(2)(ii)(E) of this section) receives (or will receive) a specific economic benefit from the state or possession or from a political subdivision of such state or possession or from an agency or instrumentality of any of the foregoing is referred to as a "dual capacity taxpayer." Dual capacity taxpayers are subject to the special rules of § 1.901–2A.

(B) Specific economic benefit. For purposes of this section and §§ 1.901–2A and 1.903–1, the term "specific economic benefit" means an economic benefit that is not made available on substantially the same terms to substantially all persons who are subject to the income tax that is generally imposed by the foreign country, or, if there is no such generally imposed income tax, an economic benefit that is not made available on substantially the same terms to the population of the country in general. Thus, a concession to extract government-owned petroleum is a specific economic benefit, but the right to travel or to ship freight on a government-owned airline is not, because the latter, but not the former, is made generally available on substantially the same terms. An economic benefit includes property; a service; a fee or other payment; a right to use, acquire or extract resources, patents or other property that a foreign country owns or controls (within the meaning of paragraph (a)(2)(ii)(D) of this section); or a reduction or discharge of a contractual obligation. It does not include the right or privilege merely to engage in business generally or to engage in business in a particular form.

(C) Pension, unemployment, and disability fund payments. A foreign levy imposed on individuals to finance retirement, old-age, death, survivor, unemployment, illness, or disability benefits, or for some substantially similar purpose, is not a requirement of compulsory payment in exchange for a specific economic benefit, as long as the amounts required to be paid by the individuals subject to the levy are not computed on a basis reflecting the respective ages, life expectancies or similar characteristics of such individuals.

(D) Control of property. A foreign country controls property that it does not own if the country exhibits substantial indicia of ownership with respect to the property, for example, by both regulating the quantity of property that may be extracted and establishing the minimum price at which it may be disposed of.

(E) Indirect receipt of a benefit. A person is considered to receive a specific economic benefit indirectly if another person receives a specific economic benefit and that other person—

(1) Owns or controls, directly or indirectly, the first person or is owned or controlled, directly or indirectly, by the first person or by the same persons that own or control, directly or indirectly, the first person; or

(2) Engages in a transaction with the first person under terms and conditions such that the first person receives, directly or indirectly, all or part of the value of the specific economic benefit.

(3) Net income tax. A foreign tax is a net income tax only if the foreign tax meets the net gain requirement in paragraph (b) of this section.

(b) Net gain requirement—(1) In general. A foreign tax satisfies the net gain requirement only if the tax satisfies the realization, gross receipts, cost recovery, and attribution requirements in paragraphs (b)(2), (3), (4), and (5) of this section, respectively, or if the foreign tax is a surtax described in paragraph (b)(6) of this section. Paragraphs (b)(2) through (6) of this section are applied with respect to a foreign tax solely on the basis of the foreign tax law governing the calculation of the foreign taxable base, unless otherwise provided, and without any consideration of the rate of tax imposed on the foreign taxable base.

(2) Realization requirement—(i) In general. A foreign tax satisfies the realization requirement if it is imposed upon one or more of the events described in paragraphs (b)(2)(i)(A) through (C) of this section. If a foreign tax meets the realization requirement in paragraphs (b)(2)(i)(A) through (C) of this section except with respect to one or more specific and defined classes of nonrealization events (such as, for example, imputed rental income from a personal residence used by the owner), and as judged based on the application of the foreign tax to all taxpayers subject to the foreign tax, the incidence and amounts of gross receipts attributable to such nonrealization events is insignificant relative to the incidence and amounts of gross receipts attributable to events covered by the foreign tax that do meet the realization requirement, then the foreign tax is treated as meeting the realization requirement in paragraph (b)(2) of this section (despite the fact that the foreign tax is also imposed on the basis of some nonrealization events, and that some persons subject to the foreign tax may only be taxed on nonrealization events).

(A) Realization events. The foreign tax is imposed upon or after the occurrence of events ("realization events") that result in the realization of income under the income tax provisions of the Internal Revenue Code.

(B) Pre-realization recapture events. The foreign tax is imposed upon the occurrence of an event before a realization event (a "pre-realization event") that results in the recapture (in whole or part) of a tax deduction, tax credit, or other tax allowance previously accorded to the taxpayer (for example, the recapture of an incentive tax credit if required investments are not completed within a specified period).

(C) Pre-realization timing difference events. The foreign tax is imposed upon the occurrence of a pre-realization event, other than one described in paragraph (b)(2)(i)(B) of this section, but only if the foreign country does not, upon the occurrence of a later event, impose tax under the same or a separate levy (a "second tax") on the same taxpayer (for purposes of this paragraph (b)(2)(i)(C), treating a disregarded entity as defined in § 301.7701–3(b)(2)(i)(C) of this chapter as a taxpayer separate from its owner), with respect to the income on which tax is imposed by reason of such pre-realization event (or, if it does impose a second tax, a credit or other comparable relief is available against the liability for such a second tax for tax paid on the occurrence of the pre-realization event) and—

(1) The imposition of the tax upon such pre-realization event is based on the difference in the fair market value of property at the beginning and end of a period;

(2) The pre-realization event is the physical transfer, processing, or export of readily marketable property (as defined in paragraph (b)(2)(ii) of this section) and the imposition of the tax upon the pre-realization event is based on the fair market value of such property; or

(3) The pre-realization event relates to a deemed distribution (for example, by a corporation to a shareholder) or inclusion (for example, under a controlled foreign corporation inclusion regime) of amounts (such as earnings and profits) that meet the realization requirement in paragraph (b)(2) of this section in the hands of the person that, under foreign tax law, is deemed to distribute such amounts.

(ii) Readily marketable property. Property is readily marketable if—

(A) It is stock in trade or other property of a kind that properly would be included in inventory if on hand at the close of the taxable year or if it is held primarily for sale to customers in the ordinary course of business, and

(B) It can be sold on the open market without further processing or it is exported from the foreign country.

* * *

(3) Gross receipts requirement—(i) Rule. A foreign tax satisfies the gross receipts requirement if it is imposed on the basis of the amounts described in paragraphs (b)(3)(i)(A) through (D) of this section.

(A) Actual gross receipts.

(B) In the case of either an insignificant nonrealization event described in the second sentence of paragraph (b)(2)(i) of this section or a realization event described in paragraph (b)(2)(i)(A) of this section that does not result in actual gross receipts, deemed gross receipts in an amount that is reasonably calculated to produce an amount that is not greater than fair market value.

(C) Deemed gross receipts in the amount of a tax deduction that is recaptured by reason of a pre-realization recapture event described in paragraph (b)(2)(i)(B) of this section.

(D) The amount of deemed gross receipts arising from pre-realization timing difference events described in paragraph (b)(2)(i)(C) of this section.

* * *

(4) Cost recovery requirement—(i) Costs and expenses that must be recovered—(A) In general. A foreign tax satisfies the cost recovery requirement if the base of the tax is computed by reducing gross receipts (as described in paragraph (b)(3) of this section) to permit recovery of the significant costs and expenses (including capital expenditures) described in paragraph (b)(4)(i)(C) of this section attributable, under reasonable principles, to such gross receipts. A foreign tax need not permit recovery of significant costs and expenses, such as certain personal expenses, that are not attributable, under reasonable principles, to gross receipts included in the foreign taxable base. A foreign tax whose base is gross receipts, with no reduction for costs and expenses, satisfies the cost recovery requirement only if there are no significant costs and expenses attributable to the gross receipts included in the foreign tax base that must be recovered under the rules of paragraph (b)(4)(i)(C)(1) of this section. See paragraph (b)(4)(iv)(A) of this section (Example 1). A foreign tax that provides an alternative cost allowance satisfies the cost recovery requirement only as provided in paragraph (b)(4)(i)(B) of this section. See paragraph (b)(4)(i)(D) of this section for rules regarding principles for attributing costs and expenses to gross receipts.

(B) Alternative cost allowances—(1) In general. Except as provided in paragraph (b)(4)(i)(B)(2) of this section, if foreign tax law does not permit recovery of one or more significant costs and expenses in computing the base of the foreign tax but provides an alternative cost allowance, the foreign tax satisfies the cost recovery requirement only if the alternative allowance permits recovery of an amount that by its terms may be greater, but can never be less, than the actual amounts of such significant costs and expenses (for example, under a provision identical to percentage depletion allowed under section 613). If foreign tax law provides an optional alternative cost allowance or an election to recover costs and expenses under an alternative method, the foreign tax satisfies the cost recovery requirement if the foreign tax law also expressly provides an option to recover actual costs and expenses. See § 1.901–2(e)(5) for rules limiting the amount of foreign income tax paid to the amount due under the option that minimizes the taxpayer's liability for foreign income tax over time. If foreign tax law provides an alternative cost allowance that does not by its terms permit recovery of an amount equal to or greater than the actual amounts of significant costs and expenses, the foreign tax does not satisfy the cost recovery requirement, even if, in practice, the amounts recovered under the alternative allowance equal or exceed the amount of actual costs and expenses.

(2) Small business exception. If foreign tax law provides an alternative method for determining the amount of costs and expenses allowed in computing the taxable base of small business enterprises, the foreign tax satisfies the cost recovery requirement if the foreign tax law contains reasonable limits on the maximum size of business enterprises to which the alternative cost allowance applies (for example, business enterprises having asset values or annual gross revenues below specified thresholds). See paragraph (b)(4)(iv)(B) of this section (Example 2).

(C) Significant costs and expenses—(1) Amounts that must be recovered. Whether a cost or expense is significant for purposes of this paragraph (b)(4)(i) is determined based on whether, for all taxpayers in the aggregate to which the foreign tax applies, the item of cost or expense constitutes a significant portion of the taxpayers' total costs and expenses. Costs and expenses (as characterized under foreign law) related to capital expenditures, interest, rents, royalties, wages or other payments for services, and research and experimentation are always treated as significant costs or expenses for purposes of this paragraph (b)(4)(i). Significant costs and expenses (such as interest expense) are not considered to be recovered by reason of the time value of money attributable to the acceleration of a tax benefit or other economic benefit attributable to the timing of the recovery of other costs and expenses (such as the current expensing of debt-financed capital expenditures). Foreign tax law is considered to permit recovery of significant costs and expenses even if recovery of all or a portion of certain costs or expenses is disallowed, if such disallowance is consistent with any principle underlying the disallowances required under the Internal Revenue Code, including the principles of limiting base erosion or profit shifting and public policy concerns. For example, a foreign tax is considered to permit recovery of significant costs and expenses if the foreign tax law limits interest deductions based on a measure of taxable income (determined either before or after depreciation and amortization), disallows deductions in connection with hybrid transactions, disallows deductions attributable to gross receipts that in whole or in part are excluded, exempt or eliminated from taxable income, or disallows certain deductions based on public policy considerations similar to those underlying the disallowances contained in section 162. See paragraph (b)(4)(iv)(C) of this section (Example 3).

(2) Amounts that need not be recovered. A foreign tax is considered to permit recovery of significant costs and expenses even if the foreign tax law does not permit recovery of any costs and expenses attributable to wage income or to investment income that is not derived from a trade or business. In addition, in determining whether a foreign tax (the "tested foreign tax") meets the cost recovery requirement, it is immaterial whether the tested foreign tax allows a deduction for other taxes that would qualify as foreign income taxes (determined without regard to whether such other tax allows a deduction for the tested foreign tax). See paragraph (b)(4)(iv)(D) and (E) of this section (Examples 4 and 5).

(3) Timing of recovery. A foreign tax law permits recovery of significant costs and expenses even if such costs and expenses are recovered earlier or later than they are recovered under the Internal Revenue Code unless the time of recovery is so much later as effectively to constitute a denial of such recovery. The amount of costs and expenses that is recovered under the foreign tax law is neither discounted nor augmented by taking into account the time value of money attributable to any acceleration or deferral of a tax benefit resulting from the foreign law cost recovery method compared to when tax would be paid under the Internal Revenue Code. Therefore, a foreign tax satisfies the cost recovery requirement if items deductible under the Internal Revenue Code are capitalized under the foreign tax law and recovered either immediately, on a recurring basis over time, or upon the occurrence of some future event (for example, upon the property becoming worthless or being disposed of), or if the recovery of items capitalized under the Internal Revenue Code occurs more or less rapidly than under the foreign tax law.

(D) Attribution of costs and expenses to gross receipts. Principles used in the foreign tax law to attribute costs and expenses to gross receipts may be reasonable even if they differ from principles that apply under the Internal Revenue Code (for example, principles that apply under section 265, 465 or 861(b) of the Internal Revenue Code). See also paragraph (b)(5) of this section for additional requirements relating to foreign tax law rules for attributing costs and expenses to gross receipts.

(ii) Consolidation of profits and losses. In determining whether a foreign tax satisfies the cost recovery requirement, one of the factors to be taken into account is whether, in computing the base of the tax, a loss incurred in one activity (for example, a contract area in the case of oil and gas exploration) in a trade or business is allowed to offset profit earned by the same person in another activity (for example, a separate contract area) in the same trade or business. If such an offset is allowed, it is immaterial whether the offset may be made in the taxable period in which the loss is incurred or only in a different taxable period, unless the period is such that under the circumstances there is effectively a denial of the ability to offset the loss against profit. In determining whether a foreign tax satisfies the cost recovery requirement, it is immaterial that no such offset is allowed if a loss incurred in one such activity may be applied to offset profit earned in that activity in a different taxable period, unless the period is such that under the circumstances there is effectively a denial of the ability to offset such loss against profit. In determining whether a foreign tax satisfies the cost recovery requirement, it is immaterial whether a person's profits and losses from one trade or business (for example, oil and gas extraction) are allowed to offset its profits and losses from another trade or business (for example, oil and gas refining and processing), or whether a person's business profits and losses and its passive investment profits and losses are allowed to offset each other in computing the base of the foreign tax. Moreover, it is immaterial whether foreign tax law permits or prohibits consolidation of profits and losses of related persons, unless foreign tax law requires separate entities to be used to carry on separate activities in the same trade or business. If foreign tax law requires that separate entities carry on such separate activities, the determination whether the cost recovery requirement is satisfied is made by applying the same considerations as if such separate activities were carried on by a single entity.

(iii) Carryovers. In determining whether a foreign tax satisfies the cost recovery requirement, it is immaterial, except as otherwise provided in paragraph (b)(4)(ii) of this section, whether losses incurred during one taxable period may be carried over to offset profits incurred in different taxable periods.

(iv) Examples. The following examples illustrate the rules of paragraph (b)(4) of this section.

(A) Example 1: Tax on gross interest income of certain residents; no deductions allowed—(1) Facts. Country X imposes a net income tax on corporations resident in Country X. Country X imposes a second tax (the "bank tax") of 1 percent on the gross amount of interest income derived by banks resident in Country X; no deductions are allowed in determining the base of the bank tax. Banks resident in Country X incur substantial costs and expenses, including interest expense, attributable to their interest income.

(2) Analysis. Because the terms of the bank tax do not permit recovery of significant costs and expenses attributable to the gross receipts included in the tax base, the bank tax does not satisfy the cost recovery requirement of paragraph (b)(4)(i) of this section.

* * *

(D) Example 4: Gross basis tax on wages—(1) Facts. A foreign country imposes payroll tax on resident employees at the rate of 10 percent of the amount of gross wages; no deductions are allowed in computing the base of the payroll tax.

(2) Analysis. Although the foreign tax law does not allow for the recovery of any costs and expenses attributable to gross receipts included in the taxable base, under paragraph (b)(4)(i)(C)(2) of this section, because the only gross receipts included in the taxable base are from wages, the payroll tax satisfies the cost recovery requirement.

(E) Example 5: No deduction for another net income tax—(1) Facts. Each of Country X and Province Y (a political subdivision of Country X) imposes a tax on resident corporations, called the "Country X income tax" and the "Province Y income tax," respectively. Each tax has an identical base, which is computed by reducing a corporation's realized gross receipts by deductions that, based on the laws of Country X and Province Y, generally permit recovery of the significant costs and expenses (including significant capital expenditures) that are attributable under reasonable principles to such gross receipts. However, the Country X income tax does not allow a deduction for the Province Y income tax for which a taxpayer is liable, nor does the Province Y income tax allow a deduction for the Country X income tax for which a taxpayer is liable.

(2) Analysis. Under paragraph (d)(1)(i) of this section, each of the Country X income tax and the Province Y income tax is a separate levy. Without regard to whether the Province Y income tax may allow a deduction for the Country X income tax, and without regard to whether the Country X income tax may allow a deduction for the Province Y income tax, both taxes would qualify as net income taxes under paragraph (a)(3) of this section. Therefore, under paragraph (b)(4)(i)(C)(2) of this section the fact that neither levy's base allows a deduction for the other levy is immaterial, and both levies satisfy the cost recovery requirement.

(5) Attribution requirement. A foreign tax satisfies the attribution requirement if the amount of gross receipts and costs that are included in the base of the foreign tax are determined based on rules described in paragraph (b)(5)(i) of this section (with respect to a separate levy imposed on nonresidents of the foreign country) or paragraph (b)(5)(ii) of this section (with respect to a separate levy imposed on residents of the foreign country).

(i) Tax on nonresidents. The gross receipts and costs attributable to each of the items of income of nonresidents of a foreign country that is included in the base of the foreign tax must satisfy the requirements of paragraph (b)(5)(i)(A), (B), or (C) of this section.

(A) Income attribution based on activities. The gross receipts and costs that are included in the base of the foreign tax are limited to gross receipts and costs that are attributable, under reasonable principles, to the nonresident's activities within the foreign country imposing the foreign tax (including the nonresident's functions, assets, and risks located in the foreign country). For purposes of the preceding sentence, attribution of gross receipts under reasonable principles includes rules similar to those for determining effectively connected income under section 864(c) but does not include rules that take into account as a significant factor the mere location of customers, users, or any other similar destination-based criterion, or the mere location of persons from whom the nonresident makes purchases in the foreign country. In addition, for purposes of the first sentence of this paragraph (b)(5)(i)(A), reasonable principles do not include rules that deem the existence of a trade or business or permanent establishment based on the activities of another person (other than an agent or other person acting on behalf of the nonresident or a pass-through entity of which the nonresident is an owner), or that attribute gross receipts or costs to a nonresident based upon the activities of another person (other than an agent or other person acting on behalf of the nonresident or a pass-through entity of which the nonresident is an owner).

(B) Income attribution based on source. The amount of gross income arising from gross receipts (other than gross receipts from sales or other dispositions of property) that is included in the base of the foreign tax on the basis of source (instead of on the basis of activities or the situs of property as described in paragraphs (b)(5)(i)(A) and (C) of this section) is limited to gross income arising from sources within the foreign country that imposes the tax, and the sourcing rules of the foreign tax law are reasonably similar to the sourcing rules that apply under the Internal Revenue Code. A foreign tax law's application of such sourcing rules need not conform in all respects to the application of those sourcing rules for Federal income tax purposes. For purposes of determining whether the sourcing rules of the foreign tax law are reasonably similar to the sourcing rules that apply under the Internal Revenue Code, the character of gross income arising from gross receipts is determined under the foreign tax law (except as provided in paragraph (b)(5)(i)(B)(3) of this section), and the following rules apply:

(1) Services. Under the foreign tax law, gross income from services must be sourced based on where the services are performed, as determined under reasonable principles (which do not include determining the place of performance of the services based on the location of the service recipient). **(b)**

(2) Royalties. A foreign tax on gross income from royalties must be sourced based on the place of use of, or the right to use, the intangible property.

(3) Sales of property. Gross income arising from gross receipts from sales or other dispositions of property (including copyrighted articles sold through an electronic medium) must be included in the foreign tax base on the basis of the rules in paragraph (b)(5)(i)(A) or (C) of this section, and not on the basis of source. In the case of sales of copyrighted articles (as determined under rules similar to § 1.861–18), a foreign tax satisfies the attribution requirement of paragraph (b)(5) of this section only if the transaction is treated as a sale of tangible property and not as a license of intangible property.

(C) Attribution based on situs of property. A foreign tax on gains of nonresidents from the sale or disposition of property, including shares in a corporation or an interest in a partnership or other pass-through entity, based on the situs of property satisfies the attribution requirement only as provided in this paragraph (b)(5)(i)(C). The amount of gross receipts from the sale or disposition of property that is included in the base of the foreign tax on the basis of the situs of real property (instead of on the basis of activities as described in paragraph (b)(5)(i)(A) of this section) may only include gross receipts that are attributable to the disposition of real property situated in the foreign country imposing the foreign tax (or an interest in a resident corporation or other entity that owns such real property) under rules reasonably similar to the rules in section 897. The amount of gross receipts from the sale or disposition of property other than shares in a corporation, including an interest in a partnership or other pass-through entity, that is included in the base of the foreign tax on the basis of the situs of property other than real property may only include gross receipts that are attributable to property forming part of the business property of a taxable presence in the foreign country imposing the foreign tax under rules that are reasonably similar to the rules in section 864(c).

(ii) Tax on residents. The base of a foreign tax imposed on residents of the foreign country imposing the foreign tax may include all of the worldwide gross receipts of the resident. The foreign tax law must provide that any allocation to or from the resident of income, gain, deduction, or loss with respect to transactions between such resident and organizations, trades, or businesses owned or controlled directly or indirectly by the same interests (that is, any allocation made pursuant to the foreign country's transfer pricing rules) is determined under arm's length principles, without taking into account as a significant factor the location of customers, users, or any other similar destination-based criterion.

* * *

(6) Surtax on net income tax. A foreign tax satisfies the net gain requirement in this paragraph (b) if the base of the foreign tax is the amount of a net income tax. For example, if a tax (surtax) is computed as a percentage of a separate levy that is itself a net income tax, then such surtax is considered to satisfy the net gain requirement.

(c) [Reserved by 87 FR 335]

(d) Separate levies—(1) In general. Each foreign levy must be analyzed separately to determine whether it is a net income tax within the meaning of paragraph (a)(3) of this section and whether it is a tax in lieu of an income tax within the meaning of § 1.903–1(b)(2). Whether a single levy or separate levies are imposed by a foreign country depends on U.S. principles and not on whether foreign tax law imposes the levy or levies pursuant to a single or separate statutes. A foreign levy is a separate levy described in this paragraph (d)(1) if it is described in paragraph (d)(1)(i), (ii), (iii), or (iv) of this section. In the case of levies that apply to dual capacity taxpayers, see also § 1.901–2A(a).

(i) Taxing authority. A levy imposed by one taxing authority (for example, the national government of a foreign country) is always separate from a levy imposed by another taxing authority (for example, a political subdivision of that foreign country), even if the base of the levy is the same.

(ii) Different taxable base. Where the base of a foreign levy is computed differently for different classes of persons subject to the levy, the levy is considered to impose separate levies with respect to each such class of persons. For example, foreign levies identical to the taxes imposed by sections 1, 11, 541, 871(a), 871(b), 881, 882, 3101 and 3111 of the Internal Revenue Code are each separate levies, because the levies are imposed on different classes of taxpayers, and the base of each of those levies contains different items than the base of each of the others. A taxable base of a separate levy may consist of a particular type of income (for example, wage income, investment income, or income from self-employment). The taxable base of a separate levy may also consist of an amount unrelated to income (for example, wage expense or assets). A separate levy may provide that items included in the base of the tax are computed separately merely for purposes of a preliminary computation and are then combined as a single taxable base. Income included in the taxable base of a separate levy may also be included in the taxable base of another levy (which may or may not also include other items of income); separate levies are considered to be imposed if the taxable bases are not combined as a single taxable base, even if the taxable bases are determined using the same computational rules. For example, a foreign levy identical to the tax imposed by section 1 is a separate levy from a foreign levy identical to the tax imposed by section 1411, because tax is imposed under each levy on a separate taxable base that is not combined with the other as a single taxable base. Where foreign tax law imposes a levy that is the sum of two or more separately computed amounts of tax, and each such amount is computed by reference to a different base, separate levies are considered to be imposed. Levies are not separate merely because different rates apply to different classes of taxpayers that are subject to the same provisions in computing the base of the tax. For example, a foreign levy identical to the tax imposed on U.S. citizens and resident alien individuals by section 1 of the Internal Revenue Code is a single levy notwithstanding that the levy has graduated rates and applies different rate schedules to unmarried individuals, married individuals who file separate returns, and married individuals who file joint returns. In addition, in general, levies are not separate merely because some provisions determining the base of the levy apply, by their terms or in practice, to some, but not all, persons subject to the levy. For example, a foreign levy identical to the tax imposed by section 11 of the Internal Revenue Code is a single levy even though some provisions apply by their terms to some but not all corporations subject to the section 11 tax (for example, section 465 is by its terms applicable to corporations described in sections 465(a)(1)(B), but not to other corporations), and even though some provisions apply in practice to some but not all corporations subject to the section 11 tax (for example, section 611 does not, in practice, apply to any corporation that does not have a qualifying interest in the type of property described in section 611(a)).

(iii) Tax imposed on nonresidents. A foreign levy imposed on nonresidents is always treated as a separate levy from that imposed on residents, even if the base of the tax as applied to residents and nonresidents is the same, and even if the levies are treated as a single levy under foreign tax law. In addition, a withholding tax (as defined in section 901(k)(1)(B)) that is imposed on gross income of nonresidents is treated as a separate levy as to each separate class of income described in section 61 (for example, interest, dividends, rents, or royalties) subject to the withholding tax. If two or more subsets of a separate class of income are subject to a withholding tax based on different income attribution rules (for example, if technical services are subject to tax based on the residence of the payor and other services are subject to tax based on where the services are performed), separate levies are considered to be imposed with respect to each subset of that separate class of income. **(d)**

(iv) Foreign levy modified by an applicable income tax treaty. A foreign levy that is limited in its application by, or is otherwise modified by, an income tax treaty to which the foreign country imposing the levy is a party is a separate levy from the levy imposed under the domestic law (without regard to the treaty) of the foreign country, and is also a separate levy from the foreign levy as modified by a different income tax treaty to which the foreign country imposing the levy is a party, even if the two treaties modify the foreign levy in exactly the same manner. Accordingly, a foreign levy paid by taxpayers that qualify for and claim benefits under an income tax treaty is a separate levy from the levy as applied to taxpayers that are ineligible for, or that do not claim, benefits under that treaty, even if the two foreign levies would apply in the same manner to a particular taxpayer, and regardless of whether the unmodified foreign levy is a foreign income tax within the meaning of paragraph (a)(1)(ii) of this section.

(2) Contractual modifications. Notwithstanding paragraph (d)(1) of this section, if foreign tax law imposing a levy is modified for one or more persons subject to the levy by a contract entered into by such person or persons and the foreign country, then the foreign tax law is considered for purposes of sections 901 and 903 to impose a separate levy for all persons to whom such contractual modification of the levy applies, as contrasted to the levy as applied to all persons to whom such contractual modification does not apply.

* * *

(e) Amount of foreign income tax that is creditable—(1) In general. Credit is allowed under section 901 for the amount of foreign income tax that is paid by the taxpayer. Under paragraph (g) of this section, the term "paid" means "paid" or "accrued," depending on the taxpayer's method of accounting for such taxes. The amount of foreign income tax paid by the taxpayer is determined separately for each taxpayer under the rules in this paragraph (e).

(2) Refunds and credits—(i) Refundable amounts. An amount remitted to a foreign country is not an amount of foreign income tax paid to the extent that it is reasonably certain that the amount will be refunded, rebated, abated, or forgiven. It is reasonably certain that an amount will be refunded, rebated, abated, or forgiven to the extent the amount exceeds a reasonable approximation of final foreign income tax liability to the foreign country. See section 905(c) and § 1.905–3 for the required redeterminations if amounts claimed as a credit (on either the cash or accrual basis) exceed the amount of the final foreign income tax liability.

(ii) Credits. Except as provided in paragraph (e)(2)(iii) of this section, an amount of foreign income tax liability is not an amount of foreign income tax paid to the extent the foreign income tax liability is reduced, satisfied, or otherwise offset by a tax credit, including a tax credit that under the foreign tax law is payable in cash only to the extent it exceeds the taxpayer's liability for foreign income tax or a tax credit acquired from another taxpayer.

(iii) Exception for overpayments and other fully refundable credits. An amount of foreign income tax paid is not reduced (or treated as constructively refunded) solely by reason of the fact that a credit is allowed (or may be allowed) for the amount paid to reduce the amount of a different separate levy owed by the taxpayer. See paragraphs (e)(2)(ii) and (e)(4) of this section. However, under paragraph (e)(2)(i) of this section (and taking into account any redetermination required under section 905(c) and § 1.905–3), an amount remitted with respect to a separate levy for a foreign taxable period that constitutes an overpayment of the taxpayer's final liability for that levy for that period, and that is refundable in cash at the taxpayer's option, is not an amount of tax paid. Therefore, if such an overpayment of one tax is applied as a credit against a different foreign income tax liability of the taxpayer for the same or a different taxable period, the credited amount of the overpayment may qualify as an amount paid of that different foreign income tax, if the credited amount does not exceed a reasonable approximation of the taxpayer's final foreign income tax liability for the taxable period to which the overpayment is applied. Similarly, if under the foreign tax law, the full amount of a tax credit is payable in cash at the taxpayer's option, the taxpayer's choice to apply all or a portion of the tax credit in satisfaction of a foreign income tax liability of the taxpayer is treated as a constructive payment of cash to the taxpayer in the amount so applied, followed by a constructive payment of the foreign income tax liability against which the credit is applied. An overpayment or other tax credit that under the foreign tax law is otherwise fully payable in cash at the taxpayer's option and that is applied in part in satisfaction of a foreign income tax liability is treated as an amount of foreign income tax paid notwithstanding that a portion of the amount otherwise payable in cash to the taxpayer is subject to a lien or otherwise seized in order to satisfy a different, pre-existing liability of the taxpayer to the foreign government or to a third party.

(iv) Examples. The following examples illustrate the rules of paragraph (e)(2) of this section.

(A) Example 1. The domestic law of Country X imposes a 25 percent tax described in § 1.903–1(b) on the gross amount of interest from sources in Country X that is received by a nonresident of Country X. Country X imposes the tax on the nonresident recipient and requires any resident of Country X that pays such interest to a nonresident to withhold and pay over to Country X 25 percent of such interest, which is applied to offset the recipient's liability for the 25 percent tax. A tax treaty between the United States and Country X modifies domestic law of Country X and provides that Country X may not tax interest received by a resident of the United States from a resident of Country X at a rate in excess of 10 percent of the gross amount of such interest. A resident of the United States may claim the benefit of the treaty only by applying for a refund of the excess withheld amount (15 percent of the gross amount of interest income) after the end of the taxable year. A, a resident of the United States, receives a gross amount of 100u (units of Country X currency) of interest income from a resident of Country X from sources in Country X in Year 1, from which 25u of Country X tax is withheld. A files a timely claim for refund of the 15u excess withheld amount. 15u of the amount withheld (25u–10u) is reasonably certain to be refunded; therefore, under paragraph (e)(2)(i) of this section 15u is not considered an amount of foreign income tax paid to Country X.

* * *

(3) Subsidies—(i) General rule. An amount of foreign income tax is not an amount of foreign income tax paid by a taxpayer to a foreign country to the extent that—

(A) The amount is used, directly or indirectly, by the foreign country imposing the tax to provide a subsidy by any means (including, but not limited to, a rebate, a refund, a credit, a deduction, a payment, a discharge of an obligation, or any other method) to the taxpayer, to a related person (within the meaning of section 482), to any party to the transaction, or to any party to a related transaction; and

(B) The subsidy is determined, directly or indirectly, by reference to the amount of the tax or by reference to the base used to compute the amount of the tax.

(ii) Subsidy. The term "subsidy" includes any benefit conferred, directly or indirectly, by a foreign country to one of the parties enumerated in paragraph (e)(3)(i)(A) of this section. Substance and not form shall govern in determining whether a subsidy exists. The fact that the U.S. taxpayer may derive no demonstrable benefit from the subsidy is irrelevant in determining whether a subsidy exists.

* * *

(4) Multiple levies—(i) In general. If, under foreign law, a taxpayer's tentative liability for one levy (the "reduced levy") is or can be reduced by the amount of the taxpayer's liability for a different levy (the "applied levy"), then the amount considered paid by the taxpayer to the foreign country pursuant to the applied levy is an amount equal to its entire liability for that applied levy (which is not considered to be reduced by the amount applied against the reduced levy), and the remainder of the total amount paid, if any, is considered paid pursuant to the reduced levy. See also paragraphs (e)(2)(ii) and (iii) of this section.

* * *

(5) Noncompulsory amounts—(i) In general. An amount remitted to a foreign country (a "foreign payment") is not a compulsory payment, and thus is not an amount of foreign income tax paid, to the extent that the foreign payment exceeds the amount of liability for foreign income tax under the foreign tax law (as defined in paragraph (g) of this section). A foreign payment does not exceed the amount of such liability if the foreign payment is determined by the taxpayer in a manner that is consistent with a reasonable interpretation and application of the substantive and procedural provisions of foreign tax law (including applicable tax treaties) in such a way as to reduce, over time, the taxpayer's reasonably expected liability under foreign tax law for foreign income tax, and if the taxpayer exhausts all effective and practical remedies, including invocation of competent authority procedures available under applicable tax treaties, to reduce, over time, the taxpayer's liability for foreign income tax (including liability pursuant to a foreign tax audit adjustment). See paragraphs (e)(5)(ii) through (v) of this section. Whether a taxpayer has satisfied its obligation to minimize the aggregate amount of its liability for foreign income taxes over time is determined without regard to the present value of a deferred tax liability or other time value of money considerations. However, a taxpayer is not required to reduce its foreign income tax liability to the extent the reasonably expected, arm's length costs of reducing the liability would exceed the amount by which the liability could be reduced. For this purpose, such costs may include an additional liability for a different foreign tax (but not U.S. taxes) that is not a foreign income tax only to the extent the amount of the additional liability is determined in a manner consistent with the rules of this paragraph (e)(5). A taxpayer is not required to alter its form of doing business, its business conduct, or the form of any business transaction in order to reduce its liability under foreign law for foreign income tax.

* * *

(6) Soak-up taxes—(i) In general. An amount remitted to a foreign country is not an amount of foreign income tax paid to the extent that liability for the foreign income tax is dependent (by its terms or otherwise) on the availability of a credit for the tax against income tax liability to another country. Liability for foreign income tax is dependent on the availability of a credit for the foreign income tax against income tax liability to another country only if and to the extent that the foreign income tax would not be imposed but for the availability of such a credit.

* * *

(f) Taxpayer—(1) In general. The person by whom tax is considered paid for purposes of sections 901 and 903 is the person on whom foreign law imposes legal liability for such tax, even if another person (e.g., a withholding agent) remits such tax. For purposes of this section, § 1.901–2A and § 1.903–1, the person on whom foreign law imposes such liability is referred to as the "taxpayer." A foreign tax of a type described in paragraph (a)(2)(ii)(C) of this section is considered to be imposed on the recipients of wages if such tax is deducted from such wages under provisions that are comparable to section 3102(a) and (b) of the Internal Revenue Code.

(2) Party undertaking tax obligation as part of transaction—(i) In general. Tax is considered paid by the taxpayer even if another party to a direct or indirect transaction with the taxpayer agrees, as a part of the transaction, to assume the taxpayer's foreign tax liability. The rules of the foregoing sentence apply notwithstanding anything to the contrary in paragraph (e)(3) of this section. See § 1.901–2A for additional rules regarding dual capacity taxpayers.

* * *

(3) Taxes imposed on combined income of two or more persons—(i) In general. If foreign tax is imposed on the combined income of two or more persons (for example, a husband and wife or a corporation and one or more of its subsidiaries), foreign law is considered to impose legal liability on each such person for the amount of the tax that is attributable to such person's portion of the base of the tax. Therefore, if foreign tax is imposed on the combined income of two or more persons, such tax is allocated among, and considered paid by, such persons on a pro rata basis in proportion to each person's portion of the combined income, as determined under foreign law and paragraph (f)(3)(iii) of this section. Combined income with respect to each foreign tax that is imposed on a combined basis is computed separately, and the tax on that combined income is allocated separately under this paragraph (f)(3)(i). If foreign law exempts from tax, or provides for specific rates of tax with respect to, certain types of income, or if certain expenses, deductions or credits are taken into account only with respect to a particular type of income, combined income with respect to such portions of the combined income is also computed separately, and the tax on that combined income is allocated separately under this paragraph (f)(3)(i). The rules of this paragraph (f)(3) apply regardless of which person is obligated to remit the tax, which person actually remits the tax, or which person the foreign country could proceed against to collect the tax in the event all or a portion of the tax is not paid. For purposes of this paragraph (f)(3), the term person means an individual or an entity (including a disregarded entity described in § 301.7701–2(c)(2)(i) of this chapter) that is subject to tax in a foreign country as a corporation (or otherwise at the entity level). In determining the amount of tax paid by an owner of a partnership or a disregarded entity, this paragraph (f)(3) first applies to determine the amount of tax paid by the partnership or disregarded entity, and then paragraph (f)(4) of this section applies to allocate the amount of such tax to the owner.

* * *

(4) Taxes imposed on partnerships and disregarded entities—(i) Partnerships. If foreign law imposes tax at the entity level on the income of a partnership, the partnership is considered to be legally liable for such tax under foreign law and therefore is considered to pay the tax for Federal income tax purposes. The rules of this paragraph (f)(4)(i) apply regardless of which person is obligated to remit the tax, which person actually remits the tax, or which person the foreign country could proceed against to collect the tax in the event all or a portion of the tax is not paid. See §§ 1.702–1(a)(6) and 1.704–1(b)(4)(viii) for rules relating to the determination of a partner's distributive share of such tax.

(ii) Disregarded entities. If foreign law imposes tax at the entity level on the income of an entity described in § 301.7701–2(c)(2)(i) of this chapter (a disregarded entity), the person (as defined in section 7701(a)(1)) who is treated as owning the assets of the disregarded entity for Federal income tax purposes is considered to be legally liable for such tax under foreign law. Such person is considered to pay the tax for Federal income tax purposes. The rules of this paragraph (f)(4)(ii) apply regardless of which person is obligated to remit the tax, which person actually remits the tax, or which person the foreign country could proceed against to collect the tax in the event all or a portion of the tax is not paid.

* * *

(g) Definitions. For purposes of this section and §§ 1.901–2A and 1.903–1, the following definitions apply.

(1) Foreign country and possession (territory) of the United States. The term foreign country means any foreign state, any possession (territory) of the United States, and any political subdivision of any foreign state or of any possession (territory) of the United States. The term possession (or territory) of the United States means American Samoa, Guam, the Commonwealth of the Northern Mariana Islands, the Commonwealth of Puerto Rico, and the U.S. Virgin Islands.

(2) Foreign levy. The term foreign levy means a levy imposed by a foreign country.

(3) Foreign tax. The term foreign tax means a foreign levy that is a tax as defined in paragraph (a)(2) of this section.

(4) Foreign tax law. The term foreign tax law means the laws of the foreign country imposing a foreign tax, including a separate levy that is modified by an applicable income tax treaty. The foreign tax law is construed on the basis of the foreign country's statutes, regulations, case law, and administrative rulings or other official pronouncements, as modified by an applicable income tax treaty.

(5) Paid, payment, and paid by. The term paid means "paid" or "accrued"; the term payment means "payment" or "accrual"; and the term paid by means "paid by" or "accrued by or on behalf of," depending on the taxpayer's method of accounting for foreign income taxes. In the case of a taxpayer that claims a foreign tax credit, the taxpayer's method of accounting for foreign income taxes refers to whether the taxpayer claims the foreign tax credit for taxes paid (that is, remitted) or taxes accrued (as determined under § 1.905–1(d)) during the taxable year. The term paid does not include foreign taxes deemed paid under section 904(c) or section 960.

(6) Resident and nonresident. The terms resident and nonresident, when used in the context of the foreign tax law of a foreign country, have the meaning provided in paragraphs (g)(6)(i) and (ii) of this section.

(i) Resident. An individual is a resident of a foreign country if the individual is liable to income tax in such country by reason of the individual's residence, domicile, citizenship, or similar criterion under such country's foreign tax law. An entity (including a corporation, partnership, trust, estate, or an entity that is disregarded as an entity separate from its owner for Federal income tax purposes) is a resident of a foreign country if the entity is liable to tax on its income (regardless of whether tax is actually imposed) under the laws of the foreign country by reason of the entity's place of incorporation or place of management in that country (or in a political subdivision or local authority thereof), or by reason of a criterion of similar nature, or if the entity is of a type that is specifically identified as a resident in an income tax treaty with the United States to which the foreign country is a party.

(ii) Nonresident. A nonresident with respect to a foreign country is any individual or entity that is not a resident of such foreign country.

(7) Taxpayer. The term taxpayer has the meaning set forth in paragraph (f)(1) of this section.

* * *

[T.D. 7918, 48 FR 46272, Oct. 12, 1983; T.D. 8372, 56 FR 56008, Oct. 31, 1991; T.D. 9416, 73 FR 40733, July 16, 2008; T.D. 9536, 76 FR 42037, July 18, 2011; T.D. 9535, 76 FR 42043, July 18, 2011; T.D. 9536, 76 FR 53819, Aug. 30, 2011; T.D. 9576, 77 FR 8125, Feb. 14, 2012; T.D. 9619, 78 FR 28489, May 15, 2013; T.D. 9634, 78 FR 54391, Sept. 4, 2013; T.D. 9959, 87 FR 335, Jan. 4, 2022; 87 FR 45019, July 27, 2022]

§ 1.901–2A Dual capacity taxpayers.

(a) Application of separate levy rules as applied to dual capacity taxpayers—(1) In

general. If the application of a foreign levy (as defined in § 1.901–2(g)(3)) is different, either by the terms of the levy or in practice, for dual capacity taxpayers (as defined in § 1.901–2(a)(2)(ii)(A)) from its application to other persons, then, unless the only such difference is that a lower rate (but the same base) applies to dual capacity taxpayers, such difference is considered to be related to the fact that dual capacity taxpayers receive, directly or indirectly, a specific economic benefit (as defined in § 1.901–2(a)(2)(ii)(B)) from the foreign country and thus to be a difference in kind, and not merely of degree. In such a case, notwithstanding any contrary provision of § 1.901–2(d), the levy as applicable to such dual capacity taxpayers is a separate levy (within the meaning of § 1.901–2(d)) from the levy as applicable to such other persons, regardless of whether such difference is in the base of the levy, in the rate of the levy, or both. In such a case, each of the levy as applied to dual capacity taxpayers and the levy as applied to other persons must be analyzed separately to determine whether it is an income tax within the meaning of § 1.901–2(a)(1) and whether it is a tax in lieu of an income tax within the meaning of § 1.903–1(a). However, if the application of the levy is neither different by its terms nor different in practice for dual capacity taxpayers from its application to other persons, or if the only difference is that a lower rate (but the same base) applies to dual capacity taxpayers, then, in accordance with § 1.901–2(d), such foreign levy as applicable to dual capacity taxpayers and such levy as applicable to other persons together constitute a single levy. In such a case, no amount paid (as defined in § 1.901–2(g)(1)) pursuant to such levy by any such dual capacity taxpayer is considered to be paid in exchange for a specific economic benefit, and such levy, as applicable in the aggregate to such dual capacity taxpayers and to such other persons, is analyzed to determine whether it is an income tax within the meaning of § 1.901–2(a)(1) or a tax in lieu of an income tax within the meaning of § 1.903–1(a). Application of a foreign levy to dual capacity taxpayers will be considered to be different in practice from application of that levy to other persons, even if no such difference is apparent from the terms of the levy, unless it is established that application of that levy to dual capacity taxpayers does not differ in practice from its application to other persons.

* * *

(b) Burden of proof for dual capacity taxpayers—(1) In general. For credit to be allowable under section 901 or 903, the person claiming credit must establish that the foreign levy with respect to which credit is claimed is an income tax within the meaning of § 1.901–2(a)(1) or a tax in lieu of an income tax within the meaning of § 1.903–1(a), respectively. Thus, such person must establish, among other things, that such levy is a tax. See § 1.901–2(a)(2)(i) and § 1.903–1(a). Where a person claims credit under section 901 or 903 for an amount paid by a dual capacity taxpayer pursuant to a foreign levy, § 1.901–2(a)(2)(i) and § 1.903–1(a), respectively, require such person to establish the amount, if any, that is paid pursuant to the distinct element of the levy that is a tax. If, pursuant to paragraph (a)(1) of this section and § 1.901–2(d), such levy as applicable to dual capacity taxpayers and such levy as applicable to other persons together constitute a single levy, then no amount paid pursuant to that levy by any such dual capacity taxpayer is considered to be paid in exchange for a specific economic benefit. Accordingly, such levy has only one distinct element, and the levy either is or is not, in its entirety, a tax. If, however, such levy as applicable to dual capacity taxpayers is a separate levy from such levy as applicable to other persons, then a person claiming credit under section 901 or 903 for an amount paid by a dual capacity taxpayer pursuant to such separate levy may establish the amount, if any, that is paid pursuant to the distinct element of the levy that is a tax only by the facts and circumstances method or the safe harbor method described in paragraph (c) of this section. If such person fails to so establish such amount, no portion of the amount that is paid pursuant to the separate levy by the dual capacity taxpayer to such foreign country shall be treated as an amount of tax. Any amount that, either by reason of application of the methods of paragraph (c) of this section or by reason of the immediately preceding sentence, is not treated as an amount of tax shall (i) be considered to have been paid in exchange for a specific economic benefit; (ii) be characterized (e.g., as royalty, purchase price, cost of sales, reduction of the proceeds of a sale, or reduction of interest income) according to the nature of the transaction and of the specific economic benefit received; and (iii) be treated according to such characterization for all purposes of chapter 1 of the Internal Revenue Code, except that any determination that an amount is not tax for purposes of section 901 or 903 by reason of application of the safe harbor method shall not be taken into account in determining whether or not such an amount is to be characterized and treated as tax for purposes of computing an allowance for percentage depletion under sections 611 and 613.

* * *

(c) Satisfaction of burden of proof—(1) In general. This paragraph (c) sets out the methods by which a person who claims credit under section 901 or 903 for an amount paid by a dual capacity taxpayer pursuant to a foreign levy that satisfies all of the criteria of section 901 or 903 other than the determination of the distinct element of the levy that is a tax and of the amount that is paid pursuant to that distinct element (a "qualifying levy") may establish such distinct element and amount. Such person must establish the amount paid pursuant to a qualifying levy that is paid pursuant to the distinct element of the levy that is a tax (which amount therefore is an amount of income tax within the meaning of § 1.901–2(a)(1) or an amount of tax in lieu of income tax within the meaning of § 1.903–1(a) (a "qualifying amount")) only by the facts and circumstances method set forth in paragraph (c)(2) of this section or the safe harbor method set forth in paragraph (c)(3) of this section. A levy is not a qualifying levy, and neither the facts and circumstances method nor the safe harbor method applies to an amount paid by a dual capacity taxpayer pursuant to a foreign levy, if it has been established pursuant to § 1.901–2(d) and paragraph (a)(1) of this section that that levy as applied to that dual capacity taxpayer and that levy as applied to persons other than dual capacity taxpayers together constitute a single levy, or if it has been established in accordance with the first sentence of paragraph (b)(2) of this section that credit is allowable by reason of a treaty for an amount paid with respect to such levy.

(2) Facts and circumstances method—(i) In general. If the person claiming credit establishes, based on all of the relevant facts and circumstances, the amount, if any, paid by the dual capacity taxpayer pursuant to the qualifying levy that is not paid in exchange for a specific economic benefit, such amount is the qualifying amount with respect to such qualifying levy. In determining the qualifying amount with respect to a qualifying levy under the facts and circumstances method, neither the methodology nor the results that would have obtained if a person had elected to apply the safe harbor method to such qualifying levy is a relevant fact or circumstance. Accordingly, neither such methodology nor such results shall be taken into account in applying the facts and circumstances method.

* * *

(3) Safe harbor method. Under the safe harbor method, the person claiming credit makes an election as provided in paragraph (d) of this section and, pursuant to such election, applies the safe harbor formula described in paragraph (e) of this section to the qualifying levy or levies to which the election applies.

* * *

(e) Safe harbor formula—(1) In general. The safe harbor formula applies to determine the distinct element of a qualifying levy that is a tax and the amount paid by a dual capacity taxpayer pursuant to such qualifying levy that is the qualifying amount with respect to such levy. Under the safe harbor formula the amount paid in a taxable year pursuant to a qualifying levy that is the qualifying amount with respect to such levy is an amount equal to:

$$(A-B-C)\times D/(1-D)$$

where: (except as otherwise provided in paragraph (e)(5) of this section):

A = the amount of gross receipts as determined under paragraph (e)(2) of this section

B = the amount of costs and expenses as determined under paragraph (e)(2) of this section

C = the total amount paid in the taxable year by the dual capacity taxpayer pursuant to the qualifying levy (the "actual payment amount")

D = the tax rate as determined under paragraph (e)(3) of this section

In no case, however, shall the qualifying amount exceed the actual payment amount; and the qualifying amount is zero if the safe harbor formula yields a qualifying amount less than zero. The safe harbor formula is intended to yield a qualifying amount that is approximately equal to the amount of generally imposed income tax within the meaning of paragraphs (a) and (b)(1) of § 1.903–1 ("general tax") of the foreign country that would have been required to be paid in the taxable year by the dual capacity taxpayer if it had not been a dual capacity taxpayer and if the base of the general tax had allowed a deduction in such year for the amount ("specific economic benefit amount") by which the actual payment amount exceeds the qualifying amount. * * *

* * *

[T.D. 7918, 48 FR 46284, Oct. 12, 1983]

§ 1.903–1 Taxes in lieu of income taxes.

(a) Overview. Section 903 provides that the term "income, war profits, and excess profits taxes" includes a tax paid in lieu of a tax on income, war profits, or excess profits that is otherwise generally imposed by any foreign country. Paragraphs (b) and (c) of this section define a tax described in section 903. Paragraph (d) of this section provides examples illustrating the application of this section. Paragraph (e) of this section sets forth the applicability date of this section. For purposes of this section and §§ 1.901–2 and 1.901–2A, a tax described in section 903 is referred to as a "tax in lieu of an income tax" or an "in lieu of tax" and the definitions in § 1.901–2(g) apply for purposes of this section. Determinations of the amount of a tax in lieu of an income tax that is paid by a person and determinations of the person by whom such tax is paid are made under § 1.901–2(e) and (f), respectively. Section 1.901–2A contains additional rules applicable to dual capacity taxpayers (as defined in § 1.901–2(a)(2)(ii)(A)).

(b) Definition of tax in lieu of an income tax—(1) In general. Paragraphs (b)(2) and (c) of this section provide the requirements for a foreign levy to qualify as a tax in lieu of an income tax. The rules of this section are applied independently to each separate levy (within the meaning of §§ 1.901–2(d) and 1.901–2A(a)). A foreign tax either is or is not a tax in lieu of an income tax in its entirety for all persons subject to the tax. It is immaterial whether the base of the in lieu of tax bears any relation to realized net gain. The base of the foreign tax may, for example, be gross income, gross receipts or sales, or the number of units produced or exported. The foreign country's reason for imposing a foreign tax on a base other than net income (for example, because of administrative difficulty in determining the amount of income that would otherwise be subject to a net income tax) is immaterial, although paragraph (c)(1) of this section generally requires a showing that the foreign country made a deliberate and cognizant choice to impose the in lieu of tax instead of a net income tax (see paragraph (c)(1)(iii) of this section).

(2) Requirements. A foreign levy is a tax in lieu of an income tax only if—

(i) It is a foreign tax; and

(ii) It satisfies the substitution requirement of paragraph (c) of this section.

(c) Substitution requirement—(1) In general. A foreign tax (the "tested foreign tax") satisfies the substitution requirement if, based on the foreign tax law, the requirements in paragraphs (c)(1)(i) through (iv) of this section are satisfied with respect to the tested foreign tax, or the tested foreign tax is a covered withholding tax described in paragraph (c)(2) of this section.

(i) Existence of generally-imposed net income tax. A separate levy that is a net income tax (as described in § 1.901–2(a)(3)) is generally imposed by the same foreign country (the "generally-imposed net income tax") that imposes the tested foreign tax.

(ii) Non-duplication. Neither the generally-imposed net income tax nor any other separate levy that is a net income tax is also imposed, in addition to the tested foreign tax, by the same foreign country on any persons with respect to any portion of the income to which the amounts (such as sales or units of production) that form the base of the tested foreign tax relate (the "excluded income"). Therefore, a tested foreign tax does not meet the requirement of this paragraph (c)(1)(ii) if a net income tax imposed by the same foreign country applies to the excluded income of any persons that are subject to the tested foreign tax, even if not all persons subject to the tested foreign tax are subject to the net income tax.

(iii) Close connection to excluded income. But for the existence of the tested foreign tax, the generally-imposed net income tax would otherwise have been imposed on the excluded income. The requirement in the preceding sentence is met only if the imposition of such tested foreign tax bears a close connection to the failure to impose the generally-imposed net income tax on the excluded income; the relationship cannot be merely incidental, tangential, or minor. A close connection must be established with proof that the foreign country made a cognizant and deliberate choice to impose the tested foreign tax instead of the generally-imposed net income tax. Such proof must be based on foreign tax law, or the legislative history of either the tested foreign tax or the generally-imposed net income tax that describes the provisions excluding taxpayers subject to the tested foreign tax from the generally-imposed net income tax. Thus, a close connection exists if the generally-imposed net income tax would apply by its terms to the excluded income, but for the fact that the excluded income is expressly excluded, and the tested foreign tax is enacted contemporaneously with the generally-imposed net income tax. A close connection also exists if the generally-imposed net income tax by its terms does not apply to, but does not expressly exclude, the excluded income, and the tested foreign tax is enacted contemporaneously with the generally-imposed net income tax. Where the tested foreign tax is not enacted contemporaneously with the generally-imposed net income tax and the generally-imposed net income tax is not amended contemporaneously with the enactment of the tested foreign tax to exclude the excluded income or to narrow the scope of the generally-imposed net income tax so as not to apply to the excluded income, a close connection can be established only by reference to the legislative history of the tested foreign tax (or a predecessor in lieu of tax). Not all income derived by persons subject to the tested foreign tax need be excluded income, provided the tested foreign tax applies only to amounts that relate to the excluded income.

(iv) Jurisdiction to tax excluded income. If the generally-imposed net income tax, or a hypothetical new tax that is a separate levy with respect to the generally-imposed net income tax, were applied to the excluded income, such generally-imposed net income tax or separate levy would meet the attribution requirement described in § 1.901–2(b)(5).

(2) Covered withholding tax. A tested foreign tax is a covered withholding tax if, based on the foreign tax law, the requirements in paragraphs (c)(1)(i) and (c)(2)(i) through (iii) of this section are met with respect to the tested foreign tax. See also § 1.901–2(d)(1)(iii) for rules treating withholding taxes as separate levies with respect to each class of income subject to the tax or with respect to each subset of a class of income that is subject to different income attribution rules.

(i) Withholding tax on nonresidents. The tested foreign tax is a withholding tax (as defined in section 901(k)(1)(B)) that is imposed on gross income of persons who are nonresidents of the foreign country imposing the tested foreign tax. It is immaterial whether the tested foreign tax is withheld by the payor or is imposed directly on the nonresident taxpayer.

(ii) Non-duplication. The tested foreign tax is not in addition to any net income tax that is imposed by the foreign country on any portion of the net income attributable to the gross income that is subject to the tested foreign tax. Therefore, a tested foreign tax does not meet the requirement of this paragraph (c)(2)(ii) if by its terms it applies to gross income of nonresidents that are also subject to a net income tax imposed by the same foreign country on the same income, even if not all nonresidents subject to the tested foreign tax are also subject to the net income tax.

(iii) Source-based attribution requirement. The income subject to the tested foreign tax satisfies the attribution requirement described in § 1.901–2(b)(5)(i)(B).

(d) Examples. The following examples illustrate the rules of this section.

(1) Example 1: Tax on gross income from services; non-duplication requirement—(i) Facts. Country X imposes a tax at the rate of 3 percent on the gross receipts of companies, wherever resident, from furnishing specified types of electronically supplied services to customers located in Country X (the "ESS tax"). No deductions are allowed in determining the taxable base of the ESS tax. In addition to the ESS tax, Country X imposes a net income tax within the meaning of § 1.901–2(a)(3) on resident companies (the "resident income tax") and also imposes a net income tax within the meaning of § 1.901–2(a)(3) on the income of nonresident companies that is attributable, under reasonable principles, to the nonresident's permanent establishment within Country X (the "nonresident income tax"). Under Country X tax law, a permanent establishment is defined in the same manner as under the 2016 U.S. Model Income Tax Convention. Both the resident income tax and the nonresident income tax, which are separate levies under § 1.901–2(d)(1)(iii), qualify as generally-imposed net income taxes. Under Country X tax law, the ESS tax applies to both resident and nonresident companies regardless of whether the company is also subject to the resident income tax or the nonresident income tax, respectively.

(ii) Analysis. Under § 1.901–2(d)(1)(iii), the ESS tax comprises two separate levies, one imposed on resident companies (the "resident ESS tax"), and one imposed on nonresident companies (the "nonresident ESS tax"). Under paragraph (c)(1)(ii) of this section, neither the resident ESS tax nor the nonresident ESS tax satisfies the substitution requirement, because by its terms the income to which the gross receipts subject to the ESS tax relate is also subject to one of the two generally-imposed net income taxes imposed by Country X. Similarly, under paragraph (c)(2)(ii) of this section, the nonresident ESS tax is not a covered withholding tax because by its terms it is imposed in addition to the nonresident income tax. The fact that nonresident taxpayers that do not have a permanent establishment in Country X are in practice subject to the nonresident ESS tax but not to the nonresident income tax on the gross receipts included in the base of the nonresident ESS tax is not relevant to the determination of whether the ESS tax meets the substitution requirement under paragraph (c)(1) of this section. Therefore, neither the resident ESS tax nor the nonresident ESS tax is a tax in lieu of an income tax.

(2) Example 2: Tax on gross income from services; attribution of income—(i) Facts. The facts are the same as those in paragraph (d)(1)(i) of this section (the facts in Example 1), except that under Country X tax law, the nonresident ESS tax is imposed only if the nonresident company does not have a permanent establishment in Country X. If the nonresident company has a Country X permanent establishment, the nonresident income tax applies to the profits attributable to that permanent establishment. In addition, the statutory language and legislative history to the nonresident ESS tax demonstrate that Country X made a cognizant and deliberate choice to impose the nonresident ESS tax instead of the nonresident income tax with respect to the gross receipts that are subject to the nonresident ESS tax.

(ii) Analysis—(A) General application of substitution requirement. The nonresident ESS tax meets the requirements in paragraphs (c)(1)(i) and (ii) of this section because Country X has two generally-imposed net income taxes and neither generally-imposed net income tax nor any other separate levy that is a net income tax is imposed by Country X on a nonresident's income to which gross receipts that form the base of the nonresident ESS tax relate (which is the excluded income). The statutory language and legislative history to the nonresident ESS tax demonstrate that Country X made a cognizant and deliberate choice not to impose the nonresident income tax on the excluded income. Therefore, the nonresident ESS tax meets the requirement in paragraph (c)(1)(iii) of this section because, but for the existence of the tested foreign tax, the nonresident income tax would otherwise have been imposed on the excluded income. However, the nonresident ESS tax does not meet the requirement in paragraph (c)(1)(iv) of this section, because if Country X had chosen to apply the nonresident income tax (rather than the nonresident ESS tax) to the excluded income, the modified nonresident income tax would fail the attribution requirement in § 1.901–2(b)(5). First, the modified tax would not satisfy the requirement in § 1.901–2(b)(5)(i)(A) because the modified tax would not apply to income attributable under reasonable principles to the nonresident's activities within the foreign country, since the modified tax is determined by taking into account the location of customers. Second, the modified tax would not satisfy the requirement in § 1.901–2(b)(5)(i)(B) because the excluded income is from services performed outside of Country X. Third, the modified tax would not satisfy the requirement in § 1.901–2(b)(5)(i)(C) because the excluded income is not from sales or dispositions of real property located in Country X or from property forming part of the business property of a taxable presence in Country X. Because the Country X nonresident income tax as applied to the excluded income would fail to meet the attribution requirement in § 1.901–2(b)(5), as required by paragraph (c)(1)(iv) of this section, the nonresident ESS tax does not satisfy the substitution requirement in paragraph (c)(1) of this section.

(B) Covered withholding tax analysis. The nonresident ESS tax meets the requirement in paragraph (c)(1)(i) of this section because there exists a generally-imposed net income tax. It also meets the requirements in paragraphs (c)(2)(i) and (ii) of this section because it is a withholding tax on gross receipts of nonresidents and the income attributable to those gross receipts is not subject to a net income tax. However, the nonresident ESS tax does not meet the requirement in paragraph (c)(2)(iii) of this section because the services income subject to the nonresident ESS tax is from electronically supplied services performed outside of Country X. See § 1.901–2(b)(5)(i)(B). Therefore, the nonresident ESS tax is not a covered withholding tax under paragraph (c)(2) of this section. Because the nonresident ESS tax does not satisfy the substitution requirement of paragraph (c) of this section, it is not a tax in lieu of an income tax.

* * *

(5) Example 5: Multiple in-lieu-of taxes—(i) Facts. Country X imposes a net income tax within the meaning of § 1.901–2(a)(3) on the income of nonresident companies that is attributable, under reasonable principles, to the nonresident's activities within Country X (the "trade or business tax"). The trade or business tax applies to all nonresident corporations that engage in business in Country X except for nonresident corporations that engage in insurance activities, which are instead subject to two different taxes ("insurance taxes"). The insurance taxes apply to nonresident corporations that engage in insurance activities that are attributable, under reasonable principles, to the nonresident's activities within Country X. The insurance taxes do not satisfy the cost recovery requirement in § 1.901–2(b)(4). The trade or business tax and the two insurance taxes were enacted contemporaneously, and the statutory language of the trade or business tax expressly excludes gross income derived by nonresident corporations engaged in insurance activities from the trade or business tax.

(ii) Analysis. The insurance taxes meet the requirements in paragraphs (c)(1)(i) and (ii) of this section because Country X has a generally-imposed net income tax, the trade or business tax, and neither the trade or business tax nor any other separate levy that is a net income tax is imposed by Country X on a nonresident's gross income to which the amounts that form the base of the insurance taxes (the "excluded income") relate. The Country X tax law expressly provides that the trade or business tax does not apply to nonresident corporations engaged in insurance activities. In addition, the two insurance taxes were enacted contemporaneously with the trade or business tax. Therefore, it is demonstrated that Country X made a cognizant and deliberate choice to impose the insurance taxes in lieu of the generally-imposed trade or business tax, and the insurance taxes meet the requirement in paragraph (c)(1)(iii) of this section. If the trade or business tax also applied to the excluded income, the trade or business tax would meet the requirement in § 1.901–2(b)(5)(i)(A), because it would apply only to income attributable, under reasonable principles, to the nonresident's activities within the foreign country. Thus, the insurance taxes meet the requirement in paragraph (c)(1)(iv) of this section. Therefore, the insurance taxes satisfy the substitution requirement in paragraph (c)(1) of this section.

* * *

[T.D. 7918, 48 FR 46272, Oct. 12, 1983; 48 FR 52033, Nov. 16, 1983; T.D. 9959, 87 FR 357, Jan. 4, 2022]

§ 1.904–1 Limitation on credit for foreign income taxes.

* * *

(b) Special computation of taxable income. For purposes of computing the limitation under paragraph (a) of this section, the taxable income in the case of an individual, estate, or trust is computed without any deduction for personal exemptions under section 151 or 642(b).

* * *

[T.D. 6500, 25 FR 11910, Nov. 26, 1960, as amended by T.D. 6789, 29 FR 19243, Dec. 31, 1964; T.D. 7294, 38 FR 33080, Nov. 30, 1973; T.D. 7490, 42 FR 30497, June 15, 1977; 42 FR 32536, June 27, 1977; T. D. 9882, 84 FR 69075, Dec. 17, 2019; T.D. 9922, 85 FR 72057, Nov. 12, 2020]

§ 1.904–4 Separate application of section 904 with respect to certain categories of income.

(a) In general. A taxpayer is required to compute a separate foreign tax credit limitation for income received or accrued in a taxable year that is described in section 904(d)(1)(A) (section 951A category income), 904(d)(1)(B) (foreign branch category income), 904(d)(1)(C) (passive category income), 904(d)(1)(D) (general category income), or paragraph (m) of this section (specified separate categories). For purposes of this section, the definitions in § 1.904–5(a)(4) apply.

(b) Passive category income—(1) In general. The term passive category income means passive income and specified passive category income.

(2) Passive income—(i) In general. The term passive income means any—

(A) Income received or accrued by any person that is of a kind that would be foreign personal holding company income (as defined in section 954(c), taking into account any exceptions or exclusions to section 954(c), including, for example, section 954(c)(3), (c)(6), (h), or (i)) if the taxpayer were a controlled foreign corporation, including any amount of gain on the sale or exchange of stock in excess of the amount treated as a dividend under section 1248;

(B) Amount includible in gross income under section 1293;

(C) Distributive shares of partnership income treated as passive category income under paragraph (n)(1) of this section, and income from the sale of a partnership interest treated as passive category income under paragraph (n)(2) of this section; or

(D) Income treated as passive category income under the look-through rules in § 1.904–5.

(ii) Exceptions. Passive income does not include any export financing interest (as defined in paragraph (h) of this section), any high-taxed income (as defined in paragraph (c) of this section), financial services income (as defined in paragraph (e)(1)(ii) of this section), or any active rents and royalties (as defined in paragraph (b)(2)(iii) of this section). In addition, passive income does not include any income that would otherwise be passive but is excluded from passive category income under § 1.904–5(b)(1) or that is assigned to a separate category other than passive category income under § 1.904–5(c)(4)(iii). See also paragraph (k) of this section for rules relating to income resourced under a tax treaty. In determining whether any income is of a kind that would be foreign personal holding company income, the rules of section 864(d)(5)(A)(i) and (6) (treating related person factoring income of a controlled foreign corporation as foreign personal holding company income that is not eligible for the export financing income exception to the separate limitation for passive income) shall apply only in the case of income of a controlled foreign corporation (as defined in section 957). Thus, income earned directly by a United States person that is related person factoring income may be eligible for the exception for export financing interest.

(iii) Active rents or royalties—(A) In general. For rents and royalties paid or accrued after September 20, 2004, passive income does not include any rents or royalties that are derived in the active conduct of a trade or business, regardless of whether such rents or royalties are received from a related or an unrelated person. Except as provided in paragraph (b)(2)(iii)(B) of this section, the principles of section 954(c)(2)(A) and the regulations under that section shall apply in determining whether rents or royalties are derived in the active conduct of a trade or business. For this purpose, the term taxpayer shall be substituted for the term controlled foreign corporation if the recipient of the rents or royalties is not a controlled foreign corporation.

(B) Active conduct of trade or business. Rents and royalties are considered derived in the active conduct of a trade or business by a United States person or by a controlled foreign corporation (or other entity to which the look-through rules apply) for purposes of section 904 (but not for purposes of section 954) if the requirements of section 954(c)(2)(A) are satisfied by one or more corporations that are members of an affiliated group of corporations (within the meaning of section 1504(a), determined without regard to section 1504(b)(3)) of which the recipient is a member. For purposes of this paragraph (b)(2)(iii)(B), an affiliated group includes only domestic corporations and foreign corporations that are controlled foreign corporations in which domestic members of the affiliated group own, directly or indirectly, at least 80 percent of the total voting power and value of the stock. For purposes of this paragraph (b)(2)(iii)(B), indirect ownership shall be determined under section 318 and the regulations under that section.

(iv) Examples. The following examples illustrate the application of this paragraph (b)(2).

(A) Example 1. For Year 1, USP, a domestic corporation, has a net foreign currency gain that would not constitute foreign personal holding company income if USP were a controlled foreign corporation because the gain is directly related to the business needs of USP. See section 954(c)(1)(D). Under paragraph (b)(2)(i)(A) of this section, the foreign currency gain is, therefore, not passive category income to USP because it is not income of a kind that would be foreign personal holding company income.

(B) Example 2. Controlled foreign corporation, CFC, is a wholly-owned subsidiary of USP, a domestic corporation. CFC is regularly engaged in the restaurant franchise business. USP licenses trademarks, tradenames, certain know-how, related services, and certain restaurant designs for which CFC pays USP an arm's length royalty. USP is regularly engaged in the development and licensing of such property. Some of the franchisees are unrelated to CFC and USP. Other franchisees are related to CFC or USP and use the licensed property outside of CFC's country of incorporation. CFC does not satisfy, but USP does satisfy, the active trade or business requirements of section 954(c)(2)(A). The royalty income earned by CFC from both its related and unrelated franchisees is foreign personal holding company income because CFC does not satisfy the active trade or business requirements of section 954(c)(2)(A) and, in addition, the royalty income from the related franchisees does not qualify for the same country exception of section 954(c)(3) or the look-through exception in section 954(c)(6).

However, all of the royalty income earned by CFC is general category income to CFC under § 1.904–4(b)(2)(iii) because USP, a member of CFC's affiliated group, satisfies the active trade or business test (which is applied without regard to whether the royalties are paid by a related person). USP's inclusion under section 951(a)(1)(A) of CFC's royalty income is general category income to USP under § 1.904–5(c)(5) and paragraph (d) of this section. The royalties received by USP are general category income to USP under § 1.904–5(b)(1) and paragraph (d) of this section.

(3) Specified passive category income means—

(i) Dividends from a DISC or former DISC (as defined in section 992(a)) to the extent such dividends are treated as income from sources without the United States;

(ii) Taxable income attributable to foreign trade income (within the meaning of section 923(b)); or

(iii) Distributions from a FSC (or a former FSC) out of earnings and profits attributable to foreign trade income (within the meaning of section 923(b)) or interest or carrying charges (as defined in section 927(d)(1)) derived from a transaction which results in foreign trade income (as defined in section 923(b)).

(c) High-taxed income—(1) In general. Income received or accrued by a United States person that would otherwise be passive income is not treated as passive income if the income is determined to be high-taxed income. Income is considered to be high-taxed income if, after allocating expenses, losses, and other deductions of the United States person to that income under paragraph (c)(2) of this section, the sum of the foreign income taxes paid or accrued, and deemed paid under section 960, by the United States person with respect to such income (reduced by any portion of such taxes for which a credit is not allowed) exceeds the highest rate of tax specified in section 1 or 11, whichever applies (and with reference to section 15 if applicable), multiplied by the amount of such income (including the amount treated as a dividend under section 78). If, after application of this paragraph (c), income that would otherwise be passive income is determined to be high-taxed income, the income is treated as general category income, foreign branch category income, section

951A category income, or income in a specified separate category, as determined under the rules of this section, and any taxes imposed on that income are considered related to the same separate category of income under § 1.904–6. If, after application of this paragraph (c), passive income is zero or less than zero, any taxes imposed on the passive income are considered related to the same separate category of income to which the passive income (if not reduced to zero or less than zero) would have been assigned had the income been treated as high-taxed income (general category, foreign branch category, section 951A category, or a specified separate category). For additional rules regarding losses related to passive income, see paragraph (c)(2) of this section. Income and taxes shall be translated at the appropriate rates, as determined under sections 986, 987 and 989 and the regulations under those sections, before application of this paragraph (c). For purposes of allocating taxes to groups of income, United States source passive income is treated as any other passive income. In making the determination whether income is high-taxed, however, only foreign source income, as determined under United States tax principles, is relevant.

* * *

(d) General category income. The term general category income means all income other than passive category income, foreign branch category income, section 951A category income, and income in a specified separate category. Any item that is excluded from the passive category under paragraph (c) or (h) of this section or § 1.904–5(b)(1) is included in general category income only to the extent that such item does not meet the definition of another separate category. General category income also includes income treated as general category income under the look-through rules referenced in § 1.904–5(a)(2).

* * *

(f) Foreign branch category income—(1) Foreign branch category income—(i) In general. Except as provided in paragraph (f)(1)(ii), (iii), or (iv) of this section, the term foreign branch category income means income of a United States person, other than a pass-through entity, that is—

(A) Income attributable to foreign branches of the United States person held directly or indirectly through disregarded entities;

(B) A distributive share of partnership income that is attributable to foreign branches held by the partnership directly or indirectly through disregarded entities, or held indirectly by the partnership through another partnership or other pass-through entity that holds the foreign branch directly or indirectly through disregarded entities; and

(C) Income from other pass-through entities determined under principles similar to those described in paragraph (f)(1)(i)(B) of this section.

(ii) Passive category income excluded from foreign branch category income. Income assigned to the passive category under paragraph (b) of this section is not foreign branch category income, regardless of whether the income is described in paragraph (f)(1)(i) of this section. Income that is treated as passive category income under the look-through rules in § 1.904–5 is also excluded from foreign branch category income, regardless of whether the income is attributable to a foreign branch. However, income that would be passive category income but for the application of section 904(d)(2)(B)(iii) (export financing interest and high-taxed income) or 904(d)(2)(C) (financial services income) and also meets the definition of foreign branch category income is foreign branch category income.

* * *

(g) Section 951A category income—(1) In general. Except as provided in paragraph (g)(2) of this section, the term section 951A category income means amounts included (directly or indirectly through a pass-through entity) in gross income of a United States person under section 951A(a).

(2) Exceptions for passive category income. Section 951A category income does not include any amounts included under section 951A(a) that are allocable to passive category income under § 1.904–5(c)(6).

* * *

(m) Income treated as allocable to a specified separate category. If section 904(a), (b), and (c) are applied separately to any category of income under the Internal Revenue Code (for example, under section 245(a)(10), 865(h), 901(j), 904(d)(6), or 904(h)(10)), that category of income is treated for all purposes of the Internal Revenue Code as if it were a separate category listed in section 904(d)(1). For purposes of this section, a separate category that is treated as if it were listed in section 904(d)(1) by reason of the first sentence in this paragraph (m) is referred to as a specified separate category.

* * *

(*o*) Separate category of section 78 gross up. The amount included in income under section 78 by reason of taxes deemed paid under section 960 is assigned to the separate category to which the taxes are allocated under 1.904–6(e).

(p) Separate category of foreign currency gain or loss. Foreign currency gain or loss recognized under section 986(c) with respect to a distribution of previously taxed earnings and profits (as described in section 959 or 1293(c)) is assigned to the separate category or categories of the previously taxed earnings and profits from which the distribution is made. See § 1.987–6(b) for rules on assigning section 987 gain or loss on a remittance from a section 987 QBU to a separate category or categories.

* * *

[T.D. 8214, 53 FR 27011, July 18, 1988; T.D. 8412, 57 FR 20644, 20645 May 14, 1992; T.D. 8412, 57 FR 45660, Oct. 2, 1992; T.D. 8556, 59 FR 37672, July 25, 1994; T.D. 8805, 64 FR 1515, Jan. 11, 1999; 64 FR 32181, June 16, 1999; T.D. 8916, 66 FR 275, Jan. 3, 2001; 66 FR 16126, March 23, 2001; T.D. 8973, 66 FR 67086, Dec. 28, 2001; T.D. 9141, 69 FR 43307, July 20, 2004; T.D. 9260, 71 FR 24530, April 25, 2006; 71 FR 48475, Aug. 21, 2006; 71 FR 77265, Dec. 26, 2006; T.D. 9368, 72 FR 72587, Dec. 21, 2007; 73 FR 15063, March 21, 2008; T.D. 9452, 74 FR 27878, June 11, 2009; T.D. 9521, 76 FR 19270, April 7, 2011; T.D. 9882, 84 FR 69077, Dec. 17, 2019; 85 FR 29323, May 15, 2020; T.D. 9922, 85 FR 72057, Nov. 12, 2020; 86 FR 54368, Oct. 1, 2021; T.D. 9959, 87 FR 360, Jan. 4, 2022; 87 FR 45020, July 27, 2022; T.D. 9994, 89 FR 82169, Oct. 10, 2024; T.D. 10016, 89 FR 100164, Dec. 11, 2024]

§ 1.904–5 Look-through rules as applied to controlled foreign corporations and other entities.

(a) Scope and definitions—(1) Look-through rules under section 904(d)(3) to passive category income. Paragraph (c) of this section provides rules for determining the extent to which dividends, interest, rents, and royalties received or accrued by certain eligible persons, and inclusions under sections 951(a)(1) and 951A(a), are treated as passive category income. Paragraph (g) of this section provides rules applying the principles of paragraph (c) of this section to foreign source interest, rents, and royalties paid by a domestic corporation to a related corporation. Paragraph (h) of this section provides rules for assigning a partnership payment to a partner described in section 707 to the passive category. Paragraph (i) of this section provides rules applying the principles of this section to assign distributions and payments from certain related entities to the passive category or to treat the distributions and payments as not in the passive category.

(2) Other look-through rules under section 904(d). Under section 904(d)(4) and paragraph (c)(4)(iii) of this section, certain dividends from noncontrolled 10-percent owned foreign corporations are treated as income in a separate category. Under section 904(d)(3)(H) and paragraph

(j) of this section, certain inclusions under section 1293 are treated as income in a separate category. Paragraph (i) of this section provides rules applying the principles of this section to assign distributions from certain related entities to separate categories.

(3) Other rules provided in this section. Paragraph (b) of this section provides operative rules for this section. Paragraph (d) of this section provides rules addressing exceptions to passive category income for certain purposes in the case of controlled foreign corporations that meet the requirements of section 954(b)(3)(A) (de minimis rule) or section 954(b)(4) (high-tax exception). Paragraph (e) of this section provides rules for characterizing a controlled foreign corporation's foreign base company income and gross insurance income when section 954(b)(3)(B) (full inclusion rule) applies. Paragraph (f) of this section modifies the look-through rules for certain types of income. Paragraph (k) of this section provides ordering rules for applying the look-through rules. Paragraph (*l*) of this section provides examples illustrating the application of certain rules in this section. Paragraphs (m) and (n) of this section provide rules related to the resourcing rules described in section 904(h).

(4) Definitions. For purposes of this section, the following definitions apply:

(i) The term controlled foreign corporation has the meaning given such term by section 957 (taking into account the special rule for certain captive insurance companies contained in section 953(c)), determined without applying section 318(a)(3)(A), (B), and (C) so as to consider a United States person as owning stock which is owned by a person who is not a United States person.

(ii) The term look-through rules means the rules described in this section that assign income to a separate category based on the separate category of the income to which it is allocable.

(iii) The term noncontrolled 10-percent owned foreign corporation has the meaning provided in section 904(d)(2)(E)(i).

(iv) The term pass-through entity means a partnership, S corporation, or any other person (whether domestic or foreign) other than a corporation to the extent that the income or deductions of the person are included in the income of one or more direct or indirect owners or beneficiaries of the person. For example, if a domestic trust is subject to Federal income tax on a portion of its income and its owners are subject to tax on the remaining portion, the domestic trust is treated as a domestic pass-through entity with respect to such remaining portion.

(v) The term separate category means, as the context requires, any category of income described in section 904(d)(1)(A), (B), (C), or (D), any specified separate category of income as defined in § 1.904–4(m), or any category of earnings and profits to which income described in such provisions is attributable.

(vi) The term United States shareholder has the meaning given such term by section 951(b) (taking into account the special rule for certain captive insurance companies contained in section 953(c)), determined without applying section 318(a)(3)(A), (B), and (C) so as to consider a United States person as owning stock which is owned by a person who is not a United States person, except that for purposes of this section, a United States shareholder includes any member of the controlled group of the United States shareholder. For purposes of this paragraph (a)(4)(vi), the controlled group is any member of the affiliated group within the meaning of section 1504(a)(1) except that "more than 50 percent" is substituted for "at least 80 percent" wherever it appears in section 1504(a)(2). When used in reference to a noncontrolled 10-percent owned foreign corporation described in section 904(d)(2)(E)(i)(II), the term United States shareholder also means a taxpayer that meets the stock ownership requirements described in section 904(d)(2)(E)(i)(II).

(b) Operative rules—(1) Assignment of income not assigned under the look-through rules. Except as provided by the look-through rules, dividends, interest, rents, and royalties received or accrued by a taxpayer from a controlled foreign corporation in which the taxpayer is a United States shareholder are excluded from passive category income. Income excluded from the passive category under this paragraph (b)(1) is assigned to another separate category (other than the passive category) under the rules in § 1.904–4.

(2) Priority and ordering of look-through rules. Except as provided in this paragraph (b)(2), to the extent the look-through rules assign income to a separate category, the income is assigned to that separate category rather than the separate category to which the income would have been assigned under § 1.904–4 (not taking into account § 1.904–4(*l*)). See paragraph (k) of this section for ordering rules for applying the look-through rules. However, passive income that is financial services income is assigned to a separate category under the rules in § 1.904–4(e)(1), (f)(1), and (*l*), regardless of whether the look-through rules otherwise would have assigned such income to the passive category.

(c) Rules for specific types of inclusions and payments—(1) Scope. Subject to the exceptions in paragraph (f) of this section, paragraphs (c)(2) through (6) (other than paragraph (c)(4)(iii) of this section) of this section provide look-through rules with respect to interest, rents, royalties, dividends, and inclusions under sections 951(a)(1) and 951A(a) that are received or accrued from a controlled foreign corporation in which the taxpayer is a United States shareholder. Paragraph (c)(4)(iii) of this section provides a look-through rule for dividends received from a noncontrolled 10-percent owned foreign corporation by a domestic corporation that is a United States shareholder in the foreign corporation.

(2) Interest—(i) In general. For purposes of this paragraph, related person interest is any interest paid or accrued by a controlled foreign corporation to any United States shareholder in that corporation (or to any other related person) to which the look-through rules of section 904(d)(3) and this section apply. Unrelated person interest is all interest other than related person interest. Related person interest is treated as passive category income to the extent it is allocable to passive category income of the controlled foreign corporation. If related person interest is received or accrued from a controlled foreign corporation by two or more persons, the amount of interest received or accrued by each person that is allocable to passive category income is determined by multiplying the amount of related person interest allocable to passive category income by a fraction. The numerator of the fraction is the amount of related person interest received or accrued by that person and the denominator is the total amount of related person interest paid or accrued by the controlled foreign corporation. * * *

* * *

(3) Rents and royalties. Any rents or royalties received or accrued from a controlled foreign corporation in which the taxpayer is a United States shareholder are treated as passive category income to the extent they are allocable to passive category income of the controlled foreign corporation under the principles of §§ 1.861–8 through 1.861–14T.

(4) Dividends—(i) Look-through rule for controlled foreign corporations. Except as provided in paragraph (d)(2) of this section, any dividend paid or accrued out of the earnings and profits of any controlled foreign corporation is treated as passive category income in proportion to the ratio of the portion of earnings and profits attributable to passive category income to the total amount of earnings and profits of the controlled foreign corporation. For purposes of this paragraph (c)(4), the term "dividend" includes any amount included in gross income under section 951(a)(1)(B) as a pro rata share of a controlled foreign corporation's increase in earnings invested in United States property.

* * *

(iii) Look-through rule for dividends from noncontrolled 10-percent owned foreign corporations—(A) In general. Except as provided in paragraph (c)(4)(iii)(B) of this section, any dividend that is distributed by a noncontrolled 10-percent owned foreign corporation and received or accrued by a domestic corporation that is a United States shareholder of such foreign corporation is treated as income in a separate category in proportion to the ratio of the portion of earnings and profits attributable to income in such category to the total amount of earnings and profits of the noncontrolled 10-percent owned foreign corporation.

(B) Inadequate substantiation. A dividend distributed by a noncontrolled 10-percent owned foreign corporation is treated as income in the separate category described in section 904(d)(4)(C)(ii) if the Commissioner determines that the look-through characterization of the dividend cannot reasonably be determined based on the available information.

(5) Inclusions under section 951(a)(1)(A). Any amount included in gross income under section 951(a)(1)(A) is treated as passive category income to the extent the amount included is attributable to income received or accrued by the controlled foreign corporation that is passive category income. All other amounts included in gross income under section 951(a)(1)(A) are treated as general category income or income in a specified separate category under the rules in § 1.904–4. For rules concerning a distributive share of partnership income, see § 1.904–4(n). For rules concerning the gross up under section 78, see § 1.904–4(*o*). For rules concerning inclusions under section 951(a)(1)(B), see paragraph (c)(4)(i) of this section.

(6) Inclusions under section 951A(a). Any amount included in gross income under section 951A(a) is treated as passive category income to the extent the amount included is attributable to income received or accrued by the controlled foreign corporation that is passive category income. All other amounts included in gross income under section 951A(a) are treated as section 951A category income or income in a specified separate category under the rules in § 1.904–4. For rules concerning a distributive share of partnership income, see § 1.904–4(n). For rules concerning the gross up under section 78, see § 1.904–4(*o*).

(7) Examples. The following examples illustrate the application of paragraph (c) of this section.

(i) Example 1—(A) Facts. CFC, a controlled foreign corporation, is a wholly-owned subsidiary of USP, a domestic corporation. In Year 1, CFC earns $100x of net income, $85x of which is general category foreign base company sales income and $15x of which is passive category foreign personal holding company income. No foreign tax is imposed on the income. CFC's income of $100x is subpart F income taxed currently to USP under section 951(a)(1)(A).

(B) Analysis. Because $15x of the subpart F inclusion is attributable to passive category income of CFC, under section 904(d)(3)(B) and paragraph (c)(5) of this section $15x of the subpart F inclusion is passive category income to USP. The remaining $85x subpart F inclusion is general category income to USP.

* * *

(d) Effect of exclusions from subpart F income—(1) De minimis amount of subpart F income. If the sum of a controlled foreign corporation's gross foreign base company income (determined under section 954(a) without regard to section 954(b)(5)) and gross insurance income (determined under section 953(a)) for the taxable year is less than the lesser of 5 percent of gross income or $1,000,000, then none of that income is treated as passive category income. In addition, if the test in the first sentence of this paragraph (d)(1) is satisfied, for purposes of paragraphs (c)(2)(ii)(D) and (E) of this section (apportionment of interest expense to passive income using the asset method), any passive assets are not treated as passive category assets but are treated as assets in the general category or a specified separate category. The determination in the first sentence of this paragraph (d)(1) is made before the application of the exception for certain income subject to a high rate of foreign tax described in paragraph (d)(2) of this section.

(2) Exception for certain income subject to high foreign tax. Except as provided in § 1.904–4(c)(7)(iii) (relating to reductions in tax upon distribution), for purposes of the dividend look-through rule of paragraph (c)(4)(i) of this section, an item of net income that would otherwise be passive category income (after application of the priority rules of § 1.904–4(*l*)) and that is received or accrued by a controlled foreign corporation is not treated as passive category income, and the earnings and profits attributable to such income is not treated as passive category earnings and profits, if the taxpayer establishes to the satisfaction of the Secretary under section 954(b)(4) that the income was subject to an effective rate of income tax imposed by a foreign country greater than 90 percent of the maximum rate of tax specified in section 11 (with reference to section 15, if applicable). Such income is treated as general category income or income in a specified separate category under the rules in § 1.904–4. The first sentence of this paragraph (d)(2) has no effect on amounts (other than dividends) paid or accrued by a controlled foreign corporation to a United States shareholder of such controlled foreign corporation to the extent those amounts are allocable to passive category income of the controlled foreign corporation.

* * *

(e) Treatment of subpart F income in excess of 70 percent of gross income—(1) Rule. If the sum of a controlled foreign corporation's gross foreign base company income (determined without regard to section 954(b)(5)) and gross insurance income for the taxable year exceeds 70 percent of the gross income, then all of the controlled foreign corporation's gross income shall be treated as foreign base company income (whichever is appropriate) and, thus, included in a United States shareholder's gross income. However, the inclusion in gross income of an amount that would not otherwise be subpart F income does not affect its character for purposes of determining whether the income is within a separate category. The determination of whether the controlled foreign corporation's gross foreign base company income and gross insurance income exceeds 70 percent of gross income is made before the exception for certain income subject to a high rate of foreign tax.

* * *

(k) Ordering rules—(1) In general. Income received or accrued by a related person to which the look-through rules apply is characterized under § 1.904–4 before amounts included from, or paid or distributed by that person and received or accrued by a related person. For purposes of determining the character of income received or accrued by a person from a related person if the payor or another related person also receives or accrues income from the recipient and the look-through rules apply to the income in all cases, the rules of paragraph (k)(2) of this section apply.

(2) Specific rules. For purposes of characterizing income under this paragraph, the following types of income are characterized in the order stated:

(i) Rents and royalties;

(ii) Interest;

(iii) Inclusions under sections 951(a)(1)(A) and 951A(a) and distributive shares of partnership income;

(iv) Dividend distributions.

If an entity is both a recipient and a payor of income described in any one of the categories described in (k)(2) (i) through (iv) of this section, the income received will be characterized before the income that is paid. In addition, the amount of interest paid or accrued, directly or indirectly, by a person to a related person shall be offset against and eliminate any interest received or accrued, directly or indirectly, by a person from that related person before application of the ordering rules of this paragraph. In a case in which a person pays or accrues interest to a related person, and also receives or accrues interest indirectly from the related person, the smallest interest payment is eliminated and the amount of all other interest payments are reduced by the amount of the smallest interest payment.

* * *

[T.D. 8214, 53 FR 27020, July 18, 1988; T.D. 8412, 57 FR 20649, May 14, 1992; T.D. 8767, 63 FR 14615, March 26, 1998; T.D. 8827, 64 FR 37677, July 13, 1999; 64 FR 58782, Nov. 1, 1999; T.D. 8916, 66 FR 278, Jan. 3, 2001; T.D. 9141, 69 FR 43307, July 20, 2004; T.D. 9260, 71 FR 24531, April 25, 2006; 71 FR 77265, Dec. 26, 2006; T.D. 9368, 72 FR 72590, Dec. 21, 2007; T.D. 9452, 74 FR 27878, June 11, 2009; T.D. 9521, 76 FR 19271, April 7, 2011; T.D. 9882, 84 FR 69091, Dec. 17, 2019; 85 FR 29323, May 15, 2020; T.D. 9908, FR 59435, Sept. 22, 2020]

§ 1.909–1 Definitions and special rules.

(a) Definitions. For purposes of section 909, this section, and §§ 1.909–2 through 1.909–5, the following definitions apply:

(1) The term section 902 corporation means any foreign corporation with respect to which one or more domestic corporations meet the ownership requirements of section 902(a) or (b).

(2) The term section 902 shareholder means any domestic corporation that meets the ownership requirements of section 902(a) or (b) with respect to a section 902 corporation.

(3) The term payor means a person that pays or accrues a foreign income tax within the meaning of § 1.901–2(f), and also includes a person that takes foreign income taxes paid or accrued by a partnership, S corporation, estate or trust into account pursuant to section 702(a)(6), section 901(b)(5) or section 1373(a).

(4) The term covered person means, with respect to a payor—

(i) Any entity in which the payor holds, directly or indirectly, at least a 10 percent ownership interest (determined by vote or value);

(ii) Any person that holds, directly or indirectly, at least a 10 percent ownership interest (determined by vote or value) in the payor; or

(iii) Any person that bears a relationship that is described in section 267(b) or 707(b) to the payor.

(5) The term foreign income tax means any income, war profits, or excess profits tax paid or accrued to any foreign country or to any possession of the United States. A foreign income tax includes any tax paid or accrued in lieu of such a tax within the meaning of section 903.

(6) The term post-1986 foreign income taxes has the meaning provided in § 1.902–1(a)(8).

(7) The term post-1986 undistributed earnings has the meaning provided in § 1.902–1(a)(9).

(8) The term disregarded entity means an entity that is disregarded as an entity separate from its owner, as provided in § 301.7701–2(c)(2)(i) of this chapter.

(9) The term hybrid partnership means a partnership that is subject to income tax in a foreign country as a corporation (or otherwise at the entity level) on the basis of residence, place of incorporation, place of management or similar criteria.

(b) Taxes paid or accrued by a partnership, S corporation or trust. Under section 909(c)(1), section 909 applies at the partner level, and similar rules apply in the case of an S corporation or trust. Accordingly, in the case of foreign income taxes paid or accrued by a partnership, S corporation or trust, taxes allocated to one or more partners, shareholders or beneficiaries (as the case may be) will be treated as split taxes to the extent such taxes would be split taxes if the partner, shareholder or beneficiary had paid or accrued the taxes directly on the date such taxes are taken into account by the partner under sections 702 and 706(a), by the shareholder under section 1373(a), or by the beneficiary under section 901(b)(5). Any such split taxes will be suspended in the hands of the partner, shareholder or beneficiary.

(c) Related income of a partnership, S corporation or trust. For purposes of determining whether related income is taken into account by a covered person, related income of a partnership, S corporation or trust is considered to be taken into account by the partner, shareholder or beneficiary to whom the related income is allocated.

(d) Application of section 909 to pre-1987 accumulated profits and pre-1987 foreign income taxes. Section 909 and §§ 1.909–1 through 1.909–5 will apply to pre-1987 accumulated profits (as defined in § 1.902–1(a)(10)(i)) and pre-1987 foreign income taxes (as defined in § 1.902–1(a)(10)(iii)) of a section 902 corporation attributable to taxable years beginning on or after January 1, 2012.

* * *

[T.D. 9710, 80 FR 7328, Feb. 10, 2015]

§ 1.909–2 Splitter arrangements.

(a) Foreign tax credit splitting event—(1) In general. There is a foreign tax credit splitting event with respect to foreign income taxes paid or accrued if and only if, in connection with an arrangement described in paragraph (b) of this section (a splitter arrangement) the related income was, is or will be taken into account for U.S. Federal income tax purposes by a person that is a covered person with respect to the payor of the tax. Foreign income taxes that are paid or accrued in connection with a splitter arrangement are split taxes to the extent provided in paragraph (b) of this section. Income (or, as appropriate, earnings and profits) that was, is or will be taken into account by a covered person in connection with a splitter arrangement is related income to the extent provided in paragraph (b) of this section.

(2) Split taxes not taken into account. Split taxes will not be taken into account for U.S. Federal income tax purposes before the taxable year in which the related income is taken into account by the payor or, in the case of split taxes paid or accrued by a section 902 corporation, by a section 902 shareholder of such section 902 corporation. Therefore, in the case of split taxes paid or accrued by a section 902 corporation, split taxes will not be taken into account for purposes of sections 902 or 960, or for purposes of determining earnings and profits under section 964(a), before the taxable year in which the related income is taken into account by the payor section 902 corporation, a section 902 shareholder of the section 902 corporation, or a member of the section 902 shareholder's consolidated group. See § 1.909–3(a) for rules relating to when split taxes and related income are taken into account.

(b) Splitter arrangements. The arrangements set forth in this paragraph (b) are splitter arrangements.

(1) Reverse hybrid splitter arrangements—(i) In general. A reverse hybrid is a splitter arrangement when a payor pays or accrues foreign income taxes with respect to income of a reverse hybrid. A reverse hybrid splitter arrangement exists even if the reverse hybrid has a loss or a deficit in earnings and profits for a particular year for U.S. Federal income tax purposes (for example, due to a timing difference).

(ii) Split taxes from a reverse hybrid splitter arrangement. The foreign income taxes paid or accrued with respect to income of the reverse hybrid are split taxes.

(iii) Related income from a reverse hybrid splitter arrangement. The related income with respect to split taxes from a reverse hybrid splitter arrangement is the earnings and profits (computed for U.S. Federal income tax purposes) of the reverse hybrid attributable to the activities of the reverse hybrid that gave rise to income included in the payor's foreign tax base with respect to which the split taxes were paid or accrued. Accordingly, related income of the reverse hybrid includes items of income or expense attributable to a disregarded entity owned by the reverse hybrid only to the extent that the income attributable to the activities of the disregarded entity is included in the payor's foreign tax base.

(iv) Reverse hybrid. The term reverse hybrid means an entity that is a corporation for U.S. Federal income tax purposes but is a fiscally transparent entity (under the principles of § 1.894–1(d)(3)) or a branch under the laws of a foreign country imposing tax on the income of the entity.

(v) Examples. The following examples illustrate the rules of paragraph (b)(1) of this section.

Example 1. (i) Facts. USP, a domestic corporation, wholly owns DE, a disregarded entity for U.S. federal income tax purposes that is organized in country A and treated as a corporation for country A tax purposes. DE wholly owns RH, a corporation for U.S. Federal income tax purposes that is organized in country A and treated as a fiscally transparent entity for country A tax purposes. Country A imposes an income tax at the rate of 30% on DE with respect to the items of income earned by RH. Prior to year 1, RH had no income for country A purposes and had no post-1986 earnings and profits for U.S. Federal income tax purposes. In year 1, RH earns 200u of income on which DE pays 60u of country A tax. Pursuant to § 1.901–2(f)(4)(ii), USP is treated as legally liable for the 60u of country A taxes paid by DE. DE has no other income. In year 2, RH earns no income and incurs no losses or expenses. At the end of year 2, RH distributes 100u to DE.

(ii) Result. (A) Split taxes and related income. Pursuant to § 1.909–2(b)(1)(iv), RH is a reverse hybrid because it is a corporation for U.S. Federal income tax purposes and a fiscally transparent entity for country A purposes. Pursuant to § 1.909–2(b)(1), RH is a covered person with respect to USP because USP wholly owns RH for U.S. Federal income tax purposes. Pursuant to § 1.909–2(b)(1)(i), there is a splitter arrangement with respect to RH because USP paid country A tax with respect to the income of RH. All 60u of taxes paid by USP in year 1 with respect to the income of RH are split taxes pursuant to § 1.909–2(b)(1)(ii). The post-1986 earnings and profits of RH are 200u as of the end of year 1. Pursuant to § 1.909–2(b)(1)(iii), the related income in year 1 is the 200u of RH's earnings and profits that are attributable to the activities that gave rise to the split taxes. No additional split taxes or related income arise in year 2.

(B) Distribution. Because DE is a disregarded entity, the 100u distribution by RH at the end of year 2 is treated as a dividend to USP. Pursuant to § 1.909–6(d)(7) and § 1.909–3(a), 100u of the 200u of related income of RH, or 50%, is taken into account by USP by reason of the 100u dividend. Accordingly, pursuant to § 1.909–6(e)(4) and § 1.909–3(a), a ratable portion of the split taxes, or 30u of taxes (50% of 60u), is no longer treated as split taxes and is taken into account by USP for U.S. Federal income tax purposes.

Example 2. (i) Facts. The facts are the same as in Example 1, except that in year 2, RH has a 100u loss for U.S. Federal income tax purposes as well as for country A tax purposes. For country A tax purposes, DE takes the 100u loss into account in year 2 and may not carry back the 100u loss to offset its country A taxable income for year 1. At the end of year 2, RH distributes 100u to DE.

(ii) Result. (A) Split taxes and related income. The split taxes and related income for year 1 are the same as in Example 1. Pursuant to § 1.909–2(b)(1)(iii), § 1.909–6(d)(1) and § 1.909–3(a), the total related income of RH is reduced to 100u (200u - 100u) in year 2 because RH incurred a 100u loss in year 2 attributable to the activities that are included in DE's country A tax base.

(B) Distribution. Because DE is a disregarded entity, the 100u distribution by RH at the end of year 2 is treated as a dividend to USP. Pursuant to § 1.909–6(d)(7) and § 1.909–3(a), 100u of the 100u of related income of RH, or 100%, is taken into account by USP by reason of the 100u dividend. Accordingly, pursuant to § 1.909–6(e)(4) and § 1.909–3(a), a ratable portion of the split taxes, or 60u of taxes (100% of 60u), is no longer treated as split taxes and is taken into account by USP for U.S. Federal income tax purposes.

(2) Loss-sharing splitter arrangements—(i) In general. A foreign group relief or other loss-sharing regime is a loss-sharing splitter arrangement to the extent that a shared loss of a U.S. combined income group could have been used to offset income of that group in the current or in a prior foreign taxable year (usable shared loss) but is used instead to offset income of another U.S. combined income group.

(ii) U.S. combined income group. The term U.S. combined income group means an individual or a corporation and all entities (including entities that are fiscally transparent for U.S. Federal income tax purposes under the principles of § 1.894–1(d)(3)) that for U.S. Federal income tax purposes combine any of their respective items of income, deduction, gain or loss with the income, deduction, gain or loss of such individual or corporation. A U.S. combined income group can arise, for example, as a result of an entity being disregarded or, in the case of a partnership or hybrid partnership and a partner, as a result of the allocation of income or any other item of the partnership to the partner. For purposes of this paragraph (b)(2)(ii), a branch is treated as an entity, all members of a U.S. affiliated group of corporations (as defined in section 1504) that file a consolidated return are treated as a single corporation, and two or more individuals that file a joint return are treated as a single individual. A U.S. combined income group may consist of a single individual or corporation and no other entities, but cannot include more than one individual or corporation. In addition, an entity may belong to more than one U.S. combined income group. For example, a hybrid partnership with two corporate partners that do not combine any of their items of income, deduction, gain or loss for U.S. Federal income tax purposes is in a separate U.S. combined income group with each of its partners.

(iii) Income and shared loss of a U.S. combined income group—(A) Income. Except as otherwise provided in this paragraph (b)(2)(iii)(A), the income of a U.S. combined income group is the aggregate amount of taxable income recognized or taken into account for foreign tax purposes by those members that have positive taxable income for foreign tax purposes. In the case of an entity that is fiscally transparent (under the principles of § 1.894–1(d)(3)) for foreign tax purposes and that is a member of more than one U.S. combined income group, the foreign taxable income of the entity is allocated between or among the groups under foreign tax law. In the case of an entity that is not fiscally transparent for foreign tax purposes and that is a member of more than one U.S. combined income group, the foreign taxable income of the entity is allocated between or among those groups based on U.S. Federal income tax principles. For example, in the case of a hybrid partnership, the foreign taxable income of the partnership is allocated between or among the groups in the manner the partnership allocates the income under section 704(b). To the extent the foreign taxable income would be income under U.S. Federal income tax principles in another year, the income is allocated between or among the groups based on how the hybrid partnership would allocate the income if the income were recognized for U.S. Federal income tax purposes in the year in which the income is recognized for foreign tax purposes. To the extent the foreign taxable income would not constitute income under U.S. Federal income tax principles in any year, the income is allocated between or among the groups in the same manner as the partnership items attributable to the activity giving rise to the foreign taxable income.

(B) Shared loss. The term shared loss means a loss of one entity for foreign tax purposes that, in connection with a foreign group relief or other loss-sharing regime, is taken into account by one or more other entities. Except as otherwise provided in this paragraph (b)(2)(iii)(B), the amount of shared loss of a U.S. combined income group is the sum of the shared losses of all members of the U.S. combined income group. In the case of an entity that is fiscally transparent (under the principles of § 1.894–1(d)(3)) for foreign tax purposes and that is a member of more than one U.S. combined income group, the shared loss of the entity is allocated between or among the groups under foreign tax law. In the case of an entity that is not fiscally transparent for foreign tax purposes and that is a member of more than one U.S. combined income group, the shared loss of the entity will be allocated between or among those groups based on U.S. Federal income tax principles. For example, in the case of a hybrid partnership, the shared loss of the partnership will be allocated between or among the groups in the manner the partnership allocates the loss under section 704(b). To the extent the shared loss would be a loss under U.S. Federal income tax principles in another year, the loss is allocated between or among the groups based on how the partnership would allocate the loss if the loss were recognized for U.S. Federal income tax purposes in the year in which the loss is recognized for foreign tax purposes. To the extent the shared loss would not constitute a loss under U.S. Federal income tax principles in any year, the loss is allocated between or among the groups in the same manner as the partnership items attributable to the activity giving rise to the shared loss.

(iv) Split taxes from a loss-sharing splitter arrangement. Split taxes from a loss-sharing splitter arrangement are foreign income taxes paid or accrued by a member of the U.S. combined income group with respect to income from the current foreign taxable year, or, in the case of a foregone carryback loss, from the prior foreign taxable year, equal to the amount of the usable shared loss of that group that offsets income of another U.S. combined income group.

(v) Related income from a loss-sharing splitter arrangement. The related income with respect to split taxes from a loss-sharing splitter arrangement is an amount of income of the individual or corporate member of the U.S. combined income group equal to the amount of income under foreign tax law of that U.S. combined income group that is offset by the usable shared loss of another U.S. combined income group.

(vi) Foreign group relief or other loss-sharing regime. A foreign group relief or other loss-sharing regime exists when an entity may surrender its loss to offset the income of one or more other entities. A foreign group relief or other loss-sharing regime does not include an allocation of loss of an entity that is a partnership or other fiscally transparent entity (under the principles of § 1.894–1(d)(3)) for foreign tax purposes or regimes in which foreign tax is imposed on combined income (such as a foreign consolidated regime), as described in § 1.901–2(f)(3).

(vii) Examples. The following examples illustrate the rules of paragraph (b)(2) of this section.

Example 1. (i) Facts. USP, a domestic corporation, wholly owns CFC1, a corporation organized in country A. CFC1 wholly owns CFC2 and CFC3, both corporations organized in country A. CFC2 wholly owns DE, an entity organized in country A. DE is a corporation for country A tax purposes and a disregarded entity for U.S. Federal income tax purposes. Country A has a loss-sharing regime under which a loss of CFC1, CFC2, CFC3 or DE may be used to offset the income of one or more of the others. Country A imposes an income tax at the rate of 30% on the taxable income of corporations organized in country A. In year 1, before any loss sharing, CFC1 has no income, CFC2 has income of 50u, CFC3 has income of 200u, and DE has a loss of 100u. Under the provisions of country A's loss-sharing regime, the group decides to use DE's 100u loss to offset 100u of CFC3's income. After the loss is shared, for country A's tax purposes, CFC2 still has 50u of income on which it pays 15u of country

A tax. CFC3 has income of 100u (200u less the 100u shared loss) on which it pays 30u of country A tax. For U.S. Federal income tax purposes, the loss sharing with CFC3 is not taken into account. Because DE is a disregarded entity, its 100u loss is taken into account by CFC2 and reduces its earnings and profits for U.S. Federal income tax purposes. Accordingly, before application of section 909, CFC2 has a loss for earnings and profits purposes of 65u (50u income less 15u taxes paid to country A less 100u loss of DE). CFC2 also has the U.S. dollar equivalent of 15u of foreign income taxes to add to its post-1986 foreign income taxes pool. CFC3 has earnings and profits of 170u (200u income less 30u of taxes) and the dollar equivalent of 30u of foreign income taxes to add to its post-1986 foreign income taxes pool.

(ii) Result. Pursuant to § 1.909–2(b)(2)(ii), CFC2 and DE constitute one U.S. combined income group, while CFC1 and CFC3 each constitute separate U.S. combined income groups. Pursuant to § 1.909–2(b)(2)(iii)(A), the income of the CFC2 U.S. combined income group is 50u (CFC2's country A taxable income of 50u). The income of the CFC3 U.S. combined income group is 200u (CFC3's country A taxable income of 200u). Pursuant to § 1.909–2(b)(2)(iii)(B), the shared loss of the CFC2 U.S. combined income group includes the 100u of shared loss incurred by DE. The usable shared loss of the CFC2 U.S. combined income group is 50u, the amount of the group's shared loss that could have otherwise offset CFC2's 50u of country A taxable income that is included in the income of the CFC2 U.S. combined income group. There is a splitter arrangement because the 50u usable shared loss of the CFC2 U.S. combined income group was used instead to offset income of CFC3, which is included in the CFC3 U.S. combined income group. Pursuant to § 1.909–2(b)(2)(iv), the split taxes are the 15u of country A income taxes paid by CFC2 on 50u of income, an amount of income of the CFC2 U.S. combined income group equal to the amount of usable shared loss of that group that was used to offset income of the CFC3 U.S. combined income group. Pursuant to § 1.909–2(b)(2)(v), the related income is the 50u of CFC3's income that equals the amount of income of the CFC3 U.S. combined income group that was offset by the usable shared loss of the CFC2 U.S. combined income group.

Example 2. (i) Facts. USP, a domestic corporation, wholly owns CFC1, a corporation organized in country B. CFC1 wholly owns CFC2 and CFC3, both corporations organized in country B. CFC2 wholly owns DE, an entity organized in country B. DE is a corporation for country B tax purposes and a disregarded entity for U.S. Federal income tax purposes. CFC2 and CFC3 each own 50% of HP1, an entity organized in country B. HP1 is a corporation for country B tax purposes and a partnership for U.S. Federal income tax purposes. All items of income and loss of HP1 are allocated for U.S. Federal income tax purposes equally between CFC2 and CFC3, and all entities use the country B currency "u" as their functional currency. Country B has a loss-sharing regime under which a loss of any of CFC1, CFC2, CFC3, DE, and HP1 may be used to offset the income of one or more of the others. Country B imposes an income tax at the rate of 30% on the taxable income of corporations organized in country B. In year 1, before any loss sharing, CFC2 has income of 100u, CFC1 and CFC3 have no income, DE has a loss of 100u, and HP1 has income of 200u. Under the provisions of country B's loss-sharing regime, the group decides to use DE's 100u loss to offset 100u of HP1's income. After the loss is shared, for country B tax purposes, CFC2 has 100u of income on which it pays 30u of country B income tax, and HP1 has 100u of income (200u less the 100u shared loss) on which it pays 30u of country B income tax. For U.S. Federal income tax purposes, the loss sharing with HP1 is not taken into account, and, because DE is a disregarded entity, its 100u loss is taken into account by CFC2 and reduces CFC2's earnings and profits for U.S. Federal income tax purposes. The 200u income of HP1 is allocated 50/50 to CFC2 and CFC3, as is the 30u of country B income tax paid by HP1. Accordingly, before application of section

909, for U.S. Federal income tax purposes, CFC2 has earnings and profits of 55u (100u income plus 100u share of HP1's income less 100u loss of DE less 30u country B income tax paid by CFC2 less 15u share of HP1's country B income tax) and the dollar equivalent of 45u of country B income tax to add to its post-1986 foreign income taxes pool. CFC3 has earnings and profits of 85u (100u share of HP1's income less 15u share of HP1's country B income taxes) and the dollar equivalent of 15u of country B income tax to add to its post-1986 foreign income taxes pool.

(ii) U.S. combined income groups. Pursuant to § 1.909–2(b)(2)(ii), because the income and loss of HP1 are combined in part with the income and loss of both CFC2 and CFC3, it belongs to both of the separate CFC2 and CFC3 U.S. combined income groups. DE is a member of the CFC2 U.S. combined income group.

(iii) Income of the U.S. combined income groups. Pursuant to § 1.909–2(b)(2)(iii)(A), the income of the CFC2 U.S. combined income group is the 200u country B taxable income of the members of the group with positive taxable incomes (CFC2's country B taxable income of 100u plus 50% of HP1's country B taxable income of 200u, or 100u). Because DE does not have positive taxable income for country B tax purposes, its 100u loss is not included in the income of the CFC2 U.S. combined income group. The income of the CFC3 U.S. combined income group is 100u (50% of HP1's country B taxable income of 200u, or 100u).

(iv) Shared loss of the U.S. combined income groups. Pursuant to § 1.909–2(b)(2)(iii)(B), the shared loss of the CFC2 U.S. combined income group is the 100u loss incurred by DE that is used to offset 100u of HP1's income. The CFC3 U.S. combined income group has no shared loss. Pursuant to § 1.909–2(b)(2)(i), the usable shared loss of the CFC2 U.S. combined income group is 100u, the full amount of the group's 100u shared loss that could have been used to offset income of the CFC2 U.S. combined income group had the loss been used to offset 100u of CFC2's country B taxable income.

(v) Income offset by shared loss. The shared loss of the CFC2 combined income group is used to offset 100u country B taxable income of HP1. Because the taxable income of HP1 is allocated 50/50 between the CFC2 and CFC3 U.S. combined income groups, the shared loss is treated as offsetting 50u of the CFC2 U.S. combined income group's income and 50u of the CFC3 U.S. combined income group's income.

(vi) Splitter arrangement. There is a splitter arrangement because 50u of the 100u usable shared loss of the CFC2 U.S. combined income group was used to offset income of the CFC3 U.S. combined income group. Pursuant to § 1.909–2(b)(2)(iv), the split taxes are the 15u of country B income tax paid by CFC2 on 50u of its income, which is equal to the amount of the CFC2 U.S. combined income group's usable shared loss that was used to offset income of another U.S. combined income group. Pursuant to § 1.909–2(b)(2)(v), the related income is the 50u of CFC3's income that was offset by the usable shared loss of the CFC2 U.S. combined income group.

(3) Hybrid instrument splitter arrangements—(i) U.S. equity hybrid instrument splitter arrangement—(A) In general. A U.S. equity hybrid instrument is a splitter arrangement if:

(1) Under the laws of a foreign jurisdiction in which the instrument owner is subject to tax, the instrument gives rise to income includible in the instrument owner's income and such inclusion results in foreign income taxes paid or accrued by the instrument owner;

(2) Under the laws of a foreign jurisdiction in which the issuer is subject to tax, the instrument gives rise to deductions that are incurred or otherwise taken into account by the issuer; and

(3) The events that give rise to income includible in the instrument owner's income for foreign tax purposes as described in paragraph (b)(3)(i)(A)(1) of this section, and to deductions for the issuer for foreign tax purposes as described in paragraph (b)(3)(i)(A)(2) of this section, do not result in an inclusion of income for the instrument owner for U.S. federal income tax purposes.

(B) Split taxes from a U.S. equity hybrid instrument splitter arrangement. Split taxes from a U.S. equity hybrid instrument splitter arrangement equal the total amount of foreign income taxes paid or accrued by the owner of the hybrid instrument less the amount of foreign income taxes that would have been paid or accrued had the owner of the U.S. equity hybrid instrument not been subject to foreign tax on income from the instrument with respect to the events described in § 1.909–2(b)(3)(i)(A).

(C) Related income from a U.S. equity hybrid instrument splitter arrangement. The related income with respect to split taxes from a U.S. equity hybrid instrument splitter arrangement is income of the issuer of the U.S. equity hybrid instrument in an amount equal to the amounts giving rise to the split taxes that are deductible by the issuer for foreign tax purposes, determined without regard to the actual amount of the issuer's income or earnings and profits for U.S. Federal income tax purposes.

(D) U.S. equity hybrid instrument. The term U.S. equity hybrid instrument means an instrument that is treated as equity for U.S. Federal income tax purposes but for foreign income tax purposes either is treated as indebtedness or otherwise entitles the issuer to a deduction with respect to such instrument.

(E) Example. (i) Facts. USP, a domestic corporation, wholly owns CFC1, which wholly owns CFC2. Both CFC1 and CFC2 are corporations organized in country A. CFC2 issues an instrument to CFC1 that is treated as indebtedness for country A tax purposes but equity for U.S. Federal income tax purposes. Under country A's income tax laws, the instrument accrues interest at the end of each month, which results in a deduction for CFC2 and an income inclusion and tax liability for CFC1 in country A. The accrual of interest does not result in an inclusion of income for CFC1 for U.S. Federal income tax purposes. Pursuant to the terms of the instrument, CFC2 makes a distribution at the end of the year equal to the amounts of interest that have accrued during the year, and such payment is treated as a dividend that is included in the income of CFC1 for U.S. Federal income tax purposes.

(ii) Result. Pursuant to § 1.909–2(b)(3)(i)(D), because the instrument is treated as equity for U.S. Federal income tax purposes but is treated as indebtedness for country A tax purposes, it is a U.S. equity hybrid instrument. Pursuant to § 1.909–2(b)(3)(i)(A)(3), because the accrual of interest under foreign law does not result in an inclusion of income of CFC1 for U.S. Federal income tax purposes, there is a splitter arrangement. The fact that the payment of the accrued amount at the end of the year pursuant to the terms of the instrument gives rise to a dividend that is included in income of CFC1 for U.S. Federal income tax purposes does not change the result because it is the accrual of interest and not the payment that gives rise to income or deductions under foreign law. The payments will be treated as a distribution of related income to the extent provided by § 1.909–3 and § 1.909–6(d).

(ii) U.S. debt hybrid instrument splitter arrangement—(A) In general. A U.S. debt hybrid instrument is a splitter arrangement if foreign income taxes are paid or accrued by the issuer of a U.S. debt hybrid instrument with respect to income in an amount equal to the interest (including original issue discount) paid or accrued on the instrument that is deductible for U.S. Federal income tax purposes but that does not give rise to a deduction under the laws of a foreign jurisdiction in which the issuer is subject to tax.

(B) Split taxes from a U.S. debt hybrid instrument splitter arrangement. Split taxes from a U.S. debt hybrid instrument splitter arrangement are the foreign income taxes paid or accrued by the issuer on the income that would have been offset by the interest paid or accrued on the U.S. debt hybrid instrument had such interest been deductible for foreign tax purposes.

(C) Related income from a U.S. debt hybrid instrument splitter arrangement. The related income from a U.S. debt hybrid instrument splitter arrangement is the gross amount of the interest income recognized for U.S. Federal income tax purposes by the owner of the U.S. debt hybrid instrument, determined without regard to the actual amount of the owner's income or earnings and profits for U.S. Federal income tax purposes.

(D) U.S. debt hybrid instrument. The term U.S. debt hybrid instrument means an instrument that is treated as equity for foreign tax purposes but as indebtedness for U.S. Federal income tax purposes.

(4) Partnership inter-branch payment splitter arrangements—(i) In general. An allocation of foreign income tax paid or accrued by a partnership with respect to an inter-branch payment as described in § 1.704–1(b)(4)(viii)(d)(3) (revised as of April 1, 2011) (the inter-branch payment tax) is a splitter arrangement to the extent the inter-branch payment tax is not allocated to the partners in the same proportion as the distributive shares of income in the CFTE category to which the inter-branch payment tax is or would be assigned under § 1.704–1(b)(4)(viii)(d) without regard to § 1.704–1(b)(4)(viii)(d)(3).

(ii) Split taxes from a partnership inter-branch payment splitter arrangement. The split taxes from a partnership inter-branch splitter arrangement equal the excess of the amount of the inter-branch payment tax allocated to a partner under the partnership agreement over the amount of the inter-branch payment tax that would have been allocated to the partner if the inter-branch payment tax had been allocated to the partners in the same proportion as the distributive shares of income in the CFTE category referred to in paragraph (b)(4)(i) of this section.

(iii) Related income from a partnership inter-branch payment splitter arrangement. The related income from a partnership inter-branch payment splitter arrangement equals the amount of income allocated to a partner that exceeds the amount of income that would have been allocated to the partner if income in the CFTE category referred to in paragraph (b)(4)(i) of this section in the amount of the inter-branch payment had been allocated to the partners in the same proportion as the inter-branch payment tax was allocated under the partnership agreement.

* * *

[T.D. 9710, 80 FR 7328, Feb. 10, 2015]

§ 1.909–3 Rules regarding related income and split taxes.

(a) Interim rules for identifying related income and split taxes. The principles of paragraphs (d) through (f) of § 1.909–6 apply to related income and split taxes in taxable years beginning on or after January 1, 2011, except that the alternative method for identifying distributions of related income described in § 1.909–6(d)(4) applies only to identify the amount of pre-2011 split taxes of a section 902 corporation that are suspended as of the first day of the section 902 corporation's first taxable year beginning on or after January 1, 2011.

(b) Split taxes on deductible disregarded payments. Split taxes include taxes paid or accrued in taxable years beginning on or after January 1, 2011, with respect to the amount of a disregarded payment that is deductible by the payor of the disregarded payment under the laws of a foreign jurisdiction in which the payor of the disregarded payment is subject to tax on related income from a splitter arrangement. The amount of the deductible disregarded payment to which this paragraph (b) applies is limited to the amount of related income from such splitter arrangement.

* * *

[T.D. 9710, 80 FR 7332, Feb. 10, 2015]

§ 1.909–4 Coordination rules.

(a) Interim rules. The principles of paragraph (g) of § 1.909–6 apply to taxable years beginning on or after January 1, 2011.

* * *

[T.D. 9710, 80 FR 7332, Feb. 10, 2015]

§ 1.909–6 Pre-2011 foreign tax credit splitting events.

(a) Foreign tax credit splitting event—(1) In general. This section provides rules for determining whether foreign income taxes paid or accrued by a section 902 corporation (as defined in section 909(d)(5)) in taxable years beginning on or before December 31, 2010 (pre-2011 taxable years and pre-2011 taxes) are suspended under section 909 in taxable years beginning after December 31, 2010, (post-2010 taxable years) of a section 902 corporation. Paragraph (b) of this section identifies an exclusive list of arrangements that will be treated as giving rise to foreign tax credit splitting events in pre-2011 taxable years (pre-2011 splitter arrangements). Paragraphs (c), (d), and (e) of this section provide rules for determining the related income and pre-2011 split taxes paid or accrued with respect to pre-2011 splitter arrangements. Paragraph (f) of this section provides rules concerning the application of section 909 to partnerships and trusts. Paragraph (g) of this section provides rules concerning the interaction between section 909 and other Internal Revenue Code (Code) provisions.

(2) Taxes not subject to suspension under section 909. Pre-2011 taxes that will not be suspended under section 909 or paragraph (a) of this section are:

(i) Any pre-2011 taxes that were not paid or accrued in connection with a pre-2011 splitter arrangement identified in paragraph (b) of this section;

(ii) Any pre-2011 taxes that were paid or accrued in connection with a pre-2011 splitter arrangement identified in paragraph (b) of this section (pre-2011 split taxes) but that were deemed paid under section 902(a) or 960 on or before the last day of the section 902 corporation's last pre-2011 taxable year;

(iii) Any pre-2011 split taxes if either the payor section 902 corporation took the related income into account in a pre-2011 taxable year or a section 902 shareholder (as defined in § 1.909–1(a)(2)) of the relevant section 902 corporation took the related income into account on or before the last day of the section 902 corporation's last pre-2011 taxable year; and

(iv) Any pre-2011 split taxes paid or accrued by a section 902 corporation in taxable years of such section 902 corporation beginning before January 1, 1997.

(3) Taxes subject to suspension under section 909. To the extent that the section 902 corporation paid or accrued pre-2011 split taxes that are not described in paragraph (a)(2) of this section, section 909 and the regulations under that section will apply to such pre-2011 split taxes for purposes of applying sections 902 and 960 in post-2010 taxable years of the section 902 corporation. Accordingly, these taxes will be removed from the section 902 corporation's pools of post-1986 foreign income taxes and suspended under section 909 as of the first day of the section 902 corporation's first post-2010 taxable year. There is no increase to a section 902 corporation's earnings and profits for the amount of any pre-2011 taxes to which section 909 applies that were previously deducted in computing earnings and profits in a pre-2011 taxable year.

(b) Pre-2011 splitter arrangements. The arrangements set forth in this paragraph (b) are pre-2011 splitter arrangements.

(1) Reverse hybrid structure splitter arrangements. A reverse hybrid structure exists when a section 902 corporation owns an interest in a reverse hybrid. A reverse hybrid is an entity that is a corporation for U.S. Federal income tax purposes but is a pass-through entity or a branch under the laws of a foreign country imposing tax on the income of the entity. As a result, the owner of the reverse hybrid is subject to tax on the income of the entity under foreign law. A pre-2011 splitter arrangement involving a reverse hybrid structure exists when pre-2011 taxes are paid or accrued by a section 902 corporation with respect to income of a reverse hybrid that is a covered person with respect to the section 902 corporation. A pre-2011 splitter arrangement involving a reverse hybrid structure may exist even if the reverse hybrid has a deficit in earnings and profits for a particular year (for example, due to a timing difference). Such taxes paid or accrued by the section 902 corporation are pre-2011 split taxes. The related income is the earnings and profits (computed for U.S. Federal income tax purposes) of the reverse hybrid attributable to the activities of the reverse hybrid that gave rise to income included in the foreign tax base with respect to which the pre-2011 split taxes were paid or accrued. Accordingly, related income of the reverse hybrid would not include any item of income or expense attributable to a disregarded entity (as defined in § 301.7701–2(c)(2)(i) of this chapter) owned by the reverse hybrid if income attributable to the activities of the disregarded entity is not included in the foreign tax base.

(2) Foreign consolidated group splitter arrangements. A foreign consolidated group exists when a foreign country imposes tax on the combined income of two or more entities. Tax is considered imposed on the combined income of two or more entities even if the combined income is computed under foreign law by attributing to one such entity the income of one or more entities. A foreign consolidated group is a pre-2011 splitter arrangement to the extent that the taxpayer did not allocate the foreign consolidated tax liability among the members of the foreign consolidated group based on each member's share of the consolidated taxable income included in the foreign tax base under the principles of § 1.901–2(f)(3) (revised as of April 1, 2011). A pre-2011 splitter arrangement involving a foreign consolidated group may exist even if one or more members has a deficit in earnings and profits for a particular year (for example, due to a timing difference). Pre-2011 taxes paid or accrued with respect to the income of a foreign consolidated group are pre-2011 split taxes to the extent that taxes paid or accrued by one member of the foreign consolidated group are imposed on a covered person's share of the consolidated taxable income included in the foreign tax base. The related income is the earnings and profits (computed for U.S. Federal income tax purposes) of such other member attributable to the activities of that other member that gave rise to income included in the foreign tax base with respect to which the pre-2011 split taxes were paid or accrued. No inference should be drawn from the treatment of foreign consolidated groups under section 909 as to the determination of the person who paid the foreign income tax for U.S. Federal income tax purposes.

(3) Group relief or other loss-sharing regime splitter arrangements—(i) In general. A foreign group relief or other loss-sharing regime exists when one entity with a loss permits the loss to be used to offset the income of one or more entities (shared loss). A pre-2011 splitter arrangement involving a shared loss exists when the following three conditions are met:

(A) There is an instrument that is treated as indebtedness under the laws of the jurisdiction in which the issuer is subject to tax and that is disregarded for U.S. Federal income tax purposes (disregarded debt instrument). Examples of a disregarded debt instrument include a debt obligation between two disregarded entities that are owned by the same section 902 corporation, two disregarded entities that are owned by a partnership with one or more partners that are section 902 corporations, a section 902 corporation and a disregarded entity that is owned by that section 902 corporation, or a partnership in which the section 902 corporation is a partner and a disregarded entity that is owned by such partnership.

(B) The owner of the disregarded debt instrument pays a foreign income tax attributable to a payment or accrual on the instrument.

(C) The payment or accrual on the disregarded debt instrument gives rise to a deduction for foreign tax purposes and the issuer of the instrument incurs a shared loss that is taken into account under foreign law by one or more entities that are covered persons with respect to the owner of the instrument.

(ii) Split taxes and related income. In situations described in paragraph (b)(3)(i) of this section, pre-2011 taxes paid or accrued by the owner of the disregarded debt instrument with respect to amounts paid or accrued on the instrument (up to the amount of the shared loss) are pre-2011 split taxes. The related income of a covered person is an amount equal to the shared loss, determined without regard to the actual amount of the covered person's earnings and profits.

(4) Hybrid instrument splitter arrangements—(i) In general. A hybrid instrument for purposes of this paragraph (b)(4) is an instrument that either is treated as equity for U.S. Federal income tax purposes but is treated as indebtedness for foreign tax purposes (U.S. equity hybrid instrument), or is treated as indebtedness for U.S. Federal income tax purposes but is treated as equity for foreign tax purposes (U.S. debt hybrid instrument).

(ii) U.S. equity hybrid instrument splitter arrangement. If the issuer of a U.S. equity hybrid instrument is a covered person with respect to a section 902 corporation that is the owner of the U.S. equity hybrid instrument, there is a pre-2011 splitter arrangement with respect to the portion of the pre-2011 taxes paid or accrued by the owner section 902 corporation with respect to the amounts on the instrument that are deductible by the issuer as interest under the laws of a foreign jurisdiction in which the issuer is subject to tax but that do not give rise to income for U.S. Federal income tax purposes. Pre-2011 split taxes paid or accrued by the section 902 corporation equal the total amount of pre-2011 taxes paid or accrued by the section 902 corporation less the amount of pre-2011 taxes that would have been paid or accrued had the section 902 corporation not been subject to tax on income from the U.S. equity hybrid instrument. The related income of the issuer of the U.S. equity hybrid instrument is an amount equal to the amounts that are deductible by the issuer for foreign tax purposes, determined without regard to the actual amount of the issuer's earnings and profits.

(iii) U.S. debt hybrid instrument splitter arrangement. If the owner of a U.S. debt hybrid instrument is a covered person with respect to a section 902 corporation that is the issuer of the U.S. debt hybrid instrument, there is a pre-2011 splitter arrangement with respect to the portion of the pre-2011 taxes paid or accrued by the section 902 corporation on income in an amount equal to the interest (including original issue discount) paid or accrued on the instrument that is deductible for U.S. Federal income tax purposes but that does not give rise to a deduction under the laws of a foreign jurisdiction in which the issuer is subject to tax. Pre-2011 split taxes are the pre-2011 taxes paid or accrued by the section 902 corporation on the income that would have been offset by the interest paid or accrued on the U.S. debt hybrid instrument had such interest been deductible for foreign tax purposes. The related income with respect to a U.S. debt hybrid instrument is the gross amount of the interest income recognized for U.S. Federal income tax purposes by the owner of the U.S. debt hybrid instrument, determined without regard to the actual amount of the owner's earnings and profits.

(c) General rules for applying section 909 to pre-2011 split taxes and related income—(1) Annual determination. The determination of related income, other income, pre-2011 split taxes, and other taxes, and the portion of these amounts that were distributed, deemed paid or otherwise transferred or eliminated must be made on an annual basis beginning with the first taxable year of the section 902 corporation beginning after December 31, 1996 (post-1996 taxable year) in which the section 902 corporation paid or accrued a pre-2011 tax with respect to a pre-2011 splitter arrangement and ending with the section 902 corporation's last pre-2011 taxable year. Annual amounts of related income and pre-2011 split taxes are aggregated for each separate pre-2011 splitter arrangement.

(2) Separate categories. The determination of annual and aggregate amounts of related income and pre-2011 split taxes with respect to each pre-2011 splitter arrangement must be made for each separate category as defined in § 1.904–4(m) of the section 902 corporation, each covered person, and any other person that succeeds to the related income and pre-2011 split taxes. In the case of a pre-2011 splitter arrangement involving a shared loss (as described in paragraph (b)(3) of this section), the amount of the related income in each separate category of the covered person is equal to the amount of income in that separate category that was offset by the shared loss for foreign tax purposes. In the case of a pre-2011 splitter arrangement involving a U.S. equity hybrid instrument (as described in paragraph (b)(4)(ii) of this section), the related income is assigned to the issuer's separate categories in the same proportions as the pre-2011 split taxes. Earnings and profits, including related income, are assigned to separate categories under the rules of §§ 1.904–4, 1.904–5, and 1.904–7. Foreign income taxes, including pre-2011 split taxes, are assigned to separate categories under the rules of § 1.904–6. A section 902 shareholder must consistently apply methodologies for determining pre-2011 split taxes and related income with respect to all pre-2011 splitter arrangements.

(d) Special rules regarding related income—(1) Annual adjustments. In the case of each pre-2011 splitter arrangement involving a reverse hybrid or a foreign consolidated group (as described in paragraphs (b)(1) and (2) of this section, respectively), a covered person's aggregate amount of related income must be adjusted each year by the net amount of income and expense attributable to the activities of the covered person that give rise to income included in the foreign tax base, even if the net amount is negative and regardless of whether the section 902 corporation paid or accrued any pre-2011 split taxes in such year.

(2) Effect of separate limitation losses and deficits. Related income is determined without regard to the application of § 1.960–1(i)(4) (relating to the effect of separate limitation losses on earnings and profits in another separate category) or section 952(c)(1) (relating to certain earnings and profits deficits).

(3) Pro rata method for distributions out of earnings and profits that include both related income and other income. If the earnings and profits of a covered person include amounts attributable to both related income and other income, including earnings and profits attributable to taxable years beginning before January 1, 1997, then distributions, deemed distributions, and inclusions out of earnings and profits (for example, under sections 301, 304, 367(b), 951(a), 964(e), 1248, or 1293) of the covered person are considered made out of related income and other income on a pro rata basis. Any reduction of a covered person's earnings and profits that results from a payment on stock that is not treated as a dividend for U.S. Federal income tax purposes (for example, pursuant to section 312(n)(7)) will also reduce related income and other income on a pro rata basis.

(4) Alternative method for distributions out of earnings and profits that include both related income and other income. Solely for purposes of identifying the amount of pre-2011 split taxes of a section 902 corporation that are suspended as of the first day of the section 902 corporation's first post-2010 taxable year, in lieu of the rule set forth in paragraph (d)(3) of this section, a section 902 shareholder may choose to treat all distributions, deemed distributions, and inclusions out of earnings and profits of a covered person as attributable first to related income. A section 902 shareholder may choose to use this alternative method on a timely filed original income tax return for the first post-2010 taxable year in which the shareholder computes an amount of foreign income taxes deemed paid with respect to a section 902 corporation that paid or accrued pre-2011 split taxes. Such choice by a section 902 shareholder is evidenced by employing the method on its income tax return; the section 902 shareholder need not file a separate statement. A section 902 shareholder that chooses this alternative method must consistently apply it with respect to all pre-2011 splitter arrangements.

(5) Distributions, deemed distributions, and inclusions of related income. Distributions, deemed distributions, and inclusions of related income (including indirectly through a partnership) to persons other than the payor section 902 corporation retain their character as related income with respect to the associated pre-2011 split taxes.

(6) Carryover of related income. Related income carries over to other corporations in the same manner as earnings and profits carry over under section 381, § 1.367(b)–7, or similar rules, and retains its character as related income with respect to the associated pre-2011 split taxes.

(7) Related income taken into account by a section 902 shareholder. Related income will be considered taken into account by a section 902 shareholder to the extent that the related income is recognized as gross income by the section 902 shareholder, or by an affiliated corporation described in paragraph (d)(9) of this section, upon a distribution, deemed distribution, or inclusion (such as under section 951(a)) out of the earnings and profits of the covered person attributable to such related income.

(8) Related income taken into account by a payor section 902 corporation. Related income will be considered taken into account by a payor section 902 corporation to the extent that:

(i) The related income is reflected in the earnings and profits of such section 902 corporation for U.S. Federal income tax purposes by reason of a distribution, deemed distribution, or inclusion out of the earnings and profits of the covered person attributable to such related income; or

(ii) The related income is reflected as a positive adjustment to the earnings and profits of such section 902 corporation for U.S. Federal income tax purposes by reason of the section 902 corporation and the covered person combining in a transaction described in section 381(a)(1) or (a)(2).

(9) Related income taken into account by an affiliated group of corporations that includes a section 902 shareholder. A section 902 shareholder will be considered to have taken related income into account if one or more members of an affiliated group of corporations (as defined in section 1504) that files a consolidated Federal income tax return that includes the section 902 shareholder takes the related income into account.

(10) Distributions of previously-taxed earnings and profits. Distributions and deemed distributions described in paragraph (d) of this section (including in the case of a section 902 shareholder that has chosen the alternative method described in paragraph (d)(4) of this section) do not include distributions of amounts described in section 959(c)(1) or (c)(2), which are distributed before amounts described in section 959(c)(3).

(e) Special rules regarding pre-2011 split taxes—(1) Taxes deemed paid pro-rata out of pre-2011 split taxes and other taxes. If the pre-2011 taxes of a section 902 corporation include both pre-2011 split taxes and other taxes, then foreign income taxes deemed paid under section 902 or 960 or otherwise removed from post-1986 foreign income taxes in pre-2011 taxable years will be treated as attributable to pre-2011 split taxes and other taxes on a pro-rata basis.

(2) Pre-2011 split taxes deemed paid in pre-2011 taxable years. Pre-2011 split taxes deemed paid in pre-2011 taxable years in connection with a dividend paid to a shareholder described in section 902(b) retain their character as pre-2011 split taxes. The section 902(b) shareholder will be treated as the payor section 902 corporation with respect to those pre-2011 split taxes.

(3) Carryover of pre-2011 split taxes. Pre-2011 split taxes that carry over to another foreign corporation, including under section 381, § 1.367(b)–7 or similar rules, retain their character as pre-2011 split taxes. The transferee foreign corporation will be treated as the payor section 902 corporation with respect to those pre-2011 split taxes.

(4) Determining when pre-2011 split taxes are no longer treated as pre-2011 split taxes. For each pre-2011 splitter arrangement, as related income is taken into account by the payor section 902 corporation or a section 902 shareholder as provided in paragraph (d) of this section, a ratable portion of the associated pre-2011 split taxes will no longer be treated as pre-2011 split taxes. In the case of a pre-2011 splitter arrangement involving a reverse hybrid or a foreign consolidated group (as described in paragraphs (b)(1) and (2) of this section, respectively), if aggregate related income is reduced to zero (other than as a result of a distribution, deemed distribution, or inclusion described in paragraph (d) of this section) or less than zero, pre-2011 split taxes will retain their character as pre-2011 split taxes until the amount of aggregate related income is positive and the related income is taken into account by the payor section 902 corporation or a section 902 shareholder as provided in paragraph (d) of this section.

(f) Rules relating to partnerships and trusts—(1) Taxes paid or accrued by partnerships. In the case of foreign income taxes paid or accrued by a partnership, the taxes will be treated as pre-2011 split taxes to the extent such taxes are allocated to one or more section 902 corporations and would be pre-2011 split taxes if the partner section 902 corporation had paid or accrued the taxes directly on the date such taxes are included by the section 902 corporation under sections 702 and 706(a). Further, any foreign income taxes subject to section 909 will be suspended in the hands of the partner section 902 corporation.

(2) Section 704(b) allocations. Partnership allocations that satisfy the requirements of section 704(b) and the regulations thereunder will not constitute pre-2011 splitter arrangements except to the extent the arrangement is otherwise described in paragraph (b) of this section (for example, a payment or accrual on a disregarded debt instrument that gives rise to a shared loss).

(3) Trusts. Rules similar to the rules of paragraph (f)(1) of this section will apply in the case of any trust with one or more beneficiaries that is a section 902 corporation.

(g) Interaction between section 909 and other Code provisions—(1) Section 904(c). Section 909 does not apply to excess foreign income taxes that were paid or accrued in pre-2011 taxable years and carried forward and deemed paid or accrued under section 904(c) in a post-2010 taxable year.

(2) Section 905(a). For purposes of determining in post-2010 taxable years the allowable deduction for foreign income taxes paid or accrued under section 164(a), the carryover of excess foreign income taxes under section 904(c), and the extended period for claiming a credit or refund under section 6511(d)(3)(A), foreign income taxes to which section 909 applies are first taken into account and treated as paid or accrued in the year in which the related income is taken into account, and not in the earlier year to which the tax relates (determined without regard to section 909).

(3) Section 905(c). If a redetermination of foreign income taxes claimed as a direct credit under section 901 occurs in a post-2010 taxable year and the foreign tax redetermination relates to a pre-2011 taxable year, to the extent such foreign tax redetermination increased the amount of foreign income taxes paid or accrued with respect to the pre-2011 taxable year (for example, due to an additional assessment of foreign tax or a payment of a previously accrued tax not paid within two years), section 909 will not apply to such taxes. If a redetermination of foreign tax paid or accrued by a section 902 corporation occurs in a post-2010 taxable year and increases the amount of foreign income taxes paid or accrued by the section 902 corporation with respect to a pre-2011 taxable year (for example, due to an additional assessment of foreign tax or a payment of a previously accrued tax not paid within two years), such taxes will be treated as pre-2011 taxes. Section 909 will apply to such taxes if they are pre-2011 split taxes and the taxes will be suspended in the post-2010 taxable year in which they would otherwise be taken into account as a prospective adjustment to the section 902 corporation's pools of post-1986 foreign income taxes.

(4) Other foreign tax credit provisions. Section 909 does not affect the applicability of other restrictions or limitations on the foreign tax credit under existing law, including, for example, the substantiation requirements of section 905(b).

* * *

[T.D. 9710, 80 FR 7332, Feb. 10, 2015]

§ 1.911–2 Qualified individuals.

(a) In general. An individual is a qualified individual if:

(1) The individual's tax home is in a foreign country or countries throughout—

(i) The period of bona fide residence described in paragraph (a)(2)(i) of this section, or

(ii) The 330 full days of presence described in paragraph (a)(2)(ii) of this section, and

(2) The individual is either—

(i) A citizen of the United States who establishes to the satisfaction of the Commissioner or his delegate that the individual has been a bona fide resident of a foreign country or countries for an uninterrupted period which includes an entire taxable year, or

(ii) A citizen or resident of the United States who has been physically present in a foreign country or countries for at least 330 full days during any period of twelve consecutive months.

(b) Tax home. For purposes of paragraph (a)(i) of this section, the term "tax home" has the same meaning which it has for purposes of section 162(a)(2) (relating to travel expenses away from home). Thus, under section 911, an individual's tax home is considered to be located at his regular or principal (if more than one regular) place of business or, if the individual has no regular or principal place of business because of the nature of the business, then at his regular place of abode in a real and substantial sense. An individual shall not, however, be considered to have a tax home in a foreign country for any period for which the individual's abode is in the United States. Temporary presence of the individual in the United States does not necessarily mean that the individual's abode is in the United States during that time. Maintenance of a dwelling in the United States by an individual, whether or not that dwelling is used by the individual's spouse and dependents, does not necessarily mean that the individual's abode is in the United States.

(c) Determination of bona fide residence. For purposes of paragraph (a)(2)(i) of this section, whether an individual is a bona fide resident of a foreign country shall be determined by applying, to the extent practical, the principles of section 871 and the regulations thereunder, relating to the determination of the residence of aliens. Bona fide residence in a foreign country or countries for an uninterrupted period may be established, even if temporary visits are made during the period to the United States or elsewhere on vacation or business. An individual with earned income from sources within a foreign country is not a bona fide resident of that country if:

(1) The individual claims to be a nonresident of that foreign country in a statement submitted to the authorities of that country, and

(2) The earned income of the individual is not subject, by reason of nonresidency in the foreign country, to the income tax of that country. If an individual has submitted a statement of nonresidence to the authorities of a foreign country the accuracy of which has not been resolved as of any date when a determination of the individual's bona fide residence is being made, then the individual will not be considered a bona fide resident of the foreign country as of that date.

(d) Determination of physical presence. For purposes of paragraph (a)(2)(ii) of this section, the following rules apply.

(1) Twelve-month test. A period of twelve consecutive months may begin with any day but must end on the day before the corresponding day in the twelfth succeeding month. The twelve-month period may begin before or after arrival in a foreign country and may end before or after departure.

(2) 330-day test. The 330 full days need not be consecutive but may be interrupted by periods during which the individual is not present in a foreign country. In computing the minimum 330 full days of presence in a foreign country or countries, all separate periods of such presence during the period of twelve consecutive months are aggregated. A full day is a continuous period of twenty-four hours beginning with midnight and ending with the following midnight. An individual who has been present in a foreign country and then travels over areas not within any foreign country for less than twenty-four hours shall not be deemed outside a foreign country during the period of travel. If an individual who is in transit between two points outside the United States is physically present in the United States for less than twenty-four hours, such individual shall not be treated as present in the United States during such transit but shall be treated as travelling over areas not within any foreign country. For purposes of this paragraph (d)(2), the term "transit between two points outside the United States" has the same meaning that it has when used in section 7701(b)(6)(C).

* * *

[T.D. 8006, 50 FR 2965, Jan. 23, 1985]

§ 1.911–3 Determination of amount of foreign earned income to be excluded.

(a) Definition of foreign earned income. For purposes of section 911 and the regulations thereunder, the term "foreign earned income" means earned income (as defined in paragraph (b) of this section) from sources within a foreign country (as defined in § 1.911–2(h)) that is earned during a period for which the individual qualifies under § 1.911–2(a) to make an election. Earned income is from sources within a foreign country if it is attributable to services performed by an individual in a foreign country or countries. The place of receipt of earned income is immaterial in determining whether earned income is attributable to services performed in a foreign country or countries.

(b) Definition of earned income—(1) In general. The term "earned income" means wages, salaries, professional fees, and other amounts received as compensation for personal services actually rendered including the fair market value of all remuneration paid in any medium other than cash. Earned income does not include any portion of an amount paid by a corporation which represents a distribution of earnings and profits rather than a reasonable allowance as compensation for personal services actually rendered to the corporation.

(2) Earned income from business in which capital is material. In the case of an individual engaged in a trade or business (other than in corporate form) in which both personal services and capital are material income producing factors, a reasonable allowance as compensation for the personal services actually rendered by the individual shall be considered earned income, but the total amount which shall be treated as the earned income of the individual from such trade or business shall in no case exceed thirty percent of the individual's share of the net profits of such trade or business.

(3) Professional fees. Earned income includes all fees received by an individual engaged in a professional occupation (such as doctor or lawyer) in the performance of professional activities. Professional fees constitute earned income even though the individual employs assistants to perform part or all of the services, provided the patients or clients are those of the individual and look to the individual as the person responsible for the services rendered.

(c) Amounts not included in foreign earned income. Foreign earned income does not include an amount:

(1) Excluded from gross income under section 119;

(2) Received as a pension or annuity (including social security benefits);

(3) Paid to an employee by an employer which is the U.S. government or any U.S. government agency or instrumentality;

(4) Included in the individual's gross income by reason of section 402(b) (relating to the taxability of a beneficiary of a nonexempt trust) or section 403(c) (relating to the taxability of a beneficiary under a nonqualified annuity or under annuities purchased by exempt organizations);

(5) Included in gross income by reason of § 1.911–6(b)(4)(ii); or

(6) Received after the close of the first taxable year following the taxable year in which the services giving rise to the amounts were performed. For treatment of amounts received after December 31, 1962, which are attributable to services performed on or before December 31, 1962, and with respect to which there existed on March 12, 1962, a right (whether forfeitable or nonforfeitable) to receive such amounts, see § 1.72–8.

(d) Determination of the amount of foreign earned income that may be excluded under section 911(a)(1)—(1) In general. Foreign earned income described in this section may be excluded under section 911(a)(1) and this paragraph only to the extent of the limitation specified in paragraph (d)(2) of this section. Income is considered to be earned in the taxable year in which the services giving rise to the income are performed. The determination of the amount of excluded earned income in this manner does not affect the time for reporting any amounts included in gross income.

(2) Limitation—(i) In general. The term "section 911(a)(1) limitation" means the amount of foreign earned income for a taxable year which may be excluded under section 911(a)(1). The section 911(a)(1) limitation shall be equal to the lesser of the qualified individual's foreign earned income for the taxable year in excess of amounts that the individual elected to exclude from gross income under section 911(a)(2) or the product of the annual rate for the taxable year (as specified in paragraph (d)(2)(ii) of this section) multiplied by the following fraction:

$$\frac{\text{The number of qualifying days in the taxable year}}{\text{The number of days in the taxable year}}$$

(ii) Annual rate for the taxable year. The annual rate for the taxable year is the rate set forth in section 911(b)(2)(A).

(3) Number of qualifying days. For purposes of section 911 and the regulations thereunder, the number of qualifying days is the number of days in the taxable year within the period during which the individual met the tax home requirement and either the bona fide residence requirement or the physical presence requirement of § 1.911–2(a). Although the period of bona fide residence must include an entire taxable year, the entire uninterrupted period of residence may include fractional parts of a taxable year. For instance, if an individual who was a calendar year taxpayer established a tax home and a residence in a foreign country as of November 1, 1982, and maintained the tax home and the residence through March 31, 1984, then the uninterrupted period of bona fide residence includes fractional parts of the years 1982 and 1984, and all of 1983. The number of qualifying days in 1982 is sixty-one. The number of qualifying days in 1983 is 365. The number of qualifying days in 1984 is ninety-one. The period during which the physical presence requirement of § 1.911–2(a)(2)(ii) is met is any twelve consecutive month period during which the individual is physically present in one or more foreign countries for 330 days and the individual's tax home is in a foreign country during each day of such physical presence. Such period may include days when the individual is not physically present in a foreign country, and days when the individual does not maintain a tax home in a foreign country. Such period may include fractional parts of a taxable year. Thus, if an individual's period of physical presence is the twelve-month period beginning June 1, 1982, and ending May 31, 1983, the number of qualifying days in 1982 is 214 and the number of qualifying days in 1983 is 151.

(e) Attribution rules—(1) In general. Foreign earned income is considered to be earned in the taxable year in which the individual performed the services giving rise to the income. If income is earned in one taxable year and received in another taxable year, then, for purposes of determining the amount of foreign earned income that the individual may exclude under section 911(a), the individual must attribute the income to the taxable year in which the services giving rise to the income were performed. Thus, any reimbursement would be attributable to the taxable year in which the services giving rise to the obligation to pay the reimbursement were performed, not the taxable year in which the reimbursement was received. For example, tax equalization payments are normally received in the year after the year in which the services giving rise to the obligation to pay the tax equalization payment were performed. Therefore, such payments will almost always have to be attributed to the prior year. Foreign earned income attributable to services performed in a preceding taxable year shall be excludable from gross income in the year of receipt only to the extent such amount could have been excluded under paragraph (d)(1) in the preceding taxable year, had such amount been received in the preceding taxable year. The taxable year to which income is attributable will be determined on the basis of all the facts and circumstances.

* * *

[T.D. 8006, 50 FR 2966, Jan. 23, 1985]

§ 1.911–4 Determination of housing cost amount eligible for exclusion or deduction.

(a) Definition of housing cost amount. The term "housing cost amount" means an amount equal to the reasonable expenses paid or incurred (as defined in section 7701(a)(25)) during the taxable year by or on behalf of the individual attributable to housing in a foreign country for the individual and any spouse or dependents who reside with the individual (or live in a second foreign household described in paragraph (b)(5) of this section) less the base housing amount as defined in paragraph (c) of this section. The housing cost amount must be reduced by the amount of any military or section 912 allowance or similar allowance excludable from gross income that is intended to compensate the individual or the individual's spouse in whole or in part for the expenses of housing during the same period for which the individual claims a housing cost amount exclusion or deduction.

(b) Housing expenses—(1) Included expenses. For purposes of paragraph (a) of this section, housing expenses include rent, the fair rental value of housing provided in kind by the employer, utilities (other than telephone charges), real and personal property insurance, occupancy taxes not described in paragraph (b)(2)(v) of this section, nonrefundable fees paid for securing a leasehold, rental of furniture and accessories, household repairs, and residential parking.

(2) Excluded expenses. Housing expenses do not include:

(i) The cost of house purchase, improvements, and other costs that are capital expenditures;

(ii) The cost of purchased furniture or accessories or domestic labor (maids, gardeners, etc.);

(iii) Amortized payments of principal with respect to an evidence of indebtedness secured by a mortgage on the taxpayer's housing;

(iv) Depreciation of housing owned by the taxpayer, or amortization or depreciation of capital improvements made to housing leased by the taxpayer;

(v) Interest and taxes deductible under section 163 or 164 or other amounts deductible under section 216(a) (relating to deduction of interest and taxes by cooperative housing corporation tenant);

(vi) The expenses of more than one foreign household except as provided in paragraph (b)(5) of this section;

(vii) Expenses excluded from gross income under section 119;

(viii) Expenses claimed as deductible moving expenses under section 217; or

(ix) The cost of a pay television subscription.

(3) Limitation. Housing expenses are taken into account for purposes of this section only to the extent attributable to housing for portions of the taxable year within the period during which the individual satisfies the requirements of § 1.911–2(a). Housing expenses are not taken into account for the period during which the value of the individual's housing is excluded from gross income under section 119, unless the individual maintains a second foreign household described in paragraph (b)(5) of this section. If an individual maintains two foreign households, only expenses incurred with respect to the abode which bears the closest relationship, not necessarily geographic, with respect to the individual's tax home shall be taken into account, unless one of the households is a second foreign household.

(4) Reasonableness. An amount paid for housing shall not be treated as reasonable, for purposes of paragraph (a) of this section, to the extent that the expense is lavish or extravagant under the circumstances.

* * *

(d) Housing cost amount exclusion—(1) Limitation. A qualified individual who has elected to exclude his or her housing cost amount may only exclude the lesser of the full amount of either the individual's housing cost amount attributable to employer provided amounts or the individual's foreign earned income for the taxable year. A qualified individual who elects to exclude his or her housing cost amount may not claim less than the full amount of the housing cost exclusion determined under this paragraph.

(2) Employer provided amounts. For purposes of this section, the term "employer provided amounts" means any amounts paid or incurred on behalf of the individual by the individual's employer which are foreign earned income included in the individual's gross income for the taxable year (without regard to section 911). Employer provided amounts include, but are not limited to, the following amounts: Any salary paid by the employer to the employee; any reimbursement paid by the employer to the employee for housing expenses, educational expenses for the individual's dependents, or as part of a tax equalization plan; the fair market value of compensation provided in kind (including lodging, unless excluded under section 119, relating to meals and lodging furnished for the convenience of the employer); and any amount paid by the employer to any third party on behalf of the employee. An individual will only have earnings that are not employer provided amounts if the individual has earnings from self-employment.

(3) Housing cost amount attributable to employer provided amounts. For the purpose of determining what portion of the housing cost amount is excludable and what portion is deductible the following rules apply. If the individual has no income from self-employment, then the entire housing cost amount is attributable to employer provided amounts and is, therefore, excludable to the extent of the limitation provided in paragraph (d)(1) of this section. If the individual only has income from self-employment, then the entire housing cost amount is attributable to non-employer provided amounts and is, therefore, deductible to the extent of the limitation provided in paragraph (e) of this section. In all other instances, the housing cost amount attributable to employer provided amounts shall be determined by multiplying the housing cost amount by the following fraction: Employer provided amounts over foreign earned income for the taxable year. The housing cost amount attributable to non-employer provided amounts shall be determined by subtracting the portion of the housing cost amount attributable to employer provided amounts from the total housing cost amount.

* * *

[T.D. 8006, 50 FR 2970, Jan. 23, 1985]

§ 1.911–6 Disallowance of deductions, exclusions, and credits.

(a) In general. No deduction or exclusion from gross income under subtitle A of the Code or credit against the tax imposed by chapter 1 of the Code shall be allowed to the extent the deduction, exclusion, or credit is properly allocable to or chargeable against amounts excluded from gross income under section 911(a). For purposes of the preceding sentence, deductions, exclusions, and credits which are definitely related (as provided in § 1.861–8), in whole or in part, to earned income shall be allocated and apportioned to foreign earned income and U.S. source earned income in accordance with the rules contained in § 1.861–8. Deductions, exclusions, and credits which are definitely related to all gross income under § 1.861–8, including deductions for interest described in § 1.861–8(e)(2)(ii), are definitely related, in whole or in part, to earned income. In the case of interest expense allocable, in whole or in part, to foreign earned income under § 1.861–8(e)(2)(ii), the expense shall normally be apportioned under option one of the optional gross income methods of apportionment (§ 1.861–8(e)(2)(v)i(A)), but without regard to conditions (1) and (2) of subdivision (vi)(A) (the fifty percent conditions). Such interest expense shall not normally be apportioned under the asset method of § 1.861–8(e)(2)(v). This is because, where section 911 is the operative section, the expense normally relates more closely to gross income generated from activities than to the amount of capital utilized or invested in activities or property. Deductions that are allocated and apportioned to foreign earned income must then be allocated and apportioned to foreign earned income that is excluded under section 911(a). If an individual has foreign earned income from both self-employment and other employment, the amount excluded under section 911(a)(1) shall be deemed to include a pro rata amount of the self-employment income and the income from other employment; thus, a pro rata portion of deductible expenses attributable to self-employment income must be disallowed. For purposes of section 911(d)(6) and this section only, deductions, exclusions, or credits which are not definitely related to any class of gross income shall not be allocable or chargeable to excluded amounts and are, therefore, deductible to the extent allowed by chapter 1 of the Code. Examples of deductions that are not definitely related to a class of gross income are personal and family medical expenses, qualified retirement contributions (but see section 219(b)(1)), real estate taxes and mortgage interest on a personal residence, charitable contributions, alimony payments, and deductions for personal exemptions. In addition, for purposes of this section, amounts excludable or deductible under section 911 or 119 shall not be allocable or chargeable to other amounts excluded under section 911(a). Thus, an individual's housing cost amount which is excludable or deductible under § 1.911–4(d) for a taxable year is not apportioned in part to the individual's foreign earned income which is excluded for such year under § 1.911–3(d). Therefore, the entire amount of such exclusion or deduction is allowed to the extent provided in § 1.911–4. This section does not affect the time for claiming any deduction, exclusion, or credit that is not allocated or apportioned to excluded amounts.

* * *

(c) Foreign taxes—(1) Amount disallowed. No deduction or credit is allowed for foreign income, war profits, or excess profits taxes paid or accrued with respect to amounts excluded from gross income under section 911. To determine the amount of disallowed foreign taxes, multiply the foreign tax imposed on foreign earned income (as defined in § 1.911–3(a)) received or accrued during the taxable year by a fraction, the numerator of which is amounts excluded under section 911(a) in such taxable year less deductible expenses properly allocated to such amounts (see paragraphs (a) and (b) of this section), and the denominator of which is foreign earned income (as defined in § 1.911–3(a)) received or accrued during the taxable year less deductible expenses properly allocated or apportioned thereto. For the purpose of determining the extent to which foreign taxes are disallowed, the housing cost amount deduction is treated as definitely related to foreign earned income that is not excluded. If the foreign tax is imposed on foreign earned income and some other income (for example earned income from sources within the United States or an amount not subject to tax in the United States), and the taxes on the other amount cannot be segregated, then the denominator equals the total of the amounts subject to tax less deductible expenses allocable to all such amounts.

(2) Definitions and special rules—(i) Taxable year. For purposes of paragraph (c)(1) of this section, the term "taxable year" means the individual's taxable year for U.S. tax purposes. Such term includes the portion of any foreign taxable year within the individual's U.S. taxable year and excludes the portion of any foreign taxable year not within the individual's U.S. taxable year.

(ii) Apportionment of foreign taxes. For purposes of this paragraph (c), foreign taxes imposed on foreign earned income shall be deemed to accrue, on a pro rata basis, to income as the income is received or accrued. The taxes so accrued shall be apportioned to the taxable year during which the income is received or accrued. This rule applies for all individuals, regardless of their method of accounting.

(iii) Effect of disallowance. The disallowance of foreign taxes under this paragraph (c) shall not affect the time for claiming any deduction or credit for foreign taxes paid. Rather, the disallowance shall only affect the amount of taxes considered paid or accrued to any foreign country.

(iv) Interest on foreign taxes. Any interest expense incurred on a liability for foreign taxes is allocated and apportioned not under this paragraph (c) but under paragraph (a) of this section to foreign earned income and then to excluded foreign earned income and to that extent disallowed as a deduction under paragraph (a). In that regard, see also § 1.861–8(e)(2) for the specific rules for allocation and apportionment of interest expense.

* * *

[T.D. 8006, 50 FR 2973, Jan. 23, 1985]

Controlled Foreign Corporations

§ 1.951–1 Amounts included in gross income of United States shareholders.

(a) In general. * * *

(4) See § 1.958–1(d) for rules regarding the ownership of stock of a foreign corporation through a domestic partnership for purposes of section 951 and for purposes of any provision that specifically applies by reference to section 951 or the regulations in this part under section 951.

* * *

[T.D. 6795, 30 FR 935, Jan. 29, 1965, as amended by T.D. 7893, 48 FR 22505, May 19, 1983; T.D. 9222, 70 FR 49866, Aug. 25, 2005; 70 FR 67906, Nov. 9, 2005; T.D. 9251, 71 FR 8944, Feb. 22, 2006; T.D. 9866, 84 FR 29337, June 21, 2019; 84 FR 44223, Aug. 23, 2019; 84 FR 53052, Oct. 4, 2019; T.D. 9960, 87 FR 3654, Jan. 25, 2022]

§ 1.951A–2 Tested income and tested loss.

* * *

(b) Definitions related to tested income and tested loss—(1) Tested income and tested income CFC. The term tested income means the excess (if any) of a controlled foreign corporation's gross tested income for a CFC inclusion year, over the allowable deductions (including taxes) properly allocable to the gross tested income for the CFC inclusion year (a controlled foreign corporation with tested income for a CFC inclusion year, a tested income CFC).

(2) Tested loss and tested loss CFC. The term tested loss means the excess (if any) of a controlled foreign corporation's allowable deductions (including taxes) properly allocable to gross tested income (or that would be allocable to gross tested income if there were gross tested income) for a CFC inclusion year, over the gross tested income of the controlled foreign corporation for the CFC inclusion year (a controlled foreign corporation without tested income for a CFC inclusion year, a tested loss CFC).

(c) Rules relating to the determination of tested income and tested loss—(1) Definition of gross tested income. The term gross tested income means the gross income of a controlled foreign corporation for a CFC inclusion year determined without regard to—

(i) Items of income described in section 952(b),

(ii) Gross income taken into account in determining the subpart F income of the corporation,

(iii) Gross income excluded from the foreign base company income (as defined in section 954) or the insurance income (as defined in section 953) of the corporation by reason of the exception described in section 954(b)(4) pursuant to an election under § 1.954–1(d)(5), or a tentative gross tested income item of the corporation that qualifies for the exception described in section 954(b)(4) pursuant to an election under paragraph (c)(7) of this section,

(iv) Dividends received by the corporation from related persons (as defined in section 954(d)(3)), and

(v) Foreign oil and gas extraction income (as defined in section 907(c)(1)) of the corporation.

(2) Determination of gross income and allowable deductions. For purposes of determining tested income and tested loss, the gross income and allowable deductions of a controlled foreign corporation for a CFC inclusion year are determined under the rules of § 1.952–2 for determining the subpart F income (as defined in section 952) of the controlled foreign corporation, except, for a controlled foreign corporation which is engaged in the business of reinsuring or issuing insurance or annuity contracts and which, if it were a domestic corporation engaged only in such business, would be taxable as an insurance company to which subchapter L of chapter 1 of the Code applies, the text "the principles of §§ 1.953–4 and 1.953–5" means "the rules of sections 953 and 954(i)" in § 1.952–2(b)(2).

(3) Allocation of deductions to gross tested income—(i) In general. Except as provided in paragraph (c)(5) of this section, any deductions of a controlled foreign corporation allowable under paragraph (c)(2) of this section are allocated and apportioned to gross tested income under the principles of section 954(b)(5) and § 1.954–1(c), by treating gross tested income that falls within a single separate category (as defined in § 1.904–5(a)(4)(v)) as a single item of gross income, separate and in addition to the items set forth in § 1.954–1(c)(1)(iii). Losses in other separate categories of income resulting from the application of § 1.954–1(c)(1)(i) cannot reduce any separate category of gross tested income, and losses in a separate category of gross tested income cannot reduce income in a category of subpart F income. In addition, deductions of a controlled foreign corporation that are allocated and apportioned to gross tested income under this paragraph (c)(3) are not taken into account for purposes of determining a qualified deficit as defined in section 952(c)(1)(B)(ii).

(ii) Coordination with the high-tax exclusion—(A) In general. In the case of a taxpayer that has made an election under paragraph (c)(7) of this section, in allocating and apportioning deductions under this paragraph (c)(3), the taxpayer must apply the rules of sections 861 through 865 and 904(d) (taking into account the rules of section 954(b)(5) and § 1.954–1(c)) in a manner that achieves results consistent with those under paragraph (c)(7) of this section.

(B) Application of consistency rule to deductions allocated and apportioned to the residual grouping in applying the high-tax exclusion. Deductions that are allocated and apportioned to the residual income group under paragraph (c)(7)(iii)(A) of this section for purposes of applying the high-tax exclusion to a controlled foreign corporation's tentative gross tested income items are allocated and apportioned for purposes of determining the controlled foreign corporation's net income in each relevant statutory grouping using a method that provides for a consistent allocation and apportionment of deductions to gross income in the relevant groupings. See §§ 1.954–1(c) and 1.960–1(d)(3) for rules relating to the allocation and apportionment of expenses for purposes of determining subpart F income, which is included in the residual grouping for purposes of applying the high-tax exclusion of sections 951A(c)(2)(A)(i)(III) and 954(b)(4) and paragraph (c)(7) of this section.

* * *

(7) Election to apply high-tax exception of section 954(b)(4)—(i) In general. For purposes of section 951A(c)(2)(A)(i)(III) and paragraph (c)(1)(iii) of this section, a tentative gross tested income item of a controlled foreign corporation for a CFC inclusion year qualifies for the exception described in section 954(b)(4) only if—

(A) An election made under paragraph (c)(7)(viii) of this section is effective with respect to the controlled foreign corporation for the CFC inclusion year; and

(B) The tentative tested income item with respect to the tentative gross tested income item was subject to an effective rate of foreign tax, as determined under paragraph (c)(7)(vi) of this section, that is greater than 90 percent of the maximum rate of tax specified in section 11.

* * *

[T. D. 9866, 84 FR 29341, 29348, June 21, 2019; T.D. 9866, 84 FR 44694, Aug. 27, 2019; T.D. 9882, 84 FR 69107, Dec. 17, 2019; T.D. 9902, 85 FR 44638, July 23, 2020; 85 FR 64040, Oct. 9, 2020; T.D. 9922, 85 FR 72070, Nov. 12, 2020; T.D. 9934, 85 FR 76975, Dec. 1, 2020; T.D. 9902, 85 FR 79853, Dec. 11, 2020; T.D. 9959, 87 FR 373, Jan. 4, 2022; 87 FR 45020, July 27, 2022; T.D. 9994, 89 FR 82169, Oct. 10, 2024]

§ 1.951A–3 Qualified business asset investment.

* * *

(h) Anti-avoidance rules related to certain transfers of property—(1) Disregard of adjusted basis in specified tangible property held temporarily—(i) In general. For purposes of determining a controlled foreign corporation's aggregate adjusted bases in specified tangible property as of the close of a quarter (tested quarter close), the adjusted basis in specified tangible property is disregarded as of the tested quarter close if the controlled foreign corporation (acquiring CFC) acquires the property temporarily before the tested quarter close with a principal purpose of increasing the deemed tangible income return of a U.S. shareholder (applicable U.S. shareholder) for a U.S. shareholder year, and the holding of the property by the acquiring CFC as of the tested quarter close would, without regard to this paragraph (h)(1)(i), increase the deemed tangible income return of the applicable U.S. shareholder for the U.S. shareholder inclusion year.

(ii) Disregard of first quarter close. The adjusted basis in specified tangible property may be disregarded under paragraph (h)(1)(i) of this section for purposes of multiple tested quarter closes that follow an acquisition and on which the acquiring CFC holds the property. However, if the holding of specified tangible property would, without regard to paragraph (h)(1)(i) of this section, increase the deemed tangible income return of an applicable U.S. shareholder because the adjusted basis in such property is taken into account for only one additional quarter close of a tested income CFC of the applicable U.S. shareholder in determining the deemed tangible income return of the applicable U.S. shareholder of the U.S. shareholder inclusion year, the adjusted basis in the property is disregarded for purposes of determining the acquiring CFC's aggregate adjusted bases in specified tangible property only as of the first tested quarter close that follows the acquisition.

(iii) Safe harbor for certain transfers involving CFCs. The holding of specified tangible property as of a tested quarter close does not increase the deemed tangible income return of an applicable U.S. shareholder within the meaning of paragraph (h)(1)(i) of this section if each of the following conditions is satisfied with respect to the acquisition and subsequent transfer of property by the acquiring CFC—

(A) A controlled foreign corporation (predecessor CFC) holds the property on a quarter close of the predecessor CFC (preceding quarter close) that occurs on the same date as the last quarter close of the acquiring CFC preceding the acquisition.

(B) A controlled foreign corporation (successor CFC) holds the property on a quarter close of the successor CFC (succeeding quarter close) that occurs on the same date as the first quarter close of the acquiring CFC following the subsequent transfer.

(C) The proportion of the stock that the applicable U.S. shareholder owns (within the meaning of section 958(a)) of the acquiring CFC on the tested quarter close does not exceed the proportion of the stock that the applicable U.S. shareholder owns of either the predecessor CFC on the preceding quarter close or the successor CFC on the succeeding quarter close; and

(D) Each of the predecessor CFC and the successor CFC is a tested income CFC for its CFC inclusion year that includes the date of the tested quarter close.

(iv) Determination of principal purpose and transitory holding—(A) Presumption for ownership less than 12 months. For purposes of paragraph (h)(1)(i) of this section, specified tangible property is presumed to be acquired temporarily with a principal purpose of increasing the deemed tangible income return of an applicable U.S. shareholder for a U.S. shareholder inclusion year if the property is held by the acquiring CFC for less than 12 months and the holding of the property by the acquiring CFC as of the tested quarter close would have the effect of increasing the deemed tangible income return of the applicable U.S. shareholder for a U.S. shareholder inclusion year. The presumption described in the preceding sentence may be rebutted only if the facts and circumstances clearly establish that the subsequent transfer of the property by the acquiring CFC was not contemplated when the property was acquired by the acquiring CFC and that a principal purpose of the acquisition of the property was not to increase the deemed tangible income return of the applicable U.S. shareholder for a U.S. shareholder inclusion year. In order to rebut the presumption, a statement must be attached to the Form 5471 filed by the taxpayer for the taxable year of the CFC in which the subsequent transfer occurs and include any information required by applicable administrative announcements, forms or instructions. The statement must explain the facts and circumstances supporting the rebuttal and be in accordance with any rules provided in forms and instructions.

(B) Presumption for ownership greater than 36 months. For purposes of paragraph (h)(1)(i) of this section, specified tangible property is presumed not to be acquired temporarily with a principal purpose of increasing the deemed tangible income return of an applicable U.S. shareholder for a U.S. shareholder inclusion year if the property is held by the acquiring CFC for more than 36 months. The presumption described in the preceding sentence may be rebutted only if the facts and circumstances clearly establish that the subsequent transfer of the property by the acquiring CFC was contemplated when the property was acquired by the acquiring CFC and that a principal purpose of the acquisition of the property was to increase the deemed tangible income return of the applicable U.S. shareholder for a U.S. shareholder inclusion year.

(v) Determination of holding period. For purposes of this paragraph (h)(1), the period during which an acquiring CFC holds specified tangible property is determined without regard to section 1223.

(vi) Treatment as single applicable U.S. shareholder. For purposes of this paragraph (h)(1), all U.S. persons that are related persons are treated as a single applicable U.S. shareholder. For purposes of the preceding sentence, U.S. persons are related if they bear a relationship described in section 267(b) or 707(b) immediately before or immediately after a transaction

* * *

[T.D. 9866, 84 FR 29341, 29351, June 21, 2019; T.D. 9956, 86 FR 52971, Sept. 24, 2021]

§ 1.952–1 Subpart F income defined.

* * *

(g) Treatment of distributive share of partnership income—(1) In general. A controlled foreign corporation's distributive share of any item of income of a partnership is income that falls within a category of subpart F income described in section 952(a) to the extent the item of income would have been income in such category if received by the controlled foreign corporation directly. For specific rules regarding the treatment of a distributive share of partnership income under certain provisions of subpart F, see §§ 1.954–1(g), 1.954–2(a)(5), 1.954–3(a)(6), and 1.954–4(b)(2)(iii).

(2) Example. The application of this paragraph (g) may be illustrated by the following example:

Example. CFC, a controlled foreign corporation, is an 80-percent partner in PRS, a foreign partnership. PRS earns $100 of interest income that is not export financing interest as defined in section 954(c)(2)(B), or qualified banking or financing income as defined in section 954(h)(3)(A), from a person unrelated to CFC. This interest income would have been foreign personal holding company income to CFC, under section 954(c), if it had received this income directly. Accordingly, CFC's distributive share of this interest income, $80, is foreign personal holding company income.

* * *

[T.D. 6795, 30 FR 938, Jan. 29, 1965, as amended by T.D. 6892, 31 FR 11144, Aug. 23, 1966; T.D. 7293, 38 FR 32802, Nov. 28, 1973; T.D. 7545, 43 FR 19652, May 8, 1978; T.D. 7862, 47 FR 56490, Dec. 17, 1982; T.D. 7893, 48 FR 22508, May 19, 1983; T.D. 7894, 48 FR 22516, May 19, 1983; T.D. 8331, 56 FR 2846, Jan. 25, 1991; T.D. 8704, 62 FR 18, Jan. 2, 1997; T.D. 9008, 67 FR 48023, July 23, 2002]

§ 1.954–1 Foreign base company income.

(a) In general—(1) Purpose and scope. Section 954 and §§ 1.954–1 and 1.954–2 provide rules for computing the foreign base company income of a controlled foreign corporation. Foreign base company income is included in the subpart F income of a controlled foreign corporation under the rules of section 952. Subpart F income is included in the gross income of a United States shareholder of a controlled foreign corporation under the rules of section 951 and thus is subject to current taxation under section 1, 11 or 55 of the Internal Revenue Code. The determination of whether a foreign corporation is a controlled foreign corporation, the subpart F income of which is included currently in the gross income of its United States shareholders, is made under the rules of section 957.

(2) Gross foreign base company income. The gross foreign base company income of a controlled foreign corporation consists of the following categories of gross income (determined after the application of section 952(b))—

(i) Foreign personal holding company income, as defined in section 954(c);

(ii) Foreign base company sales income, as defined in section 954(d);

(iii) Foreign base company services income, as defined in section 954(e);

(iv) Foreign base company shipping income, as defined in section 954(f); and

(v) Foreign base company oil related income, as defined in section 954(g).

(3) Adjusted gross foreign base company income. The term adjusted gross foreign base company income means the gross foreign base company income of a controlled foreign corporation as adjusted by the de minimis and full inclusion rules of paragraph (b) of this section.

(4) Net foreign base company income. The term net foreign base company income means the adjusted gross foreign base company income of a controlled foreign corporation reduced so as to take account of deductions (including taxes) properly allocable or apportionable to such income under the rules of section 954(b)(5) and paragraph (c) of this section.

(5) Adjusted net foreign base company income. The term adjusted net foreign base company income means the net foreign base company income of a controlled foreign corporation reduced, first, by any items of net foreign base company income excluded from subpart F income pursuant to section 952(c) and, second, by any items excluded from subpart F income pursuant to the high tax exception of section 954(b). See paragraph (d)(4)(ii) of this section. The term foreign base company income as used in the Internal Revenue Code and elsewhere in the Income Tax Regulations means adjusted net foreign base company income, unless otherwise provided.

* * *

(b) Computation of adjusted gross foreign base company income and adjusted gross insurance income—(1) De minimis and full inclusion tests—(i) De minimis test—(A) In general. Except as provided in paragraph (b)(1)(i)(C) of this section, adjusted gross foreign base company income and adjusted gross insurance income are equal to zero if the sum of the gross foreign base company income and the gross insurance income of a controlled foreign corporation is less than the lesser of—

(1) 5 percent of gross income; or

(2) $1,000,000.

(B) Currency translation. Controlled foreign corporations having a functional currency other than the United States dollar shall translate the $1,000,000 threshold using the exchange rate provided under section 989(b)(3) for amounts included in income under section 951(a).

(C) Coordination with sections 864(d) and 881(c). Adjusted gross foreign base company income or adjusted gross insurance income of a controlled foreign corporation always includes income from trade or service receivables described in section 864(d)(1) or (6), and portfolio interest described in section 881(c), even if the de minimis test of this paragraph (b)(1)(i) is otherwise satisfied.

(ii) Seventy percent full inclusion test. Except as provided in section 953, adjusted gross foreign base company income consists of all gross income of the controlled foreign corporation other than gross insurance income and amounts described in section 952(b), and adjusted gross insurance income consists of all gross insurance income other than amounts described in section 952(b), if the sum of the gross foreign base company income and the gross insurance income for the taxable year exceeds 70 percent of gross income. See paragraph (d)(6) of this section, under which certain items of full inclusion foreign base company income may nevertheless be excluded from subpart F income.

(2) Character of gross income included in adjusted gross foreign base company income. The gross income included in the adjusted gross foreign base company income of a controlled foreign corporation generally retains its character as foreign personal holding company income, foreign base company sales income, foreign base company services income, foreign base company shipping income, or foreign base company oil related income. However, gross income included in adjusted gross foreign base company income because the full inclusion test of paragraph (b)(1)(ii) of this section is met is termed full inclusion foreign base company income, and constitutes a separate category of adjusted gross foreign base company income for purposes of allocating and apportioning deductions under paragraph (c) of this section.

(3) Coordination with section 952(c). Income that is included in subpart F income because the full inclusion test of paragraph (b)(1)(ii) of this section is met does not reduce amounts that, under section 952(c), are subject to recharacterization.

(4) Anti-abuse rule—(i) In general. For purposes of applying the de minimis test of paragraph (b)(1)(i) of this section, the income of two or more controlled foreign corporations shall be aggregated and treated as the income of a single corporation if a principal purpose for separately organizing, acquiring, or maintaining such multiple corporations is to prevent income from being treated as foreign base company income or insurance income under the de minimis test. A purpose may be a principal purpose even though it is outweighed by other purposes (taken together or separately).

(ii) Presumption. Two or more controlled foreign corporations are presumed to have been organized, acquired or maintained to prevent income from being treated as foreign base company income or insurance income under the de minimis test of paragraph (b)(1)(i) of this section if the corporations are related persons, as defined in paragraph (b)(4)(iii) of this section, and the corporations are described in paragraph (b)(4)(ii)(A), (B), or (C) of this section. This presumption may be rebutted by proof to the contrary.

(A) The activities carried on by the controlled foreign corporations, or the assets used in those activities, are substantially the same activities that were previously carried on, or assets that were previously held, by a single controlled foreign corporation. Further, the United States shareholders of the controlled foreign corporations or related persons (as determined under paragraph (b)(4)(iii) of this section) are substantially the same as the United States shareholders of the one controlled foreign corporation in a prior taxable year. A presumption made in connection with the requirements of this paragraph (b)(4)(ii)(A) may be rebutted by proof that the activities carried on by each controlled foreign corporation would constitute a separate branch under the principles of § 1.367(a)–6T(g)(2) if carried on directly by a United States person.

(B) The controlled foreign corporations carry on a business, financial operation, or venture as partners directly or indirectly in a partnership (as defined in section 7701(a)(2) and § 301.7701–3 of this chapter) that is a related person (as defined in paragraph (b)(4)(iii) of this section) with respect to each such controlled foreign corporation.

(C) The activities carried on by the controlled foreign corporations would constitute a single branch operation under § 1.367(a)–6T(g)(2) if carried on directly by a United States person.

(iii) Related persons. For purposes of this paragraph (b), two or more persons are related persons if they are in a relationship described in section 267(b). In determining for purposes of this paragraph (b) whether two or more corporations are members of the same controlled group under section 267(b)(3), a person is considered to own stock owned directly by such person, stock owned with the application of section 1563(e)(1), and stock owned with the application of section 267(c). In determining for purposes of this paragraph (b) whether a corporation is related to a partnership under section 267(b)(10), a person is considered to own the partnership interest owned directly by such person and the partnership interest owned with the application of section 267(e)(3).

* * *

(d) Computation of adjusted net foreign base company income or adjusted net insurance income—(1) Application of high tax exception. Adjusted net foreign base company income (or adjusted net insurance income) equals the net foreign base company income (or net insurance income) of a controlled foreign corporation, reduced by any net item of such income that qualifies for the high tax exception provided by section 954(b)(4) and this paragraph (d). Any item of income that is portfolio interest, as described in section 881(c), does not qualify for the high tax exception. See paragraph (c)(1)(iii) of this section for the definition of the term item of income. For rules concerning the treatment for foreign tax credit purposes of amounts excluded from subpart F under section 954(b)(4), see § 1.904–4(c). For rules concerning the application of the high-tax exception of sections 954(b)(4) and 951A(c)(2)(A)(i)(III) to tentative gross tested income items, see § 1.951A–2(c)(1)(iii), (c)(3)(ii), and (c)(7) and (8). A net item of income qualifies for the high tax exception only if—

(i) An election is made under section 954(b)(4) and paragraph (d)(5) of this section to exclude the income from the computation of subpart F income; and

(ii) It is established that the net item of income was subject to foreign income taxes at an effective rate that is greater than 90 percent of the maximum rate of tax specified in section 11 for the taxable year of the controlled foreign corporation.

(2) Effective rate at which taxes are imposed. The effective rate with respect to a net item of income shall be determined separately for each controlled foreign corporation. The effective rate at which taxes are imposed on a net item of income is—

(i) The United States dollar amount of foreign income taxes paid or accrued with respect to the net item of income, determined under paragraph (d)(3) of this section; divided by

(ii) The United States dollar amount of the net item of foreign base company income or insurance income, described in paragraph (c)(1)(iii) of this section, increased by the amount of foreign income taxes referred to in paragraph (d)(2)(i) of this section.

* * *

(5) Procedure. An election made under the procedure provided by this paragraph (d)(5) is binding on all United States shareholders of the controlled foreign corporation and must be made—

(i) By the controlling United States shareholders, as defined in § 1.964–1(c)(5), by attaching a statement to such effect with their original or amended income tax returns, and including any additional information required by applicable administrative pronouncements; or

(ii) In such other manner as may be prescribed in applicable administrative pronouncements.

(6) Coordination of full inclusion and high tax exception rules. Notwithstanding paragraph (b)(1)(ii) of this section, full inclusion foreign base company income will be excluded from subpart F income if more than 90 percent of the adjusted gross foreign base company income and adjusted gross insurance company income of a controlled foreign corporation (determined without regard to the full inclusion test of paragraph (b)(1) of this section) is attributable to net amounts excluded from subpart F income pursuant to an election to have the high tax exception described in section 954(b)(4) and this paragraph (d) apply.

* * *

(g) Distributive share of partnership income—(1) Application of related person and country of organization tests. Unless otherwise provided, to determine the extent to which a controlled foreign corporation's distributive share of any item of gross income of a partnership would have been subpart F income if received by it directly, under § 1.952–1(g), if a provision of subpart F requires a determination of whether an entity is a related person, within the meaning of section 954(d)(3), or whether an activity occurred within or outside the country under the laws of which the controlled foreign corporation is created or organized, this determination shall be made by reference to such controlled foreign corporation and not by reference to the partnership.

(2) Application of related person test for sales and purchase transactions between a partnership and its controlled foreign corporation partner. For purposes of determining whether a controlled foreign corporation's distributive share of any item of gross income of a partnership is foreign base company sales income under section 954(d)(1) when the item of income is derived from the sale by the partnership of personal property purchased by the partnership from (or sold by the partnership on behalf of) the controlled foreign corporation; or the sale by the partnership of personal property to (or the purchase of personal property by the partnership on behalf of) the controlled foreign corporation (CFC-partnership transaction), the CFC-partnership transaction will be treated as a transaction with an entity that is a related person, within the meaning of section 954(d)(3), under paragraph (g)(1) of this section, if—

(i) The controlled foreign corporation purchased such personal property from (or sold it to the partnership on behalf of), or sells such personal property to (or purchases it from the partnership on behalf of), a related person with respect to the controlled foreign corporation (other than the partnership), within the meaning of section 954(d)(3); or

(ii) The branch rule of section 954(d)(2) applies to treat as foreign base company sales income the income of the controlled foreign corporation from selling to the partnership (or a third party) personal property that the controlled foreign corporation has manufactured, in the case where the partnership purchases personal property from (or sells personal property on behalf of) the controlled foreign corporation.

* * *

[T.D. 8618, 60 FR 46509, Sept. 7, 1995; 60 FR 62024, 62025, Dec. 4, 1995; T.D. 8704, 62 FR 20, Jan. 2, 1997; T.D. 8767, 63 FR 14615, March 26, 1998; T.D. 8827, 64 FR 37677, July 13, 1999; T.D. 9008, 67 FR 48023, July 23, 2002; T.D. 9883, 84 FR 63803, Nov. 19, 2019; T.D. 9882, 84 FR 69107, Dec. 17, 2019; T.D. 9902, 85 FR 44649, July 23, 2020; T.D. 9922, 85 FR 72070, Nov. 12, 2020]

§ 1.954–2 Foreign personal holding company income.

* * *

(b) Dividends, interest, rents, royalties, and annuities—(1) In general. Foreign personal holding company income includes—

(i) Dividends, except certain dividends from related persons as described in paragraph (b)(4) of this section and distributions of previously taxed income under section 959(b);

(ii) Interest, except export financing interest as defined in paragraph (b)(2) of this section and certain interest received from related persons as described in paragraph (b)(4) of this section;

(iii) Rents and royalties, except certain rents and royalties received from related persons as described in paragraph (b)(5) of this section and rents and royalties derived in the active conduct of a trade or business as defined in paragraph (b)(6) of this section; and

(iv) Annuities.

* * *

(4) Exclusion of dividends or interest from related persons—(i) In general—

(A) Corporate payor. Foreign personal holding company income received by a controlled foreign corporation does not include dividends or interest if the payor—

(1) Is a corporation that is a related person with respect to the controlled foreign corporation, as defined in section 954(d)(3);

(2) Is created or organized under the laws of the same foreign country (the country of incorporation) as is the controlled foreign corporation; and

(3) Uses a substantial part of its assets in a trade or business in its country of incorporation, as determined under this paragraph (b)(4).

(B) Payment by a partnership. For purposes of this paragraph (b)(4), if a partnership with one or more corporate partners makes a payment of interest, a corporate partner will be treated as the payor of the interest—

(1) If the interest payment gives rise to a partnership item of deduction under the Internal Revenue Code or Income Tax Regulations, to the extent that the item of deduction is allocable to the corporate partner under section 704(b); or

(2) If the interest payment does not give rise to a partnership item of deduction under the Internal Revenue Code or Income Tax Regulations, to the extent that a partnership item reasonably related to the payment would be allocated to that partner under an existing allocation under the partnership agreement (made pursuant to section 704(b)).

* * *

(5) Exclusion of rents and royalties derived from related persons—(i) In general—

(A) Corporate payor. Foreign personal holding company income received by a controlled foreign corporation does not include rents or royalties if—

(1) The payor is a corporation that is a related person with respect to the controlled foreign corporation, as defined in section 954(d)(3); and

(2) The rents or royalties are for the use of, or the privilege of using, property within the country under the laws of which the controlled foreign corporation receiving the payments is created or organized (the country of incorporation).

(B) Payment by a partnership. For purposes of this paragraph (b)(5), if a partnership with one or more corporate partners makes a payment of rents or royalties, a corporate partner will be treated as the payor of the rents or royalties—

(1) If the rent or royalty payment gives rise to a partnership item of deduction under the Internal Revenue Code or Income Tax Regulations, to the extent the item of deduction is allocable to the corporate partner under section 704(b); or

(2) If the rent or royalty payment does not give rise to a partnership item of deduction under the Internal Revenue Code or Income Tax Regulations, to the extent that a partnership item reasonably related to the payment would be allocated to that partner under an existing allocation under the partnership agreement (made pursuant to section 704(b)).

* * *

(c) Excluded rents—(1) Active conduct of a trade or business. Rents will be considered for purposes of paragraph (b)(6) of this section to be derived in the active conduct of a trade or business if such rents are derived by the controlled foreign corporation (the lessor) from leasing any of the following—

(i) Property that the lessor, through its own officers or staff of employees, has manufactured or produced, or property that the lessor has acquired and, through its own officers or staff of employees, added substantial value to, but only if the lessor, through its officers or staff of employees, is regularly engaged in the manufacture or production of, or in the acquisition and addition of substantial value to, property of such kind;

(ii) Real property with respect to which the lessor, through its own officers or staff of employees, regularly performs active and substantial management and operational functions while the property is leased;

(iii) Personal property ordinarily used by the lessor in the active conduct of a trade or business, leased temporarily during a period when the property would, but for such leasing, be idle; or

(iv) Property that is leased as a result of the performance of marketing functions by such lessor through its own officers or staff of employees located in a foreign country or countries, if the lessor, through its officers or staff of employees, maintains and operates an organization either in such country or in such countries (collectively), as applicable, that is regularly engaged in the business of marketing, or of marketing and servicing, the leased property and that is substantial in relation to the amount of rents derived from the leasing of such property.

* * *

(d) Excluded royalties—(1) Active conduct of a trade or business. Royalties will be considered for purposes of paragraph (b)(6) of this section to be derived in the active conduct of a trade or business if such royalties are derived by the controlled foreign corporation (the licensor) from licensing—

(i) Property that the licensor, through its own officers or staff of employees, has developed, created, or produced, or property that the licensor has acquired and, through its own officers or staff of employees, added substantial value to, but only so long as the licensor, through its officers or staff of employees, is regularly engaged in the development, creation, or production of, or in the acquisition and addition of substantial value to, property of such kind; or

(ii) Property that is licensed as a result of the performance of marketing functions by such licensor through its own officers or staff of employees located in a foreign country or countries, if the licensor, through its officers or staff of employees, maintains and operates an organization either in such foreign country or in such foreign countries (collectively), as applicable, that is regularly engaged in the business of marketing, or of marketing and servicing, the licensed property and that is substantial in relation to the amount of royalties derived from the licensing of such property.

* * *

(e) Certain property transactions—(1) In general—(i) Inclusions. Gain from certain property transactions described in section 954(c)(1)(B) includes the excess of gains over losses from the sale or exchange of—

(A) Property that gives rise to dividends, interest, rents, royalties or annuities, as described in paragraph (e)(2) of this section;

(B) Property that is an interest in a partnership, trust or REMIC; and

(C) Property that does not give rise to income, as described in paragraph (e)(3) of this section.

(ii) Exceptions. Gain or loss from certain property transactions described in section 954(c)(1)(B) and paragraph (e)(1)(i) of this section does not include gain or loss from the sale or exchange of—

(A) Inventory or similar property, as defined in paragraph (a)(4)(iii) of this section;

(B) Dealer property, as defined in paragraph (a)(4)(v) of this section; or

(C) Property that gives rise to rents or royalties described in paragraph (b)(6) of this section that are derived in the active conduct of a trade or business from persons that are not related persons (as defined in section 954(d)(3)) with respect to the controlled foreign corporation.

(iii) Treatment of losses. Section 1.954–1(c)(1)(ii) provides for the treatment of losses in excess of gains from the sale or exchange of property described in paragraph (e)(1)(i) of this section.

(iv) Dual character property. Property may, in part, constitute property that gives rise to certain income as described in paragraph (e)(2) of this section or, in part, constitute property that does not give rise to any income as described in paragraph (e)(3) of this section. However, property that is described in paragraph (e)(1)(i)(B) of this section cannot be dual character property. Dual character property must be treated as two separate properties for purposes of paragraph (e)(2) or (3) of this section. Accordingly, the sale or exchange of such dual character property will give rise to gain or loss that in part must be included in the computation of foreign personal holding company income under paragraph (e)(2) or (3) of this section, and in part is excluded from such computation. Gain or loss from the disposition of dual character property must be bifurcated under this paragraph (e)(1)(iv) pursuant to the method that most reasonably reflects the relative uses of the property. Reasonable methods may include comparisons in terms of gross income generated or the physical division of the property. In the case of real property, the physical division of the property will in most cases be the most reasonable method available. For example, if a controlled foreign corporation owns an office building, uses 60 percent of the building in its trade or business, and rents out the other 40 percent, then 40 percent of the gain recognized on the disposition of the property would reasonably be treated as gain that is included in the computation of foreign personal holding company income under this paragraph (e)(1). This paragraph (e)(1)(iv) addresses the contemporaneous use of property for dual purposes. For rules concerning changes in the use of property affecting its classification for purposes of this paragraph (e), see paragraph (a)(3) of this section.

(2) Property that gives rise to certain income—(i) In general. Property the sale or exchange of which gives rise to foreign personal holding company income under this paragraph (e)(2) includes property that gives rise to dividends, interest, rents, royalties or annuities described in paragraph (b) of this section, including—

(A) Property that gives rise to export financing interest described in paragraph (b)(2) of this section; and

(B) Property that gives rise to income from related persons described in paragraph (b)(4) or (5) of this section.

(ii) Gain or loss from the disposition of a debt instrument. Gain or loss from the sale, exchange or retirement of a debt instrument is included in the computation of foreign personal holding company income under this paragraph (e) unless—

(A) In the case of gain—

(1) It is interest (as defined in paragraph (a)(4)(i) of this section); or

(2) It is income equivalent to interest (as described in paragraph (h) of this section); and

(B) In the case of loss—

(1) It is directly allocated to, or treated as an adjustment to, interest income (as described in paragraph (a)(4)(i) of this section) or income equivalent to interest (as defined in paragraph (h) of this section) under any provision of the Internal Revenue Code or Income Tax Regulations; or

(2) It is required to be apportioned in the same manner as interest expense under section 864(e) or any other provision of the Internal Revenue Code or Income Tax Regulations.

(3) Property that does not give rise to income. Except as otherwise provided in this paragraph (e)(3), for purposes of this section, the term property that does not give rise to income includes all rights and interests in property (whether or not a capital asset) including, for example, forwards, futures and options. Property that does not give rise to income shall not include—

(i) Property that gives rise to dividends, interest, rents, royalties or annuities described in paragraph (e)(2) of this section;

(ii) Tangible property (other than real property) used or held for use in the controlled foreign corporation's trade or business that is of a character that would be subject to the allowance for depreciation under section 167 or 168 and the regulations under those sections (including tangible property described in § 1.167(a)–2);

(iii) Real property that does not give rise to rental or similar income, to the extent used or held for use in the controlled foreign corporation's trade or business;

(iv) Intangible property (as defined in section 936(h)(3)(B)), goodwill or going concern value, to the extent used or held for use in the controlled foreign corporation's trade or business;

(v) Notional principal contracts (but see paragraphs (f)(2), (g)(2) and (h)(3) of this section for rules that include income from certain notional principal contracts in gains from commodities transactions, foreign currency gains and income equivalent to interest, respectively); or

(vi) Other property that is excepted from the general rule of this paragraph (e)(3) by the Commissioner in published guidance. See § 601.601(d)(2) of this chapter.

* * *

[T.D. 8618, 60 FR 46517, Sept. 7, 1995; 60 FR 58731, Nov. 28, 1995; 60 FR 62025, 62026, Dec. 4, 1995; T.D. 8704, 62 FR 21, Jan. 2, 1997; T.D. 8985, 67 FR 12866, March 20, 2002; T.D. 9008, 67 FR 48024, July 23, 2002; T.D. 9039, 68 FR 4917, Jan. 31, 2003; T.D. 9141, 69 FR 43317, July 20, 2004; T.D. 9240, 71 FR 2463, Jan. 17, 2006; T.D. 9326, 72 FR 38474, July 13, 2007; T.D. 9406, 73 FR 38116, July 3, 2008; 73 FR 43863, July 29, 2008; T.D. 9525, 76 FR 26180, May 6, 2011; T.D. 9733, 80 FR 52979, Sept. 2, 2015; T.D. 9792, 81 FR 76504, Nov. 3, 2016; 81 FR 95471, Dec. 28, 2016; T.D. 9883, 84 FR 63804, Nov. 19, 2019; T.D. 9922, 85 FR 72071, Nov. 12, 2020]

§ 1.954–3 Foreign base company sales income.

(a) Income included—(1) In general—(i) General rules.

* * *

(4) Property manufactured, produced, or constructed by the controlled foreign corporation—(i) In general. Foreign base company sales income does not include income of a controlled foreign corporation derived in connection with the sale of personal property manufactured, produced, or constructed by such corporation. A controlled foreign corporation will have manufactured, produced, or constructed personal property which the corporation sells only if such corporation satisfies the provisions of paragraph (a)(4)(ii), (a)(4)(iii), or (a)(4)(iv) of this section through the activities of its employees (as defined in § 31.3121(d)–1(c) of this chapter) with respect to such property. A controlled foreign corporation will not be treated as having manufactured, produced, or constructed personal property which the corporation sells merely because the property is sold in a different form than the form in which it was purchased. For rules of apportionment in determining foreign base company sales income derived from the sale of personal property purchased and used as a component part of property which is not manufactured, produced, or constructed, see paragraph (a)(5) of this section.

(ii) Substantial transformation of property. If personal property purchased by a foreign corporation is substantially transformed by such foreign corporation prior to sale, the property sold by the selling corporation is manufactured, produced, or constructed by such selling corporation. The application of this paragraph (a)(4)(ii) may be illustrated by the following examples:

Example 1. Controlled foreign corporation A, incorporated under the laws of foreign country X, operates a paper factory in foreign country Y. Corporation A purchases from a related person wood pulp grown in country Y. Corporation A, by a series of processes, converts the wood pulp to paper which it sells for use in foreign country Z. The transformation of wood pulp to paper constitutes the manufacture or production of property for purposes of this subparagraph.

Example 2. Controlled foreign corporation B, incorporated under the laws of foreign country X, purchases steel rods from a related person which produces the steel in foreign country Y. Corporation B operates a machining plant in country X in which it utilizes the purchased steel rods to make screws and bolts. The transformation of steel rods to screws and bolts constitutes the manufacture or production of property for purposes of this subparagraph.

Example 3. Controlled foreign corporation C, incorporated under the laws of foreign country X, purchases tuna fish from unrelated persons who own fishing boats which catch such fish on the high seas. Corporation C receives such fish in country X in the condition in which taken from the fishing boats and in such country processes, cans, and sells the fish to related person D, incorporated under the laws of foreign country Y, for consumption in foreign country Z. The transformation of such fish into canned fish constitutes the manufacture or production of property for purposes of this subparagraph.

(iii) Manufacture of a product when purchased components constitute part of the property sold. If purchased property is used as a component part of personal property which is sold, the sale of the property will be treated as the sale of a manufactured product, rather than the sale of component parts, if the assembly or conversion of the component parts into the final product by the selling corporation involves activities that are substantial in nature and generally considered to constitute the manufacture, production, or construction of property. Without limiting this substantive test, which is dependent on the facts and circumstances of each case, the operations of the selling corporation in connection with the use of the purchased property as a component part of the personal property which is sold will be considered to constitute the manufacture of a product if in connection with such property conversion costs (direct labor and factory burden) of such corporation account for 20 percent or more of the total cost of goods sold. In no event, however, will packaging, repackaging, labeling, or minor assembly operations constitute the manufacture, production, or construction of property for purposes of section 954(d)(1). The application of this paragraph (a)(4)(iii) may be illustrated by the following examples:

Example 1. Controlled foreign corporation A, incorporated under the laws of foreign country X, sells industrial engines for use, consumption, and disposition outside country X. Corporation A, in connection with the assembly of such engines, performs machining and assembly operations. In addition, A Corporation purchases, from related and unrelated persons, components manufactured in foreign country Y. On a per unit basis, A Corporation's selling price and costs of such engines are as follows:

Selling price	$400
Cost of goods sold:	
Material—	
Acquired from related persons	$100
Acquired from others	40
Total material	$140
Conversion costs (direct labor and factory burden)	70

Total cost of goods sold	210
Gross profit	190
Administrative and selling expenses	50
Taxable income	140

The conversion costs incurred by A Corporation are more than 20 percent of total costs of goods sold ($70/$210 or 33 percent). Although the product sold, an engine, is not sufficiently distinguishable from the components to constitute a substantial transformation of the purchased parts within the meaning of subdivision (ii) of this subparagraph, A Corporation will be considered under this subdivision to have manufactured the product it sells.

Example 2. Controlled foreign corporation B, incorporated under the laws of foreign country X, operates an automobile assembly plant. In connection with such activity, B Corporation purchases from related persons assembled engines, transmissions, and certain other components, all of which are manufactured outside of country X; purchases additional components from unrelated persons; conducts stamping, machining, and subassembly operations; and has a substantial investment in tools, jigs, welding equipment, and other machinery and equipment used in the assembly of an automobile. On a per unit basis, B Corporation's selling price and costs of such automobiles are as follows:

Selling price	$2,500
Cost of goods sold:	
Material—	
Acquired from related persons	$1,200
Acquired from others	275
Total material	$1,475
Conversion costs (direct labor and factory burden)	25
Total cost of goods sold	1,800
Gross profit	700
Administrative and selling expenses	300
Taxable income	140

The product sold, an automobile, is not sufficiently distinguishable from the components purchased (the engine, transmission, etc.) to constitute a substantial transformation of purchased parts within the meaning of subdivision (ii) of this subparagraph. Although conversion costs of B Corporation are less than 20 percent of total cost of goods sold ($325/$1800 or 18 percent), the operations conducted by B Corporation in connection with the property purchased and sold are substantial in nature and are generally considered to constitute the manufacture of a product. Corporation B will be considered under this subdivision to have manufactured the product it sells.

Example 3. Controlled foreign corporation C, incorporated under the laws of foreign country X, purchases from related persons radio parts manufactured in foreign country Y. Corporation C designs radio kits, packages component parts required for assembly of such kits, and sells the parts in a knocked down condition to unrelated persons for use outside country X. These packaging operations of C Corporation do not constitute the manufacture, production, or construction of personal property for purposes of section 954(d)(1).

(iv) Substantial contribution to manufacturing of personal property—(a) In general. If an item of personal property would be considered manufactured, produced, or constructed (under the principles of paragraph (a)(4)(ii) or (a)(4)(iii) of this section) prior to sale by the controlled foreign corporation had all of the manufacturing, producing, and constructing activities undertaken with respect to that property prior to sale been undertaken by the controlled foreign corporation through the activities of its employees, then this paragraph (a)(4)(iv) applies. If this paragraph (a)(4)(iv) applies and if the facts and circumstances evince that the controlled foreign corporation makes a substantial contribution through the activities of its employees to the manufacture, production, or construction of the personal property sold, then the personal property sold by the controlled foreign corporation is manufactured, produced, or constructed by such controlled foreign corporation.

(b) Activities. The determination of whether a controlled foreign corporation makes a substantial contribution through the activities of its employees to the manufacture, production, or construction of the personal property sold involves, but will not necessarily be limited to, consideration of the following activities:

(1) Oversight and direction of the activities or process pursuant to which the property is manufactured, produced, or constructed (under the principles of paragraph (a)(4)(ii) or (a)(4)(iii) of this section).

(2) Activities that are considered in, but that are insufficient to satisfy, the tests provided in paragraphs (a)(4)(ii) and (a)(4)(iii) of this section.

(3) Material selection, vendor selection, or control of the raw materials, work in process or finished goods.

(4) Management of manufacturing costs or capacities (for example, managing the risk of loss, cost reduction or efficiency initiatives associated with the manufacturing process, demand planning, production scheduling, or hedging raw material costs).

(5) Control of manufacturing related logistics.

(6) Quality control (for example, sample testing or establishment of quality control standards).

(7) Developing, or directing the use or development of, product design and design specifications, as well as trade secrets, technology, or other intellectual property for the purpose of manufacturing, producing, or constructing the personal property.

(c) Application of substantial contribution test. When considering whether a controlled foreign corporation makes a substantial contribution to the manufacture, production, or construction of the personal property, the performance of any activity in paragraph (a)(4)(iv)(b) of this section will be taken into account. The performance or lack of performance of any particular activity in paragraph (a)(4)(iv)(b) of this section, or of a particular number of activities in (a)(4)(iv)(b) of this section, is not determinative. The weight accorded to the performance of any quantum of any activity (whether or not specified in paragraph (a)(4)(iv)(b) of this section) will vary with the facts and circumstances of the particular business. See paragraph (a)(4)(iv)(d) Examples 8, 10 and 11 of this section. In determining whether the activities of the controlled foreign corporation constitute a substantial contribution, there is no minimum performance threshold before an activity can be considered. The fact that other persons make a substantial contribution to the manufacture, production, or construction of the personal property prior to sale does not preclude the controlled foreign corporation from making a substantial contribution to the manufacture, construction, or production of that property through the activities of its employees. See paragraph (a)(4)(iv)(d) Example 9 of this section.

(d) Examples. The rules of this paragraph (a)(4)(iv) are illustrated by the following examples:

Example 1. No substantial contribution to manufacturing. (i) Facts. FS, a controlled foreign corporation, purchases raw materials from a related person. The raw materials are manufactured (under the principles of paragraph (a)(4)(ii) or (a)(4)(iii) of this section) into Product X by CM, an unrelated corporation, pursuant to a contract manufacturing arrangement. CM physically performs the substantial transformation, assembly, or conversion outside of FS's country of organization. Product X is sold by FS for use outside of FS's country of organization. Under the terms of the contract, FS retains the right to control the raw materials, work in process, and finished goods, and the right to oversee and direct the activities or process pursuant to which Product X is manufactured by CM. FS owns the intellectual property used in the manufacturing process. However, FS does not exercise, through its employees, its powers to control the raw materials, work in process, or finished goods, and FS does not exercise its powers of oversight and direction. Likewise, FS does not, through its employees, develop or direct the use or development of the intellectual property for the purpose of manufacturing Product X.

(ii) Result. If the manufacturing activities undertaken with respect to Product X prior to sale had been undertaken by FS through the activities of its employees, FS would have satisfied the manufacturing exception contained in paragraph (a)(4)(ii) or (a)(4)(iii) of this section with respect to Product X. Therefore, this paragraph (a)(4)(iv) applies. FS does not satisfy the test under this paragraph (a)(4)(iv) because it does not make a substantial contribution through the activities of its employees to the manufacture of Product X. Mere contractual rights to control materials, contractual rights to oversee and direct the manufacturing activities or process pursuant to which the property is manufactured, and ownership of intellectual property are not sufficient to satisfy this paragraph (a)(4)(iv). Therefore, under the facts and circumstances of the business, FS is not considered to have manufactured Product X under paragraph (a)(4)(i) of this section.

Example 2. Substantial contribution to manufacturing. (i) Facts. Assume the same facts as in Example 1, except for the following. FS, through its employees, engages in product design and quality control and controls manufacturing related logistics. Employees of FS exercise the right to oversee and direct the activities of CM in the manufacture of Product X.

(ii) Result. If the manufacturing activities undertaken with respect to Product X prior to sale had been undertaken by FS through the activities of its employees, FS would have satisfied the manufacturing exception contained in paragraph (a)(4)(ii) or (a)(4)(iii) of this section with respect to Product X. Therefore, this paragraph (a)(4)(iv) applies. Under the facts and circumstances of the business, FS satisfies the test under this paragraph (a)(4)(iv) because it makes a substantial contribution through the activities of its employees to the manufacture of Product X. Therefore, FS is considered to have manufactured Product X under paragraph (a)(4)(i) of this section. The analysis and conclusion would be the same if CM were related to FS because the relationship between CM and FS is irrelevant for purposes of applying paragraph (a)(4) of this section.

* * *

(6) Special rule applicable to distributive share of partnership income—(i) In general. To determine the extent to which a controlled foreign corporation's distributive share of any item of gross income of a partnership would have been foreign base company sales income if received by it directly, under § 1.952–1(g), the property sold will be considered to be manufactured, produced, or constructed by the controlled foreign corporation, within the meaning of paragraph (a)(4)(i) of this section, only if the manufacturing exception of paragraph (a)(4)(i) of this section would have applied to exclude the income from foreign base company sales income if the controlled foreign corporation had earned the income directly, determined by taking into account only the activities of the employees of, and property owned by, the partnership.

(ii) Example. The application of paragraph (a)(6)(i) of this section is illustrated by the following example:

Example. CFC, a controlled foreign corporation organized under the laws of Country A, is an 80 percent partner in Partnership X, a partnership organized under the laws of Country B. Partnership X performs activities in Country B that would constitute the manufacture of Product O, within the meaning of paragraph (a)(4) of this section, if performed directly by CFC. Partnership X, through its sales offices in Country B, then sells Product O to Corp D, a corporation that is a related person with respect to CFC, within the meaning of section 954(d)(3), for use within Country B. CFC's distributive share of Partnership X's sales income is not foreign base company sales income because the manufacturing exception of paragraph (a)(4) of this section would have applied to exclude the income from foreign base company sales income if CFC had earned the income directly.

(iii) Effective date. This paragraph (a)(6) applies to taxable years of a controlled foreign corporation beginning on or after July 23, 2002.

(b) Branches of controlled foreign corporation treated as separate corporations—(1) General rules for determining when to apply separate treatment—(i) Sales or purchase branch—(a) In general. If a controlled foreign corporation carries on purchasing or selling activities by or through a branch or similar establishment located outside the country under the laws of which such corporation is created or organized and the use of the branch or similar establishment for such activities has substantially the same tax effect as if the branch or similar establishment were a wholly owned subsidiary corporation of such controlled foreign corporation, the branch or similar establishment and the remainder of the controlled foreign corporation will be treated as separate corporations for purposes of determining foreign base company sales income of such corporation. See section 954(d)(2).

(b) Allocation of income and comparison of effective rates of tax. The determination as to whether such use of the branch or similar establishment has the same tax effect as if it were a wholly owned subsidiary corporation of the controlled foreign corporation shall be made by allocating to such branch or similar establishment only that income derived by the branch or establishment which, when the special rules of subparagraph (2)(i) of this paragraph are applied, is described in paragraph (a) of this section (but determined without applying subparagraphs (2), (3), and (4) of such paragraph). The use of the branch or similar establishment for such activities will be considered to have substantially the same tax effect as if it were a wholly owned subsidiary corporation of the controlled foreign corporation if the income allocated to the branch or similar establishment under the immediately preceding sentence is, by statute, treaty obligation, or otherwise, taxed in the year when earned at an effective rate of tax that is less than 90 percent of, and at least 5 percentage points less than, the effective rate of tax which would apply to such income under the laws of the country in which the controlled foreign corporation is created or organized, if, under the laws of such country, the entire income of the controlled foreign corporation were considered derived by the corporation from sources within such country from doing business through a permanent establishment therein, received in such country, and allocable to such permanent establishment, and the corporation were managed and controlled in such country.

(c) Use of more than one branch. If a controlled foreign corporation carries on purchasing or selling activities by or through more than one branch or similar establishment located outside the country under the laws of which such corporation is created or organized, then paragraph (b)(1)(i)(b) of this section shall be applied separately to the income derived by each such branch or similar establishment (by treating such purchasing or selling branch or similar establishment as if it were the only branch or similar establishment of the controlled foreign corporation and as if any such other branches or similar establishments were separate corporations) in determining whether the use of such branch or similar establishment has substantially the same tax effect as if such branch or similar establishment were a wholly owned subsidiary corporation of the controlled foreign corporation. See paragraph (b)(1)(ii)(c)(1) of this section for rules applicable to a controlled foreign corporation that carries on purchase or sales activities by or through one or more branches or similar establishments in addition to carrying on manufacturing activities by or through one or more branches or similar establishments.

(ii) Manufacturing branch—(a) In general. If a controlled foreign corporation carries on manufacturing, producing, constructing, growing, or extracting activities by or through a branch or similar establishment located outside the country under the laws of which such corporation is created or organized and the use of the branch or similar establishment for such activities with respect to personal property purchased or sold by or through the remainder of the controlled foreign corporation has substantially the same tax effect as if the branch or similar establishment were a wholly owned subsidiary corporation of such controlled foreign corporation, the branch or similar establishment and the remainder of the controlled foreign corporation will be treated as separate corporations for purposes of determining the foreign base company sales income of such corporation. See section 954(d)(2). The provisions of this paragraph (b)(1)(ii) will apply only if the controlled foreign corporation (including any branches or similar establishments of such controlled foreign corporation) manufactures, produces, or constructs such personal property within the meaning of paragraph (a)(4)(i) of this section, or carries on growing or extracting activities with respect to such personal property.

(b) Allocation of income and comparison of effective rates of tax. The determination as to whether such use of the branch or similar establishment has substantially the same tax effect as if the branch or similar establishment were a wholly owned subsidiary corporation of the controlled foreign corporation shall be made by allocating to the remainder of such controlled foreign corporation only that income derived by the remainder of such corporation, which, when the special rules of subparagraph (2)(i) of this paragraph are applied, is described in paragraph (a) of this section (but determined without applying subparagraphs (2), (3), and (4) of such paragraph). The use of the branch or similar establishment for such activities will be considered to have substantially the same tax effect as if it were a wholly owned subsidiary corporation of the controlled foreign corporation if income allocated to the remainder of the controlled foreign corporation under the immediately preceding sentence is, by statute, treaty obligation, or otherwise, taxed in the year when earned at an effective rate of tax that is less than 90 percent of, and at least 5 percentage points less than, the effective rate of tax which would apply to such income under the laws of the country in which the branch or similar establishment is located, if, under the laws of such country, the entire income of the controlled foreign corporation were considered derived by such corporation from sources within such country from doing business through a permanent establishment therein, received in such country, and allocable to such permanent establishment, and the corporation were created or organized under the laws of, and managed and controlled in, such country.

(c) Use of more than one branch—(1) Use of one or more sales or purchase branches in addition to a manufacturing branch. If, with respect to personal property manufactured, produced, constructed, grown, or extracted by or through a branch or similar establishment located outside the country under the laws of which the controlled foreign corporation is created or organized, purchasing or selling activities are carried on by or through more than one branch or similar establishment, or by or through one or more branches or similar establishments located outside such country, of such corporation, then paragraph (b)(1)(ii)(b) of this section shall be applied separately to the income derived by each such purchasing or selling branch or similar establishment (by treating such purchasing or selling branch or similar establishment as though it alone were the remainder of the controlled foreign corporation) for purposes of determining whether the use of such manufacturing, producing, constructing, growing, or extracting branch or similar establishment has substantially the same tax effect as if such branch or similar establishment were a wholly owned subsidiary corporation of the controlled foreign corporation. If this rule applies, the sales or purchase branch rules contained in paragraph (b)(1)(i) of this section do not apply. The application of this paragraph (b)(1)(ii)(c)(1) is illustrated by the following example:

Example. All activities of controlled foreign corporation conducted through sales branches and manufacturing branch. (i) Facts. FS, a controlled foreign corporation organized under the laws of country M, operates three branches. Branch A, located in country A, manufactures Product X under the principles of paragraph (a)(4)(i) of this section. Branch B, located in Country B, sells Product X manufactured by Branch A to customers for use outside of Country B. Branch C, located in Country C sells Product X manufactured by Branch A to customers for use outside of Country C. FS does not conduct any manufacturing or selling activities apart from the activities of Branches A, B and C. Country M imposes an effective rate of tax on sales income of 0%. Country A imposes an effective rate of tax on sales income of 20%. Country B imposes an effective rate of tax on sales income of 20%. Country C imposes an effective rate of tax on sales income of 18%.

(ii) Result. Pursuant to this paragraph (b)(1)(ii)(c)(1), paragraph (b)(1)(ii)(b) of this section is applied to the sales income derived by Branch B by treating Branch B as though it alone were the remainder of the controlled foreign corporation. The use of Branch B does not have the same tax effect as if Branch B were a wholly owned subsidiary of FS because the tax rate applicable to the income allocated to Branch B under paragraph (b)(1)(ii)(b) of this section (20%) is not less than 90% of, and at least 5 percentage points less than, the effective rate of tax which would apply to such income under the laws of Country A (20%), the country in which Branch A is located. In addition, paragraph (b)(1)(ii)(b) of this section is applied separately to the sales income derived by Branch C by treating Branch C as though it alone were the remainder of the controlled foreign corporation. The use of Branch C does not have the same tax effect as if Branch C were a wholly owned subsidiary of FS because the tax rate applicable to the income allocated to Branch C under paragraph (b)(1)(ii)(b) of this section (18%) is not less than 90% of, and at least 5 percentage points less than, the effective rate of tax which would apply to such income under the laws of Country A (20%), the country in which Branch A is located. Pursuant to this paragraph (b)(1)(ii)(c)(1), the rules under paragraph (b)(1)(i) of this section for determining whether a sales or purchase branch is treated as a separate corporation from the remainder of the controlled foreign corporation do not apply.

(2) Use of more than one branch to manufacture, produce, construct, grow, or extract separate items of personal property. If a controlled foreign corporation carries on manufacturing, producing, constructing, growing, or extracting activities with respect to separate items of personal property by or through more than one branch or similar establishment located outside the country under the laws of which such corporation is created or organized, then paragraphs (b)(1)(ii)(b) and (c) of this section will be applied separately to each such branch or similar establishment (by treating such manufacturing branch or similar establishment as if it were the only such branch or similar establishment of the controlled foreign corporation and as if any other such branches or similar establishments were separate corporations) for purposes of determining whether the use of such branch or similar establishment has substantially the same tax effect as if such branch or similar establishment were a wholly owned subsidiary corporation of the controlled foreign corporation. The application of this paragraph (b)(1)(ii)(c)(2) is illustrated by the following example:

Example. Multiple branches that satisfy paragraph (a)(4)(i). (i) Facts. FS is a controlled foreign corporation organized in Country M. FS operates two branches, Branch A and Branch B located in Country A and Country B, respectively. Branch A and Branch B each manufacture separate items of personal property (Product X and Product Y, respectively) within the meaning of paragraph (a)(4)(ii) or (iii) of this section. Raw materials used in the manufacture of Product X and Product Y are purchased by FS from an unrelated person. FS engages in activities in Country M to sell Product X and Product Y to a related person for use, disposition or consumption outside of Country M. Employees of FS located in Country M perform only sales functions. The effective rate of tax imposed in Country M on the income from the sales of Product X and Product Y is 10%. Country A imposes an effective rate of tax on sales income of 20%. Country B imposes an effective rate of tax on sales income of 12%.

(ii) Result. Pursuant to this paragraph (b)(1)(ii)(c)(2), paragraph (b)(1)(ii)(b) of this section is applied separately to Branch A and Branch B with respect to the sales income of FS attributable to Product X (manufactured by Branch A) and Product Y (manufactured by Branch B). Because the effective rate of tax on FS's sales income from the sale of Product X in Country M (10%) is less than 90% of, and at least 5 percentage points less than, the effective rate of tax that would apply to such income in the country in which Branch A is located (20%), the use of Branch A to manufacture Product X has substantially the same tax effect as if Branch A were a wholly owned subsidiary corporation of FS. Because the effective rate of tax on FS's sales income from the sale of Product Y in Country M (10%) is not less than 90% of, and at least 5 percentage points less than, the effective rate of tax that would apply to such income in the country in which Branch B is located (12%), the use of Branch B to manufacture Product Y does not have substantially the same tax effect as if Branch B were a wholly owned subsidiary corporation of FS. Consequently, only Branch A is treated as a separate corporation apart from the remainder of FS for purposes of determining foreign base company sales income from the sales of Product X.

(3) Use of more than one manufacturing branch, or one or more manufacturing branches and the remainder of the controlled foreign corporation, to manufacture, produce, or construct the same item of personal property—(i) In general. This paragraph (b)(1)(ii)(c)(3) applies to determine the location of manufacture, production, or construction of personal property for purposes of applying paragraph (b)(1)(i)(b) or (b)(1)(ii)(b) of this section where more than one branch or similar establishment of a controlled foreign corporation, or one or more branches or similar establishments of a controlled foreign corporation and the remainder of the controlled foreign corporation, each engage in manufacturing, producing, or constructing activities with respect to the same item of personal property which is then sold by the controlled foreign corporation. This paragraph (b)(1)(ii)(c)(3) is applied separately with respect to the income derived by each purchasing or selling branch or similar establishment or purchasing or selling remainder of the controlled foreign corporation as provided under paragraphs (b)(1)(i) and (b)(1)(ii) of this section. The location of manufacture, production, or construction is determined under paragraph (b)(1)(ii)(c)(3)(ii) of this section if one or more branches or similar establishments or the remainder of the controlled foreign corporation independently satisfies paragraph (a)(4)(i) of this section with respect to an item of personal property. The location of manufacture, production, or construction is determined under paragraph (b)(1)(ii)(c)(3)(iii) of this section if none of the branches or similar establishments or the remainder of the controlled foreign corporation independently satisfies paragraph (a)(4)(i) of this section with respect to an item of personal property, but the controlled foreign corporation as a whole makes a substantial contribution to the manufacture, production or construction of that property within the meaning of paragraph (a)(4)(iv) of this section. For purposes of this paragraph (b)(1)(ii)(c)(3), the location of any activity with respect to the manufacture, production, or construction of an item of personal property is determined under paragraph (b)(1)(ii)(c)(3)(iv) of this section. For purposes of this paragraph (b)(1)(ii)(c)(3), if multiple branches or similar establishments are located in a single jurisdiction, then the activities of those branches will be aggregated for purposes of determining whether a branch or remainder of the controlled foreign corporation satisfies paragraph (a)(4)(i) of this section.

(ii) Manufacture, production, or construction in one or more locations. If only one branch or similar establishment or only the remainder of a controlled foreign corporation independently satisfies paragraph (a)(4)(i) of this section with respect to an item of personal property, then that branch or similar establishment or the remainder of the controlled foreign corporation will be the location of manufacture, production, or construction of that property for purposes of applying paragraph (b)(1)(i)(b) or (b)(1)(ii)(b) of this section to the income from the sale of that property. See paragraph (b)(1)(ii)(c)(3)(v) Example 1 of this section. If more than one branch or similar establishment or one or more branches or similar establishments and the remainder of the controlled foreign corporation, each independently satisfy paragraph (a)(4)(i) of this section with respect to an item of personal property, then the location of manufacture, production, or construction of that property for purposes of applying paragraph (b)(1)(i)(b) or (b)(1)(ii)(b) of this section will be the location of that branch or similar establishment or the jurisdiction under the laws of which the remainder of the controlled foreign corporation is organized that satisfies paragraph (a)(4)(i) of this section and that would, after applying paragraph (b)(1)(ii)(b) of this section to such branch or similar establishment or paragraph (b)(1)(i)(b) of this section to the remainder of the controlled foreign corporation, impose the lowest effective rate of tax on the income allocated to such branch or the remainder of the controlled foreign corporation under such section (that is, either paragraph (b)(1)(i)(b) or (b)(1)(ii)(b) of this section). See paragraph (b)(1)(ii)(c)(3)(v) Example 2 of this section.

(iii) No location independently satisfies manufacturing test. If no branch or similar establishment or the remainder of the controlled foreign corporation independently satisfies paragraph (a)(4)(i) of this section with respect to an item of personal property but the controlled foreign corporation as a whole makes a substantial contribution to the manufacture, production, or construction of that property within the meaning of paragraph (a)(4)(iv) of this section, then for purposes of applying paragraph (b)(1)(i)(b) or (b)(1)(ii)(b) of this section, the location of manufacture, production, or construction with respect to the income derived by a purchasing or selling branch or similar establishment or the purchasing or selling remainder of the controlled foreign corporation in connection with the purchase or sale of that property will be the "tested manufacturing location" unless the "tested sales location" provides a greater contribution to the manufacture, production, or construction of the property. The tested manufacturing location is the location of any branch or similar establishment or remainder of the controlled foreign corporation that contributes to the manufacture, production, or construction of the personal property, if any, that would, after applying paragraph (b)(1)(ii)(b) of this section to such branch or similar establishment or paragraph (b)(1)(i)(b) of this section to the remainder of the controlled foreign corporation, be treated as a separate corporation and would impose the lowest effective rate of tax on the income allocated to such branch or similar establishment or to the remainder of the controlled foreign corporation under such section (that is, either paragraph (b)(1)(i)(b) or (b)(1)(ii)(b) of this section). The tested sales location is the location of the purchasing or selling branch or similar establishment or the remainder of the controlled foreign corporation by or through which the purchasing or selling activities are carried on with respect to the personal property. For purposes of this paragraph (b)(1)(ii)(c)(3)(iii), the contribution to the manufacture, production, or construction of the personal property by the tested sales location will be deemed to include the activities of any branch or similar establishment or remainder of the controlled foreign corporation that would not be treated as a corporation separate from the tested sales location after the application of paragraph (b)(1)(i)(b) or (b)(1)(ii)(b) of this section. For purposes of this paragraph (b)(1)(ii)(c)(3)(iii), the contribution of the tested manufacturing location to the manufacture, production, or construction of the personal property will be deemed to include any activities of any branch or similar establishment or remainder of the controlled foreign corporation that would be treated as a corporation separate from the tested sales location after the application of paragraph (b)(1)(i)(b) or (b)(1)(ii)(b) of this section. Whether the tested sales location provides a greater contribution to the manufacture, production, or construction of the personal property is determined by weighing the relative contributions to the manufacture, production, or construction of that property by the tested sales location and the tested manufacturing location under the facts and circumstances test provided in paragraph (a)(4)(iv) of this section. See paragraph (b)(1)(ii)(c)(3)(v) Examples 3, 4, 5, and 6 of this section. If the tested sales location provides a greater contribution to the manufacture, production, or construction of the personal property than the tested manufacturing location or if there is no tested manufacturing location, then the tested sales location is the location of manufacture, production, or construction of that property and the rules of paragraphs (b)(1)(i)(a) and (b)(1)(ii)(a) of this section will not apply with respect to the income derived by the tested sales location in connection with the purchase or sale of that property and the use of that purchasing or selling branch or similar establishment or the purchasing or selling remainder will not result in a branch being treated as a separate corporation for purposes of paragraph (b)(2)(ii) of this section.

(iv) Location of activity. For purposes of paragraph (b)(1)(ii)(c)(3) of this section, the location of any activity with respect to the manufacture, production, or construction of an item of personal property is the location where the employees of the controlled foreign corporation perform such activity. For example, the location of any activity concerning intellectual property is determined based on where employees of the controlled foreign corporation develop or direct the use or development of the intellectual property, not on the formal assignment of that intellectual property.

(v) Examples. The following examples illustrate the application of this paragraph (b)(1)(ii)(c)(3):

Example 1. Multiple branches contribute to the manufacture of a single product only one branch satisfies paragraph (a)(4)(i). (i) Facts. FS is a controlled foreign corporation organized in Country M. FS operates three branches, Branch A, Branch B, and Branch C, located respectively in Country A, Country B, and Country C. Branch A, Branch B, and Branch C each performs different manufacturing activities with respect to the manufacture of Product X. Branch A, through the activities of employees of FS located in Country A, designs Product X. Branch B, through the activities of employees of FS located in Country B, provides quality control and oversight and direction. Branch C, through the activities of employees of FS located in Country C, manufactures Product X (within the meaning of paragraph (a)(4)(ii) or (a)(4)(iii) of this section) using the designs developed by Branch A and under the oversight of the quality control personnel of Branch B. The activities of Branch A and Branch B do not independently satisfy paragraph (a)(4)(i) of this section. Employees of FS located in Country M purchase the raw materials used in the manufacture of Product X from a related person and control the work-in-process and finished goods throughout the manufacturing process. Employees of FS located in Country M also manage the manufacturing costs and capacities related to Product X. Further, employees of FS located in Country M oversee the coordination between the branches. The activities of the remainder of FS in Country M do not independently satisfy paragraph (a)(4)(i) of this section. Employees of FS located in Country M sell Product X to unrelated persons for use outside of Country M. The sales income from the sale of Product X is taxed in Country M at an effective rate of tax of 10%. Country C imposes an effective rate of tax of 20% on sales income.

(ii) Result. Country C is the location of manufacture for purposes of applying paragraph (b)(1)(ii)(b) of this section because only the activities of Branch C independently satisfy paragraph (a)(4)(i) of this section. The use of Branch C has substantially the same tax effect as if Branch C were a wholly owned subsidiary corporation of FS because the effective rate of tax on the sales income (10%) is less than 90% of, and at least 5 percentage points less than, the effective rate of tax that would apply to such income in the country in which Branch C is located (20%). Therefore, sales of Product X by the remainder of FS are treated as sales on behalf of Branch C. In determining whether the remainder of FS will qualify for the manufacturing exception under paragraph (a)(4)(iv) of this section, the activities of FS will include the activities of Branch A or Branch B, respectively, if each of those branches would not be treated as a separate corporation under paragraph (b)(1)(ii)(b) of this section, if that paragraph were applied independently to each of Branch A and Branch B. See paragraph (b)(2)(ii)(a) of this section.

Example 2. Multiple branches satisfy paragraph (a)(4)(i) with respect to the same product sold by the controlled foreign corporation. (i) Facts. Assume the same facts as in Example 1, except for the following. In addition to the design of Product X, Branch A also performs in Country A other manufacturing activities, including those ascribed to FS in Example 1, that are sufficient to qualify as manufacturing under paragraph (a)(4)(iv) of this section with respect to Product X. Country A imposes an effective rate of tax of 12% on sales income.

(ii) Result. Branch A and Branch C through their activities each independently satisfy the requirements of paragraph (a)(4)(i) of this section. Therefore, paragraph (b)(1)(ii)(b) of this section is applied by comparing the effective rate of tax imposed on the income from the sales of Product X against the lowest effective rate of tax that would apply to the sales income in either Country A or Country C if paragraph (b)(1)(ii)(b) of this section were applied separately to Branch A and Branch C. Country A imposes the lower effective rate of tax, and therefore, Branch A is treated as the location of manufacture for purposes of applying paragraph (b)(1)(ii)(b) of this section. The effective rate of tax in Country B is not considered because Branch B does not satisfy paragraph (a)(4)(i) of this section. Neither Branch A nor Branch C is treated as a separate corporation because the effective rate of tax on the sales income of FS from the sale of Product X (10%) is not less than 90% of, and at least 5 percentage points less than, the effective rate of tax that would apply to such income in the country in which Branch A is located (12%). Sales of Product X by the remainder of the controlled foreign corporation are not treated as made on behalf of any branch.

Example 3. Determining the location of manufacture when manufacturing activities performed by multiple branches and no branch independently satisfies paragraph (a)(4)(i). (i) Facts. FS, a controlled foreign corporation organized in Country M, purchases raw materials from a related person. The raw materials are manufactured (under the principles of paragraph (a)(4)(ii) or (a)(4)(iii) of this section) into Product X by CM, an unrelated corporation, pursuant to a contract manufacturing arrangement. CM physically performs the substantial transformation, assembly, or conversion of the raw materials in Country C. FS has two branches, Branch A and Branch B, located in Country A and Country B respectively. Branch A, through the activities of employees of FS located in Country A, designs Product X. Branch B, through the activities of employees of FS located in Country B, controls manufacturing related logistics, provides oversight and direction during the manufacturing process, and controls the raw materials and work-in-process. FS manages the manufacturing costs and capacities related to the manufacture of Product X through employees located in Country M. Further, employees of FS located in Country M oversee the coordination between the branches. Employees of FS located in Country M also sell Product X to unrelated persons for use outside of Country M. Country M imposes an effective rate of tax on sales income of 10%. Country A imposes an effective rate of tax on sales income of 20%, and Country B imposes an effective rate of tax on sales income of 24%. Neither the remainder of FS, nor any branch of FS independently satisfies paragraph (a)(4)(i) of this section. However, under the facts and circumstances of the business, FS as a whole provides a substantial contribution to the manufacture of Product X within the meaning of paragraph (a)(4)(iv) of this section.

(ii) Result. Based on the facts, neither the remainder of FS (through the activities of its employees in Country M) nor any branch of FS independently satisfies paragraph (a)(4)(i) of this section with respect to Product X, but FS, as a whole, provides a substantial contribution through the activities of its employees to the manufacture of Product X. The remainder of FS, Branch A, and Branch B each provides a contribution through the activities of employees to the manufacture of Product X. Therefore, FS must determine the location of manufacture under paragraph (b)(1)(ii)(c)(3)(iii) of this section. The tested sales location is Country M because the selling activities with respect to Product X are carried on by the remainder of FS. The location of Branch A is the tested manufacturing location because the effective rate of tax imposed on FS's sales income by Country M (10%) is less than 90% of, and at least 5 percentage points less than, the effective rate of tax that would apply to such income in Country A (20%), and Country A has the lowest effective rate of tax among the manufacturing branches that would, after applying paragraph (b)(1)(ii)(b) of this section, be treated as a separate corporation. The activities of Branch B will be included in the contribution of Branch A for purposes of determining the location of manufacture of Product X because the effective rate of tax imposed on the sales income by Country M (10%) is less than 90% of, and at least 5 percentage points less than, the effective rate of tax that would apply to such income in Country B (24%). Under the facts and circumstances of the business, the activities of the remainder of FS would not provide a greater contribution to the manufacture of Product X than the activities of Branch A and Branch B, considered together. Therefore, the location of manufacture is Country A, the location of Branch A.

Example 4. Manufacturing activities performed by multiple branches, no branch independently satisfies paragraph (a)(4)(i), selling activities carried on by remainder of the controlled foreign corporation, remainder contribution includes branch manufacturing activities. (i) Facts. The facts are the same as Example 3, except that the effective rate of tax on sales income in Country B is 12%. In addition, under the facts of the particular business, the activities of employees of FS located in Country B and Country M, if considered together, would provide a greater contribution to the manufacture of Product X than the activities of employees of FS located in Country A.

(ii) Result. Based on the facts, neither the remainder of FS (through activities of its employees in Country M) nor any branch of FS independently satisfies paragraph (a)(4)(i) of this section with respect to Product X, but FS, as a whole, provides a substantial contribution through the activities of its employees to the manufacture of Product X. The remainder of FS, Branch A, and Branch B each provide a contribution through the activities of their employees to the manufacture of Product X. Therefore, FS must determine the location of manufacture under paragraph (b)(1)(ii)(c)(3)(iii) of this section. The tested sales location is Country M because the selling activities with respect to Product X are carried on by the remainder of FS. The location of Branch A is the tested manufacturing location because the effective rate of tax imposed on FS's sales income by Country M (10%) is less than 90% of, and at least 5 percentage points less than, the effective rate of tax that would apply to such income in Country A (20%), and Branch A is the only branch that would, after applying paragraph (b)(1)(ii)(b) of this section, be treated as a separate corporation. The activities of Branch B will be included in the contribution of the remainder of FS for purposes of determining the location of manufacture of Product X because the effective rate of tax imposed on the sales income by Country M (10%) is not less than 90% of, and at least 5 percentage points less than, the effective rate of tax that would apply to such income in Country B (12%). Under a facts and circumstances analysis, considered together, the activities of Branch B and the remainder of FS would provide a greater contribution to the manufacture of Product X than the activities of Branch A. Therefore, the rules of paragraph (b)(1)(ii)(a) of this section will not apply with respect to the income derived by the remainder of FS in connection with the sale of Product X, and neither Branch A nor Branch B will be treated as a separate corporation for purposes of paragraph (b)(2)(ii) of this section.

Example 5. Manufacturing activities performed by multiple branches, no branch independently satisfies paragraph (a)(4)(i), sales carried on by remainder of the controlled foreign corporation and a sales branch. (i) Facts. The facts are the same as Example 3, except that sales of Product X are also carried on through Branch D in Country D, and Country D imposes a 16% effective rate of tax on sales income. In addition, under the facts and circumstances of the business, the activities of employees of FS located in Country A and Country M, considered together, would provide a greater contribution to the manufacture of Product X than the activities of employees of FS located in Country B.

(ii) Result. Based on the facts, neither the remainder of FS nor any branch of FS independently satisfies paragraph (a)(4)(i) of this section with respect to Product X, but FS, as a whole, provides a substantial contribution through the activities of its employees to the manufacture of Product X. The remainder of FS, Branch A, and Branch B each provide a contribution through the activities of their employees to the manufacture of Product X. Therefore, FS must determine the location of manufacture under paragraph (b)(1)(ii)(c)(3)(iii) of this section. Further, pursuant to paragraph (b)(1)(ii)(c)(1) of this section, paragraph (b)(1)(ii)(c)(3)(iii) of this section must be applied separately to the sales income derived by the remainder of FS and Branch D respectively. The results with respect to the income derived by the remainder of FS in connection with the sale of Product X in this Example 5 are the same as in Example 3. However, paragraph (b)(1)(ii)(c)(3)(iii) of this section must also be applied with respect to Branch D because the sale of Product X is also carried on through Branch D. Thus, for purposes of that sales income, the location of Branch D is the tested sales location. The location of Branch B is the tested manufacturing location because the effective rate of tax imposed on Branch D's sales income by Country D (16%) is less than 90% of, and at least 5 percentage points less than, the effective rate of tax that would apply to such income in Country B (24%), and Branch B is the only branch that would, after applying paragraph (b)(1)(ii)(b) of this section, be treated as a separate corporation. The manufacturing activities performed in Country M by the remainder of FS and the manufacturing activities performed in Country A by Branch A will be included in Branch D's contribution to the manufacture of Product X for purposes of determining the location of manufacture of Product X with respect to Branch D's sales income because the effective rate of tax imposed on the sales income by Country D (16%) is not less than 90% of, and at least 5 percentage points less than, the effective rate of tax that would apply to such income in Country M (10%) and Country A (20%). Under the facts and circumstances of the business, the activities of Branch D, Branch A, and the remainder of FS, considered together, would provide a greater contribution to the manufacture of Product X than the activities of Branch B. Therefore, the rules of paragraph (b)(1)(ii)(a) of this section will not apply with respect to the income derived by Branch D in connection with the sale of Product X and the use of Branch D to sell Product X will not result in a branch being treated as a separate corporation for purposes of paragraph (b)(2)(ii) of this section.

Example 6. Determining the location of manufacture when employees of remainder of controlled foreign corporation travel to

location of unrelated contract manufacturer to perform manufacturing activities. (i) Facts. FS, a controlled foreign corporation organized in Country M, purchases raw materials from a related person. The raw materials are manufactured (under the principles of paragraph (a)(4)(ii) or (a)(4)(iii) of this section) into Product X by CM, an unrelated corporation, pursuant to a contract manufacturing arrangement. CM physically performs the substantial transformation, assembly, or conversion of the raw materials in Country C. Employees of FS located in Country M sell Product X to unrelated persons for use outside of Country M. Employees of FS located in Country M engage in product design, manage the manufacturing costs and capacities with respect to Product X, and direct the use of intellectual property for the purpose of manufacturing Product X. Quality control and oversight and direction of the manufacturing process are conducted in Country C by employees of FS who are employed in Country M but who regularly travel to Country C. Branch A, located in Country A, is the only branch of FS. Product design with respect to Product X conducted by employees of FS located in Country A is supplemental to the bulk of the design work, which is done by employees of FS located in Country M. At all times, employees of Branch A control the raw materials, work-in-process and finished goods. Employees of FS located in Country A also control manufacturing related logistics with respect to Product X. Country M imposes an effective rate of tax on sales income of 10%. Country A imposes an effective rate of tax on sales income of 20%. Neither the remainder of FS nor Branch A independently satisfies paragraph (a)(4)(i) of this section. However, under the facts and circumstance of the business, FS as a whole (including Branch A) provides a substantial contribution to the manufacture of Product X within the meaning of paragraph (a)(4)(iv) of this section.

(ii) Result. Based on the facts, neither the remainder of FS nor Branch A independently satisfies paragraph (a)(4)(i) of this section with respect to Product X, but FS, as a whole, provides a substantial contribution through the activities of its employees to the manufacture of Product X. The remainder of FS and Branch A each provide a contribution through the activities of employees to the manufacture of Product X. Therefore, FS must determine the location of manufacture under paragraph (b)(1)(ii)(c)(3)(iii) of this section. The tested sales location is Country M because the selling activities with respect to Product X are carried on by the remainder of FS. The tested manufacturing location is the location of Branch A because the effective rate of tax imposed on the remainder of FS's sales income by Country M (10%) is less than 90% of, and at least 5 percentage points less than, the effective rate of tax that would apply to such income in Country A (20%), and Branch A is the only branch that would, after applying paragraph (b)(1)(ii)(b) of this section, be treated as a separate corporation. Although the activities of traveling employees are considered in determining whether FS, as a whole, makes a substantial contribution to the manufacture of Product X under paragraph (a)(4)(iv) of this section, the activities of the employees of FS that are performed in Country C are not taken into consideration in determining whether Country M, the jurisdiction under the laws of which FS is organized, is the location of manufacture under paragraph (b)(1)(ii)(c)(3)(iii) of this section. Activities of employees performed outside the jurisdiction in which the controlled foreign corporation is organized and outside a location in which the controlled foreign corporation maintains a branch or similar establishment, are not considered in determining the location of manufacture. Under the facts and circumstances of the business, the activities of employees of FS performed in Country M do not provide a greater contribution to the manufacture of Product X than the activities of employees of FS performed in Country A. Therefore, the location of manufacture is Country A, the location of Branch A.

(4) Use of more than one branch to manufacture, produce, construct, grow, or extract separate items of personal property. For purposes of paragraphs (b)(1)(ii)(c)(2) and (b)(1)(ii)(c)(3) of this section, an item of personal property refers to an individual unit of personal property rather than a type or class of personal property.

(2) Special rules—(i) Determination of treatment as a wholly owned subsidiary corporation. For purposes of determining under this paragraph whether the use of a branch or similar establishment which is treated as a separate corporation has substantially the same tax effect as if the branch or similar establishment were a wholly owned subsidiary corporation of a controlled foreign corporation—

(a) Treatment as separate corporations. The branch or similar establishment will be treated as a wholly owned subsidiary corporation of the controlled foreign corporation, and such branch or similar establishment will be deemed to be incorporated in the country in which it is located.

(b) Activities treated as performed on behalf of the remainder of corporation. (1) With respect to purchasing or selling activities performed by or through the branch or similar establishment, such purchasing or selling activities will, with respect to personal property manufactured, produced, constructed, grown, or extracted by the remainder of the controlled foreign corporation, be treated as performed on behalf of the remainder of the controlled foreign corporation.

(2) With respect to purchasing or selling activities performed by or through the branch or similar establishment, such purchasing or selling activities will, with respect to personal property (other than property described in paragraph (b)(2)(i)(b)(1) of this section) purchased or sold, or purchased and sold, by the remainder of the controlled foreign corporation (or any branch treated as the remainder of the controlled foreign corporation), be treated as performed on behalf of the remainder of the controlled foreign corporation.

(c) Activities treated as performed on behalf of branch. With respect to manufacturing, producing, constructing, growing, or extracting activities performed by or through the branch or similar establishment, purchasing or selling activities performed by or through the remainder of the controlled foreign corporation with respect to the personal property manufactured, produced, constructed, grown, or extracted by or through the branch or similar establishment shall be treated as performed on behalf of the branch or similar establishment.

(d) [Reserved]

(e) Tax laws to be taken into account. Tax determinations shall be made by taking into account only the income, war profits, excess profits, or similar tax laws (or the absence of such laws) of the countries involved.

(ii) Determination of foreign base company sales income. Once it has been determined under subparagraph (1) of this paragraph that a branch or similar establishment and the remainder of the controlled foreign corporation are to be treated as separate corporations, the determination of whether such branch or similar establishment, or the remainder of the controlled foreign corporation, as the case may be, has foreign base company sales income shall be made by applying the following rules:

(a) Treatment as separate corporations. The branch or similar establishment will be treated as a wholly owned subsidiary corporation of the controlled foreign corporation, and such branch or similar establishment will be deemed to be incorporated in the country in which it is located. For purposes of applying the rules of this paragraph (b)(2)(ii), a branch or similar establishment of a controlled foreign corporation treated as a separate corporation purchasing or selling on behalf of the remainder of the controlled foreign corporation under paragraph (b)(2)(ii)(b) of this section, or the remainder of the controlled foreign corporation treated as a separate corporation purchasing or selling on behalf of a branch or similar establishment of the controlled foreign corporation under paragraph (b)

(2)(ii)(c) of this section, will include the activities of any other branch or similar establishment or remainder of the controlled foreign corporation that would not be treated as a separate corporation (apart from the branch or similar establishment of a controlled foreign corporation that is treated as performing purchasing or selling activities on behalf of the remainder of the controlled foreign corporation under paragraph (b)(2)(ii)(b) of this section or the remainder of the controlled foreign corporation that is treated as performing purchasing or selling activities on behalf of the branch or similar establishment under paragraph (b)(2)(ii)(c) of this section) if the effective rate of tax imposed on the income of the purchasing or selling branch or similar establishment, or purchasing or selling remainder of the controlled foreign corporation, were tested under the principles of paragraph (b)(1)(i)(b) or (b)(1)(ii)(b) of this section against the effective rate of tax that would apply to such income if it were considered derived by such other branch or similar establishment or the remainder of the controlled foreign corporation.

(b) Activities treated as performed on behalf of the remainder of corporation. (1) With respect to purchasing or selling activities performed by or through the branch or similar establishment, such purchasing or selling activities will, with respect to personal property manufactured, produced, constructed, grown, or extracted by the remainder of the controlled foreign corporation, be treated as performed on behalf of the remainder of the controlled foreign corporation.

(2) With respect to purchasing or selling activities performed by or through the branch or similar establishment, such purchasing or selling activities will, with respect to personal property (other than property described in paragraph (b)(2)(ii)(b)(1) of this section) purchased or sold, or purchased and sold, by the remainder of the controlled foreign corporation (or any branch treated as the remainder of the controlled foreign corporation), be treated as performed on behalf of the remainder of the controlled foreign corporation.

(c) Activities treated as performed on behalf of branch. With respect to manufacturing, producing, constructing, growing, or extracting activities performed by or through the branch or similar establishment, purchasing or selling activities performed by or through the remainder of the controlled foreign corporation with respect to the personal property manufactured, produced, constructed, grown, or extracted by or through the branch or similar establishment shall be treated as performed on behalf of the branch or similar establishment.

(d) [Reserved by 76 FR 78546]

(e) Comparison with ordinary treatment. Income derived by a branch or similar establishment, or by the remainder of the controlled foreign corporation, will not be foreign base company sales income under paragraph (b) of this section if the income would not be foreign base company sales income if it were derived by a separate controlled foreign corporation under like circumstances.

(f) Priority of application. If income derived by the branch or similar establishment, or by the remainder of the controlled foreign corporation, from a transaction would be classified as foreign base company sales income of such controlled foreign corporation under section 954(d)(1) and paragraph (a) of this section, the income shall, notwithstanding this paragraph, be treated as foreign base company sales income under paragraph (a) of this section and the branch or similar establishment shall not be treated as a separate corporation with respect to such income.

(3) Inclusion of amounts in gross income of United States shareholders. A branch or similar establishment of a controlled foreign corporation and the remainder of such corporation shall be treated as separate corporations under this paragraph solely for purposes of determining the foreign base company sales income of each such corporation and for purposes of including an amount in subpart F income of the controlled foreign corporation under section 953(a). See section 954(b)(3) and paragraph (d)(4) of § 1.954–1 for rules relating to the treatment of a branch or similar establishment of a controlled foreign corporation and the remainder of such corporation as separate corporations for purposes of independently determining if the foreign base company income of each such corporation is less than 10 percent, or more than 70 percent, of its gross income. For all other purposes, however, a branch or similar establishment of a controlled foreign corporation and the remainder of such corporation shall not be treated as separate corporations. For example, if the controlled foreign corporation has a deficit in earnings and profits to which section 952(c) applies, the limitation of such section on the amount includable in the subpart F income of such corporation will apply. Moreover, income, war profits, or excess profits taxes paid by a branch or similar establishment to a foreign country will be treated as having been paid by the controlled foreign corporation for purposes of section 960 (relating to special rules for foreign tax credit) and the regulations thereunder. Also, income of a branch or similar establishment, treated as a separate corporation under this paragraph, will not be treated as dividend income of the controlled foreign corporation of which it is a branch or similar establishment.

(4) Illustrations. The application of this paragraph (b) may be illustrated by the following examples:

Example 1. Controlled foreign corporation A, incorporated under the laws of foreign country X, is engaged in the manufacturing business in such country. Corporation A negotiates sales of its products for use outside of country X through a sales office, branch B, maintained in foreign country Y. These activities constitute the only activities of A Corporation. Country X levies an income tax at an effective rate of 50 percent on the income of A Corporation derived by the manufacturing plant in country X but does not tax the sales income of A Corporation derived by branch B in country Y. Country Y levies an income tax at an effective rate of 10 percent on the sales income derived by branch B but does not tax the income of A Corporation derived by the manufacturing plant in country X. If the sales income derived by branch B were, under the laws of country X, derived from sources within country X by A Corporation, such income would be taxed by such country at an effective rate of 50 percent. In determining foreign base company sales income of A Corporation, branch B is treated as a separate wholly owned subsidiary corporation of A Corporation, the 10 percent rate of tax on branch B's income being less than 90 percent of, and at least 5 percentage points less than, the 50 percent rate. Income derived by branch B, treated as a separate corporation, from the sale by or through it for use, consumption, or disposition outside country Y of the personal property produced in country X is treated as income from the sale of personal property on behalf of A Corporation, a related person, and constitutes foreign base company sales income. The remainder of A Corporation, treated as a separate corporation, derives no foreign base company sales income since it produces the product which is sold.

Example 2. Controlled foreign corporation C is incorporated under the laws of foreign country X. Corporation C maintains branch B in foreign country Y. Branch B manufactures articles in country Y which are sold through the sales offices of C Corporation located in country X. These activities constitute the only activities of C Corporation. Country Y levies an income tax at an effective rate of 30 percent on the manufacturing profit of C Corporation derived by branch B but does not tax the sales income of C Corporation derived by the sales offices in country X. Country X does not impose an income, war profits, excess profits, or similar tax, and no tax is paid to any foreign country with respect to income of C Corporation which is not derived by branch B. If C Corporation were incorporated under the laws of country Y, the sales income of the sales offices in country X would be taxed by country Y at an effective rate of 30 percent. In determining foreign base company sales income of C Corporation, branch B is treated as a separate wholly owned subsidiary corporation of C Corporation, the zero rate of tax on the income derived by the remainder of C Corporation being less than 90 percent of, and at least 5 percentage points less than, the 30 percent rate. Branch B, treated as a separate corporation, derives no foreign base company sales income since it produces the product which is sold. Income derived by the remainder of C Corporation, treated as a separate corporation, from the sale by or through it for use, consumption, or disposition outside country X of the personal property produced in country Y is treated as income from the sale of personal property on behalf of branch B, a related person, and constitutes foreign base company sales income.

Example 3. (i) Facts. Corporation E, a controlled foreign corporation incorporated under the laws of foreign Country X, is a wholly owned subsidiary of Corporation D, also a controlled foreign corporation incorporated under the laws of Country X. Corporation E maintains Branch B in foreign Country Y. Both corporations use the calendar year as the taxable year. In 1964, Corporation E's sole activity, carried on through Branch B, consists of the purchase of articles manufactured in Country X by Corporation D, a related person, and the sale of the articles through Branch B to unrelated persons. One hundred percent of the articles sold through Branch B are sold for use outside Country X and 90% are also sold for use outside of Country Y. The income of Corporation E derived by Branch B from such transactions is taxed to Corporation E by Country X only at the time Corporation E distributes such income to Corporation D and is taxed on the basis of what the tax (a 40% effective rate) would have been if the income had been derived in 1964 by Corporation E from sources within Country X from doing business through a permanent establishment therein. Country Y levies an income tax at an effective rate of 50% on income derived from sources within such country, but the income of Branch B for 1964 is effectively taxed by Country Y at a 5% rate since under the laws of such country, only 10% of Branch B's income is derived from sources within such country. Corporation E makes no distributions to Corporation D in 1964.

(ii) Result. In determining foreign base company sales income of Corporation E for 1964, Branch B is treated as a separate wholly owned subsidiary corporation of Corporation E, the 5% rate of tax being less than 90% of, and at least 5 percentage points less than the 40% rate. Income derived by Branch B, treated as a separate corporation, from the purchase from a related person (Corporation D), of personal property manufactured outside of Country Y and sold for use, disposition, or consumption outside of Country Y constitutes foreign base company sales income. If, instead, Corporation D were unrelated to Corporation E, none of the income would be foreign base company sales income because Corporation E would be purchasing from and selling to unrelated persons and if Branch B were treated as a separate corporation it would likewise be purchasing from and selling to unrelated persons. Alternatively, if Corporation D were related to Corporation E, but Branch B manufactured the articles prior to sale under the principles of paragraph (a)(4)(iv) of this section, the income would not be foreign base company sales income because Branch B, treated as a separate corporation, would qualify for the manufacturing exception under paragraph (a)(4) of this section.

* * *

Example 8. Uniformly applicable incentive tax rate in one country. (i) Facts. FS is a controlled foreign corporation organized in Country M. FS operates one branch, Branch A, located in Country A. Branch A manufactures Product X within the meaning of paragraph (a)(4)(ii) or (a)(4)(iii) of this section. Raw materials used in the manufacture of Product X are purchased by FS from an unrelated person. FS engages in activities in Country M to sell Product X to a related person for use outside of Country M. Employees of FS located in Country M carry on only sales functions. The effective rate imposed in Country M on the income from the sale of Product X is 10%. Country A generally imposes an effective rate of tax on income of 20%, but imposes a uniformly applicable incentive rate of tax of 10% on manufacturing income and related sales income.

(ii) Result. The use of Branch A to manufacture Product X does not have substantially the same tax effect as if Branch A were a wholly owned subsidiary corporation of FS because the effective rate of tax on FS's sales income from the sale of Product X in Country M (10%) is not less than 90% of, and at least 5 percentage points less than, the effective rate of tax that would apply to such income in the country in which Branch A is located (10%). Consequently, pursuant to paragraph (b)(1)(ii)(b) of this section, Branch A is not treated as a separate corporation apart from the remainder of FS for purposes of determining foreign base company sales income.

Example 9. Manufacturing activities performed by multiple branches, no branch independently satisfies paragraph (a)(4)(i), selling activities carried on by remainder of the controlled foreign corporation, some branch manufacturing activities included in remainder contribution. (i) Facts. FS, a controlled foreign corporation organized in Country M, has three branches, Branch A, Branch B, and Branch C, located in Country A, Country B, and Country C respectively. FS purchases raw materials from a related person. The raw materials are manufactured (under the principles of paragraph (a)(4)(ii) or (a)(4)(iii) of this section) into Product X by CM, an unrelated corporation, pursuant to a contract manufacturing arrangement. CM physically performs the substantial transformation, assembly, or conversion required to manufacture Product X outside of FS's country of organization. FS manages the manufacturing costs and capacities with respect to the manufacture of Product X through employees located in Country M. Further, employees of FS located in Country M oversee the coordination between the branches. Branch A, through the activities of employees of FS located in Country A, designs Product X, controls manufacturing related logistics, and controls the raw materials and work-in-process during the manufacturing process. Branch B, through the activities of employees of FS located in Country B, provides quality control. Branch C, through the activities of employees of FS located in Country C, provides oversight and direction during the manufacturing process. Employees of FS located in Country M sell Product X to unrelated persons for use outside of Country M. Country M imposes an effective rate of tax on sales income of 10%. Country A imposes an effective rate of tax on sales income of 12%, Country B imposes an effective rate of tax on sales income of 24%, and Country C imposes an effective rate of tax on sales income of 25%. None of the remainder of FS, Branch A, Branch B, or Branch C independently satisfies paragraph (a)(4)(i) of this section. However, under the facts and circumstances of the business, FS, as a whole, provides a substantial contribution to the manufacture of Product X within the meaning of paragraph (a)(4)(iv) of this section. Under the facts and circumstances of the business, the activities of the remainder of FS and Branch A, if considered together, would not provide a greater contribution to the manufacture of Product X than the activities of Branch B and Branch C, if considered together. Under the facts and circumstances of the business, however, the activities of the employees of the remainder of FS and Branch A, if considered together, would constitute a substantial contribution to the manufacture of Product X.

(ii) Result. Based on the facts, neither the remainder of FS (through activities of its employees in Country M) nor any branch of FS independently satisfies paragraph (a)(4)(i) of this section with respect to Product X, but FS, as a whole, provides a substantial contribution through the activities of its employees to the manufacture of Product X. The remainder of FS, Branch A, Branch B, and Branch C each provide a contribution through the activities of employees to the manufacture of Product X. Therefore, FS must determine the location of manufacture under paragraph (b)(1)(ii)(c)(3)(iii) of this section. The tested sales location is Country M because the selling activities with respect to Product X are carried on by the remainder of FS. The location of Branch B is the tested manufacturing location because the effective rate of tax imposed on FS's sales income by Country M (10%) is less than 90% of, and at least 5 percentage points less than, the effective rate of tax that would apply to such income in Country B (24%), and Country B has the lowest effective rate of tax among the manufacturing branches that would, after applying paragraph (b)(1)(ii)(b) of this section, be treated as a separate corporation. The manufacturing activities performed in Country A by Branch A will be included in the contribution of the remainder of FS for purposes of determining the location of manufacture of Product X because the effective rate of tax imposed on the sales income by Country M (10%) is not less than 90% of, and at least 5 percentage points less than, the effective rate of tax that would apply to such income in Country A (12%). The manufacturing activities performed in Country C by Branch C will be included in the contribution of Branch B for purposes of determining the location of manufacture of Product X because the effective rate of tax imposed on the sales income by Country M (10%) is less than 90% of, and at least 5 percentage points less than, the effective rate of tax that would apply to such income in Country C (25%). Under the facts and circumstances of the business, the manufacturing activities of the remainder of FS and Branch A, considered together, would not provide a greater contribution to the manufacture of Product X than the activities of Branch B and Branch C, considered together. Therefore, the location of manufacture is Country B, the location of Branch B. In determining that Country B is the location of manufacture, it was determined that after applying paragraph (b)(1)(ii)(b) of this section Branch B would be treated as a separate corporation under paragraph (b)(1)(ii)(a) of this section for purposes of determining foreign base company sales income. To determine whether income from the sale of Product X is foreign base company sales income, the remainder of FS takes into account the activities of Branch A because, under paragraph (b)(2)(ii)(a) of this section, Branch A would not be treated as a separate corporation apart from FS. The remainder of FS is considered to have manufactured Product X under paragraph (a)(4)(i) of this section because the manufacturing activities of the remainder of FS and Branch A, considered together, would make a substantial contribution to the manufacture of Product X within the meaning of paragraph (a)(4)(iv) of this section. Therefore, income derived from the sale of Product X by the remainder of FS does not constitute foreign base company sales income.

* * *

[T.D. 6734, 29 FR 6392, May 15, 1964, as amended by T.D. 7545, 43 FR 32754, May 8, 1978; T.D. 7893, 48 FR 22508, May 19, 1983; T.D. 7894, 48 FR 22523, May 19, 1983; T.D. 9008, 67 FR 48025, July 23, 2002; T.D. 9438, 73 FR 79344, Dec. 29, 2008; 74 FR 11844, March 20, 2009; T.D. 9563, 76 FR 78546, Dec. 19, 2011]

§ 1.954–4 Foreign base company services income.

* * *

(b) Services performed for, or on behalf of, a related person—(1) Specific cases. For purposes of paragraph (a)(1) of this section, "services which are performed for, or on behalf of, a related person" include (but are not limited to) services performed by a controlled foreign corporation in a case where—

(i) The controlled foreign corporation is paid or reimbursed by, is released from an obligation to, or otherwise receives substantial financial benefit from, a related person for performing such services;

(ii) The controlled foreign corporation performs services (whether or not with respect to property sold by a related person) which a related person is, or has been, obligated to perform;

(iii) The controlled foreign corporation performs services with respect to property sold by a related person and the performance of such services constitutes a condition or a material term of such sale; or

(iv) Substantial assistance contributing to the performance of such services has been furnished by a related person or persons.

(2) Special rules—(i) Guaranty of performance. Subparagraph (1)(ii) of this paragraph shall not apply with respect to services performed by a controlled foreign corporation pursuant to a contract the performance of which is guaranteed by a related person, if (a) the related person's sole obligation with respect to the contract is to guarantee performance of such services, (b) the controlled foreign corporation is fully obligated to perform the services under the contract, and (c) the related person (or any other person related to the controlled foreign corporation) does not in fact (1) pay for performance of, or perform, any of such services the performance of which is so guaranteed or (2) pay for performance of, or perform, any significant services related to such services. If the related person (or any other person related to the controlled foreign corporation) does in fact pay for performance of, or perform, any of such services or any significant services related to such services, subparagraph (1)(ii) of this paragraph shall apply with respect to the services performed by the controlled foreign corporation pursuant to the contract the performance of which is guaranteed by the related person, even though such payment or performance is not considered to be substantial assistance for purposes of subparagraph (1)(iv) of this paragraph. For purposes of this subdivision, a related person shall be considered to guarantee performance of the services by the controlled foreign corporation whether it guarantees performance of such services by a separate contract of guaranty or enters into a service contract solely for purposes of guaranteeing performance of such services and immediately thereafter assigns the entire contract to the controlled foreign corporation for execution.

(ii) Application of substantial assistance test. For purposes of subparagraph (1)(iv) of this paragraph—

(a) Assistance furnished by a related person or persons to the controlled foreign corporation shall include, but shall not be limited to, direction, supervision, services, know-how, financial assistance (other than contributions to capital), and equipment, material, or supplies.

(b) Assistance furnished by a related person or persons to a controlled foreign corporation in the form of direction, supervision, services, or know-how shall not be considered substantial unless either (1) the assistance so furnished provides the controlled foreign corporation with skills which are a principal element in producing the income from the performance of such services by such corporation or (2) the cost to the controlled foreign corporation of the assistance so furnished equals 50 percent or more of the total cost to the controlled foreign corporation of performing the services performed by such corporation. The term "cost", as used in this subdivision (b), shall be determined after taking into account adjustments, if any, made under section 482.

(c) Financial assistance (other than contributions to capital), equipment, material, or supplies furnished by a related person to a controlled foreign corporation shall be considered assistance only in that amount by which the consideration actually paid by the controlled foreign corporation for the purchase or use of such item is less than the arm's length charge for such purchase or use. The total of such amounts so considered to be assistance in the case of financial assistance, equipment, material, and supplies furnished by all related persons shall be compared with the profits derived by the controlled foreign corporation from the performance of the services to determine whether the financial assistance, equipment, material, and supplies furnished by a related person or persons are by themselves substantial assistance contributing to the performance of such services. For purposes of this subdivision (c), determinations shall be made after taking into account adjustments, if any, made under section 482 and the term "consideration actually paid" shall include any amount which is deemed paid by the controlled foreign corporation pursuant to such an adjustment.

(d) Even though assistance furnished by a related person or persons to a controlled foreign corporation in the form of direction, supervision, services, or know-how is not considered to be substantial under (b) of this subdivision and assistance furnished by a related person or persons in the form of financial assistance (other than contributions to capital), equipment, material, or supplies is not considered to be substantial under (c) of this subdivision, such assistance may nevertheless constitute substantial assistance when taken together or in combination with other assistance furnished by a related person or persons which in itself is not considered to be substantial.

(e) Assistance furnished by a related person or persons to a controlled foreign corporation in the form of direction, supervision, services, or know-how shall not be taken into account under (b) or (d) of this subdivision unless the assistance so furnished assists the controlled foreign corporation directly in the performance of the services performed by such corporation.

* * *

[T.D. 6734, 29 FR 6399, May 15, 1964, as amended by T.D. 6981, 33 FR 16497, Nov. 13, 1968; T.D. 7893, 48 FR 22523, May 19, 1983; T.D. 9008, 67 FR 48025, July 23, 2002]

§ 1.956–1 Shareholder's pro rata share of the average of the amounts of United States property held by a controlled foreign corporation.

(a) Overview and scope—(1) In general. Subject to the provisions of section 951(a) and the regulations in this part, a United States shareholder of a controlled foreign corporation is required to include in gross income the amount determined under section 956 with respect to the shareholder for the taxable year but only to the extent not excluded from gross income under section 959(a)(2) and the regulations in this part. See § 1.958–1(d) for rules regarding the ownership of stock of a foreign corporation through a domestic corporation for purposes of section 956(a) * * *.

(2) Reduction for certain United States shareholders—(i) In general. For a taxable year of a controlled foreign corporation, the amount determined under section 956 with respect to each share of stock of the controlled foreign corporation owned (within the meaning of section 958(a)) by a United States shareholder is the amount that would be determined under section 956 with respect to such share for the taxable year, absent the application of this paragraph (a)(2) for the taxable year (such amount, the tentative section 956 amount, and in the aggregate with respect to all shares owned (within the meaning of section 958(a)) by the United States shareholder, the aggregate tentative section 956 amount), reduced by the amount of the deduction under section 245A, if any, that the shareholder would be allowed if the shareholder received as a distribution from the controlled foreign corporation an amount equal to the tentative section 956 amount with respect to such share on the last day during the taxable year on which the foreign corporation is a controlled foreign corporation (hypothetical distribution).

(ii) Determination of the amount of the deduction that would be allowed under section 245A with respect to a hypothetical distribution. For purposes of determining the amount of the deduction under section 245A that a United States shareholder would be allowed with respect to a share of stock of a controlled foreign corporation by reason of a hypothetical distribution, the rules in paragraphs (a)(2)(ii)(A) through (C) of this section apply—

(A) If a United States shareholder owns a share of stock of a controlled foreign corporation indirectly (within the meaning of section 958(a)(2)), then—

(1) Sections 245A(a) through (d), 246(a), and 959 apply to the hypothetical distribution as if the

United States shareholder directly owned (within the meaning of section 958(a)(1)(A)) the share;

(2) Section 245A(e) applies to the hypothetical distribution as if the distribution were made to the United States shareholder through each entity by reason of which the United States shareholder indirectly owns such share and pro rata with respect to the equity that gives rise to such indirect ownership;

(3) To the extent that a distribution treated as made to a controlled foreign corporation pursuant to the hypothetical distribution by reason of paragraph (a)(2)(ii)(A)(2) of this section would be subject to section 245A(e)(2), the United States shareholder is treated as not being allowed a deduction under section 245A by reason of the hypothetical distribution; and

(4) Section 246(c) applies to the hypothetical distribution by substituting the phrase "owned (within the meaning of section 958(a))" for the term "held" each place it appears in section 246(c);

(B) Section 246(c) applies to the hypothetical distribution by substituting "the last day during the taxable year on which the foreign corporation is a controlled foreign corporation" for the phrase "the date on which such share becomes ex-dividend with respect to such dividend" in section 246(c)(1)(A); and

(C) The hypothetical distribution is treated as attributable first to earnings and profits of the controlled foreign corporation described in section 959(c)(2), then to earnings and profits of the controlled foreign corporation described in section 959(c)(3).

* * *

[T.D. 6704, 29 FR 2600, Feb. 20, 1964, as amended by T.D. 6795, 30 FR 942, Jan. 29, 1965; T.D. 7712, 45 FR 52374, Aug. 7, 1980; T.D. 8209, 53 FR 22171, June 14, 1988; T.D. 9402, 73 FR 35582, June 24, 2008; T.D. 9530, 76 FR 36994, June 24, 2011; T.D. 9733, 80 FR 52981, Sept. 2, 2015; 80 FR 66416, Oct. 29, 2015; T.D. 9792, 81 FR 76505, Nov. 3, 2016; T.D. 9859, 84 FR 23717, May 23, 2019; 84 FR 29799, June 25, 2019; T.D. 9960, 87 FR 3654, Jan. 25, 2022]

§ 1.956–2 Definition of United States property.

* * *

(b) Exceptions—(1) Excluded property. For purposes of section 956(a) and paragraph (a) of this section, United States property does not include the following types of property held by a foreign corporation:

(i) Obligations of the United States.

(ii) Money.

(iii) Deposits with persons carrying on the banking business, unless the deposits serve directly or indirectly as a pledge or guarantee within the meaning of paragraph (c) of this section. See paragraph (e)(2) of § 1.956–1.

(iv) Property located in the United States which is purchased in the United States for export to, or use in, foreign countries. For purposes of this subdivision, property to be used outside the United States will be considered property to be used in a foreign country. Whether property is of a type described in this subdivision is to be determined from all the facts and circumstances in each case. Property which constitutes export trade assets within the meaning of section 971(c)(2) and paragraph (c)(3) of § 1.971–1 will be considered property of a type described in this subdivision.

(v) Any obligation (as defined in paragraph (d)(2) of this section) of a United States person (as defined in section 957(d)) arising in connection with the sale or processing of property if the amount of such obligation outstanding at any time during the taxable year of the foreign corporation does not exceed an amount which is ordinary and necessary to carry on the trade or business of both the other party to the sale or processing transaction and the United States person, or, if the sale or processing transaction occurs between related persons, would be ordinary and necessary to carry on the trade or business of both the other party to the sale or processing transaction and the United States person if such persons were unrelated persons. Whether the amount of an obligation described in this subdivision is ordinary and necessary is to be determined from all the facts and circumstances in each case.

(vi) Any aircraft, railroad rolling stock, vessel, motor vehicle, or container used in the transportation of persons or property in foreign commerce and used predominantly outside the United States. * * *

* * *

(viii) For taxable years beginning after December 31, 1975, the voting or nonvoting stock or obligations of an unrelated domestic corporation. For purposes of this subdivision, an unrelated domestic corporation is a domestic corporation which is neither a United States shareholder (as defined in section 951(b)) of the controlled foreign corporation making the investment, nor a corporation 25 percent or more of whose total combined voting power of all classes of stock entitled to vote is owned or considered as owned (within the meaning of section 958(b)) by United States shareholders of the controlled foreign corporation making the investment. The determination of whether a domestic corporation is an unrelated corporation is made immediately after each acquisition of stock or obligations by the controlled foreign corporations.

(ix) For taxable years beginning after December 31, 1975, movable drilling rigs or barges and other movable exploration and exploitation equipment (other than a vessel or an aircraft) when used on the Continental Shelf (as defined in section 638) of the United States in the exploration for, development, removal, or transportation of natural resources from or under ocean waters. * * *

* * *

(2) Statement required. If a United States shareholder of a controlled foreign corporation excludes any property from the United States property of such controlled foreign corporation on the ground that section 956(b)(2) applies to such excluded property, he shall attach to his return a statement setting forth, by categories described in paragraph (a)(1) of this section, the amount of United States property of the controlled foreign corporation and, by categories described in subparagraph (1) of this paragraph, the amount of such property which is excluded.

(c) Treatment of pledges and guarantees— (1) General rule. Except as provided in paragraph (c)(4) of this section, for purposes of section 956, any obligation of a United States person with respect to which a controlled foreign corporation or a partnership is a pledgor or guarantor will be considered to be held by the controlled foreign corporation or the partnership, as the case may be. See § 1.956–1(e)(2) for rules that determine the amount of the obligation treated as held by a pledgor or guarantor under this paragraph (c). For rules that treat an obligation of a foreign partnership as an obligation of the partners in the foreign partnership for purposes of section 956, see § 1.956–4(c).

(2) Indirect pledge or guarantee. If the assets of a controlled foreign corporation or a partnership serve at any time, even though indirectly, as security for the performance of an obligation of a United States person, then, for purposes of paragraph (c)(1) of this section, the controlled foreign corporation or partnership will be considered a pledgor or guarantor of that obligation. If a partnership is considered a pledgor or guarantor of an obligation, a controlled foreign corporation that is a partner in the partnership will not also be treated as a pledgor or guarantor of the obligation solely as a result of its ownership of an interest in the partnership. For purposes of this paragraph, a pledge of stock of a controlled foreign corporation representing at least 66 $^{2}/_{3}$ percent of the total combined voting power of all classes of voting stock of such corporation will be considered an indirect pledge of the assets of the controlled foreign corporation if the pledge is accompanied by one or more negative covenants or similar restrictions on the shareholder effectively limiting the corporation's discretion to dispose of assets and/or incur liabilities other than in the ordinary course of business. See § 1.956–4(d) for guidance on the treatment of indirect pledges or guarantees of an obligation of a partnership attributed to its partners under § 1.956–4(c).

(3) Illustrations. The following examples illustrate the application of this paragraph (c):

Example 1. A, a United States person, borrows $100,000 from a bank in foreign country X on December 31, 1964. On the same date controlled foreign corporation R pledges its assets as security for A's performance of A's obligation to repay such loan. The place at which or manner in which A uses the money is not material. For purposes of paragraph (b) of § 1.956–1, R Corporation will be considered to hold A's obligation to repay the bank $100,000, and, under the provisions of paragraph (e)(2) of § 1.956–1, the amount taken into account in computing R Corporation's aggregate investment in United States property on December 31, 1964, is the unpaid principal amount of the obligation on that date ($100,000).

Example 2. The facts are the same as in example 1, except that R Corporation participates in the transaction, not by pledging its assets as security for A's performance of A's obligation to repay the loan, but by agreeing to buy for $100,000 at maturity the note representing A's obligation if A does not repay the loan. Separate arrangements are made with respect to the payment of the interest on the loan. The agreement of R Corporation to buy the note constitutes a guarantee of A's obligation. For purposes of paragraph (b) of § 1.956–1, R Corporation will be considered to hold A's obligation to repay the bank $100,000, and, under the provisions of paragraph (e)(2) of § 1.956–1, the amount taken into account in computing R Corporation's aggregate investment in United States property on December 31, 1964, is the unpaid principal amount of the obligation on that date ($100,000).

Example 3. A, a United States person, borrows $100,000 from a bank on December 10, 1981, pledging 70 percent of the stock of X, a controlled foreign corporation, as collateral for the loan. A and X use the calendar year as their taxable year, in the loan agreement, among other things, A agrees not to cause or permit X Corporation to do any of the following without the consent of the bank:

(a) Borrow money or pledge assets, except as to borrowings in the ordinary course of business of X Corporation;

(b) Guarantee, assume, or become liable on the obligation of another, or invest in or lend funds to another;

(c) Merge or consolidate with any other corporation or transfer shares of any controlled subsidiary;

(d) Sell or lease (other than in the ordinary course of business) or otherwise dispose of any substantial part of its assets;

(e) Pay or secure any debt owing by X Corporation to A; and

(f) Pay any dividends, except in such amounts as may be required to make interest or principal payments on A's loan from the bank.

A retains the right to vote the stock unless a default occurs by A. Under paragraph (c)(2) of this section, the assets of X Corporation serve indirectly as security for A's performance of A's obligation to repay the loan and X Corporation will be considered a pledgor or guarantor with respect to that obligation. For purposes of paragraph (b) of § 1.956–1, X Corporation will be considered to hold A's obligation to repay the bank $100,000 and under paragraph (e)(2) of § 1.956–1, the amount taken into account in computing X Corporation's aggregate investment in United States property on December 31, 1981, is the unpaid principal amount of the obligation on that date.

Example 4. (i) Facts. USP, a domestic corporation, owns 70% of the stock of FS, a controlled foreign corporation, and a 90% interest in FPRS, a foreign partnership. X, an unrelated foreign person, owns 30% of the stock of FS. Y, an unrelated foreign person, owns a 10% interest in FPRS. There are no special allocations in the FPRS partnership agreement. FPRS borrows $100x from Z, an unrelated person. FS pledges its assets as security for FPRS's performance of its obligation to repay the $100x loan. USP's share of the $100x FPRS obligation, determined in accordance with its liquidation value percentage, is $90x. Under § 1.956–4(c), $90x of the FPRS obligation is treated as an obligation of USP for purposes of section 956.

(ii) Result. For purposes of section 956, under paragraph (c)(1) of this section, FS is considered to hold an obligation of USP in the amount of $90x, and thus is treated as holding United States property in the amount of $90x.

(4) Special rule for certain conduit financing arrangements. The rule contained in subparagraph (1) of this paragraph shall not apply to a pledge or a guarantee by a controlled foreign corporation to secure the obligation of a United States person if such United States person is a mere conduit in a financing arrangement. Whether the United States person is a mere conduit in a financing arrangement will depend upon all the facts and circumstances in each case. A United States person will be considered a mere conduit in a financing arrangement in a case in which a controlled foreign corporation pledges stock of its subsidiary corporation, which is also a controlled foreign corporation, to secure the obligation of such United States person, where the following conditions are satisfied:

(i) Such United States person is a domestic corporation which is not engaged in the active conduct of a trade or business and has no substantial assets other than those arising out of its relending of the funds borrowed by it on such obligation to the controlled foreign corporation whose stock is pledged; and

(ii) The assets of such United States person are at all times substantially offset by its obligation to the lender.

* * *

(d) Definitions—(1) Meaning of "acquired"—(i) Applicable rules. For purposes of this section—

(a) Property shall be considered acquired by a foreign corporation when such corporation acquires an adjusted basis in the property;

(b) Property which is an obligation of a United States person with respect to which a controlled foreign corporation is a pledgor or guarantor (within the meaning of paragraph (c) of this section) shall be considered acquired when the corporation becomes liable as a pledgor or guarantor or is otherwise considered a pledgor or guarantor (within the meaning of paragraph (c)(2) of this section); and * * *

[T.D. 6704, 29 FR 2601, Feb. 20, 1964, as amended by T.D. 7712, 45 FR 52374, Aug. 7, 1980; T.D. 8209, 53 FR 22171, June 14, 1988; T.D. 9008, 67 FR 48025, July 23, 2002; T.D. 9406, 73 FR 38117, July 3, 2008; T.D. 9525, 76 FR 26181, May 6, 2011; T.D. 9589, 77 FR 27614, May 11, 2012; T.D. 9761, 81 FR 20886, April 8, 2016; T.D. 9792, 81 FR 76507, Nov. 3, 2016; T.D. 9834, 83 FR 32524, July 12, 2018]

§ 1.956–4 Certain rules applicable to partnerships.

(a) Overview. This section provides rules concerning the application of section 956 to certain obligations of and property held by a partnership. Paragraph (b) of this section provides rules concerning United States property held indirectly by a controlled foreign corporation through a partnership. Paragraph (c) of this section provides rules that generally treat obligations of a foreign partnership as obligations of the partners in the foreign partnership, as well as a special rule that treats a partner that is a United States person as owing additional amounts of a partnership obligation in certain circumstances. Paragraph (d) of this section sets forth a rule concerning the application of the indirect pledge or guarantee rule to obligations of partnerships. Paragraph (e) of this section provides that obligations of a domestic partnership are obligations of a United States person. Paragraph (f) of this section provides effective and applicability dates. See §§ 1.956–1(b) and 1.956–2(c) for additional rules applicable to partnerships.

(b) Property held indirectly through a partnership—(1) General rule. For purposes of section 956, a partner in a partnership is treated as holding its attributable share of any property held by the partnership (including an obligation that the partnership is treated as holding as a result of the application of § 1.956–2(c)). A partner's attributable share of partnership property is determined under the rules set forth in paragraph (b)(2) of this section. An upper-tier partnership's attributable share of the property of a lower-tier partnership is treated as property of the upper-tier partnership for purposes of applying this paragraph (b)(1) to the partners of the upper-tier partnership. For purposes of section 956, a partner's adjusted basis in the property of the partnership equals the partner's attributable share of the partnership's adjusted basis in the property, as determined under the rules set forth in paragraph (b)(2) of this section, taking into account any adjustments to basis under section 743(b) (with respect to the partner) or section 734(b) or any similar adjustments to basis. The rules in § 1.956–1(e)(2) apply to determine the amount of an obligation treated as held by a partnership as a result of the application of § 1.956–2(c). See § 1.956–1(b) for special rules that may treat a controlled foreign corporation as holding a greater amount of United States property held by a partnership than the amount determined under this section.

(2) Methodology—(i) Liquidation value percentage—(A) Calculation. Except as otherwise provided in paragraph (b)(2)(ii) of this section, for purposes of paragraph (b)(1) of this section, a partner's attributable share of partnership property is determined in accordance with the partner's liquidation value percentage. For purposes of this paragraph (b)(2)(i) and paragraph (c)(1) of this section, the liquidation value of a partner's interest in a partnership is the amount of cash the partner would receive with respect to the interest if, on the applicable determination date, as provided in paragraph (b)(2)(i)(B) of this section, the partnership sold all of its assets for cash equal to the fair market value of such assets (taking into account section 7701(g)), satisfied all of its liabilities (other than those described in § 1.752–7), paid an unrelated third party to assume all of its § 1.752–7 liabilities in a fully taxable transaction, and then liquidated. A partner's liquidation value percentage is the ratio (expressed as a percentage) of the liquidation value of the partner's interest in the partnership divided by the aggregate liquidation value of all of the partners' interests in the partnership.

* * *

[T.D. 9792, 81 FR 76509, Nov. 3, 2016; 81 FR 95471, Dec. 28, 2016]

§ 1.957–1 Definition of controlled foreign corporation.

(a) In general. The term controlled foreign corporation means any foreign corporation of which more than 50 percent (or such lesser amount as is provided in section 957(b) or section 953(c)) of either—

(1) The total combined voting power of all classes of stock of the corporation entitled to vote; or

(2) The total value of the stock of the corporation, is owned within the meaning of section 958(a), or (except for purposes of section 953(c)) is considered as owned by applying the rules of section 958(b) and § 1.958–2, by United States shareholders on any day during the taxable year of such foreign corporation. For the definition of the term United States shareholder, see sections 951(b) and 953(c)(1)(A). For the definition of the term foreign corporation, see § 301.7701–5 of this chapter (Procedure and Administration Regulations). For the treatment of associations as corporations, see section 7701(a)(3) and §§ 301.7701–1 and 301.7701–2 of this chapter. For the definition of the term stock, see sections 958(a)(3) and 7701(a)(7). For the classification of a member in an association, joint stock company or insurance company as a shareholder, see section 7701(a)(8).

(b) Percentage of total combined voting power owned by United States shareholders—(1) Meaning of combined voting power. In determining for purposes of paragraph (a) of this section whether United States shareholders own the requisite percentage of total combined voting power of all classes of stock entitled to vote, consideration will be given to all the facts and circumstances of each case. In all cases, however, United States shareholders of a foreign corporation will be deemed to own the requisite percentage of total combined voting power with respect to such corporation—

(i) If they have the power to elect, appoint, or replace a majority of that body of persons exercising, with respect to such corporation, the powers ordinarily exercised by the board of directors of a domestic corporation;

(ii) If any person or persons elected or designated by such shareholders have the power, where such shareholders have the power to elect exactly one-half of the members of such governing body of such foreign corporation, either to cast a vote deciding an evenly divided vote of such body or, for the duration of any deadlock which may arise, to exercise the powers ordinarily exercised by such governing body; or

(iii) If the powers which would ordinarily be exercised by the board of directors of a domestic corporation are exercised with respect to such foreign corporation by a person whom such shareholders have the power to elect, appoint, or replace.

(2) Shifting of formal voting power. Any arrangement to shift formal voting power away from United States shareholders of a foreign corporation will not be given effect if in reality voting power is retained. The mere ownership of stock entitled to vote does not by itself mean that the shareholder owning such stock has the voting power of such stock for purposes of section 957. For example, if there is any agreement, whether express or implied, that any shareholder will not vote his stock or will vote it only in a specified manner, or that shareholders owning stock having not more than 50 percent of the total combined voting power will exercise voting power normally possessed by a majority of stockholders, then the nominal ownership of the voting power will be disregarded in determining which shareholders actually hold such voting power, and this determination will be made on the basis of such agreement. Moreover, where United States shareholders own shares of one or more classes of stock of a foreign corporation which has another class of stock outstanding, the voting power ostensibly provided such other class of stock will be deemed owned by any person or persons on whose behalf it is exercised or, if not exercised, will be disregarded if the percentage of voting power of such other class of stock is substantially greater than its proportionate share of the corporate earnings, if the facts indicate that the shareholders of such other class of stock do not exercise their voting rights independently or fail to exercise such voting rights, and if a principal purpose of the arrangement is to avoid the classification of such foreign corporation as a controlled foreign corporation under section 957.

* * *

[T.D. 6688, 28 FR 11631, Oct. 31, 1963; T.D. 8216, 53 FR 27510, July 21, 1988; T.D. 8618, 60 FR 46529, Sept. 7, 1995; 60 FR 62026, Dec. 4, 1995; T.D. 8704, 62 FR 21, Jan. 2, 1997]

§ 1.958–1 Direct and indirect ownership of stock.

(a) In general. Section 958(a) provides that, for purposes of sections 951 to 964 (other than sections 955(b)(1)(A) and (B) and 955(c)(2)(A)(ii) (as in effect before the enactment of the Tax Reduction Act of 1975), and 960(a)(1)), stock owned means—

(1) Stock owned directly; and

(2) Stock owned with the application of paragraph (b) of this section.

The rules of section 958(a) and this section provide a limited form of stock attribution primarily for use in determining the amount taxable to a United States shareholder under section 951(a). These rules also apply for purposes of other provisions of the Code and regulations which make express reference to section 958(a).

* * *

(d) Stock of foreign corporations owned through domestic partnerships—(1) In general. Except as otherwise provided in paragraph (d)(2) of this section, for purposes of sections 951, 951A, and 956(a), and for purposes of any provision that specifically applies by reference to any of such sections or the regulations in this part under section 951, 951A, or 956 (but only as the regulations in this part under section 956 relate to section 956(a)), a domestic partnership is not treated as owning stock of a foreign corporation within the meaning of section 958(a). For purposes of determining the persons that own stock of the foreign corporation within the meaning of section 958(a) when the preceding sentence applies, stock of a foreign corporation owned by a domestic partnership is treated in the same manner as stock of a foreign corporation owned by a foreign partnership under section 958(a)(2) and paragraph (b) of this section.

(2) Non-application for certain purposes. Paragraph (d)(1) of this section does not apply for purposes of—

(i) Determining whether any United States person is a United States shareholder (as defined in section 951(b));

(ii) Determining whether any foreign corporation is a controlled foreign corporation (CFC) (as defined in section 957(a));

(iii) Applying section 956(c) and (d);

(iv) Applying section 1248; or

(v) Determining whether any United States shareholder is a controlling domestic shareholder (as defined in § 1.964–1(c)(5)).

* * *

[T.D. 6889, 31 FR 9455, July 12, 1966, as amended by T.D. 7893, 49 FR 22509, May 19, 1983; T.D. 8955, 66 FR 37897, July 20, 2001; T.D. 9960, 87 FR 3654, Jan. 25, 2022; 87 FR 9445, Feb. 22, 2022]

§ 1.958–2 Constructive ownership of stock.

(a) In general. Section 958(b) provides that, for purposes of sections 951(b), 954(d)(3), 956(b)(2), and 957, the rules of section 318(a) as modified by section 958(b) and this section shall apply to the extent that the effect is to treat a United States person as a United States shareholder within the meaning of section 951(b), to treat a person as a related person within the meaning of section 954(d)(3), to treat the stock of a domestic corporation as owned by a United States shareholder of a controlled foreign corporation under section 956(b)(2), or to treat a foreign corporation as a controlled foreign corporation under section 957. The rules contained in this section also apply for purposes of other provisions of the Code and regulations which make express reference to section 958(b).

* * *

[T.D. 6889, 31 FR 9455, July 12, 1966, as amended by T.D. 7712, 45 FR 52375, Aug. 7, 1980; T.D. 8955, 66 FR 37897, July 20, 2001; T.D. 9883, 84 FR 63804, Nov. 19, 2019; T.D. 9908, 85 FR 59435, Sept. 22, 2020]

§ 1.962–1 Limitation of tax for individuals on amounts included in gross income under section 951(a).

(a) In general. An individual United States shareholder may, in accordance with § 1.962–2, elect to have the provisions of section 962 apply for his taxable year. In such case—

(1) The tax imposed under chapter 1 of the Internal Revenue Code on all amounts which are included in his gross income for such taxable year under section 951(a) shall (in lieu of the tax determined under section 1) be an amount equal to the tax which would be imposed under section 11 if such amounts were received by a domestic corporation (determined in accordance with paragraph (b)(1) of this section), and

(2) For purposes of applying sections 960(a) and 960(d) (relating to foreign tax credit) such amounts shall be treated as if received by a domestic corporation (as provided in paragraph (b)(2) of this section).

(3) Thus, an individual United States shareholder may elect to be subject to tax at corporate rates on amounts included in his gross income under section 951(a) and to have the benefit of a credit for certain foreign taxes paid with respect to the earnings and profits attributable to such amounts. Section 962 also provides rules for the treatment of an actual distribution of earnings and profits previously taxed in accordance with an election of the benefits of this section. See § 1.962–3.

(b) Rules of application. For purposes of this section—

(1) Application of section 11. For purposes of applying section 11 for a taxable year as provided in paragraph (a)(1) of this section in the case of an electing United States shareholder—

(i) Determination of taxable income. The term taxable income means the excess of—

(A) The sum of—

(1) All amounts required to be included in his gross income under section 951(a) for the taxable year with respect to a foreign corporation of which he is a United States shareholder, including—

(i) His section 965(a) inclusion amounts (as defined in § 1.965–1(f)(38)); and

(ii) His domestic pass-through owner shares (as defined in § 1.965–1(f)(21)) of section 965(a) inclusion amounts with respect to deferred foreign income corporations (as defined in § 1.965–1(f)(17)) of which he is a United States shareholder; plus

(2) His GILTI inclusion amount (as defined in § 1.951A–1(c)(1)) for the taxable year; plus

(3) All amounts which would be required to be included in his gross income under section 78 for the taxable year with respect to the amounts referred to in paragraph (b)(1)(i)(A)(1) and (2) of this section if the shareholder were a domestic corporation; over

(B) The sum of the following deductions, but no other deductions or amounts—

(1) His section 965(c) deduction amount (as defined in § 1.965–1(f)(42)) for the taxable year;

(2) His domestic pass-through owner shares of section 965(c) deduction amounts corresponding to the amounts referred to in paragraph (b)(1)(i)(A)(1)(ii) of this section; and

(3) The portion of the deduction under section 250 and § 1.250(a)–1 that would be allowed to a domestic corporation equal to the percentage applicable to global intangible low-taxed income for the taxable year under section 250(a)(1)(B) (including as modified by section 250(a)(3)(B)) multiplied by the sum of the amount described in paragraph (b)(1)(i)(A)(2) of this section and the amount described in paragraph (b)(1)(i)(A)(3) of this section that is attributable to the amount described in paragraph (b)(1)(i)(A)(2) of this section.

(ii) [Reserved by 85 FR 43109]

(2) Allowance of foreign tax credit—(i) In general. Subject to the applicable limitation of section 904 and to the provisions of this paragraph (b)(2), there shall be allowed as a credit against the United States tax on the amounts described in paragraph (b)(1)(i) of this section the foreign income, war profits, and excess profits taxes deemed paid under section 960(a) or section 960(d) by the electing United States shareholder with respect to such amounts.

(ii) Application of sections 960(a) and 960(d). In applying sections 960(a) and 960(d) for purposes of this paragraph (b)(2) in the case of an electing United States shareholder, the term "domestic corporation" as used in sections 960(a), 960(d), and 78, and the term "corporation" as used in sections 901 and 960(d)(2)(A) and (B), are treated as referring to such shareholder with respect to the amounts described in paragraph (b)(1)(i) of this section.

* * *

[T.D. 6858, 30 FR 13695, Oct. 28, 1965, as amended by T.D. 7413, 41 FR 12640, March 26, 1976; T.D. 9846, 84 FR 1874, Feb. 5, 2019; T.D. 9849, 84 FR 9236, March 14, 2019; T.D. 9901, 85 FR 43109, July 15, 2020]

Capital Gains and Losses

§ 1.1248–1 Treatment of gain from certain sales or exchanges of stock in certain foreign corporations.

(a) In general. (1) If a United States person (as defined in section 7701(a)(30)) recognizes gain on a sale or exchange after December 31, 1962, of stock in a foreign corporation, and if in respect of such person the conditions of subparagraph (2) of this paragraph are satisfied, then the gain shall be included in the gross income of such person as a dividend to the extent of the earnings and profits of such corporation attributable to such stock under § 1.1248–2 or 1.1248–3, whichever is applicable, which were accumulated in taxable years of such foreign corporation beginning after December 31, 1962, during the period or periods such stock was held (or was considered as held by reason of the application of section 1223, taking into account § 1.1248–8) by such person while such corporation was a controlled foreign corporation. * * *

(2) In respect of a United States person who sells or exchanges stock in a foreign corporation, the conditions referred to in subparagraph (1) of this paragraph are satisfied only if (i) such person owned, within the meaning of section 958(a), or was considered as owning by applying the rules of ownership of section 958(b), 10 percent or more of the total combined voting power of all classes of stock entitled to vote of such foreign corporation at any time during the 5-year period ending on the date of the sale or exchange, and (ii) at such time such foreign corporation was a controlled foreign corporation (as defined in section 957).

* * *

(4) For purposes of paragraph (a)(1) of this section, if a foreign partnership sells or exchanges stock of a corporation, the partners in such foreign partnership shall be treated as selling or exchanging their proportionate share of the stock of such corporation. Stock which is considered to have been sold or exchanged by a partner by reason of the application of this paragraph (a)(4) shall for purposes of applying such sentence be treated as actually sold or exchanged by such partner.

* * *

(d) Credit for foreign taxes. (1) If a domestic corporation includes an amount in its gross income as a dividend under section 1248(a) upon a sale or exchange of stock in a foreign corporation (referred to as a first tier corporation), and if on the date of the sale or exchange the domestic corporation owns directly at least 10 percent of the voting stock of the first tier corporation:

(i) The foreign tax credit provisions of sections 901 through 908 shall apply in the same manner and subject to the same conditions and limitations as if the first tier corporation on such date distributed to the domestic corporation as a dividend that portion of the amount included in gross income under section 1248(a) which does not exceed the earnings and profits of the first tier corporation attributable to the stock under § 1.1248–2 or § 1.1248–3, as the case may be, and

(ii) If on such date such first tier corporation owns directly 50 percent or more of the voting stock of a lower tier corporation described in paragraph (a)(3) of § 1.1248–2 or paragraph (a)(3) of § 1.1248–3, as the case may be (referred to as a second tier corporation), then the foreign tax credit provisions of sections 901 through 905 shall apply in the same manner and subject to the same conditions and limitations as if on such date (a) the domestic corporation owned directly that percentage of the stock in the second tier corporation which such domestic corporation is considered to own by reason of the application of section 958(a)(2), and (b) the second tier corporation had distributed to the domestic corporation as a dividend that portion of the amount included in gross income under section 1248(a) which does not exceed the earnings and profits of the second tier corporation attributable to such stock under § 1.1248–2 or § 1.1248–3, as the case may be.

(2) A credit shall not be allowed under subparagraph (1) of this paragraph in respect of taxes which are not actually paid or accrued. For the inclusion as a dividend in the gross income of a domestic corporation of an amount equal to the taxes deemed paid by such corporation under section 902(a)(1), see section 78.

* * *

(4) For purposes of paragraph (a)(1) of this section, if a foreign partnership sells or exchanges stock of a corporation, the partners in such foreign partnership shall be treated as selling or exchanging their proportionate share of the stock of such corporation. Stock which is considered to have been sold or exchanged by a partner by reason of the application of this paragraph (a)(4) shall for purposes of applying such sentence be treated as actually sold or exchanged by such partner.

* * *

[T.D. 6779, 29 FR 18130, Dec. 22, 1964, as amended by T.D. 7728, 45 FR 72650, Nov. 3, 1980; T.D. 7961, 49 FR 26225, June 27, 1984; T.D. 9345, 72 FR 41444, July 30, 2007; T.D. 9444, 74 FR 6828, Feb. 11, 2009; T.D. 9585, 77 FR 24381, April 24, 2012; T.D. 9614, 78 FR 17031, March 19, 2013; T.D. 10004, 89 FR 58285, July 18, 2024]

§ 1.1291–1 Taxation of U.S. persons that are shareholders of section 1291 funds.

(a) through (b)(2)(i) [Reserved]

(ii) Pedigreed QEF. A PFIC is a pedigreed QEF with respect to a shareholder if the PFIC has been a QEF with respect to the shareholder for all taxable years during which the corporation was a PFIC that are included wholly or partly in the shareholder's holding period of the PFIC stock.

(b)(2)(iii) and (iv) [Reserved]

(v) Section 1291 fund. A PFIC is a section 1291 fund with respect to a shareholder unless the PFIC is a pedigreed QEF with respect to the shareholder or a section 1296 election is in effect with respect to the shareholder.

(3) through (6) [Reserved]

(7) Shareholder. A shareholder is a United States person that directly owns stock of a PFIC (a direct shareholder), or that is an indirect shareholder (as defined in section 1298(a) and paragraph (b)(8) of this section), except as provided in paragraph (e) of this section. For purposes of sections 1291 and 1298, a domestic partnership or S corporation (as defined in section 1361(a)(1)) is not treated as a shareholder of a PFIC except for purposes of any information reporting requirements, including the requirement to file an annual report under section 1298(f). In addition, to the extent that a person is treated under sections 671 through 678 as the owner of a portion of a domestic trust, the trust is not treated as a shareholder of a PFIC with respect to PFIC stock held by that portion of the trust, except for purposes of the information reporting requirements of § 1.1298–1(b)(3)(i) (imposing an information reporting requirement on domestic liquidating trusts and fixed investment trusts).

(8) Indirect shareholder—(i) In general. An indirect shareholder of a PFIC is a United States person that indirectly owns stock of a PFIC. A person indirectly owns stock when it is treated as owning stock of a corporation owned by another person, including another United States person, under this paragraph (b)(8). In applying this paragraph (b)(8), the determination of a person's indirect ownership is made on the basis of all the facts and circumstances in each case; the substance rather than the form of ownership is controlling, taking into account the purposes of sections 1291 through 1298.

(ii) Ownership through a corporation—(A) Ownership through a non-PFIC foreign corporation. A person that directly or indirectly owns 50 percent or more in value of the stock of a foreign corporation that is not a PFIC is considered to own a proportionate amount (by value) of any stock owned directly or indirectly by the foreign corporation.

(B) Ownership through a PFIC. A person that directly or indirectly owns stock of a PFIC is considered to own a proportionate amount (by value) of any stock owned directly or indirectly by the PFIC. Section 1297(d) does not apply in determining whether a corporation is a PFIC for purposes of this paragraph (b)(8)(ii)(B).

(C) Ownership through a domestic corporation—(1) In general. Solely for purposes of determining whether a person satisfies the ownership threshold described in paragraph (b)(8)(ii)(A) of this section, a person that directly or indirectly owns 50 percent or more in value of the stock of a domestic corporation is considered to own a proportionate amount (by value) of any stock owned directly or indirectly by the domestic corporation.

(2) Non-duplication. Paragraph (b)(8)(ii)(C)(1) of this section does not apply to treat a United States person as owning (other than for purposes of applying the ownership threshold in paragraph (b)(8)(ii)(A) of this section) stock of a PFIC that is directly owned or considered owned indirectly within the meaning of this paragraph (b)(8) by another United States person (determined without regard to paragraph (b)(8)(ii)(C)(1)). See Example 1 of paragraph (b)(8)(iv) of this section.

(3) S corporations. The 50 percent limitation in paragraph (b)(8)(ii)(C)(1) of this section does not apply with respect to stock owned directly or indirectly by an S corporation. See paragraph (b)(8)(iii)(B) of this section for rules regarding stock owned directly or indirectly by an S corporation.

(iii) Ownership through pass-through entities—(A) Partnerships. If a foreign or domestic partnership directly or indirectly owns stock, the partners of the partnership are considered to own such stock proportionately in accordance with their ownership interests in the partnership.

(B) S Corporations. If an S corporation directly or indirectly owns stock, each S corporation shareholder is considered to own such stock proportionately in accordance with the shareholder's ownership interest in the S corporation.

(C) Estates and nongrantor trusts. If a foreign or domestic estate or nongrantor trust (other than an employees' trust described in section 401(a) that is exempt from tax under section 501(a)) directly or indirectly owns stock, each beneficiary of the estate or trust is considered to own a proportionate amount of such stock. For purposes of this paragraph (b)(8)(iii)(C), a nongrantor trust is any trust or portion of a trust that is not treated as owned by one or more persons under sections 671 through 679.

(D) Grantor trusts. If a foreign or domestic trust directly or indirectly owns stock, a person that is treated under sections 671 through 679 as the owner of any portion of the trust that holds an interest in the stock is considered to own the interest in the stock held by that portion of the trust.

(iv) Successive application. Stock considered to be owned by a person by reason of paragraphs (b)(8)(ii) or (iii) of this section is, for purposes of applying such paragraphs, considered to be actually owned by such person. Subject to the limitations provided in section 1298(a) and paragraphs (b)(8)(ii) and (b)(8)(iii) of this section, this paragraph applies by successively considering a person as actually owning its proportionate share of stock or other equity interest directly held by an entity directly owned by the person. Paragraph (b)(8)(ii)(C)(2) of this section applies after the other subparagraphs of paragraph (b)(8) of this section.

* * *

(c) Coordination with other PFIC rules.

(1), (2) [Reserved]

(3) Coordination with section 1296: distributions and dispositions. If PFIC stock is marked to market under section 1296 for any taxable year, then, except as provided in § 1.1296–1(i), section 1291 and the regulations thereunder shall not apply to any distribution with respect to section 1296 stock (as defined in § 1.1296–1(a)(2)), or to any disposition of such stock, for such taxable year.

(4) Coordination with mark to market rules under chapter 1 of the Internal Revenue Code other than section 1296—(i) In general. If PFIC stock is marked to market for any taxable year under section 475 or any other provision of chapter 1 of the Internal Revenue Code, other than section 1296, regardless of whether the application of such provision is mandatory or results from an election by the taxpayer or another person, then, except as provided in paragraph (c)(4)(ii) of this section, section 1291 and the regulations thereunder shall not apply to any distribution with respect to such PFIC stock or to any disposition of such PFIC stock for such taxable year. See §§ 1.1295–1(i)(3) and 1.1296–1(h)(3)(i) for rules regarding the automatic termination of an existing election under section 1295 or section 1296 when a taxpayer marks to market PFIC stock under section 475 or any other provision of chapter 1 of the Internal Revenue Code.

(ii) Coordination rule—(A) Notwithstanding any provision in this section to the contrary, the rule of paragraph (c)(4)(ii)(B) of this section shall apply to the first taxable year in which a United States person marks to market its PFIC stock under a provision of chapter 1 of the Internal Revenue Code, other than section 1296, if such foreign corporation was a PFIC for any taxable year, prior to such first taxable year, during the United States person's holding period (as defined in section 1291(a)(3)(A) and § 1.1296–1(f)) in such stock, and for which such corporation was not treated as a QEF with respect to such United States person.

(B) For the first taxable year of a United States person that marks to market its PFIC stock under any provision of chapter 1 of the Internal Revenue Code, other than section 1296, such United States person shall, in lieu of the rules under which the United States person marks to market, apply the rules of § 1.1296–1(i)(2) and (3) as if the United States person had made an election under section 1296 for such first taxable year.

* * *

[T.D. 8750, 63 FR 13, Jan. 2, 1998; T.D. 8870, 65 FR 5779, Feb. 7, 2000; T.D. 9123, 69 FR 24073, May 3, 2004; T.D. 9806, 81 FR 95465, Dec. 28, 2016; T.D. 9936, 86 FR 4555, Jan. 15, 2021]

§ 1.1296–1 Mark to market election for marketable stock.

(a) Definitions—(1) Eligible RIC. An eligible RIC is a regulated investment company that offers for sale, or has outstanding, any stock of which it is the issuer and which is redeemable at net asset value, or that publishes net asset valuations at least annually.

(2) Section 1296 stock. The term section 1296 stock means marketable stock in a passive foreign investment company (PFIC), including any PFIC stock owned directly or indirectly by an eligible RIC, for which there is a valid section 1296 election. Section 1296 stock does not include stock of a foreign corporation that previously had been a PFIC, and for which a section 1296 election remains in effect.

(3) Unreversed inclusions—(i) General rule. The term unreversed inclusions means with respect to any section 1296 stock, the excess, if any, of—

(A) The amount of mark to market gain included in gross income of the United States person under paragraph (c)(1) of this section with respect to such stock for prior taxable years; over

(B) The amount allowed as a deduction to the United States person under paragraph (c)(3) of this section with respect to such stock for prior taxable years.

(ii) Section 1291 adjustment. The amount referred to in paragraph (a)(3)(i)(A) of this section shall include any amount subject to section 1291 under the coordination rule of paragraph (i)(2)(ii) of this section.

(iii) Example. An example of the computation of unreversed inclusions is as follows:

Example. A, a United States person, acquired stock in Corp X, a foreign corporation, on January 1, 2005 for $150. At such time and at all times thereafter, Corp X was a PFIC and A's stock in Corp X was marketable. For taxable years 2005 and 2006, Corp X was a nonqualified fund subject to taxation under section 1291. A made a timely section 1296 election with respect to the X stock, effective for taxable year 2007. The fair market value of the X stock was $200 as of December 31, 2006, and $240 as of December 31, 2007. Additionally, Corp X made no distribution with respect to its stock for the taxable years at issue. In 2007, pursuant to paragraph (i)(2)(ii) of this section, A must include the $90 gain in the X stock in accordance with the rules of section 1291 for purposes of determining the deferred tax amount and any applicable interest. Nonetheless, for purposes of determining the amount of the unreversed inclusions pursuant to paragraph (a)(3)(ii) of this section, A will include the $90 of gain that was taxed under section 1291 and not the interest thereon.

(iv) Special rule for regulated investment companies. In the case of a regulated investment company which had elected to mark to market the PFIC stock held by such company as of the last day of the taxable year preceding such company's first taxable year for which such company makes a section 1296 election, the amount referred to in paragraph (a)(3)(i)(A) of this section shall include amounts previously included in gross income by the company pursuant to such mark to market election with respect to such stock for prior taxable years. For further guidance, see Notice 92–53 (1992–2 C.B. 384) (see also 601.601(d)(2) of this chapter).

(b) Application of section 1296 election—(1) In general. Any United States person and any controlled foreign corporation (CFC) that owns directly, or is treated as owning under this section, marketable stock, as defined in § 1.1296–2, in a PFIC may make an election to mark to market such stock in accordance with the provisions of section 1296 and this section.

(2) Election applicable to specific United States person. A section 1296 election applies only to the United States person (or CFC that is treated as a U.S. person under paragraph (g)(2) of this section) that makes the election. Accordingly, a United States person's section 1296 election will not apply to a transferee of section 1296 stock.

(3) Election applicable to specific corporation only. A section 1296 election is made with respect to a single foreign corporation, and thus a separate section 1296 election must be made for each foreign corporation that otherwise meets the requirements of this section. A United States person's section 1296 election with respect to stock in a foreign corporation applies to all marketable stock of the corporation that the person owns directly, or is treated as owning under paragraph (e) of this section, at the time of the election or that is subsequently acquired.

(c) Effect of election—(1) Recognition of gain. If the fair market value of section 1296 stock on the last day of the United States person's taxable year exceeds its adjusted basis, the United States person shall include in gross income for its taxable year the excess of the fair market value of such stock over its adjusted basis (mark to market gain).

(2) Character of gain. Mark to market gain, and any gain on the sale or other disposition of section 1296 stock, shall be treated as ordinary income.

(3) Recognition of loss. If the adjusted basis of section 1296 stock exceeds its fair market value on the last day of the United States person's taxable year, such person shall be allowed a deduction for such taxable year equal to the lesser of the amount of such excess or the unreversed inclusions with respect to such stock (mark to market loss).

(4) Character of loss—(i) Losses not in excess of unreversed inclusions. Any mark to market loss allowed as a deduction under paragraph (c)(3) of this section, and any loss on the sale or other disposition of section 1296 stock, to the extent that such loss does not exceed the unreversed inclusions attributable to such stock, shall be treated as an ordinary loss, deductible in computing adjusted gross income.

(ii) Losses in excess of unreversed inclusions. Any loss recognized on the sale or other disposition of section 1296 stock in excess of any prior unreversed inclusions will be subject to the rules generally applicable to losses provided elsewhere in the Internal Revenue Code and the regulations thereunder.

(5) Application of election to separate lots of stock. In the case in which a United States person purchased or acquired shares of stock in a PFIC at different prices, the rules of this section shall be applied in a manner consistent with the rules of § 1.1012–1.

(6) Source rules. The source of any amount included in gross income under paragraph (c)(1) of this section, or the allocation and apportionment of any amount allowed as a deduction under paragraph (c)(3) of this section, shall be determined in the same manner as if such amounts were gain or loss (as the case may be) from the sale of stock in the PFIC.

(7) Examples. The following examples illustrate this paragraph (c):

Example 1. Treatment of gain as ordinary income. A, a United States individual, purchases stock in FX, a foreign corporation that is not a PFIC, in 1990 for $1,000. On January 1, 2005, when the fair market value of the FX stock is $1,100, FX becomes a PFIC. A makes a timely section 1296 election for taxable year 2005. On December 31, 2005, the fair market value of the FX stock is $1,200. For taxable year 2005, A includes $200 of mark to market gain (the excess of the fair market value of FX stock ($1,200) over A's adjusted basis ($1,000)) in gross income as ordinary income and pursuant to paragraph (d)(1) of this section increases his basis in the FX stock by that amount.

Example 2. Treatment of gain as capital gain. The facts are the same as in Example 1. For taxable year 2006, FX does not satisfy either the asset test or the income test of section 1297(a). A does not revoke the section 1296 election it made with respect to the FX stock. On December 1, 2006, A sells the FX stock when the fair market value of the stock is $1,500. For taxable year 2006, A includes $300 of gain (the excess of the fair market value of FX stock ($1,500) over A's adjusted basis ($1,200)) in gross income as long-term capital gain because at the time of sale of the FX stock by A, FX did not qualify as a PFIC, and, therefore, the FX stock was not section 1296 stock at the time of the disposition. Further, A's holding period for non-PFIC purposes was more than one year.

Example 3. Treatment of losses as ordinary where they do not exceed unreversed inclusions. The facts are the same as in Example 1. On December 1, 2006, A sells the stock in FX for $1,100. At that time, A's unreversed inclusions (the amount A included in income as mark to market gain) with respect to the stock in FX are $200. Accordingly, for taxable year 2006, A recognizes a loss on the sale of the FX stock of $100, (the fair market value of the FX stock ($1,100) minus A's adjusted basis ($1,200) in the stock) that is treated as an ordinary loss because the loss does not exceed the unreversed inclusions attributable to the stock of FX.

Example 4. Treatment of losses as long-term capital losses. The facts are the same as in Example 3, except that FX does not satisfy either the asset test or the income test of section 1297(a) for taxable year 2006. For taxable year 2006, A's $100 loss from the sale of the FX stock is treated as long-term capital loss because at the time of the sale of the FX stock by A FX did not qualify as a PFIC, and, therefore, the FX stock was not section 1296 stock at the time of the disposition. Further, A's holding period in the FX stock for non-PFIC purposes was more than one year.

Example 5. Long-term capital loss treatment of losses in excess of unreversed inclusions. The facts are the same as in Example 3, except that A sells his FX stock for $900. At the time of A's sale of the FX stock on December 1, 2006, A's unreversed inclusions with respect to the FX stock are $200. Accordingly, the $300 loss recognized by A on the disposition is treated as an ordinary loss to the extent of his unreversed inclusions ($200). The amount of the loss in excess of A's unreversed inclusions ($100) will be treated as a long-term capital loss because A's holding period in the FC stock for non-PFIC purposes was more than one year.

Example 6. Application of section 1296 election to separate lots of stock. On January 1, 2005, Corp A, a domestic corporation, purchased 100 shares (first lot) of stock in FX, a PFIC, for $500 ($5 per share). On June 1, 2005, Corp A purchased 100 shares (second lot) of FX stock for $1,000 ($10 per share). Corp A made a timely section 1296 election with respect to its FX stock for taxable year 2005. On December 31, 2005, the fair market value of FX stock was $8 per share. For taxable year 2005, Corp A includes $300 of gain in gross income as ordinary income under paragraph (c)(1) of this section with respect to the first lot, and adjusts its basis in that lot to $800 pursuant to paragraph (d)(1) of this section. With respect to the second lot, Corp A is not permitted to recognize a loss under paragraph (c)(3) of this section for taxable year 2005. Although Corp A's adjusted basis in that stock exceeds its fair market value by $200, Corp A has no unreversed inclusions with respect to that particular lot of stock. On July 1, 2006, Corp A sells 100 shares of FX stock for $900. Assuming that Corp A adequately identifies (in accordance with the rules of § 1.1012–1(c)) the shares of FX stock sold as being from the second lot, Corp A recognizes $100 of long term capital loss pursuant to paragraph (c)(4)(ii) of this section.

(d) Adjustment to basis—(1) Stock held directly. The adjusted basis of the section 1296 stock shall be increased by the amount included in the gross income of the United States person under paragraph (c)(1) of this section with respect to such stock, and decreased by the amount allowed as a deduction to the United States person under paragraph (c)(3) of this section with respect to such stock.

(2) Stock owned through certain foreign entities. (i) In the case of section 1296 stock that a United States person is treated as owning through certain foreign entities pursuant to paragraph (e) of this section, the basis adjustments under paragraph (d)(1) of this section shall apply to such stock in the hands of the foreign entity actually holding such stock, but only for purposes of determining the subsequent treatment under chapter 1 of the Internal Revenue Code of the United States person with respect to such stock. Such increase or decrease in the adjusted basis of the section 1296 stock shall constitute an adjustment to the basis of partnership property only with respect to the partner making the section 1296 election. Corresponding adjustments shall be made to the adjusted basis of the United States person's interest in the foreign entity and in any intermediary entity described in paragraph (e) of this section through which the United States person holds the PFIC stock.

* * *

[T.D. 9123, 69 FR 24074, May 3, 2004; T.D. 9811, 82 FR 6242, Jan. 19, 2017]

Withholding of Tax on Nonresident Aliens and Foreign Corporations and Tax-Free Covenant Bonds

§ 1.1441–1 Requirement for the deduction and withholding of tax on payments to foreign persons.

(a) Purpose and scope. This section, §§ 1.1441–2 through 1.1441–9, and 1.1443–1 provide rules for withholding under sections 1441, 1442, and 1443 when a payment is made to a foreign person. This section provides definitions of terms used in chapter 3 of the Internal Revenue Code (Code) and regulations thereunder. It prescribes procedures to determine whether an amount must be withheld under chapter 3 of the Code and documentation that a withholding agent may rely upon to determine the status of a payee or a beneficial owner as a U.S. person or as a foreign person and other relevant characteristics of the payee that may affect a withholding agent's obligation to withhold under chapter 3 of the Code and the regulations thereunder. Special procedures regarding payments to foreign persons that act as intermediaries are also provided. Section 1.1441–2 defines the income subject to withholding under sections 1441, 1442, and 1443 and the regulations under these sections. Section 1.1441–3 provides rules regarding the amount subject to withholding and rules for coordinating withholding under this section with withholding under section 1445 and under chapter 4 of the Code. Section 1.1441–4 provides exemptions from withholding for, among other things, certain income effectively connected with the conduct of a trade or business in the United States, including certain compensation for the personal services of an individual. Section 1.1441–5 provides rules for withholding on payments made to flow-through entities and other similar arrangements. Section 1.1441–6 provides rules for claiming a reduced rate of withholding under an income tax treaty. Section 1.1441–7 defines the term withholding agent and provides due diligence rules governing a withholding agent's obligation to withhold. Section 1.1441–8 provides rules for relying on claims of exemption from withholding for payments to a foreign government, an international organization, a foreign central bank of issue, or the Bank for International Settlements. Sections 1.1441–9 and 1.1443–1 provide rules for relying on claims of exemption from withholding for payments to foreign tax exempt organizations and foreign private foundations.

(b) General rules of withholding—(1) Requirement to withhold on payments to foreign persons. A withholding agent must withhold 30 percent of any payment of an amount subject to withholding made to a payee that is a foreign person unless it can reliably associate the payment with documentation upon which it can rely to treat the payment as made to a payee that is a U.S. person or as made to a beneficial owner that is a foreign person entitled to a reduced rate of withholding. However, a withholding agent making a payment to a foreign person need not withhold where the foreign person assumes responsibility for withholding on the payment under chapter 3 of the Code and the regulations thereunder as a qualified intermediary (see paragraphs (e)(5) and (e)(6) of this section), as a U.S. branch of a foreign person (see paragraph (b)(2)(iv) of this section), as a withholding foreign partnership (see § 1.1441–5(c)(2)(i)), or as a withholding foreign trust (see § 1.1441–5(e)(5)(v)). When withholding under chapter 4 was applied to a payment, the withholding obligation under this section is satisfied. See § 1.1441–3(a)(2). This section (dealing with general rules of withholding and claims of foreign or U.S. status by a payee or a beneficial owner) and §§ 1.1441–4, 1.1441–5, 1.1441–6, 1.1441–8, 1.1441–9, and 1.1443–1 provide rules for determining whether documentation is required as a condition for reducing the rate of withholding on a payment to a foreign beneficial owner or to a U.S. payee and if so, the nature of the documentation upon which a withholding agent may rely in order to reduce such rate. Paragraph (b)(2) of this section prescribes the rules for the determination of who the payee is, the extent to which a payment is treated as made to a foreign payee, and reliable association of a payment with documentation. Paragraph (b)(3) of this section describes the applicable presumptions for determining the payee's status as U.S. or foreign and the payee's other characteristics (e.g., as an owner or intermediary, as an individual, partnership, corporation, etc.). Paragraph (b)(4) of this section lists the types of payments for which the 30-percent withholding rate may be reduced. Because the treatment of a payee as a U.S. or a foreign person also has consequences for purposes of making an information return under the provisions of chapter 61 of the Code and for withholding under other provisions of the Code, such as sections 3402, 3405, or 3406, paragraph (b)(5) of this section lists applicable provisions outside chapter 3 of the Code that require certain payees to establish their foreign status (e.g., in order to be exempt from information reporting). Paragraph (b)(6) of this section describes the withholding obligations of a foreign person making a payment that it has received in its capacity as an intermediary. Paragraph (b)(7) of this section describes the liability of a withholding agent that fails to withhold at the required 30-percent rate in the absence of documentation. Paragraph (b)(8) of this section deals with adjustments and refunds in the case of overwithholding. Paragraph (b)(9) of this section deals with determining the status of the payee when the payment is jointly owned. See paragraph (c)(6) of this section for a definition of beneficial owner. See § 1.1441–7(a) for a definition of withholding agent. See § 1.1441–2(a) for the determination of an amount subject to withholding. See § 1.1441–2(e) for the definition of a payment and when it is considered made. Except as otherwise provided, the provisions of this section apply only for purposes of determining a withholding agent's obligation to withhold under chapter 3 of the Code and the regulations thereunder.

(2) Determination of payee and payee's status—(i) In general. Except as otherwise provided in this paragraph (b)(2) and § 1.1441–5(c)(1) and (e)(3), a payee is the person to whom a payment is made, regardless of whether such person is the beneficial owner of the amount (as defined in paragraph (c)(6) of this section). A foreign payee is a payee who is a foreign person. A U.S. payee is a payee who is a U.S. person. Generally, the determination by a withholding agent of the U.S. or foreign status of a payee and of its other relevant characteristics (e.g., as a beneficial owner or intermediary, or as an individual, corporation, or flow-through entity) is made on the basis of a withholding certificate that is a Form W-8 or a Form 8233 (indicating foreign status of the payee or beneficial owner) or a Form W-9 (indicating U.S. status of the payee). The provisions of this paragraph (b)(2), paragraph (b)(3) of this section, and § 1.1441–5(c), (d), and (e) dealing with determinations of payee and applicable presumptions in the absence of documentation apply only to payments of amounts subject to withholding under chapter 3 of the Code (within the meaning of § 1.1441–2(a)). However, for a payment that is both an amount subject to withholding under chapter 3 and a withholdable payment under chapter 4, first apply the rules of § 1.1471–3 for determining the payee of a withholdable payment under chapter 4 and the applicable presumptions in the absence of documentation applicable to such payments. See also § 1.6049–5(d) for payments of amounts that are not subject to withholding under chapter 3 of the Code (or the regulations thereunder) but that may be reportable under provisions of chapter 61 of the Code (and the regulations thereunder). See paragraph (d) of this section for documentation upon which the withholding agent may rely in order to treat the payee or beneficial owner as a U.S. person.

See paragraph (e) of this section for documentation upon which the withholding agent may rely in order to treat the payee or beneficial owner as a foreign person. For applicable presumptions of status in the absence of documentation, see paragraph (b)(3) of this section and § 1.1441–5(d). For definitions of a foreign person and U.S. person, see paragraph (c)(2) of this section.

(ii) Payments to a U.S. agent of a foreign person. A withholding agent making a payment to a U.S. person (other than to a U.S. branch that is treated as a U.S. person pursuant to paragraph (b)(2)(iv) of this section) and who has actual knowledge that the U.S. person receives the payment as an agent of a foreign person must treat the payment as made to the foreign person. However, the withholding agent may treat the payment as made to the U.S. person if the U.S. person is a financial institution and the withholding agent has no reason to believe that the financial institution will not comply with its obligation to withhold. See paragraph (c)(5) of this section for the definition of a financial institution.

(iii) Payments to wholly-owned entities—(A) Foreign-owned domestic entity. A payment to a wholly-owned domestic entity that is disregarded for federal tax purposes under § 301.7701–2(c)(2) of this chapter as an entity separate from its owner and whose single owner is a foreign person shall be treated as a payment to the owner of the entity, subject to the provisions of paragraph (b)(2)(iv) of this section. * * *

(v) Payments to a foreign intermediary—(A) Payments treated as made to persons for whom the intermediary collects the payment. Except as otherwise provided in paragraph (b)(2)(v)(B) of this section, the payee of a payment to a person that the withholding agent may treat as a foreign intermediary in accordance with the provisions of paragraph (b)(3)(ii)(C) or (b)(3)(v)(A) of this section is the person or persons for whom the intermediary collects the payment. Thus, for example, the payee of a payment that the withholding agent can reliably associate with a withholding certificate from a qualified intermediary (defined in paragraph (e)(5)(ii) of this section) that does not assume primary withholding responsibility or a payment to a nonqualified intermediary are the persons for whom the qualified intermediary or nonqualified intermediary acts and not to the intermediary itself. See paragraph (b)(3)(v) of this section for presumptions that apply if the payment cannot be reliably associated with valid documentation. For similar rules for payments to flow-through entities, see § 1.1441–5(c)(1) and (e)(3).

(B) Payments treated as made to foreign intermediary. The payee of a payment to a person that the withholding agent may treat as a qualified intermediary is the qualified intermediary to the extent that the qualified intermediary assumes primary withholding responsibility under paragraph (e)(5)(iv) of this section for the payment. For example if a qualified intermediary assumes primary withholding responsibility under chapter 3 of the Internal Revenue Code but does not assume primary reporting or withholding responsibility under chapter 61 or section 3406 of the Internal Revenue Code and therefore provides Forms W-9 for U.S. non-exempt recipients, the qualified intermediary is the payee except to the extent the payment is reliably associated with a Form W-9 from a U.S. non-exempt recipient.

(vi) Other payees. A payment to a person described in § 1.6049–4(c)(1)(ii) that the withholding agent would treat as a payment to a foreign person without obtaining documentation for purposes of information reporting under section 6049 (if the payment were interest) is treated as a payment to a foreign payee for purposes of chapter 3 of the Code and the regulations thereunder (or to a foreign beneficial owner to the extent provided in paragraph (e)(1)(ii)(A)(6) or (7) of this section). Further, a payment that the withholding agent can reliably associate with documentary evidence described in § 1.6049–5(c)(1) relating to the payee is treated as a payment to a foreign payee. See § 1.1441–5(b)(1) and (c)(1) for payee determinations for payments to partnerships. See § 1.1441–5(e) for payee determinations for payments to foreign trusts or foreign estates.

(vii) Rules for reliably associating a payment with a withholding certificate or other appropriate documentation—(A) Generally. The presumption rules of paragraph (b)(3) of this section and §§ 1.1441–5(d) and (e)(6) and 1.6049–5(d) apply to any payment, or portion of a payment, that a withholding agent cannot reliably associate with valid documentation. Generally, a withholding agent can reliably associate a payment with valid documentation if, prior to the payment, it holds valid documentation (either directly or through an agent), it can reliably determine how much of the payment relates to the valid documentation, and it has no actual knowledge or reason to know that any of the information, certifications, or statements in, or associated with, the documentation are incorrect. * * *

* * *

(c) Definitions. The following definitions apply for purposes of sections 1441 through 1443, 1461, and regulations under those sections. For definitions of terms used in these regulations that are defined under sections 1471 through 1474, see subparagraphs (43) through (56) of this paragraph.

(1) Withholding. The term withholding means the deduction and withholding of tax at the applicable rate from the payment.

* * *

(6) Beneficial owner—(i) General rule. This paragraph (c)(6) defines the term beneficial owner for payments of income other than a payment for which a reduced rate of withholding is claimed under an income tax treaty. The term beneficial owner means the person who is the owner of the income for tax purposes and who beneficially owns that income. A person shall be treated as the owner of the income to the extent that it is required under U.S. tax principles to include the amount paid in gross income under section 61 (determined without regard to an exclusion or exemption from gross income under the Internal Revenue Code). Beneficial ownership of income is determined under the provisions of section 7701(*l*) and the regulations under that section and any other applicable general U.S. tax principles, including principles governing the determination of whether a transaction is a conduit transaction. Thus, a person receiving income in a capacity as a nominee, agent, or custodian for another person is not the beneficial owner of the income. In the case of a scholarship, the student receiving the scholarship is the beneficial owner of that scholarship. In the case of a payment of an amount that is not income, the beneficial owner determination shall be made under this paragraph (c)(6) as if the amount were income.

(d) Beneficial owner's or payee's claim of U.S. status—(1) In general. Under paragraph (b)(1) of this section, a withholding agent is not required to withhold under chapter 3 of the Code on payments to a U.S. payee, to a person presumed to be a U.S. payee in accordance with the provisions of paragraph (b)(3) of this section, or to a person that the withholding agent may treat as a U.S. beneficial owner of the payment. Absent actual knowledge or reason to know otherwise, a withholding agent may rely on the provisions of this paragraph (d) in order to determine whether to treat a payee or beneficial owner as a U.S. person.

* * *

(2) Payments for which a Form W-9 is otherwise required. A withholding agent may treat as a U.S. payee any person who is required to furnish a Form W-9 and who furnishes it in accordance with the procedures described in §§ 31.3406(d)–1 through 31.3406(d)–5 of this chapter (including the requirement that the payee furnish its taxpayer identifying number (TIN)) if the withholding agent meets all the requirements described in § 31.3406(h)–3(e) of this chapter regarding reliance by a payor on a Form W-9. Providing a Form W-9 or valid substitute form shall serve as a statement that the person whose name is on the form is a U.S. person. Therefore, a foreign person, including a U.S. branch treated as a U.S. person under paragraph (b)(2)(iv) of this section, shall not provide a Form W-9. A U.S. branch of a foreign person may establish its status as a foreign person exempt from reporting under chapter 61 and backup withholding under section 3406 by providing a withholding certificate on Form W-8.

(3) Payments for which a Form W-9 is not otherwise required. In the case of a payee who is not required to furnish a Form W-9 under section 3406 (e.g., a person exempt from reporting under chapter 61 of the Internal Revenue Code), the withholding agent may treat the payee as a U.S. payee if the payee provides the withholding agent with a Form W-9 or a substitute form described in § 31.3406(h)–3(c)(2) of this chapter (relating to forms for exempt recipients) that contains the payee's name, address, and TIN. * * *

(4) When a payment to an intermediary or flow-through entity may be treated as made to a U.S. payee. A withholding agent that makes a payment to an intermediary (whether a qualified intermediary or nonqualified intermediary), a flow-through entity, or a U.S. branch or territory financial institution described in paragraph (b)(2)(iv) of this section may treat the payment as made to a U.S. payee to the extent that, prior to the payment, the withholding agent can reliably associate the payment with a Form W-9 described in paragraph (d)(2) or (3) of this section attached to a valid intermediary, flow-through, or U.S. branch withholding certificate described in paragraph (e)(3)(i) of this section or to the extent the withholding agent can reliably associate the payment with a Form W-8 described in paragraph (e)(3)(v) of this section that evidences an agreement to treat a U.S. branch or territory financial institution described in paragraph (b)(2)(iv) of this section as a U.S. person. * * *

(e) Beneficial owner's claim of foreign status—(1) Withholding agent's reliance—(i) In general. Absent actual knowledge or reason to know otherwise, a withholding agent may treat a payment as made to a foreign beneficial owner in accordance with the provisions of paragraph (e)(1)(ii) of this section. See paragraph (e)(4)(viii) of this section for applicable reliance rules. See paragraph (b)(4) of this section for a description of payments for which a claim of foreign status is relevant for purposes of claiming a reduced rate of withholding for purposes of section 1441, 1442, or 1443. See paragraph (b)(5) of this section for a list of payments for which a claim of foreign status is relevant for other purposes, such as claiming an exemption from information reporting under chapter 61 of the Code.

(ii) Payments that a withholding agent may treat as made to a foreign person that is a beneficial owner—(A) General rule. The withholding agent may treat a payment as made to a foreign person that is a beneficial owner if it complies with the requirements described in paragraph (e)(1)(ii)(B) of this section and, then, only to the extent—

(1) That the withholding agent can reliably associate the payment with a beneficial owner withholding certificate described in paragraph (e)(2) of this section furnished by the person whose name is on the certificate or attached to a valid foreign intermediary, flow-through, or U.S. branch withholding certificate;

(2) That the payment is made outside the United States (within the meaning of § 1.6049–5(e)) with respect to an offshore obligation (within the meaning of paragraph (c)(37) of this section) and the withholding agent can reliably associate the payment with documentary evidence described in §§ 1.1441–6(c)(3) or (4), or 1.6049–5(c)(1) relating to the beneficial owner;

(3) That the withholding agent can reliably associate the payment with a valid qualified intermediary withholding certificate, as described in paragraph (e)(3)(ii) of this section, and the qualified intermediary has provided sufficient information for the withholding agent to allocate the payment to a chapter 3 withholding rate pool;

(4) That the withholding agent can reliably associate the payment with a withholding certificate described in § 1.1441–5(c)(3)(iii) or (e)(5)(iii) from a flow-through entity claiming the income is effectively connected income;

(5) That the withholding agent identifies the payee as a U.S. branch described in paragraph (b)(2)(iv) of this section, the payment to which it treats as effectively connected income in accordance with § 1.1441–4(a)(2)(ii) or (3);

* * *

(B) Additional requirements. In order for a payment described in paragraph (e)(1)(ii)(A) of this section to be treated as made to a foreign beneficial owner, the withholding agent must hold the documentation (if required) prior to the payment, comply with the electronic confirmation procedures described in paragraph (e)(4)(v) of this section (if required), and must not have been notified by the IRS that any of the information on the withholding certificate or other documentation is incorrect or unreliable. If the withholding agent has been so notified, it may rely on the withholding certificate or other documentation only to the extent provided under procedures prescribed by the IRS (see § 601.601(d)(2) of this chapter). See paragraph (b)(2)(vii) of this section for rules regarding reliable association of a payment with a withholding certificate or other appropriate documentation.

(2) Beneficial owner withholding certificate—(i) In general. A beneficial owner withholding certificate is a statement by which the beneficial owner of the payment represents that it is a foreign person and, if applicable, claims a reduced rate of withholding under section 1441. this paragraph (e)(3)(v).* * *

* * *

(5) Qualified intermediaries—(i) In general. A qualified intermediary, as defined in paragraph (e)(5)(ii) of this section, may furnish a qualified intermediary withholding certificate to a withholding agent. The withholding certificate provides certifications on behalf of other persons for the purpose of claiming and verifying reduced rates of withholding under section 1441 or 1442 and for the purpose of reporting and withholding under other provisions of the Code, such as the provisions under chapter 61 and section 3406 (and the regulations under those provisions), or for the qualified derivative dealer (if applicable). Furnishing such a certificate is in lieu of transmitting to a withholding agent withholding certificates or other appropriate documentation for the persons for whom the qualified intermediary receives the payment, including interest holders in a qualified intermediary that is fiscally transparent under the regulations under section 894. Although the qualified intermediary is required to obtain withholding certificates or other appropriate documentation from beneficial owners, payees, or interest holders pursuant to its agreement with the IRS, it is generally not required to attach such documentation to the intermediary withholding certificate. Notwithstanding the preceding sentence, a qualified intermediary must provide a withholding agent with the Forms W-9, or disclose the names, addresses, and taxpayer identifying numbers, if known, of those U.S. non-exempt recipients for whom the qualified intermediary receives reportable amounts (within the meaning of paragraph (e)(3)(vi) of this section) to the extent required in the qualified intermediary's agreement with the IRS. When a qualified intermediary is acting as a qualified derivatives dealer, the withholding certificate entitles a withholding agent to make payments with respect to potential section 871(m) transactions that are not underlying securities and dividend equivalent payments on underlying securities to the qualified derivatives dealer free of withholding. A withholding agent is required to withhold on all other U.S. source FDAP payments made to a qualified derivatives dealer as required by applicable law. Paragraph (e)(6) of this section contains detailed rules prescribing the circumstances in which a qualified intermediary can act as a qualified derivatives dealer. A person may claim qualified intermediary status before an agreement is executed with the IRS if it has applied for such status and the IRS authorizes such status on an interim basis under such procedures as the IRS may prescribe.

(ii) [Reserved]. For additional guidance, see § 1.1441–1T(e)(5)(ii).

* * *

[T.D. 6500, 25 FR 12073, Nov. 6, 1960, as amended by T.D. 6592, 27 FR 1888, Feb. 28, 1962; T.D. 6908, 31 FR 16770, Dec. 31, 1966; T.D. 7385, 40 FR 50263, Oct. 29, 1975; T.D. 7670, 45 FR 6932, Jan. 31, 1980; T.D. 8734, 62 FR 53424, Oct. 14, 1997; T.D. 8804, 63 FR 72183, 72184, 72187, Dec. 31, 1998; T.D. 8856, 64 FR 73408, 73409, 73412, Dec. 30, 1999; 65 FR 16319, March 28, 2000; T.D. 8881, 65 FR 32170, 32211, May 22, 2000; 66 FR 18188, April 6, 2001; T.D. 9023, 67 FR 70312, Nov. 22, 2002; T.D. 9253, 71 FR 13005, March 14, 2006; T.D. 9323, 72 FR 18388, April 12, 2007; T.D. 9658, 79 FR 12747, March 6, 2014; 79 FR 37182, July 1, 2014; T.D. 9734, 80 FR 56888, Sept. 18, 2015; 80 FR 75946, Dec. 7, 2015; T.D. 9808, 82 FR 2059, Jan. 6, 2017; T.D. 9815, 82 FR 8162, Jan. 24, 2017]

§ 1.1441–1T Requirement for the deduction and withholding of tax on payments to foreign persons (temporary).

* * *

(5) Qualified Intermediaries—(i) [Reserved]. For additional guidance, see § 1.1441–1(e)(5)(i).

(ii) Definition of qualified intermediary. With respect to a payment to a foreign person, the term qualified intermediary means a person that is a party to a withholding agreement with the IRS and such person is—

(A) A foreign financial institution that is a participating FFI (including a reporting Model 2 FFI), a registered deemed-compliant FFI (including a reporting Model 1 FFI), an FFI treated as a deemed-compliant FFI under an applicable IGA that is subject to due diligence and reporting requirements with respect to its U.S. accounts similar to those applicable to a registered deemed-compliant FFI under § 1.1471–5(f)(1), excluding a U.S. branch of any of the foregoing entities, or any other category of FFI identified in a qualified intermediary agreement as eligible to act as a qualified intermediary;

(B) A foreign branch or office of a U.S. financial institution or a foreign branch or office of a U.S. clearing organization that is either a reporting Model 1 FFI or agrees to the reporting requirements applicable to a participating FFI with respect to its U.S. accounts;

(C) A foreign corporation for purposes of presenting claims of benefits under an income tax treaty on behalf of its shareholders to the extent permitted to act as a qualified intermediary by the IRS; or

(D) [Reserved]. For additional guidance, see § 1.1441–1(e)(5)(ii)(D).

(E) Any other person acceptable to the IRS.

* * *

[T.D. 9658, 79 FR 12749, March 6, 2014; 79 FR 37182, July 1, 2014; T.D. 9734, 80 FR 56888, Sept. 18, 2015; 80 FR 75946, Dec. 7, 2015; T.D. 9808, 82 FR 2083, Jan. 6, 2017; T.D. 9815, 82 FR 8164, Jan. 24, 2017]

§ 1.1441–2 Amounts subject to withholding.

(a) In general. For purposes of the regulations under chapter 3 of the Internal Revenue Code, the term amounts subject to withholding means amounts from sources within the United States that constitute either fixed or determinable annual or periodical income described in paragraph (b) of this section or other amounts subject to withholding described in paragraph (c) of this section. For purposes of this paragraph (a), an amount shall be treated as being from sources within the United States if the source of the amount cannot be determined at the time of payment. See § 1.1441–3(d)(1) for determining the amount to be withheld from a payment in the absence of information at the time of payment regarding the source of the amount. Amounts subject to withholding include amounts that are not fixed or determinable annual or periodical income and upon which withholding is specifically required under a provision of this section or another section of the regulations under chapter 3 of the Internal Revenue Code (such as corporate distributions upon which withholding is required under § 1.1441–3(c)(1) that do not constitute dividend income). Amounts subject to withholding do not include—

(1) Amounts described in § 1.1441–1(b)(4)(i) to the extent they involve interest on obligations in bearer form or on foreign-targeted registered obligations (but, in the case of a foreign-targeted registered obligation, only to the extent of those amounts paid to a registered owner that is a financial institution within the meaning of section 871(h)(5)(B) or a member of a clearing organization which member is the beneficial owner of the obligation);

(2) Amounts described in § 1.1441–1(b)(4)(ii) (dealing with bank deposit interest and similar types of interest (including original issue discount) described in section 871(i)(2)(A) or 881(d));

(3) Amounts described in § 1.1441–1(b)(4)(iv) (dealing with interest or original issue discount on certain short-term obligations described in section 871(g)(1)(B) or 881(e));

(4) Amounts described in § 1.1441–1(b)(4)(xx) (dealing with income from certain gambling winnings exempt from tax under section 871(j));

(5) Amounts paid as part of the purchase price of an obligation sold or exchanged between interest payment dates, unless the sale or exchange is part of a plan the principal purpose of which is to avoid tax and the withholding agent has actual knowledge or reason to know of such plan;

(6) Original issue discount paid as part of the purchase price of an obligation sold or exchanged in a transaction other than a redemption of such obligation, unless the purchase is part of a plan the principal purpose of which is to avoid tax and the withholding agent has actual knowledge or reason to know of such plan; and

(7) Insurance premiums paid with respect to a contract that is subject to the section 4371 excise tax.

(b) Fixed or determinable annual or periodical income—(1) In general—(i) Definition. For purposes of chapter 3 of the Internal Revenue Code and the regulations thereunder, fixed or determinable annual or periodical income includes all income included in gross income under section 61 (including original issue discount) except for the items specified in paragraph (b)(2) of this section. Items of income that are excluded from gross income under a provision of law without regard to the U.S. or foreign status of the owner of the income, such as interest excluded from gross income under section 103(a) or qualified scholarship income under section 117, shall not be treated as fixed or determinable annual or periodical income under chapter 3 of the Internal Revenue Code. Income excluded from gross income under section 892 (income of foreign governments) or section 115 (income of a U.S. possession) is fixed or determinable annual or periodical income since the exclusion from gross income under those sections is dependent on the foreign status of the owner of the income. See § 1.306–3(h) for treating income from the disposition of section 306 stock as fixed or determinable annual or periodical income.

(ii) Manner of payment. The term fixed or determinable annual or periodical is merely descriptive of the character of a class of income. If an item of income falls within the class of income contemplated in the statute and described in paragraph (a) of this section, it is immaterial whether payment of that item is made in a series of payments or in a single lump sum. Further, the income need not be paid annually if it is paid periodically; that is to say, from time to time, whether or not at regular intervals. The fact that a payment is not made annually or periodically does not, however, prevent it from being fixed or determinable annual or periodical income (e.g., a lump sum payment). In addition, the fact that the length of time during which the payments are to be made may be increased or diminished in accordance with someone's will or with the happening of an event does not disqualify the payment as determinable or periodical. For this purpose, the share of the fixed or determinable annual or periodical income of an estate or trust from sources within the United States which is required to be distributed currently, or which has been paid or credited during the taxable year, to a nonresident alien beneficiary of such estate or trust constitutes fixed or determinable annual or periodical income.

(iii) Determinability of amount. An item of income is fixed when it is to be paid in amounts definitely pre-determined. An item of income is determinable if the amount to be paid is not known but there is a basis of calculation by which the amount may be ascertained at a later time. For example, interest is determinable even if it is contingent in that its amount cannot be determined at the time of payment of an amount with respect to a loan because the calculation of the interest portion of the payment is contingent upon factors that are not fixed at the time of the payment. For purposes of this section, an amount of income does not have to be determined at the time that the payment is made in order to be determinable. An amount of income described in paragraph (a) of this section which the withholding agent knows is part of a payment it makes but which it cannot calculate exactly at the time of payment, is nevertheless determinable if the determination of the exact amount depends upon events expected to occur at a future date. In contrast, a payment which may be income in the future based upon events that are not anticipated at the time the payment is made is not determinable. For example, loan proceeds may become income to the borrower when and to the extent the loan is canceled without repayment. While the cancellation of the debt is income to the borrower when it occurs, it is not determinable at the time the loan proceeds are disbursed to the borrower if the lack of repayment leading to the cancellation of part or all of the debt was not anticipated at the time of disbursement. The fact that the source of an item of income cannot be determined at the time that the payment is made does not render a payment not determinable. See § 1.1441–3(d)(1) for determining the amount to be withheld from a payment in the absence of information at the time of payment regarding the source of the amount.

(2) Exceptions. For purposes of chapter 3 of the Code and the regulations thereunder, the items of income described in this paragraph (b)(2) are not fixed or determinable annual or periodical income—

(i) Gains derived from the sale of property (including market discount and option premiums), except for gains described in paragraph (b)(3) or (c) of this section; and

(ii) Any other income that the Internal Revenue Service (IRS) may determine, in published guidance (see § 601.601(d)(2) of this chapter), is not fixed or determinable annual or periodical income.

(3) Original issue discount—(i) Amount subject to tax. An amount representing original issue discount is fixed or determinable annual or periodical income that is subject to tax under sections 871(a)(1)(C) and 881(a)(3) to the extent provided in those sections and this paragraph (b)(3) if not otherwise excluded under paragraph (a) of this section. An amount of original issue discount is subject to tax with respect to a foreign beneficial owner of an obligation carrying original issue discount upon a sale or exchange of the obligation or when a payment is made on such obligation. The amount taxable is the amount of original issue discount that accrued while the foreign person held the obligation up to the time that the obligation is sold or exchanged or that a payment is made on the obligation, reduced by any amount of original issue discount that was taken into account prior to that time (due to a payment made on the obligation). In the case of a payment made on the obligation, the tax due on the amount of original issue discount may not exceed the amount of the payment reduced by the tax imposed on any portion of the payment that is qualified stated interest.

(ii) Amounts subject to withholding. A withholding agent must withhold on the taxable amount of original issue discount paid on the redemption of an original issue discount obligation unless an exception to withholding applies (e.g., portfolio interest or treaty exception). In addition, withholding is required on the taxable amount of original issue discount upon the sale or exchange of an original issue discount obligation, other than in a redemption, to the extent the withholding agent has actual knowledge or reason to know that the sale or exchange is part of a plan the principal purpose of which is to avoid tax. If a withholding agent cannot determine the taxable amount of original issue discount on the redemption of an original issue discount obligation (or on the sale or exchange of such an obligation if the principal purpose of the sale is to avoid tax), then it must withhold on the entire amount of original issue discount accrued from the date of issue until the date of redemption (or the date the obligation is sold or exchanged) * * * as if the beneficial owner of the obligation had held the obligation since its original issue.

* * *

(d) Exceptions to withholding where no money or property is paid or lack of knowledge—(1) General rule. A withholding agent who is not related to the recipient or beneficial owner has an obligation to withhold under section 1441 only to the extent that, at any time between the date that the obligation to withhold would arise (but for the provisions of this paragraph (d)) and the due date for the filing of return on Form 1042 (including extensions) for the year in which the payment occurs, it has control over, or custody of money or property owned by the recipient or beneficial owner from which to withhold an amount and has knowledge of the facts that give rise to the payment. The exemption from the obligation to withhold under this paragraph (d) shall not apply, however, to distributions with respect to stock or if the lack of control or custody of money or property from which to withhold is part of a pre-arranged plan known to the withholding agent to avoid withholding under section 1441, 1442, or 1443. For purposes of this paragraph (d), a withholding agent is related to the recipient or beneficial owner if it is related within the meaning of section 482. Any exemption from withholding pursuant to this paragraph (d) applies without a requirement that documentation be furnished to the withholding agent. However, documentation may have to be furnished for purposes of the information reporting provisions under chapter 61 of the Code and backup withholding under section 3406. The exemption from withholding under this paragraph (d) is not a determination that the amounts are not fixed or determinable annual or periodical income, nor does it constitute an exemption from reporting the amount under § 1.1461–1(b) and (c).

(2) Cancellation of debt. A lender of funds who forgives any portion of the loan is deemed to have made a payment of income to the borrower under § 1.61–12 at the time the event of forgiveness occurs. However, based on the rules of paragraph (d)(1) of this section, the lender shall have no obligation to withhold on such amount to the extent that it does not have custody or control over money or property of the borrower at any time between the time that the loan is forgiven and the due date (including extensions) of the Form 1042 for the year in which the payment is deemed to occur. A payment received by the lender from the borrower in partial settlement of the debt obligation does not, for this purpose, constitute an amount of money or property belonging to the borrower from which the withholding tax liability can be satisfied.

* * *

(e) Payment—(1) General rule. A payment is considered made to a person if that person realizes income whether or not such income results from an actual transfer of cash or other property. For example, realization of income from cancellation of debt results in a deemed payment. A payment is considered made when the amount would be includible in the income of the beneficial owner under the U.S. tax principles governing the cash basis method of accounting. A payment is considered made whether it is made directly to the beneficial owner or to another person for the benefit of the beneficial owner (e.g., to the agent of the beneficial owner). Thus, a payment of income is considered made to a beneficial owner if it is paid in complete or partial satisfaction of the beneficial owner's debt to a creditor. In the event of a conflict between the rules of this paragraph (e)(1) governing whether a payment has occurred and its timing and the rules of § 31.3406(a)–4 of this chapter, the rules in § 31.3406(a)–4 of this chapter shall apply to the extent that the application of section 3406 is relevant to the transaction at issue.

(2) Income allocated under section 482. A payment is considered made to the extent income subject to withholding is allocated under section 482. Further, income arising as a result of a secondary adjustment made in conjunction with a reallocation of income under section 482 from a foreign person to a related U.S. person is considered paid to a foreign person unless the taxpayer to whom the income is reallocated has entered into a repatriation agreement with the IRS and the agreement eliminates the liability for withholding under this section. For purposes of determining the liability for withholding, the payment of income is deemed to have occurred on the last day of the taxable year in which the transactions that give rise to the allocation of income and the secondary adjustments, if any, took place.

* * *

[T.D. 6500, 25 FR 12073, Nov. 26, 1960, as amended by T.D. 6464, 25 FR 4239, May 12, 1960; T.D. 6592, 27 FR 1888, Feb. 28, 1962; T.D. 6841, 30 FR 9309, July 27, 1965; T.D. 6873, 31 FR 954, Jan. 25, 1966; T.D. 6908, 31 FR 16770, Dec. 31, 1966; T.D. 7977, 49 FR 36831, Sept. 20, 1984; T.D. 8734, 62 FR 53444, Oct. 14, 1997; T.D. 8804, 63 FR 72183, 72187, Dec. 31, 1998; T.D. 8856, 64 FR 73408, 73412, Dec. 30, 1999; T.D. 8881, 65 FR 32186, May 22, 2000; T.D. 9272, 71 FR 43366, Aug. 1, 2006; T.D. 9415, 73 FR 40172, July 14, 2008; 73 FR 45612, Aug. 6, 2008; T.D. 9572, 77 FR 3109, Jan. 23, 2012; 77 FR 5700, Feb. 6, 2012; T.D. 9648, 78 FR 73081, Dec. 5, 2013; T.D. 9734, 80 FR 56890, Sept. 18, 2015; T.D. 9808, 82 FR 2085, Jan. 6, 2017; T.D. 9815, 82 FR 8164, Jan. 24, 2017]

§ 1.1441–3 Determination of amounts to be withheld.

(a) General rule—(1) Withholding on gross amount. Except as otherwise provided in regulations under section 1441, the amount subject to withholding under § 1.1441–1 is the gross amount of income subject to withholding that is paid to a foreign person. The gross amount of income subject to withholding may not be reduced by any deductions, except to the extent that one or more personal exemptions are allowed as provided under § 1.1441–4(b)(6).

* * *

(c) Corporate distributions—(1) General rule. A corporation making a distribution with respect to its stock or any intermediary (described in § 1.1441–1(c)(13)) making a payment of such a distribution is required to withhold under section 1441, 1442, or 1443 on the entire amount of the distribution, unless it elects to reduce the amount of withholding under the provisions of this paragraph (c). Any exceptions from withholding provided by this paragraph (c) apply without any requirement to furnish documentation to the withholding agent. However, documentation may have to be furnished for purposes of the information reporting provisions under section 6042 or 6045 and backup withholding under section 3406. See § 1.1461–1(c) to determine whether amounts excepted from withholding under this section are considered amounts that are subject to reporting.

(2) Exception to withholding on distributions—(i) In general. An election described in paragraph (c)(1) of this section is made by actually reducing the amount of withholding at the time that the payment is made. An intermediary that makes a payment of a distribution is not required to reduce the withholding based on the distributing corporation's estimates under this paragraph (c)(2) even if the distributing corporation itself elects to reduce the withholding on payments of distributions that it itself makes to foreign persons. Conversely, an intermediary may elect to reduce the amount of withholding with respect to the payment of a distribution even if the distributing corporation does not so elect for the payments of distributions that it itself makes of distributions to foreign persons. The amounts with respect to which a distributing corporation or intermediary may elect to reduce the withholding are as follows:

(A) A distributing corporation or intermediary may elect to not withhold on a distribution to the extent it represents a nontaxable distribution payable in stock or stock rights.

(B) A distributing corporation or intermediary may elect to not withhold on a distribution to the extent it represents a distribution in part or full payment in exchange for stock.

(C) A distributing corporation or intermediary may elect to not withhold on a distribution (actual or deemed) to the extent it is not paid out of accumulated earnings and profits or current earnings and profits, based on a reasonable estimate determined under paragraph (c)(2)(ii) of this section.

(D) A regulated investment company or intermediary may elect to not withhold on a distribution representing a capital gain dividend (as defined in section 852(b)(3)(C)) or an exempt interest dividend (as defined in section 852(b)(5)(A)) based on the applicable procedures described under paragraph (c)(3) of this section.

(E) A U.S. Real Property Holding Corporation (defined in section 897(c)(2)) or a real estate investment trust (defined in section 856) or intermediary may elect to not withhold on a distribution to the extent it is subject to withholding under section 1445 and the regulations under that section. See paragraph (c)(4) of this section for applicable procedures.

(ii) Reasonable estimate of accumulated and current earnings and profits on the date of payment—(A) General rule. A reasonable estimate for purposes of paragraph (c)(2)(i)(C) of this section is a determination made by the distributing corporation at a time reasonably close to the date of payment of the extent to which the distribution will constitute a dividend, as defined in section 316. The determination is based upon the anticipated amount of accumulated earnings and profits and current earnings and profits for the taxable year in which the distribution is made, the distributions made prior to the distribution for which the estimate is made and all other relevant facts and circumstances. A reasonable estimate may be made based on the procedures described in § 31.3406(b)(2)–4(c)(2) of this chapter.

(B) Procedures in case of underwithholding. A distributing corporation or intermediary that is a withholding agent with respect to a distribution and that determines at the end of the taxable year in which the distribution is made that it underwithheld under section 1441 on the distribution shall be liable for the amount underwithheld as a withholding agent under section 1461. However, for purposes of this section and § 1.1461–1, any amount underwithheld paid by a distributing corporation, its paying agent, or an intermediary shall not be treated as income subject to additional withholding even if that amount is treated as additional income to the shareholders unless the additional amount is income to the shareholder as a result of a contractual arrangement between the parties regarding the satisfaction of the shareholder's tax liabilities. In addition, no penalties shall be imposed for failure to withhold and deposit the tax if—

(1) The distributing corporation made a reasonable estimate as provided in paragraph (c)(2)(ii)(A) of this section; and

(2) Either—

(i) The corporation or intermediary pays over the underwithheld amount on or before the due date for filing a Form 1042 for the calendar year in which the distribution is made, pursuant to § 1.1461–2(b); or

(ii) The corporation or intermediary is not a calendar year taxpayer and it files an amended return on Form 1042X (or such other form as the Commissioner may prescribe) for the calendar year in which the distribution is made and pays the underwithheld amount and interest within 60 days after the close of the taxable year in which the distribution is made.

* * *

(e) Payments other than in U.S. dollars—(1) In general. The amount of a payment made in a medium other than U.S. dollars is measured by the fair market value of the property or services provided in lieu of U.S. dollars. The withholding agent may liquidate the property prior to payment in order to withhold the required amount of tax under section 1441 or obtain payment of the tax from an alternative source. However, the obligation to withhold under section 1441 is not deferred even if no alternative source can be located. Thus, for purposes of withholding under chapter 3 of the Code, the provisions of § 31.3406(h)–2(b)(2)(ii) of this chapter (relating to backup withholding from another source) shall not apply. If the withholding agent satisfies the tax liability related to such payments, the rules of paragraph (f) of this section apply.

(2) Payments in foreign currency. If the amount subject to withholding tax is paid in a currency other than the U.S. dollar, the amount of withholding under section 1441 shall be determined by applying the applicable rate of withholding to the foreign currency amount and converting the amount withheld into U.S. dollars on the date of payment at the spot rate (as defined in § 1.988–1(d)(1)) in effect on that date. A withholding agent making regular or frequent payments in foreign currency may use a month-end spot rate or a monthly average spot rate. * * *

* * *

[T.D. 6500, 25 FR 12074, Nov. 26, 1960, as amended by T.D. 6592, 27 FR 1888, Feb. 28, 1962; T.D. 6636, 28 FR 1764, Feb. 26, 1963; T.D. 6669, 28 FR 17810, Aug. 27, 1963, T.D. 6777, 29 FR 17810, Dec. 16, 1964; T.D. 6908, 31 FR 16771, Dec. 31, 1966; T.D. 7378, 40 FR 45436, Oct. 2, 1975; T.D. 7977, 49 FR 36831, Sept. 20, 1984; T.D. 8611, 60 FR 41014, Aug. 11, 1995; T.D. 8734, 62 FR 53446, Oct. 14, 1997; T.D. 8004, 63 FR 72183, 72187, Dec. 31, 1998; T.D. 8856, 64 FR 73408, 73412, Dec. 30, 1999; T.D. 8881, 65 FR 32187, 32212, May 22, 2000; T.D. 9253, 71 FR 13006, March 14, 2006; T.D. 9572, 77 FR 3110, Jan. 23, 2012; 77 FR 5700, Feb. 6, 2012; T.D. 9648, 78 FR 73081, Dec. 5, 2013; T.D. 9658, 79 FR 12772, March 6, 2014; T.D. 9734, 80 FR 56890, Sept. 18, 2015; T.D. 9808, 82 FR 2086, Jan. 16, 2017; T.D. 9971, 87 FR 80064, Dec. 29, 2022]

§ 1.1441–4 Exemptions from withholding for certain effectively connected income and other amounts.

(a) Certain income connected with a U.S. trade or business—(1) In general. No withholding is required under section 1441 on income otherwise subject to withholding if the income is (or is deemed to be) effectively connected with the conduct of a trade or business within the United States and is includible in the beneficial owner's gross income for the taxable year. For purposes of this paragraph (a), an amount is not deemed to be includible in gross income if the amount is (or is deemed to be) effectively connected with the conduct of a trade or business within the United States and the beneficial owner claims an exemption from tax under an income tax treaty because the income is not attributable to a permanent establishment in the United States. To claim a reduced rate of withholding because the income is not attributable to a permanent establishment, see § 1.1441–6(b)

(1). This paragraph (a) does not apply to income of a foreign corporation to which section 543(a)(7) applies for the taxable year or to compensation for personal services performed by an individual. See paragraph (b) of this section for compensation for personal services performed by an individual.

(2) Withholding agent's reliance on a claim of effectively connected income—(i) In general. Absent actual knowledge or reason to know otherwise, a withholding agent may rely on a claim of exemption based upon paragraph (a)(1) of this section if, prior to the payment to the foreign person, the withholding agent can reliably associate the payment with a Form W-8 upon which it can rely to treat the payment as made to a foreign beneficial owner in accordance with § 1.1441–1(e)(1)(ii).* * *

* * *

(b) Compensation for personal services of an individual—(1) Exemption from withholding. Withholding is not required under § 1.1441–1 from salaries, wages, remuneration, or any other compensation for personal services of a nonresident alien individual if such compensation is effectively connected with the conduct of a trade or business within the United States and—

(i) Such compensation is subject to withholding under section 3402 (relating to withholding on wages) and the regulations under that section;

* * *

[T.D. 6500, 25 FR 12075, Nov. 26, 1960, as amended by T.D. 6908, 31 FR 16772, Dec. 31, 1966, T.D. 6922, 32 FR 8711, June 17, 1967; T.D. 7378, 40 FR 45436, Oct. 2, 1975; T.D. 7582, 44 FR 871, Jan. 3, 1979; T.D. 7777, 46 FR 27636, May 21, 1981; T.D. 7842, 47 FR 49842, Nov. 3, 1982; T.D. 7977, 49 FR 36832, Sept. 20, 1984; T.D. 8015, 50 FR 11856, March 26, 1985; T.D. 8288, 55 FR 3716, Feb. 5, 1990; T.D. 8734, 62 FR 53450, Oct. 14, 1997; T.D. 8004, 63 FR 72183, 72184, 72188, Dec. 31, 1998; T.D. 8856, 64 FR 73408, 73409, Dec. 30, 1999; T.D. 8881, 65 FR 32187, 32212, May 22, 2000; T.D. 9572, 77 FR 3110, Jan. 23, 2012; 77 FR 5700, Feb. 6, 2012; 77 FR 13969, March 8, 2012; T.D. 9648, 78 FR 73081, Dec. 5, 2013; T.D. 9658, 79 FR 12774, March 6, 2014; T.D. 9808, 82 FR 2087, Jan. 6, 2017]

§ 1.1441–5 Withholding on payments to partnerships, trusts, and estates.

(a) In general. This section describes the rules that apply to payments made to partnerships, trusts, and estates. Paragraph (b) of this section prescribes the rules that apply to a withholding agent making a payment to a U.S. partnership, trust, or estate. It also prescribes the obligations of a U.S. partnership, trust, or estate that makes a payment to a foreign partner, beneficiary, or owner. Paragraph (c) of this section prescribes rules that apply to a withholding agent that makes a payment to a foreign partnership. Paragraph (d) of this section provides presumption rules that apply to payments made to foreign partnerships. Paragraph (e) of this section prescribes rules, including presumption rules, that apply to a withholding agent that makes a payment to a foreign trust or foreign estate.

(b) Rules applicable to U.S. partnerships, trusts, and estates—(1) Payments to U.S. partnerships, trusts, and estates. No withholding is required under section 1.1441–1(b)(1) on a payment of an amount subject to withholding (as defined in § 1.1441–2(a)) that a withholding agent may treat as made to a U.S. payee. Therefore, if a withholding agent can reliably associate (within the meaning of § 1.1441–2(b)(vii)) a Form W-9 provided in accordance with § 1.1441–1(d)(2) or (4) by a U.S. partnership, U.S. trust, or a U.S. estate the withholding agent may treat the payment as made to a U.S. payee and the payment is not subject to withholding under section 1441 even though the partnership, trust, or estate may have foreign partners, beneficiaries, or owners. A withholding agent is also not required to withhold under section 1441 on a payment it makes to an entity presumed to be a U.S. payee under paragraphs (d)(2) and (e)(6)(ii) of this section.

(2) Withholding by U.S. payees—(i) U.S. partnerships—(A) In general. A U.S. partnership is required to withhold under § 1.1441–1 as a withholding agent on an amount subject to withholding (as defined in § 1.1441–2(a)) that is includible in the gross income of a partner that is a foreign person. Subject to paragraph (b)(2)(v) of this section, a U.S. partnership shall withhold when any distributions that include amounts subject to withholding (including guaranteed payments made by a U.S. partnership) are made. To the extent a foreign partner's distributive share of income subject to withholding has not actually been distributed to the foreign partner, the U.S. partnership must withhold on the foreign partner's distributive share of the income on the earlier of the date that the statement required under section 6031(b) is mailed or otherwise provided to the partner or the due date for furnishing the statement.

(B) Effectively connected income of partners. Withholding on items of income that are effectively connected income in the hands of the partners who are foreign persons is governed by section 1446 and not by this section. In such a case, partners in a domestic partnership are not required to furnish a withholding certificate in order to claim an exemption from withholding under section 1441(c)(1) and § 1.1441–4.

* * *

(c) Foreign partnerships—(1) Determination of payee—(i) Payments treated as made to partners. Except as otherwise provided in paragraph (c)(1)(ii) or (iv) of this section, the payees of a payment to a person that the withholding agent may treat as a nonwithholding foreign partnership under paragraph (c)(3)(i) or (d)(2) of this section are the partners (looking through partners that are foreign intermediaries or flow-through entities) as follows—

(A) If the withholding agent can reliably associate a partner's distributive share of the payment with a valid Form W-9 provided under § 1.1441–1(d), the partner is a U.S. payee;

(B) If the withholding agent can reliably associate a partner's distributive share of the payment with a valid Form W-8, or other appropriate documentation, provided under § 1.1441–1(e)(1)(ii), the partner is a payee that is a foreign beneficial owner;

(C) If the withholding agent can reliably associate a partner's distributive share of the payment with a qualified intermediary withholding certificate under § 1.1441–1(e)(3)(ii), a nonqualified intermediary withholding certificate under § 1.1441–1(e)(3)(iii), or a U.S. branch certificate under § 1.1441–1(e)(3)(v) (including one provided by a territory financial institution), then the rules of § 1.1441–1(b)(2)(v) shall apply to determine who the payee is in the same manner as if the partner's distributive share of the payment had been paid directly to such intermediary or U.S. branch or territory financial institution;

(D) If the withholding agent can reliably associate the partner's distributive share with a withholding foreign partnership certificate under paragraph (c)(2)(iv) of this section or a nonwithholding foreign partnership certificate under paragraph (c)(3)(iii) of this section, then the rules of this paragraph (c)(1)(i) or paragraph (c)(1)(ii) of this section shall apply to determine whether the payment is treated as made to the partners of the higher-tier partnership under this paragraph (c)(1)(i) or to the higher-tier partnership itself (under the rules of paragraph (c)(1)(ii) of this section) in the same manner as if the partner's distributive share of the payment had been paid directly to the higher-tier foreign partnership;

(E) If the withholding agent can reliably associate the partner's distributive share with a withholding certificate described in paragraph (e) of this section regarding a foreign trust or estate, then the rules of paragraph (e) of this section shall apply to determine who the payees are; and

(F) If the withholding agent cannot reliably associate the partner's distributive share with a withholding certificate or other appropriate documentation, the partners are considered to be the payees and the presumptions described in paragraph (d)(3) of this section shall apply to determine their classification and status.

(ii) Payments treated as made to the partnership. A payment to a person that the withholding agent may treat as a foreign partnership is treated as a payment to the foreign partnership and not to its partners only if—

(A) The withholding agent can reliably associate the payment with a withholding certificate described in paragraph (c)(2)(iv) of this section (withholding certificate of a withholding foreign partnership);

(B) The withholding agent can reliably associate the payment with a withholding certificate described in paragraph (c)(3)(iii) of this section (nonwithholding foreign partnership) certifying that the payment is income that is effectively connected with the conduct of a trade or business in the United States; or

(C) The withholding agent can treat the income as effectively connected income under the presumption rules of § 1.1441–4(a)(2)(ii) or (3)(i).

* * *

(2) Withholding foreign partnerships—(i) Reliance on claim of withholding foreign partnership status. A withholding foreign partnership is a foreign partnership that has entered into an agreement with the IRS, as described in paragraph (c)(2)(ii) of this section, with respect to distributions and guaranteed payments it makes to its partners. * * *

(ii) Withholding agreement. The IRS may, upon request, enter into a withholding agreement with a foreign partnership pursuant to such procedures as the IRS may prescribe in published guidance (see § 601.601(d)(2) of this chapter). Under the withholding agreement, a foreign partnership shall generally be subject to the applicable withholding and reporting provisions applicable to withholding agents and payors * * *.

(iii) Withholding responsibility. A withholding foreign partnership must assume primary withholding responsibility under both chapters 3 and 4 of the Code to the extent required in the withholding agreement. It is not required to provide information to the withholding agent regarding each partner's distributive share of the payment (including a withholdable payment). The withholding foreign partnership will be responsible for reporting the payments under §§ 1.1461–1(c), 1.1474–1(d), and chapter 61 of the Code and filing Form 1042 (to the extent required in the withholding agreement). A withholding agent making a payment to a withholding foreign partnership is not required to withhold any amount under chapters 3 and 4 of the Code on the payment unless it has actual knowledge or reason to know that the foreign partnership is not acting as a withholding foreign partnership with respect to the payment or has not withheld to the extent required. The withholding foreign partnership shall withhold the payments under the same procedures and at the same time as prescribed for withholding by a U.S. partnership under paragraph (b)(2) of this section, except that, for purposes of determining the partner's status, the provisions of paragraph (d)(4) of this section shall apply.

* * *

[T.D. 6500, 25 FR 12076, Nov. 26, 1960, as amended by T.D. 6238, 22 FR 4078, June 11, 1957; T.D. 6908, 31 FR 16773, Dec. 31, 1966; T.D. 7277, 38 FR 12742, May 15, 1973; T.D. 7777, 46 FR 27635, May 21, 1981; T.D. 7842, 47 FR 49842, Nov. 3, 1982; T.D. 7977, 49 FR 36834, Sept. 20, 1984; T.D. 8160, 52 FR 33933, Sept. 9, 1987; T.D. 8411, 57 FR 15241, April 27, 1992; T.D. 8734, 62

FR 53452, Oct. 14, 1997; T.D. 8804, 63 FR 72183, 72185, 72188, Dec. 31, 1998; T.D. 8856, 64 FR 73408, 73410, Dec. 30, 1999; T.D. 8881, 65 FR 32188, May 22, 2000; 66 FR 18188, April 6, 2001; T.D. 9658, 79 FR 12775, March 6, 2014; T.D. 9808, 82 FR 2088, Jan. 6, 2017]

§ 1.1441–6 Claim of reduced withholding under an income tax treaty.

(a) In general. The rate of withholding on a payment of income subject to withholding may be reduced to the extent provided under an income tax treaty in effect between the United States and a foreign country. Most benefits under income tax treaties are to foreign persons who reside in the treaty country. In some cases, benefits are available under an income tax treaty to U.S. citizens or U.S. residents or to residents of a third country. * * *

(b) Reliance on claim of reduced withholding under an income tax treaty—(1) In general. The withholding imposed under section 1441, 1442, or 1443 on any payment to a foreign person is eligible for reduction under the terms of an income tax treaty only to the extent that such payment is treated as derived by a resident of an applicable treaty jurisdiction, such resident is a beneficial owner, and all other requirements for benefits under the treaty are satisfied. See section 894 and the regulations under section 894 to determine whether a resident of a treaty country derives the income. Absent actual knowledge or reason to know otherwise, a withholding agent may rely on a claim that a beneficial owner is entitled to a reduced rate of withholding based upon an income tax treaty if, prior to the payment, the withholding agent can reliably associate the payment with a beneficial owner withholding certificate, as described in § 1.1441–1(e)(2), that contains the information necessary to support the claim, * * *

[T.D. 7157, 36 FR 25227, Dec. 30, 1971; T.D. 7842, 47 FR 49842, Nov. 3, 1982; T.D. 7977, 49 FR 36834, Sept. 20, 1984; T.D. 8734, 62 FR 53458, Oct. 14, 1997; T.D. 8804, 63 FR 72183, 72185, 72188, Dec. 31, 1998; T.D. 8856, 64 FR 73408, 73410, Dec. 30, 1999; 65 FR 16320, March 28, 2000; T.D. 8881, 65 FR 32194, May 22, 2000; T.D. 8977, 67 FR 2328, Jan. 17, 2002; T.D. 9023, 67 FR 70312, Nov. 22, 2002; T.D. 9253, 71 FR 13006, March 14, 2006; 71 FR 25748, May 2, 2006; T.D. 9648, 78 FR 73082, Dec. 5, 2013; T.D. 9658, 79 FR 12780, March 6, 2014; T.D. 9808, 82 FR 2093, Jan. 6, 2017]

§ 1.1441–7 General provisions relating to withholding agents.

(a) Withholding agent defined—(1) In general. For purposes of chapter 3 of the Internal Revenue Code and the regulations under such chapter, the term withholding agent means any person, U.S. or foreign, that has the control, receipt, custody, disposal, or payment of an item of income of a foreign person subject to withholding, * * *.

[T.D. 7977, 49 FR 36834, Sept. 20, 1984; T.D. 8611, 60 FR 41014, Aug. 11, 1995; 60 FR 55312, Oct. 31, 1995; T.D. 8734, 62 FR 53462, Oct. 14, 1997; T.D. 8804, 63 FR 72183, 72188, Dec. 31, 1998; T.D. 8856, 64 FR 73408, 73412, Dec. 30, 1999; T.D. 8881, 65 FR 32197, 32212, May 22, 2000; 66 FR 18189, April 6, 2001; T.D. 9572, 77 FR 3110, Jan. 23, 2012; 77 FR 5700, Feb. 6, 2012; 77 FR 13969, March 8, 2012; T.D. 9648, 78 FR 73082, Dec. 5, 2013; T.D. 9658, 79 FR 12782, March 6, 2014; T.D. 9734, 80 FR 56890, Sept. 18, 2015; T.D. 9808, 82 FR 2095, Jan. 6, 2017; T.D. 9815, 82 FR 8165, Jan. 24, 2017]

§ 1.1445–11T Special rules requiring withholding under § 1.1445–5 (temporary).

* * *

(d) Dispositions of interests in partnerships, trusts or estates—(1) Withholding required on disposition of certain partnership interests. Withholding is required under section 1445(e)(5) and this paragraph with respect to the disposition by a foreign partner of an interest in a domestic or foreign partnership in which fifty percent or more of the value of the gross assets consist of U.S. real property interests, and ninety percent or more of the value of the gross assets consist of U.S. real property interests plus any cash or cash equivalents. For purposes of this paragraph cash equivalents mean any asset readily convertible into cash (whether or not denominated in U.S. dollars), including, but not limited to, bank accounts, certificates of deposit, money market accounts, commercial paper, U.S. and foreign treasury obligations and bonds, corporate obligations and bonds, precious metals or commodities, and publicly traded instruments. The taxpayer on filing an income tax return for the year of the disposition may demonstrate the extent to which the gain on the disposition of the interest is not attributable to U.S. real property interests. A taxpayer is also permitted by § 1.1445–3 to apply for a withholding certificate in instances where reduced withholding is appropriate.

(2) Withholding not required—(i) Transferee receives statement that interest in partnership is not described in paragraph (d)(1). No withholding is required under paragraph (d)(1) of this section upon the disposition of a partnership interest otherwise described in that paragraph if the transferee is provided a statement, issued by the partnership and signed by a general partner under penalties of perjury no earlier than 30 days before the transfer, certifying that fifty percent or more of the value of the gross assets does not consist of U.S. real property interests, or that ninety percent or more of the value of the gross assets of the partnership does not consist of U.S. real property interests plus cash or cash equivalents.

(ii) Reliance on statement not permitted. A transferee is not entitled to rely upon a statement described in paragraph (d)(2)(i) of this section if, prior to or at the time of the transfer, the transferee either—

(A) Has actual knowledge that the statement is false, or

* * *

[T.D. 8198, 53 FR 16231, May 5, 1988; T.D. 9751, 81 FR 03421, Feb. 19, 2016]

Procedure and Administration

§ 301.7701–1 Classification of organizations for federal tax purposes.

(a) Organizations for federal tax purposes—(1) In general. The Internal Revenue Code prescribes the classification of various organizations for federal tax purposes. Whether an organization is an entity separate from its owners for federal tax purposes is a matter of federal tax law and does not depend on whether the organization is recognized as an entity under local law.

(2) Certain joint undertakings give rise to entities for federal tax purposes. A joint venture or other contractual arrangement may create a separate entity for federal tax purposes if the participants carry on a trade, business, financial operation, or venture and divide the profits therefrom. For example, a separate entity exists for federal tax purposes if co-owners of an apartment building lease space and in addition provide services to the occupants either directly or through an agent. Nevertheless, a joint undertaking merely to share expenses does not create a separate entity for federal tax purposes. For example, if two or more persons jointly construct a ditch merely to drain surface water from their properties, they have not created a separate entity for federal tax purposes. Similarly, mere co-ownership of property that is maintained, kept in repair, and rented or leased does not constitute a separate entity for federal tax purposes. For example, if an individual owner, or tenants in common, of farm property lease it to a farmer for a cash rental or a share of the crops, they do not necessarily create a separate entity for federal tax purposes.

* * *

(5) Single owner organizations. Under §§ 301.7701–2 and 301.7701–3, certain organizations that have a single owner can choose to be recognized or disregarded as entities separate from their owners.

(b) Classification of organizations. The classification of organizations that are recognized as separate entities is determined under §§ 301.7701–2, 301.7701–3, and 301.7701–4 unless a provision of the Internal Revenue Code (such as section 860A addressing Real Estate Mortgage Investment Conduits (REMICs)) provides for special treatment of that organization. For the classification of organizations as trusts, see § 301.7701–4. That section provides that trusts generally do not have associates or an objective to carry on business for profit. Sections 301.7701–2 and 301.7701–3 provide rules for classifying organizations that are not classified as trusts.

(c) Cost sharing arrangements. A cost sharing arrangement that is described in § 1.482–7 of this chapter, including any arrangement that the Commissioner treats as a CSA under § 1.482–7(b)(5) of this chapter, is not recognized as a separate entity for purposes of the Internal Revenue Code. See § 1.482–7 of this chapter for the rules regarding CSAs.

* * *

[32 FR 15241, Nov. 3, 1967, as amended by T.D. 7515, 42 FR 55612, Oct. 18, 1977; T.D. 8697, 61 FR 66588, Dec. 18, 1996; T.D. 9153, 69 FR 49810, Aug. 12, 2004; T.D. 9246, 71 FR 4816, Jan. 30, 2006; T.D. 9441, 74 FR 390, Jan. 5, 2009; T.D. 9568, 76 FR 80136, Dec. 22, 2011; T.D. 10039, 90 FR 58151, Dec 16, 2025]

§ 301.7701–2 Business entities; definitions.

(a) Business entities. For purposes of this section and § 301.7701–3, a business entity is any entity recognized for federal tax purposes (including an entity with a single owner that may be disregarded as an entity separate from its owner under § 301.7701–3) that is not properly classified as a trust under § 301.7701–4 or otherwise subject to special treatment under the Internal Revenue Code. A business entity with two or more members is classified for federal tax purposes as either a corporation or a partnership. A business entity with only one owner is classified as a corporation or is disregarded; if the entity is disregarded, its activities are treated in the same manner as a sole proprietorship, branch, or division of the owner. * * *

(b) Corporations. For federal tax purposes, the term corporation means—

(1) A business entity organized under a Federal or State statute, or under a statute of a federally recognized Indian tribe, if the statute describes or refers to the entity as incorporated or as a corporation, body corporate, or body politic;

(2) An association (as determined under § 301.7701–3);

(3) A business entity organized under a State statute, if the statute describes or refers to the entity as a joint-stock company or joint-stock association;

(4) An insurance company;

(5) A State-chartered business entity conducting banking activities, if any of its deposits are insured under the Federal Deposit Insurance Act, as amended, 12 U.S.C. 1811 et seq., or a similar federal statute;

(6) A business entity wholly owned by a State or any political subdivision thereof, or a business entity wholly owned by a foreign government or any other entity described in § 1.892–2T;

(7) A business entity that is taxable as a corporation under a provision of the Internal Revenue Code other than section 7701(a)(3); and

(8) Certain foreign entities—**(i) In general.** Except as provided in paragraphs (b)(8)(ii) and (d) of this section, the following business entities formed in the following jurisdictions:

American Samoa, Corporation
Argentina, Sociedad Anonima

Australia, Public Limited Company
Austria, Aktiengesellschaft
Barbados, Limited Company
Belgium, Societe Anonyme
Belize, Public Limited Company
Bolivia, Sociedad Anonima
Brazil, Sociedade Anonima
Canada, Corporation and Company
Chile, Sociedad Anonima
People's Republic of China, Gufen Youxian Gongsi
Republic of China (Taiwan), Ku-fen Yu-hsien Kung-szu
Colombia, Sociedad Anonima
Costa Rica, Sociedad Anonima
Cyprus, Public Limited Company
Czech Republic, Akciova Spolecnost
Denmark, Aktieselskab
Ecuador, Sociedad Anonima or Compania Anonima
Egypt, Sharikat Al-Mossahamah
El Salvador, Sociedad Anonima
Estonia, Aktsiaselts
European Economic Area/European Union, Societas Europaea
Finland, Julkinen Osakeyhtio/Publikt Aktiebolag
France, Societe Anonyme
Germany, Aktiengesellschaft
Greece, Anonymos Etairia
Guam, Corporation
Guatemala, Sociedad Anonima
Guyana, Public Limited Company
Honduras, Sociedad Anonima
Hong Kong, Public Limited Company
Hungary, Reszvenytarsasag
Iceland, Hlutafelag
India, Public Limited Company
Indonesia, Perseroan Terbuka
Ireland, Public Limited Company
Israel, Public Limited Company
Italy, Societa per Azioni
Jamaica, Public Limited Company
Japan, Kabushiki Kaisha
Kazakstan, Ashyk Aktsionerlik Kogham
Republic of Korea, Chusik Hoesa
Latvia, Akciju Sabiedriba
Liberia, Corporation
Liechtenstein, Aktiengesellschaft
Lithuania, Akcine Bendroves
Luxembourg, Societe Anonyme Malaysia, Berhad
Malta, Public Limited Company
Mexico, Sociedad Anonima
Morocco, Societe Anonyme
Netherlands, Naamloze Vennootschap
New Zealand, Limited Company
Nicaragua, Compania Anonima
Nigeria, Public Limited Company
Northern Mariana Islands, Corporation
Norway, Allment Aksjeselskap
Pakistan, Public Limited Company
Panama, Sociedad Anonima
Paraguay, Sociedad Anonima
Peru, Sociedad Anonima
Philippines, Stock Corporation
Poland, Spolka Akcyjna
Portugal, Sociedade Anonima
Puerto Rico, Corporation
Romania, Societe pe Actiuni
Russia, Otkrytoye Aktsionernoy Obshchestvo
Saudi Arabia, Sharikat Al-Mossahamah
Singapore, Public Limited Company
Slovak Republic, Akciova Spolocnost
Slovenia, Delniska Druzba.
South Africa, Public Limited Company
Spain, Sociedad Anonima
Surinam, Naamloze Vennootschap
Sweden, Publika Aktiebolag
Switzerland, Aktiengesellschaft
Thailand, Borisat Chamkad (Mahachon)
Trinidad and Tobago, Limited Company
Tunisia, Societe Anonyme
Turkey, Anonim Sirket

Ukraine, Aktsionerne Tovaristvo Vidkritogo Tipu
United Kingdom, Public Limited Company
United States Virgin Islands, Corporation
Uruguay, Sociedad Anonima
Venezuela, Sociedad Anonima or Compania Anonima

* * *

(c) Other business entities. For federal tax purposes—

(1) The term partnership means a business entity that is not a corporation under paragraph (b) of this section and that has at least two members.

(2) Wholly owned entities—(i) In general. Except as otherwise provided in this paragraph (c), a business entity that has a single owner and is not a corporation under paragraph (b) of this section is disregarded as an entity separate from its owner.

* * *

[32 FR 15241, Nov. 3, 1967, as amended by T.D. 7515, 42 FR 55612, Oct. 18, 1977; T.D. 7889, 48 FR 18805, April 26, 1983; T.D. 8475, 58 FR 28502, May 14, 1993; T.D. 8697, 61 FR 66589, Dec. 18, 1996; T.D. 8844, 64 FR 66583, Nov. 29, 1999; T.D. 9012, 67 FR 49864, Aug. 1, 2002; T.D. 9093, 68 FR 60298, Oct. 22, 2003; T.D. 9153, 69 FR 49810, Aug. 12, 2004; T.D. 9183, 70 FR 9221, Feb. 25, 2005; T.D. 9197, 70 FR 19698, April 14, 2005; T.D. 9235, 70 FR 74658, Dec. 16, 2005; T.D. 9246, 71 FR 4817, Jan. 30, 2006; T.D. 9356, 72 FR 45893, Aug. 16, 2007; T.D. 9388, 73 FR 15065, March 21, 2008; T.D. 8697, 73 FR 18442, April 4, 2008; T.D. 9388, 73 FR 21415, April 21, 2008; T.D. 9433, 73 FR 72346, Nov. 28, 2008; T.D. 9462, 74 FR 46904, Sept. 14, 2009; T.D. 9553, 76 FR 66182, Oct. 26, 2011; T.D. 9554, 76 FR 67365, Nov. 1, 2011; T.D. 9596, 77 FR 37807, June 25, 2012; T.D. 9655, 79 FR 8601, Feb. 12, 2014; T.D. 9670, 79 FR 36206, June 26, 2014; T.D. 9766 81 FR 26694, May 4, 2016; T.D. 9796, 81 FR 89851, Dec. 13, 2016; T.D. 9869, 84 FR 31479, July 2, 2019; T.D. 10026, 90 FR 3021, Jan. 14, 2025]

§ 301.7701–3 Classification of certain business entities.

(a) In general. A business entity that is not classified as a corporation under § 301.7701–2(b)(1), (3), (4), (5), (6), (7), or (8) (an eligible entity) can elect its classification for federal tax purposes as provided in this section. An eligible entity with at least two members can elect to be classified as either an association (and thus a corporation under § 301.7701–2(b)(2)) or a partnership, and an eligible entity with a single owner can elect to be classified as an association or to be disregarded as an entity separate from its owner. Paragraph (b) of this section provides a default classification for an eligible entity that does not make an election. Thus, elections are necessary only when an eligible entity chooses to be classified initially as other than the default classification or when an eligible entity chooses to change its classification. An entity whose classification is determined under the default classification retains that classification (regardless of any changes in the members' liability that occurs at any time during the time that the entity's classification is relevant as defined in paragraph (d) of this section) until the entity makes an election to change that classification under paragraph (c)(1) of this section. Paragraph (c) of this section provides rules for making express elections * * *. Paragraph (d) of this section provides special rules for foreign eligible entities. Paragraph (e) of this section provides special rules for classifying entities resulting from partnership terminations and divisions under section 708(b). Paragraph (f) of this section sets forth the effective date of this section and a special rule relating to prior periods.

(b) Classification of eligible entities that do not file an election—(1) Domestic eligible entities. Except as provided in paragraph (b)(3) of this section, unless the entity elects otherwise, a domestic eligible entity is—

(i) A partnership if it has two or more members; or

(ii) Disregarded as an entity separate from its owner if it has a single owner.

(2) Foreign eligible entities—(i) In general. Except as provided in paragraph (b)(3) of this section, unless the entity elects otherwise, a foreign eligible entity is—

(A) A partnership if it has two or more members and at least one member does not have limited liability;

(B) An association if all members have limited liability; or

(C) Disregarded as an entity separate from its owner if it has a single owner that does not have limited liability.

(ii) Definition of limited liability. For purposes of paragraph (b)(2)(i) of this section, a member of a foreign eligible entity has limited liability if the member has no personal liability for the debts of or claims against the entity by reason of being a member. This determination is based solely on the statute or law pursuant to which the entity is organized, except that if the underlying statute or law allows the entity to specify in its organizational documents whether the members will have limited liability, the organizational documents may also be relevant. For purposes of this section, a member has personal liability if the creditors of the entity may seek satisfaction of all or any portion of the debts or claims against the entity from the member as such. A member has personal liability for purposes of this paragraph even if the member makes an agreement under which another person (whether or not a member of the entity) assumes such liability or agrees to indemnify that member for any such liability.

(3) Existing eligible entities—(i) In general. Unless the entity elects otherwise, an eligible entity in existence prior to the effective date of this section will have the same classification that the entity claimed under §§ 301.7701–1 through 301.7701–3 as in effect on the date prior to the effective date of this section; except that if an eligible entity with a single owner claimed to be a partnership under those regulations, the entity will be disregarded as an entity separate from its owner under this paragraph (b)(3)(i). For special rules regarding the classification of such entities prior to the effective date of this section, see paragraph (h)(2) of this section.

(ii) Special rules. For purposes of paragraph (b)(3)(i) of this section, a foreign eligible entity is treated as being in existence prior to the effective date of this section only if the entity's classification was relevant (as defined in paragraph (d) of this section) at any time during the sixty months prior to the effective date of this section. If an entity claimed different classifications prior to the effective date of this section, the entity's classification for purposes of paragraph (b)(3)(i) of this section is the last classification claimed by the entity. If a foreign eligible entity's classification is relevant prior to the effective date of this section, but no federal tax or information return is filed or the federal tax or information return does not indicate the classification of the entity, the entity's classification for the period prior to the effective date of this section is determined under the regulations in effect on the date prior to the effective date of this section.

(c) Elections—(1) Time and place for filing—(i) In general. Except as provided in paragraphs (c)(1)(iv) and (v) of this section, an eligible entity may elect to be classified other than as provided under paragraph (b) of this section, or to change its classification, by filing Form 8832, Entity Classification Election, with the service center designated on Form 8832. * * *

* * *

(d) Special rules for foreign eligible entities—(1) Definition of relevance—(i) General rule. For purposes of this section, a foreign eligible entity's classification is relevant when its classification affects the liability of any person for federal tax or information purposes. For example, a foreign entity's classification would be relevant if U.S. income was paid to the entity and the determination by the withholding agent of the amount to be withheld under chapter 3 of the Internal Revenue Code (if any) would vary depending upon whether the entity is classified as a partnership or as an association. Thus, the classification might affect the documentation that the withholding agent must receive from the entity, the type of tax or information return to file, or how the return must be prepared. The date that the classification of a foreign eligible entity is relevant is the date an event occurs that creates an obligation to file a federal tax return, information return, or statement for which the classification of the entity must be determined. Thus, the classification of a foreign entity is relevant, for example, on the date that an interest in the entity is acquired which will require a U.S. person to file an information return on Form 5471.

(ii) Deemed relevance—(A) General rule. For purposes of this section, except as provided in paragraph (d)(1)(ii)(B) of this section, the classification for Federal tax purposes of a foreign eligible entity that files Form 8832, "Entity Classification Election", shall be deemed to be relevant only on the date the entity classification election is effective.

(B) Exception. If the classification of a foreign eligible entity is relevant within the meaning of paragraph (d)(1)(i) of this section, then the rule in paragraph (d)(1)(ii)(A) of this section shall not apply.

(2) Entities the classification of which has never been relevant. If the classification of a foreign eligible entity has never been relevant (as defined in paragraph (d)(1) of this section), then the entity's classification will initially be determined pursuant to the provisions of paragraph (b)(2) of this section when the classification of the entity first becomes relevant (as defined in paragraph (d)(1)(i) of this section).

(3) Special rule when classification is no longer relevant. If the classification of a foreign eligible entity is not relevant (as defined in paragraph (d)(1) of this section) for 60 consecutive months, then the entity's classification will initially be determined pursuant to the provisions of paragraph (b)(2) of this section when the classification of the foreign eligible entity becomes relevant (as defined in paragraph (d)(1)(i) of this section). The date that the classification of a foreign entity is not relevant is the date an event occurs that causes the classification to no longer be relevant, or, if no event occurs in a taxable year that causes the classification to be relevant, then the date is the first day of that taxable year.

* * *

[32 FR 15241, Nov. 3, 1967; T.D. 8632, 60 FR 65566, Dec. 20, 1995; T.D. 8697, 61 FR 66590, Dec. 18, 1996; 62 FR 11769, March 13, 1997; T.D. 8767, 63 FR 14619, March 26, 1998; T.D. 8827, 64 FR 37678, July 13, 1999; 64 FR 58782, Nov. 1, 1999; T.D. 8844, 64 FR 66583, Nov. 29, 1999; T.D. 8970, 66 FR 64912, Dec. 17, 2001; T.D. 9093, 68 FR 60298, Oct. 22, 2003; T.D. 9100, 68 FR 70709, Dec. 19, 2003; T.D. 9139, 69 FR 43318, July 20, 2004; T.D. 9153, 69 FR 49811, Aug. 12, 2004; T.D. 9203, 70 FR 29453, May 23, 2005; T.D. 9300, 71 FR 71045, Dec. 8, 2006; T.D. 9896, 85 FR 19857, April 8, 2020]

§ 301.7701–5 Domestic and foreign business entities.

(a) Domestic and foreign business entities. A business entity (including an entity that is disregarded as separate from its owner under § 301.7701–2(c)) is domestic if it is created or organized as any type of entity (including, but not limited to, a corporation, unincorporated association, general partnership, limited partnership, and limited liability company) in the United States, or under the law of the United States or of any State. Accordingly, a business entity that is created or organized both in the United States and in a foreign jurisdiction is a domestic entity. A business entity (including an entity that is disregarded as separate from its owner under § 301.7701–2(c)) is foreign if it is not domestic. The determination of whether an entity is domestic or foreign is made independently from the determination of its corporate or non-corporate classification. See §§ 301.7701–2 and 301.7701–3 for the rules governing the classification of entities.

* * *

[69 FR 49811, Aug. 12, 2004; T.D. 9246, 71 FR 4817, Jan. 30, 2006]

§ 301.7701–6 Definitions; person, fiduciary.

(a) Person. The term person includes an individual, a corporation, a partnership, a trust or estate, a joint-stock company, an association, or a syndicate, group, pool, joint venture, or other unincorporated organization or group. The term also includes a guardian, committee, trustee, executor, administrator, trustee in bankruptcy, receiver, assignee for the benefit of creditors, conservator, or any person acting in a fiduciary capacity.

* * *

[32 FR 15241, Nov. 3, 1967; T.D. 8697, 61 FR 66593, Dec. 18, 1996]

§ 301.7701(b)–1 Resident alien.

(a) Scope. * * * Unless the context indicates otherwise, the regulations under §§ 301.7701(b)–1 through 301.7701(b)–9 apply for purposes of determining whether a United States citizen is also a resident of the United States. (This determination may be relevant, for example, to the application of section 861(a)(1) which treats income from interest-bearing obligations of residents as income from sources within the United States.) The regulations do not apply and §§ 1.871–2 and 1.871–5 of this chapter continue to apply for purposes of the bona fide residence test of section 911. See § 1.911–2(c) of this chapter. * * *

(b) Lawful permanent resident—(1) Green card test. An alien is a resident alien with respect to a calendar year if the individual is a lawful permanent resident at any time during the calendar year. A lawful permanent resident is an individual who has been lawfully granted the privilege of residing permanently in the United States as an immigrant in accordance with the immigration laws. Resident status is deemed to continue unless it is rescinded or administratively or judicially determined to have been abandoned.

(2) Rescission of resident status. Resident status is considered to be rescinded if a final administrative or judicial order of exclusion or deportation is issued regarding the alien individual. For purposes of this paragraph, the term "final judicial order" means an order that is no longer subject to appeal to a higher court of competent jurisdiction.

(3) Administrative or judicial determination of abandonment of resident status. An administrative or judicial determination of abandonment of resident status may be initiated by the alien individual, the Immigration and Naturalization Service (INS), or a consular officer. If the alien initiates this determination, resident status is considered to be abandoned when the individual's application for abandonment (INS Form I-407) or a letter stating the alien's intent to abandon his or her resident status, with the Alien Registration Receipt Card (INS Form I-151 or Form I-551) enclosed, is filed with the INS or a consular officer. If INS replaces any of the form numbers referred to in this paragraph or § 301.7701(b)–2(f), refer to the comparable INS replacement form number. For purposes of this paragraph, an alien individual shall be considered to have filed a letter stating the intent to abandon resident status with the INS or a consular office if such letter is sent by certified mail, return receipt requested (or a foreign country's equivalent thereof). A copy of the letter, along with proof that the letter was mailed and received, should be retained by the alien individual. If the INS or a consular officer initiates this determination, resident status will be considered to be abandoned upon the issuance of a final administrative order of abandonment. If an individual is granted an appeal to a federal court of competent jurisdiction, a final judicial order is required.

(c) Substantial presence test—(1) In general. An alien individual is a resident alien if the individual meets the substantial presence test. An individual satisfies this test if he or she has been present in the United States on at least 183 days during a three year period that includes the current year. For purposes of this test, each day of presence in the current year is counted as a full day. Each day of presence in the first preceding year is counted as one-third of a day and each day of presence in the second preceding year is counted as one-sixth of a day. For purposes of this paragraph, any fractional days resulting from the above calculations will not be rounded to the nearest whole number. (See § 301.7701(b)–9(b)(2) for transitional rules for calendar years 1985 and 1986.)

(2) Determination of presence—(i) Physical presence. For purposes of the substantial presence test, an individual shall be treated as present in the United States on any day that he or she is physically present in the United States at any time during the day. (But see § 301.7701(b) 3 relating to days of presence that may be excluded.)

(ii) United States. For purposes of section 7701(b) and the regulations thereunder, the term United States when used in a geographical sense includes the states and the District of Columbia. It also includes the territorial waters of the United States and the seabed and subsoil of those submarine areas which are adjacent to the territorial waters of the United States and over which the United States has exclusive rights, in accordance with international law, with respect to the exploration and exploitation of natural resources. It does not include the possessions and territories of the United States or the air space over the United States.

(3) Current year. The term current year means any calendar year for which an alien individual is determining his or her resident status.

(4) Thirty-one day minimum. If an individual is not physically present for more than 30 days during the current year, the substantial presence test will not be applied for that year even if the three-year total is 183 or more days. For purposes of the substantial presence test, it is irrelevant that an individual was not present for more than 30 days in the first or second year preceding the current year.

(d) Application of section 7701(b) to the possessions and territories—(1) Application to aliens for purposes of mirror systems. Section 7701(b) provides the basis for determining whether an alien individual is a resident of a United States possession or territory that administers income tax laws that are identical (except for the substitution of the name of the possession or territory for the term "United States" where appropriate) to those in force in the United States, for purposes of applying such laws with respect to income tax liability incurred to such possession or territory.

(2) Non-application for bona fide resident determination. Section 7701(b) does not provide the basis for determining whether an individual (including an alien individual) is a bona fide resident of a United States possession or territory for Federal income tax purposes. For the applicable rules for making this determination, see section 937(a) and § 1.937–1 of this chapter

(e) Examples. This section may be illustrated by the following examples:

Example 1. B, an alien individual, is present in the United States for 122 days in the current year. He was present in the United States for 122 days in the first preceding calendar year and for 122 days in the second preceding calendar year. In determining his status for the current year, B counts all 122 days in the United States in the current year plus 1/3 of the 122 days in the United States in the first preceding calendar year (40 2/3 days) and 1/6 of the 122 days in the United States during the second preceding calendar year (20 1/3 days). The total of 122+40 2/3 +20 1/3 equals 183 days. B meets the substantial presence test and is a resident alien for the current year.

Example 2. C, an alien individual, is present in the United States for 25 days during the current year. She was present in the United States for 365 days during the first preceding year and 365 days during the second preceding year. The substantial presence test does not apply because C is present in the United States for fewer than 31 days during the current year.

Example 3. D, an alien individual, is present in the United States for 170 days during the current year. He was present in the United States for 30 days during the first preceding year and 30 days during the second preceding year. In determining his status for the current year, D counts all 170 days in the United States in the current year plus 1/3 of the 30 days in the United States in the first preceding calendar year (10 days) and 1/6 of the 30 days in the United States during the second preceding calendar year (5 days). The total of 170+10+5 equals 185 days. D meets the substantial presence test and is a resident alien for the current year notwithstanding the fact that he was present in the United States for fewer than 31 days in each of the two preceding years.

[T.D. 8411, 57 FR 15242, April 27, 1992; T.D. 8411, 57 FR 28612, June 26, 1992; T.D. 8411, 57 FR 37190, Aug. 18, 1992; T.D. 9194, 70 FR 18947, April 11, 2005; T.D. 9391, 73 FR 19377, April 9, 2008]

§ 301.7701(b)–2 Closer connection exception.

(a) In general. An alien individual who meets the substantial presence test may nevertheless be considered a nonresident alien for the current year if the following conditions are satisfied—

(1) The individual is present in the United States for fewer than 183 days in the current year;

(2) The individual maintains a tax home in a foreign country during the current year; and

(3) Except as provided in paragraph (e) of this section, the individual has a closer connection during the current year to a single foreign country in which he or she maintains a tax home than to the United States.

(b) Foreign country. For purposes of section 7701(b) and the regulations thereunder, the term "foreign country" when used in a geographical sense includes any territory under the sovereignty of the United Nations or a government other than that of the United States. It includes the territorial waters of the foreign country (determined in accordance with the laws of the United States), and the seabed and subsoil of those submarine areas which are adjacent to the territorial waters of the foreign country and over which the foreign country has exclusive rights, in accordance with international law, with respect to the exploration and exploitation of natural resources. It also includes the possessions and territories of the United States.

(c) Tax home—(1) Definition. For purposes of section 7701(b) and the regulations under that section, the term "tax home" has the same meaning that it has for purposes of section 162(a)(2) (relating to travel expenses while away from home). Thus, an individual's tax home is considered to be located at the individual's regular or principal (if more than one regular) place of business. If the individual has no regular or principal place of business because of the nature of the business, or because the individual is not engaged in carrying on any trade or business within the meaning of section 162(a), then the individual's tax home is the individual's regular place of abode in a real and substantial sense.

(2) Duration and nature of tax home. The tax home maintained by the alien individual must be in existence for the entire current year. The tax home must be located in the same foreign country for which the individual is claiming to have the closer connection described in paragraph (d) of this section.

(d) Closer connection to a foreign country—(1) In general. For purposes of section 7701(b) and the regulations under that section, an alien individual will be considered to have a closer connection to a foreign country than the United States if the individual or the Commissioner establishes that the individual has maintained more significant contacts with the foreign country than with the United States. In determining whether an individual has maintained more significant contacts with a foreign country than the United States, the facts and circumstances to be considered include, but are not limited to, the following—

(i) The location of the individual's permanent home;

(ii) The location of the individual's family;

(iii) The location of personal belongings, such as automobiles, furniture, clothing and jewelry owned by the individual and his or her family;

(iv) The location of social, political, cultural or religious organizations with which the individual has a current relationship;

(v) The location where the individual conducts his or her routine personal banking activities;

(vi) The location where the individual conducts business activities (other than those that constitute the individual's tax home);

(vii) The location of the jurisdiction in which the individual holds a driver's license;

(viii) The location of the jurisdiction in which the individual votes;

(ix) The country of residence designated by the individual on forms and documents; and

(x) The types of official forms and documents filed by the individual, such as Form 1078 (Certificate of Alien Claiming Residence in the United States), Form W-8 (Certificate of Foreign Status) or Form W-9 (Payer's Request for Taxpayer Identification Number).

(2) Permanent home. For purposes of paragraph (d)(1)(i) of this section, it is immaterial whether a permanent home is a house, an apartment, or a furnished room. It is also immaterial whether the home is owned or rented by the alien individual. It is material, however, that the dwelling be available at all times, continuously, and not solely for stays of short duration.

* * *

[T.D. 8411, 57 FR 15244, April 27, 1992; T.D. 8411, 57 FR 28612, June 26, 1992; T.D. 8411, 57 FR 37190, Aug. 18, 1992; 58 FR 17516, April 5, 1993]

§ 301.7701(b)–3 Days of presence in the United States that are excluded for purposes of section 7701(b).

(a) In general. In computing days of presence in the United States, an alien is considered to be present if the individual is physically present in the United States at any time during the day (see § 301.7701(b)–1(c)(2)(i)). However, for purposes of section 7701(b) and the regulations under that section, the following days shall be excluded and will not count as days of presence in the United States—

(1) Any day that an individual is present in the United States as an exempt individual;

(2) Any day that an individual is prevented from leaving the United States because of a medical condition that arose while the individual was present in the United States;

(3) Any day that an individual is in transit between two points outside the United States; and

(4) Any day on which a regular commuter residing in Canada or Mexico commutes to and from employment in the United States.

(b) Exempt individuals—(1) In general. An exempt individual is an individual who is either a—

(i) Foreign government-related individual as defined in paragraph (b)(2) of this section;

(ii) Teacher or trainee as defined in paragraph (b)(3) of this section;

(iii) Student as defined in paragraph (b)(4) of this section; or

(iv) Professional athlete as defined in paragraph (b)(5) of this section.

(2) Foreign government-related individual—(i) In general. A foreign government-related individual is an individual (and that individual's immediate family) who is temporarily present in the United States—

(A) As a full-time employee of an international organization;

(B) By reason of diplomatic status; or

(C) By reason of a visa that the Secretary of the Treasury or his or her delegate (after consultation with the Secretary of State when appropriate) determines represents full-time diplomatic or consular status. An individual described in this paragraph shall be considered to be temporarily present in the United States if the individual is not a lawful permanent resident as described in § 301.7701(b)–1(b)(1), regardless of the actual amount of time that the individual is present in the United States.

(ii) Definition of international organization. The term "international organization" means any public international organization that has been designated by the President by Executive Order as being entitled to enjoy the privileges, exemptions, and immunities provided for in the International Organizations Act (22 U.S.C. 288). An individual described in paragraph (b)(2)(i) of this section will be a full-time employee of an international organization if that individual's employment with the organization is consistent with an employment schedule of a person with a standard full-time work schedule with the organization.

(iii) Full-time diplomatic or consular status. An individual is considered to have full-time diplomatic or consular status if—

(A) The individual has been accredited by a foreign government recognized de jure or de facto by the United States;

(B) The individual intends to engage primarily in official activities for that foreign government while in the United States; and

(C) The individual has been recognized by the President, or by the Secretary of State, or by a consular officer acting on behalf of the Secretary of State, as being entitled to such status.

(3) Teacher or trainee. A teacher or trainee includes any individual (and that individual's immediate family), other than a student, who is admitted temporarily to the United States as a nonimmigrant under section 101(a)(15)(J) (relating to the admission of teachers and trainees into the United States) or section 101(a)(15)(Q) (relating to the admission of participants in international cultural exchange programs) of the Immigration and Nationality Act (8 U.S.C. 1101(a)(15)(J), (Q)) and who substantially complies with the requirements of being admitted.

(4) Student. A student is any individual (and that individual's immediate family) who is admitted temporarily to the United States as a nonimmigrant under section 101(a)(15)(F) or (M) (relating to the admission of students into the United States) or as a student under section 101(a)(15)(J) (relating to the admission of teachers and trainees into the United States) or section 101(a)(15)(Q) (relating to the admission of participants in international cultural exchange programs) of the Immigration and Nationality Act (8 U.S.C. 1101(a)(15)(F), (J), (M), (Q)) who substantially complies with the requirements of being admitted. For rules concerning taxation of certain nonresident students or trainees, see section 871(c) and § 1.871–9(a) of this chapter.

* * *

(c) Medical condition—(1) In general. An individual will not be considered present on any day that the individual intends to leave and is unable to leave the United States because of a medical condition or medical problem that arose while the individual was present in the United States. A day of presence will not be excluded if the individual, who was initially prevented from leaving, is subsequently able to leave the United States and then remains in the United States beyond a reasonable period for making arrangements to leave the United States. A day will also not be excluded if the medical condition arose during a prior stay in the United States (whether or not days of presence during the prior stay were excluded) and the alien returns to the United States for treatment of the medical condition or medical problem that arose during the prior stay.

(2) Intent to leave the United States. For purposes of paragraph (c)(1) of this section, whether an individual intends to leave the United States on a particular day will be determined based on all the facts and circumstances. Thus, if at the time an individual's medical condition or medical problem arose, the individual was present in the United States for a definite purpose which by its nature could be accomplished within the United States during a period of time that would not cause the individual to be a resident under the substantial presence test, the individual may be able to establish that he or she intended to leave the United States. However, if the individual's purpose is of such a nature that an extended period of time would be required for its accomplishment (sufficient to cause the individual to be a resident under the substantial presence test), the individual would not be able to establish the requisite intent to leave the United States. If the individual is present in the United States for no particular purpose or a purpose by its nature that does not require a specific period of time to accomplish, the determination of whether the individual has the requisite intent to leave the United States will depend on all the surrounding facts and circumstances. In the case of an individual adjudicated mentally incompetent, proof of intent to leave the United States may be determined by analyzing the incompetent's pattern of behavior prior to the adjudication of incompetence. Generally, an individual will be presumed to have intended to leave during a period of illness if the individual leaves the United States within a reasonable period of time (time to make arrangements to leave) after becoming physically able to leave.

(3) Pre-existing medical condition. A medical condition or problem will not be considered to arise while the individual is present in the United States, if the condition or problem existed prior to the individual's arrival in the United States, and the individual was aware of the condition or problem, regardless of whether the individual required treatment for the condition or problem when the individual entered the United States.

(4) Examples. The following examples illustrate the application of this paragraph (c):

Example 1. B is in a serious automobile accident in the United States on March 25. B intended to leave the United States on March 31 (as evidenced by an airline ticket), but was unable to leave on that date as a result of the injuries suffered in the accident. B recovered from the injuries and was able to leave and did leave the United States on May 31. B's presence in the United States during the period from April 1 through May 31 will not be counted as days of presence in the United States.

Example 2. The facts are the same as in Example 1, except that B's return flight (as evidenced by an airline ticket) was scheduled for May 31. Because B did not intend to leave the United States until May 31, B may not exclude any days of presence in the United States.

(d) Days in transit. An alien individual may exclude days of presence in the United States if the individual is in transit between two foreign points, and is physically present in the United States for fewer than 24 hours. For purposes of this paragraph, an individual will be considered to be in transit if the individual pursues activities that are substantially related to completing his or her travel to a foreign point of destination. For example, an alien who travels between airports in the United States in order to change planes en route to the individual's destination will be considered to be in transit. However, if the individual attends a business meeting while he or she is present in the United States, whether or not that meeting is within the confines of the airport, the individual will not be considered to be in transit. For purposes of this paragraph, the term "foreign point" means any areas that are not included within the definition of the term "United States" provided in § 301.7701(b)–1(c)(2)(ii).

(e) Regular commuters from Mexico or Canada—(1) General rule. An alien individual will not be considered to be present in the United States on days that the individual commutes to the United States from the individual's residence in Mexico or Canada if the individual regularly commutes from Mexico or Canada. An alien individual will be considered to commute regularly if the individual commutes to the individual's location of employment or self-employment in the United States from his or her residence in Mexico or Canada on more than 75% of the workdays during the working period.

(2) Definitions. (i) The term commutes means to travel to employment or self-employment and to return to one's residence within a 24-hour period.

(ii) The term workdays means days on which the individual works in the United States or Canada or Mexico.

(iii) The term working period means the period beginning with the first day in the current year on which the individual is physically present in the United States for purposes of engaging in employment or self-employment and ending on the last day in the current year on which the individual is physically present in the United States for purposes of engaging in that employment or self-employment. If the nature of the employment or self-employment is such that it requires the individual to be present in the United States only on a seasonal or cyclical basis, the working period will begin with the first day of the season or cycle on which the individual is present in the United States for purposes of engaging in that employment or self-employment and end on the last day of the season or cycle on which the individual is present in the United States for the purpose of engaging in that employment or self-employment. Thus, there may be more than one working period in a calendar year and a working period may begin in one calendar year and end in the following calendar year.

(3) Examples. The following examples illustrate the operation of this paragraph (e):

Example 1. B lives in Mexico and is employed by Corporation X in its office in Mexico. B was temporarily assigned to X's office in the United States. B's employment in the United States office began on February 1, 1988, and continued through June 1, 1988. On June 2, B resumed his employment in Mexico. On 59 days in the period beginning on February 1, 1988, and ending on June 1, 1988, B travelled each morning from his residence in Mexico to X Corporation's United States office for the purpose of engaging in his employment with X Corporation. B returned to his residence in Mexico on each of those evenings. On seven days in the period from February 1, 1988, through June 1, 1988, B worked in X's Mexico office. B is not considered to have been present in the United States on any of the days that he travelled to X's United States office for the purpose of engaging in employment with Corporation X because he commuted to his place of employment within the United States on more than 75% of the workdays during the working period (59 workdays in the United States/66 workdays in the working period=89.4%).

Example 2. C, who lives in Canada, contracted with a resort located in the United States to provide snow-skiing instructions for the resort's customers for two skiing seasons, the first beginning on November 15, 1987, and ending on March 15, 1988, and the second beginning on November 15, 1988, and ending on March 15, 1989. On 90 days in each of the two skiing seasons, C travelled in the morning from Canada to the resort to provide skiing instructions pursuant to the contract. C returned to Canada on each of those evenings. On 20 days during each of the two skiing seasons, C worked in Canada. C is not considered to have been present in the United States on any of the days that she travelled to the United States to provide ski instructions in either the first working period beginning on November 15, 1987, and ending on March 15, 1988, or the second working period beginning on November 15, 1988, and ending on March 15, 1989, because she commuted to her employment within the United States on more than 75% of the workdays during each of the working periods (90 workdays in the United States/110 workdays in the working period=81.8%).

Example 3. D, who lives in Canada, is the sole proprietor of a wholesale lumber business with offices in both the United States and Canada. Beginning on January 4, 1988, and ending on February 12, 1988, D commuted to work in his United States office on 30 days. Beginning on February 15, 1988, and ending on March 25, 1988, D commuted to work in his Canadian office on 30 days. Beginning on March 28, 1988, and ending on May 27, 1988, D commuted to work in his United States office on 45 days. Subsequent to May 27, D did not commute to the United States on any other days in 1988. D is considered to have been present in the United States on each day that he travelled to his office in the United States because D did not commute to the United States office on more than 75% of the workdays during the working period beginning on January 4, 1988, and ending on May 27, 1988 (75 workdays in the United States/105 workdays in the working period=71.4%).

(f) Determination of excluded days applies beyond year of determination. If a day of presence is excluded under this section, then that day shall not be taken into account in the current year or the first or second preceding year.

[T.D. 8411, 57 FR 15245, April 27, 1992; T.D. 8411, 57 FR 28612, June 26, 1992; T.D. 8411, 57 FR 37190, Aug. 18, 1992; T.D. 8733, 62 FR 53386, Oct. 14, 1997]

§ 301.7701(b)–4 Residency time periods.

(a) First year of residency. An alien individual who was not a United States resident during the preceding calendar year and who is a United States resident for the current year will begin to be a resident for tax purposes on the alien's residency starting date. The residency starting date for an alien who meets the substantial presence test is the first day during the calendar year on which the individual is present in the United States. The residency starting date for an alien who meets the lawful permanent resident test (green card test), described in paragraph (b)(1) of § 301.7701(b)–1, is the first day during the calendar year in which the individual is physically present in the United States as a lawful permanent resident. The residency starting date for an alien who satisfies both the substantial presence test and the green card test will be the earlier of the first day the individual is physically present in the United States as a lawful permanent resident of the United States or the first day during the year that the individual is present for purposes of the substantial presence test. (See § 301.7701(b)–9(b)(1) for the transitional rule relating to the residency starting date of an alien individual who was a lawful permanent resident in 1984. See also § 301.7701(b)–3 for days that may be excluded.)

(b) Last year of residency—(1) General rule. An alien individual who is a United States resident during the current year but who is not a United States resident at any time during the following calendar year will cease to be a resident for tax purposes on the individual's residency termination date. Generally, the residency termination date will be the last day of the calendar year.

(2) Exceptions. Notwithstanding paragraph (b)(1) of this section, the residency termination date for an alien individual who meets the substantial presence test is the last day during the calendar year that the individual is physically present in the

United States if the individual establishes that, for the remainder of the calendar year, the individual's tax home was in a foreign country and he or she maintained a closer connection (within the meaning of § 301.7701(b) 2(d)) to that foreign country than to the United States. Similarly, the residency termination date for an alien who meets the green card test is the first day during the calendar year that the alien is no longer a lawful permanent resident if the individual establishes that, for the remainder of the calendar year, his or her tax home was in a foreign country and he or she maintained a closer connection to that foreign country than to the United States. The residency termination date for an alien who satisfies both the substantial presence test and the green card test for the current year, will be the later of the first day the individual is no longer a lawful permanent resident of the United States or the last day the individual was physically present in the United States if the alien establishes that, for the remainder of the calendar year, his or her tax home was in a foreign country and he or she maintained a closer connection to that foreign country than to the United States. It is immaterial whether the individual's tax home was in the United States, or that the individual had a closer connection to the United States than to the foreign country, prior to the date of his or her departure from the United States or the date on which the individual was no longer a lawful permanent resident, whichever is applicable.

(c) Rules relating to residency starting date and residency termination date—(1) De minimis presence. An alien individual may be present in the United States for up to 10 days without triggering the residency starting date (for purposes of the substantial presence test) or extending the residency termination date (for purposes of the substantial presence test) if the individual is able to establish that, during that period, the individual's tax home was in a foreign country and he or she maintained a closer connection to that foreign country than to the United States. Days from more than one period of presence may be disregarded for purposes of determining an individual's residency starting date or termination date so long as the total is not more than 10 days. However, an individual may not disregard any days that occur in a period of consecutive days of presence, if all the days that occur during that period cannot be excluded. An individual must include days of presence for purposes of determining whether the individual meets the substantial presence test even though the days may be disregarded for purposes of determining the individual's residency starting date or residency termination date.

(2) Proration. If an individual's residency starting date does not fall on the first day of the tax year, or the individual's residency termination date does not fall on the last day of the tax year, the individual's income tax liability should be calculated in accordance with § 1.871–13 of this chapter dealing with the taxation of individuals who change residence status during the taxable year.

(3) Residency starting date for certain individuals—(i) In general. If an alien individual (who otherwise does not meet the substantial presence test or the green card test for the current year) is physically present in the United States for at least 31 consecutive days during the current year, and also for a period of continuous presence beginning with the first day of that thirty-one day period (see paragraph (c)(3)(iii) of this section), then the individual may elect to be treated as a resident during the current year. The individual's residency starting date shall be the first day of that thirty-one day period, if—

(A) The individual was not a resident of the United States under the substantial presence test or the green card test in the year preceding the current year; and

(B) The individual is a resident of the United States in the subsequent year under the substantial presence test (whether or not the individual is also a resident of the United States under the green card test).

(ii) Determination of presence. Except as otherwise provided in paragraph (c)(3)(iii) of this section, an individual shall be treated as present in the United States on any day that the individual is physically present in the United States at any time during the day.

(iii) Thirty-one day period. For purposes of this paragraph (c)(3), the term thirty-one day period means any period of 31 consecutive days during which an individual is physically present in the United States during each day of the period.

(iv) Period of continuous presence. For purposes of this paragraph (c)(3), the term continuous presence means a period of presence in the United States that includes 75 percent of the days in the current year beginning with (and including) the first day of the individual's thirty-one day period of presence. Only for purposes of the continuous presence requirement, an individual will be deemed to be present in the United States for up to 5 days on which the individual is absent from the United States. These days will not be deemed to be days of presence for purposes of the thirty-one day period of presence requirement. If an individual is present for more than one thirty-one day period of presence and satisfies the continuous presence requirement with regard to each period, the individual's residency starting date shall be the first day of the first thirty-one day period of presence. If an individual is present for more than one thirty-one day period of presence but satisfies the continuous presence requirement only for a later thirty-one day period, the individual's residency starting date shall be the first day of the later thirty-one day period of presence. For purposes of this paragraph (c)(3), days of presence that are otherwise excluded under section 7701(b)(3)(D)(i) and § 301.7701(b)–3(a)(1) (exempt individual), (a)(2) (medical condition), (a)(3) (in transit between two foreign points), and (a)(4) (regular commuter) shall not be counted as days of presence for purposes of either the thirty-one day period or continuous presence requirement.

(v) Election procedure—(A) Filing requirements. An alien individual shall make an election to be treated as a resident under paragraph (c)(3) of this section by attaching a statement (described in paragraph (c)(3)(v)(C) of this section) to the individual's income tax return (Form 1040) for the taxable year for which the election is to be in effect (the election year). The alien individual may not make this election until such time as he has satisfied the substantial presence test for the year following the election year. If an alien individual has not satisfied the substantial presence test for the year following the election year as of the due date (not including extensions) of the tax return for the election year, the alien individual may request an extension of time for filing the return until a reasonable period after he or she has satisfied such test, provided that the individual pays with his or her extension application the amount of tax he or she expects to owe for the election year computed as if he or she were a nonresident alien throughout the election year. An election made under paragraph (c)(3) of this section may not be revoked without the approval of the Commissioner or his delegate.

(B) Election on behalf of a dependent child. An individual may make an election on behalf of a dependent child (as defined in paragraphs (1) and (2) of section 152(a), without regard to section 152(b)(3)) if the individual is qualified to make an election on his or her own behalf, the child qualifies to make an election under this paragraph (c)(3), and the child is not required by section 6012 to file a United States income tax return for the year for which the election is to be effective.

(C) Statement. The statement required by paragraph (c)(3)(v)(A) of this section shall include the name and address of the alien individual and contain a signed declaration that the election is being made. If the individual is also making an election on behalf of any dependent children, then the statement must include the required information with respect to those children. The statement must specify—

(1) That the alien individual was not a resident in the year immediately preceding the election year;

(2) That the alien individual is a resident under the substantial presence test in the year following the election year;

(3) The individual's number of days of presence in the United States during the year following the election year;

(4) The date or dates of the alien individual's thirty-one day period of presence and period of continuous presence in the United States during the election year; and

(5) The date or dates of absence from the United States during the election year that are deemed to be days of presence.

(vi) Penalty for failure to comply with filing requirements—(A) General rule. If an individual fails to comply with the election procedure of paragraph (c)(3)(v) of this section, the individual must file his or her income tax return for the current year as a nonresident alien.

(B) Exception. The penalty described in paragraph (c)(3)(vi)(A) of this section shall not apply if the individual can show by clear and convincing evidence that he or she took reasonable actions to become aware of the filing requirements and significant affirmative steps to comply with the requirements. An individual who requests an extension of time to file his or her income tax return pursuant to paragraph (c)(3)(v) of this section will be considered to have taken significant affirmative steps to comply with the requirement that the individual pay his or her tax determined as if the individual were a nonresident alien if the individual paid with his or her extension application at least 90 percent of the amount of the tax the individual actually owed for the election year computed as if he or she were a nonresident alien throughout the election year.

(d) Examples. The following examples illustrate the operation of this section:

Example 1. B, a citizen of foreign country X, is an alien who has never before been a United States resident for tax purposes. B comes to the United States on January 6, 1985, to attend a business meeting and returns to country X on January 10, 1985. B is able to establish a closer connection to country X for the period January 6–10. On March 1, 1985, B moves to the United States and resides here until August 20, 1985, when he returns to country X. On December 12, 1985, B comes to the United States for pleasure and stays here until December 16, 1985 when he returns to country X. B is able to establish a closer connection to country X for the period December 12–16. B is not a United States resident for tax purposes during the following year and can establish a closer connection to country X for the remainder of calendar year 1985. B is a resident of the United States under the substantial presence test because B is present in the United States for 183 days (5 days in January plus 173 days for the period March 1–August 20 plus 5 days in December). B's residency starting date is March 1, 1985, and his residency termination date is August 20, 1985.

Example 2. The facts are the same as in Example 1, except that B remains in the United States until December 17, 1985, and is able to establish a closer connection to country X for the period December 18 through 31. B's residency termination date is December 17, 1985.

Example 3. C, a citizen of foreign country Y, is an alien who has never before been a United States resident for tax purposes. C comes to the United States for the first time on February 10, 1985, and attends a business conference until February 24, 1985, when she returns to country Y. On April 20, 1985, C enters the United States as a lawful permanent resident. On November 10, 1985, C ceases to be a lawful permanent resident but stays on in the United States until November 20, 1985 when she returns to country Y. On December 8, 1985, C comes to the United States and stays here until December 17, 1985 when she returns to country Y.

She can establish a closer connection to country Y for that period.

C is not a resident of the United States during the following calendar year and can establish a closer connection to country Y for the remainder of calendar year 1985. C qualifies as a United States resident under both the green card test and the substantial presence test. C's residency starting date under the green card test is April 20, 1985. Under the substantial presence test, C's residency starting date is February 10, 1985, because she is present for more than ten days in February and cannot take advantage of the de minimis presence rule. Therefore, C's residency starting date is February 10, 1985. C's residency termination date under the green card test is November 10, 1985. Her residency termination date under the substantial presence test is November 20, because B can disregard ten days of presence in December. Thus, her residency termination date is November 20, 1985, the later of her residency termination date under the substantial presence test or the green card test.

Example 4. The facts are the same as in Example 3, except that C is initially present in the United States on business from February 5 to February 9, 1985. C is able to establish a closer connection to country Y for that period. C may take advantage of only ten days of de minimis presence and may exclude days from a continuous period of presence only if she can exclude all the days that occur during that period. Thus, C may choose either of the following periods of residency: residency starting date February 5, 1985, and residency termination date November 20, 1985, or residency starting date April 20, 1985, and residency termination date December 17, 1985.

Example 5. D, a citizen of foreign country Z, is an alien who has never before been a United States resident for tax purposes. D comes to the United States on November 1, 1985 and is present in the United States on 31 consecutive days (from November 1 through December 1, 1985). D returns to country Z on December 1 and does not come back to the United States until December 17, 1985. He remains in the United States for the rest of the year. During 1986, D is a resident of the United States under the substantial presence test. D may elect to be treated as a resident of the United States for 1985 because he was present in the United States in 1985 for a 31 consecutive day period of presence (November 1 through December 1, 1985) and for at least 75 percent of the days following (and including) the first day of D's 31 consecutive day period of presence (46 total days of presence in the United States/61 days in the period from November 1 through December 31=75.4%). If D makes the election to be treated as a resident, his residency starting date will be November 1, 1985.

Example 6. The facts are the same as in Example 5, except that D is absent from the United States on December 24, 25, 29, 30 and 31. D may make the election to be treated as a resident for 1985 because up to five days of absence will be deemed to be days of presence for purposes of the continuous presence requirement.

Example 7. F, a citizen of foreign country M, is an alien individual who has never before been a United States resident for tax purposes. F comes to the United States on January 1, 1985 and remains in the United States through January 31, 1985, when she returns to country M. F comes back to the United States on October 1, 1985 and is present in the United States through November 1, 1985. From November 1, 1985 through December 31, 1985, F is present in the United States for 38 days. Although F satisfies two 31 consecutive day periods of presence, (January 1 through January 31 and October 1 through November 1), she satisfies the continuous presence requirement only with regard to the later period of presence (69 total days of presence/92 days in the period from October 1 through December 31=75%). Thus, if F makes the election to be treated as a resident, his residency starting date is October 1, 1985.

(e) No lapse—(1) Residency in prior year. An alien individual who was a United States resident during any part of the preceding calendar year and who is a United States resident for any part of the current year will be considered to be taxable as a resident at the beginning of the current year. For purposes of this paragraph (e)(1), it is immaterial whether an individual is considered to be a resident under the substantial presence test or the green card test.

(2) Residency in following year. An alien individual who is a United States resident for any part of the current year and who is also a United States resident for any part of the following year (regardless of whether the individual has a closer connection to a foreign country than the United States during the current year) will be taxable as a resident through the end of the current year. For purposes of this paragraph (e)(2), it is immaterial whether an individual is considered to be a resident under the substantial presence test or the green card test.

(3) Special rule. If an individual meets the green card test for the current year but is not physically present in the United States during the current year, then the individual's residency starting date shall be the first day of the following year.

(4) Example. The following example illustrates the application of this paragraph (e).

Example. B, an alien individual who is a citizen of foreign country M, comes to the United States for the first time on May 1, 1985, and remains in the United States until November 5, 1985, when he returns to country M. B comes back to the United States on March 5, 1986 as a lawful permanent resident and remains in the United States until September 10, 1986, when he ceases to be a lawful permanent resident and returns to country M. B is not a resident in calendar year 1987. B's United States residency in calendar year 1985 continues through December 31, 1985, because he is a United States resident in the following calendar year. In calendar year 1986, B's United States residency is deemed to begin on January 1, 1986 because B qualified as a resident in the preceding calendar year. Thus, B's residency period in the United States begins on May 1, 1985, and ends on September 10, 1986.

[T.D. 8411, 57 FR 15247, April 27, 1992; T.D. 8411, 57 FR 28612, June 26, 1992]

Rev. Proc. 2025–32

2025–45 I.R.B. 695

* * *

.37 *Expatriation to Avoid Tax*. For calendar year 2026, under § 877A(g)(1)(A), unless an exception under § 877A(g)(1)(B) applies, an individual is a covered expatriate if the individual's "average annual net income tax" under § 877(a)(2)(A) for the five taxable years ending before the expatriation date is more than $211,000.

.38 *Tax Responsibilities of Expatriation*. For taxable years beginning in 2026, the amount that would be includible in the gross income of a covered expatriate by reason of § 877A(a)(1) is reduced (but not below zero) by $910,000 pursuant to § 877A(a)(3).

.39 *Foreign Earned Income Exclusion*. For taxable years beginning in 2026, the foreign earned income exclusion amount under § 911(b)(2)(D)(i) is $132,900.

* * *

.60 *Revocation or Denial of Passport in Case of Certain Tax Delinquencies*. For calendar year 2026, the amount of a serious delinquent tax debt under § 7345 is $66,000.

* * *

UNITED STATES MODEL
INCOME TAX CONVENTION (February 17, 2016)

CONVENTION BETWEEN
THE GOVERNMENT OF THE UNITED STATES OF AMERICA
AND THE GOVERNMENT OF _________
FOR THE AVOIDANCE OF DOUBLE TAXATION AND THE PREVENTION OF TAX EVASION
WITH RESPECT TO TAXES ON INCOME

The Government of the United States of America and the Government of _________, intending to conclude a Convention for the elimination of double taxation with respect to taxes on income without creating opportunities for non-taxation or reduced taxation through tax evasion or avoidance (including through treaty-shopping arrangements aimed at obtaining reliefs provided in this Convention for the indirect benefit of residents of third states), have agreed as follows:

Article 1

GENERAL SCOPE

1. This Convention shall apply only to persons who are residents of one or both of the Contracting States, except as otherwise provided in this Convention.

2. This Convention shall not restrict in any manner any benefit now or hereafter accorded:

   a) by the laws of either Contracting State; or

   b) by any other agreement to which both Contracting States are parties.

3. a) Notwithstanding the provisions of subparagraph (b) of paragraph 2 of this Article:

   i) for purposes of paragraph 3 of Article XXII (Consultation) of the General Agreement on Trade in Services, the Contracting States agree that any question arising as to the interpretation or application of this Convention and, in particular, whether a taxation measure is within the scope of this Convention, shall be determined exclusively in accordance with the provisions of Article 25 (Mutual Agreement Procedure) of this Convention; and

   ii) the provisions of Article XVII (National Treatment) of the General Agreement on Trade in Services shall not apply to a taxation measure unless the competent authorities agree that the measure is not within the scope of Article 24 (Non-Discrimination) of this Convention.

   b) For the purposes of this paragraph, a "measure" is a law, regulation, rule, procedure, decision, administrative action or any similar provision or action.

4. Except to the extent provided in paragraph 5 of this Article, this Convention shall not affect the taxation by a Contracting State of its residents (as determined under Article 4 (Resident)) and its citizens. Notwithstanding the other provisions of this Convention, a former citizen or former long-term resident of a Contracting State may be taxed in accordance with the laws of that Contracting State.

5. The provisions of paragraph 4 of this Article shall not affect:

a) the benefits conferred by a Contracting State under paragraph 3 of Article 7 (Business Profits), paragraph 2 of Article 9 (Associated Enterprises), paragraph 7 of Article 13 (Gains), subparagraph (b) of paragraph 1, paragraphs 2, 3 and 6 of Article 17 (Pensions, Social Security, Annuities, Alimony and Child Support), paragraph 3 of Article 18 (Pension Funds), and Articles 23 (Relief From Double Taxation), 24 (Non-Discrimination) and 25 (Mutual Agreement Procedure); and

b) the benefits conferred by a Contracting State under paragraph 1 of Article 18 (Pension Funds), and Articles 19 (Government Service), 20 (Students and Trainees) and 27 (Members of Diplomatic Missions and Consular Posts), upon individuals who are neither citizens of, nor have been admitted for permanent residence in, that Contracting State.

6. For the purposes of this Convention, an item of income, profit or gain derived by or through an entity that is treated as wholly or partly fiscally transparent under the taxation laws of either Contracting State shall be considered to be derived by a resident of a Contracting State, but only to the extent that the item is treated for purposes of the taxation laws of such Contracting State as the income, profit or gain of a resident.

7. Where an item of income, profit or gain arising in one of the Contracting States otherwise would be entitled to the benefits of this Convention in that Contracting State and, under the law of the other Contracting State, a person's tax in respect of such item is determined by reference to the amount thereof that is remitted to or received in that other Contracting State and not by reference to the full amount thereof, then the relief to be allowed under this Convention in the first-mentioned Contracting State shall apply only to so much of the amount as is taxed in the other Contracting State.

8. Where an enterprise of a Contracting State derives income from the other Contracting State, and the first-mentioned Contracting State treats that income as attributable to a permanent establishment situated outside of that Contracting State, the benefits of this Convention shall not apply to that income if:

a) the profits that are treated as attributable to the permanent establishment are subject to a combined aggregate effective rate of tax in the first-mentioned Contracting State and the state in which the permanent establishment is situated that is less than the lesser of (i) 15 percent or (ii) 60 percent of the general statutory rate of company tax applicable in the first-mentioned Contracting State; or

b) the permanent establishment is situated in a third state that does not have a comprehensive convention for the avoidance of double taxation in force with the Contracting State from which the benefits of this Convention are being claimed, unless the first-mentioned Contracting State includes the income treated as attributable to the permanent establishment in its tax base.

However, if a resident of a Contracting State is denied the benefits of this Convention pursuant to this paragraph, the competent authority of the other Contracting State may, nevertheless, grant the benefits of this Convention with respect to a specific item of income if such competent authority determines that such grant of benefits is justified in light of the reasons such resident did not satisfy the requirements of this paragraph (such as the existence of losses). The competent authority of the Contracting State to which the request has been made shall consult with the competent authority of the other Contracting State before either granting or denying a request made under this paragraph by a resident of that other Contracting State.

Article 2

TAXES COVERED

1. This Convention shall apply to taxes on income imposed on behalf of a Contracting State irrespective of the manner in which they are levied.

2. There shall be regarded as taxes on income all taxes imposed on total income, or on elements of income, including taxes on gains from the alienation of property.

3. The existing taxes to which this Convention shall apply are:

a) in the case of __________:

b) in the case of the United States: the Federal income taxes imposed by the Internal Revenue Code (which do not include social security and unemployment taxes) and the Federal taxes imposed on the investment income of foreign private foundations.

4. This Convention also shall apply to any identical or substantially similar taxes that are imposed after the date of signature of this Convention in addition to, or in place of, the existing taxes. The competent authorities of the Contracting States shall notify each other of any significant changes that have been made in their taxation laws or other laws that relate to the application of this Convention.

Article 3

GENERAL DEFINITIONS

1. For the purposes of this Convention, unless the context otherwise requires:

a) the term "person" includes an individual, an estate, a trust, a partnership, a company, and any other body of persons;

b) the term "company" means any body corporate or any entity that is treated as a body corporate for tax purposes according to the laws of the Contracting State in which it is resident;

c) the terms "enterprise of a Contracting State" and "enterprise of the other Contracting State" mean, respectively, an enterprise carried on by a resident of a Contracting State, and an enterprise carried on by a resident of the other Contracting State; the terms also include an enterprise carried on by a resident of a Contracting State through an entity that is treated as fiscally transparent in that Contracting State;

d) the term "enterprise" applies to the carrying on of any business;

e) the term "business" includes the performance of professional services and of other activities of an independent character;

f) the term "international traffic" means any transport by a ship or aircraft, except when such transport is solely between places in a Contracting State;

g) the term "competent authority" means:

i) in __________: ----------; and

ii) in the United States: the Secretary of the Treasury or his delegate;

h) the term "__________:" means ----------;

i) the term "United States" means the United States of America, and includes the states thereof and the District of Columbia; such term also includes the territorial sea thereof and the sea bed and subsoil of the submarine areas adjacent to that territorial sea, over which the United States exercises sovereign rights in accordance with international law; the term, however, does not include Puerto Rico, the Virgin Islands, Guam or any other United States possession or territory;

j) the term "national" of a Contracting State means:

i) any individual possessing the nationality or citizenship of that Contracting State; and

ii) any legal person, partnership or association deriving its status as such from the laws in force in that Contracting State;

k) the term "pension fund" means any person established in a Contracting State that is:

i) generally exempt from income taxation in that Contracting State; and

ii) operated exclusively or almost exclusively:

A) to administer or provide pension or retirement benefits; or

B) to earn income for the benefit of one or more persons established in the same Contracting State that are generally exempt from income taxation in that Contracting State and that are operated exclusively or almost exclusively to administer or provide pension or retirement benefits;

l) the term "special tax regime" means any statute, regulation or administrative practice in a Contracting State with respect to a tax described in Article 2 (Taxes Covered) that meets all of the following conditions:

i) results in one or more of the following:

A) a preferential rate of taxation for interest, royalties, guarantee fees or any combination thereof, as compared to income from sales of goods or services;

B) a permanent reduction in the tax base with respect to interest, royalties, guarantee fees or any combination thereof, without a comparable reduction for income from sales of goods or services, by allowing:

1) an exclusion from gross receipts;

2) a deduction without regard to any corresponding payment or obligation to make a payment;

3) a deduction for dividends paid or accrued; or

4) taxation that is inconsistent with the principles of Article 7 (Business Profits) or Article 9 (Associated Enterprises); or

C) a preferential rate of taxation or a permanent reduction in the tax base of the type described in part (1), (2), (3) or (4) of subclause (B) of this clause with respect to substantially all of a company's income or substantially all of a company's foreign source income, for companies that do not engage in the active conduct of a trade or business in that Contracting State;

ii) in the case of any preferential rate of taxation or permanent reduction in the tax base for royalties, does not condition such benefits on the extent of research and development activities that take place in the Contracting State;

iii) is generally expected to result in a rate of taxation[1] that is less than the lesser of either:

A) 15 percent; or

B) 60 percent of the general statutory rate of company tax applicable in the other Contracting State;

iv) does not apply principally to:

A) pension funds;

B) organizations that are established and maintained exclusively for religious, charitable, scientific, artistic, cultural or educational purposes;

C) persons the taxation of which achieves a single level of taxation either in the hands of the person or the person's shareholders (with at most one year of deferral), that hold a diversified portfolio of securities, that are subject to investor-protection regulation in the Contracting State and the interests in which are marketed primarily to retail investors; or

D) persons the taxation of which achieves a single level of taxation either in the hands of the person or the person's shareholders (with at most one year of deferral) and that hold predominantly real estate assets; and

v) after consultation with the first-mentioned Contracting State, has been identified by the other Contracting State through diplomatic channels to the first-mentioned Contracting State as satisfying clauses (i) through (iv) of this subparagraph.

No statute, regulation or administrative practice shall be treated as a special tax regime until 30 days after the date when the other Contracting State issues a written public notification identifying the regime as satisfying clauses (i) through (v) of this subparagraph; and

m) two persons shall be "connected persons" if one owns, directly or indirectly, at least 50 percent of the beneficial interest in the other (or, in the case of a company, at least 50 percent of the aggregate vote and value of the company's shares) or another person owns, directly or indirectly, at least 50 percent of the beneficial interest (or, in the case of a company, at least 50 percent of the aggregate vote and value of the company's shares) in each person. In any case, a person shall be connected to another if, based

[1] For inclusion in an instrument reflecting an agreed interpretation: Except as provided below, the rate of taxation shall be determined based on the income tax principles of the Contracting State that has implemented the regime in question. Therefore, in the case of a regime that provides only for a preferential rate of taxation, the generally expected rate of taxation under the regime will equal such preferential rate. In the case of a regime that provides only for a permanent reduction in the tax base, the rate of taxation will equal the statutory rate of company tax generally applicable in the Contracting State to companies subject to the regime in question less the product of such rate and the percentage reduction in the tax base (with the baseline tax base determined under the principles of the Contracting State, but without regard to any permanent reductions in the tax base described in subparagraph (*l*)(i)(B)) that the regime is generally expected to provide. Therefore, a regime that generally provides for a 20 percent permanent reduction in a company's tax base would have a rate of taxation equal to the applicable statutory rate of company tax reduced by 20 percent of such statutory rate. In the case of a regime that provides for both a preferential rate of taxation and a permanent reduction in the tax base, the rate of taxation would be based on the preferential rate of taxation reduced by the product of such rate and the percentage reduction in the tax base.

on all the relevant facts and circumstances, one has control of the other or both are under the control of the same person or persons.

2. As regards the application of this Convention at any time by a Contracting State, any term not defined herein shall, unless the context otherwise requires, or the competent authorities agree to a common meaning pursuant to the provisions of Article 25 (Mutual Agreement Procedure), have the meaning that it has at that time under the law of that Contracting State for the purposes of the taxes to which this Convention applies, any meaning under the applicable tax laws of that Contracting State prevailing over a meaning given to the term under other laws of that Contracting State.

Article 4

RESIDENT

1. For the purposes of this Convention, the term "resident of a Contracting State" means any person who, under the laws of that Contracting State, is liable to tax therein by reason of his domicile, residence, citizenship, place of management, place of incorporation, or any other criterion of a similar nature, and also includes that Contracting State and any political subdivision or local authority thereof. This term does not include any person whose tax is determined in that Contracting State on a fixed-fee, "forfait" or similar basis, or who is liable to tax in respect only of income from sources in that Contracting State or of profits attributable to a permanent establishment in that Contracting State.

2. The term "resident of a Contracting State" includes:

a) a pension fund established in that Contracting State; and

b) an organization that is established and maintained in that Contracting State exclusively for religious, charitable, scientific, artistic, cultural, or educational purposes;

notwithstanding that all or part of its income or gains may be exempt from tax under the domestic law of that Contracting State.

3. Where, by reason of the provisions of paragraph 1 of this Article, an individual is a resident of both Contracting States, then his status shall be determined as follows:

a) he shall be deemed to be a resident only of the Contracting State in which he has a permanent home available to him; if he has a permanent home available to him in both Contracting States, he shall be deemed to be a resident only of the Contracting State with which his personal and economic relations are closer (center of vital interests);

b) if the Contracting State in which he has his center of vital interests cannot be determined, or if he does not have a permanent home available to him in either Contracting State, he shall be deemed to be a resident only of the Contracting State in which he has a habitual abode;

c) if he has a habitual abode in both Contracting States or in neither of them, he shall be deemed to be a resident only of the Contracting State of which he is a national;

d) if he is a national of both Contracting States or of neither of them, the competent authorities of the Contracting States shall endeavor to settle the question by mutual agreement.

4. Where by reason of the provisions of paragraph 1 of this Article a company is a resident of both Contracting States, such company shall not be treated as a resident of either Contracting State for purposes of its claiming the benefits provided by this Convention.

5. Where by reason of the provisions of paragraph 1 of this Article a person other than an individual or a company is a resident of both Contracting States, the competent authorities of the Contracting States shall by mutual agreement endeavor to determine the mode of application of this Convention to that person.

Article 5

PERMANENT ESTABLISHMENT

1. For the purposes of this Convention, the term "permanent establishment" means a fixed place of business through which the business of an enterprise is wholly or partly carried on.

2. The term "permanent establishment" includes especially:

a) a place of management;

b) a branch;

c) an office;

d) a factory;

e) a workshop; and

f) a mine, an oil or gas well, a quarry, or any other place of extraction of natural resources.

3. A building site or construction or installation project, or an installation or drilling rig or ship used for the exploration or exploitation of the sea bed and its subsoil and their natural resources, situated in one of the Contracting States constitutes a permanent establishment only if it lasts, or the activities of the rig or ship lasts, for more than twelve months. For the sole purpose of determining whether the twelve-month period referred to in this paragraph has been exceeded:

a) where an enterprise of a Contracting State carries on activities in the other Contracting State at a place that constitutes a building site or construction or installation project and these activities are carried on during periods of time that in the aggregate do not last more than twelve months; and

b) connected activities are carried on at the same building site or construction or installation project during different periods of time, each exceeding thirty days, by one or more enterprises that are connected persons with respect to the first-mentioned enterprise, these different periods of time shall be added to the periods of time during which the first-mentioned enterprise has carried on activities at that building site or construction or installation project.

4. Notwithstanding the preceding provisions of this Article, the term "permanent establishment" shall be deemed not to include:

a) the use of facilities solely for the purpose of storage, display or delivery of goods or merchandise belonging to the enterprise;

b) the maintenance of a stock of goods or merchandise belonging to the enterprise solely for the purpose of storage, display or delivery;

c) the maintenance of a stock of goods or merchandise belonging to the enterprise solely for the purpose of processing by another enterprise;

d) the maintenance of a fixed place of business solely for the purpose of purchasing goods or merchandise, or of collecting information, for the enterprise;

e) the maintenance of a fixed place of business solely for the purpose of carrying on, for the enterprise, any other activity of a preparatory or auxiliary character;

f) the maintenance of a fixed place of business solely for any combination of the activities mentioned in subparagraphs (a) through (e) of this paragraph, provided that the overall activity of the fixed place of business resulting from this combination is of a preparatory or auxiliary character.

5. Notwithstanding the provisions of paragraphs 1 and 2 of this Article, where a person—other than an agent of an independent status to whom paragraph 6 of this Article applies—is acting on behalf of an enterprise and has and habitually exercises in a Contracting State an authority to conclude contracts that are binding on the enterprise, that enterprise shall be deemed to have a permanent establishment in that Contracting State in respect of any activities that the person undertakes for the enterprise, unless the activities of such person are limited to those mentioned in paragraph 4 that, if exercised through a fixed place of business, would not make this fixed place of business a permanent establishment under the provisions of that paragraph.

6. An enterprise shall not be deemed to have a permanent establishment in a Contracting State merely because it carries on business in that Contracting State through a broker, general commission agent, or any other agent of an independent status, provided that such persons are acting in the ordinary course of their business as independent agents.

7. The fact that a company that is a resident of a Contracting State controls or is controlled by a company that is a resident of the other Contracting State, or that carries on business in that other Contracting State (whether through a permanent establishment or otherwise), shall not be taken into account in determining whether either company has a permanent establishment in that other Contracting State.

Article 6

INCOME FROM REAL PROPERTY (IMMOVABLE PROPERTY)

1. Income derived by a resident of a Contracting State from real property (immovable property), including income from agriculture or forestry, situated in the other Contracting State may be taxed in that other Contracting State.

2. The term "real property" or "immovable property" shall have the meaning which it has under the law of the Contracting State in which the property in question is situated. The term shall in any case include property accessory to real property (immovable property), livestock and equipment used in agriculture and forestry, rights to which the provisions of general law respecting landed property apply, usufruct of real property (immovable property) and rights to variable or fixed payments as consideration for the working of, or the right to work, mineral deposits, sources and other natural resources. Ships and aircraft shall not be regarded as real property (immovable property).

3. The provisions of paragraph 1 of this Article shall apply to income derived from the direct use, letting, or use in any other form of real property (immovable property).

4. The provisions of paragraphs 1 and 3 of this Article shall also apply to the income from real property (immovable property) of an enterprise.

5. A resident of a Contracting State that is liable to tax in the other Contracting State on income from real property (immovable property) situated in the other Contracting State may elect for any taxable year to compute the tax on such income on a net basis as if such income were business profits attributable to a permanent establishment in such other Contracting State. Any such election shall be binding for the taxable year of the election and all subsequent taxable years unless the competent authority of the Contracting State in which the property is situated agrees to terminate the election.

Article 7

BUSINESS PROFITS

1. Profits of an enterprise of a Contracting State shall be taxable only in that Contracting State unless the enterprise carries on business in the other Contracting State through a permanent establishment situated therein. If the enterprise carries on business as aforesaid, the profits that are attributable to the permanent establishment in accordance with the provisions of paragraph 2 of this Article may be taxed in that other Contracting State.

2. For the purposes of this Article, the profits that are attributable in each Contracting State to the permanent establishment referred to in paragraph 1 of this Article are the profits it might be expected to make, in particular in its dealings with other parts of the enterprise, if it were a separate and independent enterprise engaged in the same or similar activities under the same or similar conditions, taking into account the functions performed, assets used and risks assumed by the enterprise through the permanent establishment and through the other parts of the enterprise.

3. Where, in accordance with paragraph 2 of this Article, a Contracting State adjusts the profits that are attributable to a permanent establishment of an enterprise of one of the Contracting States and taxes accordingly profits of the enterprise that have been charged to tax in the other Contracting State, the other Contracting State shall, to the extent necessary to eliminate double taxation, make an appropriate adjustment if it agrees with the adjustment made by the first-mentioned Contracting State; if the other Contracting State does not so agree, the Contracting States shall eliminate any double taxation resulting therefrom by mutual agreement.

4. Where profits include items of income that are dealt with separately in other Articles of this Convention, then the provisions of those Articles shall not be affected by the provisions of this Article.

5. In applying this Article, paragraph 8 of Article 10 (Dividends), paragraph 5 of Article 11 (Interest), paragraph 5 of Article 12 (Royalties), paragraph 3 of Article 13 (Gains) and paragraph 3 of Article 21 (Other Income), any income, profit or gain attributable to a permanent establishment during its existence is taxable in the Contracting State where such permanent establishment is situated even if the payments are deferred until such permanent establishment has ceased to exist.

Article 8

SHIPPING AND AIR TRANSPORT

1. Profits of an enterprise of a Contracting State from the operation of ships or aircraft in international traffic shall be taxable only in that Contracting State.

2. For purposes of this Article, profits from the operation of ships or aircraft include, but are not limited to:

a) profits from the rental of ships or aircraft on a full (time or voyage) basis;

b) profits from the rental on a bareboat basis of ships or aircraft if the rental income is incidental to profits from the operation of ships or aircraft in international traffic; and

c) profits from the rental on a bareboat basis of ships or aircraft if such ships or aircraft are operated in international traffic by the lessee.

Profits derived by an enterprise from the inland transport of property or passengers within either Contracting State shall be treated as profits from the operation of ships or aircraft in international traffic if such transport is undertaken as part of international traffic.

3. Profits of an enterprise of a Contracting State from the use, maintenance, or rental of containers (including trailers, barges, and related equipment for the transport of containers) shall be taxable only in that Contracting State, except to the extent that those containers are used for transport solely between places within the other Contracting State.

4. The provisions of paragraphs 1 and 3 of this Article shall also apply to profits from participation in a pool, a joint business, or an international operating agency.

Article 9

ASSOCIATED ENTERPRISES

1. Where:

a) an enterprise of a Contracting State participates directly or indirectly in the management, control or capital of an enterprise of the other Contracting State; or

b) the same persons participate directly or indirectly in the management, control, or capital of an enterprise of a Contracting State and an enterprise of the other Contracting State;

and in either case conditions are made or imposed between the two enterprises in their commercial or financial relations that differ from those that would be made between independent enterprises, then any profits that, but for those conditions, would have accrued to one of the enterprises, but by reason of those conditions have not so accrued, may be included in the profits of that enterprise and taxed accordingly.

2. Where a Contracting State includes in the profits of an enterprise of that Contracting State, and taxes accordingly, profits on which an enterprise of the other Contracting State has been charged to tax in that other Contracting State, and the other Contracting State agrees that the profits so included are profits that would have accrued to the enterprise of the first-mentioned Contracting State if the conditions made between the two enterprises had been those that would have been made between independent enterprises, then that other Contracting State shall make an appropriate adjustment to the amount of the tax charged therein on those profits. In determining such adjustment, due regard shall be had to the other provisions of this Convention and the competent authorities of the Contracting States shall if necessary consult each other.

Article 10

DIVIDENDS

1. Dividends paid by a company that is a resident of a Contracting State to a resident of the other Contracting State may be taxed in that other Contracting State.

2. However, such dividends may also be taxed in the Contracting State of which the company paying the dividends is a resident and according to the laws of that Contracting State, but if the beneficial owner of the dividends is a resident of the other Contracting State, except as otherwise provided, the tax so charged shall not exceed:

a) 5 percent of the gross amount of the dividends if, for the twelve-month period ending on the date on which the entitlement to the dividends is determined:

i) the beneficial owner has been a company that was a resident of the other Contracting State or of a qualifying third state. The term "qualifying third state" means a state that has in effect a comprehensive convention for the avoidance of double taxation with the Contracting State of the company paying the dividends that would have allowed the beneficial owner to benefit from a rate of tax on dividends that is less than or equal to 5 percent; and

ii) at least 10 percent of the aggregate vote and value of the shares of the payor of the dividends was owned directly by the beneficial owner or a qualifying predecessor owner. The term "qualifying predecessor owner" means a company from which the beneficial owner acquired the shares of the payor of the dividends, but only if such company was, at the time the shares were acquired, a connected person with respect to the beneficial owner of the dividend, and a resident of a state that has in effect a comprehensive convention for the avoidance of double taxation with the Contracting State of the company paying the dividends that would have allowed such company to benefit from a rate of tax on dividends that is less than or equal to 5 percent. For this purpose, a company that is a resident of a Contracting State shall be considered to own directly the shares owned by an entity that:

A) is considered fiscally transparent under the laws of that Contracting State; and

B) is not a resident of the other Contracting State of which the company paying the dividends is a resident;

in proportion to the company's ownership interest in that entity; and

b) 15 percent of the gross amount of the dividends in all other cases.

This paragraph shall not affect the taxation of the company in respect of the profits out of which the dividends are paid.

3. Notwithstanding the provisions of paragraph 2 of this Article, dividends shall not be taxed in the Contracting State of which the company paying the dividends is a resident if:

a) the beneficial owner of the dividends is a pension fund that is a resident of the other Contracting State; and

b) such dividends are not derived from the carrying on of a trade or business by the pension fund or through a person that is a connected person with respect to the pension fund.

4. a) Subparagraph (a) of paragraph 2 of this Article shall not apply in the case of dividends paid by a U.S. Regulated Investment Company (RIC) or a U.S. Real Estate Investment Trust (REIT). In the case of dividends paid by a RIC, subparagraph (b) of paragraph 2 and paragraph 3 of this Article shall apply. In the case of dividends paid by a REIT, subparagraph (b) of paragraph 2 and paragraph 3 of this Article shall apply only if:

i) the beneficial owner of the dividends is an individual or pension fund, in either case holding an interest of not more than 10 percent in the REIT;

ii) the dividends are paid with respect to a class of shares that is publicly traded and the beneficial owner of the dividends is a person holding an interest of not more than 5 percent of any class of the REIT's shares; or

iii) the beneficial owner of the dividends is a person holding an interest of not more than 10 percent in the REIT and the REIT is diversified.

b) For purposes of this paragraph, a REIT shall be "diversified" if the value of no single interest in real property (immovable property) exceeds 10 percent of its total interests in real property (immovable property). For the purposes of this rule, foreclosure property shall not be considered an interest in real property (immovable property). Where a REIT holds an interest in a partnership, it shall be treated as owning directly a proportion of the partnership's interests in real property (immovable property) corresponding to its interest in the partnership.

5. In the case of the United States, notwithstanding the provisions of paragraph 2 of this Article, dividends paid by an expatriated entity and beneficially owned by a company resident in __________ that is a connected person with respect to such expatriated entity may be taxed in accordance with the law of the United States for a period of ten years beginning on the date on which the acquisition of the domestic entity is completed. For purposes of applying this paragraph:

a) no effect shall be given to any amendment to section 7874 of the Internal Revenue Code after the date of signature of this Convention; and

b) no entity shall be treated as an expatriated entity that:

i) is a connected person with respect to the domestic entity immediately after the date on which the acquisition of the domestic entity is completed; and

ii) prior to that date, was never a connected person with respect to the domestic entity.

However, an entity described in the preceding sentence shall become an expatriated entity if, subsequent to the date on which the acquisition of the domestic entity is completed, the entity joins in filing a U.S. consolidated return with either the domestic entity or another entity that was a connected person with respect to the domestic entity immediately prior to the date on which the acquisition of the domestic entity was completed.

6. Notwithstanding the provisions of paragraphs 1 and 2 of this Article, in the case of a company seeking to satisfy the requirements of paragraph 4 of Article 22 (Limitation on Benefits) regarding a dividend, if such company fails to satisfy the criteria of that paragraph solely by reason of:

a) the requirement in subclause (B) of clause (i) of subparagraph (e) of paragraph 7 of Article 22 (Limitation on Benefits) of this Convention; or

b) the requirement in clause (ii) of subparagraph (e) of paragraph 7 of Article 22 (Limitation on Benefits) that a person entitled to benefits under paragraph 5 of Article 22 (Limitation on Benefits) would be entitled to a rate of tax with respect to the dividend that is less than or equal to the rate applicable under paragraph 2 of this Article;

such company may be taxed in the Contracting State of which the company paying the dividends is a resident and according to the laws of that Contracting State. In these cases, however, the tax so charged shall not exceed the highest rate among the rates of tax to which persons described in subparagraph (e) of paragraph 7 of Article 22 (Limitation on Benefits) of this Convention (notwithstanding the requirements referred to in subparagraphs (a) and (b) of this paragraph) would have been entitled if such persons had received the dividend directly. For purposes of this paragraph, (i) such persons' indirect ownership of the shares of the company paying the dividends shall be treated as direct ownership, and (ii) a person described in clause (iii) of subparagraph (e) of paragraph 7 of Article 22 (Limitation on Benefits) shall be treated as entitled to the limitation of tax to which such person would be entitled if such person were a resident of the same Contracting State as the company receiving the dividends.

7. For purposes of this Article, the term "dividends" means income from shares or other rights, not being debt-claims, participating in profits, as well as income that is subject to the same taxation treatment as income from shares under the laws of the Contracting State of which the company making the distribution is a resident. The term does not include distributions that are treated as gain under the laws of the Contracting State of which the company making the distribution is a resident. In such case, the provisions of Article 13 (Gains) shall apply.

8. The provisions of paragraphs 1 through 6 of this Article shall not apply if the beneficial owner of the dividends, being a resident of a Contracting State, carries on business in the other Contracting State, of which the company paying the dividends is a resident, through a permanent establishment situated therein, and the holding in respect of which the dividends are paid is effectively connected with such permanent establishment. In such case the provisions of Article 7 (Business Profits) shall apply.

9. A Contracting State may not impose any tax on dividends paid by a resident of the other Contracting State, except insofar as the dividends are paid to a resident of the first-mentioned Contracting State or the dividends are attributable to a permanent establishment situated therein, nor may it impose tax on a corporation's undistributed profits, except as provided in paragraph 10 of this Article, even if the dividends paid or the undistributed profits consist wholly or partly of profits or income arising in that Contracting State.

10. a) A company that is a resident of one of the Contracting States and that has a permanent establishment in the other Contracting State or that is subject to tax in the other Contracting State on a net basis on its income that may be taxed in the other Contracting State under Article 6 (Income from Real Property (Immovable Property)) or under paragraph 1 of Article 13 (Gains) may be subject in that other Contracting State to a tax in addition to the tax allowable under the other provisions of this Convention.

b) Such tax, however, may be imposed:

i) on only the portion of the business profits of the company attributable to the permanent establishment and the portion of the income referred to in subparagraph (a) of this paragraph that is subject to tax under Article 6 (Income from Real Property (Immovable Property)) or under paragraph 1 of Article 13 (Gains) that, in the case of the United States, represents the dividend equivalent amount of such profits or income and, in the case of __________, is an amount that is analogous to the dividend equivalent amount; and

ii) at a rate not in excess of the rate specified in subparagraph (a) of paragraph 2 or paragraph 6 of this Article, but only if for the twelve-month period ending on the date on which the entitlement to the dividend equivalent amount is determined, the company has been a resident of the other Contracting State or of a qualifying third state. The term "qualifying third state" has the same meaning as in clause (i) of subparagraph (a) of paragraph 2 of this Article.

Article 11

INTEREST

1. Interest arising in a Contracting State and beneficially owned by a resident of the other Contracting State shall be taxable only in that other Contracting State.

2. Notwithstanding the provisions of paragraph 1 of this Article:

a) interest arising in __________ that is determined with reference to receipts, sales, income, profits or other cash flow of the debtor or a connected person with respect to the debtor, to any change in the value of any property of the debtor or a connected person with respect to the debtor or to any dividend, partnership distribution or similar payment made by the debtor or a connected person with respect to the debtor may be taxed in __________, and according to the laws of __________, but if the beneficial owner is a resident of the United States, the interest may be taxed at a rate not exceeding 15 percent of the gross amount of the interest;

b) interest arising in the United States that is contingent interest of a type that does not qualify as portfolio interest under the law of the United States may be taxed by the United States, but if the beneficial owner is a resident of __________, the interest may be taxed at a rate not exceeding 15 percent of the gross amount of the interest;

c) interest arising in a Contracting State and beneficially owned by a resident of the other Contracting State that is a connected person with respect to the payor of the interest may be taxed in the first-mentioned Contracting State in accordance with domestic law if such resident benefits from a special tax regime with respect to such interest in its Contracting State of residence;

d) in the case of the United States, interest paid by an expatriated entity and beneficially owned by a company resident in __________ that is a connected person with respect to such expatriated entity may be taxed in accordance with the law of the United States for a period of ten years beginning on the date on which the acquisition of the domestic entity is completed. For purposes of applying this paragraph:

i) no effect shall be given to any amendment to section 7874 of the Internal Revenue Code after the date of signature of this Convention; and

ii) no entity shall be treated as an expatriated entity that:

A) is a connected person with respect to the domestic entity immediately after the date on which the acquisition of the domestic entity is completed; and

B) prior to that date, was never a connected person with respect to the domestic entity.

However, an entity described in the preceding sentence shall become an expatriated entity if, subsequent to the date on which the acquisition of the domestic entity is completed, the entity joins in filing a U.S. consolidated return with either the domestic entity or another entity that was a connected person with respect to the domestic entity immediately prior to the date on which the acquisition of the domestic entity was completed;

e) interest arising in a Contracting State and beneficially owned by a resident of the other Contracting State that is a connected person with respect to the payor of the interest may be taxed in the first-mentioned Contracting State in accordance with domestic law if such resident benefits, at any time during the taxable year in which the interest is paid, from notional deductions with respect to amounts that the Contracting State of which the beneficial owner is resident treats as equity;

f) interest arising in a Contracting State and beneficially owned by a resident of the other Contracting State that is entitled to the benefits of this Article only by reason of paragraph 5 of Article 22 (Limitation on Benefits) may be taxed in the first-mentioned Contracting State, but the tax so charged shall not exceed 10 percent of the gross amount of the interest; and

g) interest that is an excess inclusion with respect to a residual interest in a real estate mortgage investment conduit may be taxed by each Contracting State in accordance with its domestic law.

3. Notwithstanding the provisions of paragraph 1 of this Article, in the case of a company seeking to satisfy the requirements of paragraph 4 of Article 22 (Limitation on Benefits) of this Convention regarding a payment of interest, if such company fails to satisfy the criteria of that paragraph solely by reason of:

a) the requirement in subclause (B) of clause (i) of subparagraph (e) of paragraph 7 of Article 22 (Limitation on Benefits) of this Convention; or

b) the requirement in clause (ii) of subparagraph (e) of paragraph 7 of Article 22 (Limitation on Benefits) that a person entitled to benefits under paragraph 5 of Article 22 (Limitation on Benefits) would be entitled to a rate of tax with respect to the interest that is less than or equal to the rate applicable under paragraph 2 of this Article;

such company may be taxed by the Contracting State in which the interest arises according to the laws of that Contracting State. In these cases, however, the tax so charged shall not exceed the 25 highest rate among the rates of tax to which persons described in subparagraph (e) of paragraph 7 of Article 22 (Limitation on Benefits) of this Convention (notwithstanding the requirements referred to in subparagraphs (a) and (b) of this paragraph) would have been entitled if such persons had received the interest directly. For purposes of this paragraph, a person described in clause (iii) of subparagraph (e) of paragraph 7 of Article 22 (Limitation on Benefits) shall be treated as entitled to the limitation of tax to which such person would be entitled if such person were a resident of the same Contracting State as the company receiving the interest.

4. The term "interest" as used in this Article means income from debt-claims of every kind, whether or not secured by mortgage, and whether or not carrying a right to participate in the debtor's profits, and in particular, income from government securities and income from bonds or debentures, including premiums or prizes attaching to such securities, bonds or debentures, and all other income that is subjected to the same taxation treatment as income from money lent under the law of the Contracting State in which the income arises. Income dealt with in Article 10 (Dividends) and penalty charges for late payment shall not be regarded as interest for the purposes of this Convention.

5. The provisions of paragraphs 1 through 3 of this Article shall not apply if the beneficial owner of the interest, being a resident of a Contracting State, carries on business in the other Contracting State in which the interest arises through a permanent establishment situated therein, and the debt-claim in respect of which the interest is paid is effectively connected with such permanent establishment. In such case the provisions of Article 7 (Business Profits) shall apply.

6. For purposes of this Article, interest shall be deemed to arise in a Contracting State when the payor is a resident of that Contracting State. Where, however, the person paying the interest, whether a resident of a Contracting State or not, has in a Contracting State a permanent establishment or derives profits that are taxable on a net basis in a Contracting State under paragraph 5 of Article 6 (Income from Real Property (Immovable Property)) or paragraph 1 of Article 13 (Gains), and such interest is borne by such permanent establishment or allocable to such profits, then such interest shall be deemed to arise in the Contracting State in which the permanent establishment is situated or from which such profits are derived.

7. The excess, if any, of the amount of interest allocable to the profits of a company resident in a Contracting State that are:

a) attributable to a permanent establishment in the other Contracting State (including gains under paragraph 3 of Article 13 (Gains)); or

b) subject to tax in the other Contracting State under Article 6 (Income from Real Property (Immovable Property)) or paragraph 1 of Article 13 (Gains);

over the interest paid by that permanent establishment, or in the case of profits subject to tax under Article 6 (Income from Real Property (Immovable Property)) or paragraph 1 of Article 13 (Gains), over the interest paid by that company, shall be deemed to arise in that other Contracting State and to be beneficially owned by a resident of the first-mentioned Contracting State. The tax imposed under this Article on such interest shall not exceed the rates provided in paragraphs 1 through 3 of this Article.

8. Where, by reason of a special relationship between the payor and the beneficial owner or between both of them and some other person, the amount of the interest, having regard to the debt-claim for which it is paid, exceeds the amount that would have been agreed upon by the payor and the beneficial owner in the absence of such relationship, the provisions of this Article shall apply only to the last-mentioned amount. In such case the excess part of the payments shall remain taxable according to the laws of each Contracting State, due regard being had to the other provisions of this Convention.

Article 12

ROYALTIES

1. Royalties arising in a Contracting State and beneficially owned by a resident of the other Contracting State shall be taxable only in that other Contracting State.

2. Notwithstanding the provisions of paragraph 1 of this Article:

a) a royalty arising in a Contracting State and beneficially owned by a resident of the other Contracting State that is a connected person with respect to the payor of the royalty may be taxed in the first-mentioned Contracting State in accordance with domestic law if such resident benefits from a special tax regime with respect to the royalty in its Contracting State of residence; and

b) in the case of the United States, royalties paid by an expatriated entity and beneficially owned by a company resident in __________ that is a connected person with respect to such expatriated entity may be taxed in accordance with the law of the United States for a period of ten years beginning on the date on which the acquisition of the domestic entity is completed. For purposes of applying this paragraph:

i) no effect shall be given to any amendment to section 7874 of the Internal Revenue Code after the date of signature of this Convention; and

ii) no entity shall be treated as an expatriated entity that:

A) is a connected person with respect to the domestic entity immediately after the date on which the acquisition of the domestic entity is completed; and

B) prior to that date, was never a connected person with respect to the domestic entity.

However, an entity described in the preceding sentence shall become an expatriated entity if, subsequent to the date on which the acquisition of the domestic entity is completed, the entity joins in filing a U.S. consolidated return with either the domestic entity or another entity that was a connected person with respect to the domestic entity immediately prior to the date on which the acquisition of the domestic entity was completed.

3. Notwithstanding the provisions of paragraph 1 of this Article, in the case of a company seeking to satisfy the requirements of paragraph 4 of Article 22 (Limitation on Benefits) of this Convention regarding a royalty, if such company fails to satisfy the criteria of that paragraph solely by reason of the requirement in subclause (B) of clause (i) of subparagraph (e) of paragraph 7 of Article 22 (Limitation on Benefits) of this Convention, such company may be taxed in the Contracting State of which the royalty arises and according to the laws of that Contracting State, except that the tax so charged shall not exceed the highest rate among the rates of tax to which persons described in subparagraph (e) of paragraph 7 of Article 22 (Limitation on Benefits) of this Convention (notwithstanding the requirement of subclause (B) of clause (i) of subparagraph (e) of paragraph 7 of Article 22 (Limitation on Benefits)) would have been entitled if such persons had received the royalty directly. For purposes of this paragraph, a person described in clause (iii) of subparagraph (e) of paragraph 7 of Article 22 (Limitation on Benefits) shall be treated as entitled to the limitation of tax to which such person would be entitled if such person were a resident of the same Contracting State as the company receiving the royalties.

4. The term "royalty" as used in this Article means payments of any kind received as consideration for the use of, or the right to use, any copyright of literary, artistic, scientific or other work (including cinematographic films); any patent, trademark, design or model, plan, secret formula or process; or for information concerning industrial, commercial or scientific experience.

5. The provisions of paragraphs 1 through 3 of this Article shall not apply if the beneficial owner of the royalties, being a resident of a Contracting State, carries on business in the other Contracting State in which the royalties arise through a permanent establishment situated therein and the right or property in respect of which the royalties are paid is effectively connected with such permanent establishment. In such case the provisions of Article 7 (Business Profits) shall apply.

6. Royalties shall be deemed to arise in a Contracting State when they are in consideration for the use of, or the right to use, property, information or experience in that Contracting State.

7. Where, by reason of a special relationship between the payor and the beneficial owner or between both of them and some other person, the amount of the royalties, having regard to the use, right, or information for which they are paid, exceeds the amount that would have been agreed upon by the payor and the beneficial owner in the absence of such relationship, the provisions of this Article shall apply only to the last-mentioned amount. In such case the excess part of the payments shall remain taxable according to the laws of each Contracting State, due regard being had to the other provisions of this Convention.

Article 13

GAINS

1. Gains derived by a resident of a Contracting State from the alienation of real property (immovable property) situated in the other Contracting State may be taxed in that other Contracting State.

2. For the purposes of this Article the term "real property (immovable property) situated in the other Contracting State" shall include:

   a) real property (immovable property) referred to in Article 6 (Income from Real Property (Immovable Property));

   b) where that other Contracting State is the United States, a United States real property interest; and

   c) where that other Contracting State is __________,

      i) shares, including rights to acquire shares, other than shares in which there is regular trading on a stock exchange, deriving 50 percent or more of their value directly or indirectly from real property referred to in subparagraph (a) of this paragraph situated in __________; and

      ii) an interest in a partnership or trust to the extent that the assets of the partnership or trust consist of real property situated in __________, or of shares referred to in clause (i) of this subparagraph.

3. Gains from the alienation of movable property forming part of the business property of a permanent establishment that an enterprise of a Contracting State has in the other Contracting State, including such gains from the alienation of such a permanent establishment (alone or with the whole enterprise), may be taxed in that other Contracting State.

4. Gains derived by an enterprise of a Contracting State from the alienation of ships or aircraft operated or used in international traffic or personal property pertaining to the operation or use of such ships or aircraft shall be taxable only in that Contracting State.

5. Gains derived by an enterprise of a Contracting State from the alienation of containers (including trailers, barges and related equipment for the transport of containers) used for the transport of goods or merchandise shall be taxable only in that Contracting State, unless those containers are used for transport solely between places within the other Contracting State.

6. Gains from the alienation of any property other than property referred to in paragraphs 1 through 5 of this Article shall be taxable only in the Contracting State of which the alienator is a resident.

7. Where an individual who, upon ceasing to be a resident (as determined under paragraph 1 of Article 4 (Resident)) of one of the Contracting States, is treated under the taxation law of that Contracting State as having alienated property for its fair market value and is taxed in that Contracting State by reason thereof, the individual may elect to be treated for purposes of taxation in the other Contracting State as if

the individual had, immediately before ceasing to be a resident of the first-mentioned Contracting State, alienated and reacquired such property for an amount equal to its fair market value at such time.

Article 14

INCOME FROM EMPLOYMENT

1. Subject to the provisions of Articles 15 (Directors' Fees), 17 (Pensions, Social Security, Annuities, Alimony, and Child Support) and 19 (Government Service), salaries, wages and other similar remuneration derived by a resident of a Contracting State in respect of an employment shall be taxable only in that Contracting State unless the employment is exercised in the other Contracting State. If the employment is so exercised, such remuneration as is derived therefrom may be taxed in that other Contracting State.

2. Notwithstanding the provisions of paragraph 1 of this Article, remuneration derived by a resident of a Contracting State in respect of an employment exercised in the other Contracting State shall be taxable only in the first-mentioned Contracting State if:

a) the recipient is present in the other Contracting State for a period or periods not exceeding in the aggregate 183 days for all twelve-month periods commencing or ending in the taxable year concerned;

b) the remuneration is paid by, or on behalf of, an employer who is not a resident of the other Contracting State; and

c) the remuneration is not borne by a permanent establishment that the employer has in the other Contracting State.

3. Notwithstanding the preceding provisions of this Article, remuneration described in paragraph 1 of this Article that is derived by a resident of a Contracting State in respect of an employment as a member of the regular complement of a ship or aircraft operated in international traffic shall be taxable only in that Contracting State.

Article 15

DIRECTORS' FEES

Directors' fees and other similar payments derived by a resident of a Contracting State for services rendered in the other Contracting State in his capacity as a member of the board of directors of a company that is a resident of the other Contracting State may be taxed in that other Contracting State.

Article 16

ENTERTAINERS AND SPORTSMEN

1. Notwithstanding the provisions of Article 14 (Income from Employment), income derived by a resident of a Contracting State as an entertainer, such as a theater, motion picture, radio, or television artiste, or a musician, or as a sportsman, from his personal activities as such exercised in the other Contracting State, may be taxed in that other Contracting State, except where the amount of the gross receipts derived by such entertainer or sportsman, including expenses reimbursed to him or borne on his behalf, from such activities does not exceed thirty thousand United States dollars (30,000) or its equivalent in ---------- for the taxable year of the payment.

2. Where income in respect of activities exercised by an entertainer or a sportsman in his capacity as such accrues not to the entertainer or sportsman himself but to another person, that income, notwithstanding the provisions of Article 14 (Income from Employment), may be taxed in the Contracting State in which the activities of the entertainer or sportsman are exercised unless the contract pursuant to which the personal activities are performed allows that other person to designate the individual who is to perform the personal activities.

Article 17

PENSIONS, SOCIAL SECURITY, ANNUITIES, ALIMONY, AND CHILD SUPPORT

1. a) Pensions and other similar remuneration beneficially owned by a resident of a Contracting State shall be taxable only in that Contracting State.

   b) Notwithstanding subparagraph (a) of this paragraph, the amount of any such pension or remuneration arising in a Contracting State that, when received, would be exempt from taxation in that Contracting State if the beneficial owner were a resident thereof shall be exempt from taxation in the Contracting State of which the beneficial owner is a resident.

2. a) Where an individual who is a resident of a Contracting State is a member or beneficiary of, or participant in, a pension fund established in the other Contracting State, income earned by the pension fund may not be taxed as income of that individual, unless, and then only to the extent that, it is paid to, or for the benefit of, that individual from the pension fund (and not transferred to another pension fund established in that other Contracting State in a transfer that qualifies as a tax-deferred transfer under the laws of that other Contracting State). In such case, the provisions of paragraph 1 of this Article shall apply.

   b) Where a citizen of the United States who is a resident of __________ is a member or beneficiary of, or participant in, a pension fund established in __________, the United States may not tax the income earned by the pension fund as income of the individual unless, and then only to the extent that, it is paid to, or for the benefit of, that individual from the pension fund (and not transferred to another pension fund established in __________ in a transfer that qualifies as a tax-deferred transfer under the laws of __________). In such case, the provisions of paragraph 1 of this Article, which generally is subject to paragraph 4 of Article 1 (General Scope), shall apply.

3. Notwithstanding the provisions of paragraph 1 of this Article, payments made by a Contracting State under provisions of the social security or similar legislation of that Contracting State to a resident of the other Contracting State or to a citizen of the United States shall be taxable only in the first-mentioned Contracting State.

4. Annuities derived and beneficially owned by an individual resident of a Contracting State shall be taxable only in that Contracting State. The term “annuities” as used in this paragraph means a stated sum paid periodically at stated times during a specified number of years, or for life, under an obligation to make the payments in return for adequate and full consideration (other than services rendered).

5. Alimony paid by a resident of a Contracting State to a resident of the other Contracting State shall be taxable only in that other Contracting State. The term “alimony” as used in this paragraph means periodic payments made pursuant to a written separation agreement or a decree of divorce, separate maintenance,

or compulsory support, which payments are taxable to the recipient under the laws of the Contracting State of which he is a resident.

6. Periodic payments, not dealt with in paragraph 5 of this Article, for the support of a child made pursuant to a written separation agreement or a decree of divorce, separate maintenance, or compulsory support, paid by a resident of a Contracting State to a resident of the other Contracting State, shall be exempt from tax in both Contracting States.

Article 18

PENSION FUNDS

1. Where an individual who is a member or beneficiary of, or participant in, a pension fund established in one of the Contracting States exercises an employment or self-employment in the other Contracting State:

a) contributions paid by or on behalf of that individual to the pension fund during the period that he exercises an employment or self-employment in the other Contracting State shall be deductible (or excludible) in computing the individual's taxable income in that other Contracting State; and

b) any benefits accrued under the pension fund, or contributions made to the pension fund by or on behalf of the individual's employer, during that period shall not be treated as part of the employee's taxable income and any such contributions shall be allowed as a deduction in computing the taxable income of the individual's employer in that other Contracting State.

The relief available under this paragraph shall not exceed the relief that would be allowed by the other Contracting State to residents of that Contracting State for contributions to, or benefits accrued under, a pension fund established in that Contracting State.

2. The provisions of paragraph 1 of this Article shall not apply unless:

a) contributions by or on behalf of the individual, or by or on behalf of the individual's employer, to the pension fund (or to another similar pension fund established in the same Contracting State for which the first-mentioned pension fund was substituted) were made before the individual began to exercise an employment or self-employment in the other Contracting State; and

b) the competent authority of the other Contracting State has agreed that the pension fund generally corresponds to a pension fund established in that other Contracting State.

3. a) Where a citizen of the United States who is a resident of __________ exercises an employment in __________ the income from which is taxable in __________, the contribution is borne by an employer who is a resident of __________ or by a permanent establishment situated in __________, and the individual is a member or beneficiary of, or participant in, a pension fund established in __________,

i) contributions paid by or on behalf of that individual to the pension fund during the period that the individual exercises the employment in __________, and that are attributable to the employment, shall be deductible (or excludible) in computing the individual's taxable income in the United States; and

ii) any benefits accrued under the pension fund, or contributions made to the pension fund by or on behalf of the individual's employer, during that period, and that are attributable to the employment, shall not be included in computing the employee's taxable income in the United States.

b) The relief available under this paragraph shall not exceed the lesser of:

i) the relief that would be allowed by the United States to its residents for contributions to, or benefits accrued under, a generally corresponding pension fund established in the United States; and

ii) the amount of contributions or benefits that qualify for tax relief in __________.

c) For purposes of determining an individual's eligibility to participate in and receive tax benefits with respect to a pension fund established in the United States, contributions made to, or benefits accrued under, a pension fund established in __________ shall be treated as contributions or benefits under a generally corresponding pension fund established in the United States to the extent relief is available to the individual under this paragraph.

d) This paragraph shall not apply unless the competent authority of the United States has agreed that the pension fund generally corresponds to a pension fund established in the United States.

Article 19

GOVERNMENT SERVICE

1. Notwithstanding the provisions of Articles 14 (Income from Employment), 15 (Directors' Fees), 16 (Entertainers and Sportsmen) and 20 (Students and Trainees):

a) salaries, wages and other remuneration, other than a pension, paid to an individual in respect of services rendered to a Contracting State or a political subdivision or local authority thereof shall, subject to the provisions of subparagraph (b) of this paragraph, be taxable only in that Contracting State;

b) such remuneration, however, shall be taxable only in the other Contracting State if the services are rendered in that Contracting State and the individual is a resident of that Contracting State who:

i) is a national of that Contracting State; or

ii) did not become a resident of that Contracting State solely for the purpose of rendering the services.

2. Notwithstanding the provisions of paragraph 1 of Article 17 (Pensions, Social Security, Annuities, Alimony, and Child Support):

a) any pension and other similar remuneration paid by, or out of funds created by, a Contracting State or a political subdivision or a local authority thereof to an individual in respect of services rendered to that Contracting State or subdivision or authority (other than a payment to which paragraph 3 of Article 17 (Pensions, Social Security, Annuities, Alimony, and Child Support) applies) shall, subject to the provisions of subparagraph (b) of this paragraph, be taxable only in that Contracting State;

b) such pension and other similar remuneration, however, shall be taxable only in the other Contracting State if the individual is a resident of, and a national of, that Contracting State.

3. The provisions of Articles 14 (Income from Employment), 15 (Directors' Fees), 16 (Entertainers and Sportsmen) and 17 (Pensions, Social Security, Annuities, Alimony, and Child Support) shall apply to salaries, wages and other similar remuneration, and to pensions and other similar remuneration, in respect of services rendered in connection with a business carried on by a Contracting State or a political subdivision or a local authority thereof.

Article 20

STUDENTS AND TRAINEES

1. Payments, other than remuneration for personal services, received by a student or business trainee who is, or was immediately before visiting a Contracting State, a resident of the other Contracting State, and who is present in the first-mentioned Contracting State for the purpose of his full-time education or for his full-time training, shall not be taxed in that Contracting State, provided that such payments arise outside that Contracting State, and are for the purpose of his maintenance, education or training. The exemption from tax provided by this paragraph shall apply to a business trainee only for a period of time not exceeding twelve months from the date the business trainee first arrives in the first-mentioned Contracting State for the purpose of training.

2. A student or business trainee described in paragraph 1 of this Article shall be exempt from tax by the Contracting State in which the individual is temporarily present with respect to income from personal services in an aggregate amount equal to ten thousand United States dollars (10,000) or its equivalent in ______ for the taxable year of the payment. The competent authorities of the Contracting States may adjust the amount provided in this paragraph to the extent necessary to take into account changes in the personal exemption, standard deduction or filing thresholds in the domestic laws of either Contracting State.

3. For purposes of this Article, a business trainee is an individual:

a) who is temporarily in a Contracting State for the purpose of securing training required to qualify the individual to practice a profession or professional specialty; or

b) who is temporarily in a Contracting State as an employee of, or under contract with, a resident of the other Contracting State, for the primary purpose of acquiring technical, professional or business experience from a person other than that resident of the other Contracting State (or a connected person with respect to such resident of the other Contracting State).

Article 21

OTHER INCOME

1. Items of income beneficially owned by a resident of a Contracting State, wherever arising, not dealt with in the foregoing Articles of this Convention shall be taxable only in that Contracting State.

2. Notwithstanding paragraph 1 of this Article:

a) a guarantee fee arising in a Contracting State and characterized as other income by that Contracting State and beneficially owned by a resident of the other Contracting State that is a connected person with respect to the payor of the guarantee fee may be taxed in the first-mentioned Contracting State in accordance with domestic law if such resident benefits from a special tax regime with respect to the guarantee fee in its Contracting State of residence; and

b) in the case of the United States, a guarantee fee characterized as other income paid by an expatriated entity and beneficially owned by a company resident in __________ that is a connected person with respect to such expatriated entity may be taxed in accordance with the law of the United States for a period of ten years beginning on the date on which the acquisition of the domestic entity is completed. For purposes of applying this paragraph:

i) no effect shall be given to any amendment to section 7874 of the Internal Revenue Code after the date of signature of this Convention; and

ii) no entity shall be treated as an expatriated entity that:

A) is a connected person with respect to the domestic entity immediately after the date on which the acquisition of the domestic entity is completed; and

B) prior to that date, was never a connected person with respect to the domestic entity.

However, an entity described in the preceding sentence shall become an expatriated entity if, subsequent to the date on which the acquisition of the domestic entity is completed, the entity joins in filing a U.S. consolidated return with either the domestic entity or another entity that was a connected person with respect to the domestic entity immediately prior to the date on which the acquisition of the domestic entity was completed.

3. The provisions of paragraphs 1 and 2 of this Article shall not apply to income, other than income from real property (immovable property) as defined in paragraph 2 of Article 6 (Income from Real Property (Immovable Property)), if the beneficial owner of the income, being a resident of a Contracting State, carries on business in the other Contracting State through a permanent establishment situated therein and the right or property in respect of which the income is paid is effectively connected with such permanent establishment. In such case the provisions of Article 7 (Business Profits) shall apply.

Article 22

LIMITATION ON BENEFITS

1. Except as otherwise provided in this Article and in paragraph 6 of Article 10 (Dividends), paragraph 3 of Article 11 (Interest) and paragraph 3 of Article 12 (Royalties), a resident of a Contracting State shall not be entitled to the benefits of this Convention otherwise accorded to residents of a Contracting State unless such resident is a "qualified person" as defined in paragraph 2 of this Article at the time when the benefit would be accorded.

2. A resident of a Contracting State shall be a qualified person at the time when a benefit otherwise would be accorded by this Convention if, at that time and, with respect to clause (i) of subparagraph (f) of this paragraph, on at least half of the days of any twelve-month period that includes the date when the benefit otherwise would be accorded, the resident is:

a) an individual;

b) a Contracting State, political subdivision or local authority thereof, or any agency or instrumentality of any such Contracting State, political subdivision or local authority;

c) a company, if the principal class of its shares (and any disproportionate class of shares) is regularly traded on one or more recognized stock exchanges, and either:

i) its principal class of shares is primarily traded on one or more recognized stock exchanges located in the Contracting State of which the company is a resident; or

ii) the company's primary place of management and control is in the Contracting State of which it is a resident;

d) a company, if:

i) at least 50 percent of the aggregate vote and value of the shares (and at least 50 percent of the aggregate vote and value of any disproportionate class of shares) in the company is owned directly or indirectly by five or fewer companies entitled to benefits under subparagraph (c) of this paragraph, provided that, in the case of indirect ownership, each intermediate owner is a resident of the Contracting State from which a benefit under this Convention is being sought or is a qualifying intermediate owner; and

ii) with respect to benefits under this Convention other than under Article 10 (Dividends), less than 50 percent of the company's gross income, and less than 50 percent of the tested group's gross income, is paid or accrued, directly or indirectly, in the form of payments that are deductible for purposes of the taxes covered by this Convention in the company's Contracting State of residence (but not including arm's length payments in the ordinary course of business for services or tangible property, and in the case of a tested group, not including intra-group transactions): (A) to persons that are not residents of either Contracting State entitled to the benefits of this Convention under subparagraph (a), (b), (c) or (e) of this paragraph; (B) to persons that are connected persons with respect to the company described in this subparagraph and that benefit from a special tax regime with respect to the deductible payment; or (C) with respect to a payment of interest, to persons that are connected persons with respect to the company described in this subparagraph and that benefit from notional deductions described in subparagraph (e) of paragraph 2 of Article 11 (Interest);

e) a person described in paragraph 2 of Article 4 (Resident) of this Convention, provided that:

i) in the case of a person described in subclause (A) of clause (ii) of subparagraph (k) of paragraph 1 of Article 3 (General Definitions), more than 50 percent of the person's beneficiaries, members or participants are individuals resident in either Contracting State; and

ii) in the case of a person described in subclause (B) of clause (ii) of subparagraph (k) of paragraph 1 of Article 3 (General Definitions), the earnings of such person benefit exclusively, or almost exclusively, pension funds that satisfy the requirements of clause (i) of this subparagraph; or

f) a person other than an individual, if:

i) persons that are residents of that Contracting State entitled to the benefits of this Convention under subparagraph (a), (b), (c) or (e) of this paragraph own, directly or indirectly, shares or other beneficial interests representing at least 50 percent of the aggregate vote and value (and at least 50 percent of the aggregate vote and value of any disproportionate class of shares) of the shares or other beneficial interests of such person, provided that, in the case of indirect ownership, each intermediate owner is a qualifying intermediate owner; and

ii) less than 50 percent of the person's gross income, and less than 50 percent of the tested group's gross income, is paid or accrued, directly or indirectly, in the form of payments that are deductible for purposes of the taxes covered by this Convention in the person's Contracting State of residence (but not including arm's length payments in the ordinary course of business for services or tangible property, and in the case of a tested group, not including intra-group transactions): (A) to persons that are not residents of either Contracting State entitled to the benefits of this Convention under subparagraph (a), (b), (c) or (e) of this paragraph; (B) to persons that are connected persons with respect to the person described in this subparagraph and that benefit from a special tax regime with respect to the deductible payment; or (C) with respect to a payment of interest, to persons that are connected persons with respect to the person described in this subparagraph and that benefit from notional deductions described in subparagraph (e) of paragraph 2 of Article 11 (Interest).

3. a) A resident of a Contracting State shall be entitled to benefits under this Convention with respect to an item of income derived from the other Contracting State, regardless of whether the resident is a qualified person, if the resident is engaged in the active conduct of a trade or business in the first-mentioned Contracting State, and the income derived from the other Contracting State emanates from, or is incidental to, that trade or business. For purposes of this Article, the term "active conduct of a trade or business" shall not include the following activities or any combination thereof:

i) operating as a holding company;

ii) providing overall supervision or administration of a group of companies;

iii) providing group financing (including cash pooling); or

iv) making or managing investments, unless these activities are carried on by a bank, insurance company or registered securities dealer in the ordinary course of its business as such.

b) If a resident of a Contracting State derives an item of income from a trade or business activity conducted by that resident in the other Contracting State, or derives an item of income arising in the other Contracting State from a connected person, the conditions described in subparagraph (a) of this paragraph shall be considered to be satisfied with respect to such item only if the trade or business activity conducted by the resident in the first-mentioned Contracting State to which the item is related is substantial in relation to the same or complementary trade or business activity carried on by the resident or such connected person in the other Contracting State. Whether a trade or business activity is substantial for the purposes of this paragraph shall be determined based on all the facts and circumstances.

c) For purposes of applying this paragraph, activities conducted by persons connected to a resident of a Contracting State shall be deemed to be conducted by such resident.

4. A company that is a resident of a Contracting State shall be entitled to a benefit under this Convention, regardless of whether the resident is a qualified person if, at the time when the benefit would be accorded, and on at least half of the days of a twelve-month period commencing or ending on the date when the benefit otherwise would be accorded:

a) at least 95 percent of the aggregate vote and value of its shares (and at least 50 percent of any disproportionate class of shares) is owned, directly or indirectly, by seven or fewer persons that are equivalent beneficiaries, provided that, in the case of indirect ownership, each intermediate owner is a qualifying intermediate owner; and

b) less than 50 percent of the company's gross income, and less than 50 percent of the tested group's gross income, is paid or accrued, directly or indirectly, in the form of payments that are deductible for purposes of the taxes covered by this Convention in the company's Contracting State of residence (but not including arm's length payments in the ordinary course of business for services or tangible property, and in the case of a tested group, not including intra-group transactions): (i) to persons that are not equivalent beneficiaries; (ii) to persons that are equivalent beneficiaries only by reason of paragraph 5 of this Article or of a substantially similar provision in the relevant comprehensive convention for the avoidance of double taxation; (iii) to persons that are equivalent beneficiaries that are connected persons with respect to the company described in this paragraph and that benefit from a special tax regime with respect to the deductible payment, provided that if the relevant comprehensive convention for the avoidance of double taxation does not contain a definition of a special tax regime analogous to the definition in subparagraph (*l*) of paragraph 1 of Article 3 (General Definitions), the principles of the definition provided in this Convention shall apply, but without regard to the requirement in clause (v) of that definition; or (iv) with respect to a payment of interest, to persons that are equivalent beneficiaries that are connected persons with respect to the company described in this paragraph and that benefit from notional deductions of the type described in subparagraph (e) of paragraph 2 of Article 11 (Interest).

5. A company that is a resident of a Contracting State that functions as a headquarters company for a multinational corporate group consisting of such company and its direct and indirect subsidiaries shall be entitled to benefits under this Convention with respect to dividends and interest paid by members of its multinational corporate group. A company shall be considered a headquarters company for this purpose only if:

a) such company's primary place of management and control is in the Contracting State of which it is a resident;

b) the multinational corporate group consists of companies resident in, and engaged in the active conduct of a trade or business in, at least four countries, and the trades or businesses carried on in each of the four countries (or four groupings of countries) generate at least 10 percent of the gross income of the group;

c) the trades or businesses of the multinational corporate group that are carried on in any one state other than the Contracting State of residence of such company generate less than 50 percent of the gross income of the group;

d) no more than 25 percent of such company's gross income is derived from the other Contracting State;

e) such company is subject to the same income taxation rules in its Contracting State of residence as persons described in paragraph 3 of this Article; and

f) less than 50 percent of such company's gross income, and less than 50 percent of the tested group's gross income, is paid or accrued, directly or indirectly, in the form of payments that are deductible for purposes of the taxes covered by this Convention in the company's Contracting State of residence (but not including arm's length payments in the ordinary course of business for services or tangible property or payments in respect of financial obligations to a bank that is not a connected person with respect to such company, and in the case of a tested group, not including intra-group transactions): (i) to persons that are not residents of either Contracting State entitled to the benefits of this Convention under subparagraph (a), (b), (c) or (e) of paragraph 2 of this Article; (ii) to persons that are connected persons with respect to such company and that benefit from a special tax regime with respect to the deductible payment; or (iii) with respect to a payment of interest, to persons that are connected persons with respect to such company and that benefit from notional deductions described in subparagraph (e) of paragraph 2 of Article 11 (Interest).

If the requirements of subparagraph (b), (c) or (d) of this paragraph are not fulfilled for the relevant taxable year, they shall be deemed to be fulfilled if the required ratios are met when averaging the gross income of the preceding four taxable years.

6. If a resident of a Contracting State is neither a qualified person pursuant to the provisions of paragraph 2 of this Article, nor entitled to benefits under paragraph 3, 4 or 5 of this Article, the competent authority of the other Contracting State may, nevertheless, grant the benefits of this Convention, or benefits with respect to a specific item of income, taking into account the object and purpose of this Convention, but only if such resident demonstrates to the satisfaction of such competent authority a substantial nontax nexus to its Contracting State of residence and that neither its establishment, acquisition or maintenance, nor the conduct of its operations had as one of its principal purposes the obtaining of benefits under this Convention. The competent authority of the Contracting State to which the request has been made shall consult with the competent authority of the other Contracting State before either granting or denying a request made under this paragraph by a resident of that other Contracting State.

7. For the purposes of this Article

a) the term "recognized stock exchange" means:

i) any stock exchange registered with the U.S. Securities and Exchange Commission as a national securities exchange under the U.S. Securities Exchange Act of 1934;

ii) the _______ Stock Exchange; and

iii) any other stock exchange agreed upon by the competent authorities of the Contracting States;

b) the term "principal class of shares" means the ordinary or common shares of the company, provided that such class of shares represents the majority of the aggregate vote and value of the company. If no single class of ordinary or common shares represents the majority of the aggregate vote and value of the company, the "principal class of shares" are those classes that in the aggregate represent a majority of the aggregate vote and value of the company;

c) the term "disproportionate class of shares" means any class of shares of a company, or in the case of a trust, any class of beneficial interests in such trust, resident in one of the Contracting States that entitles the shareholder or interest holder to disproportionately higher participation, through dividends, redemption payments or otherwise, in the earnings generated in the other Contracting State;

d) a company's "primary place of management and control" is in the Contracting State of which it is a resident only if:

i) the executive officers and senior management employees of the company exercise day-to-day responsibility for more of the strategic, financial and operational policy decision-making for the company and its direct and indirect subsidiaries in that Contracting State, and the staff of such persons conduct more of the day-to-day activities necessary for preparing and making those decisions in that Contracting State, than in any other state; and

ii) such executive officers and senior management employees exercise responsibility for more of the strategic, financial and operational policy decision-making for the company and its direct and indirect subsidiaries, and the staff of such persons conduct more of the day-to-day activities necessary for preparing and making those decisions, than the officers or employees of any other company;

e) the term "equivalent beneficiary" means:

i) a resident of any state, provided that:

A) the resident is entitled to all the benefits of a comprehensive convention for the avoidance of double taxation between that state and the Contracting State from which the benefits of this Convention are sought, under provisions substantially similar to subparagraph (a), (b), (c) or (e) of paragraph 2 of this Article or, when the benefit being sought is with respect to interest or dividends paid by a member of the resident's multinational corporate group, the resident is entitled to benefits under provisions substantially similar to paragraph 5 of this Article, provided that, if such convention does not contain a comprehensive limitation on benefits article, the resident would be entitled to the benefits of this Convention by reason of subparagraph (a), (b), (c) or (e) of paragraph 2 of this Article if such resident were a resident of one of the Contracting States under Article 4 (Resident) of this Convention. Notwithstanding the preceding sentence, an individual who is (1) liable to tax in his or her state of residence with respect to foreign source income or gains only on a remittance or similar basis, or (2) whose tax is determined in that Contracting State on a fixed-fee, "forfait" or similar basis, shall not be considered an equivalent beneficiary; and

B) 1) with respect to income referred to in Article 10 (Dividends), 11 (Interest) or 12 (Royalties) of this Convention, if the resident had received such income directly, the resident would be entitled under such convention, a provision of domestic law or any other international agreement, to a rate of tax with respect to such income for which benefits are being sought under this Convention that is less than or equal to the rate applicable under this Convention. Regarding a company seeking benefits under paragraph 4 of this Article with respect to dividends, for purposes of this subclause:

I) if the resident is an individual, and the company is engaged in the active conduct of a trade or business in its Contracting State of residence that is substantial in relation, and similar or complementary, to the trade or business that generated the earnings from which the dividend is paid, such individual shall be treated as if he or she were a company. Activities conducted by a person that is a connected person with respect to the company seeking benefits shall be deemed to be conducted by such company. Whether a trade or business activity is substantial shall be determined based on all the facts and circumstances; and

II) if the resident is a company (including an individual treated as a company), to determine whether the resident is entitled to a rate of tax that is less than or equal to the rate applicable under this Convention, the resident's indirect ownership of the shares of the company paying the dividends shall be treated as direct ownership; or

2) with respect to an item of income, profit or gain referred to in Article 7 (Business Profits), 13 (Gains) or 21 (Other Income) of this Convention, the resident is entitled to

benefits under such convention that are at least as favorable as the benefits that are being sought under this Convention; and

C) notwithstanding that a resident may satisfy the requirements of subclauses (A) and (B) of this clause, where the item of income, profit or gain has been derived through an entity that is treated as fiscally transparent under the laws of the Contracting State of the company seeking benefits, if the item of income, profit or gain would not be treated as the income, profit or gain of the resident under a provision analogous to paragraph 6 of Article 1 (General Scope) of this Convention had the resident, and not the company seeking benefits under paragraph 4 of this Article, itself owned the entity through which the income, profit or gain was derived by the company, such resident shall not be considered an equivalent beneficiary with respect to the item of income; and

ii) a resident of the same Contracting State as the company seeking benefits under paragraph 4 of this Article that is entitled to all the benefits of this Convention by reason of subparagraph (a), (b), (c) or (e) of paragraph 2 of this Article or, when the benefit being sought is with respect to interest or dividends paid by a member of the resident's multinational corporate group, the resident is entitled to benefits under paragraph 5 of this Article, provided that, in the case of a resident described in paragraph 5 of this Article, if the resident had received such interest or dividends directly, the resident would be entitled to a rate of tax with respect to such income that is less than or equal to the rate applicable under this Convention to the company seeking benefits under paragraph 4 of this Article; or

iii) a resident of the Contracting State from which the benefits of this Convention are sought that is entitled to all the benefits of this Convention by reason of subparagraph (a), (b), (c) or (e) of paragraph 2 of this Article, provided that all such residents' ownership of the aggregate vote and value of the shares (and any disproportionate class of shares) of the company seeking benefits under paragraph 4 of this Article does not exceed 25 percent of the total vote and value of the shares (and any disproportionate class of shares) of the company.

f) the term "qualifying intermediate owner" means an intermediate owner that is either:

i) a resident of a state that has in effect with the Contracting State from which a benefit under this Convention is being sought a comprehensive convention for the avoidance of double taxation that includes provisions addressing special tax regimes and notional deductions analogous to subparagraph (*l*) of paragraph 1 of Article 3 (General Definitions) and subparagraph (e) of paragraph 2 of Article 11 (Interest), respectively; or

ii) a resident of the same Contracting State as the company applying the test under subparagraph (d) or (f) of paragraph 2 or paragraph 4 of this Article to determine whether it is eligible for benefits under the Convention;

g) the term "tested group" means the resident of a Contracting State that is applying the test under subparagraph (d) or (f) of paragraph 2 of this Article or paragraph 4 or 5 of this Article to determine whether it is eligible for benefits under the Convention (the "tested resident"), and any company that:

i) participates as a member with the tested resident in a tax consolidation, fiscal unity or similar regime that requires members of the group to share profits or losses; or

ii) shares losses with the tested resident pursuant to a group relief or other loss sharing regime in the taxable year; and

h) the term "gross income" means gross receipts as determined in the person's Contracting State of residence for the taxable year that includes the time when the benefit would be accorded, except that where a person is engaged in a business that includes the manufacture, production or sale of goods, "gross income" means such gross receipts reduced by the cost of goods sold, and where a person is engaged in a business of providing non-financial services, "gross income" means such gross receipts reduced by the direct costs of generating such receipts, provided that:

i) except when relevant for determining benefits under Article 10 (Dividends) of this Convention, gross income shall not include the portion of any dividends that are effectively exempt from tax in the person's Contracting State of residence, whether through deductions or otherwise; and

ii) except with respect to the portion of any dividend that is taxable, a tested group's gross income shall not take into account transactions between companies within the tested group.

Article 23

RELIEF FROM DOUBLE TAXATION

1. In the case of __________, double taxation will be relieved as follows:

2. In accordance with the provisions and subject to the limitations of the law of the United States (as it may be amended from time to time without changing the general principle hereof), the United States shall allow to a resident or citizen of the United States as a credit against the United States tax on income applicable to residents and citizens:

a) the income tax paid or accrued to __________ by or on behalf of such resident or citizen; and

b) in the case of a United States company owning at least 10 percent of the voting stock of a company that is a resident of __________ and from which the United States company receives dividends, the income tax paid or accrued to __________ by or on behalf of the payor with respect to the profits out of which the dividends are paid.

For the purposes of this paragraph, the taxes referred to in subparagraph (a) of paragraph 3 and paragraph 4 of Article 2 (Taxes Covered) shall be considered income taxes.

3. For the purposes of applying paragraph 2 of this Article, an item of gross income, as determined under the law of the United States, derived by a resident of the United States that, under this Convention, may be taxed in __________ shall be deemed to be income from sources in __________.

4. Where a United States citizen is a resident of __________:

a) with respect to items of income, profit or gain that under the provisions of this Convention are exempt from United States tax or that are subject to a reduced rate of United States tax when derived by a resident of __________ who is not a United States citizen, __________ shall allow as a credit against __________ tax only the tax paid, if any, that the United States may impose under the provisions of this Convention other than taxes that may be imposed solely by reason of citizenship under paragraph 4 of Article 1 (General Scope);

b) for purposes of applying paragraph 2 to compute United States tax on those items of income, profit or gain referred to in subparagraph (a) of this paragraph, the United States shall allow as a credit against United States tax the income tax paid to __________ after the credit referred to in subparagraph (a) of this paragraph; the credit so allowed shall not reduce the portion of the United States tax that is creditable against the __________ tax in accordance with subparagraph (a) of this paragraph; and

c) for the exclusive purpose of relieving double taxation in the United States under subparagraph (b) of this paragraph, items of income, profit or gain referred to in subparagraph (a) of this paragraph shall be deemed to arise in __________ to the extent necessary to avoid double taxation of such income under subparagraph (b) of this paragraph.

Article 24

NON-DISCRIMINATION

1. Nationals of a Contracting State shall not be subjected in the other Contracting State to any taxation or any requirement connected therewith that is more burdensome than the taxation and connected requirements to which nationals of that other Contracting State in the same circumstances, in particular with respect to residence, are or may be subjected. This provision shall also apply to persons who are not residents of one or both of the Contracting States. However, for the purposes of United States taxation, United States nationals who are subject to tax on a worldwide basis are not in the same circumstances as nationals of __________ who are not residents of the United States.

2. The taxation on a permanent establishment that an enterprise of a Contracting State has in the other Contracting State shall not be less favorably levied in that other Contracting State than the taxation levied on enterprises of that other Contracting State carrying on the same activities.

3. The provisions of paragraphs 1 and 2 of this Article shall not be construed as obliging a Contracting State to grant to residents of the other Contracting State any personal allowances, reliefs, and reductions for taxation purposes on account of civil status or family responsibilities that it grants to its own residents.

4. Except where the provisions of paragraph 1 of Article 9 (Associated Enterprises), paragraph 8 of Article 11 (Interest), or paragraph 7 of Article 12 (Royalties) apply, interest, royalties, and other disbursements paid by an enterprise of a Contracting State to a resident of the other Contracting State shall, for the purpose of determining the taxable profits of such enterprise, be deductible under the same conditions as if they had been paid to a resident of the first-mentioned Contracting State. Similarly, any debts of an enterprise of a Contracting State to a resident of the other Contracting State shall, for the purpose of determining the taxable capital of the first-mentioned resident, be deductible under the same conditions as if they had been contracted to a resident of the first-mentioned Contracting State.

5. Enterprises of a Contracting State, the capital of which is wholly or partly owned or controlled, directly or indirectly, by one or more residents of the other Contracting State, shall not be subjected in the first-mentioned Contracting State to any taxation or any requirement connected therewith that is more burdensome than the taxation and connected requirements to which other similar enterprises of the first-mentioned Contracting State are or may be subjected.

6. Nothing in this Article shall be construed as preventing either Contracting State from imposing a tax as described in paragraph 10 of Article 10 (Dividends) or paragraph 7 of Article 11 (Interest).

7. The provisions of this Article shall, notwithstanding the provisions of Article 2 (Taxes Covered), apply to taxes of every kind and description.

Article 25

MUTUAL AGREEMENT PROCEDURE

1. Where a person considers that the actions of one or both of the Contracting States result or will result for such person in taxation not in accordance with the provisions of this Convention, it may, irrespective of the remedies provided by the domestic law of those Contracting States, and the time limits prescribed in such laws for presenting claims for refund, present its case to the competent authority of one or both of the Contracting States.

2. The competent authority shall endeavor, if the objection appears to it to be justified and if it is not itself able to arrive at a satisfactory solution, to resolve the case by mutual agreement with the competent authority of the other Contracting State, with a view to the avoidance of taxation that is not in accordance with this Convention. Any agreement reached shall be implemented notwithstanding any time limits or other procedural limitations in the domestic law of the Contracting States. Assessment and collection procedures shall be suspended during the period that any mutual agreement proceeding is pending.

3. The competent authorities of the Contracting States shall endeavor to resolve by mutual agreement any difficulties or doubts arising as to the interpretation or application of this Convention. They also may consult together for the elimination of double taxation in cases not provided for in this Convention. In particular the competent authorities of the Contracting States may agree:

a) to the same attribution of income, deductions, credits, or allowances of an enterprise of a Contracting State to its permanent establishment situated in the other Contracting State;

b) to the same allocation of income, deductions, credits, or allowances between persons;

c) to the settlement of conflicting applications of this Convention, including conflicts regarding:

i) the characterization of particular items of income;

ii) the characterization of persons;

iii) the application of source rules with respect to particular items of income;

iv) the meaning of any term used in this Convention;

v) the timing of particular items of income;

d) to advance pricing arrangements; and

e) to the application of the provisions of domestic law regarding penalties, fines, and interest in a manner consistent with the purposes of this Convention.

4. The competent authorities of the Contracting States may agree to increase any specific monetary amounts referred to in this Convention to reflect economic or monetary developments.

5. The competent authorities of the Contracting States may communicate with each other directly, including through a joint commission, for the purpose of reaching an agreement in the sense of the preceding paragraphs.

6. Where a person has presented a case to the competent authority of one or both of the Contracting States either:

a) pursuant to paragraph 1 of this Article on the basis that the actions of one or both of the Contracting States resulted or will result for that person in taxation not in accordance with the provisions of this Convention; or

b) on a taxpayer-specific case regarding a matter described in paragraph 3 of this Article;

and the competent authorities are unable to reach agreement to resolve that case, and the conditions described in paragraph 7 of this Article are met, the case shall be resolved through arbitration conducted in the manner prescribed by paragraphs 7 through 9 of this Article and according to any rules or procedures agreed upon by the competent authorities of the Contracting States pursuant to paragraph 10 of this Article.

7. A case shall be submitted to arbitration on the earliest date on which all of the following conditions have been satisfied:

a) tax returns have been filed with at least one of the Contracting States with respect to the taxable years at issue in the case;

b) at least two years have passed since the commencement date of such case, unless the competent authorities of the Contracting States have agreed to a different date and notified the presenter of the case of such agreement;

c) the presenter of the case has submitted a written request to the competent authority to which the case was presented for a resolution of the case through arbitration; and

d) all concerned persons and their authorized representatives or agents have submitted to the competent authorities of both Contracting States written agreements not to disclose to any other person any information received during the course of the arbitration proceeding from either Contracting State or the arbitration panel, other than the determination of the panel.

A case shall not, however, be submitted to arbitration if a decision with respect to such case has already been rendered by a court or administrative tribunal of either Contracting State, or if the competent authorities of the Contracting States have agreed prior to the date on which the arbitration otherwise would be submitted that the particular case is not suitable for resolution through arbitration.

8. For the purposes of this Article, the following definitions shall apply:

a) the term "presenter" means the person that has presented a case to the competent authority of one or both of the Contracting States either:

i) pursuant to paragraph 1 of this Article on the basis that the actions of one or both of the Contracting States result or will result for that person in taxation not in accordance with the provisions of this Convention; or

ii) on a taxpayer-specific case regarding a matter described in paragraph 3 of this Article;

b) the term "concerned person" means the presenter and all other persons, if any, whose tax liability to either Contracting State may be directly affected by a mutual agreement to resolve a case submitted to arbitration pursuant to paragraph 7 of this Article; and

c) the "commencement date" for a case means the earliest date on which the information necessary to undertake substantive consideration for a mutual agreement has been received by both competent authorities.

9. For the purposes of arbitrations under this Article, the following rules shall apply:

a) The arbitration panel shall consist of three individual members. The competent authority of each Contracting State shall select one member of the arbitration panel. In the event that the competent authority of a Contracting State fails to select a member for the arbitration panel in the manner and within the time periods agreed by the competent authorities of the Contracting States pursuant to paragraph 10 of this Article, the competent authority of the other Contracting State shall select a second member. The two members of the arbitration panel who have been selected shall select the third member, who shall serve as Chair of the arbitration panel. If the two initial members of the arbitration panel fail to select the Chair in the manner and within the time periods agreed by the competent authorities of the Contracting States pursuant to paragraph 10 of this Article, these members shall be dismissed, and each competent authority of the Contracting States shall select a new member of the arbitration panel. The Chair shall not be a national or lawful permanent resident of either Contracting State. The members appointed shall not be employees, nor have been employees within the twelve-month period prior to the date on which a case is submitted to arbitration, of the tax administration or the treasury department of the Contracting State that identified them. Furthermore, the members appointed shall not have any prior involvement with the specific matters at issue in the arbitration proceeding for which they are being considered as arbitrators.

b) The members of the arbitration panel and their staff shall be considered to be "persons or authorities" to whom information may be disclosed under Article 26 (Exchange of Information and Administrative Assistance) of this Convention.

c) All material received by a competent authority of a Contracting State in the course of, or relating to, an arbitration proceeding (including the arbitration panel's determination) shall be considered to be information exchanged between the Contracting States. Accordingly, no such information relating to an arbitration proceeding may be disclosed by the competent authorities of the Contracting States, except as permitted under Article 26 (Exchange of Information and Administrative Assistance). The competent authorities of the Contracting States shall ensure that members of the arbitration panel and their staff agree in writing to treat any information relating to the arbitration proceeding consistent with the confidentiality and nondisclosure provisions of Article 26 (Exchange of Information and Administrative Assistance) of this Convention and the applicable domestic laws of the Contracting States.

d) If at any time before the arbitration panel delivers a determination to the competent authorities of the Contracting States:

i) the competent authorities of the Contracting States reach a mutual agreement to resolve the case pursuant to this Article;

ii) the presenter of the case withdraws the request for arbitration;

iii) a decision concerning the case is rendered by a court or administrative tribunal of one of the Contracting States during the arbitration proceeding; or

iv) if any concerned person or their authorized representatives or agents violates the written nondisclosure statement required by subparagraph (d) of paragraph 7 of this Article, and the competent authorities of both Contracting States agree that such violation should result in the termination of the arbitration proceeding;

the mutual agreement procedure, including the arbitration proceeding, with respect to the case shall terminate.

e) After a case is submitted to arbitration, the presenter shall be permitted to submit to the competent authorities of both Contracting States for submission to the arbitration panel a paper setting forth the presenter's analysis and views of the case for consideration by the arbitration panel. Such submission must be submitted before the date on which the competent authorities of the Contracting States are required to submit their position papers to the arbitration panel, and shall not include any information not previously provided to the competent authorities before the case was submitted to arbitration.

f) After a case is submitted to arbitration, the competent authority of each of the Contracting States shall be permitted to submit to the arbitration panel a position paper with a proposed resolution addressing each adjustment or similar issue raised in the case, and shall simultaneously provide a copy of such position paper to the other competent authority. Such proposed resolution shall be a resolution of the entire case and shall reflect all agreements previously reached between the competent authorities of the Contracting States with respect to any adjustment or similar issue raised in the case. Such proposed resolution shall be limited to a disposition of specific monetary amounts (for example, of income, profit, gain or expense) or, where specified, the maximum rate of tax charged pursuant to the Convention for each adjustment or similar issue in the case. The competent authority of each of the Contracting States shall also be permitted to submit additional supporting papers for consideration by the arbitration panel, and shall simultaneously provide a copy of such supporting papers to the other competent authority.

g) Notwithstanding the provisions of subparagraph (e) of this paragraph, it is understood that, in the case of an arbitration proceeding concerning:

i) the tax liability of an individual for which the competent authorities have been unable to reach agreement with respect to the individual's Contracting State of residence;

ii) the taxation of the business profits of an enterprise with respect to which the competent authorities have been unable to reach an agreement on whether a permanent establishment exists; or

iii) such other issues the determination of which are contingent on resolution of similar threshold questions;

the position paper may include positions regarding clause (i), (ii) or (iii) of this subparagraph, in addition to proposed resolutions limited to specific monetary amounts (for example, of income, profit, gain or expense) or, where specified, the maximum rate of tax charged pursuant to this Convention due as a consequence of the arbitration panel's determination regarding residency, the existence of a permanent establishment or other threshold questions.

h) Where an arbitration proceeding concerns a case comprising multiple adjustments or issues each requiring a disposition of specific monetary amounts of income, profit, gain or expense or, where specified, the maximum rate of tax charged pursuant to this Convention, the position paper may propose a separate disposition for each adjustment or similar issue.

i) Each competent authority shall be permitted to submit a reply to any position paper submitted to the arbitration panel, and shall simultaneously provide the other competent authority with a copy of any such reply submitted to the arbitration panel.

j) The arbitration panel shall deliver a determination in writing to the competent authorities of the Contracting States. The determination reached by the arbitration panel in the arbitration proceeding shall be limited to one of the proposed resolutions for the case submitted by one of the competent authorities of the Contracting States for each adjustment or similar issue and any threshold questions, and shall not include a rationale or any other explanation of the determination. The determination of the arbitration panel shall have no precedential value with respect to the application of this Convention in any other case.

k) The determination of the arbitration panel with respect to a case submitted to arbitration shall constitute a resolution by mutual agreement under this Article and shall be binding on the Contracting States if it is accepted by all of the concerned persons. Unless the competent authorities of both Contracting States agree to a longer time period, the concerned persons shall have 45 days from the date they receive the determination of the arbitration panel to notify, in writing, the competent authority of the Contracting State to whom the case was presented of their acceptance of determination. In the event the case is pending in litigation, each concerned person that is a party to such litigation must also advise, within the same time frame, the relevant court of its acceptance of the determination of the arbitration panel and its intention to withdraw from the consideration of the court the issues resolved through the proceeding. If any concerned person fails to so advise the relevant competent authority and relevant court within this time frame, the determination of the arbitration panel shall be considered not to have been accepted by the concerned persons. Where the determination of the arbitration panel is not accepted, the case shall not be eligible for any subsequent further consideration by the competent authorities.

l) The fees and expenses of the members of the arbitration panel, as well as any costs incurred in connection with the proceeding by the Contracting States, shall be borne equitably by the competent authorities of the Contracting States.

10. The competent authorities of the Contracting States shall agree in writing, before the first case is submitted to arbitration, on time periods and procedures that are consistent with paragraphs 6 through 9 of this Article for:

a) establishing when information necessary to undertake substantive consideration for a mutual agreement has been received by both competent authorities for purposes of determining the commencement date, and for notifying each other when such requirement has been satisfied;

b) notifying the presenter of any agreements that a case is not suitable for resolution through arbitration, or to change the date on which a case shall be submitted to arbitration;

c) the appropriate application of arbitration in the context of a request for an advanced pricing agreement, including rules concerning the date on which a case may be submitted to arbitration;

d) obtaining the agreements of all concerned persons and their authorized representatives or agents not to disclose any information received during the course of the arbitration proceeding from the competent authority of either Contracting State or the arbitration panel, other than the determination of such panel pursuant to subparagraph (d) of paragraph 7 of this Article, and the agreements of the members of the arbitration panel and their staff to treat any information relating to the arbitration proceeding consistent with the confidentiality and nondisclosure provisions of Article 26 (Exchange of Information and Administrative Assistance), as required by subparagraph (c) of paragraph 9 of this Article;

e) the appointment of the members of the arbitration panel;

f) the submission of position papers, supporting papers and reply submissions by the competent authorities of the Contracting States to the arbitration panel;

g) the submission to the competent authorities of both Contracting States by the presenter of a paper setting forth the presenter's views and analysis of the case for consideration by the arbitration panel;

h) the delivery by the arbitration panel of its determination to the competent authorities of the Contracting States;

i) the acceptance or rejection by the concerned persons of the determination of the arbitration panel; and

j) the adoption by the arbitration panel of any additional procedures necessary for the conduct of its business.

The competent authorities of the Contracting States may mutually agree in writing to modify their agreement concerning these time periods and procedures, as needed, and may further agree in writing on such other rules, time periods and procedures as may be necessary for the effective and timely implementation of an arbitration proceeding.

Article 26

EXCHANGE OF INFORMATION AND ADMINISTRATIVE ASSISTANCE

1. The competent authorities of the Contracting States shall exchange such information as is foreseeably relevant for carrying out the provisions of this Convention or the domestic laws of the Contracting States concerning taxes of every kind imposed by a Contracting State to the extent that the taxation thereunder is not contrary to the Convention, including information relating to the assessment or collection, or administration of, the enforcement or prosecution in respect of, or the determination of appeals in relation to, such taxes. The exchange of information is not restricted by paragraph 1 of Article 1 (General Scope) or Article 2 (Taxes Covered).

2. Any information received under this Article by a Contracting State shall be treated as secret in the same manner as information obtained under the domestic law of that Contracting State and shall be disclosed only to persons or authorities (including courts and administrative bodies) involved in the assessment, collection, or administration of, the enforcement or prosecution in respect of, or the determination of appeals in relation to, the taxes referred to in paragraph 1 of this Article, or the oversight of such functions. Such persons or authorities shall use the information only for such purposes. They may disclose the information in public court proceedings or in judicial decisions. Notwithstanding the preceding sentences of this paragraph, the competent authority of the Contracting State that receives information under the provisions of this Article may, with the written consent of the Contracting State that provided the information, also make available

that information for other purposes allowed under the provisions of a mutual legal assistance treaty in force between the Contracting States that allows for the exchange of tax information.

3. In no case shall the provisions of paragraphs 1 and 2 of this Article be construed so as to impose on a Contracting State the obligation:

a) to carry out administrative measures at variance with the laws and administrative practice of that or of the other Contracting State;

b) to supply information that is not obtainable under the laws or in the normal course of the administration of that or of the other Contracting State; or

c) to supply information that would disclose any trade, business, industrial, commercial, or professional secret or trade process, or information the disclosure of which would be contrary to public policy.

4. If information is requested by a Contracting State in accordance with this Article, the other Contracting State shall use its information gathering measures to obtain the requested information, even though that other Contracting State may not need such information for its own tax purposes. The obligation contained in the preceding sentence is subject to the limitations of paragraph 3 of this Article but in no case shall such limitations be construed to permit a Contracting State to decline to supply information solely because it has no domestic interest in such information.

5. In no case shall the provisions of paragraph 3 of this Article be construed to permit a Contracting State to decline to supply information solely because the information is held by a bank, other financial institution, nominee or person acting in an agency or a fiduciary capacity or because it relates to ownership interests in a person.

6. If specifically requested by the competent authority of a Contracting State, the competent authority of the other Contracting State shall provide information under this Article in the form of depositions of witnesses and authenticated copies of unedited original documents (including books, papers, statements, records, accounts, and writings).

7. Each of the Contracting States shall endeavor to collect on behalf of the other Contracting State such amounts as may be necessary to ensure that relief granted by the Convention from taxation imposed by that other Contracting State does not inure to the benefit of persons not entitled thereto. This paragraph shall not impose upon either of the Contracting States the obligation to carry out administrative measures that would be contrary to its sovereignty, security, or public policy.

8. The requested Contracting State shall allow representatives of the requesting Contracting State to interview individuals and examine books and records in the requested Contracting State with the consent of the persons subject to examination.

9. The competent authorities of the Contracting States may develop an agreement upon the mode of application of this Article, including agreement to ensure comparable levels of assistance to each of the Contracting States, but in no case will the lack of such agreement relieve a Contracting State of its obligations under this Article.

Article 27

MEMBERS OF DIPLOMATIC MISSIONS AND CONSULAR POSTS

Nothing in this Convention shall affect the fiscal privileges of members of diplomatic missions or consular posts under the general rules of international law or under the provisions of special agreements.

Article 28

SUBSEQUENT CHANGES IN LAW

1. If at any time after the signing of this Convention, a Contracting State reduces the general statutory rate of company tax that applies with respect to substantially all of the income of resident companies with the result that such rate falls below the lesser of either (a) 15 percent or (b) 60 percent of the general statutory rate of company tax applicable in the other Contracting State, or the first-mentioned Contracting State provides an exemption from taxation to resident companies for substantially all foreign source income (including interest and royalties), the Contracting States shall consult with a view to amending this Convention to restore an appropriate allocation of taxing rights between the Contracting States. If such consultations do not progress, the other Contracting State may notify the first-mentioned Contracting State through diplomatic channels that it shall cease to apply the provisions of Articles 10 (Dividends), 11 (Interest), 12 (Royalties) and 21 (Other Income). In such case, the provisions of such Articles shall cease to have effect in both Contracting States with respect to payments to resident companies six months after the date that the other Contracting State issues a written public notification stating that it shall cease to apply the provisions of Articles 10 (Dividends), 11 (Interest), 12 (Royalties) and 21 (Other Income).

2. For the purposes of determining the general statutory rate of company tax:

a) the allowance of generally available deductions based on a percentage of what otherwise would be taxable income, and other similar mechanisms to achieve a reduction in the overall rate of tax, shall be taken into account; and

b) a tax that applies to a company only upon a distribution by such company, or that applies to shareholders, shall not be taken into account.

Article 29

ENTRY INTO FORCE

1. This Convention shall be subject to ratification in accordance with the applicable procedures of each Contracting State. The Contracting States shall notify each other in writing, through diplomatic channels when their respective applicable procedures have been satisfied.

2. This Convention shall enter into force on the date of the later of the notifications referred to in paragraph 1 of this Article. The provisions of this Convention shall have effect:

a) in respect of taxes withheld at source, for amounts paid or credited on or after the first day of the second month next following the date on which this Convention enters into force;

b) in respect of other taxes, for taxable years beginning on or after the first day of January next following the date on which this Convention enters into force.

3. Notwithstanding paragraph 2 of this Article:

a) the provisions of paragraphs 6 through 10 of Article 25 (Mutual Agreement Procedure) of this Convention shall have effect with respect to:

i) cases that are under consideration by the competent authorities as of the date on which this Convention enters into force. For such cases, the commencement date shall be the date on which this Convention enters into force; and

ii) cases that come under consideration after the date on which this Convention enters into force; and

b) the provisions of Article 26 (Exchange of Information and Administrative Assistance) shall have effect from the date of entry into force of this Convention, without regard to the taxable year to which the matter relates.

Article 30

TERMINATION

This Convention shall remain in force until terminated by a Contracting State. Either Contracting State may terminate the Convention by giving notice of termination to the other Contracting State through diplomatic channels. In such event, the Convention shall terminate on the date of such notification. Notwithstanding such termination, this Convention shall cease to have effect:

a) in respect of taxes withheld at source, for amounts paid or credited after the expiration of the six-month period beginning on the date on which notice of termination was given; and

b) in respect of other taxes, for taxable years beginning on or after the expiration of the six-month period beginning on the date on which notice of termination was given.

IN WITNESS WHEREOF, the undersigned, being duly authorized thereto by their respective Governments, have signed this Convention.

DONE at ____________in duplicate, in the English and __________languages, both texts being equally authentic, this day of, ________, 20__.

FOR THE GOVERNMENT OF	FOR THE GOVERNMENT OF
THE UNITED STATES OF AMERICA:	______________________________